UPGRADING AND REPAIRING SERVERS

Scott Mueller
Mark Edward Soper
Barrie Sosinsky

800 East 96th Street,
Indianapolis, Indiana 46240

Contents at a Glance

Upgrading and Repairing Servers

International Standard Book Number: 0-7897-2815-x

Library of Congress Catalog Card Number: 2002115889

Printed in the United States of America

First Printing: May 2006

09   08   07   06   4   3   2   1

Trademarks

Warning and Disclaimer

Bulk Sales

Que Publishing offers excellent discounts on this book when ordered in quantity for bulk purchases or special sales. For more information, please contact

U.S. Corporate and Government Sales
1-800-382-3419
corpsales@pearsontechgroup.com

For sales outside the United States, please contact

International Sales
international@pearsoned.com

Associate Publisher
Greg Wiegand

Executive Editor
Rick Kughen

Acquisitions Editor
Todd Green

Development Editor
Todd Brakke

Managing Editor
Charlotte Clapp

Project Editor
Tonya Simpson

Copy Editor
Kitty Jarrett

Indexer
Chris Barrick

Proofreader
Elizabeth Scott

Technical Editor
Robert Shimonski
Barrie Sosinsky
Shawn Porter
David Prowse

Publishing Coordinator
Sharry Lee Gregory

Book Designer
Anne Jones

Graphics
Tammy Graham
Laura Robbins

Contents

5 Memory   345

To Larry Barber, my uncle, my friend. He was never too busy to answer my questions when I was growing up, and has answered thousands of questions for students across Michigan over the years. With love and many thanks.

—Mark Soper

About the Authors

Scott Mueller is president of Mueller Technical Research (MTR), an international research and corporate training firm. Since 1982, MTR has produced the industry's most in-depth, accurate, and effective seminars, books, articles, videos, and FAQs covering PC hardware and data recovery. MTR maintains a client list that includes Fortune 500 companies, the U.S. and foreign governments, major software and hardware corporations, as well as PC enthusiasts and entrepreneurs. Scott's seminars have been presented to several thousand PC support professionals throughout the world.

Scott is best known as the author of the longest-running, most popular, and most comprehensive PC hardware book in the world, *Upgrading and Repairing PCs*, which has not only been produced in more than 16 editions but has also become the core of an entire series of books.

Scott has authored many books over the past 20+ years, including *Upgrading and Repairing PCs*, 1st through 16th and Academic editions; *Upgrading and Repairing Laptops*, 1st and 2nd editions; *Upgrading and Repairing PCs: A+ Certification Study Guide*, 1st and 2nd editions; *Upgrading and Repairing PCs Field Guide*; *Killer PC Utilities*; *The IBM PS/2 Handbook*; and *Que's Guide to Data Recovery*.

Contact MTR directly if you have a unique book, article, or video project in mind, or if you want Scott to conduct a custom PC troubleshooting, repair, maintenance, upgrade, or data-recovery seminar tailored for your organization:

Mueller Technical Research
3700 Grayhawk Drive
Algonquin, IL 60102-6325
847-854-6794
847-854-6795 Fax
scottmueller@compuserve.com
www.upgradingandrepairingpcs.com

Scott's premiere work, *Upgrading and Repairing PCs*, has sold well over 2 million copies, making it by far the most popular and longest-running PC hardware book on the market today. Scott has been featured in *Forbes* magazine and has written several articles for *Maximum PC* magazine, several newsletters, and the Upgrading and Repairing PCs website.

If you have suggestions for the next edition of this book, any comments about the book in general, or new book or article topics you would like to see covered, send them to Scott via email at scottmueller@compuserve.com or visit www.upgradingandrepairingpcs.com.

When he is not working on PC-related books or on the road teaching seminars, Scott can usually be found in the garage, working on several vehicular projects, currently including a 1999 Harley-Davidson FLHRCI Road King Classic and a 1989 Pontiac 20th Anniversary Turbo Trans Am (www.89tta.com).

Mark Edward Soper is president of Select Systems and Associates, Inc., a technical writing and training organization. Mark is a 23-year veteran of the technology field, with an extensive background in training, technical book and magazine writing, technical editing, online content development, and research. Email Mark at mark@markesoper.com.

Mark first began to work with PCs in the days of the original IBM PC, PC-XT, and PC compatibles. Mark provided sales, sales support, and technical training for these computers, as well as for Atari, TI, Commodore 64, and CP/M based systems for various retailers in Evansville, Indiana, from 1983 to 1989. Mark found the early editions of Scott Mueller's *Upgrading and Repairing PCs* a great help in both developing technical expertise and in seeing the potential to reach a larger audience by sharing that expertise in print.

Mark began his career as a technical author by writing a computer column for a local business magazine in 1988. His first breakthrough on the national scene began in 1990, when he began to write a series of articles on WordPerfect tips, tricks, and techniques for *WordPerfect Magazine* and *The WordPerfectionist*. Some of these articles involved printing issues, reflecting his long-time interest in the relationship between hardware and software.

After starting Select Systems and Associates in 1989, Mark provided training and technical services for various local and national clients in media, government, and industry. Mark continued to build his troubleshooting skills and credentials by teaching computer troubleshooting and other training classes to thousands of students from Maine to Hawaii from mid-1992 through early 1999, under contract to a New Jersey–based training company. During many of these trips, he continued to write magazine articles for publications such as *PCToday*, *PCNovice*, and *SmartComputing* on topics such as the Internet, hardware upgrades, and Windows 98 and 2000. Mark also wrote three book-length training manuals for another New Jersey–based training company in 1993, as well as shorter training manuals for various clients.

Mark has the distinction of having worked with some of the most famous authors and personalities in the technology field on various book projects, including Scott Mueller, Patrick Norton, and Leo Laporte.

In late 1998, Mark contacted Scott Mueller, dean of computer hardware authors, and began a long association, resulting in this book and many others. Mark has assisted Scott with his classic *Upgrading and Repairing PCs* series, published by Que, since the 11th edition up through the current 16th edition. Mark also provided some chapters for *Upgrading and Repairing Networks*, 2nd edition, and was a contributor to *Upgrading and Repairing Laptops*. Mark and Scott have also co-authored *Upgrading and Repairing PCs: Technician's Portable Reference* (1st and 2nd editions), *Upgrading and Repairing PCs: Field Guide* (the latest version of the *Technician's Portable Reference*), and *Upgrading and Repairing PCs: A+ Certification Study Guide*, 2nd edition, which covers the 2001 versions of the A+ Certification exams for entry-level hardware technicians. Mark also assists Scott with www.upgradingandrepairingpcs.com, the official website for the book series.

Since earning his A+ and Microsoft Certified Professional certifications in 1999, Mark has continued to work on many hardware and Windows book projects. He has been a contributor to five books in Que's Special Edition Using Windows series, including *Special Edition Using Windows Millennium*; *Special Edition Using Windows XP Home Edition*; *Special Edition Using Windows XP Home Edition, Bestseller Edition*; *Special Edition Using Windows XP Professional*; and *Special Edition Using Windows XP Professional, Bestseller Edition*. In addition to revising a number of chapters for each book, Mark's 30+ years of experience with photography and his experience with creating digital archives for several historic photo collections held by area libraries helped him write the brand-new imaging chapters for these books. Mark is also a contributor to *Windows XP Platinum Edition*.

In 2000 and 2001, Mark wrote two books on broadband Internet: *Complete Idiot's Guide to High-Speed Internet Connections* (2000), an overview of all types of broadband, and *Absolute Beginner's Guide to Cable Internet Connections* (2001), which focuses on cable modem–based services.

In mid-2001, Mark co-authored one of the first books in the TechTV series, *TechTV's Upgrading Your PC*, with Patrick Norton. Mark wrote *PC Help Desk in a Book* in 2003 and was the sole author of *TechTV's Upgrading Your PC*, 2nd edition, in late 2003.

Mark revisited the A+ Certification topic with his book *Absolute Beginner's Guide to A+ Certification*, published in February 2004 as a comprehensive study guide for the November 2003 revisions of the A+ Certification Operating Systems and Core Hardware exams. It features quick-reference tables for major topics, extensive illustrations, and detailed coverage of all Windows versions from Windows NT 4.0 through Windows XP. The companion CD features hands-on labs, a Windows command reference, additional book chapters, and a hardware supplement.

2004 was a busy year for Mark. In addition to his A+ Certification book, Mark also wrote *Easy Digital Cameras*, a visual hands-on guide to digital photography, featuring three popular brands of digital cameras, and *Absolute Beginner's Guide to Home Networking*, which covers business, educational, home control, and recreational uses for home networks, with added emphasis on security and non-PC home networking devices.

In 2005, Mark followed up his home networking book with *Absolute Beginner's Guide to Home Automation,* which shows how to control your home's lights, electronics, HVAC, and security at home and remotely through X10-compatible home control hardware from a variety of vendors. Mark also teamed up with another technology book and media veteran, Leo Laporte, to produce a new and improved edition of Mark's *PC Help Desk in a Book.* The new edition, *Leo Laporte's PC Help Desk,* published in the fall of 2005, puts Mark's and Leo's years of computer and technology experience into an easy-to-use self-diagnostic form. Symptom tables, flowcharts, and write-ups about major hardware, software, and firmware subsystems help solve computer, peripheral, and imaging device problems quickly.

In addition to book projects, Mark has also worked with ReviewNet (www.reviewnet.net/auth-gallery/authgall-soper.html), a leading screener of IT personnel for employers, to develop questions for hardware tech interviews. Mark has also written several articles for *MaximumPC* magazine, on topics such as memory technologies, BIOS tweaking, Linux for Windows users, and 64-bit Windows. Some of this material was later adapted for the books *Maximum PC Ultimate PC Performance Guide* and *Maximum PC Guide to Building a Dream PC* (published by Que). Mark is also an author for Skywire Software (www.skywiresoftware.com), a leading provider of online knowledge management and help desk services.

Mark is a graduate of Olivet Nazarene University, Bourbonnais, IL, where he graduated summa cum laude with a dual major in English and history. He has been a serious amateur photographer since 1971, and he has a growing collection of railroad and transportation photos, timetables, and other documents waiting for his attention.

Barrie Sosinsky is an author of 30 computer books and more than 400 articles on technology. He follows the server, storage, and operating systems market and has created a number of whitepapers for large corporate clients. His website TechnologyRoad.com posts articles on scientific topics, information technology, and the various projects he is working on. Sosinsky is a gadget fanatic and enjoys working on media devices of all kinds.

David Eytchison has been working in the computer industry for eight years. He has worked in technical support and network administration, and he currently works as a systems engineer for Summit Digital Networks, a system integration and consulting company in Cincinnati, Ohio. He is a Microsoft Certified Systems Engineer, a Cisco Certified Network Administrator, and a Citrix Certified Administrator, and he is A+ certified, with a degree in computer networking. He has been a technical reviewer for a variety of books on A+ Certification, networking, and Windows operating systems. He specializes in network design and installation, as well as Windows networking environments.

Ed Tittel is series editor of the Training Guide Series and the Exam Cram 2 Series, and he runs LANWrights, Inc., a training and writing firm that specializes in networking, computer security, and markup languages, in Austin, Texas. Ed has contributed to more than 100 books on various aspects of computing, including more than 50 titles on various IT certifications. He is also the originator of the Exam Cram series of IT certification books.

Acknowledgments

I want to thank God for the opportunity to work with so many talented people, past and present. They gave generously of their time and talent, even as God gives generously to all of us.

I want to thank my wife Cheryl and our children (Ed and his wife Erin, and their daughter Vivian; Kate and her husband Hugh and their boys Jarvis and Linus; Ian and his fiancée Jamie; and Jeremy). The writing of this book and the many others that preceded it could not have been possible without their love, encouragement, patience, and, yes, the technical questions that come with having a family of technology fans.

Any technology book worth reading is the product of many hands. First of all, I want to thank Scott Mueller for his more than 20 years' efforts to create the finest computer hardware reference books on the planet. I have found Scott's expertise, authoritative knowledge, and desire to keep learning an inspiration ever since I first read the original edition of *Upgrading and Repairing PCs*. Scott's research on processors, memory, hard disk interfaces, and other topics helped immensely in developing many chapters of this book, showing us the level of information and expertise necessary to cover servers in a way worthy of the *Upgrading and Repairing* brand.

I want to thank Rick Kughen at Que for the opportunity to turn the vision of an authoritative book on server technology into a reality. It's been a long road, Rick, but I hope you agree it's been worth it!

I want to thank Todd Green for overseeing this and other recent *Upgrading and Repairing* series titles. Todd, who lives not too far from Scott in the Chicagoland area, has a great vision for the series and has worked tirelessly to shepherd this book through to completion.

A great team of authors worked with me to create this book: Barrie Sosinsky, a contributing editor for *Windows IT Pro,* founder of the Sosinsky Group, a Windows Server and Sun Solaris expert with more than 30 books and hundreds of magazine articles to his credit; Ed Tittel, a contributor to more than 130 technology book titles and series editor of the *ExamCram 2* series for Que; and David Eytchison, a veteran technical editor at Que. Many thanks to Barrie, Ed, and David for outstanding material.

Our efforts are backed by a great team of publication specialists at Que, including development editor Todd Brakke, copy editor Kitty Jarrett, project editor Tonya Simpson, and publishing coordinator Sharry Gregory. Barrie Sosinsky doubled as a tech editor, joining Robert Shimonski, David Prowse, and Shawn Porter in checking technical topics for accuracy. Thanks for your work!

I'd also like to thank the associate publisher, Greg Wiegand, and the proofreaders, graphics specialists, and the rest of the gang at Que for helping this book to be the accurate, readable, and enjoyable reference book you've come to expect from Que.

—Mark Soper

We Want to Hear from You!

As the reader of this book, *you* are our most important critic and commentator. We value your opinion and want to know what we're doing right, what we could do better, what areas you'd like to see us publish in, and any other words of wisdom you're willing to pass our way.

As an associate publisher for Que Publishing, I welcome your comments. You can email or write me directly to let me know what you did or didn't like about this book—as well as what we can do to make our books better.

Please note that I cannot help you with technical problems related to the topic of this book. We do have a User Services group, however, where I will forward specific technical questions related to the book.

When you write, please be sure to include this book's title and author as well as your name, email address, and phone number. I will carefully review your comments and share them with the authors and editors who worked on the book.

Email: feedback@quepublishing.com

Mail: Greg Wiegand
          Associate Publisher
          Que Publishing
          800 East 96th Street
          Indianapolis, IN 46240 USA

Reader Services

Visit our website and register this book at www.quepublishing.com/register for convenient access to any updates, downloads, or errata that might be available for this book.

Introduction

Welcome to *Upgrading and Repairing Servers*. With networks becoming essential to business operation and more vendors than ever before selling preconfigured servers and server components that allow you to "roll your own" server, it's time for a book that provides authoritative information on servers, their components, and the network and physical environment needed to make a server-based network work for you and your company. That book is *Upgrading and Repairing Servers*. As the title implies, this book is designed to follow in the footsteps of *Upgrading and Repairing PCs* by providing the same depth and quality of information found in that tome, only tailored for the world of servers.

Many PC users, even experts, often feel that the world of servers and server-based networks is an alien one, filled with technologies and terminologies utterly different from those found on PCs. *Upgrading and Repairing Servers* is designed to help you understand that "other world" by showing you how PCs and servers are similar in some ways and by explaining clearly how, and why, they differ. Some types of current PC technology, such as Serial ATA (SATA) drives, RAID arrays, and I/O devices, are also mainstays of server design. However, other components commonly found in servers, such as SCSI drives, high-performance tape backups, rack-mounted chassis, storage area networks (SANs), fault tolerance, Gigabit and 10 Gigabit Ethernet, and redundant power supplies, are not typically found in PCs. *Upgrading and Repairing Servers* is designed to help readers who understand PC technology to apply and extend that knowledge into the world of servers. After reading this book, you will be more comfortable with server technology, understand what makes a server a server, and be ready to build, upgrade, and repair a wide variety of servers. Although Scott Mueller's *Upgrading and Repairing PCs* was the inspiration for this book and provided the basis for some of its content, *Upgrading and Repairing Servers* is much more than a rehash of its PC-oriented sibling. This book focuses on server technology. While some server components are similar (or identical) to those found in desktop computers, those technologies are often used in different ways or are far less important on a server than on a desktop. Servers also use many technologies that aren't implemented in desktop or laptop computers. *Upgrading and Repairing Servers* is designed to help you understand how servers use both PC-related and server-specific technologies and to help you master those technologies.

Book Objectives

The number-one objective of this book is to help you learn how to maintain, upgrade, and repair a server. As a consequence, *Upgrading and Repairing Servers* covers the technologies found in servers, from entry-level to enterprise-level technologies. From motherboards to memory, RAID arrays to tape backups, power supplies to server rooms, this book helps you understand how server-class technology works, how to upgrade it, and how to troubleshoot and solve problems.

Systems designed specifically as servers have been around for more than a decade, and *Upgrading and Repairing Servers* is written to help you understand the motherboard, processor, memory, and I/O technologies found in older servers (some of which might still be in use in many organizations) as well as the current technology found in the latest models.

One of the ways in which server architecture differs from PC architecture is in the emphasis on multiple and redundant components. From multiple processors and RAID drive arrays to redundant power supplies and tape backup autoloaders and libraries, *Upgrading and Repairing Servers* helps you understand why servers provide faster performance with multiple processors, how multiple-processor systems are designed for maximum performance, why redundant components are important for increased reliability, and how servers handle component failures and switch over to the redundant component.

Not every server runs an x86-compatible processor (that is, a processor that runs 32-bit Windows). This book provides extensive coverage of the Itanium, Sun SPARC and UltraSPARC, and other RISC processor architectures and their major features. An entire chapter is devoted to Sun servers and the Solaris operating system, with its unique features.

Although some servers have form factors virtually indistinguishable from that of a tower PC and might be placed in the corner of a small office, server form factors and locations are often customized to the specific needs of a server. This book helps you specify and use server-specific racks, cabinets, and closets and design the best server room for your situation.

After you read this book, you should have the knowledge to upgrade, troubleshoot, and repair almost any server system and component.

Is This Book for You?

If you work with servers or are planning to buy or build a server, this book is most definitely for you!

Upgrading and Repairing Servers is designed for people who want a thorough understanding of server hardware and how their servers work. Each section fully explains common and not-so-common problems, what causes problems, and how to handle problems when they arise. For example, you will gain an understanding of tape drive configuration and interfacing that can improve your diagnostics and troubleshooting skills. You'll develop a feel for what goes on in a system so you can rely on your own judgment and observations and not some table of canned troubleshooting steps.

Upgrading and Repairing Servers is written for people who will select, install, configure, maintain, and repair systems they or their companies use. To accomplish these tasks, you need a level of knowledge much higher than that of an average system user. You must know exactly which tool to use for a task and how to use the tool correctly. This book can help you achieve that level of knowledge.

If you want to understand and master server technology, this book is for you.

Chapter-by-Chapter Breakdown

This book is organized into chapters that cover the components of a server and its environment. While a PC might be located almost anywhere, servers are often located in a specialized environment, such as a rack mount or server room. This book covers both the components inside a server and the devices and environment outside the server chassis.

Chapter 1, "The History of Servers," helps you understand the roots of today's server technology. From the first "supercomputers" and the development of ARPAnet (the ancestor of the Internet) and Novell NetWare (the first true network operating system) to modern servers and operating systems, this chapter helps you understand where servers came from and how they're used today.

Chapter 2, "Server Microprocessors," includes detailed coverage of all the Intel and AMD processors that have been used in servers. It discusses processors designed for desktops and adapted to server use, such as the Intel Pentium II, Pentium III, Pentium 4, and Pentium D, with particular emphasis on the features that make these processors suitable for use in servers. It also discusses processors designed for use in servers—such as the Intel Pentium II Xeon, Pentium III Xeon, Xeon, Xeon MP; Itanium family; Athlon MP; Opteron; and RISC processors—showing how these processors are optimized for larger and more powerful servers and for four-way and larger configurations. This chapter also covers the roles of L1, L2, and L3 cache, along with how multiprocessor servers handle data flow. Detailed reference charts and tables of processors and processor sockets help you choose the best processor for the server task and speed needed.

Chapter 3, "Server Chipsets," provides a comprehensive discussion of server chipsets. This chapter discusses the features, processor compatibilities, applications of major server chipsets from Intel, ServerWorks, AMD, Hewlett-Packard, and other major chipset vendors. Diagrams and tables help you understand how chipsets control server architecture.

Chapter 4, "Server Motherboards and BIOS," covers server motherboard form factors, components, power supplies, system buses, embedded resources, and BIOS settings in detail. While some servers use motherboard form factors similar to those found in PCs, many use form factors designed to provide more motherboard area for the additional components found in a server, such as those developed by the Server System Infrastructure (SSI) initiative. This chapter shows you how these form factors differ and helps you understand which form factor is appropriate for a particular task. This chapter also discusses how to configure the special BIOS settings found in many servers and ends with a discussion of troubleshooting motherboard and BIOS issues.

Chapter 5, "Memory," provides a detailed discussion of server memory, including the latest in main memory specifications and error-correction technologies. Next to the processor and motherboard, the system memory is one of the most important parts of a server. It's also one of the most difficult things to understand because it is somewhat intangible, and how it works is not always obvious. This chapter helps you understand how SDRAM, DDR, and DDR-2 memory differ; why some servers use registered memory; the role of parity-checked memory in servers old and new; how different memory technologies use different methods to report speed; and how to determine the memory type of a particular memory module. You should read this chapter before you populate a new server motherboard or upgrade the memory in an existing server.

Chapter 6, "The ATA/IDE Interface," provides a detailed discussion of ATA/IDE, including types and specifications. It covers the Ultra ATA modes that allow 133MBps operation and how servers are moving to SATA for hard disk storage and are relegating ATA/IDE to optical drive support. This chapter discusses RAID arrays, as well as how to overcome the drive size limits found in some operating systems.

Chapter 7, "The SCSI Bus," discusses SCSI, the drive standard used in most servers for primary and backup storage. Both parallel SCSI (SPI and UltraSCSI) and the new Serial Attached SCSI (SAS) standard that is based on SATA are covered in detail. This chapter also covers the low-voltage differential signaling used by some of the higher-speed devices on the market, as well as the latest information on cables, terminators, SCSI configurations, and SCSI troubleshooting.

Chapter 8, "I/O System Hardware," covers USB, video displays and ports, keyboards, and optical drive technologies used in servers. It discusses troubleshooting methods, including driver, firmware, and hardware upgrades, as well as typical configurations.

Chapter 9, "Backup Operations," discusses the leading multivendor tape backup standards used in servers: Travan, DDS4, DAT 72, DLT, SDLT, and Ultrium. Detailed capacities, specifications, typical configurations, and installation instructions are provided for each type. It also discusses autoloaders and tape libraries, as well as alternative backup technologies, such as disk-to-disk (D2D), Iomega REV, and DVD. A review of backup methods and strategies, dealing with open files and backup software products and integrated utilities, completes the chapter.

Chapter 10, "Network Operations," provides a comprehensive look at network hardware, protocols, and operations. It discusses the selection, installation, advanced configuration, and hardware compatibility factors for network adapters from 10Mbps through 10 Gigabit Ethernet, Wi-Fi, and fiber based. It also covers TCP/IP protocol and troubleshooting tools for Windows, Sun, Linux, and UNIX. The chapter also includes coverage of older protocols still used in some networks, such as IPX/SPX, AppleTalk, and NetBEUI/NetBIOS.

Chapter 11, "Disk Subsystems," discusses ATA/IDE, Ultra160 and Ultra320 SCSI, and Fibre Channel disk subsystems, adapters, cables, and backplanes. Because many servers include RAID arrays, this chapter discusses the most common types of RAID arrays, from RAID 0 to RAID 10, how to upgrade an existing array, and how to troubleshoot RAID problems.

Chapter 12, "Storage Area Networks," discusses storage area network (SAN) components, configurations, use, and troubleshooting. Because SAN devices combine hard disk and network technologies, they can be challenging to work with for first-time users. This chapter helps you put SAN technology to work on your network.

Chapter 13, "Fault Tolerance," discusses the wide range of methods used to keep servers and networks running, even in the face of device or system failures. It discusses mesh configurations; RAID array rebuilding; network segmentation; redundant power supplies, fans, and memory; software maintenance; server management software; and antivirus software.

Chapter 14, "Power Protection," discusses how to protect servers from power failure with redundant power supplies, battery backup (UPS) units, and surge protection. This chapter helps you find the right UPS technology, VA rating, features, and runtime for your server. It also discusses typical UPS configurations, how to install a new UPS, and how to choose a standard or redundant power supply.

Chapter 15, "Chassis," discusses the different types of chassis (pedestal, rack mounted, wall mounted, ATX, and BTX) used for servers. Other topics include how to choose the right specifications for a particular task, how to approach chassis manage airflow and cooling issues, how to switch convertible chassis from pedestal to rack mounted, and how to remove a typical Intel server chassis.

Chapter 16, "Server Racks and Blades," discusses server rack and cabinet types. It also covers how to select a server rack by size and features, how to mount a server, and how to install a KVM switch.

Chapter 17, "Server Rooms," discusses the features needed in a server closet and data center. It also discusses planning, cable management, cooling, noise, floor elevation, safety, and security issues.

Chapter 18, "Server Platforms: Network Operating Systems," discusses major features, benefits, and licensing issues for the leading server operating systems, including Windows 2000 Server, Windows Server 2003, Novell NetWare 6.5, Sun Solaris, and Red Hat Linux. This chapter provides leading errors and solutions for each server operating system, along with guidance in selecting the best server operating system for a particular situation.

Chapter 19, "Sun Microsystems Servers," discusses the unique features of Sun's RISC-based architecture and analyzes the SPARC 32-bit and UltraSPARC architectures. It discusses each server category supported by Sun, from entry-level servers to blade servers. It also covers the Solaris operating system and its management tools, as well as methods used for integrating Sun servers into an x86 (Intel-compatible) network.

Chapter 20, "Building, Upgrading, and Deploying Servers," discusses the process of implementing a server. It also covers budgets for hardware, software, peripherals, upgrades, and network access, as well as the network's purpose, location, and size and how to install and maintain the network. A sample project plan helps you understand the process.

Chapter 21, "Server Testing and Maintenance," discusses the process of performance analysis, using both integrated and third-party tools, how to diagnose problems, and how to perform routine maintenance, such as drive testing, defragmentation, antivirus protection, and chassis/fan cleaning. It also covers how to detect problems through error logs, implement hardware redundancy, and do disaster recovery planning.

The book also contains three appendixes that provide useful background and references:

- Appendix A, "Glossary," lists server, computer, and network terms and their definitions.
- Appendix B, "List of Acronyms and Abbreviations," lists the meanings of acronyms and abbreviations you are likely to encounter as you work with servers.
- Appendix C, "Vendor List," provides an up-to-date list of server and PC vendors of systems, components, peripherals, software, and accessories.

www.upgradingandrepairingpcs.com

This book is part of the large and growing *Upgrading and Repairing* family of books:

- *Upgrading and Repairing PCs*
- *Upgrading and Repairing Laptops*
- *Upgrading and Repairing Networks*
- *Upgrading and Repairing Windows*

Written by best-selling author Scott Mueller and other leading computer authorities, this series of books is designed to make you an expert on servers, desktop PCs, laptops, networks, Windows, and other computer topics. For the latest news about *Upgrading and Repairing* books, useful articles, exclusive video clips, and reader questions and answers, be sure to visit the *Upgrading and Repairing* website at www.upgradingandrepairingpcs.com! Be sure to check this website frequently for more information on all of Scott's latest books, videos, articles, FAQs, and more!

CHAPTER 1

The History of Servers

Computer History: Pre- and Postserver

The history of servers is, naturally, a subset of the history of PCs in that the crucial events and dates that lead to the birth of electronic computing are all very similar. Consequently, the following time line is adapted from the 16th edition of the original book in this series, *Upgrading and Repairing PCs*. For time line data prior to 1960, please consult that work (we had to draw the line somewhere); only the server-specific dates and information here differ from that material.

1960	Bell Labs designs its Dataphone, the first commercial modem, specifically for converting digital computer data to analog signals for transmission across its long-distance network.
1960	The precursor to the minicomputer, DEC's PDP-1, sells for $120,000.
1961	According to *Datamation Magazine*, IBM has an 81.2% share of the computer market in 1961, the year in which it introduces the 1400 series.
1964	CDC's 6600 supercomputer, designed by Seymour Cray, performs up to three million instructions per second—a processing speed three times faster than that of its closest competitor, the IBM Stretch.
1964	IBM announces System/360, a family of six mutually compatible computers and 40 peripherals that can work together.
1964	Online transaction processing makes its debut in IBM's SABRE reservations system, set up for American Airlines.
1965	Digital Equipment Corp. introduces the PDP-8, the first commercially successful minicomputer.
1966	Hewlett-Packard enters the general-purpose computer business with its HP-2115 for computation, offering a computational power formerly found only in much larger computers.
1969	The root of what is to become the Internet begins when the U.S. Department of Defense establishes four nodes on the ARPAnet: two at University of California campuses (one at Santa Barbara and one at Los Angeles) and one each at SRI International and the University of Utah.
1971	A team at IBM's San Jose Laboratories invents the 8-inch floppy disk.
1971	The first advertisement for a microprocessor, the Intel 4004, appears in *Electronic News*.
1971	The Kenbak-1, one of the first personal computers, is advertised for $750 in *Scientific American*.
1972	Hewlett-Packard announces the HP-35 as "a fast, extremely accurate electronic slide rule" with a solid-state memory similar to that of a computer.
1972	Intel's 8008 microprocessor makes its debut.
1973	Steve Wozniak builds his "blue box," a tone generator to make free phone calls.
1973	Robert Metcalfe devises the Ethernet method of network connection at the Xerox Palo Alto Research Center (PARC).

1973	The Micral is the earliest commercial, non-kit personal computer based on a micro-processor, the Intel 8008.
1973	The TV Typewriter, designed by Don Lancaster, provides the first display of alphanumeric information on an ordinary television set.
1974	Researchers at the Xerox PARC design the Alto, the first workstation with a built-in mouse for input.
1974	Scelbi advertises its 8H computer, the first commercially advertised U.S. computer based on a microprocessor, the Intel 8008.
1975	Telenet, the first commercial packet-switching network and the civilian equivalent of ARPAnet, is born.
1975	The January edition of *Popular Electronics* features the Altair 8800, which is based on Intel's 8080 microprocessor, on its cover.
1975	The visual display module (VDM) prototype, designed by Lee Felsenstein, marks the first implementation of a memory-mapped alphanumeric video display for personal computers.
1976	Steve Wozniak designs the Apple I, a single-board computer.
1976	The 5.25-inch flexible disk drive and disk are introduced by Shugart Associates.
1976	The Cray I makes its name as the first commercially successful vector processor.
1977	Tandy Radio Shack introduces the TRS-80.
1977	Apple Computer introduces the Apple II.
1977	Commodore introduces the PET (Personal Electronic Transactor).
1978	The VAX 11/780 from Digital Equipment Corp. features the capability to address up to 4.3GB of virtual memory, providing hundreds of times the capacity of most mini-computers.
1979	Motorola introduces the 68000 microprocessor.
1979	Novell Data Systems is founded, primarily as a manufacturer of computer hardware and disk operating systems.
1979	Cromemco introduces a 19-inch rack-mounted microcomputer built around the Z80 processor that gets widely used as a network server.
1980	John Shoch, at the Xerox PARC, invents the computer "worm," a short program that searches a network for idle processors.
1980	Seagate Technology creates the first hard disk drive for microcomputers, the ST-506.
1980	The first optical data storage disk is invented; it has 60 times the capacity of a 5.25-inch floppy disk.
1981	Novell introduces its first explicit network server product family, built around the Motorola 68000 processor.
1981	Xerox introduces the Star, the first personal computer with a graphical user interface (GUI).
1981	Adam Osbourne completes the first portable computer, the Osbourne I, which weighs about 24 pounds and costs $1,795.

1981	IBM introduces its PC, igniting a fast growth in the personal computer market. The IBM PC is the grandfather of all modern PCs.
1981	Sony introduces and ships the first 3.5-inch floppy drives and disks.
1981	Philips and Sony introduce the CD-DA (compact disc–digital audio) format.
1982	Sony puts the first CD player on the market.
1983	Novell is acquired and repositioned as a network operating system company, and the first version of NetWare is introduced.
1983	Apple introduces its Lisa, which incorporates a GUI that's very similar to the one first introduced on the Xerox Star.
1983	Compaq Computer Corp. introduces its first PC clone that uses the same software as the IBM PC.
1983	Sytek implements the first version of NetBIOS for IBM.
1984	Apple Computers launches the Macintosh, the first successful mouse-driven computer with a GUI, with a single $1.5 million commercial during the 1984 Super Bowl.
1984	IBM releases the PC-AT (PC Advanced Technology), which is three times faster than original PCs and based on the Intel 286 chip. The AT introduces the 16-bit ISA bus and is the computer on which all modern PCs are based.
1984	IBM releases PC Network Technical Reference 6422916, the first formal definition of NetBIOS.
1985	Philips introduces the first CD-ROM drive.
1985	Microsoft introduces MS-NET, which morphs into the first version of Microsoft LAN Manager.
1986	Compaq announces the Desktop 386, the first computer on the market to use what was then Intel's new 386 chip.
1986	OpenNET/Microsoft Networks file sharing protocols are released; they lay the foundation for 3COM's 3+Share and, ultimately, both SMB (in 1988) and the LAN Manager network operating system (the latter comes to life as an actual product this year as well).
1987	IBM introduces its PS/2 machines, which make the 3.5-inch floppy disk drive and VGA video standard for PCs. The PS/2 also introduces the MicroChannel Architecture (MCA) bus, the first plug-and-play bus for PCs.
1987	Microsoft, Intel, and IBM release RFCs 1001 and 1002, which define NetBIOS over TCP/UDP transport concepts and methods.
1988	Microsoft releases SMB File Sharing Protocol Extensions version 2.0 (document version 3.3), which publicly unveils SMB for general use.
1988	Apple cofounder Steve Jobs, who left Apple to form his own company, unveils the NeXT.
1988	Compaq and other PC-clone makers develop Enhanced Industry Standard Architecture (EISA), which, unlike MicroChannel, retains backward compatibility with the existing ISA bus.

1988   Robert Morris's worm floods the ARPAnet. The 23-year-old Morris, the son of a computer security expert for the National Security Agency, sends a nondestructive worm through the Internet, causing problems for about 6,000 of the 60,000 hosts linked to the network.

1989   Intel releases the 486 (P4) microprocessor, which contains more than one million transistors. Intel also introduces the 486 motherboard chipsets.

1989   Compaq ships its first PC-based server product, the Compaq System Pro (also the company's first Extended ISA, or EISA, 32-bit bus machine).

1990   The World Wide Web (WWW) is born when Tim Berners-Lee, a researcher at CERN—the high-energy physics laboratory in Geneva—develops Hypertext Markup Language (HTML).

1992   Compaq introduces its first suite of server management and optimization tools (named Insight) and introduces its first low-cost server, the ProSignia.

1993   Intel Releases the Pentium 5 (P5) processor. Intel shifts from numbers to names for its chips after it learns that it's impossible to trademark a number. Intel also releases motherboard chipsets and, for the first time, complete motherboards as well.

1994   Compaq introduces the first rack-mountable server, the Rack Mountable ProLiant series.

1995   Microsoft releases Windows 95, the first mainstream 32-bit operating system, in a huge rollout.

1996   The one millionth Compaq server rolls off the company's assembly line.

1997   Intel releases the Pentium II processor, essentially a Pentium Pro with MMX instructions added.

1997   AMD introduces the K6, which is compatible with the Intel P5 (Pentium).

1997   Compaq acquires Tandem Computer (maker of the Non-Stop operating system and a proprietary, high-availability/reliability server hardware family) and begins to incorporate high-availability/reliability features into its top-of-the-line ProLiant servers.

1998   Microsoft releases Windows 98.

1998   Intel releases the Celeron, a low-cost version of the Pentium II processor. Initial versions have no L2 cache, but within a few months Intel introduces versions with a smaller but faster L2 cache.

1998   Compaq acquires Digital Equipment Corporation and also introduces first modular rack-mounted server architecture with the Compaq ProLiant 1850R server products.

1999   Intel releases the Pentium III, essentially a Pentium II with SSE (Streaming SIMD Extensions) added.

1999   AMD introduces the Athlon.

1999   The Institute of Electrical and Electronics Engineers (IEEE) officially approves the 5GHz band 802.11a 54Mbps and the 2.4GHz band 802.11b 11Mbps wireless networking standards. The Wi-Fi Alliance is formed to certify 802.11b products, ensuring interoperability.

2000	The first 802.11b Wi-Fi–certified products are introduced, and wireless networking rapidly builds momentum.
2000	Microsoft releases Windows ME (Millennium Edition) and Windows 2000.
2000	Both Intel and AMD introduce processors that run at 1GHz.
2000	AMD introduces the Duron, a low-cost Athlon with reduced size L2 cache.
2000	Intel introduces the Pentium 4, the latest processor in the Intel architecture 32-bit (IA-32) family.
2000	Sun, IBM, and Hewlett-Packard (which now includes Compaq) introduce the first blade server product families.
2001	Intel releases the Itanium processor, its first 64-bit (IA-64) processor for PCs.
2001	The industry celebrates the 20th anniversary of the release of the original IBM PC.
2001	Intel introduces the first 2GHz processor, a version of the Pentium 4. It took the industry 28.5 years to go from 108KHz to 1GHz but only 18 months to go from 1GHz to 2GHz.
2001	Microsoft releases Windows XP Home and Professional, for the first time merging the consumer (9x/Me) and business (NT/2000) operating system lines under the same code base (an extension of Windows 2000).
2001	Atheros introduces the first 802.11a 54Mbps high-speed wireless chips, allowing 802.11a products to finally reach the market.
2002	Intel releases the first 3GHz-class processor, a 3.06GHz version of the Pentium 4. This processor also introduces to desktop computing Intel's HyperThreading (HT) technology, which enables a single processor to work with two application threads at the same time.
2002	AMD formally unveils its 64-bit server processor family, Opteron.
2003	Intel releases the Pentium M, a processor designed specifically for mobile systems, offering extremely low power consumption that results in dramatically increased battery life while still offering relatively high performance. The Pentium M becomes the cornerstone of Intel's Centrino brand.
2003	AMD releases the Athlon 64, the first 64-bit processor targeted at the mainstream consumer and business markets. The Opteron 64-bit server processor also ships this year.
2003	The IEEE officially approves the 802.11g 54Mbps high-speed wireless networking standard, which uses the same 2.4GHz band as (and is backward compatible with) 802.11b. 802.11g products reach the market quickly, some even before the official standard is approved.
2004	Intel introduces a version of the Pentium 4 code-named Prescott, the first PC processor built on 90-nanometer technology.
2004	Intel introduces EM64T (Extended Memory 64 Technology), which is a 64-bit extension to Intel's IA-32 architecture. EM64T is software compatible with and targeted at the same market as the AMD Athlon 64 and is not compatible with the 64-bit Itanium.

The Rise of Client/Server Computing

Until client computers had real processing power and capability, the early client/server paradigm operated without the conventional client and server machines common in most current business environments. Rather, the early client/server model established an ad hoc definition of *client* and *server* based on which unit issued a request for information or services (thereby becoming the client) and which one responded to such requests (thereby becoming the server). This kind of capability continues to be used to this day, particularly in peer-to-peer services. Primitive implementations of this technology are also forever preserved in old reliable Internet applications, including File Transfer Protocol (FTP) and Telnet (networked virtual terminal).

Initial client/server computing centered around extremely large, expensive devices called *mainframes*. Mainframes could provide access to multiple simultaneous users by running multiple-user operating systems and were first available to big business and academia. Access to these large-scale computers for system operators and end users alike came via a terminal console (an input device and output display). Mainframe designs and concepts of yesteryear are vastly different from contemporary mainframes, and they are explored later in this chapter.

Functionality for the early mainframes consisted of business and academic applications that required no programming skill to use or maintain. This permitted business managers to create spreadsheets for ad hoc business modeling and reporting and to keep database entries for internal records, for example. The legacy applications they continue to run (and serve up) provides mainframes with their incredible staying power, often because business managers are wary of abandoning older, working systems for newer technology. Transitions from oldies but goodies into more modern equivalents can also be time-consuming and expensive, and it continues to provide a powerful argument for maintaining the mainframe as a form of status quo. When cutover from old systems to new ones is unavoidable, parallel operation is nearly always practiced during a cutover phase, so that the old system runs alongside the new one, often in complete lock-step. This is especially likely whenever costs or risks of downtime or new system failure are unacceptably high; the old system is kept up and running as a kind of "hot standby" in case anything affects the operation of the new one.

Dedicated server computing found its initial justification from the consolidation and centralization of common network resources and devices it enabled. Owing to the prohibitive cost of then-nascent technologies such as early printers, tape backups, large storage repositories, and the operational overhead involved with maintaining and operating a mainframe, business managers opted to centralize most commonly used resources and attach them to the mainframe (sometimes directly, sometimes through a variety of peripheral processing units). This eventually spurred the development of more cost-effective "minicomputer" designs, which replicated most mainframe functionality at a fraction of the cost. This affected business operations by providing higher availability and yielding higher productivity.

File and Print Services in Early Server Architectures

In the days of mainframes, an end user might work on a local copy of a given document, using a minicomputer, and then store the actual file remotely on a dedicated server or mainframe. That way, the client did most of the heavy lifting, and the mainframe or minicomputer could focus more narrowly on delivery of resources while also acting as a central repository for files and data.

It wasn't until the proliferation of personal computers—driven by the demands of a burgeoning marketplace—that the dedicated server role came to its full fruition. Though at some college campuses, research institutions, and computer manufacturers there may have been minicomputers or mainframes identified as servers (and truly playing that role) even in the 1960s, it wasn't until micro-computers became widely available in the late 1970s and early 1980s that real server-based computing got going. This led directly to the development of purpose-built computers designed to function as "network servers." Ultimately, for there to be "real servers" to deliver services, there also had to be "real clients" to demand them.

Although multiple candidates could probably vie for the title of "first network server," our research indicates that companies such as San Antonio–based Data General and Massachusetts-based Digital Equipment Corp. (also known as DEC, then as Digital) were the first companies to label their products as servers in the mid-1970s. Their initial offerings were based on typical minicomputers available at the time, and they were intended to meet price/performance needs beneath the cost and capability thresholds for mainframe computers that companies such as IBM, Sperry-Univac, Burroughs, and other "big iron" computer manufacturers offered to that market.

Over time, both Digital and Data General began to realize the value of centralizing data storage, print services, and ultimately applications, which led to widespread use of Digital PDPs and, later, VAX machines, as well as Data General Novas, MVs, and AViiOns as network servers for all kinds of uses. But all these machines started from the same basic hardware platforms and designs and were configured to include more-or-less the same kind of components. There really weren't any specific machines built exclusively for sale and use as network servers, even though many of these computers wound up playing such roles in the workplace, at colleges and research institutions, and in government facilities of all kinds.

Introduction of Specialized Servers

Originally, mainframe computers ran the gamut of operational tasks for any given organization, playing the nonspecific role of Jack-of-all-tasks. Like the hub of a wheel, a mainframe computer operated with dumb terminals acting as spokes (and users as the rim, to carry the analogy to its ultimate conclusion). As technological advancement progressed, operations saw improvements to the functional roles and functionality of existing mainframe designs. Specialization became a key design concept, with each monolithic mainframe built to deliver an even more narrowly defined and modular set of features and attributes.

On the other end of the spectrum, the workplace witnessed a profound proliferation of what came to be known as "departmental servers," as centralized functions and resources migrated closer to the individual workgroups responsible for specific organizational functions and the tasks related to their successful delivery. Because they serviced smaller groups of users who worked in smaller organizational units, these servers were perforce much smaller and less powerful than mainframes or mini-computers, but they were also much, much cheaper and therefore better suited to departmental budgets, staffing, and information processing needs. This decentralization of still somewhat centralized resources is arguably the prime impetus for network servers and all their attendant software, hardware, and peripherals as we know them today.

Consolidation of Cost and Functionality

Increasing demand for processing power and available resources, including memory capacity, storage volumes, and processors, has provoked a profound change in what describes a computer. From a precious few extremely expensive devices to a commodity present in nearly every home and office, a computer is well on its way to becoming just another building block for electronic devices, as well as a dedicated machine designed for desktop, workstation, or service roles. All these machines are also conveniently serviced by a supporting infrastructure that enables small, inexpensive servers to coexist smoothly with ultra-expensive (but far more modern) mainframes and supercomputers.

During 1970, Centronics introduced the first dot-matrix printer to the marketplace. Fast-forward a year later to the birth of the first 8-inch floppy drive, the first laser printer (developed at Xerox PARC), and a newfound file exchange service for networks: File Transfer Protocol (FTP). Then, in 1972, the compact disc (CD) was created in the United States, and interactive laser discs made their debut. Although Intel was first to market a microprocessor (the 4004) in 1971, it wasn't until a year or two later that the chip manufacturing giant produced the 8080, which defined a de facto standard that virtually all other microprocessors would follow to this very day.

In the wake of all these advancements, organizations began to see an upswing in the consolidation of computing resources as the cost of ownership reached more tolerable levels. Smaller- and medium-sized businesses found these emerging technologies more affordable, and as a result of their entry into the market, further stimulated the growth and development of better, faster, and more capable computing technologies of all kinds.

Introduction of High-Capacity RAM

Beginning in 1970, Intel produced the first high-capacity (1KB) dynamic random access memory (DRAM) solution. Hewlett-Packard introduced the HP-9800 series shortly thereafter, and these became the first commercially available computers to use such memory technology. Two short years later, Intel's PMOS DRAM IC design became the best-selling semiconductor chip on the market, surpassing magnetic core memory (a de facto standard during that period). Also in 1970, the Fairchild Corporation invented the first 256KB static random access memory (SRAM) chip.

These and other advancements started a sustained boom in the computing market and enabled the development of products better designed for small- to medium-sized business operations (and paralleled a change in equipment investments from "calculators" to "computers"). This in turn translated into vastly lower costs of ownership for computers and enhanced the development of all kinds of services and applications that promoted wider usability, greater flexibility, and rapid deployment. Scalability became the key to defining a central role in the workplace for emerging computing technologies, as the industry began to experience productivity growth and improving returns on technology investments.

The Importance of SCSI Technology

Hard disk drive improvements came by way of the conception of the small computer system interface (SCSI) protocol interface originally proposed in 1979. However, the standardization was also incredibly slow. The SCSI standard earned the approval of the American National Standards Institute in June 1986 (five years after being introduced to the X3T9.2 committee). By this time, however, the technology was already in widespread use.

Disk drive interfaces prior to SCSI were specialized components unique to particular systems, which did not lend themselves especially well to adaptability and scalability. In the world of big business, limited-capability controllers and devices were squeezed into an increasingly narrow installation base. As an interface with embedded device recognition and some level of data handling intelligence, SCSI was inherently aware of the devices attached to it, and it quickly supplanted its proprietary predecessors.

Since then, the SCSI specification has gone through several major overhauls and seen three major standards revisions. In the same year SCSI-1 was being actively developed, for example, the engineering groundwork for SCSI-2 standards were already well under way. With the addition of new command sets, wider data lines, smaller physical connectors, faster (synchronous) transfer rates, three distinct types of voltage signaling, and higher pin counts, SCSI quickly became a popular enterprise-level storage solution. You can learn more about the development and design of SCSI in Chapter 7, "The SCSI Bus."

For a long time, in fact, SCSI was the input/output (I/O) interface for storage devices of all kinds on network servers. Though personal computers went through several generations of Integrated Drive Electronics (IDE) and increased speed and capability with each succeeding one, it wasn't really until the mid-1990s that any other standard drive interfaces could compete with SCSI in terms of bandwidth, speed, or performance. That explains why SCSI completely dominated the server marketplace until 2000 or so. But SCSI has also always been considerably more expensive than consumer-oriented, lower-end interfaces. However, it continues to be used on servers where performance and reliability remain more important than price.

Also noteworthy is the official Internet SCSI (iSCSI) protocol specification, which defines a method of transacting block-level disk transfers using a TCP/IP based network. This effectively enables a given endpoint to contact a dedicated storage volume remotely and perform I/O transfers much like local disk access. Using the iSCSI protocol translates into better cost-effective centralization of storage without the added expense and cumbersome compatibility issues involved in deploying Fibre Channel equipment (typical of storage area networks).

The Development of RAID Technology

As the processor power quotient increased dramatically, the I/O subsystem needed to be beefed up in order to keep pace. Compelled by this and a growing need for high data reliability and availability, David A. Patterson led a development team of academic researchers at the University of California at Berkeley to devise what would arguably become the most valuable storage-preservation technique to date. Patterson's idea was to take a series of small, inexpensive desktop disk drives and form them in an array to provide higher I/O operations. The concept was known as a redundant array of inexpensive disks (RAID); it is covered in full detail in Chapter 11, "Disk Subsystems."

Coincidentally, IBM implemented much the same concept in its AS/400 series of minicomputers, except that IBM's concept was to mirror given data sets to provide fault-tolerant reliability. To minimize downtime—and the inconvenience of recovering lost data—IBM established a specification to provide duplication of data so that fewer operational interruptions would occur when hardware failure is imminent.

Various types of RAID configurations continue to see widespread usage in today's server world, and the technology has even become popular on the consumer front, as the latest motherboards now often support on-board ATA RAID solutions. Depending on what flavor of RAID is desired, the benefits can include improved data integrity, fault tolerance, data throughput, or storage capacity.

The Development of Standard Server Platforms

Rack-mounted server design addresses the issue of footprint. A rack-mounted case has designations such as 1U, 2U, 4U, and 42U, signifying the class and dimensions for a given application. There are 42 units total in a given rack, and each internal component must be carefully designed to fit into the tight clearances. (A 1U rack mount server stands only 1.75 inches tall.)

Compaq started this phenomenon in 1994 with the introduction of rack-mountable servers in its ProLiant product family. Other vendors quickly followed suit because the rack-mounted model worked so well for companies that typically deployed servers in equipment rooms or closets, where floor space is at a premium and machine density is therefore quite valuable. By 1998, most major PC and computer vendors (including Dell, IBM, Hewlett-Packard, and so forth) all had various rack-mounted server product offerings on the market. Ultimately, these would lead to the development of the blade server architecture, where servers on a card might maintain independent (but compact) power supplies and I/O ports, or they might instead plug in to a backplane for power, data communications, and peripherals access, thereby increasing server density further.

You can learn more about rack-mounted servers in Chapter 16, "Server Racks and Blades."

Increasing Server Sophistication, Availability, and Reliability

As servers began to assume more and more mission-critical information processing and handling roles in businesses, hardware manufacturers began to develop various ways to ensure maximum uptime and thereby increase server availability and reliability. This began at the I/O level, with the introduction of drive duplexing, where dual controller-disk drive chains could be mirrored so that a person could keep working even in the event of a drive or controller failure in either chain.

By the mid-1990s, servers with dual redundant power supplies were available, and companies such as Novell, Microsoft, and Vinca offered a variety of clever technology solutions to permit pairs or groups of servers to function in lock-step, so that if one server failed, the other server(s) would keep running, and services would continue unabated (though sometimes slowed down, especially when architectures with all components running nominally could distribute workloads and thereby deliver performance gains).

Machine clustering options extended this capability to groups of servers. By the year 2000, Microsoft and Novell offered various server clustering extensions to their network operating systems, and companies such as Hewlett-Packard, IBM, and Sun Microsystems also offered various hardware products with necessary software included to make turnkey clustering a reality. Today, it's not at all uncommon for clustered machines to serve high-traffic websites, transaction processing systems, and other high-demand, high-traffic applications. In some cases, elements of the same cluster may even be widely geographically dispersed so that a disaster or failure of an entire site does not compromise server availability.

The Development of Blade Servers

Blade servers are ultra-thin enterprise-level cases that can house one or multiple CPUs and massive quantities of memory. They're packed into tighter tolerances than typical 1U server designs, and each blade is hot-swappable, which means they can be used with servers that need to run high-availability applications. The most distinctive benefit of blade server deployment is the consolidation of resources: Storage and networking equipment is shoe-horned into a blade server chassis, which contains a single management interface. This paves the way for higher productivity and a better leveraged IT infrastructure.

The construction of a blade server is vastly different from the construction of a common rack-mountable server: Blades are more dense and compact, and key components (for example, power, networking, storage) are separate. Rack-mounted servers are generally self-contained, including power supply and drive storage (except for those that strictly use external storage volumes). Compaq is generally credited with the delivery of the first blade server products in 2000, but other players in this market (IBM, Dell, Hewlett-Packard, and others) all delivered similar products so soon after the first such offering appeared that they all must have had products in development during the same timeframe.

Today, blade servers are the preferred form factor for use in environments where high-traffic and high-demand applications and services are in use. No other approach permits as high a density of processing power in the same volume as a full-size blade server enclosure, fully populated with disk drives and other peripherals, as well as a complete complement of blade server cards. Nevertheless, standalone servers continue to be popular and widely used, particularly in small- to medium-sized businesses where high-cost, high-density blade server implementations may be overkill or too expensive to consider.

Emerging Server Hardware Trends

The following sections document several important server hardware trends that continue forward into the foreseeable future. A profound stratification of server types and capabilities is apparent, to be sure, but growth, investment, and interest in all types and strata appear strong well into the second decade of the 21st century.

Continuing Standalone Server Niches

To date, innumerable standalone devices silently and transparently work on behalf of business managers in ways that were previously only imaginable. Thanks to a healthy dose of embedded technologies, standalone servers crop up in the most unusual places, including satellite-connected retail outlets such as convenience stores and gas stations, electrical power substations, telephone company points of presence, and all kinds of networking devices, including network appliances, network attached storage servers, and so forth.

Typically, data backup servers are standalone devices in the common data center topology. There may also be a demilitarized zone for a given organization's network topology that defines single-purpose servers that provide access to their webserver, domain name services, Telnet and file transfer protocols, and others.

Parallel transaction schemes, redundant storage volumes, and multiway processing have become the modern market trend. With the advent of dual-core processors by AMD and Intel, the power once reserved for only the mightiest of enterprise solutions is now found on the desktop. RAID implementations are regular entries to the latest desktop motherboards. And dual-channel memory is nothing new to the contemporary PC.

Increasing Proliferation of Multiway Blades

Having established a strong foothold at the enterprise level, blade servers have seen a strong uptake as an alternative to the existing standard of rack-mounted servers. Midlevel and high-end deployments continue to leverage the cost-effective benefits of the blade design concept. Because they tend to create easily manageable, more efficient configurations, they lend themselves to a better IT experience.

High-Availability and Reliability Versus Cost and Transaction Speed

Network attached storage (NAS) has become a very viable and popular solution to centralizing organizational data so that it is accessible to all who need (and are authorized) to use it. Simple, pseudo-NAS devices might consist of simple bridging circuits that permit ATA-based drives to be accessible over Ethernet-based technologies. They lack the permissions capabilities and block-level data transfers of true NAS solutions, but they perform in much the same way.

However, sharing large data sets across a shared medium that is rate-limited to 10Mbps (Ethernet) can be time-consuming. Hence the adoption of Gigabit Ethernet (GigE) technologies that intimately couple storage capacity and expedient transmission rates (on the order of 100Mbps). GigE better suits high-demand enterprise environments where time-sensitive applications are at play.

Many Niches for Many Needs

Vendors such as Buffalo, D-Link, and Linksys all market devices known as media center extenders (MCEs) that arbitrate transactions between external storage archives and end-user applications. This allows a person to input video from a multitude of sources (for example, disk drives, coaxial cable,

HDTV antennas) and output it to local storage, without the assistance of a dedicated server box. This greatly simplifies the home-networking topology, which doesn't need to be a complicated mess of wires, protocols, and hardware. This class of transaction-based behavior easily typifies the client/server paradigm.

Smaller office environments, such as those at home, might contain print servers, a recent market entry that serves as a single point of access for printer resources for multiple endpoints. These small, single-purpose units relieve the network of the need for a dedicated machine (perhaps a gateway server) to operate full time in order to share a common resource among many users. Also from name-brand network equipment manufacturer Linksys is the Network Storage Link over USB 2.0 (NSLU2), which is a tiny MIPS-based core running Linux that conveniently makes USB-based storage media accessible over common Ethernet cabling.

A data center requires that mission-critical and sometimes customer-related data be backed up to some medium for potential recovery or rollback purposes. Such a data center might deploy a dedicated backup server attached to an uninterruptible power supply (UPS) and tied in to voluminous storage drives for archival purposes. This sort of modularization lends itself well to fault tolerance because a similar multipurpose server performing a myriad of duties, including backups, could wreak havoc in the event of failure. Instead, this provides a single point of failure, so that the network can continue to provide resources to its many end users and devices.

Currently, the market trend is heading toward parallelization. Dual-processor concepts have been alive and well used in the industry. Only recently has the proliferation of doubled-up devices, such as dual-core processors, dual-channel memory, and dual Ethernet, resulted in significant performance gains in contemporary applications. Eventually, more doubling up will be realized when processor core logic is able to arbitrate virtual parallelization, whereby one processor can simultaneously execute two separate operating systems.

From there, you can expect the tide to shift from software-based emulation into hardware-level emulation, relieving the system of unnecessary overhead and freeing up resources for other tasks. The advantages of utilizing this sort of technology are manifold, covering a wide and varied range of capability. As a simple example, a web farm may multiply its installation base by creating virtual servers that run FreeBSD, Linux, and Windows in tandem, without requiring rebooting into multiboot arrangements or deploying any of the various emulation packages for this purpose. Consolidating resources in this way goes a long way toward minimizing downtime and optimizing availability.

In the end, the client/server paradigm will continue to flourish, as will ad hoc peer-to-peer topologies, albeit transparently to the end user. Embedded technology is certainly the field to keep an eye on because right now that's where the most exciting new development occurs. It therefore becomes increasingly less obvious what devices constitute server hardware, as the concept of server hardware begins to blur into an even broader range of possibilities and implementations. The rest of this book concentrates on real hardware, with the greatest emphasis on systems and solutions in active use today.

CHAPTER 2

Server
Microprocessors

Server processors can be divided into three major categories:

- **CISC-based processors**—CISC (complex instruction set computer) is a processor architecture used by x86 processors such as the Xeon, Opteron, and other server and desktop processors manufactured by Intel, AMD, and other vendors. It uses variable-length instructions.

- **RISC-based processors**—RISC (reduced instruction set computer) uses a smaller number of instructions than CISC to improve processor efficiency. Server processors such as the PowerPC, Power Architecture, PA-RISC family, MIPS, Alpha, and Sun SPARC are RISC based.

- **EPIC-based processors**—EPIC (explicitly parallel instruction computer) groups instructions together into very long instruction words (VLIW), preloads the instructions most likely to be used next, and uses a technique called *predication* to run all possible code branches in parallel and discard those that are not needed, as opposed to branch prediction (used in CISC processors). Intel's Itanium server processors are EPIC based.

▶▶ Sun SPARC processors and other unique features of the Sun SPARC server platform are discussed in detail in Chapter 19, "Sun Microsystems Servers."

If you are planning to purchase a preconfigured server, you can choose from products in any of the listed categories. A bit less than half of the servers on the market fall into the "Wintel" (Intel/Intel-compatible hardware running Windows) category. Many users prefer other server platforms. Which category should you choose? Here are some considerations:

- **Lowest initial cost**—x86-based servers, because they closely resemble x86 desktop computers in general design (and often use the same components), are the least expensive to purchase and to customize.

- **Scalability**—If you need one to eight processors in a single server, any processor category can foot the bill. However, if you need a larger number of processors, you should consider a server based on RISC or EPIC technologies.

- **Operating system support**—The server operating system you prefer will have a major influence on your choice of server processor. If you prefer Linux, you can choose a platform based on virtually any current or recent server processor. However, if you prefer a different server operating system, your choices are more limited. With x86 processors, you can choose from various versions of Windows 2000 Server or Windows Server 2003, popular Linux server and enterprise-level distributions, and Sun Solaris. Itanium processors can run 64-bit versions of Windows Server 2003 and Linux. Sun SPARC processors can run Linux or Solaris. PowerPC servers from Apple can run MacOS X or Linux, while PowerPC and Power architecture servers from IBM can run Linux or AIX 5L, a proprietary version of UNIX. Hewlett-Packard PA-RISC–based Hewlett-Packard 9000 series servers use HP-UX, a proprietary version of UNIX. Hewlett-Packard AlphaServers run OpenVMS, Tru64 UNIX, or Linux.

If you are planning to "roll your own" server from motherboards and other off-the-shelf components, you can choose from processors made by Intel (Itanium 2, Xeon, Pentium D, or Pentium 4) or by AMD (Opteron). If you decide to build your own server, you will be responsible for configuring and supporting it. Thus, the biggest emphasis in this chapter is on helping you understand the features of these and earlier server-compatible x86 and Itanium processors, how they differ from each other, and the tasks each is most suited for.

This chapter also discusses the features of current RISC processors on the market from vendors other than Sun (whose products are covered in Chapter 19). If you prefer to purchase a preconfigured server, you should read this chapter and Chapter 19 to understand the differences between x86, EPIC, and RISC-based solutions. Whether you are working with an existing server or planning to build or purchase a new server, the details in these chapters will help you select, configure, and troubleshoot your system.

Server Processor Overview

The following tables provide you with a quick overview of the processor families that are considered in this chapter: Intel, AMD, Alpha, PA-RISC, MIPS, PowerPC, and Power.

Note

The Alpha, PA-RISC, and MIPS processor lines are in the process of being phased out by their respective manufacturers. However, they will continue to be available at least through 2006, and existing systems will likely require support for several years to come.

Table 2.1 lists the major specifications of Intel processors that have been used as server processors, starting with the Intel Pentium Pro. Table 2.1 includes both processors originally designed as desktop processors and those designed as server processors. Because Intel uses the same brand name for processors with distinctly different features, the code name used to refer to a particular server processor's core design is provided in parentheses.

Note

Table 2.1 excludes the 8088 through 80486 and Pentium processors, none of which are likely to be encountered today. It also excludes laptop-specific CPUs (such as the Pentium M) and the Intel Celeron family of low-cost and reduced-cache versions of the Pentium, Pentium II, Pentium III, and Pentium 4 processor families; the Celeron family is marketed exclusively as a desktop processor and is thus not likely to be encountered in a server.

Table 2.2 lists the AMD processors, starting with the AMD Athlon MP, that have been used in servers. As with Table 2.1, the core design is listed in parentheses in the Processor column.

Note

Table 2.2 omits the Pentium-equivalent K5 and K6 families; laptop-specific versions of all CPUs; the Duron and Sempron families, which are lower-performance, low-cost versions of the Athlon; and the Athlon XP and Athlon 64 processors, which are sold strictly as desktop processors.

Note

Note in Table 2.1 that the Pentium Pro processor includes 256KB, 512KB, or 1MB of full-core-speed L2 cache in a separate die within the chip. The earlier Pentium II/III processors include 512KB of half-core-speed L2 cache on the processor card. Pentium II PE and Pentium IIIE and IIIB processors include full-core-speed L2 cache integrated directly within the processor die. The later Pentium 4A includes 512KB of on-die full-core-speed L2 cache.

The transistor count figures in Table 2.1 do not include the external (off-die) 256KB, 512KB, 1MB, or 2MB L2 cache built in to the Pentium Pro, Pentium II/III, or PII/PIII Xeon, or the L3 cache in the Itanium. The external L2 cache in those processors contains an additional 15.5 million (256KB), 31 million (512KB), 62 million (1MB), or 124 million (2MB) transistors in separate chips, whereas the external 2MB or 4MB of L3 cache in the Itanium includes up to 300 million transistors.

Table 2.3 lists the major features of Alpha processors used in servers from 1996 to the present.

Table 2.1   Intel Server Processor Specifications

Processor	SMP Support[1]	Dual-Core	Process (Micron)	Clock Multiplier	Clock Speeds	Voltage	Internal Register Size
Pentium Pro	Yes	No	0.35	2x+	150–200MHz	3.3V	32-bit
Pentium II (Klamath)	Yes	No	0.35	3.5x+	233–300MHz	2.8V	32-bit
Pentium II (Deschutes)	Yes	No	0.35	3.5x+	266MHz–450MHz	2.0V	32-bit
Pentium II Xeon (Deschutes)	Yes	No	0.25	4x+	400–450MHz	2.8V	32-bit
Pentium III (Katmai)	Yes	No	0.25	4x+	600MHz	2.0V–2.05V	32-bit
Pentium III Xeon (Tanner)	Yes	No	0.25	5x+	500–550MHz	2.0V	32-bit
Pentium III (Coppermine)	Yes	No	0.18	4x+	1.133GHz	1.6V–1.75V	32-bit
Pentium IIIE Xeon (Cascades)	Yes	No	0.18	4.5x+	600–1GHz	1.65V	32-bit
Pentium III (Tualatin)	Yes	No	0.13	8.5x+	1.4GHz	1.45V	32-bit
Pentium 4 (Willamette)	No	No	0.18	3x+	2GHz	1.7V	32-bit
Xeon DP, MP (Foster)	Yes	No	0.18	3.5x+	1.4–2GHz	1.75V	32-bit
Pentium 4A (Northwood)	No	No	0.13	4x+	3.4GHZ	1.3V	32-bit
Xeon DP (Prestonia)	Yes	No	0.13	4.5x+	1.6–3.066GHz	1.5V	32-bit
Pentium 4EE (Prestonia)	No	No	0.13	8x+	3.73GHz	1.5V	32-bit
Pentium 4E (Prescott)	No	No	0.09	8x+	3.8GHz	1.3V	32-bit, 64-bit
Xeon MP (Gallatin)	Yes	No	0.13	3.75+	3.066–3.2GHz	1.475V, 1.5V	32-bit
Xeon DP (Nocona)	Yes	No	0.09	3.5x+	3.0–3.6GHz	1.25V–1.4V	64-bit
Xeon DP (Irwindale)	Yes	No	0.09	3.5x+	3.0–3.6GHz	1.25V–1.4V	64-bit
Pentium D (Smithfield)	No	Yes	0.09	3.5x+	3.2GHz	1.25V–1.4V	32-bit, 64-bit
Pentium EE (Glenwood)	No	Yes	0.09	4x	3.46GHz	1.25V–1.4V	32-bit, 64-bit
Xeon MP (Paxville)	Yes	Yes	0.09	3.5x	2.667–3GHz	1.25V–1.4V	32-bit, 64-bit
Itanium (Merced)	Yes	No	0.18	3x+	800MHz	1.6V	64-bit
Itanium 2 (McKinley)	Yes	No	0.18	3x+	1GHz	1.6V	64-bit
Itanium 2 (Madison)	Yes	No	0.13	3x+	1.67GHz	1.6V	64-bit

[1]*Key: FPU = floating-point unit (internal math coprocessor); WT = Write-Through cache (caches reads only); WB = Write-Back cache (caches both reads and writes); M = millions; Bus = processor external bus speed (motherboard speed); Core = Processor internal core speed (CPU speed); typically on-die; MMX = multimedia extensions (57 additional instructions for graphics and sound processing); 3DNow! = MMX plus 21 additional instructions for graphics and sound processing; Enh. 3DNow! = 3DNow! plus 24 additional instructions for graphics and sound processing; 3DNow! Pro = Enh. 3DNow! plus SSE instructions for graphics and sound processing; SSE = Streaming SIMD (single instruction multiple data) Extensions (MMX plus 70 additional instructions for graphics and sound processing); and SSE2 = Streaming SIMD Extensions 2 (SSE plus 144 additional instructions for graphics and sound processing); SMP = supports symmetric multi-processing (two or more processors).*

[2]*L2 cache runs at full-core speed but is contained in a separate chip die.*

Data Bus Width	Max. Memory	L1 Cache	L2 Cache	L3 Cache	Cache Speed	L2/L3 Multimedia Instructions	No. of Transistors	Date Introduced
64-bit	64GB	2×8KB	256KB, 512KB, 1MB	—	Core^2	—	5.5 million	Nov. 1995
64-bit	64GB	2×16KB	512KB	—	1/2 core	MMX	7.5 million	May 1997
64-bit	64GB	2×16KB	512KB	—	1/2 core	MMX	7.5 million	May 1997
64-bit	64GB	2×16KB	512KB, 1MB, 2MB	—	Core^2	MMX	7.5 million	June 1998
64-bit	64GB	2×16KB	512KB	—	1/2 core	SSE	9.5 million	Feb. 1999
64-bit	64GB	2×16KB	512KB, 1MB, 2MB	—	Core^2	SSE	9.5 million	Mar. 1999
64-bit	64GB	2×16KB	256KB	—	Core	SSE	28.1 million	Oct. 1999
64-bit	64GB	2×16KB	256KB, 1MB, 2MB	—	Core	SSE	28.1 million, 84 million, 140 million	Oct. 1999, May 2000
64-bit	64GB	2×16KB	512KB	—	Core	SSE	44 million	June 2001
64-bit	64GB	12+8KB	256KB	—	Core	SSE2	42 million	Nov. 2000
64-bit	64GB	12+8KB	256KB, 512KB, 1024KB	—	Core	SSE2	42 million	May 2001
64-bit	64GB	12+8KB	512KB	—	Core	SSE2	55 million	Jan. 2002
64-bit	64GB	12+8KB	512KB	0MB, 1MB, 2MB	Core	SSE2	169 million	Jan. 2002
64-bit	64GB	12+8KB	512KB	2GB	Core	SSE2	178 million	Nov. 2003
64-bit	64GB	12+16KB	1MB	—	Core	SSE3	125 million	Feb. 2004
64-bit	64GB	12+8KB	512MB	0MB, 1MB, 2MB, 4MB	Core	SSE2	178 million	Nov. 2002
64-bit	64GB	12+16KB	512MB, 1MB	1MB	Core	SSE3	125 million	Jun. 2004
64-bit	64GB	12+16KB	512MB, 1MB	2MB	Core	SSE3	169 million	Feb. 2005
64-bit	64GB	12+16KB (×2)	1MB (×2)	—	Core	SSE3	250 million	Apr. 2005
64-bit	64GB	12+16KB (×2)	1MB (×2)	—	Core	SSE3	250 million	Apr. 2005
64-bit	64GB	12+16KB (×2)	2MB (×2)	—	Core	SSE3	200 million	Oct. 2005
64-bit	16TB	2×16KB	96KB^2	2MB, 4MB	Core	MMX	25 million	May 2001
128-bit	16TB	2×16KB	256KB	1.5MB, 3MB	Core	MMX	221 million	July 2002
128-bit	16TB	2×16KB	256KB	1.5MB, 6MB	Core	MMX	410 million	June 2003

Table 2.2   AMD Server Processor Specifications

Processor	SMP Support[1]	Process (Micron)	Clock Multiplier	Maximum Clock Speeds	Voltage	Internal Register Size	Data Bus Width
AMD Athlon MP (Palomino)	Yes	0.18	5x+	1.733GHz	1.5V–1.8V	32-bit	64-bit
AMD Athlon MP (Thoroughbred)	Yes	0.13	5x+	2.133GHz	1.5V–1.8V	32-bit	64-bit
AMD Athlon MP (Barton)	Yes	0.13	5.5x+	2.133GHz	1.65V	32-bit	64-bit
AMD Opteron (SledgeHammer)	Yes	0.13	3.5x+	1.4–2.4GHz	1.55V	64-bit	128-bit
AMD Opteron 1xx (Venus)	No	0.09	3.5x+	1.8–2.8GHz	1.35–1.4V	64-bit	128-bit
AMD Opteron 2xx (Troy)	Yes	0.09	3.5x+	1.8–2.8GHz	1.35V	64-bit	128-bit
AMD Opteron 3xx (Athens)	Yes	0.09	3.5x+	1.8–2.8GHz	1.35V	64-bit	128-bit
AMD Opteron 1xx dual-core (Denmark)	No	0.09	3.5x+	1.6–2.4GHz	1.35V	64-bit	128-bit
AMD Opteron 2xx dual-core (Italy)	Yes	0.09	3.5x+	1.6–2.4GHz	1.35V	64-bit	128-bit
AMD Opteron 8xx dual-core (Egypt)	Yes	0.09	3.5x+	1.6–2.4GHz	1.35V	64-bit	128-bit

[1]Key: FPU = floating-point unit (internal math coprocessor); WT = Write-Through cache (caches reads only); WB = Write-Back cache (caches both reads and writes); M = millions; Bus = processor external bus speed (motherboard speed); Core = Processor internal core speed (CPU speed); typically on-die; MMX = multimedia extensions (57 additional instructions for graphics and sound processing; 3DNow! = MMX plus 21 additional instructions for graphics and sound processing; Enh. 3DNow! = 3DNow! plus 24 additional instructions for graphics and sound processing; 3DNow! Pro = Enh. 3DNow! plus SSE instructions for graphics and sound processing; SSE = Streaming SIMD (single instruction multiple data) Extensions (MMX plus 70 additional instructions for graphics and sound processing); and SSE2 = Streaming SIMD Extensions 2 (SSE plus 144 additional instructions for graphics and sound processing); SMP = supports symmetric multiprocessing (two or more processors).*

Table 2.3   Specifications of Alpha Server Processors, 1996–Present

Processor	Multiprocessor Support	Clock Speed	Internal Register Size	Data Bus Width	Max. Memory	L1 Cache
Alpha 21164 (EV-5)[1]	Yes	366–600MHz	64-bit	128-bit	1TB	8KB-Instructions, 8KB-Data
Alpha 21264 (EV-6)[1]	Yes	466–575MHz	64-bit	64-bit	16TB	128KB
Alpha 21264A (EV-67)[2] (.25 micron)	Yes	600–833MHz	64-bit	64-bit	16TB	128KB
Alpha 21264B (EV-68C)[3]	Yes	833MHz	64-bit	64-bit	16TB	128KB
Alpha 21264C (EV68CD)[3]	Yes	1–1.25GHz	64-bit	64-bit	16TB	128KB
Alpha 21364 (EV-7 series)[3]	Yes	1.1–1.3GHz	64-bit	64-bit	16TB	128KB

[1]These processors were built using .35-micron process technology.

[2]This processor was built using .25-micron process technology.

[3]These processors were built .18-micron process technology.

Table 2.4 lists the specifications for PA-RISC 8xxx-series server processors from 1996 to the present.

Max. Memory	L1 Cache	L2 Cache	L3 Cache	L2/L3 Cache Speed	Multimedia Instructions	No. of Transistors	Date Introduced
4GB	2×64KB	256KB	—	Core	3DNow! Pro	37.5 million	June 2001
4GB	2×64KB	256KB	—	Core	3DNow! Pro	37.2 million	Aug. 2002
4GB	2×64KB	512KB	—	Core	3DNow! Pro	54.3 million	May. 2003
1TB	2×64KB	1MB	—	Core	3DNow! Pro	105.9 million	Apr. 2003
1TB	2×64KB	1MB	—	Core	SSE3	105.9 million	May. 2004
1TB	2×64KB	1MB	—	Core	SSE3	105.9 million	May. 2004
1TB	2×64KB	1MB	—	Core	SSE3	105.9 million	May. 2004
1TB	2×64KB (×2)	1MB (×2)	—	Core	SSE3	233.2 million	Apr. 2005
1TB	2×64KB (×2)	1MB (×2)	—	Core	SSE3	233.2 million	Apr. 2005
1TB	2×64KB (×2)	1MB (×2)	—	Core	SSE3	233.2 million	Apr. 2005

L2 Cache	L3 Cache	No. of Transistors	Date Introduced
96KB	1MB to 64MB off-die	9.6 million	1996
Off-chip	—	15.2 million	1998
Off-chip	—	15.2 million	1999
Off-chip	—	15.2 million	2001
Off-chip	—	15.2 million	2001
1.75MB	—	100 million	2002

Table 2.4   Specifications of PA-RISC 8xxx Server Processors, 1996–Present

Processor	PA-RISC Version	Multi-processor Support	Maximum Clock Speed	Internal Register Size	Data Bus Width
PA-8000[1] (Onyx)	2.0	Yes	230MHz	64-bit	64-bit
PA-8200[1] (Vulcan)	2.0	Yes	300MHz	64-bit	64-bit
PA-8500[2] (Vulcan)	2.0	Yes	440MHz	64-bit	64-bit
PA-8600[2] (Landshark)	2.0	Yes	550MHz	64-bit	64-bit
PA-8700[3] (Piranha)	2.0	Yes	875MHz	64-bit	64-bit
PA-8800[4,5]	2.0	Yes	1GHz	64-bit	64-bit
PA-8900[4,5]	2.0	Yes	1.1GHz	64-bit	64-bit

[1]*These processors were built using .50-micron process technology.*
[2]*This processor was built using .25-micron process technology.*
[3]*These processors were built using .18-micron process technology.*
[4]*These processors were built using .13-micron silicon-on-insulator (SOI) process technology.*
[5]*Dual-core processor.*

Table 2.5 lists the specifications for MIPS server processors from 1994 to the present.

Table 2.5   Specifications of MIPS Server Processors, 1994–Present

Processor	Multi-processor Support	Maximum Clock Speed	Internal Register Size	Data Bus Width	Max. Memory
R10000[1]	Yes	250MHz	64-bit	64-bit	16GB
R12000[2]	Yes	400MHz	64-bit	64-bit	16GB
R14000[3]	Yes	600MHz	64-bit	64-bit	16GB
R16000[3]	Yes	700MHz	64-bit	64-bit	16GB

[1]*This processor was built using .35-micron process technology.*
[2]*This processor was built using .25-micron process technology.*
[3]*These processors were built using .13-micron process technology.*

IBM's line of Power architecture processors for the RS/6000 and p5 server lines provided the basis for the PowerPC series of processors. Table 2.6 lists the specifications for Power Architecture server processors from 1996 to the present.

Max. Memory	Max. L1 Cache	L2 Cache	No. of Transistors	Date Introduced
1TB	1MB off-chip	—	3.8 million	1996
1TB	4MB off-chip	—	3.8 million	1997
1TB	1.5MB	—	140 million	1998
1TB	1.5MB	—	140 million	1999
16TB	2.25MB	—	186 million	2001
16TB	3MB	32MB off-chip	300 million	2002
16TB	3MB	64MB off-chip	317 million	2005

L1 Cache	L2 Cache (off-chip)	No. of Transistors	Date Introduced
64KB	1–2MB	6.8 million	1994
64KB	1–8MB	6.8 million	1998
64KB	4–16MB	7.2 million	2001
64KB	4–16MB	7.2 million	2002

Table 2.6   Specifications of Power Architecture Processors, 1996–Present

Processor	Multi-processor Support	Clock Speeds	Internal Register Size	Data Bus Width	Max. Memory
Power2 SuperChip[1]	Yes	160MHz	32-bit	32-bit	4GB
Power3	Yes	200MHz	64-bit	64-bit	512GB
Power3-II[2]	Yes	375–450Hz	64-bit	64-bit	512GB
Power4 (dual-core)[3]	Yes	1.0–1.3GHz	64-bit	64-bit	256GB
Power4+[4] (dual-core)	Yes	1.2–1.7GHz	64-bit	64-bit	256GB
Power5[4] (dual-core)	Yes	1.4–1.65GHz	64-bit	64-bit	2TB
Power5+[5] (dual-core)	Yes	1.9GHz	64-bit	64-bit	2TB

[1]*Power2 was originally an eight-chip assembly.*
[2]*This processor was built using .25-micron process technology.*
[3]*This processor was built using .18-micron silicon-on-insulator (SOI) process technology.*
[4]*These processors were built using .13-micron SOI process technology.*
[5]*This processor was built using .09-micron SOI process technology.*

Table 2.7 lists the specifications for PowerPC server processors from 1995 to the present.

Note

PowerPC processors not listed are designed for use in desktop or notebook computers.

Table 2.7   Specifications of PowerPC Server Processors, 1995–Present

Processor	Multi-processor Support	Clock Speeds	Internal Register Size	Data Bus Width	Max. Memory
PowerPC 604	Yes	100–180MHz	32-bit	64-bit	4GB
PowerPC 604e	Yes	166–350MHz	32-bit	64-bit	4GB
PowerPC 740 G3 (.25 micron)	Yes	200–433MHz	32-bit	64-bit	4GB
PowerPC 750 G3 (.22 micron)	Yes	200–466MHz	32-bit	64-bit	4GB
PowerPC 750CX (SideWinder) (.18 micron)	Yes	350–550MHz	32-bit	64-bit	4GB
PowerPC 750CXe (Anaconda) (.18 micron)	Yes	400–700MHz	32-bit	64-bit	4GB
PowerPC 750FX (G3 series) (.13 micron SOI)	Yes	600–800MHz	32-bit	64-bit	4GB
PowerPC 750GX (.13 micron SOI)	Yes	800MHz–1GHz	32-bit	64-bit	4GB
PowerPC G4 7400 (.20 micron)	Yes	350–500MHz	32-bit	64-bit	4GB
PowerPC G4 7410	Yes	533MHz	32-bit	64-bit	4GB
PowerPC G4 7450	Yes	533–800MHz	32-bit	64-bit	4GB
PowerPC G4 7455	Yes	800–1.33MHz	32-bit	64-bit	4GB
PowerPC 970 (G5) 0.13 micron SOI	Yes	1.6–1.8GHz	64-bit	64-bit	4TB
PowerPC 970FX (0.09 micron)	Yes	1.4–2.7GHz	64-bit	64-bit	4TB
PowerPC 970MP (0.09 micron) (dual-core)	Yes	1.4–2.5GHz	64-bit	64-bit	4TB

L1 Cache	L2 Cache	L3 Cache	No. of Transistors	Date Introduced
160KB	Off-chip	—	15 million	1996
96KB	Off-chip	—	15 million	1998
96KB	Off-chip	—	15 million	2000
96KB	1.5MB	—	174 million	2001
96KB	1.5MB	—	184 million	2003
96KB	1.92MB	—	276 million	2003
96KB	1.92MB	—	276 million	2005

L1 Cache	L2 Cache	L3 Cache	No. of Transistors	Date Introduced
32KB	Off-chip	—	3.6 million	1995
64KB	Off-chip	—	3.6 million	1997
64KB	Off-chip	—	6.35 million	1997
64KB	Off-chip	—	6.35 million	1997
64KB	256KB	—	21.5 million	2000
64KB	256KB	—	21.5 million	2001
64KB	512KB	—	39 million	2002
64KB	1024KB	—	44 million	2004
64KB	Off-chip	—	10.5 million	1999
64KB	Off-chip	—	10.5 million	2001
64KB	256KB	—	10.5 million	2001
64KB	256KB	—	10.5 million	2002
64KB	512KB	—	52 million	2003
96KB	512KB	—	58 million	2004
96KB	1024KB	—	116 million	2005

▶▶   For an overview of Sun SPARC processors, see Table 19.1, p. 787.

▶▶   For additional information about Alpha, PA-RISC, MIPS, Power Architecture, and PowerPC processors, see "RISC-Based Server Processors," p. 130.

Server Processor Specifications

Server processors, like all other processors, can be identified by two main parameters: how wide their data path is and how fast they are. The speed of a processor is a fairly simple concept. Speed is counted in megahertz (MHz) and gigahertz (GHz), which means millions and billions, respectively, of cycles per second—and faster is better. The width of a processor is a little more complicated to discuss because three main specifications in a processor are expressed in width:

- Data I/O bus
- Address bus
- Internal registers

Note that the processor side bus (PSB) is also called the front-side bus (FSB) or CPU bus. These terms all refer to the bus that is between the CPU and the main chipset component (North Bridge or memory controller hub [MCH]). Intel uses the FSB or PSB terminology, whereas AMD uses only FSB. CPU bus is the least confusing of the terms, and it is also completely accurate.

Generally speaking, the speed of a processor can be determined by two factors:

- The internal clock speed of the processor
- The speed of the CPU bus

In terms of clock speed, the fastest server processors from each manufacturer listed in Tables 2.1–2.7 and in Chapter 19 include the following in order, from highest to lowest clock speed:

- **Intel Pentium 4**—3.8GHz (single-core)
- **Intel Pentium D, Pentium Extreme Edition**—3.2GHz (dual-core)
- **AMD Opteron 854/254/154**—2.8GHz (single-core)
- **PowerPC 970MP/G5**—2.5GHz(dual-core)
- **AMD Opteron 880/280/180**—2.4GHz (dual-core)
- **PA-8900**—2.0GHz (dual-core)
- **IBM Power5+**—1.9GHz (dual-core)
- **Sun UltraSPARC III**—1.593GHz
- **Sun UltraSPARC IV**—1.35GHz (dual-core)
- **Alpha 21364**—1.3GHz
- **MIPS R16000**—700MHz

Clock speed figures by themselves can be very misleading. Other factors, including chip architecture, the size of the address bus, single or dual-core design, the presence and size of L2 (and L3) memory cache, the speed of the processor bus, the number of processors installed, and whether the system is using SMP or NUMA multiprocessing also affect server performance.

Dual-core designs, which have become very common in the past few years, provide a huge benefit to servers because they provide virtually every benefit of multiple processors, even if the server has room for only one processor. They enable servers to handle more programs and execution threads without slowing down. For example, a single-processor server using a dual-core processor can handle multitasking almost as well as a dual-processor server. A two-way (dual-processor) server becomes the virtual equivalent of a four-way server if dual-core processors are used, and so forth. Although most dual-core processors are slightly lower in clock speed than single-core processors from the same family because of thermal issues, the increased workload, especially in server-oriented tasks, makes a dual-core processor worthwhile.

Other portions of the server design, such as system memory speeds and sizes, the speed and interfaces used for network adapters and hard disks, and the operating system used, also affect the actual throughput of a particular server.

Because a server provides services to client devices, a server's performance is measured by metrics such as the number of simultaneous clients that can be serviced and the speed at which each client receives information.

▶▶ For more information about server benchmarking, see Chapter 21, "Server Testing and Maintenance."

How can you determine what processor is installed in a server? If the server is using Windows 2000 Server or Windows Server 2003, you can use SiSoftware Sandra (available from www.sisoftware.co.uk) to determine the processor model, speed, and other information about your system, whether it is running an x86, Alpha, or Itanium processor.

To determine basic 64-bit or 32-bit compatibility with Linux or UNIX (RISC) platforms, you can use various command-line options, including the following:

- `getconf` or `file` (IBM-AIX)
- `isainfo` or `uname` (Sun Solaris)
- `uname` (Linux)

With a MacOS server, you select Apple, About This Mac.

Tip

To learn more about these commands, see the STATA FAQs "How Can I determine if my computer/OS is 64-bit?" page, at www.stata.com/support/faqs/win/64bit.html.

For more detailed information about the processor(s) in your RISC-based server, contact your hardware vendor.

The Data I/O Bus

Perhaps the most important features of a processor are the speed and width of its external data bus. This defines the rate at which data can be moved into or out of the processor, also called the *throughput*.

The processor bus discussed most often is the external data bus—the bundle of wires (or pins) used to send and receive data. The more signals that can be sent at the same time, the more data that can be transmitted in a specified interval and, therefore, the faster (and wider) the bus. Having a wider data bus is like having a highway with more lanes, which enables greater throughput. Servers that work with large databases benefit the most from wide data buses.

Data in a computer is sent as digital information consisting of a time interval in which a single wire carries a specified voltage to signal a 1 data bit or 0V to signal a 0 data bit. The more wires you have, the more individual bits you can send in the same time interval. A good way to understand this flow of information is to consider a highway and the traffic it carries. If a highway has only one lane for each direction of travel, only one car at a time can move in a certain direction. To increase traffic flow, you can add another lane in each direction so that twice as many cars pass in a specified time. You can think of an 8-bit chip as being a single-lane highway because 1 byte flows through at a time. (1 byte equals 8 individual bits.) The 16-bit chip, with 2 bytes flowing at a time, resembles a two-lane highway. You might have four lanes in each direction to move a large number of automobiles; this structure corresponds to a 32-bit data bus, which has the capability to move 4 bytes of information at a time. Taking this further, a 64-bit data bus is like an 8-lane highway moving data in and out of the chip.

All current server processors feature 64-bit (8 bytes wide) data buses. Therefore, they can transfer 64 bits of data at a time to and from the motherboard chipset or system memory.

The Address Bus

The address bus is the set of wires that carries the addressing information used to describe the memory location to which the data is being sent or from which the data is being retrieved. As with the data bus, each wire in an address bus carries a single bit of information. This single bit is a single digit in the address. The more wires (digits) used in calculating these addresses, the greater the total number of address locations. The size (or width) of the address bus indicates the maximum amount of RAM a chip can address.

Figure 2.1 shows how the data, address, and control buses relate to each other.

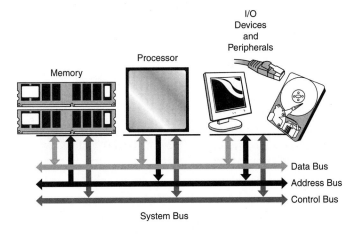

Figure 2.1   How data, address, and control buses connect the processor, memory, and I/O components of a server.

The earlier highway analogy (from the section "The Data I/O Bus") can be used to show how the address bus fits in. If the data bus is the highway, and the size of the data bus is equivalent to the number of lanes, the address bus relates to the house number or street address. The size of the address bus is equivalent to the number of digits in the house address number. For example, if you live on a street in which the address is limited to a two-digit (base 10) number, no more than 100, or 10^2, distinct addresses (00–99) can exist for that street. Add another digit, and the number of available addresses increases to 1,000 (000–999), or 10^3.

Computers use the binary (base 2) numbering system, so a two-digit number provides only four unique addresses (00, 01, 10, and 11), calculated as 2^2. A three-digit number provides only eight addresses (000–111), which is 2^3. For example, Pentium 4 processors use a 36-bit address bus that calculates as a maximum of 2^{36}, or 68,719,476,736 bytes (36GB), address locations. Table 2.8 describes the physical memory-addressing capabilities of server processors.

Table 2.8   Server Processor Memory-Addressing Capabilities

Processor Family	Address Bus	Bytes	Kilobytes (KB)	Megabytes (MB)	Gigabytes (GB)	Terabytes (TB)
Pentium, PowerPC 604 series, 7xx, 74xx series; Sun UltraSPARC II series	32-bit	4,294,967,296	4,194,304	4,096	4	—
Pentium Pro, Pentium II/Xeon, Pentium III/Xeon, Pentium 4, Xeon; Athlon MP	36-bit	68,719,476,736	67,108,864	65,536	64	—
Opteron; Alpha 21164; PA-8000–8600	40-bit	1,099,511,627,776	1,073,741,824	1,048,576	1024	1
PowerPC 970/G5 series	42-bit	4,398,046,511,104	4,294,967,296	4,194,304	4096	4
Itanium family; Alpha 21264, Alpha 21364; PA-8700–8900; R1xxxx series; UltraSPARC III, UltraSPARC IV	44-bit	17,592,186,044,416	17,179,869,184	16,777,216	16,384	16

The width of the data bus and the size of the address bus are not dependent on each other, and chip designers can use whatever size they want for each. Usually, however, chips with larger data buses have larger address buses. The sizes of the buses can provide important information about a chip's relative power, measured in two ways: The size of the data bus is an indication of the chip's information-moving capability, and the size of the address bus tells how much memory the chip can handle.

As you can see from Table 2.8, more recent server processors generally have larger address buses than older processors. Larger address buses are critical for servers that must handle very large amounts of data, particularly when working with 64-bit operating systems and extremely large data sets. While 32-bit operating systems cannot directly address more than 4GB of RAM in most situations, 64-bit operating systems can address 1TB or more RAM.

Internal Registers

The size of the internal registers indicates how much information the processor can operate on at one time and how it moves data around internally within the chip. This is sometimes also referred to as the *internal data bus*, to distinguish it from the external data bus, which connects the processor to memory. A *register* is a holding cell within the processor; for example, the processor can add numbers in two different registers, storing the result in a third register. The register size determines the size of data on which the processor can operate. The register size also describes the type of software or commands and instructions a chip can run.

As described in the following sections, server processors fall into two categories: those with 32-bit registers and those with 64-bit registers.

32-Bit Processors

Internal registers are often twice the size of the external data bus, which means the chip requires two cycles to fill a register before the register can be operated on. Server processors with a 32-bit register size and 64-bit data bus, such as the Pentium Pro and its many descendents, up through most versions of the Pentium 4 and the AMD Athlon MP, use this design.

To enable the data to be processed efficiently, most 32-bit processors use multiple 32-bit pipelines for processing information. (A *pipeline* is the section of a processor that performs calculations on data.) As a result, recent processors can perform six or more operations per clock cycle.

Although 32-bit processors have reached very high clock speeds and process information efficiently, their biggest drawback is the 4GB limit on directly addressable memory.

Note

As Table 2.8 indicates, many Intel processors use a 36-bit address bus, which translates into 64GB of addressable memory. However, most processors with a 36-bit address bus have 32-bit register sizes, which limits addressable memory to 4GB. How can a 32-bit server support more than 4GB of RAM? Windows 2000 Advanced Server and Windows Server 2003 Enterprise Edition include a translation feature called Physical Address Extension (PAE), which enables the memory above 4GB to be accessed in 4GB blocks up to 16GB. To access memory above 16GB, some database applications such as SQL Server and Oracle use special APIs called Address Windowing Extensions. These workarounds are not necessary with processors that have 64-bit registers.

64-Bit Processors

Processors with a 64-bit register size can work with programs and data that exceed the 4GB limit imposed by 32-bit architecture. Thus, these processors can be more suitable for server use than 32-bit processors in applications that require manipulation of extremely large amounts of data. However, as discussed later in this chapter, there are profound differences in how different 64-bit processor architectures work with existing 32-bit operating systems and programs. If you plan to use a 64-bit server with existing software, you need to carefully consider these differences before you choose a particular processor platform.

Current 64-bit server processors include the following:

x86-based 64-bit processors (can also run x86 32-bit software at full speed):

- AMD Opteron
- Intel Pentium D
- Intel Pentium Extreme Edition
- Intel Pentium 4 (selected models)
- Intel Xeon (selected models)

EPIC-based 64-bit processors (can also run x86 32-bit software, but not at top speed):

- Intel Itanium
- Intel Itanium 2

RISC-based 64-bit processors (compatible with 32-bit RISC-based software varies):

- Power3 and higher series
- Alpha (all models)
- PowerPC G5/970 series
- PA-RISC 8xxx series
- MIPS R4xxx and higher series
- UltraSPARC (all models)

As you can see from this list, although x86-compatible server processors with 64-bit capabilities are relatively new, 64-bit capabilities have been available since the mid-1990s in RISC-based processors. Keep in mind that a 64-bit processor can take full advantage of its architecture only when running a 64-bit operating system and 64-bit applications.

Multiple CPUs

Most of the processors discussed in this chapter support multiple-processor operation. Servers that contain multiple processors have the following major advantages:

- Superior performance when running multithreaded tasks. In this scenario, different processors can run different program threads being used by a single program. Relatively few multithreaded applications are currently available (mostly CAD, high-end graphics, and 3D rendering programs).
- Superior performance when running multiple single-threaded applications. In an environment where applications are not multithreaded, a multiprocessor system can still run individual applications on separate processors.

SMP is the multiple-CPU design used by most multiprocessor-equipped servers up to four-way designs. In a server that uses SMP, all processors use the same operating system and memory space. The operating system kernel subdivides multiple threads of a single multithreaded task or separate single-threaded tasks among the processors.

Performance Issues

At first glance, it would seem that as a single-processor system is upgraded to two or more processors, system performance would increase by the same factor as the number of processors added. The actual increase in system performance is somewhat less, however, because all processors share a common memory area and common I/O structures (expansion slots and integrated hard disk host adapters). You can estimate the overall performance boost you will obtain by adding processors to an x86 server by using the figures in Table 2.9.

Table 2.9   Processing Power in x86 Multiple-Processor Servers

Number of Processors	Processing Power[1]
1	1×
2	1.8×
4	3.5×
6	5.2×
8	6.1×

[1]Compared to the processing power of a single-processor server.

The values in Table 2.9 assume that the additional processors use the same specifications as the original processor. If faster processors are used or if other upgrades are added—such as faster Ethernet, faster ATA, SCSI drives or arrays, or more RAM—the performance improvement could be even greater, depending on the server's primary use. The results with other server processor architectures can be even better than those shown in Table 2.9, depending on the processors, operating system used, memory size, and tasks being performed.

Unfortunately, implementing a multiprocessor system doesn't guarantee improved performance. For example, a server used only for file and print sharing won't benefit from moving to a multiprocessor configuration. However, if the server performs calculations, computations, or other types of processor-intensive tasks, moving to a multiprocessor configuration can significantly improve performance.

SMP and Dual-Core Processors

A dual-core processor provides a performance boost that is similar to the performance of two single-core processors, and a pair of dual-core processors provides a performance boost similar to the performance of a four-way server running single-core processors.

With Intel, AMD, and IBM now supporting dual-core processors in their latest designs, even low-end servers can benefit from SMP multiprocessing.

NUMA Multiprocessing

Non-uniform Memory Access (NUMA) is a type of multiprocessing environment that enables processors to use memory that may be located on a remote bus.

Servers that use NUMA typically include two or more combinations of processors—cache and main memory—known as nodes. A node is comparable to the processor and memory subsystem in an SMP server. The difference is that a NUMA server has an interconnect bus between each pair of nodes, enabling the nodes to communicate with each other to share memory and data. Unlike SMP, in which all memory has the same latency, NUMA is designed to handle local memory (memory in the current node) and remote memory (memory in another node), and compensates for the longer latency that results from a node accessing remote memory. Virtually all real-world implementations of NUMA feature cache coherency, so NUMA is sometimes called ccNUMA.

NUMA is often used in the design of high-end x86 servers using the Intel Xeon MP as well as Itanium and RISC-based servers with more than four processors. Some of the current servers that support NUMA include the Hewlett-Packard Integrity rx8620, Hewlett-Packard Superdome, IBM xSeries 445, NEC Express5800, and Unisys ES7000 Aries and Orion series. These servers feature 16 to 64 processors. NUMA requires special chipset designs.

▶▶   For more information on server chipsets, see Chapter 3, "Server Chipsets."

Figure 2.2 illustrates how a typical 16-way NUMA-based system, the IBM xSeries 445, is built up from two eight-way nodes, each of which contains two four-way Xeon MP-based Central Electronics Complexes (CECs). The SMP expansion ports connect each four-processor CEC to the other CEC in the same node and to the CECs in the other node. To help reduce the effects of memory latency on performance, each CEC contains 64MB of L4 memory cache (the Xeon MP processors contains L1–L3 cache).

Upgrading to Multiple Processors

If your multiple-processor–capable x86, Itanium/Itanium 2, or RISC-based server was manufactured by a major vendor such as Dell, Hewlett-Packard, IBM, Silicon Graphics (SGI), or Sun, you can contact your vendor for additional processors. The vendor will make sure that the additional processors are compatible with your system. Servers that use a blade architecture can accommodate a large number of blades (where each blade holds a processor, memory, and support circuitry) per enclosure. For example, a Hewlett-Packard ProLiant BL10e G2 can contain up to 20 blades per enclosure. To create a more powerful server, rack mounts can be used to hold multiple enclosures.

▶▶ For more information about blade servers, see "Blade Servers," p. 725.

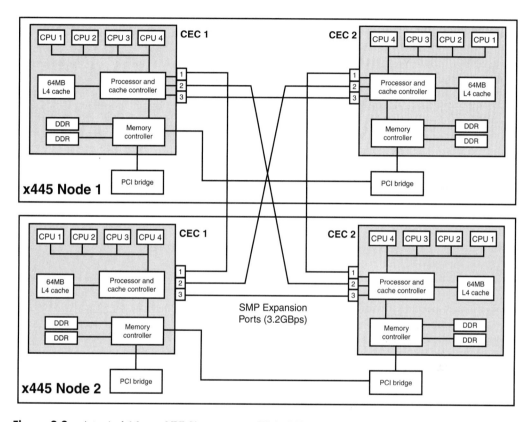

Figure 2.2   A typical 16-way NUMA system, an IBM x445.

If you built or are building your own x86 or Itanium server, you must make sure that any additional processor(s) you add will be compatible with your original processor. Use the following guidelines:

- **AMD Athlon MP**—Additional processors must run at the same clock speed as the original processor.

- **Intel Pentium II Xeon**—Additional processors should run at the same clock speed and preferably use the same processor stepping as the original processor. See http://support.intel.com/support/processors/pentiumII/xeon/24544.htm for additional information.

- **Intel Pentium III Xeon**—Additional processors should run at the same clock speed, have the same L2 cache size, and preferably use the same processor stepping as the original processor. See http://support.intel.com/support/processors/pentiumiii/xeon/sb/CS-007546.htm for additional information.

- **Intel Pentium II, Pentium III, Pentium II Xeon, Pentium III Xeon, and Xeon**—Refer to the latest specification update guide for each processor (available on the Intel website, at http://developer.intel.com) and use the DP Platform Population Matrix to determine which specific processor stepping combinations are compatible. See the document "How Do I Know Which Processors Support Dual Processing?" at http://support.intel.com/support/processors/sb/CS-007878.htm for instructions.

■ **Intel Itanium 2**—For best results, use processors with the same stepping as the original processor. These will also have the same clock speed and cache sizes. If you want to mix steppings, refer to the latest specification update guide for the Itanium 2 (available on the Intel website, at http://developer.intel.com). Search for document 251141 and go to the section "Limited Support for Mixed Steppings" for details.

■ **AMD Opteron**—You can mix and match different revisions or clock speeds of single-core processors, provided that each processor uses revision C0 or later, uses the same L2 cache size, and meets other requirements indicated in AMD's "BIOS and Kernel Developer's Guide for the AMD Athlon 64 and AMD Opteron Processors," document #26094 (section 12.8). See the AMD website, at www.amd.com, to download this document. For best results, you should use processors that have the same ordering part number (OPN). Use the same OPN for two or more dual-core Opteron processors.

If you are building a multiprocessor server, keep in mind that most x86 server motherboards support up to four processors. However, some vendors manufacture motherboards that support up to eight AMD Opteron 8xx processors through the use of a daughterboard that fits over the original motherboard's processor section. If you need a larger server, consider a preconfigured server from a major server vendor.

Tip

To identify technical information about Intel processors up through the Pentium III and Pentium III Xeon, including clock speed, stepping, onboard cache memory size, and other features, download the Intel Processor Frequency ID Utility from Intel's website, at www.intel.com/support/processors/tools/frequencyid/. For current Intel processors, including Xeon, Pentium 4, and Pentium D, use the Intel Processor Identification Utility, available from http://support.intel.com/support/processors/tools/piu/.

To identify AMD processors, download the AMD CPUInfo utility, available from the "AMD Processor Utilities and Updates" page at the AMD website, www.amd.com.

Upgrading to a Dual-Core Processor

If a system uses a motherboard that supports dual-core processors, such as motherboards based on the Intel E8500 chipset for the Xeon MP or most AMD Opteron-based systems, you can replace the existing single-core processor(s) with dual-core processors. Upgrading a one-way (single-processor) system with a dual-core processor provides a performance boost just slightly lower than what you'd receive with a dual-processor upgrade. If you want to upgrade a multiprocessor system to use dual-core processors, you should replace all of its existing single-core processors with dual-core processors.

Caution

You must check with your system or motherboard vendor to determine whether BIOS upgrades are necessary before you can use a dual-core processor on a system with a supported chipset.

Multiprocessing and Operating Systems

All modern server operating systems are designed to use two or more single-core processors or at least one dual-core processor. However, if you are considering a four-way or larger server, you need to know the maximum number of processors supported by your operating system. Table 2.10 provides a list of popular server operating systems and the number of processors they support. For UNIX implementations, see the vendor for details.

Table 2.10   SMP Support, by Operating System

Version	Maximum Number of Processors Supported
Windows	
NT Server 4.0	4
NT Server 4.0 Enterprise Edition	8
2000 Server	4
2000 Advanced Server	8
2000 Datacenter Edition	32
Server 2003 Standard Edition and Web Server Edition	2
Server 2003 Enterprise Edition	8
Server 2003 Datacenter Edition	32
Linux	
2.2x kernel	16
2.4x kernel	64
Sun Solaris	
8.0	128
9.0	128
10.0	128

Note

x86 and Itanium servers that support two-way and higher processor configurations include a BIOS option known as MPS (Multiprocessor Support). For Linux, select MPS v1.1. For Windows NT 4.0, 2000, and Windows Server 2003, select MPS v1.4 unless you have problems with this setting; use MPS v1.1 if MPS v1.4 does not work properly.

You also might need to add support for multiple processors to your operating system if you are upgrading from a single processor to a two-way or greater configuration. For Microsoft Windows, see the following documents, available from http://support.microsoft.com, for instructions and troubleshooting:

- **Windows NT 4.0**—Document numbers 156358 and 124541
- **Windows 2000**—Document number 234558
- **Windows Server 2003**—Document numbers 309283, 319091, 903006, 814607, and 824721

Depending on your Linux distribution, you may not need to do anything special to have support for SMP, or you might need to install an SMP kernel or recompile your Linux kernel to add SMP. For example, Red Hat Linux version 9 and above automatically detects SMP (two-way or larger) motherboards and automatically install kernels and boot loader entries for both one-way (single-processor) and SMP operation, and it automatically boots in SMP mode. You can use the LILO boot configuration utility to select the single-processor mode if necessary. See the documentation for your Linux distribution for details.

Cache Memory

As Tables 2.1–2.7 demonstrate, processor core speeds have increased dramatically in the past decade. Although memory speeds have increased as well during the same time period, memory speeds have not kept up with processor performance. How could you run a processor faster than the memory from which you feed it without having performance suffer terribly? The answer was cache. In its simplest terms, *cache memory* is a high-speed memory buffer that temporarily stores data the processor needs, allowing the processor to retrieve that data faster than if it came from main memory. But there is one additional feature of a cache over a simple buffer: intelligence. A cache is a buffer with a brain.

A buffer holds random data, usually on a first-in, first-out (FIFO) or first-in, last-out (FILO) basis. A cache, on the other hand, holds the data the processor is most likely to need in advance of it actually being needed. This enables the processor to continue working at either full speed or close to it without having to wait for the data to be retrieved from slower main memory. Cache memory is usually made up of static RAM (SRAM) memory integrated into the processor die, although older systems with cache also used chips installed on the motherboard.

Processors use various types of cache algorithms to determine what data to store in cache and what data to remove from cache to make room for new data. Common methods include the following:

- **Least recently used (LRU)**—This method discards the oldest data from the cache.
- **Least frequently used (LFU)**—This method discards from the cache the data that is used less often than other data.

▶▶   See "SRAM: Cache Memory," p. 348.

At least two levels of processor/memory cache are used in a modern server: Level 1 (L1) and Level 2 (L2). Some server processors such as the Itanium series and the latest Xeon models from Intel as well as some RISC-based processors also use Level 3 (L3) cache. These caches and how they function are described in the following sections.

Internal Level 1 Cache

All server processors include an integrated L1 cache and controller. This feature was first introduced to x86-compatible processors starting with the 486 family. Tables 2.1–2.7 show that, historically, server processors have featured L1 cache sizes from as little as 8KB to as much as 3MB. However, most recent server processors have L1 cache sizes ranging from 32KB to 128KB.

Note

Dual-core processors have separate L1 caches for each processor core. Most also include separate L2 caches for each core.

To understand the importance of cache, you need to know the relative speeds of processors and memory. The problem with this is that processor speed is usually expressed in MHz or GHz (millions or billions of cycles per second), whereas memory speeds are often expressed in nanoseconds (billionths of a second per cycle). Most newer types of memory express the speed in either MHz or in megabytes per second (MBps) bandwidth (throughput). Both are really time- or frequency-based measurements, and Table 5.3 in Chapter 5, "Memory," is a chart that compares them. For years, servers have had huge disparities between the speed of the processor core, the speed of the processor bus connection to memory, and the speed of the memory itself. For example, consider a server with a 3.0GHz Xeon processor with a FSB of 800MHz (200MHz×4 transfers per cycle). Typically, such a server would use

PC2700 DDR memory, which has an effective clock speed of 333MHz (166MHz×2). In this example, the processor's clock speed is 3.75 times faster than the FSB, and the FSB is 2.4 times faster than main memory. Similar comparisons can be made with virtually any server processor, whether it's x86, AMD64/EM64T, EPIC, or RISC architecture. If the processor had to get information from main memory every time it needed to process information, the processor would spend a lot of time waiting for memory.

Because L1 cache is always built in to the processor die, it runs at the full-core speed of the processor internally. *Full-core speed* means that the cache runs at the same speed as the internal processor core rather than the slower external motherboard speed. This cache is basically an area of very fast memory that is built in to the processor and used to hold some of the current working set of code and data. Cache memory can be accessed with no wait states because it is running at the same speed as the processor core.

Using cache memory reduces traditional system bottlenecks because system RAM is almost always much slower than the CPU; the performance difference between memory and CPU speed has become especially large in recent systems. Using cache memory prevents the processor from having to wait for code and data from much slower main memory, therefore improving performance. Without the L1 cache, a processor would frequently be forced to wait until system memory caught up.

Cache is even more important in modern processors because it is often the only memory in the entire system that can truly keep up with the chip. Most modern processors are clock multiplied, which means they run at a speed that is a multiple of the motherboard into which they are plugged. The Pentium 4 2.8GHz, for example, runs at a multiple of 5.25 times the true motherboard speed of 533MHz. The main memory is half this speed (266MHz) because the Pentium 4 uses a quad-pumped memory bus. Because the main memory is plugged in to the motherboard, it can run at only 266MHz maximum. The only 2.8GHz memory in such a system is the L1 and L2 caches that are built in to the processor core. In this example, the Pentium 4 2.8GHz processor has 20KB of integrated L1 cache (8KB data cache and 12KB execution trace cache) and 512KB of L2, all running at the full speed of the processor core.

▶▶ See "Memory Module Speed," p. 388.

◀◀ For cache sizes of server processors, see Tables 2.1–2.7, pp. 24–31.

If the data the processor wants is already in the internal cache, the CPU does not have to wait. If the data is not in the cache, the CPU must fetch it from the Level 2 cache or (in less sophisticated system designs) from the system bus, meaning directly from main memory.

How Cache Works

To learn how the L1 cache works, consider an analogy. In this story, you are eating food to act as the processor requesting and operating on data from memory (you're dining at a restaurant, and representing a 3GHz Xeon, by the way). The kitchen where the food is prepared represents main memory (DIMM RAM). The cache controller is represented by the waiter, and the L1 cache is represented by the table at which you are seated.

Say you start to eat at this particular restaurant every day at the same time. You come in, sit down, and order a hot dog. You can eat a bite every half second (3GHz = 0.33ns cycling). When you first arrive, you sit down, order a hot dog, and wait 3 seconds (333MHz memory speed) for the food to be produced before you can begin eating. After the waiter brings the food, you start eating at your normal rate. Pretty quickly, you finish the hot dog, so you call the waiter over and order a hamburger. Again, you wait 3 seconds while the hamburger is being produced. When it arrives, you again begin eating at full speed. After you finish the hamburger, you order a plate of fries. Again you wait, and after it is delivered 3 seconds later, you eat it at full speed. Finally, you decide to finish the meal and order cheesecake for dessert. After another 3-second wait, you can eat cheesecake at full speed. Your overall eating experience consists of mostly a lot of waiting, followed by short bursts of actual eating at full speed.

After coming into the restaurant for two consecutive nights at exactly 6 p.m. and ordering the same items in the same order each time, on the third night the waiter begins to think; "I know this guy is going to be here at 6 p.m., order a hot dog, a hamburger, fries, and then cheesecake. Why don't I have these items prepared in advance and surprise him? Maybe I'll get a big tip." So you enter the restaurant and order a hot dog, and the waiter immediately puts it on your plate, with no waiting. You then proceed to finish the hot dog, and right as you are about to request the hamburger, the waiter deposits one on your plate. The rest of the meal continues in the same fashion, and you eat the entire meal, taking two bites every second, and never have to wait for the kitchen to prepare the food. Your overall eating experience this time consists of all eating, with no waiting for the food to be prepared, due primarily to the intelligence and thoughtfulness of your waiter.

This analogy exactly describes the function of the L1 cache in the processor. The L1 cache itself is the table that can contain one or more plates of food. Without a waiter, the space on the table is a simple food buffer. When it is stocked, you can eat until the buffer is empty, but nobody seems to be intelligently refilling it. The waiter is the cache controller who takes action and adds the intelligence to decide which dishes are to be placed on the table in advance of your needing them. Like the real cache controller, he uses his skills to literally guess which food you will require next, and if and when he guesses right, you never have to wait.

Let's now say that on the fourth night, you arrive exactly on time and start off with the usual hot dog. The waiter, by now really feeling confident, has the hot dog already prepared when you arrive, so there is no waiting.

Just as you finish the hot dog, and right as he is placing a hamburger on your plate, you say "Gee, I'd really like a bratwurst now; I didn't actually order this hamburger." The waiter guessed wrong, and the consequence is that this time you have to wait the full 3 seconds as the kitchen prepares your brat. This is known as a *cache miss*, in which the cache controller did not correctly fill the cache with the data the processor actually needed next. If the system has only L1 cache, the processor must fetch data from main memory, effectively slowing down to the memory speed, when a cache miss takes place.

According to Intel, the L1 cache in most of its processors has approximately a 90% hit ratio. (Some processors, such as the Xeon, are slightly higher.) This means that the cache has the correct data 90% of the time, and consequently the processor runs at full speed—3.0GHz, in this example—90% of the time. However, 10% of the time, the cache controller guesses wrong, and the data has to be retrieved out of the significantly slower main memory, which means the processor has to wait. This essentially throttles the system back to RAM speed, which in this example is 333MHz (3.0ns). Comparable L1 performance is reported by most other server processors.

In this analogy, the processor is 9 times faster than the main memory. Memory speeds have increased from 16MHz (60ns) to 400MHz (2.5ns) or faster in the latest systems, but processor speeds have also risen, up to 3.8GHz, so even in the latest systems, memory is still 7.5 or more times *slower* than the processor. Cache makes up the difference.

The main feature of L1 cache is that it has always been integrated into the processor core, where it runs at the same speed as the core. This, combined with the hit ratio of 90% or greater, makes L1 cache very important for system performance.

Level 2 Cache

To mitigate the dramatic slowdown every time an L1 cache miss occurs, a secondary cache, L2, is employed. At one time, L2 cache was located outside the processor die. Depending on the processor, it might have been located on the motherboard or in a bulky processor cartridge (as with the Pentium II, Pentium II Xeon, and some versions of the Pentium III and Pentium III Xeon processors). In such cases, there was a slowdown when an L1 cache miss took place, but the system had the desired information in L2 cache.

However, in virtually all recent server processors (refer to Tables 2.1–2.7), L2 cache is also incorporated into the processor die, where it runs at full speed. To revisit the restaurant analogy, on-die L2 cache is like having a larger table at the restaurant where the waiter can pre-position your favorite foods. Because L2 cache is often four or more times larger than L1 cache, there's plenty of room for data (or, in our example, the hot dog, hamburger, fries, and cheesecake). As before, you take a bite every half-second, but you receive additional food just as fast from L1 cache and from L2 cache. 99% of the time, you would run at 3GHz (L1 and L2 hit ratios combined), or, in other words, the food you want is already on the table 99% of the time. You slow down to RAM speed (333MHz, or 3ns) only 1% of the time. If only restaurant performance would increase at the same rate as processor performance!

Level 3 Cache

L3 cache is the third level !of cache, and it is present in only a few very-high-performance server and high-performance workstation processors at this time. These include the Intel Pentium 4 Extreme Edition, Xeon MP, Intel Itanium family, and a few RISC-based processors.

L3 cache is checked after the processor checks L1 and then L2 cache for the necessary information. As with L2 cache, a large L3 cache improves performance by storing a larger amount of the contents of main memory for quick access by the processor. In our restaurant analogy, Level 3 cache could be compared to another food cart between the original food cart and the kitchen.

The location of the L3 cache affects its speed. If the L3 cache is off-die, it runs at a slower speed than the processor core. Consequently, the system's performance is reduced when L1 and L2 cache misses take place, but L3 cache contains the desired information. However, even in such cases, accessing L3 cache is generally faster than accessing main memory.

Processors with on-die L3 cache access it at the same speed as L1 and L2 cache. In such cases, there is little practical distinction between the operations of L2 and L3 cache.

Cache Organization

A cache stores copies of data from various main memory addresses. Because the cache cannot hold copies of the data from all the addresses in main memory simultaneously, there has to be a way to know which addresses are currently copied into the cache so that, if we need data from those addresses, it can be read from the cache rather than from the main memory. This function is performed by tag RAM, which is additional memory in the cache that holds an index of the addresses that are copied into the cache. On older systems that used external L2 cache, tag RAM was implemented as a separate SRAM chip. However, on modern servers with integrated cache, tag RAM is built in to the L1 and L2 caches in the processor die.

Each line of cache memory has a corresponding address tag that stores the main memory address of the data currently copied into that particular cache line. If data from a particular main memory address is needed, the cache controller can quickly search the address tags to see whether the requested address is currently being stored in the cache (a hit) or not (a miss). If the data is there, it can be read from the faster cache; if it isn't, it has to be read from the much slower main memory.

Various ways of organizing or mapping the tags affect how the cache works. A cache can be mapped in three different ways:

- **Fully associative**—In a fully associative mapped cache, when a request is made for data from a specific main memory address, the address is compared against all the address tag entries in the cache tag RAM. If the requested main memory address is found in the tag (a hit), the corresponding location in the cache is returned. If the requested address is not found in the address tag entries, a miss occurs, and the data must be retrieved from the main memory address instead of the cache. See Figure 2.3.

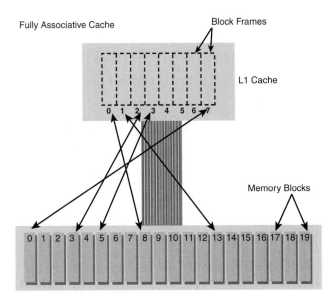

Figure 2.3   In a fully associative cache, any block can be stored in any block frame.

- **Direct mapped**—In a direct-mapped cache, specific main memory addresses are preassigned to specific line locations in the cache where they will be stored. Therefore, the tag RAM can use fewer bits because when you know which main memory address you want, only one address tag needs to be checked, and each tag needs to store only the possible addresses a given line can contain. This also results in faster operation because only one tag address needs to be checked for a given memory address. See Figure 2.4.

- **Set associative**—A set-associative cache is a modified direct-mapped cache. A direct-mapped cache has only one set of memory associations, meaning that a given memory address can be mapped into (or associated with) only a specific given cache line location. A two-way set-associative cache has two sets, so that a given memory location can be in one of two locations. A four-way set-associative cache can store a given memory address into four different cache line locations (or sets). When you increase the set associativity, the chance of finding a value increases; however, it takes a little longer because more tag addresses must be checked when you're searching for a specific location in the cache. In essence, each set in an *n*-way set-associative cache is a subcache that has associations with each main memory address. As the number of subcaches or sets increases, eventually the cache becomes fully associative—a situation in which any memory address can be stored in any cache line location. In that case, an *n*-way set-associative cache is a compromise between a fully associative cache and a direct-mapped cache. See Figure 2.5.

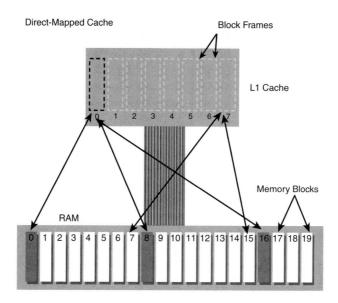

Figure 2.4 In a direct-mapped cache, specific addresses are assigned to specific cache locations.

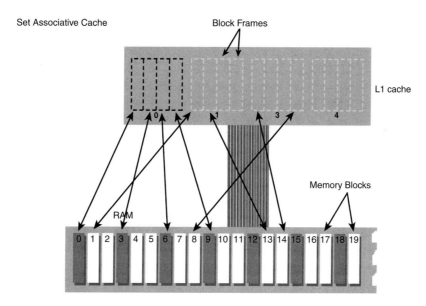

Figure 2.5 In a set-associative cache, the L1 cache is divided up into multiple memory associations.

In general, a direct-mapped cache is the fastest at locating and retrieving data from the cache because it has to look at only one specific tag address for a given memory address. However, it also results in more misses overall than the other designs. A fully associative cache offers the highest hit ratio but is the slowest at locating and retrieving the data because it has many more address tags to check through. An *n*-way set-associative cache is a compromise between optimizing cache speed and hit ratio, but the more associativity there is, the more hardware (tag bits, comparator circuits, and so on) is required, making the cache more expensive. Obviously, cache design is a series of tradeoffs, and what works best in one instance might not work best in another. Multitasking environments such as Windows are good examples of environments in which the processor needs to operate on different areas of memory simultaneously and in which an *n*-way cache can improve performance.

The organization of the cache memory in the Pentium Pro and later Pentium-class processors is called a *four-way set-associative cache*, which means that the cache memory is split into four blocks. Each block is also organized as 128 or 256 lines of 16 bytes each.

The contents of the cache must always be in sync with the contents of main memory to ensure that the processor is working with current data. Server processors use an internal write-back cache, which means that both reads and writes are cached, further improving performance over the write-through cache used by older processors.

Another feature of improved cache designs is that they are nonblocking. This is a technique for reducing or hiding memory delays by exploiting the overlap of processor operations with data accesses. A nonblocking cache enables program execution to proceed concurrently with cache misses, as long as certain dependency constraints are observed. In other words, the cache can handle a cache miss much better and enable the processor to continue doing something that is not dependent on the missing data.

The cache controller built in to the processor is also responsible for watching the memory bus when alternative processors, known as *bus masters*, are in control of the system. This process of watching the bus is referred to as *bus snooping*. If a bus master device writes to an area of memory that is also stored in the processor cache currently, the cache contents and memory no longer agree. The cache controller then marks this data as invalid and reloads the cache during the next memory access, preserving the integrity of the system.

All processor designs that support cache memory include a feature known as a translation lookaside buffer (TLB) to improve recovery from cache misses. The TLB is a table inside the processor that stores information about the location of recently accessed memory addresses. The TLB speeds up the translation of virtual addresses to physical memory addresses. To improve TLB performance, several recent processors have increased the number of entries in the TLB. Pentium 4 processors that support Hyper-Threading Technology (HT Technology) have a separate instruction TLB (iTLB) for each virtual processor thread. Some older RISC processors used the operating system to manage the TLB, but generally, especially in recent and current processors, the TLB is managed by the processor itself.

▶▶ See "Hyper-Threading Technology," p. 60.

Cache Considerations for Multiple-Processor Systems

Systems with two or more processors or with dual-core processors use cache in the same ways that single-processor systems do, but making sure that cache memory is kept up-to-date is more difficult in a multiple-processor or dual-core system. Because each of the processors in a multiple-processor system or each processor core in a dual-processor system might be working with memory locations that might also be used by other processors, there must be a method for each processor to alert others of changes to the contents of cache memory. The process of keeping cache memory up-to-date is known as *cache coherency*.

Cache coherency protocols vary widely from processor to processor. Table 2.11 lists the most widely supported cache coherency states in current server processors.

Table 2.11 Typical Cache Coherency States

Cache Coherence State	Description
Modified (also known as exclusive modified)	One processor's cache memory is up to date, but main memory has not yet been updated.
Exclusive (also known as exclusive clean)	One processor's cache memory is up to date, and main memory is up to date as well.
Shared (also known as shared clean)	Multiple processors' cache memory is up to date, as is main memory.
Invalid	No processors' cache memory is up to date.
Owned (also known as shared modified)	Combines Shared and Modified states.

Table 2.12 lists server processors and the cache coherency states they support.

Table 2.12 Selected Server Processors and Their Cache Coherency Protocols

Vendor	Processor	Cache Coherence States
AMD	Athlon MP, Opteron	Modified, Owned, Exclusive, Shared, and Invalid (MOESI)
Hewlett-Packard	Alpha (all versions)	Modified, Owned, Exclusive, Shared, and Invalid (MOESI)
IBM	PowerPC 603	Modified, Exclusive, Invalid (MEI)
IBM	PowerPC 740, 750	Modified, Exclusive, Shared, Invalid (MESI)
IBM	Power4	Enhanced MESI[1]
Intel	Pentium Pro, Pentium II/Xeon, Pentium III/Xeon, Xeon, Itanium, Itanium 2	Modified, Exclusive, Shared, Invalid (MESI)
Sun	UltraSPARC	Exclusive Modified, Shared Modified, Exclusive Clean, Shared Clean, and Invalid (MOESI)

[1]*Includes additional states in L2 and L3 caches.*

In the MESI cache coherency protocol used by some vendors, each processor snoops the memory bus to determine whether any or all processors' cache memory contains valid information or invalid information and marks the cache accordingly. The MESI protocol can lead to a performance penalty when modified data must be written back to main memory; other processors must wait until this has occurred before they can access memory.

The MOESI protocol used by Alpha, Athlon MP, Opteron, and Sun UltraSPARC reduces memory latency and improves memory performance compared to MESI. Keep in mind that the Athlon MP descends from the original AMD Athlon, which uses the EV-6 bus design originally developed for the Alpha and subsequently licensed by AMD.

To help improve cache coherency, some vendors add cache coherency filters or other cache accelerators to Intel-based systems with more than two processors. For example, the Hewlett-Packard ProLiant DL740 (4 Xeon MP processors) uses a 2MB cache accelerator feature on the motherboard. These features are not needed on AMD-based systems using up to eight-way designs because of the superior performance of MOESI caching.

Overview of x86-Compatible Servers Processors

Servers designed to run x86-compatible operating systems (such as Windows 2000 Server, Windows Server 2003, and Linux) and applications have used three different categories of processors:

■ Processors originally made for desktop computers

■ Processors derived from desktop designs but optimized for use in servers and workstations

■ Processors designed from the ground up for use in servers

Until the mid-1990s, there were no processors designed especially for use in servers running x86 software. Instead, these servers used the fastest x86 desktop processors available at the time. For example, desktop processors such as the 80286 (the first x86 processor to directly access more than 1MB of memory), the 80386 (the first x86 processor to introduce a 32-bit data bus), the 80486 (the first x86 processor with an integrated math coprocessor and an integrated L1 cache), and the Pentium (the first processor with superscalar design, running two instructions at the same time) have all been used as server processors.

The Pentium II was the first x86-compatible desktop processor to spawn an offshoot specifically designed as a server processor, the Pentium II Xeon. Ironically, the Pentium II was an offshoot of Intel's first server-oriented processor, the Pentium Pro. Successors to the Pentium II from both Intel and AMD have continued to inspire server-optimized versions:

■ The Pentium III Xeon was based on the Pentium III.

■ The Xeon was based on the Pentium 4.

■ The AMD Athlon MP was based on the Athlon.

Intel's Itanium family is the first x86-compatible processor family designed from the ground up for use in servers. However, as described in detail later in this chapter, the Itanium and Itanium 2 were not intended to be used primarily as x86-compatible processors. x86-compatibility is a convenience feature of the Itanium's design, and Itanium systems will not achieve peak performance when running x-86 operating systems or applications.

Note

x86-compatible processors are those that can run the same operating systems and applications as Intel's 8088 and newer models: MS-DOS, Windows, and so on.

The AMD Opteron was the first x86-compatible processor designed specifically for use in 64-bit servers while maintaining full-speed compatibility with existing 32-bit x86 applications.

Factors to Consider for Desktop Processors Used in Servers

Although some x86 processors used in servers, such as the Intel Xeon and Itanium series, and the AMD Athlon MP and Opteron, are designed especially for use in servers and workstations, many x86-based servers use the same processors that have been used in desktop computers.

Although processors originally designed for desktop use have been, and continue to be, used successfully in servers designed for light to moderate use, several design factors enable some desktop processors to be more successful as server processors than others:

- **L2 cache size**—Servers must provide data to and may perform active processing for multiple workstations. As with desktop processors, a larger L2 memory cache enables processor-intensive tasks to be performed more quickly.

- **The presence of L3 cache (optional)**—To further improve the performance of processor-intensive tasks, some recent server processors incorporate L3 memory cache in addition to L1 and L2 caches. Some current high-performance desktop processors also incorporate L3 cache.

- **The amount of system memory the L2 cache supports**—Servers have traditionally used larger amounts of main memory than desktop computers. The extra memory in a server enables it to process information destined for multiple workstations more quickly than through paging to and from the hard disk or disk array. Some processors used in servers have had relatively low limits on the amount of memory the integrated L2 cache supported, while others can cache larger amounts of memory. When all other factors are equal, the processor model whose L2 cache supports more main memory is the preferred processor for a server application.

- **The reliability of L2 cache**—Some older processors used in servers feature L2 cache that does not support error correcting code (ECC) error correction. ECC support, whether in main memory or in the processor cache, enables the correction of single-bit memory errors and the reporting of multibit memory errors. Because servers are responsible for the reliable delivery and storage of information used by multiple workstations, ECC support, both for main memory and for L2 cache, is very important.

- **High-speed connections to the motherboard chipset**—Much of a server's work involves data transfer between the server's own storage and workstation storage or memory. To enable this data transfer to take place as quickly as possible, a dedicated high-speed bus between the processor and the North Bridge or South Bridge or MCH or I/O controller hub chips on the motherboard is an important feature. Some chips used in servers have only one high-speed bus connection, while others have multiple bus connections for greater I/O and memory performance. Note that while the speed of the connection between the processor and chipset is a function of the chipset, if you are selecting between processors with similar FSB speeds but one processor has a faster connection to the chipset than another, the one with the faster connection is preferred.

- **Multiple-processor support**—Although some servers use only a single processor, many servers use motherboards and operating systems that can support two or more processors for better system performance. It's best to use processors that are specifically designed to support multiple-processor applications on such motherboards. Note that some processors, such as the Pentium 4, can be used only in single-processor configurations.

- **Dual-processor cores**—Processors with dual cores provide virtually every advantage of a dual-processor system while occupying only one processor socket. When two or more dual-core processors are installed in a two-way or larger server, the server has twice the number of logical CPUs and offers increased performance to match.

Note

Before the development of true dual-core processors by AMD and Intel, Intel added a sort of virtual dual-core technology to some of its Pentium 4 and Xeon processors. This technology, known as HT Technology, enables a single-processor system to emulate two processors and a two-processor system to emulate four processors. HT Technology is designed to boost performance, but whether you see a performance boost or a performance drop when HT Technology is enabled depends on the software being run on the server. Dual-core processors and multiple processors boost performance when multiple applications are in use at one time. Some of Intel's dual-core processors also feature HT Technology, but as with HT Technology implementations on single-core processors, your results may vary. When HT Technology–compatible processors are installed, HT Technology is enabled or disabled through the system BIOS.

The following sections describe which processors in a given family are the most suitable for use in servers, based on these features.

x86 Processor Modes

All Intel and Intel-compatible 32-bit and 64-bit processors, also known as x86 processors, can run in several modes. *Processor modes* refer to the various operating environments and affect the instructions and capabilities of the chip. The processor mode controls how a processor sees and manages the system memory and the tasks that use it.

As described in the following sections, there are three possible modes of operation:

- Real mode (16-bit software)
- Virtual real mode (16-bit programs within a 32-bit environment)
- Protected mode (32-bit software)

Real Mode and Virtual Real Mode

The original IBM PC included an 8088 processor that could execute 16-bit instructions using 16-bit internal registers and could address only 1MB of memory, using 20 address lines. All original PC software was created to work with this chip and was designed around the 16-bit instruction set and 1MB memory model. For example, DOS and all DOS software, Windows 1.x through 3.x, and all Windows 1.x through 3.x applications are written using 16-bit instructions. These 16-bit operating systems and applications are designed to run on an original 8088 processor.

Servers do not use real mode because it does not permit access to memory above 1MB and does not permit multitasking. Instead, if a server needs to run software that requires real mode, it does so by emulating real mode, a mode known as virtual real mode.

◀◀ See "Internal Registers," p. 35.

◀◀ See "The Address Bus," p. 34.

About the only time that a server processor runs in real mode is if a technician boots the computer with a diagnostic disk and performs tests on the computer's hardware. A diagnostic disk usually contains a DOS-based operating system and XMS memory drivers, which enable the diagnostics to test all memory in the system.

Protected (32-Bit) Mode

The Intel 386, the PC industry's first 32-bit processor, introduced an entirely new 32-bit instruction set. To take full advantage of the 32-bit instruction set, a 32-bit operating system and a 32-bit application were required. This new 32-bit mode was referred to as *protected mode*, which alludes to the fact that software programs running in that mode are protected from overwriting one another in memory. Such protection helps make the system much more crash-proof because an errant program can't very easily damage other programs or the operating system. In addition, a crashed program can be terminated while the rest of the system continues to run unaffected. Protected mode is also the native mode of subsequent x86-compatible processors up through the Pentium 4, Xeon, and Athlon MP. Server-oriented operating systems for these processors, such as Windows Server, Novell NetWare, Linux, and others, use protected mode.

64-Bit Processor Modes

When used with a 64-bit operating system, many recent x86-compatible server and desktop processors, starting with the Intel Itanium, AMD Opteron, and others, support one of two 64-bit processor modes as well as the 32-bit modes discussed previously:

- EPIC
- AMD64 (originally known as x86-64)

64-bit processors can use much more memory and disk space than 32-bit operating systems when operating in the native 64-bit mode, making them much more suitable for large databases and other applications that need large amounts of these resources.

The following sections discuss the differences between these modes.

EPIC 64-Bit Mode (Intel)

Intel's first 64-bit processor was the Itanium. The Itanium uses a processor architecture known as EPIC (Explicitly Parallel Instructional Computing), which is designed to better support multiple-processor–based systems than x86-based designs.

▶▶   See "Itanium and Itanium 2 Specifications," p. 121.

Although the Itanium family also features a backward-compatible x86 mode, the original Itanium and early versions of the Itanium 2 ran x86 operating systems and applications much more slowly than a comparable x86 server processor. The Itanium 2 "Madison," introduced in 2003, features improved x86 code compatibility for better performance with existing 32-bit applications.

Itanium-based servers have not been very popular thus far, perhaps because of the cost and the need to rewrite applications to support the EPIC architecture.

Note

The Intel Itanium family and 64-bit x86 processors such as the AMD Athlon 64/Opteron and Intel Pentium D and EM64T-compatible Pentium 4 and Xeon processors use different 64-bit architectures. Thus, 64-bit software written for one will not work on the other without being recompiled by the software vendor. This means that software written specifically for the Intel EPIC 64-bit architecture will not run on x86 64-bit processors and vice versa.

The Itanium family runs all existing 32-bit software, but to fully take advantage of the processor, a 64-bit operating system and applications are required. Microsoft has released 64-bit versions of Windows XP and Windows Server, and various versions of Linux also support the Itanium family. Current Linux distributions with Itanium support include BioBrew Linux (http://bioinformatics.org/biobrew/), White Box Linux for IA64 (http://gelato.uiuc.edu/projects/whitebox/), Debian GNU for IA64 (www.debian.org/ports/ia64/), Red Hat Enterprise Linux 4 (www.redhat.com), and SUSE Linux Enterprise 9. Several companies have released 64-bit applications for networking and workstation use.

Tip

If you use (or are considering) Linux on Itanium processors, be sure to visit the Gelato Community, at www.gelato.org, and LinuxIA64, at www.ia64-linux.org. These websites provide valuable support for Itanium servers running Linux.

AMD64 64-Bit Mode (AMD)

AMD64 (originally known as x86-64) is AMD's extension of x86 architecture into the 64-bit world. Unlike EPIC-based processors, such as the Itanium family, AMD64-based processors can run existing 32-bit x86 applications at full speed by adding two new operating modes—64-bit mode and compatibility mode—to the operating modes used by 32-bit x86 processors. Together, these two modes are known as *long mode*.

When an AMD64-compatible processor runs a 32-bit operating system, it uses protected mode, as described earlier in this chapter. Protected mode, virtual 8086 mode, and real mode are collectively known as *legacy mode* on an AMD64 processor.

Legacy mode runs about as fast on an AMD64-compatible processor as on a 32-bit processor with similar features. Thus, an AMD64-compatible processor is a much better choice for a mixed 64-bit and 32-bit software environment than an Itanium 2, which runs 32-bit x86 applications much more slowly than its native IA-64 applications. Another benefit of AMD64 is the ability to run a 32-bit operating system and switch to 64-bit operation at your own pace.

The advantages of the AMD64 architecture over the Itanium series IA-64 architecture include the following:

- You get immediate speed increases with current software.
- The command set is an extension of the x86 architecture for easier recompilation to support AMD64.
- The design of AMD64 permits a gradual movement to 64-bit processing.

Intel uses a virtually identical 64-bit instruction set known as EM64T (discussed in the next section) in a wide variety of desktop and server processors. This suggests that AMD64's approach to 64-bit compatibility will continue to be much more popular in the marketplace than IA-64.

The AMD Opteron is a server-optimized implementation of AMD64, and the AMD Athlon 64, Athlon 64 FX, and Athlon 64 x2 are desktop-optimized implementations of AMD64.

▶▶ See "AMD Opteron Processors," p. 127.

Note
For more information on the Athlon 64 family of processors, see *Upgrading and Repairing PCs*, 17th edition.

EM64T 64-Bit Mode (Intel)
Intel's EM64T 64-bit mode, introduced in 2005, is virtually identical to AMD64, except that it adds support for Intel-specific features such as SSE3 (which Opterons built on a 90-nanometer die also support) and HT Technology.

The following server processors include EM64T:

- Pentium 4 (6xx, 5x1, and 506 models)
- Pentium D (all models)
- Pentium Extreme Edition (all models)
- Xeon MP 7xxx series
- Xeon DP with 800MHz CPU bus

Intel originally used the term "Clackamas Technology" for these processors but now uses the term EM64T.

Endianess and Server Processors
Endianess refers to the method a processor uses to sequence numbers and other values.

Server processors discussed in this chapter fall into one of three categories:

- **Big-endian**—These processors store data in order, left to right, from the most significant byte (MSB) to the least significant byte (LSB). Big-endian processors discussed in this book include Sun SPARC and the PowerPC G5 (970) family.

- **Little-endian**—These processors store data in order, left to right, from LSB to MSB. x86 processors use the little-endian method.

- **Bi-endian**—These processors can store data in either order. Bi-endian processor families include Power, most PowerPC processors (except for the G5), Alpha, MIPS, PA-RISC, and Itanium.

Endianess is a concern primarily for programmers, who need to take into account the order in which data is stored in a system, and for situations in which data will be exchanged between systems that use different endian methods.

It is easier to recompile applications or move data to another processor that uses the same endian method as the application or data's original target processor. Note that most RISC server processors and the Itanium (IA64) family, which is being positioned as a replacement for the Alpha and PA-RISC processor families, feature a bi-endian design.

x86 Processor Speed Ratings

A common misunderstanding about processors is their different speed ratings. This section covers processor speed in general and then provides more specific information about Intel and AMD processors used in servers.

A computer system's clock speed is measured as a frequency, usually expressed as a number of cycles per second. A crystal oscillator controls clock speeds, using a sliver of quartz sometimes contained in what looks like a small tin container. Newer systems include the oscillator circuitry in the motherboard chipset, so it might not be a visible separate component on newer boards. As voltage is applied to the quartz, it begins to vibrate (oscillate) at a harmonic rate dictated by the shape and size of the crystal (sliver). The oscillations emanate from the crystal in the form of a current that alternates at the harmonic rate of the crystal. This alternating current is the clock signal that forms the time base on which the computer operates. A typical computer system runs millions of these cycles per second, so speed is measured in megahertz. (1Hz is equal to one cycle per second.)

Note

The Hertz was named for the German physicist Heinrich Rudolf Hertz. In 1885, Hertz confirmed the electromagnetic theory, which states that light is a form of electromagnetic radiation and is propagated as waves.

A single cycle is the smallest element of time for a processor. Every action requires at least one cycle and usually multiple cycles. To transfer data to and from memory, for example, a modern processor such as a Pentium 4 needs a minimum of three cycles to set up the first memory transfer and then only a single cycle per transfer for the next three to six consecutive transfers. The extra cycles on the first transfer typically are called *wait states*. A wait state is a clock tick in which nothing happens. This ensures that the processor isn't getting ahead of the rest of the computer.

▶▶ See "SIMMs, DIMMs, and RIMMs," p. 368.

Current server-class processors can output one to six instructions per cycle, thanks to multiple pipelines and other advances.

Different instruction execution times (in cycles) make it difficult to compare systems based purely on clock speed or number of cycles per second. How can two processors that run at the same clock rate perform differently, with one running "faster" than the other? The answer is simple: efficiency. For example, although the AMD Opteron processors have clock speeds about one-third slower than Intel Xeon processors, they perform more instructions in the same clock cycle. Thus, a "slower" Opteron is able to keep pace or even outperform a "faster" Xeon.

Although dual-core processor designs improve multitasking performance, different designs offer different levels of efficiency. The dual-core AMD Opterons incorporate a crossbar controller in the processor itself to handle communications between the cores. See Figure 2.6.

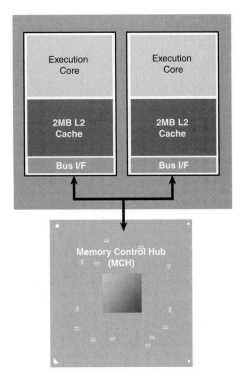

Figure 2.6   The AMD dual-core Opteron processors use the crossbar controller to transfer data between the processor cores.

However, the initial versions of Intel's dual-core processors (Pentium D and Xeon) use the MCH (North Bridge) to handle communications between the cores. See Figure 2.7.

The difference is roughly comparable to walking across a hallway to talk to a co-worker (AMD's method) compared to taking an elevator up one floor, walking to another elevator, riding down one floor, and then walking to the co-worker's office (Intel's method). Because of the inefficiencies inherent in the initial Intel design, Intel will switch to a design more similar to AMD's in dual-core processors introduced in 2006 and beyond.

Although RISC-based processors might feature slower clock speeds than recent Intel x86 or EPIC-based processors, their use of fewer processor instructions and a focus on server tasks enables them to be more efficient at handling very large numbers of clients.

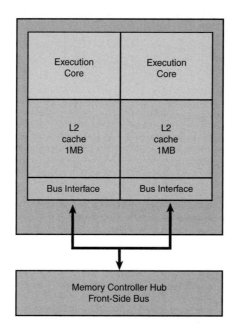

Figure 2.7 Intel's initial dual-core design uses the MCH (North Bridge equivalent) chip to manage transfers between the processor cores.

As you can see from these examples, evaluating CPU performance can be tricky. CPUs with different internal architectures execute their instructions differently and can be relatively faster at certain processes and slower at others.

Keep in mind that, unlike with PCs, server performance is less about how quickly a server performs internal operations than it is about how quickly it provides services to clients.

▶▶ For more information about server benchmarking, see Chapter 21, "Server Testing and Maintenance."

Processor Speeds Versus Motherboard Speeds

Virtually all processors used in servers, including x86, Itanium, and RISC-based processors, run the system bus and the processor core at different speeds. As mentioned earlier, the system bus is also referred to as the FSB. The effective speed of the FSB is a multiple of the actual system bus speed. For example, AMD processors perform two accesses per clock cycle, making their FSB twice the actual system bus speed. Intel processors perform four accesses per clock cycle, making their FSB four times the actual system bus speed. This is important to note for purposes of configuring the processor in the system BIOS.

▶▶ See "BIOS Setup Menus," p. 296.

RISC-based processors also use a dual-speed design, running the processor core and FSB at different speeds.

x86 Processor Features

As new processors are introduced, new features are continually added to their architectures to help improve everything from performance in specific types of applications to the reliability of the CPU as a whole. The next few sections take a look at some of these technologies, Superscalar Execution, MMX, SSE, 3DNow!, and HT Technology.

Superscalar Execution

The fifth-generation Pentium and newer processors feature multiple internal instruction execution pipelines, which enable them to execute multiple instructions at the same time. The 486 and all preceding chips can perform only a single instruction at a time. Intel calls the capability to execute more than one instruction at a time *superscalar* technology.

RISC and CISC Chips

Superscalar architecture is usually associated with high-output RISC chips. A RISC chip has a less complicated instruction set with fewer and simpler instructions. Although each instruction accomplishes less, the clock speed can be higher, which can usually increase performance. The Pentium is one of the first CISC chips to be considered superscalar. A CISC chip uses a richer, fuller-featured instruction set that has more complicated instructions. As an example, say you wanted to instruct a robot to screw in a light bulb. Using CISC instructions, you would say this:

1. Pick up the bulb.
2. Insert it into the socket.
3. Rotate clockwise until tight.

Using RISC instructions, you would say something more along the lines of this:

1. Lower hand.
2. Grasp bulb.
3. Raise hand.
4. Insert bulb into socket.
5. Rotate clockwise one turn.
6. Is bulb tight? If not, repeat step 5.
7. End.

Overall, many more RISC instructions are required to do the job because each instruction is simpler (reduced) and does less. The advantage is that there are fewer overall commands the robot (or processor) has to deal with, and it can execute the individual commands more quickly, and thus in many cases it can execute the complete task (or program) more quickly as well. The debate goes on whether RISC or CISC is really better, but in reality, there is no such thing as a pure RISC or CISC chip—it is all just a matter of definition, and the lines are somewhat arbitrary.

Intel and compatible processors have generally been regarded as CISC chips, although starting with the Pentium Pro, more recent and current Intel server processors have many RISC attributes and internally break CISC instructions down into RISC versions. Intel's Itanium processors are RISC processors.

MMX, SSE, SSE2, SSE3, 3D, and 3D Now Technologies

Intel and AMD have developed several extensions to basic x86 processor instructions. While these instructions are not important for servers, if you are considering standardizing on a particular processor for use in both server and workstation uses or are writing applications, you may want to consider which processors support particular extensions.

All these extensions are based on the concept of single instruction, multiple data (SIMD). SIMD enables one instruction to perform the same function on multiple pieces of data, similarly to a teacher telling an entire class to sit down rather than addressing each student one at a time. SIMD enables the chip to reduce processor-intensive loops common with video, audio, graphics, and animation. Table 2.13 provides an overview of these processor extensions and the processors that support them. For details about the instructions, see the documentation available for each processor at the Intel and AMD websites.

Table 2.13   Extensions to x86 Processor Instructions

Instruction Set	Vendor	Features	Server Processors Supporting Instruction Set
MMX Technology	Intel	57 instructions for processing graphics, video, and audio data	Pentium MMX and all subsequent processors, including Itanium and Itanium 2
SSE	Intel	70 instructions for processing graphics, video, and audio data; incorporates floating-point support; incorporates MMX	Pentium III, Pentium III Xeon, Itanium, Itanium 2
3D Now! Professional	AMD	Incorporates SSE commands and 3D Now! Enhanced multimedia commands	AMD Athlon MP
SSE2	Intel	Enhanced version of SSE with support for 64-bit double-precision floating-point and 8-bit through 64-bit integer operations; incorporates MMX and SSE	Pentium 4, Itanium 2 (32-bit software only when the IA32 execution layer is used), Xeon, AMD Opteron
SSE3	Intel	13 additional instructions for processing graphics, video, and audio data; incorporates MMX, SSE, and SSE2	Pentium 4 Prescott, Pentium D, Pentium Extreme Edition, Xeon (Nocoma core and newer), AMD Opteron (all 90-nanometer process)

Dynamic Execution

First used in the P6, or sixth-generation, processors, dynamic execution enables a processor to execute more instructions in parallel, so tasks are completed more quickly. This technology innovation comprises three main elements:

- **Branch prediction**—Branch prediction is a feature formerly found only in high-end mainframe processors. It enables the processor to keep the instruction pipeline full while running at a high rate of speed. A special fetch/decode unit in the processor uses a highly optimized branch prediction algorithm to predict the direction and outcome of the instructions being executed through multiple levels of branches, calls, and returns. It is similar to a chess player working out multiple strategies in advance of game play by predicting the opponent's strategy several moves into the future. By predicting the instruction outcome in advance, the instructions can be executed with no waiting.

- **Dataflow analysis**—Dataflow analysis studies the flow of data through the processor to detect any opportunities for out-of-order instruction execution. A special dispatch/execute unit in the processor monitors many instructions and can execute these instructions in an order that optimizes the use of the multiple superscalar execution units. The resulting out-of-order execution of instructions can keep the execution units busy even when cache misses and other data-dependent instructions might otherwise hold things up.

- **Speculative execution**—*Speculative execution* is the processor's capability to execute instructions in advance of the actual program counter. The processor's dispatch/execute unit uses dataflow analysis to execute all available instructions in the instruction pool and store the results in temporary registers. A retirement unit then searches the instruction pool for completed instructions that are no longer data dependent on other instructions to run or that have unresolved branch predictions. If any such completed instructions are found, the results are committed to memory by the retirement unit or the appropriate standard Intel architecture, in the order in which they were originally issued. They are then retired from the pool.

Dynamic execution essentially removes the constraint and dependency on linear instruction sequencing. By promoting out-of-order instruction execution, it can keep the instruction units working rather than waiting for data from memory. Even though instructions can be predicted and executed out of order, the results are committed in the original order so as not to disrupt or change program flow.

The Dual Independent Bus Architecture

The dual independent bus (DIB) architecture was first implemented by Intel and AMD in their sixth-generation processors (Pentium Pro, Pentium II/Xeon, Pentium III/Xeon, and Athlon MP). DIB was created to improve processor bus bandwidth and performance. Having two (dual) independent data I/O buses enables the processor to access data from either of its buses simultaneously and in parallel, rather than in a singular, sequential manner (as in a single-bus system). The main processor bus (the FSB) is the interface between the processor and the motherboard or chipset. The second (back-side) bus in a processor with DIB is used for the L2 cache, enabling it to run at much greater speeds than if it were to share the main processor bus.

▶▶ The DIB architecture is explained more fully in Chapter 3, "Server Chipsets."

Two buses make up the DIB architecture: the L2 cache bus and the main CPU bus, often called the FSB. Both buses can be used at the same time, eliminating a bottleneck there. The dual-bus architecture enables the L2 cache of the newer processors to run at full speed inside the processor core on an independent bus, leaving the main CPU bus (FSB) to handle normal data flowing in and out of the chip. The two buses run at different speeds. The FSB, or main CPU bus, is coupled to the speed of the motherboard, whereas the back-side, or L2 cache, bus is coupled to the speed of the processor core. As the frequency of processors increases, so does the speed of the L2 cache.

The key to implementing DIB was to move the L2 cache memory off the motherboard and into the processor package. L1 cache always has been a direct part of the processor die, but L2 was larger and originally had to be external. Moving the L2 cache into the processor meant that the L2 cache could run at speeds more like those of the L1 cache—much faster than the motherboard or processor bus.

DIB also enables the system bus to perform multiple simultaneous transactions (instead of singular sequential transactions), accelerating the flow of information within the system and boosting performance. Overall, DIB architecture offers up to three times the bandwidth performance over a single-bus–architecture processor.

Hyper-Threading Technology

Computers with two or more physical processors have long had a performance advantage over single-processor computers when the operating system has supported multiple processors, as with Windows NT 4.0, 2000 Server, Windows Server 2003, Linux, and Novell NetWare 6.x.

◀◀ See "Multiple CPUs," p. 37.

However, dual-processor motherboards and systems have always been more expensive than otherwise-comparable single-processor systems, and upgrading a dual-processor–capable system to dual-processor status can be difficult because of the need to match processor speeds and specifications. However, Intel's HT Technology allows a single processor to handle two independent sets of instructions at the same time. In essence, HT Technology converts a single physical processor into two virtual processors.

Intel originally introduced HT Technology in its line of Xeon processors for servers in early 2002. HT Technology enables multiprocessor servers to act as if they have twice as many processors installed. HT Technology was introduced on Xeon workstation-class processors with a 533MHz system bus and later found its way into PC processors with the Pentium 4 3.06GHz processor in late 2002.

How Hyper-Threading Works

Internally, an HT-enabled processor has two sets of general-purpose registers, control registers, and other architecture components, but both logical processors share the same cache, execution units, and buses. During operations, each logical processor handles a single thread (see Figure 2.8).

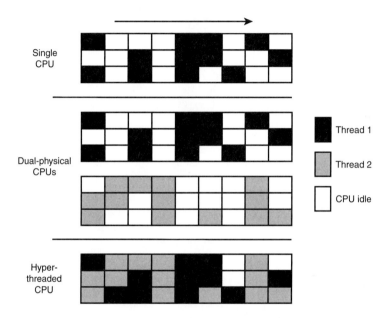

Figure 2.8   A processor with HT Technology enabled can fill otherwise-idle time with a second process, improving multitasking and performance of multithreading single applications.

Although the sharing of some processor components means that the overall speed of an HT-enabled system isn't as high as that of a true dual-processor system, speed increases of 25% or more are possible when multiple applications or a single multithreaded application is being run.

Hyper-Threading Requirements

The first HT-enabled processor was the Intel Pentium 4 3.06GHz. All faster Pentium 4 models also support HT Technology, as do all processors 2.4GHz and faster that use the 800MHz bus. However, an HT-enabled P4 processor by itself can't bring the benefits of HT Technology to a system. You also need the following:

- **A compatible motherboard (chipset)**—Your system might need a BIOS upgrade.
- **BIOS support to enable/disable HT Technology**—If your operating system doesn't support HT Technology, you should disable this feature. Application performance varies (some faster, some slower) when HT Technology is enabled. You should perform application-based benchmarks with HT Technology enabled and disabled to determine whether the applications you use benefit from using HT Technology.

■ **A compatible operating system, such as Windows Server 2003**—When HT is enabled on
these operating systems, the Device Manager shows two processors on systems with a single HT-
compatible processor or four processors on systems with dual HT-compatible processors.

Most of Intel's recent server chipsets for the Pentium 4 and Xeon support HT Technology.

▶▶   See "Intel Pentium 4 Chipsets for Single-Processor Servers," p. 180, and "Intel Xeon DP and Xeon MP Chipsets,"
p. 188, for details.

If your motherboard or server was released before HT Technology was introduced, you need a BIOS
upgrade from the motherboard or system vendor to be able to use HT Technology. Although Windows
NT 4.0 and Windows 2000 are designed to use multiple physical processors, HT Technology requires
specific operating system optimizations in order to work correctly. Linux distributions based on kernel
2.4.18 and higher also support HT Technology.

While HT Technology is designed to simulate two processors in a single physical unit, it also needs
properly written software to improve application performance. Unfortunately, many applications do
not support HT Technology, and some even slow down when HT Technology is enabled. If you find
that enabling HT Technology does not benefit server performance, you should disable it.

Dual-Core Technology

Dual-core processors include two processor cores in the same physical package, providing virtually all
the advantages of a multiple-processor computer at a cost lower than that of two matched processors.
Unlike HT Technology, dual-core processors require no support from applications.

Another advantage of dual-core processors is their ability to boost performance while maintaining the
ability to use standard-size motherboards and cases for servers. Two-way and larger servers based on
multiple single-core processors must use extended ATX or larger case designs to provide adequate
space for the additional processor socket and support circuitry. If using extended ATX or proprietary
case designs is a concern for your server environment, a dual-core CPU might fit your needs nicely.

A number of RISC-based processors developed by IBM have used dual-core designs for several years,
including IBM's Power4 (introduced in 2001) and its successors, as well as the PowerPC 970MP. AMD's
dual-core Opterons were introduced in 2005, and Intel announced dual-core Xeon MP processors for
shipment in early 2006. Dual-core Opterons can even be used as replacements for existing single-core
Opteron processors. A BIOS upgrade might be necessary on some Opteron systems. Dual-core Xeons
use the Intel E8500 chipset; older Xeon chipsets do not support dual-core Xeons.

Processor Socket and Slot Types

If you are building your own server or upgrading it with additional processors, it's very important that
you understand the processor packaging and socket, or slot type, used by your server. If you do not
know what processor socket (or slot) your server uses, you might purchase an incompatible processor
for your server. If you do not know how the processor is packaged, you might purchase an incompatible heatsink or other cooling solution.

Today, it's more important than ever before to know these details. With server processors such as the
Intel Pentium 4, AMD Opteron, and others being produced in two or more form factors at various
points of their development, the odds of buying the wrong processor or cooling solution are higher
than they once were.

The following sections put particular emphasis on Intel and AMD server processor packaging and
motherboard connectors because these are the most common processors used in build-it-yourself or
upgrade-it-yourself servers. Many processors are available in a variety of clock speeds and cache sizes,

enabling you to boost performance by swapping a faster or larger-cache-size processor for one that is slower or has a smaller cache size.

Note

Processors in RISC-type servers are generally built in to processor cartridges that contain cache memory. They are not purchased from component vendors as x86 and Itanium processors can be but are sold by the server vendor. For information about compatible processors and processor upgrades for a RISC-based server, contact your server vendor.

Overview of x86 and Itanium Server Processor and Socket Types

Intel and AMD have created a set of socket and slot designs for their processors. Each socket or slot is designed to support a different range of original and upgrade processors. Table 2.14 shows the specifications of sockets used for x86 and Itanium server processors, starting with the Intel Pentium Pro.

Table 2.14   x86 and Itanium CPU Socket and Slot Types and Specifications[1]

Socket	Pins	Layout	Voltage	Supported Processors	Introduced
Intel 686 (Pentium II/III) Class					
Socket 8	387	Dual-pattern SPGA	Auto VRM	Pentium Pro, OD	Nov. 1995
Slot 1 (SC242)	242	Slot	Auto VRM	Pentium II/III, Celeron SECC	May 1997
Socket 370	370	37×37 SPGA	Auto VRM	Celeron/Pentium III PPGA/FC-PGA	Nov. 1998
Intel Pentium 4 Class					
Socket 423	423	39×39 SPGA	Auto VRM	Pentium 4 FC-PGA	Nov. 2000
Socket 478	478	26×26 mPGA	Auto VRM	Pentium 4/ Celeron FC-PGA2	Oct. 2001
Socket T (LGA775)	775	30×33 LGA	Auto VRM	Pentium 4/ Celeron LGA775	June 2004
AMD K7 Class					
Slot A	242	Slot	Auto VRM	AMD Athlon SECC	June 1999
Socket A (462)	462	37×37 SPGA	Auto VRM	AMD Athlon/Athlon XP/MP/Duron/ Sempron PGA/FC-PGA	June 2000
AMD K8 Class					
Socket 754	754	29×29 mPGA	Auto VRM	AMD Athlon 64	Sep. 2003
Socket 939	939	31×31 mPGA	Auto VRM	AMD Athlon 64 v.2, AMD Athlon 64FX	June 2004
Socket 940	940	31×31 mPGA	Auto VRM	AMD Athlon 64FX, Opteron	April 2003
Intel/AMD Server and Workstation Class					
Slot 2 (SC330)	330	Slot	Auto VRM	Pentium II/III Xeon	April 1998

Table 2.14   Continued

Socket	Pins	Layout	Voltage	Supported Processors	Introduced
			Intel/AMD Server and Workstation Class		
Socket 603	603	31×25 mPGA	Auto VRM	Xeon (P4)	May 2001
Socket 604	604	31×25 mPGA	Auto VRM	Xeon (P4)	Oct. 2003
Socket PAC418	418	38×22 split SPGA	Auto VRM	Itanium	May 2001
Socket PAC611	611	25×28 mPGA	Auto VRM	Itanium 2	July 2002
Socket 940	940	31×31 mPGA	Auto VRM	AMD Opteron	April 2003
Socket 939	939	31×31 mPGA	Auto VRM	AMD Opteron	June 2004

¹Key: FC-PGA = flip-chip pin grid array; FC-PGA2 = FC-PGA with an Integrated Heat Spreader; OD = OverDrive (retail upgrade processors); PAC = pin array cartridge; PGA = pin grid array; PPGA = plastic pin grid array; SC242 = slot connector, 242 pins; SC330 = slot connector, 330 pins; SECC = single-edge contact cartridge; SPGA = staggered pin grid array; mPGA = micro pin grid array; VRM = voltage regulator module with variable voltage output determined by module type or manual jumpers; and Auto VRM = voltage regulator module with automatic voltage selection determined by processor voltage ID (VID) pins.

Packaging

The most common packaging type used for x86 and RISC-based processors over the past decade has been the pin grid array (PGA) design. PGA can be subdivided into several categories, reflecting advances in processor design and the never-ending quest for better cooling.

Other types of processor packaging include ball grid array (BGA) and land grid array (LGA), which are used as alternatives to PGA in some of the most recent processor designs.

Older x86 as well as Itanium and RISC processors also used various types of processor cartridges, which incorporate the processor itself and external cache memory. While x86 processors no longer use processor cartridges, some types of RISC and Itanium-based systems still use subassemblies that incorporate large amounts of cache and the processor. In some cases, a processor cartridge might incorporate two separate processors. The following sections provide details about the major types of processor packaging used on servers.

PGA and PGA Variations

PGA, which dates back to the IBM 286 processor first introduced in 1984, takes its name from the fact that the chip has a grid-like array of pins on the bottom of the package. PGA chips are inserted into sockets, which are often of a zero insertion force (ZIF) design. A ZIF socket has a lever to allow for easy installation and removal of the chip. As Figure 2.9 illustrates, PGA designs can be used for modules that contain the processor and external cache as well as for individual processors (compare Figure 2.9 to Figures 2.10 and 2.11). Figure 2.9 illustrates the front and rear view of a PGA-based processor module, the PowerPC 750.

Depending on the processor, the pins might be in standard rows and columns, as in Figure 2.9 and Figure 2.11, or might be staggered. This type of design is known as staggered PGA (SPGA). This design moves the pins closer together and decreases the overall size of the chip when a large number of pins is required. Figure 2.10 illustrates the SPGA design used by the AMD Athlon MP processor.

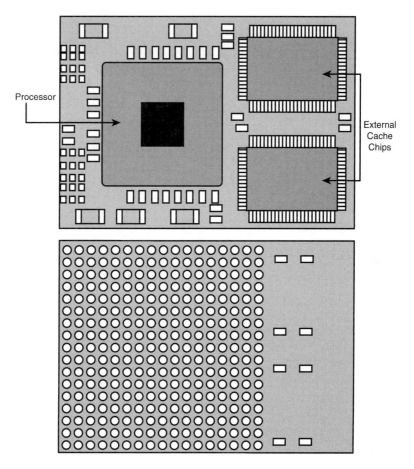

Figure 2.9 Top and bottom views of the PowerPC 750 processor module, which includes the processor and two external cache chips. The processor module connects to the system via a PGA socket.

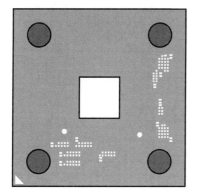 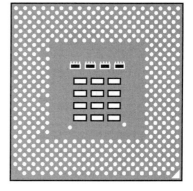

Figure 2.10 Top (left) and bottom (right) views of the Athlon MP processor. This processor uses an SPGA connector.

Several methods have been used to build PGA chips. Older PGA variations had the processor die mounted in a cavity underneath the substrate, with the top surface facing up if you turned the chip upside-down. The die was then wire-bonded to the chip package, with hundreds of tiny gold wires connecting the connections at the edge of the chip with the internal connections in the package. After the wire bonding, the cavity was sealed with a metal cover. This was an expensive and time-consuming method of producing chips, so less expensive and more efficient packaging methods were designed.

More modern processors are built on a form of flip-chip PGA (FC-PGA) packaging. This type still plugs in to a PGA socket, but the package itself is dramatically simplified. With FC-PGA, the raw silicon die is mounted facedown on the top of the chip substrate, and instead of wire bonding, the connections are made with tiny solder bumps around the perimeter of the die. The edge is then sealed with a fillet of epoxy. With the original versions of FC-PGA, you could see the backside of the raw die sitting on the chip. The Athlon MP chip shown in Figure 2.10 uses an FC-PGA design.

Unfortunately, there were some problems with attaching the heatsink to an FC-PGA chip such as an Intel Pentium III or AMD Athlon MP. The heatsink sat on the top of the die, which acted as a pedestal. If you pressed down on one side of the heatsink excessively during the installation process (such as when you were attaching the clip), you risked cracking the silicon die and destroying the chip. This was especially a problem as heatsinks became larger and heavier and the force applied by the clip became greater.

AMD decreased the risk of damage to the AMD Athlon MP and similar chips by adding rubber spacers to each corner of the chip substrate (as shown in Figure 2.10), thus preventing the heatsink from tilting excessively during installation. Still, these bumpers could compress, and it was too easy to crack the die during heatsink installation.

Intel revised its packaging with a newer FC-PGA2 version used in the newer Pentium III and all Pentium 4 and Xeon processors. It incorporates an integrated protective metal cap called a *heat spreader* that sits on top of the die, enabling larger and heavier heatsinks to be installed without any potential damage to the processor core. Ironically, the first processor for PCs to use a heat spreader was made by AMD (the K6 family). AMD has returned to the heat spreader design with its Opteron processors.

Figure 2.11 illustrates the FC-PGA2 packaging used by the Intel Xeon DP processor.

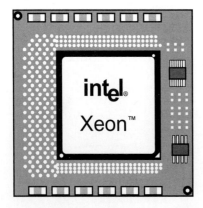 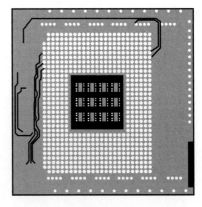

Figure 2.11 Top (left) and bottom (right) views of the Xeon DP processor. This processor uses FC-PGA2 packaging.

AMD Opteron, Intel Xeon, and Intel Pentium 4 processors also use various types of heatsink supports rather than fastening the heatsink directly to the processor socket. This helps prevent damage to the processor.

In addition to changes in the socket and arrangement of the processor core, PGA-based designs have also used various materials for the processor chip substrate. Ceramic material was common for several years, but more recent designs have used lighter-weight plastics, including some organic plastics.

Starting in the late 1990s, some processors began to use a different type of connection known as a BGA. BGA chips use small solder balls to make the connection to the socket. BGA is also used to attach DDR and newer types of memory chips to DIMM modules or graphics cards. Typically, BGA is used when chips are soldered into place, such as on a processor module, as shown in Figure 2.9.

A variation on BGA known as LGA is used by processors that use Socket 775, such as the latest version of the Intel Pentium 4, as well as the new Pentium D and Pentium Extreme Edition. LGA uses gold pads (called *lands*) on the bottom of the substrate to replace the pins used in PGA packages or the solder balls used in BGA. In socketed form, LGA allows for much greater clamping forces and therefore greater stability and improved thermal transfer (better cooling) than PGA.

Figure 2.12 illustrates the front and rear of the Pentium D, which uses an LGA design.

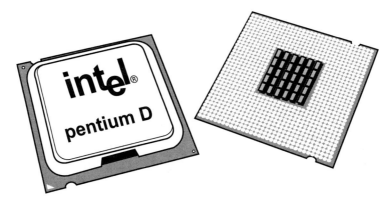

Figure 2.12   Top (left) and bottom (right) views of the Pentium D processor. This processor uses an LGA design.

Note

Although RISC-based processors typically use PGA or BGA designs, the socket is usually on a small board that also contains cache memory chips. The processor assembly is then plugged in to a slot in the server.

Single-Edge Contact Cartridge Packaging

Intel used cartridge- or board-based packaging for several of its server-class processors from 1997 through 2000. This packaging was called single-edge contact cartridge (SECC), and it consisted of the CPU and separate L2 cache chips mounted on a circuit board that looked similar to an oversized memory module and that plugged in to a slot. In some cases, the boards were covered with plastic cartridge covers.

Building the processor into a cartridge was a cost-effective method for integrating L2 cache into the processor before it was feasible to include the cache directly inside the processor die.

Intel used two types of slots for its server-class processors:

- Slot 1 was used by the Pentium II and by slot-based versions of the Pentium III. (The Pentium III was also available in a FC-PGA socket form factor.)
- Slot 2 was used by the Pentium II Xeon and Pentium III Xeon processors.

Slot 1 was also known as Slot 242, for the 242 pins in the slot connector. The connector used two different-sized sections to prevent incorrect insertion of the cartridge (see Figure 2.13). A rigid or folding frame known as a processor-retention mechanism was used to support the processor. Slot 1 supported single or two-way processor configurations.

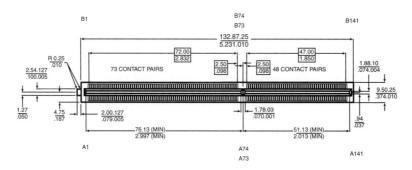

Figure 2.13   Slot 1 connector dimensions and pin layout.

Slot 2 was a more sophisticated 330-pin slot designed for the Pentium II Xeon and Pentium III Xeon processors manufactured for servers and workstations. Slot 2 supported up to four-way processing. Note that Slot 2 was also called SC330, which stands for slot connector with 330 pins (see Figure 2.14).

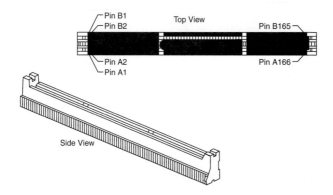

Figure 2.14   Slot 2 (SC330) connector dimensions and pin layout.

Intel later discovered less-expensive ways to integrate L2 cache into the processor core, and it no longer produces Slot 1 or Slot 2 processors. Both Slot 1 and Slot 2 processors are now obsolete, and most systems using these processors have been retired or upgraded with socket-based motherboards.

Slot 1 (SECC and SECC2) Packaging

Originally, the SECC package wrapped around three sides of the processor cartridge assembly. However, this design made cooling difficult and raised the cost of the processor. Later versions of the

Pentium II and all slot-based versions of the Pentium III used a simplified one-piece design known as SECC2.

Figure 2.15 illustrates the SECC2 design. The rectangular chips on the right side of the rear view are the cache memory chips. Note the large thermal plate used to aid in dissipating the heat from this processor. A passive or active heatsink was attached to the thermal plate. The SECC2 design used a different type of retention mechanism (the universal retention system) than the original SECC design that also worked with SECC processors.

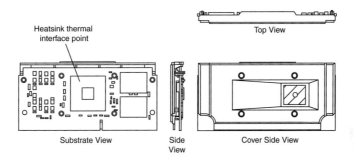

Figure 2.15　SECC2 packaging used in newer Pentium II and III processors.

Slot 2 Packaging

The Pentium II Xeon and Pentium III Xeon processors are designed in a cartridge similar to but larger than that used for the standard Pentium II/III. Figure 2.16 shows the Xeon cartridge.

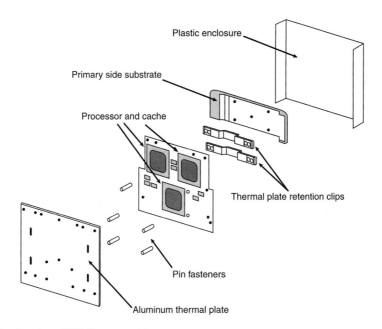

Figure 2.16　Pentium II/III Xeon cartridge.

Slot 2 versions of the Pentium II Xeon and Pentium III Xeon differ from the standard Pentium II and slot-based Pentium III mainly by virtue of having full-core–speed L2 cache, and in some versions, a larger amount of it. The additional pins allow for additional signals needed by multiple processors.

ZIF Sockets

When the Socket 1 specification used by the first 486 processors was created, manufacturers realized that if users were going to upgrade processors, they had to make the process easier. The socket manufacturers found that 100 pounds of insertion force is required to install a chip in a standard 169-pin screw Socket 1 motherboard. With this much force involved, you could easily damage either the chip or the socket during removal or reinstallation. Therefore, some motherboard manufacturers began using low insertion force (LIF) sockets, which required only 60 pounds of insertion force for a 169-pin chip. But pressing down on the motherboard with 60 to 100 pounds of force can still crack the board if it is not supported properly. A special tool is also required to remove a chip from one of these sockets. As you can imagine, even the LIF was relatively difficult to work with, and a better solution was needed if the average person was ever going to replace his or her CPU.

Manufacturers began using ZIF sockets in Socket 1 designs, and all processor sockets from Socket 2 and higher have been of the ZIF design. ZIF is required for all the higher-density sockets because the insertion force would simply be too great otherwise. ZIF sockets almost eliminate the risk involved in installing or removing a processor because no insertion force is necessary to install the chip, and no tool is needed to extract one. Most ZIF sockets are handle actuated: You lift the handle, drop the chip into the socket, and then close the handle. This design makes installing or removing a processor an easy task.

Note

Although removing a processor from a ZIF socket is simple, it is necessary to remove the heatsink from the processor before the processor itself can be removed. If the heatsink has a fan, it must be disconnected from the motherboard or other power source as well. Heatsinks for some processor types clip directly to the processor socket, and if the spring-loaded arm holding the heatsink is not released properly, the socket can be damaged. Socket 478, Socket 603/604, Socket 754, and Sockets 939 and 940 use heatsinks that are mounted on external supports, making installation and removal easier and safer.

Socket 8

Socket 8 is an SPGA socket that features 387 pins that was specifically designed for the Pentium Pro processor with integrated L2 cache. The additional pins enable the chipset to control the L2 cache integrated in the same package as the processor. Figure 2.17 shows the Socket 8 pinout.

Note

The Pentium Pro's Socket 8 is electrically compatible with Slot 1. Consequently, both Intel and third-party vendors such as PowerLeap developed Pentium II–based upgrades for Pentium Pro–based systems. These upgrades are no longer being manufactured.

Socket 370

In January 1999, Intel introduced a new socket for P6-class processors. The socket was called Socket 370, or PGA-370, because it has 370 pins and was originally designed for lower-cost PGA versions of the Celeron and Pentium III processors. Socket 370 was originally designed to directly compete in the lower-end system market, along with the Super7 platform supported by AMD and Cyrix. However,

Intel later used it for the Pentium III processor, starting in late 1999. This was possible because Intel developed improved processor designs that incorporated L2 cache in the processor core while maintaining high chip yields and low manufacturing costs. By incorporating L2 cache into the processor core, Intel was able to abandon the bulky cartridge design it used for the Pentium II and early Pentium III versions. Socket 370 versions of the Pentium III use an FC-PGA design, in which the raw die is mounted on the substrate upside-down.

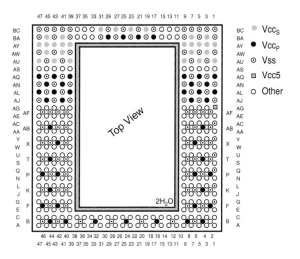

Figure 2.17   Socket 8 (Pentium Pro) pinout showing power pin locations.

The Socket 370 (PGA-370) pinout is shown in Figure 2.18.

Figure 2.18   Socket 370 (PGA-370) Pentium III/Celeron pinout (top view).

The last versions of the Pentium III use the Tualatin core design, which requires a revised socket to operate. Motherboards that can handle Tualatin-core processors are sometimes known as *Tualatin-ready* and use different chipsets from those not designed to work with the Tualatin-core processor. If you need to replace a Pentium III processor on a Socket 370 server motherboard, make sure you determine what versions of the Pentium III the board can handle. See the vendor documentation for the system or motherboard for details.

Tip

The maximum speed of the Tualatin-core Pentium III processor is 1.4GHz. Some vendors refer to their Tualatin-compatible motherboards as supporting up to 1.4GHz processors.

Socket 423

Socket 423 is a ZIF-type socket introduced in late 2000 for the original Pentium 4. Figure 2.19 shows Socket 423.

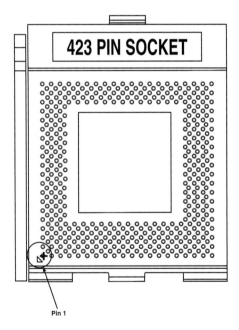

Figure 2.19   Socket 423 (Pentium 4) showing pin 1 location.

Socket 423 supports a 400MHz processor bus, which connects the processor to the MCH, which is the main part of the motherboard chipset and similar to the North Bridge in earlier chipsets. Pentium 4 processors up to 2GHz were available for Socket 423; all faster versions of the Pentium 4 use Socket 478 or Socket 775 instead.

Socket 423 uses a unique heatsink mounting method that requires standoffs attached either to the chassis or to a special plate that mounts underneath the motherboard. This was designed to support the weight of the larger heatsinks required for the Pentium 4. Because of this, many Socket 423 motherboards require a special chassis that has the necessary additional standoffs installed. Fortunately, the need for these standoffs was eliminated with the newer Socket 478 and Socket 775 for Pentium 4 processors.

The processor uses five VID pins to signal the voltage regulator module (VRM) built in to the motherboard to deliver the correct voltage for the particular CPU installed. This makes the voltage selection completely automatic and foolproof. Most Pentium 4 processors for Socket 423 require 1.7V. A small triangular mark indicates the pin-1 corner for proper orientation of the chip.

Socket 478

Socket 478 is a ZIF-type socket for the Pentium 4 introduced in late 2001. It was specially designed to support additional pins for future Pentium 4 processors and speeds over 2GHz. The heatsink mounting is different from that of the Socket 423, allowing larger heatsinks to be attached to the CPU. Figure 2.20 shows Socket 478.

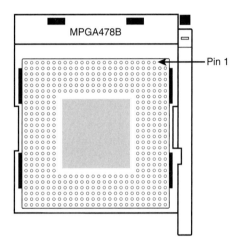

Figure 2.20   Socket 478 (Pentium 4) showing pin 1 location.

Socket 478 supports a 400MHz, 533MHz, 800MHz, or 1066MHz processor bus that connects the processor to the MCH, which is the main part of the motherboard chipset.

Socket 478 uses a different heatsink attachment method than its predecessors. Socket 478 uses a heatsink that clips directly to the motherboard, and not the CPU socket or chassis (as with Socket 423 and Socket 370). Therefore, any standard chassis can be used, and the special standoffs used by Socket 423 boards are not required. The new heatsink attachment allows for a much greater clamping load between the heatsink and processor, which aids cooling.

Socket 478 processors use five VID pins to signal the VRM built in to the motherboard to deliver the correct voltage for the particular CPU installed. This makes the voltage selection completely automatic and foolproof. A small triangular mark indicates the pin-1 corner for proper orientation of the chip.

Socket 603 and Socket 604

The Intel Xeon is based on the Pentium 4, but it supports larger amounts of on-die L2 cache. Some versions contain L3 cache. Socket 603 is used with the Intel Xeon processor in DP (dual-processor) and MP (multiple-processor) configurations. The additional pins in Socket 603 provide support for DP or MP operation at a processor bus speed of 400MHz. Figure 2.21 shows Socket 603.

Socket 604 is a variation on Socket 603, using an additional pin at location AE30. Socket 604 supports newer Xeon MP and DP processors with processor bus speeds up to 800MHz. The additional pin on Socket 604 processors prevents them from being inserted into a Socket 603 motherboard.

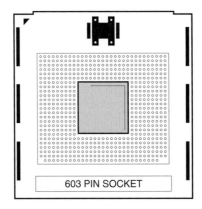

603 PIN SOCKET

Figure 2.21   Socket 603 is used by the Intel Xeon processor.

Socket 775 (Socket T)

The most recent Intel Pentium 4 processors as well as the Pentium D and Pentium Extreme Edition use a new processor socket called Socket 775 (LGA775). Originally known as Socket T, Socket 775 is unique among x86 sockets in that it uses an LGA format, so the pins are on the socket rather than the processor (see Figure 2.22). The first LGA processors were the Pentium II and Celeron processors in 1997; in those processors, LGA packaging was used for the chip mounted on the Slot 1 cartridge.

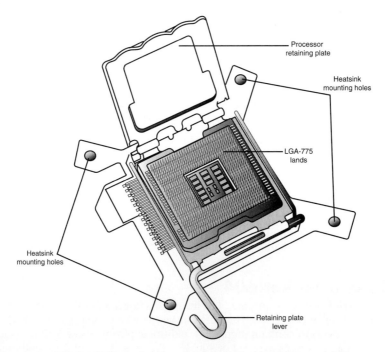

Processor retaining plate

Heatsink mounting holes

LGA-775 lands

Heatsink mounting holes

Retaining plate lever

Figure 2.22   Socket 775 (LGA775, Socket T) and its processor clamping mechanism.

LGA is really just a recycled version of what was previously called LCC (leadless chip carrier) packaging. Used way back on the 286 processor in 1984, LCC packaging had gold lands around the edge only (there were far fewer pins back then). In other ways, LGA is simply a modified version of BGA, with gold lands replacing the solder balls, making it more suitable for socketed (rather than soldered) applications. The early LCC packages were ceramic, whereas the first Pentium II LGA packages were plastic, with the package soldered to a cartridge substrate. These days (and for the future), the LGA package is organic and directly socketed instead. On a technical level, the Pentium 4 LGA chips combine several packaging technologies that have all been used in the past, including organic LGA (OLGA) for the substrate and controlled collapse chip connection (C4) flip-chip for the actual processor die.

Socket A (Socket 462)

AMD introduced Socket A, also called Socket 462, in 2000 to support the PGA versions of the Athlon and Duron processors; it also works with the Athlon XP and Athlon MP processors.

Socket A has 462 pins and 11 plugs oriented in an SPGA form (see Figure 2.23). Socket A has the same physical dimensions and layout as Socket 370; however, the location and placement of the plugs prevent Socket 370 processors from being inserted. Socket A supports 32 voltage levels from 1.100V to 1.850V, in 0.025V increments, controlled by the VID0 to VID4 pins on the processor. The automatic VRM circuitry is typically embedded on the motherboard.

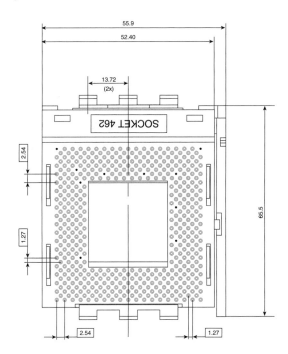

Figure 2.23   Socket A (Socket 462) Athlon/Duron layout.

There are 11 total plugged holes, including 2 of the outside pin holes at A1 and AN1. These are used to allow for keying to force the proper orientation of the processor in the socket. The pinout of Socket A is shown in Figure 2.24.

Socket 939

The AMD Opteron processor was introduced using Socket 940 (discussed in the next section), and most versions of the Opteron continue to use Socket 940. However, starting in 2005, AMD introduced a wide variety of 100-series Opterons in Socket 939. Figure 2.25 illustrates Socket 939.

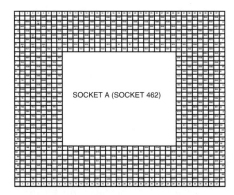

Figure 2.24   Socket A (Socket 462) pinout (top view).

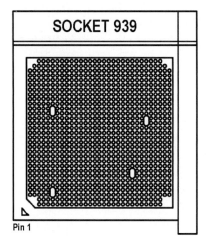

Figure 2.25   Socket 939. The cutout corner and triangle at the lower left indicate pin 1.

Socket 939, unlike Socket 940, supports standard unbuffered DDR memory. Because unbuffered DDR memory is less expensive than the registered memory used by Socket 940 versions of the Opteron, Socket 939 Opterons enable you to build a lower-cost single-processor server than do Socket 940 versions. However, note that 100-series Opterons are designed to work in single-processor configurations only. If you are planning to build a two-way or larger configuration, you must use 200-series (up to two-way) or 800-series (up to eight-way) processors, which are available only in Socket 940.

Socket 940

Socket 940 (see Figure 2.26) is used by most versions of the AMD Opteron, including all versions designed for two-way or larger configurations (200 and 800 series). Motherboards that use this socket support only registered DDR SDRAM modules in dual-channel mode.

When you compare the pinouts for Sockets 939 and 940, note that the areas without pins are different. This keying prevents you from inserting the wrong processor into the motherboard.

Both Socket 939 and Socket 940 use heatsinks that clip to a frame rather than directly to the processor socket. This enables easier heatsink installation.

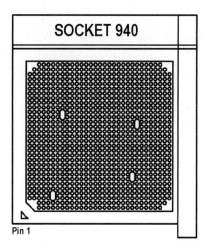

Figure 2.26   Socket 940. The cutout corner and triangle at the lower left indicate pin 1.

Pin Array Cartridge (PAC)

The original Itanium used a package called the pin array cartridge (PAC). This cartridge includes L3 cache and plugs in to a PAC418 (418-pin) socket on the motherboard and not a slot. The package is about the size of a standard index card, weighs about 6 ounces (170g), and has an alloy metal on its base to dissipate the heat (see Figure 2.27). Itanium has clips on its sides, enabling four PACs to be hung from a motherboard, both below and above.

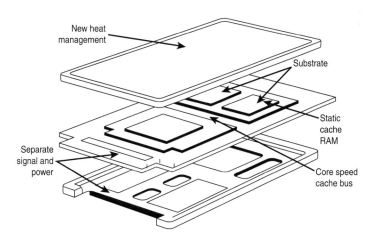

Figure 2.27   The Itanium's PAC.

The Itanium 2 uses a more compact version of the PAC, known as PAC611. See Figure 2.28.

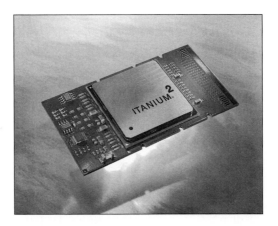

Figure 2.28   The Itanium 2 has a more compact design than the original Itanium. *(Photograph used by permission of Intel Corporation.)*

The Itanium and Itanium 2 processors both use a unique power source known as a "power pod" (see Figure 2.29). The processor slides into the edge connector on the power pod. The power pod acts as a voltage regulator (sometimes referred to as a DC/DC converter) to provide the correct power levels and power quality to the processor and its onboard cache memory. The power pod uses VID pins to specify the correct voltage for the processor. Note that the Itanium's power pod is not compatible with the Itanium 2's and vice versa.

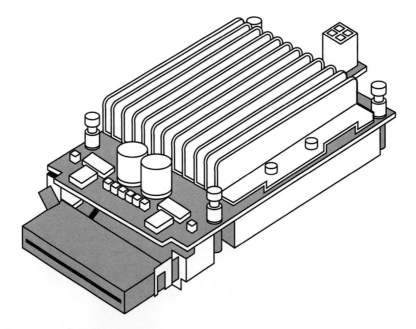

Figure 2.29   A typical power pod for the Itanium 2 processor.

A power pod for each processor socket is usually supplied with an Itanium 2 motherboard or server. If you need replacements, you should contact your motherboard or server vendor.

Operating Voltages

One trend that is clear to anybody who has been following processor design is that the operating voltages have gotten lower and lower. The benefits of lower voltage are threefold. The most obvious is that with lower voltage comes lower overall power consumption. By consuming less power, a system is less expensive to run, which is a significant issue in large corporations that use many servers.

The second major benefit is that with less voltage and therefore less power consumption, less heat is produced. Processors that run cooler can be packed into systems more tightly, and they often last longer. They also have the added advantage of helping make possible specialized server form factors, such as blade servers.

Perhaps the most important benefit, however, is that a processor running cooler on less power can be made to run faster. Lowering the voltage has been one of the key factors in enabling the clock rates of processors to go higher and higher. This is because the lower the voltage, the shorter the time needed to change a signal from low to high.

Until the release of the mobile Pentium and both desktop and mobile Pentium MMX, most processors used a single voltage level to both power the core and run the I/O circuits. Originally, most processors ran both the core and I/O circuits at 5V, which was later reduced to 3.5V or 3.3V to lower power consumption. When a single voltage is used for both the internal processor core power and the external processor bus and I/O signals, the processor is said to have a single, or unified, power plane design.

When originally designing a version of the Pentium processor for mobile or portable computers, Intel came up with a scheme to dramatically reduce the power consumption while still remaining compatible with the existing 3.3V chipsets, bus logic, memory, and other components. The result was a dual-plane, or split-plane, power design in which the processor core ran off a lower voltage while the I/O circuits remained at 3.3V. This was originally called voltage-reduction technology (VRT) and first debuted in the mobile Pentium processors released in 1996. Later, this dual-plane power design also appeared in desktop processors such as the Pentium MMX, which used 2.8V to power the core and 3.3V for the I/O circuits. Now most recent processors, including server processors, feature a dual-plane power design.

Knowing the processor voltage requirements is not a big issue with Socket 8, Socket 370, Socket 478, Socket A, Socket 603, Socket 604, Socket 754, Socket 939, Socket 940, Pentium Pro (Socket 8), Pentium II (Slot 1 or Slot 2), Itanium, or Itanium 2 processors because these sockets and slots have special VID pins the processor uses to signal to the motherboard the exact voltage requirements. This enables the voltage regulators built in to the motherboard (or connected to the processor, in the case of the Itanium and Itanium 2) to be automatically set to the correct voltage levels simply through installation of the processor.

The Pentium Pro and Pentium II processors were the first to automatically determine their voltage settings by controlling the motherboard-based voltage regulator through built-in VID pins. Those are explained in more detail later in this chapter.

▶▶ See "Pentium Pro Processors," p. 87.

▶▶ See "Pentium II Processors," p. 90.

Note that on the STD or VRE settings, the core and I/O voltages are the same; these are single-plane voltage settings. Any time a voltage other than STD or VRE is set, the motherboard defaults to a dual-plane voltage setting where the core voltage can be specifically set, while the I/O voltage remains constant at 3.3V, no matter what.

Starting with the Pentium Pro, all newer processors automatically determine their voltage settings by controlling the voltage regulator. This is done through built-in VID pins.

Heat Problems and Cooling CPUs

Heat can be a problem in any high-performance system. Higher-speed processors consume more power and therefore generate more heat. The processor is usually the single most power-hungry chip in a system, and in most situations, the fan inside a computer case is incapable of handling the load without some help.

Heatsinks

At one time, a heatsink, a special attachment for a chip that draws heat away from the chip, was needed only in systems in which processor heat was a problem. However, heatsinks have been a necessity for every processor discussed in this book. Several heatsink manufacturers are listed in Appendix C, "Vendor List."

A heatsink works like the radiator in a car, pulling heat away from the engine. In a similar fashion, a heatsink conducts heat away from the processor so it can be vented out of the system. It does this by using a thermal conductor (usually metal) to carry heat away from the processor into fins that expose a large amount of surface area to moving air. This enables the air to be heated, thus cooling the heatsink and the processor as well. Just like the radiator in a car, a heatsink depends on airflow. With no moving air, a heatsink is incapable of radiating the heat away. To keep the engine in a car from overheating when the car is not moving, auto engineers incorporate a fan. Likewise, there is always a fan somewhere inside a PC, helping to move air across the heatsink and vent it out of the system. In some name-brand systems, the fan included in the power supply is enough when combined with a special heatsink design; in most cases, though, an additional fan must be attached directly over the processor to provide the necessary level of cooling. Case fans are also typical in recent systems to assist in moving the hot air out of the system and replacing it with cooler air from the outside.

Tip

According to data from Intel, heatsink clips are the number-two destroyer of motherboards (screwdrivers are number one). When installing or removing a heatsink that is clipped on, be sure you don't scrape the surface of the motherboard. In most cases, the clips hook over protrusions in the socket, and when installing or removing the clips, it is very easy to scratch or scrape the surface of the board right below where the clip ends attach. It's a good idea to place a thin sheet of plastic underneath the edge of the clip while you work, especially if board traces that can be scratched are in the vicinity.

Heatsinks are rated for their cooling performances. Typically, the ratings are expressed as resistance to heat transfer, in degrees centigrade per watt (°C/W), where lower is better. Note that the resistance varies according to the airflow across the heatsink.

Passive Heatsinks

Passive heatsinks are basically aluminum-finned radiators that rely on airflow from an external source. Passive heatsinks don't work well unless there is some airflow across the fins, usually provided by a chassis-mounted fan that sometimes features a duct to direct airflow directly through the fins on the heatsink. Integrating a passive heatsink is difficult because you must ensure that the airflow comes from some other source; however, this can be very reliable and very cost-effective if done correctly. Some tower, pedestal, and rack-mounted chassis from major vendors such as Intel are designed to use passive heatsinks with one or more ducted chassis fans.

Figure 2.30 illustrates an aftermarket passive heatsink designed for a Xeon processor installed in a 1U rack-mounted server. It uses copper fins to provide adequate cooling, using the internal fans of the chassis that blow air past the motherboard's components.

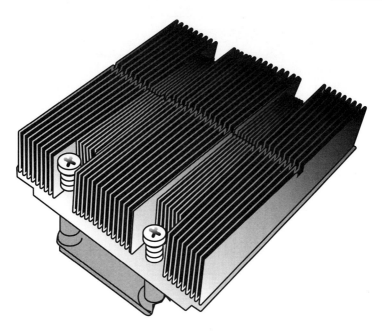

Figure 2.30   A low-profile passive heatsink for a Xeon, optimized for a 1U rack-mounted server.

Active Heatsinks

If you are building your own server or if you are using very fast processors, you will probably use active heatsinks on your processor(s). An active heatsink provides a more certain cooling solution, regardless of other airflow characteristics in the system.

To ensure a constant flow of air and more consistent performance, many heatsinks incorporate fans so they don't have to rely on the airflow within the system. Heatsinks with fans are referred to as *active* heatsinks (see Figure 2.31). An active heatsink has a power connection. Older heatsinks often used spare disk drive power connectors, but most recent heatsinks plug in to dedicated heatsink power connections found on the newer motherboards.

Tip

One of the best reasons to use the motherboard-based power connectors for the fan is that most recent system BIOS Setup programs can display the fan performance and report it to a system monitoring program. The BIOS or a system monitoring program can shut down the system if the fan fails or if its RPMs drop below a specified value. This helps prevent processor damage. On systems with a processor that supports thermal throttling, this feature can also be used to slow down the processor to avoid overheating.

The Pentium 4 design shown in Figure 2.31 uses two cams to engage the heatsink clips and place the system under tension. The force generated is 75 pounds, which produces a noticeable bow in the motherboard underneath the processor. This bow is normal, and motherboards are designed to accommodate it. The high amount of force is necessary to prevent the heavier heatsinks from pulling up on the processor during movement or shipment of the system, and it ensures a good bond for the thermal interface material (thermal grease).

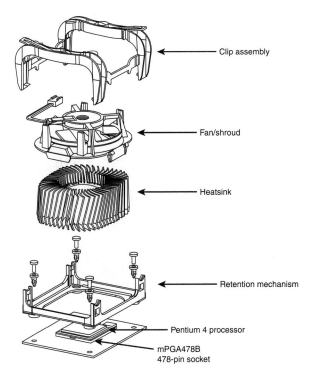

Figure 2.31   An active heatsink suitable for a Pentium 4 processor using Socket 478.

Figure 2.32 shows the design used on most AMD Opteron processors, featuring a cam and clip assembly on one side. Similar to the Pentium 4 double-cam assembly shown earlier in Figure 2.31, this design puts 75 pounds of force between the heatsink and the processor. Bowing of the motherboard is prevented in this design through the use of a special stiffening plate underneath the motherboard. The heatsink retention frame actually attaches to this plate through the board. The stiffening plate and retention frame normally come with the motherboard, but the heatsink with fan and the clip and cam assembly are included with the processor. Socket 939 and Socket 940 processors use similar designs.

Figure 2.33 shows an active heatsink arrangement on a slot-based Pentium II/III processor.

With the wide variety of processor speeds and construction on the market today, you also need to match the processor speed to the speed range of the heatsink you plan to use. Heatsinks made for faster processors have a larger cooling area, and an increasing number of them use a copper conducting plate or are made of solid copper rather than less-conductive aluminum. Figure 2.34 compares two heatsinks made for Athlon MP processors.

Note

Some Pentium 4 Socket 775 processors are sold in two forms: Some are packaged with a cooling solution suitable for ATX motherboards, and others are packaged with a cooling solution suitable for BTX motherboards. See Chapter 4, "Server Motherboards and BIOS," for more information about the differences between ATX and BTX motherboards.

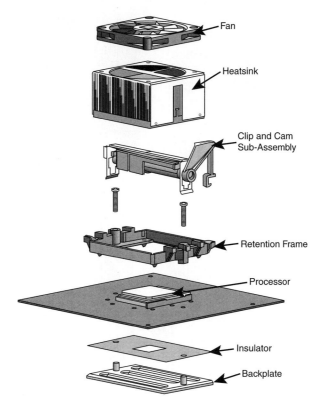

Figure 2.32   An active heatsink suitable for an Athlon 64, Athlon 64 FX, or Opteron processor using Socket 754, Socket 939, or Socket 940.

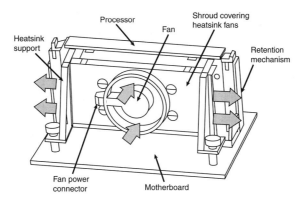

Figure 2.33   An active (fan-powered) heatsink and supports used with cartridge-type Pentium II/III processors.

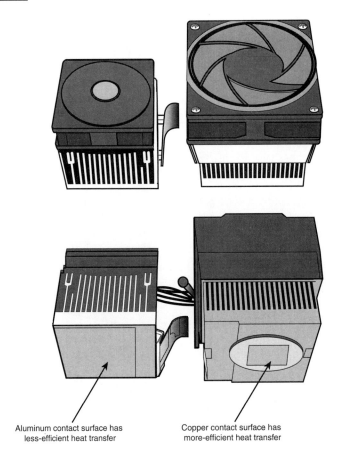

Aluminum contact surface has
less-efficient heat transfer

Copper contact surface has
more-efficient heat transfer

Figure 2.34 The all-aluminum active heatsink at left is designed for slower processors than the copper/aluminum model at right.

Processors sold as boxed or retail versions from Intel and AMD include high-quality active heatsinks designed to work under the worst possible ambient conditions. One of the main reasons to purchase boxed processors for systems that use standard motherboards is that you are guaranteed to get a high-quality heatsink with the processor, one that is designed to cool the processor under the worst conditions and that should last the life of the system. Factory-boxed processors also have long warranties that are valid only if you use the vendor-provided heatsink.

Blade Server Cooling

Depending on the product you use, the processors in your blade server might be cooled using passive coolers with very high-performance fans or more exotic technologies such as vapor cooling, which uses liquid inside a finned cooler to vaporize and transfer heat away from the processor.

Blade server vendors usually require you to purchase the appropriate cooling solution when you purchase a new blade. You can help minimize heat concerns by specifying lower-voltage versions of processors such as the Xeon and Opteron for your server blades and by adding additional air conditioning to your server room.

Heatsink Ratings and Calculations

To cool a processor, a heatsink transfers heat from the processor to the air. This capability is expressed in a figure known as *thermal resistance*, which is measured in degrees Celsius per watt (C/W). The lower the figure, the lower the thermal resistance and the more heat the heatsink can remove from the CPU.

To calculate the heatsink required for your processor, you can use this formula:

$$R_{total} = T_{case} - T_{inlet}/P_{power}$$

T_{case} is the maximum allowable CPU case temperature, T_{inlet} is the maximum allowable inlet temperature to the CPU heatsink, and P_{power} is the maximum power dissipation of the processor. For example, the Pentium 4 3.4E (Prescott) processor is rated for a maximum operating temperature of 73°C and a maximum heatsink inlet temperature of 38°C, and it has a maximum thermal output of 103 watts. This means the heatsink required to properly cool this chip needs to be rated 73°C – 38°C / 103W = 0.34°C/W. This figure includes the resistance of both the thermal interface material (thermal grease) and the heatsink itself, so if you used a thermal grease with a known resistance of 0.01°C/W, the heatsink would need to be rated at 0.33°C/W or less.

You can use another useful formula to describe processor power:

$$P_{power} = C \times V^2 \times F$$

P_{power} is the maximum power output of the processor, C is the capacitance, V^2 is the voltage squared, and F is the frequency. From this you can see that if you double the frequency of a processor, it will consume twice as much power, and if you double the voltage, the processor will consume four times as much power. Consequently, if you lower the voltage by half, it will consume only one fourth the power. These relationships are important to consider if you are overclocking your processor because a small increase in voltage will have a much more dramatic effect than a similar increase in speed.

In general, increasing the speed of a processor by 5% increases the power consumption by only the same amount. Using the previous heatsink calculation, if the processor speed was increased by 5%, the 103W processor would now draw 108.15W, and the required heatsink rating would go from 0.34°C/W to 0.32°C/W, a proportional change. In most cases, unless you are overclocking to the extreme, the existing heatsink should work. As a compromise, you can try setting the voltage on manual and dropping it a small amount to compensate, thereby reducing the power consumption. Of course, when you drop the voltage, the CPU might become unstable, so you need to test this. As you can see, changing all these settings in the interest of overclocking can take a lot of time when you consider all the testing required to ensure that everything is working properly. You have to decide whether the rewards are worth the time and energy spent on setting it up and verifying the functionality.

Note that most professional heatsink manufacturers publish their °C/W ratings, whereas many of the "boutique" heatsink vendors do not. In many cases, the manufacturers of many of the more extreme heatsinks don't do the testing that the professional manufacturers do and are more interested in the looks than the actual performance.

Installing a Heatsink

To have the best possible transfer of heat from the processor to the heatsink, most heatsink manufacturers specify some type of thermal interface material to be placed between the processor and the heatsink. This typically consists of a ceramic, alumina, or silver-based grease, but it can also be in the form of a special pad or even a type of double-stick tape. Some are called *phase-change* materials because they change viscosity (become thinner) above certain temperatures, enabling them to better flow into minute gaps between the chip and heatsink. In general, thermal greases offer higher performance than phase-change materials, but because they always have a lower viscosity, they flow more easily, can be messy to apply, and (if too much is used) can spill from the sides onto the socket and motherboard.

Typical factory-supplied active heatsinks usually include a preapplied phase-change thermal material. However, if you choose to install your own heatsink, you must make sure you have thermal grease. It is usually supplied with the heatsink, or you can use third-party products.

No matter what type you use, a thermal interface aid such as thermal grease or phase-change material can improve heatsink performance dramatically compared to installing the heatsink dry. Thermal interface materials are rated by thermal conductance (in which case higher is better) or thermal resistance (in which case lower is better). Unfortunately, several industry-standard rating scales are used to measure performance, often making product comparisons difficult. Some measure the thermal conductivity, and others measure the thermal resistance; and the scales used can vary greatly. The most commonly reported specification is thermal resistance in degrees Centigrade per watt (°C/W) for an interface layer 0.001 inch thick and 1 square inch in size. For a given material, the thinner the interface layer or the larger the area, the lower the resistance. In addition, due to other variables, such as surface roughness and pressure, it is often impossible to directly compare different materials, even if they appear to use the same ratings scale.

As a means of offering some sort of comparison, let's look at the effect on processor temperatures by using thermal interface materials of different specifications. Currently, the highest-thermal-output processor is the Pentium 4 3.4E, which is rated at 103W thermal output, with a surface area on the heat spreader of 1.5 square inches. Table 2.15 shows the rise in temperature that will result from using thermal interface materials of different C/W specifications.

Table 2.15   Thermal Interface Material Resistance Versus CPU Temperature Rise for a 103W Pentium 4 Processor

Thermal Rating (°C/W)	Temperature Rise (°C)
0.000	0.00
0.005	0.34
0.010	0.69
0.020	1.37
0.030	2.06
0.040	2.75
0.050	3.43
0.060	4.12
0.070	4.81
0.080	5.49
0.090	6.18
0.100	6.87

Most of the better thermal greases are rated from 0.005C/W to 0.02C/W per square inch, which would result in a rise of between 0.34°C and 1.37°C. Even if there were a "perfect" thermal grease available, it would reduce the CPU temperature by only less than 2°C over most of the products currently on the market. Actual tests have been done on multiple brands of thermal greases, and in most cases, the differences in temperature readings between different brands are insignificant. Most of the premium products on the market have very similar performance.

You can purchase thermal grease in small, single-use tubes or larger versions that can service multiple processor installations. Most of the recommended thermal greases include alumina or silver, which offer the lowest thermal resistances. Silver is generally the best but is significantly more expensive, and its real-world differences are very slight. One brand (Arctic Silver) has even developed a following sufficient to cause others to counterfeit the product and name. The important thing to note is that, based on calculations as well as tests, there is only a couple degrees' difference in CPU temperature under full load when substituting one brand of thermal grease for another. If you want the best, you should choose a compound with embedded silver. The next best option is alumina, and the next best is the less expensive (and somewhat less effective) ceramic-based greases.

Figure 2.35 shows the thermal interface pad or grease positioned between a processor and heatsink.

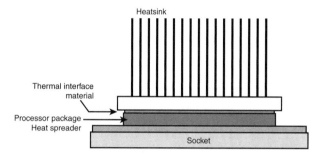

Figure 2.35   Thermal interface material helps transfer heat from the processor die to the heatsink.

Intel and AMD Processor Configurations

The following sections provide detailed information on x86 and Itanium processors used in servers. You can use these sections to help plan upgrades, determine which servers are most suitable for a particular task, decide which servers may need to be retired, and plan your next server purchase or server building project.

▶▶   For detailed information on other forms of RISC-based processors used in servers, see "RISC-Based Server Processors," p. 130.

Pentium Pro Processors

The Pentium Pro, which was introduced in November) 1995 and became widely available in 1996, was the first x86 processor developed primarily for use as a server processor. Because it was optimized for 32-bit processing, it actually performed more slowly than the existing Pentium when running 16-bit applications. In addition to single-processor designs, various vendors developed two-way, four-way, and eight-way configurations. As Table 2.16 indicates, the Pentium Pro processor was available with 256KB, 512KB, or 1MB of full-speed L2 cache. The larger cache sizes were favored for server applications.

Table 2.16 lists the general specifications for various models of the Pentium Pro. Table 2.17 lists specifications by processor model.

Table 2.16   Pentium Pro General Specifications

Introduction date	November 1995
Maximum rated speeds	150MHz, 166MHz, 180MHz, 200MHz
CPU	2.5x, 3x

Table 2.16   Continued

Internal registers	32-bit
External data bus	64-bit
Memory address bus	36-bit
Addressable memory	64GB
Virtual memory	64TB
Integral L1 cache size	8KB code, 8KB data (16KB total)
Integrated L2 cache bus	64-bit, full-core speed
Socket/Slot	Socket 8
Physical package	387-pin dual cavity PGA
Package dimensions	2.46 (6.25cm)×2.66 (6.76cm)
Math coprocessor	Built-in FPU
Power management	System Management Mode (SMM)
Operating voltage	3.1V or 3.3V

Table 2.17   Pentium Pro Processor Specifications, by Processor Model

Pentium Pro Processor (200MHz) with 1MB Integrated Level 2 Cache	
Introduction date	August 18, 1997
Clock speed	200MHz
FSB speed	66MHz
CPU clock ratio	3x
Number of transistors	5.5 million (0.35-micron process), plus 62 million in 1MB L2 cache (0.35-micron)
Cache memory	8Kx2 (16KB) L1, 1MB core-speed L2
Die size	0.552 (14.0mm)
Pentium Pro Processor (200MHz)	
Introduction date	November 1, 1995
Clock speed	200MHz
FSB speed	66MHz
CPU clock ratio	3x
Number of transistors	5.5 million (0.35-micron process), plus 15.5 million in 256KB L2 cache (0.6-micron), or 31 million in 512KB L2 cache (0.35-micron)
Cache memory	8Kx2 (16KB) L1, 256KB or 512KB core-speed L2
Die size	0.552 inch per side (14.0mm)
Pentium Pro Processor (180MHz)	
Introduction date	November 1, 1995
Clock speed	180MHz
FSB speed	60MHz
CPU clock ratio	3x
Number of transistors	5.5 million (0.35-micron process), plus 15.5 million in 256KB L2 cache (0.6-micron)
Cache memory	8Kx2 (16KB) L1, 256KB core-speed L2
Die size	0.552 inch per side (14.0mm)

Table 2.17   Continued

Pentium Pro Processor (166MHz)	
Introduction date	November 1, 1995
Clock speed	166MHz
FSB speed	66MHz
CPU clock ratio	2.5x
Number of transistors	5.5 million (0.35-micron process), plus 31 million in 512KB L2 cache (0.35-micron)
Cache memory	8Kx2 L1, 512KB core-speed L2
Die size	0.552 inch per side (14.0mm)
Pentium Pro Processor (150MHz)	
Introduction date	November 1, 1995
Clock speed	150MHz
FSB speed	60MHz
CPU clock ratio	2.5x
Number of transistors	5.5 million (0.6-micron process), plus 15.5 million in 256KB L2 cache (0.6-micron)
Cache memory	8Kx2 speed L2
Die size	0.691 inch per side (17.6mm)

Figure 2.36 shows the underside of the Pentium Pro processor with 256KB of L2 cache, and Figure 2.37 shows the underside of the Pentium Pro processor with 1MB of L2 cache.

Figure 2.36   Pentium Pro processor with 256KB L2 cache; the cache is on the left side of the processor die. (*Photograph used by permission of Intel Corporation.*)

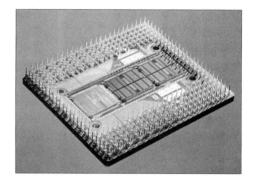

Figure 2.37   Pentium Pro processor with 1MB L2 cache; the cache is in the center and right portions of the die. (*Photograph used by permission of Intel Corporation.*)

The main processor die includes a 16KB split L1 cache with an 8KB two-way set-associative cache for primary instructions and an 8KB four-way set-associative cache for data. The Pentium Pro introduced the DIB architecture used in subsequent processors from Intel and AMD. Two buses made up the DIB architecture: the L2 cache bus (contained entirely within the processor package) and the processor-to-main memory system bus. The speed of the dedicated L2 cache bus on the Pentium Pro was equal to the full-core speed of the processor. This was accomplished by embedding the cache chips directly into the Pentium Pro package, as shown in Figures 2.36 and 2.37. The DIB processor bus architecture addressed processor-to-memory bus bandwidth limitations. It offered up to three times the performance bandwidth of the single-bus, "Socket 7"–generation processors, such as the Pentium.

Pentium II Processors

The Pentium II processor, introduced in May 1997, was designed, in part, as a lower-cost follow-up to the Pentium Pro. Instead of using expensive on-die full-speed L2 cache, as in the Pentium Pro, the Pentium II's 512KB of L2 cache is off-die, attached to the processor assembly, and runs at half the processor's core speed. Because the Pentium II was aimed primarily at the desktop processor market, it was not designed to scale above a two-way configuration. The Pentium II Xeon was used for more powerful server configurations. However, many two-way Pentium II servers were built for entry-level tasks. The Pentium II uses Slot 1, rather than Socket 8, as was used by the Pentium Pro.

Although the Pentium II was suitable for use in single- or dual-processor server configurations, some versions were better optimized for this task than others. Table 2.18 lists only the Pentium II processor versions that can cache up to 4GB of RAM and support ECC L2 cache. Versions that cache only 512MB of RAM drop in performance if more than 512MB of RAM is installed, and versions that lack ECC support in L2 cache might cache corrupt memory contents, causing system errors or a system crash when cache memory is accessed.

Table 2.18   Pentium II Processor Identification Information[1]

S-Spec	Core Stepping	CPUID Bus Speed	Core/ Cache Size (MHz)	L2 Cache Type (MB)	L2 Package	CPU
SL35V[2,3]	dA1	0651h	300/66	512	ECC	SECC 3.00
SL2QH[2,3]	dA1	0651h	333/66	512	ECC	SECC 3.00
SL2S5[3,5]	dA1	0651h	333/66	512	ECC	SECC 3.00
SL2ZP[3,5]	dA1	0651h	333/66	512	ECC	SECC 3.00
SL2ZQ[3,5]	dA1	0651h	350/100	512	ECC	SECC 3.00
SL2S6[3,5]	dA1	0651h	350/100	512	ECC	SECC 3.00
SL2S7[3,5]	dA1	0651h	400/100	512	ECC	SECC 3.00
SL2SF[2,3]	dA1	0651h	350/100	512	ECC	SECC 3.00
SL2SH[2,3]	dA1	0651h	400/100	512	ECC	SECC 3.00
SL2VY[2,3]	dA1	0651h	300/66	512	ECC	SECC 3.00
SL33D[2,3]	dB0	0652h	266/66	512	ECC	SECC 3.00
SL2YK[2,3,5]	dB0	0652h	300/66	512	ECC	SECC 3.00
SL2WZ[2,3,5]	dB0	0652h	350/100	512	ECC	SECC 3.00
SL2YM[2,3,5]	dB0	0652h	400/100	512	ECC	SECC 3.00
SL37G[2,3,4]	dB0	0652h	400/100	512	ECC	SECC2 OLGA
SL2WB[2,3,5]	dB0	0652h	450/100	512	ECC	SECC 3.00
SL37H[2,3]	dB0	0652h	450/100	512	ECC	SECC2 OLGA
SL2W7[3,5]	dB0	0652h	266/66	512	ECC	SECC 2.00
SL2W8[3,5]	dB0	0652h	300/66	512	ECC	SECC 3.00
SL2TV[3,5]	dB0	0652h	333/66	512	ECC	SECC 3.00

Table 2.18   Continued

S-Spec	Core Stepping	CPUID Bus Speed	Core/ Cache Size (MHz)	L2 Cache Type (MB)	L2 Package	CPU
SL2U3[3,5]	dB0	0652h	350/100	512	ECC	SECC 3.00
SL2U4[3,5]	dB0	0652h	350/100	512	ECC	SECC 3.00
SL2U5[3,5]	dB0	0652h	400/100	512	ECC	SECC 3.00
SL2U6[3,5]	dB0	0652h	400/100	512	ECC	SECC 3.00
SL2U7[3,5]	dB0	0652h	450/100	512	ECC	SECC 3.00
SL356[3,5]	dB0	0652h	350/100	512	ECC	SECC2 PLGA
SL357[3,5]	dB0	0652h	400/100	512	ECC	SECC2 OLGA
SL358[3,5]	dB0	0652h	450/100	512	ECC	SECC2 OLGA
SL37F[2,3,5]	dB0	0652h	350/100	512	ECC	SECC2 PLGA
SL3FN[3,5]	dB0	0652h	350/100	512	ECC	SECC2 OLGA
SL3EE[3,5]	dB0	0652h	400/100	512	ECC	SECC2 PLGA
SL3F9[2,3]	dB0	0652h	400/100	512	ECC	SECC2 PLGA
SL38M[2,3,5]	dB1	0653h	350/100	512	ECC	SECC 3.00
SL38N[2,3,5]	dB1	0653h	400/100	512	ECC	SECC 3.00
SL36U[3,5]	dB1	0653h	350/100	512	ECC	SECC 3.00
SL38Z[3,5]	dB1	0653h	400/100	512	ECC	SECC 3.00
SL3D5[2,3]	dB1	0653h	400/100	512	ECC	SECC2 OLGA

[1]Key: CPUID = the internal ID returned by the CPUID instruction; ECC = error correcting code; OLGA = organic land grid array; PLGA = plastic land grid array; SECC = single-edge contact cartridge; and SECC2 = single-edge contact cartridge, revision 2.

[2]This is a boxed Pentium II processor with an attached fan heatsink.

[3]This processor has an enhanced L2 cache, which can cache up to 4GB of main memory. Other standard PII processors can cache only up to 512MB of main memory.

[4]This is a boxed Pentium II OverDrive processor with an attached fan heatsink, designed for upgrading Pentium Pro (Socket 8) systems.

[5]This part operates only at the specified clock multiplier frequency ratio at which it was manufactured. It can be overclocked only by increasing the bus speed.

◄◄ See "Single-Edge Contact Cartridge Packaging," p. 67, for processor package and slot details and pictures.

Pentium II Xeon

The Pentium II Xeon, introduced in June 1998, is an advanced version of the Pentium II that was designed to support up to eight-way operation, featuring larger and faster L2 cache than the standard Pentium II. The Pentium II Xeon uses Slot 2, rather than Slot 1, as with the Pentium II.

◄◄ See "Single-Edge Contact Cartridge Packaging," p. 67, for processor package and slot details and pictures.

The Pentium II Xeon processors were produced in four variations—with 256KB, 512KB, 1MB, or 2MB of L2 cache. Even more significant than the size of the cache is its speed. All the cache memory in the Pentium II Xeon processors runs at the full-core speed. This is difficult to do, considering that the cache chips are separate chips on the board in Slot 2–based versions. The original Pentium II Xeon processors had 7.5 million transistors in the main processor die. The L2 cache in all Pentium II Xeon processors has a full 64GB RAM address range and supports ECC.

Table 2.19 provides the specifications of the Pentium II Xeon.

Table 2.19   Pentium II Xeon Specifications

S-Spec	Core Steppings	CPUID	Core Speed (MHz)	Bus Speed (MHz)	L2 Cache Size (KB)
SL2RH	B0	0652h	400	100	512
SL344	B0	0652h	400	100	512
SL2NB	B0	0652h	400	100	1024
SL345	B0	0652h	400	100	1024
SL34H	B1	0653h	400	100	512
SL35N	B1	0653h	400	100	512
SL35P	B1	0653h	400	100	1024
SL34J	B1	0653h	400	100	1024
SL354[1]	B1	0653h	450	100	512
SL36W[1]	B1	0653h	450	100	512
SL2XJ[1]	B1	0653h	450	100	512
SL33T[1]	B1	0653h	450	100	512
SL33U[1]	B1	0653h	450	100	1024
SL2XK[1]	B1	0653h	450	100	1024
SL2XL[1]	B1	0653h	450	100	2048
SL33V[1]	B1	0653h	450	100	2048

[1]*Error checking and correcting (ECC) for the L2 cache transactions cannot be disabled on these processors.*

Table 2.20   Intel Pentium III Processor Variations[1]

Speed (MHz)	Bus Speed (MHz)	Multiplier	Boxed CPU S-Spec	OEM CPU S-Spec	Stepping	CPUID	L2 Cache
450	100	4.5x	SL3CC	SL364	kB0	0672	512K
450	100	4.5x	SL37C	SL35D	kC0	0673	512K
500	100	5x	SL3CD	SL365	kB0	0672	512K
500	100	5x	SL365	SL365	kB0	0672	512K
500	100	5x	SL37D	SL35E	kC0	0673	512K
500E	100	5x	SL3R2	SL3Q9	cA2	0681	256K
500E	100	5x	SL45R	SL444	cB0	0683	256K
533B	133	4x	SL3E9	SL3BN	kC0	0673	512K
533EB	133	4x	SL3SX	SL3N6	cA2	0681	256K
533EB	133	4x	SL3VA	SL3VF	cA2	0681	256K
533EB	133	4x	SL44W	SL3XG	cB0	0683	256K
533EB	133	4x	SL45S	SL3XS	cB0	0683	256K

Pentium III Processors

The Pentium III processor, introduced in 1999, is an improved version of the Pentium II processor, supporting higher clock speeds and higher memory speeds. Early versions of the Pentium III used the same SECC2 cartridge packaging and Slot 1 connector used by the Pentium II.

◄◄   See "Single-Edge Contact Cartridge Packaging," p. 67, for processor package and slot details and pictures.

Later versions of the Pentium III switched to an FC-PGA packaging compatible with Socket 370 (a development of the socket design originally created for use with the Celeron).

All versions of the Pentium III that contain 512KB of L2 cache can be used in multiple-processor configurations. However, late releases of the Pentium III that use the .13-micron process with 256KB of L2 cache onboard (code-named Tualatin) are not compatible with multiple-processor configurations. Pentium III–based servers are configured as single-processor or two-way systems.

Note

Although a few servers with four physical Pentium III processors onboard exist, such as the NEC Express5800 320La, these systems use the third and fourth processors as redundant spares for the first two processors.

Table 2.20 lists the technical specifications for the various models of the Pentium III processor.

L2 Speed	Max. Temp. (C)	Voltage	Max. Power (W)	Process (Microns)	Transistors	Package
225	90	2.00	25.3	0.25	9.5M	SECC2
225	90	2.00	25.3	0.25	9.5M	SECC2
250	90	2.00	28.0	0.25	9.5M	SECC2
250	90	2.00	28.0	0.25	9.5M	SECC2
250	90	2.00	28.0	0.25	9.5M	SECC2
500	85	1.60	13.2	0.18	28.1M	FC-PGA
500	85	1.60	13.2	0.18	28.1M	FC-PGA
267	90	2.05	29.7	0.25	9.5M	SECC2
533	85	1.65	14.0	0.18	28.1M	SECC2
533	85	1.65	14.0	0.18	28.1M	FC-PGA
533	85	1.65	14.0	0.18	28.1M	SECC2
533	85	1.65	14.0	0.18	28.1M	FC-PGA

Table 2.20   Intel Pentium III Processor Variations[1]

Speed (MHz)	Bus Speed (MHz)	Multiplier	Boxed CPU S-Spec	OEM CPU S-Spec	Stepping	CPUID	L2 Cache
550	100	5.5x	SL3FJ	SL3F7	kC0	0673	512K
550E	100	5.5x	SL3R3	SL3QA	cA2	0681	256K
550E	100	5.5x	SL3V5	SL3N7	cA2	0681	256K
550E	100	5.5x	SL44X	SL3XH	cB0	0683	256K
550E	100	5.5x	SL45T	N/A	cB0	0683	256K
600	100	6x	SL3JT	SL3JM	kC0	0673	512K
600E	100	6x	SL3NA	SL3H6	cA2	0681	256K
600E	100	6x	SL3NL	SL3VH	cA2	0681	256K
600E	100	6x	SL44Y	SL43E	cB0	0683	256K
600E	100	6x	SL45U	SL3XU	cB0	0683	256K
600E	100	6x	N/A	SL4CM	cC0	0686	256K
600E	100	6x	N/A	SL4C7	cC0	0686	256K
600B	133	4.5x	SL3JU	SL3JP	kC0	0673	512K
600EB	133	4.5x	SL3NB	SL3H7	cA2	0681	256K
600EB	133	4.5x	SL3VB	SL3VG	cA2	0681	256K
600EB	133	4.5x	SL44Z	SL3XJ	cB0	0683	256K
600EB	133	4.5x	SL45V	SL3XT	cB0	0683	256K
600EB	133	4.5x	SL4CL	SL4CL	cC0	0686	256K
600EB	133	4.5x	N/A	SL46C	cC0	0686	256K
650	100	6.5x	SL3NR	SL3KV	cA2	0681	256K
650	100	6.5x	SL3NM	SL3VJ	cA20	681	256K
650	100	6.5x	SL452	SL3XK	cB0	0683	256K
650	100	6.5x	SL45W	SL3XV	cB0	0683	256K
650	100	6.5x	N/A	SL4CK	cC0	0686	256K
650	100	6.5x	N/A	SL4C5	cC0	0686	256K
667	133	5x	SL3ND	SL3KW	cA2	0681	256K
667	133	5x	SL3T2	SL3VK	cA2	0681	256K
667	133	5x	SL453	SL3XL	cB0	0683	256K
667	133	5x	SL45X	SL3XW	cB0	0683	256K
667	133	5x	N/A	SL4CJ	cC0	0686	256K
667	133	5x	N/A	SL4C4	cC0	0686	256K
700	100	7x	SL3SY	SL3S9	cA2	0681	256K
700	100	7x	SL3T3	SL3VL	cA2	0681	256K
700	100	7x	SL454	SL453	cB0	0683	256K
700	100	7x	SL45Y	SL3XX	cB0	0683	256K
700	100	7x	SL4M7	SL4CH	cC0	0686	256K
700	100	7x	N/A	SL4C3	cC0	0686	256K
733	133	5.5x	SL3SZ	SL3SB	cA2	0681	256K

L2 Speed	Max. Temp. (C)	Voltage	Max. Power (W)	Process (Microns)	Transistors	Package
275	80	2.00	30.8	0.25	9.5M	SECC2
550	85	1.60	14.5	0.18	28.1M	FC-PGA
550	85	1.60	14.5	0.18	28.1M	SECC2
550	85	1.60	14.5	0.18	28.1M	SECC2
550	85	1.60	14.5	0.18	28.1M	FC-PGA
300	85	2.00	34.5	0.25	9.5M	SECC2
600	82	1.65	15.8	0.18	28.1M	SECC2
600	82	1.65	15.8	0.18	28.1M	FC-PGA
600	82	1.65	15.8	0.18	28.1M	SECC2
600	82	1.65	15.8	0.18	28.1M	FC-PGA
600	82	1.7	15.8	0.18	28.1M	FC-PGA
600	82	1.7	15.8	0.18	28.1M	SECC2
300	85	2.05	34.5	0.25	9.5M	SECC2
600	82	1.65	15.8	0.18	28.1M	SECC2
600	82	1.65	15.8	0.18	28.1M	FC-PGA
600	82	1.65	15.8	0.18	28.1M	SECC2
600	82	1.65	15.8	0.18	28.1M	FC-PGA
600	82	1.7	15.8	0.18	28.1M	FC-PGA
600	82	1.7	15.8	0.18	28.1M	SECC2
650	82	1.65	17.0	0.18	28.1M	SECC2
650	82	1.65	17.0	0.18	28.1M	FC-PGA
650	82	1.65	17.0	0.18	28.1M	SECC2
650	82	1.65	17.0	0.18	28.1M	FC-PGA
650	82	1.7	17.0	0.18	28.1M	FC-PGA
650	82	1.7	17.0	0.18	28.1M	SECC2
667	82	1.65	17.5	0.18	28.1M	SECC2
667	82	1.65	17.5	0.18	28.1M	FC-PGA
667	82	1.65	17.5	0.18	28.1M	SECC2
667	82	1.65	17.5	0.18	28.1M	FC-PGA
667	82	1.7	17.5	0.18	28.1M	FC-PGA
667	82	1.7	17.5	0.18	28.1M	SECC2
700	80	1.65	18.3	0.18	28.1M	SECC2
700	80	1.65	18.3	0.18	28.1M	FC-PGA
700	80	1.65	18.3	0.18	28.1M	SECC2
700	80	1.65	18.3	0.18	28.1M	FC-PGA
700	80	1.7	18.3	0.18	28.1M	FC-PGA
700	80	1.7	18.3	0.18	28.1M	SECC2
733	80	1.65	19.1	0.18	28.1M	SECC2

Table 2.20   Continued

Speed (MHz)	Bus Speed (MHz)	Multiplier	Boxed CPU S-Spec	OEM CPU S-Spec	Stepping	CPUID	L2 Cache
733	133	5.5x	SL3T4	SL3VM	cA2	0681	256K
733	133	5.5x	SL455	SL3XN	cB0	0683	256K
733	133	5.5x	SL45Z	SL3XY	cB0	0683	256K
733	133	5.5x	SL4M8	SL4CG	cC0	0686	256K
733	133	5.5x	SL4KD	SL4C2	cC0	0686	256K
733	133	5.5x	SL4FQ	SL4CX	cC0	0686	256K
750	100	7.5x	SL3V6	SL3WC	cA2	0681	256K
750	100	7.5x	SL3VC	SL3VN	cA2	0681	256K
750	100	7.5x	SL456	SL3XP	cB0	0683	256K
750	100	7.5x	SL462	SL3XZ	cB0	0683	256K
750	100	7.5x	SL4M9	SL4CF	cC0	0686	256K
750	100	7.5x	SL4KE	SL4BZ	cC0	0686	256K
800	100	8x	SL457	SL3XR	cB0	0683	256K
800	100	8x	SL463	SL3Y3	cB0	0683	256K
800	100	8x	SL4MA	SL4CE	cC0	0686	256K
800	100	8x	SL4KF	SL4BY	cC0	0686	256K
800EB	133	6x	SL458	SL3XQ	cB0	0683	256K
800EB	133	6x	SL464	SL3Y2	cB0	0683	256K
800EB	133	6x	SL4MB	SL4CD	cC0	0686	256K
800EB	133	6x	SL4G7	SL4XQ	cC0	0686	256K
800EB	133	6x	SL4KG	SL4BX	cC0	0686	256K
850	100	8.5x	SL47M	SL43F	cB0	0683	256K
850	100	8.5x	SL49G	SL43H	cB0	0683	256K
850	100	8.5x	SL4MC	SL4CC	cC0	0686	256K
850	100	8.5x	SL4KH	SL4BW	cC0	0686	256K
866	133	6.5x	SL47N	SL43G	cB0	0683	256K
866	133	6.5x	SL49H	SL43J	cB0	0683	256K
866	133	6.5x	SL4MD	SL4CB	cC0	0686	256K
866	133	6.5x	SL4KJ	SL4BV	cC0	0686	256K
866	133	6.5x	SL5B5	SL5QE	cD0	068A	256K
900	100	9x	N/A	SL4SD	cC0	0686	256K
933	133	7x	SL47Q	SL448	cB0	0683	256K
933	133	7x	SL49J	SL44J	cB0	0683	256K
933	133	7x	SL4ME	SL4C9	cC0	0686	256K
933	133	7x	SL4KK	SL4BT	cC0	0686	256K
933	133	7x	N/A	SL5QF	cD0	068A	256K
1000B	133	7.5x	SL4FP	SL48S	cB0	0683	256K
1000B	133	7.5x	SL4C8	SL4C8	cC0	0686	256K

L2 Speed	Max. Temp. (C)	Voltage	Max. Power (W)	Process (Microns)	Transistors	Package
733	80	1.65	19.1	0.18	28.1M	FC-PGA
733	80	1.65	19.1	0.18	28.1M	SECC2
733	80	1.65	19.1	0.18	28.1M	FC-PGA
733	80	1.7	19.1	0.18	28.1M	FC-PGA
733	80	1.7	19.1	0.18	28.1M	SECC2
733	80	1.7	19.1	0.18	28.1M	SECC2
750	80	1.65	19.5	0.18	28.1M	SECC2
750	80	1.65	19.5	0.18	28.1M	FC-PGA
750	80	1.65	19.5	0.18	28.1M	SECC2
750	80	1.65	19.5	0.18	28.1M	FC-PGA
750	80	1.7	19.5	0.18	28.1M	FC-PGA
750	80	1.7	19.5	0.18	28.1M	SECC2
800	80	1.65	20.8	0.18	28.1M	SECC2
800	80	1.65	20.8	0.18	28.1M	FC-PGA
800	80	1.7	20.8	0.18	28.1M	FC-PGA
800	80	1.7	20.8	0.18	28.1M	SECC2
800	80	1.65	20.8	0.18	28.1M	SECC2
800	80	1.65	20.8	0.18	28.1M	FC-PGA
800	80	1.7	20.8	0.18	28.1M	FC-PGA
800	80	1.7	20.8	0.18	28.1M	SECC2
800	80	1.7	20.8	0.18	28.1M	SECC2
850	80	1.65	22.5	0.18	28.1M	SECC2
850	80	1.65	22.5	0.18	28.1M	FC-PGA
850	80	1.7	22.5	0.18	28.1M	FC-PGA
850	80	1.7	22.5	0.18	28.1M	SECC2
866	80	1.65	22.9	0.18	28.1M	SECC2
866	80	1.65	22.9	0.18	28.1M	FC-PGA
866	80	1.7	22.5	0.18	28.1M	FC-PGA
866	80	1.7	22.5	0.18	28.1M	SECC2
866	80	1.75	26.1	0.18	28.1M	FC-PGA
900	75	1.7	23.2	0.18	28.1M	FC-PGA
933	75	1.7	25.5	0.18	28.1M	SECC2
933	75	1.7	24.5	0.18	28.1M	FC-PGA
933	75	1.7	24.5	0.18	28.1M	FC-PGA
933	75	1.7	25.5	0.18	28.1M	SECC2
933	77	1.75	27.3	0.18	28.1M	FC-PGA
1000	70	1.7	26.1	0.18	28.1M	SECC2
1000	70	1.7	26.1	0.18	28.1M	FC-PGA

Table 2.20   Continued

Speed (MHz)	Bus Speed (MHz)	Multiplier	Boxed CPU S-Spec	OEM CPU S-Spec	Stepping	CPUID	L2 Cache
1000B	133	7.5x	SL4MF	N/A	cC0	0686	256K
1000	100	10x	SL4BR	SL4BR	cC0	0686	256K
1000	100	10x	SL4KL	N/A	cC0	0686	256K
1000B	133	7.5x	SL4BS	SL4BS	cC0	0686	256K
1000B	100	10x	N/A	SL5QV	cD0	068A	256K
1000B	133	7.5x	SL5DV	N/A	cD0	068A	256K
1000B	133	7.5x	SL5B3	SL5B3	cD0	068A	256K
1000B	133	7.5x	SL52R	SL52R	cD0	068A	256K
1000B	133	7.5x	SL5FQ	N/A	cD0	068A	256K
1100	100	11x	N/A	SL5QW	cD0	068A	256K
1133	133	8.5x	SL5LT	N/A	tA1	06B1	256K
1133	133	8.5x	SL5GQ	SL5GQ	tA1	06B1	256K
1133-S	133	8.5x	SL5LV	N/A	tA1	06B1	512K
1133-S	133	8.5x	SL5PU	SL5PU	tA1	06B1	512K
1200	133	9x	SL5GN	SL5GN	tA1	06B1	256K
1200	133	9x	SL5PM	N/A	tA1	06B1	256K
1266-S	133	9.5x	SL5LW	SL5QL	tA1	06B1	512K
1333	133	10x	N/A	SL5VX	tA1	06B1	256K
1400-S	133	10.5x	SL657	SL5XL	tA1	06B1	512K

[1]Key: CPUID = the internal ID returned by the CPUID instruction; ECC = error correcting code; FC-PGA = flip-chip pin grid array; FC-PGA2 = flip-chip pin grid array, revision 2; SECC = single-edge contact cartridge; and SECC2 = single-edge contact cartridge, revision 2.

Pentium III Xeon

The Pentium III Xeon is an improved version of the Pentium II Xeon. Initial versions with external L2 cache chips included 9.5 million transistors. The Pentium III Xeon, like the Pentium III, later switched to on-die L2 cache. However, unlike the standard Pentium III, the Pentium III Xeon continued to use a slot-based design.

When the Pentium III versions with on-die cache were released, the transistor count went up to 28.1 million transistors in the 256KB cache version, 84 million transistors in the 1MB cache version, and a whopping 140 million transistors in the latest 2MB cache version, setting an industry record at the time. The high transistor counts are due to the on-die L2 cache, which is very transistor intensive. As with the Pentium II Xeon, the L2 cache in all Pentium III Xeon processors has a full 64GB RAM address range and supports ECC.

To improve reliability over that of the Pentium II Xeon, the Pentium III Xeon has an SMBus interface and a thermal sensor. These are used along with the additional signals in the SC330 connector to monitor the processor's operation.

L2 Speed	Max. Temp. (C)	Voltage	Max. Power (W)	Process (Microns)	Transistors	Package
1000	70	1.7	26.1	0.18	28.1M	FC-PGA
1000	70	1.7	26.1	0.18	28.1M	SECC2
1000	70	1.7	26.1	0.18	28.1M	SECC2
1000	70	1.7	26.1	0.18	28.1M	SECC2
1000	75	1.75	29.0	0.18	28.1M	FC-PGA
1000	75	1.75	29.0	0.18	28.1M	FC-PGA
1000	75	1.75	29.0	0.18	28.1M	FC-PGA
1000	75	1.75	29.0	0.18	28.1M	FC-PGA
1000	75	1.75	29.0	0.18	28.1M	FC-PGA
1100	77	1.75	33.0	0.18	28.1M	FC-PGA
1133	69	1.475	29.1	0.13	44M	FC-PGA2
1133	69	1.475	29.1	0.13	44M	FC-PGA2
1133	69	1.45	27.9	0.13	44M	FC-PGA2
1133	69	1.45	27.9	0.13	44M	FC-PGA2
1200	69	1.475	29.9	0.13	44M	FC-PGA2
1200	69	1.475	29.9	0.13	44M	FC-PGA2
1266	69	1.45	29.5	0.13	44M	FC-PGA2
1333	69	1.475	29.9	0.13	44M	FC-PGA2
1400	69	1.45	29.9	0.13	44M	FC-PGA2

Most versions of the Pentium III Xeon use SC330 (Slot 2) or an improved version known as SC330.1. However, a few late-model Pentium III Xeon processors use a 495-pin SECC connector in a proprietary cartridge. These were used as OEM products in multiprocessor-capable servers such as the Dell PowerEdge 4400. Dell configures the processors to run as primary or secondary processors, so you must order processors for this and similar models from Dell. Table 2.21 lists the specifications of all Pentium III Xeon processors.

Table 2.21   Pentium III Xeon Specifications

S-Spec Number	Step	Processor Signature	Core Speed (MHz)	FSB Speed (MHz)	L2 Size (KB)	Slot or Socket Type
SL2XU	B0	0672h	500	100	512	SC330
SL2XV	B0	0672h	500	100	1024	SC330
SL2XW	B0	0672h	500	100	2048	SC330
SL385	C0	0673h	500	100	512	SC330
SL386	C0	0673h	500	100	1024	SC330
SL387	C0	0673h	500	100	2048	SC330
SL3C9	B0	0672h	500	100	512	SC330
SL3CA	B0	0672h	500	100	1024	SC330

Table 2.21   Continued

S-Spec Number	Step	Processor Signature	Core Speed (MHz)	FSB Speed (MHz)	L2 Size (KB)	Slot or Socket Type
SL3CB	B0	0672h	500	100	2048	SC330
SL3D9	C0	0673h	500	100	512	SC330
SL3DA	C0	0673h	500	100	1024	SC330
SL3DB	C0	0673h	500	100	2048	SC330
SL3AJ	C0	0673h	550	100	512	SC330
SL3CE	C0	0673h	550	100	1024	SC330
SL3CF	C0	0673h	550	100	2048	SC330
SL3FK[1]	C0	0673h	550	100	512	SC330
SL3FR[1]	C0	0673h	550	100	512	SC330
SL3LM	C0	0673h	550	100	512	SC330
SL3LN	C0	0673h	550	100	1024	SC330
SL3LP	C0	0673h	550	100	2048	SC330
SL3TW	C0	0673h	550	100	1024	SC330
SL3Y4	C0	0673h	550	100	512	SC330
SL3BJ	A2	0681h	600	133	256	SC330.1
SL3BK	A2	0681h	600	133	256	SC330.1
SL3SS	A2	0681h	600	133	256	SC330.1
SL3WM	B0	0683h	600	133	256	SC330.1
SL3WN	B0	0683h	600	133	256	SC330.1
SL3BL	A2	0681h	667	133	256	SC330.1
SL3DC	A2	0681h	667	133	256	SC330.1
SL3ST	A2	0681h	667	133	256	SC330.1
SL3WP	B0	0683h	667	133	256	SC330.1
SL3WQ	B0	0683h	667	133	256	SC330.1
SL3U4[2]	A0	06A0h	700	100	1024	SC330.1
SL3U5[2]	A0	06A0h	700	100	1024	SC330.1
SL3WZ[2]	A0	06A0h	700	100	2048	SC330.1
SL3X2[2]	A0	06A0h	700	100	2048	SC330.1
SL49P	A1	6A1h	700	100	1024	SC330.1
SL49Q	A1	6A1h	700	100	1024	SC330.1
SL49R	A1	6A1h	700	100	2048	SC330.1
SL49S	A1	6A1h	700	100	2048	SC330.1
SL4GD[3]	A0	06A0h	700	100	1024	SC330.1
SL4GE[3]	A0	06A0h	700	100	1024	SC330.1
SL4GF[3]	A0	06A0h	700	100	2048	SC330.1
SL4GG[3]	A0	06A0h	700	100	2048	SC330.1
SL4R3	A1	6A1h	700	100	2048	SC330.1
SL4RZ	A1	6A1h	700	100	1024	SC330.1
SL4XU	B0	6A4h	700	100	1024	SC330.1

Table 2.21   Continued

S-Spec Number	Step	Processor Signature	Core Speed (MHz)	FSB Speed (MHz)	L2 Size (KB)	Slot or Socket Type
SL4XV	B0	6A4h	700	100	1024	SC330.1
SL4XW	B0	6A4h	700	100	2048	SC330.1
SL4XX	B0	6A4h	700	100	2048	SC330.1
SL5D4	B0	6A4h	700	100	1024	SC330.1
SL5D5	B0	6A4h	700	100	2048	SC330.1
SL3SF	A2	0681h	733	133	256	SC330.1
SL3SG	A2	0681h	733	133	256	SC330.1
SL3SU	A2	0681h	733	133	256	SC330.1
SL3WR	B0	0683h	733	133	256	SC330.1
SL3WS	B0	0683h	733	133	256	SC330.1
SL4H6	C0	0686h	733	133	256	SC330.1
SL4H7	C0	0686h	733	133	256	495-pin SECC
SL3V2	A2	0681h	800	133	256	SC330.1
SL3V3	A2	0681h	800	133	256	SC330.1
SL3VU	A2	0681h	800	133	256	SC330.1
SL3WT	B0	0683h	800	133	256	SC330.1
SL3WU	B0	0683h	800	133	256	SC330.1
SL4H8	C0	0686h	800	133	256	SC330.1
SL4H9	C0	0686h	800	133	256	495-pin SECC
SL3WV	B0	0683h	866	133	256	SC330.1
SL3WW	B0	0683h	866	133	256	SC330.1
SL4HA	C0	0686h	866	133	256	SC330.1
SL4HB	C0	0686h	866	133	256	495-pin SECC
SL4PZ	B0	0683h	866	133	256	SC330.1
SL4U2	C0	0686h	866	133	256	SC330.1
SL4XY	B0	6A4h	900	100	2048	SC330.1
SL4XZ	B0	6A4h	900	100	2048	SC330.1
SL5D3	B0	6A4h	900	100	2048	SC330.1
SL3WX	B0	0683h	933	133	256	SC330.1
SL3WY	B0	0683h	933	133	256	SC330.1
SL4HC	C0	0686h	933	133	256	495-pin SECC
SL4HD	C0	0686h	933	133	256	495-pin SECC
SL4R9	C0	0686h	933	133	256	SC330.1
SL4HE	C0	0686h	1000	133	256	495-pin SECC
SL4HF	C0	0686h	1000	133	256	495-pin SECC
SL4Q2	C0	0686h	1000	133	256	495-pin SECC

[1]*Processors validated for use in two-way systems only.*

[2]*Should not be mixed with processors designated by footnote 3 due to differences in AGTL+ reference voltage.*

[3]*Should not be mixed with processors designated by footnote 2 due to differences in AGTL+ reference voltage.*

Pentium 4 Processors

The Pentium 4, introduced in 2000, is the most popular of Intel's current desktop processors. Like its predecessors, it has also been adapted for use in single-processor low-end servers. However, unlike the Pentium II and Pentium III, the Pentium 4 does not support multiple-processor configurations. Initially, the Pentium 4 was produced in a Socket 423 version (originally code-named Willamette), but updated versions used Socket 478, with the most recent steppings designed for use with Socket 775.

Internally, the Pentium 4 introduces a new architecture Intel calls *NetBurst* microarchitecture, which is more a marketing term than a technical one. Intel uses NetBurst to describe hyper-pipelined technology, a rapid execution engine, a high-speed (400MHz, 533MHz, or 800MHz) system bus, and an execution trace cache. The hyper-pipelined technology doubles the instruction pipeline depth compared to the Pentium III, which means more and smaller steps are required to execute instructions. Even though this might seem less efficient, it enables much higher clock speeds to be more easily attained. The rapid execution engine enables the two integer arithmetic logic units (ALUs) to run at twice the processor core frequency, which means instructions can execute in half a clock cycle. The 400MHz/533MHz/800MHz system bus is a quad-pumped bus running on a 100MHz/133MHz/200MHz system clock, transferring data four times per clock cycle. The execution trace cache is a high-performance L1 cache that stores approximately 12,000 decoded micro-operations. This removes the instruction decoder from the main execution pipeline, increasing performance.

The high-speed processor bus is most notable of the Pentium 4's features. Technically speaking, the processor bus is a 100MHz, 133MHz, or 200MHz quad-pumped bus that transfers four times per cycle (4x), for a 400MHz, 533MHz, or 800MHz effective rate. Because the bus is 64 bits (8 bytes) wide, this results in a throughput rate of 3200MBps, 4266MBps, or 6400MBps. The Pentium 4 Extreme Edition offers a 1066MHz processor bus, which offers a throughput of 8528MBps.

Table 2.22 Pentium 4 Processor Information[1]

CPU Speed (GHz)	Bus Speed (MHz)	Bus Speed (GBps)	HT Support	Boxed S-Spec	OEM S-Spec	Stepping	CPUID
1.30	400	3.2	No	SL4QD	SL4SF	B2	0F07h
1.30	400	3.2	No	SL4SF	SL4SF	B2	0F07h
1.30	400	3.2	No	SL5GC	SL5FW	C1	0F0Ah
1.40	400	3.2	No	SL4SC	SL4SG	B2	0F07h
1.40	400	3.2	No	SL4SG	SL4SG	B2	0F07h
1.40	400	3.2	No	SL4X2	SL4WS	C1	0F0Ah
1.40	400	3.2	No	SL5N7	SL59U	C1	0F0Ah
1.40	400	3.2	No	SL59U	SL59U	C1	0F0Ah
1.40	400	3.2	No	SL5UE	SL5TG	D0	0F12h
1.40	400	3.2	No	SL5TG	SL5TG	D0	0F12h
1.50	400	3.2	No	SL4TY	SL4SH	B2	0F07h
1.50	400	3.2	No	SL4SH	SL4SH	B2	0F07h
1.50	400	3.2	No	SL4X3	SL4WT	C1	0F0Ah
1.50	400	3.2	No	SL4WT	SL4WT	C1	0F0Ah
1.50	400	3.2	No	SL5TN	SL5SX	D0	0F12h

Power Supply Issues

The Pentium 4 requires a lot of electrical power, and most Pentium 4 motherboards therefore use a VRM that is powered from 12V instead of 3.3V or 5V, as with previous designs. By using 12V power, more 3.3V and 5V power is available to run the rest of the system, and the overall current draw is greatly reduced with the higher voltage as a source. PC power supplies generate a more than adequate supply of 12V power, but the ATX motherboard and power supply design originally allotted only one pin for 12V power (each pin is rated for only 6 amps), so additional 12V lines were necessary to carry this power to the motherboard.

The fix appears in the form of a third power connector, called the ATX12V connector. This new connector is used in addition to the standard 20-pin ATX power supply connector and 6-pin auxiliary (3.3/5V) connector. Fortunately, the power supply itself doesn't need a redesign; there is more than enough 12V power available from the drive connectors. To utilize this, companies such as PC Power and Cooling sell an inexpensive ($8) adapter that converts a standard Molex-type drive power connector to the ATX12V connector. Typically, a 300-watt (the minimum recommended) or larger power supply has more than adequate levels of 12V power for both the drives and the ATX12V connector.

If a power supply is less than the 300-watt minimum recommended, you need to purchase a replacement ATX12V power supply.

▶▶ For illustrations of the ATX12V connector, see "ATX Power Supply Standards," p. 248.

Pentium 4 Versions

The various Pentium 4 versions, including thermal and power specifications, are shown in Table 2.22.

L2 Cache	L3 Cache	Max. Temp	Max. Power	Socket	Process	Transistors	Processor Model Number
256K	0K	69°C	48.9W	423	180nm	42M	N/A
256K	0K	69°C	48.9W	423	180nm	42M	N/A
256K	0K	70°C	51.6W	423	180nm	42M	N/A
256K	0K	70°C	51.8W	423	180nm	42M	N/A
256K	0K	70°C	51.8W	423	180nm	42M	N/A
256K	0K	72°C	54.7W	423	180nm	42M	N/A
256K	0K	72°C	55.3W	478	180nm	42M	N/A
256K	0K	72°C	55.3W	478	180nm	42M	N/A
256K	0K	72°C	55.3W	478	180nm	42M	N/A
256K	0K	72°C	55.3W	478	180nm	42M	N/A
256K	0K	72°C	54.7W	423	180nm	42M	N/A
256K	0K	72°C	54.7W	423	180nm	42M	N/A
256K	0K	73°C	57.8W	423	180nm	42M	N/A
256K	0K	73°C	57.8W	423	180nm	42M	N/A
256K	0K	73°C	57.8W	423	180nm	42M	N/A

Table 2.22   Continued

CPU Speed (GHz)	Bus Speed (MHz)	Bus Speed (GBps)	HT Support	Boxed S-Spec	OEM S-Spec	Stepping	CPUID
1.50	400	3.2	No	SL5N8	SL59V	C1	0F0Ah
1.50	400	3.2	No	SL5UF	SL5TJ	D0	0F12h
1.50	400	3.2	No	SL5TJ	SL5TJ	D0	0F12h
1.50	400	3.2	No	SL62Y	SL62Y	D0	0F12h
1.60	400	3.2	No	SL4X4	SL4WU	C1	0F0Ah
1.60	400	3.2	No	SL5UL	SL5VL	D0	0F12h
1.60	400	3.2	No	SL5VL	SL5VL	D0	0F12h
1.60	400	3.2	No	SL5UW	SL5US	C1	0F0Ah
1.60	400	3.2	No	SL5UJ	SL5VH	D0	0F12h
1.60	400	3.2	No	SL5VH	SL5VH	D0	0F12h
1.60	400	3.2	No	SL6BC	SL679	E0	0F13h
1.60	400	3.2	No	SL679	SL679	E0	0F13h
1.60A	400	3.2	No	SL668	SL668	B0	0F24h
1.70	400	3.2	No	SL57V	SL57W	C1	0F0Ah
1.70	400	3.2	No	SL57W	SL57W	C1	0F0Ah
1.70	400	3.2	No	SL5TP	SL5SY	D0	0F12h
1.70	400	3.2	No	SL5N9	SL59X	C1	0F0Ah
1.70	400	3.2	No	SL5UG	SL5TK	D0	0F12h
1.70	400	3.2	No	SL5TK	SL5TK	D0	0F12h
1.70	400	3.2	No	SL62Z	SL62Z	D0	0F12h
1.70	400	3.2	No	SL6BD	SL67A	E0	0F13h
1.70	400	3.2	No	SL67A	SL67A	E0	0F13h
1.80	400	3.2	No	SL4X5	SL4WV	C1	0F0Ah
1.80	400	3.2	No	SL5UM	SL5VM	D0	0F12h
1.80	400	3.2	No	SL5VM	SL5VM	D0	0F12h
1.80	400	3.2	No	SL5UV	SL5UT	C1	0F0Ah
1.80	400	3.2	No	SL5UK	SL5VJ	D0	0F12h
1.80	400	3.2	No	SL5VJ	SL5VJ	D0	0F12h
1.80	400	3.2	No	SL6BE	SL67B	E0	0F13h
1.80	400	3.2	No	SL67B	SL67B	E0	0F13h
1.80A	400	3.2	No	SL63X	SL62P	B0	0F24h
1.80A	400	3.2	No	SL62P	SL62P	B0	0F24h
1.80A	400	3.2	No	SL68Q	SL66Q	B0	0F24h
1.80A	400	3.2	No	SL66Q	SL66Q	B0	0F24h
1.90	400	3.2	No	SL5WH	SL5VN	D0	0F12h
1.90	400	3.2	No	SL5VN	SL5VN	D0	0F12h
1.90	400	3.2	No	SL5WG	SL5VK	D0	0F12h

L2 Cache	L3 Cache	Max. Temp	Max. Power	Socket	Process	Transistors	Processor Model Number
256K	0K	73°C	57.9W	478	180nm	42M	N/A
256K	0K	73°C	57.9W	478	180nm	42M	N/A
256K	0K	73°C	57.9W	478	180nm	42M	N/A
256K	0K	71°C	62.9W	478	180nm	42M	N/A
256K	0K	75°C	61.0W	423	180nm	42M	N/A
256K	0K	75°C	61.0W	423	180nm	42M	N/A
256K	0K	75°C	61.0W	423	180nm	42M	N/A
256K	0K	75°C	60.8W	478	180nm	42M	N/A
256K	0K	75°C	60.8W	478	180nm	42M	N/A
256K	0K	75°C	60.8W	478	180nm	42M	N/A
256K	0K	75°C	60.8W	478	180nm	42M	N/A
256K	0K	75°C	60.8W	478	180nm	42M	N/A
512K	0K	66°C	46.8W	478	130nm	55M	N/A
256K	0K	76°C	64.0W	423	180nm	42M	N/A
256K	0K	76°C	64.0W	423	180nm	42M	N/A
256K	0K	76°C	64.0W	423	180nm	42M	N/A
256K	0K	76°C	63.5W	478	180nm	42M	N/A
256K	0K	76°C	63.5W	478	180nm	42M	N/A
256K	0K	76°C	63.5W	478	180nm	42M	N/A
256K	0K	73°C	67.7W	478	180nm	42M	N/A
256K	0K	73°C	67.7W	478	180nm	42M	N/A
256K	0K	73°C	67.7W	478	180nm	42M	N/A
256K	0K	78°C	66.7W	423	180nm	42M	N/A
256K	0K	78°C	66.7W	423	180nm	42M	N/A
256K	0K	78°C	66.7W	423	180nm	42M	N/A
256K	0K	77°C	66.1W	478	180nm	42M	N/A
256K	0K	77°C	66.1W	478	180nm	42M	N/A
256K	0K	77°C	66.1W	478	180nm	42M	N/A
256K	0K	77°C	66.1W	478	180nm	42M	N/A
512K	0K	67°C	49.6W	478	130nm	55M	N/A
512K	0K	67°C	49.6W	478	130nm	55M	N/A
512K	0K	67°C	49.6W	478	130nm	55M	N/A
512K	0K	67°C	49.6W	478	130nm	55M	N/A
256K	0K	73°C	69.2W	423	180nm	42M	N/A
256K	0K	73°C	69.2W	423	180nm	42M	N/A
256K	0K	75°C	72.8W	478	180nm	42M	N/A

Table 2.22 Continued

CPU Speed (GHz)	Bus Speed (MHz)	Bus Speed (GBps)	HT Support	Boxed S-Spec	OEM S-Spec	Stepping	CPUID
1.90	400	3.2	No	SL5VK	SL5VK	D0	0F12h
1.90	400	3.2	No	SL6BF	SL67C	E0	0F13h
1.90	400	3.2	No	SL67C	SL67C	E0	0F13h
2.0	400	3.2	No	SL5TQ	SL5SZ	D0	0F12h
2.0	400	3.2	No	SL5UH	SL5TL	D0	0F12h
2.0	400	3.2	No	SL5TL	SL5TL	D0	0F12h
2.0A	400	3.2	No	SL5ZT	SL5YR	B0	0F24h
2.0A	400	3.2	No	SL5YR	SL5YR	B0	0F24h
2.0A	400	3.2	No	SL68R	SL66R	B0	0F24h
2.0A	400	3.2	No	SL66R	SL66R	B0	0F24h
2.0A	400	3.2	No	SL6E7	SL6GQ	C1	0F27h
2.0A	400	3.2	No	SL6GQ	SL6GQ	C1	0F27h
2.0A	400	3.2	No	SL6QM	SL6PK	D1	0F29h
2.20	400	3.2	No	SL5ZU	SL5YS	B0	0F24h
2.20	400	3.2	No	SL5YS	SL5YS	B0	0F24h
2.20	400	3.2	No	SL68S	SL66S	B0	0F24h
2.20	400	3.2	No	SL66S	SL66S	B0	0F24h
2.20	400	3.2	No	SL6E8	SL6GR	C1	0F27h
2.20	400	3.2	No	SL6GR	SL6GR	C1	0F27h
2.20	400	3.2	No	SL6QN	SL6PL	D1	0F29h
2.26	533	4.3	No	SL683	SL67Y	B0	0F24h
2.26	533	4.3	No	SL67Y	SL67Y	B0	0F24h
2.26	533	4.3	No	SL6ET	SL6D6	B0	0F24h
2.26	533	4.3	No	SL6EE	SL6DU	C1	0F27h
2.26	533	4.3	No	SL6DU	SL6DU	C1	0F27h
2.26	533	4.3	No	SL6Q7	SL6PB	D1	0F29h
2.40	400	3.2	No	SL67R	SL65R	B0	0F24h
2.40	400	3.2	No	SL65R	SL65R	B0	0F24h
2.40	400	3.2	No	SL68T	SL66T	B0	0F24h
2.40	400	3.2	No	SL66T	SL66T	B0	0F24h
2.40	400	3.2	No	SL6E9	SL6GS	C1	0F27h
2.40	400	3.2	No	SL6GS	SL6GS	C1	0F27h
2.40A	533	4.3	No	SL7E8	SL7E8	C0	0F33h
2.40B	533	4.3	No	SL684	SL67Z	B0	0F24h
2.40B	533	4.3	No	SL67Z	SL67Z	B0	0F24h
2.40B	533	4.3	No	SL6EU	SL6D7	B0	0F24h
2.40B	533	4.3	No	SL6EF	SL6DV	C1	0F27h

L2 Cache	L3 Cache	Max. Temp	Max. Power	Socket	Process	Transistors	Processor Model Number
256K	0K	75°C	72.8W	478	180nm	42M	N/A
256K	0K	75°C	72.8W	478	180nm	42M	N/A
256K	0K	75°C	72.8W	478	180nm	42M	N/A
256K	0K	74°C	71.8W	423	180nm	42M	N/A
256K	0K	76°C	75.3W	478	180nm	42M	N/A
256K	0K	76°C	75.3W	478	180nm	42M	N/A
512K	0K	68°C	52.4W	478	130nm	55M	N/A
512K	0K	68°C	52.4W	478	130nm	55M	N/A
512K	0K	68°C	52.4W	478	130nm	55M	N/A
512K	0K	68°C	52.4W	478	130nm	55M	N/A
512K	0K	69°C	54.3W	478	130nm	55M	N/A
512K	0K	69°C	54.3W	478	130nm	55M	N/A
512K	0K	74°C	54.3W	478	130nm	55M	N/A
512K	0K	69°C	55.1W	478	130nm	55M	N/A
512K	0K	69°C	55.1W	478	130nm	55M	N/A
512K	0K	69°C	55.1W	478	130nm	55M	N/A
512K	0K	69°C	55.1W	478	130nm	55M	N/A
512K	0K	70°C	57.1W	478	130nm	55M	N/A
512K	0K	70°C	57.1W	478	130nm	55M	N/A
512K	0K	70°C	57.1W	478	130nm	55M	N/A
512K	0K	70°C	56.0W	478	130nm	55M	N/A
512K	0K	70°C	56.0W	478	130nm	55M	N/A
512K	0K	70°C	56.0W	478	130nm	55M	N/A
512K	0K	70°C	58.0W	478	130nm	55M	N/A
512K	0K	70°C	58.0W	478	130nm	55M	N/A
512K	0K	70°C	58.0W	478	130nm	55M	N/A
512K	0K	70°C	57.8W	478	130nm	55M	N/A
512K	0K	70°C	57.8W	478	130nm	55M	N/A
512K	0K	70°C	57.8W	478	130nm	55M	N/A
512K	0K	70°C	57.8W	478	130nm	55M	N/A
512K	0K	71°C	59.8W	478	130nm	55M	N/A
512K	0K	71°C	59.8W	478	130nm	55M	N/A
1M	0K	69°C	89.0W	478	90nm	125M	N/A
512K	0K	70°C	57.8W	478	130nm	55M	N/A
512K	0K	70°C	57.8W	478	130nm	55M	N/A
512K	0K	70°C	57.8W	478	130nm	55M	N/A
512K	0K	71°C	59.8W	478	130nm	55M	N/A

Table 2.22   Continued

CPU Speed (GHz)	Bus Speed (MHz)	Bus Speed (GBps)	HT Support	Boxed S-Spec	OEM S-Spec	Stepping	CPUID
2.40B	533	4.3	No	SL6DV	SL6DV	C1	0F27h
2.40B	533	4.3	No	SL6QP	SL6PM	D1	0F29h
2.40C	800	6.4	Yes	SL6WR	SL6WF	D1	0F29h
2.40C	800	6.4	Yes	SL6Z3	SL6Z3	M0	0F25h
2.50	400	3.2	No	SL6EB	SL6GT	C1	0F27h
2.50	400	3.2	No	SL6GT	SL6GT	C1	0F27h
2.50	400	3.2	No	SL6QQ	SL6QQ	D1	0F29h
2.53	533	4.3	No	SL685	SL682	B0	0F24h
2.53	533	4.3	No	SL682	SL682	B0	0F24h
2.53	533	4.3	No	SL6EV	SL6D8	B0	0F24h
2.53	533	4.3	No	SL6EG	SL6DW	C1	0F27h
2.53	533	4.3	No	SL6DW	SL6DW	C1	0F27h
2.53	533	4.3	No	SL6Q9	SL6PD	D1	0F29h
2.60	400	3.2	No	SL6HB	SL6GU	C1	0F27h
2.60	400	3.2	No	SL6GU	SL6GU	C1	0F27h
2.60	400	3.2	No	SL6QR	SL6QR	D1	0F29h
2.60B	533	4.3	No	SL6S3	SL6S3	C1	0F27h
2.60B	533	4.3	No	SL6QA	SL6PE	D1	0F29h
2.60C	800	6.4	Yes	SL6WS	SL6WH	D1	0F29h
2.60C	800	6.4	Yes	SL78X	N/A	D1	0F29h
2.66	533	4.3	No	SL6DX	SL6DX	C1	0F27h
2.66	533	4.3	No	SL6EH	N/A	C1	0F27h
2.66	533	4.3	No	SL6S3	SL6S3	C1	0F27h
2.66	533	4.3	No	SL6SK	N/A	C1	0F27h
2.66	533	4.3	No	SL6PE	SL6PE	D1	0F29h
2.66	533	4.3	No	SL6QA	N/A	D1	0F29h
2.66	533	4.3	No	SL7E9	N/A	C0	0F33h
2.66	533	4.3	No	SL7YU	N/A	D0	0f34h
2.66	533	4.3	No	SL85U	N/A	E0	0F41H
2.80	400	3.2	No	N/A	SL7EY	D1	0F29h
2.80	533	4.3	No	SL6K6	SL6HL	C1	0F27h
2.80	533	4.3	No	SL6HL	SL6HL	C1	0F27h
2.80	533	4.3	No	SL6SL	SL6S4	C1	0F27h
2.80	533	4.3	No	SL6S4	SL6S4	C1	0F27h
2.80	533	4.3	No	SL6QB	SL6PF	D1	0F29h
2.80C	533	4.3	No	N/A	SL7PK	E0	0F41h
2.80C	533	4.3	No	SL88G	SL88G	E0	0F41h

L2 Cache	L3 Cache	Max. Temp	Max. Power	Socket	Process	Transistors	Processor Model Number
512K	0K	71°C	59.8W	478	130nm	55M	N/A
512K	0K	74°C	66.2W	478	130nm	55M	N/A
512K	0K	74°C	66.2W	478	130nm	55M	N/A
512K	0K	72°C	74.5W	478	130nm	55M	N/A
512K	0K	72°C	61.0W	478	130nm	55M	N/A
512K	0K	72°C	61.0W	478	130nm	55M	N/A
512K	0K	72°C	61.0W	478	130nm	55M	N/A
512K	0K	71°C	59.3W	478	130nm	55M	N/A
512K	0K	71°C	59.3W	478	130nm	55M	N/A
512K	0K	71°C	59.3W	478	130nm	55M	N/A
512K	0K	72°C	61.5W	478	130nm	55M	N/A
512K	0K	72°C	61.5W	478	130nm	55M	N/A
512K	0K	72°C	61.5W	478	130nm	55M	N/A
512K	0K	72°C	62.6W	478	130nm	55M	N/A
512K	0K	72°C	62.6W	478	130nm	55M	N/A
512K	0K	75°C	69.0W	478	130nm	55M	N/A
512K	0K	74°C	66.1W	478	130nm	55M	N/A
512K	0K	74°C	66.1W	478	130nm	55M	N/A
512K	0K	74°C	66.1W	478	130nm	55M	N/A
512K	0K	74°C	66.1W	478	130nm	55M	N/A
512KB	0K	73°C	66.1W	478	130nm	55M	N/A
512KB	0K	73°C	66.1W	478	130nm	55M	N/A
512KB	0K	74°C	66.1W	478	130nm	55M	N/A
512KB	0K	74°C	66.1W	478	130nm	55M	N/A
512KB	0K	74°C	66.1W	478	130nm	55M	N/A
512KB	0K	74°C	66.1W	478	130nm	55M	N/A
1M	0K	73.1°C	103W	478	90nm	125M	N/A
1M	0K	69.1°C	84W	775	90nm	125M	505
1M	0K	67.7°C	84W	775	90nm	125M	505
512KB	0K	75°C	68.4W	478	130nm	55M	N/A
512K	0K	75°C	68.4W	478	130nm	55M	N/A
512K	0K	75°C	68.4W	478	130nm	55M	N/A
512K	0K	75°C	68.4W	478	130nm	55M	N/A
512K	0K	75°C	68.4W	478	130nm	55M	N/A
512K	0K	75°C	69.7W	478	130nm	55M	N/A
1M	0K	69.1°C	89.0W	478	90nm	125M	N/A
1M	0K	69.1°C	89.0W	478	90nm	125M	N/A

Table 2.22 Continued

CPU Speed (GHz)	Bus Speed (MHz)	Bus Speed (GBps)	HT Support	Boxed S-Spec	OEM S-Spec	Stepping	CPUID
2.80	800	6.4	Yes	SL6WJ	SL6WJ	D1	0F29h
2.80	800	6.4	Yes	SL6WT	SL6WT	D1	0F29h
2.80	800	6.4	Yes	SL6Z5	N/A	M0	0F25h
2.80	800	6.4	Yes	SL7E2	SL7E2	D0	0f34h
2.80	800	6.4	Yes	SL7E3	SL7E3	D0	0f34h
2.80	800	6.4	Yes	N/A	SL7J5	D0	0f34h
2.80	800	6.4	Yes	SL7KA	SL7KA	D0	0f34h
2.80	800	6.4	Yes	N/A	SL7J5	D0	0f34h
2.80	800	6.4	Yes	N/A	SL7PL	E0	0F41h
2.80	800	6.4	No	N/A	SL7PT	E0	0F41h
2.80	800	6.4	Yes	N/A	SL88H	E0	0F41h
2.80	800	6.4	Yes	SL8HX	SL8HX	E0	0F41h
2.80A	533	4.3	No	SL7K9	SL7K9	D0	0f34h
2.80A	533	4.3	No	SL7D8	SL7D8	C0	0F33h
2.80C	800	6.4	Yes	SL78Y	N/A	D1	0F29h
2.80E	800	6.4	Yes	SL79K	SL79K	C0	0F33h
2.93	533	6.4	No	N/A	SL7YV	D0	0f34h
2.93	533	6.4	No	N/A	SL85V	E0	0F41h
3.0	800	6.4	Yes	SL6WU	SL6WK	D1	0F29h
3.0	800	6.4	Yes	SL78Z	N/A	D1	0F29h
3.0	800	6.4	Yes	SL7BK	N/A	M0	0F25h
3.0	800	6.4	Yes	SL7E4	SL7E4	D0	0f34h
3.0	800	6.4	Yes	SL7KB	SL7KB	D0	0f34h
3.0	800	6.4	Yes	SL7PM	SL7PM	E0	0F41h
3.0	800	6.4	Yes	SL7PU	SL7PU	E0	0F41h
3.0	800	6.4	Yes	SL7Z9	SL7Z9	N0	0F43h
3.0	800	6.4	Yes	SL88J	N/A	E0	0F41h
3.00	800	6.4	Yes	SL7KK	SL7KK	D0	0f34h
3.00	800	6.4	Yes	SL7J6	SL7J6	D0	0f34h
3.0E	800	6.4	Yes	SL79L	SL79L	C0	0F33h
3.06	533	4.3	Yes	SL6K7	SL6JJ	C1	0F27h
3.06	533	4.3	Yes	SL6JJ	SL6JJ	C1	0F27h
3.06	533	4.3	Yes	SL6SM	SL6S5	C1	0F27h
3.06	533	4.3	Yes	SL6S5	SL6S5	C1	0F27h
3.06	533	4.3	Yes	SL6QC	SL6PG	D1	0F29h
3.06	533	4.3	No	N/A	SL87L	E0	0F41h
3.20	800	6.4	Yes	SL6WE	SL6WG	D1	0F29h

L2 Cache	L3 Cache	Max. Temp	Max. Power	Socket	Process	Transistors	Processor Model Number
512K	0K	75°C	69.7W	478	130nm	55M	N/A
512K	0K	75°C	69.7W	478	130nm	55M	N/A
512k	0K	73°C	76.0W	478	130nm	55M	N/A
1M	0K	69.1°C	89.0W	478	90nm	125M	N/A
1M	0K	69.1°C	89.0W	478	90nm	125M	N/A
1M	0K	67.7°C	84.0W	775	90nm	125M	520
1M	0K	69.1°C	89.0W	478	90nm	125M	N/A
1M	0K	67.7°C	84.0W	775	90nm	125M	520
1M	0K	69.1°C	89.0W	775	90nm	125M	N/A
1M	0K	67.7°C	84.0W	775	90nm	125M	505
1M	0K	69.1°C	89.0W	478	90nm	125M	N/A
1M	0K	67.7°C	84.0W	775	90nm	125M	521[2]
1M	0K	69.1°C	89.0W	478	90nm	125M	N/A
1M	0K	69°C	89.0W	478	90nm	125M	N/A
512K	0K	75°C	69.7W	478	130nm	55M	N/A
1M	0K	69°C	89.0W	478	90nm	125M	N/A
1M	0K	67.7°C	84.0W	775	90nm	125M	515
1M	0K	67.7°C	84.0W	775	90nm	125M	515
512K	0K	70°C	81.9W	478	130nm	55M	N/A
512K	0K	70°C	81.9W	478	130nm	55M	N/A
512k	0K	66°C	82.0W	478	130nm	55M	N/A
1M	0K	69.1°C	89.0W	478	90nm	125M	N/A
1M	0K	69.1°C	89.0W	478	90nm	125M	N/A
1M	0K	69.1°C	89.0W	478	90nm	125M	N/A
1M	0K	67.7°C	84.0W	775	90nm	125M	530J
2MB	0K	67.7°C	84.0W	775	90nm	169M	630[2]
1M	0K	69.1°C	89.0W	478	90nm	125M	N/A
1M	0K	67.7°C	84.0W	775	90nm	125M	530
1M	0K	67.7°C	84.0W	775	90nm	125M	530
1M	0K	69°C	89.0W	478	90nm	125M	N/A
512K	0K	69°C	81.8W	478	130nm	55M	N/A
512K	0K	69°C	81.8W	478	130nm	55M	N/A
512K	0K	69°C	81.8W	478	130nm	55M	N/A
512K	0K	69°C	81.8W	478	130nm	55M	N/A
512K	0K	69°C	81.8W	478	130nm	55M	N/A
1M	0K	67.7°C	84.0W	775	90nm	125M	519
512K	0K	70°C	82.0W	478	130nm	55M	N/A

Table 2.22   Continued

CPU Speed (GHz)	Bus Speed (MHz)	Bus Speed (GBps)	HT Support	Boxed S-Spec	OEM S-Spec	Stepping	CPUID
3.20	800	6.4	Yes	SL792	N/A	D1	0F29h
3.20	800	6.4	Yes	SL79M	SL79M	C0	0F33h
3.20	800	6.4	Yes	SL7B8	SL7B8	C0	0F33h
3.20	800	6.4	Yes	SL7E5	SL7E5	D0	0f34h
3.20	800	6.4	Yes	SL7J7	SL7J7	D0	0f34h
3.20	800	6.4	Yes	SL7KC	SL7KC	D0	0f34h
3.20	800	6.4	Yes	SL7KL	SL7KL	D0	0f34h
3.20	800	6.4	Yes	SL7LA	SL7LA	D0	0f34h
3.20	800	6.4	Yes	SL7PN	SL7PN	E0	0F41h
3.20	800	6.4	Yes	SL7PW	SL7PW	E0	0F41h
3.20	800	6.4	Yes	N/A	SL7PX	E0	0F41h
3.20	800	6.4	Yes	SL7Z8	SL7Z8	E0	0F43h
3.20	800	6.4	Yes	SL88K	N/A	E0	0F41h
3.2EE	800	6.4	Yes	SL7AA	SL7AA	M0	0F25h
3.40	800	6.4	Yes	SL793	SL793	D1	0F29h
3.40	800	6.4	Yes	SL7AJ	SL7AJ	C0	0F33h
3.40	800	6.4	Yes	SL7B9	N/A	C0	0F33h
3.40	800	6.4	Yes	SL7E6	SL7E6	D0	0f34h
3.40	800	6.4	Yes	SL7J8	SL7J8	D0	0f34h
3.40	800	6.4	Yes	SL7KD	SL7KD	E0	0F41h
3.40	800	6.4	Yes	SL7KM	SL7KM	D0	0f34h
3.40	800	6.4	Yes	SL7LH	SL7LH	D0	0f34h
3.40	800	6.4	Yes	N/A	SL7PP	E0	0F41h
3.40	800	6.4	Yes	SL7PY	SL7PY	E0	0F41h
3.40	800	6.4	Yes	N/A	SL7PZ	E0	0F41h
3.40	800	6.4	Yes	SL7RR	SL7RR	M0	0F25h
3.40	800	6.4	Yes	SL7Z7	SL7Z7	N0	0F43h
3.4EE	800	6.4	Yes	SL7CH	SL7CH	M0	0F25h
3.4EE	800	6.4	Yes	SL7GD	SL7GD	M0	0F25h
3.46EE	1066	8.5	Yes	SL7NF	SL7NF	M0	0F25h
3.46EE	1066	8.5	Yes	N/A	SL7RT	M0	0F25h
3.60	800	6.4	Yes	SL7J9	SL7J9	D0	0f34h
3.60	800	6.4	Yes	N/A	SL7KN	D0	0f34h
3.60	800	6.4	Yes	SL7L9	SL7L9	D0	0f34h
3.60	800	6.4	Yes	N/A	SL7NZ	E0	0F41h
3.60	800	6.4	Yes	SL7Q2	SL7Q2	E0	0F41h
3.60	800	6.4	Yes	SL8J6	SL8J6	E0	0F41h

L2 Cache	L3 Cache	Max. Temp	Max. Power	Socket	Process	Transistors	Processor Model Number
512K	0K	70°C	82.0W	478	130nm	55M	N/A
1MB	0K	73.2°C	103.0W	478	90nm	125M	N/A
1MB	0K	73.2°C	103.0W	478	90nm	125M	N/A
1MB	0K	69.1°C	89.0W	478	90nm	125M	N/A
1MB	0K	67.7°C	84.0W	775	90nm	125M	540
1MB	0K	69.1°C	89.0W	478	90nm	125M	N/A
1MB	0K	67.7°C	84.0W	775	90nm	125M	540
1MB	0K	67.7°C	103.0W	775	90nm	125M	N/A[3]
1MB	0K	73.2°C	103.0W	775	90nm	125M	N/A
1MB	0K	67.7°C	84.0W	775	90nm	125M	540J
1MB	0K	67.7°C	84.0W	775	90nm	125M	540[3]
2MB	0K	67.7°C	84.0W	775	90nm	169M	640[2]
1MB	0K	69.1°C	89.0W	478	90nm	125M	N/A
512K	2M	64°C	92.1W	478	130nm	178M	N/A
512K	0K	70°C	89.0W	478	130nm	55M	N/A
1M	0K	73°C	103.0W	478	90nm	125M	N/A
1M	0K	73.2°C	103.0W	478	90nm	125M	N/A
1M	0K	73.2°C	103.0W	478	90nm	125M	N/A
1M	0K	72.8°C	115.0W	775	90nm	125M	550
1M	0K	73.2°C	103.0W	478	90nm	125M	N/A
1M	0K	72.8°C	115.0W	775	90nm	125M	550
1M	0K	72.8°C	115.0W	775	90nm	125M	N/A[3]
1M	0K	73.2°C	103.0W	478	90nm	125M	N/A
1M	0K	67.7°C	84.0W	775	90nm	125M	550J
1M	0K	67.7°C	84.0W	775	90nm	125M	550[3]
512K	2M	66°C	109.6W	775	130nm	169M	N/A
2MB	0K	67.7°C	84.0W	775	90nm	125M	650[2]
512K	2M	68°C	102.9W	478	130nm	178M	N/A
512K	2M	66°C	109.6W	775	130nm	178M	N/A
512K	2M	66°C	110.7W	775	130nm	178M	N/A
512K	2M	66°C	110.7W	775	130nm	178M	N/A
1M	0K	72.8°C	115.0W	775	90nm	125M	560
1M	0K	72.8°C	115.0W	775	90nm	125M	560
1M	0K	72.8°C	115.0W	775	90nm	125M	560[3]
1M	0K	72.8°C	115.0W	775	90nm	125M	560[3]
1M	0K	72.8°C	115.0W	775	90nm	125M	560J
1M	0K	72.8°C	115.0W	775	90nm	125M	N/A[2]

Table 2.22   **Continued**

CPU Speed (GHz)	Bus Speed (MHz)	Bus Speed (GBps)	HT Support	Boxed S-Spec	OEM S-Spec	Stepping	CPUID
3.60	800	6.4	Yes	SL7Z5	SL7Z5	N0	0F43h
3.80	800	6.4	Yes	SL7P2	SL7P2	E0	0F41h
3.80	800	6.4	Yes	SL82U	SL82U	E0	0F41h
3.80	800	6.4	Yes	N/A	SL8J7	E0	0F41h
3.80	800	6.4	Yes	N/A	SL7Z3	N0	0F43h

[1]*HT = Hyper-Threading Technology; and EE = Extreme Edition.*
[2]*This processor supports Intel Extended Memory 64 Technology (EM64T) and Execute Disable Bit (NX).*
[3]*This processor supports Intel Extended Memory 64 Technology (EM64T).*

A Pentium 4 processor is shown in Figure 2.38.

Figure 2.38   A Pentium 4 FC-PGA2 processor.

Xeon Processors

Xeon processors are based on the Pentium 4 and are designed, as their predecessors, for multiple-processor applications.

The Xeon processors based on the original 32-bit version of Pentium 4 desktop processor are divided into two categories:

- **Xeon DP**—The Xeon DP with 256KB L2 cache is designed for workstations; the Xeon DP with 512KB up to 2MB of L2 is designed for use in single- or dual-processor servers.
- **Xeon MP**—The Xeon MP is designed for use in up to eight-way servers.

Figure 2.39 shows the front and rear views of the Xeon MP processor.

L2 Cache	L3 Cache	Max. Temp	Max. Power	Socket	Process	Transistors	Processor Model Number
2MB	0K	72.8°C	115.0W	775	90nm	125M	660[2]
1M	0K	72.8°C	115.0W	775	90nm	125M	N/A[2]
1M	0K	72.8°C	115.0W	775	90nm	125M	570J
1M	0K	72.8°C	115.0W	775	90nm	125M	N/A[2]
2MB	0K	72.8°C	115.0W	775	90nm	125M	670[2]

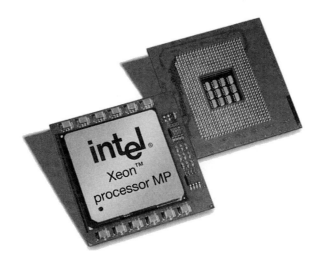

Figure 2.39 The Intel Xeon MP processor is based on the Intel Pentium 4 but is designed for use in up to eight-way servers. *(Photograph used by permission of Intel Corporation.)*

Table 2.23 provides essential details about the Xeon processors.

Table 2.23   Intel Xeon Processors for Workstations and Servers

S-Spec	Core Stepping	Processor Signature	CPU Core Speed (GHz)	FSB Speed (MHz)	L2 Size (KB)	L3 Size (MB)	HT Technology	Socket Type
SL4XU	B0	6AH4	.7	100	1024	—	No	Slot 2
SL4WX	C1	0F0Ah	1.4	400	256	—	No	603-pin
SL56G	C1	0F0Ah	1.4	400	256	—	No	603-pin
SL4WY	C1	0F0Ah	1.5	400	256	—	No	603-pin
SL4ZT	C1	0F0Ah	1.5	400	256	—	No	603-pin
SL5TD	D0	0F12h	1.5	400	256	—	No	603-pin
SL5U6	D0	0F12h	1.5	400	256	—	No	603-pin

Table 2.23   Continued

S-Spec	Core Stepping	Processor Signature	CPU Core Speed (GHz)	FSB Speed (MHz)	L2 Size (KB)	L3 Size (MB)	HT Technology	Socket Type
SL6GV	C1	0F27H	1.6	400	512	—	Yes	604-pin
SL6XK	D1	0F29H	1.6	400	512	—	Yes	604-pin
SL56H	C1	0F0Ah	1.7	400	256	—	No	603-pin
SL56N	C1	0F0Ah	1.7	400	256	—	No	603-pin
SL5TE	D0	0F12h	1.7	400	256	—	No	603-pin
SL5U7	D0	0F12h	1.7	400	256	—	No	603-pin
SL5Z8	B0	0F24h	1.8	400	512	—	Yes	603-pin
SL622	B0	0F24h	1.8	400	512	—	Yes	603-pin
SL6EL	C1	0F27H	1.8	400	512	—	Yes	603-pin
SL6JX	C1	0F27H	1.8	400	512	—	Yes	603-pin
SL6W3	D1	0F29H	1.8	400	512	—	Yes	603-pin
SL6YS	D1	0F29H	1.8	400	512	—	Yes	603-pin
SL5TH	D0	0F12h	2	400	256	—	No	603-pin
SL5U8	D0	0F12h	2	400	256	—	No	603-pin
SL5Z9	B0	0F24h	2	400	512	—	Yes	603-pin
SL623	B0	0F24h	2	400	512	—	Yes	603-pin
SL6EM	C1	0F27H	2	400	512	—	Yes	603-pin
SL6JY	C1	0F27H	2	400	512	—	Yes	603-pin
SL6W6	D1	0F29H	2	400	512	—	Yes	603-pin
SL6XL	D1	0F29H	2	400	512	—	Yes	604-pin
SL6YT	D1	0F29H	2	400	512	—	Yes	603-pin
SL6NP	C1	0F27H	2	533	512	—	Yes	604-pin
SL6RQ	C1	0F27H	2	533	512	—	Yes	604-pin
SL6VK	D1	0F29H	2	533	512	—	Yes	604-pin
SL6YM	D1	0F29H	2	533	512	—	Yes	604-pin
SL72C	M0	0F25H	2	533	512	—	Yes	604-pin
SL73K	M0	0F25H	2	533	512	—	Yes	604-pin
SL73L	M0	0F25H	2	533	512	—	Yes	604-pin
SL5ZA	B0	0F24h	2.2	400	512	—	Yes	603-pin
SL624	B0	0F24h	2.2	400	512	—	Yes	603-pin
SL6EN	C1	0F27H	2.2	400	512	—	Yes	603-pin
SL6JZ	C1	0F27H	2.2	400	512	—	Yes	603-pin
SL6W7	D1	0F29H	2.2	400	512	—	Yes	603-pin
SL6YU	D1	0F29H	2.2	400	512	—	Yes	603-pin
SL65T	B0	0F24h	2.4	400	512	—	Yes	603-pin
SL687	B0	0F24h	2.4	400	512	—	Yes	603-pin

Table 2.23   Continued

S-Spec	Core Stepping	Processor Signature	CPU Core Speed (GHz)	FSB Speed (MHz)	L2 Size (KB)	L3 Size (MB)	HT Technology	Socket Type
SL6EP	C1	0F27H	2.4	400	512	—	Yes	603-pin
SL6K2	C1	0F27H	2.4	400	512	—	Yes	603-pin
SL6W8	D1	0F29H	2.4	400	512	—	Yes	603-pin
SL6YV	D1	0F29H	2.4	400	512	—	Yes	603-pin
SL6GD	C1	0F27H	2.4	533	512	—	Yes	604-pin
SL6NQ	C1	0F27H	2.4	533	512	—	Yes	604-pin
SL6VL	D1	0F29H	2.4	533	512	—	Yes	604-pin
SL6YN	D1	0F29H	2.4	533	512	—	Yes	604-pin
SL72D	M0	0F25H	2.4	533	512	—	Yes	604-pin
SL74T	D1	0F29H	2.4	533	512	—	Yes	604-pin
SL6EQ	C1	0F27H	2.6	400	512	—	Yes	603-pin
SL6K3	C1	0F27H	2.6	400	512	—	Yes	603-pin
SL6W9	D1	0F29H	2.6	400	512	—	Yes	603-pin
SL6YW	D1	0F29H	2.6	400	512	—	Yes	603-pin
SL6GF	C1	0F27H	2.66	533	512	—	Yes	604-pin
SL6NR	C1	0F27H	2.66	533	512	—	Yes	604-pin
SL6NR	D1	0F29H	2.66	533	512	—	Yes	604-pin
SL6VM	D1	0F29H	2.66	533	512	—	Yes	604-pin
SL72E	M0	0F25H	2.66	533	512	—	Yes	604-pin
SL73M	M0	0F25H	2.66	533	512	—	Yes	604-pin
SL6M7	C1	0F27H	2.8	400	512	—	Yes	603-pin
SL6MS	C1	0F27H	2.8	400	512	—	Yes	603-pin
SL6WA	D1	0F29H	2.8	400	512	—	Yes	603-pin
SL6YX	D1	0F29H	2.8	400	512	—	Yes	603-pin
SL6Z8	B1	0F25H	2.8	400	512	2	Yes	603-pin
SL6GG	C1	0F27H	2.8	533	512	—	Yes	604-pin
SL6NS	C1	0F27H	2.8	533	512	—	Yes	604-pin
SL6VN	D1	0F29H	2.8	533	512	—	Yes	604-pin
SL6VN	D1	0F29H	2.8	533	512	—	Yes	604-pin
SL6YQ	D1	0F29H	2.8	533	512	—	Yes	604-pin
SL72F	M0	0F25H	2.8	533	512	—	Yes	604-pin
SL73N	M0	0F25H	2.8	533	512	—	Yes	604-pin
SL7D5	M0	0F25H	2.8	533	512	1	Yes	604-pin
SL7D5	M0	0F25H	2.8	533	512	1	Yes	604-pin
SL7DV	D0	0f34H	2.8	800	1024	—	Yes	604-pin
SL7HF	D0	0f34H	2.8	800	1024	—	Yes	604-pin

Table 2.23 Continued

S-Spec	Core Stepping	Processor Signature	CPU Core Speed (GHz)	FSB Speed (MHz)	L2 Size (KB)	L3 Size (MB)	HT Technology	Socket Type
SL7PD	E0	0F41H	2.8	800	1024	—	Yes	604-pin
SL7TB	E0	0F41H	2.8	800	1024	—	Yes	604-pin
SL6YY	D1	0F29H	3	400	512	—	Yes	603-pin
SL6VW	C1	0F27H	3	400	1024	—	Yes	603-pin
SL6X4	C1	0F27H	3	400	1024	—	Yes	603-pin
SL7EW	C0	0F41H	3	667	512	8	Yes	604-pin
SL7DW	D0	0f34H	3	800	1024	—	Yes	604-pin
SL7HG	D0	0f34H	3	800	1024	—	Yes	604-pin
SL7PE	E0	0F41H	3	800	1024	—	Yes	604-pin
SL7TC	E0	0F41H	3	800	1024	—	Yes	604-pin
SL7ZF	N0	0F43H	3	800	2048	—	Yes	604-pin
SL8ZQ	N0	0F43H	3	800	2048	—	Yes	604-pin
SL84U	A0	0F41H	3.16	667	1024	—	Yes	604-pin
SL6GH	C1	0F27H	3.06	533	512	—	Yes	604-pin
SL6RR	C1	0F27H	3.06	533	512	—	Yes	604-pin
SL6VP	D1	0F29H	3.06	533	512	—	Yes	604-pin
SL6YR	D1	0F29H	3.06	533	512	—	Yes	604-pin
SL72G	M0	0F25H	3.06	533	512	1	Yes	604-pin
SL73P	M0	0F25H	3.06	533	512	1	Yes	604-pin
SL72Y	M0	0F25H	3.2	533	512	1	Yes	604-pin
SL73Q	M0	0F25H	3.2	533	512	1	Yes	604-pin
SL7AE	M0	0F25H	3.2	533	512	2	Yes	604-pin
SL7BW	M0	0F25H	3.2	533	512	2	Yes	604-pin
SL7DX	D0	0F34H	3.2	800	1024	—	Yes	604-pin
SL7HH	D0	0F34H	3.2	800	1024	—	Yes	604-pin
SL7PF	E0	0F41H	3.2	800	1024	—	Yes	604-pin
SL7TD	E0	0F41H	3.2	800	1024	—	Yes	604-pin
SL7ZE	N0	0F43H	3.2	800	2048	—	Yes	604-pin
SL8ZP	N0	0F43H	3.2	800	2048	—	Yes	604-pin
SL8EY	C0	0F41H	3.33	667	512	8	Yes	604-pin
SL7DY	D0	0F34H	3.4	800	1024	—	Yes	604-pin
SL7HJ	D0	0F34H	3.4	800	1024	—	Yes	604-pin
SL7PG	E0	0F41H	3.4	800	1024	—	Yes	604-pin
SL7TE	E0	0F41H	3.4	800	1024	—	Yes	604-pin
SL7ZD	N0	0F43H	3.4	800	512	2	Yes	604-pin
SL7ZK	N0	0F43H	3.4	800	512	2	Yes	604-pin

Table 2.23   Continued

S-Spec	Core Stepping	Processor Signature	CPU Core Speed (GHz)	FSB Speed (MHz)	L2 Size (KB)	L3 Size (MB)	HT Technology	Socket Type
SL7DZ	D0	0F34H	3.6	800	1024	—	Yes	604-pin
SL7HK	D0	0F34H	3.6	800	1024	—	Yes	604-pin
SL7PH	E0	0F41H	3.6	800	1024	—	Yes	604-pin
SL7VF	E0	0F41H	3.6	800	1024	—	Yes	604-pin
SL7ZC	N0	0F43H	3.6	800	512	2	Yes	604-pin
SL7ZJ	N0	0F43H	3.6	800	512	2	Yes	604-pin
SL84W	A0	0F41H	3.66	667	1024	—	Yes	604-pin

The Xeon MP is designed for use in servers with more than two processors. All versions of the Xeon MP features L1, L2, and L3 caches; use Socket 603; and feature HT Technology.

Table 2.24 lists the different versions of the 32-bit Xeon MP processor.

Table 2.24   Xeon MP Specifications

S-Spec	Core Stepping	Processor Signature	Core Speed (GHz)	Data Bus (MHz)	L2 Cache Size (KB)	L3 Cache Size (KB)	HT Technology
SL5FZ	C0	0F11h	1.4	400	256	512	Yes
SL5RV	C0	0F11h	1.4	400	256	512	Yes
SL5G2	C0	0F11h	1.5	400	256	512	Yes
SL5RW	C0	0F11h	1.5	400	256	512	Yes
SL6GZ	A0	0F22h	1.5	400	512	1024	Yes
SL6KB	A0	0F22h	1.5	400	512	1024	Yes
SL5G8	C0	0F11h	1.6	400	256	1024	Yes
SL5S4	C0	0F11h	1.6	400	256	1024	Yes
SL6H2	A0	0F22h	1.9	400	512	1024	Yes
SL6KC	A0	0F22h	1.9	400	512	1024	Yes
SL66Z	A0	0F22h	2	400	512	2048	Yes
SL6KD	A0	0F22h	2	400	512	2048	Yes
SL6YJ	B1	0F25h	2	400	512	1024	Yes
SL6Z6	B1	0F25h	2	400	512	1024	Yes
SL7A5	C0	0F26h	2.2	400	512	2048	Yes
SL6Z2	B1	0F25h	2.5	400	512	1024	Yes
SL6Z7	B1	0F25h	2.5	400	512	1024	Yes
SL79Z	C0	0F26h	2.7	400	512	2048	Yes
SL6YL	B1	0F25h	2.8	400	512	2048	Yes
SL79V	C0	0F26h	3	400	512	4096	Yes

Xeon DP with EM64T Support

Just as recent versions of the Pentium 4 incorporate EM64T support so they can run 64-bit applications, the Xeon DP is also available with 64-bit support (see Table 2.25). EM64T is Intel's implementation of the 64-bit extensions originally developed by AMD for its Opteron and Athlon 64 and 64FX processors. These processors also support Execute Disable Bit (XDB) to stop buffer-overrun virus attacks and Enhanced SpeedStep Technology.

Table 2.25   Xeon DP with EM64T Specifications[1]

Core Speed (GHz)	Data Bus (MHz)	L2 Cache Size (KB)	L3 Cache Size (KB)	HT Technology	Dual-Core Support	Processor Number
2.80GHz	800MHz	2MB	—	Yes	—	—
2.8GHz	800MHz	4MB	—	Yes	Yes	—
3GHz	800MHz	2MB	—	Yes	—	—
3.2GHz	800MHz	2MB	—	Yes	—	—
3.4GHz	800MHz	2MB	—	Yes	—	—
3.6GHz	800MHz	2MB	—	Yes	—	—
3.8GHz	800MHz	2MB	—	Yes	—	—

[1]For S-Spec numbers and other details, see the Intel website (www.intel.com).

Xeon MP with EM64T Support

In 2005, Intel announced a new series of Xeon MP processors with Intel's Extended Memory 64 Technology (EM64T) support. EM64T is Intel's implementation of the 64-bit extensions originally developed by AMD for its Opteron and Athlon 64 and 64FX processors. Xeon MP processors with EM64T have the following specifications:

- 1MB of on-die L2 cache

- Socket 604 (except as noted in Table 2.26)

- 4MB or 8MB of on-die L3 cache; 8MB is twice the size of the largest L3 cache available in the 32-bit Xeon MP product line, and very few 32-bit Xeon MPs featured 4MB. 8MB is very close to the L3 cache size used by the Itanium 2 and makes the Xeon MP a better choice for network servers that need to support a mixture of 32-bit and 64-bit applications.

- Clock speeds of 2.83GHz to 3.66GHz, compared to 3GHz for the 32-bit versions of the Xeon MP

- 667MHz FSB; this is significantly faster than the 400MHz FSB used by 32-bit versions of the Xeon MP.

- 7xxx-series processors that feature dual-core designs, enabling a four-way processor, for example, to have performance similar to that of an eight-way single-core processor.

Table 2.26 lists the specifications for these processors.

Table 2.26   64-bit Xeon MP Specifications[1]

Core Speed (GHz)	Data Bus (MHz)	L2 Cache Size (KB)	L3 Cache Size (KB)	HT Technology	Dual-Core Support	Processor Number
2.66GHz	667MHz	2MB	—	Yes	Yes	7020[2]
2.8GHz	800MHz	2MB	—	Yes	Yes	7030
2.83GHz	667MHz	1MB	—	Yes	—	—
3GHz	667MHz	4MB	—	Yes	Yes	7040
3GHz	800MHz	4MB	—	Yes	Yes	7041
3.16GHz	667MHz	1MB	—	Yes	—	—
3.33GHz	667MHz	1MB	—	Yes	—	—
3.66GHz	667MHz	1MB	—	Yes	—	—
2.66GHz	667MHz	1MB	4MB	Yes	—	—
2.66GHz	667MHz	1MB	8MB	Yes	—	—
2.83GHz	667MHz	1MB	4MB	Yes	—	—
2.83GHz	667MHz	1MB	8MB	Yes	—	—
3.00GHz	667MHz	1MB	4MB	Yes	—	—
3.00GHz	667MHz	1MB	8MB	Yes	—	—
3.16GHz	667MHz	1MB	4MB	Yes	—	—
3.16GHz	667MHz	1MB	8MB	Yes	—	—
3.33GHz	667MHz	1MB	4MB	Yes	—	—
3.33GHz	667MHz	1MB	8MB	Yes	—	—
3.66GHz	667MHz	1MB	4MB	Yes	—	—
3.66GHz	667MHz	1MB	8MB	Yes	—	—

[1]For S-Spec numbers and other details, see the Intel website (www.intel.com).
[2]This processor plugs in to Socket T (LGA775).

Processors in the 7xxx series support Intel's virtualization technology, which enables a system to run different operating systems and applications in logical partitions. In other words, one server can act like two or more servers.

Single-core processors are supported by Intel's E8500 chipset, and dual-core processors require Intel's E8501 chipset. (See Chapter 3 for details.)

Itanium and Itanium 2 Processors

Introduced in 2001, the Itanium was the first processor in Intel's IA-64 (Intel Architecture 64-bit) product family, and it incorporated innovative performance-enhancing architecture techniques, such as prediction and speculation. It and its newer sibling, the Itanium 2 (introduced in 2002), are the highest-end processors from Intel and are designed for the enterprise server market. In fact, Hewlett-Packard (which co-developed the Itanium series with Intel) has decided to retire its RISC-based AlphaServer and Hewlett-Packard 9000 servers and their processors (Alpha and PA-RISC) in favor of Itanium 2–based systems.

Note

To learn more about the Hewlett-Packard's Business Systems Evolution programs for moving users of AlphaServer and PA-RISC products to Itanium 2-based platforms, go to www.hp.com/products1/evolution/.

The Itanium family represents the eight-generation processors in the Intel family. Even more significantly, Itanium uses a different chip architecture than the x86-based processors discussed in previous sections.

Itanium Architecture

Intel and Hewlett-Packard began jointly working on the Itanium processor in 1994, although the first Itaniums were not released until 2001. Itanium is the first microprocessor based on the IA-64 specification, which is also supported by Itanium 2. IA-64 is a completely different processor design that uses Very Long Instruction Words (VLIW), instruction prediction, branch elimination, speculative loading, and other advanced processes for enhancing parallelism from program code. The Itanium series features elements of both CISC and RISC design.

The Itanium series incorporates a design architecture Intel calls EPIC, which enables the processor to execute *parallel instructions*—that is, several instructions at the same time. In the Itanium and Itanium 2, three instructions can be encoded in one 128-bit word so that each instruction has a few more bits than today's 32-bit instructions. The extra bits let the chip address more registers and tell the processor which instructions to execute in parallel. This approach simplifies the design of processors with many parallel-execution units and should let them run at higher clock rates. In other words, besides being capable of executing several instructions in parallel within the chip, the Itanium can be linked to other Itanium chips in a parallel processing environment. The Itanium 2 also supports parallel processing.

Besides having new features and running a completely new 64-bit instruction set, Itanium and Itanium 2 feature full backward compatibility with the current 32-bit Intel x86 software. In this way, they support 64-bit instructions while retaining full compatibility with today's 32-bit applications. Full backward compatibility means the Itanium and Itanium 2 can run all existing applications as well as any new 64-bit applications. Unfortunately, because this is not the native mode for the processor, performance is not as good when executing 32-bit instructions as it is with the Pentium 4 and earlier chips.

Tip

If you need to run 32-bit x86 software on an Itanium 2 processor, make sure your operating system supports the IA-32 Execution Layer (IA-32 EL) technology. IA-32 EL improves performance of 32-bit software on the Itanium 2 processor. Operating systems that include or support IA-32 EL include Windows Server 2003 Enterprise Edition, Windows Server 2003 Datacenter Edition, Windows XP 64-bit Edition, and most current Linux distributions that support Itanium 2.

To download IA-32 EL for Red Hat Enterprise Linux 4; Red Hat Enterprise Linux 3 UP5; Red Hat Enterprise 3 UP4; SUSE Enterprise Server 9 SP1; or SUSE Enterprise Server Linux SP1, Kernel 2.6, go to the "IA-32 Execution Layer" page, at www.intel.com/cd/software/products/asmo-na/eng/219773.htm. To download the latest version of the IA-32 EL for Windows Server 2003, go to www.microsoft.com/windowsserver2003/64bit/ipf/ia32el.mspx.

For more information about IA-32 EL technology for Windows and Linux operating systems, see www.intel.com/design/itanium/downloads/25431803.pdf.

To use the IA-64 instruction set, programs must be recompiled for the new instruction set. The Itanium and Itanium 2 are currently supported by these operating systems: Microsoft Windows (XP 64-bit Itanium Edition and Windows Server 2003 for Itanium-based systems), Linux (from four distributor companies: Red Hat, SUSE, Caldera, and Turbo Linux), and two UNIX versions (Hewlett-Packard's HP-UX and IBM's AIX). Hewlett-Packard's fault-tolerant NonStop operating system also supports IA-64.

In September 2005, the Itanium Solutions Alliance was formed by founding sponsors Bull, Fujitsu, Fujitsu Siemens Computers, Hitachi, Hewlett-Packard, Intel, NEC, SGI, and Unisys. Charter members include BEA, Microsoft, Novell, Oracle, Red Hat, SAP, SAS, and Sybase. The alliance's goals include helping software vendors more easily move their applications to IA-64 and providing information about existing IA-64 applications and industry-specific solutions. You can learn more at www.itanium-solutionsalliance.org.

Although the creation of the Itanium Solutions Alliance is a helpful development, the high cost of Itanium 2–based solutions and their relatively poor performance when running existing x86 code make them suitable primarily for very large enterprise networks that are running native IA-64 applications. You can build your own Itanium 2–based server by using motherboards from vendors such as Supermicro (www.supermicro.com), but if you're looking at four-way or smaller solutions, you're likely to be better off with an AMD Opteron or Intel Xeon EMT64-based solution.

Itanium and Itanium 2 Specifications

The following features apply to both Itanium and Itanium 2 processors:

- They have 16TB of physical memory addressing (44-bit address bus).
- They have full 32-bit instruction compatibility in hardware.
- They use EPIC technology, which enables up to 20 operations per cycle.
- They have two integer and two memory units that can execute four instructions per clock.
- They have two FMAC (floating-point multiply accumulate) units with 82-bit operands.
- Each FMAC unit is capable of executing two floating-point operations per clock.
- Two additional MMX units are capable of executing two single-precision floating-point operations each.
- A total of eight single-precision floating-point operations can be executed every cycle.
- They have 128 integer registers, 128 floating-point registers, 8 branch registers, and 64 predicate registers.

The Itanium 2 also has the following features:

- 400MHz, 533MHz, or 667MHz CPU bus (versus 266MHz for Itanium)
- 128-bit wide CPU bus (versus 64-bit for Itanium)

The Itanium and Itanium 2's technical details are listed in Table 2.27; Itanium versions are listed in Table 2.28, and Itanium 2 versions are listed in Table 2.29.

Table 2.27   Intel Itanium and Itanium 2 Technical Details

Processor	Processor Speed	L2 Cache	L3 Cache Size	FSB Speed	Memory Bus Width	Bandwidth	Number of Transistors
Itanium	733MHz, 800MHz	96KB	2MB[1] or 4MB[1]	266MHz	64-bit	2.1GBps	25 million (core), 150 or 300 million (cache)
Itanium 2	900MHz	256KB	1.5MB[2]	400MHz	128-bit	6.4GBps	221 million
Itanium 2	1GHz[3], 1.3GHz[3]	256KB	3MB[2]	400MHz	128-bit	6.4GBps	221 million
Itanium 2	1.4GHz[4]	256KB	1.5MB	400MHz	128-bit	6.4GBps	221 million
Itanium 2	1.6GHz[4]	256KB	3MB	400MHz, 533MHz	128-bit	6.4GBps, 8.5GBps	500 million
Itanium 2	1.4GHz, 1.5GHz[5], 1.6GHz[4]	256KB	4MB[2]	400MHz	128-bit	6.4GBps	410 million
Itanium 2	1.5GHz, 1.6GHz[5]	256KB	6MB[2]	400MHz	128-bit	6.4GBps	500 million
Itanium 2	1.66GHz[5]	256KB	6MB[2]	667MHz	128-bit	10.6GBps	500 million
Itanium 2	1.6GHz[5]	256KB	9MB[2]	400MHz	128-bit	6.4GBps	592 million
Itanium 2	1.66GHz[5]	256KB	9MB[2]	667MHz	128-bit	10.6GBps	592 million

[1]*On-cartridge, full-speed unified 128 bits wide.*

[2]*On-die, full-speed unified 128 bits wide.*

[3]*Also available in low-voltage version.*

[4]*Optimized for dual-processor operation (DP Optimized).*

[5]*Optimized for multiple-processor operation.*

Table 2.28   Intel Itanium Processor Models

S-Spec/ QDF Number	Core Stepping	CPUID	Core Clock Speed (MHz)	FSB Speed (MHz)	L3 Size (MB)
SL4LT	C0	0007000604h	733	266	2
SL4LS	C0	0007000604h	733	266	4
SL5VS	C1	0007000704h	733	266	2
SL5VT	C1	0007000704h	733	266	4
SL6RH	C2	0007000804h	733	266	2
SL4LR	C0	0007000604h	800	266	2
SL4LQ	C0	0007000604h	800	266	4
SL5VU	C1	0007000704h	800	266	2
SL5VW	C1	0007000704h	800	266	4
SL6RK	C2	0007000804h	800	266	2
SL6RL	C2	0007000804h	800	266	4

Table 2.29 Intel Itanium 2 Processor Models

S-Spec Number	Processor Stepping	CPUID1	Core Clock Speed (MHz)	FSB Speed (MHz)	L3 Size (MB)	Code Name
SL67W	B3	001F000704h	900	400	1.5	McKinley
SL6P6	B3	001F000704h	900	400	1.5	McKinley
SL754	B1	001F010504h	1000	400	1.5	Deerfield
SL67U	B3	001F000704h	1000	400	1.5	McKinley
SL6P5	B3	001F000704h	1000	400	1.5	McKinley
SL67V	B3	001F000704h	1000	400	3	McKinley
SL6P7	B3	001F000704h	1000	400	3	McKinley
SL6XD	B1	001F010504h	1300	400	3	Madison
SL7SD	A1	001F020104h	1300	400	3	Madison
SL8CY	A2	001F020204h	1300	400	3	Madison
SL76K	B1	001F010504h	1400	400	1.5	Madison
SL7FP	B1	001F010504h	1400	400	3	Madison
SL6XE	B1	001F010504h	1400	400	4	Madison
SL8CX	A2	001F020204h	1500	400	4	Madison
SL7ED	A1	001F020104h	1500	400	4	Madison
SL6XF	B1	001F010504h	1500	400	6	Madison
SL7FQ	B1	001F010504h	1600	400	3	Madison
SL7EC	A1	001F020104h	1600	400	3	Madison
SL8CW	A2	001F020204h	1600	400	3	Madison
SL8CV	A2	001F020204h	1600	400	6	Madison
SL7EB	A1	001F020104h	1600	400	6	Madison
SL87H	A1	001F020104h	1600	400	9	Madison
SL8CU	A2	001F020204h	1600	400	9	Madison
SL7EF	A1	001F020104h	1600	533	3	Madison
SL8CZ	A2	001F020204h	1600	533	3	Madison
SL8JK	A2	001F020204h	1660	667	6	Madison
SL8JJ	A2	001F020204h	1660	667	9	Madison

Itanium 2 versions with 1.5MB or 3MB of L3 cache are designed for use in single- or dual-processor systems, and versions with 6MB and 9MB of L3 cache are designed for use in multiple-processor systems. Generally, you should use only the same stepping for a multiple-processor configuration. However, Intel has tested the following combinations:

- SL7SD and SL8CY
- SL7ED and SL8CX
- SL7EC and SL8CW
- SL7EB and SL8CV
- SL87H and SL8CU
- SL7EF and SL8CZ

Itanium and Itanium 2 were initially based on 0.18-micron technology. The 0.13-micron Madison and low-voltage Deerfield versions of the Itanium 2 were officially introduced in 2003. The Deerfield is a low-voltage version of Madison. As with other processors using smaller technologies, the switch to 0.13-micron technology allows for higher core clock speeds and larger memory caches.

AMD Athlon MP Processors

AMD's first server-class processor was the Athlon MP, based on the AMD Athlon and Athlon XP. Introduced in 2001, the Athlon MP supports up to two-way configurations and was a popular choice for cost-sensitive "white box" servers, including rack-mounted servers, before the development of the AMD Opteron processor. The leading vendor of Athlon MP–based motherboards for servers and workstations is Tyan (www.tyan.com).

There are four major models of the Athlon MP:

- The Athlon MP Model 6 is derived from the AMD Athlon Model 4, code-named Thunderbird.
- The Athlon MP Model 6 OPGA is derived from the AMD Athlon XP Model 6, code-named Palomino.
- The Athlon MP Model 8 is derived from the AMD Athlon XP Model 8, code-named Thoroughbred.
- The Athlon MP Model 10 is also derived from the AMD Athlon XP Model 8 but features 512KB of L2 cache.

The Athlon MP Model 6 OPGA, Athlon MP Model 8, and Athlon MP Model 10 use the same plus (+) numbering scheme introduced by the Athlon XP rather than the actual clock speed of the processor for the model number. We've never found this type of numbering system useful (although AMD continues to use it with its Opteron and other current processor lines). It is more useful to look at the processors' actual features, which are shown in Table 2.30.

All Athlon MP processors use the same Socket A (Socket 462) interface introduced for the AMD Athlon.

Table 2.30   Athlon MP Processors

Model	Model Number	Actual Clock Speed (MHz)	L2 Cache Size (KB)	Core Voltage (V DC)	Typical Thermal Power (W)	Max. Die Temperature (°Celsius)
Model 6	1000	1000	256	1.75	41.3	95
Model 6	1200	1200	256	1.75	49.1	95
Model 6 OPGA	1500+	1333	256	1.75	53.8	95
Model 6 OPGA	1600+	1400	256	1.75	56.3	95
Model 6 OPGA	1800+	1533	256	1.75	58.9	95
Model 6 OPGA	1900+	1600	256	1.75	58.9	95
Model 6 OPGA	2000+	1667	256	1.75	58.9	95
Model 6 OPGA	2100+	1733	256	1.75	58.9	95
Model 8	2000+	1667	256	1.60	52.8	90
Model 8	2200+	1800	256	1.65	54.5	90
Model 10	2600+	2000	512	1.60	47.2	90
Model 10	2800+	2133	512	1.60	47.2	90

As Table 2.30 shows, the AMD Athlon MP Model 10 is the best of the four Athlon MP models for two reasons: Model 10 variants feature double the L2 cache of previous versions, and Model 10 variants run cooler than other versions. The AMD Opteron (described in the next section) has largely replaced the Athlon MP and offers a much wider range of motherboard support.

An Athlon MP processor is shown in Figure 2.40.

Figure 2.40   The AMD Athlon MP processor is a dual-processor–capable version of the AMD Athlon and Athlon XP processors. *(Photograph used by permission of AMD Corporation.)*

AMD Opteron Processors

The AMD Opteron, introduced in 2003, was the first 64-bit processor to provide a seamless, no-compromise transition between current 32-bit operating systems and applications and 64-bit operating systems and applications. Unlike the Intel Itanium and Itanium 2, which provide relatively poor x86 performance because their native 64-bit mode (IA-64) uses a different processor architecture, the Opteron uses a fully compatible 64-bit extension of x86 architecture known as AMD64.

◄◄   For more information about the differences between IA-64 and AMD64, see "64-Bit Processor Modes," p. 52.

The Opteron has a second major distinction: It was the first x86-compatible processor with an integrated memory controller. The Opteron uses matched pairs of DDR memory for dual-channel memory access, enabling very high memory performance and very low latency when accessing memory.

Figure 2.41 illustrates an AMD Opteron processor.

Figure 2.41   The AMD Opteron family can be scaled up to eight-way servers in its 800-series version. *(Photograph used by permission of AMD Corporation.)*

The Opteron is divided into three series: the 100 Series (single-processor systems), 200 Series (one- or two-way systems), and 800 Series (up to eight-way systems). The following are the major features of single-core Opteron processors:

- 128KB L1 cache
- 1MB L2 cache
- Initial clock speeds of 1.4GHz–2.2GHz
- Three 6.4MBps HyperTransport links to the chipset
- 940-pin socket (most 100, all 200 and 800 series)
- 939-pin socket (some 100 series)
- Integrated memory controller
- 128-bit plus ECC dual-channel memory bus
- Maximum addressable memory of 1TB (40-bit physical) and 256TB (48-bit virtual)
- AMD64 architecture

Socket 940 versions of the Opteron require registered memory. In 2005, AMD introduced 100 series Opteron processors in Socket 939. Socket 939 uses standard DDR memory, enabling you to build a lower-cost single-processor server than with Socket 940 processors.

Opteron processors are available in three wattage ranges:

- Standard Opteron processors use from 82.1 to 92.6 watts of power, depending on clock speed and manufacturing technology.
- HE processors use 55 watts of power.
- EE processors use 30 watts of power.

HE and EE processors are recommended for use in rack-mounted or blade servers, as well as in other environments in which processor cooling can be difficult.

AMD Opteron processors are available in single-core and dual-core versions. Single-core versions were originally manufactured using a .13-micron silicon-on-insulator (SOI) process, but recent versions have switched to a .09-micron (90-nanometer) SOI process. Table 2.31 cross-references model numbers and clock speeds for various single-core AMD Opteron models.

Table 2.31   AMD Single-Core Opteron Processors

Clock Speed (GHz)	Single Processor	Dual Processor	Multiprocessor
1.4	140[1]	240[1]	840[1]
1.6	142	242[2]	842[2]
1.8	144[2,4]	244[2]	844[2]
2.0	146[3,4]	246[2,3]	846[2,3]
2.2	148[4]	248[2,3]	848[2,3]
2.4	150[4]	250[2,3]	850[2,3]

Table 2.31 Continued

Clock Speed (GHz)	Single Processor	Dual Processor	Multiprocessor
2.6	152[4]	252[5]	852[5]
2.8	154[6]	254[5]	854[5]

[1]*EE (30W) low-power version also available.*
[2]*Manufactured in .13- and .09-micron versions.*
[3]*HE (55W) low-power version also available.*
[4]*Socket 939 (.09-micron) version available.*
[5]*Manufactured in .09-micron version only.*
[6]*Available only in Socket 939 version.*

You can build an Opteron-based server with up to eight processors, and Opteron-based servers are also available from most major server vendors.

Dual-Core Opteron Processors

From the beginning, AMD's Opteron processors for servers were designed for dual-core operation, with space in the original design for an integrated crossbar memory controller. Dual-core processors enable you to have the virtual equivalent of a two-way server in a low-cost single-processor model. Larger server configurations also benefit.

◀◀ To learn more about the benefits of multiple processors and dual-core processors, see "Multiple CPUs," p. 37.

AMD introduced dual-core Opteron processors in 2005; all dual-core Opterons use the .09-micron SOI manufacturing process. Any Opteron motherboard that supports .09-micron Opteron processors is a candidate for an upgrade to a dual-core processor. You can contact your motherboard or server vendor for details. A BIOS upgrade may be necessary on some models.

Caution

Because of the dual-core design, the dual-core Opteron 175 and 180 processors require 110W. This is 15 watts more than the maximum for single-core or other dual-core Opteron processors. Make sure your server offers adequate cooling.

All dual-core Opterons offer 2MB of L2 cache (1MB per core), and versions are available for both Socket 940 (200 and 800 series) and Socket 939 (100 series). Some Socket 940 versions are available in the reduced-wattage HE series.

Table 2.32 cross-references model numbers and clock speeds for dual-core Opteron processors.

Table 2.32 AMD Dual-Core Opteron Processors

Clock Speed (GHz)	Single Processor	Dual Processor	Multiprocessor
1.6	—	260[1]	860[1]
1.8	165[2]	265[1]	865[1]
2.0	170[2]	270[1]	870[1]
2.2	175[2]	275	875
2.4	180[2]	280	880

[1]*HE (55W) low-power version also available.*
[2]*Available only in Socket 939 version.*

If you are already using an Opteron-based server that supports upgrading to dual-core processors, you can significantly improve the performance of your server by swapping processors. If you are building a server, using dual-core processors from the start provides you with better multitasking and the ability to handle greater loads, which can help you use your current hardware longer before upgrading.

RISC-Based Server Processors

Historically, RISC-based servers have dominated the eight-way and larger server categories. RISC-based servers are so named because their processors use a design known as reduced instruction set computer (RISC). RISC processors use customized instruction sets tailored to the tasks the processor is designed to do, separate instruction and data caches, instruction pipelining, and superscalar operation to permit multiple instructions to be performed at the same time.

At one time, the differences in performance between RISC and CISC designs such as x86 processors was profound. However, starting with sixth-generation processors such as the Pentium Pro and its many descendents, x86 processors have adopted many RISC techniques to improve performance. The EPIC processor architecture used by the Itanium family has elements of both RISC and CISC designs. At the same time, the clock speeds of Itanium 2 processors have matched those offered by the fastest RISC processors, and x86 processors offer considerably faster clock speeds.

Note

When gauging processor performance, pure clock speed is only one factor in gauging a chip's overall performance.

As a result of the performance gains in x86-based chips, several families of RISC-based processors, including the Alpha, PA-RISC, and MIPS R1xxxx will be phased out in the next year or two. While RISC technologies dominate embedded computing, RISC is no longer the undisputed champion of network servers. For this reason, much of this book is focused on Intel and AMD-based system designs. The following sections provide additional details about major RISC-based sever processor families.

Alpha

The Alpha processor family is often referred to as the DEC Alpha because it was originally developed by one-time powerhouse Digital Equipment Corporation in 1992 as the Alpha 21064. The code name EV applied to various Alpha designs is short for "extended VAX," as the Alpha was originally intended to run DEC's VAX operating system.

Major features of the Alpha architecture include the following:

- Native 64-bit design from the start; other 64-bit RISC chips are developments of 32-bit designs
- Built-in math coprocessor
- Out-of-order execution (starting with the 21264 EV6 processor of 1998)
- EV6 bus licensed to AMD and used for the AMD Athlon, Athlon MP, and other processors

The success of the AMD Athlon family indicates the fundamental strength of the Alpha design as well as its biggest weakness: The Alpha uses a short, very efficient pipeline, which makes it able to handle frequent changes in instructions and data. However, the shorter the pipeline, the harder it is to scale the processor to higher clock speeds. Consequently, while the Alpha processor offered very competitive clock speeds in the late 1990s, it fell behind compared to other RISC designs such as PowerPC or x86 and Itanium 2–based chips.

However, the major reason for Hewlett-Packard's decision to stop selling AlphaServers in 2006 is that Hewlett-Packard has three 64-bit server platforms. Hewlett-Packard had already decided to phase out its PA-RISC 8x00-based platforms, such as the Hewlett-Packard 9000 and Superdome series, because of its co-development with Intel of the Itanium processor family. When Hewlett-Packard purchased Compaq in 2001, Hewlett-Packard found itself with another unwanted RISC processor family that Compaq had already decided to abandon by 2004. In effect, Hewlett-Packard's purchase of Compaq gave the Compaq/Hewlett-Packard AlphaServer line a two-year reprieve that is now coming to an end. The latest AlphaServers use the 21364 processor.

Compaq, and now Hewlett-Packard, have offered AlphaServers in four product lines, as detailed in Table 2.33:

- **DS**—Entry-level (1 or 2 processors)
- **ES**—Midrange (4 to 8 processors)
- **GS**—High-end (8 to 32 processors)
- **SC**—Server clusters

Table 2.33   Compaq/Hewlett-Packard AlphaServers

AlphaServer System	Base Processor/Chip	Max. CPUs	Max. Clock Speed
DS Series			
DS10	21264	1	600MHz
DS10L	21264	1	600MHz
DS20E	21264	2	833MHz or 667MHz
DS20L	21264	2	833MHz
DS25	21264	2	1GHz
ES Series			
ES40	21264	4	667MHz or 833MHz
ES45	21264	4	1GHz or 1.25GHz
ES47	21364	4	1GHz
ES80	21364	8	1GHz
GS Series			
GS80	21264	8	1.25GHz
GS160	21264	16	1.25GHz
GS1280	21364	16	1.15GHz
GS320	21264	32	1.25GHz
SC Series			
SC20	21264	256	833MHz
SC45	21264	4096	1.25GHz

Hewlett-Packard is not the only source for AlphaServers or workstations, however. Microway (www.microway.com) offers customized Alpha-powered systems that use the 21264 Alpha processor. Microway took over support and warranty service for non–Hewlett-Packard Alpha systems in 2001 when API (a joint venture between Compaq and Samsung, started in 1998 to manufacture and support Alpha processors and systems) quit the Alpha business.

◄◄   For technical details of the differences in Alpha processors, see Table 2.3, p. 26.

PA-RISC 8xxx

Hewlett-Packard's PA-RISC 8000, introduced in 1996, was the first 64-bit version of its PA-RISC processor line, which was first used in the original 32-bit form in the Hewlett-Packard 3000 minicomputer line starting around 1989.

The PA-RISC 8xxx family has undergone only relatively minor design changes since it was first introduced. The major features of the PA-RISC 8000 include the following:

- Two separate instruction caches to permit fast and slow instructions to be executed separately
- Pipelining
- Superscalar execution
- No on-chip L1 cache

Improvements added to later versions include the following:

- Better branch prediction and larger cache (PA-8200)
- Onboard L1 cache, bigger branch history table, and translation lookaside buffer (PA-8500)
- Faster clock speeds with improved cache design (PA-8600)
- Even faster clock speeds with data prefetch and larger translation lookaside buffer (PA-8700)
- Dual-core design with off-chip L2 cache and faster bus (PA-8800)
- Faster L2 cache with improved error detection and correction (PA-8900)

Hewlett-Packard uses the Hewlett-Packard 9000 brand for its PA-RISC–based server product line. Current Hewlett-Packard 9000 servers are listed in Table 2.34

Table 2.34   Current Hewlett-Packard 9000 Servers

Model	Processor	Processor Range
		High-end
Superdome	PA-8900, Itanium 2[1]	4-32, 4-64, 12-128
		Midrange
rp7420-16	PA-8900 or PA-8800	2-16
rp8420-32	PA-8900 or PA-8800	2-32
		Entry-level
rp3410-2	PA-8900	1-2
rp3440-4	PA-8900	1, 2, or 4
rp4410-4	PA-8900	1, 2, or 4
rp4440-8	PA-8900	2, 4, 6, or 8

[1]*Can be mixed in the same server within separate hard partitions.*

For more information about current Hewlett-Packard servers, see the Hewlett-Packard website, at www.hp.com.

For more information about PA-RISC hardware and software, past and present, see the OpenPA website, at www.openpa.net.

◀◀   For technical details of PA-RISC 8xxx processors, see Table 2.4, p. 28.

MIPS R1xxxx

Although the MIPS R-series is associated with SGI, it was actually developed by MIPS Computer Systems in 1985. SGI bought MIPS in 1991 after MIPS ran into financial trouble during the development of the world's first 64-bit microprocessor, the R4000. After several other 64-bit processors were developed in various series, the R10000 processor was introduced in 1995 as an improved version of the R8000 and was used by many companies besides SGI.

The R10000 processor has the following major features:

- Superscalar design
- Out-of-order execution
- Improved integer performance (compared to the R8000)

SGI had planned to switch from MIPS to Itanium processors in the late 1990s, but when the Itanium was delayed, SGI was forced to continue to develop the R10000 design with subsequent versions:

- Faster clock speeds due to reduced die size (R12000)
- DDR SDRAM support in off-chip cache and faster FSB (R14000)
- Larger data and instruction caches and further die shrink for even greater speed (R16000)

Currently, SGI uses the MIPS R16000 in its SGI Origin 350 technical servers and Origin 3000 super-computers. These systems, which run SGI's IRIX implementation of UNIX, offer highly modular and expandable designs and more closely resemble server clusters in a box than a conventional multi-processor server. For more information, visit www.sgi.com/products/servers/origin/.

The other major vendor currently offering MIPS-based servers is Hewlett-Packard. Its NonStop S-series line of high-availability servers uses matched pairs of R12000, R14000, or R16000 processors running in lockstep, depending on the model. See www.hp.com for details.

Both Hewlett-Packard and SGI are expected to eventually move completely to Itanium-class processors for their entire product lines. Most of SGI's current servers have already moved to Itanium 2, and Hewlett-Packard is transitioning its AlphaServer and Hewlett-Packard 9000 (PA-RISC) users to Itanium 2 systems. Hewlett-Packard also offers a line of NonStop servers that use Itanium 2 processors.

◄◄   For technical details of the MIPS 1xxxxx series of processors, see Table 2.5, p. 28.

◄◄   For more information about Itanium, see "Itanium and Itanium 2 Processors," p. 121.

Power Architecture

The most successful RISC processor vendor appears to be IBM. It continues to develop two distinct families of RISC-based processors: the PowerPC, discussed in the following section, and the PowerPC's big brother, Power Architecture (discussed in this section).

Power Architecture processors are known as Power*x* processors, ranging from the original 32-bit Power1 (RIOS) processor used by the RS/6000 line of servers and computers in 1990 to the current Power5+.

Early Power processors used multichip designs. However, the Power2 SuperChip (also known as the P2SC) was the first single-chip Power Architecture processor, and it was the last to feature 32-bit operation. Its major features included the following:

- Superscalar operation
- Two integer and two floating-point calculation units
- Additional math instructions

The Power3 added the following:

■ 64-bit instructions derived from the PowerPC, making the Power3 compatible with both 32-bit and 64-bit instructions

The Power4 added the following:

■ Support for AS/400 instructions (derived from AS/400-specific PowerPC chip projects), enabling the Power4 to run in both RS/6000 and AS/400 systems

■ Dual-processor cores

■ Instruction grouping to put related instructions together for faster operation

The Power5 adds the following:

■ Improved L3 cache speed

■ Dynamic thread prioritizing (The processor determines which process threads need the most attention and uses dynamic resource balancing to keep conflicting programs on different processor cores.)

■ Simultaneous multithreading (SMT) (The processor runs two processes at the same time on the same processor core; this is a similar concept to Intel's HT Technology.)

■ Processor virtualization (This enables multiple operating systems and applications to run on a single server.)

The Power5+ is a die-shrunk version of the Power5.

Current eServer Open Power and System p5 IBM servers that use Power chips are listed in Table 2.35. Power chips are also used in other product lines, including the iSeries integrated business system.

Table 2.35   IBM Power Servers

Model	Processor	Processor Range
eServer Open Power[1]		
710 Express	Power5	1–2
710	Power5	1–2
720 Express	Power5	2, 4
720	Power5	1, 2, 4
System p5[2]		
505	Power5	1–2
510	Power5	1–2
520	Power5+	1–2
550	Power5+	2, 4
550Q	Power5+	4, 8
570 Express	Power5	2–8
570	Power5	2–16
575	Power5	8, 16

Table 2.35   Continued

Model	Processor	Processor Range
		System p5[2]
590	Power5	8–32
595	Power5	16–64

[1]*Runs Linux (Red Hat or SUSE).*

[2]*Runs AIX 5L (IBM implementation of UNIX) or Linux (Red Hat or SUSE).*

◀◀ For technical details of the IBM Power2 SuperChip through Power5 series of processors, see Table 2.6, p. 30.

PowerPC

The PowerPC chip family, originally introduced in 1992, is based on the Power Architecture Power family. PowerPC chips were originally developed as single-chip versions of the multichip Power1 processor that could be used in other IBM products in a cooperative effort between IBM, Apple, and Motorola.

The 32-bit PowerPC chip 604 was used in several servers manufactured by Apple, Motorola, and IBM, among others. Windows NT was available for early PowerPC systems but was quickly discontinued.

The 604's major features included the following:

- Four-instruction superscalar execution
- SMP (dual-processor) support

The 604e added larger instruction and data caches.

The 740 and 750 are members of the G3 family and were the first commercially successful 64-bit PowerPC chips:

- The 740 lacks support for L2 cache.
- The 750 can use L2 cache on the processor cartridge.

Both also support 32-bit PowerPC code and were used in Apple PowerMac G3 servers.

The 7400 processor (also known as the G4) was manufactured by Freescale (Motorola's former processor division) and was co-designed by Motorola and Apple. IBM did not participate in its design. The G4/7400's major features include the following:

- 32/64-bit operation
- AltiVec "Velocity Engine" vector processing unit
- Improved SMP
- 64-bit math coprocessor

The G4/7400 was used in Apple PowerMac servers.

The latest PowerPC processor family, the 970, is also known as the G5. It was developed by IBM. Major features of the G5/970 include the following:

- IBM's Power4 processor core
- Integrated AltiVec vector processing unit

The 970FX is a die-shrunk version of the 970. The 970MP is a dual-core version. All 970-family processors have been used in Apple PowerMac G5 xServe servers. The 970 is also used by IBM's BladeCenter JS20 server blade.

The long-term future of PowerPC chips at the server level is questionable because Apple has switched to Intel Core processors for its latest Macintosh products. However, PowerPC chips continue to be popular in video game and embedded applications, and IBM may continue to use them in its own server products.

For more information about PowerPC processors, see the IBM website, at www.ibm.com, and the Freescale website, at www.freescale.com. For more information about PowerPC-based servers, see the Apple website, at www.apple.com.

◄◄ For technical details of the PowerPC series of processors, see Table 2.7, p. 30.

Processor Replacement/Upgrades

It's possible to upgrade the processor in most x86-based servers to obtain better performance, either by adding a faster version of an existing processor or, in some cases, by moving to a new processor family (such as upgrading from a single-core to a dual-core processor).

To maximize the performance of a single-processor server, you can almost always upgrade to the fastest processor your particular board will support. Because of the varieties of processor sockets and slots—not to mention voltages, speeds, and other potential areas of incompatibility—you should consult with your motherboard or system manufacturer to see whether a higher-speed processor will work in your board. Usually, that can be determined by the type of socket or slot on the motherboard, but other things, such as the voltage regulator and BIOS, can be deciding factors as well.

For example, if your motherboard uses Socket 604, you might be able to upgrade to the fastest version of the Intel Xeon. Before purchasing a new CPU, you should verify that the motherboard has proper bus speed, voltage settings, and ROM BIOS support for the new chip.

Caution

If you are upgrading processors in a multiple-processor server, the replacement processors must have identical steppings or at least have been tested for proper operation in a multiple-processor environment. See "Upgrading to Multiple Processors," earlier in this chapter, for links to vendor documentation with specific recommendations for mixing steppings.

If a BIOS upgrade is available for your server or server motherboard, you should install it before installing an additional processor or upgrading the processor. Otherwise, the system might not recognize the processor.

If you are unable to install a faster processor directly into your system, you can try one of the available third-party solutions, including adapters that can help first-generation Socket 423 Pentium 4 motherboards use Socket 478 processors, faster Socket 370 processors for older Slot 1 motherboards, and so on. Rather than purchase processors and adapters separately, you should generally purchase them together in a module from companies such as PowerLeap (see Appendix C).

Caution

If you want to use an adapter-based solution for upgrading a multiple-processor server, you need to make sure the adapter has been designed to work in a multiple-processor mode. For example, the PowerLeap PL-P3/SMP upgrade for Slot 1 Pentium II/Pentium III–based systems is designed to work in dual-processor systems, but the PowerLeap PL-iP3/T is designed for use in single-processor systems.

Upgrading the processor can, in some cases, double the performance of a system. However, if you already have the fastest processor that will fit a particular socket, you need to consider other alternatives. In that case, you should look into a complete motherboard change, which would let you upgrade to a motherboard that supports the latest version of your preferred server processor.

If your chassis design is not proprietary and your system uses an industry-standard ATX, BTX, or SSI motherboard design, you should change the motherboard and processor rather than try to find an upgrade processor that will work with your existing board.

Tip

If you want to upgrade to a dual-processor configuration by replacing your motherboard, you need to be sure to compare the form factor of the new motherboard to the space in your current case. Many dual-processor motherboards use the Extended ATX form factor, which supports a motherboard up to 12 inches wide by 13 inches long. Some ATX cases can't handle boards of this size or might not offer adequate cooling or clearance for processors and heatsinks.

Also, make sure your existing power supply matches the ATX or SSI standards. If not, you might not be able to replace the motherboard.

▶▶ See "ATX Motherboards," p. 228.

▶▶ See "SSI Form Factor Specifications," p. 234.

▶▶ See "BTX Motherboards," p. 241.

▶▶ See "Power Supplies and Connectors," p. 247.

Processor Installation Procedures

If you are installing a processor or processors into a new motherboard, you should install them before you install the motherboard into the system. If you are upgrading a system with a replacement or additional processor, you should remove the motherboard from the system before performing the upgrade. There are two reasons to work with the motherboard out of the system for processor upgrades:

- Processor configuration
- Avoiding damage to the motherboard

Some older motherboards have jumpers that control both the CPU speed and the voltage supplied to it. If these are set incorrectly, the system might not operate at all, might operate erratically, or might even damage the CPU. If you have any questions about the proper settings, you should contact the vendor that sold you the board before making any jumper changes.

◀◀ See "Operating Voltages," p. 79.

With some processors, especially those that use Socket 370 or Socket A (Socket 462), you need to use a great deal of force to clip the heatsink to the socket or release the heatsink from the socket. The amount of force required can damage the motherboard if the motherboard is not removed from the system and placed on a surface that supports the processor socket area of the motherboard. Newer processors use different heatsink installation methods that require less force.

To install a processor and heatsink, you can use one of the procedures described in the following sections, depending on your processor type.

Installing Socketed Processors

To install socketed processors, follow these steps:

1. Find pin 1 on the processor; it is usually denoted by a corner of the chip being marked by a dot or bevel.

2. Find the corresponding pin 1 of the ZIF socket for the CPU on the motherboard; it is usually marked on the board or with a bevel in one corner of the socket. Be sure the pins on the processor are straight and not bent; if they are bent, the chip will not insert properly into the socket. If necessary, use small needle-nose pliers or a hemostat to carefully straighten any pins. Don't bend them too much, or they might break off, ruining the chip.

3. Insert the CPU into the ZIF socket by lifting the release lever until it is vertical. Then align the pins on the processor with the holes in the socket and drop it into place. If the processor does not seem to want to drop in all the way, remove it to check for proper alignment and any possibly bent pins. When the processor is fully seated in the socket, push the locking lever on the socket down until it latches to secure the processor (see Figure 2.42).

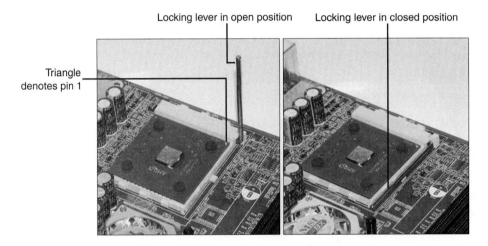

Figure 2.42   The lever on a ZIF socket locks the processor into the socket when lowered. Note the triangle on the corner of the processor, denoting pin 1.

Heatsinks made for Socket 370, Socket A, and Socket 423 clip to the socket itself (see Figure 2.43), and heatsinks made for Socket 478, Socket 775, Socket 603/604, Socket 939, and Socket 940 clip to various types of retaining mechanisms built in to the motherboard or case (see Figure 2.44).

You need to be careful when attaching the clip to the socket, especially with Socket 370 or Socket A heatsink clips; you don't want it to scrape against the motherboard, which can damage circuit traces or components. You also need to keep the heatsink steady on the chip while attaching the clips, so you should not move, tilt, or slide the heatsink while you attach it. Most heatsinks have a preapplied thermal pad (also known as a phase-change pad); to prepare this type of heatsink, you remove the protective tape before installing the heatsink. For heatsinks that don't include a thermal pad, you need to put a dab of heatsink thermal transfer compound (normally a white-colored grease; some vendors of high-performance heatsinks use a silver-based compound such as Arctic Silver instead) on the CPU before installing the heatsink. This prevents any air gaps and enables the heatsink to work more efficiently. If the CPU has an active heatsink (with a fan), you need to plug the fan power connector in to one of the fan connectors supplied on the motherboard (see Figure 2.45). Optionally, some heatsinks use a disk drive power connector for fan power.

Screwdriver positioning retaining clip on other side of socket

Retaining clip to be secured to lug on socket

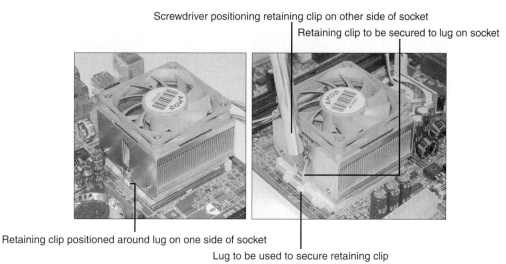

Retaining clip positioned around lug on one side of socket

Lug to be used to secure retaining clip

Figure 2.43   Attaching a heatsink to a socketed processor. The retaining clip is spring-loaded, so it must be positioned with a screwdriver or similar tool that can push the clip down and swing it into place.

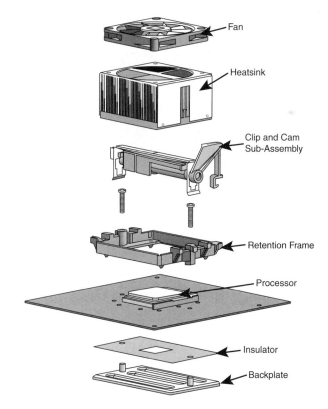

Fan

Heatsink

Clip and Cam
Sub-Assembly

Retention Frame

Processor

Insulator

Backplate

Figure 2.44   The Socket 754/939/940 active heatsink uses a clip and cam subassembly and retention frame to hold the heatsink in place.

Heatsink fan
power connector

Figure 2.45 Attaching the heatsink fan power connector to the motherboard.

Installing Slot-Based Processors

To install slot-based processors, follow these steps:

1. Make sure you have the processor, the universal retention mechanism brackets with included fasteners (if they are not built in to the motherboard already), and the heatsink supports. Most slot-based processors come with either an active or a passive heatsink already installed. Position the two universal retention mechanism brackets on either side of the processor slot so that the holes in the brackets line up with the holes in the motherboard (see Figure 2.46).

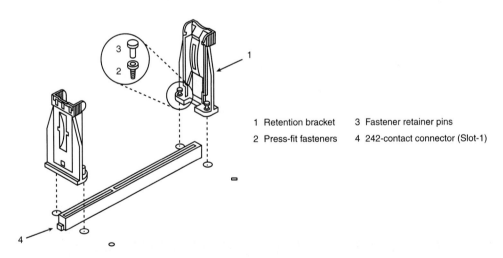

1 Retention bracket   3 Fastener retainer pins
2 Press-fit fasteners   4 242-contact connector (Slot-1)

Figure 2.46 Universal retention mechanism for slot-based processors. *(Illustration used by permission of Intel Corporation.)*

2. Push the included fasteners through the mounting holes in the retention bracket and the motherboard until you feel them snap into place.

3. Insert the fastener retainer pins through the holes in the fastener to lock them into place.

4. Slide the processor/heatsink down between the brackets until it is firmly seated in the slot. The latches on the top sides of the processor lock into place when the processor is fully seated.

5. Install the heatsink supports into the holes provided in the motherboard and processor.

◀◀ If you are installing a Pentium II or Pentium III Xeon, see "Single-Edge Contact Cartridge Packaging," p. 67.

After installing either type of processor, you should refer to the motherboard manufacturer's manual to set the jumpers, if any, to match the CPU you are going to install. Look for the diagram of the motherboard to find the jumper location, and look for the tables for the correct settings for your CPU. If the CPU supplied was already installed on the motherboard, the jumpers should already be correctly set for you, but it is still a good idea to check them.

Note

Most recent systems use a BIOS-based configuration method instead of jumper blocks or DIP switches to configure the processor. To complete the configuration process, you start the computer, start the BIOS Setup program, and select the correct options for clock multiplier, frequency, voltage, and other settings required by the particular system BIOS in use. You need to be sure to save the changes when exiting the BIOS Setup program.

Some systems, particularly those that use rack-mounted form factors or blade-based components, use passive heatsinks and cooling ducts instead of heatsinks with integrated fans to cool the processor(s). When installing or upgrading processors in such systems, you need to be sure to remove the cooling duct before attempting to remove the existing processor. If you are installing an additional processor, you should contact the vendor to determine whether you need to install an additional cooling duct for the second processor.

Some multiprocessor servers use terminator boards (essentially a processor cartridge with special circuits inside instead of a processor) to fill empty processor slots on a multiprocessor motherboard. With these servers, you need to remove the terminator board before attempting to install a new processor.

Hardware Compatibility with Server Platforms

Intel and AMD server-class processors are supported by Windows Server 2000, Windows Server 2003, Novell Netware 6.x, x86-compatible Linux distributions, SCO UnixWare 7.1.x, and Sun Solaris for x86. It might be necessary to download and install service packs, patches, or updates to fully support the newest processors, particularly if your server's operating system was introduced before your processor model was developed.

RISC-based servers are supported by the vendor's UNIX implementation and sometimes by various Linux distributions as well. See the vendor's website for details.

▶▶ For more information about server operating systems, see Chapter 18, "Server Platforms: Network Operating Systems."

Troubleshooting and Documenting Your Server's CPU

Whether your server was built by a major vendor and arrived in your hands as a preconfigured system or you built it yourself, you need accurate documentation about the server's onboard hardware. You can obtain this documentation through the following sources:

- For preconfigured servers from major vendors such as IBM, Hewlett-Packard/Compaq, Gateway, Dell, Sun, SGI, and others, contact the vendor. Vendor websites usually offer model-specific technical support documentation.

- For white-box servers built from components, you need to determine the vendor for each component (processor, chipset, motherboard, hard disk, SCSI, network adapter, and so forth) and contact each vendor. Component vendor websites typically offer model-specific documentation.

Note

If you are not satisfied with the technical documentation available from a server vendor, you can sometimes obtain technical documentation from the server's OEM component vendors. Note that in some cases, a server vendor might use modified components that are not the same as those the component vendor sells at retail or to other companies.

Even if you received excellent documentation with your server or server components, keep in mind that updated versions might be available for download. You should check for documentation updates before attempting to determine whether a particular server or component is suitable for a given task.

▶▶ For more information about server benchmarking and maintenance, see Chapter 21, "Server Testing and Maintenance."

Processor Bugs

All processors can contain design defects or errors. Processor bugs aren't new: Some of Intel's first 32-bit processors, 386s, were unable to perform 32-bit math correctly. Chips that could perform 32-bit math properly were stamped at the factory with a double-sigma marking. However, the most notorious processor bug was the 1994 FDIV bug in early Intel Pentiums. This bug caused some floating-point calculations to produce errors. Intel ended up replacing affected processors. Although this example might be the only example that the average computer user might remember of a buggy processor, in reality, all types of microprocessors can have various types of errors, including the following:

- Power management problems
- Memory compatibility issues
- Cache coherency or lockup issues on multiple-processor systems

You can often avoid the effects of a given bug by implementing hardware or software workarounds. Intel documents these bugs and workarounds well for its processors in its processor Specification Update manual, which is available from Intel's website (http://developer.intel.com). AMD provides information for its processors in its Revision Guide for each processor, available from the AMD website (www.amd.com).

Unlike the Intel 386 and Pentium bugs, bugs in recent processors usually don't result in the generation of spurious data. However, they can result in system slowdowns, system lockups, or other issues that are detrimental to reliable server performance. Because there is no trade-in policy for processors—and even if there were, you'd be trading in a processor with one set of bugs for a processor with another set—three methods have been adopted to counteract processor bugs:

- Operating system patches and updates
- BIOS updates
- Processor updates

Processor Updates

The need for processor updates became obvious in 1994, when the Intel Pentium processor was determined to have an error in its floating-point processor. At the time, the only way to solve such a significant problem was to replace the chip with one that had the bug fixed or to create software or BIOS-based workarounds. Starting with the Pentium Pro processor and continuing through current models, Intel introduced a method of fixing bugs by altering the microcode in the processor. *Microcode* is essentially a set of instructions and tables in the processor that control how the processor operates. These processors incorporate a feature called *reprogrammable microcode*, which enables certain types of bugs to be worked around via microcode updates. The microcode updates reside in the motherboard ROM BIOS and are loaded into the processor by the motherboard BIOS during the POST. Each time the system is rebooted, the fix code is reloaded, ensuring that it will have the bug fix installed any time the processor is operating.

Intel provides the updated microcode for a given processor to the motherboard manufacturer so it can incorporate the microcode into the flash ROM BIOS for the board. This is one reason it is important to install the most recent motherboard BIOS anytime you install a new processor. If your processor is newer than your motherboard ROM BIOS code, it probably doesn't include updated microcode to support your processor. In that case, you should visit the website of your motherboard manufacturer so you can download and install the latest BIOS update for your motherboard.

BIOS Updates

Because the BIOS controls all standard onboard hardware, including the processor, it has a vital role in determining how well your processors work. If your server's BIOS does not recognize a new processor you plan to install, you must update the BIOS before performing the processor upgrade. However, if you notice any other problems with the processor, including unexplained lockups or slowdowns, you should check out the server or motherboard vendor's list of BIOS fixes to determine whether any of them apply to your situation. If you find a BIOS update that applies, download and install it. If possible, test your server in a non-production setting for a while to determine whether the new BIOS update has solved the problem or whether it has introduced new problems.

CHAPTER 3

Server Chipsets

The story of modern servers is as much the story of specialized chipsets as it is the story of specialized processors and motherboards. The chipset *is* the motherboard; therefore, any two server boards with the same chipsets are functionally identical unless the vendor has added features to those provided by the chipset or removed support for certain chipset features.

Note

You will sometimes find server motherboards that use the same chipset but differ in their integrated features. Vendors might add additional chips to support additional features, such as a second 10Mbps Ethernet, 100Mbps Fast Ethernet, or 1000Mbps Gigabit Ethernet port. A vendor might also choose not to support some optional features in a given chipset.

Server Chipsets Overview

The chipset typically contains the processor bus interface (called the front-side bus [FSB]), memory controllers, bus controllers, I/O controllers, and more. All the circuits on the motherboard are contained within the chipset. If the CPU is like the engine in your car, the chipset represents the car's chassis. It is the framework in which the engine rests and is its connection to the outside world. The chipset is the frame, suspension, steering, wheels and tires, transmission, driveshaft, differential, and brakes. The chassis in your car is what gets the power to the ground, allowing the vehicle to start, stop, and corner.

In a typical server, the chipset represents the connection between the processor and everything else. In most cases, the processor can't talk to memory modules, adapter boards, devices, and so on without going through the chipset.

Note

The AMD Opteron processors for servers and workstations incorporate memory controllers. Thus, chipsets that support Opteron processors do not contain memory controllers.

Because the chipset controls the interface or connections between the processor and everything else, the chipset ends up dictating which type of processor you have; how fast it will run; how fast each bus will operate; the speed, type, and amount of memory you can use; and more.

In fact, the chipset might be the single most important component in a system, possibly even more important than the processor. Systems with faster processors can be outperformed by systems with slower processors but better chipsets, much like how a car with less power might win a race through better cornering, acceleration, and braking. When deciding on an x86 server, whether it is prebuilt or assembled from parts, it is a good idea to start by choosing the chipset first because the chipset decision dictates the processor, memory, I/O, and expansion capabilities.

Although server chipsets are designed to perform the same types of tasks as desktop chipsets, the feature set included in a typical server chipset emphasizes stability rather than performance, as with a typical desktop chipset. Server-specific chipset features such as support for error-correcting code (ECC) memory, advanced error correction for memory, system management, and a lack of overclocking options demonstrate the emphasis on stability.

Although servers use x86, Itanium, and a variety of RISC processors, this chapter focuses on chipsets used in x86 and Itanium-based servers. There are several reasons for this. When you select an x86 or Itanium processor as the basis for a server, you can typically select from motherboards based on several chipsets that offer different levels of performance and features, either as part of a preconfigured server or as a component of a custom-built server. Many motherboards offer third-party chipsets, which provides additional flexibility in your final selection. However, when you select a server with a RISC processor, the chipset and motherboard are almost always produced by the same vendor that produced the processor. In addition, a single chipset is usually used to support a particular processor model. Product differentiation on a RISC-based server is based far less on the chipset than on factors such as the number of processors, memory size, and form factor.

Server Chipset History

When IBM created the first PC motherboards, it used several discrete (separate) chips to complete the design. Besides the processor and optional math coprocessor, many other components were required to complete the system, with each component requiring its own separate chip.

Table 3.1 lists all the primary chip components used on the original PC/XT and AT motherboards.

Table 3.1   Primary Chip Components on PC/XT and AT Motherboards

Chip Function	PC/XT Version	AT Version
Processor	8088	80286
Math coprocessor (floating-point unit)	8087	80287
Clock generator	8284	82284
Bus controller	8288	82288
System timer	8253	8254
Low-order interrupt controller	8259	8259
High-order interrupt controller	—	8259
Low-order DMA controller	8237	8237
High-order DMA controller	—	8237
CMOS RAM/real-time clock	—	MC146818
Keyboard controller	8255	8042

In addition to the processor/coprocessor, a six-chip set was used to implement the primary motherboard circuit in the original PC and XT systems. IBM later upgraded this to a nine-chip design in the AT and later systems, mainly by adding more interrupt and DMA controller chips and the nonvolatile CMOS RAM/real-time clock chip.

All these motherboard chip components came from Intel or an Intel-licensed manufacturer, except the CMOS/clock chip, which came from Motorola. Building a clone or copy of one of these IBM systems required all these chips plus many smaller, discrete logic chips to glue the design together—totaling 100 or more individual chips. This kept the price of a motherboard high and left little room on the board to integrate other functions.

A chipset integrates the functions of two or more discrete chips into a single chip. The first PC chipset was developed by Chips and Technologies, which developed the first PC chipset in 1986.

The Chips and Technologies 82C206 integrated all the functions of the main motherboard chips in an AT-compatible system. This chip included the functions of the 82284 clock generator, 82288 bus controller, 8254 system timer, dual 8259 interrupt controllers, dual 8237 DMA controllers, and even the MC146818 CMOS/clock chip. Besides the processor, virtually all the major chip components on a PC motherboard could now be replaced by a single chip. Four other chips augmented the 82C206, acting as buffers and memory controllers, thus completing virtually the entire motherboard circuit with five total chips. Later, the four chips augmenting the 82C206 were replaced by a new set of only three chips, and the entire set was called the New Enhanced AT (NEAT) CS8221 chipset. This was later followed by the 82C836 Single Chip AT (SCAT) chipset, which finally condensed all the chips in the set down to a single chip.

Intel did not enter the desktop and server chipset business until 1994, which was when the first true server-class processor, the Intel Pentium, was introduced. Although Novell NetWare and other early network operating systems had supported processors from the 8088 through 486 families, those systems did not provide feature support for multiple processors or other hallmarks of modern server design. Starting with the Pentium, chipsets from Intel and other vendors made multiprocessor servers possible.

Although Intel has several other rivals in the desktop chipset business, none of them (VIA Technologies, AcerLabs/ALi, SiS, nVidia, or ATI) are significant rivals to Intel in the manufacture of server chipsets for Intel processors. However, Intel is not alone in supplying server chipsets for its processors. Starting in 1997, ServerWorks (a Broadcom company originally known as Reliance Computer Corporation) introduced its first server chipsets for Intel processors. Today, ServerWorks is the second major supplier of server chipsets for Intel-based servers, with Intel continuing in first place.

Although Advanced Micro Devices (AMD) had made desktop processors for many years, it did not become a significant factor in server chipsets until the development of the Athlon MP processor, its first processor to support SMP operation. AMD now also makes Opteron processors for use in up to four-way servers and produces server chipsets for use with both processor families. Third-party vendors are producing Opteron-compatible chipsets that support up to eight processors.

Sun Microsystems uses two distinct types of architecture in its servers. Its proprietary SPARC-based servers use an equally proprietary motherboard architecture, while its AMD-based Sun Fire X-series and V40z servers use AMD 8000 chipsets.

▶▶   For more information about Sun servers using the SPARC architecture, see Chapter 19, "Sun Microsystems Servers."

Differences Between Server and Desktop Chipsets

Although some chipsets are used for both servers and desktop PCs, and many chipsets are used for both servers and workstations, there are several differences between server and desktop chipsets. Server chipsets generally include the following features not found on desktop chipsets:

- **Support for system management software**—System management software programs such as IBM Tivoli and CA Unicenter TNG enable a system administrator to determine the condition of a server and take action if memory, processor, or other essential components operate outside normal parameters or fail completely.

- **Support for error correction**—The ability to detect and correct some types of memory and data errors is an essential feature for any server chipset. Depending on the chipset, error correction might include support for ECC memory, hardware memory scrubbing, chipkill, and ECC support in the North Bridge/South Bridge or hub interface.

Note

Hardware memory scrubbing checks the reliability of the memory subsystem during idle periods and informs the system management software in use of any memory modules that are causing noncorrectable memory errors. Chipkill supports error correction of up to 4 bits per memory module and shuts down memory modules that create too many memory errors while keeping the system operating, using the remainder of the memory modules. Server processors' cache memory often supports ECC as well. For details, see Chapter 2, "Server Microprocessors."

- **Support for registered memory**—Registered memory, also known as buffered memory, incorporates buffers for greater reliability. However, registered memory is slower than unbuffered memory and is more expensive.

- **Support for multiple processors**—Although some entry-level servers support only one processor, most servers can be expanded to two or more processors for improved performance.

- **Support for 64-bit and 66MHz PCI expansion slots**—Most servers feature 66MHz/64-bit PCI expansion slots for use with SCSI and iSCSI drive array host adapters and Gigabit Ethernet network adapters, as well as the more common 33MHz/32-bit PCI slots widely used on desktop computers.

- **Support for PCI-X expansion slots**—Many recent server chipsets support PCI-X expansion slots as well as PCI expansion slots. The high-performance (up to 133MHz, 64-bit) PCI-X expansion bus is particularly well suited to high-performance SCSI RAID arrays and Gigabit Ethernet adapters, and it is backward compatible with PCI cards. Depending on the server chipset, PCI-X support might be provided by an additional chip in the chipset or might be integrated into the South Bridge (I/O controller hub [ICH]) component of the chipset. PCI-X slots are backward compatible with PCI slots.

- **Support for PCI-Express expansion slots**—PCI-Express, the newest and fastest member of the PCI family, is supported on some of the newest servers. The exact grouping of lanes per slot varies from chipset to chipset. Typically, servers with PCI-Express support might offer PCI-Express x1 and x4, and some also feature x8 slots. Each PCI-Express lane (x) features a throughput of 250MBps. Thus, a PCI-Express x4 slot has a throughput of 1GBps, which is about the same as that offered by 133MHz, 64-bit PCI-X slots.

Although server chipsets typically have many features not found in desktop chipsets, they also lack some features that are common to most desktop chipsets. For example, audio and advanced video/graphics features are not necessary on servers, and thus it's not surprising that most server chipsets lack support for onboard audio, don't support AGP or PCI-Express video cards, and might not support Microsoft's gaming API, DirectX (which is the case with some ServerWorks chipsets).

Although server motherboards often support integrated SCSI and PCI or low-end AGP video, these features are not native to a server's chipset but are provided by discrete chips from other vendors. (See Figure 3.1, later in this chapter, for a typical example of a motherboard with onboard SCSI and VGA support.)

The North Bridge and South Bridge Architectures

Most of Intel's earlier chipsets (and, until recently, virtually all non-Intel chipsets) are broken into a multitiered architecture incorporating the North Bridge and South Bridge components, as well as a Super I/O chip:

- **North Bridge**—North Bridge is so named because it is the connection between the high-speed processor bus (running at speeds from 66MHz to as high as 800MHz in recent designs) and slower buses, such as AGP, PCI, PCI-X, and PCI-Express. The North Bridge is what the chipset is named after, meaning that, for example, what we call the E7505 chipset is derived from the fact that the actual North Bridge chip part number for that set is E7505. Many vendors now use other terms, such as memory controller hub (MCH; Intel) for the North Bridge chip.

- **South Bridge**—South Bridge was originally named because it is the bridge between the PCI bus (66/33MHz) and the even slower ISA bus (8MHz). On older systems, the PCI bus was used to connect the North and South Bridge chips, but on most recent systems, a dedicated bus such as Intel's Accelerated Hub Architecture or the AMD-developed HyperTransport bus is used for the connection between the North and South Bridge chips. Note that the South Bridge chip is often referred to by other names in recent chipset designs; for example, Intel now uses the term I/O controller hub.

■ **Super I/O chip**—This is a separate chip attached to the ISA bus that is not really considered part of the chipset and often comes from a third party, such as National Semiconductor or Standard MicroSystems Corp. (SMSC). The Super I/O chip contains the logic for legacy ports such as keyboard, PS/2 mouse, serial, and parallel ports, all combined into a single chip. Note that most recent South Bridge chips also include Super I/O functions (such chips are known as Super-South Bridge chips), so most recent motherboards no longer include a separate Super I/O chip.

Figure 3.1 shows a typical dual Socket 370 motherboard using North Bridge/South Bridge architecture, the ServerWorks Super P3TDL3, with the locations of all major chips and components identified.

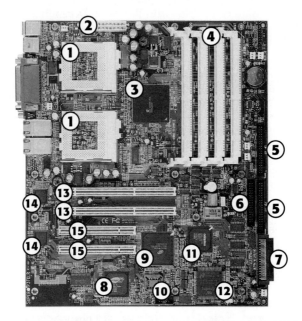

1. Dual Socket 370 processor sockets	9. ServerWorks OSB4/OSB5 South Bridge chip
2. ATX power supply connector	10. BIOS chip
3. ServerWorks CNB30LE North Bridge chip	11. Adaptec AIC-7892 Ultra 160 SCSI chip
4. Sockets for registered ECC SDRAM memory	12. National Semiconductor Super I/O chip
5. ATA/IDE port (2)	13. PCI (64-bit/66MHz) slots
6. Floppy drive port	14. Intel 82559 Ethernet chips
7. SCSI port	15. PCI (32-bit/33MHz) slots
8. ATI RageXL video chip	

Figure 3.1   A typical dual Socket 370 (Pentium III) server motherboard, showing component locations.

The North Bridge is sometimes referred to as the PAC (PCI/AGP controller). It is essentially the main component of the motherboard and is the only motherboard circuit besides the processor that normally runs at full motherboard (processor bus) speed. Most modern chipsets use a single-chip North Bridge; however, some of the older chipsets actually consist of up to three individual chips to make up the complete North Bridge circuit.

The South Bridge is the lower-speed component in the chipset and has always been a single individual chip. The South Bridge is a somewhat interchangeable component in that different North Bridge chips are often designed to use the same South Bridge component. This modular design of the chipset allows for lower cost and greater flexibility for motherboard manufacturers. Similarly, many vendors produce several versions of pin-compatible South Bridge chips with different features to enable more flexible and lower-cost manufacturing and design. The South Bridge connects to the 33MHz PCI bus and contains the interface or bridge to the 8MHz ISA bus (if present). It also typically contains dual ATA/IDE hard disk controller interfaces, one or more USB interfaces, and, in later designs, even the CMOS RAM and real-time clock functions. In older designs, the South Bridge contained all the components that make up the ISA bus, including the interrupt and DMA controllers.

The third motherboard component, the Super I/O chip, is connected to the 8MHz ISA bus or the low-pin-count (LPC) bus and contains all the legacy ports that are built in to a motherboard. For example, most Super I/O chips contain the serial ports, parallel port, floppy controller, and keyboard/mouse interface. Optionally, they might contain the CMOS RAM/clock, IDE controllers, and game port interface as well. Systems that integrate IEEE 1394 and SCSI ports use separate chips for these port types, as in Figure 3.1.

Most recent motherboards that use North Bridge/South Bridge chipset designs incorporate a Super-South Bridge, which incorporates the South Bridge and Super I/O functions into a single chip. Additional features, such as the onboard SCSI and VGA video found on the motherboard shown in Figure 3.1, are provided by third-party chips. Although SCSI chips used on server motherboards usually support high-performance SCSI (Ultra160 or Ultra320) and might also support SCSI RAID arrays, VGA video support is usually at a minimal level. For example, the ATI Rage XL video chip used in the motherboard shown in Figure 3.1 supports only 8MB of video memory and lacks advanced 3D graphics performance. Because a server's video is typically used only for monitoring and diagnostics, advanced features are not needed.

Figure 3.2 illustrates the block diagram of the motherboard shown in Figure 3.1. Note that the 33MHz 32-bit PCI bus is used as the connection between North and South Bridge chips as well as for expansion slots. Also, USB 1.1 ports on this system are used only for low-speed (1.5MBps) input devices, such as keyboards and mouse devices.

Intel Hub Architecture

The newer 8xx, 9xx, 72xx, 73xx, 85xx, and the E75xx series server chipsets from Intel use hub architectures in which the former North Bridge chip is now called a MCH and the former South Bridge is called an ICH. Rather than being connected through the PCI bus, as in a standard North Bridge/South Bridge design, they are connected via a dedicated hub interface that is much faster than PCI.

Hub architectures offer a couple advantages over traditional North Bridge/South Bridge designs:

- **Much greater speed**—266MBps up to 2GBps (based on version), compared to 133MBps PCI bus.
- **Reduced PCI loading**—The hub interface is independent of PCI and doesn't share or steal PCI bus bandwidth for chipset or Super I/O traffic. This improves performance of all other PCI bus–connected devices because the PCI bus is not involved in those transactions.

The MCH interfaces between the high-speed processor bus (1066/800/533/400MHz) and video buses such as AGP (up to 533MHz) or PCI-Express x8 (2GBps) or x16 (4GBps), if present. Some systems connect a PCI-X hub (133MHz) to the PCI-Express x8 bus. The ICH interfaces between the ATA (IDE) ports (66/100MHz), the SATA ports (150MBps or faster), and the PCI bus (33MHz). If PCI-Express x1 slots (250MBps) are present, they are usually interfaced via the ICH. Some systems also connect PCI-X slots (100/133MHz) to the ICH.

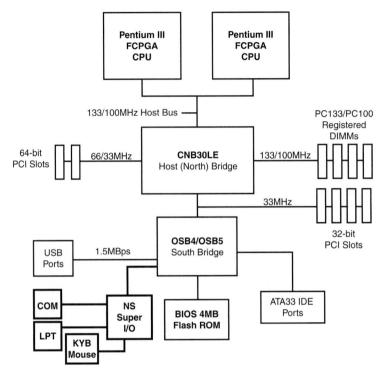

Figure 3.2   The North Bridge/South Bridge architecture used by the motherboard shown in Figure 3.1.

The ICH also includes an LPC bus, consisting basically of a stripped 4-bit-wide version of PCI designed primarily to support the motherboard ROM BIOS and Super I/O chips. By using the same 4 signals for data, address, and command functions, only 9 other signals are necessary to implement the bus, for a total of only 13 signals. This dramatically reduces the number of traces connecting the ROM BIOS chip and Super I/O chips in a system as compared to the 98 ISA bus signals necessary for older North Bridge/South Bridge chipsets that used ISA as the interface to those devices. The LPC bus has a maximum bandwidth of 16.67MBps, which is much faster than ISA and more than enough to support devices such as ROM BIOS and Super I/O chips.

Intel server chipsets for Pentium 4, Xeon, and Itanium use two different versions of hub architecture:

- Hub Interface 1.5 (HI 1.5)
- Direct Media Interface (DMI or HI 2.0)

HI 1.5 supports a 266MBps connection between the MCH and ICH chips, while DMI supports a 1MBps connection in each direction. HI 1.5 is an updated version of Intel's original Accelerated Hub Architecture (AHA) that was introduced with its first 8xx-series chipsets for Pentium III processors.

Table 3.2 cross-references the hub architectures and Intel server chipsets that use a particular hub architecture.

Table 3.2   Intel Server Chipsets and Hub Architectures

Hub Architecture	Maximum Speed	Chipsets
Hub Interface 1.5	266MBps	E7210, E7320, E7520, E7525, E8500
Direct Media Interface (Hub Interface 2.0)	2GBps[1]	E7500, E7501, E7505, E8870

[1]*1GBps in each direction; DMI supports bidirectional (full-duplex) operation.*

Figure 3.3 shows a typical Intel server motherboard that uses hub architecture—the SE7320SP2.

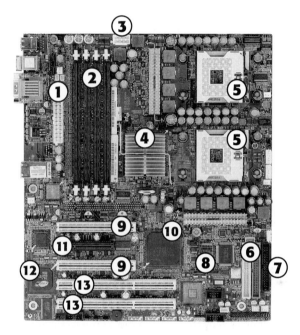

1. SSI 24-pin power supply connector	8. Serial ATA host adapters
2. DDR SDRAM memory sockets	9. PCI (32-bit/33MHz) slots
3. Processor power connector	10. ICH5 I/O Controller Hub
4. E7320 Memory Controller Hub (with Heatsink)	11. PCI-Express x4 slot
5. Dual Socket 604 processor sockets	12. ATI RageXL video chip
6. ATA/IDE host adapters	13. PCI-X (64-bit/66MHz) slots
7. Floppy drive port	

Figure 3.3   A typical dual Socket 6040 (Xeon) server motherboard, showing component locations.

Figure 3.4 illustrates the block diagram of the motherboard shown in Figure 3.4. When you compare this to Figure 3.2, note that the PCI and PCI-X buses are connected to the ICH.

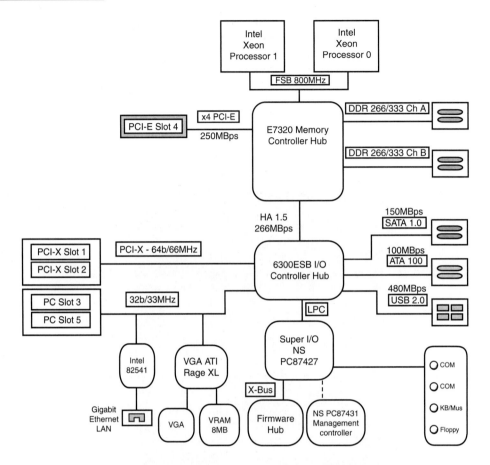

Figure 3.4 The hub architecture used by the motherboard shown in Figure 3.3.

VIA V-Link

V-Link is bus technology that VIA Technologies created to compete with Intel's Hub Architecture. VIA Technologies designed the V-Link architecture to connect its North Bridge and South Bridge chips at speeds matching or exceeding those of Intel Hub Architecture, using a dedicated 8-bit data bus. It is currently implemented in three versions:

- **4x V-Link**—4x V-Link transfers data at 266MBps (4×66MHz), which is twice the speed of PCI and matches the speed of Intel's HI 1.5 hub architectures. 4x V-Link was used on the Apollo Pro266, a dual-processor-capable chipset for Intel Pentium III processors.

- **8x V-Link**—8x V-Link transfers data at 533MBps (4×133MHz), which is twice the speed of Intel's HI 1.5 hub architecture.

- **Ultra V-Link**—Ultra V-Link transfers data at 1GBps, which is four times the speed of Intel's HI 1.5 hub architecture and half the speed of Intel's latest DMI hub architecture.

▶▶ See "VIA Technologies Chipsets for Intel Server Processors," p. 202.

All VIA South Bridge chips in the VT82xx series support V-Link. The first chipsets to use V-Link were VIA's 266-series chipsets for the Pentium III, Pentium 4, and Athlon processor families. VIA's newer chipsets also use V-Link. Although VIA is best known as a desktop and portable chipset vendor, some of its chipsets are used in Athlon-based server motherboards made by various companies.

The ServerWorks Inter Module Bus (IMB)

Most recent ServerWorks chipsets for Intel server processors use a unique high-performance interconnect between the North Bridge and the 64-bit PCI bridge. This interconnect, known as the Inter Module Bus (IMB), is a high-speed serialized data bus. The speed of IMB varies with the chipset, as shown in Table 3.3.

Table 3.3   ServerWorks IMB Performance, by Chipset

Chipset	Processors	Maximum Number of Processors	I/O Bandwidth per Channel	Number of Channels	Aggregate Bandwidth
HE-SL Champion	Pentium III Xeon	Two	1GBps	One	1GBps
HE Champion	Pentium III Xeon	Four	1GBps	One	1GBps
GC-SL Grand Champion	Xeon	Two	3.2GBps	One	3.2GBps
GC-LE Grand Champion	Xeon	Two	3.2GBps	Two	6.4GBps
GC-HE Grand Champion	Xeon	Four	1.6GBps per channel	Three	4.8GBps

The Champion models' thin IMB performance of 1GBps is sufficient to support Pentium III Xeon processors, which feature 100/133MHz FSB and PC100/133 registered memory. However, the faster performance of Xeon processors, which are based on the Pentium 4 design, demands faster connections. The GC-SL and GC-LE Grand Champion chipsets support Xeon processors with 400MHz or 533MHz FSB connections. The GC-LE's greater memory bandwidth is preferable for use with systems that use multiple 64-bit PCI cards. The GC-HE Grand Champion supports up to four processors, compared to up to two for other Grand Champion models. However, because these processors have FSB speeds of only 400MHz, 4.8GBps of memory bandwidth is adequate to support their operation.

▶▶   See "Broadcom ServerWorks Chipsets for Intel Processors," p. 196.

HyperTransport

AMD's Opteron and other 64-bit AMD processors (Athlon 64, Athlon 64 X2, Turion, and Socket 754 Sempron) use HyperTransport as their interconnection between the processor and the chipset. HyperTransport is also used by most chipsets for these processors as the interconnect between chipset components.

Although HyperTransport is sometimes referred to as "AMD HyperTransport," its original developer, AMD, released HyperTransport to the HyperTransport Consortium (www.hypertransport.org) in 2001. Besides AMD, other founding members include Sun Microsystems, Apple Computer, Broadcom (the parent company of ServerWorks), Cisco Systems, NVIDIA, and Transmeta. The consortium now manages and develops HyperTransport interface technology for use in server and PC chipsets, processors, and other technologies.

How HyperTransport Works

HyperTransport uses low-voltage differential signaling (LVDS) over high-speed connections of varying widths to perform low-latency transfers. HyperTransport is a full-duplex interconnect technology, supporting simultaneous two-way connections between chips. HyperTransport supports asymmetrical connections to provide appropriate bandwidth for different applications. For example, an Opteron processor uses a 16-bit-wide Side A HyperTransport connection to a HyperTransport bridge chip that supports PCI, PCI-X, or PCI-Express connections. However, the bridge chip might use an 8-bit-wide Side B HyperTransport connection to the HyperTransport hub that supports USB and other slower ports.

Note

Connections to the host are known as Side A connections. Connections to the next chip in the chipset are known as Side B connections. HyperTransport speeds are rated in megatransfers (MT) per second.

Tunnels, Bridges, and Hubs

Chips used between the host (processor) and the hub (equivalent to South Bridge) are known as *tunnel chips* because they pass HyperTransport signals through to the next device. A tunnel chip can provide a direct connection to a device, such as the AMD-8151 AGP 3.0 graphics tunnel, or it can provide bridges (interconnects) to bus types such as PCI, PCI-X, and PCI-Express. HyperTransport devices use independent data streams to carry traffic between the host, tunnel chips, and the hub. When a chip receives a data stream, it determines whether it is the intended target; if it is not, it passes the data stream to the next chip.

Figure 3.5 shows the block diagram for a typical server configuration using components of the AMD-8000 chipset. Note that the AMD-8000 does not include a North Bridge. That is because the AMD Opteron processor contains its own memory controller rather than relying on a memory controller in the chipset.

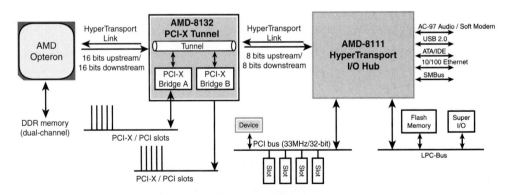

Figure 3.5   A typical implementation of HyperTransport on a server using an AMD Opteron processor.

Four-Way and Eight-Way Server Chipsets

Although chipsets designed for single-processor and dual-processor servers are similar in many ways to desktop chipsets, the greater complexity of four-way and eight-way servers that use Intel processors requires the use of more specialized chips than the multipurpose North Bridge/South Bridge or MCH and ICH designs used for single-processor or two-way servers.

A chipset designed for a four-way or eight-way server typically uses several chips to interface and control memory instead of a traditional North Bridge, and it might use specialized chips to provide PCI expansion slot support instead of or along with a traditional South Bridge.

▶▶ See "The Intel 450NX Chipset," p. 173.

▶▶ See "The Intel (Corollary) Profusion Chipset," p. 175.

▶▶ See "Broadcom ServerWorks Chipsets for Intel Processors," p. 196.

▶▶ See "IBM Chipsets for Intel Server-Class Processors," p. 204.

▶▶ See "Hewlett-Packard Server Chipsets for Intel Processors," p. 210.

Criteria for Real-World Server Chipsets

Let's examine the leading chipsets used in servers, starting with those used in Pentium Pro–based servers and working all the way through to the latest Xeon, Itanium, Athlon MP, and Opteron chipsets.

In the following sections, the chipsets discussed in detail meet the following real-world server criteria:

- Chipsets that are designed for processors other than the Pentium 4, Pentium D, and Pentium Extreme Edition (which do not support symmetric multiprocessing [SMP]) must support SMP (two or more processors).

- All chipsets, at least, support parity-checked memory or, preferably, ECC memory. Although some vendors sell server motherboards or systems that use chipsets that lack parity or ECC support, you can't consider such systems to be true servers. Because a server is called on to provide mission-critical information to the organization, you need to use technology in your server that ensures that data is reliable.

- Both server and workstation chipsets are discussed because many so-called workstation chipsets are also used in entry-level server installations.

This is the simplest way to summarize what makes a server chipset: If it acts like a server chipset and has been (or can be) used as a server chipset by Intel or a third-party motherboard or system vendor, it *is* a server chipset.

Comparison of System and Component Bus Speeds

The system chipset is the conductor that controls the orchestra of system components, enabling each to have its turn on its respective bus. Table 3.4 shows the widths, speeds, data cycles, and overall bandwidth of virtually all PC buses.

Table 3.4   Bandwidth and Detailed Comparison of Most PC Buses and Interfaces[1]

Bus Type	Bus Width (Bits)	Bus Speed (MHz)	Data Cycles per Clock	Bandwidth (MBps)
Legacy PC/XT/AT Bus Designs				
8-bit ISA (PC/XT)	8	4.77	1/2	2.39
8-bit ISA (AT)	8	8.33	1/2	4.17
16-bit ISA (AT-Bus)	16	8.33	1/2	8.33
EISA bus	32	8.33	1	33
VL-bus	32	33	1	133

Table 3.4 Continued

Bus Type	Bus Width (Bits)	Bus Speed (MHz)	Data Cycles per Clock	Bandwidth (MBps)
Micro Channel Architecture Buses				
MCA-16	16	5	1	10
MCA-32	32	5	1	20
MCA-16 streaming	16	10	1	20
MCA-32 streaming	32	10	1	40
MCA-64 streaming	64	10	1	80
MCA-64 streaming	64	20	1	160
Floppy Drive Interfaces				
DD floppy interface	1	0.25	1	0.03125
HD floppy interface	1	0.5	1	0.0625
ED floppy interface	1	1	1	0.125
Laptop/Notebook Buses				
PC-Card (PCMCIA)	16	10	1	20
CardBus	32	33	1	133
PCI-Based Buses				
LPC bus	4	33	1	16.67
PCI	32	33	1	133
PCI 66MHz	32	66	1	266
PCI 64-bit	64	33	1	266
PCI 66MHz/64-bit	64	66	1	533
PCI-X 66	64	66	1	533
PCI-X 133	64	133	1	1,066
PCI-X 266	64	266	1	2,133
PCI-X 533	64	533	1	4,266
PCI-Express 1.0, 1 lane	1	2,500	0.8	250
PCI-Express 1.0, 4 lanes	4	2,500	0.8	1,000
PCI-Express 1.0, 16 lanes	16	2,500	0.8	4,000
PCI-Express 1.0, 32 lanes	32	2,500	0.8	8,000
Chipset Interconnects				
Intel hub interface (HI 1.5)	8	66	4	266
Intel Direct Media Interface (HI 2.0)	8	266	4	2000
AMD HyperTransport 2x2	2	200	2	100
AMD HyperTransport 4x2	4	200	2	200
AMD HyperTransport 8x2	8	200	2	400
AMD HyperTransport 16x2	16	200	2	800
AMD HyperTransport 32x2	32	200	2	1,600
AMD HyperTransport 2x4	2	400	2	200

Table 3.4   Continued

Bus Type	Bus Width (Bits)	Bus Speed (MHz)	Data Cycles per Clock	Bandwidth (MBps)
Chipset Interconnects				
AMD HyperTransport 4x4	4	400	2	400
AMD HyperTransport 8x4	8	400	2	800
AMD HyperTransport 16x4	16	400	2	1,600
AMD HyperTransport 32x4	32	400	2	3,200
AMD HyperTransport 2x8	2	800	2	400
AMD HyperTransport 4x8	4	800	2	800
AMD HyperTransport 8x8	8	800	2	1,600
AMD HyperTransport 16x8	16	800	2	3,200
AMD HyperTransport 10x8 2.0	16	1000	2	4,000
AMD HyperTransport 32x8	32	800	2	6,400
ATI A-Link	16	66	2	266
SiS MuTIOL	16	133	2	533
SiS MuTIOL 1G	16	266	2	1,066
VIA V-Link 4x	8	66	4	266
VIA V-Link 8x	8	66	8	533
VIA Ultra V-Link	8	66	16	1,066
Accelerated Graphics Port Versions				
AGP-1X	32	66	1	266
AGP-2X	32	66	2	533
AGP-4X	32	66	4	1,066
AGP-8X	32	66	8	2,133
Legacy Ports				
RS-232 Serial	1	0.1152	1/10	0.01152
RS-232 Serial HS	1	0.2304	1/10	0.02304
IEEE 1284 Parallel	8	8.33	1/6	1.38
IEEE 1284 EPP/ECP	8	8.33	1/3	2.77
USB Ports				
USB 1.1/2.0 low-speed	1	1.5	1	0.1875
USB 1.1/2.0 full-speed	1	12	1	1.5
USB 2.0 high-speed	1	480	1	60
IEEE-1394 (FireWire) Ports				
IEEE 1394a S100	1	100	1	12.5
IEEE 1394a S200	1	200	1	25
IEEE 1394a S400	1	400	1	50
IEEE 1394b S800	1	800	1	100
IEEE 1394b S1600	1	1600	1	200

Table 3.4   Continued

Bus Type	Bus Width (Bits)	Bus Speed (MHz)	Data Cycles per Clock	Bandwidth (MBps)
		ATA/IDE Ports		
ATA PIO-4	16	8.33	1	16.67
ATA-UDMA/33	16	8.33	2	33
ATA-UDMA/66	16	16.67	2	66
ATA-UDMA/100	16	25	2	100
ATA-UDMA/133	16	33	2	133
		Serial ATA (SATA) ports		
SATA-150	1	750	2	150
SATA-300	1	1500	2	300
SATA-600	1	3000	2	600
		SCSI Ports		
SCSI	8	5	1	5
SCSI Wide	16	5	1	10
SCSI Fast	8	10	1	10
SCSI Fast/Wide	16	10	1	20
SCSI Ultra	8	20	1	20
SCSI Ultra/Wide	16	20	1	40
SCSI Ultra 2	8	40	1	40
SCSI Ultra 2/Wide	16	40	1	80
SCSI Ultra 3 (Ultra160)	16	40	2	160
SCSI Ultra 4 (Ultra320)	16	80	2	320
		DRAM speeds		
FPM DRAM	64	22	1	177
EDO DRAM	64	33	1	266
		Synchronous DRAM (SDRAM) Speeds		
PC66 SDRAM DIMM	64	66	1	533
PC100 SDRAM DIMM	64	100	1	800
PC133 SDRAM DIMM	64	133	1	1,066
		DDR SDRAM Speeds		
PC1600 DDR DIMM (DDR200)	64	100	2	1,600
PC2100 DDR DIMM (DDR266)	64	133	2	2,133
PC2700 DDR DIMM (DDR333)	64	167	2	2,666
PC3200 DDR DIMM (DDR400)	64	200	2	3,200
PC3500 DDR (DDR433)	64	216	2	3,466
PC3700 DDR (DDR466)	64	233	2	3,733
		DDR2 SDRAM speeds		
PC2-3200 DDR2 (DDR2-400)	64	200	2	3,200
PC2-4300 DDR2 (DDR2-533)	64	267	2	4,266

Table 3.4 Continued

Bus Type	Bus Width (Bits)	Bus Speed (MHz)	Data Cycles per Clock	Bandwidth (MBps)
		DDR2 SDRAM speeds		
PC2-5400 DDR2 (DDR2-667)	64	333	2	5,333
PC2-6400 DDR2 (DDR2-800)	64	400	2	6,400
		Rambus DirectRAM (RDRAM) Speeds		
RIMM1200 RDRAM (PC600)	16	300	2	1,200
RIMM1400 RDRAM (PC700)	16	350	2	1,400
RIMM1600 RDRAM (PC800)	16	400	2	1,600
RIMM2100 RDRAM (PC1066)	16	533	2	2,133
RIMM2400 RDRAM (PC1200)	16	600	2	2,400
RIMM3200 RDRAM (PC800)	32	400	2	3,200
RIMM4200 RDRAM (PC1066)	32	533	2	4,266
RIMM4800 RDRAM (PC1200)	32	600	2	4,800
		Processor FSB Speeds		
66MHz Pentium Pro/II/III/Xeon FSB	64	66	1	533
100MHz Pentium Pro/II/III/Xeon FSB	64	100	1	800
133MHz Pentium III/Xeon FSB	64	133	1	1,066
200MHz Athlon FSB	64	100	2	1,600
266MHz Athlon FSB	64	133	2	2,133
333MHz Athlon FSB	64	167	2	2,666
400MHz Athlon FSB	64	200	2	3,200
533MHz Athlon FSB	64	267	2	4,266
400MHz Pentium 4/Xeon FSB	64	100	4	3,200
533MHz Pentium 4/Xeon FSB	64	133	4	4,266
800MHz Pentium 4/Xeon FSB	64	200	4	6,400
1066MHz Pentium 4 FSB	64	267	4	8,533
266MHz Itanium FSB	64	133	2	2,133
400MHz Itanium 2 FSB	128	100	4	6,400

[1]*Key: ISA, EISA, VL-Bus, and MCA are no longer used in current motherboard designs; ISA = Industry Standard Architecture, also known as the PC/XT (8-bit) or AT-Bus (16-bit); LPC = low pin count bus; DD floppy = Double Density (360/720KB) floppy; HD floppy = High Density (1.2/1.44MB) floppy; ED floppy = Extra-high Density (2.88MB) floppy; EISA = Extended ISA (32-bit ISA); VL-Bus = VESA (Video Electronics Standards Association) local bus (ISA extension); MCA = MicroChannel Architecture (IBM PS/2 systems); PC-Card = 16-bit PCMCIA (Personal Computer Memory Card International Association) interface; CardBus = 32-bit PC-Card; Hub Interface = Intel 8xx chipset bus; HyperTransport = AMD chipset bus; V-Link = VIA Technologies chipset bus; MuTIOL = Silicon Integrated System chipset bus; PCI = Peripheral Component Interconnect; AGP = Accelerated Graphics Port; RS-232 = Standard Serial port, 115.2Kbps; RS-232 HS = High Speed Serial port, 230.4Kbps; IEEE 1284 Parallel = Standard Bidirectional Parallel Port; IEEE 1284 EPP/ECP = Enhanced Parallel Port/Extended Capabilities Port; USB = universal serial bus; ATA PIO = AT Attachment (also known as IDE) Programmed I/O; ATA-UDMA = AT Attachment Ultra DMA; SCSI = Small computer system interface; FPM = Fast Page Mode, based on X-3-3-3 (1/3 max) burst mode timing on a 66MHz bus; EDO = Extended Data Out, based on X-2-2-2 (1/2 max) burst mode timing on a 66MHz bus; SDRAM = synchronous dynamic RAM; RDRAM = Rambus dynamic RAM; DDR = double data rate SDRAM; DDR2 = next-generation DDR; and CPU FSB = processor front-side bus.*

Note that many of the buses use multiple data cycles (transfers) per clock cycle to achieve greater performance. Therefore, the data transfer rate is higher than it would seem for a given clock rate, which provides an easy way to make an existing bus go faster in a backward-compatible way.

The Processor Bus

The processor bus (also called the FSB) is the communication pathway between the CPU and the motherboard chipset (specifically, the North Bridge or MCH). This bus runs at the full motherboard speed—typically between 200MHz and 800MHz in modern systems, depending on the particular board and chipset design.

Most recent one- or two-way servers use bus designs similar to those shown in Figures 3.5 and 3.6. Figure 3.6 shows the bus design for a typical dual-processor Intel Xeon server running at 800MHz CPU (FSB) using the E7525 chipset.

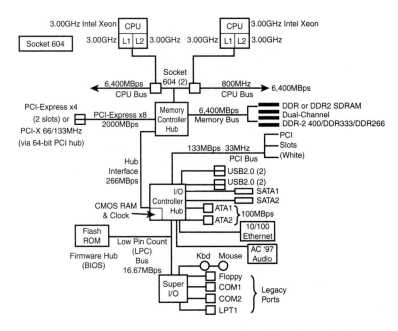

Figure 3.6 A typical bus design for a recent two-way server based on the Intel Xeon processor.

A system running an AMD Opteron processor has a different bus design from the one shown in Figure 3.6:

■ The Opteron uses an integrated dual-channel DDR memory controller rather than the traditional North Bridge/MCP design shown in Figure 3.6.

■ The Opteron uses three HyperTransport tunnels to carry traffic between the processor and the chipset. Compare Figures 3.5 and 3.6 to get a better sense of these differences.

Because the purpose of the processor bus is to get information to and from the CPU at the fastest possible speed, this bus typically operates at faster than any other bus in the system. The bus consists of electrical circuits for data, addresses (the address bus, which is discussed in the following section), and control purposes. Most processors since the original Pentium have a 64-bit data bus, so they transfer 64 bits (8 bytes) at a time over the CPU bus.

The processor bus operates at the same base clock rate as the CPU does externally. This can be misleading because most CPUs these days run at a higher clock rate internally than they do externally. For example, an AMD Athlon 64 3800+ system has a processor that runs at 2.4GHz internally but only 400MHz externally, whereas a Pentium 4 3.4GHz runs at 3.4GHz internally but only 800MHz externally. In newer systems, the actual processor speed is some multiple (2x, 2.5x, 3x, and higher) of the processor bus.

The processor (FSB) speeds are largely governed by the speed of memory. While memory speeds have increased since the first x86 PCs were introduced 25 years ago, internal processor speeds have gone up by a much higher rate.

◀◀   See "x86 Processor Speed Ratings," p. 55.

▶▶   See "Memory Types Overview," p. 359.

The processor bus is tied to the external processor pin connections and can transfer 1 bit of data per data line every cycle. Most modern processors transfer 64 bits (8 bytes) of data at a time.

To determine the transfer rate for the processor bus, you multiply the data bus width (64 bits or 8 bytes for a Pentium III/4 or Xeon or Athlon MP/Athlon 64) by the clock speed of the bus (the same as the base or unmultiplied clock speed of the CPU). For example, if you are using a Xeon 3.6GHz processor that runs on an 800MHz processor bus, you have a maximum instantaneous transfer rate of roughly 6400MBps. You get this result by using the following formula:

   800MHz × 8 bytes (64 bits) = 6400MBps

With slower versions of the Xeon, you get either this:

   533.33MHz × 8 bytes (64 bits) = 4266MBps

or this:

   400MHz × 8 bytes (64 bits) = 3200MBps

With Socket A (Athlon MP), you get this:

   333.33MHz × 8 bytes (64 bits) = 2667MBps

or this:

   266.66MHz × 8 bytes (64 bits) = 2133MBps

or this:

   200MHz × 8 bytes (64 bits) = 1600MBps

With Slot 2 (Pentium III Xeon), you get this:

   133.33MHz × 8 bytes (64 bits) = 1066MBps

or this:

   100MHz × 8 bytes (64 bits) = 800MBps

This transfer rate, often called the *bandwidth*, of the processor bus represents the maximum speed at which data can move. Refer to Table 3.4 for a more complete list of various processor bus bandwidths.

The Memory Bus

The memory bus is used to transfer information between the CPU and main memory—the RAM in the system. This bus is connected to the motherboard chipset North Bridge or MCH chip in most server designs. (AMD Opteron processors incorporate the memory controller.) Depending on the type of memory the chipset (and therefore motherboard) is designed to handle, the North Bridge runs the memory bus at various speeds. The best solution is if the memory bus runs at the same speed as the processor bus. Systems that use PC133 SDRAM have a memory bandwidth of 1066MBps, which is the same as the 133MHz CPU bus. Pentium 4 or Xeon systems with the 533MHz bus run dual-channel DDR PC2100 or PC2700 modules, which match or exceed the throughput of the 4266MBps processor bus.

Running memory at the same speed as the processor bus means you don't need to have cache memory on the motherboard.

Note

The main memory bus must transfer data in the same width as the processor bus. This defines the size of what is called a *bank* of memory, at least when dealing with anything except RDRAM. Memory banks and their widths relative to processor buses are discussed in the section "Memory Banks" in Chapter 5, "Memory."

The SCSI Bus

Although hardly any PCs have integrated SCSI ports, many servers have one or more integrated SCSI ports. SCSI (pronounced "scuzzy") is a general-purpose interface with its roots in SASI (Shugart Associates System Interface). SCSI is a popular interface for attaching high-speed disk drives, RAID arrays, and tape drives to high-end network servers. SCSI is a bus that supports as many as 7 or 15 total devices. Multichannel adapters exist that can support up to 7 or 15 devices per channel.

For more information about SCSI devices and configuration, see Chapter 7, "The SCSI Bus."

About Intel Chipsets

You can't talk about server chipsets today without discussing Intel because the company currently owns the vast majority of the Intel server processor chipset market. It is interesting to note that we probably have Compaq (now part of Hewlett-Packard) to thank for forcing Intel into the chipset business in the first place!

The event that really started it all was the introduction of the EISA bus that Compaq designed in 1989. At that time, Compaq had shared the EISA bus with other manufacturers in an attempt to make it a market standard. However, Compaq refused to share its EISA bus chipset—a set of custom chips necessary to implement this bus on a motherboard.

Intel decided to fill the chipset void for the rest of the PC manufacturers wanting to build EISA bus motherboards. As is well known today, the EISA bus only found short-term market support as part of a niche server business in the early 1990s, but ultimately it failed to become a market success. This opened the door for Intel, which now had a taste of the chipset business that it apparently wouldn't forget.

With the introduction of the 286 and 386 processors, Intel became impatient with how long it took the other chipset companies to create chipsets around its new processor designs; this delayed the introduction of motherboards that supported the new processors. For example, it took more than two years after the 286 processor was introduced for the first 286 motherboards to appear and just over a year after the 386 had been introduced for the first 386 motherboards to appear. Intel couldn't sell its processors in volume until other manufacturers made motherboards that would support them, so it thought that by developing motherboard chipsets for a new processor in parallel with the new processor, it could jumpstart the motherboard business by providing ready-made chipsets for the motherboard manufacturers to use.

After introducing the 420 series chipsets along with its 486 processor in April 1989, Intel realized it controlled over 90% of the components on a typical motherboard because it made both processors and chipsets. What better way to ensure that motherboards were available for its Pentium processor when it was introduced than by making its own motherboards as well and having these boards ready on the new processor's introduction date?

When the first Pentium processor debuted in 1993, Intel also debuted the 430LX chipset, as well as a fully finished motherboard. Now, besides the chipset companies being upset, the motherboard companies weren't too happy, either. Intel was not only the major supplier of parts needed to build finished boards (processors and chipsets) but was now building and selling the finished boards as well. By 1994, Intel dominated the processor and chipset markets for desktop PCs. By the late 1990s, through a combination of internally developed chipsets and shrewd acquisitions, such as Intel's purchase of Corollary, the original developer of Intel's Profusion 8-way chipset, Intel also dominated the processor and chipset markets for entry-level dual and four-way servers.

Now as Intel develops new processors, it develops chipsets and motherboards simultaneously, which means they can be announced and shipped in unison. This eliminates the delay between introducing new processors and waiting for motherboards and systems capable of using them, which was common in the industry's early days.

Starting with the 486 in 1989, Intel began a pattern of numbering its chipsets as shown in Table 3.5.

Table 3.5   Intel Chipset Model Numbers

Chipset Number	Processor Family Supported
420xx	P4 (486)
430xx	P5 (Pentium) North Bridge/South Bridge architecture
440xx	P6 (Pentium Pro/PII/PIII) North Bridge/South Bridge architecture
8xx	P6/P7 (PII/PIII/P4) with hub architecture
9xx	P7 (Pentium 4, Pentium D) with hub architecture and PCI-Express
450xx	P6 server (Pentium Pro/PII Xeon/PIII Xeon)
460xx	Xeon MP server
E72xx	Xeon DP workstation or server with hub architecture
E73xx	Xeon DP server with hub architecture
E75xx	Xeon DP workstation or server with hub architecture
E85xx	Xeon MP server with hub architecture and PCI-Express
460xx	Itanium processor
E88xx	Itanium 2 processor with hub architecture

The chipset numbers listed in Table 3.5 are abbreviations of the actual chipset numbers stamped on the individual chips. For example, the 945G chipset supports the Pentium D and Pentium 4 and consists of two main parts: the 82945G Graphics MCH (GMCH, which replaces the North Bridge and includes integrated video) and an 82801GR ICH (ICH7R, which replaces the South Bridge).

Tip

In many cases, the North Bridge/GMCH/MCH chip on recent motherboards is covered up with a passive or active heatsink, and some motherboards also use a heatsink on the South Bridge or ICH chip. To determine the chipset used in these systems, you can watch for motherboard information some systems display at startup. Alternatively, you can use a third-party hardware reporting program such as SiSoftware Sandra (www.sisoftware.co.uk).

Intel Pentium Pro/II/III Chipsets for Servers

Intel was the leading vendor of chipsets for its P6 processor families, which included the Pentium Pro, Pentium II, and Pentium III. Table 3.6 shows the Intel chipsets used on Pentium Pro motherboards. All the chipsets shown in Table 3.6 were designed to be suitable for use in server applications. However, most systems using these chipsets have been retired.

Table 3.6   Intel Pentium Pro Motherboard Chipsets (North Bridge)[1]

Feature	450KX	450GX	440FX
Codename	Mars	Orion	Natoma[2]
Date introduced	Nov. 1995	Nov. 1995	May 1996
Bus speed	66MHz	66MHz	66MHz
SMP (dual CPUs)	Yes	Yes (up to 4)[3]	Yes
Memory types	FPM	FPM	FPM/EDO/BEDO
Parity/ECC	Both	Both	Both
Maximum memory	1GB	4GB	1GB
L2 cache type	In CPU	In CPU	In CPU
Maximum cacheable	1GB	1GB	1GB
PCI support	2.0	2.0	2.1
AGP support	No	No	No
AGP speed	n/a	n/a	n/a
South Bridge	PIIX3	PIIX3	PIIX3

[1]Key: AGP = accelerated graphics port; BEDO = burst EDO; EDO = extended data out; FPM = fast page mode; Pburst = pipeline burst (synchronous); PCI = peripheral component interconnect; PIIX = PCI ISA IDE Xcelerator; SDRAM = synchronous dynamic RAM; SIO = system I/O; and SMP = symmetric multiprocessing (multiple processors).

[2]Also supports Pentium II processor.

[3]Some vendors, such as ALR (Revolution 6x6), used the chipset's 2-bit CPU addressing scheme to create six-processor servers (two sets of three processors each).

Note

PCI 2.1 supports concurrent PCI operations.

Intel Pentium II/III chipsets that were suitable for use in servers are shown in Tables 3.7 and 3.8. 4xx series chipsets incorporate a North Bridge/South Bridge architecture (Table 3.7), whereas 8xx series chipsets support the newer and faster hub architecture. P6/P7 (Pentium III, Pentium 4, and Xeon) processor chipsets using hub architecture are shown in Table 3.8.

Table 3.7   P6 Processor Chipsets Using North Bridge/South Bridge Architecture

Feature	440FX	440LX	440BX	440GX	450NX
Codename	Natoma	None	None	None	None
Date introduced	May 1996	Aug. 1997	April 1998	June 1998	June 1998
Part numbers	82441FX, 82442FX	82443LX	82443BX	82443GX	82451NX, 82452NX, 82453NX, 82454NX
Bus speed	66MHz	66MHz	66/100MHz	100MHz	100MHz
Supported processors	PII	PII	PII/III[1]	PII/III, Xeon	PII/III, Xeon
Maximum Number of CPUs supported	Two	Two	Two	Two	Four
Memory types supported	FPM/EDO/ BEDO	FPM/EDO/ SDRAM	SDRAM	SDRAM	FPM/EDO
Parity/ECC	Both	Both	Both	Both	Both
Maximum memory	1GB	1GB EDO/ 512MB SDRAM	1GB	2GB	8GB
Memory banks	4	4	4	4	4
PCI version	2.1	2.1	2.1	2.1	2.1
AGP support	No	AGP 2x	AGP 2x	AGP 2x	No
South Bridge	82371SB (PIIX3)	82371AB (PIIX4)	82371EB (PIIX4E)	82371EB (PIIX4E)	82371EB (PIIX4E)

[1]This chipset also supports Celeron.

Table 3.8   P6 (Pentium III) Server Processor Chipsets Using Hub Architecture[1]

Feature	820	820E	840
Codename	Camino	Camino	Carmel
Date introduced	Nov. 1999	June 2000	Oct. 1999
Part number	82820	82820	82840
Bus speed	66MHz, 100MHz, 133MHz	66MHz, 100MHz, 133MHz	66MHz, 100MHz, 133MHz
Supported processors	Celeron, Pentium II/III	Celeron, Pentium II/III	Pentium III, Xeon
SMP (dual CPUs)	Yes	Yes	Yes
Memory types	RDRAM	RDRAM	RDRAM
Memory speeds	PC800	PC800	PC800, dual-channel
Parity/ECC	Both	Both	Both
Maximum memory	1GB	1GB	4GB
Memory banks	2	2	3×2
PCI support	2.2	2.2	2.2

Table 3.8   Continued

Feature	820	820E	840
PCI speed/ width	33MHz/32-bit	33MHz/32-bit	33MHz/32-bit
AGP slot	AGP 4x	AGP 4x	AGP 4x
Integrated video	No	No	No
South Bridge (ICH)	82801AA (ICH)	82801BA (ICH2)	82801AA (ICH)

[1]*Key: AGP = accelerated graphics port; ICH = I/O controller hub; Pburst = pipeline burst (synchronous); PCI = peripheral component interconnect; and RDRAM = Rambus Direct RAM.*

Note

Pentium Pro, Celeron, and Pentium II/III CPUs have their secondary caches integrated into the CPU package. Therefore, cache characteristics for these machines are not dependent on the chipset but on the processor instead.

Most recent Intel chipsets for single-processor or dual-processor servers are designed as two-part systems, using a North Bridge (MCH or GMCH in hub-based designs) and a South Bridge (ICH in hub-based designs) component. Often the same South Bridge or ICH component can be used with several different North Bridge (MCH or GMCH) chipsets. Table 3.9 shows a list of all the Intel South Bridge components used with P6-class processors and their capabilities. The ICH2 is also used as part of some of the first seventh-generation (Pentium 4) Intel chipsets.

Table 3.9   Intel South Bridge/ICH Chips for P6 Class CPUs[1]

Feature	SIO	PIIX	PIIX3	PIIX4	PIIX4E	ICH0	ICH	ICH2
Part number	82378IB/ZB	82371FB	82371SB	82371AB	82371EB	82801AB	82801AA	82801BA
IDE support	None	BMIDE	BMIDE	UDMA-33	UDMA-33	UDMA-33	UDMA-66	UDMA-100
USB support	None	None	1C/2P	1C/2P	1C/2P	1C/2P	1C/2P	2C/4P
CMOS/clock	No	No	No	Yes	Yes	Yes	Yes	Yes
ISA support	Yes	Yes	Yes	Yes	Yes	No	No	No
LPC support	No	No	No	No	No	Yes	Yes	Yes
Power management	SMM	SMM	SMM	SMM	SMM/ACPI	SMM/ACPI	SMM/ACPI	SMM/ACPI

[1]*Key: SIO = system I/O; PIIX = PCI ISA IDE (ATA) Xcelerator; ICH = I/O controller hub; USB = universal serial bus version 1.x; 1C/2P = 1 controller, 2 ports; 2C/4P = 2 controllers, 4 ports; IDE = Integrated Drive Electronics (ATA = AT attachment); BMIDE = bus master IDE (ATA); UDMA = Ultra DMA IDE (ATA); ISA = industry standard architecture bus; LPC = low-pin-count bus; SMM = system management mode; and ACPI = advanced configuration and power interface.*

The following sections examine the server-class chipsets for P6 processors up through the Pentium III.

The Intel 450KX/GX (Mars/Orion) Chipsets

The first chipsets to support the Pentium Pro were the 450KX and GX. Although both are commonly known as Orion, the 450KX was originally known as Mars. The 450KX was designed for networked or standalone workstations and is also suitable for low-end servers; the more powerful 450GX was designed for servers. The GX server chipset was particularly suited to the server role because it supports up to four Pentium Pro processors for SMP servers, up to 8GB of four-way interleaved memory with ECC or parity, and two bridged PCI buses. Some vendors, such as ALR, with its Revolution 6x6, designed systems that could use up to six processors using the GX chipset. The 450KX is the low-end server or workstation (standalone user) version of Orion and, as such, it supports fewer processors (one or two) and less memory (1GB) than the GX. The 450GX and 450KX both have full support for ECC memory—a requirement for server and workstation use.

◄◄ See "Pentium Pro Processors," p. 87.

The 450GX and 450KX North Bridge comprises four individual chip components: an 82454KX/GX PCI bridge, an 82452KX/GX data path (DP), an 82453KX/GX data controller (DC), and an 82451KX/GX memory interface controller (MIC). Options for QFP or BGA packaging were available on the PCI Bridge and the DP. BGA uses less space on a board.

Note

Quad flat pack (QFA) is a method used for surface-mounting a chip to a board. Chips that use QFA packaging have leads on all four sides of the chip. Ball grid array (BGA) chips use solder balls on the underside of the chip.

The 450's high reliability was obtained through ECC from the Pentium Pro processor data bus to memory. Reliability is also enhanced through parity protection on the processor bus, control bus, and all PCI signals. In addition, single-bit error correction is provided, thereby avoiding server downtime because of spurious memory errors caused by cosmic rays.

►► See "Parity and ECC," p. 389.

Until the introduction of the following 440FX chipset, these chipsets were used almost exclusively in fileservers. After the debut of the 440FX, the expensive Mars/Orion chipsets all but disappeared due to their complexity and high cost.

The Intel 440FX (Natoma) Chipset

The first popular mainstream P6 (Pentium Pro or Pentium II) motherboard chipset was the 440FX, which was codenamed Natoma. Intel designed the 440FX to be a lower-cost and somewhat higher-performance replacement for the 450KX workstation chipset. Although the 440FX was designed for use in workstation applications, it was also used as a low-end server chipset by numerous vendors. It offered better memory performance through support of EDO memory, which the prior 450KX lacked.

►► See "Early Server RAM Types: DRAM, EDO DRAM, and SDRAM," p. 361.

The 440FX uses half the number of components that the previous Intel chipset used. It offers additional features, such as support for the PCI 2.1 (concurrent PCI) standard, support for USB 1.1 ports, and reliability through ECC.

The concurrent PCI processing architecture maximizes system performance with simultaneous activity on the CPU, PCI, and ISA buses. Concurrent PCI provides increased bandwidth to better support 2D/3D graphics, video and audio, and processing for host-based applications. ECC memory support delivers improved reliability to business system users.

The main features of this chipset included the following:

- Support for up to 1GB of EDO memory
- Full 1GB cacheability (based on the processor because the L2 cache and tag are in the CPU)
- Support for USB 1.1
- Support for bus master IDE
- Support for full parity/ECC memory

The 440FX consists of a two-chip North Bridge. The main component is the 82441FX PCI bridge and memory controller, along with the 82442FX data bus accelerator for the PCI bus. This chipset uses the PIIX3 82371SB South Bridge chip that supports high-speed bus master DMA IDE interfaces and USB, and it acts as the bridge between the PCI and ISA buses. Figure 3.7 illustrates the design of the 440FX.

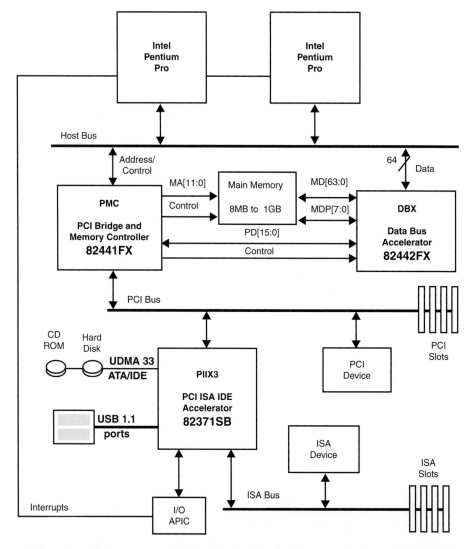

Figure 3.7   System block diagram using the Intel 440FX chipset.

Note that the 440FX was the first P6 chipset to support EDO memory, but it lacked support for the faster SDRAM memory. Also, the PIIX3 South Bridge used with this chipset does not support the faster Ultra DMA IDE hard drives.

The 440FX was the chipset used on the first Pentium II motherboards, which have the same basic architecture as the Pentium Pro. The Pentium II was released several months before the chipset that was supposedly designed for it was ready, so early PII motherboards used the older 440FX chipset. However, this chipset was never designed with the Pentium II in mind, whereas the newer 440LX was optimized specifically to take advantage of the Pentium II architecture. When the 440LX was introduced, the 440FX was quickly superseded.

The Intel 440LX Chipset

The 440LX quickly took over in the marketplace after it was introduced in August 1997. This was the first chipset to really take full advantage of the Pentium II processor. The 440LX chipset was the first Intel Pentium II chipset to use a single-chip North Bridge design, setting a design standard that would be followed by subsequent designs. The 82443LX North Bridge chip incorporated the features that required two chips in its immediate predecessor, the 440BX, and added support for two then-new technologies, AGP video and 66MHz synchronous DRAM (SDRAM). The 440LX's South Bridge, the PIIX4, was also a new design, adding support for Ultra DMA 33 ATA/IDE drives.

◀◀ See "Pentium II Processors," p. 90.

The 440LX chipset's major features included the following:

- Single-chip North Bridge design (82443LX chip)
- Support for the (then-new) AGP video card bus
- Support for 66MHz SDRAM memory
- Support for the Ultra DMA ATA/IDE interface (UDMA/33)
- Support for USB 1.1 ports

The 440LX's design was flexible enough to support all types of Pentium II systems, from two-way servers to desktop computers. It was the most popular chipset for Pentium II systems from late 1997 through spring 1998.

The Intel 440BX Chipset

The Intel 440BX chipset, introduced in April 1998, was the first chipset to run the processor host bus (often called the FSB) at 100MHz. The 440BX was designed specifically to support the faster Pentium II/III processors at 350MHz and higher. The main change from the previous 440LX to the BX is that the 440BX chipset improves performance by increasing the bandwidth of the system bus from 66MHz to 100MHz. Because the chipset can run at either 66MHz or 100MHz, it allows one basic motherboard design to support all Pentium II/III processor speeds based on either the 66MHz or 100MHz processor bus.

Here are the Intel 440BX highlights:

- Support for 100MHz SDRAM (PC100); the now-common PC133 RAM can also be installed, but it will still run at just 100MHz
- Support for both 100MHz and 66MHz system and memory bus designs
- Support for up to 1GB of memory in up to four banks (four DIMMs)
- Support for ECC memory
- Support for ACPI power management

◀◀ See "Pentium III Processors," p. 93.

▶▶ See "ACPI," p. 290.

The Intel 440BX consists of a single North Bridge chip called the 82443BX host bridge/controller, paired with a new 82371EB PCI-ISA/IDE Xcelerator (PIIX4E) South Bridge chip. This South Bridge adds support for the ACPI specification version 1.0 to the features of its predecessor, the PIIX4. Figure 3.8 shows a typical system block diagram using the 440BX.

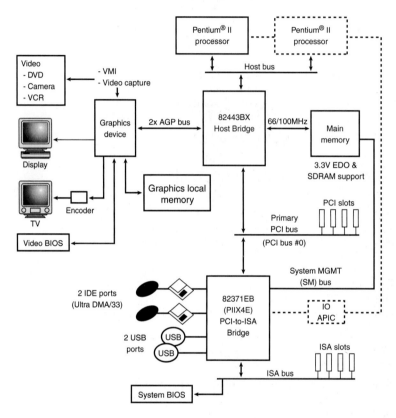

Figure 3.8   System block diagram using the Intel 440BX chipset.

The 440BX was a popular one-way and two-way server chipset during 1998 and into 1999. It offered superior performance and high reliability through the use of ECC, SDRAM, and DIMMs.

The Intel 440GX Chipset

The Intel 440GX AGP set was the first chipset optimized for high-volume midrange workstations and lower-cost servers, and it was Intel's first chipset for the server/workstation version of the Pentium II, the Pentium II Xeon. The 440GX also supports the Pentium III Xeon processor. The 440GX is essentially a version of the 440BX that has been upgraded to support the Slot 2 (also called SC330) processor slot for the Pentium II/III Xeon processor. The 440GX can still be used in Slot 1 designs, as well. It also supports up to 2GB of memory, twice that of the 440BX. Other than these items, the 440GX is essentially the same as the 440BX. Because the 440GX is core compatible with the 440BX, motherboard manufacturers could quickly and easily modify their existing Slot 1 440BX board designs into Slot 1 or 2 440GX designs.

The main features of the 440GX include the following:

- Support for Slot 1 and Slot 2
- Support for 100MHz system bus
- Support for up to 2GB of SDRAM memory

This chipset allows for lower-cost, high-performance workstations and servers using the Slot 2–based Xeon processors.

◄◄ See "Pentium II Xeon," p. 91.

◄◄ See "Pentium III Xeon," p. 98.

The Intel 450NX Chipset

The 450NX chipset (originally known as the 440NX) was designed for multiprocessor systems and standard high-volume servers based on the Pentium II/III Xeon processor. The Intel 450NX chipset consists of four components: the 82454NX PCI expander bridge (PXB), 82451NX memory and I/O bridge controller (MIOC), 82452NX RAS/CAS generator (RCG), and 82453NX data path multiplexer (MUX). As Table 3.10 shows, a full implementation of the 450NX uses two or more of the PXB, RCG, and MUX chips.

Table 3.10   Details of the 450NX Chipset

Component Part Number	Component Name	How Used	Number of Chips in Chipset
82451NX	Memory and I/O bridge controller (MIOC)	Controls and buffers data traffic flowing between the system bus, PCI bus, and system memory.	1
82454NX	PCI expander bridge (PXB)	Provides interfacing between the MIOC and the PCI bus.	2
82452NX	RAS/CAS generator (RCG)	Converts memory requests from the MIOC for use by up to four banks of DRAM.	2
82453NX	Data path multiplexer (MUX)	Supports memory interleaving and staging between memory and the MIOC.	4
82371EB	PIIX4E	Used as a South Bridge chip.	1

The 450NX supports up to four Pentium II/III Xeon processors at 100MHz. Two dedicated PCI expander bridges can be connected via the expander bus. Each PXB provides two independent 32-bit, 33MHz PCI buses, with an option to link the two buses into a single 64-bit, 33MHz bus.

Figure 3.9 shows a typical high-end server block diagram using the 450NX chipset.

The 450NX supports one or two memory cards. Each card incorporates an RCG chip and two MUX chips, in addition to the memory DIMMs. Up to 8GB of memory is supported in total.

The primary features of the 450NX include the following:

- Slot 2 (SC330) processor bus interface at 100MHz
- Support for up to four-way processing

- Support for two dedicated PCI expander bridges
- Support for up to four 32-bit PCI buses or two 64-bit PCI buses

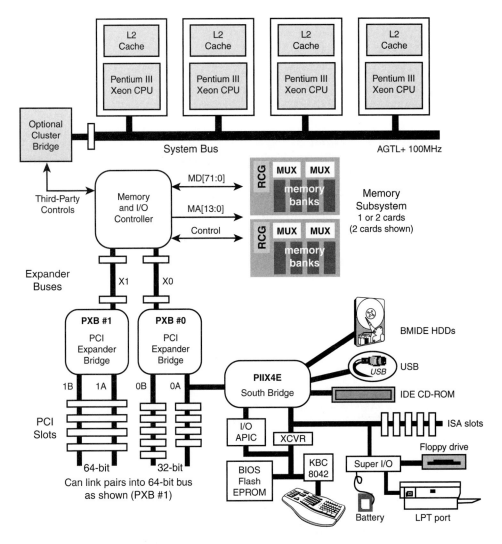

Figure 3.9   High-end server block diagram using the Intel 450NX chipset.

The 450NX chipset does not support AGP because high-end video is not an issue in network fileservers.

Fujitsu also used the 450NX chipset, to develop its TeamServer M800i series. This eight-way server used two 450NX chipsets linked by Fujitsu's Synfinity interconnect technology and non-uniform memory access (NUMA) memory architecture to create what is, in effect, a tightly coupled computer cluster in a single unit.

◄◄   See "NUMA Multiprocessing," p. 38.

The Intel (Corollary) Profusion Chipset

The Profusion chipset, which supports eight-way Pentium III Xeon servers, is extremely different from most other Intel chipsets for servers. As we have seen, most Intel chipsets for Pentium II/III Xeon servers use some form of the North Bridge/South Bridge chipset architecture originally developed for use with the Intel 486 processor. However, the greater complexity of four-way and larger multiprocessor server architectures using Intel processors requires the use of several specialized chips.

Intel's first chipset to use multiple specialized chips was the 450NX for four-way Pentium II/III Xeon servers (see the section "The Intel 450NX Chipset," earlier in this chapter). Profusion's design, originally developed by Corollary in cooperation with Compaq (now a Hewlett-Packard brand), is even more sophisticated than the 450NX's because of the added challenge of supporting eight processors. Although Corollary began developing the Profusion chipset in 1996, the first systems that used Profusion were not released until late 1999, after Intel purchased Corollary in late 1997, making it a wholly owned subsidiary, and released the chipset to server developers in June 1998.

The Profusion chipset creates a five-port (dual memory banks, dual processor buses, and I/O bus) non-blocking crossbar switch using two components:

- One memory access controller (MAC) chip, which also provides a three-way processor bus bridge, support for up to 32GB of SDRAM, and TAG SDRAM management

- One data interface buffer (DIB) chip, which also provides three processor bus data ports with ECC support, two SDRAM data ports with ECC support, and concurrent data transfer on all ports and 64 cache line buffers

These two chips form a five-way crossbar switch that handles data flow between the processors, memory, and I/O bus. The combination of MAC and DIB chips in the Profusion chipset replaces the physical switch often used in other eight-way SMP architectures to interface the processors with memory and I/O bridge connections to system RAM and I/O devices such as PCI slots and PCI/ISA ports. Figure 3.10 illustrates how the MAC and DIB chips work together.

Other components of the Profusion chipset include the following:

- A 64-bit PCI bus bridge chip, the PB64 (also co-developed by Corollary and Compaq), which supports up to 8 66MHz, 64-bit PCI bus masters and up to 16 33MHz, 64-bit PCI bus masters. Up to 4 PB64 chips can be used to provide redundancy and to provide support for mixed PCI speeds. Typically, 1 of the PB64 chips is devoted to 33MHz PCI slots, and the others provide support for 66MHz slots.

- Cache coherency filters (also known as cache accelerators), which are used to improve cache memory performance on eight-way systems; one is required for each four-processor section of an eight-way configuration. A four-way system does not need a cache coherency filter.

- A South Bridge chip (Intel's PXII4E) to provide support for keyboard, mouse, USB, and serial and parallel ports.

The crossbar switch and support for multiple PCI bus bridge chips enable servers based on Profusion to handle memory, processor, cache coherency, and PCI bridge failures while continuing to operate.

Figure 3.11 shows a block diagram of a typical eight-way system based on the Profusion chipset.

From late 1999 through 2001, the Profusion chipset was the leading eight-way server chipset used with Intel server-class processors. Although the Profusion chipset itself has been discontinued, an improved version of the chipset was developed by Compaq (now owned by Hewlett-Packard) for use in servers using the Xeon MP processor. This chipset, the Hewlett-Packard F8, is covered later in this chapter, in the section "The F8 Chipset for Xeon MP."

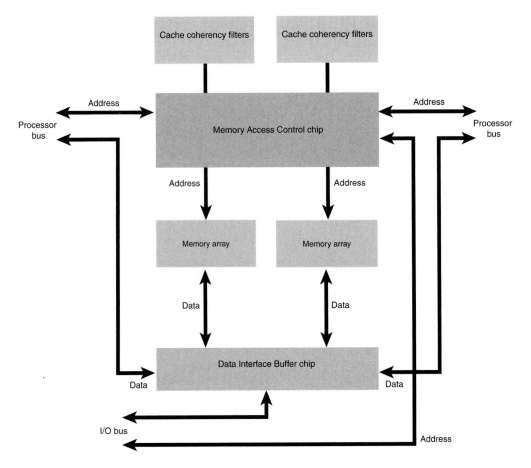

Figure 3.10 The Profusion chipset's MAC and DIB chips form a five-way crossbar switch.

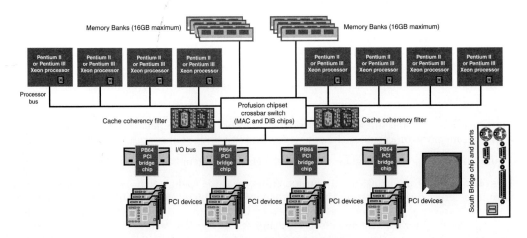

Figure 3.11 Block diagram of a typical system based on the Profusion chipset.

The Intel 820 and 820E Chipsets

The Intel 8xx series chipsets introduced in 1999 represent a major departure from the **4xx-series** chipsets previously used by Intel for its one-way and two-way servers. The 4xx-series **chipsets used the** North Bridge/South Bridge design, which use the 133MBps PCI bus to carry signals be**tween the com**ponents. The 8xx-series chipsets replace the North Bridge with an MCH, and the South **Bridge with an** ICH. Intel 8xx systems replace the PCI bus interconnection between chipset compon**ents with a** 266MBps dedicated bus known variously as the Accelerated Hub Architecture (AHA) **or, in later sys**tems, Hub Architecture 1.5.

◀◀ See "Intel Hub Architecture," p. 151.

The Intel 820 chipsets were designed to support Slot 1 or Socket 370 processors, **such as the Pentium** III and Celeron. The 820 chipset was the first to support RDRAM memory technology, **a 133MHz sys**tem bus, and 4x AGP.

The 82820 MCH provides the processor, memory, and AGP interfaces. Two **versions are available: One** supports a single processor (82820), and the other supports two processors **(82820DP), making the** 820E suitable for use in low-end two-way servers. Either is designed to work **with the same 82801 ICH** as used with the other 800-series chipsets, such as the 810 and 840. The 820 **chipset also uses the** 82802 firmware hub (FWH) for BIOS storage and for the Intel random **number generator (RNG).**

The 820 chipset was designed to use RDRAM memory, which has a **maximum throughput of up to** 1.6GBps. The 820 supports PC600, PC700, and PC800 RDRAM, deli**vering up to 1.6GBps of theoretical** memory bandwidth in the PC800 version. PC800 RDRAM is a 400MHz bus **running double-clocked** and transferring 16 bits (2 bytes) at a time (2×400MHz×2 bytes = 1.6GBps). **Two RIMM sockets are** available to support up to 1GB of total system memory.

The AGP interface in the 820 enables graphics controllers to access main **memory at AGP 4x speed,** which is about 1GB per second—twice that of previous AGP **2x platforms.**

820 chipset features include the following:

- Single- or dual- (820E) processor support
- 100/133MHz processor bus
- Intel 266MBps hub interface
- PC800 RDRAM RIMM memory support
- AGP 4x support
- ATA-100 (820E) or ATA-66 interface
- Intel RNG
- LPC interface
- AC '97 controller
- One (820) or two (820E) USB 1.1 buses with either two or four ports, **respectively**

The 820 chipset consists of three main components, with a few optional ex**tras. The main component** is the 82820 (single-processor) or 82820DP (dual-processor) MCH, which is a 324 BGA chip. That is paired with an 82801 ICH, which is a 241 BGA chip. Finally, it has the 82802 firmware hub (FWH), which is really just a fancy flash ROM BIOS chip. Optionally, there can be an 82380AB PCI-ISA bridge that is used only if the board is equipped with ISA slots.

The newer 820E version uses an updated 82801BA ICH2, which supports ATA-100 and incorporates dual USB controllers with two ports each, for a total of four USB ports. Although the 820E supports dual processors, few, if any, dual-processor 820E motherboards were ever built.

The Intel 840 Chipset

The Intel 840 was a high-end chipset designed for use in high-performance multiprocessor systems using Slot 1, Slot 2 (Xeon processor), or Socket 370 processors. The 840 chipset uses the same hub architecture and modular design as the rest of the 800 family of chipsets, with some additional components that enable more performance. Figure 3.12 shows a photo of the Intel 840 chipset.

Figure 3.12   Intel 840 chipset, showing the 82840 (MCH), 82801 (ICH), 82802 (FWH), 82803 (MRH-R), 82804 (MRH-S), and 82806 (P64H) chips. (Photograph used by permission of Intel Corporation.)

As with the other 800 series chipsets, the 840 has three main components:

- **82840 MCH**—This provides graphics support for AGP 2x/4x, dual RDRAM memory channels, and multiple PCI bus segments for high-performance I/O. Equivalent to the North Bridge in older chipset designs.

- **82801 ICH**—This is the equivalent to the South Bridge in older chipset designs, except that it connects directly to the MCH component via the high-speed Intel Hub Architecture bus. The ICH supports 32-bit PCI, IDE controllers, and dual USB 1.1 ports.

- **82802 FWH**—This is basically an enhanced flash ROM chip that stores system BIOS and video BIOS, as well as an Intel RNG. The RNG provides truly random numbers to enable stronger encryption, digital signing, and security protocols.

In addition to the core components, parts are available for scaling up to a more powerful design. Three additional components shown in Figure 3.12 can be added:

- **82806 64-bit PCI controller hub (P64H)**—Supports 64-bit PCI slots at speeds of either 33MHz or 66MHz. The P64H connects directly to the MCH using Intel Hub Architecture, providing a dedicated path for high-performance I/O. This is the first implementation of the 66MHz 66-bit PCI on a PC motherboard chipset, allowing for a PCI bus four times faster than the standard 32-bit 33MHz version.

- **82803 RDRAM-based memory repeater hub (MRH-R)**—Converts each memory channel into two memory channels for expanded memory capacity.

- **82804 SDRAM-based memory repeater hub (MRH-S)**—Translates the RDRAM protocol into SDRAM-based signals for system memory flexibility. This is used only in 840 systems that support SDRAM.

Figure 3.13 shows the 840 chipset architecture.

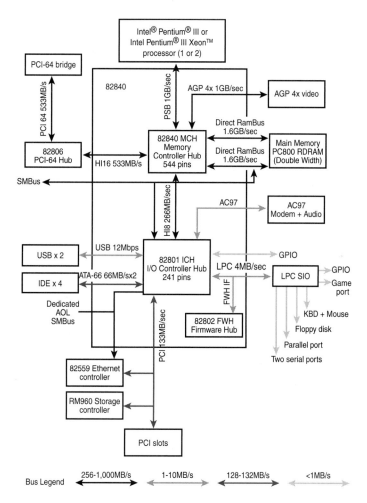

Figure 3.13   Intel 840 chipset architecture.

840 chipset features include the following:

- Support for one or two Pentium III or Pentium III Xeon processors
- 100/133MHz processor bus
- Dual RDRAM memory channels, operating simultaneously and providing up to 3.2GBps memory bandwidth (requires 82803 chip)
- 16-bit wide implementation of Intel Hub Architecture (HI16), which enables high-performance concurrent PCI I/O with the optional P64H component
- AGP 4x
- Prefetch cache, unique to the 840 chipset, which enables highly efficient data flow and helps maximize system concurrency
- Intel RNG
- USB 1.1 support

Optionally, network interface and RAID controller interface chips could be added as well. Both Intel and third-party vendors have used the 840 chipset to build dual-processor server motherboards.

Intel Pentium 4 Chipsets for Single-Processor Servers

Although Intel supported .multiple-processor configurations for its Pentium, Pentium II, and Pentium III processors and produced server-class chipsets for all three processor families, its primary multiple-processor (two-way and higher) platforms have been the various members of the Xeon family:

- Pentium II Xeon
- Pentium III Xeon
- Xeon DP (based on the Pentium 4)
- Xeon MP (based on the Pentium 4)

Starting with the Pentium 4, Intel discontinued supporting multiple-processor configurations for its desktop processors. Although Intel continues to support features such as ECC memory and relatively large amounts of RAM (2GB or higher) in some of its Pentium 4 chipsets and sells some entry-level server boards that use the Pentium 4, its primary server platforms are the Xeon (which is based on the Pentium 4 but which uses Socket 603 and Socket 604 and supports up to eight processors in its Xeon MP version) and Itanium family (Intel's first 64-bit processors). If you want to build a multiprocessor server based on Intel processors today, you need to use the Xeon DP, Xeon MP, or Itanium 2 processors. Xeon DP supports up to two-way designs, while Xeon MP and Itanium 2 also support four-way and larger designs.

Tip

If you want the low cost of a single-processor server but want to enjoy virtually all the advantages of two processors in an Intel-based platform, you can select servers based on the dual-core Pentium D or Pentium Extreme Edition processors.

Although some third-party chipsets have been used for entry-level Pentium 4–based servers, some of Intel's 8xx- and 9xx-series chipsets have achieved widespread support in both Intel and third-party server motherboards and systems (see Table 3.11).

Table 3.11   Intel 8xx- and 9xx-Series (Pentium 4) Chipsets Suitable for Use in Servers

Feature	845	845E	875P	925X	955X	975X
Codename	Brookdale	Brookdale-E	Canterwood	Alderwood	Glenwood	Glenwood
Date introduced	September 2001 (SDRAM); Jan 2002 (DDR)	May 2002	April 2003	June 2004	April 2005	November 2005
Part number	82845	82845E	82875	82925X	82955X	82975X
SMP (dual CPUs)	No	No	No	No	No	No
Bus speeds 1066/800MHz	400MHz	533/400MHz	800/533MHz	800MHz	1066/ 800MHz	
Memory types	PC133 SDRAM, DDR 200/266 SDRAM	DDR 200/266 SDRAM	DDR333/ 400 dual-channel	DDR2 533/ 400MHz dual-channel	DDR2 667/ 533MHz, dual-channel	DDR2 667/ 533MHz, dual-channel
Parity/ECC support	ECC	ECC	ECC	ECC	ECC	ECC
Maximum memory	2GB (PC2100 DDR); 3GB (PC133 SDRAM)	2GB	4GB	4GB	8GB	8GB
Memory banks	2 (PC2100); 3 (PC133)	2	2	2	2	2
GigE (Gigabit Ethernet) support[1]	No	No	Yes[1]	Yes	Yes[2]	Yes[2]
PCI version	2.2	2.2	2.2	2.2	2.3	2.3
PCI support	33MHz/32-bit	33MHz/ 32-bit	33MHz/ 32-bit	33MHz/ 32-bit	33MHz/ 32-bit	33MHz/ 32-bit
PCI-Express support	No	No	No	x1, x16	x1, x16	x1, x16 (dual)
Video support	AGP 4x (1.5V)	AGP 4x (1.5V)	AGP 8x	x16	x16	x16
MCH/ICH Interconnect speed	266MBps	266MBps	2GBps	2GBps	2GBps	2GBps
ICH (South Bridge)	ICH2	ICH4	ICH5/ICH5R	ICH6R	ICH7R	ICH7R

[1]*GigE connects directly to MCH/GMCH chip, bypassing the PCI bus. It is implemented via an optional Intel 82547E1 Gigabit connection chip.*

[2]*GigE connects directly to ICH.*

Note that compared to midrange and high-end server chipsets made for the Pentium II Xeon and Pentium III Xeon, the 8xx- and 9xx-series server chipsets lack support for 64-bit PCI expansion slots. This prevents servers based on these chipsets from supporting very high-performance Ultra320 SCSI RAID arrays because the host adapters for such arrays requires 64-bit 66MHz PCI or 133MHz PCI-X expansion slots. Given the lack of dual-processor support inherent in the Pentium 4 processor design and the lack of 64-bit PCI support in the Pentium 4 chipsets used by servers, it's appropriate that Intel's server motherboards using these chipsets are identified as Entry [level] Server Boards.

More advanced single-processor Pentium 4 servers from Intel and third parties use the E72xx chipsets, which combine server-specific features with some of the latest developments found in the 8xx and 9xx chipsets for desktop computers. Table 3.12 compares the features of the E7210, E7221, and E7230 chipsets.

Table 3.12   E72xx Chipsets for Pentium 4–Based Servers

Feature	E7210	E7221	E7230
HT Technology support	Yes	Yes	Yes
FSB speeds supported	800/533MHz	800/533MHz	1066/800MHz
EMT64 (64-bit OS/apps) support	—	Yes	Yes
MCH/ICH Interconnect	HI 1.5	DMI	DMI
Interconnect speed	266MBps	2GBps	2GBps
Dual-channel DDR 333/400 memory	Yes	Yes	—
Dual-channel DDR2 memory	—	Yes	Yes
ECC support	Yes	Yes	Yes
Integrated graphics	—	Yes	—
Number of ATA/IDE ports	1	1	1
SATA with optional RAID 0,1	Yes	—	—
SATA with optional RAID 0, 1, 0+1	—	Yes	Yes
Number of SATA ports	2	4	4
SATA speed	150MBps	150MBps	300MBps
PCI-Express x8 support	—	Yes	Yes
PCI-Express x1 support	—	Yes	Yes
PCI-X/PCI hot-swap	—	Yes	Yes
PCI-X bridge	Yes	Yes	Yes
Number of USB 2.0 ports	4	8	8
GigE (Gigabit Ethernet) support	Yes	—	Yes
ICH	6300ESB	ICH6R	ICH7R

Note

Although the E7210 chipset was designed for the Pentium 4, some vendors have used it to create motherboards that support dual Xeon processors.

The 955X and 975X chipsets in Table 3.11 also support the dual-core Pentium D and Pentium Extreme Edition processors. The E7230 in Table 3.12 chipset also supports the dual-core Pentium D processor.

Table 3.13 compares the features of the ICH chips used by the chipsets listed in Tables 3.11 and 3.12.

Table 3.13   ICH Chips for Pentium 4 Server-Capable Chipsets[1]

Feature	ICH2	ICH4	ICH5	ICH5R	ICH6R	6300ESB	ICH7	ICH7R
Part number	82801BA	82801DB	82801EB	82801ER	82801FR	6300ESB	80801GB	80801GR
ATA support	UDMA-100	UDMA-100	UDMA-100	UDMA-100	UDMA-100	UDMA-100	UDMA-100	UDMA-100
SATA support	No	No	SATA-150	SATA-150	SATA-150	SATA-150	SATA-300	SATA-300
SATA RAID	No	No	No	RAID 0, 1	RAID 0, 1, 0+1	RAID 0, 1	No	RAID 0, 1, 0+1
USB support	2C/4P	3C/6P	4C/8P	4C/8P	4C/8P	2C/4P	4C/8P	4C/8P
USB 2.0	No	Yes	Yes	Yes	Yes	Yes	Yes	Yes
CMOS/clock	Yes	Yes	Yes	Yes	Yes	Yes	Yes	Yes
PCI support	2.2	2.2	2.3	2.3	2.3, PCI-Express	2.2, PCI-X	2.3, PCI-Express	2.3, PCI-Express
ISA support	No	No	No	No	No	No	No	No
LPC support	Yes	Yes	Yes	Yes	Yes	Yes	No	No
Power management	SMM / ACPI 1.0	SMM/ ACPI 1.0	SMM 2.0/ ACPI 1.0	SMM 2.0/ ACPI 1.0	SMM 2.0 / ACPI 1.0	SMM 2.0/ ACPI 1.0	SMM 2.0/ ACPI 1.0	SMM 2.0/ ACPI 1.0
Ethernet	No	10/100	10/100	10/100	10/100	No	GigE (via PCI-Express x1)	GigE (via PCI-Express x1)

[1]*Key: ICH = I/O controller hub; USB = universal serial bus; xC/xP = number of controllers/number of ports; ATA = AT attachment (IDE); UDMA = Ultra DMA ATA; ISA = industry-standard architecture bus; LPC = low-pin-count bus; SMB = system management bus; and ACPI = advanced configuration and power interface.*

The Intel 845 Family of Chipsets

The 845 family of chipsets is widely used by both Intel and third-party motherboard makers for both entry-level servers and desktop computers. If you purchased a Pentium 4 system from late 2001 through mid-2003, it probably used some version of the 845 chipset. The 845, codenamed Brookdale during its development, was the first Pentium 4 chipset from Intel to support low-cost SDRAM instead of expensive RDRAM. Subsequent variations support DDR SDRAM at speeds up to DDR333, ATA-100, and USB 2.0.

The 845-series chipset is suitable for use in servers, including the 845 and 845E models. All members of the 845 family use the same hub-based architecture developed for the 8xx family, but they also have onboard audio and support the communications and networking riser (CNR) card for integrated modem and 10/100 Ethernet networking. However, they differ in their support for different types and amounts of memory, integrated graphics, external AGP support, and which ICH chip they use.

Although the original version of the 845 supported only PC133 SDRAM memory, the so-called 845D model (a designation used by review sites but not by Intel) also supports 200/266MHz DDR SDDRAM. The Intel 845's 82845 MCH supports Socket 478–based Celeron or Pentium 4 processors and can support up to two DDR SDRAM modules or three standard SDRAM modules (depending on the motherboard). When DDR SDRAM is used, the 845 supports either 200MHz (PC2100) or 266MHz (PC2700) memory speeds, with an FSB speed of 400MHz. The 845 also supports ECC error correction when parity-checked memory modules are used and offers an AGP 4x video slot, but it has no onboard video.

The 845 uses the same ICH2 chip (82801-BA) used by the Intel 850 and 850E chipsets in Rambus-based systems and the 815EP in low-cost SDRAM-based systems. The ICH2 supports ATA-100 hard disk interfacing, basic AC '97 sound, and four USB 1.1 ports.

The 845E is an updated version of the 845D with ECC error correction and support for 533MHz FSB, and it uses the enhanced ICH4 82801DB, which offers six USB 2.0 ports as well as integrated networking and enhanced 20-bit audio.

Figure 3.14 compares the system block diagrams of the 845 and 845E models.

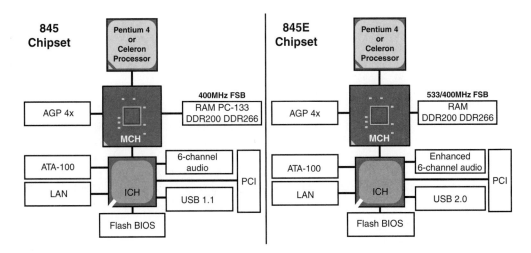

Figure 3.14   The 845E (right) adds support for faster FSB speeds, memory, and USB 2.0 to the basic 845 chipset architecture (left).

The Intel 875P Chipset

The Intel 875P chipset, codenamed Canterwood during its development, was introduced in April 2003. The 875P chipset supports Intel's Hyper-Threading (HT) Technology, so it fully supports 3.06GHz and faster Pentium 4s, including the newer Prescott (90nm) core versions.

For faster memory access, the 875P supports four standard or ECC memory modules (up to 4GB total) using DDR333 or DDR400 memory in a dual-channel mode, and it offers a new Turbo mode that uses a faster path between DDR400 memory and the MCH to boost enhanced performance. Because multiple memory modules aren't always the same size or type, the 875P also features a new dynamic mode that optimizes system memory when different types or sizes of memory are used at the same time. The 875P also includes both SATA and RAID support and uses the same ICH5/ICH5R family used by the 865 series.

The Intel 925X Chipset

The Intel 925X chipset, codenamed Alderwood before its release, was released in 2004 as a replacement for the 875P Canterwood chipset. Unlike its predecessor, the 925X supports only DDR2 memory (up to 4GB maximum). The 925X supports the Pentium 4 Extreme Edition and the Pentium 4 processors in Socket 775 form factors.

The 925X supports PCI-Express x1 and PCI-Express x16 (video) as well as PCI version 2.3 expansion slots. It supports the LGA 775 processor socket and the Intel Prescott Pentium 4 core and uses the ICH6 family of South Bridge replacements detailed in Table 3.13. The 925X is widely used for single-processor server motherboards.

Intel 955X and 975X (Glenwood) Chipset Family

The Intel "Glenwood" chipset family, released in 2005, includes two members, the 955X and 975X. These chipsets are the first to support Intel's new dual-core Pentium D processors, and they also support the new high-performance single-core Pentium Extreme Edition processors as well as existing Pentium 4 HT Technology processors that use Socket 775. Although Intel categorizes these chipsets as "Entry-Level Workstation" and "Performance PC" chipsets, some vendors use these chipsets for single-processor workstation/server designs.

Although these chipsets are numbered in different series, most of their features are identical. Both support FSB speeds of 800MHz and 1066MHz and support up to four DDR2 667/533MHz memory modules (two pairs of dual-channel modules), for a maximum memory size of 8GB. Both support ECC memory, a must for server operation, and both use the ICH7 family of ICH chips listed in Table 3.13.

The 955X and 975X differ from each other in their video support. The 955X supports a single PCI-Express x16 video card, whereas the 975X supports two PCI-Express video cards in x8 mode, such as the ATI CrossFire series of graphics cards.

Alternatives to 955X/975X–Based Servers

Although you can use 955X or 975X chipsets in a server motherboard, servers don't need the high-performance graphics support they provide. Motherboards based on the E7230 chipset provide support for more memory than the 955X and 975X, optional support for PCI-X, and matrix RAID storage. The E7230's PCI slots can be used for video.

The E7210 Chipset

The Intel E7210 chipset, codenamed Canterwood-ES, during its development, was introduced in February 2004. Like the 875P, the E7210 supports Socket 478 Pentium 4 processors, including those featuring Intel's HT Technology and 800MHz FSB. It supports both Northwood (130 nm) and Prescott (90nm) core versions at clock speeds up to 3.4GHz.

The E7210 supports four standard or ECC memory modules (up to 4GB total) using DDR400 or DDR333 memory modules in a dual-channel configuration. The E7210 uses the 6300ESB ICH rather than the ICH5/ICH5R series used by the 8xx-series of server/workstation/desktop computer chipsets. The 6300ESB includes integrated support for PCI version 2.2 and 66MHz PCI-X slots. The E7210 supports up to two SATA (SATA) and two ATA-100 (ATA/IDE) drives, as well as four USB 2.0 ports. The PCI-X slots can be used for high-performance Gigabit Ethernet network adapters and SCSI RAID host adapters.

Figure 3.15 compares the architecture of the 875P and E7210 chipsets.

The E7221 Chipset

The Intel E7221 chipset, codenamed Copper River during its development, was introduced in September 2004. The E7221 supports Socket 775 Pentium 4 processors, enabling it to use the fastest and newest Pentium 4 processor designs on the market. The E7221 also supports Intel Extended Memory 64 Technology (EM64T), enabling systems based on this processor to support 64-bit operating systems such as Windows Server 2003 x64 Edition and various Linux distributions, as well as 32-bit operating systems, at full processor speed.

The E7210 supports four standard or ECC memory modules (up to 4GB total), using DDR2-533/400 or DDR400/333 memory modules in a dual-channel configuration. The E7210's MCH features a PCI-Express x8 interface. The PCI-Express x8 interface also supports the 6702PXH 64-bit PCI hub component of the chipset. When the 6702PXH chip is used as part of the E7221 chipset, the system also supports PCI-X expansion slots running at 64MHz or 133MHz.

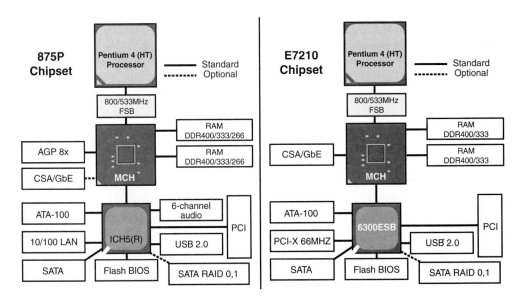

Figure 3.15   The E7210 (right) is based on the 875P (left) but adds support for PCI-X expansion slots.

The E7221 uses the ICH6R ICH, the same ICH used by the Intel 9xx desktop chipsets. The ICH6R provides SATA, PCI-Express x1, USB 2.0, PCI, and ATA-100 interfaces, and it connects to the MCH via the high-speed DMI interface. The E7221 is essentially a workstation and server version of the 9xx chipset.

The architecture of the E7221 chipset is shown in Figure 3.16.

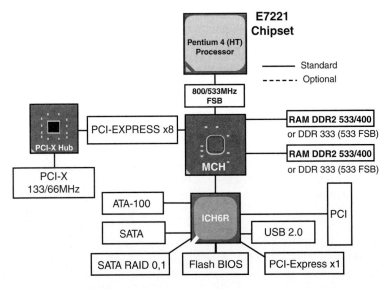

Figure 3.16   The E7221 is based on the Intel 9xx chipsets, featuring PCI-Express.

The E7230 Chipset

The E7230 chipset, originally codenamed Mukilteo, was introduced in July 2005. Its basic design is similar to that of the E7221 chipset, but with several enhancements designed to support the newest processor and storage technologies.

The E7230 is the first Intel server chipset to support the dual-core Pentium D processor, enabling a single-processor server to have performance virtually the same as that of a two-way server, but at a lower cost. The E7230 also supports Intel matrix storage technology, enabling simultaneous RAID 0 (striping) and RAID 1 (mirroring) with only two disk drives and PCI-Express x8, x4, and x1 cards. By adding the 6702PXH 64-bit PCI-X hub, PCI-X cards, such as network and SCSI RAID adapters, are also supported.

The E7230 also supports Socket 775 Pentium 4 processors with HT Technology, Execute Disable Bit, and Intel Extended Memory 64 Technology (EM64T). The E7230 features a maximum memory size of 8GB, using only DDR2 memory modules in 667/533/400MHz speeds, arranged in a dual-channel configuration.

The E7230 uses the ICH7R ICH, the same ICH used by the Intel 955X and 975X desktop chipsets. The ICH7R provides SATA Matrix storage RAID, PCI-Express x1, USB 2.0, PCI, and ATA-100 interfaces, and it connects to the MCH via the high-speed DMI interface.

Intel ICH Chips for 9xx and E72xx Chipsets

Intel has used the ICH5, ICH5R, ICH6R, 6300ESB, and ICH7R ICH chips with its 8xx, 9xx, and E72xx chipsets for the Pentium 4. The following sections provide additional details about these chips.

The ICH5 and ICH5R I/O Controllers

ICH5 and ICH5R (RAID) are the Intel ICHs for its AHA and HI 1.5 hub-based architecture, which is the equivalent of the South Bridge in Intel's hub-based architecture introduced with the 800 series of chipsets.

ICH5 and ICH5R feature four USB 2.0 controllers with eight external ports, two ATA-100 ports, and two SATA-150 ports. ICH5R models add support for RAID 0 (striping) and RAID 1 (mirroring) on the SATA ports. ICH5 and ICH5R also support the PCI 2.3 bus and include an integrated 10/100 Ethernet LAN controller.

Note

RAID 1 (mirroring) support for ICH5R-equipped motherboards requires the installation of the latest version of the Intel Application Accelerator, RAID Edition. In some cases, you might also need to install the latest edition of the Intel RAID Option ROM first. For more information and to download driver and option ROM updates, go to http://support.intel.com/support/chipsets/iaa_raid/.

The 6300ESB I/O Controller

The 6300ESB I/O controller used in the E7210 chipset integrates support for four PCI-X 66MHz slots. It also features support for four PCI 2.2 slots, two SATA-150 ports (including RAID), four USB 2.0 ports, two ATA-100 ports, and AC '97 integrated audio.

The ICH6R I/O Controller

ICH6R is the RAID version of the Intel ICH used by the 9xx series of desktop chipsets as well as by the E7221 server/workstation chipset. ICH6R features four USB 2.0 controllers with eight external ports, one ATA-100 port, one 10/100 Ethernet port, four PCI-Express x1 slots, and four SATA-150 ports. The SATA ports support RAID 0, 1, and 10. The ICH6R also features high-definition audio.

The ICH7 and ICH7R I/O Controllers

ICH7 and ICH7R are the latest versions of Intel's ICH chips. They are based on ICH6/6R, but also feature 10/100/1000 Ethernet and SATA-300 ports. The ICH7R version features Matrix storage technology, which supports simultaneous RAID 0 and RAID 1 on two drives, and also supports RAID 0+1 support with four drives.

Intel Xeon DP and Xeon MP Chipsets

The Intel Xeon DP and Xeon MP processors are workstation and server-class processors based on the Pentium 4 processor, but they use a larger socket (Socket 603/604) and use the E75xx series of chipsets. The E75xx chipsets are improved versions of the 860 chipset, which was the first Xeon DP chipset.

The Intel 860 Chipset

The Intel 860 was a high-performance chipset designed for the first Socket 603 (Pentium 4–based) Xeon processors for DP workstations. The 860 uses the same ICH2 as the Intel 850 but uses a different MCH—the 82860, which supports one or two Socket 603 ("Foster") Xeon processors. The other major features of the 82860 are similar to those of the 82850, including support for dual 400MHz RDRAM memory channels with a 3.2GBps bandwidth and a 400MHz system bus. The 82860 MCH also supports 1.5V AGP 4x video cards at a bandwidth exceeding 1GBps.

The 860 chipset uses a modular design, in which its two core chips can be supplemented by the 82860AA (P64H) 66MHz PCI controller hub and the 82803AA MRHR. The 82860AA supports 64-bit PCI slots at either 33MHz or 66MHz, and the 82803AA converts each RDRAM memory channel into two, which doubles memory capacity. Thus, whether a particular 860-based motherboard offers 64-bit or 66MHz PCI slots or dual-channel RDRAM memory depends on whether these supplemental chips are used in its design.

The 860 chipset was replaced by the E7500 Plumas chipset in 2002.

The Intel E7500 Chipset

The Intel E7500 chipset, codenamed Plumas, was introduced in March 2002. It supports up to two Xeon processors with 512KB L2 cache, 400MHz FSB, and Intel HT Technology. The E7500's design is simpler than that used by the 860 because by 2002, Intel was no longer supporting RDRAM in new systems.

The E7500 chipset includes the MCH and the ICH3-S ICH. To achieve 66MHz/64-bit PCI and 133MHz PCI-X support, the E7500 can be used with up to three optional P64H2 (82870P2) chips, an improved version of the P64H chip that is an optional part of the 860 chipset. Note that the E7500's MCH connects directly to memory, rather than to MRHR chips as with the 860. The E7500's design is simpler than that used by the 860, because by 2002 Intel was no longer supporting RDRAM in new systems. The E7500 supports up to 16GB of dual-channel DDR200 registered ECC SDRAM memory (up to eight modules). Its Intel x4 single-device data correction (SDDC) can correct up to four errors per memory module for better system reliability. Hub Architecture 2.0 provides a 2GBps bidirectional connection between the E7500 MCH and each P64H2 chip.

The E7500, and its sibling, the E7501 (described in the next section), have been used in many two-way servers.

The Intel E7501 Chipset

The Intel E7501 chipset, codenamed Plumas 533, was introduced in November 2002. It represents an improved version of the E7500, differing primarily in support for the 533MHz FSB versions of Xeon processors and support for dual-channel DDR266 memory. The E7501 also uses the same P64H2 and ICH-3S chips as the E7500.

Figure 3.17 depicts the architecture of the E7501 chipset.

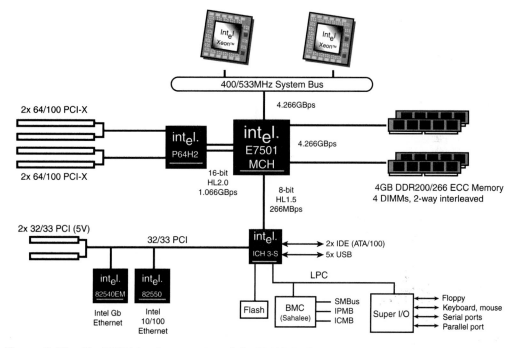

Figure 3.17   The E7501 is a faster version of the E7500; both support two Xeon processors.

The Intel E7505 Chipset

The Intel E7505 chipset, codenamed Placer, was introduced in November 2002. It supports up to two Xeon processors with 512KB L2 cache, 533MHz FSB, and Intel HT Technology.

The E7505 supports 1.5V AGP 1x–8x and AGP Pro cards (but not the nonstandard 3.5V versions of AGP once sold by some vendors), and it uses the ICH4. To achieve 66MHz/64-bit PCI and 133MHz PCI-X support, the E7505 can be used with up to three optional P64H2 (82870P2) chips. The E7505 uses the ICH4. The E7505 has been used in many two-way server and workstation designs.

Figure 3.18 illustrates the architecture of the E7505 chipset.

The Intel E7520 and E7320 Chipsets

The Intel E7520 chipset, codenamed Lindenhurst, was introduced in August 2004. Its companion, the E7320 chipset, codenamed Lindenhurst VS, was introduced at the same time. Both chipsets support up to two 64-bit (EM64T) Xeon processors with 2MB L2 cache, 800MHz FSB, and Intel HT Technology or Xeon processors with 1MB L2 cache and 800MHz FSB.

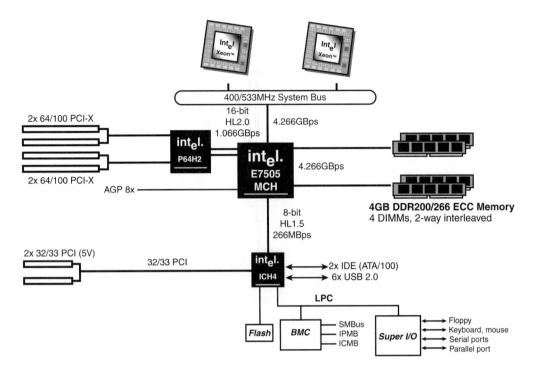

Figure 3.18   The E7505 supports AGP 8x, making it suitable for workstation as well as server applications.

These chipsets support dual-channel DDR2-400 or DDR 333/266 memory and can be used with either the ICH5R or 6300ESB ICHs.

The E7520 differs from the less-expensive E7320 by offering memory mirroring as well as DMA support in the memory subsystem. Both chipsets support ECC memory, X4 SDDC, and hub interface ECC for reliable memory access.

▶▶   See "Advanced Error Correction Technologies," p. 391.

The E7520 includes three PCI-Express x8 interfaces, and the E7320 includes one PCI-Express x8 interface. The x8 interfaces can be configured as two PCI-Express x4 interfaces, which act as hosts for optional 6700 PXH 64-bit PCI hubs that provide 66MHz PCI-X or PCI interfaces with hot-plug support. The E7520 also supports the IOP332 I/O processor chip (codenamed Dobson), designed for high-performance RAID implementations. Figure 3.19 illustrates a typical block diagram for a system running an E7520/6300ESB chipset.

The Intel E8500 Chipset

The Intel E8500 chipset, codenamed Twin Castle before its release, was introduced in April 2005. It supports up to four of the latest dual-core Xeon MP processors as well as existing single-core processors, and it supports Intel's EM64T extensions, enabling this chipset to support 64-bit or 32-bit server operating systems. When dual-core Xeon MP processors are used, the system is essentially an eight-way system.

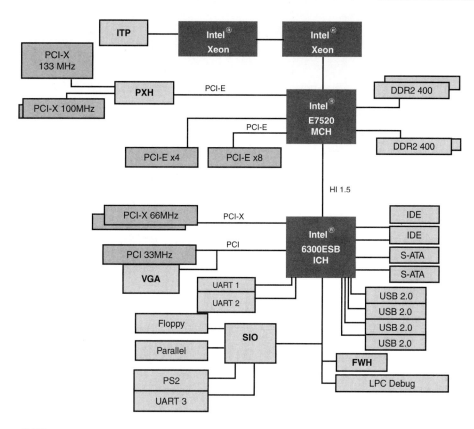

Figure 3.19   The E7520 supports PCI-X and PCI-Express interfaces, enabling it to operate with the latest high-speed I/O boards for SCSI RAID, networking, and other applications.

The E8500 chipset includes the following components:

- E8500 North Bridge
- E8500 XMB
- 6700PXH 64-bit PCI hub (supports PCI and PCI-X slots up to 133MHz)
- ICH5 (equivalent to the South Bridge)

Despite Intel's use of the term "North Bridge," the E8500 uses a hub architecture to connect to the ICH5.

The E8500 North Bridge supports PCI-Express, providing three x8 lanes and four 1x lanes. PCI-Express support enables the E8500 to use newly emerging and forthcoming PCI-Express interfaces for high-speed networking, SCSI RAID arrays, and other server-optimized components.

The E8500 supports DDR266, DDR333, and DDR-2 400 memory via one or more high-speed IMI connections to the 8500's XMB memory bridge chips (see Figure 3.20). It supports registered ECC DIMMS and features memory RAID (similar to memory mirroring) and demand and patrol scrubbing to detect and repair memory problems. If it encounters a memory problem that cannot be repaired, it marks the bad location so that it will not be used in the future. The IMI interconnect runs at 2.67GBps inbound and 5.33GBps outbound.

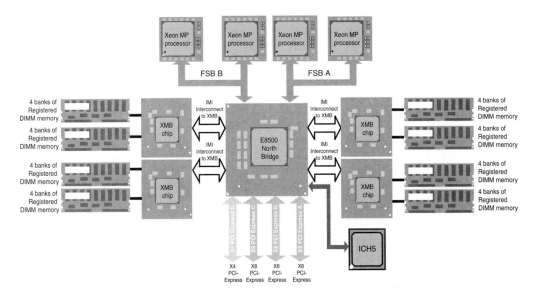

Figure 3.20   The E8500 combines the hub architecture of the 8xx-series chipsets with specialized memory controller and PCI-Express bridge chips to support a powerful four-way architecture.

Intel Itanium and Itanium 2 Chipsets

Intel's first 64-bit server processors are the Itanium and Itanium 2 processor families. The 64-bit architecture of these processors is a completely different architecture than the 32-bit or x64 extensions to 32-bit processor architectures supported by the Intel Pentium series and AMD Athlon series. (See Chapter 2 for more information.)

Intel's first chipset for the Itanium, the 460GX, was introduced in June 2001, coinciding with the initial release of the Itanium processor. The 460GX chipset included 10 components, enabling developers to customize Itanium systems for use as workstations with AGP4x graphics or as servers with up to four Itanium processors. The original Itanium was quickly replaced by the Itanium 2 because the Itanium's lengthy development time basically made it obsolete by the time it was delivered. The Itanium 2 offers faster clock speeds and larger memory caches than the original Itanium.

The current Intel Itanium 2 chipset is the E8870, which supports up to four Itanium 2 processors. When equipped with the E8870SP scalability port switch component, the E8870 supports up to eight Itanium 2 processors. The E8870 was introduced in August 2002.

The following sections provide detailed information about these chipsets.

The Intel 460GX Chipset for Itanium

The Intel 460GX chipset, the first (and only) chipset developed by Intel for the first-generation Itanium processor, was scarcely a chipset in the established sense of the term. Instead of using a relatively small number of versatile chips, the Intel 460GX seemed to use a different chip for almost every significant task performed outside the processor. As a result, the 460GX chipset includes a total of 10 components:

- **82461GX**—The System Address Controller (SAC) interfaced memory and control lines between memory and the Itanium processors via the MAC chips.

- **82462GX**—The System Data Path Controller (SDC) interfaced data lines between memory and the Itanium processors via the MDC chips.

- **82463GX**—The Memory Address Controller (MAC) connected system memory to the SAC.

- **82464GX**—The Memory Data Controller (MDC) connected system memory to the SDC.

- **82465GX**—The Graphics Expansion Bus (GXB) provided an AGP 4x expansion slot (for workstation use).

- **82466GX**—The Wide and Fast PCI Expansion Bus (WXB) supported two independent 66MHz, 64-bit PCI interfaces to the SAC.

- **82467GX**—The PCI eXpander Bridge (PXB) provided two 32-bit, 33MHz PCI interfaces or a single 64-bit, 33MHz PCI interface to the SAC.

- **82468GX**—The I/O and Firmware Bridge (IFB) provided a PCI-to-ISA bridge, USB ports, the interface to the FWH, the interface to the Super I/O chip, and other support functions. It connected to the PXB.

- **82802AC**—The Firmware Hub (FWH) stored firmware (BIOS) and security features. It connected to the IFB.

- **82094AA**—The Programmable Interrupt Device (PID) was an interrupt controller with steering capabilities. It was actually an NEC-developed part (NEC #UPD66566S1-016).

Figure 3.21 illustrates the architecture of a four-way system using the 460GX chipset.

Very few servers were built using the Itanium processor or the 460GX chipset. However, the 460GX chipset is significant for being the most complex Intel chipset to date.

The Intel E8870 Chipset for Itanium 2

The Itanium 2 processor rapidly replaced the original Itanium processor, and because of major changes in its design, a brand-new chipset was needed. The E8870 was introduced at the same time as the Itanium 2, and it continues to be Intel's only Itanium 2–compatible chipset. (Other vendors have also produced Itanium 2 chipsets.)

Note

The E8870 was designed during the period in which Intel had selected RDRAM as its preferred memory technology. However, by the time the E8870 was introduced, it had become obvious that RDRAM was more expensive than DDR SDRAM and did not offer performance commensurate with its higher cost. Thus, Intel decided to add a DDR memory hub component to the E8870 to convert DDR SDRAM signals to RDRAM signals compatible with the SNC's built-in memory controller. While this adds several chips to typical E8870 implementations, servers based on the E8870 can now use reasonably priced registered DDR SDRAM instead of expensive RDRAM.

Unlike the 460GX, the E8870 (also known as the 870) uses Intel's modern hub architecture along with specialized support chips. The E8870's components include the following:

- **E8870**—The Scalable Node Controller (SNC) provides memory controller and system bus interfacing services. It can be connected to the SPS for scaling to dual-node (eight-way) implementations, or it can connect to the SIOH for single-node (four-way and smaller) implementations. It receives DDR memory signals through connections to DMH chips.

- **E8870DM**—The DDR Memory Hub (DMH) translates two DDR channels into the native quad-channel Rambus memory bus on the SNC.

- **E8870IO**—The Server Input/Output Hub (SIOH) provides an HI 1.5 (266Mbps) connection to the ICH4 and provides dual HI 2.0 (1Gbps) connections to the P64H2 PCI-X bridges.

- **82870P2**—The 64-bit PCI/PCI-X Controller (P64H2) supports 64-bit PCI-X slots running at 133MHz. (PCI-X also supports PCI devices.) It can be used to support Intel Gigabit Ethernet and Intel I/O processor chips.

- **82801DB**—The ICH (ICH4) supports USB 2.0, ATA/IDE, and other legacy ports.

- **80802AC**—The Firmware Hub (FWH) supports BIOS and security features.

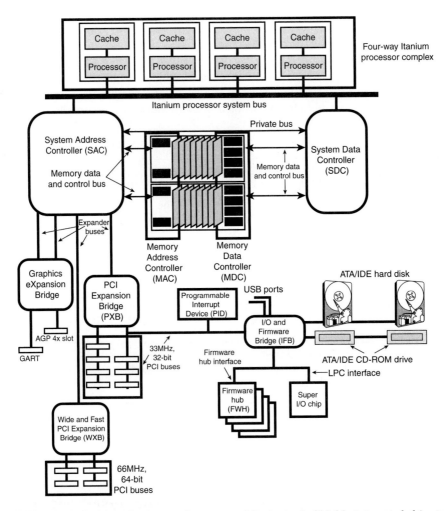

Figure 3.21   The 460GX used many single-purpose chips instead of highly integrated chips to support the original Itanium processor.

These components are used in four-way Itanium implementations; each four-way implementation is known as a *node*. However, an additional component, known as the E8870SP, the Scalability Port Switch (SPS), is used to connect two nodes into an eight-way implementation. The SPS was introduced after the initial release of the E8870 chipset.

Figure 3.22 illustrates the architecture of a typical four-way Itanium 2 system using the E8870, and Figure 3.23 illustrates how the SPS is used to enable eight-way processing.

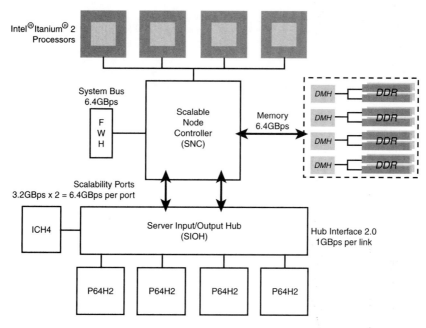

Figure 3.22   The E8870's architecture in a typical four-way implementation.

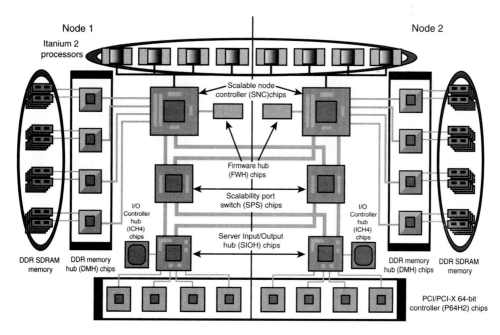

Figure 3.23   The E8870's architecture when SPS chips are used to create a two-node (eight-way) system. Note that one SPS chip is used for each node.

Broadcom ServerWorks Chipsets for Intel Processors

Starting in 1997, ServerWorks (a Broadcom company originally known as Reliance Computer Corporation) introduced its first server chipsets for Intel processors. Today, ServerWorks is second only to Intel as the major supplier of server chipsets for Intel-based servers.

Early ServerWorks chipsets included the ServerSet I (also known as the Champion 1.0 chipset) and the ServerSet II. ServerSet I supported up to six Pentium Pro processors and featured two 32-bit PCI buses. ServerSet II supported up to four Pentium II Xeon processors and featured a 64-bit PCI bus. These chipsets were discontinued several years ago.

Current ServerWorks chipsets support the Pentium III Xeon and Xeon DP and MP (based on Pentium 4) processors. Although ServerWorks uses the North Bridge and South Bridge terminology for its chipsets, its current chipsets also include memory controller and I/O bridge chips. Thus, ServerWorks chipsets more closely resemble E7xxx-series Intel chipsets than Intel's 8xx or 9xx chipsets.

Several major motherboard and system builders, including Intel, have used Champion- and Grand Champion–series chipsets for multiprocessor server motherboards and systems.

Note

For more information about ServerWorks chipsets, see the Broadcom website, at www.broadcom.com.

ServerWorks Chipsets for Intel Pentium III Xeon Processors

ServerWorks currently makes three chipsets for the Pentium III Xeon processors:

- **Champion HE (also known as Champion Enterprise)**—Supports up to four processors with 100MHz FSB; the North Bridge is the NB6536 2.0HE.
- **Champion HE-SL (also known as Champion Volume)**—Supports up to two processors with 133/100MHz FSB; the North Bridge is the NB6576.
- **Champion LE (also known as Champion Entry)**—Supports up to two processors with 133/100MHz FSB; the North Bridge is the NB6635 3.0LE.

Originally, this series of chipsets was known as the ServerSet III series.

All three North Bridge chips can be paired with either the OSB4 or CSB5 South Bridge chip to form a chipset. The OSB4 features UDMA/33 ATA/IDE hard disk host adapter, USB 1.1 ports, and an LPC connection to a Super I/O chip. The CSB5 features an UDMA/100 ATA/IDE hard disk host adapter, USB 1.1 ports, and an LPC connection to a Super I/O chip. Most motherboards that use a Champion-series chipset use SCSI-based hard disks or RAID arrays instead of ATA hard disks, so there is little practical difference between these South Bridge chips.

Table 3.14 provides an overview of the Champion series of chipsets for the Pentium III Xeon processor.

Table 3.14   Champion Chipsets for Pentium III Xeon

Chipset Model Number	Chipset Model Name	Processors Supported	Number of Processors	Compatible South Bridge chips	Memory Controller Chip	I/O Bridge Chips
HE	Champion Enterprise	PIII Xeon 100MHz FSB	4	OSB4, CSB5	MADP	CIOB-20
HE-SL	Champion Volume	PIII Xeon 133/ 100MHz FSB	2	OSB4, CSB5	—	CIOB-20
LE	Champion Entry	PIII Xeon 133/ 100MHz FSB	2	OSB4, CSB5	—	—

The Champion LE Chipset

The Champion LE chipset is the simplest of the current Champion series, using only North Bridge and South Bridge chips. For greater reliability than with desktop-adapted chipsets, Champion LE, like all current ServerWorks server chipsets, uses registered memory.

Champion LE supports two 64-bit/66MHz PCI expansion slots via the South Bridge chip. However, if you need additional 64-bit slots, Champion LE is not a suitable choice. Thus, Champion LE is best suited to basic dual-processor server applications.

The Champion HE-SL Chipset

Although the Champion HE-SL chipset supports two processors, as does the Champion LE, it is a more powerful and flexible chipset. It supports AGP 2x graphics, and ECC registered memory must be installed in matched pairs to support memory interleaving for better memory performance.

However, the most significant improvement in Champion HE-SL over its Champion LE sibling is its support for both 3.3V (66MHz) and 5V (33MHz) 64-bit PCI slots. This comes via the third component in the HE-SL chipset, the CIOB20 I/O bridge. The CIOB20 (also known as the NB6555 IO Bridge 2.0 chip), provides a 64-bit PCI bridge between the North Bridge and 64-bit PCI slots. The connection to the North Bridge uses ServerWorks's own Inter Module Bus (IMB) high-speed connection. IMB runs at 1GBps, which is four times faster than Intel's Hub Architecture 1.0 or 1.5 or the VIA V-Link 4x interconnections.

If you need to use several PCI cards (33MHz or 66MHz) in a server, the Champion HE-SL is a better choice than the Champion LE.

The Champion HE Chipset

The Champion HE is the most powerful of the Champion series. It supports four Pentium III Xeon processors and uses a fourth ServerWorks chipset component, the MADP memory controller chip. In a four-way configuration, four MADP chips are used, but in a two-way configuration, only one MADP chip is used (see Figure 3.24).

The MADP chip supports memory interleaving for better memory performance in both two-way and four-way configurations.

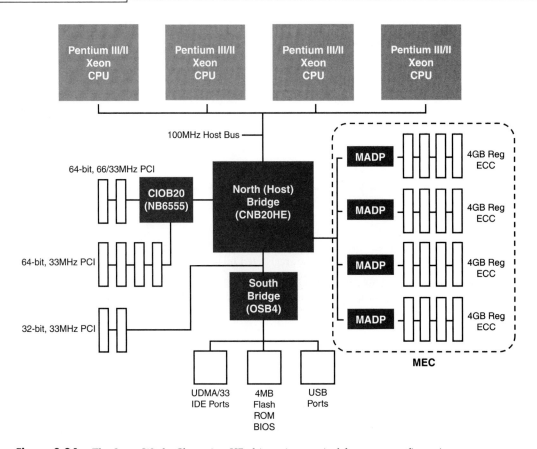

Figure 3.24   The ServerWorks Champion HE chipset in a typical four-way configuration.

ServerWorks Chipsets for Intel Xeon Processors

ServerWorks currently makes three chipsets for the Xeon processors based on the Pentium 4:

- **Grand Champion HE (also known as Grand Champion Enterprise)**—Supports up to four processors with 400MHz FSB; the North Bridge chip is called CMIC-HE.

- **Grand Champion LE (also known as Grand Champion Volume)**—Supports up to two processors with 533/400MHz FSB; the North Bridge chip is called CMIC-SL.

- **Grand Champion SL (also known as Grand Champion Entry)**—Supports up to two processors with 533/400MHz FSB; the North Bridge chip is called CMIC-LE.

Originally, this series of chipsets was to be known as the ServerSet IV series.

All three North Bridge chips can be paired with either the CSB5 or CSB6 South Bridge chip to form a chipset. The CSB6 is the most advanced South Bridge chip used by any ServerWorks chipset to date. It includes three ATA-100 ATA/IDE host adapters; support for ATA RAID 0, 1, and 5; 64-bit PCI bus; 400MBps connection to the North Bridge; and USB 1.1 ports.

Table 3.15 provides an overview of the Grand Champion series of chipsets for Xeon processors.

Table 3.15   Grand Champion Chipsets for Intel Xeon

Chipset Model Number	Chipset Model Name	Processors Supported	Number of Processors	Compatible South Bridge Chips	Memory Controller Chip	I/O Bridge Chips
GC-HE	Grand Champion Enterprise	Xeon 400MHz FSB	4	CSB5, CSB6	REMC	CIOB-E, CIOB-ES, CIOB-X, CIOB-X2
GC-LE	Grand Champion Volume	Xeon 533/ 400MHz FSB	2	CSB5, CSB6	—	CIOB-E, CIOB-X2
GC-SL	Grand Champion Entry	Xeon 533/ 400MHz FSB	2	CSB5, CSB6	—	CIOB-X2

The GC-SL (Grand Champion Entry) Chipset

The Grand Champion SL chipset is the simplest of the current Grand Champion series. Its North Bridge chip incorporates a single IMB I/O interface and a single Thin-IMB interface to the South Bridge. It supports up to 4GB of RAM. RAM contents are protected with 128-bit ECC and spare memory technologies. The optional CIOB-E bridge provides Gigabit Ethernet support, while the optional CIOB-X2 I/O bridge provides PCI-X support up to 133MHz. In its basic North Bridge/South Bridge configuration, Grand Champion SL is suitable for basic server designs. However, when the CIOB-X2 PCI-X bridge is added, it is also suitable for midrange server designs.

The GC-LE (Grand Champion LE) Chipset

The dual-processor Grand Champion LE is designed to handle four times the memory (16GB) of the Grand Champion SL. It also supports two CIOB-X2 PCI-X I/O bridge chips, enabling a motherboard to have up to six PCI-X 100/66MHz cards, up to three PCI-X 133MHz cards or a mix of PCI-X cards and onboard devices. Thus, if you need support for several PCI-X cards, or a mix of PCI-X cards, a high-speed integrated SCSI host adapter and a Gigabit Ethernet adapter as in Figure 3.25, the Grand Champion GC-LE chipset is a better choice than the GC-SL.

Figure 3.25 illustrates the block diagram of a typical server using the GC-LE chipset.

The GC-HE (Grand Champion HE) Chipset

The Grand Champion HE is the most powerful of the Grand Champion series. It supports four Xeon MP processors and incorporates three IMB I/O interfaces for the fastest memory interfacing of any GC-series ServerWorks chipset. With support for up to 64GB of memory, its memory contents are protected with 128-bit ECC, chipkill, spare memory, memory mirroring, and hot-plug memory card support technologies. The GC-HE uses five REMC memory controller chips in a four-way configuration: four in the data path and a fifth one in the address path.

Figure 3.26 illustrates a four-way implementation of the GC-HE chipset.

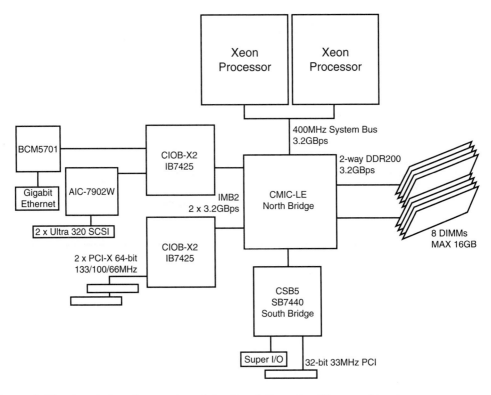

Figure 3.25   A typical implementation of the Grand Champion LE server chipset.

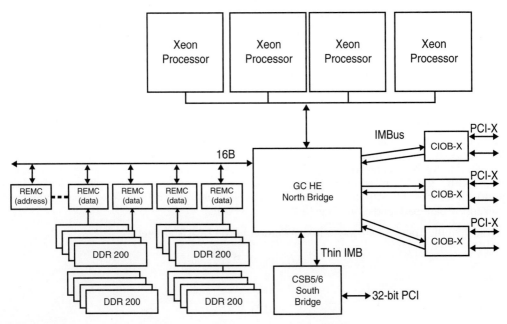

Figure 3.26   A typical implementation of the Grand Champion HE server chipset.

ServerWorks South Bridge and Support Chips

All ServerWorks Champion and Grand Champion chipsets contain South Bridge chips, and many of them also contain I/O bridge and memory controller chips. The South Bridge chips used by ServerWorks chipsets support ATA/IDE, PCI, and legacy I/O devices. Table 3.16 provides more information about the South Bridge chips used with Champion and Grand Champion chipsets.

Table 3.16   Champion/Grand Champion South Bridge Chips

South Bridge	Compatible With	ATA/IDE Support	USB	PCI Support	Speed of Connection to North Bridge
OSB4	HE, HE-SL, LE	ATA-33	USB 1.1	32-bit	33MHz/32-bit PCI bus
CSB5	GC-HE, GC-LE, GC-SL, HE, HE-SL, LE	ATA-33	USB 1.1	32-bit	33MHz/32-bit PCI bus (Champion series); Thin IMB at 200MBps (Grand Champion series)
CSB6	GC-HE, GC-LE, GC-SL	ATA-100 with ATA RAID 0, 1, and 5support	USB 1.1	64-bit	Thin IMB at 400Mbps

The I/O bridge chips provide support for PCI-X slots and, in some versions, Gigabit Ethernet. Table 3.17 provides more information about the I/O bridges used by the Champion and Grand Champion chipsets.

Table 3.17   Champion/Grand Champion I/O Bridge Chips

I/O Bridge	Compatible With	PCI-X Support	Gigabit Ethernet Support
CIOB-X	GC-HE	Dual PCI-X 33/66/100MHz	—
CIOB-X2	GC-LE, GC-SL	Dual PCI-X 33/66/100/133MHz	—
CIOB-E	GC-LE, GC-SL	Dual PCI-X 33/66/100/133MHz	Dual GigE Copper
CIOB-ES	GC-LE, GC-SL	Dual PCI-X 33/66/100/133MHz	Dual GigE copper with integrated SerDes[1]
CIOB20	HE, HE-SL	Dual PCI 33/66MHz	—

[1]*Serializer Deserializer (SerDes) interface is used to convert serial to parallel data and vice versa. SerDes (also known as SERDES) interfaces are used as part of many Gigabit Ethernet installations and other high-speed connections.*

The high-end HE and GC-HE chipsets also use memory controller chips to provide support for memory interleaving. Memory interleaving divides memory into banks, permitting memory to be accessed more quickly for improved performance. Table 3.18 provides more information about these chips.

Table 3.18   Champion/Grand Champion Memory Controller Chips

Memory Controller Chip	Chip Name	Compatible With	Features	Configuration
REMC	Reliability Enhanced Memory Controller	GC-HE	Supports two-way and four-way memory interleaving	Four chips in data path; one in address path (provides multiple copies of address and control signals)
MADP	Memory Address Data Path Controller	HE	Supports two-way and four-way memory interleaving	Four chips in a four-way configuration, one chip in a two-way configuration

Other Third-Party Server Chipsets for Intel Processors

Although Intel and ServerWorks are the major producers of server-class chipsets for Intel server processors, they are not the only producers of these chipsets.

Other vendors, including VIA Technologies, IBM, and Hewlett-Packard have also produced server-class chipsets for Intel processors from the Pentium Pro and Pentium II through the Itanium 2. The following sections discuss the offerings from these companies.

VIA Technologies Chipsets for Intel Server Processors

Although VIA Technologies built a variety of chipsets for the P6 family of processors, only the following have been used in one-way and two-way servers:

■ Apollo Pro 133A with VIA 694MP North Bridge (two-way servers) with VIA VT82694X (one-way servers)

■ Apollo Pro 266/266T

Table 3.19 provides an overview of these chipsets.

Table 3.19   VIA Server-Class Chipset for P6 Processors

Feature	Apollo Pro 133A	Apollo Pro 266/266T
Part number	VT82694X or VT82C694MP	VT8633
Bus speed	66, 100, 133MHz	66, 100, 133MHz
Supported processors	Pentium II, III	Pentium III(Tualatin)
Form factor	Slot 1, Socket 370	Socket 370
SMP (dual CPUs)	Yes (with VT82C694MP NB only)	Yes
Memory types	PC66, 100, 133 SDRAM, EDO	PC100, 133 SDRAM, DDR200, 266
Parity/ECC	Yes	No
Maximum memory	4GB	4GB
PCI support	2.2	2.2
PCI speed/ width	33MHz/32-bit	33MHz/32-bit

Table 3.19   Continued

Feature	Apollo Pro 133A	Apollo Pro 266/266T
AGP slot	2x, 4x	2x, 4x
Integrated video	No	No
South Bridge	VT82C596B or VT82C686A	VT8233C[1]

[1]*Supports VIA 4x V-Link 266MHz high-speed interconnect between North Bridge and South Bridge.*

Although some of VIA Technologies Pentium 4–class chipsets are also compatible with the Xeon, litigation has discouraged motherboard makers from adopting them for server-class motherboards.

The VIA Technologies Apollo Pro 133A Chipset

The VIA Apollo Pro133A chipset was a North Bridge/South Bridge chipset designed to support Slot 1 and Socket 370 processors such as the Intel Pentium III, Intel Celeron, and VIA Cyrix III. The Apollo Pro133A is based on the previous Pro133, with additional features added. Note that there are actually two versions of this chipset. The original version was released in fall 1999 and supported single-processor installations and used the VIA 694 North Bridge. In spring 2000, VIA Technologies developed a dual-processor–compatible version using the 694MP North Bridge.

Features of the Apollo Pro133A include the following:

- AGP 4x graphics bus support
- 133/100/66MHz processor bus support
- PC-133 SDRAM memory interface
- UltraATA/66 interface
- Support for four USB 1.1 ports
- AC '97 link for audio and modem
- Hardware monitoring
- Power management

The VIA Apollo Pro133A chipset was a two-chip set consisting of the VT82C694X North Bridge controller (single-CPU version) or VT82C694MP North Bridge controller (dual-CPU version) and a choice of a VT82C596B or VT82C686A South Bridge controller.

Table 3.20 provides an overview of the features of the South Bridge chips used in the Apollo Pro 133A chipset.

Table 3.20   VIA South Bridge Chips Used with Apollo Pro 133A

South Bridge Chip	Number of USB 1.1 Ports	ATA Support	Integrated Sound	Integrated Super I/O
VT82C586A	—	ATA-33	No	No
VT82C596B	4	ATA-66	AC '97	Yes

A number of vendors produced dual-processor server motherboards using the Apollo Pro 133A chipset.

The VIA Technologies Apollo Pro266 Chipset

The VIA Apollo Pro266 is a high-performance North Bridge/South Bridge chipset designed to support Socket 370 processors, including the Pentium III. The Apollo Pro266 was the first chipset from VIA to replace the traditional PCI (133MBps) connection between North Bridge and South Bridge chips with VIA's 4x V-Link interconnect, which runs at 266MBps. The Apollo Pro 266 was introduced in late 2000.

Features of the Apollo Pro266 include the following:

- AGP 2x/4x graphics bus support
- 133/100/66MHz processor bus support
- PC-100/133 SDRAM and PC200/266 DDR SDRAM memory interface
- ATA-100 IDE interface
- Support for six USB 1.1 ports
- Integrated AC '97 six-channel audio
- Integrated MC '97 modem
- Integrated 10/100BASE-T Ethernet and 1/10MHz Home PNA networking
- Hardware monitoring
- ACPI/On Now! power management
- VIA 4x (266MBps) V-Link North Bridge/South Bridge interconnect

The VIA Apollo Pro266 chipset was a two-chip set consisting of the 552-pin BGA VT8633 North Bridge controller and the 376-pin BGA VT8233 South Bridge controller. The Apollo Pro266T is an updated version of this chipset that supports Pentium III Tualatin processors. Figure 3.27 shows the architecture of the Apollo Pro266 chipset.

Because of the V-Link high-speed interconnect between the North Bridge and South Bridge, PCI is managed by the South Bridge. This is similar to the way in which Intel Hub Architecture works, and this basic architecture has been followed by all subsequent VIA chipsets that use V-Link architecture.

The Apollo Pro 266 and 266T (Tualatin-compatible version) chipsets have been used by a variety of vendors to produce both standard ATX form factor and various types of single-board–computer servers using one or two processors.

IBM Chipsets for Intel Server-Class Processors

IBM has produced several chipsets for its own lines of Intel server-class processors:

- **XA-32 (Summit)**—Supports 32-bit Xeon processors.
- **XA-32 second-generation**—Supports 32-bit Xeon processors.
- **XA-64**—Supports Itanium 2 processors.
- **XA-64e (Hurricane)**—Supports 64-bit Xeon processors. The following sections provide details of these chipsets.

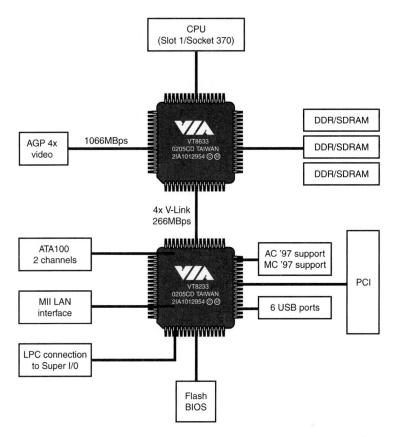

Figure 3.27   Apollo Pro266 chipset architecture.

The XA-32 Chipset for Xeon MP/DP

IBM's XA-32 chipset, codenamed Summit, was first fully implemented in the IBM @server xSeries 440, released in September 2002. This chipset, developed by the IBM Microelectronics Division in Austin, Texas, has the following major features:

- Support for Xeon MP Foster processors for two-way, four-way, or eight-way implementations
- Support for Xeon DP Prestonia processors for two-way or four-way implementations (the XA-32 chipset permits four-way operation with Xeon DP processors, although Intel designed the Xeon DP for single- or two-way operation only)
- Support for memory mirroring, chipkill, and Memory ProteXion features for memory reliability
- Support for 64-bit PCI-X slots at 133MHz, 100MHz, and 66MHz speeds

The components of the XA-32 chipset include the following:

- **The Cyclone memory controller**—Each four-way installation requires a memory controller. The memory controller is located in the SMP expansion module.
- **The Twister processor and cache controller**—Each eight-way installation requires a cache controller. The processor and cache controller is located in the SMP expansion module.

■ **Two Winnipeg PCI bridges**—The PCI bridges are connected to the Cyclone memory controller. Typically, one PCI bridge is used for interfacing to 133MHz and 100MHz PCI-X slots, and the other PCI bridge is used for interfacing to 66MHz PCI-X slots, video, USB, keyboard/mouse, SCSI, Gigabit Ethernet, and other I/O devices, as well as the Remote Expansion I/O (RXE) port. The RXE port connects to the optional RXE-100 enclosure, which supports 12 PCI-X slots.

Figures 3.28 and 3.29 show the major components of the XA-32 chipset in a 4-way (top) and 8-way (bottom) configuration, respectively. Each 8-way configuration is called a *node*, and two nodes can be connected via the SMP expansion ports to create a 16-way processor complex.

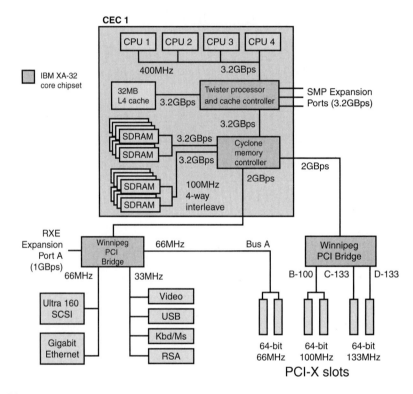

Figure 3.28 Four-way configuration using the IBM XA-32 chipset.

The XA-32 Second-Generation Chipset for Xeon MP/DP

The second generation of the IBM XA-32 chipset is used in IBM xSeries servers such as the x365, x445, and x455. It has the following major differences from the original XA-32:

■ Improved Cyclone memory controller (version 3.0) for lower memory latency than in the original XA-32 chipset.

■ Improved Winnipeg PCI bridges (version 4.0) that support 133MHz PCI-X expansion slots.

■ Support for Gallatin versions of the Xeon MP processor. Gallatin versions of the Xeon MP run at speeds up to 3GHz.

◀◀ See "Xeon Processors," p. 114.

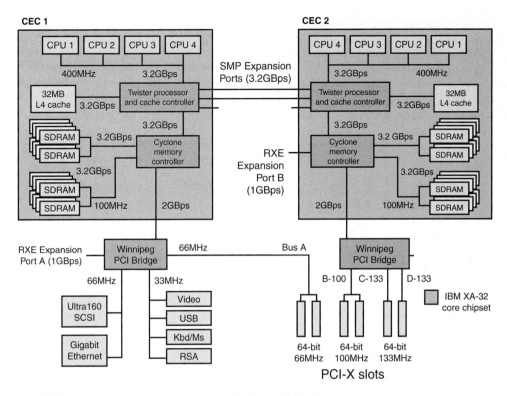

Figure 3.29 Eight-way configurations using the IBM XA-32 chipset.

The block diagram shown in Figure 3.28 applies to both original and second-generation XA-32–based systems.

The XA-64 Chipset for Itanium 2

The IBM XA-64 chipset, codenamed Summit, was first used in the xSeries 450 server released in mid-2003. It was developed by the IBM Microelectronics Division. It has the following major features:

- Support for one to four Itanium 2 Madison processors
- Support for memory mirroring, chipkill, and Memory ProteXion features for memory reliability
- Support for 64-bit PCI-X slots at 133MHz, 100MHz, and 66MHz speeds

The components of the XA-64 chipset include the following:

- **The Cyclone memory controller**—The memory controller is located in the memory-board assembly.
- **The Tornado processor and cache controller**—The processor and cache controller is located in the processor board assembly. It connects to the processors as well as to 64MB of L4 cache, a feature IBM calls XceL4 Server Accelerator Cache.

- **Two Winnipeg PCI bridges**—The PCI bridges are connected to the Cyclone memory controller. Typically, one PCI bridge is used for interfacing to 133MHz and 100MHz PCI-X slots, and the other PCI bridge is used for interfacing to 66MHz PCI-X slots, video, USB, keyboard/mouse, SCSI, Gigabit Ethernet, and other I/O devices, as well as the RXE port. The RXE port connects to the optional RXE-100 enclosure, which supports 12 PCI-X slots.

Figure 3.30 shows the major components of the XA-64 chipset in a four-way configuration.

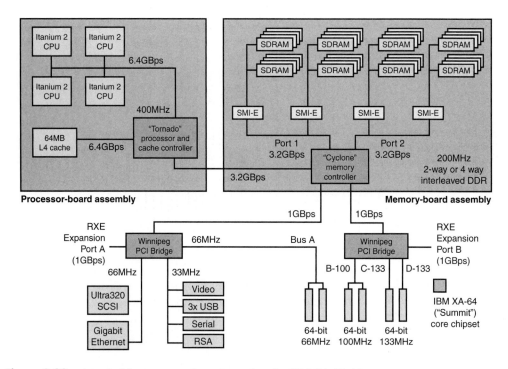

Figure 3.30 A typical four-way configuration using the IBM XA-64 chipset.

The XA-64e Chipset for 64-Bit Xeon Processors

IBM's XA-64e chipset, codenamed Hurricane, is used in Xeon EM64T-compatible IBM @servers such as the xSeries 366. This chipset, developed by the IBM Microelectronics Division in Austin, Texas, has the following major features:

- Support for one to four Xeon MP Cranford processors supporting EM64T (Intel's term for 64-bit extensions to IA-32 architecture)

- Support for memory mirroring (works with hot-swapping), chipkill, and Memory ProteXion features for memory reliability

- Support for memory hot-swapping or hot-adding (hot-adding requires that memory mirroring be disabled)

- Support for 64-bit PCI-X 2.0 Active PCI slots running at 266MHz.

◀◀ See "Xeon MP with EM64T Support," p. 120.

The components of the XA-64e chipset include the following:

- **The Hurricane memory and I/O controller**—The memory controller provides a one-chip interface between the processor(s), memory, and the Winnipeg PCI-X bridge chips. Memory is plugged in to SMI2 memory cards (see Figure 3.31).

- **Two Calgary PCI-X 2.0 bridges**—The PCI bridge chips are connected to the Hurricane memory and I/O controller. Typically, one PCI bridge is used to interface to four of the PCI-X 2.0 slots, and the other PCI bridge is used for interfacing to two PCI-X 2.0 slots, video, USB 2.0 ports, RAID, Gigabit Ethernet, and South Bridge chips. PCI-X 2.0 slots run at speeds up to 266MHz.

Figure 3.31 shows the major components of the XA-64e chipset in a four-way configuration.

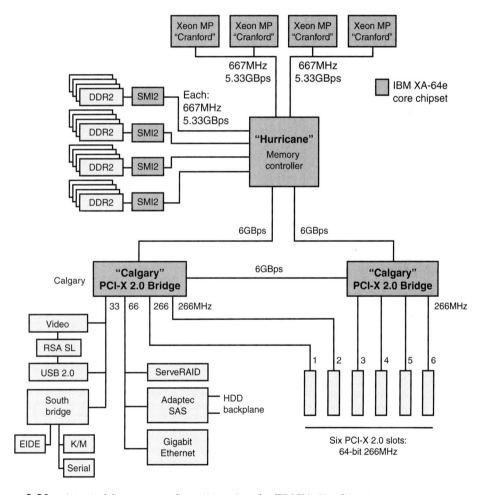

Figure 3.31 A typical four-way configuration using the IBM XA-64e chipset.

Hewlett-Packard Server Chipsets for Intel Processors

In addition to using server chipsets from third-party vendors, Hewlett-Packard has developed two distinct lines of chipsets for its servers:

■ The F8 (an improved version of the Corollary/Compaq Profusion chipset) supports Xeon MP processors.

■ The zx1 is the first of a line of chipsets that support PA-RISC or Itanium-family–equipped Hewlett-Packard servers in the Superdome (originally Half Dome) family.

The following sections discuss the major features of these chipsets.

The F8 Chipset for Xeon MP

The Hewlett-Packard F8 chipset was developed by Compaq as a follow-on to the eight-way Corollary chipset co-developed by Corollary and Compaq. Hewlett-Packard obtained the F8 chipset as part of its merger with Compaq. The F8 chipset is used in the Hewlett-Packard ProLinea DL740 and DL760-series eight-way servers.

The F8 chipset's major features include the following:

■ Support for eight Xeon MP processors

■ Dual-channel memory supporting PC133 SDRAM

■ Support for PCI and PCI-X expansion slots

■ Hot-plug RAID memory

■ Up to 64GB of addressable memory

The F8 chipset has the following major components:

■ **Five F8 dual memory controllers**—Four are used for data and one is used to store parity information. Each is connected to a memory cartridge containing up to eight DIMMs of dual-channel PC133 SDRAM using cache-line interleaving for better performance. Memory can be hot-plugged (in or out) without shutting down the server, and the memory controllers can correct single-bit and double-bit memory errors as well as correct DIMM failures.

■ **One F8 crossbar switch**—The crossbar switch handles traffic running at 400 megatransfers per second between the memory controllers, processors, and the PCI bridges. It uses multiple buffers and 128 cache lines to manage eight-way traffic.

■ **One F8 cache coherence filter**—A cache coherence filter connected to the crossbar switch prevents unnecessary traffic between L2 caches in different processors.

■ **Up to four PCI-X bridges with PCI hot-plug controllers**—Each bridge supports two 64-bit PCI-X bus segments, and each segment can be configure to run in 33/66MHz PCI mode or 66/100MHz PCI-X mode.

Figure 3.32 illustrates the major components of the F8 chipset.

The zx1 Chipset for Itanium 2 McKinley

The Hewlett-Packard zx1 Pluto chipset for the Itanium 2 processor uses only two or three chips, making it the simplest chipset available for the Itanium 2 processor. However, although the zx1 is designed to work in one-way and two-way workstation configurations as well as in two-way and four-way server applications, it does not support eight-way implementations.

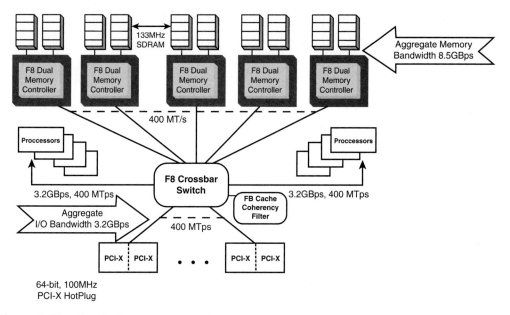

Figure 3.32   The F8 chipset supports eight-way Xeon MP processors.

Note

The Hewlett-Packard zx1 also supports some PA-RISC processors made by Hewlett-Packard. In fact, some Hewlett-Packard servers can be converted from one processor type to the other.

The Hewlett-Packard zx1 chipset has the following components in two-way configurations:

- **Hewlett-Packard chipset and memory I/O controller**—This chip connects memory and processors to each other. This is designed for DDR SDRAM memory, unlike the E8870, which uses translator hubs.

- **Hewlett-Packard chipset I/O adapter**—This chip can be used as a bridge to an AGP 4x slot for workstation uses, PCI-X slots up to 133MHz, and for various types of I/O, including ATA/IDE, USB, SCSI, and networking.

When used in a four-way server implementation, two Hewlett-Packard zx1 scalable memory adapter chips are added to the chipset to connect the greater number of memory banks supported, and additional Hewlett-Packard Chipset I/O adapters are used to support additional 66MHz PCI-X devices. Some of Hewlett-Packard's latest servers based on the zx1 incorporate two Itanium 2 processors in the mx2 dual processor module, enabling the chipset to support eight-way implementations.

Figure 3.33 illustrates a typical two-way (workstation/server) implementation of the zx1 chipset, and Figure 3.34 shows a typical four-way server implementation.

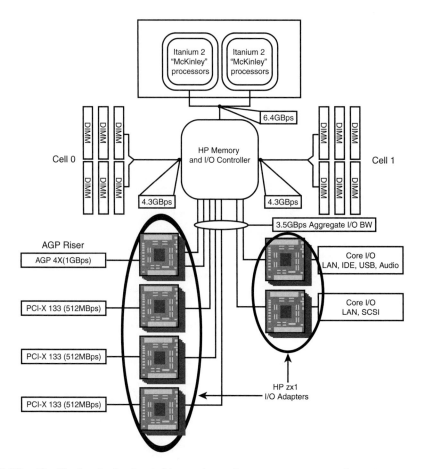

Figure 3.33 The Hewlett-Packard zx1 chipset, shown here in a two-way configuration, uses two or three chips, depending upon the number of processors supported.

The sx1000 Pinnacles Chipset

The Hewlett-Packard Super-Scalable Processor chipset sx1000, codenamed Pinnacles, supports eight-way or higher implementations. Like the zx1, it can use single- or dual-processor cartridges. However, compared to other Itanium 2 chipsets, it has several distinct features:

■ The sx1000 uses a cell architecture: Each cell comprises a cell controller chip and eight memory buffer chips. Each cell can contain four CPU modules and up to 32 PC133 registered SDRAM modules. The cell controller chip connects directly to the PCI-X system bus adapter, which connects to PCI-X bridge chips. See Figure 3.35.

■ sx1000-based servers include 2, 4, 8, or 16 cells. (Each cell includes four or eight processors, depending on whether single- or dual-processor cartridges are used; see Figure 3.36.)

■ When four or more cells are connected together, one or more crossbar switches are used. One crossbar switch is used for each group of four cells (16 processor sockets). For example, in a 64-socket system, four crossbar switches would be used.

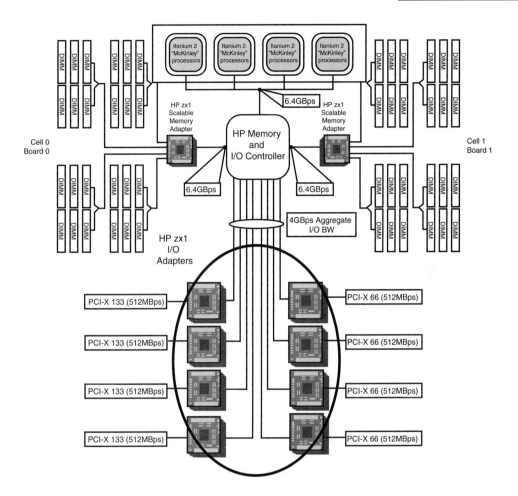

Figure 3.34   A four-way configuration of the Hewlett-Packard zx1 chipset.

Note

Hewlett-Packard uses the term *cell* to refer to a component that contains processors, control chips, and memory modules in an easily swappable package. The cell architecture design used by servers such as the sx1000 permits the server to be upgraded from a RISC-based processor such as the PA-8700 to the Intel Itanium 2 by swapping cells.

Figure 3.35 illustrates the block diagram of a four-way or eight-way sx1000 cell board. A four-way cell board uses four standard Itanium 2 processors, while an eight-way cell board uses four Hewlett-Packard mx2 processor cartridges, each of which contains two Itanium 2 processors along with 32MB L4 memory cache.

Figure 3.36 illustrates the block diagram of an mx2 processor cartridge.

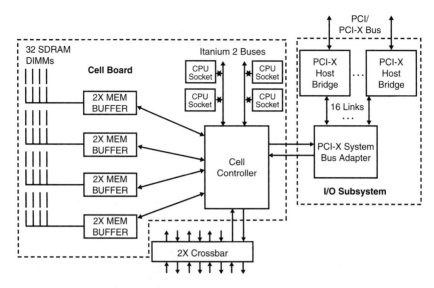

Figure 3.35   The block diagram of a cell board from a Hewlett-Packard sx1000 chipset.

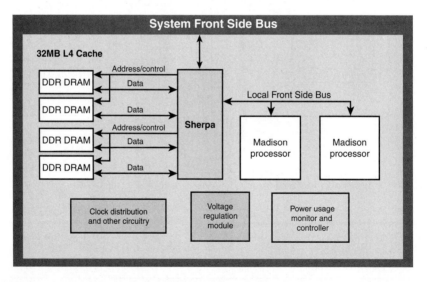

Figure 3.36   The block diagram of an mx2 processor cartridge.

The sx1000 is designed to be highly scalable to handle server tasks of virtually any size and complexity.

AMD Athlon MP and Opteron Server-Class Chipsets

The original AMD Athlon Slot A processor was not commonly used in servers for two reasons:

- It was never certified for SMP (dual-processor) operation
- There were no dual-processor chipsets that supported the processor.

However, after the Athlon design was shifted to Socket 462 (also known as Socket A), AMD developed an SMP-compatible version of the processor known as the Athlon MP. This processor was supported by AMD's AMD-760MP chipset, which was the first major chipset on the market to support DDR SDRAM memory.

However, development of server-class chipsets for AMD processors didn't become widespread until the development of the AMD Opteron, the first 64-bit processor capable of also running existing 32-bit IA-32 applications at full speed. Both AMD and third-party chipmakers have developed a number of chipsets for the Opteron. Unlike the most powerful chipsets made for Intel processors, which are almost always limited to preconfigured servers from major vendors, motherboards built for Opteron processors are widely available for "build-your-own" server builders.

The following sections discuss the various server-class chipsets available for AMD processors in greater detail.

The AMD-760 Family of Chipsets

The AMD-760 chipset, introduced in October 2000, is notable as the first chipset to support DDR SDRAM memory. The AMD-760 chipset consists of the AMD-761 system controller (North Bridge) in a 569-pin plastic ball-grid array (PBGA) package and the AMD-766 peripheral bus controller (South Bridge) in a 272-pin PBGA package.

The AMD-761 North Bridge features the AMD Athlon system bus, DDR-SDRAM system memory controller with support for either PC1600 or PC2100 memory, AGP 4x controller, and PCI bus controller. The 761 allows for 200MHz or 266MHz processor bus operation and supports the newer Athlon chips that use the 266MHz processor bus (also called the FSB).

The AMD-766 South Bridge includes a USB controller, dual UDMA/100 ATA/IDE interfaces, and the LPC bus for interfacing newer Super I/O and ROM BIOS components.

The AMD-760 chipset includes the following features:

- AMD Athlon 200/266MHz processor bus
- Dual-processor support
- PCI 2.2 bus with up to six masters
- AGP 2.0 interface that supports 4x mode
- PC1600 or PC2100 DDR SDRAM with ECC
- Support for a maximum of 2GB buffered or 4GB registered DDR SDRAM
- ACPI power management
- ATA-100 support
- USB controller
- LPC bus for Super I/O support

The AMD-760MP chipset, which uses the AMD-762 North Bridge chip, is a development of the basic AMD-760 design that supports dual-processor Athlon MP systems. It differs from the standard 760 chipset in the following ways:

- Supports dual AMD Athlon MP processors with 200/266MHz processor bus speeds
- Supports up to 4GB PC2100 DDR (registered modules)
- Supports 33MHz PCI slots in 32-bit and 64-bit widths

The AMD-760MPX chipset uses the same AMD-762 North Bridge chip as the AMD-760MP to support multiple Athlon MP processors, but it uses the AMD-768 peripheral bus controller (South Bridge) chip. It differs from the 760MP chipset in the following ways:

- The AMD-762 North Bridge chip is used to support two 66MHz 32/64-bit PCI slots.
- The AMD-768 South Bridge chip is used to support 33MHz/32-bit PCI slots.

The 760MPX chipset is a better choice for a server because of its support for 66MHz and 64-bit PCI slots, whereas the 760MP is a suitable choice for a workstation.

Figure 3.37 illustrates the 760MPX's architecture.

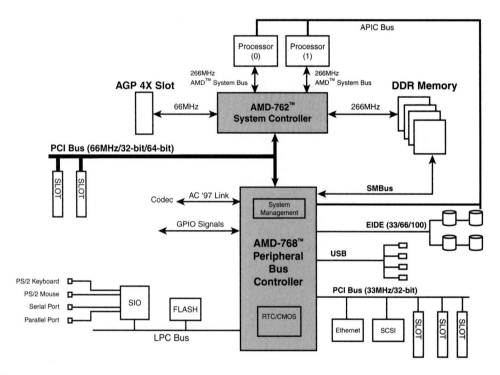

Figure 3.37   AMD-760MPX chipset block diagram.

The 760MP and 760MPX chipsets continue to be popular choices for AMD-based workstations and servers that use the Athlon MP processor.

AMD Opteron Chipsets

The AMD Opteron is unique among x86-compatible server processors in having an integrated memory controller. Servers based on the Opteron can be scaled from single-processor to eight-way servers without ever needing any type of specialized memory controller or cache coherence controller. The integrated memory controller in the Opteron supports registered DDR memory, including ECC memory. By integrating the memory controller in the processor, AMD has made it possible for chipset vendors to produce simpler chipsets for Opteron than for earlier AMD-based or Intel-based servers.

The Opteron also features a HyperTransport bus between components. HyperTransport is a high-speed point-to-point interface somewhat similar to the Intel Hub Architecture discussed earlier in this chapter.

◀◀   See "HyperTransport," p. 155.

Because the Opteron contains integrated memory controllers, it's possible to build a server that contains only an ICH (South Bridge) chip in its chipset. Also, the use of HyperTransport interconnects enables chips from different vendors to be combined in a variety of ways to create a specific motherboard design. Therefore, Table 3.21 is broken down into chipset component categories. For additional details, see the sections that follow Table 3.21.

An Opteron-based system can combine various brands of chips together into a customized solution. For example, a server can use the NVIDIA nForce Professional 2200 along with an AMD 8131 or 8132 PCI-X bridge to support PCI-Express, PCI-X, and PCI cards.

Depending upon the features of a system I/O controller, it can be used by itself to create a motherboard. For example, the nForce Professional 2200, the AMD 8111, or the ServerWorks HT1000 can be used to provide disk, legacy ports, and PCI support.

This ability to mix and match chipset products from various vendors is not exactly new. Vendors such as ULi (formerly Acer Labs) have long produced South Bridge chips compatible with various vendors' North Bridge chips. However, because of the combination of a common industry standard (HyperTransport) for chip interconnects and the location of the memory controllers in the Opteron processors, Opteron-based systems provide unparalleled flexibility in motherboard chipset design. The AMD-8000, nForce Professional, and ServerWorks HT-2000/HT-1000 chipsets are all popular choices for Opteron-based servers and server motherboards.

The AMD 8000 Chipset

The AMD 8000 is AMD's first chipset designed for the Athlon 64 and Opteron families. Its architecture is substantially different from the North Bridge/South Bridge or hub-based architectures we are familiar with from the chipsets designed to support Pentium II/III/4/Celeron and AMD Athlon/Athlon XP/Duron processors.

The AMD-8000 chipset is sometimes referred to as the AMD-8151 because the AMD-8151 provides the connection between the Athlon 64 or Opteron processor and the AGP video slot, the task normally performed by the North Bridge or MCH hub in other chipsets. The name of the North Bridge or MCH hub chip is usually applied to the chipset. However, AMD refers to the AMD-8151 chip as the AGP Graphics tunnel chip because its only task is to provide a high-speed connection to the AGP slot on the motherboard. Consequently, the AMD-8151 is usually not used on Opteron motherboards used for servers. The other components of the AMD-8000 chipset include the AMD-8111 HyperTransport I/O hub (South Bridge), the AMD-8131 PCI-X tunnel chip, and the AMD-8132 PCI-X 2.0 tunnel chip.

The AMD-8151 AGP Graphics tunnel chip has the following major features:

■ Support for AGP 2.0/3.0 (AGP 1x–8x) graphics cards

■ 16-bit up/down HyperTransport connection to the processor

■ 8-bit up/down HyperTransport connection to downstream chips

Table 3.21 Chipset Logic for Opteron Server Platforms

Chip Model	Category	AGP Video	PCI-Express	PCI-X Bridge	PCI-X 2.0 Bridge	USB 2.0 Ports
AMD						
8151	AGP 3.0 Tunnel	8x	—	—	—	—
8131	PCI-X Tunnel	—	—	Yes	—	—
8132	PCI-X 2.0 Tunnel	—	—	—	Yes	—
8111	I/O Hub (South Bridge)	—	—	—	—	6 ports
NVIDIA						
nForce Professional 2200	Single-chip chipset	—	20 lanes	—	—	10 ports
nForce Professional 2050	Single-chip chipset	—	x16, x1, x1, x1, x1	—	—	—
ServerWorks (Broadcom)						
HT2000	System I/O Controller	—	17 lanes (up to four controllers)	Yes	—	— (two ports)
HT1000	System I/O Controller	—	—	Yes	—	4 ports

The AMD-8111 HyperTransport I/O hub (South Bridge) chip's major features include the following:

- PCI 2.2–compliant PCI bus (32-bit, 33MHz) for up to eight devices
- AC '97 2.2 audio (six-channel)
- Six USB 1.1/2.0 ports (three controllers)
- Two ATA/IDE host adapters supporting up to ATA-133 speeds
- RTC
- LPC bus
- Integrated 10/100 Ethernet
- 8-bit up/down HyperTransport connection to upstream chips

The AMD-8131 HyperTransport PCI-X tunnel chip's major features include the following:

- Two PCI-X bridges (A & B) supporting up to five PCI bus masters each
- PCI-X transfer rates up to 133MHz
- PCI 2.2 33MHz and 66MHz transfer rates
- Independent operational modes and transfer rates for each bridge
- 8-bit up/down HyperTransport connection to upstream and downstream chips

The newest member of the AMD 8000 chipset family, the AMD-8132 PCI-X 2.0 tunnel chip, offers PCI-X 2.0 transfer rates up to 266MHz. Other features are similar to those of the AMD-8131.

Figure 3.38 shows the architecture of the AMD 8000 chipset in a typical two-way server implementation.

Ethernet	ATA/SATA	RAID Levels	Audio Support	PCI Support
—	—	—	—	—
—	—	—	—	Yes
—	—	—	—	Yes
10/100	ATA-133	—	AC '97 6-channel	Yes
10/100/1000	ATA-133, SATA-300	RAID 0, 1, 0+1 (can span ATA and SATA)	AC '97 8-channel HDA	Yes
10/100/1000	ATA-133, SATA-300	RAID 0, 1, 0+1	—	—
10/100/1000	—	—	—	—
—	ATA-100, SATA-50	RAID 0, 1, 0+1, 5	—	Yes

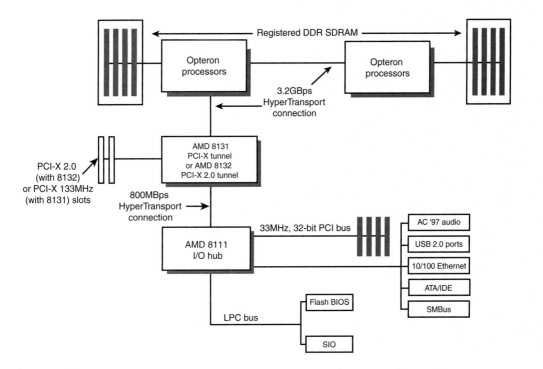

Figure 3.38   Block diagram of the AMD 8000 chipset in a typical server implementation.

The NVIDIA nForce Professional 2000 Series of Chipsets

NVIDIA is no stranger to the AMD Opteron and AMD Athlon 64 processors: Its nForce 3–series chipsets for the AMD Athlon 64 are among the most popular and best-performing chipsets available. However, NVIDIA did not release its first chipsets optimized for Opteron-based servers, the nForce Professional 2000 series, until January 2005.

Like other recent nForce chipsets, the nForce Professional chipsets feature a highly integrated single-chip design. The initial offerings include the following:

- nForce Professional 2200
- nForce Professional 2050

Both chipsets feature the following:

- HyperTransport connections to Opteron processors and other components
- PCI-Express
- SATA RAID 0, 1, and 0+1
- Native Gigabit Ethernet with hardware firewall
- Support for up to eight-way or higher implementations
- Support for dual-core Opteron processors
- Second-generation SATA (3GBps)

The 2200 also features support for up to 10 USB 2.0 ports, 20 flexible PCI-Express lanes, 8-channel AC '97 audio, ATA-133, and a 33MHz, 32-bit PCI interface. The 2200's implementation of RAID can include both SATA and ATA/IDE drives in the same array. The 2050 lacks USB, PCI, and ATA-133 support; supports an x16 PCI-Express slot and four x1 slots; and does not have onboard audio.

Although neither the 2200 nor 2050 chipsets support PCI-X slots natively, they support connections to other Opteron-compatible chipset components via HyperTransport. As a result, some vendors have combined the AMD 8131 or 8132 chips with the 2200 or 2050 chips to produce systems with PCI-X support.

The ServerWorks HT Series of Chipsets

Broadcom's ServerWorks division released its first logic chips for Opteron systems, the HT-2000 and HT-1000, in April 2005. The HT-2000 I/O controller combines support for two PCI-X slots or integrated devices, a two-port Gigabit Ethernet controller, and 17-lane PCI-Express support (with up to four PCIe controllers) in a single chip. The HT-2000 provides 16x HyperTransport upstream connections at up to 2GHz to the host and 8x HyperTransport downstream connections at up to 1.6GHz to the HT-1000 I/O controller or other chips. A single HT-2000 chip supports up to two Opteron processors. A four-way platform uses two HT-2000 chips, and an eight-way platform uses four HT-2000 chips. With any number of HT-2000, a single HT-1000 I/O controller is used to provide support for other components.

The companion HT-1000 controller supports two PCI-X slots, as well as 32-bit PCI slots; USB 2.0 ports; one ATA/IDE and up to four SATA drives; SATA RAID levels 0, 1, 0+1, and 5; and an LPC bus. Because of its versatile design, the HT-1000 I/O controller can also be used by itself for entry-level two-way servers, providing an 8x HyperTransport connection to the host.

Figure 3.39 illustrates an advanced two-way configuration using the HT-2000 and HT-1000 and a basic two-way configuration using the HT-1000 by itself.

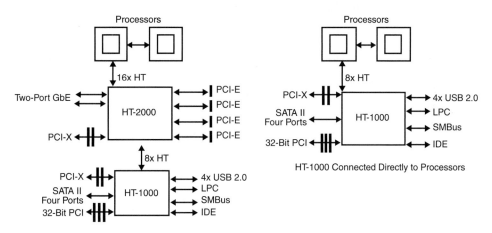

Figure 3.39 Block diagram of the ServerWorks HT-2000/HT-1000 chipset in typical advanced (left) and basic (right) two-way server implementations.

Determining Hardware Compatibility with Server Platforms

Before you purchase or build a new server or upgrade an existing server, it's very important that you determine whether the server is compatible with both of the following:

- The onboard or external hardware you need to use with that server
- The operating system you are using (or intend to use) with that server

The following sections describe how you can best determine this information.

Determining Operating System Compatibility

If you are buying a new server or building one from scratch (a very real possibility today, especially if you want to create a single-processor to four-way server), you need to verify the compatibility of your server or server motherboard with the operating system you plan to use with it.

If you are purchasing an already-built server, this is relatively simple. Server vendors usually offer a variety of preconfigured systems that include validated operating systems. However, if you are planning to build your own server from scratch or by upgrading an existing system, you need to be more careful. The following sections describe methods and resources you can use to determine that your hardware is ready to run the server operating system of your choice.

▶▶ See "Server NOSs," p. 758.

Determining Windows Compatibility

Windows Server 2003 is the "king of the hill" in server operating systems today. Most vendors of server-class hardware from motherboards to PCI-X cards list Windows Server 2003 compatibility on their websites. You can also verify compatibility for specific hardware with the Windows Server Catalog. You can click the link available at the "Products Designed for Microsoft Windows—Windows Catalog and HCL" page at www.microsoft.com/whdc/hcl/default.mspx to check compatibility with Windows Server 2003 and Windows 2000 Server.

If you need drivers for existing hardware, you should make sure you understand what version of Windows Server 2003 you need drivers for:

- The standard 32-bit versions of Windows Server 2003 use the same drivers as Windows XP Professional.

- The x64 edition designed for Intel EM64T and AMD Opteron processors requires specially written 64-bit drivers.

- Itanium 2–based servers use the 64-bit edition of Windows Server 2003; this uses different 64-bit drivers than the x64 edition.

Determining Linux Compatibility

Many hardware vendors now provide drivers for various versions or distributions of Linux on their websites. However, you should first visit the Linux distribution vendor's website to consult the latest catalog of certified and compatible hardware.

In some cases, you might need to use an open-source driver for certain hardware. You should be sure to note where the driver came from and check for updates.

Determining Sun Solaris Compatibility

Sun maintains a list of compatible hardware for Sun Solaris 9 and 10 on its website. You can search the Sun Solaris hardware compatibility list at www.microsoft.com/whdc/hcl/default.mspx.

If you need a driver for a particular device, you should follow the link provided. The compatibility notes list any problems with the driver.

Integration with Bus Types

Generally, current server operating systems can be used with the most common bus types on the market, including PCI, USB, PCI-X, PCI-Express, and AGP. As with any other computer hardware item, driver support is necessary before a particular bus or component will work.

If you are coming from a desktop computer background, you have probably noticed that some server chipsets use older ICH or South Bridge chips than their desktop counterparts and that many of them use older and slower memory types than those found in the latest desktop computers. The most likely reason for this is to assure stability. Although desktop users can accept a certain amount of instability in return for better performance, servers must be stable, even if it means using "last year's" chipset component.

Conclusions, Troubleshooting, and Documentation

Choosing the right server platform for your project is essential to achieving a server solution that will be satisfactory today and will be able to grow with your needs. Here are some methods that will help you avoid problems and diagnose them when they appear:

- **Gather system and chipset-specific documentation for your platform.** You can find countless pages of documentation from chipset and system vendors, most of it available online in HTML or PDF format. You should download as much of this information as possible and order anything not available electronically in paper or CD-ROM format.

- **Familiarize yourself with the features and limitations of your server platform.** The chipset *is* the server! If the chipset isn't designed to work with a particular type of memory or with a particular processor type, you must do without that particular change or consider an upgrade.

- **Use the troubleshooting and technical resources provided by the operating system and hardware vendors.** Some vendors provide downloadable programs that can be used to check compatibility or perform tests on components.

- **Keep your information up-to-date.** Don't forget to download specification updates for your system and chipset.

- **If you use a search engine to locate solutions, there are a couple ways you can save your information for easier access.** You can use the Save as PDF option in Adobe Acrobat 5.0 or greater to create a PDF (Acrobat Reader) version of a web page. With Internet Explorer, you can choose Save as Web Archive to save all the contents of a web page in a single file.

CHAPTER 4

Server Motherboards and BIOS

Without a doubt, the most important component in a PC server is the main board or motherboard. Some companies refer to the motherboard as a system board or planar. (The terms *motherboard, main board, system board*, and *planar* are interchangeable.) This chapter examines the various types of motherboards available for servers and those components typically contained on the motherboard and motherboard interface connectors.

Motherboard Types and Form Factors

Several common form factors are used for server motherboards. The *form factor* refers to the physical dimensions (size and shape) as well as certain connector, screw holes, and other positions that dictate into which type of case the board will fit. Some are true standards (meaning that all boards with that form factor are interchangeable), whereas others are not standardized enough to allow for interchangeability. Unfortunately, these nonstandard form factors preclude any easy upgrade or inexpensive replacement, which generally means they should be avoided. The most commonly known obsolete motherboard form factors used for servers include the following:

- Baby-AT
- Full-size AT
- WTX

The most commonly known current and emerging motherboard form factors used for servers include the following, listed according to form factor type:

Small form factor:

- SSI TEB (Thin Electronics Bay)
- microATX (AT Extended)
- microBTX (Balanced Technology Extended)

Tower and pedestal:

- microATX
- microBTX
- ATX
- Extended ATX
- BTX
- SSI CEB (Compact Electronics Bay)
- SSI EEB (Entry-Level Electronics Bay)
- SSI MEB (Midrange Electronics Bay)
- Proprietary designs (large x86-based; Itanium and RISC-based designs)

Rack-mounted:

- PICMG (PCI Industrial Computer Manufacturers Group)
- SSI CEB
- SSI TEB
- Blade servers

Note that some form factors fall into more than one category.

Before 1996, low-cost servers that used industry-standard form factors typically used motherboards based on the Baby-AT form factor, a reduced-size version of the AT motherboard used in the IBM AT PC introduced in 1984. Starting in 1996, standards-based server motherboards began to use the ATX form factor, the larger extended ATX, or, in rare instances, the reduced-size microATX design. Starting in 2005, servers based on the BTX form factor were introduced. BTX is an evolutionary development of ATX that provides for better thermal management of high-performance systems.

Although ATX and extended ATX are the most common server platforms for low-cost entry-level servers, starting in the late 1990s, Intel, in cooperation with Dell, IBM, and Silicon Graphics (SGI), developed a series of form factors especially designed for servers. These form factors are known collectively as Server System Infrastructure (SSI), and they support small form factor, pedestal, and rack-mounted servers. SSI form factors are used widely in entry-level servers based on x86 processors.

Other server form factors considered in this chapter include the PICMG family of standards, which are used primarily in specialized industries such as telecommunications, blade servers, and various proprietary designs used for high-capacity rack-mounted and pedestal servers. Although there are no de facto or official standards for blade servers, blade server designs represent a significant development in server architecture.

Some server form factors developed since the replacement of Baby-AT by newer designs have already been superseded. The SSI MEB form factor was designed to support up to four-way slot-mounted processors such as the Pentium III Xeon. With the development of more compact socketed processors, most vendors no longer use SSI MEB in its original form. Although some vendors use motherboards that have the same dimensions as SSI MEB, the motherboards are now designed for up to eight-way socketed server processors, such as the AMD Opteron. WTX was designed for workstations and medium-duty servers but never became popular. WTX motherboards today actually fit in Extended ATX cases.

Because most x86-based servers on the market today use one of the industry-standard form factors listed in this section, you can upgrade such servers by replacing the motherboard. You can replace an ATX motherboard with a more advanced ATX motherboard, an SSI EEB motherboard with a more advanced SSI EEB motherboard, and so forth. As long as the chassis and power supply provide the necessary thermal and power requirements for the new processors and memory installed on the new motherboard, you can create a like-new server as an alternative to purchasing a brand-new server platform. If you are building your own server, you need to make sure you use an industry-standard form factor. (Each of these form factors is discussed in more detail in the following sections.)

Form factors affect how much internal hardware a server can contain, and, in some cases, whether or how easily a server can be rack-mounted. Generally, servers based on SSI, PICMG, or blade server form factors are designed for or can be converted to rack-mounted form factors.

Tip

If you are planning to switch from a pedestal to a rack-mounted server in the next 24 months or less, purchase a pedestal server that can be converted to a rack-mounted server. Many vendors make pedestal servers or chassis that also support rack-mounting.

Anything that does not fit into one of the industry-standard form factors should be considered proprietary. Although it is possible to build up to an eight-way server by using off-the-shelf server components, the reality is that many four-way and larger servers are proprietary. If you need an eight-way or larger server, you should evaluate the vendor-provided upgrade paths available if you plan to use the server long enough to need a new generation of memory or processor options. Also, you should determine how spare parts are provided. Can you obtain them from more than one source, or must you use the vendor's own service department? These considerations will help you find the best fit in terms of serviceability and long life for a server you cannot upgrade with standard components.

ATX Motherboards

Although some vendors built servers based on the original IBM XT and AT motherboard form factors (AT and Baby-AT) from the 1980s through the mid-1990s, all servers using these form factors are long obsolete, and most of them have been replaced. Thus, the first form factor we consider in detail is the ATX form factor.

Intel initially released the official ATX specification in July 1995. It was written as an open specification for the industry. ATX boards didn't hit the market in force until mid-1996, when they rapidly began replacing Baby-AT boards in new systems. The ATX specification was updated to version 2.01 in February 1997, 2.03 in May 2000, 2.1 in June 2002, and 2.2 in February 2004. Intel publishes these detailed specifications so other manufacturers can use the interchangeable ATX design in their systems. The current specifications for ATX and other current motherboard types are available online from the Desktop Form Factors site: www.formfactors.org. ATX is the most popular motherboard form factor for new entry-level and midrange servers through at least 2006. An ATX system will be upgradable for many years to come, exactly as Baby-AT was in the past.

Note

Although many major server OEMs build machines that appear to meet the ATX form factor specifications, they may use proprietary cases or power supply designs to limit your upgrade options. If you want maximum flexibility, consider building your own server, based on ATX or SSI form factors.

The major features of an ATX motherboard include the following:

- **Built-in double high external I/O connector panel**—The rear portion of the motherboard includes a stacked I/O connector area that is 6.25 inches wide by 1.75 inches tall. This enables external connectors to be located directly on the board and negates the need for cables running from internal connectors to the back of the case as with Baby-AT designs.

- **Single main keyed internal power supply connector**—Most versions of ATX use a keyed 20-pin connector. However, some recent systems now use a 24-pin version of this connector. (Some high-end power supplies can be used with either motherboard connection.) Some systems use additional connectors.

▶▶ See "Power Supplies and Connectors," p. 247.

- **Relocated CPU and memory (compared to Baby AT)**—The CPU and memory are located next to the power supply, which is where the primary system fan is located. There is room for a CPU and a heatsink and fan combination of up to 2.8 inches in height, as well as more than adequate side clearance provided in that area.

About Cooling

Virtually any server today requires more cooling than the fan in the power supply can provide. This could come in the form of a secondary case-mounted fan or an active heatsink on the processor with an integral fan.

Intel and AMD supply processors with attached high-quality (ball bearing) fans for CPUs sold to smaller vendors. These are so-called boxed processors because they are sold in single-unit box quantities instead of cases of 100 or more, like the raw CPUs sold to the larger vendors. Boxed CPUs include active heatsinks to ensure proper cooling. They are the best choice if you are building your own server because of the long warranty coverage and because the active heatsink helps ensure proper cooling.

When they put high-quality fans on these boxed processors, Intel and AMD can put a warranty on the boxed processors that is independent of the system warranty. Larger vendors have the engineering talent to select the proper passive heatsink, thus reducing the cost of the system as well as increasing reliability. With an OEM non-boxed processor, the warranty is with the system vendor and not the processor manufacturer directly.

Heatsink mounting instructions are usually included with a motherboard if non-boxed processors are used. Servers that use proprietary processor cards or cartridges might combine a passive heatsink with a high-performance fan and duct system for cooling.

- **Relocated internal I/O connectors**—The internal I/O connectors for the floppy and hard disk drives are relocated to be near the drive bays and out from under the expansion board slot and drive bay areas. Therefore, internal cables to the drives can be much shorter, and accessing the connectors does not require card or drive removal.

- **Improved cooling**—The CPU and main memory are designed and positioned to improve overall system cooling. However, most servers require additional cooling fans for the CPU and chassis. Note that the ATX specification originally specified that the ATX power supply fan blows into the system chassis instead of outward. This reverse flow, or positive pressure design, pressurizes the case and minimizes dust and dirt intrusion. Later, the ATX specification was revised to allow the more normal standard flow, which negatively pressurizes the case by having the fan blow outward. Because the specification technically allows either type of airflow, and because some overall cooling efficiency is lost with the reverse flow design, most power supply manufacturers provide ATX power supplies with fans that exhaust air from the system, otherwise called a negative pressure design. See Chapter 15, "Chassis," for more detailed information.

Figure 4.1 shows the ATX system layout and chassis features of a typical entry-level server, as you would see them looking sideways in a tower with the side panel removed. Notice how virtually the entire motherboard is clear of the drive bays and how the devices such as CPU, memory, and internal drive connectors are easy to access and do not interfere with the bus slots. Also notice how the processor is positioned near the power supply.

The ATX motherboard shape is basically a Baby-AT design rotated sideways 90°. Compared to a Baby-AT design, the expansion slots are now parallel to the shorter side dimension and do not interfere with the CPU, memory, or I/O connector sockets (see Figure 4.2). There are actually two basic sizes used by ATX-based servers:

- A full-size ATX board is 12 inches wide by 9.6 inches deep (305mm×244mm). See Figure 4.2.
- An Extended ATX board is 12 inches wide by 13.05 inches deep (305mm×332mm).

MiniATX was once an official specification, but starting with ATX 2.1, it was dropped. Extended ATX was never part of the official ATX specification. Because it is substantially deeper than either ATX or MiniATX, an Extended ATX motherboard will not fit in some of the smaller ATX cases. Be sure to check with the case vendor if you are building a server based on an Extended ATX board or if you are upgrading an existing server.

Although the case holes are similar to those in the Baby-AT case, cases for Baby-AT and ATX are generally incompatible. The ATX power supply design is identical in physical size to the standard slimline power supply used with Baby-AT systems; however, they also use different connectors and supply different voltages.

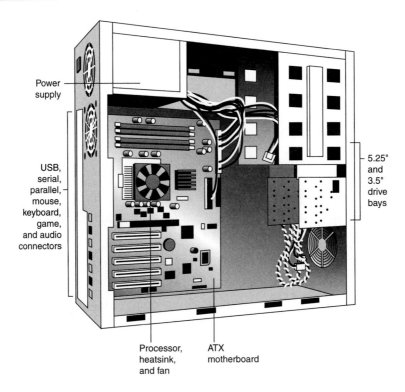

Power supply

USB,
serial,
parallel,
mouse,
keyboard,
game,
and audio
connectors

5.25"
and
3.5"
drive
bays

Processor,
heatsink,
and fan

ATX
motherboard

Figure 4.1   When mounted inside the case, the ATX motherboard is oriented so that the CPU socket is near the power supply fan and case fan (if the case includes one).

If you are considering replacing the motherboard in an existing server, the best way to tell if it has an ATX-family motherboard design without removing the lid is to look at the back of the system. Two distinguishing features identify ATX. One is that the expansion boards plug directly in to the motherboard. There is usually no riser card, as with LPX or NLX form factors, so the slots are perpendicular to the plane of the motherboard. Also, ATX boards have a unique double-high connector area for all the built-in connectors on the motherboard (see Figure 4.3 and Table 4.1). This is located just to the side of the bus slot area and can be used to easily identify an ATX board.

Table 4.1   Built-in Ports Usually Found on ATX Server Motherboards[1]

Port Description	Connector Type	PC99 Connector Color
PS/2 mouse port	6-pin mini-DIN	Green
PS/2 keyboard port	6-pin mini-DIN	Purple
USB ports	Dual Stack USB	Black
Parallel port	25-pin D-submini	Burgundy
Serial port	9-pin D-submini	Teal
VGA analog video port	15-pin HD D-submini	Dark blue
10/100/1000 Ethernet LAN	8-pin RJ-45	Black
SCSI (not shown in Figure 4.3)	50/68-pin HD SCSI	Black

[1]Key: DIN = Deutsches Institut für Normung e.V.; USB = universal serial bus; VGA = video graphics array; LAN = local area network; RJ = registered jack; and SCSI = small computer system interface.

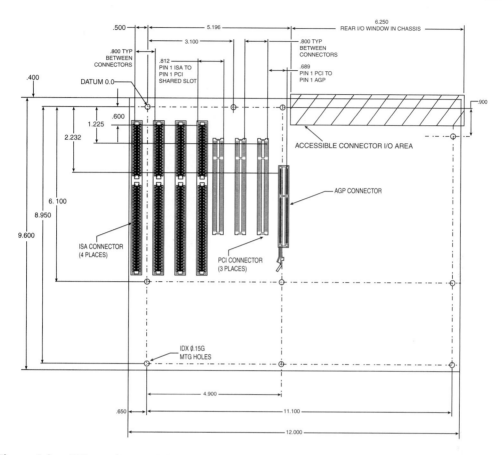

Figure 4.2   ATX specification 2.2 motherboard dimensions.

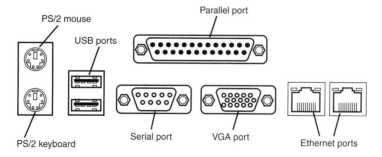

Figure 4.3   ATX motherboard and rear panel connections from a typical server with dual Ethernet ports and integrated video.

Note

Most ATX motherboards feature connectors with industry-standardized color codes (shown in Table 4.1). This makes plugging in devices much easier and more foolproof: You merely match up the colors. For example, most keyboards have a cable with a purple plug, whereas most mouse devices have a cable with a green plug. Even though the keyboard and mouse connectors on the motherboard appear the same (both are 6-pin mini-DIN types), their color-coding matches the plugs on the respective devices. Thus, to plug them in properly, you merely insert the purple plug into the purple connector and the green plug into the green connector. This saves you from having to bend down to try to decipher small labels on the connectors to ensure that you get them right.

The ATX Riser

In December 1999, Intel introduced a riser card design modification for ATX motherboards. The design includes the addition of a 22-pin (2×11) connector to one of the PCI slots on the motherboard, along with a two- or three-slot riser card that plugs in. The riser enables two or three PCI cards to be installed, but it does not support AGP. The ATX riser design enables ATX motherboards to be used in 1U or 2U rack-mounted systems. Figure 4.4 shows an example of a riser card installation on an ATX-family motherboard. Note that if you use a riser card, you cannot use the remaining slots on the motherboard.

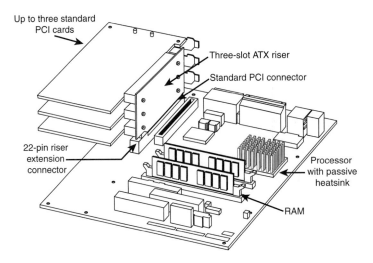

Up to three standard PCI cards

Three-slot ATX riser

Standard PCI connector

22-pin riser extension connector

Processor with passive heatsink

RAM

Figure 4.4   A three-slot ATX riser implementation on a MicroATX motherboard.

On motherboards that use a 22-pin extension connector, the riser is usually installed in line with PCI slot 6, which is the second one from the right; the slots are usually numbered from right to left (facing the board), starting with 7 as the one closest to the processor. It's useful to know the slot numbering scheme used by your server's motherboard in case of conflicts or card failures; check your system or motherboard documentation for details. The pinout of the ATX 22-pin riser extension connector is shown in Figure 4.5.

The PCI connector that is in line with the riser extension connector is just a standard PCI slot; none of the signals are changed.

Signal	Pin	Pin	Signal
Ground	B1	A1	PCI_GNT1#
PCI_ CLK1	B2	A2	Ground
Ground	B3	A3	PCI_GNT2#
PCI_REQ1#	A4	B4	Ground
Ground	A5	B5	PCI_CLK3
PCI_CLK2	A6	B6	RISER_ID1
Ground	A7	B7	Reserved
PCI_REQ2#	A8	B8	RISER_ID2
Ground	A9	B9	NOGO
PC/PCI_DREQ#	A10	B10	+12V
PC/PCI_DGNT#	A11	B11	SER_IRQ

Figure 4.5   An ATX 22-pin riser extension connector pinout.

Some multislot riser cards can be plugged in to standard PCI slots: They use cables and special connectors to provide power and signaling to the second or third slots in a riser card. Some recent systems now support risers for PCI, PCI-X, and PCI-Express cards. PCI-X is backward compatible with PCI, so a PCI-X riser card can be used with either type of card. PCI-Express uses a different slot design and thus a different riser design.

Systems that use the riser are generally low-profile designs. Therefore, they don't fit normal PCI or AGP cards in the remaining (non-riser-bound) slots. Although the ATX riser standard was originally developed for use with low-end boards—which have integrated video, sound, and network support—many rack-mounted servers are also using the ATX riser because these boards also have most of their required components already integrated. In fact, the ATX riser appears to be more popular for rack-mounted servers than for the originally intended target market of slimline desktop systems.

Note

A slimline case is a case that is thinner than a normal case. A standard ATX tower case is about 7 to 7.5 inches wide, and a slimline case is 2 or so inches narrower.

ATX riser cards, compatible cases, and compatible motherboards are available from a variety of vendors, which means you can build your own slimline ATX system.

The WTX Form Factor

WTX was a board and system form factor developed for the midrange workstation market; however, most vendors making workstations and servers have used the ATX form factor. WTX went beyond ATX and defined the size and shape of the board and the interface between the board and chassis, as well as required chassis features.

WTX was first released in September 1998 (1.0) and updated in February 1999 (1.1). The specification and other information on WTX used to be available at www.wtx.org; however, WTX has been officially discontinued, and there will be no further updates.

WTX motherboards have a maximum width of 14 inches (356mm) and a maximum length of 16.75 inches (425mm), which is significantly larger than ATX. There are no minimum dimensions, so board designers are free to design smaller boards as long as they meet the mounting criteria. The additional space provided by the WTX form factor provides room for two or more processors and other onboard equipment needed in a workstation or server design. Although WTX is no longer an official form factor, a number of server and workstation motherboard vendors, such as Tyan, MSI, and SuperMicro, continue to build products that use it. In practice, current systems using WTX-sized motherboards are basically extensions of the ATX architecture.

WTX motherboards use different power connectors than ATX motherboards. Originally, WTX motherboards used a 24-pin power connector that supplied only 5V and 3.3V power to the motherboard and a separate 22-pin power connector that supplied 12V power and control signals.

Modern WTX motherboards still use a 24-pin primary power connector, but the connector might use the EPS12V (also known as the Superset ATX or SSI) standard or the older ATX-GES standard. Both ATX-GES and EPS12V provide 3.3V, 5V, and 12V power to the motherboard, but the pinouts are completely different. EPS12V motherboards also use an 8-pin power connector to provide additional 12V power to the processor(s).

▶▶ See "Power Supplies and Connectors," p. 247.

SSI Form Factor Specifications

Another ATX-derived form factor is the Server System Infrastructure (SSI) group of specifications that Intel developed in cooperation with Dell, IBM, and Silicon Graphics. The SSI initiative, which began in 1998, provides the following specifications for power supplies:

- EPS12V—Entry-level power supply
- EPS1U—Nonredundant power supply for 1U rack-mounted servers
- EPS2U—Nonredundant power supply for 2U rack-mounted servers
- ERP12V—Redundant power supply for pedestal-mounted servers
- ERP2U—Redundant power supply for 2U rack-mounted servers
- PSMI—Power Supply Management Interface

▶▶ For more information about these specifications, see "Power Supplies and Connectors," p. 247.

The SSI initiative provides the following current specifications for electronic bays (chassis):

- CEB—Compact Electronics Bay (supports 1U or larger rack-mounted or pedestal servers); see Figure 4.7 in the next section
- TEB—Thin Electronics Bay (optimized for 1U/2U rack-mounted servers)
- EEB—Entry-Level Electronics Bay (optimized for pedestal-mounted servers)

Although the SSI MEB specification is no longer current (it was designed to support slot-mounted processors), some vendors produce motherboards in this form factor to support four-way and larger servers. See Figure 4.8 in the next section.

Table 4.2 compares the dimensions and other features of SSI motherboard form factors with ATX motherboard form factors.

Table 4.2 ATX and SSI Motherboard Form Factors Compared

Form Factor	Dimensions	Maximum Number of Expansion Slots	Notes
ATX	12 in. (304.8mm) wide, 9.6 in. (244mm) deep	7	—
Extended ATX	12 in. (304.8mm) wide, 13.05 in. (332mm) deep	7	Deeper version of ATX; might not fit into some smaller ATX chassis; check chassis internal dimensions
SSI CEB 1.01	12 in. (304.8mm) wide, 10.5 in. (226.7mm) deep	7	Most slots are omitted in 1U rack-mounted versions and are replaced by a riser card
SSI TEB 2.11	12 in. (304.8mm) wide, 13 in. (330mm) deep	1	Uses a riser card in 1U/2U implementations
SSI EEB 3.61	12 in. (304.8mm) wide, 13 in. (330mm) deep	7	Same dimensions as Extended ATX; 1U/2U optimized versions may omit some slots
SSI MEB	13 in. (330mm) wide, 16 in. (406.4mm) deep	10	Some vendors misidentify this formfactor as SSI EEB; check the actual dimensions of the motherboard to verify the form factor

Note

For details on current and older versions of SSI specifications and information about products that meet those specifications, see the SSI website, at www.ssiforum.org.

Table 4.3 provides examples of current products that correspond to each SSI form factor.

Table 4.3 Typical Products Based on SSI Chassis and Motherboard Form Factors

Product Type	SSI CEB	SSI TEB	SSI EEB	SSI MEB
Motherboard	Giga-Byte GA-9IVDT (www.giga-byte.com)	Intel SE7520JR2 (www.intel.com)	MSI MS-9161-040 (www.msicomputer.com)	Tyan Thunder K8QS Pro (S4882) (www.tyan.com)
Chassis	CIDesign RS 1204 or RS 1400 (1U) (www.cidesign.com)	Intel SR2400 (2U) or SR1400 (1U) (www.intel.com)	AIPIPC RMC3F2-XP (3U) (www.aicipc.com)	RMC48-T82 (5U) (www.rackmount.net)

The EEB Form Factor

The EEB form factor has essentially the same shape as the Extended ATX form factor: 12 inches by 13 inches (305mm×330mm). Mounting holes used by EEB are the same as those used by ATX specification version 2.1. The I/O connector cluster is also the same as that for ATX. However, EEB supports a 24-pin power connector, following the EPS12V standard rather than the 20-pin ATX power connector standard used on older ATX motherboards. Like ATX, EEB supports up to seven expansion slots.

Another difference between EEB and ATX is EEB's inclusion of an 8-pin 12V power connector for processor power and a 4-pin connector for cooling fans. The additional pin provides control as well as voltage, ground, and sensing features found in 3-pin fan connectors on ATX motherboards. The EEB standard recommends at least five motherboard fan connectors and as many as eight in rack-mounted implementations.

The EEB 24-pin main power connector, 8-pin 12V power connector, and 4-pin cooling fan pinouts are illustrated in Figure 4.6.

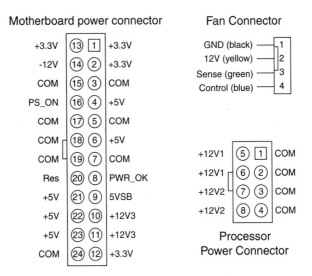

Figure 4.6   SSI EEB motherboard (top), processor (lower right), and fan (upper right) power connectors.

The CEB Form Factor

The CEB form factor is similar to the EEB form factor, but the maximum motherboard dimensions are reduced to 12 inches×10.5 inches (305mm×267mm). Thus, CEB falls between the ATX and EEB form factors in overall dimensions. It uses the same mounting holes as ATX specification version 2.2. The same power and fan connectors shown in Figure 4.6 are also part of the CEB specification.

Figure 4.7 illustrates a typical SSI CEB-compatible motherboard that is optimized for rack-mounted use compared to a typical ATX motherboard. Note the empty spaces reserved for PCI and PCI-X expansion slots; this model uses a riser card for add-on cards. Similar models designed for pedestal servers include the expansion slots not shown in this example.

As you can see from Figure 4.7, an SSI-CEB and an ATX motherboard can have similar features. However, the SSI-CEB motherboard generally has provision for more memory sockets than an ATX motherboard and is a slightly different size (refer to Table 4.2).

The TEB Form Factor

Unlike other SSI specifications, the latest version of the TEB specification, version 2.11, is tailored to the requirements of Intel 64-bit Xeon processors and motherboards based on the E7320, E7520, and E7525 chipsets. TEB is a specification optimized for 1U and 2U rack-mounted servers.

◀◀   See "The Intel E7520 and E7320 Chipsets," p. 189.

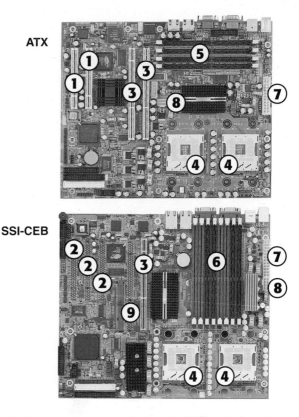

ATX

SSI-CEB

1. 32-bit PCI slots
2. Spaces reserved for 32-bit PCI slots (not installed)
3. PCI-X slots
4. Xeon processor sockets
5. Memory sockets (ATX)
6. Memory socket (SSI EEB)
7. ATX12V 24-pin power connectors
8. Processor power connectors
9. Space reserved for PCI-X slot (not installed)

Figure 4.7 A typical dual-CPU ATX motherboard (top) compared to an SSI CEB motherboard optimized for 1U/2U rack-mounting (bottom).

The size of a TEB version 2.11 motherboard is the same as that used by the latest version of EEB: 12 inches by 13 inches (305mm×330mm). Mounting holes used by TEB are the same as those used by ATX specification version 2.1. TEB, unlike EEB and CEB, uses a riser card slot that supports up to three 2U cards or one 1U card rather than multiple PCI, PCI-X, or PCI-Express slots. The riser card connector type is not defined, so a motherboard designer can choose the appropriate type of riser card and slot to use for the job. TEB motherboards use the same power and fan connectors supported by EEB and CEB motherboards (refer to Figure 4.6). TEB motherboards for 2U rack-mounted servers use the same type of I/O port cluster as ATX motherboards, while 1U rack-mounted servers use a thinner version.

The MEB Form Factor

MEB was designed in 1999, at a time when most server processors used bulky Slot 1 or Slot 2 designs. Thus, the MEB form factor has dimensions of 13 inches (330mm) by 16 inches (406.4mm), and it supports up to 10 expansion slots, as well as a memory riser board slot. This standard is now officially obsolete, but some vendors continue to build products based on the MEB standard, primarily for four-way systems.

Note

Some vendors mislabel MEB form factor motherboards as corresponding to the EEB 3.5 standard. To avoid confusion, you should look at the actual dimensions of the motherboard in question. If you are considering motherboards that correspond to the Extended ATX, EEB, or MEB form factors, you should be sure to get a list of recommended enclosures from the motherboard vendor. MEB form factor motherboards do not fit into ATX cases.

Figure 4.8 compares a typical ATX server motherboard (left) to an MEB server motherboard (right).

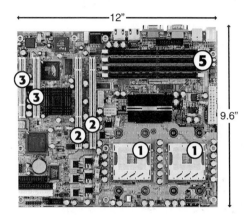
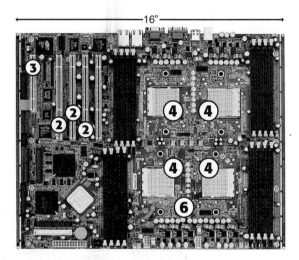

1. Dual Xeon processor sockets
2. PCI-X expansion slots
3. PCI expansion slots
4. Four-way Opteron processor sockets
5. DDR sockets for i7501 motherboard
6. DDR sockets for K8QS motherboard

Figure 4.8   The Tyan Tiger i7501 (S2723) motherboard (left) uses the ATX form factor, whereas the Tyan Thunder K8QS Pro (S4882) motherboard (right) uses the SSI MEB form factor. *Photos courtesy of Tyan Computer Corporation.*

Backplane Systems

Ever since the first IBM PC was introduced in 1981, the vast majority of PCs and servers have placed major components such as the processor (CPU), chipset, and memory on the motherboard. Expansion slots were used for I/O and display devices. However, some servers and PCs have used a different type of design, known as a *backplane system*. These systems do not have a motherboard in the true sense of the word. In a backplane system, the components typically found on a motherboard are located instead on one or more expansion adapter cards plugged in to slots.

In these systems, the board with the slots is called a *backplane*, rather than a *motherboard*. Systems that use this type of construction are called *backplane systems*. Backplane systems enable faster swapping of failed components than motherboard-based systems, easier upgrading to faster processors and memory (you swap a single board to make the change), and greater reliability in industrial environments.

Backplane systems come in two main types: passive and active. In a *passive* backplane, the main backplane board does not contain any circuitry at all except for the bus connectors and maybe some buffer and driver circuits. All the circuitry found on a conventional motherboard is contained on one or more expansion cards installed in slots on the backplane. Some backplane systems use a passive design that incorporates the entire system circuitry into a single mothercard. The mothercard is essentially a complete motherboard designed to plug in to a slot in the passive backplane. The passive backplane/mothercard concept enables you to easily upgrade the entire system by changing one or more cards. The major examples of passive backplane systems in use today include PICMG-based single-board computers and various types of blade servers.

In an *active* backplane, the main backplane board contains bus control and usually other circuitry as well. Most active backplane systems contain all the circuitry found on a typical motherboard except for the processor complex. The *processor complex* is the circuit board that contains the main system processor and any other circuitry directly related to it, such as clock control, cache, and so forth. The processor's complex design enables the user to easily upgrade the system later to a new processor type by changing one card. In effect, it amounts to a modular motherboard with a replaceable processor section. Although servers built by IBM, Compaq, and ALR (later absorbed into Gateway) have used this type of design, this type of backplane design is no longer used due to the expense of proprietary processor boards and the advent of easy industry-standard processor upgrades through zero insertion force (ZIF) sockets.

PICMG Backplanes

PICMG has developed a series of specifications for passive-backplane computers for industrial use, including servers. These specifications are listed in Table 4.4.

Table 4.4 PICMG Specifications

PICMG Version	Name	Features/Notes
1.0	PCI/ISA	Single-board computers that support PCI and ISA buses. The current revision is 2.0.
1.2	ePCI-X	Single-board computers that support one or two PCI/PCI-X buses.
2.0	CompactPCI	Eurocard (VME bus) form factor for network and telecommunications nodes in rack-mounted (U) applications
3.0	AdvancedTCA	Advanced Telecommunications Architecture (ATCA); optimized for rack-mounted (U) telecommunications systems.

Passive backplane systems with mothercards (often called single-board computers [SBCs]) are by far the most popular backplane design. They are used in industrial or laboratory-type systems and are rack mountable. They usually have a large number of slots and extremely heavy-duty power supplies; they also feature high-capacity, reverse flow cooling designed to pressurize the chassis with cool, filtered air. Many passive backplane systems, such as the one pictured in Figure 4.9, adhere to the ePCI-X passive backplane form factor standard set forth by PICMG. You can get more information about these standards from PICMG's website, at www.picmg.org.

Figure 4.9 shows a typical dual-Xeon single-board computer used in PICMG 1.2 ePCI-X passive backplane systems. Figure 4.10 shows a rack-mounted chassis with a passive backplane.

Blade Servers

Blade servers are the latest development of passive-backplane technology. Multiple server blades of various types can be connected to a single blade server enclosure.

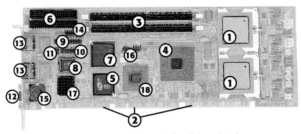

1. Xeon processors (2)
2. PICMG 1.2 interface to backplane
3. DIMM memory sockets (2)
4. Intel E7501 North Bridge/MCH
5. ATI Rage XL graphics chip
6. ATA/IDE host adapters
7. ICH3-S South Bridge/ICH
8. System BIOS chip
9. Floppy controller
10. Parallel port header
11. PS/2 and keyboard header
12. VGA port
13. 10/100/1000 Ethernet ports (2)
14. Serial port headers (2)
15. CR-2032 battery
16. USB headers (2)
17. Intel 82546EB gigabit Ethernet chip
18. Intel P64H2 PCI/PCI-X Hub

Figure 4.9 A typical Xeon PICMG single-board computer. This single card provides PCI and PCI-X interfacing; integrated video; 2 Gigabit Ethernet (10/100/1000) network interfaces; and normal parallel, serial, ATA/IDE, USB, and floppy interfaces.

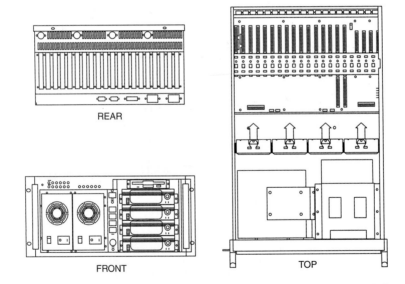

Figure 4.10 A rack-mounted chassis with passive backplane.

A server blade is a self-contained computer that contains one or more processors, memory, and storage. It differs from a PICMG single-board computer in several ways:

■ You can have multiple server blades in a single enclosure, while only one PICMG single-board computer can occupy a backplane. This enables you to place a larger number of servers into a standard rack-mounted enclosure.

■ A server blade does not have traditional I/O ports, such as serial, parallel, USB, and VGA ports. Depending on the enclosure, keyboard, video, and mouse (KVM) and other ports might be located on the rear of the enclosure, or all management and I/O might be performed via a network connection.

- Server blades are hot-swappable to reduce downtime and permit quick provisioning of an enclosure.
- Some blades perform network, storage, or management functions, enabling you to combine different types of blades in a single enclosure to customize the performance of your server.
- Some blade server enclosures offer swappable modules at the rear of the enclosure for I/O, networking, and KVM. Although these modules are not hot-swappable, they permit a great deal of customization.

Typical sizes for blade servers include 1U (1.75 inches high) and 3U (5.25 inches high); 3U and larger units permit more flexibility in storage solutions.

Figure 4.11 illustrates two of the many different server blades available, and Figure 4.12 illustrates a blade server enclosure.

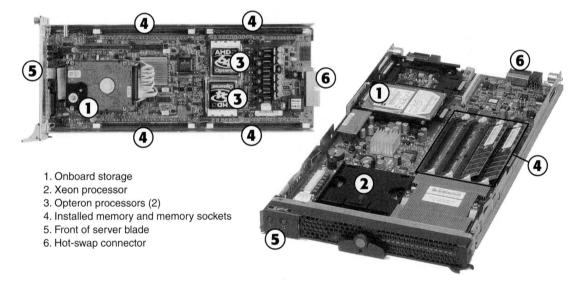

1. Onboard storage
2. Xeon processor
3. Opteron processors (2)
4. Installed memory and memory sockets
5. Front of server blade
6. Hot-swap connector

Figure 4.11 Some typical server blades.

Figures 4.11 and 4.12 make it clear that, unlike traditional and rack-mounted servers that use motherboards or PICMG single-board computers, there is no true standard for blade server technology. Each developer of blade servers uses its own proprietary design for the blades, the chassis, and the I/O and network modules.

▶▶ To learn more about the development of blade servers and major blade vendors, see "Blade Servers," p. 725. The Sun Microsystems blade server product line is discussed in "Blade Servers," p. 791.

BTX Motherboards

BTX is a motherboard form factor specification Intel originally released in September 2003, with a 1.0a update in February 2004. BTX may eventually replace the venerable ATX form factor while addressing ever-increasing component power and cooling requirements, as well as enabling improved circuit routing and more flexible chassis designs.

1. Thumbscrews for rapid removal of server blades
2. Handles for easy insertion and removal of server blades
3. Status lights (top) and USB ports (bottom)

Figure 4.12   A typical fully populated server blade chassis.

BTX represents a completely new form factor that is not backward compatible with ATX or other designs. A full-size BTX board is 17% larger than an ATX board, allowing room for more integrated components onboard. The I/O connectors, slots, and mounting holes are in different locations than with ATX, requiring new chassis designs. However, the power supply interface connectors are the same as in the latest ATX12V specifications, and newer ATX, TFX, SFX, CFX, and LFX power supplies can be used. The latter two power supply form factors were specifically created to support compact and low-profile BTX systems.

The primary advantages of BTX include the following:

- **Optimized inline component layout and routing**—The major components (processor and memory modules) are aligned front to back, allowing connections between components and I/O connectors to run unobstructed.

- **Optimized airflow path**—BTX allows for a condensed system design and an optimized, unobstructed airflow path for efficient system cooling with fewer fans and lower acoustics.

- **Support and retention module (SRM)**—BTX offers mechanical support for heavy heatsinks. It also helps to prevent board flexing or damaging of board components and traces during shipping and handling.

- **Scalable board dimensions**—Flexible board sizes enable developers to use the same components for a variety of system sizes and configurations.

- **Flexible, compatible power supply designs**—Connectors are shared with recent ATX designs; smaller, more efficient power supply form factors can be used for small form factor systems, whereas standard ATX12V power supplies can be used for larger tower configurations.

BTX includes three definitions of motherboard size, as shown in Table 4.5.

Table 4.5 BTX Motherboard Form Factors

Form Factor	Maximum Width	Depth	Maximum Area	Size Compared to BTX
BTX	12.8 in. (325mm)	10.5 in. (267mm)	134 sq. in. (867 sq. cm)	—
microBTX	10.4 in. (264mm)	10.5 in. (267mm)	109 sq. in. (705 sq. cm)	19% smaller
picoBTX	8.0 in. (203mm)	10.5 in. (267mm)	84 sq. in. (542 sq. cm)	37% smaller

Each board has the same basic screw hole and connector placement requirements. So if you have a case that fits a full-size BTX board, you can also mount a MicroBTX or picoBTX board in that same case (see Figure 4.13). Obviously, if you have a smaller case designed for MicroBTX or picoBTX, you can't put the larger MicroBTX or BTX boards in that case.

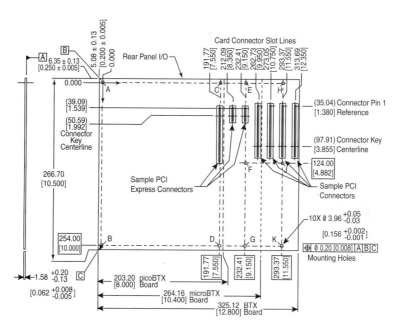

Figure 4.13 BTX specification 1.0a motherboard dimensions.

BTX requires up to 10 mounting holes and supports up to seven slots, depending on the size, as shown in Table 4.6.

Table 4.6 BTX Motherboard Mounting Holes

Board Size	Mounting Holes	Maximum Slots
BTX	A, B, C, D, E, F, G, H, J, K	7
microBTX	A, B, C, D, E, F, G	4
picoBTX	A, B, C, D	1

BTX also clearly specifies volumetric zones around the motherboard to prevent any interference from the chassis or internal components, such as drives, which allows for maximum interchangeability without physical interference or fit problems.

With processors exceeding 100W in thermal output, as well as voltage regulators, motherboard chipsets, and video cards adding to the thermal load in a system, BTX was designed to allow all the high-heat-producing core components to be mounted inline from front to back so that a single high-efficiency thermal module (heatsink) can cool the system. This eliminates the need for an excessive number of fans. The thermal module includes a heatsink for the processor, a high-efficiency fan, and a duct to direct airflow through the system. Extra support for the thermal module is provided under the board via a support and retention module (SRM), which provides structural support for heatsinks that are much heavier than allowed in ATX designs. The thermal module pulls air directly from the front of the case over the processor and memory for better cooling than with ATX systems.

BTX uses the same power connectors as in the latest ATX12V v2.x power supply form factor specifications, including a 24-pin main connector for the board and a 4-pin ATX12V connector for the CPU voltage regulator module. The particular power supply form factor used depends mostly on the chassis selected.

A typical tower system has components arranged as shown in Figure 4.14.

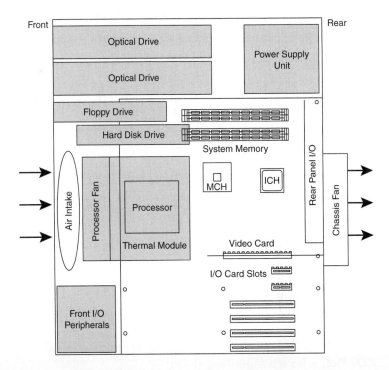

Figure 4.14   BTX tower chassis layout.

From Figure 4.14, you can see that the main heat-producing core components are centrally located inline from front to rear, allowing the most efficient thermal design. Air flows from front to rear through the center, cooling the processor, motherboard chipset, memory, and video card.

To support the heavy processor heatsink and thermal module assembly, an SRM is mounted under the board. The SRM is essentially a metal plate affixed to the chassis under the board, and the thermal module is bolted directly to the SRM instead of to the motherboard. This helps carry the weight of the module and prevents excessive loads from being applied to the processor and motherboard, especially during the shipping and handling of the system.

The BTX I/O connector area is similar to ATX, except that it is at the opposite side of the rear of the board. The size of the area is slightly shorter but wider than ATX, allowing a large number of interfaces and connectors to be built in to the motherboard.

As of early 2006, only a few BTX servers were available in the marketplace. It remains to be seen whether BTX will replace ATX at some point or will become unnecessary as both Intel and AMD introduce lower-wattage processors in 2006 and beyond.

Proprietary Server Designs

Proprietary server designs aren't limited to the world of blade servers. Many four-way and almost all eight-way or larger servers use proprietary designs. There are several reasons for this:

- These systems are designed for upgrading at a processor, memory, and storage level rather than a motherboard level.
- Motherboard form factors such as ATX and its server offshoots, such as SSI, are not suitable for very large systems.
- ATX, BTX, and SSI standards do not support hot-swapping of processors and memory.
- ATX, BTX, and SSI do not support fault-tolerant system designs.

For these reasons, proprietary designs have been and will continue to be popular. All servers running RISC processors are, by definition, proprietary. Itanium-based processors also use proprietary designs. However, systems running x86 processors might also feature proprietary designs. Table 4.7 lists some of the major proprietary server designs available from major vendors.

Table 4.7   x86 and Itanium 2-Based Proprietary Server Designs1

Product Family	Form Factor Type2	Processors2	Processors Supported	Other Features2
		Hewlett-Packard (www.hp.com)		
ProLiant DL	Rack-mounted (1U–7U)	1–8	AMD Opteron; Intel Xeon MP, DP; Pentium D; Pentium 4	Hot-swap RAID memory cartridges, iLO, hot-swap redundant power
Integrity RX series	Rack-mounted (1U–4U)	1–8	Intel Itanium 2	MX2 dual-processor cartridges; QuickFind LED panel for troubleshooting
Integrity Superdome	Pedestal	2–64	Intel Itanium 2	Up to 128 CPUs if mx2 dual-processor cartridges are used; hot-swap PCI-X, redundant power supplies, multiple operating systems canrun in a single server

Table 4.7   Continued

Product Family	Form Factor Type2	Processors2	Processors Supported	Other Features2
Stratus (www.stratus.com)				
ftServer W series	Pedestal or rack-mounted	2–4	Intel Xeon	Fault-tolerant (two systems in one) runs Windows Server 2003
NEC Solutions America (www.necsam.com)				
Express5800 series	Pedestal or rack-mounted	2–4	Intel Xeon	Fault-tolerant (two systems in one) runs Windows Server 2003; uses technology licensed from Stratus
Dell (www.dell.com)				
PowerEdge 18xx and higher	Pedestal or rack-mounted	1–4	Intel Xeon	Hot-pluggable components
IBM (www.ibm.com)				
xSeries 455	Rack-mounted	1–4	Itanium 2	Memory mirroring; hot-swap PCI-X slots; hot-swap SCSI hard disks; self-healing memory and redundant fans and power supplies
xSeries 460	Rack-mounted	4–32	Xeon (64-bit)	Hot-swap memory and memory mirroring; hot-swap PCI-X slots; predicts failures to allow maintenance before component failure takes place
xSeries 260	Pedestal	4	Xeon (64-bit)	Hot-swap memory and memory mirroring; hot-swap PCI-X slots; predicts failures to allow maintenance before component failure takes place

[1]*Key: iLO = Integrated Lights-Out Management.*
[2]*Varies by model; check vendor's website for details.*

One of the benefits of considering proprietary server designs is the greater emphasis on redundancy and hot-swapping of defective hardware that is possible. While many midrange and high-end servers feature various levels of fault-tolerant design, such as hot-swap memory, fans, and drives, it's still possible for a failure in another part of the server to cripple the unit or shut it down entirely. If your business depends on true 24×7×365 reliability from a server, you might want to consider a server that replicates every major component and processes information in parallel. This type of server is known as a *fault-tolerant server*.

Fault-Tolerant Servers

Because fault-tolerant servers process information in parallel, using two or three replicated systems in one, a failure in one part of the server does not cause data loss or even require a shutdown; the parallel components continue to work and provide the information needed.

Major vendors of fault-tolerant servers include Stratus, NEC, and Hewlett-Packard. Their products are discussed in the following sections.

Stratus ftServer and Continuum Servers

Stratus (www.stratus.com) offers several lines of fault-tolerant servers:

- The ftServer W series runs Windows Server 2003 and supports Xeon processors. It offers up to four-way fault-tolerant operation.

- The ftServer T series runs Red Hat Enterprise Linux and supports Xeon processors. It offers up to four-way fault-tolerant operation.

- The ftServer V series runs Stratus's own VOS operating system. Stratus provides migration tools and support to move existing applications to VOS. The V Series also supports Xeon processors and offers up to four-way fault-tolerant operation.

- The Stratus Continuum series runs VOS; the Continuum 400 also runs HP-UX (the Hewlett-Packard version of UNIX).

The ftServer W and T series are roughly comparable to the NEC Express5800 series (discussed in the next section). Because they run Windows Server 2003 or Linux, they would be easy to add to any network already running those operating systems.

NEC Express5800 Series

NEC (www.necsam.com) offers a line of fault-tolerant servers known as the Express5800 series. The Express5800 series offers both Linux and Windows Server 2003–based systems with up to four-way Xeon processors. The Express5800 series uses technology licensed from Stratus.

Hewlett-Packard Integrity NonStop Series

Hewlett-Packard (www.hp.com) offers a line of fault-tolerant servers known as the Integrity NonStop series. The Integrity NonStop series, introduced in 2005, differs from the previous NonStop series because it uses Intel Itanium 2 processors, whereas the previous NonStop servers used Silicon Graphics MIPS S88000 processors.

Hewlett-Packard refers to its fault-tolerant design as NonStop Advanced Architecture (NSAA). NSAA is designed to provide fault tolerance at both software and hardware levels. Therefore, Integrity NonStop servers run a specially designed operating system and applications.

The Integrity NonStop series is designed to handle much larger server tasks than the Stratus W or T series or the NEC Express5800 series, with scalability up to 4,080 processors and up to 64TB of memory.

Power Supplies and Connectors

Servers based on the ATX or microATX form factors generally use an ATX power supply, while pedestal servers based on one of the SSI form factors generally use an EPS12V power supply. Servers that use proprietary form factors, as well as many slimline 1U and 2U servers, use various form factors. The following sections deal with standard types of power supplies and connectors, including ATX, ATX12, and EPS12V, among others.

ATX Power Supply Standards

ATX power supplies were originally designed for use in desktop computers, and they are also widely used in entry-level tower and slimline servers. ATX power supply standards include the following:

- **ATX version 2.03**—Older entry-level tower servers
- **ATX12V**—More recent entry-level tower servers
- **ATX1U**—1U slimline servers
- **ATX2U**—2U slimline servers

The following sections provide information on these power supply standards.

ATX/ATX12V Power Supplies and Connectors

Motherboards that support the ATX version 2.03 power supply use a 20-pin main power connector, as shown in Figure 4.15.

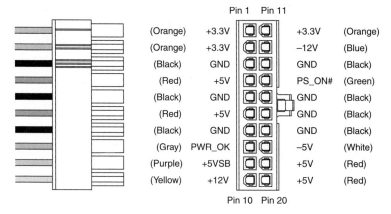

Figure 4.15—The ATX version 2.03 power supply connector uses a positive-locking plug to secure the power supply cable.

Some servers may also feature a 6-pin auxiliary power connector, as shown in Figure 4.16. This additional connector provides additional 3.3V and 5V power to the motherboard. ATX power supplies with ratings of 250 watts or more feature this connector, but if your motherboard does not feature this connector, you can just leave the auxiliary power connector unconnected.

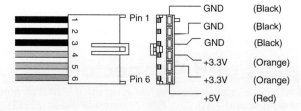

Figure 4.16 ATX auxiliary power connector.

Most recent servers that use ATX power supplies also feature a 4-pin connector called the ATX12V connector, shown in Figure 4.17. This connector provides additional 12V power to meet the requirements of newer processors, such as the Pentium 4.

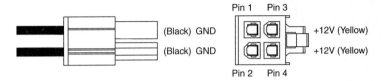

Figure 4.17   An ATX12V power connector.

Power supplies that feature the ATX12V connector shown in Figure 4.17 are known as ATX12V power supplies. Most ATX power supplies on the market today, particularly those with 300w or higher ratings, meet ATX12V standards. ATX12V version 1.x power supplies also include the 6-pin auxiliary connector, although most recent servers do not use it.

Figure 4.18 illustrates a typical ATX12V v1.x power supply. Note the 4-pin floppy and hard disk power cables shown above the 20-pin main power supply cable.

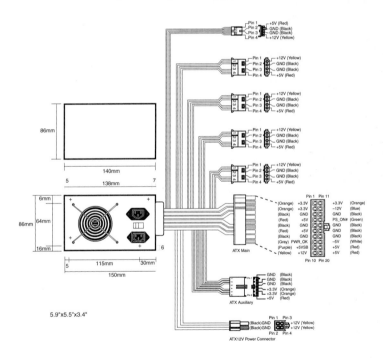

Figure 4.18   An ATX12V v1.x power supply.

The ATX12V version 2.0 power supply standard was introduced in 2003. The 6-pin auxiliary connector was discontinued, and the main power connector was enlarged from 20 pins to 24 pins, using the Molex 39-01-2240 connector. ATX12V version 2.0 and newer connectors also feature integrated power supply connectors for SATA drives, which are increasingly common today. Figure 4.19 compares the 20-pin ATX and 24-pin ATX12V version 2.x power supply connectors to each other. The 24-pin

ATX12V version 2.x connector uses the same physical connectors as the ATX-GES and EPX12V power supply connectors used in multiple-processor servers.

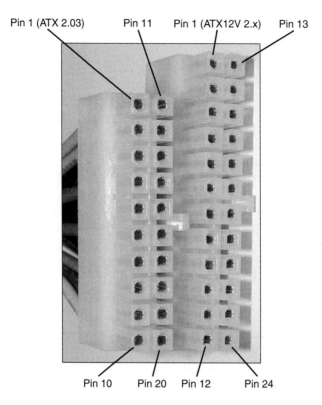

Figure 4.19 The ATX 2.03 power supply connector (left) and ATX12V 2.x power supply connector (right).

Figure 4.20 compares the motherboard connectors and pinouts used by these power supplies.

Tip

If your server uses the 20-pin ATX power supply connector, you can use the newer ATX12V v2.x power supply by using a 20-pin–to–24-pin adapter. Many power supply vendors ship such an adapter with their ATX12V v2.x power supplies, or you can purchase it separately.

ATX1U/2U Rack-Mounted Power Supplies

Rack-mounted servers use a variety of power supply standards. Although most 1U and 2U servers use the power supply standards developed by the SSI Forum, some use the ATX1U and ATX2U power supply standards discussed in this section.

▶▶ See "SSI Rack-Mounted Power Supply Standards," p. 253.

ATX 20-pin power connector (top view)

Orange	+3.3v	1		11	+3.3v	Orange
Orange	+3.3v	2		12	-12v	Blue
Black	Ground	3		13	Ground	Black
Red	+5v	4		14	PS-On	Green
Black	Ground	5		15	Ground	Black
Red	+5v	6		16	Ground	Black
Black	Ground	7		17	Ground	Black
Gray	Power Good	8		18	-5v	White
Purple	+5v Standby	9		19	+5v	Red
Yellow	+12v	10		20	+5v	Red

ATX 12V version 2.x 24-pin power connector
(top view)

Orange	+3.3v	1		13	+3.3v	Orange
Orange	+3.3v	2		14	-12v	Blue
Black	Ground	3		15	Ground	Black
Red	+5v	4		16	PS-On	Green
Black	Ground	5		17	Ground	Black
Red	+5v	6		18	Ground	Black
Black	Ground	7		19	Ground	Black
Gray	Power Good	8		20	NC	White
Purple	+5v Standby	9		21	+5v	Red
Yellow	+12v	10		22	+5v	Red
Yellow	+12v	11		23	+5v	Red
Orange	+3.3v	12		24	Ground	Black

Figure 4.20 Pinouts for the ATX2.03/ATX12V v1.x (top) and ATX12V 2.x (bottom) power supplies.

The ATX1U and ATX2U power supply standards use the same 20-pin ATX power supply, floppy, and hard disk power connectors used by the ATX 2.03 and ATX12V v1.x power supply standards (refer to Figure 4.14). Some 200w and larger ATX1U power supplies also feature the 4-pin ATX12V power supply connector (refer to Figure 4.17), while ATX2U power supplies feature the 6-pin auxiliary power supply connector shown in Figure 4.15.

Figure 4.21 illustrates typical ATX1U and ATX2U power supplies.

Typical ATX1U power supplies use two 40mm fans for cooling, one at the front and one at the back. Typical ATX2U power supplies use a 60mm fan for cooling.

SSI Power Supply Standards

The SSI Forum has developed a series of power supply and connector form factors designed for use in various types of servers. These include the following:

- EPS12V—Nonredundant power supply for pedestal-mounted servers
- ERP12V—Redundant power supply for pedestal-mounted servers
- EPS1U—Nonredundant power supply for 1U rack-mounted servers
- EPS2U—Nonredundant power supply for 2U rack-mounted servers
- ERP2U—Redundant power supply for 2U rack-mounted servers
- PSMI—Power Supply Management Interface

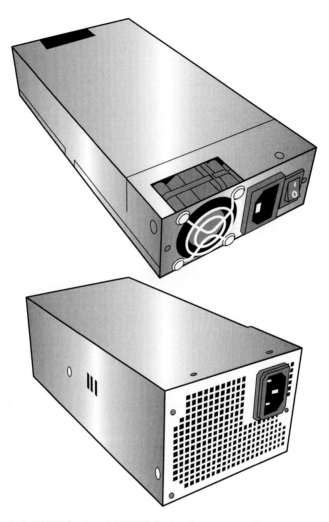

Figure 4.21   Typical ATX1U (top) and ATX2U (bottom) power supplies.

The following sections provide details of these power supplies and connectors.

SSI Pedestal Power Supply and Connector Standards

The ATX12V v2.x power supply standard discussed earlier in this chapter is actually based on the SSI Forum's EPS12V standard, one of the power supply standards developed by the SSI Forum for use in servers.

◀◀   See "SSI Form Factor Specifications," p. 234.

Because both standards are sponsored in part by Intel, it should not be surprising that features from the SSI EPS power supply standard should eventually find their way into the ATX standard. The EPS12V and ATX12V v2.x power supplies use the same 24-pin connector and the same pinout (refer to Figures 4.18 and 4.19). However, the EPS12V power supply differs from the ATX12V v2.x power supply by providing an 8-pin 12V connector rather than the 4-pin 12V connector shown in Figure 4.17. The additional 12V lines provide sufficient 12V power for multiple-processor motherboards. (Recent and current processors use voltage regulators powered by 12V lines rather than 5V lines as with older processors.)

Note

For motherboards equipped with a 4-pin 12V connector, you can plug the 8-pin cable into the 4-pin connector without needing an adaptor.

An EPS12V power supply closely resembles an ATX12V v2.0 power supply except that an EPS12V unit is somewhat deeper. An ATX power supply has a maximum depth of 140mm, while an EPS12V power supply can be as much as 230mm deep. Because an EPS12V power supply can be used in place of an ATX power supply if the chassis permits, some vendors refer to EPS12V power supplies as "extended ATX" power supplies. If you want to use an EPS12V power supply in a server chassis designed for ATX hardware, check the space available for the power supply and compare it to the depth of the EPS12V power supply you are considering.

ERP12V power supplies use the same connectors and form factor as EPS12V power supplies, but they contain two or, occasionally, three removable power supply modules. Generally, each module has its own AC power cord. By connecting each module to a different circuit, you have protection against AC power failure as well as against power supply module failure.

▶▶ For more information about redundant power supplies, see "Redundant Power Supplies (RPSs)," p. 675.

SSI Rack-Mounted Power Supply Standards

Although the EPS12V power supply can be considered a "supersized" power supply in both features and form factors, EPS power supply standards for rack-mounted 1U and 2U servers feature much different form factors. While the EPS1U and EPS2U power supplies use the same 24-pin main power connector and other power connectors used by the EPS12V power supply, they feature slimmer form factors designed to fit in rack-mounted cabinets and provide adequate cooling.

Typical EPS1U power supply designs feature a trio of 40mm fans: one at the front of the power supply and two at the rear. Typical EPS2U power supply designs feature a 60mm fan. See Figure 4.22.

SSI has also developed the ERP2U standard for redundant 2U rack-mounted power supplies. Essentially, an ERP2U power supply contains two removable power supply modules similar in size to the ESP1U power supply shown in Figure 4.22. A folding handle can be flipped upright to enable each module to be removed. ERP2U power supplies use the same connectors as other SSI power supplies. See Figure 4.23 for a typical example.

ATX GES and WTX Power Supply Connectors

Although all recent x86 server motherboards with 24-pin connections are designed to use either ATX12V v2.x or EPS12V power supplies, some servers use one of two other power supply standards:

- AMD developed the ATX GES power supply standard to support its first server-class processor, the Athlon MP, when used in dual-processor (two-way) configurations.
- Some servers based on the Intel 860 chipset used a version of the WTX power supply standard.

Caution

Because the ATX GES and WTX power supplies use different pinouts than the ATX12V and EPS12V power supplies, if you install an ATX GES or WTX-compatible power supply in a server designed to use ATX12V v2.x or EPS12V, or vice versa, you will damage the motherboard and power supply.

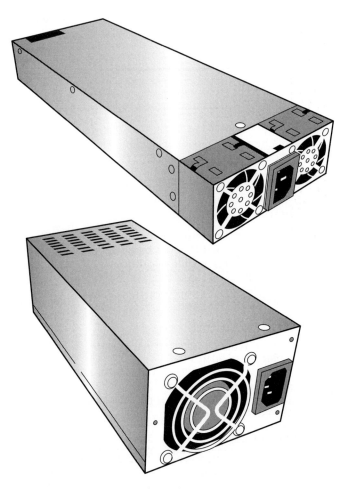

Figure 4.22   Typical EPS1U (top) and EPS2U (bottom) power supplies.

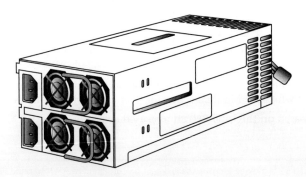

Figure 4.23   Rear view of a typical ERP2U redundant power supply.

The WTX power supply pinout listed in Table 4.8 was used primarily by motherboards based on the Intel 860 chipset and the first-generation Xeon processor based on the Pentium 4. These motherboards include the Tyan S2608 (Thunder i860), Iwill DP400, and MSI MS-6508. These motherboards also used a 6-pin CPU power supply connector to provide additional power for the motherboard's CPU power regulator.

The ATX GES power supply standard shown in Table 4.8 was used by the Tyan Thunder K7 (S2452 series) and Tyan Thunder K7X (S2468 series) motherboards made for the AMD Athlon MP processor. Note that the Tyan Thunder K7X Pro uses an EPS12V power supply.

Table 4.8 compares the pinouts of the ATX-GES, WTX, and EPS12V/ATX12V v2.x 24-pin primary power connectors.

Table 4.8   ATX-GES, EPS12V, and WTX 24-Pin Primary Power Connector Pinouts

Pin #	ATX-GES	EPS12V ATX12V	WTX	Pin #	ATX-GES	EPS12V ATX12V	WTX
1	+5V red	+3.3V orange	+3.3V orange	13	+5V red	+3.3V orange and brown	+3.3V orange
2	+5V red	+3.3V orange	+3.3V orange	14	+5V red	-12V blue	+3.3V orange
3	GND black	GND black	+3.3V orange (Sense)	15	GND black	GND black	GND black
4	GND black	+5V red	GND black	16	+5V SB purple	PS-On green	GND black
5	PS-On green	GND black	GND black	17	-12V blue	GND black	+5V red
6	GND black	+5V red	+5V red	18	GND black	GND black	+5V red
7	+3.3V orange + orange	GND black	+5V red (AUX)	19	+3.3V orange	GND black	+5V red
8	+3.3V orange	Pwr-OK gray	GND black	20	+3.3V orange	-5V white	-12V blue
9	GND black	+5V SB purple	GND black	21	+3.3V orange	+5V red	+12V yellow
10	GND black	+12V yellow	GND black	22	GND black	+5V red	+12V yellow
11	+12V yellow	+12V yellow	PC	23	GND black	+5V red	PSON
12	+12V yellow	+3.3V orange	FAN C	24	+12V yellow	GND black	FAN M

If you need to replace the power supply in a server, be sure to verify what standard it uses. Some power supply vendors list specific motherboards or system compatibility information on their websites to help you select the correct power supply.

Note

The ATX GES power supply also uses an 8-pin processor power connector: Pin 1 provides +5V, pin 2 is used for power good, pins 3–5 provides ground, and pins 6–8 provide +12V. The WTX power supply also uses a 6-pin processor power connector: pins 1–3 provide +12V, and pins 4–6 are signal grounds.

Server Motherboard Components

As the previous section indicates, the power supply is a very important part of server design. Power supply designs have been developed in conjunction with motherboard designs to make sure there is enough power to operate the many components built in to, or plugged in to, modern server motherboards.

Most modern server motherboards have at least the following major components on them:

- Processor socket(s)/slot(s)
- Chipset (North Bridge/South Bridge or memory and I/O controller hubs)
- Super I/O chip
- ROM BIOS (Flash ROM/firmware hub)
- DIMM/RIMM (RAM memory) sockets
- PCI/PCI-X/PCI-Express bus slots
- CPU voltage regulator
- Battery
- Integrated PCI or low-end AGP video
- Integrated Fast (10/100) or Gigabit (10/100/1000) Ethernet

Many boards also have Serial ATA (SATA) or SCSI RAID interfaces onboard.

These standard components are discussed in the following sections.

Processor Sockets and Slots

Server motherboards often support two or more processors. Depending on the server and processor type, the processor might be installed in a ZIF socket for easy insertion and removal, a single-processor cartridge, or a proprietary multiprocessor cartridge. Most recent servers use socketed processors, but a few high-end servers use proprietary processor cartridges. For example, the Hewlett-Packard Integrity rx and Superdome series can use either standard Intel Itanium 2 processors or proprietary mx2 two-processor cartridges.

Typically, systems based on the ATX, BTX, and SSI motherboard form factors support up to four processors. Most systems with more than four processors use proprietary motherboard designs. Note that servers that use proprietary motherboards (primarily four-way or larger) often use proprietary processor boards. The processor board might provide enhanced cooling features not present with standard processor sockets. See the vendor's instructions for adding or removing processors in servers that use processor boards or cartridges.

◄◄   See "Processor Socket and Slot Types," p. 62.

Single Versus Dual-/Multiple-Processor Sockets

One of the factors that influences what motherboard to use in a server is the number of processors you want it to support initially and in the future. A standard ATX motherboard can support up to two socketed processors. However, if more processors are needed, larger form factors must be used. Table 4.9 lists the maximum number of processors supported by industry-standard form factors.

Table 4.9   The Number of Processors Supported by Motherboard Form Factors

Form Factor	Maximum Number of Processors
ATX	2
Extended ATX	2
WTX	2
BTX	2

Table 4.9   Continued

Form Factor	Maximum Number of Processors
PICMG PCI-ISA	2
SSI EEB	4[1]
SSI CEB	2
SSI MEB	4[1]

[1]*Some vendors support up to eight processors in this form factor with proprietary daughtercards.*

Note that the number of processors supported by a blade server is the number of processors per blade multiplied by the number of server blades per chassis. Thus, if a chassis can support 10 server blades, and each server blade can hold two processors, the blade server chassis contains up to 20 processors.

Chipsets and Super I/O Chips

Although several server motherboards might have the same form factor, the processors, memory types, and other features they support are controlled by the chipset used by the motherboard designer. The chipset *is* the motherboard; therefore, any two boards with the same chipsets are functionally identical unless the vendor has added features to those provided by the chipset or removed support for certain chipset features.

The chipset contains the processor bus interface (called front-side bus [FSB]), memory controllers, bus controllers, I/O controllers, and more. All the circuits of the motherboard are contained within the chipset. Because the chipset controls all the major features of the system, including the processor, we recommend selecting the chipset as the first part of the server selection process.

Chipsets designed with server use in mind vary from desktop PC chipsets in several ways, including the following:

- Support for memory-reliability technologies such as error-correcting-code (ECC) and registered SDRAM and DDR RAM
- Support for PCI-X expansion slots (a faster, wider version of PCI that supports 64-bit operation and speeds up to 133MHz); PCI-X is backward compatible with PCI
- Support for two-way and higher processor counts (when feasible); the ability to run multiple-processor configurations is affected by the processor used. For example, the Pentium 4, Pentium D, and AMD Opteron 1xx series support single-processor configurations only, and the Xeon DP and Opteron 2xx series support dual-processor configurations. The Xeon MP and Opteron 8xx support higher numbers of processors.

Major chipset vendors for servers include Intel, ServerWorks, AMD, and nVidia. See Chapter 3, "Server Chipsets," for more information.

The third major chip on many server motherboards is called the Super I/O chip. This is a chip that integrates legacy devices such as floppy controllers and serial, parallel, PS/2 mouse, and keyboard ports. Increasingly, the South Bridge chip incorporates the Super I/O chip's functions.

Memory: SIMM/DIMM/RIMM/SDRAM/DDR

You should consider the type and speed of memory used by a particular server or server-class motherboard when you select or build a server. Server memory differs from desktop PC memory in several ways:

■ Many servers still use PC100 or PC133 SDRAM rather than the newer DDR memory. Because its use is no longer widespread and less of it is produced, SDRAM memory is actually now more expensive than DDR memory. If you are upgrading multiple servers, the additional cost could be significant.

■ Most servers use registered memory rather than the unbuffered memory used by desktop PCs. Registered memory contains a small buffer chip to improve signal strength, which is very important for memory reliability in large modules.

■ Virtually all servers include ECC features in the chipset and BIOS. ECC uses the parity bit to correct single-bit memory errors and report larger memory errors. Many high-end servers include additional memory-reliability features such as hot-swapping memory and memory scrubbing.

Registered ECC memory modules are more expensive than the normal unbuffered, non-parity memory used by desktop PCs, but the extra reliability provided by these features makes the extra cost worthwhile.

The most common types of memory used by servers include the following:

■ PC100 or PC133 registered SDRAM with ECC

■ Various speeds of registered DDR SDRAM with ECC

■ Various speeds of registered DDR2 SDRAM with ECC

Older servers might use one of these types of memory:

■ PC66 registered SDRAM with ECC

■ Rambus RDRAM with ECC

■ EDO DRAM with ECC

For more information about memory types, see Chapter 5, "Memory."

Expansion Slots: ISA, PCI, AGP, and Others

Although today's servers have more integrated devices than ever before, the number and type(s) of expansion slots available is still an important factor to consider when building or buying a server.

The most common expansion slot types found on recent servers include the following:

■ PCI—Although desktop computers normally use only the 32-bit/33MHz version of PCI, servers often use 64-bit/66MHz slots (which are backward compatible with 32-bit/33MHz versions).

■ PCI-X—PCI-X runs at much faster speeds than PCI, making it an excellent choice for high-performance network adapters or RAID host adapters. PCI-X slots are backward compatible with PCI cards.

If you support or find yourself working on older servers, particularly those used in industrial applications, you might also encounter systems that still support ISA and EISA slots. On the other end of the spectrum, PCI-Express is an emerging technology found in some of the latest servers. Eventually you can expect it to replace PCI and PCI-X.

Finally, there's AGP. Although AGP is a very important bus type for desktop PCs, it is seldom found in servers except for low-end systems also suitable for workstation use.

The following sections discuss these slot designs in greater detail.

ISA Slots

Industry Standard Architecture (ISA) is the bus architecture that was introduced as an 8-bit bus with the original IBM PC in 1981; it was later expanded to 16 bits with the IBM PC/AT in 1984. ISA is the basis of the modern PC and was the primary architecture used in the vast majority of PC systems until the late 1990s. It might seem amazing that such a presumably antiquated architecture was used for so long, but it provided reliability, affordability, and compatibility, plus this old bus is still faster than many of the peripherals connected to it.

Note

The ISA bus hasn't been seen in either standard servers or desktop PCs for several years. However, it continues to be used in industrial computer (PICMG) designs. That said, it is expected to eventually fade away from those systems as well.

Two versions of the ISA bus exist, based on the number of data bits that can be transferred on the bus at a time. The older version is an 8-bit bus; the newer version is a 16-bit bus. The original 8-bit version ran at 4.77MHz in the PC and XT, and the 16-bit version used in the AT ran at 6MHz and then 8MHz. Later, the industry as a whole agreed on an 8.33MHz maximum standard speed for 8-/16-bit versions of the ISA bus for backward compatibility. Some systems have the capability to run the ISA bus faster than this, but some adapter cards do not function properly at higher speeds. ISA data transfers require anywhere from two to eight cycles. Therefore, the theoretical maximum data rate of the ISA bus is about 8MBps, as the following formula shows:

8.33MHz × 2 bytes (16 bits) ÷ 2 cycles per transfer = 8.33MBps

The bandwidth of the 8-bit bus would be half this figure (4.17MBps). Remember, however, that these figures are theoretical maximums. Because of I/O bus protocols, the effective bandwidth is much lower—typically by almost half. Even so, at about 8MBps, the ISA bus is still faster than many of the peripherals connected to it, such as serial ports, parallel ports, floppy controllers, keyboard controllers, and so on.

Figure 4.24 describes the pinouts for the full 16-bit ISA expansion slot (8-bit ISA cards plug in to the top portion of the slot only), and Figure 4.25 shows how the additional pins are oriented in the expansion slot.

The dimensions of a typical AT expansion board are as follows:

- 4.8 inches (121.92mm) high
- 13.13 inches (333.5mm) long
- 0.5 inches (12.7mm) wide

The EISA Bus

The EISA standard was developed primarily by Compaq in 1988. EISA was the company's attempt at taking over future development of the PC bus from IBM. Compaq formed the EISA committee, a non-profit organization designed specifically to control development of the EISA bus, and provided the bus designs freely to other vendors. Unfortunately, very few EISA adapters were ever developed. Those that were developed centered mainly around disk array controllers and server-type network cards.

The EISA bus was essentially a 32-bit version of ISA that provided full backward compatibility with 8-bit or 16-bit ISA cards. EISA cards use automatic configuration via software.

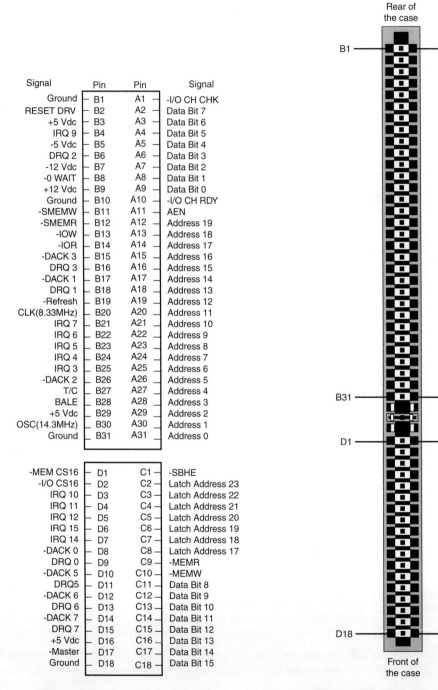

Signal	Pin		Pin		Signal
Ground	B1		A1		-I/O CH CHK
RESET DRV	B2		A2		Data Bit 7
+5 Vdc	B3		A3		Data Bit 6
IRQ 9	B4		A4		Data Bit 5
-5 Vdc	B5		A5		Data Bit 4
DRQ 2	B6		A6		Data Bit 3
-12 Vdc	B7		A7		Data Bit 2
-0 WAIT	B8		A8		Data Bit 1
+12 Vdc	B9		A9		Data Bit 0
Ground	B10		A10		-I/O CH RDY
-SMEMW	B11		A11		AEN
-SMEMR	B12		A12		Address 19
-IOW	B13		A13		Address 18
-IOR	B14		A14		Address 17
-DACK 3	B15		A15		Address 16
DRQ 3	B16		A16		Address 15
-DACK 1	B17		A17		Address 14
DRQ 1	B18		A18		Address 13
-Refresh	B19		A19		Address 12
CLK(8.33MHz)	B20		A20		Address 11
IRQ 7	B21		A21		Address 10
IRQ 6	B22		A22		Address 9
IRQ 5	B23		A23		Address 8
IRQ 4	B24		A24		Address 7
IRQ 3	B25		A25		Address 6
-DACK 2	B26		A26		Address 5
T/C	B27		A27		Address 4
BALE	B28		A28		Address 3
+5 Vdc	B29		A29		Address 2
OSC(14.3MHz)	B30		A30		Address 1
Ground	B31		A31		Address 0

Signal	Pin		Pin		Signal
-MEM CS16	D1		C1		-SBHE
-I/O CS16	D2		C2		Latch Address 23
IRQ 10	D3		C3		Latch Address 22
IRQ 11	D4		C4		Latch Address 21
IRQ 12	D5		C5		Latch Address 20
IRQ 15	D6		C6		Latch Address 19
IRQ 14	D7		C7		Latch Address 18
-DACK 0	D8		C8		Latch Address 17
DRQ 0	D9		C9		-MEMR
-DACK 5	D10		C10		-MEMW
DRQ5	D11		C11		Data Bit 8
-DACK 6	D12		C12		Data Bit 9
DRQ 6	D13		C13		Data Bit 10
-DACK 7	D14		C14		Data Bit 11
DRQ 7	D15		C15		Data Bit 12
+5 Vdc	D16		C16		Data Bit 13
-Master	D17		C17		Data Bit 14
Ground	D18		C18		Data Bit 15

Figure 4.24 Pinouts for the 16-bit ISA bus.

Figure 4.25 The ISA 16-bit bus connector.

The EISA bus added 90 new connections (55 new signals plus grounds) without increasing the physical connector size of the 16-bit ISA bus. At first glance, the 32-bit EISA slot looks a lot like the 16-bit ISA slot. However, the EISA adapter has two rows of stacked contacts. The first row is the same type used in 16-bit ISA cards; the other, thinner row extends from the 16-bit connectors. Therefore, ISA cards can still be used in EISA bus slots. Although this compatibility was not enough to ensure the popularity of EISA buses, it is a feature that was carried over into the desktop VL-Bus standard that followed. The physical specifications of an EISA card are as follows:

- 5 inches (127mm) high
- 13.13 inches (333.5mm) long
- 0.5 inches (12.7mm) wide

The EISA bus can handle up to 32 bits of data at an 8.33MHz cycle rate. Most data transfers require a minimum of two cycles, although faster cycle rates are possible if an adapter card provides tight timing specifications. The maximum bandwidth on the bus is 33MBps, as the following formula shows:

$$8.33\text{MHz} \times 4 \text{ bytes (32 bits)} = 33\text{MBps}$$

Figure 4.26 describes the pinouts for the EISA bus. Figure 4.27 shows the locations of the pins; note that some pins are offset to allow the EISA slot to accept ISA cards. Figure 4.28 shows the card connector for the EISA expansion slot.

PCI, PCI-X, and PCI-Express

In early 1992, recognizing the need to overcome weaknesses in the ISA and EISA buses, Intel spearheaded the creation of another industry group: the PCI Special Interest Group (PCI-SIG). This group was formed with the same goals as the VESA group in relation to the PC bus.

The PCI bus specification was released in June 1992 as version 1.0 and since then, it has undergone several upgrades. Table 4.10 shows the various releases of PCI.

Table 4.10   PCI Specifications

PCI Specification	Release Date	Major Change
PCI 1.0	June 1992	Original 32/64-bit specification
PCI 2.0	April 1993	Defined connectors and expansion boards
PCI 2.1	June 1995	66MHz operation, transaction ordering, latency changes
PCI 2.2	Jan. 1999	Power management, mechanical clarifications
PCI-X 1.0	Sept. 1999	133MHz operation, addendum to 2.2
Mini-PCI	Nov. 1999	Small form factor boards, addendum to 2.2
PCI 2.3	March 2002	3.3V signaling, low-profile add-in cards
PCI-X 2.0	July 2002	266MHz and 533MHz operation, supports subdivision of 64-bit data bus into 32-bit or 16-bit segments for use by multiple devices, 3.3V/1.5V signaling
PCI-Express 1.0	July 2002	2.5GBps per lane per direction, using 0.8V signaling, resulting in 250MBps per lane; designed to eventually replace PCI 2.x in PC and server systems

Servers typically offer a mixture of PCI and PCI-X or PCI-X and PCI-Express slots. The specifications for different types of PCI slots are listed in Table 4.11.

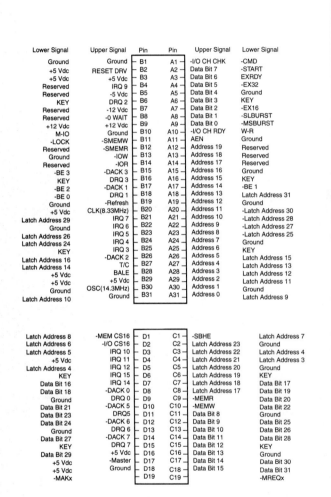

Lower Signal	Upper Signal	Pin	Pin	Upper Signal	Lower Signal
Ground	Ground	B1	A1	-I/O CH CHK	-CMD
+5 Vdc	RESET DRV	B2	A2	Data Bit 7	-START
+5 Vdc	+5 Vdc	B3	A3	Data Bit 6	EXRDY
Reserved	IRQ 9	B4	A4	Data Bit 5	-EX32
Reserved	-5 Vdc	B5	A5	Data Bit 4	Ground
KEY	DRQ 2	B6	A6	Data Bit 3	KEY
Reserved	-12 Vdc	B7	A7	Data Bit 2	-EX16
Reserved	-0 WAIT	B8	A8	Data Bit 1	-SLBURST
+12 Vdc	+12 Vdc	B9	A9	Data Bit 0	-MSBURST
M-IO	Ground	B10	A10	-I/O CH RDY	W-R
-LOCK	-SMEMW	B11	A11	AEN	Ground
Reserved	-SMEMR	B12	A12	Address 19	Reserved
Ground	-IOW	B13	A13	Address 18	Reserved
Reserved	-IOR	B14	A14	Address 17	Reserved
-BE 3	-DACK 3	B15	A15	Address 16	Ground
KEY	DRQ 3	B16	A16	Address 15	KEY
-BE 2	-DACK 1	B17	A17	Address 14	-BE 1
-BE 0	DRQ 1	B18	A18	Address 13	Latch Address 31
Ground	-Refresh	B19	A19	Address 12	Ground
+5 Vdc	CLK(8.33MHz)	B20	A20	Address 11	-Latch Address 30
Latch Address 29	IRQ 7	B21	A21	Address 10	-Latch Address 28
Ground	IRQ 6	B22	A22	Address 9	-Latch Address 27
Latch Address 26	IRQ 5	B23	A23	Address 8	-Latch Address 25
Latch Address 24	IRQ 4	B24	A24	Address 7	Ground
KEY	IRQ 3	B25	A25	Address 6	KEY
Latch Address 16	-DACK 2	B26	A26	Address 5	Latch Address 15
Latch Address 14	T/C	B27	A27	Address 4	Latch Address 13
+5 Vdc	BALE	B28	A28	Address 3	Latch Address 12
+5 Vdc	+5 Vdc	B29	A29	Address 2	Latch Address 11
Ground	OSC(14.3MHz)	B30	A30	Address 1	Ground
Latch Address 10	Ground	B31	A31	Address 0	Latch Address 9

Latch Address 8	-MEM CS16	D1	C1	-SBHE	Latch Address 7
Latch Address 6	-I/O CS16	D2	C2	Latch Address 23	Ground
Latch Address 5	IRQ 10	D3	C3	Latch Address 22	Latch Address 4
+5 Vdc	IRQ 11	D4	C4	Latch Address 21	Latch Address 3
Latch Address 4	IRQ 12	D5	C5	Latch Address 20	Ground
KEY	IRQ 15	D6	C6	Latch Address 19	KEY
Data Bit 16	IRQ 14	D7	C7	Latch Address 18	Data Bit 17
Data Bit 18	-DACK 0	D8	C8	Latch Address 17	Data Bit 19
Ground	DRQ 0	D9	C9	-MEMR	Data Bit 20
Data Bit 21	-DACK 5	D10	C10	-MEMW	Data Bit 22
Data Bit 23	DRQ5	D11	C11	Data Bit 8	Ground
Data Bit 24	-DACK 6	D12	C12	Data Bit 9	Data Bit 25
Ground	DRQ 6	D13	C13	Data Bit 10	Data Bit 26
Data Bit 27	-DACK 7	D14	C14	Data Bit 11	Data Bit 28
KEY	DRQ 7	D15	C15	Data Bit 12	KEY
Data Bit 29	+5 Vdc	D16	C16	Data Bit 13	Ground
+5 Vdc	-Master	D17	C17	Data Bit 14	Data Bit 30
+5 Vdc	Ground	D18	C18	Data Bit 15	Data Bit 31
-MAKx		D19	C19		-MREQx

Figure 4.26   Pinouts for the EISA bus.

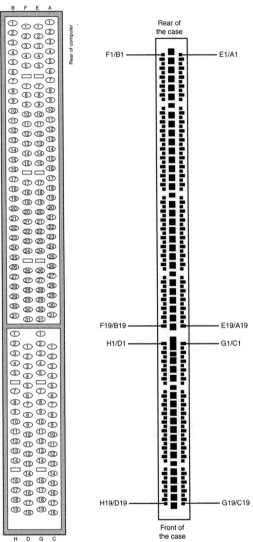

Figure 4.27
Pin locations
inside the EISA
bus connector.

Figure 4.28   The EISA bus
connector.

Table 4.11   PCI Bus Types

PCI Bus Type	Bus Width (Bits)	Bus Speed (MHz)	Data Cycles per Clock	Bandwidth (MBps)
PCI	32	33	1	133
PCI 66MHz	32	66	1	266
PCI 64-bit	64	33	1	266
PCI 66MHz/64-bit	64	66	1	533
PCI-X 64	64[1]	66	1	533
PCI-X 100	100[1]	66	1	800
PCI-X 133	64[1]	133	1	1,066
PCI-X 266	64[1]	133	2	2,132
PCI-X 533	64[1]	133	4	4,266
PCI-Express[2]	1	2,500	0.8	250
PCI-Express[2]	16	2,500	0.8	4,000
PCI-Express[2]	32	2,500	0.8	8,000

[1]*Bus width on PCI-X devices can be shared by multiple 32-bit or 16-bit devices.*

[2]*PCI-Express uses 8b/10b encoding, which transfers 8 bits for every 10 bits sent and can transfer 1–32 bits at a time, depending on how many lanes are in the implementation.*

Aiding performance is the fact that the PCI bus can operate concurrently with the processor bus; it does not supplant it. The CPU can be processing data in an external cache while the PCI bus is busy transferring information between other parts of the system; this is a major design benefit of the PCI bus.

The PCI specification identifies three board configurations, each designed for a specific type of system with specific power requirements; each specification has a 32-bit version and a longer 64-bit version. The 5V specification is for stationary computer systems (using PCI 2.2 or earlier versions), the 3.3V specification is for portable systems (also supported by PCI 2.3), and the universal specification is for motherboards and cards that work in either type of system. 64-bit versions of the 5V and universal PCI slots are found primarily on server motherboards. The PCI-X 2.0 specifications for 266 and 533 versions support 3.3V and 1.5V signaling; this corresponds to PCI version 2.3, which supports 3.3V signaling. PCI-X slots also support PCI cards.

Unlike older card designs, such as ISA and EISA, PCI does not use jumper blocks or DIP switches for configuration. Instead, software or a Plug and Play (PnP) BIOS does the configuration. This was the model for the Intel PnP specification. True PnP systems are capable of automatically configuring the adapters.

PCI-SIG developed PCI-Express during 2001–2002, based on the 3GIO draft high-speed bus specification originally developed by the Arapahoe Work Group (a work group led primarily by Intel). The initial PCI-Express 1.0 specification was released in 2002. However, the first systems to use PCI-Express slots did not appear until 2004.

The key features of PCI-Express are as follows:

- Compatibility with existing PCI enumeration and software device drivers
- Physical connection over copper, optical, or other physical media to allow for future encoding schemes

- Maximum bandwidth per pin, which allows small form factors, reduced cost, simpler board designs and routing, and reduced signal integrity issues

- An embedded clocking scheme, which enables easy frequency (speed) changes compared to synchronous clocking

- Bandwidth (throughput) that can increase easily with frequency and width (lane) increases

- Low latency, suitable for applications that require isochronous (time-sensitive) data delivery, such as streaming video

- Hot-plugging and hot-swapping capabilities

- Power management capabilities

PCI-Express, like other high-speed interfaces, such as SATA, USB 2.0, and IEEE 1394 (FireWire or i.LINK), uses a serial bus for signaling. A serial bus sends 1 bit at a time over a single wire at very high speeds. Serial bus signaling avoids the problems caused by parallel buses such as PCI and PCI-X, which must synchronize multiple bits sent simultaneously and may have problems with jitter or propagation delays.

PCI-Express is a very fast serial bus design that is backward compatible with current PCI parallel bus software drivers and controls. In PCI-Express, data is sent full-duplex (that is, via simultaneously operating one-way paths) over two pairs of differentially signaled wires called a *lane*. Each lane allows for about 250MBps throughput in each direction initially, and the design allows for scaling from 1 to 2, 4, 8, 16, or 32 lanes. The most common configurations in PCs and servers are x1 (one lane), x4, and x16.

For example, a high-bandwidth configuration with eight lanes allowing 8 bits to be sent in each direction simultaneously would allow up to 2000MBps bandwidth (each way) and use a total of only 40 pins (32 for the differential data pairs and 8 for control). Future increases in signaling speed could increase that to 8000MBps each way over the same 40 pins. This compares to PCI, which has only 133MBps bandwidth (one way at a time) and requires more than 100 pins to carry the signals. For expansion cards, PCI-Express takes on the physical format of a smaller connector that appears adjacent to any existing PCI slots on the motherboard. Figure 4.29 shows how PCI-Express x1 and x16 slots compare to 33MHz PCI and 133MHz PCI-X expansion slots.

PCI-Express uses an IBM-designed 8-bit–to–10-bit encoding scheme, which allows for self-clocked signals that easily allow future increases in frequency. The starting frequency is 2.5GHz, and the specification allows increasing up to 10GHz in the future, which is about the limit of copper connections. By combining frequency increases with the capability to use up to 32 lanes, PCI-Express will be capable of supporting future bandwidths up to 32GBps.

PCI-Express is designed to augment and eventually replace many of the buses currently used in PCs and servers. In addition, it will replace video interfaces such as AGP and act as a mezzanine bus to attach other interfaces, such as SATA, USB 2.0, IEEE 1394b, Gigabit Ethernet, and more. Currently, PCI-Express is used alongside PCI-X and PCI slots, as Figure 4.29 suggests.

Because PCI-Express can be implemented over cables as well as onboard, it can be used to create systems constructed with remote "bricks" that contain the bulk of the computing power. Imagine the motherboard, processor, and RAM in one small box, hidden under a table, with the video, disk drives, and I/O ports in another box, sitting out on a table within easy reach. This will enable a variety of flexible PC form factors to be developed in the future without compromising performance.

For more information on PCI-Express, you can consult the PCI-SIG website (www.pcisig.org).

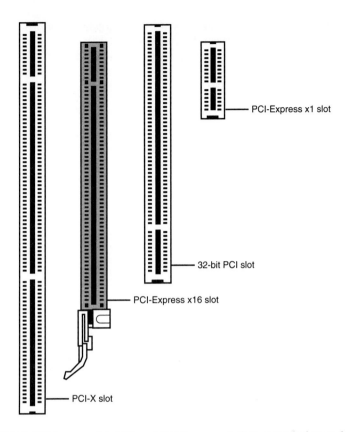

PCI-Express x1 slot

32-bit PCI slot

PCI-Express x16 slot

PCI-X slot

Figure 4.29   PCI-X, PCI-Express x16, PCI, and PCI-Express x1 slots compared to each other.

The AGP Bus

The AGP bus was created in 1996 by Intel specifically for high-performance graphics and video support. Although the PnP BIOS treats AGP like a PCI slot in terms of IRQ and other hardware resources, it uses different connectors and is otherwise separate from PCI.

Table 4.12 lists the various versions of AGP that have been developed for PCs. Although you might find AGP slots in some servers, systems with AGP slots are primarily workstation or PC systems. Currently, servers don't need anything other than basic 2D GUI graphics for system management, and therefore most servers use PCI-based graphics, such as the ATI Rage XL, on the motherboard.

Table 4.12   AGP Versions and Specifications

AGP Version	Speed	Voltage	Notes
1.0	1x, 2x	3.3V	Not compatible with AGP 1.5V slots
2.0	4x	1.5V	Systems with universal AGP sockets can accept AGP 1x/2x cards
3.0	8x	1.5V	Systems with universal AGP sockets can accept AGP 1x/2x cards

We recommend using AGP video in a server only if you cannot use PCI video—for example, if you run out of PCI slots and your server does not incorporate video. If you need to use AGP video, keep in mind the differences between AGP slots:

■ Most recent AGP video cards are designed to conform to the AGP 4X or AGP 8X specification, each of which runs on only 1.5 volts.

■ Most older motherboards with AGP 2X slots are designed to accept only 3.3V cards.

If you plug a 1.5V card in to a 3.3V slot, both the card and motherboard could be damaged, so special keys have been incorporated into the AGP specification to prevent such disasters. Normally, the slots and cards are keyed such that 1.5V cards fit only in 1.5V sockets, and 3.3V cards fit only in 3.3V sockets. However, universal sockets do exist that accept either 1.5V or 3.3V cards. The keying for the AGP cards and connectors is dictated by the AGP standard, as shown in Figure 4.30.

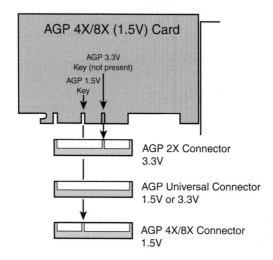

Figure 4.30   AGP 4X/8X (1.5V) card and AGP 3.3V, universal, and 1.5V slots.

As you can see from Figure 4.30, AGP 4X or 8X (1.5V) cards fit only in 1.5V or universal (3.3V or 1.5V) slots. Due to the design of the connector and card keys, a 1.5V card cannot be inserted into a 3.3V slot.

Caution

Some AGP 4x/8x-compatible motherboards require you to use 1.5V AGP 4x/8x cards only; be sure to check compatibility between the motherboard and the AGP card you want to buy to avoid problems. Some AGP 4x/8x-compatible slots use the card retention mechanism shown in Figure 4.31. Note that AGP 1x/2x slots have a visible divider not present on the newer AGP 4x/8x slot. AGP 4x slots can also accept AGP 8x cards and vice versa.

Server/workstation motherboards with AGP slots might use a variation known as AGP Pro, now in version 1.1a. AGP Pro defines a slightly longer slot with additional power pins at each end to drive bigger and faster AGP cards that consume more than 25 watts of power, up to a maximum of 110 watts. AGP Pro slots are backward compatible, meaning that a standard AGP card can plug in, and a number of motherboard vendors have used AGP Pro slots rather than AGP 4x slots in their products. Because AGP Pro slots are longer, an AGP 1x/2x card can be incorrectly inserted into the slot, which could damage it, so some vendors supply a cover or an insert for the AGP Pro extension at the rear of the slot. This protective cover or insert should be removed only if you want to install an AGP Pro card.

Figure 4.31 compares the standard AGP 1x/2x, AGP 4x, and AGP Pro slots.

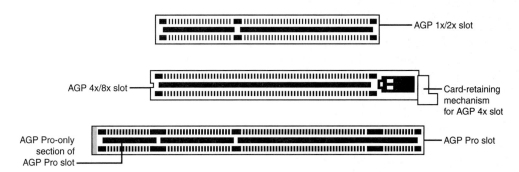

Figure 4.31 AGP standard (1x/2x), AGP 4x, and AGP Pro slots compared. AGP 4x and AGP Pro can accept AGP 1x, 2x, and 4x cards. AGP 4x and AGP Pro slots can also accept AGP 8x cards.

CPU Voltage Regulators

Because virtually all x86 processors run on a fraction of 3.3V DC (the lowest power level available from a server's power supply), server and PC motherboards alike feature voltage regulators. Occasionally the voltage regulator is built in to a removable daughtercard, but in most cases, the voltage regulator is built in to the motherboard. The voltage regulator uses a series of capacitors and coils and is usually located near the processor socket(s) or slot(s). Figure 4.32 shows the location of a typical voltage regulator on a typical server motherboard.

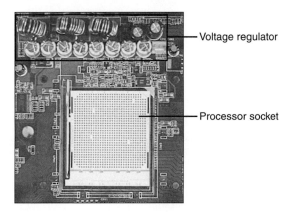

Figure 4.32 Voltage regulator components on a typical server motherboard.

If you plan to use an aftermarket active or passive heatsink to cool your processor(s), you should be sure to check the clearance between the processor socket(s) and the voltage regulator's components. Some voltage regulators are located so close to the processor socket(s) that extra-large heatsinks cannot be used.

BIOS Chips

The BIOS chip in any given server might take one of the following forms:

- A socketed chip
- A surface-mounted chip

The BIOS chip provides the interface between the operating system and the motherboard's onboard hardware. In virtually any server built in the past decade, the BIOS chip's contents can be updated through software. BIOSs that support software updating are known as flash BIOS chips.

BIOS settings are stored in a separate chip known as the CMOS chip or as the nonvolatile RAM/real-time clock (NVRAM/RTC) chip.

▶▶ For more information on configuring the system BIOS, see "ROM BIOS," p. 286.

CMOS Battery

A small battery on the motherboard, often called the CMOS battery, maintains the BIOS settings stored in the CMOS and maintains clock timing when the server is turned off.

If the CMOS battery's voltage falls below minimum amounts, the system clock loses time, and eventually CMOS settings are lost. When that happens, the BIOS returns to its default settings the next time power is restored. Most recent servers use the same CR2032 3V lithium watch battery used by most recent desktop PCs. However, some older servers use other battery types, including rechargeable Ni-Cad battery packs or chips that incorporate battery and CMOS RAM/RTC. See your server or motherboard manual for details.

Figure 4.33 shows a BIOS chip and CMOS battery on a typical server motherboard.

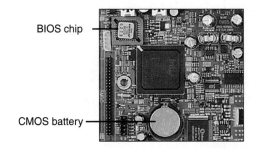

BIOS chip

CMOS battery

Figure 4.33   Voltage regulator components on a typical server motherboard.

System Resources

System resources are the communications channels, addresses, and other signals hardware devices use to communicate on the bus of an x86 or Itanium-based server. At their lowest level, these resources typically include the following:

- Memory addresses
- IRQ (interrupt request) channels
- DMA channels
- I/O port addresses

These are listed roughly in the order in which you would experience problems with them. Memory conflicts are perhaps the most troublesome of these and certainly the most difficult to fully explain and overcome. Memory conflicts are discussed in Chapter 5. This chapter focuses on the other resources listed here, in the order in which you will likely have problems with them.

Historically, IRQs have caused more problems than DMAs because they are in much higher demand; virtually all cards use IRQ channels. Fewer problems exist with DMA channels because fewer cards use them: DMA channels are only used by legacy devices, and there are usually more than enough channels to go around. I/O ports are used by all hardware devices on the bus, but there are technically 64KB of them, which means there are plenty to go around.

If you are managing a modern server that uses PnP configuration, hardware resources are configured automatically for you. However, if you are working with older servers that use ISA cards or use non-PnP operating systems such as Windows NT 4.0, you are responsible for ensuring that each hardware device has nonconflicting resources.

These resources are required and used by many components of a system. Adapter cards need these resources to communicate with the system and accomplish their purposes. Not all adapter cards have the same resource requirements. A serial communications port, for example, needs an IRQ channel and an I/O port address, whereas most network cards use an IRQ channel and an I/O port address, and some also use a 16KB block of memory addresses. As a system's complexity increases, the chance for resource conflicts increases, particularly if your system does not use PnP configuration. Modern servers with several additional devices can really push the envelope and become a configuration nightmare for the uninitiated. Sometimes under these situations the automatic configuration capability of PnP can get confused or fail to optimally configure resources so that everything will work.

There are two major methods that you can use for managing PnP configuration:

■ A server with a PnP BIOS can usually be configured to use the operating system's PnP configuration or to use its own PnP handlers. If the BIOS is configured not to use a PnP operating system, the BIOS's own PnP handlers will be used to manage PnP hardware.

■ If the BIOS is configured to use a PnP operating system, such as Windows 2000 Server, Windows Server 2003, or recent Linux distributions (particularly those based on kernel 2.4 or later), the operating system will be responsible for managing PnP hardware.

Depending on which type of PnP handler you are using and the operating system, you might be able to modify resource assignments by using the PnP software that comes with the card (typically used by ISA cards with PnP configuration options) or the Device Manager in Windows 2000 Server and Windows Server 2003. Thus, you can sometimes improve on a default configuration by making some changes. Even if the automatic configuration gets confused (which happens more often than it should), fortunately, in almost all cases, a logical way to configure the system exists—when you know the rules.

IRQ

IRQ channels, or hardware interrupts, are used by various hardware devices to signal the motherboard that a request must be fulfilled. This procedure is the same as a student raising his hand to indicate that he needs attention.

These interrupt channels are represented by wires on the motherboard running to the slot connectors and to onboard devices. When a particular interrupt is invoked, a special routine takes over the system, which first saves all the CPU register contents in a stack and then directs the system to the interrupt vector table. This vector table contains a list of memory addresses that correspond to the interrupt channels. Depending on which interrupt was invoked, the program corresponding to that channel is run.

The pointers in the vector table point to the address of whatever software driver is used to service the card that generated the interrupt. For a network card, for example, the vector might point to the address of the network drivers that have been loaded to operate the card; for a hard disk controller, the vector might point to the BIOS code that operates the controller.

After the particular software routine finishes performing whatever function the card needed, the interrupt control software returns the stack contents to the CPU registers, and the system then resumes whatever it was doing before the interrupt occurred.

Through the use of interrupts, a system can respond to external events in a timely fashion. Each time a serial port presents a byte to the system, an interrupt is generated to ensure that the system reads that byte before another comes in. Keep in mind that in some cases a port device—in particular, a modem with a 16550 or higher UART chip—might incorporate a byte buffer that allows multiple characters to be stored before an interrupt is generated.

Hardware interrupts are generally prioritized by their numbers; with some exceptions, the highest-priority interrupts have the lowest numbers. Higher-priority interrupts take precedence over lower-priority interrupts by interrupting them. As a result, several interrupts can occur in a system concurrently, with each interrupt nesting within another.

Interrupts are handled in two ways:

- Edge triggered
- Level triggered

The ISA and EISA buses use *edge-triggered* interrupt sensing, in which an interrupt is sensed by a changing signal sent on a particular wire located in the slot connector. A different wire corresponds to each possible hardware interrupt. Because the motherboard can't recognize which slot contains the card that used an interrupt line and therefore generated the interrupt, confusion results if more than one card is set to use a particular interrupt. Each interrupt, therefore, is usually designated for a single hardware device. The only documented interrupt sharing supported by the ISA/EISA bus was the assignment of COM 1 and COM 3 to IRQ 4 and COM 2 and COM 4 to IRQ 3. However, this "sharing" was valid only if COM 1 and COM 3 (or COM 2 and COM 4) were not in use at the same time. Any attempt to use two devices set to the same IRQ crashed the system.

On the other hand, devices connected to the PCI bus (which also includes PCI-X, PCI Express, AGP slots and USB and IEEE 1394 ports) can share interrupts. The real problem is that there are technically two sets of hardware interrupts in the system: PCI interrupts and ISA interrupts. For PCI cards to work in a PC or server, the PCI interrupts are first mapped to ISA interrupts, which are then configured as non-shareable. Consequently, early PCI users continued to have problems with IRQs.

Fortunately, PCI IRQ steering was introduced starting with Windows 95 OSR 2.x and is part of Windows 2000 Server and Windows Server 2003. PCI IRQ steering allows a plug-and-play operating system such as Windows to dynamically map, or "steer," PCI cards (which almost all use PCI INTA#) to standard PC interrupts and allows several PCI cards to be mapped to the same interrupt. You can find more information on PCI IRQ steering in the section "PCI Interrupts," later in this chapter.

Hardware interrupts are sometimes referred to as *maskable interrupts*, which means the interrupts can be masked or turned off for a short time while the CPU is used for other critical operations. It is up to the system BIOS and programs to manage interrupts properly and efficiently for the best system performance. The following sections discuss the IRQs that any standard devices use, as well as what might be free in your system.

Table 4.13 shows the typical uses for interrupts in the 16-bit ISA and 32-bit PCI/AGP buses and lists them in priority order from highest to lowest. The obsolete ISA and EISA buses used a similar IRQ map.

Note

32-bit and 64-bit cards also use 16-bit IRQs (9–15).

Table 4.13   16/32-Bit ISA/PCI/AGP Default and Typical Interrupt Assignments

IRQ	Standard Function	Bus Slot	Card Type	Recommended Use
0	System Timer	No	—	—
1	Keyboard Controller	No	—	—
2	Second IRQ Controller Cascade	No	—	—
8	Real-Time Clock	No	—	—
9	Available (as IRQ2 or IRQ9)	Yes	8/16-bit	Network Card[1]
10	Available	Yes	16-bit	USB[1]
11	Available	Yes	16-bit	SCSI Host Adapter[1]
12	Mouse Port/Available	Yes	16-bit	Mouse Port
13	Math Coprocessor	No	—	—
14	Primary IDE	Yes	16-bit	Primary IDE (hard disks)
15	Secondary IDE	Yes	16-bit	Second IDE (CD-ROM/Tape)
3	Serial 2 (COM2:)	Yes	8/16-bit	COM2:/Internal Modem
4	Serial 1 (COM1:)	Yes	8/16-bit	COM1:
5	Sound/Parallel 2 (LPT2:)	Yes	8/16-bit	Sound Card
6	Floppy Controller	Yes	8/16-bit	Floppy Controller
7	Parallel 1 (LPT1:)	Yes	8/16-bit	LPT1:

[1]*Typical usage; may vary from system to system.*

Notice that interrupts 0, 1, 2, 8, and 13 are not on the bus connectors and are not accessible to adapter cards. Interrupts 8, 10, 11, 12, 13, 14, and 15 are from the second interrupt controller and are accessible only by boards that use the 16-bit extension connector because that is where those wires are located. IRQ9 is rewired to the 8-bit slot connector in place of IRQ2, so IRQ9 replaces IRQ2 and, therefore, is available to 8-bit cards, which treat it as though it were IRQ2. IRQs used by 16-bit ISA cards are also used by newer expansion bus types such as PCI, PCI-X, AGP, and PCI Express.

If you are managing an older server that uses ISA or EISA cards, or even a server that uses onboard legacy devices such as serial and parallel ports, the likelihood of IRQ conflicts is greater than on servers that use only PCI/AGP/PCI-X/PCI Express slots and onboard PCI devices.

PCI Interrupts

The PCI bus supports hardware interrupts (IRQs) that can be used by PCI devices to signal to the bus that they need attention. The four PCI interrupts are called INTA#, INTB#, INTC#, and INTD#. These INTx# interrupts are *level sensitive*, which means the electrical signaling enables them to be shared among PCI cards. In fact, all single-device or single-function PCI chips or cards that use only one interrupt must use INTA#. This is one of the rules in the PCI specification. If additional devices are within a chip or onboard a card, the additional devices can use INTB# through INTD#. Because there are very few multifunction PCI chips or boards, practically all the devices on a given PCI bus share INTA#.

Before the development of PCI IRQ steering, PCI interrupts had to be mapped to ISA interrupts. Because ISA interrupts cannot be shared, the result was that each PCI card using INTA# on the PCI bus was mapped to a different non-shareable ISA interrupt. For example, you could have a system with four PCI slots and four PCI cards installed, each using PCI interrupt INTA#. These cards would each be mapped to a different available ISA interrupt request, such as IRQ9, IRQ10, IRQ11, or IRQ5 in most cases.

PCI IRQ steering enables multiple PCI-bus devices to share a single IRQ. In addition to using a compatible operating system, such as Windows 2000 Server or Windows Server 2003, the system BIOS must also support IRQ steering.

Generally, the BIOS assigns unique IRQs to PCI devices. Although Windows has the capability to change these settings, it typically does not do so automatically, except where necessary to eliminate conflicts. If there are insufficient free IRQs to go around, IRQ steering allows Windows to assign multiple PCI devices to a single IRQ, thus enabling all the devices in the system to function properly. Without IRQ steering, Windows begins to disable devices after it runs out of free IRQs to assign.

On systems running Windows 2000 Server 2000 and Windows Server 2003, IRQ steering is obvious in the Device Manager: Multiple PCI devices would be listed with the same IRQ. You can have several PCI devices mapped to the same ISA IRQ only in the following situations:

- If no ISA devices are using the IRQ
- If the BIOS and operating system support PCI IRQ steering
- If PCI IRQ steering is enabled

Advanced Programmable Interrupt Controller (APIC)

As a replacement for the traditional pair of 8259 interrupt controllers, Intel developed APIC in the mid-1990s. Although all processors since the original Pentium contain an APIC, an APIC must also be present in the motherboard's chipset, and the BIOS and operating system must also support APIC. APIC support is present on most recent motherboards, and it is also supported by Windows 2000 Server, Windows Server 2003, and recent Linux distributions. You can enable or disable APIC support in the system BIOS.

APIC provides support for multiple processors, but it is also used on single-processor computers. The major benefit of APIC for a single-processor system is support for virtual PCI IRQs above 15. Most APIC implementations support virtual IRQs up to 24. Although Windows 2000 tends to place PCI IRQs into the traditional ISA range of 0–15, even when APIC is enabled, Windows Server 2003 and Linux distributions with APIC support make full use of APIC services when installed on a system with APIC enabled. On Windows Server 2003, APIC limits IRQ sharing to enable devices to perform better with fewer conflicts. For example, on one typical Windows system with APIC enabled (see Figure 4.34), PCI IRQs are assigned thus:

- PCI IRQ 16: onboard audio / AGP graphics (shared)
- PCI IRQ 17: add-on card USB 1.1 controller (non-shared)
- PCI IRQ 18: add-on card USB 1.1 controller (non-shared)
- PCI IRQ 19: 10/100 Ethernet adapter / add-on card USB 2.0 controller (shared)
- PCI IRQ 21: onboard USB 1.1 controllers (3) / onboard USB 2.0 controller (shared)

Note that APIC must be enabled in the system BIOS when Windows 2000 Server or Windows Server 2003 is installed to make APIC services available.

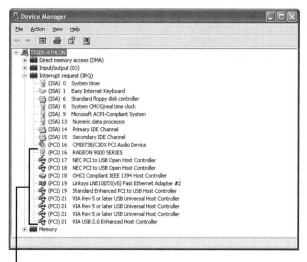

Interrupts generated by APIC are assigned to
PCI/AGP/PCI-X/PCI Express slots and devices.

Figure 4.34   The IRQ map for a typical system with APIC support.

Note

The default view used by Device Manager in Windows 2000, Windows Server 2003, and client operating systems displays devices by type. To view IRQs and other hardware resources such as DMA, I/O port addresses, and memory addresses, select View, Resources by Type.

Linux Interrupt Handling

Linux handles PCI interrupts differently than Windows 2000 Server or Windows Server 2003. Linux does not assign IRQs to devices until they are actually used. To ensure that Linux has assigned IRQs to all onboard devices, you should use each onboard device as soon as Linux is installed.

To view Linux IRQ usage, you can use the command-line program cat/procs/interrupts. Each IRQ in use is listed by its IRQ number. Each IRQ number displays the type of interrupt controller used to generate the IRQ and the device that is using the IRQ.

Unlike Windows 2000 Server and Windows Server 2003, Linux is not designed to share IRQs. If two or more IRQs are listed as using the same IRQ when you run cat/procs/interrupts, you have an IRQ conflict unless the devices are using the same add-on card. To resolve the conflict, see the following tip.

Tip

To fix conflicts between cards on a modern x86 server that uses a PnP BIOS or operating system, try the following:

1. Disable the BIOS setting for PnP operating system, particularly if you use Linux. If you use Windows 2000 Server or Windows Server 2003 and this setting is already disabled, try enabling it.

2. Select the option to clear the Enhanced System Configuration Data (ESCD) settings in the BIOS and restart the system. The system will reconfigure PnP cards.

3. If you have conflicts between cards in different slots or between cards and onboard devices, move one of the conflicting cards to a different slot.

4. Disable unused legacy ports such as integrated parallel and serial ports. This can enable the BIOS to use the IRQs reserved for those ports for PCI and other non-legacy devices.

Recent Linux distributions also support APIC, enabling you to use PCI interrupts above 15, if APIC is enabled in the system BIOS. If APIC is enabled, each PCI device is likely to be assigned to its own IRQ, eliminating conflicts. Linux is not designed to support IRQ sharing, so the use of APIC on a Linux-based server is even more essential to avoid IRQ problems. Note that APIC is fully supported in Linux kernel v2.6 and higher.

The PCI bus enables two types of devices to exist: bus masters (initiators) and slaves (targets). A *bus master* is a device that can take control of the bus and initiate a transfer. The *slave* device is the intended destination of the transfer. Most PCI devices can act as both masters and slaves, and to be compliant with the PC'97 and newer system design guides, all PCI slots must support bus master cards.

The PCI bus is an arbitrated bus: A central arbiter (part of the PCI bus controller in the motherboard chipset) governs all bus transfers, giving fair and controlled access to all the devices on the bus. Before a master can use the bus, it must first request control from the central arbiter, and then it is granted control for only a specified maximum number of cycles. This arbitration allows equal and fair access to all the bus master devices, prevents a single device from hogging the bus, and prevents deadlocks because of simultaneous multiple device access. In this manner, the PCI bus acts much like a local area network (LAN), albeit one that is contained entirely within the system and runs at a much higher speed than conventional external networks between PCs.

DMA Channels

Communications devices that must send and receive information at high speeds use DMA channels. A serial port does not use a DMA channel, but an ISA-based SCSI adapter often does, as does a parallel port using ECP or EPP/ECP modes. DMA channels can sometimes be shared if the devices are not the type that would need them simultaneously. However, there is hardly any need to share DMA channels on a system that has no ISA or EISA slots.

Note

There are several types of DMA in a modern PC. The DMA channels referred to in this section involve the ISA bus. Other buses, such as the ATA/IDE bus used by hard drives, have different DMA uses. The DMA channels explained here don't involve your ATA/IDE drives, even if they are set to use DMA or Ultra DMA transfers.

Since the introduction of the 286 CPU, the ISA bus has supported eight DMA channels, with seven channels available to the expansion slots. Similar to the expanded IRQ lines described earlier in this chapter, the added DMA channels were created by cascading a second DMA controller to the first one. DMA channel 4 is used to cascade channels 0–3 to the microprocessor. Channels 0–3 are available for 8-bit transfers, and channels 5–7 are for 16-bit transfers only. Table 4.14 shows the typical uses for the DMA channels on a typical x86 or Itanium server.

Table 4.14   16-Bit ISA Default DMA Channel Assignments as Used on x86 and Itanium Servers

DMA	Standard Function	Bus Slot	Card Type	Transfer	Recommended Use
0	Available	Yes	16-bit	8-bit	Available[1]
1	Available	Yes	8/16-bit	8-bit	Available[1]
2	Floppy Disk Controller	Yes	8/16-bit	8-bit	Floppy Controller
3	Available	Yes	8/16-bit	8-bit	LPT1: in ECP or EPP/ECP Mode
4	First DMA Controller Cascade	No	—	16-bit	—
5	Available	Yes	16-bit	16-bit	Available[1]
6	Available	Yes	16-bit	16-bit	Available
7	Available	Yes	16-bit	16-bit	Available

[1]*Available on servers that don't have integrated audio or whose integrated audio does not emulate the Sound Blaster Pro sound card.*

In Table 4.14, DMA channels 0, 1, and 5 would be assigned to audio if the server had an ISA sound card or a PCI sound card or integrated audio that emulates the Creative Labs Sound Blaster Pro. However, these DMA channels are listed as available because most servers do not have onboard or card-based audio.

I/O Port Addresses

A computer's I/O ports enable communications between devices and software in the system. They are equivalent to two-way radio channels. If you want to talk to the serial port, you need to know on which I/O port (radio channel) it is listening. Similarly, if you want to receive data from the serial port, you need to listen on the same channel on which it is transmitting.

Unlike IRQs and DMA channels, systems have an abundance of I/O ports. There are 65,535 ports to be exact—numbered from 0000h to FFFFh—which is an artifact of the Intel processor design more than anything else. Even though most devices use up to 8 ports for themselves, with that many to spare, you won't run out anytime soon. The biggest problem you have to worry about is setting two devices to use the same port. Most modern plug-and-play systems resolve any port conflicts and select alternative ports for one of the conflicting devices.

One confusing issue is that I/O ports are designated by hexadecimal addresses similar to memory addresses. They are not memory; they are ports. The difference is that when you send data to memory address 1000h, it gets stored in your SIMM or DIMM memory. If you send data to I/O port address 1000h, it gets sent out on the bus on that "channel," and anybody listening in could then "hear" it. If nobody is listening to that port address, the data reaches the end of the bus and is absorbed by the bus-terminating resistors.

Driver programs primarily interact with devices at the various port addresses. The driver must know which ports the device is using to work with it, and vice versa. That is not usually a problem because the driver and device come from the same company.

Motherboard and chipset devices are usually set to use I/O port addresses 0h–FFh, and all other devices use 100h–FFFFh. Table 4.15 shows the commonly used motherboard and chipset-based I/O port usage.

Table 4.15   Motherboard and Chipset-Based Device Port Addresses

Address (Hex)	Size	Description
0000–000F	16 bytes	Chipset–8237 DMA 1
0020–0021	2 bytes	Chipset–8259 interrupt controller 1
002E–002F	2 bytes	Super I/O controller configuration registers
0040–0043	4 bytes	Chipset–Counter/Timer 1
0048–004B	4 bytes	Chipset–Counter/Timer 2
0060	1 byte	Keyboard/mouse controller byte - reset IRQ
0061	1 byte	Chipset–NMI, speaker control
0064	1 byte	Keyboard/mouse controller, CMD/STAT byte
0070, bit 7	1 bit	Chipset–Enable NMI
0070, bits 6:0	7 bits	MC146818–Real-time clock, address
0071	1 byte	MC146818–Real-time clock, data
0078	1 byte	Reserved–Board configuration
0079	1 byte	Reserved–Board configuration
0080–008F	16 bytes	Chipset–DMA page registers
00A0–00A1	2 bytes	Chipset–8259 interrupt controller 2
00B2	1 byte	APM control port
00B3	1 byte	APM status port
00C0–00DE	31 bytes	Chipset–8237 DMA 2
00F0	1 byte	Math Coprocessor Reset Numeric Error

To find out exactly which port addresses are being used on your motherboard, consult the board documentation or look up the settings in the Windows Device Manager.

Bus-based devices typically use the addresses from 100h up. Table 4.16 lists the commonly used bus-based device addresses and some common adapter cards and their settings.

Table 4.16   Bus-Based Device Port Addresses

Address (Hex)	Size	Description
0130–0133	4 bytes	Adaptec SCSI adapter (alternate)
0134–0137	4 bytes	Adaptec SCSI adapter (alternate)
0168–016F	8 bytes	Fourth IDE interface
0170–0177	8 bytes	Secondary IDE interface
01E8–01EF	8 bytes	Third IDE interface
01F0–01F7	8 bytes	Primary IDE/AT (16-bit) hard disk controller
0200–0207	8 bytes	Gameport or joystick adapter
0210–0217	8 bytes	IBM XT expansion chassis
0220–0233	20 bytes	Creative Labs Sound Blaster 16 audio (default)
0230–0233	4 bytes	Adaptec SCSI adapter (alternate)
0234–0237	4 bytes	Adaptec SCSI adapter (alternate)

Table 4.16   Continued

Address (Hex)	Size	Description
0238–023B	4 bytes	MS bus mouse (alternate)
023C–023F	4 bytes	MS bus mouse (default)
0240–024F	16 bytes	SMC Ethernet adapter (default)
0240–0253	20 bytes	Creative Labs Sound Blaster 16 audio (alternate)
0260–026F	16 bytes	SMC Ethernet adapter (alternate)
0260–0273	20 bytes	Creative Labs Sound Blaster 16 audio (alternate)
0270–0273	4 bytes	Plug and Play I/O read ports
0278–027F	8 bytes	Parallel port 2 (LPT2)
0280–028F	16 bytes	SMC Ethernet adapter (alternate)
0280–0293	20 bytes	Creative Labs Sound Blaster 16 audio (alternate)
02A0–02AF	16 bytes	SMC Ethernet adapter (alternate)
02C0–02CF	16 bytes	SMC Ethernet adapter (alternate)
02E0–02EF	16 bytes	SMC Ethernet adapter (alternate)
02E8–02EF	8 bytes	Serial port 4 (COM4)
02EC–02EF	4 bytes	Video, 8514, or ATI standard ports
02F8–02FF	8 bytes	Serial port 2 (COM2)
0300–0301	2 bytes	MPU-401 MIDI port (secondary)
0300–030F	16 bytes	SMC Ethernet adapter (alternate)
0320–0323	4 bytes	XT (8-bit) hard disk controller
0320–032F	16 bytes	SMC Ethernet adapter (alternate)
0330–0331	2 bytes	MPU-401 MIDI port (default)
0330–0333	4 bytes	Adaptec SCSI adapter (default)
0334–0337	4 bytes	Adaptec SCSI adapter (alternate)
0340–034F	16 bytes	SMC Ethernet adapter (alternate)
0360–036F	16 bytes	SMC Ethernet adapter (alternate)
0366	1 byte	Fourth IDE command port
0367, bits 6:0	7 bits	Fourth IDE status port
0370–0375	6 bytes	Secondary floppy controller
0376	1 byte	Secondary IDE command port
0377, bit 7	1 bit	Secondary floppy controller disk change
0377, bits 6:0	7 bits	Secondary IDE status port
0378–037F	8 bytes	Parallel Port 1 (LPT1)
0380–038F	16 bytes	SMC Ethernet adapter (alternate)
0388–038B	4 bytes	Audio–FM synthesizer
03B0–03BB	12 bytes	Video, Mono/EGA/VGA standard ports
03BC–03BF	4 bytes	Parallel port 1 (LPT1) in some systems
03BC–03BF	4 bytes	Parallel port 3 (LPT3)
03C0–03CF	16 bytes	Video, EGA/VGA standard ports

Table 4.16 Continued

Address (Hex)	Size	Description
03D0–03DF	16 bytes	Video, CGA/EGA/VGA standard ports
03E6	1 byte	Third IDE command port
03E7, bits 6:0	7 bits	Third IDE status port
03E8–03EF	8 bytes	Serial port 3 (COM3)
03F0–03F5	6 bytes	Primary floppy controller
03F6	1 byte	Primary IDE command port
03F7, bit 7	1 bit	Primary floppy controller disk change
03F7, bits 6:0	7 bits	Primary IDE status port
03F8–03FF	8 bytes	Serial port 1 (COM1)
04D0–04D1	2 bytes	Edge/level triggered PCI interrupt controller
0530–0537	8 bytes	Windows sound system (default)
0604–060B	8 bytes	Windows sound system (alternate)
0678–067F	8 bytes	LPT2 in ECP mode
0778–077F	8 bytes	LPT1 in ECP mode
0A20–0A23	4 bytes	IBM Token-Ring adapter (default)
0A24–0A27	4 bytes	IBM Token-Ring adapter (alternate)
0CF8–0CFB	4 bytes	PCI configuration address registers
0CF9	1 byte	Turbo and reset control register
0CFC–0CFF	4 bytes	PCI configuration data registers
FF00–FF07	8 bytes	IDE bus master registers
FF80–FF9F	32 bytes	Universal serial bus
FFA0–FFA7	8 bytes	Primary bus master IDE registers
FFA8–FFAF	8 bytes	Secondary bus master IDE registers

To find out exactly what your devices are using, you should consult the documentation for the device or look up the device in the Windows Device Manager. Note that the documentation for some devices might list only the starting address instead of the full range of I/O port addresses used.

Figure 4.35 shows a portion of the I/O port address map for a typical 32-bit Windows system. Note that some I/O port address ranges appear to have a conflict, such as 03B0–03FBB, which is used by the chipset's AGP controller and the installed video card (RADEON 9000). However, this is not a conflict but actually indicates that the I/O port address range is used to communicate between the devices listed.

Virtually all devices on the system buses use I/O port addresses. Most of these are fairly standardized, which means conflicts or problems do not often occur with these settings.

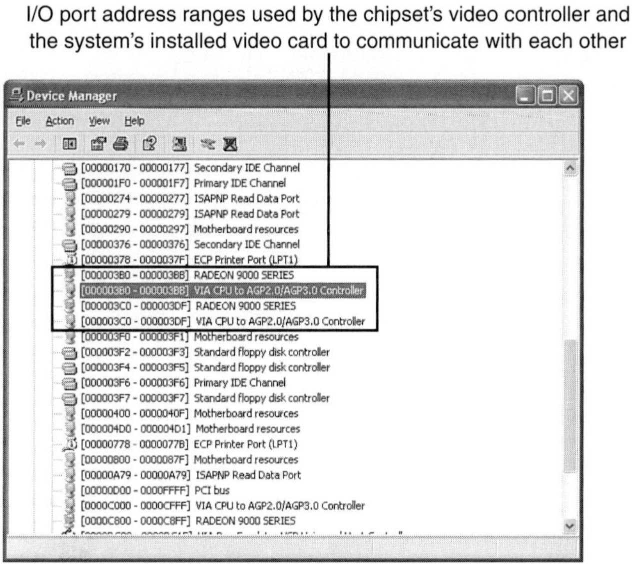

I/O port address ranges used by the chipset's video controller and
the system's installed video card to communicate with each other

Figure 4.35   A portion of a system's I/O port address, as displayed by the Windows Device Manager.

Embedded and Integrated Components

There are a variety of connectors on a modern motherboard. Figure 4.36 shows connector locations on a typical motherboard. Note that Figure 4.36 combines features from several different motherboards; you might not see every feature on a particular motherboard. Several of these connectors, such as power supply connectors, serial and parallel ports, and keyboard/mouse connectors, are covered in other chapters.

This section provides figures and tables that show the configurations and pinouts of most of the other interface and I/O connectors you will find.

One of the biggest problems many people overlook when building and upgrading systems is the front panel connections. Connectors that don't match between the motherboard and chassis are one of the small but frustrating things that can be problematic in an otherwise smooth upgrade or system build. Unfortunately, there is no single standard in use for front panel connectors on servers. The de facto standard for front panel connections in servers is the SSI front panel I/O connector shown in Figure 4.37. Motherboards that fully adhere to one of the current SSI standards (CEB, EEB, and TEB) use this I/O connector. Note that this I/O connector is often located on the left edge of the motherboard, as viewed from the front, rather than on the front edge, as with many desktop motherboards.

This is a much larger connector than the 10-pin keyed header defined by the "Intel Front Panel I/O Connectivity Guide" first developed in 2000 and followed by Intel and some other desktop PC makers. The SSI front panel connector supports additional LEDs used for system faults, activity and fault lights for up to two onboard NICs, temperature sensor, system ID, NMI, SMBus, and chassis intrusion. These features are very important for server management. Most current Intel server motherboards use the SSI connector.

Other major brands of server motherboards, however, use different connector standards, and sometimes a single brand of server uses more than one front panel connector standard on different models. See the manual for a particular server or server motherboard to determine the pinout and features supported.

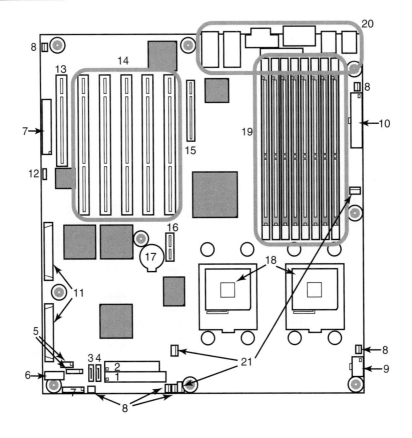

Figure 4.36   Typical motherboard connectors on a dual-processor server.

1. ATA/IDE
2. Floppy interface
3. Primary SATA
4. Secondary SATA
5. USB header pins
6. COM header pins
7. Front-panel headers
8. CPU Fan (3-pin) headers
9. CPU power (8-pin)
10. EPS12V (24-pin) power
11. Wide SCSI (68-pin) ports (2)

12. Speaker
13. PCI slot
14. PCI-X slot
15. PCI-Express x4 slot
16. PCI-Express x1 slot
17. CR-2032 battery socket
18. CPU sockets (2)
19. Memory sockets (8)
20. Rear I/O port cluster
21. Case fan (4-pin) headers

Tip

If your server uses SATA drives connected to an add-on card rather than the motherboard's integrated host adapter, the front drive access light will not operate. This light is normally connected to pins 7 and 9 of the SSI front panel connections shown in Figure 4.37 or to the equivalent pins on servers that use a different front panel connection standard. To enable the HDD activity light to operate when SATA drives connected to an add-on card are in use, connect the HDD activity light to the SATA adapter card, if possible. See the documentation for your server's SATA host adapter card to determine whether the card has a connector for HDD activity lights.

Figure 4.37   Front panel connections specified by SSI server standards.

To adapt the connectors in a chassis to those on a motherboard, in some cases you might need to change the connector ends by removing the terminals and reinserting them into different positions. For example, in a chassis that uses a 3-pin power LED connection and a motherboard with only a 2-pin connection, you have to remove one of the terminals, reinsert it into the middle position on the 3-pin connector, and then plug the connector in to the motherboard so that two pins are mated and the third empty position is hanging off the end of the connector. Fortunately, the terminals are easy to remove by merely lifting a latch on the side of the connector and then sliding the terminal and wire back out. When the terminal is inserted, the latch automatically grabs the terminal and locks it into position. To minimize the need to adapt connectors, you should use a chassis recommended by your server motherboard vendor.

Many server motherboards include front panel USB connectors, which are designed to be connected to front-mounted USB connectors in the chassis. The standard uses a single 10-pin keyed connector to provide two USB connections. The pinout of a standard dual USB motherboard header connector is shown in Figure 4.38 and Table 4.17.

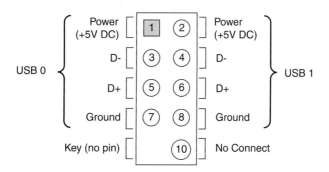

Figure 4.38   Front panel dual-USB header connector configuration.

Table 4.17   Front Panel USB Header Connector Pinout

Description	Signal Names	Pin	Pin	Signal Names	Description
Port 0 +5V	USB0_PWR	1	2	USB1_PWR	Port 1 +5V
Port 0 Data-	USB_D0-	3	4	USB_D1-	Port 1 Data-
Port 0 Data+	USB_D0+	5	6	USB_D1+	Port 1 Data+
Port 0 Ground	GND	7	8	GND	Port 1 Ground
No pin	Key	9	10	NC/Shield	No Connect/Shield

Many chassis includes multiple inline connectors for the dual-USB–to–front panel connection instead of a single keyed connector. An example of this is shown in Figure 4.39.

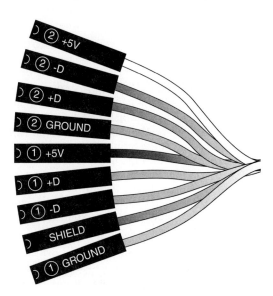

Figure 4.39   Front panel USB cable using multiple individual non-keyed connectors.

Using the multiple individual connectors shown in Figure 4.39, you would have to plug each individual connector in to the proper pin. Some internal chassis USB cables use two 5-pin inline connectors, in which case you just need to ensure that you don't put them on backward. You should consult your motherboard and chassis manual for more information if you are unsure about your particular connections.

Caution

If your chassis uses multiple individual non-keyed connections, you must be sure to connect them properly to the connector on the motherboard. If you connect them improperly, you can cause a short circuit to occur that can damage the motherboard or any USB peripherals you plug in to the front panel connectors. Higher-quality motherboards usually have self-healing fuses on the power signals, which can prevent damage if such a situation occurs. You might want to tape the cables together before inserting them to keep them in the right sequence.

Other miscellaneous connectors might appear on server motherboards as well; several are shown in Tables 4.18–4.24.

Table 4.18   Battery Connector

Pin	Signal	Pin	Signal
1	Gnd	3	KEY
2	Unused	4	+4 to 6V

Table 4.19   LED and Keylock Connector

Pin	Signal	Pin	Signal
1	LED Power (+5V)	4	Keyboard Inhibit
2	KEY	5	Gnd
3	Gnd		

Table 4.20   Speaker Connector

Pin	Signal	Pin	Signal
1	Ground	3	Board-Mounted Speaker
2	KEY	4	Speaker Output

Table 4.21   Chassis Intrusion (Security) Pin-Header

Pin	Signal Name
1	Ground
2	CHS_SEC

Table 4.22   Wake on LAN Pin-Header

Pin	Signal Name
1	+5 VSB
2	Ground
3	WOL

Table 4.23   Wake on Ring Pin-Header

Pin	Signal Name
1	Ground
2	RINGA

Table 4.24   SMB (I²C) Connector

Pin	Signal Name
1	Clock
2	SMB Data
3	N/A
4	N/A
5	N/A

Most modern server motherboards have five or more fan connectors for use with the processor fan(s), rear chassis fan, front chassis fan, and voltage regulator (power) fan(s) (see Tables 4.25 and 4.26). They all generally use the same 3-pin connector, with the third pin providing a tachometer signal for optional speed monitoring. If the motherboard is capable of monitoring the fan speed, it can sound an alarm when the fans begin to slow down due to bearing failure or wear. The alarm sound can vary, but it normally comes from the internal speaker and might be an ambulance siren–type sound. Some systems use both 3-pin and 4-pin fan connectors; the extra pin provides support for pulse width modulation (PWM) fan speed control via the system BIOS, enabling the fan to run faster or slower, as needed, to provide adequate system cooling.

Table 4.25   Three-Pin Fan Power Connectors

Pin	Signal Name
1	Ground
2	+12V
3	Sense tachometer

Table 4.26   Four-Pin Fan Power Connectors

Pin	Signal Name
1	Ground
2	+12V
3	Sense tachometer
4	PWM (thermal management) control via BIOS

Note that pins 1 through 3 of the 4-pin fan headers in Table 4.26 are the same as the pinouts in Table 4.25. Even though some motherboards have both types of fan headers (see Figure 4.36 for an example), you should use all the same type of fan if you enable thermal management control in the system BIOS.

Caution

Do not place a jumper on the fan connector; serious board damage will result if the 12V is shorted to ground.

SCSI, ATA/IDE, and SATA

Unlike desktop PCs, which use primarily ATA/IDE or SATA interfaces for hard disks, most servers use SCSI interfaces for hard disks, including RAID arrays. As a result, a typical server may feature one or two 68-pin SCSI connectors on the motherboard, with corresponding SCSI host adapter chips.

Servers use ATA/IDE host adapters primarily for optical (CD, DVD) drives. Depending on the chipset, ATA/IDE host adapters might run at typical UDMA speeds up to UDMA-100 or UDMA-133, or they might run at much slower PIO speeds.

Some recent servers use SATA ports in place of SCSI ports. In most cases, the SATA ports can be operated in a RAID 0 (striping) or RAID 1 (mirroring) configuration. If four SATA ports (and drives) can be connected to the motherboard, RAID 0+1 can be used for speed and safety. Some servers also support the new SAS (Serial Attached SCSI) standard, which supports both SAS and SATA drives.

The configuration of ATA/IDE and SATA host adapters on a server motherboard is performed through the system BIOS. Depending on the motherboard, SCSI and SAS host adapters might be enabled or disabled via the system BIOS or via jumpers on the motherboard. Note that the system or option BIOS is used to configure SATA or SCSI drives in a RAID array and to configure SCSI settings.

If SATA, SCSI, or SAS drives are supported by an add-on adapter, the adapter's BIOS is used to configure the interface and drives.

▶▶ For more information about ATA/IDE and SATA drives and interfaces, see Chapter 6, "The ATA/IDE Interface."

▶▶ For more information about SCSI and SAS drives and interfaces, see Chapter 7, "The SCSI Bus."

NICs, Modems, and Wireless NICs

Depending on the server, a network adapter (NIC) might be plugged in to a PCI, PCI-X, or PCI-Express x1 slot or might be located on the motherboard. Older servers with integrated NICs usually feature a 10/100 Ethernet RJ-45 port, while current servers with integrated NICs might feature a 10/100/1000 Ethernet RJ-45 port. Servers with two NIC ports can be used as routers without the addition of an additional NIC.

Although wireless networks using the IEEE 802.11 (Wi-Fi) family of standards are extremely common, there are virtually no servers with integrated wireless Ethernet NICs. Dial-up modems are also quite scarce on servers. Although servers designed for communications might feature one or more RJ-11 telephone jacks, these are normally used for connections to telephone switches rather than by analog modems.

Legacy Ports (Serial, Parallel, Keyboard, and Mouse)

Although legacy ports (serial, parallel, PS/2 keyboard, and PS/2 mouse) are fading away in current desktop and notebook computer designs, these ports are still virtually universal in server designs. There are several reasons for the continued popularity of legacy ports:

■ Most KVM (keyboard, video, mouse) switches, which are often used to permit a single keyboard, mouse, and display to control multiple systems, support legacy ports plus VGA.

▶▶ For more information about KVM switches, see "KVM Switches," p. 497.

■ Serial ports enable a server to be controlled via an ASCII terminal or a Telnet connection from a remote PC.

■ Parallel ports support dot-matrix and laser/LED printers for use in printing status reports.

Note that some server systems and motherboards omit the parallel port but usually include the other legacy ports listed here.

Servers that use ATX or other ATX-derived motherboard form factors provide access to legacy ports via the port cluster at the rear of the motherboard. PICMG-based single-board computers might place some legacy ports on the rear bracket, while others might be located on header cables. Although proprietary server designs vary in their legacy port locations, virtually all of them place the legacy ports at the rear of the system.

USB and IEEE 1394

USB ports are quite common on servers, but the level of USB support varies by server. Older servers might support USB 1.1 devices only, while most recent servers also support USB 2.0 devices.

If you plan to use USB input devices (mouse and keyboard), you need to be sure to verify that USB legacy support is available and enabled in the system BIOS. See "CMOS Settings and Specifications," later in this chapter, for details.

Although most recent and current servers support USB 2.0 devices, most servers do not support USB devices such as floppy or flash memory drivers as boot devices. If your system does not support USB drives as boot devices and you plan to use floppy disk–based diagnostic or testing software, you should specify a traditional floppy-controller–based 1.44MB floppy drive as part of your server's configuration or use bootable CD-based diagnostic and testing programs. To determine whether your server can boot from a USB drive, check the server's BIOS configuration.

Although USB ports are common on servers, the only servers that incorporate IEEE 1394 ports are Macintosh servers. Servers can use IEEE 1394 ports for high-speed external storage.

ROM BIOS

BIOS stands for *basic input/output system*, and it consists of low-level software that controls the system hardware and acts as an interface between the operating system and the hardware. Most people know the term BIOS by another name: *device drivers*, or just *drivers*. In other words, the BIOS is a collection of all the drivers in a system. BIOS is essentially the link between hardware and software in a system. The system BIOS is contained in a ROM chip on the motherboard that also contains the power-on self-test (POST) program and a bootstrap loader. The BIOS directs the bootstrap loader to look for an operating system (OS) in any one of various drive locations. After the OS was loaded, the bootstrap program could call on the low-level routines (device drivers) in the BIOS to interact with the system hardware.

Motherboard BIOS

Every server with an x86 or Itanium processor must have a special chip that contains software called the ROM BIOS. This ROM chip contains the startup programs and drivers used to get the system running and act as the interface to the basic hardware in the system. When you turn on a system, the POST in the BIOS also tests the major components in the system. In addition, you can run a setup program to store system configuration data in the CMOS memory, which is powered by a battery on the motherboard. This CMOS RAM is often called NVRAM because it runs on about 1 millionth of an amp of electrical current and can store data for years when powered by a tiny lithium battery.

The BIOS is a collection of programs embedded in one or more chips, depending on the design of the computer. That collection of programs is the first thing loaded when you start the computer, even before the operating system. The BIOS in most x86 and Itanium servers has four main functions:

- **POST**—The POST tests the computer's processor, memory, chipset, video adapter, disk controllers, disk drives, keyboard, and other crucial components. It uses various methods to indicate problems, including beep codes, onscreen error messages, and status/problem codes output to a particular I/O port address.
- **Setup**—The system configuration and setup program is usually a menu-driven program that you activate by pressing a special key during the POST. It enables you to configure the motherboard and chipset settings, along with the date and time, passwords, disk drives, and other basic

system settings. You can also control the power-management settings and boot-drive sequence from the BIOS Setup, and on some systems, you can configure CPU timing and clock-multiplier settings.

- **Bootstrap loader**—The bootstrap loader is a routine that reads the first physical sector of various disk drives, looking for a valid master boot record (MBR). If it finds one that meets certain minimum criteria (ending in the signature bytes 55AAh), the code within is executed. The MBR program code then continues the boot process by reading the first physical sector of the bootable volume, which is the start of the volume boot record (VBR). The VBR then loads the first operating system startup file, and the operating system is then in control and continues the boot process.

- **BIOS**—BIOS is the collection of drivers used to act as a basic interface between the operating system and the hardware when the system is booted and running. When running Windows in Safe Mode or Linux/UNIX in single-user mode, you are running almost solely on ROM-based BIOS drivers because none are loaded from disk.

The system ROM BIOS is loaded into upper memory (that is, memory between 640KB and 1MB) when the system is started, as are BIOS chips on the video adapter and other adapter ROM BIOS chips used in the system. Figure 4.40 shows a map of the first megabyte of memory in a PC; notice that the upper memory areas are reserved for adapter card and motherboard RAM or ROM BIOS at the end of the first megabyte.

If you are working with legacy (ISA/EISA) hardware that uses RAM or ROM BIOS chips, you need to make sure each device that uses RAM or ROM uses a non-overlapping section of upper memory. PnP hardware, BIOS, and operating systems automatically place RAM and ROM chips into nonconflicting memory addresses.

ROM BIOS Hardware

The main ROM BIOS is contained in a ROM chip on the motherboard, but adapter cards with ROMs contain auxiliary BIOS routines and drivers needed by the particular card, especially for cards that must be active early in the boot process, such as video cards. Cards that don't need drivers active during boot (such as sound cards) typically don't have ROM because those drivers can be loaded from the hard disk later in the boot process.

Because the BIOS is the main portion of the code stored in ROM, we often call the ROM the *ROM BIOS*. Adapter card ROMs, such as those used for video, SCSI, add-on ATA cards, and network cards for diskless workstations, are automatically scanned and read by the motherboard ROM during the early part of the boot process—during the POST. The motherboard ROM scans a special area of RAM reserved for adapter ROMs (addresses C0000–DFFFFh), looking for 55AAh signature bytes, which indicates the start of a ROM.

All adapter ROMs must start with 55AAh; otherwise, the motherboard won't recognize them. The third byte indicates the size of the ROM in 512-byte units called *paragraphs*, and the fourth byte is the actual start of the driver programs. The motherboard ROM uses the size byte for testing purposes. The motherboard ROM adds all the bytes in the ROM and divides the sum by the number of bytes. The result should produce a remainder of 100h. Thus, when creating a ROM for an adapter, a programmer typically uses a "fill" byte at the end to get the checksum to come out right. Using this checksum, the motherboard tests each adapter ROM during the POST and flags any that appear to have been corrupted.

The motherboard BIOS automatically runs the programs in any adapter ROMs it finds during the scan. You see this in most systems when you turn on the system, and during the POST you see the video card BIOS and other BIOS chips, such as SATA, ATA/SATA RAID, and SCSI, initialize and display onscreen messages.

```
      . = RAM
      G = Graphics Mode Video RAM
      M = Monochrome Text Mode Video RAM
      C = Color Text Mode Video RAM
      V = Video adapter ROM BIOS
      a = Reserved for other adapter board ROM
      r = Additional Motherboard ROM BIOS in some systems
      R = Motherboard ROM BIOS


      Conventional (Base) Memory

            : 0---1---2---3---4---5---6---7---8---9---A---B---C---D---E---F---
      000000: ................................................................
      010000: ................................................................
      020000: ................................................................
      030000: ................................................................
      040000: ................................................................
      050000: ................................................................
      060000: ................................................................
      070000: ................................................................
      080000: ................................................................
      090000: ................................................................

      Upper Memory Area (UMA)

            : 0---1---2---3---4---5---6---7---8---9---A---B---C---D---E---F---
      0A0000: GGGGGGGGGGGGGGGGGGGGGGGGGGGGGGGGGGGGGGGGGGGGGGGGGGGGGGGGGGGGGGGG
      0B0000: MMMMMMMMMMMMMMMMMMMMMMMMMMMMMMMMCCCCCCCCCCCCCCCCCCCCCCCCCCCCCCCC
            : 0---1---2---3---4---5---6---7---8---9---A---B---C---D---E---F---
      0C0000: VVVVVVVVVVVVVVVVVVVVVVVVVVVVVVVVaaaaaaaaaaaaaaaaaaaaaaaaaaaaaaaa
      0D0000: aaaaaaaaaaaaaaaaaaaaaaaaaaaaaaaaaaaaaaaaaaaaaaaaaaaaaaaaaaaaaaaa
            : 0---1---2---3---4---5---6---7---8---9---A---B---C---D---E---F---
      0E0000: rrrrrrrrrrrrrrrrrrrrrrrrrrrrrrrrrrrrrrrrrrrrrrrrrrrrrrrrrrrrrrrr
      0F0000: RRRRRRRRRRRRRRRRRRRRRRRRRRRRRRRRRRRRRRRRRRRRRRRRRRRRRRRRRRRRRRRR
```

Figure 4.40   PC memory map showing ROM BIOS.

ROM Shadowing

ROM chips, by their nature, are very slow, with access times of 150ns (nanoseconds, or billionths of a second), compared to DRAM access times of less than 10ns on the newest systems. Because of this, in virtually all systems, the ROMs are *shadowed*, which means they are copied into DRAM chips at startup to allow faster access during normal operation. The shadowing procedure copies the ROM into RAM and then assigns that RAM the same address as the ROM originally used, disabling the actual ROM in the process. This makes the system seem as though it has ROM running at the same speed as RAM.

The performance gain from shadowing is often very slight, and it can cause problems if it is not set up properly. Therefore, in most cases, it is wise to shadow only the motherboard (and maybe the video card BIOS) and leave the others alone.

Typically, shadowing is useful only when running 16-bit operating systems, such as DOS or Windows 3.x. When running a 32-bit or 64-bit operating system, such as Windows Server 2000, Windows Server 2003, or Linux, shadowing is virtually useless because those operating systems do not use the 16-bit ROM code while running. Instead, those operating systems load 32-bit or 64-bit drivers into RAM, which replace the 16-bit BIOS code used only during system startup.

Shadowing controls are found in the CMOS Setup program in the motherboard ROM, which is covered in more detail later in this chapter.

EEPROM/Flash ROM

For over a decade, virtually all x86-based servers have used a BIOS chip with EEPROM or flash ROM technology. These chips can be erased and reprogrammed with software, unlike older technologies that required the chip to be removed from the motherboard for replacement or reprogramming.

If your server is having problems with hardware controlled by the BIOS, such as processor or memory upgrades, onboard ports or expansion slots, check with the system or motherboard manufacturer to see if a BIOS upgrade is available and if it solves the problems the server is experiencing.

Caution

Even if a BIOS upgrade is available for your server, don't install it blindly. Keep in mind that BIOS upgrades can cause problems as well as solve them. If possible, test the BIOS upgrade on a non-production server before upgrading other servers of the same type.

Be sure to follow the manufacturer's instructions for performing the BIOS upgrade. A failed BIOS upgrade will prevent your system from working.

▶▶ See "Upgrading a Flash BIOS," p. 314, for more information on updating your PC motherboard flash ROMs.

Many other devices have flash ROMs; for example, you can update the flash ROM code (often called *firmware*) in network routers (which act as DHCP servers and frequently run Linux), wireless access points, rewritable CD and DVD drives, and even some digital cameras. Installing flash ROM or firmware upgrades is as easy as downloading a file from the device manufacturer's website and running the update program included in the file.

Flash ROM updates can also be used to add new capabilities to existing peripherals, such as modems and rewriteable DVD or CD drives, to meet the latest standards; for example, you can update a modem from X2 or K56Flex to V.90 or V.92 or add support for the latest types of media to a rewriteable drive.

BIOS Types

The system ROM BIOS is not the only BIOS chip found in a typical server. The following sections briefly discuss additional BIOS chips and BIOS types and how they work.

PnP BIOS

Traditionally, installing and configuring devices in PCs has been a difficult process. During installation, the user is faced with the task of configuring the new card by selecting the IRQ, I/O ports, and DMA channel. In the past, users were required to move jumpers or set switches on the add-in cards to control these settings. They needed to know exactly which resources were already in use so they could find a set of resources that did not conflict with the devices already in the system. If a conflict existed, the system might not boot, and the device might fail or cause the conflicting hardware to fail.

PnP technology is designed to prevent configuration problems and provide users with the capability to easily expand a PC. With PnP, the user simply plugs in the new card, and the system configures it automatically for proper operation.

PnP is composed of three principal components:

- PnP BIOS
- Extended System Configuration Data (ESCD)
- PnP operating system

The PnP BIOS initiates the configuration of the PnP cards during the bootup process. If the cards were previously installed, the BIOS reads the information from ESCD, initializes the cards, and boots the system. During the installation of new PnP cards, the BIOS consults the ESCD to determine which system resources are available and needed for the add-in card. If the BIOS is capable of finding sufficient available resources, it configures the card. However, if the BIOS is incapable of locating sufficient available resources, the PnP routines in the operating system complete the configuration process. During the configuration process, the configuration registers (in flash BIOS) on the card and the ESCD are updated with the new configuration data.

PnP Device IDs

Every PnP device must contain a PnP device ID to enable the operating system to uniquely recognize the device so it can load the appropriate driver software. Each device manufacturer is responsible for assigning the PnP ID for each product and storing it in the hardware.

Each manufacturer of PnP devices is assigned an industry-unique, three-character vendor ID. The device manufacturer is responsible for assigning a unique product ID to each individual product model. After an ID is assigned to a product model, it must not be assigned to any other product model manufactured by the same company (that is, one that uses the same vendor ID).

ACPI

ACPI, which stands for Advanced Configuration and Power Interface, defines a standard method for integrating power management as well as system configuration features throughout an x86 or Itanium server, including the hardware, operating system, and application software. ACPI goes far beyond the previous standard, called Advanced Power Management (APM), which consists mainly of processor, hard disk, and display control. ACPI controls not only power but also all the PnP hardware configuration throughout the system. With ACPI, system configuration (PnP) as well as power management configuration is no longer controlled via the BIOS Setup; it is controlled entirely within the operating system instead.

ACPI enables system designers to implement a range of power management features with various hardware designs while using the same operating system driver. ACPI also uses the PnP BIOS data structures and takes control over the PnP interface, providing an operating-system–independent interface for configuration and control. ACPI is supported by Windows 2000 Server, Windows 2003 Server, and Linux.

During the system setup and boot process, Windows versions that support ACPI perform a series of checks and tests to determine whether the system hardware and BIOS support ACPI. If support for ACPI is either not detected or found to be faulty, the system typically reverts to standard APM control, but problems can also cause a lockup with a blue screen with an ACPI error code.

The ACPI error codes are described in Table 4.27.

Table 4.27   ACPI Error Codes

Error Code	Description
1xxx	Indicates an error during the initialization phase of the ACPI driver and usually means the driver can't read one or more of the ACPI tables
2xxx	Indicates an ACPI machine language (AML) interpreter error
3xxx	Indicates an error within the ACPI driver event handler
4xxx	Indicates a thermal management error
5xxx	Indicates a device power management error

Virtually all these errors are the result of partial or incomplete ACPI implementations or incompatibilities in either the BIOS or device drivers. If you encounter any of these errors, you should contact your motherboard manufacturer for an updated BIOS or the device manufacturers for updated drivers.

However, ACPI problems don't always trigger error messages. If your server won't come out of standby mode, make sure the option Allow This Device to Bring the Computer Out of Standby is enabled in the Power Management tab of the Device Manager properties sheet for devices such as network adapters, keyboards, and mouse devices. With a network adapter, you should also enable the option Allow the Computer to Turnoff This Device to Save Power if the network adapter does not work properly after the server does not come out of standby mode. Do not select the Only Allow Management Stations option on a server. Enabling this option prevents the server from responding to requests from clients if the server goes into standby mode (see Figure 4.41).

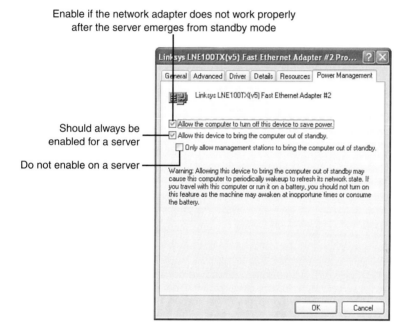

Figure 4.41   Configuring a network adapter so it will wake a server from standby mode.

Initializing a PnP Device

One responsibility of a PNP BIOS during POST is to isolate and initialize all PnP cards and assign each a valid card select number (CSN). After CSNs are assigned, the system BIOS can then designate resources to the cards. The BIOS is responsible only for the configuration of boot devices; all the remaining PnP devices can be configured dynamically by the operating system software.

The following steps outline a typical flow of a PnP BIOS during the POST:

1. Disable all configurable devices.

2. Identify all PnP devices.

3. Construct a resource map of resources that are statically allocated to devices in the system.

4. Enable input and output devices.

5. Perform ISA ROM scan.

6. Configure the boot device.

7. Enable PnP ISA and other configurable devices.

8. Start the bootstrap loader.

If the loaded operating system is PnP compliant, it takes over management of the system resources. Any unconfigured PnP devices are configured by the appropriate system software or the PnP operating system.

At this point, the operating system is loaded and takes control over PnP system resources. Using the Device Manager in the operating system, the user can control any PnP devices.

Although PnP is often thought of as a Windows-specific technology, PnP configuration and device management are also performed by recent Linux distributions.

Other BIOS Chips

The PnP BIOS is built in to the system BIOS. However, other types of devices are supported by separate BIOS chips. If the device is built in to the motherboard, the BIOS chip is also located on the motherboard. If the device plugs in to a card slot, the BIOS chip is located on the card. These BIOS chips are mapped to the system's memory map at various locations between 640KB and 1MB.

Typical device BIOS chips include the following:

■ **Video BIOS**—This chip controls the display of error and status messages onscreen during system startup. If the server uses a graphical operating system such as Windows 2000 Server or Windows Server 2003, video BIOS services are replaced by the operating system's video driver.

■ **SCSI adaptor BIOS**—The SCSI adapter BIOS is used to initialize SCSI hard disks and configure SCSI boot options. During system startup, an onscreen message prompts the user to open the SCSI configuration menu to make changes. Some systems feature a SCSI BIOS that works in conjunction with special SCSI host adapters. Various types of server motherboards use BIOS settings or jumper blocks to enable or disable onboard SCSI.

■ **NIC Wake-on-LAN (WOL)**—WOL is a common feature of both integrated NICs and NICs in add-on card slots used in servers. The setting used for WOL determines whether LAN activity will wake up a system. WOL is configured through the system BIOS Setup program, but if a WOL-capable NIC is used on a system, the WOL patch cable from the NIC must be connected to a WOL connection on the motherboard before WOL can be used with that NIC.

■ **SMART Hard Disk Monitoring**—Self-Monitoring, Analysis, and Recording Technology (SMART) is a self-diagnostic feature commonly supported on ATA/IDE and SATA hard disks. If SMART monitoring is enabled in the system BIOS, drives with SMART functions are checked for proper operation during the POST process, and problems are reported. To detect SMART failures after initial startup, you need to use a monitoring program supported by the server's operating system.

■ **RAID BIOS**—Many recent servers support onboard RAID, particularly with high-performance SATA or SCSI hard disks. Although in some cases a special configuration program is used to configure the RAID array, most servers with onboard RAID use a BIOS-based configuration program. See your system or RAID adapter's documentation for details.

Note

With Windows 2000 Server and Windows 2003 Server, you must load a driver during installation to enable most types of motherboard-based and all types of add-on–card RAID to operate. This is also required for support of SCSI host adapters. For details, see the section "ATA/SATA RAID Configurations for Server Platforms" in Chapter 6, "The ATA/IDE Interface."

System Management Features

Servers often need to be managed remotely, and IT staff need to determine when a server has problems before those problems cause a server to fail. As a result, several types of server management have been developed.

Many servers support System Management Bus (SMBus) management, developed by Intel in 1995 and based on an earlier Philips standard known as I^{2}C. SMBus uses a two-wire serial-signaling connection to transmit information about temperature, intrusion detection, and battery charge to an external monitor. SMBus version 1.x was designed to support motherboard-based devices. However, SMBus version 2.x also supports add-on cards.

Many recent servers now support a newer, more advanced type of cross-platform system management standard known as the Intelligent Platform Management Interface (IPMI), which was developed by Intel, Hewlett-Packard, Dell, and NEC in 1999.

IPMI enables server status and management to occur, whether a server is running or shut down. Starting with version 1.5, IPMI can use direct serial, network, or serial over network connections for management and alert messages. IPMI incorporates SMBus signaling and sensors, and it interfaces with existing SMBus host controllers to permit the existing SMBus management infrastructure to continue to be used.

To learn more about SMBus, see the System Management Interface Forum, website, at www.smbus.com. To learn more about IPMI, see the Intel IPMI website, at www.intel.com/design/servers/ipmi/.

Intel's Advanced Server Management Interface (ASMI) is a 120-pin motherboard connector that supports integrated KVM over IP for remote server management and other features. ASMI supports the IPMI management standard. Some server and KVM vendors such as Avocent (www.avocent.com) and Raritan (www.raritan.com) are using ASMI or proprietary daughtercards to add KVM support to existing and forthcoming servers.

BIOS Manufacturers

Several popular BIOS manufacturers in the market today supply the majority of motherboard and system manufacturers with the code for their ROM chips. This section discusses the various available versions.

The leading manufacturers of server BIOS today include American Megatrends (AMI) and Phoenix Technologies. Phoenix also owns Award Software. The current Phoenix First BIOS software is based on Award BIOS version 6.x, and the current Phoenix First BIOS Pro software is based on Phoenix BIOS version 4.x.

There are various ways to determine what BIOS brand and version is being used by a particular server or server motherboard:

- Turn on the server and watch for BIOS version messages, such as the example shown in Figure 4.42.

BIOS vendor and version

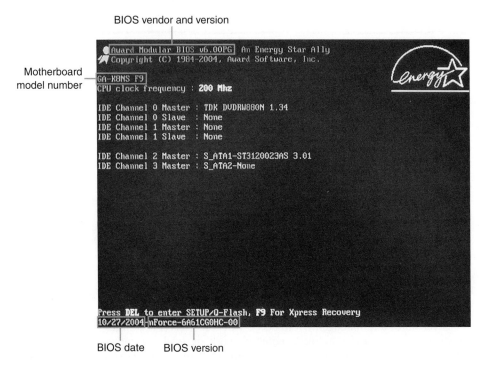

Motherboard
model number

BIOS date   BIOS version

Figure 4.42 A typical power-on display indicating BIOS vendor, motherboard model number and chipset, and BIOS version.

- Check the technical specifications for the server or motherboard. This information may be included in the documentation, or it might need to be obtained from the vendor's website. The vendor's website will also list the available BIOS versions for a particular server or system. Note that preconfigured systems are less likely to display the name of the BIOS vendor at startup or list the name in their documentation than third-party server motherboard vendors.

- Use a utility such as SiSoftware Sandra Lite (www.sisoftware.co.uk). Belarc Advisor (www.belarc.com), or eSupport BIOS Agent (www.esupport.com; eSupport also sells BIOS upgrades) to display BIOS vendor and version.

Note that because of BIOS customization, BIOS upgrades are provided by the system or motherboard vendor or by third-party companies specializing in BIOS upgrades, not by the original BIOS vendor.

If you need to troubleshoot a server, it's important to know the BIOS vendor and version number of the BIOS used by that server. Error codes and messages vary by BIOS vendor, and different versions of a BIOS for a particular server may affect compatibility. If you prefer the features and error reporting functions of a particular BIOS vendor, you may prefer to specify systems or motherboards that use your favorite BIOS.

Table 4.28 lists the BIOS vendors used by a selection of current x86 and Itanium-based server motherboards made by Intel and other major vendors.

Table 4.28   Selected Server Motherboards and BIOS Vendors

Model Number	BIOS Vendor	Processor Type
Asus (www.asus.com.tw)		
K8N-DRE	AMI	Opteron
NCLV-DS	AMI	Xeon
Intel (www.intel.com)		
SE7520AF2, SE7525GP2, SE7320SP2	AMI	Xeon
SE7210TP1	AMI	Pentium 4
SR870BN4	AMI	Itanium 2
Iwill (www.iwill.com.tw)		
DK88	AMI	Opteron
DN800-L	AMI	Xeon
SuperMicro (www.supermicro.com)		
X6DH3-G2	Phoenix	Xeon
P4QH8	AMI	Xeon
i2DML-iG2	AMI	Itanium 2
S2QR6	AMI	Pentium III
Tyan (www.tyan.com)		
S3870	AMI	Opteron
S5360	Phoenix	Xeon
S5161	Phoenix	Pentium 4
S5112	Award	Pentium 4

For more information about Phoenix and Award BIOS, visit www.phoenix.com. For more information about AMI BIOS, visit www.ami.com.

Tip

If you support servers and clients that use several BIOS types, consider adding Phil Croucher's *The BIOS Companion* to your bookshelf or PDF file collection. This book provides detailed BIOS options and configuration information for today's leading BIOS. You can purchase various editions from Amazon.com and other bookstores, but for the most up-to-date (and least expensive) edition, I suggest ordering the PDF (Adobe Acrobat) version of *The BIOS Companion* from Electrocution.com.

Accessing the Motherboard BIOS

If you want to run the BIOS Setup program, you usually have to reboot the system and press a particular key or key combination during the POST. Normally, the correct key to press is displayed onscreen momentarily during the POST. If it flashes past too quickly to read, you can try pressing the Pause key on the keyboard when it appears. This freezes the system, allowing you to read the display. Pressing any other key (such as the spacebar) un-pauses the system and allows the POST to continue. The major vendors have standardized the following keystrokes to enter the BIOS Setup in recent systems:

- **AMI BIOS**—Press Delete during POST.
- **Phoenix BIOS (FirstBIOS Pro)**—Press F2 during POST.

- **Award BIOS (FirstBIOS)**—Press Delete or Ctrl+Alt+Esc during POST.
- **Microid Research (MR) BIOS**—Press Esc during POST.

If your system does not respond to one of these common keystroke settings, you might have to contact the manufacturer or read the system documentation to find the correct keystrokes.

The following are some unique keystrokes:

- **Older Phoenix BIOS**—Boot to a safe mode DOS command prompt and then press Ctrl+Alt+Esc or Ctrl+Alt+S.
- **Compaq**—Press F10 during POST.

When you are at the BIOS Setup main screen, you usually find a main menu that allows access to other menus and submenus of different sections or screens. The following sections cover typical BIOS menus and submenus found on typical servers running Intel or AMD processors. Even if you are familiar with the BIOS settings used on typical desktop computers, the following sections will be useful to you because servers often feature different settings than those used on desktop computers.

CMOS Settings and Specifications

After you enter the BIOS (CMOS) Setup menu, you can view current system settings and configuration and make changes to most settings. Some BIOS Setup listings are read-only, such as current fan RPM and motherboard/processor voltage readouts.

BIOS Setup Menus

Most modern BIOSs offer a menu bar at the top of the screen when you're in the BIOS Setup that controls navigation through the various primary menus. A typical menu bar offers the choices shown in Table 4.29.

Note

Because most common server BIOSs use similar settings but the exact order and features vary, the following tables focus on the setup programs used by an Intel Xeon-based server and an AMD-based Opteron server.

Because the BIOS is customized by the motherboard manufacturer, even the same BIOS can offer different options for different boards. The settings covered here help you get a general idea of the type of settings to expect and how the BIOS Setup settings affect your server's operation.

Table 4.29   Typical Server BIOS Setup Menus

Setup Menu Screen	Description
Intel SE7520AF2 Server Board	
Main	Displays BIOS, processor, and memory information. Sets date and time.
Advanced	Contains the following submenus: Processor—Displays processor information and configures processor settings. IDE Configuration—Configures ATA/IDE and SATA host adapter and drive settings. Floppy Configuration—Configures the floppy controller and drive. Super I/O Configuration—Configures serial ports. Memory Configuration—Displays installed memory and configures memory handling. USB Configuration—Configures USB host adapter and device settings. PCI Configuration—Configures onboard PCI devices such as SCSI, video, NIC, and option ROMs.

Table 4.29   Continued

Setup Menu Screen	Description
	Intel SE7520AF2 Server Board
Boot	Specifies boot options via the following submenus:
	Boot Settings Cfg—Configures various boot settings.
	Boot Device Priority—Sets the order in which drives are used as boot devices by device type and specified drive (uses submenus for hard disk, removable drive, and ATAPI CD-ROM drives).
Security	Specifies passwords and security features.
Server	Configures system management, redirection of display output to a terminal, and other server-specific options via submenus.
Exit	Saves or discards changes to the setup program options.
	Tyan Thunder K8SE Motherboard
Main	Displays BIOS, processor, and memory information. Sets date and time.
Advanced	Specifies access to the same submenus as for the Intel SE7520AF2 server board (see first part of table); configures operating system type and configuration data reset.
Memory	Sets memory size, memory caching, and memory addresses to cache.
Security	Specifies passwords and security features.
Boot	Specifies boot options and boot sequence.
Power	Specifies power management features.
Exit	Saves or discards changes to the setup program options.

Choosing each of these selections takes you to another menu with more choices. The following sections examine the choices available in a typical server motherboard.

The Main Menu

The standard CMOS Setup menu dates back to the 286 days, when the complete BIOS Setup consisted of only one menu. In the standard menu, you can set the system clock and record hard disk and floppy drive parameters and the basic video type. Newer BIOSs have more complicated setups with more menus and submenus, so the main menu is often fairly sparse compared to those in older systems.

The main menu in a modern system reports system information such as the BIOS date and version, the processor type and speed, and the amount of memory. The main menu can also be used to set the system date and time.

Table 4.30 shows a typical main menu.

Table 4.30   Typical Main Menu Settings

Setting	Options	Description
BIOS Version	—	Displays the version of the BIOS.
BIOS(Build) Date	—	Displays the date of the BIOS.
Processor (CPU) Type	—	Displays the processor type.
Processor Speed	—	Displays the processor speed.
Count	—	Displays the number of installed processors.

Table 4.30   Continued

Setting	Options	Description
(Installed) Memory	—	Displays the total amount of RAM.
Extended Memory	—	Displays the memory size, starting at 1MB.
Language	English (default)	Specifies the current default language used by the BIOS. You can select other languages listed as needed.
System Time	Hour:minute:second	Specifies the current time.
System Date	Month/day/year	Specifies the current date.

Some systems report a single value for installed memory, whereas others provide a separate display for extended memory. (Extended memory is the memory beyond the first megabyte in the system.)

You can't change any values in the memory fields; they are only for your information because they are automatically counted up by the system. If the memory count doesn't match what you have installed, a problem has likely occurred with some of the memory: It is defective, is not fully seated or properly installed, or is a type that is incompatible with your system. Most server BIOSs have one or more beep codes that alert you to memory problems.

The Advanced Menu

The Advanced menu is a doorway to submenus for setting advanced features that are available through the motherboard chipset. This part of your BIOS Setup is specific to the particular chipset the motherboard uses. Many chipsets are available on the market today, and each has unique features. The chipset setup is designed to enable the user to customize these features and control some of the chipset settings. Table 4.31 shows the typical Advanced submenus available.

Table 4.31   Typical Advanced BIOS Submenus

Submenu	Description
Processor Configuration	Displays processor information, such as cache sizes; configures processor settings.
Hammer Configuration	Configures AMD Opteron features.
PCI Configuration	Configures the IRQ priority of individual PCI slots.
Boot Configuration	Configures PnP, resets PnP configuration data, and configures the NumLock key.
Peripheral Configuration	Configures peripheral ports and devices.
IDE (ATA) Drive Configuration	Configures IDE and SATA devices.
Floppy Configuration	Configures the floppy drive.
Event Log Configuration	Configures event logging.
Video Configuration	Configures video features.
USB Configuration	Configures USB support.
Chipset Configuration	Configures advanced chipset features.
Fan Control Configuration	Configures fan operation.
Hardware Monitoring	Monitors system temperatures, voltages, and fan speeds.
Server	Configures system management and other server-specific functions.
System Management	Displays serial and part numbers for major components.
Serial Console	Configures console redirection options.
Event Log	Configures logging of system and BIOS events.

The following sections discuss these options. Note that different systems might list these options in different orders or might omit or combine some submenus.

The Processor and Hammer Configuration Submenus

Table 4.32 lists settings used by a typical Processor Configuration submenu used by a server running an Intel chipset and processor.

Table 4.32   Typical Processor Configuration Submenu Options

Option	Settings	Description
Frequency	—	Specifies processor speed.
FSB Speed	—	Specifies processor FSB speed.
CPUID[1]	—	Specifies the CPUID for the installed processor.
Cache L1[1]	—	Specifies the L1 cache size.
Cache L2[1]	—	Specifies the L2 cache size.
Cache L3[1]	—	Specifies the L3 cache size (if included in processor).
Hardware Prefetcher	Enabled and Disabled	Improves performance on some systems if enabled.
Hyper-Threading	Enabled and Disabled	Supported on Intel P4 or Xeon/XeonMP processors only; enable if using a Hyper-Threading (HT Technology)–compatible operating system.

[1]*Listed separately for each processor installed on the motherboard.*

If your server uses AMD Opteron processors, you're likely to see a Hammer Configuration submenu (Table 4.33) instead of the Processor Configuration submenu.

Table 4.33   Typical Hammer Configuration Submenu Options

Option	Settings	Description
Memhole Mapping	Hardware, Software, and Disabled	Configures the PCI memory hole.
HT-LDT Frequency	(in MHz) 800, 200, 400, 600, and 1000	Specifies the speed of HyperTransport connections.
MTRR Mapping	Discrete and Continuous	Configures mapping of transfers to and from PCI or AGP video.

Advanced ECC Memory Configuration Settings

Servers that feature ECC memory error correction offer an option to enable or disable ECC. More advanced types of error correction require additional BIOS options. Table 4.34 lists typical ECC and advanced ECC BIOS settings. Depending on the server, these options might be found in various menus or submenus.

Table 4.34   Typical ECC/Advanced ECC Submenu Options

Option	Settings	Description
ECC	Enabled and Disabled	Configures ECC memory correction; requires ECC modules, if enabled.
ECC Scrub Redirect	Enabled, Disabled, and Foreground	When enabled, allows ECC scrubber to correct memory errors detected during normal operation.
4-bit ECC (Chip-Kill)	Enabled and Disabled	Enables 4-bit ECC (Chip-Kill); corrects up to 4-bit memory errors.
DCACHE ECC Scrub	Various	Configures background scrubbing rates for DCACHE.
L2 ECC Scrub	Various	Configures background scrubbing rates for L2 cache.
Dram ECC Scrub	Various	Configures background scrubbing rates for system memory.

The I/O Device Configuration Submenu

The I/O Device Configuration submenu is used to configure legacy I/O devices built in to the motherboard, such as serial ports, parallel ports, and sometimes others. Note that some motherboards place these options on two or more submenus.

Table 4.35 shows a typical I/O Device Configuration submenu's options.

Table 4.35   Typical I/O Device Configuration Submenu Options

Option	Settings	Description
Serial Port A	Auto,[1] Disabled[2], and Enabled[1]	Configures serial port A. Auto-assigns the first free COM port (normally COM 1) I/O addresses 3F8h and IRQ4.
Base I/O Address	3F8h (default), 2F8h, 3E8h, and 2E8h	Specifies the base I/O address for serial port A.
Interrupt	IRQ 4 (default) and IRQ 3	Specifies the interrupt for serial port A.
Serial Port B	Auto,[1] Disabled[2], and Enabled[1]	Configures serial port B. Auto-assigns the second free COM port (normally COM 2) I/O addresses 2F8h and IRQ3.
Base I/O Address	3F8h, 2F8h, (default) 3E8h, and 2E8h	Specifies the base I/O address for serial port B.
Interrupt	IRQ 4 and IRQ 3 (default)	Specifies the interrupt for serial port B.
Parallel Port	Auto (default), Enabled, and Disabled[2]	Configures the parallel port. Auto-assigns I/O addresses 378h and IRQ7.
Mode	Output Only, Bi-directional (default), EPP, and ECP[3]	Selects the mode for the parallel port. EPP is Extended Parallel Port mode, a high-speed, bidirectional mode. ECP is Enhanced Capabilities Port mode, another high-speed, bidirectional mode.
Base I/O Address	378 (default) and 278	Specifies the base I/O address for the parallel port.
Interrupt	IRQ 7 (default) and IRQ 5	Specifies the interrupt for the parallel port.
DMA	DMA 3 (default) and DMA 1	Specifies the DMA channel for the parallel port.

[1]*Some systems use Enable as the default setting, whereas others use Auto.*

[2]*You should disable the serial and parallel ports if they are not being used because doing so frees up those resources for other devices.*

[3]*EPP and ECP are IEEE 1284–compliant modes and require the use of an IEEE 1284–compliant printer cable.*

The Integrated Device Configuration Submenu

The Integrated Device Configuration submenu is used to configure newer I/O devices built in to the motherboard, such as USB ports, SATA ports, RAID arrays, and integrated NIC boot ROMs. Note that some motherboards place these options on different menus, such as the Advanced menu or the USB Configuration submenu.

Table 4.36 shows settings for typical Integrated Device Configuration submenu options.

Table 4.36   Typical Integrated Device Configuration Submenu Options

Option	Settings	Description
USB Control	USB 1.1+2.0, USB 1.1, and Disabled	Configures, enables, and disables onboard USB ports.
USB Legacy	Enabled and Disabled	Configures USB support for keyboard and mouse.
RAID Controller[1]	Enabled and Disabled	Enables or disables the listed SATA or ATA RAID host adapter.
Onboard LAN Boot ROM[1]	Disabled and Enabled	Enables or disables the boot ROM for the listed onboard NIC.
Interrupt Mode	APIC and 8259/PIC	Selects interrupt mode. APIC supports ACPI power management.

[1]Each controller or NIC ROM present is listed separately.

The USB Configuration Submenu

Some systems use the USB Configuration submenu to configure USB ports and devices. When present, this submenu might also contain a submenu used to configure specific USB mass-storage devices.

Table 4.37 lists typical options from a USB Configuration submenu, and Table 4.38 lists typical USB mass storage configuration settings.

Table 4.37   Typical USB Configuration Submenu Options

Option	Settings	Description
USB Function	Enabled and Disabled	Enables and disables onboard USB ports.
USB Legacy	Auto, Keyboard only, Keyboard and mouse, and Disabled	Configures USB support for keyboard and mouse.
Port 64/60 Emulation	Enabled and Disabled	When enabled, provides complete USB legacy support for non-USB–aware operating systems
USB 2.0 Controller	Enabled and Disabled	Enables USB 2.0 support; if disabled, USB ports run in USB 1.1 mode only.
USB 2.0 Mode	FullSpeed (12Mbps) and HiSpeed (480Mbps)	Selects USB operating speed. Select HiSpeed for USB 2.0-specific devices.

Table 4.38   Typical USB Mass Storage Device Submenu Options

Option	Settings	Description
USB Mass Storage Reset Delay	Varies	Specifies the amount of time, in seconds, for POST to wait for device after start command.
(Device #x)[1] Emulation Type	Auto, Floppy, Forced FDD, Hard Disk, and CD/DVD	Auto-sets devices under 530MB as floppy; others as hard disk. Use Forced FDD to boot hard disk-formatted drives as if they were floppies.

[1]*A separate listing is used for each USB mass storage device detected.*

The PCI Configuration Submenus

The PCI Configuration submenus are used to configure PCI slots, to configure onboard PCI devices such as video, and to set aside hardware resources needed by legacy ISA devices. Hardly any systems have all the options shown in Table 4.39.

Table 4.39   Typical PCI Configuration Submenu Options

Option	Settings	Description
PCI Slot # Option ROM[1]	Enable and Disable	Enable to use option ROMs on NICs, SCSI host adapters, and other add-on cards.
Enable Master[1]	Disable and Enable	Enable to make the specified slot a bus master.
Onboard SCSI	Enable and Disable	Enable if SCSI devices are used.
SCSI ROM Mode	RAID 0 and RAID 1/1e	RAID 0 (integrated striping); RAID 1/1e (integrated mirroring/integrated mirroring enhanced); change only if you are prepared to rebuild the RAID array.
Onboard Video	Enable and Disable	Disable only if you use a PCI or other graphics card.
Dual Monitor Video	Disable and Enable	Enable if you want to use a PCI card along with internal video for a dual-display setup.
Integrated NIC[2]	Enable and Disable	Disable only if you plan to use a NIC in an add-on card slot.
Integrated NIC ROM[2]	Enable and Disable	Enable if you want to boot from the integrated NIC rather than from onboard drives.
PCI Slot[1] Frequency	Auto, PCI-X 133 (MHz), PCI-X 100, PCI-X 66, PCI 66, and PCI 33	Many systems configure PCI-X slot speeds via motherboard jumpers rather than via the system BIOS.

[1]*Each PCI slot and its options are listed separately.*
[2]*If more than one NIC is built in to the motherboard, each is listed separately.*

Table 4.40 lists typical options for setting aside resources needed by legacy ISA devices.

Table 4.40   Typical PCI/PnP Configuration Options

Option	Settings	Description
UMB Region[1]	Available and Reserved	Select Reserved if a legacy (non-PnP) ISA device uses the UMB area for option RAM or ROM.
ISA IRQ Resource Exclusion[2]	Available and Reserved	Select Reserved if a legacy (non-PnP) ISA device uses the specified IRQ.

[1]*Each UMB region (C800-CBFF, CC00-CFFF, D000-D3FF, D400-D7FF, D800-D8FF, DC00-DFFF) is listed separately.*
[2]*Each ISA IRQ (3, 4, 5, 7, 9, 10, 11, 15) is listed separately.*

◀◀   For more information about ISA IRQ usage, see "IRQ," p. 269.

To make IRQs 3, 4, and 7 available, if needed, for PCI or other PnP devices you disable the serial ports (IRQs 3 and 4) and the parallel port (IRQ 7) if these ports are not used.

The ATA (IDE) Hard Disk Drive Configuration Submenu

You use the ATA Configuration submenu for configuring ATA and SATA devices, such as hard drives, CD-ROM drives, LS-120 (SuperDisk) drives, tape drives, and so on. Table 4.41 shows typical ATA Configuration submenu options for a typical modern server motherboard. Note that depending on the system, these options might be found on different menus.

Table 4.41   Typical ATA Interface Configuration Settings[1]

Option	Settings	Description
ATA Configuration	Enhanced (default), Disabled, and Legacy[2]	Enhanced causes all SATA and PATA resources to be enabled. PATA resources to resources to be disabled.
Legacy ATA Channels	PATA Pri Only, PATA Sec Only, PATA Pri and Sec, SATA P0/P1 Only, SATA P0/P1, PATA Sec, and SATA P0/P1, PATA Pri	Configures PATA and SATA resources for operating systems requiring legacy ATA operation. This feature is present only when the ATA Configuration option is set to Legacy.
PCI ATA Bus Master	Enabled (default) and Disabled	Enables/disables the use of DMA for hard drive BIOS INT13 reads and writes.
Hard Disk Pre-Delay	Various	Specifies the hard disk drive predelay, in seconds.
PATA or SATA RAID[3]	Disabled (default) and Enabled	Configures RAID support.
Large Disk Access	DOS and Other	Use DOS for Windows; use Other for Linux, Novell, and others.

[1]*Key: PATA = parallel ATA (also known as ATA or ATA/IDE); SATA = Serial ATA; Pri = Primary; Sec = Secondary; P0 = SATA connector 0; and P1 = SATA connector 1.*
[2]*Legacy causes up to two ATA channels to be enabled for operating systems that require legacy ATA operation.*
[3]*From this menu, you can also select the SATA or PATA drive you need to configure. See Table 4.42 for settings.*

The hard disk predelay function delays accessing drives that are slow to spin up. Some drives are not ready when the system begins to look for them during boot, which causes the system to display Fixed Disk Failure messages and fail to boot. Setting this delay allows time for the drive to become ready before continuing the boot. Of course, this slows down the boot process, so if your drives don't need this delay, it should be disabled.

The ATA/SATA Drive Configuration Submenus

The ATA/SATA Drive Configuration submenus are for configuring each ATA or SATA device. Of all the BIOS Setup menus, the hard disk settings are by far the most important. In fact, they are the most important of all the BIOS settings. Most modern servers have one or two ATA/IDE host adapters; each host adapter supports two drives. Many modern servers also incorporate two or more SATA host adapters; each host adapter supports one drive. Some servers include up to eight SATA host adapters.

Most modern BIOSs have an autodetect feature that enables automatic configuration of ATA or SATA drives. If this is available, in most cases you should use it because it will prevent confusion in the future. With the Auto setting, the BIOS sends a special Identify Drive command to the drive, which responds with information about the correct settings. From this, the BIOS can automatically detect the specifications and optimal operating mode of almost all ATA and SATA hard drives. When you select Auto for a hard drive, the BIOS redetects the drive specifications during POST every time the system boots. You could swap drives with the power off, and the system would automatically detect the new drive the next time it was turned on.

In addition to the Auto setting, most older BIOSs offered a standard table of up to 47 drive types with specifically prerecorded parameters. Each defined drive type has a specified number of cylinders, number of heads, write precompensation factor, landing zone, and number of sectors. This was often used many years ago, but it is rarely used today because virtually no drives today conform to the parameters on those drive type lists.

Another option is to select a setting called User or User Defined, which is where you can enter the specific drive CHS (Cylinder, Head, and Sector) parameters into the proper fields. These parameters are saved in the CMOS RAM and reloaded every time the system is powered up.

Most BIOSs today offer control over the drive translation settings if the type is set to User and not Auto. Usually, two translation settings are available: Standard and LBA. Standard, or LBA-disabled, is used only for drives of 528MB or less, where the maximum number of cylinders, heads, and sectors are 1,024, 16, and 63, respectively. Because most drives today are larger, this setting is rarely used.

LBA (logical block addressing) is used for virtually all ATA drives that are larger than 528MB. Note that systems from 1997 and earlier are usually limited to a maximum drive size of 8.4GB unless they have a BIOS upgrade. Systems from 1998 and later usually support drives up to 136.9GB; systems from 2002 and beyond usually support drives beyond 137GB (48-bit LBA support), although a BIOS upgrade might be necessary. During drive access, the ATA controller transforms the data address described by sector, head, and cylinder number into a physical block address, significantly improving data transfer rates.

Table 4.42 shows the ATA and SATA drive settings found in a typical modern server BIOS.

Table 4.42   Typical ATA and SATA Drive Settings

Option	Settings	Description
Drive Installed	—	Displays the type of drive installed.
Type	Auto (default) and User	Specifies the ATA configuration mode. Auto-reads settings from the ATA/ATAPI/SATA device. User allows settings to be changed.
Maximum Capacity	—	Displays the drive capacity.
LBA/Large Mode	Auto (default) and Disabled	Displays whether automatic translation mode is enabled for the hard disk.
Block Mode[1]	Auto (default) and Disabled	Displays whether automatic multiple-sector data transfers are enabled.

Table 4.42   Continued

Option	Settings	Description
32-bit Data Transfer	Disabled and Enabled	Enable for faster transfer; disable if Enable is not reliable.
Transfer Mode	Auto (default), 0, 1, 2, 3, and 4	Sets Programmed I/O mode.
Ultra DMA Mode[2]	Auto Mode 2 Mode 3 Mode 4 Mode 5	 33MHz 66MHz 100MHz 133MHz
SMART	Auto (default), Disabled, and Enabled	Enables/disables SMART. Auto-enables SMART if it is supported by the drive.
Cable Detected	—	Displays the type of cable connected to the PATA interface: 40-conductor or 80-conductor. 80-conductor is required for UDMA Mode 3 or higher.
ARMD (ATAPI Removable Media Device) Emulation Type	Floppy	This is displayed only when an LS-120 SuperDisk drive is connected.

[1]*Also known as multi-sector transfers on some systems.*

[2]*Some systems also list single-word DMA (SWDMA) and multi-word DMA (MWDMA) settings.*

Setting the drive type to Auto causes the other values to be automatically configured correctly. You should do this for virtually all standard system configurations. When set to Auto, the BIOS sends an Identify command to the drive, causing it to report back all the options and features found on that drive. Using this information, the BIOS then automatically configures all the settings on this menu for maximum performance with that drive, including selecting the fastest possible transfer modes and other features.

For hard drives, the only option available other than Auto is User. When set to User, the other choices are made available and are not automatically set. This can be useful for somebody who wants to "play" with these settings, but in most cases, all you will get by doing so is lower performance and possibly even trouble in the form of corrupted data or a nonfunctional drive. User should be used only if a drive was originally prepared with a set of values different from those recognized automatically with the default Auto configuration setting.

The Boot Menu

You use the Boot menu for setting the boot features and the boot sequence (through submenus). If your operating system includes a bootable CD—Windows Server 2003, for example—you use this menu to change the boot drive order so the BIOS checks your CD drive before your hard drive for boot files. Table 4.43 shows the functions and settings available on a typical motherboard.

Table 4.43   Typical Boot Menu Settings

Option	Settings	Description
Silent Boot	Enabled (default) and Disabled	Enabled displays the OEM graphic instead of POST messages. Disabled displays normal POST messages.
Add-On ROM Display Mode	Enabled (default) and Disabled	Enables/disables the splash screen for add-in cards.

Table 4.43   Continued

Option	Settings	Description
Fast Boot	Enabled (default) and Disabled	Enables the computer to boot with or without running certain POST tests.
USB Boot	Enabled (default) and Disabled	Enables/disables booting from USB devices.
Boot Device Priority	—	Selects a submenu that specifies the boot sequence from the available types of boot devices.

By using the Boot menu, you can configure which devices your system boots from and in which order the devices are sequenced. From this menu, you can also access Hard Drive and Removable Devices submenus, which enable you to configure the ordering of these devices in the boot sequence. For example, you can set hard drives to be the first boot choice, and then in the hard drive submenu, you can decide to boot from the secondary drive first and the primary drive second. Normally, the default with two drives would be the other way around.

Some recent systems also enable you to boot from external USB drives, such as Zip or LS-120 SuperDisk drives.

The Boot Device Priority Submenu

You use the Boot Device Priority submenu to select the order in which boot devices will be read to start the system. Table 4.44 shows the options found on a typical motherboard.

Table 4.44   Boot Device Priority Submenu Options

Option	Settings	Description
1st Boot Device	Removable (Floppy)	Specifies the boot sequence according to the device type.
2nd Boot Device	Hard Drive device	Specifies the boot sequence according to the device type.
3rd Boot Device	ATAPI CD-ROM device	Specifies the boot sequence according to the device type.

Depending on the system, there might be as few as three or many more boot devices available. Some systems, primarily those that use late-model Intel chipsets, feature additional submenus in which you can select boot device priority for each drive type. Some systems offer an option to boot from any bootable drive in the system at startup time. Generally, systems with this option use the F12 key to activate a boot menu.

When you install an operating system for the first time, or if you need to run other CD-based diagnostics, you should set the first boot device as the CD-ROM or other optical drive. With this setting, you can boot from your operating system or diagnostics CD. The hard disk should generally be configured as the second boot device, unless you occasionally need to boot from a floppy disk to run diagnostics programs. In such cases, the floppy and CD-ROM should be listed before the hard disk.

The Maintenance/Health/Fan Control and Monitor Menus

The Maintenance menu has many names, but it typically displays motherboard and processor voltage levels, processor temperature, and fan speeds. System management software can monitor this information after the system starts, and network or SMBus management programs and devices can monitor it remotely. Table 4.45 lists typical settings in the Maintenance menu.

Table 4.45   Maintenance/PC Health/Fan Control Menu Options

Option	Settings	Description
CPU VCore	—	Displays voltage going to the CPU core.
VBAT	—	Displays current battery voltage.
+3.3V	—	Displays current voltage on 3.3V circuit.
+5V	—	Displays current voltage on 5.0V circuit.
+12V	—	Displays current voltage on 12V circuit.
DDR	—	Displays current DDR memory voltage.
CPUx Fan Speed1	—	Displays CPUx fan speed (RPM).
System Fanx Speed1	—	Displays System Fanx fan speed (RPM).
CPUx Temperature1	—	Displays the temperature of the listed processor.
Fan Speed Control	Enabled and Disabled	Enable to control fans through temperature sensors.

[1]Each CPU fan and system fan connected to the motherboard is listed here. Replace x with the actual CPU or system fan number.

Some systems also list temperatures for other areas inside the chassis.

Power Management Settings

Table 4.46 shows the typical power settings found in a managed system.

Table 4.46   Typical Power Settings for a Managed System

Option	Settings	Description
ACPI	—	Selects a submenu that sets the ACPI power management options.
After Power Failure (AC Link)	Last State (default), Stay Off, and Power On	Specifies the mode of operation if an AC power loss occurs. Last State restores the computer to the power state it was in before the power loss. Stay Off keeps the computer powered off until the power button is pressed. Power On boots the computer when power is restored.
Power Button	On/Off and Wake/Sleep	Specifies how the front panel power button operates.
Spread Spectrum	Enabled and Disabled	Disable to improve system stability; enable to help pass EMI/RFI emissions tests.

Security Settings

Most BIOSs include two passwords for security: the supervisor and user passwords. These passwords help control who is allowed to access the BIOS Setup program and who is allowed to boot the computer. The supervisor password is also called a setup password because it controls access to the setup program. The user password is also called a system password because it controls access to the entire system.

If a supervisor password is set, a password prompt is displayed when an attempt is made to enter the BIOS Setup menus. When entered correctly, the supervisor password gives unrestricted access to view and change all the setup options in the setup program. If the supervisor password is not entered or is entered incorrectly, access to view and change setup options in the setup program is restricted.

If the user password is set, the password prompt is displayed before the computer boots up. The password must be entered correctly before the system is allowed to boot. Note that if only the supervisor password is set, the computer boots without asking for a password because the supervisor password controls access only to the BIOS Setup menus. If both passwords are set, the password prompt is displayed at boot time, and either the user or the supervisor password can be entered to boot the computer. In most systems, the password can be up to seven or eight characters long.

If you forget the password, most systems have a jumper on the board that allows all passwords to be cleared. This means that for most systems, the password security also requires that the system case be locked to prevent users from opening the cover and accessing the password-clear jumper. This jumper is often not labeled on the board for security reasons, but it can be found in the motherboard or system documentation.

If you know the password and can get into the BIOS Setup, you can also clear a password by entering the BIOS Setup and selecting the Clear Password function. If no clear function is available, you can still clear the password by selecting the Set Password function and pressing Enter (for no password) at the prompts.

Table 4.47 shows the security functions in a typical server's BIOS Setup.

Table 4.47   Typical Security Settings

Option	Settings	Description
Supervisor Password	—	Displays supervisor password.
User Password	—	Displays user password.
Set Supervisor Password	—	Specifies the supervisor password.
Set User Password	—	Specifies the user password.
Password Check	Setup and User	Specifies level to check password.
Password on Boot	Enable and Disable	Specifies when to check password.
Password Check	Full (default), No Access, View Only, and Limited	Sets the user access rights to the BIOS Setup utility. Full allows the user to change all fields except the supervisor password. No Access prevents user access to the BIOS Setup utility. View Only allows the user to view but not change the BIOS Setup utility fields. Limited allows the user to change some fields.
Chassis Intrusion	Disabled (default), Log; Log, notify once; and Log, notify until cleared	Disabled disables chassis intrusion; Log logs the intrusion in the event log. Log, notify once halts the system during POST, and the user must press F4 to continue, the intrusion flag is cleared, and the event log is updated. Log, notify until cleared halts the system during POST, and the user must enter the BIOS Setup Security menu and select Clear Chassis Intrusion Status to clear the chassis intrusion flag.

To clear passwords if the password is forgotten, most motherboards have a password-clear jumper or switch. If you can't find the documentation for your board and aren't sure how to clear the passwords, you can try removing the battery for a minute or so to clear the CMOS RAM. It can take that long for the CMOS RAM to clear on some systems because they have capacitors in the circuit that retain a charge. Note that this also erases all other BIOS settings, including the hard disk settings, so you should record them beforehand.

Event Logging, Console Redirection, and System Management Settings

Unlike desktop PCs, servers are usually managed remotely. To enable remote management at the console level, most servers include a BIOS menu for console redirection (also called remote management). Table 4.48 lists typical console redirection menu options.

Table 4.48   Console Redirection Menu Options

Option	Settings	Description
BIOS Redirection Port (COM Port Address)	Disabled, Serial A, and Serial B	Specifies COM (serial) port used for remote management.
Baud Rate	Varying rates from 300bps up to 115.2Kbps	Specifies the serial port transmission rate; theusual defaults are 9600bps and 19.2Kbps.
Flow Control	None, CTS/RTS (Hardware), XON/XOFF (Software), and CTS/RTS+CD (Modem)	Specifies the type of flow control used to manage the connection.
Remote Access	Enable and Disable	Enables or disables remote access to server.
Terminal Type	PC-ANSL, PC-ANSI 7-bit, VT100 8-bit, VT100+, VT100, and VT-UTF8	Specifies the type of terminal or terminal emulation mode on a remote PC used for remote management.

Note that all settings in the Console Redirection menu must be the same as those used by the ASCII terminal, modem, or PC terminal emulation software used to receive the redirected information. If the baud rate, flow control, or terminal type settings don't match at both ends of the connection, the terminal will see garbage onscreen.

Note that console redirection will fail if the specified serial (COM) port has been disabled in the system BIOS.

Many servers provide an Event Log menu in the system BIOS. The event log stores POST errors so they can be reviewed for clues to system problems. Table 4.49 lists typical Event Log menu options. In Table 4.49, DMI refers to the Desktop Management Interface standard developed by the Distributed Management Task Force (www.dmtf.org).

Table 4.49   Event Log Menu Options

Option	Settings	Description
DMI Event Log (BIOS Event Logging)	Disabled and Enabled	When enabled, stores POST errors in the event log.
Clear Event Log	Yes and No	When set to Yes, clears the event log when the system restarts.
View DMI Event Log	Press Enter key	Opens the log for viewing.
Mark DMI Events as Read	Press Enter key	Specifies that the log has been read.
Event Log Capacity	Space Available and Full	Indicates whether the log is full.
Event Log	Valid and Invalid	Indicates whether the log is valid.

Some BIOSs with event logging offer additional options for specifying the types of events logged, such as ECC, PCI, PCI Express, System Bus, Hub Interface, and Memory Buffer. Events can also be viewed by a DMI-compliant management program such as Intel's LANDesk Client Manager.

Note that some systems have the Console Redirection and Event Log menus as submenus under a Server menu that offers additional management options. Some servers also include a System Management menu that lists serial numbers of onboard components and MAC addresses for onboard NICs.

Additional BIOS Options

Some systems have additional features in their BIOS Setup screens that might not be found in all BIOSs. Some of the most common features you might see are listed in Table 4.50.

Table 4.50   Additional BIOS Options

Option	Description
System BIOS Cacheable	Allows caching of the system BIOS ROM at F0000h–FFFFFh, resulting in better system performance when 16-bit applications are run. If any program writes to this memory area, a system error can result.
Video BIOS Cacheable	Allows caching of the video BIOS ROM at C0000h–C7FFFh, resulting in better video performance when 16-bit applications are run. If any program writes to this memory area, a system error can result.
Video RAM Cacheable	Selecting Enabled allows Video Memory Cache Modecaching of the video memory (RAM) at A0000h–AFFFFh, resulting in better video performance when 16-bit applications are run. If any program writes to this memory area, a memory access error can result. Uncacheable Speculative Write-Combining (USWC) mode is the same as Enabled on some systems.
Delayed Transaction	The chipset has an embedded 32-bit posted write buffer to support delay transaction cycles. Select Enabled to support compliance with PCI specification version 2.1.
Virus Warning	When enabled, you receive a warning message if a program attempts to write to the boot sector or the partition table of the hard disk drive. If you get this warning during normal operation, you should run an antivirus program to see whether an infection has occurred. This feature protects only the master boot sector, not the entire hard drive. Note that programs that usually write to the master boot sector, such as FDISK, can trigger the virus warning message.
Quick Power On Self Test	When enabled, this reduces the amount of time required to run the POST. A quick POST skips certain steps, such as the memory test. If you trust your system, you can enable the quick POST, but in most cases, you should leave it disabled so you get the full-length POST version.
Swap Floppy Drive	This field is functional only in systems with two floppy drives. Selecting Enabled assigns physical drive B: to logical drive A: and physical drive A: to logical drive B:.
Boot Up Floppy Seek	When enabled, the BIOS tests (seeks) floppy drives to determine whether they have 40 or 80 tracks. Only 360KB floppy drives have 40 tracks; drives with 720KB, 1.2MB, and 1.44MB capacity all have 80 tracks. Because very few modern PCs have 40-track floppy drives, you can disable this function to save time.
PS/2 Mouse Function Control	If your system has a PS/2 (motherboard) mouse port and you install a serial or USB pointing device, select Disabled.

Table 4.50   Continued

Option	Description
ROM Shadowing	ROM chips are typically very slow, around 150ns (nanoseconds), and operate only 8 bits at a time, whereas RAM runs 60ns or even 10ns or less and is either 32 bits or 64 bits wide in most systems. Shadowing is the copying of BIOS code from ROM into RAM, where the CPU can read the BIOS drivers at the higher speed of RAM. This has little effect on GUI-based systems such as Windows.
Operating Frequency	Some motherboards enable you to select the FSB and CPU clock multiplier speeds within the BIOS rather than through the normal motherboard-based DIP switches or jumper blocks. Select this option to enable customized settings for the CPU Clock Multiplier and CPU Frequency options.
CPU Frequency	This option enables you to vary the CPU FSB frequency from the default 66MHz, 100MHz, or 133MHz to higher values, which enables you to over clock the system.
CPU Clock Multiplier	This option enables you to vary the CPU clock multiplier from its default values to higher values *if* the CPU is not multiplier-locked. Recent and current Intel CPUs ignore nonstandard CPU clock multiplier settings, but AMD Athlon and Duron CPUs can be overclocked with this option.
CPU Vcore Setting	This option enables you to vary the core voltage of the CPU to improve the stability of the system during overclocking or to install CPUs not specifically supported by the default Automatic voltage settings.
Quiet Boot	System does not display POST information.
Boot-Time Diagnostic Screen	System displays POST information.

Default, Fail-Safe, Optimized, and Custom Settings

The Exit menu is for exiting the setup program, saving changes, and loading and saving defaults. Table 4.51 shows the typical selections found in most motherboard BIOSs.

Table 4.51   Typical Exit Menu Settings

Option	Description
Exit Saving Changes	Exits and saves the changes in CMOS RAM.
Exit Discarding Changes	Exits without saving any changes made in the BIOS Setup.
Load Optimal Defaults	Loads the factory (optimal) default values for all the setup options.
Load Custom Defaults[1]	Loads the custom defaults for setup options.
Save Custom Defaults[1]	Saves the current values as custom defaults in CMOS RAM. Normally, the BIOS reads the saved setup values from CMOS RAM. If this memory is corrupted, the BIOS reads the custom defaults. If no custom defaults are set, the BIOS reads the factory defaults from the flash ROM.
Discard Changes	Discards changes without exiting setup. The option values present when the computer was turned on are used.

[1]*Not present on all systems.*

After you have selected an optimum set of BIOS Setup settings, you can save them by using the Save Custom Defaults option. This enables you to quickly restore your settings if they are corrupted or lost.

All BIOS settings are stored in CMOS RAM memory, which is powered by a battery attached to the motherboard.

Considerations for BIOS Upgrades

The following are some of the primary functions of a ROM BIOS upgrade; the exact features and benefits of a particular BIOS upgrade depend on the system:

- Added support for newer-type and faster-speed processors
- Fast POST for decreasing boot times
- Support for Ultra DMA/100 or Ultra DMA/133 ATA drives
- Support for ATA hard drives greater than 8.4GB or 137GB (48-bit LBA)
- Support for SATA drives
- Support for a preboot environment and recovery software in the host protected area (HPA)
- PnP support and compatibility
- Correction of calendar-related and leap-year bugs
- Correction of known bugs or compatibility problems with certain hardware and application or operating system software
- Support for ACPI power management
- Enhanced DMI support
- Support for temperature monitoring and fan speed monitoring and control
- Support for legacy USB devices (keyboards and mouse devices)
- Support for chassis intrusion detection

If you install newer hardware or software and follow all the instructions properly, but you can't get it to work, specific problems might exist with the BIOS that an upgrade can fix. This is especially true with newer operating systems. Because these problems are random and vary from board to board, it pays to periodically check the board manufacturer's website to see whether any updates are posted and what problems they fix. Because new hardware and software that are not compatible with your system could cause it to fail, you should check the BIOS upgrades available for your system before you install new hardware or software, particularly processors.

Where to Get a BIOS Update

For most BIOS upgrades, you must download the upgrade from the motherboard or system vendor's website. BIOS manufacturers do not offer BIOS upgrades because the BIOSs in motherboards do not actually come from them. In other words, although you think you have a Phoenix, AMI, or Award BIOS, you really don't. Instead, you have a custom version of one of these BIOSs that was licensed by your server motherboard or system manufacturer and uniquely customized for its board. Therefore, you must get any BIOS upgrades from the motherboard or system manufacturer or from a third-party source because they must be customized for your board or system as well.

Tip

If you cannot get a BIOS upgrade from your server motherboard or system vendor, you may be able to obtain one from a third-party vendor. However, before you order one, compare the cost of a BIOS upgrade to the cost of a new server motherboard. If you have a low-end server motherboard based on the ATX form factor, it might be less expensive to purchase a new motherboard than to purchase a BIOS upgrade.

If you decide to buy a new motherboard, keep in mind that you will probably need to perform a repair install to enable the operating system to recognize and install drivers for the new motherboard's chipset and onboard hardware.

Before you buy a new motherboard, make sure your existing operating system license will work with the new motherboard. If it will not, you will also need to purchase a new operating system license. Be sure to look at the hidden costs of purchasing a new motherboard versus purchasing a replacement BIOS if you cannot get a BIOS upgrade from the original vendor.

Determining the BIOS Version

When seeking a BIOS upgrade for a particular motherboard (or system), you need to know the following information:

- The make and model of the motherboard (or system)
- The version of the existing BIOS
- The type of CPU

You usually can identify the BIOS you have by watching the screen when the system is first powered up. It helps to turn on the monitor first because some take a few seconds to warm up, and the BIOS information is often displayed for only a few seconds.

Note

Many newer PCs do not display the typical POST screen. Instead, many show a logo for the motherboard or PC manufacturer, which is usually referred to as a *splash screen*. To enter BIOS Setup, you must press a key or keys (specific to the BIOS manufacturer). See the section "Accessing the Motherboard BIOS," earlier in this chapter, for more information. You might hear some in the industry refer to displaying a manufacturer's logo instead of the default POST screen as a *quiet boot*.

Tip

Look for any copyright notices or part number information. Sometimes you can press the Pause key on the keyboard to freeze the POST, which allows you to take your time to write down the information. You can then press any other key to cause the POST to resume.

You can often find BIOS ID information in the BIOS Setup screens. eSupport also offers the downloadable BIOS Agent, which you can use to determine this information, as well as the motherboard chipset and Super I/O chip the motherboard uses. When you have this information, you should be able to contact the motherboard manufacturer to see whether a new BIOS is available for the system. If you go to the website, check whether a version exists that is newer than the one you have. If so, you can download it and install it in your system.

Backing Up Your BIOS

Many BIOS upgrade programs enable you to make a backup of your current BIOS version before you install a new version. You should use this option, when available, in case the updated BIOS does not work as well as the previously installed version.

Backing Up BIOS CMOS Settings

A motherboard BIOS upgrade usually wipes out the BIOS Setup settings in the CMOS RAM. Therefore, you should record these settings, especially the important ones, such as hard disk parameters. The easiest way to record your BIOS setup parameters is to use a digital camera with a close-up setting to photograph each setup screen. Don't forget to scroll if necessary to see all the settings on a particular screen and to take an additional picture of the settings not displayed on the first screen. Use your digital camera's LCD display rather than the optical viewfinder to make sure you don't cut off part of the image.

Upgrading a Flash BIOS

Virtually all PCs built since 1996 include flash ROM to store the BIOS. Flash ROM is a type of EEP-ROM chip you can erase and reprogram directly in the system without special equipment. Older EPROMs required a special UV light source and an EPROM programmer device to erase and reprogram them, whereas flash ROM can be erased and rewritten without even being removed from the system. On many recent systems, flash ROM is not a separate chip but might be incorporated into the South Bridge chip.

Using flash ROM enables you to download ROM upgrades from a website or receive them on disk; you can then load the upgrade into the flash ROM chip on the motherboard without removing and replacing the chip. Depending on the server, you might need to create a bootable floppy with the new BIOS image and update program, or you might be able to install the update from within the operating system.

Note that motherboard manufacturers do not notify you when they upgrade the BIOS for a particular board. You must periodically log on to their websites to check for updates. Flash updates are usually free.

Before proceeding with a BIOS upgrade, you must first locate and download the updated BIOS from your motherboard or system manufacturer. Log on to its website and follow the menus to the BIOS updates page; then select and download the new BIOS for your motherboard.

Note

If a flash BIOS upgrade is identified as being for only certain board revisions of a particular model, you need to be sure to determine that it will work with your motherboard before you install it. You might need to open your system and look for a revision number on the motherboard or for a particular component. You can check the vendor's website for details.

If the BIOS upgrade must be installed from a bootable floppy disk, the upgrade is usually contained in a self-extracting archive file that can initially be downloaded to your hard drive, but it must be extracted and copied to a floppy before the upgrade can proceed. Different motherboard manufacturers have slightly different procedures and programs to accomplish a flash ROM upgrade, so you should read the directions included with the update. If the upgrade can be installed from within Windows, see the manufacturer's instructions to learn how to extract and install the BIOS upgrade.

Tip

Before you start the flash BIOS upgrade process, you should disconnect all USB devices except for your keyboard and mouse. On some systems, leaving USB drives connected prevents a BIOS upgrade from working properly.

If you have Byte Merge enabled in an Award BIOS or a FirstBIOS-based system, you need to disable this feature before you perform the BIOS upgrade. On some systems, leaving Byte Merge enabled during a BIOS upgrade can destroy the BIOS. You can reenable this feature after you complete the upgrade.

If the BIOS Setup is performed with a bootable floppy disk, the first step in the upgrade after downloading the new BIOS file is to enter the CMOS Setup and write down or record your existing CMOS settings because they will be erased during the upgrade. Then you need to create a DOS boot floppy and uncompress or extract the BIOS upgrade files to the floppy from the file you downloaded. Next, you reboot with the newly created upgrade disk and follow the menus for the actual reflash procedure. If necessary, you can change the BIOS boot order so that the floppy disk drive is listed before the hard disk. Many servers offer different versions of the flash bootable disk and BIOS loader, depending on the operating system in use.

During the actual BIOS update, you will be reminded not to shut off system power or restart the system until the update is finished. If the BIOS does not finish updating, see the section "Flash BIOS Recovery," later in this chapter, for suggestions on how to recover.

After the BIOS upgrade is complete, remove the floppy disk and restart the system. Enter the BIOS setup program and reset options to the settings you used with the old BIOS. If you have questions about new or changed options in the updated BIOS, check your vendor's website for help.

Note

If you encounter a CMOS checksum error or other problems after rebooting, try rebooting the system again. CMOS checksum errors require that you enter Setup, check and save your settings, and exit Setup a second time.

Some systems use a single downloadable executable file that contains the BIOS loader program and replacement BIOS code.

If you find that the updated BIOS causes problems, you should revert to the version you used previously. Most server system and motherboard vendors permit you to download older versions, or you can reinstall your older version if the update program made a backup copy for you.

Flash BIOS Recovery

When you performed the flash reprogramming, you should have seen a warning message onscreen similar to the following:

```
The BIOS is currently being updated. DO NOT REBOOT OR POWER DOWN until the
update is completed (typically within three minutes)...
```

If you fail to heed this warning or something interrupts the update procedure, you will be left with a system that has a corrupted BIOS. This means you will not be able to restart the system and redo the procedure, at least not easily. Depending on the motherboard, you might have to replace the flash ROM chip with one that was preprogrammed by the motherboard manufacturer or from a vendor such as BIOSMAN (www.biosman.com), which provides replacement BIOS chips containing the same BIOS code as that provided by your motherboard vendor. This is an unfortunate necessity because your board will be nonfunctional until a valid ROM is present.

In some of the latest systems, the flash ROM is soldered into the motherboard so it can't be replaced, rendering the reprogramming idea moot. Figure 4.43 illustrates typical socketed and soldered ROM chips on server motherboards.

However, this doesn't mean that the only way out is a complete motherboard replacement. Most motherboards with soldered-in flash ROMs have a special BIOS recovery procedure that can be performed. This hinges on a special non-erasable part of the flash ROM that is reserved for this purpose.

In the unlikely event that a flash upgrade is interrupted catastrophically, the BIOS might be left in an unusable state. You should check the documentation for your system to determine whether the system's BIOS supports flash recovery and how to perform a BIOS recovery.

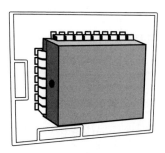 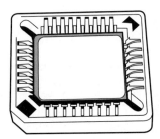

Figure 4.43   Socketed and soldered ROM BIOS chips.

Some servers use a two-chip BIOS to enable BIOS recovery. Changes are made to the secondary BIOS chip, leaving the BIOS code in the primary section alone so it can be used as a backup in case of failure. This feature is sometimes known as the rolling BIOS.

With either BIOS recovery or rolling BIOS technology, it may be necessary to adjust a chip on the motherboard to enable or configure recovery options. See your server or motherboard documentation for details.

Troubleshooting BIOS and System Problems

When an x86-based system is first powered on, the system runs a POST. If errors are encountered during the POST, you usually see a text error message displayed onscreen. Errors that occur very early in the POST might happen before the video card is initialized. These types of errors can't be displayed, so the system uses two other alternatives for communicating the error message. One is beeping—the system beeps the speaker in a specific pattern that indicates which error has occurred.

The other alternative is to send a hexadecimal error code to I/O port address 80h, which can be read by a special card in one of the bus slots. When the ROM BIOS is performing the POST, in most systems the results of these tests are continuously sent to I/O Port 80h so they can be monitored by special diagnostics cards called POST cards (see Figure 4.44). These tests sometimes are called *manufacturing tests* because they were designed for testing systems on the assembly line without video displays attached.

A POST card has a two-digit hexadecimal display used to report the number of the currently executing test routine. Before executing each test, a hexadecimal numeric code is sent to the port and then the test is run. If the test fails and locks up the machine, the hexadecimal code of the last test being executed remains on the card's display.

POST cards are available from vendors such as JDR (www.jdr.com), Ultra-X (www.uxd.com), eSupport (www.esupport.com), and many others. A PCI POST card will work in any system with PCI or PCI-X slots. Some ISA POST cards are still available, but you should purchase them only if you are maintaining legacy servers with ISA or EISA slots.

Figure 4.44   A typical POST card with two-digit hexadecimal code display (left) and a POST card in operation (right).

Many tests are executed in a system before the video display card is enabled, especially if the display is EGA or VGA. Therefore, many errors can occur that would lock up the system before the system could possibly display an error code through the video system. Because not all these errors generate beep codes, to most normal troubleshooting procedures, a system with this type of problem (such as a memory failure in Bank 0) would appear completely "dead." By using one of the commercially available POST cards, however, you can often diagnose the problem.

These codes are completely BIOS dependent because the card does nothing but display the codes sent to it. Some BIOSs have more detailed POST procedures and therefore send more informative codes. You can purchase POST cards from JDR Microdevices or other sources; they are available in both ISA and PCI bus versions.

For simple but otherwise fatal errors that can't be displayed onscreen, most of the BIOS versions also send audio codes that can be used to help diagnose such problems. The audio codes are similar to POST codes, but they are read by listening to the speaker beep rather than by using a special card.

The following sections detail the text error codes for all the popular BIOS versions and their beep codes.

Error Messages

During the boot process on an x86 or Itanium processor, the bootstrap loader routine in the motherboard ROM BIOS reads the first physical sector of each of the bootable drives or devices, which is cylinder 0, head 0, sector 1 in CHS mode or logical block address 0 in LBA mode. The code from the first sector is loaded into RAM, and the last 2 bytes are checked to see whether they match a signature value of 55AAh. If the signature bytes match, that tells the ROM that the first sector contains a valid MBR and that the ROM can continue by transferring control to the MBR code.

If the last 2 bytes of the first physical sector do not match 55AAh, the ROM continues by checking the first physical sector of the next bootable device in the boot sequence until it either finds one with a valid MBR or runs out of devices to check. If after checking all the drives or devices in the boot sequence, none are found to have the proper signature bytes indicating a valid MBR, the ROM invokes an interrupt 18h that calls a subroutine that displays an error message. The specific text or wording of the message varies according to the ROM manufacturer and version. The messages are detailed in the following section.

ROM BIOS Messages Indicating Boot Failure (No Valid MBR Found)

If a hard disk is not properly defined in the system BIOS, you might see an error message similar to one of the following when you start the server:

- Boot failure... (AMI BIOS)
- Insert Boot Media into selected Boot Device (AMI BIOS)
- Reboot and select proper Boot device (AMI BIOS)
- DISK BOOT FAILURE, INSERT SYSTEM DISK AND PRESS ENTER (AWARD BIOS)
- Operating system not found (Phoenix BIOS)
- No boot device available - strike F1 to retry boot, F2 for setup utility (Phoenix BIOS)
- No boot sector on fixed disk - strike F1 to retry boot, F2 for setup utility (Phoenix BIOS)

These and similar error messages indicate that the system could not locate the startup (boot) files on the default boot device. However, such a message could also mean that you left a nonbootable floppy disk in drive A: if the floppy disk is listed before the hard disk in the boot sequence for your server. Before rerunning the BIOS setup to verify that you have properly configured your hard disks, remove any floppy disk found in drive A: and restart your computer.

Note

For a more complete list of startup error messages, see the documentation for your server or server motherboard. Or see the following documents:

- AMI BIOS v8 error messages—www.ami.com/support/doc/AMIBIOS8-error-messages.pdf
- PhoenixBIOS 4.0 Revision 6 User's Manual—Go to www.phoenix.com/en/Customer+Services/White+Papers-Specs/Other+Platform+Products/default.htm and select from User Guides
- AwardBIOS Setup Utility—Go to www.phoenix.com/en/Customer+Services/White+Papers-Specs/Other+Platform+Products/default.htm and select from User Guides

If the system was not trying to boot from a floppy drive, these error messages could indicate that the hard disk is not properly defined in the system BIOS. For example, if the hard disk is configured as user defined but incorrect values for cylinders, heads, or other settings such as LBA (required for ATA/IDE and SATA drives over 8.4GB) are not properly listed, the BIOS will not check the correct part of the hard disk for boot files and will not be able to start the operating system. Or, if the hard disk is listed as "not present" or its host adapter (particularly in the case of a SATA, an ATA RAID, or a SCSI host adapter) has been disabled in the system BIOS, the system will not be able to locate the hard disk and will not be able to start the system.

If you determine that the startup hard disk and its host adapter have been properly configured in the system BIOS or by the SCSI BIOS, the hard disk may not have been prepared by the operating system. Or, if the system previously booted from the hard disk, it might indicate that the hard disk's MBR has been corrupted.

You can repair a corrupt MBR by using the following programs:

- Fixmbr (Windows NT/2000/Server 2003)
- lilo (Linux)
- fdisk -u (UNIX)

Review the documentation for your operating system for details and cautions.

Audio and Video Codes

Different system BIOS chips use different types of audio (beep) and video (text) error codes to indicate serious system problems. The following sections list these error codes for the most common BIOSs.

AMI BIOS POST Error Codes

Table 4.52   AMI BIOS POST Beep Codes[1]

Number of Beeps	Error Description	Action
1	Memory Refresh Error	Clean the memory contacts and reseat the modules. Remove all modules except the first bank. Replace the memory, power supply, and motherboard.
2	Memory Parity Error	Clean the memory contacts and reseat the modules. Remove all modules except the first bank. Replace the memory, power supply, and motherboard.
3	Base 64KB Memory Error	Clean the memory contacts and reseat the modules. Remove all modules except the first bank. Replace the memory, power supply, and motherboard.
4	Timer Error	Check for proper motherboard installation, loose screws, foreign objects causing shorts, and overtightened screws. Replace the motherboard.
5	Processor Error	Check for proper motherboard installation, loose screws, foreign objects causing shorts, and overtightened screws. Make sure the processor and heatsink are installed properly; remove and reseat them. Replace the processor. Replace the motherboard.
6	8042 - Gate A20 Error	Check for proper motherboard installation, loose screws, foreign objects causing shorts, and overtightened screws. Replace the keyboard, motherboard, and processor.
7	Processor Exception Interrupt Error	Make sure the processor and heatsink are installed properly; remove and reseat them. Replace the processor. Replace the motherboard.
8	Display Memory Read/Write Error	Check the video card for proper installation. Try replacing the video card memory, and replace the video card. Replace the motherboard.
9	ROM Checksum Error	Try reseating the motherboard ROM chip. Try reflashing the motherboard ROM. Replace the motherboard.
10	CMOS Shutdown Register Read/Write Error	Replace the CMOS battery. Replace the motherboard.
11	Cache Memory Bad	Make sure cache settings in BIOS Setup are properly configured. Replace the processor. Replace the motherboard.
1 long, 3 short	Conventional/Extended Memory Error	Clean the memory contacts and reseat the modules. Remove all modules except the first bank. Replace the memory, power supply, and motherboard.
1 long, 8 short	Display/Retrace Error	Check the video card for proper installation. Try replacing the video card memory. Replace the video card. Replace the motherboard.

[1]*AMI BIOS codes used by permission of American Megatrends, Inc.*

If you have a POST card, you can find the AMI BIOS POST checkpoint codes in the documentation for your POST card or by downloading this file from the AMI website, at www.ami.com/support/doc/ AMIBIOS-codes.pdf.

Award BIOS and Phoenix FirstBIOS POST Error Codes

Currently, only one standard beep code exists in the Award BIOS (also known as the Phoenix FirstBIOS). A single long beep followed by two short beeps indicates that a video error has occurred and that the BIOS cannot initialize the video screen to display any additional information. If multiple or continuous beeps occur with an Award BIOS, this usually indicates problems with the power supply or memory.

Table 4.53   Award BIOS/Phoenix FirstBIOS POST Beep Codes

Beeps	Error Description	Action
1 long, 2 short	Video Card Error	Check the video card for proper installation. Try replacing the video card memory and replace the video card. Replace the motherboard.
1 long, 3 short	Video Card Error	Check the video card for proper installation. Try replacing the video card memory and replace the video card. Replace the motherboard.
Continuous beeps	Memory Error	Clean the memory contacts and reseat the modules. Remove all modules except the first bank. Replace the memory, power supply, and motherboard.

If you have a POST card, you can find the Award BIOS and Phoenix FirstBIOS POST checkpoint codes at www.uxd.com/award.html (versions 4.x–5.x PnP) and www.uxd.com/award2.html (version 6.x).

Table 4.54   Award BIOS POST Onscreen Error Messages

Message	Description
BIOS ROM checksum error - System halted	The checksum of the BIOS code in the BIOS chip is incorrect, indicating that the BIOS code might have become corrupt. Contact your system dealer to replace the BIOS.
CMOS battery failed	The CMOS battery is no longer functional. Contact your system dealer for a replacement battery.
CMOS checksum error - Defaults loaded	The checksum of CMOS is incorrect, so the system loads the default equipment configuration. A checksum error can indicate that CMOS has become corrupt. This error might have been caused by a weak battery. Check the battery and replace it if necessary.
CPU at *nnnn*	Displays the running speed of the CPU.
Display switch is set incorrectly	The display switch on the motherboard can be set to either monochrome or color. This message indicates that the switch is set to a different setting than indicated in Setup. Determine which setting is correct and then either turn off the system and change the jumper or enter setup and change the video selection.
Press ESC to skip memory test	The user can press Esc to skip the full memory test.

Table 4.54   Continued

Message	Description
Floppy disk(s) fail	Cannot find or initialize the floppy drive controller or the drive. Make sure the controller is installed correctly. If no floppy drives are installed, be sure the Diskette Drive selection in setup is set to NONE or AUTO.
HARD DISK initializing. Please wait a moment	Some hard drives require extra time to initialize.
HARD DISK INSTALL FAILURE	Cannot find or initialize the hard drive controller or the drive. Make sure the controller is installed correctly. If no hard drives are installed, be sure the Hard Drive selection in setup is set to NONE.
Hard disk(s) diagnosis fail	The system might run specific disk diagnostic routines. This message appears if one or more hard disks return an error when the diagnostics run.
Keyboard error or no keyboard present	Cannot initialize the keyboard. Make sure the keyboard is attached correctly and no keys are pressed during POST. To purposely configure the system without a keyboard, set the Error Halt condition in setup to HALT ON ALL, BUT KEYBOARD. The BIOS then ignores the missing keyboard during POST.
Keyboard is locked out - Unlock the key	This message usually indicates that one or more keys have been pressed during the keyboard tests. Be sure no objects are resting on the keyboard.
Memory Test:	This message displays during a full memory test, counting down the memory areas being tested.
Memory test fail	If POST detects an error during memory testing, additional information appears, giving specifics about the type and location of the memory error.
Override enabled - Defaults loaded	If the system can't boot using the current CMOS configuration, the BIOS can override the current configuration with a set of BIOS defaults designed for the most stable, minimal-performance system operations.
Press TAB to show POST screen	System OEMs might replace Phoenix's AwardBIOS POST display with their own proprietary displays. Including this message in the OEM display permits the operator to switch between the OEM display and the default POST display.
Primary master hard disk fail	POST detects an error in the primary master IDE hard drive.
Primary slave hard disk fail	POST detects an error in the secondary master IDE hard drive.
Resuming from disk, Press TAB to show POST screen	Phoenix Technologies offers a save-to-disk feature for notebook computers. This message might appear when the operator restarts the system after a save-to-disk shutdown.
Secondary master hard disk fail	POST detects an error in the primary slave IDE hard drive.
Secondary slave hard disk fail	POST detects an error in the secondary slave IDE hard drive.

Phoenix BIOS POST Error Codes

Phoenix FirstBIOS Pro is based on Phoenix BIOS 6.x. It uses different beep codes than earlier versions.

Table 4.55 Phoenix BIOS 5.x and Earlier POST Beep Codes[1]

Beeps	Error Description	Action
1-2	Video Card Error	Check the video card for proper installation. Try replacing the video card memory and replace the video card. Replace the motherboard.
1-3	CMOS RAM Read/Write Error	Replace the CMOS battery. Replace the motherboard.
1-1-4	ROM Checksum Error	Try reseating the motherboard ROM chip. Try reflashing the motherboard ROM. Replace the motherboard.
1-2-1	Timer Error	Check for proper motherboard installation, loose screws, foreign objects causing shorts, and overtightened screws. Replace the motherboard.
1-2-2	DMA Initialization Error	Check for proper motherboard installation, loose screws, foreign objects causing shorts, and overtightened screws. Replace the motherboard.
1-2-3	DMA Page Register Read/ Write Error	Check for proper motherboard installation, loose screws, foreign objects causing shorts, and overtightened screws. Replace the motherboard.
1-3-1	RAM Refresh Verification Error	Clean the memory contacts and reseat the modules. Remove all modules except the first bank. Replace the memory. Replace the power supply. Replace the motherboard.
1-3-3	First 64KB RAM Multibit Data Line Error	Clean the memory contacts and reseat the modules. Remove all modules except the first bank. Replace the memory, power supply, and motherboard.
1-3-4	First 64KB RAM Odd/Even Logic Error	Clean the memory contacts and reseat the modules. Remove all modules except the first bank. Replace the memory, power supply, and motherboard.
1-4-1	First 64KB RAM Address Line Error	Clean the memory contacts and reseat the modules. Remove all modules except the first bank. Replace the memory, power supply, and motherboard.
1-4-2	First 64KB RAM Parity Error	Clean the memory contacts and reseat the modules. Remove all modules except the first bank. Replace the memory. Replace the power supply. Replace the motherboard.
2-x-x	First 64KB RAM Error	Clean the memory contacts and reseat the modules. Remove all modules except the first bank. Replace the memory. Replace the power supply. Replace the motherboard.
3-1-1	Slave DMA Register Error	Check for proper motherboard installation, loose screws, foreign objects causing shorts, and overtightened screws. Replace the motherboard.
3-1-2	Master DMA Register Error	Check for proper motherboard installation, loose screws, foreign objects causing shorts, and overtightened screws. Replace the motherboard.
3-1-3	Master Interrupt Mask Register Error	Check for proper motherboard installation, loose screws, foreign objects causing shorts, and overtightened screws. Replace the motherboard.

Table 4.55   Continued

Beeps	Error Description	Action
3-1-4	Slave Interrupt Mask Register Error	Check for proper motherboard installation, loose screws, foreign objects causing shorts, and overtightened screws. Replace the motherboard.
3-2-4	Keyboard Controller Error	Check for proper motherboard installation, loose screws, foreign objects causing shorts, and overtightened screws. Replace the keyboard. Replace the motherboard. Replace the processor.
3-3-4	Screen Initialization Error	Check the video card for proper installation. Try replacing the video card memory and replace the video card. Replace the motherboard.
3-4-1	Screen Retrace Error	Check the video card for proper installation. Try replacing the video card memory and replace the video card. Replace the motherboard.
3-4-2	Video ROM Error	Check the video card for proper installation. Try replacing the video card memory and replace the video card. Replace the motherboard.
4-2-1	Timer Interrupt Error	Check for proper motherboard installation, loose screws, foreign objects causing shorts, and overtightened screws. Replace the motherboard.
4-2-2	Shutdown Error	Check for proper motherboard installation, loose screws, foreign objects causing shorts, and overtightened screws. Replace the keyboard. Replace the motherboard. Replace the processor.
4-2-3	Gate A20 Error	Check for proper motherboard installation, loose screws, foreign objects causing shorts, and overtightened screws. Replace the keyboard. Replace the motherboard. Replace the processor.
4-2-4	Unexpected Interrupt In Protected Mode	Check for a bad expansion card. Check for proper motherboard installation, loose screws, foreign objects causing shorts, and overtightened screws. Replace the motherboard.
4-3-1	RAM Address Error >FFFh	Clean the memory contacts and reseat the modules. Remove all modules except the first bank. Replace the memory. Replace the power supply. Replace the motherboard.
4-3-3	Interval Timer Channel 2 Error	Check for proper motherboard installation, loose screws, foreign objects causing shorts, and overtightened screws. Replace the motherboard.
4-3-4	Real Time Clock Error	Replace the CMOS battery. Replace the motherboard.
4-4-1	Serial Port Error	Reset the port configuration in BIOS Setup. Disable the port.
4-4-2	Parallel Port Error	Reset the port configuration in BIOS Setup. Disable the port.
4-4-3	Math Coprocessor Error	Check for proper motherboard installation, loose screws, foreign objects causing shorts, and overtightened screws. Make sure the processor and heatsink are installed properly; remove and reseat them. Replace the processor. Replace the motherboard.

Table 4.55   Continued

Beeps	Error Description	Action
Low 1-1-2	System Board Select Error	Check for proper motherboard installation, loose screws, foreign objects causing shorts, and overtightened screws. Make sure the processor and heatsink are installed properly; remove and reseat them. Replace the processor. Replace the motherboard.
Low 1-1-3	Extended CMOS RAM Error	Replace the CMOS battery. Replace the motherboard.

[1]*Second and third codes can be 1–4 beeps each, indicating different failed bits within the first 64KB of RAM.*

Table 4.56   Phoenix BIOS 6.x and Later POST Beep Codes

Beeps	Error Description	Description/Action
1-2-2-3	BIOS ROM Checksum Error	Try reseating the motherboard ROM chip. Try reflashing the motherboard ROM. Replace the motherboard.
1-3-1-1	DRAM Refresh Error	Clean the memory contacts and reseat the modules. Remove all modules except the first bank. Replace the memory. Replace the power supply. Replace the motherboard.
1-3-1-3	8742 Keyboard Controller Error	Check for proper motherboard installation, loose screws, foreign objects causing shorts, and overtightened screws. Replace the keyboard. Replace the motherboard. Replace the processor.
1-3-4-1	Memory Address Line Error	Clean the memory contacts and reseat the modules. Remove all modules except the first bank. Replace the memory. Replace the power supply. Replace the motherboard.
1-3-4-3	Memory Low Byte Data Error	Clean the memory contacts and reseat the modules. Remove all modules except the first bank. Replace the memory. Replace the power supply. Replace the motherboard.
1-4-1-1	Memory High Byte Data Error	Clean the memory contacts and reseat the modules. Remove all modules except the first bank. Replace the memory. Replace the power supply. Replace the motherboard.
2-1-2-3	ROM Copyright Error	Try reseating the motherboard ROM chip. Try reflashing the motherboard ROM. Replace the motherboard.
2-2-3-1	Unexpected Interrupts	Check for a bad expansion card. Check for proper mother board installation, loose screws, foreign objects causing shorts, and overtightened screws. Replace the motherboard.
1-2	Video Card Error	Check the video card for proper installation. Try replacing the video card memory and replace the video card. Replace the motherboard.

If you are using a POST card, you can find the Phoenix BIOS v4 POST codes at www.uxd.com/phoenix.html.

IBM BIOS POST Error Codes

Table 4.57   IBM BIOS Beep Codes[1]

Audio Code	Sound Graph	Description
1 short beep	•	Normal POST—system okay
2 short beeps	••	POST error—error code on display
No beep		Power supply, system board
Continuous beep	—————	Power supply, system board
Repeating short beeps	••••••	Power supply, system board
1 long, 1 short beep	—•	System board
1 long, 2 short beeps	—••	Video adapter (MDA/CGA)
1 long, 3 short beeps	—•••	Video adapter (EGA/VGA)
3 long beeps	———	3270 keyboard card

[1]*IBM BIOS beep and alphanumeric error codes used by permission of IBM.*

Table 4.58   IBM BIOS POST/Diagnostics Display Error Codes[1]

Code	Description
1xx	System board errors
2xx	Memory (RAM) errors
3xx	Keyboard errors
4xx	Monochrome display adapter (MDA) errors
4xx	PS/2 system board parallel port errors
5xx	Color graphics adapter (CGA) errors
6xx	Floppy drive/controller errors
7xx	Math coprocessor errors
9xx	Parallel printer adapter errors
10xx	Alternate parallel printer adapter errors
11xx	Primary async communications (Serial COM1:) errors
12xx	Alternate async communications (Serial COM2:, COM3:, and COM4:) errors
13xx	Game control adapter errors
14xx	Matrix printer errors
15xx	Synchronous data link control (SDLC) communications adapter errors
16xx	Display station emulation adapter (DSEA) errors (5520, 525x)
17xx	ST-506/412 fixed disk and controller errors
18xx	I/O expansion unit errors
19xx	3270 PC attachment card errors
20xx	Binary synchronous communications (BSC) adapter errors
21xx	Alternate BSC adapter errors
22xx	Cluster adapter errors
23xx	Plasma monitor adapter errors

Table 4.58   Continued

Code	Description
24xx	EGA or VGA errors
25xx	Alternate EGA errors
26xx	XT or AT/370 370-M (memory) and 370-P (processor) adapter errors
27xx	XT or AT/370 3277-EM (emulation) adapter errors
28xx	3278/79 emulation adapter or 3270 connection adapter errors
29xx	Color/graphics printer errors
30xx	Primary PC network adapter errors
31xx	Secondary PC network adapter errors
32xx	3270 PC or AT display and programmed symbols adapter errors
33xx	Compact printer errors
35xx	Enhanced display station emulation adapter (EDSEA) errors
36xx	General-purpose interface bus (GPIB) adapter errors
37xx	System board SCSI controller errors
38xx	Data acquisition adapter errors
39xx	Professional graphics adapter (PGA) errors
44xx	5278 display attachment unit and 5279 display errors
45xx	IEEE interface adapter (IEEE 488) errors
46xx	A real-time interface coprocessor (ARTIC) multiport/2 adapter errors
48xx	Internal modem errors
49xx	Alternate internal modem errors
50xx	PC-convertible LCD errors
51xx	PC-convertible portable printer errors
56xx	Financial communication system errors
70xx	Phoenix BIOS/chipset unique error codes
71xx	Voice communications adapter (VCA) errors
73xx	3.5-inch external disk drive errors
74xx	IBM PS/2 display adapter (VGA card) errors
74xx	8514/A display adapter errors
76xx	4216 PagePrinter adapter errors
84xx	PS/2 speech adapter errors
85xx	2MB XMA memory adapter or XMA adapter/A errors
86xx	PS/2 pointing device (mouse) errors
89xx	MIDI adapter errors
91xx	IBM 3363 write-once read multiple (WORM) optical drive/adapter errors
96xx	SCSI adapter with cache (32-bit) errors
100xx	Multiprotocol adapter/A errors
101xx	300/1200bps internal modem/A errors
104xx	ESDI or MCA IDE fixed disk or adapter errors
107xx	5.25-inch external disk drive or adapter errors

Table 4.58   Continued

Code	Description
112xx	SCSI adapter (16-bit without cache) errors
113xx	System board SCSI adapter (16-bit) errors
129xx	Processor complex (CPU board) errors
149xx	P70/P75 plasma display and adapter errors
152xx	XGA display adapter/A errors
164xx	120MB internal tape drive errors
165xx	6157 streaming tape drive or tape attachment adapter errors
166xx	Primary token-ring network adapter errors
167xx	Alternate token-ring network adapter errors
180xx	PS/2 wizard adapter errors
185xx	DBCS Japanese display adapter/A errors
194xx	80286 memory-expansion option memory-module errors
200xx	Image adapter/A errors
208xx	Unknown SCSI device errors
209xx	SCSI removable disk errors
210xx	SCSI fixed disk errors
211xx	SCSI tape drive errors
212xx	SCSI printer errors
213xx	SCSI processor errors
214xx	SCSI WORM drive errors
215xx	SCSI CD-ROM drive errors
216xx	SCSI scanner errors
217xx	SCSI magneto optical drive errors
218xx	SCSI jukebox changer errors
219xx	SCSI communications errors
243xxxx	XGA-2 adapter/A errors
1998xxxx	Dynamic configuration select (DCS) information codes
199900xx	Initial microcode load (IML) error
199903xx	No bootable device, initial program load (IPL) errors
199904xx	IML-to-system mismatch
199906xx	IML (boot) errors

[1]*IBM BIOS beep and alphanumeric error codes used by permission of IBM.*

Troubleshooting Other Server Platforms

Although most x86 and Itanium-based servers use BIOS beep codes and error messages to indicate problems, other types of servers use different methods for solving startup and system problems. The following sections highlight the methods used on some of the most popular advanced server platforms.

IBM Light Path Diagnostics

Several of IBM's server product lines include Light Path Diagnostics. Light Path Diagnostics monitors major subsystems inside the server, including the following:

- Disk drives
- Memory
- Power supplies
- CPUs
- Voltage regulator modules
- PCI buses
- Processor mismatches and failures
- Temperature alerts
- Non-redundancy alerts
- System board failure

The front of each server features a signal light that illuminates if any component monitored by Light Path Diagnostics has failed. Inside the server, a Light Path Diagnostics panel indicates which subsystem has failed. When the server is disassembled, an LED indicates which component has failed. Because most servers have multiple components in a particular category, such as memory modules, the ability of Light Path Diagnostics to indicate exactly the component that has failed saves a great deal of time in bringing a failed server back into operation. On a BladeCenter server, Light Path Diagnostics also features a location LED, which can be illuminated remotely by the system administrator to indicate which server blade needs attention.

The implementation of Light Path Diagnostics varies by server model. See the documentation for the particular IBM server for details.

Hewlett-Packard's RX Series Integrity Server LEDs

Hewlett-Packard's RX series of Integrity servers feature LEDs at various points throughout the system that can be used to track down problems. The front panel LEDs indicate whether a management processor is installed, how the system is being managed, power status, and system status. If a fault is detected, use the LED arrays around the system to determine the problem. LEDs provide status for the following:

- System (bulk) power supplies
- PCI-X power supply
- System and PCI I/O fans and cooling status
- Internal cell board power
- PCI-X card slots
- Core I/O power
- MP I/O power

Configuring and Troubleshooting Sun SPARC Systems with EEPROM

Sun SPARC servers use EEPROM chips to store system configuration information. If this information is corrupted or missing, the system is unable to start. To view or change the current EEPROM settings, use the eeprom command from the OK prompt. You must be a superuser to run eeprom. Note that the eeprom command also works with x86-based Sun servers running Solaris; these systems use a file in the boot area to simulate EEPROM storage.

The eeprom command can be used to control and display many system features, including the following:

- Enabling/disabling ACPI power management (x86-based SPARC servers only)
- Configuring the console device
- Boot configuration
- Terminal emulation
- System diagnostics
- Error recovery options
- Input device configuration
- Hardware revision and update information
- Network settings (MAC address, network booting, and others)
- Path to the operating system
- Screen configuration
- Security settings
- TTY settings
- Memory testing

For examples and details, see the system administration commands section of the documentation for your server's version of Solaris.

Troubleshooting and Managing Hewlett-Packard Servers

Hewlett-Packard manufactures several server lines, including AlphaServer, Hewlett-Packard Integrity, and Hewlett-Packard 9000. Hewlett-Packard's Technical Documentation page (http://docs.hp.com/en/index.html) provides links to hardware documentation, operating system support, and hardware diagnostics for its server and other product lines.

Hewlett-Packard AlphaServers are managed with the AlphaServer Management Station (AMS) program. Some components of AMS can be run from a client workstation running Windows, and others are run directly on the AlphaServer's own console.

AMS permits you to work with server hardware and disk partitions, display events, view warnings, and perform other tasks. For more information, see the documentation supplied with your AlphaServer or available at Hewlett-Packard's website.

Hewlett-Packard Integrity and Hewlett-Packard 9000 servers use the Integrated Lights-Out (ILO) management processor to manage and troubleshoot the operations of these servers. For more information about using ILO, see the documentation provided with these servers or visit the Hewlett-Packard website.

Upgrading Versus Replacing Motherboards

Depending on your server's form factor, you may have two ways to improve its performance:

■ Keep the current motherboard but add or upgrade components such as memory, processors, or system BIOS.

■ Replace the motherboard with one that supports faster and newer processor, RAM, and I/O technologies.

The options available to you depend in large measure on the server's form factor. If the server uses a standard form factor, such as ATX or SSI, many motherboard upgrades should be available. However, if the system uses a proprietary form factor (as with RISC-based servers and some large x86-based servers), you can upgrade components but not the motherboard itself.

If your server offers both types of upgrade options, what is the best option to choose? The following sections discuss the benefits and drawbacks of each approach.

Memory, CPU, BIOS, and Component Upgrades

If you replace components such as memory, processor(s), system BIOS, or other components with faster or more capable versions while keeping the current server motherboard, you need to consider a number of advantages and disadvantages.

Consider these advantages:

■ You can probably keep the current preloaded operating system and applications. These files are sometimes referred to as the *server image*, or *preload*.

■ You probably won't be required to purchase a new operating system license unless you add additional processors or switch from single-core to dual-core processors. (Contact your operating system vendor for details.)

■ You can get your server back into action more quickly because you don't need to reinstall the operating system (unless you move from a single processor to a two-way or higher configuration).

Consider these disadvantages:

■ You will not be able to move to faster technologies that are often integrated into the latest systems, such as Gigabit Ethernet and SATA RAID unless you use add-on cards in PCI, PCI-X, or PCI-Express slots.

■ You might be limited in your choice of processors and memory modules if your server no longer uses current-production processors and memory.

Motherboard Replacement

If you replace the motherboard, you need to consider a number of advantages and disadvantages.

Consider these advantages:

■ If you choose a motherboard that's compatible with some of your existing components, you can move toward better system performance at your own pace.

■ You can move to newer I/O technologies such as SATA, SATA RAID, PCI-X, and PCI-Express.

■ You can move to faster processors, including dual-core processors.

■ You can move to faster memory technologies, such as DDR and DDR-2.

Consider these disadvantages:

- You will probably need to replace a preloaded operating system license with a new license. (Most preloads are tied to a particular motherboard.)

- You will need to perform at the very least a repair installation and, more likely, a complete reinstallation of your operating system because of changes in the chipset and components.

- It will take substantially longer to put the server back into working order than with upgraded components because you must back up data before swapping the motherboard, remove components and the old motherboard, install the new motherboard, replace components, and reinstall or repair install the operating system.

The bottom line is that for shorter downtime and fewer hassles, you should upgrade your existing server motherboard. For a longer operating lifespan and greater access to new technologies, you should replace your server motherboard.

Troubleshooting Server Motherboards and BIOS

Servers store the vital records for your business (or your clients' businesses). When a server goes down, it's essential to get it up and working again. The following sections discuss some of the best ways to troubleshoot problems related to motherboards.

Troubleshooting by Replacing Parts

You can troubleshoot a server in several ways, but in the end, it often comes down to simply reinstalling or replacing parts. That is why you should normally use a simple "known-good spare" technique that requires very little in the way of special tools or sophisticated diagnostics. In its simplest form, say you have two identical servers sitting side-by-side. One of them has a hardware problem; in this example, let's say one of the memory modules (DIMMs) is defective. Depending on how and where the defect lies, this could manifest itself in symptoms ranging from a completely dead system to one that boots up normally but crashes when running the operating system or a particular application. You observe that the system on the left has the problem but the system on the right works perfectly; they are otherwise identical. The simplest technique for finding the problem would be to swap parts from one system to another, one at a time, retesting after each swap. At the point when the DIMMs were swapped, upon powering up and testing (in this case testing is nothing more than allowing the system to boot up and run some of the installed applications), the problem has now moved from one system to the other. Knowing that the last item swapped over was the DIMM, you have just identified the source of the problem! This does not require an expensive ($2,000 or more) DIMM test machine or any diagnostics software. Because components such as DIMMs are not economical to repair, replacing the defective DIMM provides the needed solution.

Although this example is very simplistic, replacing parts is often the quickest and easiest way to identify a problem component as opposed to specifically testing each item with diagnostics. What if you don't have an identical system? You can maintain an inventory of known-good spare parts. These are parts that have been previously used, are known to be functional, and can be used to replace a suspicious part in a problem machine. However, this is different from new replacement parts because, when you open a box containing a new component, you really can't be 100% sure that it works. In some situations, you may replace a defective component with another (unknown to you) defective *new* component, and the problem remains. Not knowing that the new part you just installed was also defective, you could waste a lot of time checking other parts that are not the problem. This technique is also effective because few parts are needed to make up an entry-level server, and the known-good parts don't always have to be the same (for example, a lower-end NIC can be substituted in a system to verify that the original card had failed).

If you are troubleshooting a server that uses a proprietary architecture, such as one that uses processor or memory cartridges, blade-based components, and so on, we recommend that you pull temporary replacements for swapping from an identical system to avoid compatibility problems.

Troubleshooting Using the Bootstrap Approach

Another variation on the replacing-parts theme is the bootstrap approach, which is especially good for what seems to be a dead system. In this approach, you take the system apart to strip it down to the bare minimum necessary, functional components and test it to see whether it works. For example, you might strip down a server to the chassis/power supply, bare motherboard, CPU (with heatsink), one bank of RAM, and the display and then power it up to see whether it works. In that stripped configuration, you should see the POST or splash (logo) screen on the display, verifying that the motherboard, CPU, RAM, onboard video, and display are functional. If a keyboard is connected, you should see the three LEDs (Capslock, Scrlock, and Numlock) flash within a few seconds after power-on. This indicates that the CPU and motherboard are functioning because the POST routines are testing the keyboard. After you get the system to a minimum of components that are functional, you should reinstall or add one part at a time, testing the system each time you make a change to verify that it still works and that the part you added or changed is not the cause of a problem. Essentially, you rebuild the system from scratch, using the existing parts, but you do it one step at a time.

Many times, problems are caused by corrosion on contacts or connectors, so the mere act of disassembling and reassembling a server will "magically" repair it. In some cases, you may disassemble, test, and reassemble systems only to find no problems after the reassembly. How can merely taking a system apart and reassembling it repair a problem? Although it might seem that nothing was changed and everything is installed exactly as it was before, in reality, simply unplugging and replugging renews all the slot and cable connections between devices, which is often all the system needs.

Some useful troubleshooting tips include the following:

- Eliminate unnecessary variables or components that are not pertinent to the problem.
- Reinstall, reconfigure, or replace only one component at a time.
- Test after each change you make.
- Keep a detailed record (write it down) of each step you take.
- Don't give up! Every problem has a solution.
- If you hit a roadblock, take a break or work on another problem. A fresh approach the next day often reveals things you overlooked.
- Don't overlook the simple or obvious. Double- and triple-check the installation and configuration of each component.
- Keep in mind that the power supply is one of the most failure-prone parts in a server, as well as one of the most overlooked components. A high-output known-good spare power supply is highly recommended to use for testing suspect systems that use standard ATX or SSI form factors. For servers based on proprietary form factors, swap a power supply from a known-working system for testing.
- Cables and connections are major causes of problems, so keep replacements of all types on hand.

Before starting any system troubleshooting, you should perform a few basic steps to ensure a consistent starting point and to isolate the failed component:

1. Turn off the server and any peripheral devices. Disconnect all external peripherals from the system, except for the keyboard and video display.
2. Make sure the server is plugged in to a properly grounded power outlet.

3. If the server can be managed locally, make sure the keyboard and video displays are connected to the system. Turn on the video display and turn up the brightness and contrast controls to at least two-thirds of the maximum. Some displays have onscreen controls that might not be intuitive. Consult the display documentation for information on how to adjust these settings. If you can't get any video display but the system seems to be working, try moving the video card to a different slot or try a different video card or monitor.

4. To enable the system to boot from a hard disk, make sure no floppy disk is in the floppy drive. Or put a known-good bootable floppy with diagnostics on it in the floppy drive for testing.

5. Turn on the system. Observe the power supply, chassis fans (if any), and lights on either the system front panel or power supply. If the fans don't spin and the lights don't light, the power supply or motherboard might be defective.

6. Observe the POST. If no errors are detected, the system beeps once and boots up. Errors that display onscreen (*nonfatal* errors) and that do not lock up the system display a text message that varies according to BIOS type and version. Record any errors that occur and refer to the tables earlier in this chapter for help with text error messages or beep codes.

7. Confirm that the operating system loads successfully.

Problems During the POST

Problems that occur during the POST are usually caused by incorrect hardware configuration or installation. Actual hardware failure is a far less-frequent cause. If you have a POST error, check the following:

- Are all cables correctly connected and secured?

- Are the configuration settings correct in setup for the devices you have installed? In particular, ensure that the processor, memory, and hard drive settings are correct.

- Is the motherboard configured properly? Most recent systems use BIOS-based configuration settings for processor speeds and clock multipliers, so you might need to enter the BIOS setup program to check and change configurations. If the motherboard uses jumper blocks or DIP switches for some or all configuration, check those as well.

- Are all resource settings on add-in boards and peripheral devices set so that no conflicts exist (for example, two add-in boards sharing the same interrupt)?

- Is the power supply set to the proper input voltage (110V–120V or 220V–240V)?

- Are adapter boards and disk drives installed correctly?

- Is a bootable hard disk (properly partitioned and formatted) installed? (This may not apply to some systems.)

- Does the BIOS support the drive you have installed, and if so, are the parameters entered correctly?

- Is a bootable floppy disk installed in drive A:?

- Are all memory SIMMs or DIMMs installed correctly? Try reseating them and moving them around in different slots.

- Is the operating system properly installed?

Problems Running Software

Problems running application software (especially new software) are usually caused by or related to the software itself or are due to the fact that the software is incompatible with the system. Here is a list of items to check in that case:

- Check whether the system meets the minimum hardware requirements for the software. Check the software documentation to be sure.
- Ensure that the software is correctly installed. Reinstall it if necessary.
- Check to see that the latest drivers are installed.
- Scan the system for viruses using the latest antivirus software.

Resource Conflicts

Problems related to add-in boards are usually related to improper board installation or resource (interrupt, DMA, or I/O address) conflicts. You need to be sure to check drivers for the latest versions and ensure that the card is compatible with your system and the operating system version you are using.

Sometimes adapter cards can be picky about which slot they are running in. Despite the fact that, technically, a PCI or ISA adapter should be able to run in any of the slots, minor timing or signal variations sometimes occur from slot to slot. Simply moving a card from one slot to another can make a failing card begin to work properly. Sometimes moving a card works just by the inadvertent cleaning (wiping) of the contacts that takes place when removing and reinstalling the card, but in other cases you can duplicate the problem by inserting the card back into its original slot. When all else fails, you should try moving the cards around. Because some motherboards share a single IRQ between two PCI slots or between a PCI and an AGP slot, changing one of the PCI cards to another slot can resolve conflicts.

Caution

Note that PCI cards become slot specific after their drivers are installed. So if you move the card to another slot, the PnP resource manager sees it as if you have removed one card and installed a new one. You must therefore install the drivers all over again for that card. You should not move a PCI card to a different slot unless you are prepared with all the drivers at hand to perform the driver installation. ISA cards don't share this quirk because the system is not aware of which slot an ISA card is in.

Special Server Problems

If problems occur after a system has been running and without any hardware or software changes having been made, a hardware fault has possibly occurred. Here is a list of items to check in that case:

- Try reinstalling the software that has crashed or refuses to run.
- Try clearing CMOS RAM (many systems use a jumper on the motherboard to clear CMOS) and running setup.
- Check for loose cables, a marginal power supply, or other random component failures.
- Check to see if a transient voltage spike, power outage, or brownout might have occurred. Symptoms of voltage spikes include a flickering video display, unexpected system reboots, and the system not responding to user commands. Reload the software and try again.
- Try reseating the memory modules (SIMMs, DIMMs, or RIMMs).

The following sections answer some of the most frequently asked troubleshooting questions.

When I power on the system, I see the power LED light and hear the fans spin, but nothing else ever happens.

The fact that the LEDs illuminate and fans spin indicates that the power supply is partially working, but that does not exclude it from being defective. This is a classic "dead" system, which can be caused by almost any defective hardware component.

Power supplies seem to have more problems than most other components, so you should immediately use a multimeter to measure the outputs at the power supply connectors and ensure that they are within the proper 5% tolerances of their rated voltages. Even if the voltage measurements check out, you should swap in a high-quality, high-power, known-good spare supply and retest. If that doesn't solve the problem, you should revert to the bootstrap approach mentioned earlier, which is to strip the system down to just the chassis/power supply, motherboard, CPU (with heatsink), one bank of RAM (one DIMM), and a video card and display. If the motherboard now starts, begin adding the components you removed, one at a time, retesting after each change. If the symptoms remain, use a POST card (if you have one) to see whether the board is partially functional and where it stops. Also, try replacing the video card, RAM, CPU, and finally the motherboard, and verify the CPU and (especially) the heatsink installation.

The system beeps when I turn it on, but there is nothing on the screen.

The beep indicates a failure detected by the ROM POST routines. Look up the beep code in the table corresponding to the ROM version in your motherboard. This can typically be found in the motherboard manual; however, you can also find the beep codes for the most popular AMI, Award, and Phoenix BIOS earlier in this chapter.

I see STOP or STOP ERROR in Windows NT/2000/2003.

Many things, including corrupted files, viruses, incorrectly configured hardware, and failing hardware, can cause Windows STOP errors. The most valuable resource for handling any error message displayed by Windows is the Microsoft Knowledge Base (MSKB), an online compendium of more than 250,000 articles covering all Microsoft products. You can visit the Knowledge Base at http://support. microsoft.com, and from there you can use the search tool to retrieve information specific to your problem.

For example, say you are receiving Stop 0x0000007B errors in Windows Server 2003. In this case, you should visit the Knowledge Base and enter the error message in the search box. In this case, you can type stop 7B error Windows Server 2003 in the box, and the Knowledge Base gives you two articles, one of which is Microsoft Knowledge Base article number 324103, titled "HOW TO: Troubleshoot "Stop 0x0000007B" Errors in Windows XP." When you click this link, you are taken to the article at http://support.microsoft.com/default.aspx?scid=kb;en-us;324103, which has a complete description of the problem and solutions for Windows XP and related operating systems (Windows Server 2003 is based on Windows XP). The article states that this error could be caused by the following:

- Boot-sector viruses
- Device driver issues
- Hardware issues
- Other issues

The article explains each issue and solution in detail. All things considered, the Knowledge Base is a valuable resource for dealing with any problems related to or reported by any version of Windows or any other Microsoft software.

I'm having other types of Windows problems.

This is another example where the Microsoft Knowledge Base comes to the rescue. For example, assume that you can't shut down your Windows Server 2003–based server. By searching for `shutdown problems Windows Server 2003`, (substitute the version of Windows you are using), you can quickly find several articles that can help you troubleshoot this type of problem. This problem has been caused by bugs in motherboard ROM (try upgrading your motherboard ROM to the latest version), bugs in the various Windows versions (visit www.windowsupdate.com and install the latest fixes, patches, and service packs), and configuration or hardware problems. The Knowledge Base articles provide more complete explanations of the Windows issues.

I'm having problems with Linux.

Because there are many different Linux distributions in use, there are several places to check for help with Linux-related problems of all types. In addition to checking the official website for your Linux distribution, try these additional resources:

- **www.debian-administration.org**—For administrators of Debian GNU/Linux–based distributions
- **www.aboutdebian.org**—For users of Debian GNU/Linux and related distributions
- **www.linuxquestions.org**—Forums, tutorials, podcasts, and other help
- **http://linux-nfs.org**—Help for using the Network File System with Linux, including client and server patches, bugs, and FAQs
- **www.apachefriends.org**—Help for users of the Apache webserver
- **www.linux.org**—News, distributions, tutorials, and other help for Linux users
- **www.tdlp**—The Linux Documentation Project is full of FAQs and how-tos
- **http://linux-ip.net/html/linux-ip.html**—A useful guide to Linux networking with TCP/IP

I'm having problems with UNIX.

UNIX implementations, unlike Linux, are proprietary to a particular hardware platform. However, many commands are the same or are very similar across different UNIX platforms. In addition to checking with your hardware vendor for help with your UNIX implementation, try the following websites:

- **www.unix.com**—The UNIX Forums provide general and distribution-specific help with most versions of UNIX, including Sun Solaris, HP-UX, AIX, SCO, and BSD, as well as OS X (Apple), and Linux.
- **www.tek-tips.com**—The Tek-Tips website has help for various UNIX-based operating systems. Select Forums, MIS/IT, Operating Systems - UNIX Based to find version-specific help for virtually all UNIX distributions as well as FreeBSD.
- **www.osdata.com/kind/unix.htm**—The UNIX page at OSdata.com provides links to extensive coverage of specific UNIX implementations. Information such as features, FAQs, links to official and third-party websites, and other help is provided for each implementation.

The power button won't turn off the system.

Servers that use the ATX, BTX, or SSI form factors use power supply designs in which the case power switch is connected to the motherboard and not directly to the power supply. This enables the motherboard and operating system to control system shutdown, preventing an unexpected loss of power that could cause data loss or file system corruption. However, if the system experiences a problem and becomes frozen or locked up in some way, the motherboard might not respond to the power button, meaning it does not send a shutdown signal to the power supply. It might seem that you will have to pull the plug to power off the system, but fortunately, a forced shutdown override is provided. You merely press and hold down the system power button (usually on the front of the chassis) for a minimum of 4 seconds, and the system should power off. The only drawback is that because this type of shutdown is forced and under the control of the motherboard or operating system, unsaved data can be lost, and some file system corruption could result. You should therefore run Chkdsk in Windows XP to check and correct any file-system issues after a forced shutdown.

If the system fails to power up after you perform an internal upgrade, make sure the front panel power switch cable is properly connected to the appropriate header pins on the motherboard.

For servers that use proprietary form factors, see the system documentation to determine how the power switch operates and how to shut down a system if the power switch fails. Note that in some situations, the power switch might be connected to AC power rather than to DC power. Be sure to disconnect the system from all external power to prevent electric shock.

The modem doesn't work.

First verify that the phone line is good and that you have a dial tone. Then check and, if necessary, replace the phone cable from the modem to the wall outlet. If the modem is integrated into the motherboard, check the BIOS Setup to ensure that the modem is enabled. Try clearing the ESCD in the BIOS Setup. This forces the PnP routines to reconfigure the system, which can resolve any conflicts. If the modem is internal and you aren't using the COM1/COM2 serial ports integrated into the motherboard (as for an external modem), try disabling the serial ports to free up additional system resources. Also try removing and reinstalling the modem drivers, ensuring that you are using the most recent drivers from the modem manufacturer. If that doesn't help, try physically removing and reinstalling the modem. If the modem is internal, install it in a different slot. If the modem is external, make sure it has power and is properly connected to the serial or USB port on the PC. Try replacing the external modem power brick and the serial/USB cable. Finally, if you get this far and the modem still doesn't work, try replacing the modem and finally the motherboard.

Note that modems are very susceptible to damage from nearby lightning strikes. Consider adding lightning arrestors or surge suppressors on the phone line running to the modem and unplug the modem during storms. If the modem has failed after a storm, you can be almost certain that it has been damaged by lightning. The strike might have damaged the serial port or motherboard in addition to the modem. Any items damaged by lightning will most likely need to be replaced.

The keyboard doesn't work.

The two primary ways to connect a keyboard to a server are via the standard keyboard port (usually called a PS/2 port) and via USB. One problem is that many older systems that have USB ports cannot use a USB keyboard because USB support is provided by the operating system—for instance, if the motherboard has a USB port but does not include USB Legacy Support in the BIOS. This support is specifically for USB keyboards (and mouse devices) and was not common in servers until 1998 or later. Many servers that had such support in the BIOS still had problems with the implementation; in other words, they had bugs in the code that prevented the USB keyboard from working properly. If you are having problems with a USB keyboard, check to ensure that USB Legacy Support is enabled in the BIOS. If you are still having problems, make sure you have installed the latest BIOS for your motherboard and any Windows updates from Microsoft. Some older systems never could properly use a USB keyboard, in which case they should change to a PS/2 keyboard instead. Some keyboards feature both USB and PS/2 interfaces, which offer the flexibility to connect to almost any system.

If a PS/2 keyboard is having problems, the quickest way to verify whether the problem is the keyboard or the motherboard is to replace the keyboard with a known-good spare. In other words, borrow a working keyboard from another system and try it. If it still doesn't work, the keyboard controller on the motherboard is most likely defective, which means the entire board must be replaced.

The monitor appears completely garbled or unreadable.

A completely garbled screen is most often due to improper, incorrect, or unsupported settings for the refresh rate, resolution, or color depth. Using incorrect drivers can also cause this. To check the configuration of the video card or onboard video, the first step is to power on the system and verify whether you can see the POST or the system splash screen and enter the BIOS Setup. If the screen looks fine during the POST but goes crazy after Windows starts to load, the problem is almost certainly due to an incorrect setting or configuration of the card. To resolve this, boot a system running Windows 2000 Server or Windows Server 2003 in VGA mode (hold down the F8 function key as Windows starts to load and select VGA mode from the special startup menu listing). This bypasses the current video driver and settings and places the system in the default VGA mode supported by the BIOS on the video card. When the Windows desktop appears, right-click the desktop, select Properties, and then either reconfigure the video settings or change drivers, as necessary.

If the problem occurs from the moment you turn on the system, a hardware problem definitely exists with the video card, cable, or monitor. First, replace the monitor with another one; if the cable is detachable, replace that, too. If replacing the monitor and cable does not solve the problem, the video card or integrated video is probably defective. If the motherboard uses integrated video, replace it with a PCI card. If it uses a video card, move the video card to a different slot. If video continues to malfunction, replace the card.

The image on the display is distorted (bent), shaking, or wavering.

This can often be caused by problems with the power line, such as an electric motor, an air conditioner, a refrigerator, or another device causing interference. Try replacing the power cord, plugging the monitor and/or the system in to a different outlet, or moving it to a different location entirely. This problem can also be caused by local radio transmitters such as a nearby radio or television station or two-way radios being operated in the vicinity of the system. If the monitor image is bent and discolored, it could be due to the shadow mask being magnetized. Turn the monitor on and off repeatedly; this causes the built-in degaussing coil around the perimeter of the tube to activate in an attempt to demagnetize the shadow mask. If this seems to work partially but not completely, you might need to obtain a professional degaussing coil from an electronics or TV service shop to demagnetize the mask. Next, replace the monitor cable, try a different (known-good) monitor, and, finally, replace the video card.

I installed an upgraded processor, but it won't work.

First, make sure the motherboard supports the processor that is installed. Also make sure you are using the latest BIOS for your motherboard; check with the motherboard manufacturer to see whether any updates are available for download and install them if any are available. Check the jumper settings (on older boards) or BIOS Setup screens to verify that the processor is properly identified and set properly with respect to the FSB (or CPU bus) speed, clock multiplier, and voltage settings. Make sure the processor is set to run at its rated speed and is not overclocked. If any of the CPU settings in the BIOS Setup are on manual override, set them to automatic instead. Then reseat the processor in the socket. Next, make sure the heatsink is properly installed and you are using thermal interface material (that is, thermal grease) at the mating junction between the CPU and heatsink.

Just because a processor fits in the socket (or slot) on your motherboard does not mean it will work. For a processor to work in a system, the following are required:

- **The CPU must fit in the socket.** Because processors with different specifications sometimes use the same socket but the pinout might vary, you must make sure the motherboard supports the processor type as well as the pinout. For example, the Pentium D processor uses the same Socket LGA775 as late-model Pentium 4 processors, but most Pentium 4 server motherboards are not compatible with the Pentium D.

- **The motherboard must support the voltage required by the CPU.** Modern motherboards set voltages by reading voltage ID (VID) pins on the processor and then setting the onboard voltage regulator module (VRM) to the appropriate settings. Older boards might not support the generally lower voltage requirements of newer processors.

- **The motherboard ROM BIOS must support the CPU.** Modern boards read the CPU to determine the proper FSB (or CPU bus) speed settings as well as the clock multiplier settings for the CPU. Many CPUs have different requirements for cache settings and initialization, as well as for bug fixes and workarounds.

- **The motherboard chipset must support the CPU.** In some cases, specific chipset models or revisions might be required to support certain processors.

Before purchasing an upgraded processor for a system, you should first check with the motherboard manufacturer to see whether your board supports the processor. If so, it will meet all the requirements listed previously. Often, BIOS updates are available that enable newer processors to be supported in older boards, beyond what was originally listed in the manual when the board was new. The only way to know for sure is to check with the motherboard manufacturer for updated information regarding supported processors for a particular board.

The system runs fine for a few minutes but then freezes or locks up.

This is the classic symptom of a system that is overheating. Most likely the CPU(s) may be overheating, but other components, such as the memory or motherboard chipset, could also be overheating. If the system is custom built from standard components, the design might be insufficient for proper cooling, and bigger heatsinks, more fans, or other solutions might be required. If the system was working fine but now is exhibiting this problem, check to see whether the problem started after any recent changes were made. If so, the change that was made could be the cause of the problem. If no changes were made, most likely something such as a cooling fan has either failed or is starting to fail.

Most modern servers have several fans, one or two inside the power supply, one on the CPU (or positioned to blow on the CPU), and optionally others for the chassis. Slimline 1U and 2U servers often use arrays of multiple small-diameter internal fans. Verify that any and all fans are properly installed and spinning. They should not be making grinding or growling noises, which usually indicate bearing failure. Many newer systems have thermostatically controlled fans; in these systems, it is normal for the fan speeds to change with the temperature. Make sure that the chassis is several inches from walls and that the fan ports are unobstructed. Try removing and reseating the processor; then reinstall the CPU heatsink with new thermal interface material. Check the power supply and verify that it is rated sufficiently to power the system (most should be 300 watts or more). Use a digital multimeter to verify the voltage outputs of the power supply, which should be within ±5% of the rated voltage at each pin. Try replacing the power supply with a high-quality replacement or known-good spare.

I am experiencing intermittent problems with the hard drive(s).

Many entry-level servers use ATA (commonly called ATA/IDE or PATA) interface drives, which consist of a drive and integrated controller, a ribbon cable, and a host adapter circuit in the motherboard.

Typically, intermittent problems are found with the cable and the drive; it is far more rare that the host adapter fails or exhibits problems. Many problems occur with the cables. ATA drives use either 40-conductor or 80-conductor cables, with one 40-pin connector at each end and optionally one in the middle. Drives supporting transfer rates higher than ATA33 (33MBps or Ultra DMA Mode 2) must use 80-conductor cables. Check the cable to ensure that it is not cut or damaged; then try unplugging and replugging it in to the drive and motherboard. Check to see that the cable is not more than 18 inches (46cm) in length because that is the maximum allowed by the ATA specification. This is especially important when you are using the faster ATA100 or ATA133 transfer rates. Try replacing the cable with a new 80-conductor 18 inches version.

If replacing the cable does not help, replace the drive with a spare, install an OS, and test it to see whether the problem remains. If the problem does remain, the problem is with the motherboard, which most likely needs to be replaced.

SATA drives use a jacketed cable that is thicker but much narrower than ATA/IDE cables. If the SATA cable is folded or creased, replace it. Make sure the SATA cable is tightly connected to the host adapter and the drive.

SCSI drives use cables that resemble ATA/IDE but are wider. In addition to cable problems, SCSI drives and devices can also fail because of conflicting device ID numbers and termination issues.

If the drive continues to fail after you replace the data cables or connect it to another system, the problem is most likely with your original drive. You can simply replace it or try testing, formatting, and reinstalling to see whether the drive can be repaired. To do this, you need the low-level format or test software provided by the drive manufacturer. See the following websites for diagnostic and testing software:

- **Maxtor (includes former Quantum hard disk products)**—www.maxtor.com (In December 2005 Seagate announced plans to merge with Maxtor in the second half of 2006.)
- **Seagate**—www.seagate.com
- **Western Digital**—www.wdc.com
- **Hitachi (includes former IBM hard disk products)**—www.hitachigst.com

The system won't boot up; the screen says `Missing operating system`.

When your system boots, it reads the first sector from the hard disk—called the MBR—and runs the code contained in that sector. The MBR code then reads the partition table (also contained in the MBR) to determine which partition is bootable and where it starts. Then it loads the first sector of the bootable partition—called the VBR—which contains the operating system–specific boot code. However, before executing the VBR, the MBR checks to ensure that the VBR ends with the signature bytes `55AAh`. The MBR displays the `Missing operating system` message if it finds that the first sector of the bootable partition (the VBR) does not end in `55AAh`.

Several things can cause this to occur, including the following:

- **The drive parameters entered in the BIOS Setup are incorrect or corrupted.** These are the parameters that define the drive that you entered in the BIOS Setup, and they're stored in a CMOS RAM chip powered by a battery on the motherboard. Incorrect parameters cause the MBR program to translate differently and read the wrong VBR sector, thus displaying the `Missing operating system` message. A dead CMOS battery can also cause this because it loses or corrupts the stored drive translation and transfer mode parameters. In fact, a dead battery is one of the more likely causes. To repair, check, and replace the CMOS battery, run the BIOS Setup, go to the hard drive parameter screen, and enter the correct drive parameters. Note that most drive parameters should be set to Auto or Autodetect.

- **The drive is not yet partitioned and formatted on this system.** This is a normal error if you try to boot the system from the hard disk before the OS installation is complete. Boot to an OS startup disk (floppy or CD) and run the setup program, which prompts you through the partitioning and formatting process during the OS installation.

- **The MBR and/or partition tables are corrupt.** This can be caused by boot sector viruses, among other things. To repair the MBR on an x86-based server using Windows 2000 Server or Windows Server 2003, insert the original Windows distribution CD and shut down the computer. Turn on the computer and select the option to boot from the CD. Select Repair and the option to run the Recovery Console. Log in to the system and use the FIXBOOT and FIXMBR commands to rewrite boot files and fix the MBR. Exit the Recovery Console and restart the system. See the Microsoft Knowledge Base article 326215 at http://support.microsoft.com for details for Windows Server 2003, or see article 229716 for Windows 2000 Server. If you use Linux, see "All About Linux: How to Repair a Corrupt MBR and boot into Linux," at http://linuxhelp. blogspot.com/2005/11/how-to-repair-corrupt-mbr-and-boot.html. For other distributions or for UNIX versions, see your operating system's documentation for help.

The system is experiencing intermittent memory errors.

If the memory was recently added or some other change was made to the system, you should undo that addition/change to see whether it is the cause. If it's not, remove and reseat all memory modules. If the contacts look corroded, clean them with contact cleaner and then apply contact enhancer for protection. Check the memory settings in the BIOS Setup; generally, all settings should be on automatic settings. Some BIOS setup programs refer to Automatic as "by SPD" or something similar (the SPD is the serial presence detect chip that stores the default memory timing settings on DIMM modules). Next, upgrade to the latest BIOS for your motherboard and remove all memory except one bank. Then run only one bank of memory, but in the second or third bank position. A socket can develop a problem, and most motherboards do not require that the sockets be filled in numeric order. Also, replace the remaining module with one of the others that was removed, a new module, or a known-good spare. Note that if your motherboard uses pairs of memory (as in a dual-channel or redundant arrangement), you might need to use two or more modules.

If you get this far, the problem is most likely either the motherboard or the power supply—or possibly some other component in the system. Remove other components from the system to see whether they are causing problems. Reseat the CPU and replace the power supply with a high-quality new unit or a known-good spare. Finally, try replacing the motherboard.

The system locks up frequently and sometimes reboots on its own.

This is one of the classic symptoms of a power supply problem. The power supply is designed to send a special Power_Good signal to the motherboard when it has passed its own internal tests and outputs are stable. If this signal is dropped, even for an instant, the system resets. Problems with the power good circuit cause lockups and spontaneous rebooting. This can also be caused if the power at the wall outlet is not correct. Verify the power supply output with a digital multimeter; all outputs should be within ±5% of the rated voltages. Use a tester for the wall outlet to ensure that it is properly wired and verify that the voltage is near 120V. Replace the power cord or power strip between the power supply and wall outlet.

Unfortunately, the intermittent nature makes this problem difficult to solve. If the problem is not with the wall outlet power, check the power connection(s) between the power supply and the motherboard. If your server uses a standard 20- or 24-pin ATX- or SSI-style connector, intermittent operation can be caused by not snapping the connector into place. Shut off the system and verify that the connector is fully inserted and locked into place. If the system uses multiple power connectors (which is common with some types of redundant power supplies), make sure each connector is completely inserted and locked in place (if the connector features a locking mechanism).

If the system continues to perform erratically, determine whether you have another system of the same type that is working properly and swap the suspect power supply from the failing system into another system. If the system performs properly after you swap power supplies, the original power supply is defective and should be replaced. If the problem stays with the original system, other power-related components, such as the power-supply paralleling board (PSPB) used on some Dell servers, redundant power supply modules, or internal power cables, may be defective. Continue to swap suspect for known-working parts until you determine the source of the problem. If the problem stops after you swap out a part, the swapped part has failed and should be replaced.

If the system continues to run erratically after you swap all parts of the power supply/distribution system, consider other components, such as memory modules, the processor, or the motherboard. Reseat the CPU and reinstall the heatsink with new thermal interface material. Then reseat the memory modules, run only one bank of memory, and replace the motherboard if all other options fail.

If you must replace the power supply, try to get a larger-wattage-rated unit if possible. This is easy to do if the server uses a standard form factor, such as ATX12V. If the server uses a proprietary power supply form factor, you might not be able to get a higher-rated unit.

I installed a 200GB ATA/IDE drive in my server, but it is recognizing only 137GB.

Motherboard ROM BIOSs have been updated throughout the years to support larger and larger ATA/IDE drives. BIOSs older than August 1994 are typically limited to drives of up to 528MB, whereas BIOSs older than January 1998 are limited to 8.4GB. Most BIOSs dated 1998 or newer support drives up to 137GB, and those dated September 2002 or newer should support drives larger than 137GB. These are only general guidelines; to accurately determine this for a specific system, you should check with your motherboard manufacturer. If your server's BIOS does not support the full capacity of your hard disk, try these solutions:

- Check with the server motherboard or system vendor for a BIOS upgrade that provides 48-bit LBA support.
- If a BIOS upgrade is not available, install a PCI host adapter that provides 48-bit LBA support, such as the Promise Ultra100 TX2, Ultra133 TX2, or most current ATA RAID adapters from various vendors. Connect the drive to the host adapter, which contains its own BIOS.

Do *not* use the dynamic drive overlay or similar boot code replacement options offered by a hard disk vendor's installation programs. These options do not work with Windows Server 2003 or with Linux, and in any event, they create a nonstandard disk configuration.

If you are using Windows 2000 Server, make sure you have Service Pack 3 or greater installed. Windows Server 2003 has native 48-bit LBA support. Linux distributions based on the Linux kernel 2.4.20 or greater, such as Red Hat Linux 9, SUSE Linux 9, and Mandriva (Mandrake) Linux 9.2 and newer versions also have native 48-bit LBA support.

You should also download and install the latest versions of the correct motherboard/chipset drivers for your hardware and operating system from your hardware vendor's website.

Note that if you use an external USB or IEEE 1394 hard disk, 48-bit LBA support is not an issue; the hardware in the external enclosure takes care of handling the drive's entire capacity.

My CD-ROM/DVD drive doesn't work.

CD and DVD drives are some of the most failure-prone components in a PC. It is not uncommon for one to suddenly fail after a year or so of use.

If you are having problems with a drive that was just installed, check the installation and configuration of the drive. Check the jumper settings on the drive. If you're using an 80-conductor cable, the drive should be jumpered to Cable Select; if you're using a 40-conductor cable, the drive should be set to either master or slave (depending on whether it is the only drive on the cable). Check the cable to ensure that it is not nicked or cut and is a maximum of 18 inches long (the maximum allowed by the ATA specification). Replace the cable with a new one or a known-good spare, preferably using an 80-conductor cable. Make sure the drive power is connected and verify that power is available at the connector by using a digital multimeter. Also make sure the BIOS Setup is set properly for the drive and verify that the drive is detected during the boot process. Finally, try replacing the drive and, if necessary, the motherboard.

If the drive had already been installed and was working before, first read different discs, preferably commercial-stamped discs rather than writable or rewritable ones. Then try the procedures listed previously.

My USB port or device doesn't work.

Make sure you have enabled the USB ports in the BIOS Setup. Make sure your operating system supports USB; Windows NT 4 does not support USB ports, whereas Windows 2000 and Windows Server 2003 do have USB support. Then remove any hubs and plug the device directly in to the root hub connections on your system. Replace the cable. Many USB devices require additional power, so ensure that your device has an external power supply connected if one is required. Replace the power supply.

I installed an additional memory module, but the system doesn't recognize it.

Verify that the memory is compatible with your motherboard. Many subtle variations exist in memory types that can appear to be identical on the surface. Just because it fits in the slot does not mean the memory will work properly with your system. Check your motherboard manual for the specific type of memory your system requires and possibly for a list of supported modules. You can visit www.crucial.com and use its memory selector to determine the exact type of memory for a specific system or motherboard. Also note that all motherboards have limits to the amount of memory they support, and many boards today support only up to 512MB or 1GB. Again, consult the motherboard manual or manufacturer for information on the limits for your board.

If you are sure you have the correct type of memory, follow the memory troubleshooting steps listed previously for intermittent memory problems.

I installed a new drive, but it doesn't work, and the drive LED remains lit.

This is the classic symptom for a cable plugged in backward. Both ATA and floppy drives are designed to use cables with keyed connectors; however, some cables are available that lack this keying, which means they can easily be installed backward. When the cable is installed backward into either the motherboard or the drive, the LED on the drive remains lit and the drive does not function. In some cases, this can also cause the entire system to freeze. Check the cables to ensure that they are plugged in properly at both ends; the stripe on the cable indicates pin-1 orientation. On the drive, pin 1 is typically oriented toward the power connector. On the motherboard, look for orientation marks silk-screened on the board or observe the orientation of the other cables plugged in (all cables follow the same orientation).

While I was updating my BIOS, the system froze, and now the system is dead.

This can occur when a flash ROM upgrade goes awry. Fortunately, most motherboards have a recovery routine that can be enabled via a jumper on the board. When enabled, the recovery routine causes the system to look for a floppy with the BIOS update program on it. If you haven't done so already, you need to download an updated BIOS from the motherboard manufacturer and follow its directions for placing the BIOS update program on a bootable floppy. Then set the BIOS recovery mode via the jumper on the motherboard, power on the system, and wait until the procedure completes. It usually takes up to 5 minutes, and you might hear beeping to indicate the start and end of the procedure. When the recovery is complete, turn off the system and restore the recovery jumper to the original (normal) settings.

If your motherboard does not feature BIOS recovery capability, you might have to send the board to the manufacturer for repair.

I installed a PCI video card in an older system with PCI slots, and it doesn't work.

The PCI bus has gone through several revisions; most older slots are 2.0 type, and most newer cards need 2.1 or later PCI slots. The version of PCI your system has is dictated by the motherboard chipset. If you install a newer video or other PCI card that requires 2.1 slots in a system with 2.0 slots, often the system won't boot up or operate at all.

If you check the chipset reference information in Chapter 3, you might be able to determine which revision of PCI slots your motherboard has by knowing which chipset it has. If this is your problem, the only solution is to change either the card or motherboard so that they are both compatible.

The Importance of Documentation

Whether you're building a server from the ground (motherboard) up or using a preconfigured server, you need to make sure you have all the documentation you can get for the hardware on board. At a minimum, this should include the following:

- The system or motherboard/BIOS manual
- The technical specifications for components such as the processor, memory, and add-on cards
- Additional documentation for system hardware, such as whitepapers, addenda, and so forth

You can usually download a PDF version if you don't have the original paper copy of this information or if you didn't receive detailed information with your system.

If you have problems with your system, especially after a hardware upgrade, you should check with the system or motherboard vendor to determine whether you need a BIOS upgrade.

You need to be sure to keep the original operating system license documents, including serial numbers, CDs, and so forth. If you need to reinstall or repair the operating system at some point, this information is vital.

CHAPTER 5

Memory

This chapter discusses memory from both physical and logical points of view. First, we'll examine what memory is, where it fits into the server architecture, and how it works. Then we'll look at the various types of memory, their speeds, and the packaging of the chips and memory modules you can buy and install.

Memory Basics

Memory is the workspace for a server's processor. It is a temporary storage area where the programs and data being operated on by the processor must reside. Memory storage is considered temporary because the data and programs remain there only as long as the server has electrical power or is not reset. Before the server is shut down or reset, any data that has been changed should be saved to a more permanent storage device (usually a hard disk) so it can be reloaded into memory in the future.

Memory is often called *RAM*, for *random access memory*. RAM's contents are volatile, requiring frequent power refreshes to remain valid. Main memory is called RAM because you can randomly (as opposed to sequentially) access any location in memory. This designation is somewhat misleading and often misinterpreted. Read-only memory (ROM), for example, is also randomly accessible, yet it is usually differentiated from system RAM because ROM, unlike RAM, maintains its contents without power and can't normally be written to. Disk memory is also randomly accessible, but we don't consider that RAM, either.

Over the years, the definition of RAM has changed from being a simple acronym to referring to the primary memory workspace the processor uses to run programs, which is usually constructed of a type of chip called dynamic RAM (DRAM). One of the characteristics of DRAM chips (and, therefore, RAM in general) is that they store data dynamically, which really has two meanings. One meaning is that the information can be written to RAM repeatedly at any time. The other has to do with the fact that DRAM requires the data to be refreshed (essentially rewritten) every 15ms (milliseconds) or so. A type of RAM called static RAM (SRAM) does not require this periodic refreshing. An important characteristic of RAM in general is that data is stored only as long as the memory has electrical power.

When we talk about a computer's memory, we usually mean the RAM or physical memory in the system (the memory modules used to temporarily store currently active programs and data). It's important not to confuse memory with *storage*, which refers to things such as disk and tape drives (although they can be used as a substitute for RAM called *virtual memory*).

RAM can refer to both the physical chips/modules that make up memory in a system and the logical mapping and layout of that memory. *Logical mapping* and *layout* refer to how the memory addresses are mapped to actual chips and what address locations contain which types of system information.

Memory temporarily stores programs when they are running, along with the data being used by those programs. RAM chips are sometimes termed *volatile storage* because when you turn off a computer or an electrical outage occurs, whatever is stored in RAM is lost unless it's been saved to a local hard disk or other storage device or the server's hard disk. Because of the volatile nature of RAM, many computer users make it a habit to save their work frequently. (Some software applications can do timed backups automatically.) Launching a computer program from either local or network storage brings files into RAM, and as long as they are running, computer programs reside in RAM. The CPU executes programmed instructions in RAM and also stores results in RAM. The server transmits data to onboard storage or to connected workstations that request the information.

Physically, the *main memory* in a system is a collection of chips or modules containing chips that are usually plugged in to the motherboard. These chips or modules vary in their electrical and physical designs and must be compatible with the system into which they are being installed in order to function properly. This chapter discusses the various types of chips and modules that can be installed in different systems.

Next to the processor and motherboard, memory can be one of the most expensive components in a modern PC, although the total amount of money spent on memory for a typical system has declined over the past few years. Server memory generally sells for about $200 per gigabyte. It is somewhat more expensive than desktop memory because it supports data-protection and reliability features such as parity/error correcting code (ECC) and a signal buffer. (Memory that uses a signal buffer chip is known as *registered* memory.)

If you build a new server, you can't expect to be able to use just any existing server memory in your inventory. Similarly, if you upgrade the motherboard in an existing server, it's likely that the new motherboard will not support the old motherboard's memory. Therefore, you need to understand all the various types of memory on the market today so you can best determine which types are required by which systems and thus more easily plan for future upgrades and repairs.

To better understand physical memory in a system, you should see where and how it fits into the system. Three main types of physical memory are used in modern systems:

- Read-only memory (ROM)
- Dynamic random access memory (DRAM)
- Static random access memory (SRAM)

ROM

ROM is a type of memory that can permanently or semipermanently store data. It is called *read-only* because it is either impossible or difficult to write to. ROM is also often referred to as *nonvolatile memory* because any data stored in ROM remains there, even if the power is turned off. Therefore, ROM is an ideal place to put a server's startup instructions (that is, the software that boots the system).

Note that ROM and RAM are not opposites, as some people seem to believe. They are both simply types of memory. In fact, ROM could be classified as technically a subset of the system's RAM. In other words, a portion of the system's RAM address space is mapped into one or more ROM chips. This is necessary to contain the software that enables the PC to boot up; otherwise, the processor would have no program in memory to execute when it was powered on.

◀◀ For more information on ROM, see "Motherboard BIOS," p. 286.

The main ROM BIOS is contained in a ROM chip on the motherboard, but there are also adapter cards with ROM on them as well. ROM on adapter cards contains auxiliary BIOS routines and drivers needed by the particular card, especially for those cards that must be active early in the boot process, such as video cards. Cards that don't need drivers active at boot time typically don't have ROM because those drivers can be loaded from the hard disk later in the boot process.

Most systems today use a type of ROM called *electrically erasable programmable ROM (EEPROM)*, which is a form of flash memory. Flash is a truly nonvolatile memory that is rewritable, enabling users to easily update the ROM or firmware in their motherboards or any other components (video cards, SCSI cards, peripherals, and so on).

DRAM

DRAM is the type of memory chip used for most of the main memory in a modern PC. The main advantages of DRAM are that it is very dense, meaning you can pack a lot of bits into a very small chip, and it is inexpensive, which makes purchasing large amounts of it affordable.

The memory cells in a DRAM chip are tiny capacitors that retain a charge to indicate a bit. The problem with DRAM is that it is dynamic. Because of its design, DRAM must be constantly refreshed; otherwise, the electrical charges in the individual memory capacitors drain, and the data is lost. A refresh occurs when the system memory controller takes a tiny break and accesses all the rows of data in the memory chips. Most systems have a memory controller (which is built in to the North Bridge portion of the motherboard chipset of most servers or is found in the processor on the AMD Opteron), which is set for an industry-standard refresh rate of 15ms. This means that every 15ms, all the rows in the memory chip are automatically read to refresh the data.

◄◄ See "Server Chipsets Overview," p. 146.

Unfortunately, refreshing memory takes processor time away from other tasks because each refresh cycle takes several CPU cycles to complete. A few servers allow you to alter the refresh timing parameters via the CMOS Setup, but be aware that increasing the time between refresh cycles to speed up your system can allow some of the memory cells to begin draining, which can cause random soft memory errors to appear. (A *soft error* is a data error that is not caused by a defective chip.)

On a server using ECC memory, the server will automatically correct a single-bit soft error without any user intervention. A soft error involving two or more memory bits would trigger an error message. Servers using advanced ECC (chipkill) can correct up to four bit errors in the same memory module. However, a few low-end servers don't use ECC memory. On those servers, any type of memory error would cause the system to lock up and require a restart. Unsaved data would be lost. It is usually safer to stick with the recommended or default refresh timing. Because refreshing consumes less than 1% of a modern system's overall bandwidth, altering the refresh rate has little effect on performance. It is almost always best to use default or automatic settings for any memory timings in the BIOS Setup. Most servers don't allow changes to memory timings and are permanently set to automatic settings. On an automatic setting, the motherboard reads the timing parameters out of the serial presence detect (SPD) ROM found on the memory module and sets the cycling speeds to match. Even if you're accustomed to altering memory settings on desktop PCs to boost performance, such changes often require a lot of experimentation to find a balance between performance and stability. With a server, you should always opt for stability over a relatively minute gain in performance.

The transistor for each DRAM bit cell reads the charge state of the adjacent capacitor. If the capacitor is charged, the cell is read to contain a 1; no charge indicates a 0. The charge in the tiny capacitors is constantly draining, which is why the memory must be refreshed constantly. Even a momentary power interruption, or anything that interferes with the refresh cycles, can cause a DRAM memory cell to lose the charge and therefore the data. If this happens in a running system, it can lead to blue screens, global protection faults, corrupted files, and any number of system crashes. Therefore, you should use battery backup systems (UPS devices) and high-quality surge suppressors on your servers.

DRAM is used in desktop and server systems because it is inexpensive, and the chips can be densely packed, so a lot of memory capacity can fit in a small space. Unfortunately, DRAM is also slow, typically much slower than the processor. For this reason, many types of DRAM architectures have been developed to improve performance. These architectures are covered later in this chapter.

SRAM: Cache Memory

Another distinctly different type of memory exists that is significantly faster than most types of DRAM. SRAM is so named because it does not need the periodic refresh rates that DRAM needs. Because of how SRAM is designed, not only are refresh rates unnecessary, but SRAM is much faster than DRAM and much more capable of keeping pace with modern processors.

SRAM is available in access times of 2ns (nanoseconds) or less, so it can keep pace with processors running 500MHz or faster. This is because of the SRAM design, which calls for a cluster of six transistors for each bit of storage. The use of transistors but no capacitors means that refresh rates are not necessary because there are no capacitors to lose their charges over time. As long as there is power, SRAM remembers what is stored. Unfortunately, SRAM is too expensive and too large to use as main memory.

However, SRAM is a perfect choice for memory caching. Cache memory runs at speeds close to or equal to the processor speed and is the memory the processor usually directly reads from and writes to. During read operations, the data in the high-speed cache memory is resupplied from the lower-speed main memory or DRAM in advance. Cache memory is built in to all modern server processors, starting with the Pentium and Pentium Pro.

Cache effectiveness is expressed as a *hit ratio*, which is the ratio of cache hits to total memory accesses. A *hit* occurs when the data the processor needs has been preloaded into the cache from the main memory, meaning that the processor can read it from the cache. A cache *miss* occurs when the cache controller does not anticipate the need for a specific address and the desired data is not preloaded into the cache. In the case of a miss, the processor must retrieve the data from the slower main memory instead of the faster cache. Anytime the processor reads data from main memory, the processor must wait longer because the main memory cycles at a much slower rate than the processor. If a processor with integral on-die cache is running at 3400MHz (3.4GHz), both the processor and the integral cache would be cycling at 0.29ns, while the main memory would most likely be cycling 8.5 times more slowly, at 2.5ns (200MHz DDR). Therefore, the memory would be running at only a 400MHz equivalent rate. So, every time the 3.4GHz processor read from main memory, it would effectively slow down 8.5-fold to only 400MHz! The slowdown is accomplished by having the processor execute *wait states*, which are cycles in which nothing is done; the processor essentially cools its heels while waiting for the slower main memory to return the desired data. Obviously, you don't want your processors slowing down, so cache function and design become more important as system speeds increase.

To minimize the processor being forced to read data from the slow main memory, two or three stages of cache usually exist in a modern system: called Level 1 (L1), Level 2 (L2), and Level 3 (L3). The L1 cache is also called the *integral*, or *internal*, *cache* because it has always been built directly in to the processor as part of the processor die (the raw chip). Therefore, the L1 cache always runs at the full speed of the processor core and is the fastest cache in any system.

L1 cache has been a part of all processors since the Intel 386. To improve performance, later processor designs from Intel (starting with the Pentium Pro of 1995) and AMD (starting with the K6-III of 1999) included the L2 cache as a part of the processor die (earlier systems used the L2 cache on the motherboard). Although the Pentium Pro included L2 cache in the processor core, running at full speed, this was a very expensive processor to build, and Intel switched over to slot-based designs for the Pentium II, Pentium II Xeon, and early versions of the Pentium III and Pentium III Xeon, a design also used by the original AMD Athlon. These processors placed L2 cache in separate chips from the processor core, and the L2 cache ran at half the speed (or sometimes a bit less) of the processor core.

However, by late 1999, with the introduction of the Pentium III Coppermine and Pentium III Xeon (Advanced Transfer Cache) processors, all of Intel's subsequent processors for servers as well as desktops have placed full-speed L2 cache in the processor core. Likewise, AMD's Socket A Athlon (first introduced in 2000) and Athlon MP server processors led AMD's return to on-die full-speed L2 cache. Today, all server (as well as desktop) processors use on-die L2 cache. In chips with on-die L2, the cache runs at the full core speed of the processor and is much more efficient than older designs that placed L2 cache outside the processor core. For details, see Chapter 2, "Server Microprocessors."

On-die L3 cache has been present in high-end workstation and server processors such as the Xeon and Itanium families since 2001. Having more levels of cache helps mitigate the speed differential between the fast processor core and the relatively slow motherboard and main memory. L2 and L3 cache is faster and is accessed much more quickly than main memory. Thus, virtually all motherboards designed for processors with built-in cache don't have any cache on the board; the entire cache is contained in the processor or processor module instead. The key to understanding both cache and main memory is to see where they fit in the overall system architecture.

Chapter 4, "Server Motherboards and BIOS," provides diagrams showing recent systems with different types of cache memory. Table 5.1 illustrates the need for and function of cache memory in modern systems.

Table 5.1   The Relationship Between L1 (Internal) Cache, L2 (External) Cache, and Main Memo

CPU Type	Pentium	Pentium Pro	Pentium II, Pentium II Xeon	Pentium III Xeon
CPU speed	233MHz	200MHz	450MHz	933MHz
L1 cache speed	4.3ns (233MHz)	5.0ns (200MHz)	2.2ns (450MHz)	1.07ns (933MHz)
L1 cache size	16KB	32KB	32KB	32KB
L2 cache type	Onboard	On-chip	On-chip	Onboard
CPU/L2 speed ratio	—	1/1	1/2	1/2
L2 cache speed	15ns (66MHz)	5ns (200MHz)	4.4ns (225MHz)	2.14ns (466.5MHz)
L2 cache size	Varies 1	256KB 2	512K	256KB 3
CPU bus speed	66MHz	66MHz	100MHz	133MHz
Memory bus speed	60ns (16MHz)	60ns (16MHz)	10ns (100MHz)	7.5ns (133MHz)

[1]The L2 cache is on the motherboard, and its size depends on which board is chosen and how much memory is installed.
[2]The Pentium Pro was also available with 512KB and 1024KB L2 cache.
[3]The Pentium III Xeon was also available with 512KB, 1024KB, and 2048KB L2 cache.
[4]Dual-core versions of the Opteron have 1024KB L2 cache per core.
[5]The Pentium 4 is also available with 256KB and 512KB L2 cache.
[6]The Xeon is also available with 512KB and 1024KB L2 cache. Some models also include L3 cache.

Starting with the Pentium Pro and Pentium II, the processor sets the amount of main memory that can be cached (that is, the *cacheability limit*). The Pentium Pro and some of the earlier Pentium IIs can address up to 64GB but only cache up to 512MB. The later Pentium IIs and all Pentium III and Pentium 4 processors can cache up to 4GB. All the server-oriented Xeon processors can cache up to 64GB. On current servers, all installed memory is cacheable.

The System Logical Memory Layout

The original PC had a total of 1MB of addressable memory, and the top 384KB of that was reserved for use by the system. Placing that reserved space at the top (between 640KB and 1024KB instead of at the bottom, between 0KB and 640KB) led to what is often called the *conventional memory barrier*. The constant pressures on system and peripheral manufacturers to maintain compatibility by never breaking from the original memory scheme of the first PC has resulted in a system memory structure that is (to put it kindly) a mess. Almost two decades after the first PC was introduced, even the newest Xeon-based servers are limited in many important ways by the memory map of the first PCs.

Although most server-based operating systems operate in *protected mode*, which uses memory above 1MB, the area between 640KB and 1024KB can be a problem when you're configuring servers because this area is used for ROM BIOS chips on the motherboard and add-on cards, and it is used for RAM mapping used by video chipsets.

Diagnostics software, by nature, must talk to the hardware directly. This means that little intensive diagnostics testing can be done while a protected-mode operating system such as Windows or Linux is running. For system testing, you usually have to boot from a DOS floppy. Many of the higher-end hardware diagnostics programs include their own special limited 16-bit operating systems, so they can more easily access memory areas that DOS would use. With Windows 2000 Server, Windows XP, and Windows Server 2003, you can format a floppy disk with MS-DOS startup files by selecting that option from the Format menu in My Computer.

ern Servers

Athlon MP 2200+	Opteron 250	Pentium 4 560	Xeon
1.8GHz	2.4GHz	3.6GHz	3.8GHz
0.56ns (1.8GHz)	0.42ns (2.4GHz)	0.278ns (3.6GHz)	0.263ns (3.8GHz)
128KB	128KB	16KB	16KB
On-die	On-die	On-die	On-die
1/1	1/1	1/1	1/1
0.56ns (1.8GHz)	0.42ns (2.2GHz)	0.278ns (3.6GHz)	0.263ns (3.8GHz)
256KB	1MB *4*	1MB *5*	2MB *6*
266MHz	333MHz	800MHz	800MHz
3.8ns (266MHz)	3.0ns (333MHz)	1.25ns (800MHz)	1.25ns (800MHz)

The point of all this is that although you might not be running DOS very much these days, at least for system configuration and installation, as well as for high-level hardware diagnostics testing, data recovery, and so forth, you might still have to boot to a 16-bit OS occasionally. When you are in that mode, the system's architecture changes, less memory is accessible, and some of the software you are running (16-bit drivers and most application code) must fight over the first 1MB or even 640KB for space.

The system memory areas discussed in this chapter, including the 384KB at the top of the first megabyte, which is used for video, adapter BIOS, and motherboard BIOS, as well as the remaining extended memory, are all part of the PC hardware design. They exist whether you are running 16-bit, 32-bit or 64-bit software; however, the limitations on their use in 16-bit (real) mode are much more severe.

32-bit operating systems such as Windows 9x, Windows 2000, Windows XP, Linux, and Windows Server, as well as their 64-bit offshoots, automatically manage the use of RAM, which means you don't have to interact with and manage this memory yourself as you often did with 16-bit operating systems.

The following sections are intended to give you an understanding of the server's hardware memory layout, which is consistent no matter which operating system you use. The only things that change are how the operating system uses and manages these areas.

From a server management standpoint, the most critical area of memory is the upper memory area (UMA). Although most servers now use PCI, AGP, and PCI-Express add-on cards that support plug-and-play auto-configuration of RAM and ROM addresses and other hardware resources, some older servers, particularly those used in industrial applications, still use ISA cards. Many ISA cards require manual configuration of their hardware resources. Thus, this chapter focuses on understanding the UMA and the devices that use UMA resource:

- Upper memory area (UMA)
- Video RAM memory (part of UMA)
- Adapter ROM and special-purpose RAM (part of UMA)
- Motherboard ROM BIOS (part of UMA)

Figure 5.1 shows the logical address locations for a 16-bit or higher system. If the processor is running in real mode, only the first megabyte is accessible. If the processor is in protected mode, either the full 16MB, 4,096MB, or 65,536MB is accessible. Each symbol is equal to 1KB of memory, and each line or segment is 64KB. This map shows the first 2MB of system memory.

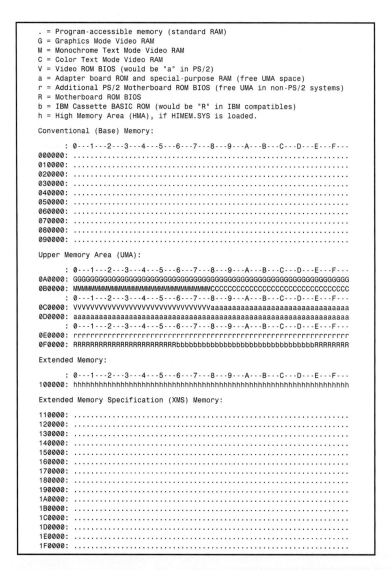

Figure 5.1 The logical memory map of the first 2MB of system memory.

◄◄ See "x86 Processor Modes," and "64-bit Processor Modes," p. 52.

Note

To save space, this map stops after the end of the second megabyte. In reality, however, this map continues to the maximum of addressable memory.

Upper Memory Area (UMA)

The term *UMA* describes the reserved 384KB at the top of the first megabyte of system memory on a PC/XT and the first megabyte on an AT-type system. This memory has the addresses from A0000 through FFFFF. The way the 384KB of upper memory is used breaks down as follows:

- **The first 128KB after conventional memory is called *video RAM*.** It is reserved for use by video adapters, whether built into the motherboard or plugged into a card slot. When text and graphics are displayed onscreen, the data bits that make up those images reside in this space. Video RAM is allotted the address range A0000–BFFFF.

- **The next 128KB is reserved for the adapter BIOS that resides in ROM chips on some adapter boards plugged in to the bus slots or for SCSI or other integrated adapters such as Serial ATA or ATA/SATA RAID.** Most VGA-compatible video adapters use the first 32KB of this area for their onboard BIOS. Any other adapters installed can use the rest. Many network adapters also use this area for special-purpose RAM called *shared memory*. Adapter ROM and special-purpose RAM is allotted the address range C0000–DFFFF.

- **The last 128KB of memory is reserved for motherboard BIOS (the basic input/output system, which is stored in read-only RAM chips or ROM).** The power-on self-test (POST) and bootstrap loader, which handles your system at boot-up until the operating system takes over, also reside in this space. Most systems use only the last 64KB (or less) of this space, leaving the first 64KB or more free for remapping with memory managers. Some systems also include the CMOS Setup program in this area. The motherboard BIOS is allotted the address range E0000–FFFFF.

Not all the 384KB of reserved memory is fully used on most 16-bit and higher systems. For example, according to the PC standard, reserved video RAM begins at address A0000, which is right at the 640KB boundary. Normally, it is used for VGA graphics modes, whereas the monochrome and color text modes use B0000–B7FFF and B8000–BFFFF, respectively. Older non-VGA adapters used memory only in the B0000 segment. Different video adapters use varying amounts of RAM for their operations, depending mainly on the mode they are in. To the processor, however, it always appears as the same 128KB area, no matter how much RAM is really on the video card. This is managed by bank-switching areas of memory on the card in and out of the A0000–BFFFF segments.

The remainder of the memory in this area is reserved for motherboard and option ROM and for RAM memory on other types of add-on cards. Protected-mode operating systems do not load drivers into this area, as was common with DOS. The amount of free UMA space varies from system to system, depending mostly on the adapter cards installed on the system. For example, most video adapters, SCSI adapters, and some network adapters require some of this area for built-in ROM or special-purpose RAM use.

Video RAM Memory

A video adapter installed in a system uses a portion of the system's first megabyte of memory to hold graphics or character information for display, but this typically is used or active only when in basic VGA mode.

Whether the video adapter is built into the motherboard, part of the motherboard chipset, or plugs into an expansion slot, all modern video adapters emulate a standard VGA adapter card. The video BIOS appears in the first 32KB of segment C000. The built-in video circuit in these systems can in many cases be disabled with a switch or jumper, or sometimes by simply plugging in a video card. When the built-in VGA acts as though it were a separate card, disabling it allows a new adapter to be installed without any compatibility problems that might arise if the video drivers were incorporated into the motherboard BIOS.

Adapter ROM and Special-Purpose RAM Memory

The second 128KB of the UMA, beginning at segment C000, is reserved for the software programs, or BIOS, on the adapter boards plugged in to the system slots. These BIOS programs are stored on special chips known as ROM. Most adapters today use EEPROM or flash ROM, which can be erased and reprogrammed right in the system, without requiring the removal of the chip or card. Updating flash ROM is as simple as running the update program you get from the manufacturer and following the directions onscreen. It pays to check periodically with your card manufacturers to see whether they have flash ROM updates for their cards.

ROM is useful for semipermanent programs that must always be present while the system is running, and especially for booting. On a server, the most likely devices to use this address space include SCSI BIOS, ATA RAID or SATA RAID BIOS, and some network adapter cards (BIOS or RAM).

Thanks to plug-and-play configuration used by PCI devices and supported by recent server operating systems such as Windows 2000 Server and newer versions, there is little need to worry about ROM conflicts. However, if you are managing an older server using Windows NT 4.0, you might need to manually configure adapter cards with onboard BIOS ROM or option RAM to avoid conflicts. If these systems use ISA cards, you might need to adjust DIP switches or jumpers to set address ranges. With PCI cards, you can use a configuration program provided by the card vendor.

Hard Disk Controller and SCSI Host Adapter BIOS

The UMA addresses C0000–DFFFF are also used for the built-in BIOS contained on many hard drive and SCSI controllers. Table 5.2 lists the amount of memory and the addresses commonly used by the BIOS contained on hard drive adapter cards.

Table 5.2   Memory Addresses Used by Various Hard Drive Adapter Cards

Disk Adapter Type	Onboard BIOS Size	BIOS Address Range
Most enhanced IDE adapters	16KB	C8000–CBFFF
ATA RAID or SATA RAID adapters	16KB	C8000–CBFFF
Some SCSI host adapters	16KB	C8000–CBFFF or DC000–DFFFF

Note that integrated SCSI or ATA/SATA RAID adapters also use these same ranges. However, if the ATA or SATA RAID function is integrated into the motherboard's South Bridge chip, the standard motherboard BIOS rather than an add-on BIOS configures the host adapter, and no additional BIOS address space is used.

The hard drive or SCSI adapter card used on a particular system might use a different amount of memory, but it is most likely to use the memory segment beginning at C800 because this address is considered part of the IBM standard for personal computers. Virtually all the disk controller or SCSI adapters today that have onboard BIOS allow the BIOS starting address to be easily moved in the C000 and D000 segments. The locations listed in Table 5.2 are only the default addresses that most of these cards use. If the default address is already in use by another card, you have to consult the documentation for the new card to see how to change the BIOS starting address to avoid any conflicts.

Figure 5.2 shows a sample memory map for an Adaptec AHA-2940 SCSI adapter.

```
. = Empty Addresses
G = Video Graphics Array (VGA) Adapter Graphics Mode Video RAM
M = VGA Monochrome Text Mode Video RAM
C = VGA Color Text Mode Video RAM
V = Standard VGA Video ROM BIOS
S = SCSI Host Adapter ROM BIOS
R = Standard Motherboard ROM BIOS

       : 0---1---2---3---4---5---6---7---8---9---A---B---C---D---E---F---
0A0000: GGGGGGGGGGGGGGGGGGGGGGGGGGGGGGGGGGGGGGGGGGGGGGGGGGGGGGGGGGGGGGGGG
0B0000: MMMMMMMMMMMMMMMMMMMMMMMMMMMMMMMMMMMCCCCCCCCCCCCCCCCCCCCCCCCCCCCCCCC
       : 0---1---2---3---4---5---6---7---8---9---A---B---C---D---E---F---
0C0000: VVVVVVVVVVVVVVVVVVVVVVVVVVVVVVVVVV..............................
0D0000: .............................................SSSSSSSSSSSSSSSSS
       : 0---1---2---3---4---5---6---7---8---9---A---B---C---D---E---F---
0E0000: ...............................................................
0F0000: RRRRRRRRRRRRRRRRRRRRRRRRRRRRRRRRRRRRRRRRRRRRRRRRRRRRRRRRRRRRRRRRR
```

Figure 5.2 Adaptec AHA-2940U SCSI adapter default memory use.

Network Adapters

Network adapter cards can also use upper memory in segments C000 and D000. The exact amount of memory used and the starting address for each network card vary with the card's type and manufacturer. Some network cards do not use any memory at all. A network card might have two primary uses for memory:

- IPL (initial program load or boot) ROM
- Shared memory (RAM)

IPL ROM is usually an 8KB ROM that contains a bootstrap loader program that enables the system to boot directly from a file server on the network. This enables the removal of all disk drives from the PC, creating a diskless workstation. Because no floppy or hard disk is in the system to boot from, IPL ROM gives the system the instructions necessary to locate an image of the operating system on the file server and load it as though it were on an internal drive. Network adapters that include IPL ROM are usually identified as supporting PXE (preboot execution environment).

Shared memory refers to a small portion of RAM contained on the network card that is mapped into the PC's UMA. This region is used as a memory window onto the network and offers rapid data transfer from the network card to the system. Network adapters that do not use shared memory use DMA or programmed I/O (PIO) transfers to move data to and from the network adapter. However, most high-performance adapters use shared memory. Depending on the adapter, the shared memory range is usually 16KB in size and can be located at any user-selected 4KB increment of memory in segments C000 or D000 in conventional memory. Some network adapters use memory addresses above 1MB to avoid conflicts with other devices.

Motherboard BIOS Memory

The last 128KB of reserved memory is used by the motherboard BIOS. The BIOS programs in ROM control the system during the boot-up procedure and remain as drivers for various hardware in the system during normal operation. Because these programs must be available immediately, they can't be loaded from a device such as a disk drive.

◄◄   See Chapter 4, "ROM BIOS," p. 286.

Both segments E000 and F000 in the memory map are considered reserved for the motherboard BIOS, but only some systems actually use this entire area. Most 16-bit or greater systems use all F000 for the BIOS and might decode but not use any of segment E000. By decoding an area, the motherboard essentially grabs control of the addresses, which precludes installing any other hardware in this region. In other words, configuring adapter cards to use this area isn't possible. This is why most adapters that use memory simply do not allow any choices for memory use in segment E000. Figure 5.3 shows the motherboard ROM BIOS memory use of most 16-bit or greater systems.

```
. = Empty Addresses
R = Standard Motherboard ROM BIOS

        : 0---1---2---3---4---5---6---7---8---9---A---B---C---D---E---F---
0E0000: ................................................................
0F0000: RRRRRRRRRRRRRRRRRRRRRRRRRRRRRRRRRRRRRRRRRRRRRRRRRRRRRRRRRRRRRRRRRR
```

Figure 5.3   The motherboard ROM BIOS memory use of most systems.

Note that the standard system BIOS uses only segment F000 (64KB).

Extended Memory

As mentioned previously in this chapter, the memory map on a system based on a 286 or higher processor can extend beyond the 1MB boundary that exists when the processor is in real mode. For a system to address memory beyond the first megabyte, the processor must be in protected mode. *Extended memory* is basically all memory past the first megabyte, and it can be accessed only while the processor is in protected mode.

Systems based on the Pentium Pro, Pentium II, and newer 32-bit server processors have a limit of 64GB (65,536MB, using 36-bit addressing) of system memory.

Note

36-bit memory addressing is enabled through a method called *physical address extension (PAE)*. PAE is an Intel-provided memory address extension that enables support of up to 64GB of physical memory for applications running on most 32-bit Intel Pentium Pro and later processors. PAE enables the processor to expand the number of bits that can be used to address physical memory from 32 bits to 36 bits, but it requires operating system support as well. Support for PAE is provided only in server-oriented operating systems such as Windows 2000 and later versions of the Advanced Server and Datacenter Server operating systems. Without PAE support, memory addressing is limited to 32 bits, or 4GB of physical RAM.

Preventing ROM BIOS Memory Conflicts and Overlap

As explained previously, C000 and D000 are reserved for use by adapter-board ROM and RAM. If two adapters have overlapping ROM or RAM addresses, usually neither board operates properly. Each board functions if you remove or disable the other one, but they do not work together.

This type of conflict is most likely to occur on servers running Windows NT 4.0 or servers that use ISA-slot expansion cards or integrated ISA devices that do not support plug-and-play configuration. To resolve conflicts, you can change the actual memory locations to be used with jumpers or switches or the adapter card or by using the adapter card's driver software. This type of conflict can cause problems for troubleshooters. You must read the documentation for each adapter to find out which memory addresses the adapter uses and how to change the addresses to allow coexistence with another adapter. Most of the time, you can work around these problems by reconfiguring the board or by changing jumpers, switch settings, or software-driver parameters. This type of change enables the two boards to coexist and stay out of each other's way.

Similarly, if you must configure adapter boards manually, you must ensure that adapter boards do not use the same IRQ, DMA channel, or I/O port address. You can easily avoid adapter board memory, IRQ, DMA channel, and I/O port conflicts by creating a chart or template that mocks up the system configuration by penciling on the template the resources already used by each installed adapter. You end up with a picture of the system resources and the relationship of each adapter to the others. With Windows NT 4.0, you must ensure that the resources Windows lists for the device are those it actually uses. You should print out all the settings in your system before and after you make modifications to see what is changed. This can help you anticipate conflicts and ensures that you configure each adapter board correctly the first time. The template also becomes important documentation when you consider new adapter purchases because new adapters must be configurable to use the available resources in your system.

Plug-and-play server operating systems such as Windows 2000 Server and Windows Server 2003 feature the Device Manager, which can be used to view and print out device settings, and most servers running these operating systems no longer contain ISA cards. These systems resolve almost all potential conflicts automatically by dynamically reconfiguring hardware to use nonconflicting memory address ranges.

◄◄ See "System Resources," p. 268.

ROM Shadowing

Virtually all 386 and higher systems enable you to use what is termed *shadow memory* for the motherboard and possibly some adapter ROM as well. Shadowing essentially moves the programming code from slow ROM chips into fast 32-bit system memory. Shadowing slow ROM by copying its contents into RAM can greatly speed up these BIOS routines—sometimes making them four to five times faster.

Note that shadowing ROM is not very important when running a 32-bit operating system, such as Windows NT, Windows 2000 Server, or Windows Server 2003. This is because those operating systems use the 16-bit BIOS driver code only during booting; then they load 32-bit replacement drivers into faster extended memory and use them. Therefore, shadowing normally affects only DOS or other 16-bit software and operating systems. Because of this, some people are tempted to turn off the Video BIOS shadowing feature in the BIOS Setup. Unfortunately, doing so does not gain you any memory back (you've lost it anyway), and it in fact makes the system slightly slower to boot up and somewhat slower when in Windows safe mode. The 16-bit BIOS video driver code is used at those times.

Adapter Memory Configuration and Optimization

Adapter boards use upper memory for their BIOS and as working RAM. If two boards attempt to use the same BIOS area or RAM area of upper memory, a conflict occurs that can keep the system from booting. In most cases, the plug-and-play software in the operating system ensures that such cards are automatically reconfigured so that they are not in conflict; however, sometimes problems can occur, and you must step in and manually resolve a conflict. The following sections cover ways to avoid these potential unresolved conflicts and how to troubleshoot if they do occur. In addition, these sections discuss moving adapter memory to resolve conflicts and provide some ideas on optimizing adapter memory use.

How to Determine What Adapters Occupy the UMA

You can determine which adapters are using space in upper memory in the following two ways:

- Study the documentation for each adapter on your system to determine the memory addresses they use.
- Use a software utility or the Device Manager in your operating system to determine which UMAs your adapters are using.

The simplest way (although by no means always the most foolproof) is to use a software utility to determine the UMAs used by the adapters installed on your system. You use the Device Manager in Windows 2000 Server or Windows Server 2003. You access it through the System properties sheet in the Control Panel. Device Manager examines your system configuration and determines not only the upper memory used by your adapters but also the IRQs used by each of these adapters.

True plug-and-play systems also shut down one of the cards involved in a conflict to prevent a total system lockup. This could cause Windows to boot in safe mode.

After you run Device Manager, or another utility to determine your system's upper memory configuration, you should make a printout of the memory addresses used. Thereafter, you can quickly refer to the printout when you are adding a new adapter to ensure that the new board does not conflict with any devices already installed on your system.

Different Linux distributions use different methods of viewing and controlling hardware. For example, SUSE uses a hardware configuration utility called YaST. Red Hat Fedora uses a collection of tools stored in the System Settings submenu. Mandriva (formerly Mandrake) uses the drakconf or hard-drake2 tools. See the documentation for your Linux distribution for details.

Moving Adapter Memory to Resolve Conflicts

Plug-and-play–based operating systems such as Windows 2000, Windows XP, and Windows Server 2003, as well as recent versions of Linux, automatically reallocate memory locations and other settings on plug-and-play hardware. Consequently, it's rare to encounter an adapter memory conflict. If necessary, you can move a card with a conflicting resource to another expansion slot.

However, if you support older servers that use a non–plug-and-play operating system, such as Windows NT 4.0, or servers that contain ISA cards, you might need to manually configure cards to avoid conflicts.

After you identify a conflict or potential conflict by using one of the two methods discussed in the previous section, you might have to reconfigure one or more of your adapters to move the upper memory space used by a problematic adapter.

Most non–plug-and-play adapter boards make moving adapter memory a somewhat simple process in which you simply change a few jumpers or switches to reconfigure the board. With plug-and-play cards in a non–plug-and-play system, you can use the configuration program that comes with the board to make the changes. The following steps help you resolve most problems that arise because adapter boards conflict with one another:

1. Determine the upper memory addresses currently used by your adapter boards and write them down.

2. Determine whether any of these addresses are overlapping, which results in a conflict.

3. Consult the documentation for your adapter boards to determine which boards can be reconfigured so that all adapters have access to unique memory addresses.

4. Configure the affected adapter boards so that no conflict in memory addresses occurs.

For example, if one adapter uses the upper memory range C8000–CBFFF and another adapter uses the range CA000–CCFFF, you have a potential address conflict. One of them must be changed. Note that plug-and-play cards running in a plug-and-play–based operating system and motherboard allow these changes to be made directly from the Windows Device Manager.

Memory Types Overview

The earliest servers used DRAM. The fastest DRAM speed was 60ns. The lower the ns rating, the faster the memory. (This can be confusing if you're accustomed to the newer method of expressing memory speeds in MHz or throughput [MBps].) A *nanosecond* is defined as one billionth of a second—a very short time indeed. To put some perspective on that, the speed of light is 186,282 miles (299,792 kilometers) per second in a vacuum. In one billionth of a second, a beam of light travels a mere 11.80 inches, or 29.98 centimeters—less than the length of a typical ruler!

To convert access time in nanoseconds to MHz, you use the following formula:

1 / nanoseconds × 1,000 = MHz

To convert from MHz to nanoseconds, you use the following inverse formula:

1 / MHz × 1,000 = nanoseconds

Although 60ns might seem very fast, it converts to about 16.7MHz, or less than 1/100 of the speed of recent server processors. Standard DRAM was used in servers up through about 1998. A slightly faster form of DRAM, known as extended data out (EDO) DRAM, was developed in the mid-1990s and was used in some servers as well. Although EDO DRAM's clock speed was also 60ns, it had improved memory access internally, to provide slightly faster throughput.

When we compare the speed of typical server processors in the mid-1990s to DRAM or EDO DRAM memory, it's obvious that the memory was actually slowing down system performance. For example, consider a Pentium Pro processor running at 200MHz. 200MHz is equivalent to 5ns. In other words, the processor was 12 times faster than memory (60/5=12)!

With faster processors in use by 1996–1997, such as the Pentium II and the Pentium II Xeon, the mismatch between processor speed and memory speed became even more lopsided. For example, a 300MHz Pentium II runs at the equivalent of 3.3ns—more than 18 times faster than the 60ns memory used in early models!

By 2000, servers were using memory types based on a new standard, called SDRAM (synchronous DRAM). 100MHz memory (PC100) and 133MHz memory (PC133) were the most common. Starting in early 2001, double data rate (DDR) memory of 200MHz and 266MHz become popular, along with 800MHz Rambus DRAM (RDRAM). In 2002, standard 333MHz DDR memory arrived, and in 2003, the speeds increased to 400MHz. The fastest current memory is DDR2, now available at 400MHz, 533MHz, 667MHz, and 1000MHz.

System memory timing is a little more involved than simply converting nanoseconds to megahertz. The transistors for each bit in a memory chip are most efficiently arranged in a grid, using a row-and-column scheme to access each transistor. All memory accesses involve selecting a row address and then a column address and then transferring the data. The initial setup for a memory transfer where the row and column addresses are selected is a necessary overhead referred to as *latency*. The access time for memory is the cycle time plus latency for selecting the row and column addresses. For example, SDRAM memory rated at 133MHz (7.5ns) typically takes five cycles to set up and complete the first transfer (5×7.5ns = 37.5ns) and then perform three additional transfers with no additional setup. Thus, four transfers take a total of eight cycles, or an average of about two cycles per transfer.

Over the development life of the PC, memory has had a difficult time keeping up with the processor, requiring several levels of high-speed cache memory to intercept processor requests for the slower main memory. Table 5.3 shows the progress and relationship between system board (motherboard) speeds in servers and the most common types and speeds of main memory or RAM used and how these changes have affected total bandwidth.

Table 5.3   DRAM Memory Module and Bus Standards/Bandwidth (Past, Current, and Future)[1]

Module Standard	Module Format	Chip Type	Clock Speed (MHz)	Cycles per Clock	Bus Speed (MT/s)	Bus Width (Bytes)	Transfer Rate (MBps)
Fast Page Mode and EDO DRAM							
FPM	SIMM	60ns	22	1	22	8	177
EDO	SIMM	60ns	33	1	33	8	266
SDR DRAM							
PC66	SDR DIMM	10ns	66	1	66	8	533
PC100	SDR DIMM	8ns	100	1	100	8	800
PC133	SDR DIMM	7/7.5ns	133	1	133	8	1,066
DDR DRAM							
PC1600	DDR DIMM	DDR200	100	2	200	8	1,600
PC2100	DDR DIMM	DDR266	133	2	266	8	2,133
PC2700	DDR DIMM	DDR333	166	2	333	8	2,667
PC3200	DDR DIMM	DDR400	200	2	400	8	3,200
PC4000	DDR DIMM	DDR500	250	2	500	8	4,000
DDR2 DRAM							
PC2-3200	DDR2 DIMM	DDR2-400	200	2	400	8	3,200
PC2-4300	DDR2 DIMM	DDR2-533	266	2	533	8	4,266
PC2-5400	DDR2 DIMM	DDR2-667	333	2	667	8	5,333
Rambus RIMM							
RIMM1600	RIMM-16	PC800	400	2	800	2	1,600
RIMM2100	RIMM-16	PC1066	533	2	1,066	2	2,133
RIMM2400	RIMM-16	PC1200	600	2	1,200	2	2,400
RIMM3200	RIMM-32	PC800	400	2	800	4	3,200
RIMM4200	RIMM-32	PC1066	533	2	1,066	4	4,266
RIMM4800	RIMM-32	PC1200	600	2	1,200	4	4,800

[1]*Key: MT/s = megatransfers per second; MBps = megabytes per second; ns = nanoseconds (billionths of a second); FPM = Fast Page Mode; EDO = extended data out; SIMM = single inline memory module; DIMM = dual inline memory module; RIMM = Rambus inline memory module; SDR = single data rate; and DDR = double data rate.*

Generally, a system works best when the throughput of the memory bus matches the throughput of the processor bus. Compare the memory bus transfer speeds (bandwidth) to the speeds of the processor bus shown in Table 5.4, and you see that some of the memory bus rates match some of the processor bus rates. In most cases, the type of memory that matches the CPU bus transfer rate is the best type of memory for systems with that type of processor.

Table 5.4   Processor Bus Bandwidth[1]

CPU Bus Type	Clock Speed (MHz)	Cycles per Clock	Bus Speed (MT/s)	Bus Width (bytes)	Bandwidth (MBps)
133MHz Pentium III Xeon FSB	133	1	133	8	1,066
333MHz Athlon MP FSB	166	2	333	8	2,667
400MHz Opteron FSB	200	2	400	8	3,200
667MHz Itanium 2 FSB	166	4	667	8	5,336
800MHz Xeon FSB	200	4	800	8	6,400

[1]Key: FSB = front side bus; MBps = megabytes per second; and MT/s = megatransfers per second.

Because the processor is fairly well insulated from directly dealing with main memory by the L1 and L2 caches, memory performance has often lagged behind the performance of the processor bus. Systems using RDRAM, SDRAM, DDR, and DDR2 SDRAM have memory bus performance equaling that of the processor bus. When the speed of the memory bus equals the speed of the processor bus, memory performance is optimum for that system.

Early Server RAM Types: DRAM, EDO DRAM, and SDRAM

Standard DRAM was used in early servers up through about 1996. This memory is accessed through a technique called *paging*. Normal memory access requires that a row-and-column address be selected, which takes time. Paging enables faster access to all the data within a given row of memory by keeping the row address the same and changing only the column. If a memory address is needed from a range of memory outside the current page, wait states are added to the memory access cycle.

Fast Page Mode DRAM

Early servers took advantage of a feature called *burst mode* to speed up access to adjacent memory locations. A typical burst mode access of standard DRAM is expressed as *x-y-y-y*, where *x* is the time for the first access (latency plus cycle time), and *y* represents the number of cycles required for each consecutive access. Standard 60ns DRAM normally runs 5-3-3-3 burst mode timing. This means the first access takes a total of five cycles (on a 66MHz system bus, this is about 75ns total or 5×15ns cycles), and the consecutive cycles take three cycles each (3×15ns = 45ns). As you can see, the actual system timing is somewhat less than the memory is technically rated for. Without the bursting technique, memory access would be 5-5-5-5 because the full latency would be necessary for each memory transfer.

Memory that uses paging and burst mode is referred to as *Fast Page Mode (FPM)* DRAM. FPM DRAM was the leading type of memory used in Pentium and Pentium Pro-class systems until 1995.

EDO DRAM

In 1995, a newer type of memory called extended data out (EDO) DRAM became available for Pentium and newer servers. EDO, a modified form of FPM memory patented by Micron Technologies, is sometimes referred to as *Hyper Page mode*. EDO memory consists of specially manufactured chips that allow a timing overlap between successive accesses. The name *extended data out* refers specifically to the fact that unlike with FPM, the data output drivers on the chip are not turned off when the memory controller removes the column address to begin the next cycle. This enables the next cycle to overlap the previous one, saving approximately 10ns per cycle and providing a real-world performance boost of about 5% over FPM DRAM.

Intel server-class chipsets built in the 1995–1998 period that support EDO include the 430HX (Triton II), 440FX (Natoma), 440LX, and 450NX (originally known as the 440NX). After this time, Intel servers began to use RDRAM or other, newer memory technologies.

◄◄   See "Intel Pentium Pro/II/III Chipsets for Servers," p. 166.

SDRAM

SDRAM, short for *synchronous DRAM*, is a type of DRAM that runs in synchronization with the memory bus. SDRAM delivers information in very high-speed bursts, using a high-speed, clocked interface. SDRAM removes most of the latency involved in asynchronous DRAM because the signals are already in synchronization with the motherboard clock.

As with EDO RAM, chipset must support SDRAM memory for it to be usable in your system. The first Intel server-class chipset to support SDRAM was the 440LX, which also supported EDO DRAM. Other Intel Pentium II/III/Xeon-class chipsets to support SDRAM included the 440BX and 440GX. SDRAM support has also been a popular choice for many third-party chipsets. See Chapter 3, "Server Chipsets," for details.

SDRAM performance is dramatically improved over that of FPM or EDO RAM. Because SDRAM is still a type of DRAM, the initial latency is the same, but overall cycle times are much faster than with FPM or EDO. SDRAM timing for a burst access would be 5-1-1-1, meaning that four memory reads would complete in only 8 system bus cycles, compared to 11 cycles for EDO and 14 cycles for FPM. This makes SDRAM almost 20% faster than EDO. Besides being capable of working in fewer cycles, SDRAM is also capable of supporting up to 133MHz (7.5ns) system bus cycling.

SDRAM is sold in dual inline memory module (DIMM) form and is often rated by megahertz speed rather than by nanosecond cycling time, which was confusing during the change from FPM and EDO DRAM.

To meet the stringent timing demands of its chipsets, Intel created specifications for SDRAM called PC66, PC100, and PC133. To meet the PC100 specification, 8ns chips are usually required. Normally, you would think 10ns would be considered the proper rating for 100MHz operation, but the PC100 specification calls for faster memory to ensure that all timing parameters are met.

In May 1999, the Joint Electron Device Engineering Council (JEDEC) created a specification called PC133. JEDEC achieved this 33MHz speed increase by starting with the PC100 specification and tightening up the timing and capacitance parameters. The faster PC133 quickly caught on as the most popular version of SDRAM for any systems running a 133MHz processor bus. The original chips used in PC133 modules were rated for exactly 7.5ns, or 133MHz; later ones were rated at 7.0ns, or 143MHz. These faster chips were still used on PC133 modules, but they allowed for improvements in column address strobe latency (abbreviated as CAS or CL), which somewhat improves overall memory cycling time.

JEDEC

JEDEC is the semiconductor engineering standardization body of the Electronic Industries Alliance (EIA), a trade association that represents all areas of the electronics industry. JEDEC was originally created in 1960, and it governs the standardization of all types of semiconductor devices, integrated circuits, and modules. JEDEC has about 300 member companies, including memory, chipset, and processor manufacturers, as well as practically any company involved in manufacturing computer equipment using industry-standard components.

The idea behind JEDEC is simple: to create industry standards for memory technology. For example, if one company were to create a proprietary memory technology, other companies that wanted to manufacture components compliant with that memory would have to pay license fees, assuming that the company that owned the memory was interested in licensing at all. Parts would be more proprietary in nature, causing problems with interchangeability or sourcing reasonably priced replacements. In addition, those companies licensing the technology would have no control over future changes or evolutions made by the owner company.

JEDEC prevents this type of scenario for memory by getting all the memory manufacturers to work together to create shared industry standards covering memory chips and modules. JEDEC-approved standards for memory can then be freely shared by all the member companies, and no one single company has control over a given standard or any of the companies producing compliant components. FPM, SDRAM, DDR SDRAM, and DDR2 SDRAM are examples of JEDEC memory standards used in PCs, whereas EDO and RDRAM are proprietary examples. You can learn more about JEDEC standards for memory and other semiconductor technology at www.jedec.org.

Table 5.5 shows the timing, rated chip speeds, and standard module speeds for various SDRAM DIMMs.

Table 5.5   SDRAM Timing, Actual Speed, and Rated Speed

Timing	Rated Chip Speed	Standard Module Speed
15ns	66MHz	PC66
10ns	100MHz	PC66
8ns	125MHz	PC100
7.5ns	133MHz	PC133
7.0ns	143MHz	PC133

Table 5.6 shows the standard SDRAM module types and resulting bandwidths.

Table 5.6   SDRAM Module Types and Bandwidths[1]

Module Standard	Module Format	Chip Type	Clock Speed (MHz)	Cycles per Clock	Bus Speed (MT/s)	Bus Width (Bytes)	Transfer Rate (MBps)
PC66	SDR DIMM	10ns	66	1	66	8	533
PC100	SDR DIMM	8ns	100	1	100	8	800
PC133	SDR DIMM	7/7.5ns	133	1	133	8	1,066

[1]Key: MT/s = megatransfers per second; MBps = megabytes per second; ns = nanoseconds (billionths of a second); DIMM = dual inline memory module; and SDR = single data rate.

▶▶ See "SIMMs, DIMMs, and RIMMS," p. 368.

Caution

At one time, PC133 memory was backward compatible with PC100 memory. However, current PC133 memory uses different sizes of memory chips than those used by PC100 modules. If you use servers that require PC100 memory, you should not attempt to use PC133 memory in them unless the memory is specifically identified by the vendor as being compatible with your system. You can use the online memory configurators provided by most major memory vendors to ensure that you get the right memory for your server.

DDR SDRAM, DDR2-SDRAM, and RDRAM

Current servers use DDR SDRAM, DDR2 SDRAM, and in some cases RDRAM. The following sections discuss these memory technologies in detail, as these are the memory technologies you'll be most likely to encounter in building and servicing servers.

DDR SDRAM

Double data rate (DDR) SDRAM memory is a JEDEC-created standard that is an evolutionary upgrade of standard SDRAM in which data is transferred twice as quickly. Instead of doubling the actual clock rate, DDR memory achieves the doubling in performance by transferring twice per transfer cycle: once at the leading (falling) edge and once at the trailing (rising) edge of the cycle. This effectively doubles the transfer rate, even though the same overall clock and timing signals are used.

DDR SDRAM was first used for graphics cards, and starting in 2001, it began to show up in PCs, although Intel did not officially support DDR until early 2002. Most recent server designs use DDR SDRAM.

DDR DIMMs come in a variety of speeds or throughput ratings and normally run on 2.5 volts. They are basically an extension of the standard SDRAM DIMMs, redesigned to support double clocking, where data is sent on each clock transition (twice per cycle) rather than once per cycle, as with standard SDRAM. To eliminate confusion with DDR, regular SDRAM is often called single data rate (SDR). Table 5.7 compares the various types of standard DDR SDRAM modules used in servers. As you can see, the raw chips are designated by their speed, in megatransfers per second, whereas the modules are designated by their approximate throughput, in megabytes per second.

Table 5.7   DDR SDRAM Module Types and Bandwidths[1]

Module Standard	Module Format	Chip Type	Clock Speed (MHz)	Cycles per Clock	Bus Speed (MT/s)	Bus Width (Bytes)	Transfer Rate (MBps)
PC1600	DDR DIMM	DDR200	100	2	200	8	1,600
PC2100	DDR DIMM	DDR266	133	2	266	8	2,133
PC2700	DDR DIMM	DDR333	166	2	333	8	2,667
PC3200	DDR DIMM	DDR400	200	2	400	8	3,200
PC4000	DDR DIMM	DDR500	250	2	500	8	4,000
PC4300	DDR DIMM	DDR533	266	2	533	8	4,266

[1]*Key: MT/s = megatransfers per second; MBps = megabytes per second; DIMM = dual inline memory module; and DDR = double data rate.*

The bandwidths listed in Tables 5.6 and 5.7 are per module. Many recent server and desktop chipsets support dual-channel DDR memory, in which two DDR DIMMs are installed at one time and function as a single bank with double the bandwidth of a single module. For example, the Intel E7320 and

E7221 server chipsets use dual-channel DDR memory. The E7320 supports the 800MHz front side bus (FSB) version of the 64-bit Xeon processor, and the E7221 supports Pentium 4 processors with the 800MHz FSB. Both processors transfer 8 bytes (64 bits) at a time, for a bandwidth of 6,400MBps (800×8 = 6,400). With an 800MHz FSB processor installed, these boards use standard PC3200 modules, installed two at a time (dual-channel), for a total bandwidth of 6,400MBps (3,200MBps × 2 = 6,400MBps). This design allows the memory bus throughput to match the CPU bus throughput exactly, resulting in the best possible performance. Note that the AMD Opteron processor's integrated memory controller also supports dual-channel DDR memory. You can optimize PC design by ensuring that the CPU bus and memory bus both run at exactly the same speeds (meaning bandwidth, not megahertz), so that data can move synchronously between the buses without delays.

DDR2 SDRAM

JEDEC and its members began working on the DDR2 specification in April 1998 and published the standard in September 2003. DDR2 chip and module production actually began in mid-2003 (mainly samples and prototypes), and the first chipsets, motherboards, and systems supporting DDR2 appeared in mid-2004. DDR2 is supported by many of the newest server chipsets, such as the Intel E7221.

DDR2 SDRAM is simply a faster version of conventional DDR-SDRAM memory: It achieves higher throughput by using differential pairs of signal wires to allow faster signaling without noise and interference problems. DDR2 is still double data rate, just like DDR, but the modified signaling method enables higher speeds to be achieved, with more immunity to noise and cross-talk between the signals. The additional signals required for differential pairs add to the pin count; DDR2 DIMMs have 240 pins, compared to the 184 pins of DDR. The original DDR specification tops out at 400MHz, whereas DDR2 starts at 400MHz and goes up to 533MHz, 800MHz, and 1000MHz. Table 5.8 shows the various DDR2 module types and bandwidth specifications.

Table 5.8   DDR2 SDRAM Module Types and Bandwidths[1]

Module Standard	Module Format	Chip Type	Clock Speed (MHz)	Cycles per Clock	Bus Speed (MT/s)	Bus Width (Bytes)	Transfer Rate (MBps)
PC2-3200	DDR2 DIMM	DDR2-400	200	2	400	8	3,200
PC2-4300	DDR2 DIMM	DDR2-533	266	2	533	8	4,266
PC2-5400	DDR2 DIMM	DDR2-667	333	2	667	8	5,333
PC2-6400	DDR2 DIMM	DDR2-800	400	2	800	8	6,400

[1]Key: MT/s = megatransfers per second; MBps = megabytes per second; DIMM = dual inline memory module; and DDR = double data rate.

In addition to providing greater speeds and bandwidth, DDR2 has other advantages. It uses lower voltage than conventional DDR (1.8V versus 2.5V), so power consumption and heat generation are reduced. Because of the greater number of pins required on DDR2 chips, the chips typically use fine-pitch ball grid array (FBGA) packaging rather than the thin small outline package (TSOP) chip packaging used by most DDR and conventional SDRAM chips. FPGA chips are connected to the substrate (meaning the memory module, in most cases) via tightly spaced solder balls on the base of the chip.

DDR2 DIMMs resemble conventional DDR DIMMs but have more pins and slightly different notches to prevent confusion or improper application. DDR2 memory module designs incorporate 240 pins, significantly more than conventional DDR or standard SDRAM DIMMs.

RDRAM

Rambus DRAM (RDRAM) is a fairly radical memory design found in high-end PC systems and servers from late 1999 through 2002. Intel signed a contract with Rambus in 1996, ensuring that it would support RDRAM into 2001. After 2001, Intel continued to support RDRAM in existing systems, but new chipsets and motherboards primarily shifted to DDR SDRAM, and all Intel chipsets and motherboards since that time have been designed for either conventional DDR or DDR2. RDRAM standards had been proposed that will support faster processors through 2006; however, without Intel's commitment to future chipset development and support, very few RDRAM-based systems were sold in 2003, and almost none after that. Due to the lack of industry support from chipset and motherboard manufacturers, RDRAM will most likely not play a big part in future PCs or servers.

With RDRAM, Rambus developed what is essentially a chip-to-chip memory bus, with specialized devices that communicate at very high rates of speed, a technology originally introduced for the Nintendo 64 and Sony PlayStation 2 game systems.

Conventional memory systems that use FPM/EDO or SDRAM are known as *wide-channel systems*. They have memory channels as wide as the processor's data bus, which for the Pentium and up is 64 bits. The DIMM is a 64-bit wide device, which means data can be transferred to it 64 bits (or 8 bytes) at a time.

RDRAM devices, on the other hand, are narrow-channel devices. They transfer data only 16 bits (2 bytes) at a time (plus 2 optional parity bits), but at much faster speeds. This is a shift away from a more parallel to a more serial design and is similar to what is happening with other evolving buses in the PC.

16-bit single-channel Rambus inline memory modules (RIMMs) originally ran at 800MHz, so the overall throughput is 800×2, or 1.6GB per second for a single channel—the same as for PC1600 DDR SDRAM. Pentium 4–based desktops and servers using Rambus memory typically used two banks simultaneously, creating a dual-channel design capable of 3.2GBps, which matches the bus speed of the original Pentium 4 processors. The RDRAM design features less latency between transfers because they all run synchronously in a looped system and in only one direction.

Newer RIMM versions run at 1,066MHz or 1,200MHz in addition to the original 800MHz rate and are available in single-channel, 16-bit versions as well as multiple-channel, 32-bit versions, for throughputs up to 4.8GBps per module.

A single Rambus memory channel can support up to 32 individual RDRAM devices (the RDRAM chips), and more if buffers are used. Each individual chip is serially connected to the next on a package called a RIMM, but all memory transfers are done between the memory controller and a single device, not between devices. The individual RDRAM chips are contained on RIMMs, and a single channel typically has three RIMM sockets. The RDRAM memory bus is a continuous path through each device and module on the bus, with each module having input and output pins on opposite ends. Therefore, any RIMM sockets not containing a RIMM must be filled with a continuity module to ensure that the path is completed. The signals that reach the end of the bus are terminated on the motherboard.

Each RDRAM chip on a RIMM1600 essentially operates as a standalone module sitting on the 16-bit data channel. Internally, each RDRAM chip has a core that operates on a 128-bit wide bus split into eight 16-bit banks running at 100MHz. In other words, every 10ns (100MHz), each RDRAM chip can transfer 16 bytes to and from the core. This internally wide yet externally narrow high-speed interface is the key to RDRAM. The overall wait before a memory transfer can begin (latency) is only one cycle, or 2.5ns maximum. RDRAM is also a low-power memory system. RDRAM modules use only 2.5V and support power management.

As discussed previously, RDRAM chips are installed in modules called RIMMs. A RIMM is similar in size and physical form to current DIMMs, but RIMMs and DIMMs are not interchangeable. RIMMs are available in module sizes up to 1GB or more and can be added to a system one at a time because each individual RIMM technically represents multiple banks to a system. They have to be added in pairs if your motherboard implements dual-channel RDRAM and you are using 16-bit wide RIMMs.

An RDRAM memory controller with a single Rambus channel supports up to three RIMM modules according to the design. However, most motherboards implement only two modules per channel to avoid problems with signal noise.

RIMMs are available in three primary speed grades, with three different width versions in each grade. The 16-bit versions are usually run in a dual-channel environment, so they have to be installed in pairs, with each one of the pairs in a different set of sockets. Each set of RIMM sockets on such boards is a channel. The 32-bit version incorporates multiple channels within a single device and is therefore designed to be installed individually, eliminating the requirement for matched pairs. Table 5.9 compares the various types of RDRAM modules. Note that the once-common names for RIMM modules, such as PC800, have been replaced by names that reflect the actual bandwidth of the module to avoid confusion with DDR memory.

Table 5.9   RDRAM Module Types and Bandwidth[1]

Module Standard	Module Format	Chip Type	Clock Speed (MHz)	Cycles per Clock	Bus Speed (MT/s)	Bus Width (Bytes)	Transfer Rate (MBps)
				16-Bit RDRAM			
RIMM1600	RIMM-16	PC800	400	2	800	2	1,600
RIMM2100	RIMM-16	PC1066	533	2	1,066	2	2,133
RIMM2400	RIMM-16	PC1200	600	2	1,200	2	2,400
				32-Bit RDRAM			
RIMM3200	RIMM-32	PC800	400	2	800	4	3,200
RIMM4200	RIMM-32	PC1066	533	2	1,066	4	4,266
RIMM4800	RIMM-32	PC1200	600	2	1,200	4	4,800

[1]*Key: MT/s = megatransfers per second; MBps = megabytes per second; and RIMM = Rambus inline memory module.*

One of the reasons that RIMMs were formerly favored by Intel is that their throughput matched the throughput of the original 400MHz Pentium 4 and Xeon processor buses. However, with the rise of dual-channel DDR and DDR2 memory and processor buses up to 800MHz and beyond, DDR and DDR2 memory provide the throughput needed, making them the best choices for modern server platforms.

Memory Modules

The CPU and motherboard architecture (chipset) dictates a particular computer's physical memory capacity and the types and forms of memory that can be installed. Over the years, two main changes have occurred in computer memory: It has gradually become faster and wider. The CPU and the memory controller circuitry indicate the speed and width requirements. In most cases, the server chipset's North Bridge contains the memory controller. For this reason, Intel chipsets based on hub architecture call this chip the *memory controller hub* chip. However, AMD Opteron processors incorporate the memory controller into the processor itself.

Even though a system might physically support a given amount of memory, the type of software you run could dictate whether all the memory can be used.

The first modern server-class processors (Pentium and Pentium-MMX) had 32 address lines, enabling them to use up to 4GB of memory; the Pentium Pro, Pentium II/III, and 4, and Xeon as well as the AMD Athlon family (including the Athlon 64), have 36 address lines and can manage an impressive 64GB. The Opteron uses 40-bit addressing, allowing up to 1TB of physical RAM. Itanium and Itanium 2 processors feature 44-bit addressing, which allows for up to 16TB (terabytes) of physical RAM!

◄◄   See "Server Processor Specifications," p. 32.

In reality, the actual limit on today's server-class processors isn't the processor's memory-address capability. Instead, it's the cost of memory, in addition to the limitations of real-world server and memory design.

SIMMs, DIMMs, and RIMMs

Starting in the mid-1980s, motherboard designs using socketed or soldered individual memory chips (often referred to as *dual inline package [DIP]* chips) on systems began to be replaced by motherboards designed to use small circuit boards that had multiple memory chips soldered to them. The benefits of this approach included faster system assembly, increased reliability, and easier replacement of failed modules.

The first generation of memory modules used a design known as a *single inline memory module (SIMM)*. For memory storage, most modern systems have adopted SIMMs, DIMMs, or RIMMs as an alternative to individual memory chips. These small boards plug in to special connectors on a motherboard or memory card. The individual memory chips are soldered to the module, so removing and replacing them is impossible. Instead, you must replace the entire module if any part of it fails. The module is treated as though it were one large memory chip.

One type of SIMMs, three main types of DIMMs, and one type of RIMM have been used in servers. The various types are often described by their pin count, memory row width, or memory type.

SIMMs, for example, were available in two main physical types—30-pin (8 bits plus an option for 1 additional parity bit) and 72-pin (32 bits plus an option for 4 additional parity bits)—with various capacities and other specifications. Most servers used the 72-pin version. The 30-pin SIMMs were physically smaller than the 72-pin versions, and either version could have chips on one or both sides. SIMMs were widely used from the late 1980s to the late 1990s and have become obsolete.

DIMMs are available in three main types. DIMMs usually hold standard SDRAM or DDR SDRAM chips and are distinguished by different physical characteristics. A standard DIMM has 168 pins, one notch on either side, and two notches along the contact area. The notches enabled the module to be keyed for motherboards using SDRAM DIMMs or for the much rarer EDO DRAM DIMMs. A DDR DIMM, on the other hand, has 184 pins, two notches on each side, and only one offset notch along the contact area. A DDR2 DIMM has 240 pins, two notches on each side, and one notch in the center of the contact area. All DIMMs are either 64 bits (non-ECC/parity) or 72 bits (parity or ECC) wide (data paths). The main physical difference between SIMMs and DIMMs is that DIMMs have different signal pins on each side of the module. That is why they are called *dual* inline memory modules, and why with only 1 inch of additional length, they have many more pins than a SIMM.

Double-Sided Memory Modules

There is confusion among users and even in the industry regarding the terms *single-sided* and *double-sided* with respect to memory modules. In truth, the single- or double-sided designation actually has *nothing* to do with whether chips are physically located on one or both sides of the module, and it has *nothing* to do with whether the module is a SIMM or DIMM (meaning whether the connection pins are single- or double-inline). Instead, the terms *single-sided* and *double-sided* are used to indicate whether the module has one or two banks of memory chips installed. A double-banked DIMM module has two complete 64-bit-wide banks of chips logically stacked so that the module is twice as deep (that is, has twice as many 64-bit rows). In most (but not all) cases, this requires chips to be on both sides of the module; therefore, the term *double-sided* has often been used to indicate that a module has two banks, even though that is technically incorrect. Single-banked modules (incorrectly referred to as *single-sided*) can have chips physically mounted on both sides of the module, and double-banked modules (incorrectly referred to as *double-sided*) can have chips physically mounted on only one side. It's a good idea to use the terms *single-banked* and *double-banked* instead of *single-sided* and *double-sided* because they are much more accurate and easily understood. Note that some systems cannot use double-banked modules.

RIMMs also have different signal pins on each side. Three different physical types of RIMMs are available: a 16/18-bit version with 184 pins, a 32/36-bit version with 232 pins, and a 64/72-bit version with 326 pins. Each of these plugs in to the same sized connector, but the notches in the connectors and RIMMs are different, to prevent mismatches. A given board will accept only one type. By far the most common type is the 16/18-bit version. The 32-bit version was introduced in late 2002, and the 64-bit version was introduced in 2004 but has never been produced.

A standard 16/18-bit RIMM has 184 pins, one notch on either side, and two notches centrally located in the contact area. 16-bit versions are used for non-ECC applications, whereas the 18-bit versions incorporate the additional bits necessary for ECC. Servers using RIMMs normally use the 18-bit versions.

Figures 5.4 through 5.9 show a typical 30-pin (8-bit) SIMM (seldom used in servers, by the way), 72-pin (32-bit) SIMM, 168-pin SDRAM DIMM, 184-pin DDR SDRAM (64-bit) DIMM, 240-pin DDR2 DIMM, and 184-pin RIMM, respectively. The pins are numbered from left to right and are connected through to both sides of the module on the SIMMs. The pins on the DIMM are different on each side, but on a SIMM, each side is the same as the other and the connections carry through. Note that all dimensions are in both inches and millimeters (in parentheses), and modules are generally available in ECC versions with 1 extra ECC (or parity) bit for every 8 data bits (multiples of 9 in data width) or versions that do not include ECC support (multiples of 8 in data width).

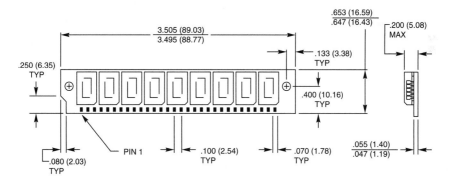

Figure 5.4 A typical 30-pin SIMM.

All these memory modules are fairly compact, considering the amount of memory they hold, and are available in several capacities and speeds. Table 5.10 lists the various capacities available for SIMMs, DIMMs, and RIMMs.

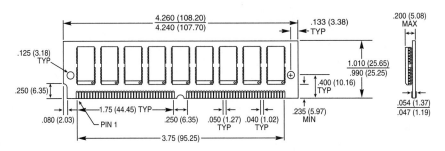

Figure 5.5   A typical 72-pin SIMM.

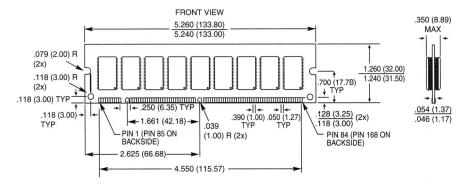

Figure 5.6   A typical 168-pin SDRAM DIMM.

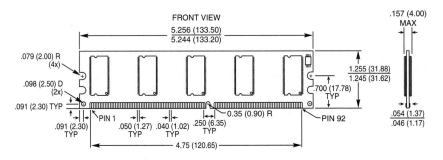

Figure 5.7   A typical 184-pin DDR SDRAM DIMM.

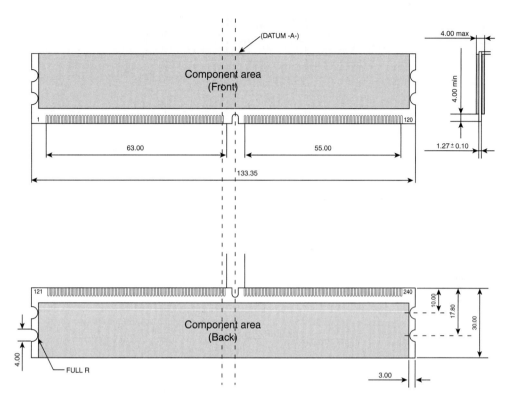

Figure 5.8   A typical 240-pin DDR2 DIMM.

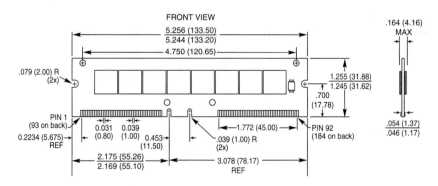

Figure 5.9   A typical 184-pin RIMM.

Table 5.10   SIMM, DIMM, and RIMM Capacities

Capacity	Standard	Parity/ECC
	30-Pin SIMM	
256KB	256KB×8	256KB×9
1MB	1MB×8	1MB×9
4MB	4MB×8	4MB×9
16MB	16MB×8	16MB×9
	72-Pin SIMM	
1MB	256KB×32	256KB×36
2MB	512KB×32	512KB×36
4MB	1MB×32	1MB×36
8MB	2MB×32	2MB×36
16MB	4MB×32	4MB×36
32MB	8MB×32	8MB×36
64MB	16MB×32	16MB×36
128MB	32MB×32	32MB×36
	168/184-Pin DIMM/DDR DIMM	
8MB	1MB×64	1MB×72
16MB	2MB×64	2MB×72
32MB	4MB×64	4MB×72
64MB	8MB×64	8MB×72
128MB	16MB×64	16MB×72
256MB	32MB×64	32MB×72
512MB	64MB×64	64MB×72
1,024MB	128MB×64	128MB×72
2,048MB	256MB×64	256MB×72
4,096MB	512MB×64	512MB×72
	240-Pin DDR2 DIMM	
256MB	32MB×64	32MB×72
512MB	64MB×64	64MB×72
1,024MB	128MB×64	128MB×72
2,048MB	256MB×64	256MB×72
4,096MB	512MB×64	512MB×72
	184-Pin RIMM	
64MB	32MB×16	32MB×18
128MB	64MB×16	64MB×18
256MB	128MB×16	128MB×18
512MB	256MB×16	256MB×18
1,024MB	512MB×16	512MB×18

SIMMs, DIMMs, DDR/DDR2 DIMMs, and RIMMs of each type and capacity are available in various speed ratings. You should consult your motherboard documentation for the correct memory speed and type for your system. It is usually best for the memory speed (also called *throughput* or *bandwidth*) to match the speed of the processor data bus (also called the *FSB*).

If a system requires a specific speed, you can almost always substitute faster speeds if the one specified is not available. Generally, no problems occur in mixing module speeds, as long as you use modules equal to or faster than what the system requires. Because there's little price difference between the various speed versions, buying faster modules than are necessary for a particular application might make them more usable in a future system that could require the faster speed.

Because DIMMs and RIMMs have onboard SPD that reports their speed and timing parameters to the system, most systems run the memory controller and memory bus at the speed matching the slowest DIMM/RIMM installed. Most DIMMs contain either SDRAM or DDR SDRAM memory chips.

Note

A *bank* is the smallest amount of memory needed to form a single row of memory addressable by the processor. It is the minimum amount of physical memory that is read or written by the processor at one time and usually corresponds to the data bus width of the processor. If a processor has a 64-bit data bus, a bank of memory is also 64 bits wide. If the memory is interleaved or runs dual-channel, a virtual bank is formed that is twice the absolute data bus width of the processor.

You can't always replace a module with a higher-capacity unit and expect it to work. Systems might have specific design limitations for the maximum capacity of module they can take. A larger-capacity module works only if the motherboard is designed to accept it in the first place. You should consult your system documentation to determine the correct capacity and speed to use.

Registered SDRAM and DDR DIMMs

SDRAM and DDR DIMMs are available in unbuffered and registered versions. Most desktop and some entry-level server motherboards are designed to use *unbuffered* modules, which allow the memory controller signals to pass directly to the memory chips on the module with no interference. This is not only the least expensive design but also the fastest and most efficient. Its only drawback is that the motherboard designer must place limits on how many modules (that is, module sockets) can be installed on the board and possibly also limit how many chips can be on a module. So-called double-sided modules that really have two banks of chips (twice as many as normal) on board might be restricted on some systems in certain combinations.

Systems designed to accept extremely large amounts of RAM, including most servers, often require registered modules. A *registered module* uses an architecture that has register chips on the module that act as an interface between the actual RAM chips and the chipset. The registers temporarily hold data passing to and from the memory chips and enable many more RAM chips to be driven or otherwise placed on the module than the chipset could normally support. This allows for motherboard designs that can support many modules and enables each module to have a larger number of chips. In general, registered modules are required by server or workstation motherboards designed to support more than 1GB or 2GB of RAM. The important thing to note is that you can use only the type of module your motherboard (or chipset) is designed to support.

To provide the space needed for the buffer chip, a registered DIMM is often taller than a standard DIMM. Figure 5.10 compares a typical registered DIMM to a typical unbuffered DIMM.

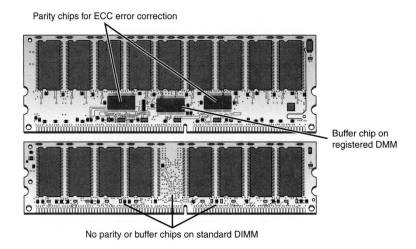

Parity chips for ECC error correction

Buffer chip on registered DMM

No parity or buffer chips on standard DIMM

Figure 5.10 A typical registered DIMM is taller than a typical unbuffered DIMM to provide room for buffer and parity/ECC chips.

Tip

If you are installing registered DIMMs in a slim-line or blade server, clearance between the top of the DIMM and the case might be a problem in some situations. Some vendors sell low-profile registered DIMMs that are about the same height as an unbuffered DIMM. You should use this type of DIMM if your system does not have enough headroom for standard registered DIMMs. Some vendors sell only this type of DIMM for particular systems.

SIMM Pinouts

Table 5.11 shows the interface connector pinouts for standard 72-pin SIMMs. These SIMMs also include a special presence detect table that shows the configuration of the presence detect pins on various 72-pin SIMMs. The motherboard uses the presence detect pins to detect exactly what size and speed SIMM is installed. Industry-standard 30-pin SIMMs do not have a presence detect feature, but IBM did add this capability to its modified 30-pin configuration. Note that all SIMMs have the same pins on both sides of the module.

Table 5.11   Standard 72-Pin SIMM Pinout

Pin	SIMM Signal Name	Pin	SIMM Signal Name	Pin	SIMM Signal Name
1	Ground	25	Data Bit 22	49	Data Bit 8
2	Data Bit 0	26	Data Bit 7	50	Data Bit 24
3	Data Bit 16	27	Data Bit 23	51	Data Bit 9
4	Data Bit 1	28	Address Bit 7	52	Data Bit 25
5	Data Bit 17	29	Address Bit 11	53	Data Bit 10

Pin	SIMM Signal Name	Pin	SIMM Signal Name	Pin	SIMM Signal Name
6	Data Bit 2	30	+5 Vdc	54	Data Bit 26
7	Data Bit 18	31	Address Bit 8	55	Data Bit 11
8	Data Bit 3	32	Address Bit 9	56	Data Bit 27
9	Data Bit 19	33	Address Bit 12	57	Data Bit 12
10	+5 Vdc	34	Address Bit 13	58	Data Bit 28
11	Presence Detect 5	35	Parity Data Bit 2	59	+5 Vdc
12	Address Bit 0	36	Parity Data Bit 0	60	Data Bit 29
13	Address Bit 1	37	Parity Data Bit 1	61	Data Bit 13
14	Address Bit 2	38	Parity Data Bit 3	62	Data Bit 30
15	Address Bit 3	39	Ground	63	Data Bit 14
16	Address Bit 4	40	Column Address Strobe 0	64	Data Bit 31
17	Address Bit 5	41	Column Address Strobe 2	65	Data Bit 15
18	Address Bit 6	42	Column Address Strobe 3	66	EDO
19	Address Bit 10	43	Column Address Strobe 1	67	Presence Detect 1
20	Data Bit 4	44	Row Address Strobe 0	68	Presence Detect 2
21	Data Bit 20	45	Row Address Strobe 1	69	Presence Detect 3
22	Data Bit 5	46	Reserved	70	Presence Detect 4
23	Data Bit 21	47	Write Enable	71	Reserved
24	Data Bit 6	48	ECC Optimized	72	Ground (Gnd)

Notice that a 72-pin SIMM uses a set of four or five pins to indicate its type to the motherboard. These presence detect pins are either grounded or not connected to indicate the type of SIMM to the motherboard. Presence detect outputs must be tied to the ground through a 0-ohm resistor or jumper on the SIMM—to generate a high logic level when the pin is open or a low logic level when the motherboard grounds the pin. This produces signals the memory interface logic can decode. If the motherboard uses presence detect signals, a POST procedure can determine the size and speed of the installed SIMMs and adjust control and addressing signals automatically. This enables autodetection of the memory size and speed.

In many ways, the presence detect pin function is similar to the industry-standard DX coding used on modern 35mm film rolls to indicate the ASA (speed) rating of the film to the camera. When you drop the film into the camera, electrical contacts can read the film's speed rating via an industry-standard configuration.

Table 5.12 shows the JEDEC industry-standard presence detect configuration listing for the 72-pin SIMM family. As discussed earlier in this chapter, JEDEC is an organization of U.S. semiconductor manufacturers and users that sets semiconductor standards.

Table 5.12   Presence Detect Pin Configurations for 72-Pin SIMMs[1]

Size	Speed	Pin 67	Pin 68	Pin 69	Pin 70	Pin 11
1MB	100ns	Gnd	—	Gnd	Gnd	—
1MB	80ns	Gnd	—	—	Gnd	—
1MB	70ns	Gnd	—	Gnd	—	—
1MB	60ns	Gnd	—	—	—	—

Table 5.12 Continued

Size	Speed	Pin 67	Pin 68	Pin 69	Pin 70	Pin 11
2MB	100ns	—	Gnd	Gnd	Gnd	—
2MB	80ns	—	Gnd	—	Gnd	—
2MB	70ns	—	Gnd	Gnd	—	—
2MB	60ns	—	Gnd	—	—	—
4MB	100ns	Gnd	Gnd	Gnd	Gnd	—
4MB	80ns	Gnd	Gnd	—	Gnd	—
4MB	70ns	Gnd	Gnd	Gnd	—	—
4MB	60ns	Gnd	Gnd	—	—	—
8MB	100ns	—	—	Gnd	Gnd	—
8MB	80ns	—	—	—	Gnd	—
8MB	70ns	—	—	Gnd	—	—
8MB	60ns	—	—	—	—	—
16MB	80ns	Gnd	—	—	Gnd	Gnd
16MB	70ns	Gnd	—	Gnd	—	Gnd
16MB	60ns	Gnd	—	—	—	Gnd
16MB	50ns	Gnd	—	Gnd	Gnd	Gnd
32MB	80ns	—	Gnd	—	Gnd	Gnd
32MB	70ns	—	Gnd	Gnd	—	Gnd
32MB	60ns	—	Gnd	—	—	Gnd
32MB	50ns	—	Gnd	Gnd	Gnd	Gnd

[1]Key: — = no connection (open); Gnd = ground; Pin 67 = presence detect 1; Pin 68 = presence detect 2; Pin 69 = presence detect 3; Pin 70 = presence detect 4; and Pin 11 = presence detect 5.

Unfortunately, unlike in the photographic film industry, not everybody in the computer industry follows established standards, and presence detect signaling is not a standard throughout the PC industry. Different system manufacturers sometimes use different configurations for what is expected on these four pins. Many Compaq, IBM PS/2 systems, and Hewlett-Packard (HP) systems that used 72-pin SIMMs had nonstandard definitions for these pins. If you service very old servers that use 72-pin memory, don't assume that it can always be interchanged. Table 5.13 shows how IBM defined these pins.

Table 5.13 Presence Detect Pins for IBM 72-Pin SIMMs[1]

67	68	69	70	SIMM Type	IBM Part Number
—	—	—	—	Not a valid SIMM	N/A
Gnd	—	—	—	1MB 120ns	N/A
—	Gnd	—	—	2MB 120ns	N/A
Gnd	Gnd	—	—	2MB 70ns	92F0102
—	—	Gnd	—	8MB 70ns	64F3606
Gnd	—	Gnd	—	Reserved	N/A

67	68	69	70	SIMM Type	IBM Part Number
—	Gnd	Gnd	—	2MB 80ns	92F0103
Gnd	Gnd	Gnd	—	8MB 80ns	64F3607
—	—	—	Gnd	Reserved	N/A
Gnd	—	—	Gnd	1MB 85ns	90X8624
—	Gnd	—	Gnd	2MB 85ns	92F0104
Gnd	Gnd	—	Gnd	4MB 70ns	92F0105
—	—	Gnd	Gnd	4MB 85ns	79F1003 (square notch) L40-SX
Gnd	—	Gnd	Gnd	1MB 100ns	N/A
Gnd	—	Gnd	Gnd	8MB 80ns	79F1004 (square notch) L40-SX
—	Gnd	Gnd	Gnd	2MB 100ns	N/A
Gnd	Gnd	Gnd	Gnd	4MB 80ns	87F9980
Gnd	Gnd	Gnd	Gnd	2MB 85ns	79F1003 (square notch) L40SX

[1]Key: — = no connection (open); Gnd = ground; Pin 67 = presence detect 1; Pin 68 = presence detect 2; Pin 69 = presence detect 3; and Pin 70 = presence detect 4.

Although servers that use SIMMs are most likely to be outdated, you should keep these differences in mind if you are salvaging parts to keep an older server in service or if you must order memory for a server that uses SIMMs.

SIMM pins might be tin- or gold-plated. The plating on the module pins must match that on the socket pins, or corrosion will result.

Caution

To have the most reliable system, you must install modules with gold-plated contacts into gold-plated sockets and modules with tin-plated contacts into tin-plated sockets only. If you mix gold contacts with tin sockets, or vice versa, you are likely to experience memory failures from six months to one year after initial installation because a type of corrosion know as *fretting* takes place. This was a major problem with 72-pin SIMM-based systems because some memory and motherboard vendors opted for tin sockets and connectors, while others opted for gold. According to connector manufacturer AMP's "Golden Rules: Guidelines for the Use of Gold on Connector Contacts" (available at www.amp.com/products/technology/aurulrep.pdf) and "The Tin Commandments: Guidelines for the Use of Tin on Connector Contacts" (available at www.amp.com/products/technology/sncomrep.pdf), you should match connector metals. Commandment 7 from the Tin Commandments specifically states "Mating of tin-coated contacts to gold-coated contacts is not recommended."

If you are maintaining systems with mixed tin/gold contacts in which fretting has already taken place, use a wet contact cleaner. After cleaning, to improve electrical contacts and help prevent corrosion, you should use a liquid contact enhancer and lubricant called Stabilant 22 from D.W. Electrochemicals when installing SIMMs or DIMMs. Its website (www.stabilant.com/llsting.htm) has detailed application notes on this subject that provide more technical details.

DIMM Pinouts

Table 5.14 shows the pinout configuration of a 168-pin registered SDRAM DIMM. Note again that the pins on each side of the DIMM are different. All pins should be gold-plated.

Table 5.14   168-Pin SDRAM DIMM Pinouts[1]

Pin	Signal	Pin	Signal	Pin	Signal	Pin	Signal
1	Gnd	43	Gnd	85	Gnd	127	Gnd
2	Data Bit 0	44	Do Not Use	86	Data Bit 32	128	Clock Enable 0
3	Data Bit 1	45	Chip Select 2#	87	Data Bit 33	129	Chip Select 3#
4	Data Bit 2	46	I/O Mask 2	88	Data Bit 34	130	I/O Mask 6
5	Data Bit 3	47	I/O Mask 3	89	Data Bit 35	131	I/O Mask 7
6	+3.3V	48	Do Not Use	90	+3.3V	132	Reserved
7	Data Bit 4	49	+3.3V	91	Data Bit 36	133	+3.3V
8	Data Bit 5	50	—	92	Data Bit 37	134	—
9	Data Bit 6	51	—	93	Data Bit 38	135	—
10	Data Bit 7	52	Parity Bit 2	94	Data Bit 39	136	Parity Bit 6
11	Data Bit 8	53	Parity Bit 3	95	Data Bit 40	137	Parity Bit 7
12	Gnd	54	Gnd	96	Gnd	138	Gnd
13	Data Bit 9	55	Data Bit 16	97	Data Bit 41	139	Data Bit 48
14	Data Bit 10	56	Data Bit 17	98	Data Bit 42	140	Data Bit 49
15	Data Bit 11	57	Data Bit 18	99	Data Bit 43	141	Data Bit 50
16	Data Bit 12	58	Data Bit 19	100	Data Bit 44	142	Data Bit 51
17	Data Bit 13	59	+3.3V	101	Data Bit 45	143	+3.3V
18	+3.3V	60	Data Bit 20	102	+3.3V	144	Data Bit 52
19	Data Bit 14	61	—	103	Data Bit 46	145	—
20	Data Bit 15	62	—	104	Data Bit 47	146	—
21	Parity Bit 0	63	Clock Enable 1	105	Parity Bit 4	147	REGE[2]
22	Parity Bit 1	64	Gnd	106	Parity Bit 5	148	Gnd
23	Gnd	65	Data Bit 21	107	Gnd	149	Data Bit 53
24	—	66	Data Bit 22	108	—	150	Data Bit 54
25	—	67	Data Bit 23	109	—	151	Data Bit 55
26	+3.3V	68	Gnd	110	+3.3V	152	Gnd
27	WE#	69	Data Bit 24	111	CAS#	153	Data Bit 56
28	I/O Mask 0	70	Data Bit 25	112	I/O Mask 4	154	Data Bit 57
29	I/O Mask 1	71	Data Bit 26	113	I/O Mask 5	155	Data Bit 58
30	Chip Select 0#	72	Data Bit 27	114	Chip Select 1#	156	Data Bit 59
31	Do Not Use	73	+3.3V	115	RAS#	157	+3.3V
32	Gnd	74	Data Bit 28	116	Gnd	158	Data Bit 60
33	Address Bit 0	75	Data Bit 29	117	Address Bit 1	159	Data Bit 61
34	Address Bit 2	76	Data Bit 30	118	Address Bit 3	160	Data Bit 62
35	Address Bit 4	77	Data Bit 31	119	Address Bit 5	161	Data Bit 63
36	Address Bit 6	78	Gnd	120	Address Bit 7	162	Gnd
37	Address Bit 8	79	Clock 2	121	Address Bit 9	163	Clock 3
38	Address Bit 10	80	—	122	Bank Address 0	164	—

Pin	Signal	Pin	Signal	Pin	Signal	Pin	Signal
39	Bank Address 1	81	SPD Write Protect	123	Address Bit 11	165	SPD Address 0
40	+3.3V	82	SPD Data	124	+3.3V	166	SPD Address 1
41	+3.3V	83	SPD Clock	125	Clock 1	167	SPD Address 2
42	Clock 0	84	+3.3V	126	Reserved	168	+3.3V

[1]*Key: Gnd = ground; SPD = serial presence detect; — = no connection; and REGE = register enable.*
[2]*No connection in an unbuffered DIMM.*

A DIMM uses a completely different type of presence detect than a SIMM, called *SPD*. SPD consists of a small EEPROM, or flash memory, chip on the DIMM that contains specially formatted data indicating the DIMM's features. This serial data can be read via the serial data pins on the DIMM, and it enables the motherboard to autoconfigure to the exact type of DIMM installed.

DIMMs for PC-based servers use 3.3V power and might be unbuffered or registered. DIMMs made for Macintosh computers use a 5V buffered design. Keying in the socket and on the DIMM prevents the insertion of 5V DIMMs into a 3.3V slot or vice versa. See Figure 5.11.

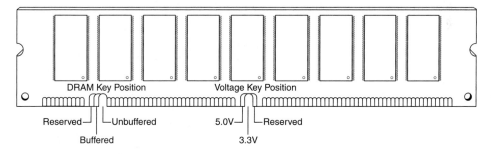

Figure 5.11   168-pin DRAM DIMM notch key definitions.

DDR DIMM Pinouts

Table 5.15 shows the pinout configuration of a 184-pin DDR SDRAM DIMM. Note again that the pins on each side of the DIMM are different. All pins are typically gold-plated.

Table 5.15   184-Pin DDR DIMM Pinouts[1]

Pin	Signal	Pin	Signal	Pin	Signal	Pin	Signal
1	Reference +1.25V	47	Data Strobe 8	93	Gnd	139	Gnd
2	Data Bit 0	48	Address Bit 0	94	Data Bit 4	140	Data Strobe 17
3	Gnd	49	Parity Bit 2	95	Data Bit 5	141	Address Bit 10
4	Data Bit 1	50	Gnd	96	I/O +2.5V	142	Parity Bit 6
5	Data Strobe 0	51	Parity Bit 3	97	Data Strobe 9	143	I/O +2.5V
6	Data Bit 2	52	Bank Address 1	98	Data Bit 6	144	Parity Bit 7
7	+2.5 V	53	Data Bit 32	99	Data Bit 7	145	Gnd
8	Data Bit 3	54	I/O +2.5 V	100	Gnd	146	Data Bit 36
9	—	55	Data Bit 33	101	—	147	Data Bit 37

Table 5.15   Continued

Pin	Signal	Pin	Signal	Pin	Signal	Pin	Signal
10	—	56	Data Strobe 4	102	—	148	+2.5V
11	Gnd	57	Data Bit 34	103	Address Bit 13	149	Data Strobe 13
12	Data Bit 8	58	Gnd	104	I/O +2.5V	150	Data Bit 38
13	Data Bit 9	59	Bank Address 0	105	Data Bit 12	151	Data Bit 39
14	Data Strobe 1	60	Data Bit 35	106	Data Bit 13	152	Gnd
15	I/O +2.5V	61	Data Bit 40	107	Data Strobe 10	153	Data Bit 44
16	Clock 1	62	I/O +2.5V	108	+2.5V	154	RAS#
17	Clock 1#	63	WE#	109	Data Bit 14	155	Data Bit 45
18	Gnd	64	Data Bit 41	110	Data Bit 15	156	I/O +2.5V
19	Data Bit 10	65	CAS#	111	Clock Enable 1	157	S0#
20	Data Bit 11	66	Gnd	112	I/O +2.5V	158	S1#
21	Clock Enable 0	67	Data Strobe 5	113	Bank Address 2	159	Data Strobe 14
22	I/O +2.5V	68	Data Bit 42	114	Data Bit 20	160	Gnd
23	Data Bit 16	69	Data Bit 43	115	Address Bit 12	161	Data Bit 46
24	Data Bit 17	70	+2.5V	116	Gnd	162	Data Bit 47
25	Data Strobe 2	71	S2#	117	Data Bit 21	163	S3#
26	Gnd	72	Data Bit 48	118	Address Bit 11	164	I/O +2.5V
27	Address Bit 9	73	Data Bit 49	119	Data Strobe 11	165	Data Bit 52
28	Data Bit 18	74	Gnd	120	+2.5V	166	Data Bit 53
29	Address Bit 7	75	Clock 2#	121	Data Bit 22	167	FETEN
30	I/O +2.5V	76	Clock 2	122	Address Bit 8	168	+2.5V
31	Data Bit 19	77	I/O +2.5V	123	Data Bit 23	169	Data Strobe 15
32	Address Bit 5	78	Data Strobe 6	124	Gnd	170	Data Bit 54
33	Data Bit 24	79	Data Bit 50	125	Address Bit 6	171	Data Bit 55
34	Gnd	80	Data Bit 51	126	Data Bit 28	172	I/O +2.5V
35	Data Bit 25	81	Gnd	127	Data Bit 29	173	—
36	Data Strobe 3	82	+2.5VID	128	I/O +2.5V	174	Data Bit 60
37	Address Bit 4	83	Data Bit 56	129	Data Strobe 12	175	Data Bit 61
38	+2.5V	84	Data Bit 57	130	Address Bit 3	176	Gnd
39	Data Bit 26	85	+2.5V	131	Data Bit 30	177	Data Strobe 16
40	Data Bit 27	86	Data Strobe 7	132	Gnd	178	Data Bit 62
41	Address Bit 2	87	Data Bit 58	133	Data Bit 31	179	Data Bit 63
42	Gnd	88	Data Bit 59	134	Parity Bit 4	180	I/O +2.5V
43	Address Bit 1	89	Gnd	135	Parity Bit 5	181	SPD Address 0
44	Parity Bit 0	90	SPD Write Protect	136	I/O +2.5V	182	SPD Address 1
45	Parity Bit 1	91	SPD Data	137	Clock 0	183	SPD Address 2
46	+2.5V	92	SPD Clock	138	Clock 0#	184	SPD +2.5V

[1]Key: Gnd = ground; SPD = serial presence detect; and — = no connection.

DDR DIMMs use a single key notch to indicate voltage, as shown in Figure 5.12.

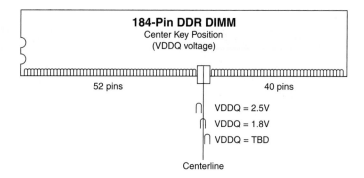

Figure 5.12   184-pin DDR SDRAM DIMM keying.

A 184-pin DDR DIMM uses two notches on each side to enable compatibility with both low- and high-profile latched sockets. Note that the key position is offset with respect to the center of the DIMM to prevent it from being inserted in the socket backward. The key notch is positioned to the left, centered, or to the right of the area between pins 52 and 53. The position indicates the I/O voltage for the DDR DIMM and prevents the installation of the wrong type into a socket that might damage the DIMM.

DDR2 DIMM Pinouts

Table 5.16 shows the pinout configuration of a 240-pin DDR2 SDRAM DIMM. Pins 1–120 are on the front side, and pins 121–240 are on the back. All pins should be gold-plated.

Table 5.16   240-Pin DDR2 DIMM Pinouts

Pin	Signal	Pin	Signal	Pin	Signal	Pin	Signal
1	VREF	61	A4	121	VSS	181	VDDQ
2	VSS	62	VDDQ	122	DQ4	182	A3
3	DQ0	63	A2	123	DQ5	183	A1
4	DQ1	64	VDD	124	VSS	184	VDD
5	VSS	65	VSS	125	DM0	185	CK0
6	-DQS0	66	VSS	126	—	186	-CK0
7	DQS0	67	VDD	127	VSS	187	VDD
8	VSS	68	—	128	DQ6	188	A0
9	DQ2	69	VDD	129	DQ7	189	VDD
10	DQ3	70	A10/-AP	130	VSS	190	BA1
11	VSS	71	BA0	131	DQ12	191	VDDQ
12	DQ8	72	VDDQ	132	DQ13	192	-RAS
13	DQ9	73	-WE	133	VSS	193	-CS0
14	VSS	74	-CAS	134	DM1	194	VDDQ
15	-DQS1	75	VDDQ	135	—	195	ODT0
16	DQS1	76	-CS1	136	VSS	196	A13
17	VSS	77	ODT1	137	CK1	197	VDD
18	—	78	VDDQ	138	-CK1	198	VSS

Table 5.16 Continued

Pin	Signal	Pin	Signal	Pin	Signal	Pin	Signal
19	—	79	SS	139	VSS	199	DQ36
20	VSS	80	DQ32	140	DQ14	200	DQ37
21	DQ10	81	DQ33	141	DQ15	201	VSS
22	DQ11	82	VSS	142	VSS	202	DM4
23	VSS	83	-DQS4	143	DQ20	203	—
24	DQ16	84	DQS4	144	DQ21	204	VSS
25	DQ17	85	VSS	145	VSS	205	DQ38
26	VSS	86	DQ34	146	DM2	206	DQ39
27	-DQS2	87	DQ35	147	—	207	VSS
28	DQS2	88	VSS	148	VSS	208	DQ44
29	VSS	89	DQ40	149	DQ22	209	DQ45
30	DQ18	90	DQ41	150	DQ23	210	VSS
31	DQ19	91	VSS	151	VSS	211	DM5
32	VSS	92	-DQS5	152	DQ28	212	—
33	DQ24	93	DQS5	153	DQ29	213	VSS
34	DQ25	94	VSS	154	VSS	214	DQ46
35	VSS	95	DQ42	155	DM3	215	DQ47
36	-DQS3	96	DQ43	156	—	216	VSS
37	DQS3	97	VSS	157	VSS	217	DQ52
38	VSS	98	DQ48	158	DQ30	218	DQ53
39	DQ26	99	DQ49	159	DQ31	219	VSS
40	DQ27	100	VSS	160	VSS	220	CK2
41	VSS	101	SA2	161	—	221	-CK2
42	—	102	—	162	—	222	VSS
43	—	103	VSS	163	VSS	223	DM6
44	VSS	104	-DQS6	164	—	224	—
45	—	105	DQS6	165	—	225	VSS
46	—	106	VSS	166	VSS	226	DQ54
47	VSS	107	DQ50	167	—	227	DQ55
48	—	108	DQ51	168	—	228	VSS
49	—	109	VSS	169	VSS	229	DQ60
50	VSS	110	DQ56	170	VDDQ	230	DQ61
51	VDDQ	111	DQ57	171	CKE1	231	VSS
52	CKE0	112	VSS	172	VDD	232	DM7
53	VDD	113	-DQS7	173	—	233	—
54	—	114	DQS7	174	—	234	VSS
55	—	115	VSS	175	VDDQ	235	DQ62
56	VDDQ	116	DQ58	176	A12	236	DQ63

Pin	Signal	Pin	Signal	Pin	Signal	Pin	Signal
57	A11	117	DQ59	177	A9	237	VSS
58	A7	118	VSS	178	VDD	238	VDDSPD
59	VDD	119	SDA	179	A8	239	SA0
60	A5	120	SCL	180	A6	240	SA1

A 240-pin DDR2 DIMM uses two notches on each side to enable compatibility with both low- and high-profile latched sockets. The connector key is offset with respect to the center of the DIMM to prevent it from being inserted into the socket backward. The key notch is positioned in the center of the area between pins 64 and 65 on the front (184/185 on the back), and there is no voltage keying because all DDR2 DIMMs run on 1.8V.

RIMM Pinouts

RIMM modules and sockets are gold-plated and designed for 25 insertion/removal cycles. A 16/18-bit RIMM has 184 pins, split into two groups of 92 pins on opposite ends and sides of the module. Table 5.17 shows the pinout configuration of a RIMM.

Table 5.17   RIMM Pinout[1]

Pin	Signal	Pin	Signal	Pin	Signal	Pin	Signal
A1	Gnd	B1	Gnd	A47	—	B47	—
A2	LData Bit A8	B2	LData Bit A7	A48	—	B48	—
A3	Gnd	B3	Gnd	A49	—	B49	—
A4	LData Bit A6	B4	LData Bit A5	A50	—	B50	—
A5	Gnd	B5	Gnd	A51	VREF	B51	VREF
A6	LData Bit A4	B6	LData Bit A3	A52	Gnd	B52	Gnd
A7	Gnd	B7	Gnd	A53	SPD Clock	B53	SPD Address 0
A8	LData Bit A2	B8	LData Bit A1	A54	+2.5V	B54	+2.5V
A9	Gnd	B9	Gnd	A55	SDA	B55	SPD Address 1
A10	LData Bit A0	B10	Interface Clock+	A56	SVDD	B56	SVDD
A11	Gnd	B11	Gnd	A57	SPD Write Protect	B57	SPD Address 2
A12	LCTMN	B12	Interface Clock-	A58	+2.5V	B58	+2.5V
A13	Gnd	B13	Gnd	A59	RSCK	B59	RCMD
A14	LCTM	B14	—	A60	Gnd	B60	Gnd
A15	Gnd	B15	Gnd	A61	Rdata Bit B7	B61	RData Bit B8
A16	—	B16	LROW2	A62	Gnd	B62	Gnd
A17	Gnd	B17	Gnd	A63	Rdata Bit B5	B63	RData Bit B6
A18	LROW1	B18	LROW0	A64	Gnd	B64	Gnd
A19	Gnd	B19	Gnd	A65	Rdata Bit B3	B65	RData Bit B4
A20	LCOL4	B20	LCOL3	A66	Gnd	B66	Gnd
A21	Gnd	B21	Gnd	A67	Rdata Bit B1	B67	RData Bit B2
A22	LCOL2	B22	LCOL1	A68	Gnd	B68	Gnd
A23	Gnd	B23	Gnd	A69	RCOL0	B69	RData Bit B0

Table 5.17 Continued

Pin	Signal	Pin	Signal	Pin	Signal	Pin	Signal
A24	LCOL0	B24	LData Bit B0	A70	Gnd	B70	Gnd
A25	Gnd	B25	Gnd	A71	RCOL2	B71	RCOL1
A26	LData Bit B1	B26	LData Bit B2	A72	Gnd	B72	Gnd
A27	Gnd	B27	Gnd	A73	RCOL4	B73	RCOL3
A28	LData Bit B3	B28	LData Bit B4	A74	Gnd	B74	Gnd
A29	Gnd	B29	Gnd	A75	RROW1	B75	RROW0
A30	LData Bit B5	B30	LData Bit B6	A76	Gnd	B76	Gnd
A31	Gnd	B31	Gnd	A77	—	B77	RROW2
A32	LData Bit B7	B32	LData Bit B8	A78	Gnd	B78	Gnd
A33	Gnd	B33	Gnd	A79	RCTM	B79	—
A34	LSCK	B34	LCMD	A80	Gnd	B80	Gnd
A35	VCMOS	B35	VCMOS	A81	RCTMN	B81	RCFMN
A36	SOUT	B36	SIN	A82	Gnd	B82	Gnd
A37	VCMOS	B37	VCMOS	A83	Rdata Bit A0	B83	RCFM
A38	—	B38	—	A84	Gnd	B84	Gnd
A39	Gnd	B39	Gnd	A85	Rdata Bit A2	B85	RData Bit A1
A40	—	B40	—	A86	Gnd	B86	Gnd
A41	+2.5V	B41	+2.5V	A87	Rdata Bit A4	B87	RData Bit A3
A42	+2.5V	B42	+2.5V	A88	Gnd	B88	Gnd
A43	—	B43	—	A89	Rdata Bit A6	B89	RData Bit A5
A44	—	B44	—	A90	Gnd	B90	Gnd
A45	—	B45	—	A91	Rdata Bit A8	B91	RData Bit A7
A46	—	B46	—	A92	Gnd	B92	Gnd

[1]Key: — = no connection (open); Gnd = ground; Pin 67 = presence detect 1; Pin 68 = presence detect 2; Pin 69 = presence detect 3; and Pin 70 = presence detect 4.

A 16/18-bit RIMM is keyed with two notches in the center. This prevents backward insertion and prevents the wrong type (voltage) of RIMM from being used in a system. To allow for changes in RIMM designs, three keying options are possible in the design (see Figure 5.13). The left key (indicated as "DATUM A" in Figure 5.13) is fixed in position, but the center key can be in three different positions, spaced 1mm or 2mm to the right, indicating different types of RIMMs. The current default is Option A, as shown in Figure 5.13 and Table 5.18, which corresponds to 2.5V operation.

Table 5.18 Possible Keying Options for RIMMs

Option	Notch Separation	Description
A	11.5mm	2.5V RIMM
B	12.5mm	Reserved
C	13.5mm	Reserved

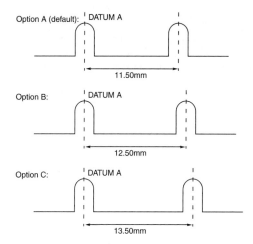

Figure 5.13 RIMM keying options.

A RIMM incorporates an SPD device, which is essentially a flash ROM onboard. This ROM contains information about the RIMM's size and type, including detailed timing information for the memory controller. The memory controller automatically reads the data from the SPD ROM to configure the system to match the RIMMs installed.

Figure 5.14 shows a typical RIMM installation. Note that RIMM sockets not occupied by a module cannot be left empty but must be filled with a continuity module (essentially a RIMM module without memory). This enables the memory bus to remain continuous from the controller through each module (and, therefore, each RDRAM device on the module) until the bus finally terminates on the motherboard.

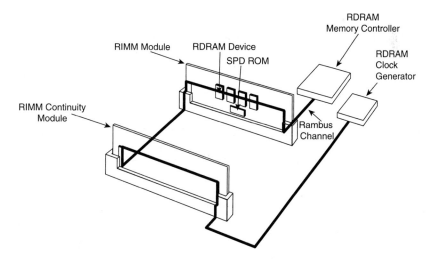

Figure 5.14 Typical RDRAM bus layout showing a RIMM and one continuity module.

Determining a Memory Module's Size and Features

Most memory modules are labeled with a sticker indicating the module's type, speed rating, and manufacturer. If you are attempting to determine whether existing memory can be used in a new server, or if you need to replace memory in an existing server, this information can be very useful.

If you have memory modules that are not labeled, however, you can still determine the module type, speed, and capacity if the memory chips on the module are clearly labeled. For example, assume that you have a memory module with chips labeled thus:

MT46V64M8TG-75

By using an Internet search engine such as Google and entering the number from one of the memory chips, you can usually find the datasheet for the memory chips. Note for a registered memory module that you want to look up the part number for the memory chips (usually eight or more chips) rather than the buffer chips on the module (one to three, depending on the module design).

In this example, the part number turns out to be a Micron memory chip that decodes like this:

MT = Micron Technologies (the memory chip maker)

46 = DDR SDRAM

V = 2.5V DC

64M8 = 8 million rows × 8 (equals 64) × 8 banks (often written as 64MB × 8)

TG = 66-pin TSOP chip package

–75 = 7.5ns @ CL2 latency (DDR 266)

The full datasheet for this example is located at http://download.micron.com/pdf/datasheets/dram/ddr/512MBDDRx4x8x16.pdf.

From this information, we can determine that the module has the following characteristics:

- The module runs at DDR266 speeds, using standard 2.5V DC voltage.
- The module has a latency of CL2, so it can be used on any system that requires CL2 or slower latencies.
- Each chip has a capacity of 512Mb (64×8=512).
- Each chip contains 8 bits. It takes 8 bits to make a byte, so the capacity of the module can be calculated by grouping the memory chips on the module into groups of 8. If each chip contains 512MB, a group of 8 means that the module has a size of 512MB (512Mb×8=512MB). A dual-bank module has two groups of 8 chips for a capacity of 1GB (512Mb×8×=1024MB, or 1GB).

If the module has 9, instead of 8, memory chips (or 18 instead of 16), the additional chips are used for parity checking and support ECC error correction on servers with this feature.

To determine the size of the module in megabytes or gigabytes and to determine whether the module supports ECC, count the memory chips on the module and compare this number to Table 5.19. Note that the size of each memory chip in Mb is the same as the size in MB if the memory chips use an 8-bit design.

Table 5.19   Module Capacity Using 512Mb (64Mb × 8) Chips

Number of Chips	Number of Bits in Each Bank	Module Size	Supports ECC	Single or Dual-Bank
8	64	512MB	No	Single
9	72	512MB	Yes	Single
16	64	1GB	No	Dual
18	72	1GB	Yes	Dual

The additional chip used by each group of 8 chips provides parity checking, which is used by the ECC function on most server motherboards to correct single-bit errors.

A registered module will contain full-sized memory chips plus additional chips for ECC/parity and buffering. These chips are usually smaller in size and located near the center of the module, as shown in Figure 5.10.

Note

Some modules use 16-bit-wide memory chips. In such cases, only 4 chips are needed for single-bank memory (5 with parity/ECC support) and 8 for double-bank memory (10 with parity/ECC support). These memory chips use a design listed as *capacity* × 16, such as 256Mbx16.

You can also see this information if you look up the manufacturer, the memory type, and the organization in a search engine. For example, this web search:

Micron "64 Meg x 8" DDR DIMM

locates a parts list for Micron's 512MB and 1GB modules at www.micron.com/products/modules/ddrs-dram/partlist.aspx?pincount=184-pin&version=Registered&package=VLP%20DIMM. The Comp. Config column lists the chip design for each chip on the module.

As you can see, with a little detective work, you can determine the size, speed, and type of a memory module, even if the module isn't marked, as long as the markings on the memory chips themselves are legible.

Tip

If you are unable to decipher a chip part number, you can use the HWiNFO or SiSoftware Sandra program to identify your memory module, as well as many other facts about your computer, including chipset, processor, empty memory sockets, and much more. You can download shareware versions of HWiNFO from www.hwinfo.com and SiSoftware Sandra from www.sisoftware.net.

Memory Banks

Memory chips (DIPs, SIMMs, SIPPs, and DIMMs) are organized in banks on motherboards and memory cards. You should know your memory bank layout and position on the motherboard and memory cards.

You need to know the bank layout when adding memory to a system. In addition, memory diagnostics report error locations by byte and bit addresses, and you must use these numbers to locate which bank in your system contains the problem.

The banks usually correspond to the data bus capacity of the system's microprocessor. Table 5.20 shows the widths of individual banks, based on the type of server processor used and whether the chipset operates in single-channel or dual-channel mode.

Table 5.20   Memory Bank Widths on Various Systems

Processor	Data Bus	Memory Bank Size (No Parity)	Memory Bank Size (Parity/ECC)	30-Pin SIMMs Per Bank	72-Pin SIMMs per Bank	DIMMs per Bank
Pentium Pro, PII, Xeon, Pentium III, PIII Xeon, P4, Athlon MP, Xeon(single-channel mode), Itanium	64-bit	64 bits	72 bits	8[1]	2[2]	1
P4, Xeon, Opteron (dual-channel mode), Itanium 2	64-bit	128-bit[3]	144-bit[3]	—	—	2

[1]*Very few, if any, motherboards using this type of memory were made for these processors.*

[2]*72-pin SIMMs were used by some systems running Pentium Pro, Pentium, and Pentium II and Pentium II Xeon processors; they were replaced by SDRAM and newer types of DIMMs.*

[3]*These systems require matched pairs of memory to operate in dual-channel mode. If a single module or two different-sized modules are used, the system runs in single-channel mode.*

DIMMs are ideal for Pentium and higher systems because the 64-bit width of the DIMM exactly matches the 64-bit width of the Pentium processor data bus. Therefore, each DIMM represents an individual bank, and DIMMs can be added or removed, one at a time. Note that for dual-channel operation, matched pairs of DIMMs must be inserted into the appropriate slots on the motherboard. Note that the Itanium 2 runs only in dual-channel mode.

The physical orientation and numbering of the memory module sockets used on a motherboard is arbitrary and determined by the board's designers, so documentation covering your system or card is handy, particularly if you want to take advantage of the additional performance available from running recent server designs in dual-channel mode.

Memory Module Speed

When you replace a failed memory module or install a new module as an upgrade, you typically must install a module of the same type and speed as the others in the system. You can substitute a module with a different speed, but only if the replacement module's speed is equal to or faster than that of the other modules in the system.

Some people have had problems when mixing modules of different speeds. With the wide variety of motherboards, chipsets, and memory types, few ironclad rules exist. When in doubt as to which speed module to install in your system, you should consult the motherboard documentation for more information.

Substituting faster memory of the same type doesn't result in improved performance if the system still operates the memory at the same speed. Systems that use DIMMs or RIMMs can read the speed and timing features of the module from a special SPD ROM installed on the module and then set chipset (memory controller) timing accordingly. In these systems, you might see an increase in performance by installing faster modules, to the limit of what the chipset will support.

To place more emphasis on timing and reliability, Intel and JEDEC standards govern memory types that require certain levels of performance. A number of common symptoms result when the system memory has failed or is simply not fast enough for the system's timing. The usual symptoms are frequent parity check errors or a system that does not operate at all. The POST might report errors, too. If you're unsure of which chips to buy for your system, you should contact the system manufacturer or a reputable chip supplier.

▶▶ See "Parity Checking," p. 390.

Parity and ECC

Part of the nature of memory is that it inevitably fails. Memory failures are usually classified as two basic types: hard fails and soft errors.

The best understood memory failures are *hard fails*, in which the chip is working and then, because of some flaw, physical damage, or other event, becomes damaged and experiences a permanent failure. Fixing this type of failure normally requires replacing some part of the memory hardware, such as the chip, SIMM, or DIMM. Hard error rates are known as *HERs*.

The other, more insidious, type of failure is the *soft error*, which is a nonpermanent failure that might never recur or could occur only at infrequent intervals. (Soft fails are effectively "fixed" by powering the system off and back on.) Soft error rates are known as *SERs*.

Problems with early memory chips were caused by alpha particles, a very weak form of radiation coming from trace radioactive elements in chip packaging. Although this cause of soft errors was eliminated years ago, cosmic rays have proven to be a major cause of soft errors, particularly as memory chip densities have increased.

Although cosmic rays and other radiation events are the biggest cause of soft errors, soft errors can also be caused by the following:

- **Power glitches or noise on the line**—This can be caused by a defective power supply in the system or by defective power at the outlet.

- **Incorrect type or speed rating**—The memory must be the correct type for the chipset and match the system access speed.

- **Radio frequency interference (RFI)**—RFI is caused by radio transmitters in close proximity to the system, which can generate electrical signals in system wiring and circuits. Keep in mind that the increased use of wireless networks, keyboards, and mouse devices can lead to a greater risk of RFI.

- **Static discharges**—Static discharge causes momentary power spikes, which alter data.

- **Timing glitches**—In a timing glitch, data doesn't arrive at the proper place at the proper time, causing errors. They are often caused by improper settings in the BIOS Setup, by memory that is rated slower than the system requires, or by overclocked processors and other system components.

- **Heat buildup**—High-speed memory modules run hotter than older modules. Note that RDRAM RIMM modules were the first memory to include integrated heat spreaders, and many high-performance DDR and DDR2 memory modules now include heat spreaders to help fight heat buildup.

Most of these problems don't cause chips to permanently fail (although bad power or static can damage chips permanently), but they can cause momentary problems with data.

Although soft errors are regarded as an unavoidable consequence of desktop and portable computer operation, system lockups are absolutely unacceptable for servers and other mission-critical systems. The best way to deal with this problem is to increase the system's fault tolerance. This means implementing ways of detecting and possibly correcting errors in PC systems.

Historically, early PCs and servers used a type of fault tolerance known as *parity checking*, while more recent servers use fault-tolerance methods that actually correct memory errors.

Parity Checking

One standard that IBM set for the industry is that the memory chips in a bank of nine each handle 1 bit of data: 8 bits per character plus 1 extra bit, called the *parity bit*. The parity bit enables memory-control circuitry to keep tabs on the other 8 bits—a built-in cross-check for the integrity of each byte in the system. If the circuitry detects an error, the computer stops and displays a message, informing the user of the malfunction. In a GUI operating system, a parity error generally manifests itself as a locked system. Upon reboot, the BIOS should detect the error and display the appropriate error message.

SIMMs and DIMMs are available both with and without parity bits. Originally, all PC systems used parity-checked memory to ensure accuracy. Although desktop PCs began to abandon parity-checking in 1994 (saving 10% to 15% on memory costs), servers continue to use parity checking. Parity can't correct system errors, but because parity can detect errors, it can make the user aware of memory errors when they happen. This has two basic benefits:

- Parity guards against the consequences of faulty calculations based on incorrect data.
- Parity pinpoints the source of errors, which helps with problem resolution, thus improving system serviceability.

Let's look at how parity checking works and then examine in more detail the successor to parity checking, called ECC, which can not only detect but correct memory errors on-the-fly.

How Parity Checking Works

IBM originally established the odd parity standard for error checking. As the 8 individual bits in a byte are stored in memory, a parity generator/checker, which is either part of the CPU or located in a special chip on the motherboard, evaluates the data bits by adding up the number of 1s in the byte. If an even number of 1s is found, the parity generator/checker creates a 1 and stores it as the ninth bit (the parity bit) in the parity memory chip. That makes the sum for all 9 bits (including the parity bit) an odd number. If the original sum of the 8 data bits is an odd number, the parity bit created would be a 0, keeping the sum for all 9 bits an odd number. The basic rule is that the value of the parity bit is always chosen so that the sum of all 9 bits (8 data bits plus 1 parity bit) is stored as an odd number. If the system used even parity, the example would be the same, except the parity bit would ensure an even sum. It doesn't matter whether even or odd parity is used; the system uses one or the other, and it is completely transparent to the memory chips involved. Remember that the 8 data bits in a byte are numbered 0 1 2 3 4 5 6 7. The following examples might make it easier to understand:

```
Data bit number:  0 1 2 3 4 5 6 7  Parity bit
Data bit value:   1 0 1 1 0 0 1 1  0
```

In this example, because the total number of data bits with a value of 1 is an odd number (5), the parity bit must have a value of 0 to ensure an odd sum for all 9 bits.

Here is another example:

```
Data bit number:  0 1 2 3 4 5 6 7  Parity bit
Data bit value:   1 1 1 1 0 0 1 1  1
```

In this example, because the total number of data bits with a value of 1 is an even number (6), the parity bit must have a value of 1 to create an odd sum for all 9 bits.

When a system reads memory back from storage, it checks the parity information. If a (9-bit) byte has an even number of bits, that byte must have an error. The system can't tell which bit has changed or whether only a single bit has changed. If 3 bits changed, for example, the byte still flags a parity-check error; if 2 bits changed, however, the bad byte could pass unnoticed. Because multiple bit errors (in a single byte) are rare, this scheme gives a reasonable and inexpensive ongoing indication that memory is good or bad.

Parity error messages vary by system, but usually include a reference to parity check or NMI (non-maskable interrupt). Most systems that use parity checking do not halt the CPU when a parity error is detected; instead, they display an error message and offer the choice of rebooting the system or continuing as though nothing happened. Although you don't need to reboot a system after a parity error, it makes sense to do so because the contents of memory might be corrupted. Obviously, parity checking is not sufficient fault tolerance for servers.

ECC

ECC goes a big step beyond simple parity error detection. Instead of just detecting an error, ECC allows a single-bit error to be corrected, which means the system can continue without interruption and without corrupting data. Older implementations of ECC can only detect, not correct, double-bit errors. Because studies have indicated that approximately 98% of memory errors are the single-bit variety, the most commonly used type of ECC is one in which the attendant memory controller detects and corrects single-bit errors in an accessed data word (double-bit errors can be detected but not corrected). This type of ECC is known as *single-bit error-correction–double-bit error detection (SEC-DED)* and requires an additional 7 check bits over 32 bits in a 4-byte system and an additional 8 check bits over 64 bits in an 8-byte system. Consequently, you can use parity-checked (36-bit SIMM or 72-bit DIMM) memory in any system that supports ECC memory (as most recent servers do), and the system will use the parity bits for ECC mode. RIMMs are installed in singles or pairs, depending on the chipset and motherboard. They must be 18-bit or 36-bit versions if parity/ECC is desired.

ECC entails the memory controller calculating the check bits on a memory-write operation, performing a comparison between the read and calculated check bits on a read operation, and, if necessary, correcting bad bits. ECC has a slight effect on memory write performance. This is because the operation must be timed to wait for the calculation of check bits and, when the system waits for corrected data, reads. On a partial-word write, the entire word must first be read, the affected byte(s) rewritten, and then new check bits calculated. This turns partial-word write operations into slower read-modify writes. Fortunately, this performance hit is very small, on the order of a few percent at maximum, so the tradeoff for increased reliability is good.

An ECC-based system is a good choice for servers, workstations, or mission-critical applications in which the cost of a potential memory error outweighs the additional memory and system cost to correct it, along with ensuring that it does not detract from system reliability. If you value your data and use your system for important (to you) tasks, you want ECC memory, assuming, of course, that your system supports it. You should check the specifications for a new server or server motherboard to ensure that it supports ECC.

Advanced Error Correction Technologies

Although single-bit ECC is useful for entry-level servers with memory below 4GB, today's high-capacity servers (some of which have memory sizes up to 64GB) and higher memory module capacities (1GB and larger) need more effective error correction technologies.

Many recent servers support Advanced ECC (also known as ChipKill), which differs from standard ECC in its ability to correct up to 4-bit errors that take place within the same memory module. Early versions of Advanced ECC/ChipKill required special Advanced ECC memory modules, but current implementations support standard parity/ECC memory modules.

Another method used on high-end servers is hot-plug RAID memory. This technology uses five memory controllers to create a memory array, similar in concept to a RAID 5 disk array. Four of the controllers store memory data in a striped fashion, while the fifth controller stores parity information. If memory connected to one of the memory controllers used for data fails, it can be removed and replaced without taking down the server. The contents of the original memory are rebuilt from the striped data and parity information in the other modules.

Memory scrubbing is another technique many recent servers use. Memory scrubbing tests memory during idle periods for errors and, if possible, corrects them. If correction is not possible, the system informs the operator that the memory module that has failed.

If you are building or purchasing a midrange or high-end server, you should find out which types of advanced memory error correction technologies are used and choose hardware that provides the best combination of performance and reliability for your needs.

Installing RAM Upgrades

Adding memory to a system is one of the most useful upgrades you can perform and also one of the least expensive. Boosting a server's available memory is an excellent way to get more performance out of an older server rather than replacing it, and it enables you to support more clients in a given configuration without reducing performance. More memory enables servers to handle a greater number of requests in a given time and provide faster data throughput by increasing the workspace available for data.

For example, a study commissioned by Crucial Technology found that a webserver upgraded from 512MB of RAM to 2GB of RAM increased the number of HTTP requests per second and MBps data throughput by more than 70%. Upgrading from 512MB to 4GB provided a performance increase of more than 800% compared to the 512MB baseline and more than 400% compared to the performance at 2GB. (See the study at www.crucial.com/library/server_memory_benchmark_tests.asp for more information.)

The following sections discuss adding memory, including selecting memory, installing memory, and testing the installation.

Upgrade Options and Strategies

There are two options for adding server memory:

- Adding memory to vacant slots on your motherboard or memory cartridge
- Replacing your current server's memory with higher-capacity memory

Note

Some servers, primarily very high-end servers, don't use conventional motherboards with traditional memory sockets. Instead, they use modular designs that include proprietary memory cartridges. The memory cartridge, rather than the motherboard, is where memory is installed. To upgrade memory in a cartridge-based system, you remove the cartridge, add additional memory (or remove and then add memory), and replace it in the system.

To determine the current amount of memory in your system, you can use system analysis programs such as SiSoftware Sandra (www.sisoftware.net) or the memory-analysis utilities provided by major memory vendors. These programs help you determine the amount of memory currently installed as well as whether your system has empty sockets you can use for upgrades or whether you must remove low-capacity memory to make room for larger modules.

To determine at what point you should add memory, you can use the Performance Monitor (Perfmon.msc) that is built into Windows NT Server, Windows 2000 Server, Windows 2000, Professional, Windows XP, and Windows Server 2003. You can launch it remotely or from the server's own console. To check memory usage, you select Memory as the Performance object and enable the following counters:

- **Pages/Sec**—This counter measures the number of times per second that the system uses virtual (swapfile) memory rather than physical memory. A value above 20 indicates a potential problem. Check virtual memory settings; if the counter remains above 20, install more memory.

- **Committed Bytes and Available Bytes**—Committed Bytes tracks virtual memory in use; Available Bytes tracks physical memory available. Add more memory if you run short of Available Bytes.

- **Cache Bytes**—Measures amount of RAM uses for file system cache. Add more RAM if this amount exceeds 4MB.

Linux users can run the command-line tool vmstat on their servers to view memory, CPU, and other factors affecting performance. If vmstat reveals a lot of paging happening frequently, add more RAM to your server. System Performance Monitor 2 (http://sourceforge.net/projects/cspm/) is a graphical performance monitor developed from Complete System Performance Monitor 2.

Although you can consult your system documentation to determine what memory to use, the original documentation shipped with your system or server motherboard might not take into account BIOS upgrades or memory products released after the system was designed that are compatible with the system. For those reasons, you should use the memory configuration tools available on most memory vendors' websites. Given the price of server memory and the critical timing factors involved in memory operation, you want to make sure you choose memory that is designed to work in your system.

If you need to replace a defective memory module and do not have the system documentation, you can determine the correct module for your system by inspecting the modules that are already installed. Each module has markings that indicate its capacity and speed. (RAM capacity and speed are discussed in detail earlier in this chapter.)

If you do not have the documentation for your system and the manufacturer does not offer technical support, you can open your system case and carefully write down the markings that appear on your memory chips. Then contact a module vendor, such as Kingston, Micron (Crucial), or PNY, for help in determining the proper memory modules for your system. Adding the wrong modules to a system can make it as unreliable as leaving a defective module installed and trying to use the system in that condition.

Selecting and Installing Memory

Installing extra memory on your motherboard is an easy way to add memory to your server. Most systems have at least one vacant memory module socket where you can install extra memory to speed up your computer.

If your system requires dual-channel memory, as some high-performance systems do, you must use two identical memory modules (of the same size, speed, and type). Many recent servers provide the option to run in dual-channel mode. If you install a single module or install two modules that aren't the same size or have the same performance, the system will run in a lower-performance single-channel mode.

Purchasing Memory

When you purchase memory, you need to consider several issues. Some are related to the manufacturing and distribution of memory, whereas others depend on the type of memory you are purchasing. The following sections discuss some of the issues you should consider when purchasing memory.

Suppliers

Many companies sell memory, but only a few companies actually *make* memory. In addition, only a few companies make memory chips, but many more companies make memory modules such as SIMMs, DIMMs, and RIMMs. Most of the companies that make the actual RAM chips also make modules containing their own chips. Other companies, however, strictly make modules; these companies purchase memory chips from several chip makers and then produce modules with these chips. Finally, some companies don't make either the chips or modules. Instead, they purchase modules made by other companies and relabel them.

You can think of memory modules made by the chip manufacturers as first-party modules, and you can think of those made by module (but not chip) manufacturers as second-party modules. Finally, those that are simply relabeled first- or second-party modules under a different name can be called third-party modules. It's a good idea to purchase first- or second-party modules if you can because they are better documented. In essence, they have a better pedigree, and their quality is generally more assured. Furthermore, purchasing from a first or second party eliminates one or more middlemen in the distribution process.

First-party manufacturers (that make both the chips and the modules) include Micron (www.crucial.com), Infineon (formerly Siemens), Samsung, Mitsubishi, Toshiba, NEC, and others. Second-party companies (that make the modules but not the chips) include Kingston, Viking, PNY, Simple Tech, Smart, Mushkin, and OCZ Technologies.

At the third-party level, you are not purchasing from a manufacturer but from a reseller or remarketer. Most of the large manufacturers don't sell small quantities of memory to individuals, but some have set up factory outlet stores where individuals can purchase as little as a single module. One of the largest memory manufacturers in the world, Micron, sells direct to the consumer (see www.crucial.com). Because you are buying direct, the pricing at these outlets is often highly competitive with the second- and third-party suppliers.

Considerations in Purchasing DIMMs

When purchasing DIMMs, these are the main things to consider:

- Do you need SDR or DDR versions?
- Do you need ECC or non-ECC?
- Do you need registered or standard (unbuffered) versions?
- What speed grade do you need?
- Do you need a particular CAS latency?

Currently, DIMMs come in SDR (SDRAM), DDR, and DDR2 versions. Most servers use DDR, but there are some servers now on the market using DDR2 memory. SDRAM, DDR, and DDR2 modules are not interchangeable because they use completely different signaling and have different notches to prevent mismatches. Generally, servers use ECC versions, and servers designed to support very large amounts of memory might require registered DIMMs (registered DIMMs also include ECC support). Registered DIMMs contain their own memory registers (buffer chips), enabling the module to hold more memory than a standard DIMM. DIMMs come in a variety of speeds, with the rule that you can always substitute a faster one for a slower one, but not vice versa. As an example, if your system requires PC2100 DDR DIMMs, you can install faster PC2700 DDR DIMMs but not slower PC1600 versions.

Another speed-related issue is CAS latency (sometimes called CL). This is expressed in a number of cycles, with lower numbers indicating higher speeds (fewer cycles). A lower CAS latency shaves a cycle off a burst mode read, which marginally improves memory performance. SDR DIMMs are available in CL3 or CL2 versions, with CL2 being faster. DDR DIMMs are available in CL2.5 or CL2 versions, with CL2 being the faster and better version in that case. You can mix DIMMs with different CAS latency ratings, but the system usually defaults to cycling at the slower speeds of the lowest common denominator.

Considerations in Purchasing RIMMs

When purchasing RIMMs, these are the main things to consider:

- Do you need 184-pin (16/18-bit) or 232-pin (32/36-bit) versions?
- Do you need ECC or non-ECC?
- What speed grade do you need?

RIMMs are available in 184-pin and 232-pin versions, and although they appear to be the same size, they are not interchangeable. Differences exist in the notches that prevent mismatches. High-reliability systems might want or need ECC versions, which have extra ECC bits. As with other memory types, you can mix ECC and non-ECC types, but when you do, the system can't use the ECC capability.

Replacing Modules with Higher-Capacity Versions

If all the memory module slots on a motherboard are occupied, your best option is to remove an existing bank of memory and replace it with higher-capacity modules. For example, if you have a motherboard that supports two DIMM modules (each representing one bank on a processor with a 64-bit data bus), you could remove one of them and replace it with a higher-capacity version. For example, if you have two 256MB modules, giving a total of 512MB, you could remove one of the 256MB modules and replace it with a 512MB unit, in which case you'd then have a total of 768MB of RAM.

However, just because higher-capacity modules are available that are the correct pin count to plug in to your motherboard, you shouldn't automatically assume that the higher-capacity memory will work. Your system's chipset and BIOS set limit the capacity of the memory you can use. You should check your system or motherboard documentation to see which size modules work with it before purchasing new RAM. You should also make sure you have the latest BIOS for your motherboard when installing new memory.

If your system supports dual-channel memory, you must use matched pairs of DDR or DDR2 modules (depending on which type your system supports) and install them in the correct location on the motherboard to achieve the superior memory performance that dual-channel access offers. You should see your server or motherboard manual for details.

Installing Memory

This section discusses installing memory—specifically DIMM modules. It also covers the problems you are most likely to encounter and how to avoid them. Finally, it provides information on configuring your system to use new memory.

When you install or remove memory, you are most likely to encounter the following problems:

- Electrostatic discharge (ESD)
- Improperly seated modules
- Incorrect memory configuration settings in the BIOS Setup

To prevent ESD when you install sensitive memory chips or boards, you shouldn't wear synthetic-fiber clothing or leather-soled shoes, which promote the generation of static charges. You should remove any static charge you are carrying by touching the system chassis before you begin, or, better yet, wear a good commercial grounding strap on your wrist. You can order one from any electronics parts store. A grounding strap consists of a conductive wristband grounded at the other end through a 1-Megohm resistor by a wire clipped to the system chassis. Be sure the system you are working on is unplugged.

Caution

Be sure to use a properly designed commercial grounding strap; do not make one yourself. Commercial units have a 1-Megohm resistor that serves as protection if you accidentally touch live power. The resistor ensures that you do not become the path of least resistance to the ground and therefore become electrocuted. An improperly designed strap can cause the power to conduct through you to the ground, possibly killing you.

Follow this procedure to upgrade memory on a typical server:

1. Shut down the server and unplug it. As an alternative to unplugging it, you can turn off the power supply using the on/off switch on the rear of some power supplies. Wait about 10 seconds for any remaining current to drain from the motherboard.

2. Open the system. See the system or case instructions for details.

3. Connect the wrist strap to a metal portion of the system chassis, such as the frame. Make sure the metal plate on the inside of the wrist strap is tight against the skin of your wrist.

4. Move obstructions inside the case, such as cables or wires, out of the way of the memory modules and empty sockets. If you must remove a cable or wire, note its location and orientation.

5. If you need to remove an existing DIMM or RIMM, flip down the ejector tab at each end of the module and lift the module straight up out of the socket. Note the keying on the module.

6. Note the specific locations needed if you are inserting modules to operate in dual-channel mode. The sockets used for dual-channel memory might use a different-colored plastic to distinguish them from other sockets, or you might need to see the server.

7. To insert a DIMM or RIMM module into a socket, make sure the ejector tabs are flipped down on the socket you plan to use. DIMMs and RIMMs are keyed by notches along the bottom connector edge that are offset from the center so they can be inserted in only one direction, as shown in Figure 5.15.

8. Push down on the DIMM or RIMM until the ejector tabs lock into place in the notch on the side of the module. It's important that you not force the module into the socket. If the module does not slip easily into the slot and then snap into place, it is probably not oriented or aligned correctly. Forcing the module could break it or the socket. When installing RIMMs, you need to fill any empty RIMM sockets with continuity modules. Refer to Figure 5.14 for details.

9. Replace any cables or wires you disconnected.

10. Close up the system.

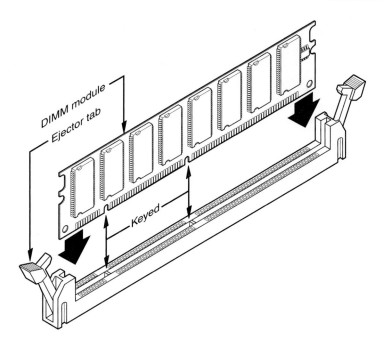

Figure 5.15 DIMM keys match the protrusions in the DIMM sockets. DDR DIMM and RIMM keys are similar but not exactly the same.

11. Reconnect system power or turn on the power supply.

12. Restart the computer.

After adding memory and putting the system back together, you might have to run the BIOS Setup and resave with the new amount of memory being reported. Most newer systems automatically detect the new amount of memory and reconfigure the BIOS Setup settings for you. Most newer systems also don't require setting any jumpers or switches on the motherboard to configure it for your new memory.

After configuring your system to work properly with the additional memory, you might want to run a memory-diagnostics program to ensure that the new memory works properly. Some are run automatically for you. At least two and sometimes three memory-diagnostics programs are available for all systems. In order of accuracy, these programs are as follows:

- POST
- Disk-based advanced diagnostics software

The POST is used every time you power up the system.

Many additional diagnostics programs are available from aftermarket utility software companies.

Common Server Configurations and Features

Various generations of servers have used different types of memory. The following sections provide an overview, by memory type. For the details of the memory used by your server, you should check your system documentation or look up your server's chipset in Chapter 3. Chapter 3 also provides information about processor types supported and other features of these chipsets.

Server Chipsets and Memory Types Used

Although SDRAM memory is no longer the most common type of desktop memory, some servers continue to use it. Just as the most common type of desktop memory is currently DDR, most servers also use DDR memory. Some recent servers use DDR2 memory, and a few, primarily older servers, use RDRAM. Table 5.21 provides a quick reference to server chipsets and the memory types they support. Note that some chipsets support two or more types of memory. In such cases, you should check the documentation for the particular system or motherboard using that chipset to determine what type of memory it uses.

Table 5.21   Memory Types Supported by Major Server Chipsets

Chipset Model	Supports SDRAM	Supports DDR SDRAM	Supports DDR2 SDRAM
Acer Labs			
Aladdin Pro II[1-3]	Yes	—	—
Hewlett-Packard			
F8	Yes	—	—
sx1000 "Pinnacles"	Yes	—	—
zx1	—	Yes	—
IBM			
XA-32	Yes	—	—
XA-32 second generation	—	Yes	—
XA-64	—	Yes	—
XA-64e	—	Yes	—
Intel			
440LX	Yes	—	—
440BX	Yes	—	—
440GX	Yes	—	—
450NX	Yes	—	—
Corollary[4]	Yes	—	—
460GX	Yes	—	—
845	Yes	Yes	—
845P	—	Yes	—
875P	—	Yes	—
E7210	—	Yes	—
E7221	—	Yes	Yes
E7500	—	Yes	—
E7501	—	Yes	—
E7505	—	Yes	—
E7520	—	Yes	Yes
E7320	—	Yes	Yes
E8500	—	Yes	Yes
E8870	—	Yes	—

Chipset Model	Supports SDRAM	Supports DDR SDRAM	Supports DDR2 SDRAM
ServerWorks			
Champion HE	Yes	—	—
Champion HE-SL	Yes	—	—
Champion LE	Yes	—	—
Grand Champion HE	—	Yes	—
Grand Champion LE	—	Yes	—
Grand Champion SL	—	Yes	—
VIA Technologies			
Apollo Pro133A	Yes	—	2
VIA Apollo Pro266	Yes	Yes	—

[1] *Also supports FPM DRAM.*

[2] *Also supports EDO DRAM.*

[3] *Acer Labs is now ULi.*

[4] *This chipset was originally co-developed by Compaq and Profusion.*

To determine the specific speeds and types of memory, or to determine whether a particular server uses SDRAM or another type of memory if it uses chipsets compatible with more than one type of RAM, you should see the system documentation or use a hardware analysis program such as SiSoftware Sandra or HWiNFO.

Chipsets for AMD Opteron and DDR Memory

The AMD Opteron processor incorporates the memory controller in the processor, rather than in the North Bridge or memory controller hub, as do other chipsets. The AMD Opteron's integrated memory controller supports DDR memory. Thus, every server based on Opteron processors supports DDR memory.

Servers That Use RDRAM Memory

Relatively few server-class systems used RDRAM memory. Systems based on the following chipsets used RDRAM memory:

- Intel 820
- Intel 840 (note that some systems based on this chipset used SDRAM, thanks to a memory repeater hub chip)
- Intel 850
- Intel 850e

Note that Intel no longer supports RDRAM memory for server or desktop chipsets. Although a few other chipset vendors continue to support RDRAM, most notably Silicon Information Systems (SiS), there are no SiS-based servers to date.

Troubleshooting Memory Problems

Memory problems can be difficult to troubleshoot. For one thing, computer memory is still mysterious to people because it is a kind of "virtual" thing that can be hard to grasp. The other difficulty is that memory problems can be intermittent and often look like problems with other areas of a system, even software. The following sections show some simple troubleshooting steps you can take if you suspect that you are having a memory problem.

To troubleshoot memory, you first need some memory-diagnostics testing programs. You already have several of them. Every motherboard BIOS has a memory-diagnostics program in the POST that runs when you first turn on the system. You probably also have a memory-diagnostics program on a utility disk that came with your system. Many commercial diagnostics programs are available on the market, and almost all of them include memory tests.

When the POST runs, it not only tests memory but also counts it. The count is compared to the count taken the last time BIOS Setup was run; if these counts are different, an error message is issued. As the POST runs, it writes a pattern of data to all the memory locations in the system and reads that pattern back to verify that the memory works. If any failure is detected, you see or hear a message. Audio messages (beeping) are used for critical, or "fatal," errors that occur in areas that are important for the system's operation. If the system can access enough memory to at least allow video to function, you see error messages instead of hearing beep codes.

Note

Visit the Upgrading and Repairing Servers web page (accessible from www.upgradingandrepairingpcs.com) to download detailed listings of the BIOS beep and other error codes, which are specific to the type of BIOS you have.

If your system makes it through the POST with no memory error indications, there might not be a hardware memory problem, or the POST might not be able to detect the problem. Intermittent memory errors are often not detected during the POST, and other subtle hardware defects can be difficult for the POST to catch. The POST is designed to run quickly, so its testing is not nearly as thorough as it could be. On many recent systems, memory testing is disabled by default to permit faster startup. That is why you often have to boot from a DOS or diagnostic disk and run a true hardware diagnostic to do more extensive memory testing. These types of tests can be run continuously and be left running for days, if necessary, to hunt down an elusive intermittent defect.

Still, even these programs do only pass/fail type testing; that is, all they can do is write patterns to memory and read them back. They can't determine how close the memory is to failing—only whether it worked. For the highest level of testing, the best thing to have is a dedicated memory test machine, usually called a *memory module tester*. This type of device enables you to insert a module and test it thoroughly at a variety of speeds, voltages, and timings, so you can determine for certain whether the memory is good or bad. Versions of these testers are available to handle all types of memory, from older SIMMs to the latest DDR and DDR2 DIMMs or RIMMs. Defective modules can work in some systems (slower ones) but not others, so the *same* memory test program may fail the module in one machine but pass it in another. In a module tester, such a problem is always identified as bad, right down to the individual bit, and the tester even tells the actual speed of the device, not just its rating. Companies that offer memory module testers include Tanisys (www.tanisys.com), CST (www.simmtester.com), and Innoventions (www.memorytest.com). They can be expensive, but for a professional in the PC repair business, using one of these memory module testers is the only way to go.

After your operating system is running, memory errors can still occur, and they are typically accompanied by error messages. These are the most common error messages:

- **Parity errors**—This type of error message indicates that the parity-checking circuitry on the motherboard has detected a change in memory since the data was originally stored.

◄◄   See "How Parity Checking Works," p. 390.

- **General or global protection faults**—This is a general-purpose error message, indicating that a program has been corrupted in memory, usually resulting in immediate termination of the application. This can also be caused by buggy or faulty programs.

- **Fatal exception errors**—Error codes are returned by a program when an illegal instruction has been encountered, invalid data or code has been accessed, or the privilege level of an operation is invalid.

- **Divide-by-zero error**—This is a general-purpose error message, indicating that division by 0 was attempted or the result of an operation does not fit in the destination register.

If you are encountering any of these errors, they could be caused by defective or improperly configured memory, but they could also be caused by software bugs (especially drivers), bad power supplies, static discharges, close proximity to radio transmitters, timing problems, and more.

If you suspect that these types of problems are caused by memory, there are ways to test the memory to determine whether that is the problem (as discussed earlier in this section). Most of this testing involves running one or more memory test programs.

Testing Memory

Many people make a critical mistake when they run memory testing software. For example, many people run memory tests with the system caches enabled. This effectively invalidates memory testing because most systems have what is called a *write-back cache*. This means that data written to the main memory is first written to the cache. Because a memory test program first writes data and then immediately reads it back, the data is read back from the cache, not from the main memory. This makes the memory test program run very quickly, but all it tests is the cache. The bottom line is that if you test memory with the cache enabled, you aren't really writing to the SIMM/DIMMs, but only to the cache. Before you run any memory test programs, you need to be sure your cache is disabled. The system will run very slowly when you do this, and the memory test will take much longer to complete, but you will be testing your actual RAM, not the cache.

The following steps enable you to effectively test and troubleshoot your system RAM. Figure 5.16 provides a boiled-down procedure to help you step through the process quickly.

1. Power up the system and observe the POST. If the POST completes with no errors, basic memory functionality has been tested. If errors are encountered, go to the defect isolation procedures.

2. Restart the system and enter your BIOS (or CMOS) Setup. In most systems, you do this by pressing the F2, Delete, or Esc key during the POST but before the boot process begins (see the onscreen prompts or system/motherboard documentation for details). When you're in BIOS Setup, verify that the memory count is equal to the count that has been installed. If the count does not match what has been installed, go to the defect isolation procedures.

3. Find the BIOS Setup options for cache and set all cache options to Disabled. Save the settings and reboot to a DOS-formatted system disk (floppy) that contains the diagnostics program of your choice. Note that some diagnostic disks are self-booting (that is, they contain their own operating systems). If your system came with a diagnostics disk, you can use that, or you can use one of the many commercial PC diagnostics programs on the market, such as PC-Technician by Windsor Technologies (which comes in self-booting form) or others.

4. Follow the instructions that came with your diagnostic program to have it test the system base and extended memory. Most programs have a mode that enables them to loop the test—that is, to run it continuously—which is great for finding intermittent problems. If the program encounters a memory error, proceed to the defect isolation procedures.

5. If no errors are encountered in the POST or in the more comprehensive memory diagnostic, your memory has tested okay in hardware. Be sure at this point to reboot the system, enter the BIOS Setup, and reenable the cache. The system will run very slowly until the cache is turned back on.

6. If you are having memory problems, yet the memory still tests okay, you might have a problem that is undetectable by simple pass/fail testing, or the problem could be caused by software or one of many other defects or problems in your system. You might want to bring the memory to a SIMM/DIMM tester for a more accurate analysis. Most PC repair shops have such testers. You should also check the software (especially drivers, which might need to be updated), power supply, and system environment for problems such as static and radio transmitters.

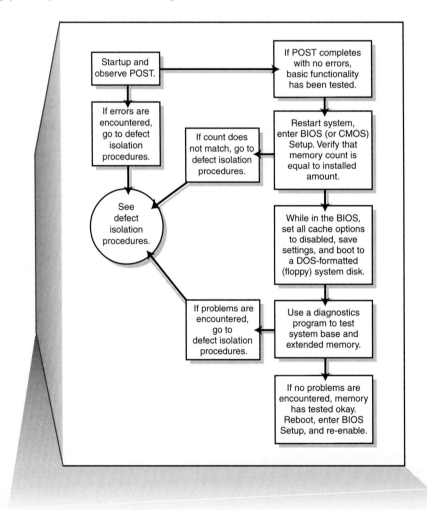

Figure 5.16   Testing and troubleshooting memory.

First, let's cover the memory testing and troubleshooting procedures:

Memory Defect Isolation Procedures

If you have identified an actual memory problem that is being reported by the POST or disk-based memory diagnostics, you can use the following steps and Figure 5.17 to identify or isolate which SIMM or DIMM in the system is causing the problem:

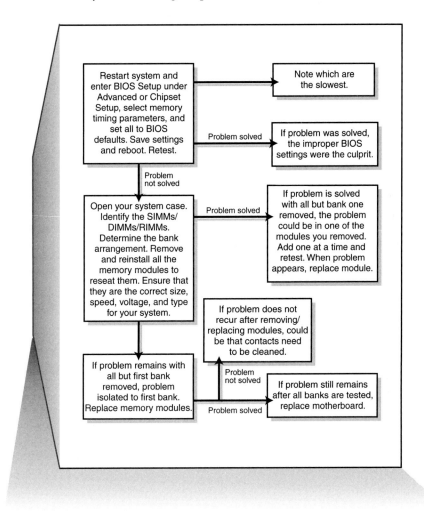

Figure 5.17   Follow these steps if you are still encountering memory errors after completing the steps in Figure 5.16.

1. Restart the system and enter the BIOS Setup. Look for a menu called something like Advanced or Chipset Setup for memory timing parameters. Select BIOS or Setup defaults, which are usually the slowest settings. Save the settings, reboot, and retest, using the testing and troubleshooting procedures listed in "Testing Memory," earlier in this chapter. If the problem has been solved, improper BIOS settings were the problem. If the problem remains, you likely have defective memory, so continue to the next step.

2. Open the system so you have physical access to the SIMMs/DIMMs/RIMMs on the motherboard. Identify the bank arrangement in the system. For example, Pentium systems use 64-bit banks, which means two SIMMs or one DIMM per bank. Systems that support dual-channel memory use matched pairs of modules. Pentium 4 systems require two 184-pin RIMMs at a time (in separate channels) or a single 232-pin RIMM if the system uses that type. Using the manual or the legend silk-screened on the motherboard, identify which modules correspond to which banks.

3. Remove all the memory except the first bank and retest, using the troubleshooting and testing procedures listed in "Testing Memory," earlier in this chapter. If the problem remains with all but the first bank removed, the problem has been isolated to the first bank, which must be replaced. With a dual-channel system, you can swap down to a single module for troubleshooting. However, afterward you should restore the matched pair to the system.

4. Replace the memory in the first bank, preferably with known good spare modules (or others that you have removed and retest). If the problem *still* remains after testing all the memory banks (and finding them all to be working properly), it is likely that the motherboard itself is bad (with the problem probably in one of the memory sockets). Replace the motherboard and retest.

5. At this point, the first (or previous) bank has tested good, so the problem must be in the remaining modules that have been temporarily removed. Install the next bank of memory and retest. If the problem resurfaces now, the memory in that bank is defective. Continue testing each bank until you find the defective module.

6. Repeat step 5 until all remaining banks of memory are installed and have been tested. If the problem does not resurface after you remove and reinstall all the memory, the problem was likely intermittent or caused by poor conduction on the memory contacts. Often simply removing and replacing memory can resolve problems because of the self-cleaning action between the module and the socket during removal and reinstallation.

CHAPTER 6

The ATA/IDE Interface

The interface used to connect hard disk and optical drives to a modern PC is typically called *IDE (Integrated Drive Electronics)*; however, the true name of this interface is *ATA (AT Attachment)*. The ATA designation refers to the fact that this interface was originally designed to connect a combined drive and controller directly to the 16-bit bus found in the 1984 vintage IBM AT (Advanced Technology) and compatible computers. The AT bus is otherwise known as the ISA (Industry Standard Architecture) bus. Although ATA is the official name of the interface, *IDE* is a marketing term originated by some of the drive manufacturers to describe the drive/controller combination used in drives with the ATA interface. *IDE* refers to the fact that the interface electronics or controller is built in to the drive and is not a separate board, as with earlier drive interfaces. Although the correct name for the particular IDE interface we most commonly use is technically ATA, many persist in using the IDE designation today. If you are being picky, you could say that *IDE* refers generically to any drive interface in which the controller is built in to the drive, whereas *ATA* refers to the specific implementation of IDE that is used in most PCs.

ATA is used to connect not only hard disks, but also optical (CD-ROM and DVD-ROM) drives, high-capacity SuperDisk or Zip drives, and tape drives. Even so, ATA is still thought of primarily as a hard disk interface, and it evolved directly from the separate controller and hard drive interfaces that were used prior to ATA. This chapter covers the standard parallel version of ATA as well as the newer Serial ATA (SATA) interfaces; it also briefly mentions the original interfaces from which ATA evolved.

Although virtually every server contains one or more ATA interfaces, the parallel ATA (PATA) interface is used primarily for CD-ROM and DVD-ROM optical drives on midrange and high-end servers. These servers typically use the SCSI interface for hard disks. However, the newer SATA interface is being used by all levels of servers for hard disk interfacing.

Origins of IDE

Any drive with an integrated controller could be called an IDE drive, although normally when we say *IDE*, we really mean the specific version of IDE called ATA. No matter what you call it, combining the drive and controller greatly simplifies installation because there are no separate power or signal cables that run from the controller to the drive. Also, when the controller and drive are assembled as a unit, the number of total components is reduced, signal paths are shorter, and the electrical connections are more noise resistant. This results in a more reliable and less expensive design than is possible when a separate controller, connected to the drive by cables, is used, as was the case with the early ST412, ST506, and ESDI interfaces used by PCs and early servers in the 1980s.

Placing the controller, including the digital-to-analog encoder/decoder (endec), on the drive offers an inherent reliability advantage over interfaces with separate controllers, such as the ST506 and ESDI. Reliability is increased because the digital-to-analog data encoding is performed directly on the drive in a tight, noise-free environment. The timing-sensitive analog information does not have to travel along crude ribbon cables that are likely to pick up noise and insert propagation delays into the signals. The integrated configuration enables increases in the clock rate of the encoder and the storage density of the drive.

Integrating the controller and drive also frees the controller and drive engineers from having to adhere to the strict guidelines imposed by the earlier interface standards. Engineers can design what essentially are custom drive and controller implementations because no other controller will ever have to be connected to the drive. The resulting drive and controller combinations can offer higher performance than earlier standalone controller and drive setups. IDE drives are sometimes called drives with embedded controllers.

The earliest IDE drives were called *hardcards* and were nothing more than hard disks and controllers bolted directly together and plugged in to a slot as a single unit. Companies such as the Plus

Development Division of Quantum attached a small 3.5-inch drive (either ST-506/412 or ESDI) directly to a standard controller. The drive/controller assembly was then plugged in to an ISA bus slot as though it were a normal disk controller card. To improve reliability and free up the expansion slot blocked by the relatively thick card-and-drive combination, several companies got the idea to redesign the controller, to replace the logic board assembly on a standard hard disk and then mount it in a standard drive bay just like any other drive. Because the built-in controller in these drives still needed to plug directly in to the expansion bus, just like any other controller, a cable was run between the drive and one of the slots. This is the origin of IDE.

IDE Variations

There have been four main types of IDE interfaces, based on three bus standards:

- SATA
- PATA (based on the 16-bit AT-bus, also called ISA)
- XT IDE (based on 8-bit ISA, obsolete)
- MCA IDE (based on 16-bit Micro Channel, obsolete)

Of these, only the PATA and SATA versions are used today. PATA and SATA have evolved with newer, faster, and more powerful versions. The newer versions of PATA are referred to as ATA-2 and higher. They are also sometimes called EIDE (Enhanced IDE), Fast ATA, Ultra ATA, or Ultra DMA (UDMA). Even though PATA has hit the end of the evolutionary road with ATA-7, SATA picks up where PATA leaves off and offers greater performance, higher reliability, easier installation, lower cost, and an established roadmap for future upgrades.

Note

It is important to note that only the ATA IDE interface has been standardized by the industry. The XT and MCA IDE interfaces were never adopted as industrywide standards and never became very popular. These interfaces were only used from 1987 to 1993 and only in IBM PS/2 (and some early ThinkPad) systems.

In most modern server systems, you find one or more PATA connectors on the motherboard, and systems that offer ATA RAID have two additional PATA connectors, which can be used for an ATA RAID array or for additional ATA drives running as independent devices. If your motherboard does not have one of these connectors and you want to attach an ATA drive to your system, you can purchase an adapter card that adds an ATA interface (or two) to a system via the PCI or PCI-X bus slots. Some of the cards offer additional features, such as an onboard ROM BIOS or cache memory.

Because only the PATA and SATA versions of IDE are in use today, this chapter focuses on them.

Note

Many people who use systems with ATA connectors on the motherboard believe that a hard disk controller is built in to their motherboard, but in a technical sense, the controller is actually in the drive. Although the integrated ATA ports on a motherboard are often referred to as *controllers*, they are more accurately called *host adapters* (although you rarely hear this term). A host adapter can be thought of as a device that connects a controller to a bus.

PATA is a 16-bit parallel interface, meaning that 16 bits are transmitted simultaneously down the interface cable. A serial interface called SATA was officially introduced in late 2000 and began appearing in systems starting in 2003. SATA sends 1 bit down the cable at a time, enabling thinner and smaller cables to be used and providing higher performance due to the higher cycling speeds allowed.

SATA is a completely new and updated physical interface design, while remaining compatible on the software level with PATA. (Throughout this book, *ATA* refers to both the parallel and serial versions, whereas PATA and SATA refer to the specific versions, as indicated.) Figure 6.1 shows how the power and data cables used by SATA compare in size to those used by PATA.

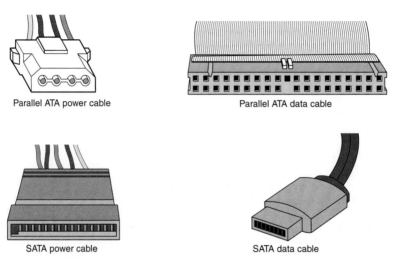

Parallel ATA power cable   Parallel ATA data cable

SATA power cable   SATA data cable

Figure 6.1 SATA data cables (lower right) are much smaller than those used by PATA (upper right), whereas the power cables (left) are similar in size.

The primary advantage of ATA drives over the older, separate controller-based interfaces and newer host bus interface alternatives, such as USB, SCSI, and IEEE 1394 (i.LINK or FireWire), is cost. Because the separate controller or host adapter is eliminated and the cable connections are simplified, ATA drives cost much less than a standard controller-and-drive combination.

▶▶ See "ANSI SCSI Standards," p. 449.

▶▶ See "USB," p. 468.

In terms of performance, ATA drives are often some of the highest-performance drives available, but they can also be among the lowest-performance drives. This apparent contradiction is a result of the fact that all ATA drives are different. You can't make a blanket statement about the performance of ATA drives because each drive is unique. The high-end models, however, offer performance equal to or superior to that of any other type of drive on the market for a single-user, single-tasking operating system. However, because of the simplicity of the ATA design, PATA in particular is not suitable for midrange or high-end server designs. PATA is adequate for entry server designs, though.

Note

Many people are confused about 16- versus 32-bit bus connections and 16- versus 32-bit hard drive connections. A PCI bus connection allows for a 32-bit (and possibly 64-bit, in some versions) connection between the bus and the ATA host interface, which is typically in the motherboard chipset South Bridge or I/O Controller Hub (ICH) chip. However, the actual PATA interface between the host connector on the motherboard and the drive (or drives) itself is only a 16-bit interface. Thus, in a PATA drive configuration, you are still getting only 16-bit transfers between the drive and the motherboard-based host interface. Even so, the clock speeds of the ATA interface are high enough that one or two hard drives normally can't supply the controller enough data to saturate even a 16-bit channel. The same is true with SATA, which—although it transmits only 1 bit at a time—does so at extremely high speeds.

ATA Standards

Today, the ATA interface is controlled by an independent group of representatives from major PC, drive, and component manufacturers. This group, called Technical Committee T13 (www.t13.org), is responsible for all standards related to the PATA and SATA storage interfaces. Technical Committee T13 is a part of the InterNational Committee on Information Technology Standards (INCITS; www.incits.org), which operates under rules approved by the American National Standards Institute (ANSI; www.ansi.org), a governing body that sets rules that control nonproprietary standards in the computer industry as well as many other industries. A second group, called the Serial ATA Working Group (now the Serial ATA International Organization [SATA-IO; www.serialata.org]) was formed to initially create the SATA standards, which are then passed on to Technical Committee T13 for refinement and official publication under ANSI. The current ATA-7 standard incorporates both PATA and SATA standards and represents the end of the road for PATA because ATA-8 and beyond will contain only SATA standards.

The rules under which these committees operate are designed to ensure that voluntary industry standards are developed through the consensus of people and organizations in the affected industries. INCITS specifically develops information processing system standards; ANSI approves the process under which they are developed and then publishes them. Because Technical Committee T13 is essentially a public organization, all the working drafts, discussions, and meetings of Technical Committee T13 are open for all to see.

Copies of any of the published standards can be purchased from ANSI or Global Engineering Documents (see the vendor list in Appendix C, "Vendor List"). Draft versions of the standards can be downloaded from Technical Committee T13 and SATA-IO websites.

The ATA interface has evolved into several successive standard versions:

- ATA-1
- ATA-2 (also called Fast ATA, Fast ATA-2, and EIDE)
- ATA-3
- ATA-4 (Ultra ATA/33)
- ATA-5 (Ultra ATA/66)
- ATA-6 (Ultra ATA/100)
- ATA-7 (Ultra ATA/133 or SATA)
- SATA-8 (SATA II)

Since ATA-1, newer versions of the ATA interface and complementary BIOS have supported larger and faster drives, as well as different types of devices other than hard disks. ATA-2 and later have improved the original ATA interface in five main areas:

- Secondary two-device channel
- Increased maximum drive capacity
- Faster data transfer
- ATAPI (AT Attachment Packet Interface)
- SATA (Serial ATA)

Each newer version of ATA is backward compatible with the previous versions. In other words, older ATA-1 or ATA-2 devices work fine on ATA-6 and ATA-7 interfaces. ATA-7 includes both PATA and

SATA, but SATA-8 is serial only. Newer versions of ATA are normally built on older versions and with few exceptions can be thought of as extensions of the previous versions. This means that ATA-7, for example, is generally considered equal to ATA-6, with the addition of some features.

Table 6.1 breaks down the various ATA standards. The following sections describe all the ATA versions in more detail.

Table 6.1   ATA Standards[1]

Standard	Year Pro- posed	Year Published	Year With- drawn	PIO Modes	DMA Modes	UDMA Modes	Parallel Speed (MBps)	Serial Speed (MBps)	Features
ATA-1	1988	1994	1999	0–2	0	—	8.33	—	Drives support up to 136.9GB; BIOS issues not addressed
ATA-2	1993	1996	2001	0–4	0–2	—	16.67	—	Faster PIO modes; CHS/LBA BIOS translation defined up to 8.4GB; PC Card
ATA-3	1995	1997	2002	0–4	0–2	—	16.67	—	SMART; improved signal integrity; LBA support mandatory; eliminated single-word DMA modes
ATA-4	1996	1998	—	0–4	0–2	0–2	33.33	—	Ultra-DMA modes; ATAPI; BIOS support up to 136.9GB
ATA-5	1998	2000	—	0–4	0–2	0–4	66.67	—	Faster UDMA modes; 80-pin cable with autodetection

Standard	Year Pro- posed	Year Published	Year With- drawn	PIO Modes	DMA Modes	UDMA Modes	Parallel Speed (MBps)	Serial Speed (MBps)	Features
ATA-6	2000	2002	—	0–4	0–2	0–5	100	—	100MBps UDMA mode; extended drive and BIOS sup- port up to 144PB
ATA-7	2001	2004	—	0–4	0–2	0–6	133	150	133MBps UDMA mode; SATA
SATA-8	2004	—	—	—	—	—	—	300	SATA II

[1]Key: SMART = Self-Monitoring, Analysis, and Reporting Technology; ATAPI = AT Attachment Packet Interface; MB = megabytes; GB = gigabytes; PB = petabytes; CHS = Cylinder, Head, Sector; LBA = logical block address; PIO = pro- grammed I/O; DMA = direct memory access; and UDMA = Ultra DMA (direct memory access).

Virtually all recent servers support ATA-6 or newer ATA standards, so the following sections discuss these standards in greater detail.

ATA-6/ATAPI

The ATA-6 standard includes Ultra ATA/100 (also called UDMA/100), which increases the Ultra ATA burst transfer rate by reducing setup times and increasing the clock rate. As with ATA-5, the faster modes require the improved 80-conductor cable (refer to Figure 6.6, later in this chapter, for a com- parison of the original 40-conductor and current 80-conductor PATA cables). Using the ATA/100 mode requires both a drive and a motherboard interface that supports that mode.

Work on ATA-6 began in 2000, and the standard was finished and officially published in 2002, as ANSI NCITS 361-2002, "AT Attachment - 6 with Packet Interface."

The major changes or additions in the standard include the following:

- UDMA Mode 5 was added, which allows 100MBps (called UDMA/100, Ultra ATA/100, or just ATA/100) transfers. This requires an 80-conductor cable.

- The sector count per command was increased from 8 bits (256 sectors, or 131KB) to 16 bits (65,536 sectors, or 33.5MB), allowing larger files to be transferred more efficiently.

- LBA addressing was extended from 2^{28} to 2^{48} (281,474,976,710,656) sectors, supporting drives up to 144.12PB (petabytes = quadrillion bytes). Vendors often refer to this feature as *48-bit LBA*, or *greater than 137GB support*; Maxtor refers to this feature as *Big Drive*.

- CHS addressing was made obsolete; drives must use 28-bit or 48-bit LBA addressing only.

Besides adding the 100MBps UDMA Mode 5 transfer rate, ATA-6 also extended drive capacity greatly— and just in time. ATA-5 and earlier standards supported drives of up to only 137GB in capacity, which became a limitation because larger drives were becoming available. Commercially available 3.5-inch drives exceeding 137GB were introduced during 2001, but they were originally available only in SCSI versions because SCSI doesn't share the same limitations as ATA. With ATA-6, the sector addressing limit was extended from 2^{28} sectors to 2^{48} sectors. This means that LBA addressing previously could use only 28-bit numbers, but with ATA-6, LBA addressing can use larger 48-bit numbers, if necessary. With 512 bytes per sector, this raises the maximum supported drive capacity to 144.12PB, which is equal to more than 144.12 quadrillion bytes. Note that the 48-bit addressing is optional and necessary only for drives larger than 137GB. Drives 137GB or smaller can use either 28-bit or 48-bit addressing.

ATA-7/ATAPI

The primary addition in ATA-7 is another transfer mode for PATA, called UDMA Mode 6, that allows for data transfers up to 133MBps. As with UDMA Mode 5 (100MBps) and UDMA Mode 4 (66MBps), the use of an 80-conductor cable is required. Slower speeds don't require the 80-conductor cable, although they do work with it and an 80-conductor cable is always preferred over the 40-conductor type.

Another major change in the specification is the inclusion of the SATA 1.0 specification into ATA-7. This makes SATA an official part of the ATA standard. Work on ATA-7 began in 2001, and the standard was finished and officially published in 2004.

Note that although the throughput has been increased from the drive controller (on the drive) to the motherboard via the UDMA modes, most ATA drives—even those capable of UDMA Mode 6 (133MBps) from the drive to the motherboard—still have an average maximum sustained transfer rate while reading data of under 60MBps. This means that although newer ATA drives can transfer at speeds up to 133MBps from the circuit board on the drive to the motherboard, data from the drive media (platters) through the heads to the circuit board on the drive moves at less than half that rate. For that reason, running a drive capable of UDMA Mode 6 (133MBps) on a motherboard capable of only UDMA Mode 5 (100MBps) really doesn't slow things down much, if at all. Likewise, upgrading your ATA host adapter from one that does 100MBps to one that can do 133MBps doesn't help much if your drive reads data off the disk platters at only half that speed. When selecting a drive, remember that the media transfer rate is far more important than the interface transfer rate because the media transfer rate is the limiting factor.

ATA-8

In 2004, work began on SATA-8, which is a new ATA standard based on ATA-7. The following are the main features of SATA-8:

- The development of separate SATA and PATA versions of the standard
- The replacement of read-long/write-long functions
- Improved host protected area (HPA) management

The most dramatic change is the development of separate PATA and SATA standards. ATA8 for PATA drives is known as ATA8-APT (ATA/ATAPI Parallel Transport), while ATA8 for SATA drives is known as ATA8-AST (ATA/ATAPI Serial Transport). The main benefit of this change is to allow new features and functions to be made available in ATA8-SPT–compliant SATA drives while providing a PATA-specific standard that can be used as a reference. By creating separate standards for PATA and SATA, the result is a clearer and more concise description of the SATA standard. ATA8-APT is virtually identical to the PATA-specific content of ATA-7. Basically, any PATA drive compliant with ATA-7 is also compliant with ATA8-APT. It is expected that both versions of the ATA8 standard will be finalized and officially published in 2006.

ATA Features and Resource Allocations

Although ATA drives are now following two divergent paths in terms of hardware (PATA and SATA), they have the ATA-7 command set in common. The following sections discuss the different ATA standards and the ATA command set.

PATA

PATA and SATA have unique specifications and requirements regarding the physical interface, cable, and connectors. The following sections detail the unique features of PATA.

PATA I/O Connector

The PATA interface connector is normally a 40-pin header-type connector with pins spaced 0.1 inch (2.54mm) apart, and it is generally keyed, to prevent the possibility of installing it upside down (see Figures 6.2 and 6.3). There are two methods of creating a keyed connector:

- Pin 20 might be removed from the male connector and the matching pin 20 on the female cable connector is blocked, which prevents the user from installing the cable backward.

- Some cables incorporate a protrusion on the top of the female cable connector that fits into a notch in the shroud surrounding the mating male connector on the device.

Some cables use both keying methods. The use of keyed connectors and cables is highly recommended. Plugging in an ATA cable backward normally doesn't cause any permanent damage; however, it can lock up a system and prevent it from running.

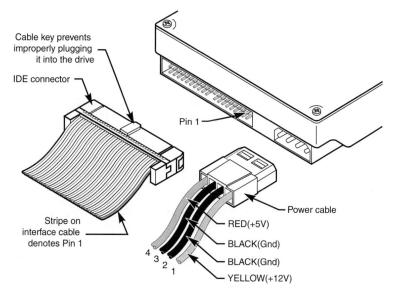

Figure 6.2   Typical PATA (IDE) hard drive connectors.

Table 6.2 shows the standard 40-pin PATA (IDE) interface connector pinout. Note that although PATA drives corresponding to the ATA-5 and later standards use an 80-conductor (80-wire) cable, the connector and pinout remain the same as those shown in Figures 6.2 and 6.3.

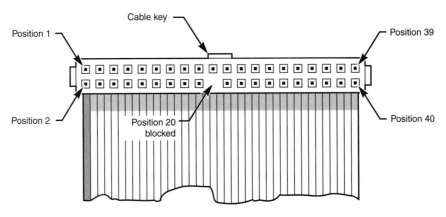

Figure 6.3 PATA (IDE) 40-pin interface connector detail.

Table 6.2   40-Pin PATA Connector

Signal Name	Pin	Pin	Signal Name
-RESET[1]	1	2	GROUND
Data Bit 7	3	4	Data Bit 8
Data Bit 6	5	6	Data Bit 9
Data Bit 5	7	8	Data Bit 10
Data Bit 4	9	10	Data Bit 11
Data Bit 3	11	12	Data Bit 12
Data Bit 2	13	14	Data Bit 13
Data Bit 1	15	16	Data Bit 14
Data Bit 0	17	18	Data Bit 15
GROUND	19	20	KEY (pin missing)
DRQ 3	21	22	GROUND
-IOW	23	24	GROUND
-IOR	25	26	GROUND
I/O CH RDY	27	28	CSEL:SPSYNC[2]
-DACK 3	29	30	GROUND
IRQ 14	31	32	Reserved[3]
Address Bit 1	33	34	-PDIAG
Address Bit 0	35	36	Address Bit 2
-CS1FX	37	38	-CS3FX
-DA/SP	39	40	GROUND
+5V (Logic)	41	42	+5V (Motor)
GROUND	43	44	Reserved

[1]Note that a - preceding a signal name (such as with -RESET) indicates that the signal is "active low."
[2]Pin 28 is usually cable select, but some older drives could use it for spindle synchronization between multiple drives.
[3]Pin 32 was defined as -IOCS16 in ATA-2 but is no longer used.

The 2.5-inch drives found in notebook/laptop-size computers and in server blades typically use a smaller, unitized 50-pin header connector with pins spaced only 2.0mm apart. The main 40-pin part of the connector is the same as the standard PATA connector (except for the physical pin spacing), but there are added pins for power and jumpering. The cable that plugs in to this connector typically has 44 pins, carrying power as well as the standard ATA signals. The jumper pins usually have a jumper on them (the jumper position controls cable select, master, or slave settings). Figure 6.4 shows the unitized 50-pin connector used on the 2.5-inch PATA drives in laptop and notebook computers and in server blades.

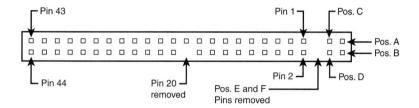

Figure 6.4   50-pin unitized PATA connector detail (used on 2.5-inch notebook/laptop/server blade PATA drives with a 44-pin cable).

Note the jumper pins at positions A–D and that the pins at positions E and F are removed. A jumper is usually placed between positions B and D to set the drive for cable select operation. On this connector, pin 41 provides +5V power to the drive logic (circuit board), pin 42 provides +5V power to the motor (2.5-inch drives use 5V motors, unlike larger drives that typically use 12V motors), and pin 43 provides a power ground. The last pin (44) is reserved and not used.

Table 6.3 shows the 50-pin unitized PATA interface connector pinout, which is used on most 2.5-inch (laptop or notebook computer/server blade) drives.

Table 6.3   50-Pin Unitized PATA 2.5-Inch (Notebook/Laptop/Server Blade Drive) Connector Pinout

Signal Name	Pin	Pin	Signal Name
Jumper pin	A	B	Jumper pin
Jumper pin	C	D	Jumper pin
KEY (pin missing)	E	F	KEY (pin missing)
-RESET[1]	1	2	GROUND
Data Bit 7	3	4	Data Bit 8
Data Bit 6	5	6	Data Bit 9
Data Bit 5	7	8	Data Bit 10
Data Bit 4	9	10	Data Bit 11
Data Bit 3	11	12	Data Bit 12
Data Bit 2	13	14	Data Bit 13
Data Bit 1	15	16	Data Bit 14
Data Bit 0	17	18	Data Bit 15
GROUND	19	20	KEY (pin missing)
DRQ 3	21	22	GROUND
-IOW	23	24	GROUND

Table 6.3   Continued

Signal Name	Pin	Pin	Signal Name
-IOR	25	26	GROUND
I/O CH RDY	27	28	CSEL
-DACK 3	29	30	GROUND
IRQ 14	31	32	Reserved
Address Bit 1	33	34	-PDIAG
Address Bit 0	35	36	Address Bit 2
-CS1FX	37	38	-CS3FX
-DA/SP	39	40	GROUND
+5V (Logic)	41	42	+5V (Motor)
GROUND	43	44	Reserved

[1]*Note that a - preceding a signal name (such as with -RESET) indicates that the signal is "active low."*

Not All Cables and Connectors Are Keyed

Many lower-cost board and cable manufacturers leave out the keying; this was particularly true with the now-outdated 40-conductor ATA cables. Cheaper motherboards often don't have pin 20 removed on their ATA connectors; consequently, they don't supply a cable with pin 20 blocked. If they don't use a shrouded connector with a notch and a corresponding protrusion on the cable connector, no keying exists, and the cables can be inserted backward. Fortunately, in most cases, the only consequence of this is that the device won't work until the cable is attached with the correct orientation.

Note that some systems do not display any video until the ATA drives respond to a spin-up command, which they can't receive if the cable is connected backward. So, if you connect an unkeyed ATA drive to your computer, turn on the computer, and it seems as if the system is locked up (you don't see anything onscreen), you should check the ATA cable. (See Figure 6.6, later in this chapter, for examples of unkeyed and keyed ATA cables.)

In rare situations in which you are mixing and matching items, you might encounter a cable with pin 20 blocked (as it should be) and a board with pin 20 still present. In that case, you can break off pin 20 from the board—or for the more squeamish, remove the block from the cable or replace the cable with one without the blocked pin. Some cables have the block permanently installed as a part of the connector housing, in which case you must use a different cable or break off pin 20 on the board or device end.

The simple rule of thumb is that pin 1 should be oriented toward the power connector on the device, which normally corresponds to the stripe on the cable.

PATA I/O Cables

A 40-conductor ribbon cable is specified to carry signals between the bus adapter circuits and the drive (controller). To maximize signal integrity and eliminate potential timing and noise problems, the cable should not be longer than 18-inches, although testing shows that 80-conductor cables up to 27 inches in length can be used reliably.

Note that ATA drives supporting the higher-speed transfer modes, such as programmed I/O (PIO) Mode 4 or any of the UDMA modes, are especially susceptible to cable integrity problems and cables that are too long. If the cable is too long, you can experience data corruption and other maddening errors. This is manifested in problems reading from or writing to the drive. In addition, any drive that uses UDMA Mode 5 (66MBps transfer rate), Mode 6 (100MBps transfer rate), or Mode 7 (133MBps transfer rate) must use a special, higher-quality 80-conductor cable; the extra conductors are grounds to reduce noise. You should also use this type of cable if your drive is running at UDMA Mode 2 (33MBps) or slower because it can't hurt and can only help. It's a good idea to keep a high-quality 80-conductor ATA cable in your toolbox for testing drives where you suspect cable integrity or cable length problems. Figure 6.5 shows the typical ATA cable layout and dimensions.

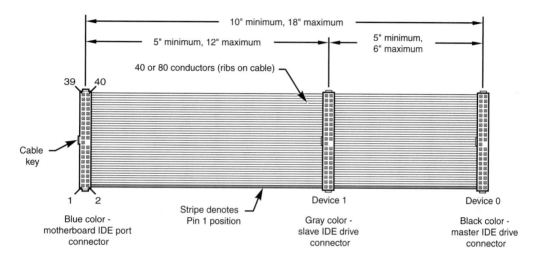

Figure 6.5   PATA (IDE) cable, with 40-pin connectors and either 40- or 80-conductor cables. (Additional wires are grounded in 80-conductor versions.)

Note

Most 40-conductor cables do not color-code the connectors, whereas virtually all 80-conductor cables do color-code the connectors.

Two primary variations of PATA cables are used today: one with 40 conductors and one with 80 conductors (see Figure 6.6). Both use 40-pin connectors, and the additional wires in the 80-conductor version are simply wired to ground. The additional conductors are designed to reduce noise and interference and are required when setting the interface to run at 66MBps (ATA/66) or faster. The drive and host adapter are designed to disable the higher-speed ATA/66, ATA/100, or ATA/133 modes if an 80-conductor cable is not detected. In such cases, you might see a warning message when you start your computer if an ATA/66 or faster drive is connected to a 40-conductor cable. The 80-conductor cable can also be used at lower speeds; although this is unnecessary, it improves the signal integrity. Therefore, it is the recommended version, no matter which drive you use.

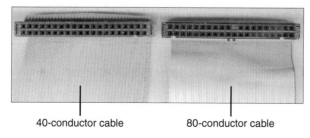

40-conductor cable   80-conductor cable

Figure 6.6   40-conductor (left) and 80-conductor (right) PATA cables.

Note

How do you tell an 80-conductor cable from a 40-conductor cable? Each conductor in a ribbon cable can be seen as a rib or ridge in the cable. You need to count the ridges (conductors) in the cable. If you count only 40, it must be a 40-conductor cable, and if you count to 80, well…you get the idea. If you observe the two cables side-by-side, the difference is clear: The 80-conductor cable has an obviously smoother, less ridged appearance than the 40-conductor cable.

Note in Figure 6.6 that the keying on the 80-conductor cable is designed to prevent backward installation. Note also that the poorly constructed 40-conductor cable shown in this example lacks keying. Most good 40-conductor cables include the keying; however, because it is optional, many cheaply constructed versions do not include it. Keying was made mandatory for all 80-conductor cables as part of the standard.

Longer Cables and Rounded Cables

The official PATA standard limits cable length to 18 inches; however, many of these cables that are sold are longer, up to even 36 inches or more in length. Why would people sell cables longer than 18 inches if the standard doesn't allow it? Well, just because something is for sale doesn't mean it conforms to the standards and will work properly.

Improperly designed, poorly manufactured, and nonconforming items are for sale all the time. Still, many people have used the longer cables, and their systems seem to work fine, but there have also been numerous cases in which using longer cables has caused problems.

It turns out that you can use longer 80-conductor cables reliably up to 27 inches in length, but 40-conductor cables should remain limited to 18 inches, just as the standard indicates. In fact, an attempt was made to change the PATA standard to allow 27-inch cables. Read www.t13.org/technical/e00151r0.pdf, and you'll see data from a proposal that shows "negligible differences in Ultra DMA Mode 5 signal integrity between a 27-inch, 80-conductor cable and an 18-inch, 80-conductor cable." This extended cable design was actually proposed in October 2000, but it was never incorporated into the standard. Even though it was never officially approved, the information presented in this proposal is empirical evidence for allowing the use of 80-conductor cables up to 27 inches in length.

Regardless of their length, in general you should not use "rounded" ATA cables. A rounded design is popular with case modders working on high-performance desktop PCs, but it has not been approved in the ATA standard, and there is some evidence that these cables can cause problems with cross-talk and noise. The design of 80-conductor cables is such that a ground wire is interspersed between each data wire in the ribbon, and rounding the cable causes some of the data lines to run parallel or adjacent to each other at random, thereby causing cross-talk and noise and resulting in signal errors. Signal errors are unacceptable in a mission-critical environment such as a server.

There is an interview with Rahul Sood, the chief technology officer of Voodoo PC (www.voodoopc.com), a popular system builder, in the March 2004 issue of *CPU* (www.computerpoweruser.com). In the *CPU* interview, Sood said, "I don't agree with rounded cables, I never have. SATA cables are great, of course, but rounded [PATA] cables are a different story because there is potential for noise. Any benchmarks that I've run on any of the rounded cables that we've tested show either errors generating over time or they're slower than good quality flat IDE cables."

Of course, many people are using rounded cables with success, but electrical engineers and the ATA standard don't encourage their use. It is best to stick with 80-conductor ribbon cables of 27 inches or less in length.

Tip

If you are concerned about the airflow problems that can result from flat cables, you can try these two solutions:

■ Carefully fold (but do not crease!) ATA cables to reduce excess length after you install them and secure the folded section with a nylon cable tie.

■ Replace PATA drives with SATA drives, which use a very small rounded cable natively.

PATA Signals

This section describes in more detail some of the most important PATA signals having to do with drive configuration and installation. Understanding these signals is important in understanding how the drive operates and, in turn, understanding how the cable select feature works, for example.

As mentioned earlier in this chapter, pin 20 is used as a key pin for cable orientation, and it is not connected to the interface. This pin should be missing from any ATA connectors, and the cable should have the pin 20 hole in the connector plugged off to prevent the cable from being plugged in backward.

Pin 39 carries the drive active/slave present (DASP) signal, which is a dual-purpose, time-multiplexed signal. During power-on initialization, this signal indicates whether a slave drive is present on the interface. After that, each drive asserts the signal to indicate that it is active. Early drives could not multiplex these functions and required special jumper settings to work with other drives. Standardizing this function to allow for compatible dual-drive installations is one of the features of the ATA standard. This is why some drives require a slave present (SP) jumper, whereas others do not.

Pin 28 carries the cable select (CSEL) signal. In some older drives, it could also carry a spindle synchronization (SPSYNC) signal, but that is not commonly found on newer drives. The CSEL function is the most widely used and is designed to control the designation of a drive as master (drive 0) or slave (drive 1), without requiring jumper settings on the drives. If a drive sees the CSEL as being grounded, the drive is a master; if CSEL is open, the drive is a slave.

Standard 80-wire cables support CSEL. The connector at the far end of the cable from the host adapter connection has the CSEL line connected through, indicating a master drive; the connector at the middle of the cable has the CSEL line open (showing that the conductor is interrupted or removed), making the drive at that end the slave.

PATA Dual-Drive Configurations

Dual-drive PATA installations can be problematic because each drive has its own controller, and both controllers must function while being connected to the same bus. There has to be a way to ensure that only one of the two controllers will respond to a command at a time.

The ATA standard provides the option of operating on the AT bus with two drives in a daisy-chained configuration. The primary drive (drive 0) is called the *master*, and the secondary drive (drive 1) is called the *slave*. You designate a drive as being master or slave by setting a jumper or switch on the drive or by using a special line in the interface called the *cable select (CS or CSEL) pin* and setting the CS/CSEL jumper on the drive.

When only one drive is installed, the controller responds to all commands from the system. When two drives (and, therefore, two controllers) are installed, both controllers receive all commands from the system. Each controller must then be set up to respond only to commands for itself. In this situation, one controller must be designated as the master and the other as the slave. When the system sends a command for a specific drive, the controller on the other drive must remain silent while the selected controller and drive are functioning. When you set the jumper to master or slave, you can also enable discrimination between the two controllers by setting a special bit (the DRV bit) in the drive/head register of a command block.

Configuring ATA drives can be simple, which is the case with most single-drive installations. Or it can be troublesome, especially when it comes to mixing two (primarily older) drives from different manufacturers on a single cable.

Most ATA drives can be configured with four possible settings:

- Master, single-drive
- Master, dual-drive
- Slave, dual-drive
- Cable select

Many drives simplify this to three settings: master, slave, and cable select. Because each ATA drive has its own controller, you must specifically tell one drive to be the master and the other to be the slave. No functional difference exists between the two, except that the drive that's specified as the slave will assert a DASP signal after a system reset informs the master that a slave drive is present in the system. The master drive then pays attention to the drive select line, which it otherwise ignores. Telling a drive that it's the slave also usually causes it to delay its spin-up for several seconds to allow the master to get going and thus to lessen the load on the system's power supply.

Until the ATA specification, no common implementation for drive configuration was in use. Some drive companies even used different master/slave methods for different models of drives. Because of these incompatibilities, some drives work together only in a specific master/slave or slave/master order. This situation mostly affects older IDE drives introduced before the ATA specification, but it has been known to take place with certain combinations of newer ATA drives.

Most drives that fully follow the ATA specification now need only one jumper (master/slave) for configuration. A few also need a slave present jumper, as well. Table 6.4 shows the jumper settings required by most ATA drives.

Table 6.4   Jumper Settings for Most ATA-Compatible Drives on Standard (Non–Cable Select) Cables

Jumper Name	Single Drive	Dual-Drive Master	Dual-Drive Slave
Master (M/S)	On	On	Off
Slave present (SP)	Off	On	Off
Cable select (CS/CSEL)	Off	Off	Off

Note

If a CS cable is used, the CS jumper should be set to On, and all others should be set to Off. The cable connector then determines which drive will be master or slave.

Figure 6.7 shows the jumpers on a typical ATA drive.

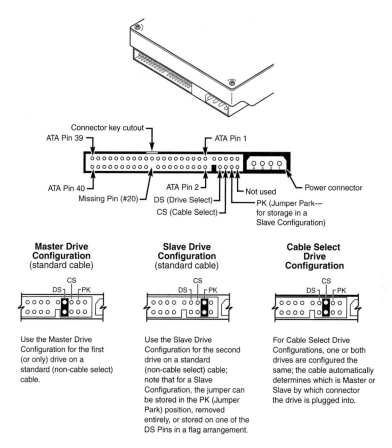

Figure 6.7 PATA (IDE) drive jumpers for most drives.

The master jumper indicates that the drive is a master or a slave. Some drives also require a slave present jumper, which is used only in a dual-drive setup and is installed only on the master drive—which is somewhat confusing. This jumper tells the master that a slave drive is attached. With many PATA drives, the master jumper is optional and can be left off. Installing this jumper doesn't hurt in these cases and can eliminate confusion; you should install the jumpers listed here. Note that most Western Digital drives have a fourth jumper option: single drive. This is actually a "no-jumper" configuration in which the jumper is removed or parked across two pins horizontally so no circuit is completed. Western Digital drives that specify removing the jumper in a single-drive configuration do not work properly if the master jumper is applied. However, in a dual-drive configuration, the jumpers on Western Digital drives work as listed in Table 6.4.

Note

Some drives have these jumpers on the drive circuit board on the bottom of the drive, and they therefore might not be visible on the rear. Some vendors provide a jumper guide on the top of the drive, while others require you to look up the jumpering in drive documentation.

To eliminate confusion over master/slave settings, most newer systems now use the cable select option. Cable select requires an 80-wire UDMA cable (these cables have all the wires except pin 28 running from the motherboard connector to both drive connectors. Pin 28 is used for cable select and is connected to one of the drive connectors (labeled master) and not to the other (labeled slave). Both drives are then configured in cable select mode via the CS jumper on each drive.

With cable select, the drive that receives signals on pin 28 automatically becomes the master, and the other becomes the slave. Most cables implement this by removing the metal insulation displacement bit from the pin-28 hole, which can be difficult to see at a glance. Other cables have a section of pin 28 visibly cut from the cable somewhere along the ribbon. Because this is such a minor modification to the cable and can be difficult to see, cable select cables typically have the connectors labeled master, slave, and system, indicating that the cable controls these options rather than the drive. All 80-conductor Ultra ATA cables are designed to use cable select.

With cable select, you simply set the CS jumper on all drives and then plug the drive you want to be the master in to the connector labeled master on the cable, and you plug the drive you want to be the slave in to the connector labeled slave.

The only downside to using cable select is that it can restrict how the cable is routed or where you mount the drive that is to be master versus slave because they must be plugged in to specific cable connector positions.

Caution

Although it's possible to connect two PATA or ATAPI drives to the same PATA host adapter, you should not connect a tape backup drive or optical drive to the same host adapter as the hard disk. PATA isn't as intelligent an interface as SCSI, and connecting drives that will be used at the same time to the same host adapter limits read and write throughput. However, it's okay to connect drives that will not be used at the same time, such as a tape backup and an optical drive, to the same PATA host adapter.

PATA PIO Transfer Modes

ATA-2 and ATA-3 defined the first of several higher-performance PIO modes for transferring data over the PATA interface, to and from the drive. These faster modes were the main part of the newer specifications and were the main reason they were initially developed.

The PIO mode determines how fast data is transferred to and from the drive, using PIO transfers. In the slowest possible mode—PIO Mode 0—the data cycle time can't exceed 600ns (nanoseconds). In a single cycle, 16 bits are transferred into or out of the drive, making the theoretical transfer rate of PIO Mode 0 (600ns cycle time) 3.3MBps, whereas PIO Mode 4 (120ns cycle time) achieves a 16.6MBps transfer rate.

Table 6.5 shows the PIO modes, with their respective transfer rates.

Table 6.5   PIO Modes and Transfer Rates[1]

PIO Mode	Bus Width (Bits)	Cycle Speed (ns)	Bus Speed (MHz)	Cycles per Clock	Transfer Rate (MBps)	ATA Specification
0	16	600	1.67	1	3.33	ATA-1
1	16	383	2.61	1	5.22	ATA-1
2	16	240	4.17	1	8.33	ATA-1
3	16	180	5.56	1	11.11	ATA-2[2]
4	16	120	8.33	1	16.67	ATA-2

[1]*Key: ns = nanoseconds and MB = megabytes.*

[2]*ATA-2 was also referred to as EIDE (Enhanced IDE) or Fast ATA.*

Most motherboards with ATA-2 or greater support incorporate dual ATA connectors. Most of the motherboard chipsets include the ATA interface in their South Bridge components, which in most systems is tied to the PCI bus.

When interrogated with an `Identify Drive` command, a hard disk returns, among other things, information about the PIO and DMA modes it is capable of using. Most enhanced BIOSs automatically set the correct mode to match the capabilities of the drive. If you set a mode faster than the drive can handle, data corruption results.

ATA-2 and newer drives also perform Block Mode PIO, which means they use the `Read Multiple` and `Write Multiple` commands, which greatly reduce the number of interrupts sent to the host processor. This lowers the overhead, and the resulting transfers are even faster.

PATA DMA Transfer Modes

ATA drives also support *direct memory access (DMA)* transfers. Unlike with PIO, DMA transfers, are performed directly between drive and memory, without using the CPU as an intermediary. This has the effect of offloading much of the work of transferring data from the processor, in effect allowing the processor to do other things while the transfer is taking place.

There are two distinct types of DMA: single-word (8-bit) and multiword (16-bit) DMA. Single-word DMA modes were removed from the ATA-3 and later specifications and are obsolete. DMA modes are also sometimes called *busmaster* ATA modes because they use a host adapter that supports busmastering. Ordinary DMA relies on the legacy DMA controller on the motherboard to perform the complex task of arbitration, grabbing the system bus and transferring the data. In the case of busmastering DMA, all this is done by a higher-speed logic chip in the host adapter interface (which is also on the motherboard).

Systems that use the Intel PIIX (PCI IDE ISA eXcelerator) and later South Bridge chips (or third-party equivalents) have the capability of supporting busmaster ATA. The single-word and double-word busmaster ATA modes and transfer rates are shown in Tables 6.6 and 6.7.

Table 6.6   Single-Word (8-bit) DMA Modes and Transfer Rates

8-bit DMA Mode	Bus Width (Bits)	Cycle Speed (ns)	Bus Speed (MHz)	Cycles per Clock	Transfer Rate (MBps)	ATA Specification
0	16	960	1.04	1	2.08	ATA-1[1]
1	16	480	2.08	1	4.17	ATA-1[1]
2	16	240	4.17	1	8.33	ATA-1[1]

[1]Single-word (8-bit) DMA modes were removed from the ATA-3 and later specifications.

Table 6.7   Multiword (16-bit) DMA Modes and Transfer Rates

16-bit DMA Mode	Bus Width (Bits)	Cycle Speed (ns)	Bus Speed (MHz)	Cycles per Clock	Transfer Rate (MBps)	ATA Specification
0	16	480	2.08	1	4.17	ATA-1
1	16	150	6.67	1	13.33	ATA-2[1]
2	16	120	8.33	1	16.67	ATA-2[1]

[1]ATA-2 was also referred to as EIDE (Enhanced IDE) or Fast ATA.

Note that double-word DMA modes are also called busmaster DMA modes by some manufacturers. Unfortunately, even the fastest double-word DMA Mode 2 results in the same 16.67MBps transfer speed as PIO Mode 4. However, even though the transfer speed is the same as that of PIO, because DMA offloads much of the work from the processor, overall system performance is higher. Even so, multiword DMA modes were never very popular and have been superseded by the newer UDMA modes supported in devices that are compatible with ATA-4 through ATA-7.

Table 6.8 shows the UDMA modes now supported in the ATA-4 through ATA-7 specifications. Note that in order to use this feature, you need to install the correct drivers for your host adapter and version of Windows.

Table 6.8   UDMA Support in ATA-4 Through ATA-7[1]

UDMA Mode	Bus Width (Bits)	Cycle Speed (ns)	Bus Speed (MHz)	Cycles per Clock	Transfer Rate (MBps)	ATA Specification
0	16	240	4.17	2	16.67	ATA-4
1	16	160	6.25	2	25.00	ATA-4
2	16	120	8.33	2	33.33	ATA-4
3	16	90	11.11	2	44.44	ATA-5
4	16	60	16.67	2	66.67	ATA-5
5	16	40	25.00	2	100.00	ATA-6
6	16	30	33.00	2	133.00	ATA-7

[1]*ATA-4 UDMA Mode 2 is sometimes called Ultra ATA/33 or ATA-33, ATA-5 UDMA Mode 4 is sometimes called Ultra ATA/66 or ATA-66, ATA-6 UDMA Mode 5 is sometimes called Ultra ATA/100 or ATA-100, and ATA-7 UDMA Mode 6 is sometimes called Ultra ATA/133 or ATA-133.*

Note that hardly any systems ever supported the 44.44Mbps UDMA Mode 3 transfer rate and that UDMA Mode 4 and higher transfer rates require 80-conductor cables.

Some of the older UMDA Mode 4 and UDMA Mode 5 drives require you to run a special utility to configure the drive to run at UDMA Mode 4 or faster speeds. For details, see the documentation for your hard disk drive.

SATA

Although ATA8-APT is a forthcoming PATA drive standard, it contains no improvements in performance over ATA-7. Sending data at rates faster than 133MBps down a parallel ribbon cable is fraught with all kinds of problems because of signal timing, electromagnetic interference (EMI), and other integrity problems. The solution is SATA, which is an evolutionary replacement for the venerable PATA physical storage interface. SATA is software-compatible with PATA, which means it fully emulates all the commands, registers, and controls so that existing software can run on the new architecture without any changes. In other words, the existing BIOSs, operating systems, and utilities that work on PATA also work on SATA.

Of course, PATA and SATA do differ physically—that is, you can't plug PATA drives in to SATA host adapters and vice versa unless you use a signal converter. The physical changes are all for the better because SATA uses much smaller and thinner cables, with only seven conductors, that are easier to route inside the PC and easier to plug in, with smaller, redesigned cable connectors. The interface chip designs are also improved, with far fewer pins and lower voltages. These improvements are all designed to eliminate the design problems inherent in PATA.

Figure 6.8 shows the official SATA-IO logo used to identify most SATA devices.

Figure 6.8 The SATA-IO official logo, which is used to identify SATA devices.

Although SATA won't immediately replace PATA, most new servers and server motherboards include SATA interfaces alongside PATA interfaces. In many cases, the traditional duo of PATA host adapters is reduced to one, while two or more SATA host adapters are used. Eventually, SATA will replace PATA as the de facto standard internal storage device interface found in servers. As current motherboard designs indicate, the transition from ATA to SATA is a gradual one, and during this transition, PATA capabilities will continue to be available. With more than a 10-year history, PATA devices will likely continue to be available even after most servers have switched to SATA. Because of the higher native performance and greater growth potential of SATA, some servers now feature SATA interfaces in place of SCSI interfaces.

Development for SATA started when the SATA Working Group effort was announced at the Intel Developer Forum in February 2000. The initial members of the SATA Working Group included APT Technologies, Dell, IBM, Intel, Maxtor, Quantum, and Seagate. The first SATA 1.0 draft specification was released in November 2000 and was officially published as a final specification in August 2001. The SATA II extensions to this specification, which make SATA suitable for network storage, were released in October 2002.

The SATA Working Group was incorporated in July 2004 into the SATA-IO. SATA-related standards and draft standards can be downloaded from www.sata-io.com. Note that the specification formerly known as SATA II is now known as Extensions to SATA 1.0a; see the SATA-IO website for the latest revision.

Systems using SATA were first released in late 2002; they used discrete PCI interface boards and chips. SATA was finally integrated directly into the motherboard chipset in April 2003, with the introduction of the Intel ICH5 (I/O controller hub) chipset component. Since then, most new desktop and server motherboard chipsets have included SATA.

The performance of SATA is impressive, although current hard drive designs can't fully take advantage of its bandwidth. Three variations of the standard have been proposed, and they all use the same cables and connectors; they differ only in transfer rate performance. Currently, only the first two speeds are available, with higher speeds coming in the future. Table 6.9 shows the specifications for the current and future proposed SATA versions; the next-generation 300MBps version was introduced in 2005, and the 600MBps version is expected in 2007.

Table 6.9   SATA Transfer Modes

Serial ATA Type	Signal Rate (GBps)	Bus Width (bits)	Bus Speed (MHz)	Data Cycles per Clock	Bandwidth (MBps)
SATA-150	1.5	1	1,500	1	150
SATA-300	3.0	1	3,000	1	300
SATA-600	6.0	1	6,000	1	600

Note

Extensions to Serial ATA 1.0a (formerly called SATA II) is not the same as SATA 3GB/sec. While 3GB/sec is the standard transfer rate for Extensions to SATA 1.0a, other parts of the extended specifications might or might not be supported by a particular drive. See "ATA8-AST," p. 429, for more about extended SATA specifications.

From Table 6.9, you can see that SATA sends data only a single bit at a time. The cable used has only seven wires (four signal and three ground) and is a very thin design, with keyed connectors only 14mm (0.55-inch) wide on each end. This eliminates problems with airflow compared to the wider PATA ribbon cables. Each cable has connectors only at each end, and each cable connects the device directly to the host adapter (typically on the motherboard). There are no master/slave settings because each cable supports only a single device. The cable ends are interchangeable; the connector on the motherboard is the same as on the device, and both cable ends are identical. Maximum SATA cable length is 1 meter, which is considerably longer than the 18-inch maximum for PATA. Even with this thinner, longer, and less-expensive cable, you initially get transfer rates of 150MBps (nearly 13% greater than those of PATA/133). Extensions to SATA 1.0a supports 300MBps, and even 600MBps is possible.

SATA uses a special encoding scheme called *8B/10B* to encode and decode data sent along the cable. The 8B/10B transmission code was originally developed (and patented) by IBM in the early 1980s for use in high-speed data communications. This encoding scheme is now used by many high-speed data transmission standards, including Gigabit Ethernet, Fibre Channel, and FireWire. The main purpose of the 8B/10B encoding scheme is to guarantee that there are never more than four 0s (or 1s) transmitted consecutively. This is a form of run length limited (RLL) encoding called RLL 0,4, in which the 0 represents the minimum and the 4 represents the maximum number of consecutive 0s in each encoded character.

8B/10B encoding also ensures that there are never more than six or fewer than four 0s (or 1s) in a single encoded 10-bit character. Because 1s and 0s are sent as voltage changes on a wire, this ensures that the spacing between the voltage transitions sent by the transmitter is fairly balanced, with a more regular and steady stream of pulses. This presents a steadier load on the circuits, increasing reliability. The conversion from 8-bit data to 10-bit encoded characters for transmission leaves several 10-bit patterns unused. Many of these additional patterns are used to provide flow control, delimit packets of data, perform error checking, or perform other special functions.

SATA Cables and Connectors

The physical transmission scheme for SATA uses *differential NRZ (nonreturn to zero)*. This uses a balanced pair of wires, each carrying ±0.25V. The signals are sent differentially: If one wire in the pair carries +0.25V, the other wire carries –0.25V, where the differential voltage between the two wires is always 0.5V. So, for a given voltage waveform, the opposite voltage waveform is sent along the adjacent wire. Differential transmission minimizes electromagnetic radiation and makes the signals easier to read on the receiving end.

A 15-pin power cable and power connector is optional with SATA, providing 3.3V power in addition to the 5V and 12V provided via the industry-standard 4-pin device power connectors. Although it has 15 pins, this new power connector design is only 24mm in diameter. With 3 pins designated for each of the 3.3V, 5V, and 12V power levels, enough capacity exists for up to 4.5 amps of current at each voltage, which is plenty for even the most power-hungry drives. For compatibility with existing power supplies, SATA drives can be made with the original, standard 4-pin device power connector or the new 15-pin SATA power connector—or both. If the drive doesn't have the type of connector you need, you can get an adapter to convert from one type to the other.

Figure 6.9 shows what SATA signal and power connectors look like.

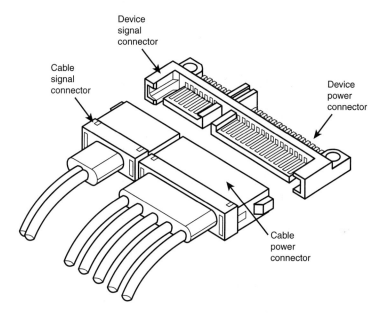

Figure 6.9   SATA signal and power connectors on a typical SATA hard drive.

Figure 6.10 shows SATA and PATA host adapters on a typical motherboard.

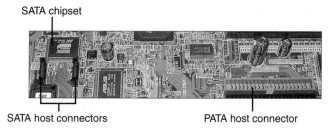

Figure 6.10   A motherboard with SATA and PATA host adapters.

The pinouts for the SATA data and optional power connectors are shown in Tables 6.10 and 6.11, respectively.

Table 6.10   SATA Data Connector Pinout[1,2]

Signal Pin	Signal	Description
S1	Gnd	First mate
S2	A+	Host Transmit +
S3	A-	Host Transmit -
S4	Gnd	First mate
S5	B-	Host Receive -
S6	B+	Host Receive +
S7	Gnd	First mate

[1]All pins are in a single row, spaced 1.27mm apart.

[2]All ground pins are longer so they will make contact before the signal/power pins to allow hot plugging.

Table 6.11   SATA Optional Power Connector Pinout[1-3]

Power Pin	Signal	Description
P1	+3.3V	3.3V power
P2	+3.3V	3.3V power
P3	+3.3V	3.3V power
P4	Gnd	First mate
P5	Gnd	First mate
P6	Gnd	First mate
P7	+5V	5V power
P8	+5V	5V power
P9	+5V	5V power
P10	Gnd	First mate
P11	Gnd	First mate
P12	Gnd	First mate
P13	+12V	12V power
P14	+12V	12V power
P15	+12V	12V power

[1]All pins are in a single row, spaced 1.27mm (.050-inch) apart.

[2]All ground pins are longer so they will make contact before the signal/power pins to allow hot plugging.

[3]Three power pins are used to carry 4.5 amps, the maximum current for each voltage.

SATA Configuration

Configuring SATA devices is also much simpler than configuring PATA devices because the master/slave or cable select jumper settings used with PATA are not necessary.

BIOS Setup for SATA drives is also quite simple. Because SATA is based on ATA, autodetection of drive settings on systems with SATA connectors is performed in the same way as on PATA systems.

Depending on the system, SATA interfaces might be enabled by default or might need to be enabled in the BIOS Setup program.

◀◀ See "The Integrated Device Configuration Submenu," p. 301.

Although add-on SATA host adapters and converters for connecting PATA drives to SATA motherboards are available for desktop PCs, they aren't recommended for servers because these adapters can fail or become disconnected from SATA data cables. This problem can lead to lower reliability, something most server environments cannot afford to leave to chance.

Most recent servers and server motherboards now feature two or more integrated SATA host adapters.

ATA8-AST

As with PATA, SATA was designed to be the primary storage interface used inside a PC and was not initially designed to be used as an external interface. However, with the Extensions to SATA 1.0a (formerly known as SATA II)—and also known as ATA8-AST—now under development, SATA will evolve to include external connections, storage enclosures with multiple drives, and port multipliers that allow up to 15 SATA drives to be connected to a single SATA port. The external connection is designed to support four lanes, with 300MBps per lane, for a total of 1200MBps. This competes with external SCSI for RAID enclosures but most likely won't compete with general-purpose high-speed external device interfaces, such as USB 2.0 and IEEE 1394 (i.LINK/FireWire). Because of the lower cost and smaller size of the internal cables, there is little doubt that SATA will replace PATA in both desktop and laptop systems over the next few years. It could also become common in servers as another way to connect high-performance external drives.

You don't need to wait for ATA8-AST to be formally adopted to enjoy some of its benefits. Some current SATA hardware supports the following ATA8-AST features:

- Native command queuing
- A 300MBps maximum transfer rate
- Hot-swapping

Note that both the host adapter and drive must support a particular ATA8-AST feature in order for it to be used.

Advanced Host Controller Interface

SATA was designed not only as a replacement for PATA but also as an interface that would evolve into something with many more capabilities and features than its predecessor. Initially, compatibility with PATA was one of the most important features of SATA because it enabled a smooth and easy transition from one to the other. This compatibility extends to the driver level, allowing SATA devices to use the same BIOS-level drivers and software as legacy PATA devices.

Although the intent of SATA was to allow an easy transition from PATA, it was also designed to allow future growth and expansion of capabilities. To accomplish this, an enhanced software interface called the Advanced Host Controller Interface (AHCI) was initially developed by the AHCI Contributor Group, a group chaired by Intel and originally consisting of AMD, Dell, Marvell, Maxtor, Microsoft, Red Hat, Seagate, and StorageGear. The AHCI Contributor Group released a preliminary version of AHCI v0.95 in May 2003 and released the final specification in 2004.

AHCI provides a standard, high-performance interface to system driver/operating system software for discovering and implementing such advanced SATA features as command queuing, hot-swapping, and power management. AHCI was integrated into SATA-supporting chipsets in 2004 and is supported by AHCI drivers for Windows. ACHI features are included in ATA8-AST.

SATA Transfer Modes

SATA transfers data in a completely different manner from PATA. As indicated previously, the transfer rates are 150MBps, 300MBps, and 600MBps, with most drives today using the 150MBps rate. However, because SATA is designed to be backward compatible with PATA, some confusion can result because SATA drives can report and emulate PATA mode settings for backward compatibility.

For example, many motherboards detect and report a SATA drive as supporting UDMA Mode 5 (ATA/100), which is a PATA mode that operates at 100MBps. This is obviously incorrect because even the slowest SATA mode (SATA-150) is 150MBps, and UDMA modes simply do not apply to SATA drives.

PATA and SATA are completely different electrical and physical specifications, but SATA does *emulate* PATA in a way that makes it completely software transparent. In fact, the PATA emulation in SATA specifically conforms to the ATA-5 specification.

This is especially apparent in the IDENTIFY DEVICE command used by the autodetect routines in the BIOS to read the drive parameters. The SATA specification indicates that many of the items returned by IDENTIFY DEVICE are to be set as indicated for ATA-5/ATAPI, including available UDMA modes and settings.

SATA was designed to be fully software compatible with ATA-5/ATAPI, which is why a SATA drive can report in some ways as if it were PATA or running in PATA modes, even though it isn't.

ATA Features

The ATA standards have gone a long way toward eliminating incompatibilities and problems with interfacing IDE drives to ISA/PCI bus systems. The ATA specifications define the signals on the 40-pin connector, the functions and timings of these signals, cable specifications, and so on. The following sections cover ATA commands; the host protected area used for system recovery software; and ATAPI interfacing for optical, removable-media, and tape drives.

ATA Commands

One of the best features of the ATA interface is the enhanced command set. The ATA interface was modeled after the WD1003 controller that IBM used in the original AT system. All ATA drives must support the original Western Digital (WD) command set (eight commands), with no exceptions, which is why ATA drives are so easy to install in systems today. All IBM-compatible systems have built-in ROM BIOS support for the WD1003, so they essentially support ATA as well.

In addition to supporting all the WD1003 commands, the ATA specification added numerous other commands to enhance performance and capabilities. These commands are an optional part of the ATA interface, but several of them are used in most drives available today and are very important to the performance and use of ATA drives in general.

Perhaps the most important is the Identify Drive command. This command causes the drive to transmit a 512-byte block of data that provides all details about the drive. Through this command, any program (including the system BIOS) can find out exactly which type of drive is connected, including the drive manufacturer, the model number, the operating parameters, and even the serial number of the drive. Many modern BIOSes use this information to automatically receive and enter the drive's parameters into CMOS memory, eliminating the need for the user to enter these parameters manually during system configuration. This arrangement helps prevent mistakes that can later lead to data loss when the user no longer remembers what parameters he or she used during setup.

The Identify Drive data can tell you many things about your drive, including the following:

- The number of logical block addresses available, using LBA mode
- The number of physical cylinders, heads, and sectors available in P-CHS mode
- The number of logical cylinders, heads, and sectors in the current translation L-CHS mode
- The transfer modes (and speeds) supported
- The manufacturer and model number
- The internal firmware revision
- The serial number
- The buffer type/size, indicating sector buffering or caching capabilities

Two other important commands are Read Multiple and Write Multiple. These commands permit multiple-sector data transfers and, when combined with block-mode PIO capabilities in the system, can result in incredible data transfer rates that are many times faster than single-sector PIO transfers. Some older systems require you to select the correct number of sectors supported by the drive, but most recent systems automatically determine this information for you. Note that some BIOSs refer to Read Multiple as "block mode."

Many other enhanced commands are available, and there is even room for a given drive manufacturer to implement vendor-unique commands. Certain vendors often create such commands for their own unique features. Often, vendor-unique commands control features such as low-level formatting and defect management. This is why low-level format (LLF) programs can be so specific to a particular manufacturer's ATA drives and why many manufacturers make their own LLF programs available.

The Host Protected Area

Most PCs sold today include some form of automated product recovery or restoration feature that allows a user to easily restore the operating system and other software on the system to the state it was in when the system was new. Originally, this was accomplished via one or more product recovery CDs containing automated scripts that reinstalled all the software that came preinstalled on the system when it was new.

Unfortunately, the CDs could be lost or damaged, they were often problematic to use, and including them by default cost manufacturers a lot of money. This prompted PC manufacturers to move the recovery software to a hidden partition of the boot hard drive. Although this wastes some space on the drive, the recovery software normally fits on from one to four CDs, which occupies 1GB–3GB of drive space. With 60GB or larger drives, this amounts to 5% or less of the total space. Still, storing this information on the hidden partition was less than satisfactory because the partition could easily be damaged or overwritten by partitioning software or other utilities, so there was no way to make it secure.

In 1996, Gateway proposed a change to the ATA-4 standard under development that would allow a space called the *host protected area (HPA)* to be reserved on a drive. This change was ratified, and the HPA feature set was incorporated into the ATA-4 specification that was published in 1998. A separate BIOS firmware interface specification called Protected Area Run Time Interface Extension Services (PARTIES) was initiated in 1999 that defined services an operating system could use to access the HPA. The PARTIES standard was completed and published in 2001 as NCITS 346-2001, "Protected Area Run Time Interface Extension Services."

The HPA works by using the optional ATA SET MAX ADDRESS command to make the drive appear to the system as a slightly smaller drive. Anything from the new max address (that is, the newly reported end of the drive) to the true end of the drive is considered the HPA and is accessible only using PAR-TIES commands. This is more secure than having a hidden partition because any data past the end of the drive simply cannot be seen by any normal application, or even a partitioning utility such as PartitionMagic or Partition Commander. Still, if you want to remove the HPA, you can use some options in the BIOS Setup or separate commands to reset the max address, thus exposing the HPA. At that point, you can run a utility such as PartitionMagic or Partition Commander to resize the adjacent partition to include the extra space that was formerly hidden and unavailable.

Most new systems using Phoenix FirstBIOS come with their recovery software and diagnostics in the HPA because this is part of the new Phoenix FirstBIOS core managed environment (CME), which is used by a large number of OEMs (including IBM) on most desktop and laptop systems starting in 2003.

ATAPI

The ATAPI standard is designed to provide the commands necessary for devices such as CD-ROM and DVD drives, removable media drives such as SuperDisk and Zip drives, and tape drives that plug in to an ordinary ATA (IDE) connector. The principal advantage of ATAPI hardware is that it's cheap and works with your current adapter. All modern ATA CD-ROM drives support the ATAPI protocols, and generally the terms *ATA* and *ATAPI* are synonymous. In other words, an ATAPI CD-ROM is an ATA CD-ROM and vice versa.

Caution

Starting in 1998, most systems began supporting the Phoenix El Torito specification, which enables booting from ATAPI CD or DVD drives. Systems without El Torito support in the BIOS can't boot from an ATAPI CD or DVD drive. Even with ATAPI support in the BIOS, you must still load a driver to use ATAPI under DOS or Windows; an ATAPI driver is supplied with all recent Windows and Linux versions. Most recent server operating systems, including Windows 2000 Server and Windows Server 2003, include bootable CDs for easy installation.

You should normally keep ATA devices you will be accessing simultaneously on separate channels. Because ATA does not typically support overlapping access, when one drive is being accessed on a given channel, the other drive on the same channel can't be accessed. By keeping the CD-ROM or DVD drive and hard disk on separate channels, you can more effectively overlap accessing between them.

This is easy to do if your server uses SCSI or SATA hard disks for storage and has a single CD or DVD drive. The CD or DVD drive is the only ATA device in the system, so it cannot interfere with hard disk storage. However, this can be trickier on a server that uses ATA drives for both hard disk storage and optical drives. In such cases, you need to be sure to use one ATA host adapter for the hard disk and a separate one for the CD or DVD drive. If you are using PATA drives in a RAID array, they are connected to a special ATA host adapter designated as a RAID adapter. You can use the non-RAID ATA adapter for the CD or DVD drive.

If you must put a PATA hard disk and CD or DVD drive on the same cable, you should set PATA hard drives as masters (Device 0) and parallel ATAPI drives as slaves (Device 1).

ATA Drive Capacity Limitations

ATA interface versions up through ATA-5 suffered from a drive capacity limitation of about 137GB (billion bytes). Depending on the BIOS used, this limitation could be further reduced to 8.4GB, or even as low as 528MB. This is due to limitations in both the BIOS and the ATA interface, which, when combined, create even further limitations. To understand these limits, you have to look at the BIOS (software) and ATA (hardware) interfaces together.

Note

In addition to the BIOS/ATA limitations discussed in this section, various operating system limitations also exist, as described later in this chapter.

When dealing with ATA drives, you face limitations of the ATA interface itself as well as limitations of the BIOS interface used to talk to the drive. A summary of these limitations is shown in Table 6.12.

The following sections detail the differences between the various sector addressing methods and the limitations related to using them.

Prefixes for Decimal and Binary Multiples

You may be unfamiliar with the MiB (mebibyte), GiB (gibibyte), and so on designations used in this section and throughout the rest of the book. They are part of a standard designed to eliminate confusion between decimal- and binary-based multiples, especially in computer systems. Standard SI (system international, or metric system) units are based on multiples of 10. This worked well for most things, but not for computers, which operate in a binary world, where most numbers are based on powers of 2. This has resulted in different meanings being assigned to the same prefix; for example 1KB (kilobyte) could mean either 1,000 (10^3) bytes or 1,024 (2^{10}) bytes. To eliminate confusion, in December 1998 the International Electrotechnical Commission (IEC) approved as an international standard the prefix names and symbols for binary multiples used in data processing and transmission. Some of these prefixes are shown in Table 6.13.

Under the IEC standard terminology, 1MB (megabyte) would be 1,000,000 bytes, whereas 1MiB (mebibyte) would be 1,048,576 bytes.

Note

For more information on these industry-standard decimal and binary prefixes, check out the National Institute of Standards and Technology (NIST) website, at http://physics.nist.gov/cuu/Units/prefixes.html.

BIOS Limitations

Motherboard ROM BIOS has been updated throughout the years to support larger and larger drives. Table 6.14 shows the most important relative dates when drive capacity limits were changed.

Table 6.12   ATA/IDE Capacity Limitations for Various Sector Addressing Methods[1]

Sector Addressing Method	Total Sectors Calculation	Maximum Total Sectors
CHS: BIOS w/o TL	1024×16×63	1,032,192
CHS: BIOS w/bit-shift TL	1024×240×63	15,482,880
CHS: BIOS w/LBA-assist TL	1024×255×63	16,450,560
CHS: BIOS INT13h	1024×256×63	16,515,072
CHS: ATA-1/ATA-5	65536×16×255	267,386,880
LBA: ATA-1/ATA-5	2^{28}	268,435,456
LBA: ATA-6+	2^{48}	281,474,976,710,656
LBA: EDD BIOS	2^{64}	18,446,744,073,709,551,616

[1]*Key: BIOS = basic input/output system; CHS = cylinder head sector; LBA = logical block (sector) address; w/ = with; w/o = without; TL = translation; INT13h = interrupt 13 hex; EDD = Enhanced Disk Drive specification (Phoenix/ATA); MB = megabytes; MiB = mebibytes; GB = gigabytes; GiB = gibibytes; PB = petabyte; PiB = pebibytes; ZB = zettabytes; and ZiB = zebibytes.*

Table 6.13   Standard Prefix Names and Symbols for Binary Multiples

Decimal Prefixes

Factor	Symbol	Name	Value
10^3	K	Kilo	1,000
10^6	M	Mega	1,000,000
10^9	G	Giga	1,000,000,000
10^{12}	T	Tera	1,000,000,000,000
10^{15}	P	Peta	1,000,000,000,000,000
10^{18}	E	Exa	1,000,000,000,000,000,000
10^{21}	Z	Zetta	1,000,000,000,000,000,000,000

Table 6.14   Dates of Changes to Drive Capacity Limitations in the ROM BIOS

BIOS Date	Capacity Limit
August 1994	528MB
January 1998	8.4GB
September 2002	137GB

BIOSes dated September 2002 or newer should support drives larger than 137GB. Table 6.14 gives only general guidelines; to accurately determine the capacity limit for a specific system, you should check with your motherboard manufacturer. You can also use the BIOS Wizard utility at www.unicore.com/bioswiz/index2.html, which can tell you the BIOS date from your system and specifically whether your system supports the Enhanced Disk Drive (EDD) specification (which means drives over 8.4GB).

Maximum Capacity (Bytes)	Capacity (Decimal)	Capacity (Binary)
528,482,304	528.48MB	504.00MiB
7,927,234,560	7.93GB	7.38GiB
8,422,686,720	8.42GB	7.84GiB
8,455,716,864	8.46GB	7.88GiB
136,902,082,560	136.90GB	127.50GiB
137,438,953,472	137.44GB	128.00GiB
144,115,188,075,855,872	144.12PB	128.00PiB
9,444,732,965,739,290,427,392	9.44ZB	8.00ZiB

Binary Prefixes

Factor	Symbol	Name	Derivation	Value
2^{10}	Ki	Kibi	Kilobinary	1,024
2^{20}	Mi	Mebi	Megabinary	1,048,576
2^{30}	Gi	Gibi	Gigabinary	1,073,741,824
2^{40}	Ti	Tebi	Terabinary	1,099,511,627,776
2^{50}	Pi	Pebi	Petabinary	1,125,899,906,842,624
2^{60}	Ei	Exbi	Exabinary	1,152,921,504,606,846,976
2^{70}	Zi	Zebi	Zettabinary	1,180,591,620,717,411,303,424

Generally, any server currently in use should support at least the EDD (8.4GB–137GB) standard. You should upgrade the motherboard BIOS on a server that cannot support a hard disk greater than 8.4GB. Although other fixes such as using a BIOS upgrade card with onboard ATA/IDE ports or a software fix have been used on desktop systems, they are not suitable for servers.

Increasing ATA Drive Size: CHS and LBA Modes

There are two primary methods to address (or number) sectors on an ATA drive. The first method is called CHS (cylinder head sector), after the three respective coordinate numbers used to address each sector of the drive. The second method is called LBA (logical block address), and it uses a single number to address each sector on a drive. CHS was derived from the way drives were physically constructed (and is how they work internally), whereas LBA evolved as a simpler and more logical way to number the sectors, regardless of the internal physical construction.

CHS access limits the size of a hard disk to 528MB (decimal) or 504MiB. To overcome this limitation, the EDD specification was released by BIOS maker Phoenix Technologies in 1994. It specifies three ways to overcome the 528MB CHS barrier:

- Use BIOS INT13h extensions supporting 64-bit LBA
- Bit-shift geometric CHS translation
- LBA-assist geometric CHS translation

The method for dealing with the CHS problem was called *translation* because it enabled additional subroutines in the BIOS to translate CHS parameters from ATA maximums to BIOS maximums (and vice versa). In an effort to make its methods standard among the entire PC industry, Phoenix released the EDD document publicly and allowed the technology to be used free of charge, even among its competitors, such as American Megatrends (AMI) and Award. The T13 committee in charge of ATA subsequently adopted the EDD standard and incorporated it into official ATA documents.

Although a few vendors standardized on the bit-shift method of translation (also known as Large, or Extended, CHS in BIOS Setup), LBA-assist (better known as LBA mode) became the de facto standard for translating drives greater than 528MB. Note that a BIOS configured in LBA mode cannot properly read a drive prepared using Large mode because the methods of capacity translation are different.

Problems with the implementation of Extended CHS translation caused several additional drive capacity barriers, including the 2.1GB barrier and the 4.2GB barrier. LBA mode avoids these problems.

For drives over 8.4GB, CHS geometry is no longer translated into LBA geometry, but the drive is accessed in a purely LBA mode. This feature was introduced in 1998 as part of the EDD standard.

The 8.4GB Barrier

Although CHS translation breaks the 528MB barrier, it runs into another barrier at 8.4GB. Supporting drives larger than 8.4GB requires leaving CHS behind and changing to LBA addressing at the BIOS level. Although, the ATA interface had always supported LBA addressing, even in the original ATA-1 specification, it had been optional, but the main problem was that there was no LBA support at the BIOS interface level. You could set LBA-assist translation in the BIOS Setup, but all that did was convert the drive LBA numbers to CHS numbers at the BIOS interface level.

Phoenix Technologies recognized that the BIOS interface needed to move from CHS to LBA early on and, beginning in 1994, it published the BIOS Enhanced Disk Drive Specification (EDD) specification, which addressed this problem with new extended INT13h BIOS services that worked with LBA rather than with CHS addresses.

To ensure industrywide support and compatibility for these new BIOS functions, in 1996, Phoenix turned this document over to the InterNational Committee on Information Technology Standards (INCITS) T13 technical committee for further enhancement and certification as the EDD standard. Starting in 1998, most of the other BIOS manufacturers began installing EDD support in their BIOSs, enabling BIOS-level LBA mode support for ATA drives larger than 8.4GB. This support arrived just in time because ATA drives of that size and larger became available the same year.

The EDD specification describes new extended INT13h BIOS commands that allow LBA addressing up to 2^{64} sectors, which results in a theoretical maximum capacity of more than 9.44ZB (zettabytes, or quadrillion bytes). That is the same as saying 9.44 trillion GB: 9.44×10^{21} bytes, or, to be more precise, 9,444,732,965,739,290,427,392 bytes! This is *theoretical* capacity because even though by 1998 the BIOS could handle up to 2^{64} sectors, ATA drives were still using only 28-bit addressing (2^{28} sectors) at the ATA interface level. This limited an ATA drive to 268,435,456 sectors, which was a capacity of

137,438,953,472 bytes, or 137.44GB. Thus, the 8.4GB barrier had been broken, but another barrier remained at 137GB because of the 28-bit LBA addressing used in the ATA interface.

By using the new extended INT13h 64-bit LBA mode commands at the BIOS level as well as the existing 28-bit LBA mode commands at the ATA level, no translation would be required, and the LBA numbers would be passed unchanged. The combination of LBA at the BIOS and ATA interface levels meant that the clumsy CHS addressing could finally be laid to rest. This also means that when you install an ATA drive larger than 8.4GB in a PC that has an EDD-capable BIOS (1998 or newer), both the BIOS and the drive are automatically set to use LBA mode.

An interesting quirk is that to allow backward compatibility when you boot an older operating system that doesn't support LBA mode addressing (DOS or the original release of Windows 95, for example), most drives larger than 8.4GB report 16,383 cylinders, 16 heads, and 63 sectors per track, which is 8.4GB. For example, this enables a 120GB drive to be seen as an 8.4GB drive by older BIOSes or operating systems. It sounds strange, but having a 120GB drive being recognized as an 8.4GB drive is better than not having it work at all. (If you want to install a drive larger than 8.4GB into a system dated before 1998, the recommended solution is a motherboard BIOS upgrade.)

The 137GB Barrier and Beyond

By 2001, the 137GB barrier had become a problem because 3.5-inch hard drives were poised to breach that capacity level. The solution came in the form of ATA-6, which was being developed during that year. To enable the addressing of drives of greater capacity, ATA-6 upgraded the LBA functions from using 28-bit numbers to using larger 48-bit numbers.

The ATA-6 specification extends the LBA interface such that it can use 48-bit sector addressing. This means that the maximum capacity is increased to 2^{48} (281,474,976,710,656) total sectors. Each sector stores 512 bytes, so this results in a maximum drive capacity of just over 144PB (petabytes, or quadrillion bytes)—which should be sufficient for years to come.

Because, according to Moore's Law, hard disk drives have been doubling in capacity every 1.5–2 years, and considering that 200GB+ ATA drives were available in late 2003, it will probably take us until between the years 2031 and 2041 to reach the 144PB barrier (assuming that hard disk technology hasn't been completely replaced by then).

The 137GB barrier has proven a bit more complicated than previous barriers because, in addition to considering BIOS issues, we must also consider operating system issues. Internal ATA drives larger than 137GB require 48-bit LBA (logical block address) support. This support absolutely needs to be provided in the OS, but it can also be provided in the BIOS. It is best if both the OS and BIOS support it, but it can be made to work if only the OS does.

Windows versions that are suitable for server use and include 48-bit LBA support include the following:

- Windows 2000 Server with Service Pack 3 (SP3) or later; SP4 or later is recommended for best performance
- Windows XP with SP1 or later
- Windows Server 2003

To have 48-bit LBA support in the BIOS requires either of the following:

- A motherboard BIOS with 48-bit LBA support (most of those dated September 2002 or later)
- An ATA host adapter card with onboard BIOS that includes 48-bit LBA support

If your motherboard BIOS does not have LBA support and an update is not available from your motherboard manufacturer, you can use a card to provide 48-bit LBA support. Vendors that offer 48-bit LBA support plus additional ATA, SATA, or ATA/SATA RAID host adapters include SIIG (www.siig.com) and Promise Technology (www.promisetech.com). These cards provide 48-bit LBA support for connected hard disk drives.

Note that if you have both BIOS and OS support, you can simply install and use the drive as you would any other. If you have no BIOS support but you do have OS support, portions of the drive past 137GB are not recognized or accessible until the OS is loaded. If you are installing the OS to a blank hard drive and booting from an original Windows XP (pre-SP1) CD-ROM or earlier, you need to partition and install up to the first 137GB of the drive at installation time. After installing the OS and then the SP1 update, you can either partition the remainder of the drive, using standard partitioning software, or use a third-party partitioning program such as PartitionMagic or Partition Commander to resize the first partition to use the full drive. If you are booting from a Windows XP SP1 or later CD-ROM, you can recognize and access the entire drive during the OS installation and partition the entire drive as a single partition greater than 137GB, if you want.

Finally, you should keep in mind that the versions of Windows 2000 and Windows XP prior to those listed earlier in this section do not provide native support for ATA (PATA and SATA) hard drives that are larger than 137GB. However, Windows Server 2003 has native support for 48-bit LBA.

Operating System and Other Software Limitations

If you use older software, including utilities, applications, or even operating systems that rely exclusively on CHS parameters, they will see all drives over 8.4GB as 8.4GB only. In this case, you need not only a newer BIOS but also newer software designed to handle the direct LBA addressing to work with drives over 8.4GB.

Table 6.15 lists server operating system limitations with respect to drives over 8.4GB.

Table 6.15   Server Operating System Limitations

Operating System	Limits for Hard Drive Size
Windows NT	Windows NT 3.5x does not support drives greater than 8.4GB. Windows NT 4.0 does support drivers greater than 8.4GB; however, when a drive larger than 8.4GB is being used as the primary bootable device, Windows NT does not recognize more than 8.4GB. Microsoft has released SP4 to correct this problem.
Windows 2000/XP	Windows 2000/XP supports drives greater than 8.4GB.
Windows Server 2003	Windows Server 2003 includes 48-bit LBA mode, so it can support drives over 137GB (as well as smaller drives).
OS/2 Warp	Some versions of OS/2 are limited to a boot partition size of 3.1GB or 4.3GB. IBM has a Device Driver Pack upgrade that enables the boot partition to be as large as 8.4GB. The HPFS file system in OS/2 supports drives up to 64GB.
Novell	NetWare 5.0 or later supports drives greater than 8.4GB.
Linux	The Ext2 file system (the default file system in all recent and current Linux distributions) supports partitions up to 4TB, with a maximum file size of 2GB.

In the case of operating systems that support drives over 8.4GB, the maximum drive size limitations are dependent on the BIOS and hard drive interface standard, not on the OS. In those cases, other limitations come into play for the volumes (partitions) and files that can be created and managed by the various operating systems. These limitations are dependent on not only the operating system involved but also the file system used for the volume. Table 6.16 shows the minimum and maximum volume (partition) size and file size limitations of the various Windows server operating systems. As noted in the previous section, the original version of Windows XP, as well as Windows 2000/NT or Windows 95, 98, or Me, does not currently provide native support for ATA hard drives that are larger than 137GB. You need to use Windows XP and ensure that you have SP1 or later installed to use an ATA drive over 137GB. This does not affect drives using USB, FireWire, SCSI, or other interfaces.

Table 6.16   Operating System Volume/File Size Limitations, by File System[1]

Limitation (File System)	FAT16	FAT32	NTFS
Min. Volume Size (NT/2000/XP)	2.092MB	33.554MB	1.000MB
Max. Volume Size (NT/2000/XP)	4.294GB	8.796GB	281.475TB
Max. File Size (all)	4.294GB	4.294GB	16.384TB

[1]*Key: MB = megabytes; GB = gigabytes; and TB = terabytes.*

Common ATA Configurations for Server Platforms

Although SCSI hard disks have traditionally been used in midrange and high-end server platforms, ATA-based hard disks continue to be popular in entry-level servers. The superior performance and easier configuration offered by SATA hard disks make them a suitable choice for both entry-level and many midrange server implementations. The following sections provide recommendations for using ATA drives in a server platform.

ATA/ATAPI Configurations for Server Platforms

If you decide to use PATA hard disks in an entry-level server, you need to configure your server as follows:

- Connect the hard disk to the primary PATA (40-pin) connector on the motherboard.
- Connect the CD or DVD optical drive used for program loading or for creating backups to the secondary PATA connector on the motherboard.
- Choose a hard disk with a 7200RPM spin rate and an 8MB cache for best performance.
- Use 80-wire UDMA cables on both drives to permit maximum speed operation.
- Be sure to install the appropriate UDMA drivers in the operating system.

Note that most commercial entry-level servers no longer use PATA hard disks, although ATAPI CD and DVD drives continue to be popular.

SATA Configurations for Server Platforms

As noted earlier in this chapter, SATA drives have largely replaced PATA hard disks in entry-level servers, and they have made inroads into the midrange server market as well.

To improve reliability and performance, you should consider using SATA hard disks that meet the following standards:

- 7200RPM or 10,000RPM spin rates; drives with 10,000RPM spin rates are recommended when access time is more important than high capacity (10,000RPM spin rate drives are currently limited to 150GB per drive, while 7200RPM drives are available in capacities up to 500GB)
- 8MB or larger cache; some 16MB cache drives are now available

- Support for command queuing (tagged or native) to improve throughput; the type of command queuing supported must also be supported by the SATA host adapter used by the system

- Designed for higher reliability; look at factors such as MTBF, thermal management, and warranty

Each SATA hard disk uses a separate host adapter.

ATA/SATA RAID Configurations for Server Platforms

RAID, which stands for redundant array of independent (or inexpensive) disks, was designed to improve the fault tolerance and performance of computer storage systems. RAID was first developed at the University of California at Berkeley in 1987, and it was designed so that a group of smaller, less expensive drives could be interconnected with special hardware and software to make them appear as a single, larger drive to the system. By using multiple drives to act as one drive, fault tolerance and performance could be increased.

Initially, RAID was conceived to simply enable all the individual drives in the array to work together as a single, larger drive with the combined storage space of all the individual drives added together. However, this actually reduced reliability and didn't do much for performance, either. For example, if you had four drives connected in an array acting as one drive, you would be four times as likely to experience a drive failure than if you used just a single, larger drive. To improve its reliability and performance, the Berkeley scientists proposed six levels (corresponding to different methods) of RAID. These levels provide varying emphasis on fault tolerance (reliability), storage capacity, or performance—or a combination of the three.

An organization called the RAID Advisory Board (RAB) was formed in July 1992 to standardize, classify, and educate on the subject of RAID. RAB has developed specifications for RAID, a conformance program for the various RAID levels, and a classification program for RAID hardware.

Currently, RAB defines seven standard RAID levels, RAID 0–6. RAID is typically implemented by a RAID controller board, although software-only implementations are possible (but not recommended). The levels are as follows:

- **RAID Level 0: Striping**—File data is written simultaneously to multiple drives in the array, which act as a single, larger drive. This level offers high read/write performance but very low reliability. It requires a minimum of two drives.

- **RAID Level 1: Mirroring**—Data written to one drive is duplicated on another, providing excellent fault tolerance (if one drive fails, the other is used and no data is lost) but no real increase in performance compared to using a single drive. It requires a minimum of two drives (and has the same capacity as one drive).

- **RAID Level 2: Bit-level ECC**—Data is split 1 bit at a time across multiple drives, and error correction codes (ECCs) are written to other drives. It is intended for storage devices that do not incorporate ECC internally (all SCSI and ATA drives have internal ECC). It provides high data rates with good fault tolerance, but large numbers of drives are required, and no commercial RAID 2 controllers or drives without ECC are available on the market.

- **RAID Level 3: Striped with parity**—This level combines RAID Level 0 striping with an additional drive that is used for parity information. This RAID level is really an adaptation of RAID Level 0 that sacrifices some capacity, for the same number of drives. However, it also achieves a high level of data integrity or fault tolerance because data can usually be rebuilt if one drive fails. It requires a minimum of three drives (two or more for data and one for parity).

- **RAID Level 4: Blocked data with parity**—This level is similar to RAID 3, except data is written in larger blocks to the independent drives, offering faster read performance with larger files. It requires a minimum of three drives (two or more for data and one for parity).

- **RAID Level 5: Blocked data with distributed parity**—This level is similar to RAID 4, but it offers improved performance by distributing the parity stripes over a series of hard drives. It requires a minimum of three drives (two or more for data and one for parity).

- **RAID Level 6: Blocked data with double distributed parity**—This level is similar to RAID 5, except parity information is written twice, using two different parity schemes, to provide even better fault tolerance in case of multiple drive failures. It requires a minimum of four drives (two or more for data and two for parity).

- **RAID Level 10 (RAID 1+ 0): Striping plus mirroring**—This level is a combination of RAID 1 (mirroring) and RAID 0 (striping). Provides higher performance than RAID 1. It requires a minimum of four drives (two for mirroring; two for striping).

Additional RAID levels exist that are not supported by RAB but that are instead custom implementations by specific companies.

Note

Note that a higher RAID level number doesn't necessarily mean increased performance or fault tolerance; the numbered order of the RAID levels is entirely arbitrary.

At one time, virtually all RAID controllers were SCSI based, meaning that they used SCSI drives. For a professional setup, SCSI RAID is definitely the best choice because it combines the advantages of RAID with the advantages of SCSI—an interface that was already designed to support multiple drives. Now, however, ATA RAID controllers are available that allow for even less expensive RAID implementations. These ATA RAID controllers are typically used in single-user systems for performance rather than reliability increases.

Most ATA RAID implementations are much simpler than the professional SCSI RAID adapters used on network file servers. ATA RAID is designed more for an individual who is seeking performance or simple drive mirroring for redundancy. When they're set up for performance, ATA RAID adapters run RAID Level 0, which incorporates data striping. Unfortunately, RAID 0 also sacrifices reliability, such that if one drive fails, all data is lost. With RAID 0, performance scales up with the number of drives you add to the array. If you use four drives, you don't necessarily have four times the performance of a single drive, but you can get close to that for sustained transfers. Some overhead is still involved in the controller performing the striping, and issues still exist with latency—that is, how long it takes to find the data—but performance with RAID is higher than what any single drive could normally achieve.

When they're set up for reliability, ATA RAID adapters generally run RAID Level 1, which is simple drive mirroring. All data written to one drive is written to the other. If one drive fails, the system can continue to work on the other drive. Unfortunately, this does not increase performance at all, and it also means you get to use only half of the available drive capacity. In other words, you must install two drives, but you get to use only one (the other is the mirror). However, in an era of high capacities and low drive prices, this is not a significant issue. If you want to eliminate a lot of bulky cable, consider SATA RAID, which uses the narrow SATA cables shown in Figure 6.1, earlier in this chapter.

Combining performance with fault tolerance requires using one of the other RAID levels, such as RAID Level 3 or RAID Level 5. For example, virtually all professional RAID controllers used in network file servers are designed to use RAID Level 5. Controllers that implement RAID Level 5 are more expensive, and at least three drives must be connected. To improve reliability, but at a lower cost, many of the ATA RAID controllers enable combinations of the RAID levels—such as 0 and 1 combined (also known as RAID 10). This usually requires four drives, two of which are striped together in a RAID Level 0 arrangement, which is then redundantly written to a second set of two drives in a

RAID Level 1 arrangement. This enables you to have approximately double the performance of a single drive, and you have a backup set, in case one of the primary sets fails. Many recent servers include four SATA host adapters with RAID functionality, enabling SATA RAID 0+1 implementations.

Today, you can get PATA or SATA RAID controllers from companies such as Arco Computer Products, Iwill, Promise Technology, and HighPoint. A typical low-cost ATA RAID controller enables up to four drives to be attached, and you can run them in RAID Level 0, 1, or 0+1 mode. Remember that performance suffers somewhat when you run two drives (master/slave) on a single PATA channel because only one drive can transfer on the cable at a time, which cuts performance in half. Four-channel PATA RAID cards are available, but most new RAID cards are moving to SATA, which doesn't have the master/slave channel sharing problems of PATA. SATA RAID cards use a separate SATA data channel (cable) for each drive, allowing maximum performance. You should use SATA RAID cards for best performance.

If you are looking for an ATA RAID controller (or a motherboard with an integrated ATA RAID controller), you should look for the following:

- RAID levels supported (most support 0, 1, and 0+1, although some ATA RAID 5 card products are now available)
- Two or four channels (for best performance, you should use four channels with four devices using PATA)
- Support for ATA/100 or ATA/133 speeds for PATA
- Support for 33MHz or 66MHz PCI slots (some servers have 66MHz slots)
- SATA RAID implementations for maximum performance, ease of installation, and reliability

If you want to experiment with RAID inexpensively, you can implement RAID without a custom controller when using certain higher-end (often server-based) operating systems. For example, the Windows NT/2000 and Windows XP or Windows Server 2003 operating systems provide a software implementation for RAID, using both striping and mirroring. In these operating systems, you use the Disk Administrator tool to set up and control the RAID functions, as well as to reconstruct the volume after a failure occurs. Normally, though, if you are building a server and want the ultimate in performance and reliability, you should look for SATA or SCSI RAID controllers that support RAID Level 3 or Level 5.

Tip

The best solutions for RAID are SATA and SATA RAID implementations that are native to the motherboard chipset's South Bridge or I/O controller hub chip. When Windows 2000 Server or Windows Server 2003 is installed on a system with native SATA or SATA RAID support, there is no need to press the F6 key when you're prompted to install a driver from a floppy disk. With add-on SATA and ATA/SATA RAID add-on cards or motherboard implementations using a separate SATA host adapter chip, you must press F6 when prompted to install the appropriate driver from a floppy disk.

The latest type of RAID array, RAID^n, developed by Inostor, a division of Tandberg Data, combines special software that can specify the number of drives used for replacements. A RAID^n array designed to protect against the failure of up to four drives uses only 7 drives (4 for data and 3 for parity), compared to 10 drives for a RAID 5+1 array (4 data, 1 parity; 4 mirrored data; 1 mirrored parity). Currently, RAID^n arrays are available only in Inostor network attached storage (NAS) devices, but RAID^n software is designed to be portable to other operating systems.

▶▶   For more about RAID, see "Introduction to RAID," p. 600.

Using NAS

As an alternative to expanding internal server storage by adding ATA, SATA, or SCSI hard disks to a server (a concept often referred to as *direct attached storage* [DAS]), you can connect a network attached storage (NAS) device to your network. Each NAS device has its own IP address, and an NAS device contains one or more hard disks that can be accessed directly from the network.

The first company to develop an NAS device was Auspex, which introduced the first NAS shortly after being founded in 1987. Although the company went bankrupt in June 2003, its technology was sold to other firms. Using NAS devices continues to be a popular method of expanding network storage, and many companies now build NAS devices.

In addition to hard disks, an NAS device contains one or more processors to handle I/O, network, and data storage and retrieval tasks. Although a given NAS device might contain a processor similar to that used by a desktop PC or server, an NAS device is not a PC or a server. Instead, it is a specialized storage appliance.

The benefits of expanding network storage by using an NAS device include the following:

- **No server downtime**—You can connect an NAS device to the network without disrupting existing servers.
- **Easier configuration**—In most cases, you can configure the NAS from a web browser on a client PC. The client PC logs in to the NAS device's built-in webserver. Some NAS devices use Windows Storage Server 2003.
- **Easy rack-mounting**—Many NAS devices fit in a 1U or 2U form factor.
- **Easy backup**—Some NAS devices, including autoloaders, support direct disk-to-disk or disk-to-tape backups. Some NAS devices can be used as network backup appliances (NBAs) for other servers.
- **Wide range of RAID options**—RAID options vary by product and vendor, but most vendors offer RAID 0, RAID 1, RAID 0+1, RAID 4, and RAID 5. Some offer additional RAID options.

The following are the shortcomings of NAS storage:

- **The speed of storage is limited by the speed of the network**—For best results, an NAS should be connected to a Gigabit Ethernet network, with all clients using Gigabit Ethernet adapters.
- **As the name implies, NAS is for network storage only**—If you use thin clients that remotely store applications, applications must be stored on a server, not on an NAS.
- **NAS storage can be more difficult to secure than server-based storage**—For maximum protection, NAS devices should be protected by antivirus programs made especially for NAS, such as Symantec AntiVirus ScanEngine. Also, networks that use NAS devices should be protected from public access by firewall devices.

If you need speeds significantly faster than NAS can provide (about 32MBps sustained transfer rate with a Gigabit Ethernet network) and prefer more security options, you should consider a storage area network (SAN) installation.

▶▶ For more about SANs, see Chapter 12, "Storage Area Networks."

Troubleshooting ATA and SATA Hard Disks

ATA and SATA hard disks are more reliable today than in the past, but problems with them can still affect a server's ability to run reliably. Problems can occur during drive configuration and during operation. The following sections describe typical problems and solutions.

CMOS/BIOS, Startup Problems

Some of the most common problems to be aware of during the installation of ATA and SATA hard disks include the following:

- **Using the wrong parameters for the hard disk**—For reliable installation, you should use the autoconfiguration option in the system BIOS/CMOS Setup program. Doing so ensures that the correct geometry, LBA mode setting, and UDMA mode setting will be used for each drive.

- **Failing to enable SATA host adapters**—Many systems disable onboard SATA host adapters by default. If you plan to use SATA hard disks connected to onboard SATA host adapters, you must enable the SATA host adapters in the system BIOS/CMOS Setup program.

- **Failing to install SATA, SATA RAID, or ATA RAID host adapter drivers during Windows installation**—If the host adapter uses a discrete chip on the motherboard or an add-on card (instead of being built into the motherboard's South Bridge or I/O controller hub), Windows will not be able to use the drive if you don't provide the driver when prompted (see Figure 6.11).

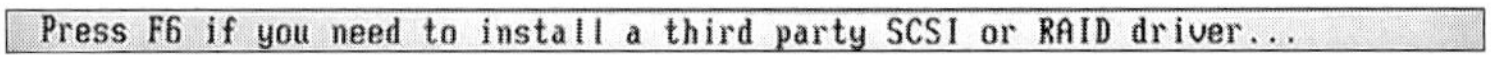

```
Press F6 if you need to install a third party SCSI or RAID driver...
```

Figure 6.11   This prompt appears extremely early in the installation process for Windows Server 2003 as well as Windows 2000 and Windows XP.

- **Disabling onboard SMART detection of hard disk problems**—Most recent systems support SMART, as do most system management programs. Making sure SMART is enabled is cheap insurance against hard disk failure.

If you plan to use an onboard RAID array for ATA or SATA hard disks, you need to be sure to follow the system or motherboard vendor's instructions. Many systems with onboard ATA or SATA RAID use a so-called "soft RAID" configuration that requires you to run a RAID Setup application from disk to prepare the RAID array for use.

If you decide to convert a single-drive installation into a RAID array, you need to make sure to make a full backup of the drive first. Although some recent RAID implementations do not wipe out existing data, the possibility of data loss remains.

If your ATA RAID, SATA RAID, or SATA host adapter uses an add-on card host adapter or your motherboard has a separate SATA or SATA/ATA RAID host adapter chip, you should have received a driver floppy disk with your host adapter or motherboard. When you see the prompt to press F6 during the installation of Windows (see Figure 6.11), you need to press F6 and provide the driver disk. Otherwise, the server's SATA, SATA RAID, or ATA RAID host adapter card or onboard host adapter will not work and the drives connected to it cannot be accessed.

If you miss this prompt, you need to restart your computer and restart the installation process, and you will have another chance to provide the needed driver.

BSODs and Other Postinstallation Problems

The notorious blue screen of death (BSOD) or STOP errors associated with serious problems in Windows 2000, Windows Server 2003, and Windows XP are sometimes caused by problems with ATA or SATA hard disks or device drivers. Some of these errors include the following:

- **STOP 0x0000000A (IRQL_NOT_LESS_OR_EQUAL)**—This error can be caused by a variety of faulty device drivers or firmware problems. If this error occurs after you update ATA or SATA device drivers, you should restart Windows in Safe Mode and roll back to the previous driver.

- **STOP 0x0000001E (KMODE_EXCEPTION_NOT_HANDLED)**—This error can be caused by running short of disk space. You need to remove unneeded temporary files or outdated system restore files.

- **STOP 0x00000024 (NTFS_FILE_SYSTEM)**—This error can be caused by problems with ATA, SATA, or SCSI hard disks, cables, or drivers. You need to replace cables and check drivers. You should use error checking (CHKDSK) to test all hard disks.

- **STOP 0x0000002E (DATA_BUS_ERROR)**—One of the less likely causes for this error is hard disk corruption. You should use error checking (CHKDSK) and enable the option to repair file system errors to test all hard disks.

- **STOP 0x00000077 (KERNEL_STACK_INPAGE_ERROR)**—You can use CHKDSK (error checking) on the paging hard disk to check for bad sectors.

- **STOP 0x0000007A (KERNEL_STACK_DATA_ERROR)**—You can check the I/O status code to help troubleshoot this error:

  - **STATUS_DEVICE-DATA_ERROR**—You should use CHKDSK (error checking) on the paging hard disk to check for bad sectors.

  - **STATUS_DEVICE_NOT_CONNECTED**—You should check the BIOS/CMOS configuration for hard disks; you should also check drive power and data cables.

  - **STATUS_IO_DEVICE_ERROR**—You should check the host adapter configuration; you should also check drive power and data cables. This error can also be caused by failing to install the appropriate driver after pressing F6.

◀◀ See "CMOS/BIOS, Startup Problems," p. 444, for details.

- **STOP 0x0000007B (INACCESSIBLE_BOOT_DEVICE)**—Windows can't locate the system partition or boot volume. You need to make sure correct drivers for ATA or SATA host adapters have been loaded.

- **STOP 0x000000ED (UNMOUNTABLE_BOOT_VOLUME)**—This error can be caused by trying to use a 40-wire ATA/IDE cable with a drive configured in firmware or system BIOS/CMOS to use 80-wire (UDMA 66 or faster) mode. You should use an 80-wire UDMA 66 cable.

Note that most of these errors can also be caused by other problems. For full details on each error and suggested solutions, go to http://support.microsoft.com and look up the specific STOP error.

If you use SMART-enabled hard disks and have SMART monitoring enabled in the system BIOS, you should back up and replace any drives that display SMART errors during startup or during operation. Note that you must have system management software that supports SMART monitoring to see errors after server startup.

CHAPTER 7

The SCSI Bus

Small Computer System Interface (SCSI; pronounced "scuzzy") is a general-purpose interface used for connecting many types of devices to a PC. This interface has its roots in SASI (Shugart Associates System Interface). SCSI is very flexible; it is not just a disk interface, but is a systems-level interface that allows many types of devices to be connected, including scanners and printers. SCSI's primary use today is as a host adapter for high-performance hard disk, tape-backup, and RAID arrays on servers.

SCSI is a bus that supports as many as 7 or 15 total devices. Multichannel adapters exist that can support up to 7 or 15 devices per channel. The SCSI *host adapter* might be installed as a PCI or as a PCI-Express card, or it might be built in to the motherboard.

The host adapter functions as the gateway between the SCSI bus and the PC system bus. Each device on the bus has a SCSI controller chip built in. The SCSI host adapter does not talk directly with actual devices such as hard disks; instead, it talks to the SCSI interface controller that is built in to the drive.

A single SCSI bus can support as many as 8 or 16 physical units, usually called SCSI *IDs*. One of these units is the SCSI host adapter in the PC; the other 7 or 15 can be other peripherals. You can have hard disks, a tape backup, or other devices connected to a single SCSI host adapter. Most systems can support up to 4 host adapters, each with up to 15 devices, for a total of 60 devices. There are even dual-channel adapters that could double that figure.

SCSI is a fast interface, generally suited to high-performance workstations, servers, or anywhere ultimate performance for a storage system interface is needed. The latest SCSI version, Ultra 5 (Ultra640), supports transfer speeds of up to 640MBps. By comparison, parallel ATA (PATA; also known as ATA/IDE) transfers at speeds up to 133MBps, first-generation Serial ATA (SATA) transfers at 150MBps, and 3G (second-generation) SATA transfers at 300MBps. Note that these figures are raw interface transfer speeds; the speeds of individual devices are normally much lower.

The real advantage of the SCSI bus over ATA/IDE is seen when multiple devices share the bus. Multiple SCSI devices can overlap reads and writes and more fully utilize the higher bandwidth available. The slower ATA buses allow only one or two devices, making higher throughputs unnecessary because they would be unusable.

When you purchase a SCSI device such as a SCSI hard disk, you are usually purchasing the device, device controller, and SCSI interface controller in one circuit; the device is ready to connect directly to the SCSI bus. This type of drive is usually called an *embedded* SCSI device because the SCSI interface is built in. For example, most SCSI hard drives are technically the same as or similar to their ATA counterparts except for the addition of the SCSI interface controller circuits (normally a single chip) added to the logic board. Your system cannot talk directly to the device controller as though it were plugged in to the system bus, as it could on a standard ATA drive. Instead, communications go through the SCSI host adapter installed in the system bus, then to the SCSI interface controller on the drive logic board, and finally to the device controller (also on the logic board) and disk drive. You can access the drive only through the SCSI protocols.

SCSI originally became popular in the PC-based workstation and server market because of the performance and expandability it offers. One block that stalled acceptance of SCSI in the early PC marketplace was the lack of a complete standard; the SCSI standard was originally designed by one company and then turned into a committee-controlled public standard, where it eventually became comprehensive and complete. Since then, no single manufacturer has controlled it.

Note

Low-end SCSI host adapters, such as those bundled with image scanners or rewritable CD or DVD drives, are not suitable for use with multiple SCSI devices and also lack support for bootable SCSI hard disks. These stripped-down host adapters are designed to support only the device they are packaged with. However, a full-featured SCSI host adapter can support multiple devices, and most SCSI host adapters sold at retail also support booting from a SCSI hard disk.

SCSI drives are controlled with a special SCSI BIOS that is built in to the SCSI host adapter; on servers with an integrated SCSI host adapter, the SCSI BIOS is incorporated into the system BIOS.

ANSI SCSI Standards

The SCSI standard defines the physical and electrical parameters of a parallel I/O bus used to connect computers and peripheral devices in daisy-chain fashion. The standard supports devices such as disk drives, tape drives, and CD-ROM drives. The original SCSI standard (ANSI X3.131-1986) was approved in 1986, SCSI-2 was approved in 1994, and the first portions of SCSI-3 were approved in 1995. Note that SCSI-3 has evolved into an enormous standard with numerous sections and is an evolving, growing standard still very much under development. Because it has been broken down into multiple standards, there really is no single SCSI-3 standard.

The SCSI bus is defined as a standard by ANSI (the American National Standards Institute), specifically by a committee currently known as T10. T10 is a technical committee of the InterNational Committee on Information Technology Standards (INCITS, pronounced "insights"). INCITS is accredited by ANSI and operates under rules approved by ANSI. These rules are designed to ensure that voluntary standards are developed by the consensus of industry groups. INCITS develops information-processing system standards, whereas ANSI approves the processes under which they are developed and publishes them. Working draft copies of all SCSI-related standards can be downloaded from the T10 Technical Committee site (www.t10.org).

Most companies indicate that their host adapters follow both the ANSI X3.131-1986 (SCSI-1) and the X3.131-1994 (SCSI-2) standards. Note that because virtually all parts of SCSI-1 are supported in SCSI-2, most SCSI-1 devices are also considered SCSI-2 by default. Many manufacturers advertise that their devices are SCSI-2, but this does not mean they support any of the additional optional features that were incorporated in the SCSI-2 revision. For example, an optional part of the SCSI-2 specification includes a fast synchronous mode that doubles the standard synchronous transfer rate from 5MBps to 10MBps. This Fast SCSI transfer mode can be combined with 16-bit Wide SCSI for transfer rates of up to 20MBps. An optional 32-bit version was defined in SCSI-2, but component manufacturers have shunned it as too expensive. In essence, 32-bit SCSI was a stillborn specification, as it was withdrawn from the SCSI-3 standard. Most SCSI implementations are 8-bit standard SCSI or 16-bit Fast/Wide SCSI. Even devices that support none of the Fast or Wide modes can still be considered SCSI-2.

SCSI-3 is broken down into a number of standards. The SCSI Parallel Interface (SPI) standard controls the parallel interconnection between SCSI devices, which is mostly what we are talking about here. So far, five versions of SPI have been created: SPI, SPI-2, SPI-3, SPI-4, and SPI-5.

What can be confusing is that several terms can be used to describe each of the newer SPI standards, as shown in Table 7.1.

Table 7.1   SPI Standards

SCSI-3 Standard	Also Known As	Speed	Throughput
SPI	Ultra SCSI	Fast-20	20/40MBps
SPI-2	Ultra 2 SCSI	Fast-40	40/80MBps
SPI-3	Ultra 3 SCSI or Ultra160(+)	Fast-80DT	160MBps
SPI-4	Ultra 4 SCSI or Ultra320	Fast-160DT	320MBps
SPI-5	Ultra 5 SCSI or Ultra640	Fast-320DT	640MBps

To add to the confusion, SPI-3 or Ultra 3 SCSI is also called Ultra160 or Ultra160+, SPI-4 or Ultra 4 SCSI is also called Ultra320, and SPI-5 or Ultra 5 SCSI is also called Ultra640. The Ultra160 designation refers to any device that includes the first three of the five main features from the Ultra 3 SCSI specification. Ultra160+ refers to any device that supports all five main features of Ultra 3 SCSI. Ultra320 and Ultra640 include all the features of Ultra160+ as well as several additional features.

Table 7.2 shows the maximum transfer rates for the SCSI bus at various speeds and widths and the cable types required for the specific transfer widths.

Table 7.2   SCSI Types, Data-Transfer Rates, and Cables[1]

SCSI Standard	SCSI Technology	Marketing Term	Clock Speed (MHz)	Transfer Width	ST/DT
SCSI-1	Async	Asynchronous	5	8-bit	ST
SCSI-1	Fast-5	Synchronous	5	8-bit	ST
SCSI-2	Fast-5/Wide	Wide	5	16-bit	ST
SCSI-2	Fast-10	Fast	10	8-bit	ST
SCSI-2	Fast-10/Wide	Fast/Wide	10	16-bit	ST
SCSI-3/SPI	Fast-20	Ultra	20	8-bit	ST
SCSI-3/SPI	Fast-20/Wide	Ultra/Wide	20	16-bit	ST
SCSI-3/SPI-2	Fast-40	Ultra 2	40	8-bit	ST
SCSI-3/SPI-2	Fast-40/Wide	Ultra 2/Wide	40	16-bit	ST
SCSI-3/SPI-3	Fast-80DT	Ultra 3 (Ultra160)	40[5]	16-bit	DT
SCSI-3/SPI-4	Fast-160DT	Ultra 4 (Ultra320)	80[5]	16-bit	DT
SCSI-3/SPI-5[6]	Fast-320DT	Ultra 5 (Ultra640)	160[5]	16-bit	DT

Note

The A cable listed in Table 7.2 is the standard 50-pin SCSI cable, whereas the P cable is a 68-pin cable designed for 16-bit transfers. High-voltage differential (HVD) signaling was never popular and is now considered obsolete. Low-voltage differential (LVD) signaling is used in the Ultra 2 and Ultra 3 modes to increase performance and cable lengths. Pinouts for the cable connections are listed in this chapter in Tables 7.4–7.7 (starting on p. 468), and you can see the connectors in Figures 7.7–7.9 (starting on p. 476).

SCSI is both forward and backward compatible, meaning you can run faster devices on buses with slower host adapters or vice versa. In each case, the entire bus runs at the lowest-common-denominator speed. Thus, although you can mix and match different speeds of devices on the same bus, you should place fast devices on a separate SCSI adapter (or connector, if you use dual-bus adapters) from slower devices. In fact, as stated earlier, virtually any SCSI-1 device can also legitimately be called SCSI-2 (or even SCSI-3) because most of the improvements in the later versions are optional. Of course, you can't take advantage of the faster modes on an older, slower host adapter. By the same token, you can purchase an Ultra 3–capable SCSI host adapter and still run older standard SCSI devices. You can even mix standard 8-bit and 16-bit (Wide) devices on the same bus, using cable adapters.

Transfer Speed (MB/s)	Max. No. Devices[2]	Cable Type	Max. Length (SE)	Max. Length (HVD)	Max. Length (LVD)
4	7	A (50-pin)	6m	25m	—
5	7	A (50-pin)	6m	25m	—
10	15	P (68-pin)	6m	25m	—
10	7	A (50-pin)	3m	25m	—
20	15	P (68-pin)	3m	25m	—
20	7	A (50-pin)	3/1.5m[3]	25m	—
40	7	P (68-pin)	3/1.5m[3]	25m	—
40	7	A (50-pin)	—	—	12m[4]
80	15	P (68-pin)	—	—	12m[4]
160	15	P (68-pin)	—	—	12m[4]
320	15	P (68-pin)	—	—	12m[4]
640	15	P (68-pin)	—	—	10m[7]

[1]Cable lengths are in meters: 25m = 80ft., 12m = 40ft., 6m = 20ft., 3m = 10ft., 1.5m = 5ft; SE = single-ended signaling, HVD = high-voltage differential signaling (obsolete), LVD = low-voltage differential signaling, SPI = SCSI Parallel Interface (part of SCSI-3), ST = single transition (one transfer per clock cycle), and DT = double transition (two transfers per clock cycle; 16-bit only).

[2]Not including the host adapter.

[3]Ultra SCSI cable total length is restricted to 1.5m if more than three devices exist on the bus (not including the host adapter). A maximum of seven devices is allowed.

[4]A 25m cable can be used if only one device exists (point-to-point interconnect).

[5]Ultra 3 (Ultra160), Ultra 4 (Ultra320), and Ultra 5 (Ultra640) SCSI transfer twice per clock cycle and are 16-bit only.

[6]No Ultra640 products have been produced to date.

[7]For Ultra 5 (Ultra640) only, cable length is restricted to 2m using ribbon cable, and a 20m cable can be used if only one device exists (point-to-point interconnect).

Modern SCSI hard disks and tape backups suitable for servers correspond to SCSI-3 (SPI-3, SPI-4, and SPI-5) standards. However, to understand SCSI, it is also helpful to review the original SCSI-1 and follow-on SCSI-2 implementations. The following sections provide more details.

SCSI-1

SCSI-1 was the first implementation of SCSI and was officially known as ANSI X3.131-1986. The major features of SCSI-1 are as follows:

- 8-bit parallel bus
- 5MHz asynchronous or synchronous operation
- 4MBps (asynchronous) or 5MBps (synchronous) throughput
- 50-pin cables with low-density pin-header internal and Centronics-style external connectors
- Single-ended (SE) unbalanced transmission
- Passive termination
- Optional bus parity

SCSI-1 is now considered obsolete; in fact, the standard has been withdrawn by ANSI and replaced by SCSI-2.

SCSI-2

SCSI-2 is officially known as ANSI X3.131-1994. The SCSI-2 specification is essentially an improved version of SCSI-1, with some parts of the specification tightened and several new features and options added. Normally, SCSI-1 and SCSI-2 devices are compatible, but SCSI-1 devices ignore the additional features in SCSI-2.

Some of the changes in SCSI-2 are very minor. For example, SCSI-1 allows SCSI bus parity to be optional, whereas parity must be implemented in SCSI-2. (Parity is an extra bit that is sent as a verification bit to ensure that the data is not corrupted.) Another requirement of SCSI-2 is that initiator devices, such as host adapters, provide terminator power to the interface; most devices already did so, though.

SCSI-2 also added several optional features:

- Fast SCSI (10MHz)
- Wide SCSI (16-bit transfers)
- Command queuing
- New commands
- High-density, 50-pin cable connectors
- Active (Alternative 2) termination for improved SE transmission
- HVD transmission (incompatible with SE on the same bus) for longer bus lengths

Wide SCSI enables parallel data transfers at a bus width of 16 bits. The wider connection requires a new cable design. The standard 50-conductor, 8-bit cable is called the A cable. SCSI-2 originally defined a special 68-conductor B cable that was supposed to be used in conjunction with the A cable for 32-bit transfers. However, because of a lack of industry support and the added expenses involved, 32-bit SCSI was never actually implemented and was finally removed as part of the SCSI-3 specifications. Therefore, two different types of SCSI cables are now available: the A cable and the P cable. An

A cable is any SCSI cable with a 50-pin connector, whereas a P cable is any SCSI cable with 68-pin connectors. You need a P cable if you are connecting a Wide SCSI device and want it to work in 16-bit mode. The P cable was not officially included in the standard until SCSI-3.

Fast SCSI refers to high-speed synchronous transfer capability. Fast SCSI achieves a 10MBps transfer rate on the standard 8-bit SCSI cabling. When combined with a 16-bit Wide SCSI interface, this configuration results in data transfer rates of 20MBps (called Fast/Wide).

The high-density connectors for SCSI-2 enable smaller, more efficient connector and cable designs.

In SCSI-1, an initiator device, such as a host adapter, was limited to sending one command per device. In SCSI-2, the host adapter can send as many as 256 commands to a single device, which will store and process those commands internally before responding on the SCSI bus. The target device can even resequence the commands to enable the most efficient execution or performance possible. This is especially useful in multitasking environments, such as 32-bit Windows versions, which can take advantage of this feature.

SCSI-2 made the Common Command Set (CCS) that was being used throughout the industry an official part of the standard. The CCS was designed mainly for disk drives and did not include specific commands designed for other types of devices. In SCSI-2, many of the old commands are reworked, and several new commands are added. New command sets are added for CD-ROMs, optical drives, scanners, communications devices, and media changers (jukeboxes).

The single-ended SCSI bus depends on very tight termination tolerances to function reliably. Unfortunately, the original 132-ohm passive termination defined in the SCSI-1 documentation was not designed for use at the higher synchronous speeds now possible. These passive terminators, which are sometimes built in to SCSI devices (they are activated with jumper blocks or a built-in switch), can cause signal reflections to generate errors when transfer rates increase or when more devices are added to the bus. SCSI-2 defines an active (voltage-regulated) terminator that lowers termination impedance to 110 ohms and improves system integrity. Note that LVD SCSI requires special LVD terminators. If you use SE terminators on a bus with LVD devices, they either won't work or, if they are multimode devices, will default to SE operation.

These features are not required; they are optional under the SCSI-2 specification. If you connect a standard SCSI host adapter to a Fast SCSI drive, for example, the interface will work, but only at standard SCSI speeds.

SCSI-3

SCSI-3 is a term used to describe a set of SCSI standards currently being developed. Unlike SCSI-1 and SCSI-2, SCSI-3 is not one document that covers all the layers and interfaces of SCSI; it is instead a collection of documents that cover the primary commands, specific command sets, and electrical interfaces and protocols. The command sets include hard disk interface commands, commands for tape drives, commands for RAID, and other commands. In addition, an overall SCSI Architectural Model (SAM) exists for the physical and electrical interfaces, as does a SPI standard that controls the form of SCSI most commonly used. Each document within the standard is now a separate publication with its own revision level; for example, within SCSI-3, five versions of SPI have been published. Usually, we don't refer to SCSI-3 anymore as a specific interface and instead refer to the specific subsets of SCSI-3, such as SPI-3 (Ultra 3 SCSI).

The main additions to SCSI-3 include the following:

- Ultra 2 (Fast-40) SCSI
- Ultra 3 (Fast-80DT) SCSI

- Ultra 4 (Fast-160DT) SCSI
- Ultra 5 (Fast-320DT) SCSI
- New LVD signaling
- Elimination of HVD signaling

Breaking SCSI-3 into many smaller individual standards has enabled the standard as a whole to develop more quickly. The individual standards can now be published more quickly rather than waiting for an entire large standard to be approved.

Figure 7.1 shows the main parts of the SCSI architecture today.

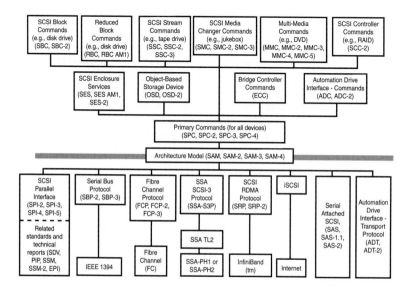

Figure 7.1   SCSI architecture.

The most recent changes or additions to SCSI include the Ultra320 (Ultra 4) and Ultra640 (Ultra 5) SCSI standards, which have taken the performance of SCSI up to 320MBps and 640MBps. Ultra 2 SCSI and beyond also include the LVD electrical interface standard, which enables greater cable lengths. The older HVD signaling has also been removed from the standard.

A number of people are confused about the speed variations in SCSI. Part of the problem is that speeds are quoted as either clock speeds (MHz) or transfer speeds. With 8-bit transfers, you get 1 byte per transfer, so if the clock is 40MHz (Fast-40 or Ultra 2 SCSI), the transfer speed is 40MBps. On the other hand, if you are using a Wide (16-bit) interface, the transfer speed doubles to 80MBps, even though the clock speed remains at 40MHz. With Fast-80DT, the bus speed technically remains at 40MHz; however, two transfers are made per cycle, resulting in a throughput speed of 160MBps. The same is true for Ultra 4 SCSI, which runs at 80MHz, transfers 2 bytes at a time, and has two transfers per cycle, for a throughput of 320MBps. Ultra 5 doubles the clock speed again, running at 160MHz, transferring 2 bytes at a time, two times per cycle, for a throughput of 640MBps.

Finally, confusion exists because SCSI speeds or modes are often discussed using either the official terms—such as Fast-10, Fast-20, Fast-40, Fast-80DT, and Fast-160DT—or the equivalent marketing terms, such as Fast, Ultra, Ultra 2, Ultra 3 (also called Ultra160), and Ultra 4 (Ultra320). Refer to Table 7.2 for a complete breakdown of SCSI official terms, marketing terms, and speeds.

The further evolution of the most commonly used form of SCSI is defined under the SPI standards within SCSI-3. The SPI standards are detailed in the following sections.

SPI (Ultra SCSI)

The SPI standard, published in 1995, is the first SCSI standard that fell under the SCSI-3 designation. The SPI standard is officially known as ANSI/INCITS 253-1995 (formerly ANSI X3.253-1995). SPI is also called Ultra SCSI by most marketing departments, and it defines the parallel bus electrical connections and signals. A separate document, called the SCSI Interlocked Protocol (SIP), defines the parallel command set. SIP was included in the later SPI-2 and SPI-3 revisions and is no longer carried as a separate document. These are the main features added in SPI:

- Fast-20 (Ultra) speeds (20MBps or 40MBps)
- 68-pin P cable and connectors defined for Wide SCSI

SPI initially included speeds up to Fast SCSI (10MHz), which enabled transfer speeds up to 20MBps using a 16-bit bus. Later, Fast-20 (20MHz), commonly known as Ultra SCSI, was added through an addendum document (ANSI/INCITS 253-1995 Amendment 1), allowing a throughput of 40MBps on a 16-bit bus (commonly called Ultra/Wide).

SPI-2 (Ultra2 SCSI)

SPI-2 is also called Ultra 2 SCSI and was officially published in 1998 as ANSI/INCITS 302-1998 (formerly ANSI X3.302-1998). SPI-2 adds several features to the prior versions:

- Fast-40 (Ultra 2) speeds (40MBps or 80MBps)
- LVD signaling
- Single connector attachment (SCA-2) connectors
- A 68-pin very-high-density connector (VHDC)

The most notable of these is a higher speed, called Fast-40, which is commonly called Ultra 2 SCSI and runs at 40MHz. On a narrow (8-bit) bus, this results in 40MBps throughput, whereas on a Wide (16-bit) bus, this results in 80MBps throughput and is commonly referred to as Ultra 2/Wide.

To achieve these speeds, a new electrical interface, called LVD, must be used. The slower single-ended electrical interface is good only for speeds up to Fast-20; Fast-40 mode requires LVD operation. The LVD signaling also enables longer cable lengths: up to 12 meters with multiple devices or 25 meters with only one device. LVD and SE devices can share the same cable, but in that case, the bus runs in SE mode and is restricted in length to as little as 1.5 meters in Fast-20 mode. LVD operation requires special LVD-only or LVD/SE multimode terminators. If multimode terminators are used, the same terminators work on either SE or LVD buses.

The SPI-2 standard also includes SIP and defines the SCA-2 80-pin connector for hot-swappable drive arrays. There is also a new 68-pin (VHDC), which is smaller than the previous types.

SCSI Signaling

"Normal," or standard, SCSI uses a signaling technique called SE signaling. SE signaling is a low-cost technique, but it also has performance and noise problems.

SE signaling is also called *unbalanced signaling* because each signal is carried on a pair of wires, usually twisted to help reduce noise. With SE, one of the pair is grounded—often to a common ground for all signals—and the other carries the actual voltage transitions. It is up to a receiver at the other end of the cable to detect the voltage transitions, which are really just changes in voltage.

Unfortunately, this type of unbalanced signaling is very prone to problems with noise, electromagnetic interference, and ground leakage; these problems get worse the longer the cable is. This is why Ultra SCSI was limited to such short maximum bus lengths—as little as 1.5 meters.

When SCSI was first developed, a signaling technique called HVD signaling was also introduced into the standard. Differential signaling, also known as *balanced signaling*, is still done with a pair of wires. In fact, the first in the pair carries the same type of signal that single-ended SCSI carries. The second in the pair, however, carries the logical inversion of that signal. The receiving device detects the difference between the pair (hence the name *differential*). By using the wires in a balanced pair, the receiver no longer needs to detect voltage magnitude, only the differential between voltages in two wires. This is much easier for circuits to do reliably, which makes them less susceptible to noise and enables greater cable length. Therefore, differential SCSI can be used with cable lengths of up to 25 meters, whereas single-ended SCSI is good only for 6 meters maximum, or as little as 1.5 meters in the faster modes.

HVD was hardly ever used in PCs and has been replaced by LVD. A few HVD SCSI host adapters remain on the market, but HVD signaling is obsolete and was removed from SCSI-3 standards.

Most LVD devices are actually multimode devices, designed to work in SE mode as well as LVD. Therefore, all multimode LVD/SE SCSI devices can be used on either LVD or SE SCSI buses. However, when on a bus with even one other SE device, all the LVD devices on the bus run only in SE mode. Because SE mode supports only SCSI speeds of up to 20MHz (Fast-20 or Ultra SCSI) and cable lengths of up to 1.5 or 3 meters, the devices also work only at that speed or lower; you also might have problems with longer cables. Although you can purchase an Ultra 3 SCSI multimode LVD/SE drive and install it on a SCSI bus along with SE devices, you will certainly be wasting the capabilities of the faster device. Fortunately, SE SCSI devices are largely obsolete, and in any case are not suitable for use in servers.

Note that all Ultra 2, Ultra 3, and faster devices support LVD signaling because that is the only way they can be run at the Ultra 2 (40MHz) or Ultra 3 (80MHz) speeds. Ultra SCSI (20MHz) or slower devices can support LVD signaling, but in most cases, LVD is synonymous with Ultra 2 or Ultra 3 only.

Table 7.2, earlier in this chapter, lists all the SCSI speeds and maximum lengths for each speed, using the supported signaling techniques for that speed.

Because the connectors are the same for SE, HVD, LVD, or multimode SE/LVD devices, and because putting an HVD device on any bus with SE or LVD devices causes damage, it is good to be able to tell them apart. One way is to look for a special symbol on the unit; the industry has adopted different universal symbols for single-ended and differential SCSI. Figure 7.2 shows these symbols.

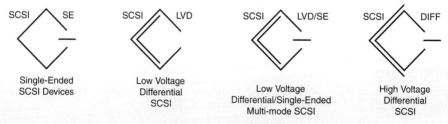

Figure 7.2   Universal symbol icons identifying SE, LVD, multimode LVD/SE, and HVD devices.

If you do not see such symbols, you can tell whether you have an HVD device by using an ohmmeter to check the resistance between pins 21 and 22 on the device connector:

- On a single-ended or LVD device, the pins should be tied together and also tied to the ground.

- On an HVD device, the pins should be open or have significant resistance between them.

Although you will blow up stuff if you plug HVD devices into LVD or SE buses, this generally should not be a problem because virtually all devices used in the PC environment are SE, LVD, or LVD/SE. HVD has essentially been rendered obsolete because it has been removed from the SCSI standard with Ultra 3 SCSI (SPI-3).

SPI-3 (Ultra 3 SCSI [Ultra160])

SPI-3, also known as Ultra 3 or Ultra160 SCSI, was published in 2000 and builds on the previous standard primarily by doubling the speed to Fast-80DT (double transition). This results in a maximum throughput of 160MBps. These are the main features added to SPI-3:

- DT clocking
- Cyclic redundancy checking (CRC)
- Domain validation
- Packetization
- Quick Arbitrate and Select (QAS)

DT clocking sends data on both the rising and falling edges of the REQ/ACK clock. This enables Ultra 3 SCSI to transfer data at 160MBps, while still running at a bus clock rate of 40MHz. This mode is defined for 16-bit bus use only.

CRC is a form of error checking incorporated into Ultra 3 SCSI. Previous versions of SCSI use simple parity checking to detect transmission errors. CRC is a much more robust form of error-detection capability that is far superior for operation at higher speeds.

Domain validation allows better negotiation of SCSI transfer speeds and modes. With prior SCSI versions, when the bus is initialized, the host adapter sends an INQUIRY command at the lowest 5MHz speed to each device to determine which data transfer rate the device can use. The problem is that, even though both the host adapter and device might support a given speed, there is no guarantee that the interconnection between the devices will reliably work at that speed. If a problem occurs, the device becomes inaccessible. With domain validation, after a maximum transfer speed is negotiated between the host and device, it is then tested at that rate. If errors are detected, the rate is stepped down until the connection tests error-free. This is similar to how modems negotiate transmission speeds before communicating and really improves the flexibility and perceived reliability of SCSI.

Packetization is a protocol that enables information to be transferred between SCSI devices in a much more efficient manner. Traditional parallel SCSI uses multiple bus phases to communicate different types of information between SCSI devices: one for command information, two for messages, one for status, and two for data. In contrast, packetized SCSI communicates all this information by using only two phases: one for each direction. This dramatically reduces the command and protocol overhead, especially as higher and higher speeds are used.

Packetized SCSI is fully compatible with traditional parallel SCSI, which means packetized SCSI devices can reside on the same bus as traditional SCSI devices. As long as the host adapter supports packetization, it can communicate with one device using packets and another using the traditional protocol. Not all Ultra 3 or Ultra160 SCSI devices include packetization support, however. Ultra 3 devices that support packetization are typically referred to as Ultra160+ SCSI.

QAS is a feature in Ultra 3 SCSI that reduces arbitration time by eliminating bus free time. QAS enables a device to transfer control of the bus to another device without an intervening BUS FREE phase. SCSI devices that support QAS report that capability in the INQUIRY command.

Ultra160 and Ultra160+

Because the five main new features of Ultra 3 SCSI are optional, drives could claim Ultra 3 capability and not have a consistent level of functionality. To ensure truth in advertising and a minimum level of performance, a group of manufacturers got together and created a substandard within Ultra 3 SCSI that requires a minimum set of features. These are called Ultra160 and Ultra160+ because both indicate 160MBps throughput. They are technically not an official part of the SPI-3 standard, but they do guarantee that certain specifications will be met and certain performance levels will be attained.

Ultra160 is a specific implementation of Ultra 3 (SPI-3) SCSI that includes the first three additional features of Ultra3 SCSI:

- Fast-80DT clocking for 160MBps operation
- CRC
- Domain validation

Ultra160 SCSI runs in LVD mode and is backward compatible with all Ultra 2 SCSI (LVD) devices. The only caveat is that no SE devices must be on the bus. When Ultra 2 and Ultra160 (Ultra 3) devices are mixed, each device can operate at its full-rated speed, independent of the other. The bus will dynamically switch from single- to double-transition mode to support the differences in speeds.

Ultra160+ adds the other two features, ensuring a full implementation of Ultra 3:

- Packetization
- QAS

To determine whether a particular Ultra160 device actually meets Ultra160+ standards, you can check its specifications for support of packetization and QAS features.

Ultra160 host adapters are available in 32-bit and 64-bit PCI and PCI-Express x4 form factors and in single-channel and two-channel models. You use the two-channel models to support up to 30 devices and to provide separate channels for different speeds of devices.

SPI-4, or Ultra 4 SCSI (Ultra320)

SPI-4, also known as Ultra 4 or Ultra320 SCSI, was published in 2002 as ANSI/INCITS 362-2002, and it has all the same features as Ultra 3 (Ultra160) SCSI plus several new features to ensure reliable data transmission at twice the speed.

Ultra320 SCSI integrates both the packetization and QAS features from Ultra160+ SCSI as mandatory features. Ultra320 SCSI then adds the following new features:

- **Transfer speed**—Ultra320 transfers data 2 bytes (16 bits) at a time at 80MHz using DT cycling, meaning it transfers twice per cycle (Hz). This results in a burst transfer rate of 320MBps.

- **Read/write data streaming**—This minimizes the overhead for queued data transfers by enabling a device to send one data stream queue-tag packet followed by multiple data packets. Previously, only one data packet could be sent with each queue-tag packet. Write performance is also increased because there are fewer bus turnarounds from data in to data out.

- **Flow control**—This allows a target device to indicate when the last packet of a data stream will be transferred, which enables the initiator to terminate the data prefetch or begin flushing data buffers sooner than previously possible.

At the high 80MHz DT signaling speeds used with Ultra320, problems were discovered with high-frequency roll-off (signal degradation) and skew (timing variations) in the cables and logic boards. To compensate for this, Ultra320 can use one of two methods: write precompensation (WPC) in the transmitters or adjustable active filters (AAF) in the receivers. WPC alters the transmitted signals by driving the first bit after a clock transition harder than the subsequent bits. WPC can be turned off if receivers with AAF are used instead, because they are capable of compensating for roll-off and skew problems in the transmission line at the receiving end. With AAF, a special training pattern with low- and high-frequency signals is sent before each data transfer to allow the receiver to dynamically adjust for the high-frequency roll-off and skew problems. AAF is considered the best method because it is dynamic and automatically adjusts to compensate for the particular conditions in the bus at the time of each data transfer. Because of this, the faster Ultra640 standard requires AAF, and WPC is not an option.

Ultra320 host adapters require 64-bit 133MHz PCI-X or PCI-Express x4 expansion slots, making them incompatible with very low-end servers. However, most midrange and entry-level servers include multiple PCI-X slots (which can also be used by PCI cards), and the newest designs often feature PCI-Express x4 expansion slots along with, or instead of, PCI-X slots. Although the SPI-5 (Ultra640) standard was published in 2003, it appears that Ultra320 products will be the last, and fastest, SPI-based products to be produced.

SPI-5, or Ultra 5 SCSI (Ultra640)

SPI-5, also known as Ultra 5 or Ultra640 SCSI, was published in 2003 as ANSI/INCITS 367-2003, and it is twice as fast as the Ultra 4 (Ultra320) standard. Its major features include the following:

- Signal and clock speeds are doubled (160MHz, 2 bytes per transfer, and two transfers per cycle).
- WPC is no longer allowed.
- AAF is required.
- The AAF receiver adjusts the clocking for both the rising and falling edges of the signal.
- The AAF training pattern is changed to compensate for crosstalk effects.
- Cable length is restricted to 2m using a multidrop ribbon cable, or up to 20m for a shielded cable if only one device exists (point-to-point interconnect).

With Ultra640 SCSI, ribbon cables are restricted to 2m in total length. This is because ribbon cable has high crosstalk, or signal noise transfer, between adjacent wires. The maximum length for a shielded cable bus is 10m, or 20m if a single device is connected.

No products have been developed supporting SPI-5 standards. Instead, the SCSI storage industry is switching its emphasis for very high-end performance to Serial Attached SCSI (SAS). Because SAS uses the same basic physical layer and connections as SATA, SAS is becoming the next step in both SCSI and high-end SATA solutions. See the next section for details.

SAS

With parallel SCSI reaching the end of the road with the development of Ultra320 and the introduction of the moribund Ultra640 standard, the T10 committee decided to look into serial architecture as a possible solution for future SCSI implementations. Starting in 2002, the committee began work on a future serial SCSI standard. Rather than reinvent the wheel, it decided to adopt the same signaling, cable, and connector designs as used in SATA and combine the SCSI command protocol with a somewhat modified SATA physical layer design. The result was called SAS and was officially published in 2003 as ANSI/INCITS 376-2003. An extension featuring incremental enhancements and fixes is called SAS 1.1 and is currently under development.

SAS was designed to leverage the cost economies of the SATA physical interface, cable, and connector designs while preserving the robust software and reliability of SCSI. SAS was designed as an extendable standard with future increases in speed and performance in mind. As with SATA, the serial interface is self-clocking, which allows data rates to be more easily pushed higher and higher. The main features of SAS include the following:

■ 300MBps point-to-point connections are possible, with up to 1200MBps also possible, and future backward-compatible enhancements are expected.

■ Wide-port devices will allow multiple serial connections, multiplying the bandwidth available by the number of connections.

■ SAS utilizes the robust and refined (20 years in development) SCSI protocol.

■ SAS supports both 300MBps SAS and 150MBps SATA drives, enabling a motherboard or host adapter with SAS connectors to support both SAS and SATA drives.

The most important feature of SAS is that it actually supports two types of drives. SATA drives can be attached for low-cost storage, and true SAS drives can be attached for higher-performance systems. The SAS connector design enables both SAS and SATA drives to be plugged in; however, it is impossible to plug an SAS drive in to a SATA interface. Because the SATA connector signals are a subset of SAS signals, SATA drives will operate on SAS host adapters. SAS drives, on the other hand, will not operate on SATA adapters. The SAS connectors are specially keyed to prevent plugging them in to SATA host adapters.

SAS uses three protocols, each for transferring different types of data, depending on which type of device is being accessed:

■ **Serial SCSI Protocol (SSP)**—SSP sends SCSI commands to SAS devices.

■ **SCSI Management Protocol (SMP)**—SMP sends management information to expanders.

■ **SATA Tunneled Protocol (STP)**—STP sends SATA commands to SATA devices.

By including these protocols, SAS provides full compatibility with existing SCSI devices and applications software as well as SATA devices and software. Combined with the backward compatibility of SAS and SATA physical connections, this enables SAS to operate as a universal interconnection for both SAS and SATA devices. If SAS is onboard, a user could upgrade his or her system from SATA to SAS by either replacing the SATA drive with an SAS drive or by keeping the SATA drive and adding the SAS drive to the system and using both simultaneously. To further ensure compatibility, in 2003, the SCSI Trade Association (STA) and the SATA II Working Group announced a partnership to enable system-level compatibility with SAS and SATA hard drives.

SAS is designed for extremely high bandwidth. Data transfer rates start at 3GBps (300MBps), with a roadmap enabling increases up to 12GBps (1200MBps), which is nearly four times that of Ultra320 SCSI. In addition, SAS is a point-to-point connection that allows full bandwidth to each drive rather than sharing it among multiple drives, as does parallel SCSI. Devices can also use wide-port connections, meaning they can have multiple connections to a single device. The total bandwidth available in that case is multiplied by the total number of connections to the device.

Internal connections use cables up to 1 meter long; these are similar to SATA cables except that they have a modified connector key (see Figure 7.3).

Table 7.3 shows the pinouts of the SAS host adapter and device connectors.

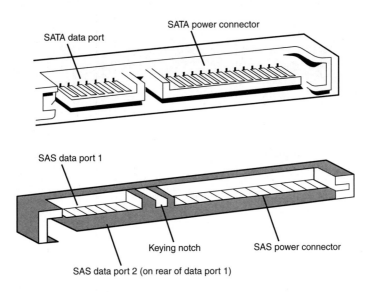

Figure 7.3   A SATA internal hard disk drive connector compared to a SAS internal drive connector.

Table 7.3   Pinouts for SAS Host and Device Connectors

Host Connector		Device Connector	
Pin	**Signal**	**Pin**	**Signal**
S1[1]	Ground	S1	Ground
S2	TP+	S2	RP+
S3	TP-	S3	RP-
S4	Ground	S4	Ground
S5	RP-	S5	TP-
S6	RP+	S6	TP+
S7	Ground	S7	Ground
		S8[2]	Ground
		S9	RS+
		S10	RS-
		S11	Ground
		S12	TS-
		S13	TS+
		S14	Ground

[1]*S1–S7 = primary physical interface*
[2]*S8–S14 = secondary phy (no connects on SAS single-phy drives, SATA drives, and narrow cables).*

External SAS connections, on the other hand, use InfiniBand-type cables that support four physical connections, along with an adapter that allows four internal connections to be mated to the external cable via an open expansion slot. The device connector looks a lot like the connector on a SATA drive; however, it also features a key and optional secondary signals for wide-port device connections. Figure 7.4 shows a typical external SAS cable and adapter.

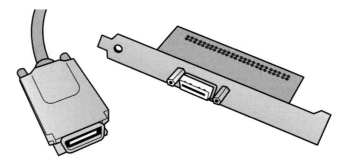

Figure 7.4   SAS external cable (left) and adapter (right). The adapter uses an empty expansion slot.

The design of the host connector enables both SATA and SAS cables to be attached. The pinout of each connection uses seven pins, and the pinout is identical to the SATA pinout.

Figure 7.5 shows the icon used to identify SAS devices and connections that are compliant with the SAS standard.

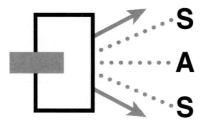

Figure 7.5   SAS icon.

A key feature of SAS is expandability. Devices called *expanders* enable SAS to be scaled up to connect large numbers of drives. Expanders are essentially low-cost switches that enable up to 128 individual point-to-point connections to be made; a total of up to 16,384 SAS devices can be connected via multiple expanders to a single host. In contrast, parallel SCSI imposes a limit of 15 devices per SCSI chain and severely limits total cable length. Figure 7.6 shows how expanders enable great flexibility in connections between SAS initiator devices (such as host adapters) and SAS target devices (such as SAS or SATA drives).

Although the SAS specification was released in October 2003, prototype SAS adapters and drives were first demonstrated by Seagate and Hewlett-Packard in March 2003. Motherboards with onboard SAS host adapters have been available since late summer 2005, and all the major disk drive manufacturers have announced plans to develop SAS disk drives; SAS allows existing SATA drives to be used as well.

RAID Arrays

Most servers, especially at levels above the workgroup, use SCSI drives rather than ATA drives because of their superior performance. You can enhance performance and data reliability further by creating a drive array. RAID technologies are used by both SCSI and ATA drives. Current SCSI-based RAID products primarily support Ultra320 and Ultra160 drives and are used in traditional servers and rack-mounted computers. For a complete description of RAID levels and terminologies, see Chapter 6, "The ATA/IDE Interface."

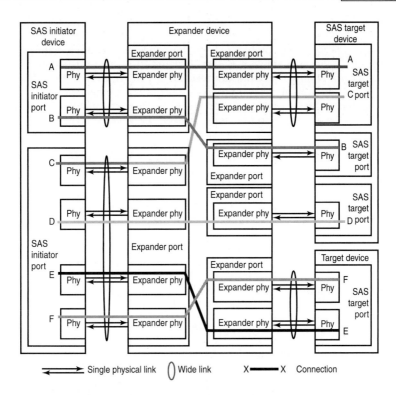

Figure 7.6   Typical SAS expander connection diagram. Note that each expander, SAS initiator port, and SAS target port has a unique SAS address. Connections E and F represent a wide SAS initiator port with two concurrent connections to a wide SAS port.

Tip

When you install Windows 2000, Windows XP, or Windows Server 2003 on a system with SCSI drives, make sure you press F6 when prompted to install a third-party SCSI or RAID driver. The driver must be on a floppy disk.

Fibre Channel SCSI

Fibre Channel SCSI is a specification for a serial interface using a Fibre Channel physical and protocol characteristic with a SCSI command set. It can achieve 200MBps or 400MBps over either fiber or coaxial cable of several kilometers in length. Fibre Channel is designed for long-distance connectivity (such as several kilometers) and connecting multiple systems, and it has become a popular choice for storage area networks (SANs) and server clusters. Fibre Channel SCSI complements, rather than replaces, Ultra160 and Ultra320 SCSI, which are designed for direct connection to servers.

200MBps versions of Fibre Channel SCSI use the gigabit interface connector (GBIC), whereas 400MBps versions use either the small form factor pluggable (SFP) connector for optical connections or the high-speed serial data connector (HSSDC) for copper cable. (These connectors are shown later in this chapter, in Figures 7.11–7.13.)

Because SAS and iSCSI offer much the same performance and benefits of Fibre Channel at a much lower cost, it is expected that SAS and iSCSI will replace Fibre Channel in many high-end server applications.

iSCSI

Another variation on SCSI, iSCSI, combines the performance of SCSI drives with Ethernet networking up to gigabit speeds. Because iSCSI uses Ethernet to transport data between systems, iSCSI storage can be located anywhere an Ethernet network can reach, including Internet access. In addition, iSCSI storage enables secure remote storage for computers that could be hundreds of kilometers away. Because iSCSI data can be routed the same way any other type of Ethernet data can be routed, it enables data to be transported even when some connections between the server and the storage devices are unavailable.

Eventually, iSCSI is expected to replace Fibre Channel in uses such as network attached storage (NAS), SANs, and storage clusters. Similarly to Fibre Channel, iSCSI cards can be purchased in both copper-wire and fiber-optic versions to match the Ethernet network already in use. iSCSI storage arrays are available in rack-mounted form factors for easy installation in data centers.

iSCSI host adapters for copper (CAT5 and greater UTP cable) support 1Gbps (Gigabit Ethernet) transfer rates and also support Fast Ethernet (100Mbps) transfer rates. For best performance, you should use a 64-bit PCI slot, PCI-X slot or PCI-Express slot, although most are backward compatible with 32-bit PCI slots. The process of setting up an iSCSI host adapter requires the user to configure the card's parameters, identify the target drives by IP address or DNS name, specify the port number, configure login information, configure routing tables, and store configuration information in the host adapter's non-volatile RAM. For details, see the documentation for a particular iSCSI host adapter.

SCSI Cables and Connectors

The SCSI standards are very specific when it comes to cables and connectors. However, because of the long development process for SCSI devices and standards, there are many different SCSI cables and connectors. Devices that support Wide SCSI, including parallel SCSI (SPI) host adapters and drives made for servers, use 68-pin or 80-pin connectors, but SCSI devices that support the original 8-bit Narrow SCSI specification use various 50-pin connectors, such as the 50-position unshielded pin header connector for internal SCSI connections and the 50-position shielded Centronics latch-style connectors for external connections. Some nonstandard Narrow SCSI implementations also used a DB-25F connector that is physically identical to that for a parallel port.

The shielded Centronics-style connector shown in Figure 7.7 is also called Alternative 2 in the official specification. Passive or active termination (active is preferred) is specified for both single-ended and differential buses. The 50-conductor bus configuration is defined in the SCSI-2 standard as the A cable. SCSI-2 added the high-density, 50-position, D-shell connector option for the A cable connectors. This connector (shown in Figure 7.8) is now called Alternative 1. Very few, if any, SCSI hard disk or tape backup drives used on servers today use Narrow SCSI connections.

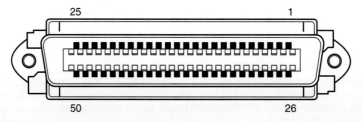

Figure 7.7   Low-density, 50-pin SCSI device connector.

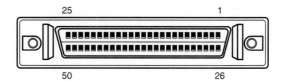

Figure 7.8   High-density, 50-pin SCSI device connector.

A new 68-conductor P cable was developed as part of the SCSI-3 specification. Shielded and unshielded high-density D-shell connectors are specified for both the A and P cables. The shielded high-density connectors use a squeeze-to-release latch rather than the wire latch used on the Centronics-style connectors. Active termination for single-ended buses is specified, providing a high level of signal integrity. Figure 7.9 shows the 68-pin, high-density SCSI connector.

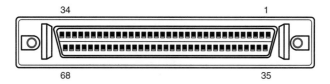

Figure 7.9   High-density, 68-pin SCSI device connector.

Drive arrays normally use special SCSI drives with what is called an 80-pin Alternative-4 connector that is capable of Wide SCSI and also includes power signals. Drives with the 80-pin connector are usually *hot-swappable*—that is, they can be removed and installed with the power on—in drive arrays. The 80-pin Alternative-4 connector is shown in Figure 7.10.

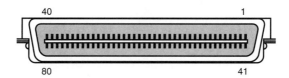

Figure 7.10   80-pin Alternative-4 SCSI device connector.

Fibre Channel SCSI devices running at 200MBps can connect to various types of devices, depending on the GBIC module installed in the host adapter. The module could use a subscriber connector (SC) for fiber-optic cable, an HSSDC for copper cable, or a DB-9 connector for copper cable. The GBIC module can be removed from the host adapter, as shown in Figure 7.11. 400MBps devices can connect to the HSSDC connector shown in Figure 7.12 if copper wire is used, or they can connect to the modular small form factor pluggable (SFP) connector shown in Figure 7.13 if fiber-optic cable is used.

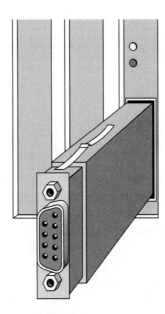

Figure 7.11 The GBIC module used for 200MBps versions of Fibre Channel can accept DB-9 (shown), SC, or HSSDC modules.

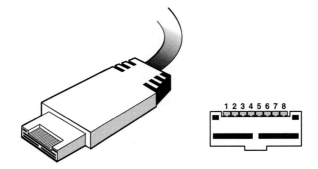

Figure 7.12 The HSSDC used for 400MBps versions of Fibre Channel over copper wire.

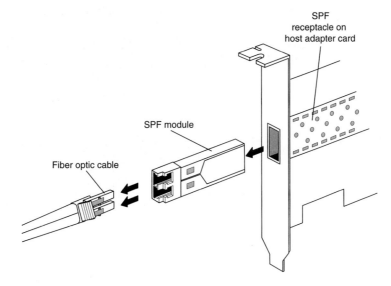

Figure 7.13   The SFP module used for 400MBps versions of Fibre Channel over fiber-optic cable.

Parallel SCSI Cable and Connector Pinouts

This section details the pinouts of the various SCSI cables and connectors. Two electrically different versions of SCSI exist: SE and differential. These two versions are electrically incompatible and must not be interconnected; otherwise, damage will result. Fortunately, very few differential SCSI applications are available in the PC industry, so you will rarely (if ever) encounter one. Within each electrical type (SE or differential), there are basically two SCSI cable types:

- A cable (Narrow 8-bit SCSI)
- P cable (16-bit Wide SCSI)

Although the 50-pin A cable was the most common cable in earlier SCSI-1 and SCSI-2 installations, it does not support today's high-speed SCSI implementations for servers. In servers, you most often find the 68-pin P cable originally developed for SCSI-2 Wide (16-bit) devices. If you need to install a standard (Narrow) SCSI device on the same SCSI bus that you use for Wide devices, you can use adapters that convert P cable connectors to accept A cables.

SCSI cables used for external drives are specially shielded, with the most important high-speed signals carried in the center of the cable and the less important, slower ones in two additional layers around the perimeter. A typical SCSI cable is constructed as shown in Figure 7.14.

This specialized construction is what makes SCSI cables so expensive, as well as thicker than other types of cables. Note that this specialized construction is necessary only for external SCSI cables. Cables used to connect devices inside a shielded enclosure (such as inside a PC) can use much less expensive ribbon cables.

The A cables can have pin-header–type (internal) connectors or external shielded connectors, each with a different pinout. The P cables feature the same connector pinout on both internal and external cable connections.

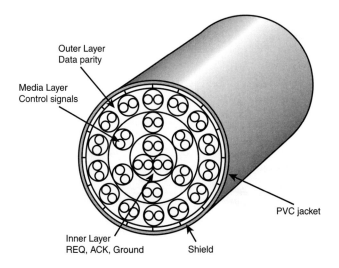

Figure 7.14   A cross-section of a typical SCSI cable.

LVD SCSI Cables and Connectors

Virtually all recent servers with integrated or add-on SCSI host adapters support LVD signaling. Table 7.4 lists the pinouts for a 68-pin LVD P cable. Note that in the P cable, the RESERVED lines are left open in SCSI devices and the bus terminator assemblies. A hyphen preceding a signal name indicates that the signal is Active Low.

Table 7.4   P Cable (LVD) Internal or External Shielded Connectors

Signal Name	Pin	Pin	Signal Name
+DB12	1	35	-DB(12)
+DB13	2	36	-DB(13)
+DB14	3	37	-DB(14)
+DB15	4	38	-DB(15)
+DBP1	5	39	-DB(Parity 1)
+DB0	6	40	-DB(0)
+DB1	7	41	-DB(1)
+DB2	8	42	-DB(2)
+DB3	9	43	-DB(3)
+DB4	10	44	-DB(4)
+DB5	11	45	-DB(5)
+DB6	12	46	-DB(6)
+DB7	13	47	-DB(7)

Signal Name	Pin	Pin	Signal Name
+P_CRCA	14	48	-P_CRCA
GROUND	15	49	GROUND
DIFFSENSE	16	50	GROUND
TERMPWR	17	51	TERMPWR
TERMPWR	18	52	TERMPWR
RESERVED	19	53	RESERVED
GROUND	20	54	GROUND
+ATN	21	55	-ATN
GROUND	22	56	GROUND
+BSY	23	57	-BSY
+ACK	24	58	-ACK
+RST	25	59	-RST
+MSG	26	60	-MSG
+SEL	27	61	-SEL
+C/D	28	62	-C/D
+REQ	29	63	-REQ
+I/O	30	64	-I/O
+DB8	31	65	-DB(8)
+DB9	32	66	-DB(9)
+DB10	33	67	-DB(10)
+DB11	34	68	-DB(11)

SE SCSI Cables and Connectors

SE SCSI cables and connectors use the pinouts listed in Tables 7.5 and 7.6 (the same pinouts used by HVD SCSI cables and connectors). Although servers don't incorporate SE-only host adapters, both integrated (embedded) and add-on card LVD SCSI host adapters are designed to work with both LVD and SE devices. To avoid slowing down LVD devices, SE devices should be connected to a separate bus from the one hosting LVD devices.

The A cable is available in both internal unshielded and external shielded configurations. A hyphen preceding a signal name indicates that the signal is Active Low. The RESERVED lines have continuity from one end of the SCSI bus to the other. In an A cable bus, the RESERVED lines should be left open in SCSI devices (but may be connected to ground) and are connected to ground in the bus terminator assemblies.

Table 7.5   A-Cable (SE) Internal Unshielded Header Connector

Signal	Pin	Pin	Signal
GROUND	1	2	-DB(0)
GROUND	3	4	-DB(1)
GROUND	5	6	-DB(2)
GROUND	7	8	-DB(3)
GROUND	9	10	-DB(4)
GROUND	11	12	-DB(5)
GROUND	13	14	-DB(6)
GROUND	15	16	-DB(7)
GROUND	17	18	-DB(Parity)
GROUND	19	20	GROUND
GROUND	21	22	GROUND
RESERVED	23	24	RESERVED
Open	25	26	TERMPWR
RESERVED	27	28	RESERVED
GROUND	29	30	GROUND
GROUND	31	32	-ATN
GROUND	33	34	GROUND
GROUND	35	36	-BSY
GROUND	37	38	-ACK
GROUND	39	40	-RST
GROUND	41	42	-MSG
GROUND	43	44	-SEL
GROUND	45	46	-C/D
GROUND	47	48	-REQ
GROUND	49	50	-I/O

Table 7.6   A-Cable (SE) External Shielded Connector

Signal	Pin	Pin	Signal
GROUND	1	26	-DB(0)
GROUND	2	27	-DB(1)
GROUND	3	28	-DB(2)
GROUND	4	29	-DB(3)
GROUND	5	30	-DB(4)
GROUND	6	31	-DB(5)
GROUND	7	32	-DB(6)
GROUND	8	33	-DB(7)
GROUND	9	34	-DB(Parity)
GROUND	10	35	GROUND
GROUND	11	36	GROUND
RESERVED	12	37	RESERVED
Open	13	38	TERMPWR
RESERVED	14	39	RESERVED
GROUND	15	40	GROUND
GROUND	16	41	-ATN
GROUND	17	42	GROUND
GROUND	18	43	-BSY
GROUND	19	44	-ACK
GROUND	20	45	-RST
GROUND	21	46	-MSG
GROUND	22	47	-SEL
GROUND	23	48	-C/D
GROUND	24	49	-REQ
GROUND	25	50	-I/O

HVD SCSI Signals

HVD SCSI is not normally used in a PC environment but is very popular with minicomputer installations because of the very long bus lengths that are allowed. This has changed with the introduction of LVD signaling for SCSI, bringing the benefits of differential signaling to lower-end and more mainstream SCSI products.

Differential signaling uses drivers on both the initiator and target ends of the bus and makes each signal work in a push/pull arrangement rather than a signal/ground arrangement, as with standard SE SCSI. This enables much greater cable lengths and eliminates some of the problems with termination.

Almost all PC peripherals produced since SCSI was introduced have been SE types. These are incompatible with HVD devices, although HVD devices can be used on an SE bus with appropriate (and expensive) adapters. This is possible because HVD cables use the same pinouts as SE cables (refer to Tables 7.5 and 7.6). The LVD devices, on the other hand, can be used on an SE bus if they are multimode devices, in which case they switch into SE mode. If all devices—including the host adapter—support LVD mode, all the devices switch into that mode, and much longer cable lengths and higher speeds can be used. The normal limit for an SE SCSI bus is 1.53 meters maximum and up to 20MHz. If run in LVD mode, the maximum bus length goes up to 12 meters, and speeds can go up to 80MHz. HVD SCSI supports bus lengths of up to 25 meters.

Almost all modern SCSI hard disks are Ultra 2 or Ultra 3 devices, which means that by default they are also LVD or multimode LVD/SE devices.

Expanders

SCSI expanders separate a SCSI bus into more than one physical segment, each of which can have the full SCSI cable length for that type of signaling. They provide a complete regeneration of the SCSI bus signals, allowing greater cable lengths and incompatible devices to essentially share the same bus. An expander can also be used to separate incompatible parts of a SCSI bus—for example, to keep SE and HVD SCSI devices in separate domains.

Expanders are transparent to the software and firmware on the bus, and they don't take up a device ID. They are usually capable of providing termination if located at the end of a bus segment, or they can have termination disabled if they are in the middle of a bus segment.

Figure 7.15 illustrates the interior of a typical SCSI expander. Note that a SCSI expander is usually housed in a protective shell. The dime at the lower right provides an indication of the relative size of the expander.

Configuration jumpers

AMP 171826-4 connector
for four-pin 3.5-inch floppy
drive-type power cable

Connectors for SCSI cables

Figure 7.15   The interior of a typical SCSI expander.

Because of their expense (often more than $100 each), expanders are not normally used except in extreme situations in which no other alternative remains. In most cases, it is better to stick within the recommended cable and bus length requirements and keep incompatible devices, such as HVD devices, off a standard SE or LVD bus.

SCSI Termination

Because a SCSI bus carries high-speed electrical signals, it can be affected by electrical reflections that might occur within any transmission line system. A terminator is designed to minimize the potential for reflections or noise on the bus, as well as to create the proper load for the bus transmitter circuits. Terminators are placed at each end of the bus to minimize these problems.

Despite the simple rules that only two terminators must be on the bus, and they must be at each end, termination are still the most common cause of problems in SCSI installations.

Several types of SCSI terminators are available, depending on the bus signaling and speed requirements:

- Passive
- Active (also called Alternative-2)
- Forced perfect termination (FPT): FPT-3, FPT-18, and FPT-27
- HVD termination
- LVD termination

The first three of these are used on single-ended SCSI buses only. Passive terminators use a passive network of 220-ohm and 330-ohm resistors to control bus termination. They should be used only in Narrow (8-bit) SCSI buses running at 5MHz. Passive terminators allow signal fluctuations in relation to the terminator power signal on the bus. Usually, passive terminating resistors suffice over short distances, such as 1 meter or less, but for longer distances or higher speeds, active termination is a real advantage. Active termination is required with Fast SCSI.

Passive terminators can be plugged in to the unused SCSI port or be built in to many low-speed SCSI devices, such as scanners, optical drives, and removable-media drives. On such devices, you can activate or deactivate built-in passive termination with jumper blocks, a toggle switch, or some other form of selector switch, depending on the device. Figure 7.16 shows the schematic of a typical passive terminator.

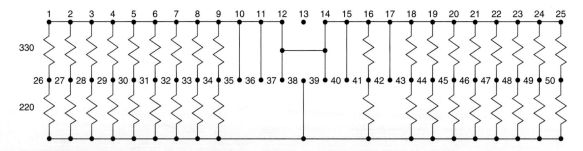

Figure 7.16   Passive SCSI terminator schematic.

Active terminators use built-in voltage regulator ICs combined with 110-ohm resistors. An active terminator actually has one or more voltage regulators to produce the termination voltage, rather than resistor voltage dividers alone. This arrangement helps ensure that the SCSI signals are always terminated to the correct voltage level. Active terminators often have some type of LED indicating the termination activity. The SCSI-2 specification recommends active termination on both ends of the bus and requires active termination whenever Fast or Wide SCSI devices are used. Most high-performance host adapters have an "auto-termination" feature, so if it is the end of a chain, it terminates itself. Figure 7.17 shows the schematic of a typical active terminator.

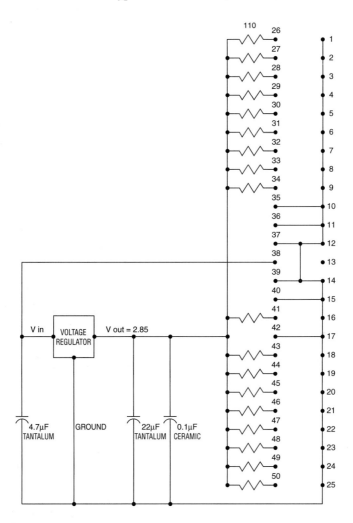

Figure 7.17   Active SCSI terminator schematic.

A variation on active termination is available for single-ended buses: FPT. FPT is an even better form of active termination, in which diode clamps are added to eliminate signal overshoot and undershoot. The trick is that instead of clamping to +5 and ground, these terminators clamp to the output of two regulated voltages. This arrangement enables the clamping diodes to eliminate signal overshoot and undershoot, especially at higher signaling speeds and over longer distances. FPT is technically not found in the SCSI specifications but is a superior type of termination for SE applications that experience high levels of electrical noise.

FPT terminators are available in several versions. FPT-3 and FPT-18 versions are available for 8-bit standard SCSI (Figure 7.18 shows the schematic for an FTP-18 terminator), whereas the FPT-27 is available for 16-bit (Wide) SCSI. The FPT-3 version forces the three most highly active SCSI signals on the 8-bit SCSI bus to be perfect, whereas the FPT-18 forces all the SCSI signals on the 8-bit bus except grounds to be perfect. FPT-27 also forces all the 16-bit Wide SCSI signals except grounds to be perfect.

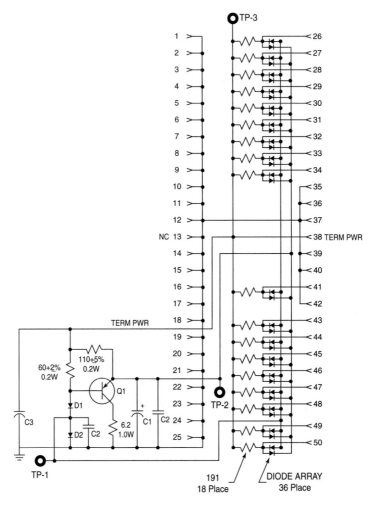

Figure 7.18   FPT18 SCSI terminator schematic.

HVD buses require HVD terminators, constructed using a passive network of 330-ohm/150-ohm/330-ohm resistors. The only choice is that the terminator matches the cable or device connection. The same is true for LVD buses. They require LVD terminators for the bus to function properly. One twist is that special LVD/SE (active) multimode terminators are available. These function as LVD types on an LVD bus and as active types on an SE bus. Note that if any SE devices are on the bus, the bus functions in SE mode and never uses LVD mode, severely limiting bus length and performance. If any SE-only terminators or SE devices are on the bus, the bus defaults into SE mode.

▶▶   See "SCSI Drive/Device Configuration," p. 475.

Note

Several companies make high-quality terminators for the SCSI bus, including East/West Manufacturing Enterprises, Inc. (formerly Aeronics) and the Data Mate division of Methode. Both of these companies make a variety of terminators. EWME is well noted for some unique FPT versions that are especially suited to problem configurations that require longer cable runs or higher signal integrity. One of the best investments you can make in any SCSI installation is in high-quality cables and terminators. Contact information for both of these companies is in the vendor list in Appendix C, "Vendor List."

Special terminators are also required for LVD and HVD SCSI, so if you are using those interfaces, you need to be sure your terminators are compatible.

With LVD or HVD buses, you don't have much choice in terminator types, but for SE buses, you have at least three choices.

Tip

The best rule for terminators, as well as for cables, is to get the best you can. You should *never* use passive terminators; instead, use active or, if you want the best in reliability and integrity, use only FPT.

SCSI Drive/Device Configuration

SCSI drives and devices are not too difficult to configure, but they are more complicated than ATA drives. The SCSI standard controls the way the drives must be set up. You need to set up a couple items when you configure a SCSI drive:

- SCSI ID setting (0–7 or 0–15)
- Terminating resistors

The SCSI ID setting is very simple. Up to 7 SCSI devices can be used on a single Narrow SCSI bus or up to 15 devices on a Wide SCSI bus, and each device must have a unique SCSI ID address. There are 8 or 16 addresses, respectively, and the host adapter takes 1 address, so the rest are free for up to 7 or 15 SCSI peripherals. Most SCSI host adapters are factory-set to ID 7 or 15, which is the highest-priority ID. All other devices must have unique IDs that do not conflict with one another. Some host adapters boot only from a hard disk set to a specific ID. Older Adaptec host adapters required the boot hard disk to be ID 0; newer ones can boot from any ID.

Setting the ID usually involves changing jumpers on the drive. If the drive is installed in an external chassis, the chassis might have an ID selector switch that is accessible at the rear. This selector makes ID selection a simple matter of pressing a button or rotating a wheel until the desired ID number appears. If no external selector is present, you must open the external device chassis and set the ID via the jumpers on the drive.

On 50-pin and 68-pin SCSI drives, three jumpers are required to set the SCSI ID; 80-pin SCA drives used in SCSI RAID arrays usually receive the SCSI ID from the host adapter.

The particular ID selected is actually derived from the binary representation of the jumpers themselves. One example is setting all three ID jumpers to off, which results in a binary number of 000b, which translates to an ID of 0. A binary setting of 001b equals ID 1, 010b equals 2, 011b equals 3, and so on. (The lowercase b indicates binary numbers.)

Unfortunately, the jumpers can appear either forward or backward on the drive, depending on how the manufacturer set them up. To keep things simple, the following tables list all the various ID jumper settings. Table 7.7 shows the settings for drives that order the jumpers with the most significant bit (MSB) to the left; Table 7.8 shows the settings for drives that have the jumpers ordered so that the MSB is to the right. Note that Tables 7.7 and 7.8 list configurations for Wide SCSI (68-pin interface) hard disks. For Narrow SCSI hard disks, you can disregardSCSI IDs from 8 to 15; these drives do not support SCSI IDs higher than 7.

Table 7.7   SCSI ID Jumper Settings with the MSB to the Left[1]

SCSI	ID	Jumper	Settings	
0	0	0	0	0
1	0	0	0	1
2	0	0	1	0
3	0	0	1	1
4	0	1	0	0
5	0	1	0	1
6	0	1	1	0
7	0	1	1	1
8	1	0	0	0
9	1	0	0	1
10	1	0	1	0
11	1	0	1	1
12	1	1	0	0
13	1	1	0	1
14	1	1	1	0
15	1	1	1	1

Table 7.8   SCSI ID Jumper Settings with the MSB to the Right

SCSI	ID	Jumper	Settings	
0	0	0	0	0
1	1	0	0	0
2	0	1	0	0
3	1	1	0	0
4	0	0	1	1
5	1	0	1	0
6	0	1	1	0
7	1	1	1	0
8	0	0	0	1
9	1	0	0	1
10	0	1	0	1
11	1	1	0	1
12	0	0	1	1
13	1	0	1	1
14	0	1	1	1
15	1	1	1	1

[1] 1 = jumper on; 0 = jumper off. Narrow SCSI drives support only SCSI IDs from 0 to 7.

SCSI termination is very simple. Termination is required at both ends of the bus; there are no exceptions. If the host adapter is at one end of the bus, it must have termination enabled. If the host adapter is in the middle of the bus, and if both internal and external bus links are present, the host adapter must have its termination disabled, and the devices at each end of the bus must have terminators installed. As mentioned earlier, the majority of problems with SCSI installations are the result of improper termination.

Figure 7.19 shows a representation of a SCSI bus with several devices attached. In this case, the host adapter is at one end of the bus, and a hard disk is at the other. For the bus to work properly, those devices must be terminated, whereas the others do not have to be.

When installing an external SCSI device, you usually find the device in a storage enclosure with both input and output SCSI connectors, so you can use the device in a daisy-chain. If the enclosure is at the end of the SCSI bus, an external terminator module most likely will have to be plugged in to the second (outgoing) SCSI port to provide proper termination at that end of the bus (see Figure 7.20).

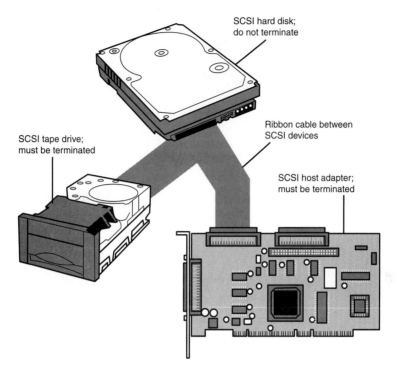

Figure 7.19 SCSI bus daisy-chain connections; the first and last devices must be terminated.

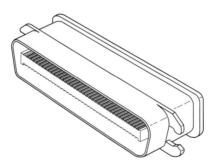

Figure 7.20 External SCSI device terminator.

Note that an external terminator often looks like the end of a SCSI cable. External terminator modules are available in a variety of connector configurations, including pass-through designs, which are necessary if only one port is available. Pass-through terminators are also commonly used in internal installations in which the device does not have built-in terminating resistors. Many hard drives use pass-through terminators for internal installations to save space on the logic-board assembly (see Figure 7.21).

The pass-through models are required when a device is at the end of the bus and only one SCSI connector is available.

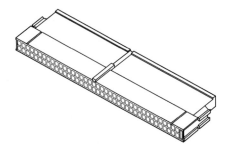

Figure 7.21   Internal pin-header connector pass-through SCSI terminator.

Other configuration items on a SCSI drive can be set via jumpers. Following are several of the most common additional settings:

- Start on Command (delayed start), also known as Delay Spin
- SCSI Parity
- Terminator Power
- SCSI Synchronous Negotiation
- No Wide
- Write Protection

These configuration items are described in the following sections.

Start on Command (Delayed Start)

If you have multiple drives installed in a system, it is wise to set them up so that not all the drives start to spin immediately when the system is powered on. A hard disk drive can consume three or four times more power during the first few seconds after power-on than during normal operation. The motor requires this additional power to get the platters spinning quickly. If several drives are drawing all this power at the same time, the power supply can be overloaded, which can cause the system to hang or have intermittent startup problems.

Nearly all SCSI drives provide a way to delay drive spinning so this problem does not occur. When most SCSI host adapters initialize the SCSI bus, they send out a command called Start Unit to each of the ID addresses in succession. By setting a jumper on the hard disk, you can prevent the disk from spinning until it receives the Start Unit command from the host adapter. Because the host adapter sends this command to all the ID addresses in succession, from the highest-priority address (ID 7) to the lowest (ID 0), the higher-priority drives can be made to start first, with each lower-priority drive spinning up sequentially. Because some host adapters do not send the Start Unit command, some drives might simply delay spin-up for a fixed number of seconds rather than wait for a command that will never arrive.

If drives are installed in external chassis with separate power supplies, you need not implement the delayed-start function. This function is best applied to internal drives that must be run from the same power supply that runs the system. For internal installations, you should set Start on Command (delayed start) even if you have only one SCSI drive; this setting eases the load on the power supply by spinning the drive up after the rest of the system has full power. This method is especially good for portable systems and other systems in which the power supply is limited. (Note that the jumper is sometimes referred to as Delay Spin.)

Some older SCSI host adapters do not support Start on Command or Delay Spin option on the hard disk. In those cases, you should see if the hard disk supports a feature called Stagger Spin. Stagger Spin has the same effect as Start on Command or Delay Spin, except that no support is needed for this command from the SCSI host adapter.

SCSI Parity

SCSI parity checking is a limited form of error checking that helps ensure that all data transfers are reliable. Virtually all host adapters support SCSI parity checking, so the SCSI Parity option should be enabled on every device that supports it. The only reason it exists as an option is that some older host adapters do not work with SCSI parity, so the parity must be turned off.

Most recent SCSI hard disk drives do not support SCSI parity settings, but some tape backup drives do.

Terminator Power

The terminators at each end of the SCSI bus require power from at least one device on the bus. In most cases, the host adapter supplies this terminator power; in some cases, however, it does not. For example, parallel port SCSI host adapters typically do not supply terminator power. It is not a problem if more than one device supplies terminator power because each source is diode protected. For simplicity's sake, many people often configure all devices to supply terminator power. If no device supplies terminator power, the bus is not terminated correctly and will not function properly.

SCSI Synchronous Negotiation

The SCSI bus can run in two modes: asynchronous (the default) and synchronous. The bus actually switches modes during transfers through a protocol called *synchronous negotiation*. Before data is transferred across the SCSI bus, the sending device (called the *initiator*) and the receiving device (called the *target*) negotiate how the transfer will take place. If both devices support synchronous transfers, they will discover this fact through the negotiation, and the transfer will take place at the faster synchronous rate.

Unfortunately, some older devices do not respond to a request for synchronous transfer and can actually be disabled when such a request is made. For this reason, both host adapters and devices that support synchronous negotiation often have a jumper that can be used to disable this negotiation so it can work with older devices. By default, all devices today should support synchronous negotiation, and this function should be enabled.

No Wide

Modern SCSI hard disks are almost always designed to run in Wide (16-bit) mode. Some Wide SCSI hard disks feature a jumper called No Wide. When enabled, No Wide configures the drive to run in Narrow (8-bit) mode. You should not use this option unless you must use a Narrow SCSI host adapter on your server.

Write Protection

Some SCSI hard disks have an optional Write Protection jumper. When it is enabled, the drive is a read-only drive. You can use this setting to keep an image of your server's primary drive on a read-only hard disk for quick restoration or for development purposes.

Plug and Play SCSI

Plug and Play (PnP) SCSI was originally released in April 1994. This specification enables SCSI device manufacturers to build PnP peripherals that are automatically configured when used with a PnP operating system. This enables you to easily connect or reconfigure external peripherals, such as hard disk drives, backup tapes, and CD-ROMs.

To connect SCSI peripherals to the host PC, the specification requires a PnP SCSI host adapter. PnP add-in cards enable a PnP operating system to automatically configure software device drivers and system resources for the host bus interface.

The PnP SCSI specification includes these technical highlights:

- A single cable connector configuration
- Automatic termination of the SCSI bus
- SCAM (SCSI Configured AutoMagically) automatic ID assignment (Note that this was removed in the SPI-3 revision of the SCSI standard. However, most current SCSI drives support an optional cable connection for automatic ID assignment.)
- Full backward compatibility of PnP SCSI devices with the installed base of SCSI systems

Note

AutoMagically is not a misspelling. The word is actually used in the official name for the original specification, which the X3T9.2 committee designated X3T9.2/93-109r5.

Each SCSI peripheral you add to your SCSI bus (other than hard disk drives) requires an external driver to make the device work. Hard disks are the exception; driver support for them is typically provided as part of the SCSI host adapter BIOS. These external drivers are specific not only to a particular device but also to the host adapter.

Two types of standard host adapter interface drivers have become popular, greatly reducing this problem. By having a standard host adapter driver to write to, peripheral makers can more quickly create new drivers that support their devices and then talk to the universal host adapter driver. This arrangement eliminates dependence on one particular type of host adapter. These primary or universal drivers link the host adapter and operating system.

The Advanced SCSI Programming Interface (ASPI) is currently the most popular universal driver, with most peripheral makers writing their drivers to talk to ASPI. (The *A* in ASPI used to stand for Adaptec, the company that introduced it, but other SCSI device vendors have licensed the right to use ASPI with their products.) All recent and current Windows versions, starting with Windows 9x and Windows NT, provide automatic ASPI support for several SCSI host adapters.

Future Domain (now merged into Adaptec) and NCR created another interface driver, called the Common Access Method (CAM). CAM is an ANSI-approved protocol that enables a single driver to control several host adapters. CAM is widely used by UNIX operating systems for SCSI device interfacing using open-source drivers.

Major SCSI host adapter vendors feature drivers customized for various Linux distributions. You should see your host adapter vendor's website for details. Note that if your host adapter vendor does not support your host adapter with a driver, an open-source driver might be available.

SCSI Configuration Troubleshooting

When you are installing a chain of devices on a single SCSI bus, the installation can get complicated very quickly. If you have a problem during installation, you should check the following first:

- Make sure you are using the latest BIOS from your motherboard manufacturer. Some have had problems with their PCI bus slots not working properly.
- Make sure that all SCSI devices attached to the bus are powered on.

- Make sure that all SCSI cables and power cables are properly connected. Try removing and reseating all the connectors to be sure.

- Check that the host adapter and each device on each SCSI bus channel has a unique SCSI ID setting.

- Make sure the SCSI bus is terminated properly. Remember that there should be only two terminators on the bus, one at each end. All other terminations should be removed or disabled.

- If your system BIOS setup has settings for controlling PCI bus configuration, make sure the PCI slot that contains the SCSI adapter is configured for an available interrupt. If your system is PnP, use the Windows Device Manager to check and possibly change the resource configuration.

- If you have a SCSI hard disk installed and your system will not boot from the SCSI drive, there can be several causes for this problem. Note that if both SCSI and non-SCSI disk drives are installed in your computer, in almost all cases, the non-SCSI drive is the boot device. If you want to boot from a SCSI drive, check the boot sequence configuration in your BIOS. If your system allows it, change the boot sequence to allow SCSI devices to boot first. If your system does not allow this type of changes, try removing the non-SCSI drives from your system.

If the system has only SCSI disk drives and still doesn't boot, check the following:

- Be sure your computer's BIOS Setup drive configuration is set to No Drives Installed. The PC BIOS supports only ATA (also called IDE) drives; if you set this to No Drives, the system will then try to boot from another device, such as SCSI.

- Make sure the drive is partitioned and that a primary partition exists. Use the Windows Disk Management tool in Windows 2000/XP/Server 2003 to check.

- Make sure the boot partition of the boot hard disk is set to active. This can be checked or changed with the Disk Management program.

- As a last resort, you can try backing up all data on the SCSI hard disk and then perform a low-level format with the Format utility that is built in to or included with the host adapter.

Here are some tips for getting your setup to function quickly and efficiently:

- **Add one device at a time**—Rather than plugging numerous peripherals into a single SCSI card and then trying to configure them at the same time, you should start by installing the host adapter and a single hard disk. Then you can continue installing devices one at a time, checking to ensure that everything works before moving on.

- **Keep good documentation**—When you add a SCSI peripheral, write down the SCSI ID address and any other switch and jumper settings, such as SCSI Parity, Terminator Power, and Delayed or Remote Start. For the host adapter, record the BIOS addresses, interrupt, DMA channel, and I/O Port addresses used by the adapter, and any other jumper or configuration settings (such as termination) that might be important to know later. Note that some of the configuration tasks performed on the latest SCSI host adapters are performed through the SCSI configuration program that is built in to the SCSI BIOS.

- **Use proper termination**—Each end of the bus must be terminated, preferably with active or FPT terminators. With Fast SCSI-2 and newer devices, you must use active terminators rather than the cheaper passive types. If you have only internal or external devices on the bus, the host adapter and last device on the chain should be terminated. If you have external and internal devices on the chain, you generally terminate the first and last of these devices, but not the SCSI host adapter (which is in the middle of the bus).

■ **Use high-quality shielded SCSI cables**—You need to be sure your cable connectors match your devices. You should use high-quality shielded cables, and observe the SCSI bus-length limitations. You should also use cables designed for SCSI use, and, if possible, stick to the same brand of cable throughout a single SCSI bus. Different brands of cables have different impedance values; this situation sometimes causes problems, especially in long or high-speed SCSI implementations.

Following these simple tips will help minimize problems and help ensure a trouble-free SCSI installation.

SCSI Versus ATA Performance: Advantages and Limitations

Modern operating systems are multitasking, and unlike ATA devices, SCSI devices (with all their additional controller circuitry) function independently of one another. Therefore, data can be read and written to any of the SCSI devices simultaneously. This enables smoother multitasking and increased overall data throughput. The most advanced operating systems, such as Windows NT/2000/XP, even allow drive striping. A *striped drive set* is two or more drives that appear to the user as one drive. Data is split between the drives equally, again increasing overall throughput. Increased fault tolerance and performance are readily implemented and supported in SCSI drive arrays.

Ultra4 (Ultra320) SCSI drives offer advantages compared with ATA. Ultra320 SCSI is 140% faster than UltraATA/133, which has a maximum data rate of 133MBps. Ultra320 SCSI also fully supports multitasking and can significantly improve system performance in servers running Windows NT or Windows Server 2000/2003. ATA limits cable lengths to 0.5 meters, effectively eliminating the ability to connect remote or external devices, whereas Ultra4 (Ultra320) SCSI allows external connections of up to 12 meters or more in length. Also note that ATA allows only 2 devices per cable, whereas Ultra320 SCSI can connect up to 15 devices. Finally, the domain validation feature of Ultra320 SCSI enables noise and other problems on the bus to be handled properly, whereas with ATA, if a problem occurs with the connection (and that is more common at the UltraATA/100 and 133 speeds), the ATA drives simply fail.

ATA drives have much less command overhead for a given sector transfer than do SCSI drives. In addition to the drive-to-controller command overhead that both ATA and SCSI must perform, a SCSI transfer involves negotiating for the SCSI bus; selecting the target drive; requesting data; terminating the transfer over the bus; and converting the logical data addresses to the required cylinder, head, and sector addresses. This arrangement gives ATA an advantage in sequential transfers handled by a single-tasking operating system. In a multitasking system that can take advantage of the extra intelligence of the SCSI bus, SCSI can have a performance advantage.

SCSI drives offer significant architectural advantages over ATA and other drives. Because each SCSI drive has its own embedded disk controller that can function independently from the system CPU, the computer can issue simultaneous commands to every drive in the system. Each drive can store these commands in a queue and then perform the commands simultaneously with other drives in the system. The data could be fully buffered on the drive and transferred at high speed over the shared SCSI bus when a time slot is available.

Although ATA drives also have their own controllers, they do not normally operate simultaneously, and command queuing is not supported. In effect, the dual controllers in a dual-drive ATA installation work one at a time so as not to step on each other.

ATA does not fully support overlapped, multitasked I/O, which enables a device to take on multiple commands and work on them independently and in an order different from which they were received, releasing the bus for other devices to use. The ATA bus instead waits for each command to be completed before the next one can be sent.

As you can see, SCSI has some advantages over ATA, especially where expansion is concerned, and also with regard to support for multitasking operating systems. Unfortunately, it also costs more to implement.

One final advantage of SCSI is in the portability of external devices. It is easy to quickly move an external SCSI CD-ROM, tape drive, scanner, or even a hard disk to another system. This allows moving peripherals more freely between systems and can be a bonus if you have several systems with which you might want to share a number of peripherals. Installing a new external SCSI device on a system is easier because you normally do not need to open it up.

Of course, moving an external SCSI device from one system to another is not nearly as easy as it would be with a USB or FireWire (IEEE 1394) device, which is one reason the latter two (especially USB) are catching on in the mainstream market. USB and FireWire devices are PnP and hot-swappable, allowing you to attach or remove a device with the power on. Plus, no device ID or other configuration is necessary. Narrow and Wide SCSI devices must normally be attached with the device and system power turned off; they also must be configured to use a unique device ID and have proper termination set for existing and new devices.

If you are considering a SCSI-based server, you need to be prepared for sticker shock: SCSI hard disks are considerably more expensive than ATA/IDE or SATA hard disks with comparable capacities. Despite the faster transfer rates claimed by Ultra SCSI 160 and higher speed grades versus ATA/IDE (133MBps) and SATA (150MBps and 300MBps), there's hardly any difference in effective performance between ATA/IDE and SCSI hard disks with comparable designs (same size buffer and rotational rate). If you are building a single-drive server and plan to use external USB or FireWire hard disks for backup, you don't need the extra expense of SCSI because you won't see a comparable difference in performance. However, SCSI hard disks made especially for servers have much higher spin rates than any ATA/IDE or most SATA hard disks: 10,000 to 15,000 rpm, versus 7,200 for typical ATA/IDE or SATA hard disks. The higher spin rate improves single-drive performance.

The biggest performance benefits with SCSI come with SCSI-based RAID arrays and SCSI tape backup drives. Because a SCSI host adapter can handle multiple overlapping read and write commands more efficiently than ATA/IDE, its performance with these types of high-end applications and hardware makes SCSI worthwhile.

Recommended SCSI Host Adapters, Cables, and Terminators

Adaptec's adapters are a good choice because they work well and come with the necessary formatting and operating software. Windows NT/2000/XP/Server 2003 all feature built-in support for Adaptec SCSI adapters. This support is a consideration in many cases because it frees you from having to deal with additional drivers.

For maximum performance, you should use the fastest slot available for your SCSI host adapter card. For example, if your motherboard has PCI-Express x4 slots, you should use them. If you don't have PCI-Express x4 but you have PCI-X slots (which run at up to 133MHz), you should use a PCI-X SCSI host adapter. If your motherboard does not have PCI-Express x4 or PCI-X slots, but has 64-bit/66MHz PCI slots, you should use a 64-bit/66MHz PCI SCSI host adapter. If you want to add SAS support to a motherboard that lacks SAS host adapters, you can choose from PCI-Express or PCI-X host adapters. PCI-Express is faster than PCI-X, but PCI-Express is supported by only some of the very latest servers.

◄◄ See "PCI, PCI-X, and PCI-Express," p. 261.

Like all modern PCI adapters, PnP is supported, meaning virtually all functions on the card can be configured and set through software. This means no more digging through manuals or looking for interrupt, DMA, I/O port, and other jumper settings; everything is controlled by software and saved in a flash memory module on the card. The following are some features found on recent SCSI cards:

- Complete configuration utility built in to the adapter's ROM
- Software-configurable IRQ, ROM addresses, DMA, I/O port addresses, SCSI parity, SCSI ID, and other settings
- Software-selectable automatic termination (no resistors to pull out!)
- Enhanced BIOS support for up to 15 drives
- No drivers required for more than two hard disks
- Drive spin-up on a per-drive basis available
- Boots from any SCSI ID

Adaptec has full PnP support on all its SCSI adapters. These adapters are either automatically configured in any PC that supports the PnP specification or can be configured manually through supplied software in non-PnP systems. The PnP SCSI adapters are highly recommended because they can be configured without opening up the PC. All functions are set by software, and there are no jumpers or switches to attend to. Most peripheral manufacturers write drivers for Adaptec's cards first, so you do not have many compatibility or driver-support problems with Adaptec cards.

For SCSI cables, CS Electronics (www.scsi-cables.com) are good because this company can supply or custom-manufacture virtually any SCSI cable or adapter. It can also supply a wide range of terminators, as can a company called East/West Manufacturing Enterprises, Inc. (formerly Aeronics), which is also worth a look (www.ewme.com).

CHAPTER 8

I/O System Hardware

Although most server activity is network centered, I/O ports and devices still have important functions to perform in a server. I/O ports such as USB and video ports enable local control and monitoring of a server. Keyboards enable commands to be entered during server setup and for maintenance and troubleshooting. With the addition of keyboard-video-mouse (KVM) switches, a single keyboard, mouse, and display can be used to manage multiple servers. CD and DVD drives can be used for installing applications and for backup of low-end servers.

To make your server as reliable and useful as possible, it's important that you understand when I/O hardware might need driver and firmware updates, how to specify the right mix of I/O hardware for a particular server and its mission, and how to troubleshoot that hardware. This chapter is designed to help you master the I/O hardware your servers use.

USB

Universal serial bus (USB) ports have become the single most important I/O ports built into both desktop PCs and servers. Since their introduction in the late 1990s, USB ports have largely replaced serial and parallel ports (however, PS/2 mouse and PS/2 keyboard ports are still around for legacy purposes). USB ports are also used for data-intensive I/O devices, such as external hard disks, rewritable CD and DVD drives, tape backups and scanners. USB ports are also used for signaling connections to battery-backup (UPS) units.

USB is an external peripheral bus standard designed to provide plug-and-play capability for attaching peripherals externally to the PC. USB eliminates the need for special-purpose ports, reduces the need to use special-purpose I/O cards (thus reducing the need to reconfigure the system with each new device added), and saves important system resources, such as interrupts (IRQs), because regardless of the number of devices attached to a system's USB ports, only one IRQ is required. PCs equipped with USB enable peripherals to be automatically recognized and configured as soon as they are physically attached, without the need to reboot or run setup. USB allows up to 127 devices to run simultaneously on a single bus, with peripherals such as monitors and keyboards acting as additional hubs. USB cables, connectors, hubs, and peripherals can be identified by icons, as shown in Figure 8.1. Note the plus symbol added to the upper icon, which indicates that the port supports USB 2.0 (also called Hi-Speed USB) in addition to the standard 1.x support. However, most current equipment seldom uses the plus sign to mark USB 2.0–compatible ports.

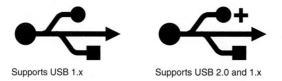

Supports USB 1.x   Supports USB 2.0 and 1.x

Figure 8.1   Icons used to identify USB cables, connectors, hubs, and peripherals.

Intel pioneered USB, and all its PC chipsets, starting with the PIIX3 South Bridge chipset component (introduced in February 1996), have included USB support. Other chipset vendors have followed suit, making USB as common on servers, desktops, and notebook PCs as serial and parallel ports once were.

Six other companies initially worked with Intel in developing USB: Compaq, Digital, IBM, Microsoft, NEC, and Northern Telecom. Together, these companies have established the USB Implementers Forum (USB-IF; see www.usb.org) to develop, support, and promote USB architecture.

The USB-IF formally released USB 1.0 in January 1996, USB 1.1 in September 1998, and USB 2.0 in April 2000. The 1.1 revision was mostly a clarification of some issues related to hubs and other areas of the specification. Most devices and hubs should be 1.1 compliant, even if they were manufactured before the release of the 1.1 specification. The bigger changes were reserved for USB 2.0, which runs at speeds up to 40 times faster than the original USB specification, while maintaining full backward compatibility with USB 1.1. USB ports can be retrofitted to older computers that lack built-in USB connectors through the use of either an add-on PCI card (for desktop computers) or a PC Card on Cardbus-compatible notebook computers. You can also use USB 2.0 add-on cards to update older systems that have only USB 1.1 on their motherboards. Since mid-2002, virtually all motherboards have included four or more USB 2.0 ports as standard.

USB Specifications

USB 1.1 runs at 12Mbps (1.5MBps) over a simple four-wire connection. The bus supports up to 127 devices, connected to a single root hub, and uses a tiered-star topology, built on expansion hubs that can reside in the PC, any USB peripheral, or even standalone hubs.

Note that although the standard allows up to 127 devices to be attached, they all must share the 1.5MBps bandwidth, meaning that adding active devices slows down the bus. In practical reality, few people have more than 8 devices attached at any one time.

USB 2.0 (also called Hi-Speed USB) is a backward-compatible extension of the USB 1.1 specification that uses the same cables, connectors, and software interfaces but runs up to 40 times faster than the original USB 1.0 and 1.1 versions. The higher speed enables higher-performance peripherals, such as high-resolution web/videoconferencing cameras, scanners, and printers, to be connected externally with the same easy plug-and-play installation of current USB peripherals. From the end user's point of view, USB 2.0 works exactly the same as 1.1—only faster. All existing USB 1.1 devices work in a USB 2.0 bus because USB 2.0 supports all the slower-speed connections. USB data rates are shown in Table 8.1.

Table 8.1   USB Data Rates

Interface	Speed	Speed
USB 1.1 (low speed)	1.5Mbps	0.1875MBps
USB 1.1 (full speed)	12Mbps	1.5MBps
USB 2.0 (high speed)	480Mbps	60MBps

USB devices are considered either functions, hubs, or both. *Functions* are the individual devices that attach to the USB, such as a keyboard, mouse, camera, printer, telephone, and so on. *Hubs* provide additional attachment points, allowing for the use of more hubs and devices. The initial ports in the PC system unit are called the *root hub*, and they are the starting point for the USB. Most motherboards have two or more USB ports, any of which can be connected to functions or additional hubs. Some systems place one or two of the USB ports in the front of the computer, which is very convenient for devices used only occasionally, such as a USB keychain drive. External hubs (also called *generic hubs*) are essentially wiring concentrators, and through a star-type topology, they allow the attachment of multiple devices. Each attachment point is referred to as a *port*. Most hubs have either four or eight ports, and more are possible. For more expandability, you can connect additional hubs to the ports on an existing hub to a maximum of five levels. A hub controls both the connection and distribution of power to each of the connected functions.

Although USB 1.1 is not as fast at data transfer as FireWire or SCSI, it is still more than adequate for the types of peripherals for which it is designed. Current servers incorporate USB 2.0 ports, enabling support of USB 2.0 and USB 1.1 devices at their maximum speeds. One of the additional benefits of USB 2.0 is its capability to handle concurrent transfers, which enables your USB 1.1 devices to transfer data at the same time as USB 2.0 devices, without tying up the USB bus.

Table 8.2 lists the requirements for USB 2.0 support for current Windows versions used in servers.

Table 8.2   USB 2.0 Support Requirements for Windows Server/Windows XP

Windows Version	Requirement for USB 2.0 Support
Windows 2000	Install Service Pack 4
Windows XP	Install Service Pack 1 or greater
Windows Server 2003	Native support is included

USB 2.0 support is increasingly important for servers because DDS-4 and DAT-72 tape backups are now available in USB 2.0 form factors. If you need to add USB 2.0 support to an older server, you can install an add-on USB 2.0 card. You should use the drivers provided with the card or available from the card vendor if the operating system's drivers do not support the card.

Tip

Some vendors disable USB 2.0 support in the server motherboard's default BIOS configuration. In such cases, the onboard USB ports function as USB 1.1 ports only. Be sure to enable USB 2.0 support in the system BIOS Setup and save changes if you want to use USB 2.0 devices with your server.

◀◀   See "The USB Configuration Submenu," p. 301, for details.

How can you tell which devices support USB 1.1 and which support the USB 2.0 standard? USB-IF, which owns and controls the USB standard, introduced logos in late 2000 for products that have passed its certification tests. The logos are shown in Figure 8.2.

Figure 8.2   The USB-IF USB 1.1–compliant logo (left) compared to the USB-IF USB 2.0–compliant logo (right).

As you can see from Figure 8.2, USB 1.1 is also known simply as USB, and USB 2.0 is also known as Hi-Speed USB.

USB Connectors

Four main styles of connectors are specified for USB: Series A, Series B, Mini-A, and Mini-B connectors. The Series A connectors are used for upstream connections between a device and the host or a hub. The USB ports on motherboards and hubs are usually Series A connectors. Series B connectors are designed for the downstream connection to a device that has detachable cables, such as a printer or tape backup drive. Mini connectors (which feature smaller, but electrically identical versions of the full size connectors) are used primarily for hubs and consumer-grade USB devices rather than those designed for use with servers.

The physical USB plugs (especially the mini plugs) are small and, unlike a typical serial or parallel cable, the plug is not attached by screws or thumbscrews. There are no pins to bend or break, making USB devices very user friendly to install and remove. The USB plug shown in Figure 8.3 snaps into place on the USB connector.

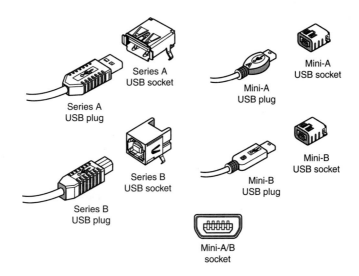

Figure 8.3 USB Series A and Series B plugs and receptacles.

Tables 8.3 and 8.4 show the pinouts for the USB connectors and cables. Most systems with USB connectors feature one or two pairs of Series A plugs on the rear of the system. Some also feature one or two pairs on the front of the system for ease of use with items that are not permanently connected.

Table 8.3   USB Connector Pinouts for Series A and Series B Connectors

Pin	Signal Name	Wire Color	Comment
1	Vbus	Red	Bus power
2	-Data	White	Data transfer
3	+Data	Green	Data transfer
4	Ground	Black	Cable ground
Shell	Shield	—	Drain wire

Table 8.4   USB Connector Pinouts for Mini-A and Mini-B Connectors

Pin	Signal Name	Wire Color	Comment
1	Vbus	Red	Bus power
2	-Data	White	Data transfer
3	+Data	Green	Data transfer

Table 8.4   Continued

Pin	Signal Name	Wire Color	Comment
4	ID[1]	—	A/B identification[2]
4	Ground	Black	Cable ground
Shell	Shield	—	Drain wire

[1]ID is connected to ground in a Mini-A plug and not connected (open) in a Mini-B plug.
[2]Used to identify a Mini-A from a Mini-B connector to the device.

USB support is also required in the BIOS for devices such as keyboards and mouse devices. This support is included in all newer systems with USB ports built in. Aftermarket PCI and PC Card boards are also available for adding USB to systems that don't include it as standard on the motherboard.

USB Installation and Troubleshooting

USB conforms to Intel's Plug and Play (PnP) specification, including hot-plugging, which means that you can plug in devices dynamically, without powering down or rebooting the system. You simply plug in the device, and the USB controller in the PC detects the device and automatically determines and allocates the required resources and drivers.

One interesting feature of USB is that, with certain limitations, attached devices can be powered by the USB bus. The plug-and-play aspects of USB enable the system to query the attached peripherals as to their power requirements and issue a warning if available power levels are exceeded. You can determine the amount of power available to each port in a USB root or generic hub and the amount of power required by a USB peripheral by using the Windows Device Manager (see Figure 8.4).

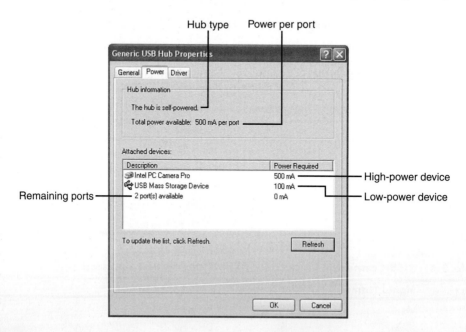

Figure 8.4   The Power tab of the properties sheet for a USB generic hub lists the available power and power usage, by device.

Devices that use more than 100mA must be connected to a root hub or a self-powered generic hub. Devices that use 100mA or less can be connected to bus-powered hubs, such as those built in to some keyboards and monitors.

Tip

If a device plugged in to a self-powered hub stops working, you should check the power source for the self-powered hub—it might have failed or been disconnected. In such cases, a self-powered hub becomes a bus-powered hub, providing only 100mA per port instead of the 500mA per port available in self-powered mode.

For maximum reliability, I recommend that you connect all USB devices used on a server to a root hub (a port built into the server's motherboard) instead of using an external hub. There are usually enough USB ports on recent servers to make this possible. If you need to add additional ports, plug a USB 2.0 card into a PCI or PCI-X expansion slot.

Another benefit of the USB specification is self-identifying peripherals. This feature greatly eases installation because you don't have to set unique IDs or identifiers for each peripheral—USB handles that automatically. Keep in mind that you can plug in USB devices at any time. However, to prevent data loss when unplugging "hot" USB drives and storage devices, you need to use the Eject Hardware or Safely Remove Hardware feature in the Windows system tray: You need to click the device, select Stop, click OK, and wait for the system to indicate that the device has been stopped before you remove it.

Note

It's a myth that you don't need to install a driver for a USB device before you connect it to a system. Although Windows Server 2000, Windows 2000 Professional, Windows XP, and Windows Server 2003 include many USB drivers, they don't support all USB devices, especially those introduced after the operating system was released.

If the server doesn't recognize the USB device when you plug it in, you need to provide the driver floppy disk or CD (if it contains drivers for your operating system version) or download a driver from the vendor's website and install it. If you use USB devices with a Linux server, it's often necessary to download a driver from the vendor's website or from an open-source developer.

Video and Monitors

Although many servers are managed remotely after they are installed, a server's video port has a variety of functions:

- During initial configuration, video is used to display the BIOS configuration so it can be adjusted as necessary.
- During server startup, video is used to display hardware and operating system status and error messages.
- During normal operation, video is used to monitor operation and display error and status messages.

The video subsystem of a server consists of two main components:

- **Monitor (or video display)**—The monitor can be a CRT or an LCD panel, or any device that accepts VGA or DVI signals, such as a data projector.
- **Video adapter (also called the video card or graphics adapter)**—Most servers use a PCI-level discrete video chip that is built in to the motherboard, but some servers feature an AGP or a PCI-Express x16 slot.

The following sections describe video display and adapter technologies used in servers, including CRT and LCD displays, integrated graphics, graphics cards, and KVM switches.

CRT and LCD Monitors

A monitor can use one of several display technologies. The original display technology, and still the most popular until recently, is cathode ray tube (CRT) technology—the same technology traditionally used in television sets. A newer display technology, borrowed from laptop manufacturers, is liquid crystal display (LCD). LCD monitors, often referred to as flat-panel displays, have low-glare, completely flat screens and low power requirements (5W versus nearly 100W for an ordinary monitor). The color quality of an active-matrix LCD panel actually exceeds that of most CRT displays.

LCD displays are rapidly replacing CRTs for several reasons, including lower space requirements, cooler operation, and lower operating costs.

Although CRTs are still less expensive than LCD displays, a low-end LCD (14- or 15-inch diagonal measurement) is not much more expensive than a 17-inch CRT, which is comparable in actual viewable screen area to a 15-inch LCD. Larger 17-inch and 19-inch LCDs, which are useful for multi-windowed server monitoring, are far more compact, run cooler, and consume far less electricity than comparably sized CRTs. Also, most LCDs can be hung on the wall and are light enough to be placed almost anywhere.

Table 8.5 compares the typical resolutions of mainstream LCD monitors to those of mainstream CRT monitors that have comparable viewable areas. Note that a CRT's viewable area is smaller than its actual size, so an 18.1-inch LCD has a viewable area that's slightly larger than a typical 19-inch CRT.

Table 8.5   LCD and CRT Resolutions Compared

LCD Size (Inches)	LCD Resolution	CRT Size (Inches)	CRT Viewable Area (Inches)	CRT Maximum Resolution
15	1024×768	17	16	1024×768 1280×1024 1600×1200[1]
17	1280×1024	—	—	—
18.1	1280×1024	19	18	1600×1200 1920×1440[1]
19	1280×1024	—	—	—
20.1	1600×1200	21	20	1600×1200 1920×1440[1]

[1]*Available on high-end monitors only.*

As you can see from Table 8.5, you need a 20.1-inch or larger LCD panel to achieve resolutions above 1280×1024, although most 18-inch CRT displays can achieve 1600×1200.

How CRT Display Technology Works

A CRT consists of a vacuum tube enclosed in glass. One end of the tube contains an electron gun assembly that projects three electron beams, one each for the red, green, and blue phosphors used to create the colors you see onscreen; the other end contains a screen with a phosphorous coating.

When heated, the electron gun emits a stream of high-speed electrons that are attracted to the other end of the tube. Along the way, a focus control and deflection coil steer the beam to a specific point on the phosphorous screen. When struck by the beam, the phosphor glows. This light is what you see when you watch TV or look at your computer screen. A metal plate called a *shadow mask* is used to align the electron beams; it has slots or holes that divide the red, green, and blue phosphors into groups of three (one of each color). Various types of shadow masks affect picture quality, and the distance between each group of three (the *dot pitch*) affects picture sharpness.

The phosphor chemical has a quality called *persistence*, which indicates how long this glow remains onscreen. Persistence is what causes a faint image to remain on a TV screen for a few seconds after you turn off the set. The scanning frequency of the display specifies how often the image is refreshed. With a good match between persistence and scanning frequency, the image has less flicker (which occurs when the persistence is too low) and no ghost images (which occur when the persistence is too high).

The electron beam moves very quickly, sweeping the screen from left to right in lines from top to bottom, in a pattern called a *raster*. The *horizontal scan rate* refers to the speed at which the electron beam moves laterally across the screen.

During its sweep, the beam strikes the phosphor wherever an image should appear onscreen. The beam also varies in intensity to produce different levels of brightness. Because the glow begins to fade almost immediately, the electron beam must continue to sweep the screen to maintain an image—a practice called *redrawing*, or *refreshing*, the screen.

Most current CRT displays have an ideal refresh rate (also called the *vertical scan frequency*) of about 85Hz, which means the screen is refreshed 85 times per second. Refresh rates that are too low cause the screen to flicker, contributing to eyestrain. The higher the refresh rate, the better for your eyes.

It is important that the refresh rates expected by your monitor match those produced by your video card. If the rates are mismatched, you do not see an image and can actually damage your monitor. Generally speaking, video card refresh rates cover a higher range than most monitors. For this reason, the default refresh rate used by most video cards is relatively low (usually 60Hz) to avoid monitor damage. On a system running Windows 2000 Server or Windows Server 2003, the refresh rate for the current resolution can be adjusted through the Windows Display properties sheet. You click the Settings tab and then click Advanced. Next, you click the Monitor tab and select the refresh rate desired from the list. Finally, you click Apply and then OK.

Note

Linux distributions use XFree86 to control the Linux GUI. Some Linux distribution vendors provide customized tools for tweaking screen resolution, graphics card, and monitor choices. For example, Red Hat provides the X Configurator, and SUSE Linux provides graphics options in its YaST SUSE setup tool. See the documentation for your Linux distribution for details. You can also use the standard XFree86 **XF86Setup** program to select and configure your video card, monitor, and input hardware. **XF86Setup** is run from the command line but brings up a series of menus. You can also use the command-line **xf86config** program to set up your video hardware. However, **xf86config** is not as easy to use as **XF86Setup**. For a tutorial on the use of **XF86Setup** and **xf86config**, go to www.control-escape.com/linux/x.html.

How LCD Technology Works

In an LCD, a polarizing filter creates two separate light waves. The polarizing filter allows light waves that are aligned only with the filter to pass through. After passing through the polarizing filter, the remaining light waves are all aligned in the same direction. Aligning a second polarizing filter at a right angle to the first causes all those waves to be blocked. Changing the angle of the second polarizing filter causes the amount of light allowed to pass to be changed. It is the role of the liquid crystal cell to change the angle of polarization and control the amount of light that passes. The liquid crystals are rod-shaped molecules that flow like a liquid. They enable light to pass straight through, but an electrical charge alters their orientations and the orientation of light passing through them.

Note that LCD monitors usually have a relatively narrow refresh rate range of 60Hz to 75Hz. However, because of the way that LCD displays receive signals, they never flicker. Improvements in viewing angles in recent LCD displays make it easier to see the contents of an LCD display from different angles.

In a color LCD, an additional filter has three cells for each pixel—one each for displaying red, green, and blue—with a corresponding transistor for each cell. The red, green, and blue cells, which make up a pixel, are sometimes referred to as *subpixels*. The ability to control each cell individually has enabled Microsoft to develop a new method of improving LCD text quality known as ClearType, which is supported in Windows XP and Windows Server 2003.

Dead Pixels

A so-called *dead pixel* is one in which the red, green, or blue cell is stuck on or off. (Failures in the on state are more common than failures in the off state.) In particular, pixels that fail when on are very noticeable on a dark background, such as bright red, green, or blue dots. Although even a few of these can be distracting, manufacturers vary in their warranty policies regarding how many dead pixels are required before you can get a replacement display. Some vendors look at both the total number of dead pixels and their locations. Fortunately, improvements in manufacturing quality make it less and less likely that you will see a screen with dead pixels either on your desktop or in your notebook computer display.

Although there is no tried-and-true way to repair bad pixels, there might be a simple fix that can help. In some cases you can repair bad pixels by gently tapping on the screen at the pixel location. This seems to work in many cases, especially in cases in which the pixel is always illuminated instead of dead (dark).

Integrated Graphics

Although desktop PCs have progressed from PCI to AGP to PCI-Express x16 graphics to manage the increasing complexity of high-resolution 2D and full-motion 3D displays, servers do not need high-speed graphics. The server's display subsystem only needs to do the following:

- Display startup messages
- Display the Windows desktop or other operating system interface, such as the Linux command line or GUI
- Display diagnostic and monitoring programs

For this reason, most servers use PCI-level discrete graphics chips such as the ATI Rage XL with 4MB or 8MB of graphics memory (most vendors use the 8MB version). 4MB of graphics memory is sufficient to support 24-bit color (more than 4 million colors) at resolutions up to 1280×1024, while 8MB of graphics memory is sufficient to support 24-bit color at resolutions up to 1600×1200.

Integrated graphics use the traditional VGA port shown in Figure 8.5; the VGA pinouts are shown in Table 8.6.

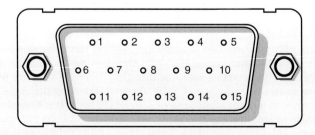

Figure 8.5   The VGA connector used for SVGA and other VGA-based standards.

Table 8.6 The Standard 15-Pin VGA Connector Pinout

Pin #	Function	Direction
1	Red video	Out
2	Green video	Out
3	Blue video	Out
4	Monitor ID 2	In
5	TTL Ground (monitor self-test)	—
6	Red analog ground	—
7	Green analog ground	—
8	Blue analog ground	—
9	Key (plugged hole)	—
10	Synch Ground	—
11	Monitor ID 0	In
12	Monitor ID 1	In
13	Horizontal Synch	Out
14	Vertical Synch	Out
15	Monitor ID 3	In

On the VGA cable connector that plugs in to a VGA port, pin 9 is often pinless. Pin 5 is used only for testing purposes, and pin 15 is rarely used. To identify the type of monitor connected to a system, some manufacturers use the presence or absence of the monitor ID pins in various combinations.

The VGA port is supported by the standard VGA cable used by both CRT and most LCD displays and by the KVM switches frequently used in server rooms.

▶▶ For more information about KVM switches, see "KVM Switches," p. 497.

PCI, AGP, and PCI-Express Graphics Cards

The Rage XL and similar PCI-level discrete graphics chips used for integrated video in servers were designed in the late 1990s and do not support multiple monitors. If a multiple-monitor solution is needed for a particular server (to enable the display of more monitoring or diagnostic programs, for example), onboard graphics can be disabled, and a dual-head 32-bit 33MHz PCI graphics card can be installed in a PCI or PCI-X expansion slot.

Some server motherboards and systems are also designed for use as workstations. Such systems are likely to have a high-speed AGP or PCI-Express video card slot instead of integrated video.

◀◀ See "PCI, PCI-X, and PCI-Express," p. 261, and "AGP Bus," p. 265, for more information about these high-speed expansion slot designs.

If you decide to install an AGP video card rather than use a PCI card, keep in mind the following support issues:

- You need to properly configure AGP settings in the system BIOS, such as AGP speed (1x, 2x, 4x, 8x), AGP graphics aperture, and AGP timings. See Table 8.8, in the following section.

- If you use a non-Intel chipset, you might need to install an AGP GART driver provided by the chipset vendor.

- AGP cards are more expensive than PCI cards. While AGP cards provide greater performance in 3D and high-end 2D applications such as video or photo editing, the additional complexity of AGP BIOS and software settings is not necessary for a server.

Although a PCI-Express video card does not require special system BIOS settings as an AGP card does, it is much more expensive than a PCI card or a low-end AGP card, and the additional performance it offers is not necessary in a server environment.

The bottom line? You should stick with integrated PCI graphics if your server platform offers it, and you should use a PCI card rather than an AGP or PCI-Express card if you need to add a video card (unless you run out of PCI or PCI-X slots). PCI video cards are simple to configure and offer adequate performance at minimal cost.

Video Installation and Configuration

Video installation and configuration vary greatly according to the type of video used by the server. If a server uses a motherboard-integrated graphics chip such as the ATI Rage XL, the graphics chip is automatically detected during operating system installation. All recent server operating systems have native drivers for the ATI Rage XL and similar PCI-based discrete graphics chips. In a worst-case scenario, such chips can use standard VGA graphics drivers. Although standard VGA graphics drivers don't offer 3D acceleration, this is a moot point because servers don't use—and thus don't need—3D graphics.

To install a video card in your server, follow the steps listed in Table 8.7 for the type of card you're using. If you are building a server, note that you cannot install add-on cards until the server motherboard has been secured in the case. You should see the documentation for your server or motherboard to determine whether you need to disable onboard video manually before installing a video card or whether installing a video card automatically disables onboard video.

Table 8.7   Installing a Video Card in a Server

Step #	Instructions	PCI	AGP	PCI-Express
1.	Remove the slot cover that corresponds to the slot. Save the screw that secures the slot cover for reuse.	Yes	Yes	Yes
2.	Open the slot-locking mechanism at the end of the slot furthest from the rear of the system.	No	Yes	Yes
3.	Push the card straight down into the slot.	Yes	Yes	Yes
4.	Fasten the card into place with the screw used to hold the slot cover in place (step 1).	Yes	Yes	Yes
5.	Connect auxiliary power to cards that have additional power connectors. Use Y-splitters to free up power connectors, if necessary.	No	Yes	Yes
6.	After the server hardware is completely installed, start the system and enter the BIOS Setup program (see "Accessing the Motherboard BIOS" in Chapter 4, "Server Motherboards and BIOS," for details).	No	Yes	Yes
7.	Configure the AGP or PCI-specific portions of the BIOS Setup program as listed in Table 8.8. The exact location and terminology for these settings varies from system to system. Save changes and exit.	Yes	Yes	Yes
8.	If the card is detected as standard VGA during the operating system installation or system startup, install the appropriate drivers.	Yes	Yes	Yes

Table 8.8 lists some typical BIOS configuration settings for AGP cards. For other AGP options besides the ones listed in Table 8.8, you should keep the default settings. They have little effect on display speed for standard Windows applications.

Table 8.8   Typical BIOS Setup Options for AGP Cards

BIOS Setup Option	Recommended Setting(s)
AGP Speed	Same as the rated card speed; use AGP 4x for AGP 8x cards if the 8x setting is not available
AGP Aperture Size	Same as the amount of onboard video on the AGP card; no less than 32MB is recommended
Primary Video Adapter	AGP (select PCI if you install a PCI card instead of AGP)

If you plan to use a single monitor with onboard or add-on video, you connect the VGA cable from the monitor to the VGA port on the motherboard or add-on card. If you need to use two monitors on a dual-headed PCI, AGP, or PCI-Express video card, note that most of these cards include one VGA and one DVI-I (analog/digital) port. You use a DVI-I/VGA adapter to enable VGA cables from both monitors to connect to the card. If one of the displays has a DVI cable, you should not use the DVI-I–to-VGA adapter; instead, you should plug the DVI cable directly in to the DVI-I port on the video card.

To enable dual-display capabilities in Windows, you use the Settings tab on the Display properties sheet. With some cards, it might be necessary to first enable dual-display mode through an advanced setting, which you can access by clicking the Advanced button on the Settings tab.

KVM Switches

KVM switches are very useful devices if you need to manage more than one server. A KVM switch enables you to manage two or more servers (or desktop PCs, for that matter) with a single keyboard, video cable, and mouse.

Typical KVM switches range in size from 2-port (controls two PCs or servers) up to 16-port (controls 16 PCs or servers) switches. Expansion devices available for some KVM switches enable them to control as many as 64 to 256 servers from a single keyboard, display, and monitor.

Figure 8.6 shows a typical two-port KVM switch. Note that the PS/2 keyboard, PS/2 mouse, and VGA cables for each managed unit are grouped together at the right. You connect your keyboard, mouse, and LCD or CRT display to the control box at left.

Depending on the KVM switch you use, you might switch between managed units by using keyboard commands or a selector switch, or the unit might automatically cycle between units.

Basic KVM units support only the PS/2 mouse, PS/2 keyboard, and VGA ports shown in Figure 8.6. However, more advanced KVM units also support audio, and some support USB mouse devices and keyboards. Some users report that USB-based KVM switches work acceptably well with Windows but might not work as well with Linux.

Table 8.9 provides a list of features to consider before you purchase a KVM switch for your server room.

Figure 8.6   A typical two-port KVM switch.

Table 8.9   KVM Features

Feature	Considerations
Maximum number of servers to manage	Your KVM switch should support at least the number of servers you need to manage. If you expect the number of servers to increase in the future, you should look for an expandable KVM switch.
PS/2 mouse	Almost all KVM switches support PS/2 mouse and similar pointing devices. Note that some specify particular pointing devices, so you need to check compatibility carefully.
PS/2 keyboard	Almost all KVM switches support PS/2 keyboards. If you need to use programmable keys to support special functions, you should make sure the KVM switch supports these functions.
Video	The maximum resolution and vertical refresh rate supported by KVM switches varies by model. If you need to support resolutions above 1280×1024 or refresh rates above 75Hz, you should make sure the KVM switch supports the video mode(s) you want to use.
Audio	Some KVM switches support audio. Audio support is typically limited to stereo output and microphone input. If you need audio output from servers for diagnostics or reporting purposes, you should make sure your KVM switch supports audio.
USB	Some KVM switches support USB keyboards and mouse devices. Some users of these switches report slow performance when switching between systems. Unless you cannot use PS/2 mouse devices and keyboards on the system that monitors your servers, you should avoid USB-based KVM switches.
Distance between servers and the monitoring PC	Conventional KVM wire bundles (three wires between each monitored server and the control box) can become bulky and difficult to manage as the number of managed servers grows. If you need to manage more than 16 systems, or if you find it difficult to manage wiring for a smaller number of systems, you should consider a CAT5 KVM solution. CAT5-based KVM switches use CAT5 cables in a daisy-chain between monitored systems.

Video/Display Troubleshooting

Solving most graphics adapter and monitor problems is fairly simple, although costly, because replacing the adapter or display is the normal procedure. However, before you take this step, you need to be sure that you have exhausted all your other options. One embarrassingly obvious fix to monitor display problems that many users overlook is to adjust the controls on the monitor, such as contrast and brightness. Most monitors today have a control panel on the front of the unit, and other adjustments might be possible as well.

You should always examine the monitor case, documentation, and manufacturer's website or other online services for the locations of adjustment controls. Most recent CRT and LCD monitors use front-mounted controls with onscreen display (OSD).

A defective or dysfunctional adapter or display is usually replaced as a single unit rather than being repaired. Except for specialized CAD or graphics workstation–oriented adapters, virtually all of today's adapters cost more to service than to replace. In addition, the documentation required to service the hardware properly is not always available. You can't get schematic diagrams, parts lists, wiring diagrams, and other documents for most adapters or monitors. Also, virtually all adapters now are constructed with surface-mount technology that requires a substantial investment in a rework station before you can remove and replace these components by hand. You can't use a $25 pencil-type soldering iron on these boards! Note that the least expensive way to fix a problem with onboard video in a typical server is to install a PCI video card. You should keep a few PCI video cards on hand for this purpose. Although vendors still sell PCI video cards, you can also get them from Pentium and Pentium II-class systems as they are retired from service, or you can purchase them from vendors that specialize in surplus or used hardware.

Servicing monitors is a slightly different proposition. Although a display is often replaced as a whole unit, some displays—particularly 20-inch or larger CRTs and most LCD panels—might be cheaper to repair than to replace. If you decide to repair a monitor, your best bet is to either contact the company from which you purchased the display or contact a company that specializes in monitor depot repair. If your CRT monitor has a 15-inch diagonal measurement or less, you should consider replacing it with a unit that is 17 inches or larger because repair costs on small monitors come close to replacement costs, and large monitors aren't much more expensive these days. If a CRT monitor fails, you should consider replacing it with an LCD display to save space, reduce heat, and reduce power consumption.

Note

Depot repair means you send in your display to repair specialists who either fix your particular unit or return an identical unit they have already repaired. This is usually done for a flat-rate fee; in other words, the price is the same, no matter what the depot has done to repair your actual unit.

Because you usually get a different (but identical) unit in return, they can ship out your repaired display immediately on receiving the one you sent in, or even in advance, in some cases. This way, you have the least amount of downtime and can receive the repaired display as quickly as possible. In some cases—for example, if your particular monitor is unique or one the depot doesn't have in stock—you must wait while they repair your specific unit.

Troubleshooting a failed monitor is relatively simple. If your display goes out, for example, a swap with another monitor can confirm that the display is the problem. If the problem disappears when you change the display, the problem is almost certainly in the original display or the cable; if the problem remains, it is likely in the video adapter or server itself.

Many of the better-quality, late-model monitors have built-in self-diagnostic circuitry. You should check your monitor's manual for details. Using this feature, if it's available, can help you determine whether the problem is really in the monitor, in a cable, or somewhere else in the system. If self-diagnostics produce an image onscreen, you should look to other parts of the video subsystem for your problem.

The monitor cable can sometimes be the source of display problems. A bent pin in the DB-15 connector that plugs in to the video adapter can prevent the monitor from displaying images, or it can cause color shifts. Most of the time, you can repair the connector by carefully straightening the bent pin with needle-nosed pliers. A loose cable or DVI/VGA adapter can also cause color shifts; you should tighten the cable and adapter securely.

If you use a KVM switch, note when you see problems with video. If you see problems viewing all computers, the cable from the KVM switch to the managing system might be damaged or loose. If most systems look okay, but one or two have problems, you should check the video cable that runs from those systems to the KVM switch.

If the pin breaks off or the connector is otherwise damaged, you can sometimes replace the monitor cable. Some monitor manufacturers use cables that disconnect from the monitor and video adapter, whereas others are permanently connected. Depending on the type of connector the device uses at the monitor end, you might have to contact the manufacturer for a replacement.

If you use KVM switches, you should use models that have fully detachable cables. Some low-cost units have built-in cables, and with one of these units, if the cable breaks or fails, the entire unit must be serviced or replaced.

If you narrow down the problem to the display, you should consult the documentation that came with the monitor or call the manufacturer for the location of the nearest factory repair depot. Third-party depot repair service companies are also available to repair most displays (that are no longer covered by warranty); their prices are often much lower than factory service. Check the vendor list in Appendix C, "Vendor List," for several companies that do depot repair of computer monitors and displays.

Caution

You should *never* attempt to repair a CRT monitor yourself. Touching the wrong component can be fatal. The display circuits can hold extremely high voltages for hours, days, or even weeks after the power is shut off. A qualified service person should discharge the CRT and power capacitors before proceeding.

With most displays, you are limited to making simple adjustments. On color displays, the necessary adjustments can be quite formidable if you lack experience. You should use the OSD controls to adjust color, brightness, picture size, and other settings. To quickly adjust an LCD, you can try the auto-tune feature that is available on many models. Even factory service technicians often lack proper documentation and service information for newer models; they usually exchange your unit for another and repair the defective one later. You should never buy a monitor for which no local factory repair depot is available.

If you have a problem with a display or an adapter, it pays to call the manufacturer, which might know about the problem and make repairs available. Sometimes, when manufacturers encounter numerous problems with a product, they offer free repair or replacement, or make other generous offers that you never know about unless you call.

Remember, also, that many of the problems you might encounter with modern video adapters and displays are related to the drivers that control these devices rather than to the hardware. You need to be sure you have the latest and proper drivers before you attempt to have the hardware repaired; a solution might already be available.

Troubleshooting Monitors

The following sections provide solutions for the most common problems you might encounter with CRT and LCD displays.

Problem

No picture.

Solution

If the LED on the front of the monitor is yellow or flashing green, the monitor is in power-saving mode. Move the mouse or press Alt+Tab on the keyboard and wait up to 1 minute to wake up the system if the system is turned on.

If the LED on the front of the monitor is green, the monitor is in normal mode (receiving a signal), but the brightness and contrast are set incorrectly; adjust them.

If no lights are lit on the monitor, check the power and power switch. Check the surge protector or power director to ensure that power is going to the monitor. Replace the power cord with a known-working spare, if necessary. Retest. Replace the monitor with a known-working spare to ensure that the monitor is the problem.

Check data cables at the monitor and video card end.

Problem

Jittery picture quality.

Solution

For all monitors, check cables for tightness at the video card and the monitor (if removable):

- Remove the extender cable and retest with the monitor plugged directly in to the video card. If the extended cable is bad, replace it.
- Check the cables for damage; replace as needed.
- If problems are intermittent, check for interference. (Microwave ovens near monitors can cause severe picture distortion when turned on.)

For LCD monitors only, use display-adjustment software or onscreen menus to reduce or eliminate pixel jitter and pixel swim.

For CRT monitors only, check refresh-rate settings; reduce them until acceptable picture quality is achieved:

- Use onscreen picture adjustments until an acceptable picture quality is achieved.
- If problems are intermittent and can be "fixed" by waiting or gently tapping the side of the monitor, the monitor power supply is probably bad or has loose connections internally. Service or replace the monitor.

Troubleshooting Video Cards and Drivers

Problem

Display works at startup and in system BIOS Setup but not in Windows.

Solution

If you have acceptable picture quality at system boot but no picture in Windows, most likely you have an incorrect or corrupted video driver installed in Windows. Boot Windows 2000 Server or Windows Server 2003 in VGA mode. If VGA mode works, get the correct driver for the video card and reinstall it.

If you have overclocked your card with a manufacturer-supplied or third-party utility, you might have set the speed too high. Restart the system in safe mode and reset the card to run at its default speed. If you have adjusted the speed of AGP/PCI slots in the BIOS Setup program, restart the system, start the BIOS Setup program, and reset the AGP and PCI slots to run at the normal speed.

Problem

Can't replace the built-in video card with an add-on PCI or AGP video card.

Solution

Check with the video card and system vendors for a list of acceptable replacement video cards. Try another video card with a different chipset. Check the BIOS or motherboard for jumper or configuration settings to disable built-in video. Place the add-on card in a different PCI slot. Be sure the card is fully inserted into the PCI, PCI-Express, or AGP slot.

Problem

Can't select the desired color depth and resolution combination.

Solution

Verify that the card is properly identified in Windows and that the card's memory is working properly. Use diagnostic software provided by the video card or chipset maker to test the card's memory. If the hardware is working properly, check for new drivers. Use the vendor's drivers rather than the ones provided with Windows.

Problem

Can't select the desired refresh rate.

Solution

Verify that the card and monitor are properly identified in Windows. Obtain updated drivers for the card and monitor.

Problem

Can't adjust the OpenGL or Direct3D (DirectX) settings.

Solution

Install the graphic card or chipset vendor's latest drivers instead of using the drivers included with Microsoft Windows. Standard Microsoft drivers often don't include 3D or other advanced dialog boxes.

Audio Devices

Most servers do not include onboard audio, nor is there a reason to add a sound card to most servers. If your server has onboard audio but you don't plan to use it, you can disable it in the system BIOS. If you want to know more about audio hardware used in desktop PCs, see the latest edition of *Upgrading and Repairing PCs*.

◄◄   See "The Integrated Device Configuration Submenu," p. 301, for details on disabling unneeded onboard devices such as onboard audio.

Keyboards

Keyboards are useful on servers primarily during software installation and when running diagnostic programs. Virtually all servers include PS/2 keyboard and USB ports, enabling you to use a low-cost PS/2 or USB keyboard for entering commands.

Types of Keyboards

Servers can use any of the numerous models of 104-key Windows keyboards, as well as the older, but still serviceable, 101/102-key PS/2 keyboards. Although keyboards with features such as ergonomic design and specialized keys for Internet access and multimedia can also be used, there is no need to install specialized keyboard drivers. The standard keys are sufficient for server setup, configuration, and management.

A USB keyboard can also be used, particularly if the keyboard will be used with a server that's running Windows 2000 Server or Windows Server 2003. USB keyboards don't work as well as PS/2 keyboards on KVM switches if a non-Windows server operating system such as Linux is in use. If you use a USB keyboard on a server, you need to be sure the USB legacy mode is enabled in the system BIOS so you can perform setup, startup, and command-line tasks with the keyboard.

◄◄   See "The USB Configuration Submenu," p. 301, for USB Legacy mode configuration.

Keyboard Maintenance

One of the best ways to keep a keyboard in top condition is periodic cleaning. As preventive mainte-nance, you should vacuum the keyboard weekly, or at least monthly. When vacuuming, you should use a soft brush attachment to dislodge dust and other debris.

Many keyboards have keycaps that can come off easily. If you're not careful when vacuuming, you'll have to dig the keycaps out of the vacuum cleaner. You should use a small, handheld vacuum cleaner made for cleaning computers and sewing machines; these have enough suction to get the job done, with little risk of removing your keycaps.

You can also use canned compressed air to blow the dust and dirt out of your keyboard instead of using a vacuum. Before you dust a keyboard with the compressed air, turn the keyboard upside down so that the particles of dirt and dust collected inside can fall out.

On all keyboards, each keycap is removable, which can be handy if a key sticks or acts erratically. For example, a common problem is a key that does not work every time you press it. This problem usu-ally results from dirt or other items like hair or food collecting under the key. An excellent tool for removing keycaps on almost any keyboard is the U-shaped chip puller included in many computer toolkits. You simply slip the hooked ends of the tool under the keycap, squeeze the ends together to grip the underside of the keycap, and lift. (IBM sells a tool designed specifically for removing keycaps from its keyboards, but the chip puller works even better.) After removing the cap, spray some com-pressed air into the space under the cap to dislodge the dirt. Then replace the cap and check the action of the key.

On some keyboards, when you remove a keycap, you are actually detaching the entire key from the keyswitch. You need to be careful during the removal or reassembly of your keyboard to avoid breaking switches. The classic IBM/Lexmark-type keyboards (now made by Unicomp) use a removable keycap that leaves the actual key in place, enabling you to clean under the keycap without risking breaking the switches. If your keyboard doesn't have removable keycaps, you should consider using cleaning wands with soft foam tips to clean beneath the keycaps.

Spills can be a problem with keyboards, too. If you spill a soft drink or cup of coffee into a keyboard, you do not necessarily have a disaster. Many keyboards that use membrane switches are spill resistant. However, you should immediately (or as soon as possible) disconnect the keyboard and flush it out with distilled water and allow it to dry completely before attempting to reuse it.

However, you might prefer to replace the keyboard with a new one. Given the low cost of today's keyboards, it is easier and faster to replace a liquid-damaged keyboard than to clean it.

Tip

If you expect spills or excessive dust or dirt because of the environment or conditions in which the PC is used, you can purchase a thin membrane skin that molds over the top of the keyboard, protecting it from liquids, dust, and other contaminants. These skins are generally thin enough so that they don't interfere too much with the typing or action of the keys.

Keyboard Troubleshooting

The first time to check for keyboard problems is at initial server startup. The signal lights on the keyboard should blink just after power-on. If they don't, chances are the keyboard or the keyboard port is not working.

Keyboard errors are usually caused by two simple problems:

- Defective cables
- Stuck keys

(Other, more difficult, intermittent problems can arise, but they are much less common than these two.) Defective cables are easy to spot if the failure is not intermittent. If the keyboard stops working altogether or if every keystroke results in an error or incorrect character, the cable is likely the culprit.

To determine whether the keyboard cable is at fault, swap the original keyboard with a known-working spare (most keyboards today do not have easily-removable cables). If the keyboard uses the PS/2 port, turn off the system before swapping keyboards. If the problem persists, the keyboard port itself is probably at fault. If the keyboard was plugged into the PS/2 port, try plugging a USB keyboard into the server.

Many times you first discover a problem with a keyboard because the system has an error during the power-on self-test (POST). Many systems use error codes in a 3*xx* numeric format to distinguish the keyboard. If you encounter any such errors during the POST, you should write them down. Some BIOS versions do not use cryptic numeric error codes; they simply state something such as the following:

```
Keyboard stuck key failure
```

This message is usually displayed by a system with a Phoenix BIOS if a key is stuck. Unfortunately, the message does not identify which key it is!

If your system displays a 3*xx* error preceded by a two-digit hexadecimal number, the number is the scan code of a failing or stuck keyswitch. For example, 1c 301 indicates the Enter key is stuck (1c is the Enter key's scan code; 301 indicates a stuck key).

If you don't want to (or can't) swap the keyboard for a known-working keyboard, you can look up the scan code at the *Upgrading and Repairing Servers* website at www.upgradingandrepairingpcs.com to determine which key is the culprit. By removing the keycap of the offending key and cleaning the switch, you can often solve the problem.

Make sure that your keyboard is plugged tightly in to the keyboard socket. If a KVM switch is used, make sure the cables between the switch and managed servers and those between the switch and the PC used for management are tightly connected.

CD-ROM, CD-RW, and DVD Drives

Your server should include a CD-ROM, CD-RW, or rewritable DVD drive. The following are some of the benefits of including these types of optical drives in a server:

- Easy installation of server operating systems, service packs, and drivers from CD media
- Image or file-by-file backup to rewriteable media (particularly with DVD media) if you choose a rewritable DVD drive

The following sections are designed to help you choose the right optical drive for your server installation.

Specifications

Optical drive standards for computers can be divided into two major types:

- **CD (CD-ROM, CD-R, CD-RW)**—The maximum capacity of these drives is 703MB (80-minute CD-R media).
- **DVD (DVD-ROM, DVD-RAM, DVD-RW, DVD-R, DVD-R DL, DVD+RW, DVD+R, DVD+R DL)**—The maximum capacity of these drives for single-layer media is 4.7GB; for dual-layer media the maximum capacity is 8.5GB.

A CD-ROM drive can read any of the listed CD formats, although a universal disc format (UDF) reader program might be required to enable data to be read from CD-RW media created using drag-and-drop applications such as DirectCD, InCD, DLA, and others. Currently, all Windows Server–based operating systems are distributed on CD media, as are commercial Linux distributions. Downloadable Linux distributions are usually provided as International Organization for Standardization (ISO) CD images and must be burned to a recordable CD before installation.

If you plan to use other types of backup media for backing up server data, a CD-ROM drive is sufficient for now. However, in most cases, a DVD-ROM drive is about the same price as a CD-ROM drive, and using a DVD-ROM drive in a server enables you to read both CD and single-layer DVD media. In the near future, it's possible that vendors might start distributing business applications or operating systems on DVD media. Some PC games are already available on DVD.

When hard disk drives were 10GB or smaller, backing up data with a rewritable CD drive using CD-RW or CD-R media made sense. However, with even entry-level servers now featuring 40GB or larger hard disks, rewritable CD drives are typically inadequate.

Although some server vendors might offer combo DVD-ROM/CD-RW drives, you're better off getting a dual-layer rewritable DVD drive if you plan to use DVD media for backups. Such drives can write to almost any DVD or CD media. (However, most do not support DVD-RAM.) Keep in mind that even if you use dual-layer media, you have a native capacity of 8.5GB (but data compression can store up to twice this amount on the media). For drives over 40GB, you should consider using disk-to-disk or tape backup units.

▶▶ For more information about server backup technologies and strategies, see Chapter 9, "Backup Operations."

CD/DVD Interfaces

Early optical drives (CD-ROM, CD-R, and CD-RW) used various categories of the SCSI interface. Although SCSI continues to be a popular choice for high-speed RAID arrays in all types of servers, SCSI optical drives have not been produced for several years.

Virtually all CD and DVD optical drives currently on the market use the Advanced Drive Electronics/AT Attachment (ATA/IDE also known as parallel ATA [PATA] or Enhanced IDE [EIDE]) interface. If a server uses ATA/IDE for the hard disk and for optical drive interfacing, you should connect the hard disk to the primary ATA/IDE interface on the motherboard and the optical drive to the secondary ATA/IDE interface to improve throughput.

◄◄ See "ATA Standards," p. 409 and "PATA," p. 413, for details on the ATA/IDE interface.

A few high-end rewritable DVD drives now use the Serial ATA (SATA) interface discussed in Chapter 6, "The ATA/IDE Interface." Although SATA uses thin data cables and offers higher potential throughput, rewritable DVD drives using the SATA interface, while more expensive than ATA/IDE drives, offer little or no additional performance.

CD/DVD Host Adapters

Virtually every server has at least one PATA 40-pin host adapter on the motherboard. This can be used for an ATA/IDE-based CD or DVD drive. If the server also uses a PATA hard disk, it's preferable to place the hard disk and host adapter on separate cables rather than connect them as master and slave on a single cable. Although each PATA host adapter can support two drives, throughput is faster when each drive is located on its own host adapter.

Many recent servers have a mix of PATA and SATA host adapters, or a mix of PATA and SCSI host adapters. In such cases, the 40-pin PATA port can be used for a CD or DVD drive, and the SATA or SCSI host adapters can be used for hard disks.

CD/DVD Installation and Troubleshooting

You install CD and DVD drives the same way you install any other drive that uses the same interface. In the case of PATA drives, the drive is jumpered as master or slave if a 40-pin cable is used. If the superior 80-pin cable is used, cable select is the preferable jumpering method. No jumpering is required in the case of SATA optical drives; you just plug the drive in to power and data cables.

◄◄ See "SATA," p. 424 for details on the Serial ATA interface.

If a rewritable DVD or CD drive will be used for data backups, compatible backup software must be installed after the drive is installed. See the vendor list on this book's CD-ROM for examples of server backup products.

Caring for Optical Media

By far the most common causes of problems with optical discs and drives are scratches, dirt, and other contamination. Small scratches or fingerprints on the bottom of a disc should not affect performance because the laser focuses on a point inside the actual disc, but dirt or deep scratches can interfere with reading a disc.

To remedy this type of problem, you can clean the bottom surface of a disc with a soft cloth, but you need to be careful not to scratch the surface in the process. The best technique is to wipe the disc in a radial fashion, using strokes that start from the center of the disc and emanate toward the outer edge. This way, any scratches will be perpendicular to the tracks rather than parallel to them, minimizing the interference they might cause. You can use any type of solution on the cloth to clean the disc, so long as it will not damage plastic. Most window cleaners are excellent at removing fingerprints and other dirt from discs and don't damage the plastic surface.

If a disc has deep scratches, you might be able to buff or polish them out. The Skip Doctor device made by Digital Innovations (see www.skipdoctor.com) can be used to make the polishing job easier.

Most people are careful about the bottom of discs because that is where the laser reads, but the top is actually more fragile. This is because the lacquer coating on top of the disc is very thin, normally only 6–7 microns (0.24–0.28 thousandths of an inch). You should write on discs only with felt tip pens that have compatible inks, such as a Sharpie or a Staedtler Lumocolor, or other markers specifically sold for writing on CDs. In any case, remember that scratches or dents on the top of a disc are more fatal than those on the bottom.

Read errors can also occur when dust accumulates on the read lens of an optical drive. You can try to clean out the drive and lens with a blast of canned compressed air or by using a drive cleaner (which can be purchased at most stores that sell audio CDs).

If your discs and your drive are clean, but you still can't read a particular disc, your trouble might be due to disc capacity. Many older CD-ROM drives are unreliable when they try to read the outermost tracks of newer discs, where the last bits of data are stored. You're most likely to run into this problem with a CD that contains a lot of data. If you have this problem, you might be able to solve it with a firmware or driver upgrade for your CD-ROM drive, but you may have to replace the drive.

If you have problems reading a particular brand or type of recordable or rewritable disc in some drives but not others, you might have a poor drive/media match. You should use the media types and brands recommended by the drive vendor. You should test backup media in other drives to ensure the backup can be read in case of emergency. If you have problems reading media on another system, you might want to reduce the burn speed; media written at slower burn speeds can be easier for some drives to read. As an alternative, some vendors supply utility software with their rewritable drives that enables the strength of the recording laser to be varied (for example, Plextor's PlexTools Professional's VariRec; see www.plextor.com for details).

If you are having problems with only one particular disc and not the drive in general, you might find that your difficulties are in fact caused by a defective disc. You should see whether you can exchange the disc for another to determine whether that is indeed the cause.

Handling Failure to Read a CD/DVD

If your drive fails to read a CD or DVD, you can try the following solutions:

- Check for scratches on the disc data surface.
- Check the drive for dust and dirt; use a cleaning disc.
- Make sure the drive shows up as a working device in System Properties.
- Try a disc that you know works.
- Restart the computer (the magic cure-all).
- Remove the drive from Device Manager in Windows, allow the system to redetect the drive, and then reinstall the drivers (in a plug-and-play–based system).

Handling Failure to Read CD-R and CD-RW Discs in a CD-ROM or DVD Drive

If your CD-ROM or DVD drive fails to read CD-R and CD-RW discs, you can try the following solutions:

- Check compatibility; some very old 1x CD-ROM drives can't read CD-R media. Replace the drive with a newer, faster, cheaper model.
- Many early-model DVD drives can't read CD-R and CD-RW media; check compatibility.

- The CD-ROM drive must be MultiRead compatible to read CD-RW because of the lower reflectivity of the media; replace the drive.

- If some CD-Rs but not others can be read, check the media color combination to see whether some color combinations work better than others; change the brand of media.

- Record the media at a slower speed. The pits/lands created at faster speeds sometimes can't be read by older drives.

- If you are trying to read a packet-written CD-R created with Adaptec/Roxio DirectCD or Drag to Disk on a CD-ROM drive, reinsert the media into the original drive, eject the media, and select the option Close to Read on Any Drive.

- Download and install a UDF reader that is compatible with the packet-writing software used to create the CD-RW on the target computer. If you are not sure how the media was created, try using the universal UDF reader/media repair program called FixUDF! (also included as part of WriteCD-RW! Pro) from Software Architects. WriteDVD! Pro includes the similar FixDVD! UDF reader/media repair program for DVD drives.

Handling Failure to Read a Rewritable DVD in a DVD-ROM Drive or Player

If your DVD-ROM or DVD player fails to read a rewritable DVD, you can try the following solutions:

- Reinsert the DVD-RW media into the original drive and finalize the media. Make sure you don't need to add any more data to the media if you use a first-generation (DVD-R 2x/DVD-RW 1x) drive because you must erase the entire disc to do so. You can unfinalize media written by second-generation DVD-R 4x/DVD-RW 2x or faster drives. See your DVD-RW disc-writing software instructions or help file for details.

- Reinsert the DVD+RW media into the original drive and change the compatibility (bit) setting to emulate DVD-ROM. Check with the drive vendor for details.

- Make sure the media contains more than 521MB of data. Some drives can't read media that contains a small amount of data.

Handling Failure to Create a Writable DVD

If you can't create a writable DVD but the drive can be used with CD-R, CD-RW, or rewritable DVD media, you can try the following solutions:

- Make sure you are using the correct media. +R and –R media can't be interchanged unless the drive is a DVD±R/RW dual-mode drive.

- Be sure you select the option to create a DVD project in your mastering software. Some CD/DVD-mastering software defaults to the CD-R setting.

- Select the correct drive as the target. If you have both rewritable DVD and rewritable CD drives on the same system, be sure to specify the rewritable DVD drive.

- Try a different disc.

- Contact the mastering software vendor for a software update.

Handling Failure to Write to CD-RW or DVD-RW 1x Media

If you can't write to CD-RW or DVD-RW 1x media, you can try the following solutions:

- Make sure the media is formatted. Use the format tool provided with the UDF software to prepare the media for use.

- If the media was formatted, verify that it was formatted with the same or a compatible UDF program. Different packet-writing programs support different versions of the UDF standard. You should use the same UDF packet-writing software on the computers you use or use drives that support the Mount Rainier standard.

- Make sure the system has identified the media as CD-RW or DVD-RW. Eject and reinsert the media to force the drive to redetect it.

- Contact the packet-writing software vendor for a software update.

- The disc might have been formatted with Windows XP's own limited CD writing software instead of a true UDF packet-writing program. In this case, erase the disc with Windows XP after transferring any needed files from the media; then format it with your preferred UDF program.

- Contact the drive vendor for a firmware update. Be sure to follow the drive vendor's instructions carefully. A failed firmware update renders the drive useless.

Handling Problems with an ATAPI CD-ROM or a Rewritable CD or a DVD Drive Running Slowly

AT Attachment Packet Interface (ATAPI) is a term used to refer to CD-ROM or other optical or removable-media drives that connect to an ATA/IDE interface. If your ATAPI CD-ROM or rewritable CD or DVD drive performs poorly, you can check the following items:

- Check whether the drive is set as the slave to your hard disk; move the drive to the secondary PATA host adapter, if possible.

- Your PIO (programmed I/O) or Ultra DMA (UDMA) mode might not be set correctly for your drive in the BIOS; check the drive specs and use autodetect in BIOS for the best results.

◄◄ See "The ATA/SATA Drive Configuration Submenus," p. 304, for details on autodetecting ATA/IDE and SATA hard disk drives.

- Check that you are using busmastering drivers on compatible systems; install the appropriate drivers for the motherboard's chipset and the operating system in use.

- Make sure buffer underrun-prevention settings are enabled in the CD or DVD mastering program.

- Make sure the latest drive firmware is installed.

Handling Trouble Reading CD-RW Discs on a CD-ROM Drive

If you can't read CD-RW discs in your CD-ROM drive, you can try the following solutions:

- Check the vendor specifications to see whether your drive is MultiRead compliant. Some drives are not.

- If your drive is MultiRead compliant, try the CD-RW disc on a known-compliant CD-ROM drive (a drive with the MultiRead feature).

- Insert CD-RW media back into the original drive and check it for problems with the packet-writing software program's utilities.

- Insert CD-RW media back into the original drive and eject the media. Use the right-click Eject command in My Computer or Windows Explorer to properly close the media.

- Create a writable CD or DVD to transfer data to a computer that continues to have problems reading rewritable media.

Handling Trouble Reading CD-R Discs on DVD Drive

If your DVD drive can't read a CD-R disc, check to see that the drive is MultiRead2 compliant because noncompliant DVDs can't read CD-R media. Newer DVD drives generally support reading CD-R media.

Hardware Drivers

Using stable hardware drivers made for your hardware and operating system is essential to successful server operation. During the initial installation of a server operating system, onboard hardware is normally detected, and drivers are provided from the operating system CD, where possible.

In some cases, particularly if the motherboard or other installed hardware is more recent than the operating system version being installed, some drivers need to be installed after the initial installation process.

Drivers can be installed in any of the following ways:

■ Most hardware includes a driver CD. Depending on the hardware, it might be necessary to run an installation program on the CD before connecting the hardware. This is particularly common with USB devices and video cards that are not already supported by installed drivers.

■ Windows Server and Windows 2000/XP prompt the user for the location of drivers after a new plug-and-play device is detected. If the driver files are on an accessible local or network drive, you can use the Browse button to direct Windows to the driver location to complete installation.

■ Windows XP, starting with Service Pack 2, and Windows Server 2003 can use Windows Update to obtain device drivers when a new plug-and-play device has been detected. You can modify this behavior through Group Policy settings.

Note that Windows Server 2003 can use many, but not all, Windows XP drivers. These versions of Windows are also compatible with most Windows 2000 (Server or Professional) drivers.

For Linux installations, if the drivers for a particular device are not included as part of the distribution, you should check with the hardware vendor for compatible drivers. Note that different vendors' distributions and different versions of a particular Linux distribution usually require different drivers. If the hardware vendor does not have a driver, a driver might have been developed by an independent open-source developer. You should be sure to follow the instructions provided with the driver for building and installing the driver.

To update a driver in Windows, you open the Device Manager and then open the properties sheet for the device. You click Driver Details to see the current driver version and files. Then you click Update and follow the prompts to install an updated driver. You can click Rollback to revert to an earlier driver if a newer driver fails. If a faulty driver causes the system to fail to start normally, you can use safe mode to restart the system and then access the Device Manager (safe mode loads very few drivers); then you use Rollback. To remove a driver in Windows, you click Uninstall from the Driver tab of the device's properties sheet.

By default, Windows Server 2003 warns you if you attempt to install unsigned device drivers. To prevent installation of unsigned device drivers, you click Driver Signing on the Hardware tab of the System properties sheet and change the default action from Warn to Block. Although unsigned device drivers might cause system instability, in some cases, using an unsigned driver is the only way to get a particular hardware device to operate in Windows.

Firmware and Hardware Upgrades

The operation of I/O devices in a server can be greatly affected by the firmware used to control them. For built-in I/O devices such as USB ports, keyboard ports, and so forth, the firmware in question is the system BIOS. The system BIOS is used to configure and control these ports. If you have problems with built-in I/O ports and devices, you should check with your server or server motherboard vendor to see if a BIOS upgrade is available.

The performance of CD and DVD drives is also affected by a drive's built-in firmware. Although CD-ROM and DVD-ROM drives generally don't have upgradeable firmware, rewritable CD and DVD drives do. Firmware upgrades for CD and DVD drives can improve a drive's compatibility with certain brands, types, and speeds of media, and they can improve mastering or drag-and-drop reliability.

Obtaining Firmware Upgrades

To obtain a system BIOS or optical drive firmware upgrade, you can visit the vendor's website. It's important that you review the technical notes carefully to determine which upgrade you need for your device and what problems it solves. Generally, you should not install a firmware upgrade if you are satisfied with your system or drive performance or stability.

Adding or Replacing Onboard Ports/Devices

With the high degree of integration available in today's servers, it's most desirable to use onboard I/O ports and devices when they are suitable to your purposes. However, it might be necessary to use add-on I/O cards to improve the operation of a particular server. For example, if you decide to use a USB 2.0 backup device such as an external hard disk or tape drive, but your server has only USB 1.1 ports, you should install a USB 2.0 PCI card to get maximum performance. If you need to free up system resources, you can disable the onboard USB 1.1 ports in the system BIOS if they are not in use. However, given the fact that both onboard and add-on USB ports are PCI devices that can share IRQs, this is typically not a significant problem.

Similarly, if you want to install a RAID array in a system that does not have an onboard RAID controller, you need to install a RAID-capable ATA/IDE (PATA), SATA, or SCSI host adapter. Again, you can disable no-longer-needed host adapters in the system BIOS if necessary.

Whether you add additional I/O ports or replace onboard ports with newer, faster devices, you should try to use add-on cards that are compatible with digitally signed device drivers. Unsigned device drivers can lead to system failures, which are unacceptable in a server. You should contact the vendor of a particular add-on card to determine whether the card uses a standard Windows Server driver or whether a vendor-provided driver must be used. If a vendor-provided driver must be used, you should favor cards whose vendors provide digitally signed drivers.

Common I/O Device Configurations in Servers

Most typical servers use the following I/O devices discussed earlier in this chapter:

- PS/2 keyboard and mouse
- CD-ROM or DVD-ROM drive connected to an onboard ATA/IDE (PATA) host adapter
- Onboard PCI video

These devices are found in virtually all servers, and they provide more-than-adequate performance for the task. In addition to or instead of these, in some cases you might need the following devices:

- A USB keyboard and mouse instead of those that interface with the server by using a PS/2 connection. This is a desirable option if you don't want to keep a mouse and keyboard attached to the server at all times. USB devices, unlike PS/2 devices, can be hot-swapped. However, although USB-compatible KVM switches exist, they might not work as well as PS/2-based KVM switches, particularly in a mixed Windows Server/Linux environment.

- An add-on PCI, AGP, or PCI-Express video card in place of onboard PCI video. If your server does not have onboard video, or if the onboard video fails, you need to install some type of video card to be able to configure and monitor the system. You should use the least-expensive and simplest video card possible: a PCI card. If you need dual-display functionality, dual-head PCI cards are available.

- A rewritable DVD drive in place of a CD-ROM or DVD-ROM drive. You should make this substitution if you plan to use the DVD drive to perform data backups.

Determining Hardware Compatibility

If you use Windows Server 2000 or 2003, the easiest way to determine whether a particular I/O or other component is compatible with your operating system is to visit the Windows Server Catalog site at www.microsoft.com/windows/catalog/server/. After you select the Hardware tab, you can browse or search the major categories and subcategories listed in Table 8.10.

Table 8.10   Windows Server Hardware Categories

Major Category	Subcategories
Cameras and Video	Analog TV Tuners Digital TV Tuners Motherboard Video Chipsets Video/Web Cameras Video Capture Cards Video Cards
Cluster Solutions	Cluster Solution Geographically Dispersed Cluster Solution
Input Devices	Keyboards (USB, Wireless, PS/2) Mice (USB, Wireless, PS/2) Pressure-Sensitive Pens SmartCard Readers Touch Pads Trackball
Monitors	CRT LCD Flat Panel
Networking and Modems	ATM Adapters Cable Modems Datacenter Driver Tested DSL Modems External Modems ISDN Modems LAN Cards Modem Cards Modem Motherboard Chipsets Motherboard LAN Chipsets WAN Devices
Printers	Dot Matrix Laser Solid Ink

Major Category	Subcategories
Scanners	Flatbed Scroll Fed
Servers	Datacenter Server Server
Sound	Sound Cards (includes chipset-integrated and discrete motherboard-based audio)
Storage	CD-DVD Drives[1] Hard Disk Drives Media Changer Devices RAID Storage[1] Removable Media Drives Storage Adapters and Controllers[1] Tape Drives
Other Hardware	1394 Controllers Biometrics Cardbus/PCMCIA Controllers Keyboard Video Mouse Switches Miscellaneous Multiport Serial Adapters UPS (Uninterruptible Power Supply) USB Controllers USB Hubs

[1]*Includes one or more subcategories.*

To see listings of iSCSI hardware that is compatible with Windows Server 2003, Windows 2000, and Windows XP, click the iSCSI Hardware Devices link on the Hardware tab.

Note that the Windows Server listing for each supported hardware item is very specific about which Windows Server 2000 or 2003 version(s) is supported by a particular hardware device and the driver and ROM BIOS (when applicable) versions tested. To ensure trouble-free operation, you should follow the recommendations given there.

Although the decentralized nature of Linux (multiple vendors publishing multiple distributions) makes a "one-stop" listing of compatible hardware difficult to achieve, some individual Linux vendors are making an attempt to list compatible hardware:

- Visit the Red Hat Hardware Catalog at http://bugzilla.redhat.com/hwcert/.
- Visit the Mandriva (formerly Mandrake) Linux Hardware Database at www.mandrivalinux.com/en/hardware.php3.

For general help with Linux hardware compatibility, see these sites:

- The Linux-drivers.org website offers a page of links to various compatibility lists (most are in English, but a few are in German), at www.linux-drivers.org.
- The Linux Online, Inc., "Linux Hardware Compatibility HOWTO" listing at www.linux.org/docs/ldp/howto/Hardware-HOWTO/ is a collection of links, organized by hardware categories, that help you configure and troubleshoot various types of hardware for all types of Linux distributions.

To save time, you should also visit the Linux Incompatibility List at http://leenooks.com/1, particularly if you are attempting to configure an existing server as a Linux platform.

Troubleshooting and Documentation

To troubleshoot your server's I/O hardware, you should consider the following:

- Is the device on the compatibility list for the server operating system you use? If not, check with the vendor to see if a compatible driver is available. If a driver is not available, replace the device with a compatible item.

- If the device is running under Windows Server and is a plug-and-play item, open the properties sheet for the item in Device Manager and remove the item listing. Then select Rescan to enable Device Manager to rediscover the device and reload new drivers.

- If removing and reinstalling the device in Device Manager doesn't work, check the properties sheet in Device Manager for an error code. For Windows 2000 Server versions, Windows XP, and Windows Server 2003, see Knowledge Base article 125174, at http://support.microsoft.com, for a list of error codes and suggested solutions.

- Replace suspect hardware with known-working hardware, preferably an identical item, and retest.

For specific help in troubleshooting particular types of I/O hardware, see the following sections:

- "USB Installation and Troubleshooting," p. 490.
- "Video/Display Troubleshooting," p. 499.
- "Keyboard Troubleshooting," p. 504.
- "CD/DVD Installation and Troubleshooting," p. 506.

If some of your hardware devices did not come with technical documentation, you can visit the vendors' websites for downloadable manuals and technical notes. This information is usually in Adobe Reader (PDF) format, so you must use Adobe Reader or Adobe Acrobat to view it.

To determine the manufacturer and model number of already-installed hardware without disassembling a computer, you can use a system information program such as SiSoftware Sandra (available from www.sisoftware.net).

CHAPTER 9

Backup Operations

Data backup involves transferring files from a system's primary storage to a different local or network device. Unlike simple file copying performed using the server operating system's file management system, backup programs (either those built into operating systems or purchased separately) perform file compression and, optionally, encryption during the backup. As a result, backed-up files must be restored before they can be used. Timely and well-organized data backups enable a business to recover from hardware failure, user error, or other threats to the contents of a server's hard disk.

While data backup is at least moderately important for individual PCs, it is a critical task for a server. Depending on the amount of new data generated and stored on a server, a weekly backup routine is often the absolute minimum recommended, and daily backups are often in order.

Backups provide additional benefits, as well. In addition to recording a copy of current information, backups can be used to move older and infrequently used data from hard disk to tape storage, giving the server's hard disk more capacity for newer and more frequently accessed information.

Historically, a popular method for backing up full hard disks or modified files has been using a tape backup drive. Although tape backups are no longer the only way to back up a server, tape backups remain the most popular method. This chapter discusses tape, removable-media drives such as Iomega REV drives, rewritable DVDs, and disk-to-disk backups to help you determine which type of storage technology is right for you.

This chapter examines the various types of tape and other backup drives on the market. It begins by looking at tape backup units, describing the capacities of different drives, the system requirements for installation and use of a tape drive, tape libraries, tape backup upgrades, backup strategies, and common backup applications.

Tape Backup Units

A tape backup drive is the most simple and efficient device for creating a full backup of a hard disk if the tape is large enough. With a tape backup drive installed in a computer, you insert a tape into the drive, start your backup software, and select the drive and files you want to back up. The backup software copies your selected files onto the tape while you attend to other business. Later, when you need to retrieve some or all of the files from the backup tape, you insert the tape in the drive, start your backup program, and select the files you want to restore. The tape backup drive takes care of the rest of the job.

Tape drives come in a variety of industry-standard as well as some proprietary formats. This chapter covers the major industry-standard formats:

- **Travan**—Travan is a development of the QIC and QIC-Wide family of low-cost, entry-level tape backup drives. Travan drives can handle data up to 40GB at 2:1 compression.

- **DAT (digital audio tape)**—This is a newer technology than QIC and its offshoots, and it uses digital data storage (DDS) technology to store data up to 72GB at 2:1 compression (DAT 72). DAT drives are often referred to as DDS drives for this reason.

- **DLT (digital linear tape)**—DLT drives use servo-based linear recording, writing one track the length of the tape, repositioning the head to a new track, and then writing another track as the tape is wound in the opposite direction.

- **SDLT (Super DLT)**—SDLT is a development of DLT designed to handle higher-capacity drives. It uses laser-guided magnetic recording (LGMR) to boost tape capacity and other technologies to improve capacity, speed, and reliability. Current SDLT drives can store up to 600GB (2:1 compression).

- **Ultrium**—Ultrium uses dual-servo tracks and a nonvolatile RAM (NVRAM) chip in each cartridge to enhance data reliability. Current LTO-3 drives store up to 800GB (2:1 compression).

Note

A *servo track* is a prewritten track that is used to ensure that data is written in a readable manner. Ultrium and several other types of tape backup technologies use servo tracks.

Most current tape drives and all tape libraries support LVD SCSI interfaces, although some also support USB, ATA/IDE, Narrow SCSI, and FireWire interfaces. The following sections provide details.

Travan

Travan is a family of quarter-inch tape drives and cartridges that 3M (now Imation) developed in 1994. Travan was designed to support backward compatibility with certain QIC and QIC-Wide tape cartridges and to boost capacity and reliability.

Note

QIC was the Quarter-Inch Cartridge Drive Standards, Inc., trade association, which developed standards for quarter-inch tape drives and media starting in the early 1980s. QIC-Wide was a Sony-developed technology that was based on QIC MC standards but used a wider (8mm) tape.

Although the QIC trade association became inactive in 1997, the QIC website is still online, at www.qic.org. The information provided there can be useful if you need to determine drive and media compatibility for QIC tape backups in your archives or need to retrieve files from a `.qic` backup file.

Travan drives, unlike larger tape backups, fit into a 3.5-inch form factor. Travan drives maintain backward compatibility with various QIC standards and provide backup capabilities up to 20GB uncompressed and 40GB at 2:1 compression. Table 9.1 provides a guide to the Travan family tree. Note that the only current versions of Travan are Travan 20 (NS-20, TR-5) and Travan 40 (TR-7).

Table 9.1　The Travan Family of Cartridges

Travan Cartridge (previous name)	Capacity, Native/2:1 Compression	Read/Write Compatible With	Read Compatible With
Travan-1 (TR-1)	400MB/800MB	QIC-80, QW5122	QIC-40
Travan-3 (TR-3)	1.6GB/3.2GB	TR-2, QIC-3020, QIC-3010, QW-3020XLW, QW-3010XLW	QIC-80, QW-5122, TR-1
Travan 8GB (Travan 4/TR-4)	4GB/8GB	Travan 8, QIC-3080, QIC-Wide (3080)	QIC-80, QIC-3010, QIC-Wide (3010), QIC-3020, QIC-Wide (3020), TR-1, TR-3
Travan NS-8[1]	4GB/8GB	TR-4, QIC-3080	QIC-Wide (3080)
Travan 20[2] (Travan TR-5, Travan NS-20)	10GB/20GB	—	Travan 8GB, QIC-3095
Travan 40[2] (Travan TR-7, Travan-NS40)	20GB/40GB	—	Travan 20

[1]*This cartridge can be used in place of the Travan 8GB (TR-4); the same cartridge can be used on either NS8 or TR-4 drives.*
[2]*This drive and cartridge also supports Travan NS technology.*

Nonstandard versions of Travan technology included the 5GB Tecmar/Iomega DittoMax, 5GB Hewlett-Packard/Colorado, 6.6GB AIWA Bolt, 7GB Tecmar/Iomega DittoMax, 10GB Tecmar DittoMax, and 14GB Hewlett-Packard/Colorado. These drives are basically orphans and should be used only to recover archival data stored on media that cannot be read on a standard Travan drive.

Note

Backward compatibility can vary with drive; consult the manufacturer to verify backward compatibility issues before purchasing any drive.

Current Travan Drives and Media

Travan NS drives (Travan NS-8, Travan 20, and Travan 40) use a dual-head design that permits verification during the data writing process instead of requiring the user to rewind the tape and reread it for verification, as with older Travan, QIC, and QIC-Wide drives. Travan NS drives also use hardware-based data compression for faster backups instead of software-based data compression, as with older Travan products.

Travan 20 and 40 drives are currently available from Quantum, thanks to Quantum's 2005 acquisition of Certance (formerly Seagate Removable Storage Solutions LLC). Travan 40GB drives are available in internal ATA/IDE and external USB 2.0 form factors. Travan 20 drives are available in internal ATA/IDE and SCSI-2 and external USB 2.0 form factors.

Certance/Quantum model numbers include the following:

- CTM40, for Travan 40 media.
- CTM20, for Travan20 media.
- CTMCL, which is the cleaning cartridge model (this cartridge also works with Travan-8, NS-8, and Travan 20 drives).

Media is available from Quantum and from many other vendors, including Dell, IBM, Imation, Sony, and Seagate. Figure 9.1 illustrates a typical Travan 20 or Travan 40 data cartridge. Before backing up to this type of media, you need to make sure the cartridge's write-protect switch is open (unlocked) for recording. When you've completed a backup, you should close the write-protect switch to prevent accidental overwriting on a cartridge that contains archival data.

Installing a Travan 20/40 Physical Drive

Travan 20 and 40 ATAPI (ATA/IDE) and SCSI-2 drives can be installed in a 3.5-inch or 5.25-inch drive bay. If a 5.25-inch drive bay is used, you use a mounting bracket kit like the one shown in Figure 9.2. The mounting bracket kit provides the large faceplate needed to completely cover the 5.25-inch drive bay opening and extends the sides of the drive so that the drive can be mounted in the larger drive bay. If the case uses drive rails, you attach them to the sides of the mounting bracket kit.

Travan 20 and 40 USB drives do not require special installation and can be connected to any USB 2.0 port. These drives can be used with USB 1.1 ports, but performance will be severely limited.

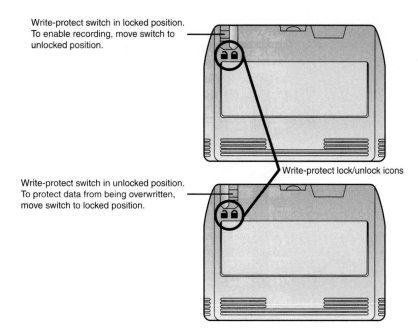

Write-protect switch in locked position. To enable recording, move switch to unlocked position.

Write-protect lock/unlock icons

Write-protect switch in unlocked position. To protect data from being overwritten, move switch to locked position.

Figure 9.1   Setting a Travan 20 or 40 cartridge's write-protect switch.

Configuration for Travan ATAPI Drives

Travan 20 and Travan 40 drives cannot be used on the same ATA/IDE cable as an ATA/IDE hard disk and should always be connected to a separate cable. However, the second cable can also host an ATAPI CD-ROM, DVD-ROM, or other removable-media ATAPI drive. By using a separate cable for the tape backup and hard disk drive, the tape backup can run at maximum speed and will not interfere with the hard disk during backup or restoration operations.

Although Travan 40 drives have four sets of jumpers on the rear of the drive (see Figure 9.3), only the rightmost two are used. You remove the jumper block to configure the drive as a slave when the drive is installed on the same cable as another ATAPI drive. You insert the jumper block into the rightmost set of jumpers to configure the drive as master. If an 80-wire Ultra ATA cable is used, you can insert the jumper into the Cable Select jumper one position to the left from the Master jumper.

Travan 20 drives use the traditional three-position jumper (Master, Slave, Cable Select) used by most other ATA/IDE and ATAPI drives. The jumpers are mounted on the bottom of the drive rather than at the rear.

Configuring Travan 20 SCSI-2 Drives

Travan 20 SCSI-2 drives are designed to work on Narrow SCSI (50-pin) interfaces rather than the 68-pin LVD SCSI interfaces used by most SCSI-interface tape backups for servers. The drive uses a standard 50-pin SCSI-2 ribbon cable. The configuration jumper pins are located on the bottom of the drive. They permit the drive to be configured for any SCSI ID between 0 and 7 and are also used to enable or disable termination, provide termination power, and enable parity checking (see Figure 9.4).

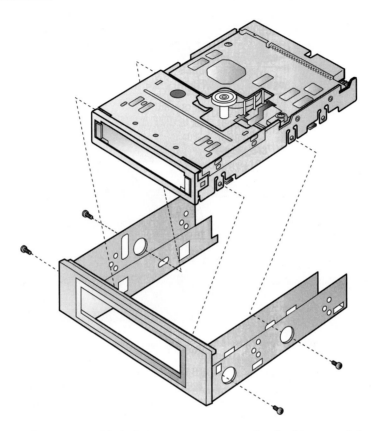

Figure 9.2 Installing a Travan 20 or 40 drive into a mounting bracket kit to permit installation in a 5.25-inch drive bay.

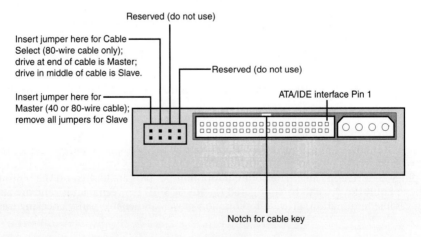

Figure 9.3 Jumper selections for a Travan 40 ATAPI drive.

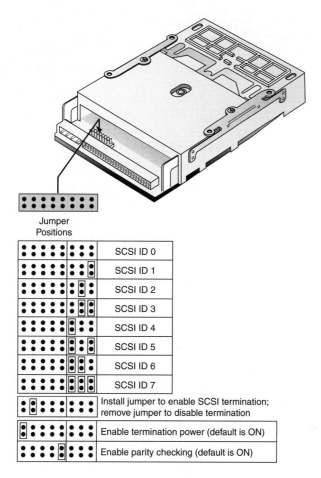

Jumper
Positions

• • • • • • • •	SCSI ID 0
• • • • • • • ▪	SCSI ID 1
• • • • • ▪ • •	SCSI ID 2
• • • • • ▪ • ▪	SCSI ID 3
• • • • ▪ • • •	SCSI ID 4
• • • • ▪ • • ▪	SCSI ID 5
• • • • ▪ ▪ • •	SCSI ID 6
• • • • ▪ ▪ • ▪	SCSI ID 7
• ▪ • • • • • •	Install jumper to enable SCSI termination; remove jumper to disable termination
▪ • • • • • • •	Enable termination power (default is ON)
• • • ▪ • • • •	Enable parity checking (default is ON)

Figure 9.4   SCSI configuration for a Travan 20 SCSI-2 tape backup drive. Note that the drive is upside-down in this view.

Termination power and parity checking are enabled by default. If another device on the SCSI daisy chain, such as a hard disk, is already configured to provide termination power, you need to disable the tape backup's termination power setting. If double bus termination power is present, backup problems can result. Parity checking should always be left enabled to ensure reliable backups; you should disable it only for diagnostic purposes.

If the drive is located at the end of the SCSI daisy-chain (that is, at the end of the cable), you insert the termination jumper. If the drive is located elsewhere in the daisy-chain, you remove the termination jumper.

Travan Software Drivers and Utility Programs

The Travan 20 and Travan 40 drives currently sold at retail include Yosemite TapeWare XE Server/Workstation backup software. This backup program supports the following server operating systems for ATAPI drives: Windows NT 4.0, Windows 2000 Server, Windows Server 2003, and Linux for ATAPI drives; and Windows 2000 Server and Windows Server 2003 for USB drives.

For third-party backup software support, you should go to the software vendor's website or use the Quantum compatibility guide that is available at www.quantum.com/ServiceandSupport/CompatibilityGuides/Index.aspx.

If you plan to use Travan 40 ATAPI drives with the built-in backup programs in Windows NT 4 or in Windows 2000 Server/Windows Server 2003, you can download drivers from www.quantum.com/ServiceandSupport/SoftwareandDocumentationDownloads/Travan40ATAPI/Index.aspx. These versions of Windows have native support for Travan 20.

TapeRX diagnostics for Travan 20 and Travan 40 drives are available for Windows, Linux, NetWare, and Solaris, from www.quantum.com/ServiceandSupport/SoftwareandDocumentationDownloads/Travan40USB2.0/Index. aspx.

DDS-3, DDS-4, and DAT72 Tape Drives

Of the many high-performance] tape drives on the market, a great choice for use with entry-level to midrange servers is the DAT/DDS tape drive family because of its combination of performance, capacity, reliability, and reasonable price. Current members of the DDS family include the following:

- **DDS-3 (DAT 24)**—DDS-3 has a slightly larger capacity (12GB native/24GB at 2:1 compression) than Travan 20. SCSI-2 versions are read/write compatible with DDS-1 (1.3/2.6GB for 60 minutes or 2.0/4.0GB for 90-minute tapes) and DDS-2 (4.0/8.0GB) media. SCSI-2 versions are sold by Quantum, Hewlett-Packard, IBM, and Dell. External USB 2.0 versions, sold only by Hewlett-Packard, are read/write compatible with DDS-2 media.

- **DDS-4 (DAT 40)**—DDS-4 has a 20GB native/40GB at 2:1 compression capacity, which is double the capacity of Travan 20 and equal to Travan GB. It is read/write compatible with DDS-3 media. Quantum DDS-4 drives use the Ultra 2 SCSI LVD interface, while Hewlett-Packard DDS-4 drives use the SCSI-2 interface. Both are available in internal and external form factors. Hewlett-Packard also produces USB 2.0 drives in both internal and external form factors.

- **DAT 72**—The newest member of the DAT/DDS family, DAT 72 drives have a 36GB native/72GB at 2:1 compression capacity. They are read/write compatible with DDS-4 and DDS-3 media.

Note

Some DDS-4 drives are also read compatible with DDS-2 media, which means they can be used in place of older drives for retrieving existing backups. Some DDS-4 drives are also read/write compatible with DDS-2 media, which means they can reuse DDS-2 media. It's important to check media compatibility with the drive manufacturer for details.

DDS and DAT 72 drives use helical scan recording. The read/write heads used in helical scan recording are mounted on a drum and write data at a slight angle to the tape, using a mechanism highly reminiscent of that in a VCR. The entire surface of the tape is used to store data, enabling more data to be placed in a given length of tape than with the linear recording techniques that the QIC and Travan family of drives use.

Table 9.2 lists current DDS-3, DDS-4, and DAT 72 drives, interfaces, and form factors, by manufacturer. Vendors such as IBM and Dell are not listed; they do not manufacture DDS and DAT drives but instead re-label drives from other vendors. Sony, the originator of the DDS standard, no longer makes DDS drives.

Table 9.2   Interfaces and Form Factors for DDS-3, DDS-4, and DAT 72 Drives

Interface and Form Factor	DDS-3	DDS-4	DAT 72
SCSI-2 (50-pin, SE) internal[1]	Hewlett-Packard, Quantum	—	—
SCSI-2 (50-pin, SE) external[1]	Hewlett-Packard, Quantum	—	—
USB 2.0 internal[2]	Hewlett-Packard	Hewlett-Packard	Hewlett-Packard
USB 2.0 external[2]	Hewlett-Packard	Hewlett-Packard	Hewlett-Packard
Ultra SCSI (68-pin LVD) internal[3,4]	—	Hewlett-Packard, Quantum	Hewlett-Packard, Quantum
Ultra SCSI (68-pin LVD) external[3,4]	—	Hewlett-Packard, Quantum	Hewlett-Packard, Quantum
Ultra SCSI hot-plug	—	Hewlett-Packard	Hewlett-Packard

[1]*DAT 24 drives can be connected to 50-pin or 68-pin SCSI host adapters that support SE operation.*

[2]*Hewlett-Packard's USB 2.0 drives use a native USB 2.0 controller rather than a bridged design for enhanced performance.*

[3]*Quantum and Hewlett-Packard's DDS-4 and DAT 72 drives work in either SE or LVD environments. LVD is recommended for best performance.*

[4]*Hewlett-Packard recommends Ultra160 LVD or Ultra320LVD for best performance with DDS-4 and DAT 72 drives.*

In 2006 and 2007, the next generation of DAT/DDS, DAT 160 (80GB native/160GB 2:1 compression) should be released. For a complete road map of DAT/DDS technology, visit the DAT Manufacturers Group website, at www.datmgm.com.

Quantum and Hewlett-Packard-Specific DDS/DAT 72 Features

Quantum's DDS-3, DDS-4, and DAT 72 drives feature a combination of technologies called TapeShield that are designed to protect drives and data:

- A sealed chamber for the head-to-tape interface
- A continuous-contact capstan cleaner
- A sapphire media-cleaning blade that removes debris from the tape before it contaminates the drive

These improvements enable DAT 72 drives to run 10 times longer in dusty conditions than similar drives that don't have these features. DDS-3, DDS-4, and DAT 72 drives from Quantum also feature SmartShield, which uses multiple reads to improve data recovery when reading from out-of-spec or weak recorded tapes.

Hewlett-Packard's DAT 72 drives include self-cleaning features and One Button Disaster Recovery, an easy-to-use disaster-recovery feature designed to restore a system to its most recent backed-up condition with the press of a button. This feature is supported on several Hewlett-Packard ProLiant servers. See http://h18006.www1.hp.com/products/storageworks/drs/index.html for compatibility information and technical notes.

DDS and DAT 72 Media

DDS and DAT 72 media is labeled with one of the logos shown in Figure 9.5. Current drive manufacturers recommend (of course!) their own brand of media. If you prefer a third-party brand, you need to make sure it supports the appropriate DDS or DAT level.

Figure 9.5 DDS and DAT 72 logos. When used on media, the DDS logo (top) is accompanied by a number that lists the DDS version (middle).

Even though DAT/DDS drives are more expensive than Travan drives with similar capacities, the drive's design is such that the cost of media is lower. For example, a DDS-4 data cartridge is about US$10 in single quantities, compared to about US$50 for a typical Travan 40 data cartridge in single quantifies. A DAT 72 cartridge is about US$23 in single quantities. Over time, a DDS-4 or DAT 72 drive is far less expensive to operate than a Travan 40 drive because of the sharply lower media cost.

Configuring and Installing a Quantum DDS/DAT 72 Tape Backup

Quantum DDS-3, DDS-4, and DAT 72 SCSI drives are designed to work with many different server operating systems, not just Windows. Consequently, installation and configuration of these drives is much more complex than with a Travan drive.

Before installing any drive, you need to install the software drivers provided with the drive. If additional software is needed, you should download it from the support page for the drive. You can download drivers for Windows, Linux, and other operating systems; TapeRX diagnostics; and firmware updates. To download these files, you select the drive type from the Quantum Software and Documentation Downloads page, at www.quantum.com/ServiceandSupport/SoftwareandDocumentationDownloads/index.aspx.

A Quantum DDS or DAT 72 internal SCSI drive has several sets of jumpers or DIP switches:

- The SCSI device ID jumpers are usually located at the rear of an internal drive. Quantum drives use a default SCSI ID of 6.
- Jumpers for enabling or disabling parity and termination power are usually located next to the SCSI device ID jumpers.
- DIP switches for advanced settings, such as data compression, operating system compatibility, SCSI Wide or Narrow, and others, are located at the bottom of the drive.

You configure external drives in the following ways:

- You configure SCSI device IDs by using a switch on the rear of the drive. A small window shows the current device ID. You press buttons above and below the window to select a different device ID. Quantum drives use a default SCSI ID of 6, and Hewlett-Packard drives use a default SCSI ID of 3.
- DIP switches for advanced settings, such as data compression, operating system compatibility, SCSI Wide or Narrow, and others, are located at the bottom of the drive under a small access panel.

Figures 9.6 and 9.7 show examples of these jumpers and switches.

Note

Depending on the drive, documentation for a Quantum DDS or DAT 72 drive might be labeled Seagate, Certance, or Quantum. Seagate was the original manufacturer of most of these drives, before it spun off its tape drive division as Certance. Quantum then purchased Certance in 2005.

Generally, DIP switches 1 through 4 and 9 should be left in their default ON position. However, depending on the server operating system you use, you might need to adjust the position of DIP switches 5 through 8 and 10. The default ON setting shown in Figure 9.7 configures these drives to support Windows NT 4.0, Windows 2000 Server, Windows 2003 Server, Windows 98, Windows Me, and Windows XP.

Table 9.3 lists the appropriate configurations for other operating systems.

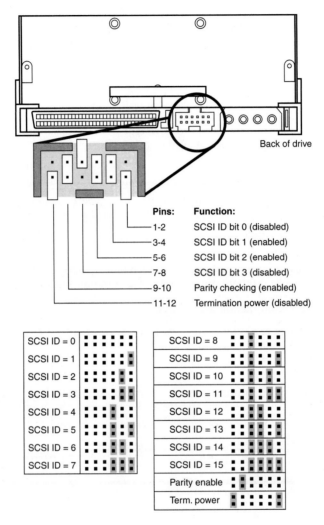

Figure 9.6   The default SCSI Device ID, parity checking, and termination power jumper settings for Quantum internal DDS-4 and DAT 72 drives.

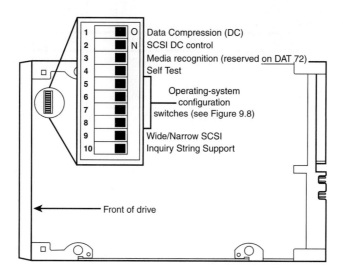

Figure 9.7 Default settings for advanced tape drive configuration DIP switches on Quantum internal and external DDS-4 and DAT 72 drives.

Table 9.3 Operating System–Specific DIP Switch Settings for Quantum DDS-4 and DAT 72 Internal SCSI Tape Backup Drives

Host OS	Driver	SW5	SW6	SW7	SW8	SW10
Windows NT 4[1]	STDAT4.SYS (Seagate)	On	On	On	On	On
Windows NT 4[1]	4mmDAT.SYS (Microsoft)	On	On	On	On	Off
Novell 4.11[1]	TAPEDAI	Off	On	On	Off	Off
Novell 4.11[1]	NWTAPE.CDM (pre 11/3/99)	Off	On	On	Off	Off
Novell 4.11[1]	NWTAPE.CDM (after 11/3/99)	On	On	On	On	Off
Novell 5.x[1]	NWTAPE.CDM (pre 11/3/99)	Off	On	On	Off	Off
Novell 5.x[1]	NWTAPE.CDM (post 11/3/99)	On	On	On	On	Off
DEC UNIX	—	Off	On	On	On	—
Sun UNIX	—	On	Off	On	On	—
SGI	—	On	On	On	On	—
HP-UX	—	On	On	Off	On	—
IBM AIX	—	On	Off	On	Off	—
Linux	—	On	On	On	On	—

Table 9.3   Continued

Host OS	Driver	SW5	SW6	SW7	SW8	SW10
SCO (ODT and Open Server)[2]	—	Off	On	On	Off	—
SCO UNIXWare 7.x[2]	—	On	On	On	On	—

[1]*Listings for Windows NT 4 and Novell 4.x and 5.x assume use of the native backup applet.*

[2]*Setting for the ODT and Open Server versions of the SCO OS assume that installation is done using the* MAKDEV *utility.*

Internal DDS-3 drives use a 10-position DIP switch on the underside of the drive for SCSI ID and other configuration settings. The SCSI ID can also be configured with DIP switches on the rear of the drive. For details, see http://downloads.quantum.com/Certance/manuals/userguides/user_guide_stdx24000n_en.pdf.

You use external terminators with Quantum internal SCSI tape backups if the drive is at the end of the SCSI daisy-chain. Quantum internal drives fit into half-height 5.25-inch drive bays. All external SCSI tape backups from any vendor require termination if the drive is at the end of the SCSI daisy-chain.

Configuring and Installing a Hewlett-Packard DDS or DAT 72 Tape Backup Drive

Hewlett-Packard provides a CD containing its StorageWorks Library and Tape Tools with its drives. If the CD contains drivers for your operating system, you should install the appropriate drivers. If a driver for your operating system is not supplied with the drive, you can download updates from the Hewlett-Packard website. To determine software compatibility with a particular Hewlett-Packard tape backup drive, you can go to www.hp.com/go/connect, click Tape Backup, and then click Software Compatibility. Next, you click the entry for each combination of drive and operating system for compatibility details and links to driver updates. Unlike Quantum's SCSI DDS and DAT 72 drives, which depend on a combination of software drivers and DIP switches to configure a drive for a particular operating system, Hewlett-Packard tape drives use software drivers.

To configure the SCSI Device ID on an internal drive, you use the jumper blocks on the rear of the drive. Hewlett-Packard SCSI tape drives are generally configured using Device ID 3; if you need to change the default ID, refer to Table 7.6 in Chapter 7, "The SCSI Bus." The jumpers used to configure the device ID are numbered 1 through 4, from right to left. Other jumpers should not be moved from their default locations. You configure external drives using push buttons to select SCSI IDs. Hewlett-Packard DDS-3 drives support SCSI IDs 0 through 7; Hewlett-Packard DDS-4 and DAT 72 drives use a Wide SCSI interface and support SCSI IDs 0 through 15.

Figure 9.8 illustrates the location of the SCSI ID jumper blocks and external switch on a Hewlett-Packard DDS-3, DDS-4, or DAT 72 drive.

You use external terminators with Hewlett-Packard SCSI tape backups if the drive is at the end of the SCSI daisy-chain. Hewlett-Packard internal drives fit into half-height 5.25-inch drive bays.

To install a Hewlett-Packard USB 2.0 drive, you connect the drive to a USB 2.0 port built into the server or an add-on card. For best performance, you should not connect the drive to a USB 2.0 hub.

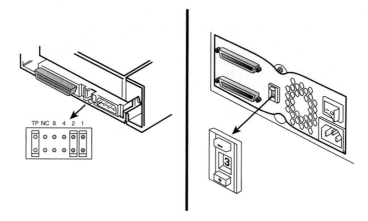

Figure 9.8 Configuring the SCSI ID on an Hewlett-Packard internal (left) and external (right) tape drive.

DLT and SDLT

Digital linear tape (DLT) technology was originally developed by Digital Equipment Corporation (DEC) in 1991. DEC sold its DLT business to Quantum in 1994, and since then, DLT and its higher-capacity sibling, Super DLT (SDLT), have become some of the leading high-end tape backup technologies. Both DLT and SDLT drives are manufactured and sold by many vendors, including ADIC, Hewlett-Packard, IBM, Overland Storage, Quantum, and Tandberg Data.

DLT segments the tape into parallel horizontal tracks and records data by streaming the tape across a single stationary head at 100 inches to 150 inches per second during read/write operations. This is in dramatic contrast to traditional helical-scan technology used by DDS and DAT 72 drives, in which the data is recorded in diagonal stripes, with a rotating drumhead, while a much slower tape motor draws the media past the recording head.

The result is a very durable drive and a robust medium. DLT drive heads have a minimum life expectancy of 15,000 hours under worst-case temperature and humidity conditions. DLTtape III has a life expectancy of 500,000 passes, and DLTtape IIIXT and DLTtape IV double the life expectancy to 1 million passes.

SDLT uses several technologies to increase capacity and reliability over those of the already-impressive DLT standards. These include laser-guided magnetic recording (LGMR), a pivoting optical servo on the backside of the media, thin-film magneto-resistive cluster heads for tape reading and writing, high-efficiency PRML channels for greater recording density, improved media coating, and a positive engagement tape-leading buckling mechanism.

SDLT drives can read SDLT and DLT media up to six generations back. This enables you to replace older, smaller drives with newer, larger drives without losing access to older backups.

Note

SDLT and DLT media use different head cleaning cartridges because of the differences in recording head and media technologies between DLT and SDLT.

Current DLT and SDLT Drives and Media

Although DLT drives have previously been available in capacities as low as 10GB native/20GB at 2:1 compression (DLT-2000), the smallest-capacity DLT drive currently on the market is the DLT VS80, which has a capacity of 40GB/80GB (2:1 compression). Table 9.4 lists the specifications for current DLT and SDLT drives. All current DLT and SDLT drives are designed to connect to Wide SCSI (68-pin) interfaces.

Table 9.4   Current DLT and SDLT Drives

Drive	Standard	Native /Compressed Capacity (2:1)	Interface	Form Factors	Read Compatible With	Read/Write Compatible With
DLT VS80	DLTtapeIV	40GB/80GB	Wide Ultra 2 SCSI	Internal, external, 1U rack-mounted	DLT-4000	DLT1
DLT VS160	DLTtape VS1	80GB/160GB	Ultra 160 SCSI	Internal, external, 1U rack-mounted	DLT1, DLT VS80	
SDLT 320	SDLTtape I	160GB/320GB	Wide Ultra 2 SCSI, HVD, Ultra SCSI	Internal, external, 2U rack-mounted	DLT 8000, DLT 7000, DLT 4000, DLT 1, DLT VS80	SDLT 220
SDLT 600	SDLT Tape II	300GB/600GB	Ultra 160 SCSI	Internal, external, 2U rack-mounted	SDLT 320, SDLT 220, DLT VS80	

DLT media is available in three families: DLTtape III, DLTtape IIIXT, and DLTtape IV. Current installations of DLT drives are most likely to support DLTtape IV. This media can also be read by SDLT drives. SDLT media is available in two families: Super DLTtape I (SDLTtape I) and Super DLTtape II (SDLTtape II). Table 9.5 lists the specifications for DLT and SDLT media.

Table 9.5   DLT and SDLT Media

Drive Type	Native/Compressed (2:1) Capacity	Transfer Rate Native/Compressed	Tape Length
DLTtape III			
DLT-2000	10/20GB	1.5/3MBps	1,200 ft.
DLTtape IIIXT			
DLT-2000XT	15/30GB	1.25/2.5MBps	1,828 ft.
DLTtape IV			
DLT-4000	20/40GB	1.5/3MBps	1,828 ft.
DLT-7000	35/70GB	5/10MBps	1,828 ft.
DLT-8000, DLT1, VS80	40/80GB	8/16MBps	1,828 ft.
DLTtape VS1			
VS-160	80/160GB	8/16MBps	1,847 ft.

Drive Type	Native/Compressed (2:1) Capacity	Transfer Rate Native/Compressed	Tape Length
	Super DLTtape I		
SDLT 220 (SDLT1)	110/220GB	11/22MBps	1,833.5 ft.
SDLT 320	160/320GB	16/32MBps	1,833.5 ft.
	Super DLTtape II		
SDLT 600	300/600GB	36/72MBps	2,066 ft.

Configuring and Installing DLT and SDLT Drives

Compared to DDS and DAT72 /tape drives, the configuration of current DLT and SDLT drives is relatively simple. The software drivers used by DLT and SDLT drives are used to optimize these drives' operations with different operating systems rather than the configuration jumpers used by DDS and DAT72 tape drives. The only hardware setting used by current DLT and SDLT tape drives is the SCSI device ID. For internal drives, you use jumper blocks on the rear of the drive to configure the SCSI device ID. For external drives, you use push buttons to set the device ID. Figure 9.9 illustrates typical DLT drives, the Quantum DLT VS80 in its external and internal versions, and the SCSI device ID settings used on these drives. For other drives, see the documentation.

As with any SCSI drive, if a tape drive is the last drive in the daisy-chain, it must be terminated. With external drives, you connect an external terminator to the second connector on the drive (refer to Figure 9.9). To terminate an internal drive, you connect the terminator/ to the data cable connector at the next position past the drive.

LTO Ultrium

LTO Ultrium is the highest-performing and highest-capacity open standard tape backup system currently available for servers. Ultrium was developed by the Linear Tape-Open (LTO) Technology organization, co-founded by Hewlett-Packard, Seagate, and IBM in 1997. Originally, LTO developed two standards: Ultrium (optimized for high capacity) and Accelis (optimized for high speed). Accelis was never adopted, in large measure because Ultrium provided comparable speeds at higher capacities. Thus, Ultrium and LTO are sometimes used interchangeably. The first Ultrium drives (LTO-1) were released in 2000. Currently, LTO-1, LTO-2, and LTO-3 drives are available from many vendors, including Hewlett-Packard, IBM, Quantum, and Tandberg Data.

Note

To learn more about Ultrium and LTO, visit the LTO Technology organization website, at www.lto.org

LTO Ultrium technology divides a 384-track half-inch tape into four data bands, separated by servo bands. Each read/write head contains eight elements. Two servo bands are used simultaneously to provide accurate head positioning and to overcome any flaws in the media. Tape is written bidirectionally at very high speeds. Each data band is written in the opposite direction from the previous band to help avoid cross-talk between data bands.

Each Ultrium cartridge contains a NVRAM chip that provides calibration and other information. The drive reads this information and uses it to help operate the cartridge in an optimal manner. This information can also be read by an RF receiver before the cartridge is inserted into a tape drive. As with other current tape backup technologies, Ultrium uses the read-while-write method of data verification. If data cannot be verified, it is rewritten on another portion of the tape during backup.

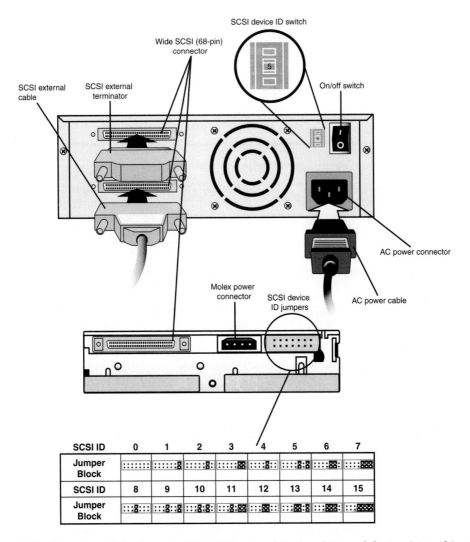

Figure 9.9   Rear views of the Quantum DLT VS80 external (top) and internal (bottom) tape drives.

LTO Ultrium Drives and Media

Ultrium products are currently available in three generations: LTO-1, LTO-2, and LTO-3. Each generation doubles the native and 2:1 compressed capacity compared to the previous generation, and each generation also significantly increases the compressed transfer rate. Table 9.6 lists current Ultrium drives from major vendors.

Table 9.6 Current LTO Ultrium Drives[1]

Standard	Drive	Recommended SCSI Interface	Form Factor
		Hewlett-Packard	
LTO-1	Ultrium 215	Ultra 2 Wide or faster	Half-height internal, external
	Ultrium 230	Ultra 2 Wide or faster	Full-height internal, external
	Ultrium 232	Ultra 2 Wide or faster	Half-height internal, external
LTO-2	Ultrium 448	Ultra 160 or Ultra320	Half-height internal, external
	Ultrium 460	Ultra160 or Ultra320	Full-height internal, external
LTO-3	Ultrium 960	Ultra320	Full-height internal, external
		IBM	
LTO-1[2]	3580 L11, H11	Ultra160	External
	3580 L13, H13	Ultra160	External
LTO-2[2]	3580 L23, H23	Ultra160	External
LTO-3	3580 L3H	Ultra160	External
	3580 L33	Ultra160	External
		Quantum	
LTO-2	LTO-2 HH	Ultra160	Half-height internal, external, 1U rack-mounted
LTO-2	LTO-2	Ultra160	Full-height internal, external, 2U rack-mounted
LTO-3	LTO-3	Ultra160	Full-height internal, external, 2U rack-mounted
		Tandberg Data	
LTO-1	240LTO	Ultra160	Full-height internal, external
LTO-2	420LTO	Ultra160	Half-height internal, external
	440LTO	Ultra160	Full-height internal, external
LTO-3	840LTO	Ultra160	Full-height internal, external

[1]*All LTO Ultrium drives are designed to connect to 68-pin (Wide) SCSI interfaces.*

[2]*H versions of this model are designed to connect to HVD SCSI interfaces*

Note

Full-height LTO drives offer faster performance than half-height versions.

Table 9.7 lists the specifications for each LTO Ultrium standard. As this table indicates, LTO-3 drives are read/write compatible with LTO-2 media and can read LTO-1 media. LTO-2 drives are read/write compatible with LTO-1 media. As LTO continues to be developed, forthcoming drives are expected to continue to feature read/write compatibility with the previous generation and read compatibility two generations back. Backward compatibility makes it easier to move up to higher-capacity drives without the necessity to convert existing backup data to a new drive format.

Table 9.7   LTO Ultrium Specifications

LTO Ultrium Generation	Native/ Compressed Capacity (2:1)	Transfer Rate (2:1 compression)[1]	Read/Write Compatible With	Read Compatible With
LTO-1	100/200GB	30–54MBps	—	—
LTO-2	200/400GB	48–70MBps	LTO-1	—
LTO-3	400/800GB	136–160MBps	LTO-2	LTO-1

[1]*Transfer rate varies with drive model; see the specifications for a particular drive for details.*

Configuring and Installing LTO Ultrium Drives

As with DLT and SDLT drives, configuring LTO Ultrium SCSI drives is relatively simple. With external drives, you use push buttons to set the device ID. With internal drives, you use jumper blocks on the rear of the drive to configure the SCSI device ID (see Figure 9.9 for examples of both types of drives). See the drive's documentation for specific jumper configurations.

If a drive is the last drive in the daisy-chain, it must be terminated. With external drives, you connect an external terminator to the second connector on the drive. To terminate an internal drive, you connect the terminator to the data cable connector at the next position past the drive.

Before connecting a drive to your system, you should install the drivers included with the drive. You can visit the vendor's support site to download updated drivers.

Tape Autoloaders

If tape capacity had kept pace with hard disk capacity, it would be easy to make backups: You could just install a single blank tape in the tape backup and start the process. Then you could label it when you're finished and put it aside for storage. However, in many cases today, a single backup requires multiple tapes:

- Even entry-level servers today might use large ATA/IDE or SATA hard disks that range in capacity from 100GB to as much as 500GB. SCSI and SAS hard disks are now available in 300GB sizes. Most tape backups discussed in this chapter have capacities smaller than these extremes, even when a 2:1 compression ratio is assumed.

- Multidisk SCSI or SATA RAID arrays might have capacities approaching the terabyte (1,000GB) range, which exceeds even the capacity of LTO-3 Ultrium tape backups (800GB at 2:1 compression).

To avoid the need to manually load tapes for a multiple-tape backup, you can consider a tape autoloader. An autoloader is an external device that contains a single tape backup drive and holds anywhere from 8 to 16 tape cartridges. When the first cartridge is full, the autoloader removes it and inserts another. The process is repeated until the backup task is finished. Tape autoloaders are available in DDS/DAT, DLT, SDLT, and LTO-Ultrium formats. Most vendors that sell individual tape drives also sell autoloaders, and autoloaders are also manufactured by companies that incorporate third-party tape drives. Figure 9.10 illustrates a typical autoloader for DLT cartridges.

Autoloader Drives and Media

Table 9.8 lists the specifications for the most common autoloaders based on the drives covered earlier in this chapter.

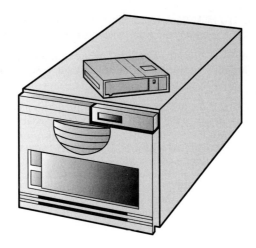

Figure 9.10 A typical 8-slot autoloader for DLT cartridges.

Table 9.8   Autoloaders Based on DDS/DAT, DLT, SDLT, and LTO Technologies

Tape Media Supported	Number of Tape Cartridges	Native Capacity	Compressed Capacity (2:1 Compression)
SDLT 600	8	2400GB	4800GB
	16	4800GB	9600GB
SDLT 320	8	1280GB	2560GB
	16	2560GB	5120GB
DLT VS160	16	1280GB	2560GB
	8	640GB	1280GB
DLT1	16	640GB	1280GB
DLT VS80	8	320GB	640GB
LTO-3	8	3200GB	6400GB
LTO-2	16	3200GB	6400GB
	10	2000GB	4000GB
	8	1600GB	3200GB
LTO-1	16	1600GB	3200GB
	10	1000GB	2000GB
	8	800GB	1600GB
DAT 72	6	216GB	434GB
DDS-4	6	180GB	360GB

The media used by an autoloader is the same as that used by a single tape drive, using the same technology. Autoloaders have trays or cassettes that hold the media when not in use. To simplify calculation of native and compressed capacities, you should use the same size and type of media for each cartridge, even if the drive can read and write to more than one size of media.

Installing Autoloaders

Many autoloaders are designed and configured for rack installation. A 2U-sized rack is normally used. A team of two people should work together to install the unit into a rack: one to hold the unit, and the other to fasten the unit to a rack. Some autoloaders are designed to work in a full-height 5.25-inch drive bay, and others can be placed on a desktop.

Most autoloaders use Ultra160 SCSI interfaces, but some are available in 2Gbps Fibre Channel interfaces as well. For best performance, autoloaders as well as single tape backup drives should be connected to a separate SCSI channel from SCSI drives or RAID arrays.

If the vendor recommends it, you should connect the autoloader to a slot-based SCSI host adapter rather than to a SCSI RAID or integrated SCSI host adapter. If necessary, you should install the recommended SCSI host adapter into the server before continuing. You need to be sure to terminate the autoloader if it is the last (or only) device on the SCSI bus. Generally, this requires that you attach the appropriate type of terminator to the unused SCSI connector on the rear of the autoloader.

When you fill the autoloader's magazine with data cartridges, you need to make sure each cartridge is not write-protected. Some autoloaders require you to insert the cartridges one at a time. Others use multicartridge inserts. If the unit is a dual-capacity 8/16 cartridge unit, you must use a magazine blank and a single eight-cartridge magazine or else two magazines of eight cartridges each.

The front panel is used to perform most initial setup and management tasks. Depending on the autoloader, typical options might include the following:

- The SCSI device ID for the drive
- The SCSI device ID for the autoloader (if it requires its own device ID)
- Date/time and time zone information
- Cartridge changing mode
- Cleaning tape location and settings
- Which magazine to use (on dual-magazine units)
- Passwords and security settings
- Installation of system updates
- Other device-specific settings, such as network configuration and compression

Even if you plan to use remote network management for an autoloader, you must first configure devices that support remote management with the appropriate IP address and other network configuration settings.

Some autoloaders, particularly those made for DAT 72 and DDS-4 media, might require you to configure the drive with DIP switches and a back panel option switch if you plan to use a Linux or other non-Windows operating system with the autoloader. Typically, the default setting supports Windows operating systems.

If the autoloader includes a web-based management interface, you need to connect an RJ-45 cable from your network to the RJ-45 (Ethernet) port on the rear of the autoloader. After you use the front panel to configure the autoloader, you can log in to the autoloader's IP address and perform most of the management tasks you can also perform through the device's front panel controls. Some of the tasks you will find particularly useful to perform remotely include cartridge inventory, cleaning the drive (if a cleaning cartridge is installed), moving a cartridge, viewing drive usage statistics, running diagnostic tests, and configuring a single IP address or range of IP addresses authorized to manage the drive. Note that autoloaders can also be configured to work in an Auto Clean mode if a cleaning cartridge is installed.

Autoloader Troubleshooting

Autoloaders are a good bit more complex than single tape backup units. To troubleshoot a unit, you use the front-panel display or remote management. If the device stores log files, you should examine them, which typically requires you to log in to the unit remotely. If the vendor provides diagnostic software, you should run it to determine problems. Note that the diagnostic software provided with the unit might not be compatible with some operating systems. You can visit the vendor's website for the latest versions.

You need to verify that the autoloader works with your tape backup application. For some backup software, whether built in to the operating system or provided by a third party, you might need to install patches or updates to enable it to work with an autoloader. You can check the autoloader vendor's website for compatibility information and links to update files.

You need to be sure to check SCSI-specific settings, such as device IDs (each device on a particular SCSI bus must have a unique SCSI ID), cabling, and termination.

You also need to check the signal lights on the front of the unit, which are used to report various problems. The patterns of flashing lights or, on some units, the color of the LED, are used to indicate various problems. You should see your unit's documentation for details.

If the drive is not using the latest firmware and you are having problems, you should update the firmware.

Tape Libraries and Enterprise Units

As the previous section discusses, tape autoloaders enable you to automate tape backup and archiving to handle the backup requirements of large hard disks. However, if you are responsible for an enterprise-level server, an autoloader might not provide enough capacity or sufficient management options to be suitable. In such cases, you should consider a tape library.

A tape library resembles an autoloader, but with the following differences:

- **Number of drives**—An autoloader has only one drive, whereas a tape library usually has two or more drives. Some enterprise-level tape libraries sold by IBM, for example, support up to 192 drives.

- **Number of cartridges**—Entry-level tape libraries usually support 24 or more slots for data or other cartridges. Some enterprise-level tape libraries can support more than 500 slots.

- **Library partitioning**—A library can be partitioned into two or more logical libraries. Each library can be used as a virtual backup destination or source for a different server or department.

- **Expandability**—Most tape libraries are modular, enabling multiple modules to be managed as a single logical unit.

- **Manageability**—Tape libraries are designed for remote network management.

- **Support for Fibre Channel–based storage area networks (SANs) as well as SCSI interfacing**—Fibre Channel is a high-speed (up to 4Gbps) connection between servers and shared storage devices such as tape drives and libraries. Fibre Channel can use optical fiber, coaxial cable, and UTP cable.

- **Availability of a mail slot**—A mail slot is a special slot that does not require that all cartridge be re-inventoried when the cartridge is added to or removed from this slot. The mail slot is a good location to use for the cleaning cartridge.

Tape libraries are normally based on the largest and fastest tape backups available in a particular technology. These are the most common choices:

- LTO Ultrium (LTO-2 and LTO-3)
- SDLT (SDLT 600 and SDLT 320)

Some tape libraries support only one type of drive, but others support mixing LTO Ultrium and SDLT drives in the same unit. This is useful because LTO-3 Ultrium and SDLT 600 media are now available in a special write-once, read-many (WORM) format. Thus, you could partition a tape library could to write data for permanent archiving to the drive using WORM tape media and data for backup and later reuse and replacement to the library's other drive, using standard rewritable tape.

Installing Tape Libraries

Tape libraries usually require some assembly. You might need to install the entry/exit port (used to move cartridges), support legs, and a conversion kit to convert a tabletop unit into a rack-mounted unit. Some libraries also require you to install the tape drives and to add additional power supplies for redundancy or to provide necessary power for a larger number of tape drives.

Tape libraries, unlike tape autoloaders, usually include one or more onboard SCSI host adapters in a mini-PCI form factor. The SCSI host adapter is used to run the library's robot tape loading/unloading/movement mechanism. If the tape library will be partitioned into two or more logical libraries, additional SCSI host adapters are needed in the library (see Figure 9.11).

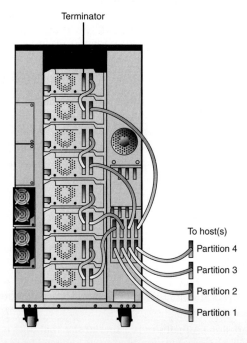

Figure 9.11   A tape library configured as four logical libraries.

Depending on the size of the tape library, one host adapter might be used to run one or more drives. Each tape drive in a tape library, as well as the library itself, requires a SCSI device ID. For example, a tape library with two tape drives requires three unique SCSI device IDs. Special short patch cables are used for daisy-chaining SCSI drives to each other.

You use the front panel to configure the SCSI device IDs, other SCSI settings (mode, bus parity, and so forth), Fibre Channel options, library partitioning, reserved slot(s) for cleaning cartridges, TCP/IP network settings, front panel and media security locks, and magazine access (for loading or removing cartridges). You also use the front panel for viewing and changing system settings such as cartridge access mode, automatic cleaning, cartridge mapping (displays cartridge names), emulation (necessary to enable some backup programs to operate with certain libraries), and library maintenance (rebooting, updating firmware, and so forth). If a tape library is connected to a Fibre Channel switch, one cable from the switch is connected to the library, and a separate cable from the switch is connected to each drive built in to the tape library.

To permit remote management, you connect an RJ-45 Ethernet port in the tape library to an RJ-45 cable from your network. To manage the tape library via a web browser, you enter the IP address assigned to the unit and provide a password to log in to the unit. You can normally perform most configuration options through the web browser.

To create a library partition, you must specify which SCSI or Fibre Channel host adapter card will control access and specify which tape cartridge slots and drives are assigned to that partition.

A tape library requires at least one and sometimes more AC power cords. You need to be sure to provide an AC outlet with adequate power to run the tape library.

Tape Library Troubleshooting

Learning to troubleshoot a tape library requires that you familiarize yourself with the methods your library server uses for reporting problems. The front-panel LCD display is often used to display problem messages and error codes, for example. If you use remote access, you should check the documentation to determine whether some problems are only reported through the front-panel LCD display. Before you can control the robot remotely, you might need to configure it for remote access.

Cartridges are identified by unique bar codes. If the system is unable to locate a particular cartridge, you should check the bar code labels on each cartridge. Any labels that are worn or dirty should be replaced. If the labels are clean, you need to make sure the laser and lens used to read the bar code is not dirty or blocked by debris. You can use the bar code statistics readout to determine failure rates.

You can use other reports to find additional problems. On the first sign of a problem, you should try resetting the library. If problems recur, you should contact the company for help.

Alternatives to Tape Backup

Although tape backup has long been the leading solution for backing up servers, it might not be appropriate for your situation, particularly if you have a relatively small server hard disk or don't require automation. The following sections discuss the leading alternatives to tape backup:

- Disk-to-disk backup
- Iomega REV
- DVD-rewritable

After discussing these alternatives, we take a look at the limitations of these methods.

Disk-to-Disk (D2D) Backup

As an alternative to tape backup, many users of desktop PCs and entry-level servers now use some form of D2D backup. The most common type of D2D backup involves the use of an external IEEE 1394 or USB 2.0–based hard disk equipped with backup software. "One button" backup drives can start the backup program automatically as soon as the drive is plugged in to the system and powered up.

For drives with relatively small amounts of changing data to back up, a low-end D2D backup using an external hard disk makes a great deal of sense. External hard disks are now available with capacities as high as 500GB. External drives with capacities of 300GB or larger are big enough to permit a full backup and many incremental backups of a typical 160GB entry-level server hard disk.

Unlike tape backups, which require that the tape be advanced to a particular point before a restore process can begin, restorations from a D2D backup can begin instantaneously.

D2D backup is not limited to USB 2.0 or IEEE 1394 drives, however. Network-based backup appliances are available for backing up multiple stations on a network. In addition to traditional backup programs that can also be used in a D2D backup process, special D2D software is now available from several sources.

IBM introduced Tivoli Continuous Data Protection (CDP) for Files in 2005 for Windows 2000 Server, Windows XP, and Windows Server 2003. CDP backs up changed files to a variety of local and network drives in real-time and periodically backs up data to a remote file server or Tivoli Storage Manager. For more information, see www-306.ibm.com/software/tivoli/products/continuous-data-protection/. Microsoft also released System Center Data Protection Manager (DPM) D2D program in 2005. DPM supports Windows Server 2003 on servers or NAS storage devices. DPM tracks and stores byte-level changes to server files and offers scheduled replication. For more information, see www.microsoft.com/windowsserversystem/dpm/default.mspx. Traditional backup programs are also available in D2D versions.

▶▶ For more information about D2D backup programs, see "Third-Party Backup Software," p. 551.

High-end disk-based backup devices that emulate tape libraries are also available. These devices enable a backup to be performed directly to a large hard disk array. Later, backup files can be transferred to tape for archiving operations, enabling the backup drive to be reused.

Iomega REV

Although current tape technologies such as LTO, SDLT, and DAT 72 are much faster than their predecessors, tape drives are still hampered by their linear technology that requires sequential access to data. To find a particular area of a tape to use for backup or restoration, you must move the tape past the recording head. Even though some recent tape technologies store certain information about a particular cartridge in the cartridge's NVRAM, it still takes time to rewind the tape and advance it to a particular location.

If only certain files need to be restored, the user must wait as the tape is advanced to the first file, the file is read and restored to disk, the tape is advanced to the next file, and so forth. To replace outdated files on a tape, the tape must be rewritten.

In contrast, removable-media storage provides random, rather than sequential, access to files and easy replacement, when necessary, of outdated information. However, traditional removable-media storage such as Zip, rewritable CD, and even rewritable DVD do not have capacities comparable to even entry-level server hard disks.

Iomega's REV removable-media drive is designed to provide capacity comparable to that of DAT 72 or DLT VS80 tape drives while providing faster read and write access. REV uses 35GB hard-disk-type removable-media cartridges that Iomega refers to as *removable rigid disks (RRDs)*. Unlike older technologies such as Zip, REV's RRD cartridges provide a sealed, air-filtered environment for read/write heads and electronics. The RRD media in a REV cartridge spins at 4,200RPM. While this is significantly slower than desktop ATA/IDE hard disks, this spin rate is comparable to that of many laptop ATA/IDE hard disks. In drag-and-drop file transfer tests, REV drives offer comparable transfer rates to 30GB ATA/IDE hard disks with files up to 64KB in size, and they are much faster with files of 1MB or larger. The maximum data transfer is up to 25MBps.

Iomega REV Capacity

The native capacity of any Iomega REV drive is 35GB. Iomega claims a maximum compressed capacity of 90GB (2.6:1), based on testing performed with the Calgary Corpus data set. However, most users will not see this level of data compression in most real-world operations. The reason is that the files used in the Calgary Corpus were primarily text files. As any time spent using PKZip, WinZip, or the built-in Zip-compatible Windows XP archiving feature will tell you, text files can be compressed up to 90% smaller than normal. However, a great deal of the data on today's systems is already compressed data, such as JPEG photos, PDF files, MP3 and WMA audio files, zip and cab archives, and so forth. A better estimate for compression performance is to assume a maximum capacity of 70GB (2:1 compression), as is assumed by most third-party backup products.

Note

The Calgary Corpus data set was developed in 1990 by Tim Bell and Ian Witten. It can be downloaded from www.data-compression.info/Corpora/CalgaryCorpus/.

A newer data set used for compression testing is the Canterbury Corpus. It can be downloaded from http://corpus.canterbury.ac.nz/index.html. This corpus was developed in 1997. You might want to try both with your favorite backup or archiving programs to see how the results differ.

Iomega REV Drives

Iomega offers a wide variety of drive interfaces for REV, enabling you to choose a drive for almost any type of internal or external host adapter. Table 9.9 lists available models. Note that all drives include Iomega Automatic Backup Pro for Windows 2000 and XP.

Table 9.9   Iomega REV Drive Versions

Interface	Form Factor	Third-Party Backup Software Included
USB 2.0	Desktop	—
ATA/IDE (ATAPI)	3.5-inch or 5.25-inch internal	—
1394a/FireWire 400[1]	Desktop	Dantz Retrospect Express for Mac
SCSI external[2]	Desktop	Yosemite TAPEWARE for REV
SCSI internal[2]	3.5-inch or 5.25-inch internal	Yosemite TAPEWARE for REV
SATA internal	3.5-inch or 5.25-inch internal	—

[1]*Compressed capacity of 70GB when Dantz Restrospect Express is used.*
[2]*Ultra160 LVD interface.*

REV is supported by many third-party server backup applications. To determine whether you need updates, you can visit your backup application vendor's website. Some vendors offer bundles including REV drives, media, and a backup application. Note that the NT Backup utility that is built in to Windows 2000 Server and Windows Server 2003 cannot span a backup to multiple REV cartridges unless Firestreamer-RM is installed.

▶▶ See the tip on p. 543 for details on using Firestreamer-RM to span a backup to multiple rewritable DVDs.

Note

For users of larger hard disks who need an autoloader, REV is also available in a 10-cartridge autoloader format. The REV Autoloader 1000 is a desktop device with a native capacity of 350GB and a compressed capacity of 700GB (2:1 compression). It includes CA BrightStor ARCServe Backup OEM edition for a single server, and it connects to a server via a 68-pin LVD SCSI connection. Options include a bar code reader, a remote management unit, and 2U rack-mounted hardware.

DVD Rewritable/Recordable

If you need to perform backup on a budget, you can use a rewritable DVD drive. Usually, dual-layer (DL) rewritable DVD drives can be substituted for DVD-ROM or rewritable CD drives when a server is first configured, or they can be added later. The native capacity of single-layer DVD media is 4.7GB. If you use DL media, each disc can hold 8.5GB.

DVD rewritable media is a good choice for backups of work-in-progress because the media can be erased and rewritten later. Conversely, DVD recordable provides durable archival storage. Most server backup programs designed for small and medium businesses support DVD rewritable/recordable drives. Note that the NT Backup utility that is built in to Windows 2000 Server and Windows Server 2003 cannot span a backup to multiple rewritable DVDs or CDs unless Firestreamer-RM is installed.

▶▶ See the tip on p. 543 for details on using Firestreamer-RM to span a backup to multiple rewritable DVDs.

Limitations of Tape Alternatives

Tape alternatives have some limitations compared to tape backups, including the following:

- **The problem of creating a long-term backup archive**—If you use D2D backups, you can back up your server quickly, but you should move the backups to archival tape media at some point. Thus, you should not look upon D2D as a total replacement for tape. If you use an external USB 2.0 or IEEE 1394a hard disk as a low-cost D2D backup for an entry-level server, you will eventually run out of disk space unless you move the backup files to other media such as DVD. To determine whether this is feasible, you should look at the backup files created on the external drive to see if they are small enough to move to DVD (4.7GB or less for standard DVD; 8.5GB for DL DVD).

- **Capacity limitations**—If you need to back up a large hard disk or RAID array, a network-based D2D backup solution can be more expensive than some autoloaders. The Iomega REV is most comparable to tape, but its capacity is roughly that of DAT 72. It would take several REV cartridges to back up a 160GB or larger drive on an entry-level or midrange server. If you use DVD media, it will take quite a few DVDs to back up even an entry-level server's 40GB or 80GB hard disk. Unlike tape or Iomega REV, DVD backups cannot be automated; you must insert each additional DVD disc after the previous one is filled.

- **Software support**—Although D2D, REV, and rewritable DVD drives are supported by many third-party backup utilities, you might need to upgrade your current backup program to obtain support for new types of hardware. You should be sure to check compatibility with your existing backup software before adding tape alternatives or switching from tape.

Upgrading Tape Backup Units

You can upgrade a tape backup drives (or tape alternative) to fix problems with the operation or performance in three ways:

- Driver upgrades
- Firmware updates
- Hardware upgrades

The following sections discuss these methods.

Driver Upgrades

Even though most tape backup drives (except for so-called bare drives) include a CD or DVD that contains drivers for major operating systems, you should go to the drive vendor's website and check for updates even before you install the driver CD or DVD. This is a good idea for several reasons:

- If you are using a recently released operating system or service pack, the drivers included with the backup unit might not support your software. You should download and install updates if necessary.

- Even if the installation media supports your operating system, there might be bugs or shortcomings in the version supplied with the backup unit. The latest versions on the website should be used in place of older versions.

- Diagnostic utilities on the installation media might also have been replaced with newer versions, or they might not support your particular operating system. However, the website often has the drivers needed for less-common server operating systems.

Firmware Updates

Just as firmware updates improve a server's ability to work with newer processors and memory and to correct various other problems, firmware updates can also solve problems for users of tape backup drives and other backup hardware.

A backup hardware vendor's website has the latest firmware updates. Note that firmware updates are customized to the particular server operating system in use. For example, if you need to update the firmware for a tape backup, an autoloader, or a library connected to a Linux server, you should make sure you download and install the Linux version of the firmware.

You should not install any firmware update unless it solves specific problems that you have with your system. If a firmware update fails, your drive or other backup device must be serviced.

Hardware Upgrades

Hardware upgrades can help improve the performance of your tape backup or other backup device. This does not always mean an upgrade to the backup device itself. For example, upgrading to a faster SCSI host adapter in the server (for example, Ultra320 rather than Ultra160) can improve performance for many midrange and high-end tape backups, autoloaders, and libraries.

Most SCSI-based tape backups and autoloaders recommend, if not require, that the backup device be on a separate bus from other SCSI devices. If you're using the same SCSI bus to run the tape backup and other SCSI devices (such as the server drive), adding an additional SCSI host adapter (Ultra160 or Ultra320, in most cases) for use by the tape backup will boost performance even more.

If you use a tape autoloader that can handle 16 cartridges, but you only use 8, adding the additional hardware needed to handle another 8 cartridges can help make backups easier. With more cartridges online, you won't need to change them as often. You should upgrade the tape drive for faster and higher-capacity backups. If the autoloader didn't include a bar code reader initially, you should add one for easier organization of large backup sets.

A tape library upgrade can include installation of additional SCSI host adapters to partition the library into multiple logical libraries, replacing SCSI with Fibre Channel, and swapping slower, lower-capacity tape drives for faster, higher-capacity drives.

To find out what the upgrade options are for a particular tape drive, autoloader, or library, you should check the vendor's website for technical documents.

Backup Operations

No matter what type of tape or tape alternative you choose for server backups, you need to understand how backup and restoration processes work and what can go wrong during either process. Typically, backup processes involve making a full backup, followed by one of various backup types that record only changes to files. For the greatest reliability, you should verify a backup upon completion. It's important to keep in mind that a backup must be restored before the files it contains can be used, although in most cases you have the option of restoring all files in a backup or ones that you select.

A successful backup involves the following steps:

1. Choosing a backup solution that supports your operating system and backup hardware.

2. Installing or configuring options for open file backup, client backup, and other options to maximize the ability to recover from data loss.

3. Selecting a full backup as the first backup operation you perform on the server. Make a backup copy, if needed, in case of disaster.

4. Verifying the backup.

5. Safely storing your disaster recovery backup for future use.

6. Performing differential or incremental backups on a regular basis. Differential backups are recommended because a smaller amount of media must be restored to recover from a system crash.

7. Rotating and replacing tape or removable-media cartridges to enable permanent storage of the most valuable data and prevent media failure and consequent data loss.

8. Cleaning the tape drive when recommended by the vendor.

9. Testing the ability to restore the backup. Ideally, you should attempt to restore a disaster recovery backup to a duplicate server. However, at the very least, you should attempt to restore selected files to another folder on your hard disk.

The following sections provide additional details regarding the backup process.

Backup Strategies

The term *backup strategy* refers to the decisions you make about subjects such as the following:

- What files to back up
- What method to use to back them up
- How often files should be backed up
- What to do about open files

The following sections discuss backup strategies, helping you to choose the best backup strategies for your network.

Full Backups and Disaster Recovery Backups

A full backup records all information on the server's hard disk, including data files, applications, operating system files, and the system registry or other configuration details (often referred to as the *system state*). A full backup should be performed as soon as a server is first configured into operating condition. With Windows 2003 Server, the option in Windows NT Server backup option All Information on This Computer sets up a full backup.

When a full backup is performed, many backup programs provide the option to create a disaster recovery backup. A disaster recovery backup usually involves the creation of one or more bootable floppy disks or a bootable CD. The bootable media is used to start the restoration process without the need to reinstall an operating system first.

Windows 2003 Server's integrated NT Backup utility includes a form of disaster recovery known as the Automated System Recovery (ASR) Wizard. ASR can be used to restore a working system from local storage. ASR makes a floppy disk that is used to guide the restoration process in conjunction with the original Windows 2003 Server CD. Note that ASR restores only system files needed to restart the system. Application and data files must be restored separately, unless you specified the Back Up All Information On My Computer option when you ran the ASR backup.

When a file or folder is first created, its archive bit (one of several file/folder attributes) is turned on. After a full backup, the archive bit is cleared (turned off). Understanding the role of the archive bit is essential to understanding the differences between other types of backups.

Differential Backups

It is not necessary to create a full backup every time you back up your system. Instead, you should back up only changed files. One method offered by most backup programs is a differential backup. A differential backup backs up all files that have changed since the last full backup was performed. Files that are newly created or have been changed turn on the archive bit, but a differential backup, unlike a full backup, does not clear the archive bit.

On a server that experiences many newly created or changed files, differential backups can take almost as much time as full backups. However, unlike incremental backups (discussed in the next section), only the last differential backup needs to be restored after a full backup is restored to restore a system to its latest backed-up configuration.

For example, assume that a server required 4 tapes for its initial full backup. The first differential backup might require only one tape, but because archive bits aren't changed, each differential backup is likely to take more media. However, even if the last differential backup required 7 tapes, the total number of tapes required to restore the backup would only be 11 (4 from the full backup plus 7 from the last differential backup). In most cases, you use fewer tape cartridges to restore your system to its last backed-up state with a differential backup because you only need to restore the full backup plus the last differential backup.

Incremental Backups

The other major method used for changed-file-only backups after a full backup is performed is the incremental backup. In an incremental backup, only files changed since the last full or incremental backup are stored. When a file is backed up using the incremental method, the archive bit set when the file was first created or was edited is cleared.

Incremental backups are much quicker to perform and require fewer tape cartridges or other media than differential backups. However, to restore a system to operation after a system crash, you must restore both the full backup and then all incremental backups made in the meantime. For example, assume that a full backup required two tape cartridges, and each incremental backup (performed weekly) required one backup cartridge. If the server crashed after a three-month period, you would need to restore about 16 tapes: 4 from the initial full backup and 12 (1 per week) incremental backup tapes, in order from oldest to newest. Even if each incremental backup used only part of a tape, that's a lot of media to restore.

Open File Backups

Open files create a major problem for reliable server backup. In recent times, servers are frequently running around the clock, 24/7, to provide access to files at any time, day or night. Thus, instead of there being several hours of inactivity during which all data files could be closed, backups are often performed while a server is providing data to some users.

Traditional backup programs cannot back up open files, meaning that the most important (or most used) files might not be backed up at all. To make certain that important files are backed up, server backup programs often include or can be upgraded with open file backup features. If your current backup program does not include or cannot be upgraded with open file backup, you should consider upgrading to a version that does support open file backup, especially if you must run backup while users are accessing files.

One method of performing open file backup is the Volume Shadow Copy Service (VSS) included in Windows 2003 Server.

Volume Shadow Copy Service (Snapshots)

Windows 2003 Server includes VSS as a method of backing up open files. VSS also protects files from accidental deletion or replacement on network shares.

VSS is supported on NTFS volumes only. It is enabled through a drive's properties menu. You click the Shadow Copies tab to enable or configure VSS for a particular drive. You can store VSS copies on the same drive letter or, preferably, a different drive letter.

The drive used for shadow copies must have at least 100MB of free space. You can limit the space used for shadow copies, but keep in mind that Windows 2003 Server can maintain up to 64 versions of each file. If you are not concerned about disk space, you should not limit the size of the shadow copy storage area. Windows deletes the oldest files if space becomes limited.

After a server has VSS enabled, you must install the Windows shadow copy client, which is available in the `\System32\twclient\x86` folder located in the server's system (`\Windows` or `\WinNT`) folder. This client will work with Windows XP Professional. For Windows XP Professional and Windows 2000 clients, you can obtain a shadow copy client from www.microsoft.com/windowsserver2003/downloads/shadowcopyclient.mspx. You must use Windows Installer 2.0 or later to install the client.

After the client has been installed, a new tab called Previous Versions shows up in the properties sheet for network shared folders and files stored in folders on volumes running VSS.

To retrieve deleted files, you go to the network shared folder, open it, right-click an empty area, select Properties, and click the Previous Versions tab. Then you select the version and copy or drag it to the user's PC.

To retrieve a previous version of a corrupted or overwritten file, you right-click the file, select Properties, click Previous Versions, and select Restore (to replace current version) or Copy. If you select Copy, you need to choose a location for the file.

To recover a deleted folder, you open the folder that contained the deleted folder, right-click an empty area in that folder, select Properties, and click Previous Versions. Then you choose Copy to copy the folder and all contents to a location you specify. Next, you click Restore to recover the folder and all contents to the current folder.

If you use NTBackup as your server's backup utility, you need to run NTBackup from the command line to enable or disable backup of volume shadow copies. To enable backup of volume shadow copies, you use `ntbackup/SNAP: on`; to disable volume shadow copy backup, you use `ntbackup/snap: off`.

Deciding Which Backup Methods to Use

As you can see from the previous sections, a full backup is not the only backup method you should depend on. You should supplement a full backup with some type of changed-file backups, and, for extra security, implement volume shadow copies if you use Windows 2003 Server. For most users, a combination of full and differential backups produces the easiest type of backup to manage and restore.

One easy method for combining full with differential backups is known as the grandfather, father, son (GFS) method. GFS assumes daily backups on a weekly cycle. Before starting GFS, you should have a full backup. Then you create daily differential backups Monday through Friday and a new full backup on Saturday. The daily differential backups are known as the son, and the weekly full backup is the father. You repeat this weekly. The full backup on the last Saturday of the month (the grandfather) is considered a monthly backup and should be placed into permanent storage. You replace its media with new media.

Verification and Restoration

A backup of any type is worthless if it can't be restored. To make sure a backup can be restored, you should use verification. Modern tape backup systems covered earlier in this chapter perform read-after-write verification to make sure that data can be read immediately after it is written to tape. If a particular file cannot be read, the drive will write it again.

File Verification in Backup Programs

Note that read-after-write verification is not supported on D2D or removable-media backups. In such cases, you should select the option to verify data after backup in your backup application. You might want to use this option the first time you run a tape backup as well to assure yourself that the backup is valid.

With tape backup, the verify after backup option rewinds the tape to the beginning and compares each backed-up file to the file on the source drive, using some type of checksum comparison. If more than one tape was used for the backup, the first tape must be inserted, followed by each subsequent tape. If multiple removable-media or DVD discs are used, the first cartridge or disc must be inserted when prompted, followed by each subsequent cartridge or disc. D2D backups are the fastest and easiest to verify because the backup media does not need to be rewound or inserted.

If you see errors during verification, you should note which files caused the error. If the files were open during backup, you need to enable open file backup with third-party backup software or volume shadow copy backup with Windows 2003 Server and NTBackup. If the file was not open but could not be verified, you might have problems with the source drive or with your media. In that case, you should schedule a disk check with the option to fix file system errors and repair bad sectors. Then you should rerun the backup process and specify backup of only files that did not verify. If problems persist after disk checking, you should clean the tape drive and try a different brand of media.

Restoring Files from a Backup

If a file is damaged, overwritten, or deleted, you can restore it from backup media. You start the backup program and select the option to restore specified files. To ensure that you are restoring the latest version of a data file, you start the restoration process from the latest backup set. Normally, the backup program stores a catalog of each backup. However, if the backup catalog is lost, it can usually be re-created from the backup media.

After the catalog is retrieved or re-created for the latest backup, you need to locate the file(s) to be restored and select them for restoration. The backup device will locate the files, and the backup program will write the files back to their original locations. If you are restoring a good file to replace a damaged or incorrect file, you will be prompted to permit the replacement.

Restoring a Crashed Server Using Disaster Recovery

If you need to restore a crashed server, the easiest way to restore it is if you made a disaster recovery backup. Most modern backup programs support disaster recovery, which creates a full backup of the system and bootable media, enabling a "bare metal" recovery of the system to an empty hard disk. Depending on the backup program, a disaster recovery backup might be based on an image backup or a file-by-file backup.

You use the bootable CD or DVD you created to start the process. You insert your backup media when prompted until the system has been restored. Then you restore your daily backups. If you used the differential method, you need to restore only the last differential backup.

Restoring a Crashed Server Using ASR

If you used the ASR feature with Windows 2003 Server and need to restore from an ASR backup, you start the system with the Windows 2003 Server CD. When you see the prompt Press F2 to Run Automated System Recovery, you press the F2 key. Then you insert the ASR floppy disk. The system drive (usually the C: drive) is formatted by ASR. Afterward, a file copy process begins to restore a basic working copy of Windows 2003 Server. After the system reboots, the ASR Wizard starts and asks you where the ASR backup is located. After you specify the location, ASR restores information from your backup to your system drive.

After ASR is finished, you should restore other backups needed to complete the restoration of your system (such as the last full backup of non-system drives plus the most recent differential backup, or all incremental backups).

Restoring a Crashed Server Without Disaster Recovery or ASR

If you need to restore a crashed server without disaster recovery or ASR, follow this process:

1. Partition and format the drive where you plan to reinstall the operating system.
2. Reinstall the operating system.
3. Reinstall the backup software.
4. Restore the most recent full backup.
5. Restore the most recent differential backup or all incremental backups.

As you can see, it's much easier and faster to take advantage of disaster recovery backups, or, at the very least, ASR backups, than to restore a system from scratch.

Hardware Compatibility

A full system backup, including disaster recovery and ASR backup, is designed to be restored back to the same system. If you are restoring a backup due to hard disk failure, you should make sure the replacement hard disk is the same type and size, or larger, than the original. The rest of the hardware is the same as before, so the backup will be restored to identical hardware.

It's a bit tougher if you must replace a failed server. In such cases, you should use a server that's the same model or, for white box built-it-yourself servers, use a server with the same motherboard, video card, and other add-on cards. If you use hardware with different specifications, the restoration might fail, or the system might not be bootable afterward.

Backup and Restoration Troubleshooting and Documentation

If you are having problems with backing up or restoring data, you need to first identify your problem from the following sections and then follow the steps for the solutions they provide.

Tape Retensioning

The solutions for many problems with tape-based backup devices involve retensioning one or more of the drive tapes. *Retensioning* a tape is the process of fast-forwarding and then rewinding the tape to ensure that there is even tension on the tape and rollers throughout the entire tape travel. Retensioning is recommended as a preventive maintenance operation when using a new tape or after an existing tape has been exposed to temperature changes or shock (for example, dropping the tape). Retensioning restores the proper tension to the media and removes unwanted tight spots that can develop.

The following are some general rules for retensioning:

- Retension any tapes that have not been used for more than a month or two.
- Retension tapes if you have errors reading them.
- Retension any tapes that have been dropped.
- In some cases, you might need to perform a retension operation several times to achieve the proper effect. Most tape drive or backup software includes a retension feature as a menu selection.

Backup or Restore Operation Failure

If your tape drive suffers a backup or restore operation failure, follow these steps:

1. Make sure you are using the correct type of tape cartridge.
2. Remove and replace the cartridge.

3. Restart the system.

4. Retension the tape.

5. Try a new tape.

6. Clean the tape heads.

7. Make sure all cables are securely connected.

8. Rerun the confidence test that checks data transfer speed with a blank tape. (This test overwrites any data that is already on the tape.)

Bad Block or Other Types of Media Errors

To troubleshoot bad block or other types of media errors, follow these steps:

1. Retension the tape.

2. Clean the heads.

3. Try a new tape.

4. Restart the system.

5. Try initializing the tape.

6. Perform a secure erase on the tape. (Previous data will no longer be retrievable from the tape.)

System Lockup or Freeze While Running Tape Backup

If your system locks up or freezes while running a tape backup, follow these steps:

1. Ensure that your system meets at least the minimum requirements for both the tape drive and the backup software.

2. For ATA/IDE (ATAPI) tape drives, make sure the tape drive is using a different host adapter than the hard disk. Set the CD or DVD drive to master and the tape drive to slave if both are using the same ATA/IDE port.

3. For SCSI tape drives, check device IDs, particularly if a new SCSI device has been installed since the last time the tape drive was used. Note that most vendors recommend that the tape drive be on a separate bus from the system's SCSI hard disk or SCSI RAID array.

4. Check the BIOS boot sequence; ensure that it is not set to ATAPI (tape/CD-ROM) devices if the tape drive is configured as a master device or as a slave with no master.

5. Make sure the hard drive has sufficient free space; most backup programs temporarily use hard drive space as a buffer for data transfer.

6. Hard drive problems can cause the backup software to lock up. Check your hard disk for errors by using CHKDSK or a comparable utility.

7. Check for viruses.

8. Check for previous tape drive installations; ensure that any drivers from previous installations are removed.

9. Restart the server in VGA mode. If the problem does not recur, contact your graphics board manufacturer for an updated video driver.

10. Disable antivirus programs and Advanced Power Management.

11. Try the tape drive on another computer system and different operating system, or try swapping the drive, card, and cable with known-good, working equipment. Start by swapping the cables.

Other Tape Drive Problems

The following are some other issues that might cause problems in general with tape backups:

- Corrupted data or ID information on the tape.
- Incorrect BIOS (CMOS) settings.
- Networking problems (outdated network drivers and so on).
- A tape that was recorded by another tape drive. If the other drive can still read the tape, this might indicate a head-alignment problem or an incompatible environment.

If you use a third-party backup program with disaster recovery enabled, make sure the boot floppies or boot CD-ROM are clearly labeled with the date and system name. If possible, store them with the media used to create the disaster recovery backup.

If you use ASR, make sure the date and system name are marked clearly on the ASR floppy. If possible, store the floppy with the media used to create the ASR backup.

Common Backup Software Applications

Backup applications abound, both those built in to server operating systems and those available from third parties. The following sections help you find the right backup software for your network.

Native Operating System Software

Most server operating systems include some type of backup software designed to support tape backup drives:

- **Windows NT 4.0, Windows 2000 Server, and Windows Server 2003: NTBackup**—NTBackup for Windows Server 2003 can be used to restore data backed up with NTBackup for Windows 2000 Server. NTBackup can be run in a wizard mode, an advanced mode, or a command-line mode.
- **Linux and UNIX: tar**—tar is a command-line utility that supports backups to tape drives as well as to archive files on a hard disk (see www.unixpress.com/cactus/lonetar/lonetar.html).
- **Novell Netware 4.x and 5.x: SBackup and Enhanced SBackup**—Some 4.x versions of NetWare include the sbackup.nlm (Netware Loadable Module), while later versions of 4.x and NetWare 5.x use Enhanced SBackup (SBCON).

Although many servers use integrated backup software, the desire for enhanced features such as support of autoloaders, tape libraries, and newer backup hardware and better disaster recovery options have led to the development of many third-party alternatives.

Third-Party Backup Software

The following are some of the leading third-party backup and disaster recovery programs for major server operating systems:

- **BrightStor ARCserve Backup (Computer Associates)**—This is a family of backup products for Windows and Linux servers and clients. It supports optional agents for disaster recovery, Windows and NetWare open files, tape libraries, SANs, tape RAID, image backup, online backups, and other functions.
- **Lone-TAR (Lone Star Software Corporation)**—Lone-TAR is a replacement for the UNIX and Linux tar command, offering menus, bit-level verification, and other advanced features. Companion products offer disaster recovery (Rescue-Ranger) and a graphical user interface (LTX).

- **NovaNet (NovaStor Corporation)**—NovaNet is designed to support cross-platform (Windows, Linux, NetWare) server and client backups. It supports plug-ins that provide open file management, disaster recovery, cluster and SQL server backups, and other services.

- **Retrospect (EMC Dantz)**—Retrospect 7 is a family of backup applications for Windows servers. Various versions support client backup and D2D backup, among others. Add-ons provide for open file backup, disaster recovery, support for tape autoloaders and libraries, and support for SQL Server or Exchange Server installations.

- **Symantec LiveState Recovery (Symantec)**—LiveState Recovery is a family of applications designed to support disaster recovery to Windows or other types of servers and desktops.

- **Veritas Backup Exec (Symantec)**—Backup Exec is a family of server backup applications for Windows servers. It supports D2D as well as tape backup, web-based file retrieval, and remote backup of Linux and UNIX servers, and there is a version that provides continuous protection for Windows servers.

Troubleshooting Backup Programs

The wrong time to discover that there's a problem with your tape backup system is when it fails. The following sections can help you solve problems in advance.

Backup Product Compatibility

Make sure that the backup software you use is designed to be compatible with your server (and client) operating systems, your backup hardware, and, if possible, your existing backups.

Some backup products are designed exclusively for Windows. Others support a mixture of Windows, Linux, and NetWare servers. In some cases, you can use remote agents to back up non-Windows servers using the backup device connected to the Windows server. While this enables you to standardize on a single backup program, it can increase network traffic significantly.

If you use Microsoft Exchange Server or SQL Server, consider backup programs or add-ons made especially for those server services. Many standard server backup programs are not optimized to back up those servers.

If network clients often store critical data on their local hard disks, consider a backup program that is designed to back up clients as well as servers. This is a built-in feature of some backup programs, but it is an extra-cost option in others.

From the standpoint of hardware, most commercial backup programs support tape drives and leading removable-media and DVD drives. It might be necessary to download updates to assure support. However, if you want to use an autoloader, a tape library, or a D2D backup device, you might need to purchase an extra-cost agent, plug-in, or update from your backup software vendor. When you consider the cost of your backup software, be sure to calculate the cost of any add-ons needed to support your hardware or network configuration.

If you upgrade to a newer version of the same vendor's backup software, you should be able to retrieve your existing backups with the new software version. However, don't assume that you can do so. Ask before upgrading.

Tip

Backup software vendor NovaStor (www.novastor.com) offers unique solutions for issues caused by moving from an older backup system to a new one: What to do with the data on the older tapes? NovaStor's TapeCopy 2.1 software enables you to move data archives from your outmoded SCSI, ATA/IDE, USB, or FireWire tape backup to a new tape drive or library. You can also use it to make hard disk copies of your tapes and to duplicate a backup tape on a similar drive. If you need to move data to a different operating system, NovaXchange provides cross-platform data transfer between different types of tape drives and libraries, operating systems, and architectures. See the website for details.

Backup Software Patches and Updates

Be sure to visit your backup software vendor's website to find the latest patches and updates for your backup software. If you use the backup software that is integrated in the operating system, visit your operating system vendor's website.

CHAPTER 10

Network Operations

By definition, servers provide network services to other computers. All servers—from small, general-purpose servers such as Windows Small Business Server (SBS) servers, to domain controller (DC) servers, to enterprisewide application servers, such as an Exchange, Oracle, or SQL Server servers—rely heavily on their network I/O subsystem to maintain acceptable performance. Indeed, in the current architecture of the modern computer, network I/O is seen to be a primary performance bottleneck. That's why the network protocols used, how the network interfaces are configured, the hardware employed, and the monitoring software used are of critical concern to any server administrator and to an enterprise IT department's bottom line. We'll touch on these topics in this chapter.

High-speed server networking must support areas as diverse as the following:

- Multimedia streaming
- Server-to-server clustering
- Server-to-storage communication
- Wireless LAN (WLAN) networking

Each of these applications makes different demands on a server, and each has given rise to different networking standards. These areas of networking are cutting-edge technologies, and thus many of the newer hardware standards that are meant to support them are works in progress. In addition, many new networking standards are cross-fertilized with other standards. Thus, in this chapter you will encounter areas of technology replete with acronyms that you need to know.

Vendors take three approaches to the problem of improving and optimizing network throughput:

- Make network components faster.
- Separate different types of network traffic onto separate network infrastructures.
- Manage the network infrastructure to eliminate bottlenecks and route traffic appropriately.

The first approach is exemplified by the introduction of Gigabit Ethernet (GigE) into the network over the past couple years. GigE is a faster standard that is overlaid on earlier, slower Ethernet technologies. GigE is backward compatible with Fast Ethernet (100BaseTX) and even slow Ethernet (10BaseT); thus it preserves your investment in infrastructure, such as CAT5 cabling and network management software.

The second approach is often referred to as "out-of-band" networking, with an example being Fibre Channel storage area networks (SANs) and storage interconnect technologies such as Giganet's cLAN, Myrinet, InfiniBand, Virtual Interface Architecture (VIA), Tandem ServerNet, and others. An out-of-band network, as differentiated from an in-band network such as your Ethernet infrastructure, is meant to direct specialized network traffic off your communications network and to offload processing from your server's CPU(s).

Backup traffic, for example, can saturate an Ethernet network, making all other traffic painfully slow. So out-of-band technologies are meant to be self-contained. That is, network adapters that support VIA, for example, expect to talk to other network adapters that support VIA; these networking standards are not generally interoperable with other standards, but sometimes they are.

This chapter includes a discussion of the Fibre Channel networking standard. Fibre Channel is really a server-storage interconnect technology that utilizes the SCSI interface. (The reason that SCSI doesn't qualify for inclusion in this chapter is that it is limited in terms of both cable length and the number of attachment points available.) Fibre Channel fiber-optic cables, on the other hand, can be used over several kilometers, if needed, with dozens of attachments on a Fibre Channel loop and tens of thousands of possible connections in a Fibre Channel fabric.

You will also find emerging standards such as iSCSI, which spans two different mainstream I/O technologies. iSCSI takes SCSI data traffic that would go between the server and the separated storage and sends the data over specialized parallel SCSI cables, packaged or wrapped inside an Ethernet frame. The Ethernet traffic is then sent over a packet-switching Ethernet network between two dedicated iSCSI network interface cards (NICs), using a CAT5 cable infrastructure. Because the traffic is now TCP/IP traffic, the network runs can cover long distances and are both managed and fault tolerant. That is, with iSCSI, the data is encapsulated into a TCP/IP wrapper and is a standard TCP/IP frame. You can use your standard Ethernet network management tools to manage iSCSI traffic, and because TCP/IP is a routed fabric architecture, it is redundant in the sense that it can survive path failures and be retransmitted and rerouted as necessary.

iSCSI offers a cost-effective way for small and midsize servers to send storage data over an enterprise's Ethernet network, and it has the added bonus of letting you leverage your staff's experience in TCP/IP networking.

iSCSI gives you the block-level access and storage I/O intelligence of SCSI, but it transforms your SCSI storage devices from server attached to network attached, which means they can be managed, partitioned, and allocated to servers and applications much more efficiently. iSCSI also provides much better reliability and availability than does regular SCSI. As with Fibre Channel SANs, there's no need to take down a server to add storage to an iSCSI SAN, and after it is added, that storage can be made available to any SAN-attached server.

When you consider the fact that higher-speed networking tasks—such as server-to-server connections, server-to-storage server communications, backbone transmissions, or any kind of networking that involves data transmission—fan out from a high-speed computer, you realize that you need to you learn about the newer interface technologies that are introduced in this chapter.

Network Interface Cards (NICs)

NICs and networking protocols aren't as sexy a topic as microprocessors and motherboards. They don't come with code names of mountains, cities, or rivers, nor are they supported by a team of blue-faced men doing wild drum antics. Instead, reading about NICs is a little like reading about plumbing. However, your network interface can make all the difference when you are trying to squeeze the last drop of value from a $15,000 quad-processor server. Network interface technologies are therefore one of the most active areas of server hardware development today.

Types of NICs

NICs run the gamut from costing $15 for 10/100BaseTX Fast Ethernet cards up to being very specialized high-speed multi-gigabit cards costing upward of $1,500. These more expensive cards perform special functions, such as TCP/IP offloading.

Note

TCP/IP offloading takes the TCP/IP processing that your CPU does and offloads the TCP/IP stack onto a specialized and optimized application-specific integrated circuit (ASIC) on the network card.

You don't want to spend tens of thousands of dollars on a departmental server and then sip through a straw the data the server produces or consumes. That's why server administrators always opt for and recommend superior networking equipment for reliable and dependable connectivity.

When you network a modern server or set of servers, you need to put aside some of your older, hard-won PC networking skills. Long gone are the days of the 16-bit ISA (Industry Standard Architecture) bus, or even IBM's proprietary 32-bit MCA (Microchannel Architecture) or EISA (Enhanced ISA) networking cards. They are history as far as server technologies are concerned, although you may from time to time find them in legacy server systems.

You can also forget about networking connections such as BNC or AUI type connectors. Technologies that relied on those connections are also a thing of the past but are also still seen from time to time on production networks. Apple and Novell held out a long time with their protocols and standards AppleTalk and IPX/SPX, but both have given way to TCP/IP in lieu of proprietary systems and technology. While client systems are overwhelmingly supplied these days with 32-bit PCI Ethernet cards and RJ-45 connectors, server networking employs many different networking standards and will almost always have multiple network interfaces running at the same time (called *multihoming*). In *multihoming*, a computer has two or more network addresses, where each address is identified by its own NIC. Multihoming is most often used to communicate with different networks, often to provide a physical and protocol isolation between the two networks. A firewall or proxy server is an example of a dual-homed system.

Table 10.1 summarizes the different NICs available today.

Table 10.1 The Network Interface Cards Available Today

NIC Type	Interface	Speed
2G, 4G, and 10G Ethernet	PCI-X	≥2000Mbps (fibre)
Fast Ethernet	PCI, PCI-X, USB	100Mbps max (copper)
Gigabit Ethernet	PCI, PCI-X	1000Mbps max (copper)
802.11a	PCI, USB	54Mbps max
802.11b	PCI, USB	11Mbps max
802.11g	PCI, USB	54Mbps max
Super G or Double G (802.11g)	PCI, USB	110Mbps max
Fibre Channel, single channel	PCI, USB	100MBps
Fibre Channel, dual channel	PCI, USB	200MBps

Ethernet

Ethernet (along with its variations) is by far the most predominant networking hardware standard in use today. This is the case for several reasons, but the fact that the hardware tends to be relatively inexpensive and easy to find, native support from all operating systems, and the reliability of TCP/IP over Ethernet have all contributed to the widespread support of Ethernet.

There are three Ethernet standards:

- **10BaseT, or standard Ethernet**—This slow-speed standard isn't used much in server technology, but it is sometimes used to connect a server with a cable modem, a DSL modem, a printer, or another low-speed peripheral. It is possible to purchase external Ethernet connectors that are 10BaseT standard and plug them in to a USB port, but those devices aren't used in the server market.

- **100BaseT, or Fast Ethernet**—Most 100BaseT cards are sold as 10/100 32-bit PCI form factor cards. The predominant networking cards in use today are of this type, with a price range of $15 to $20. It is possible to buy PCMCIA or PC Cards of this type, but their use tends to be very rare in the server market.

- **1000BaseT, or Gigabit Ethernet (GigE)**—GigE is an emerging standard that is widely used in server applications. You can buy 10/100/1000 Ethernet cards as 32- and 64-bit PCI cards. The 32-bit cards are a commodity product, with NICs costing in the range of $20 to $40.

■ **100Base-VGAnyLAN**—This is a technology that is closely related to Ethernet. It runs at 100Mbps and is a former IEEE 802.12 standard. The VG stands for "voice grade" and means that this standard can work over UTP wiring. The AnyLAN part of the name is meant to indicate that this particular standard will work with Ethernet, Token Ring, and other networking standards.

Most server motherboards ship with at least one Ethernet port, and nearly all these ports (and the aforementioned cards) use the RJ-45 connector type. The newer motherboards tend to ship with onboard GigE built in. Figure 10.1 shows a dual-homed server motherboard.

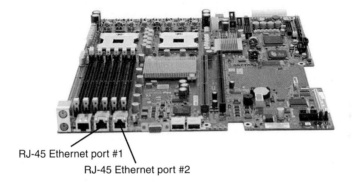

RJ-45 Ethernet port #1 \
RJ-45 Ethernet port #2

Figure 10.1   A dual-homed network server board.

Unless you are working with older equipment, it is best to use GigE NICs in your servers. The cost of NICs that support GigE isn't much more than the cost of those that support Fast Ethernet, and as the technology gets more widespread, the cost of hubs and switches will continue to decrease. As it is, the cost of GigE hubs and switches is quite reasonable, around $10 to $40 per port. The main difference in pricing is between unmanaged (but autosensing) ports and managed (and intelligent) ports. The intelligence here relates to the inclusion of special algorithms to manage traffic as well as techniques for increasing the speed accuracy of data going through the port.

Fibre Channel

Fibre Channel is today's preferred interconnection technology for high-speed server storage I/O connections. The current speeds (called *throughput*) range between 1Gbps and 2Gbps (gigabits per second). Fibre Channel may become less popular in the next few years as faster Ethernet technologies arrive, but for the foreseeable future, you can expect Fibre Channel to be strongly supported, if for no other reason than that it's a highly reliable technology.

Note

To read further details about Fibre Channel, go to the Fibre Channel Industry Association (FICA) website, at www.fibrechannel.org. FICA is the industry standards group for Fibre Channel vendors. It writes the standard specification and does plug fests—meetings at which vendors get to test their equipment against other vendors' equipment—among other things. To see what the future has in store for Fibre Channel, you may want to take a look at the road map at www.fibrechannel.org/OVERVIEW/Roadmap.html.

The majority of SANs are built using Fibre Channel technology. Because Chapter 12, "Storage Area Networks," describes SANs in some detail, this section takes a brief look at the NIC hardware used. More and more server administrators are being asked to integrate storage server technologies, and Fibre Channel host bus adapters (HBAs) are something you may be asked to install and support. (An HBA is the Fibre Channel equivalent of a NIC.)

▶▶ See Chapter 12, "Storage Area Networks," for more information on Fibre Channel technologies.

The name for an HBA or another Fibre Channel device with an address is a *node*, and a Fibre Channel node offers multiple ports or listening channels, just as you find in TCP/IP devices. A Fibre Channel node comes with a unique 64-bit worldwide name (see www.t13.org/docs2002/e02136r1.pdf) that is assigned by the card's manufacturer. In a switched-fabric network, a port is assigned a 24-bit ID; in an arbitrated loop network, a port is assigned an 8-bit address. In both cases, these addresses are dynamically assigned, and when the two SAN Fibre Channel network types are interconnected, the 8-bit address is translated to 24 bits for compatibility.

A *channel*, as first described in mainframe interconnects, is a dedicated interconnect pipe. Because Fibre Channel is often the next step up from direct attached storage (DAS) SCSI, you will often see the two technologies compared and differentiated. Fibre Channel provides longer wire lengths, more ports, and greater remote administration possibilities. An arbitrated loop can provide theoretical support for up to 127 ports, and a switched-fabric network can support 2^{24}, or 16,777,216, ports. Latency issues reduce these theoretical results significantly, to perhaps 50 ports for an arbitrated loop and 15,000 for a switched-fabric network.

A Fibre Channel HBA is most often found as a PCI card (as shown in Figure 10.2) and is driven in Windows by a SCSIPort or Storport minidriver. It is common to see Fibre Channel HBAs with dual ports to provide additional fault tolerance. Fibre Channel HBAs connect to either fiber-optic or copper cable; the former is faster, and the latter is cheaper. Copper has a range of around 30m (or 100 feet), whereas optical cable can work up to 2km for multimode or 10km for single-mode cable. You will also find that copper cable is more susceptible to crosstalk, while optical cable requires a conversion between light and electrical signals as it traverses switches and HBAs.

Figure 10.2 Fibre Channel NICs look similar to Ethernet NICs but use optical cabling.

In terms of connections, Fibre Channel HBAs are not standardized connections. Depending on the technology type, you will find any of the following: Gigabit interface converters (GBICs), Gigabit link modules (GLMs), small form factor (SFF) adapters, and media interface adapters. Therefore, when selecting a Fibre Channel HBA, it is important to know what type of SAN you are going to connect it to.

Wireless Ethernet (Wi-Fi)

Wireless Ethernet, or Wi-Fi, is based on the IEEE 802.11 standard for radio frequency (RF) broadcasts. A Wi-Fi NIC is both a sender and a receiver of radio signals. 802.11 standards operate at different radio frequencies. The 802.11b standard operates at 900MHz (where some older phones operate), and while the 802.11g standard operates at 2GHz (where newer wireless phones and microwave ovens operate). Wi-Fi lets you do away with wires entirely. However, you still need at least one wired connection to connect to the Internet, so at least one of your wireless devices must be a router with a connection to your ISP's modem or a similar gateway device.

Other important issues in Wi-Fi are interoperability standards (e.g. 802.11a versus 802.11g), coverage areas, and security concerns. Still, there is a lot of interest in adding Wi-Fi capabilities to servers as well as all other computers, no matter the pros and cons.

From the standpoint of wireless NICs, there is no differentiation yet between adding a Wi-Fi Ethernet card to a server and adding that card to a PC. The main issue with adding Wi-Fi to a general-purpose server is whether you can find the appropriate drivers or management software to work with your card. The speed of the connection may also become a bottleneck because wireless network speeds have yet to break significant ground in the backbone area of networks. Because the backbone is where production servers are most likely to be located, this is a significant drawback.

You can add Wi-Fi networking to a server by installing a PCI card, an external USB device, or even a PC Card with an adapter. None of the wireless standards is considered a high-throughput network interface, which is why Wi-Fi technology doesn't really get much discussion when it comes to server networking standards, so you don't find many servers that have Wi-Fi.

The trend in wireless networking has been to market special-purpose wireless devices in the form of wireless routers or wireless access points. You buy these devices as appliances and then connect to these standards through a network card or a hub. This is a much more common and cost-effective approach to creating a server-based Wi-Fi solution than simply adding a Wi-Fi PCI card to a server.

The most important consideration when adding Wi-Fi to a server is the selection of the wireless protocol. If you intend to stream large files or multiple files to a set of clients, then your server needs to connect wirelessly using one of the faster wireless standards. 802.11b is not sufficient, and 802.11g or 802.11a may be only marginally effective. You might want to install one of the newest protocols or use technologies such as double-speed 802.11g that several vendors offer. It is always best with Wi-Fi technology to minimize the number of different vendors' products you use. You will almost certainly find that a technology such as D-Links's Super G might be compatible with NetGear's Super G but will almost certainly have problems attaining the rated throughput when connected to a Linksys Wireless-G with SpeedBooster product.

Hardware Compatibility

While on the surface a NIC might not seem like very exotic technology, it is an essential part of network services for your computer. The last few years have seen the speeds of new NICs rise dramatically. Often new NICs are the first kinds of add-in cards that take advantage of new bus interface standards. This section looks at the kinds of NICs that are on the market today. The following are the most common form factors for server NIC interfaces:

- **Onboard network interfaces**—*Onboard* (also known as *integrated*) means that the networking chip is located on the motherboard and that you plug your network cable directly in to the motherboard itself. A NIC's chipset is inexpensive and can be easily integrated onto a server motherboard. At this point, nearly every motherboard on the market offers an onboard LAN function.

- **PCI cards**—Fast Ethernet and Gigabit Ethernet cards are widely available as a 32-bit or 64-bit PCI card. The PCI bus is an autoconfiguring standard that operates at 33MHz and includes a bus-mastering feature that allows a card to command the bus's bandwidth (temporarily) and offload CPU processing onto the PCI card's ASIC.

- **PCI-X cards**—PCI-X is an extension of the PCI standard. Version 2.0 of this standard comes in two versions: PCI-X 266 and PCI-X 533. IBM and Hewlett-Packard started including this standard in servers in 2004. Part of the attraction of PCI-X is that it is backward compatible with PCI cards. To read further details about the PCI-X standard and to learn about current events, go to the PCI SIG site, at www.pcisig.com/specifications/pcix_20/. PCI SIG is the industry standards group for this technology.

◀◀ PCI-X is covered in more detail in "Expansion Slots: ISA, PCI, AGP, and Others," p. 258.

- **PCI Express**—PCI Express is another extension of the PCI bus that is supported by both Intel and Dell. PCI Express is much faster than PCI-X; it currently runs at speeds of up to 2.5GHz. Eventually, the PCI Express road map extends outward to a 40GHz bus speed. The PCI Express standard is supported by the PCI SIG industry group (see www.pcisig.com/home) and will, in time, replace PCI just as PCI replaced the ISA bus.

Although external adapters, or PC Cards (with or without adapters, such as IDE adapters), are available, they aren't commonly used with servers.

The Heritage of PCI Express

Unlike PCI, which is a parallel bus structure, PCI Express is a serial bus structure that arises out of work done on server chip interconnect technology. PCI Express is an evolution of previous standards, including Next-Generation I/O (NGIO) and Future I/O, which were merged to form the InfiniBand interconnect standard. In 2001, Intel began promoting its Arapahoe technology, which became branded as 3GIO (Third-Generation I/O) and was adopted by the PCI SIG.

PCI Express is better known for server interconnect technology than for networking, and it didn't appear integrated on server motherboards until 2006. Eventually, a variant of PCI Express is expected to replace the Southbridge I/O chip on today's motherboards, which will create opportunities for technologies such as FireWire replacement.

PCI, PCI-X, and PCI Express are all related hardware standards. There are currently as many as 10 different types of PCI slots on motherboards. PCI itself is available as the following:

- The original PCI standard
- Wide PCI
- Fast/wide PCI (in two voltage standards)

PCI-X is available as the following:

- A standard PCI-X slot
- The Narrow PCI-X slot type

Finally, the emerging PCI Express standard supports four different channel depths:

- PCI Express x1
- PCI Express x4
- PCI Express x8
- PCI Express x16

Figure 10.3 shows some pictures of the different kinds of PCI slots.

PCI Express x16

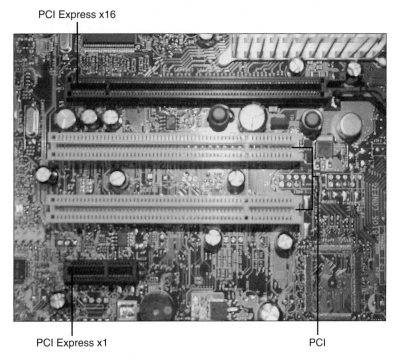

PCI Express x1   PCI

Figure 10.3   Different PCI package types.

For PCI Express, the number refers to the number of channels, and this is also a measure of the expected throughput of the board. The x1 and x4 standards appeared first, and the x8 and x16 cards appeared shortly thereafter.

Of the aforementioned standards, the two high-performance options that are the most commonly available are 64-bit/66MHz PCI and PCI-X. The problem with both of these standards is that you may only find one or two of these kinds of card interfaces on a server motherboard. PCI-X comes in several different channel widths, including 1x, 4x, and 16x, and you may need to use the higher-performance slot to support an enhanced graphics board (or something else). Therefore, you might want to consider breakout boxes or PCI expansion systems of the type sold by Magma Mobility Electronics (see www.mobl.com/expansion/pci/7slot6466/#) if you need to provide enhanced I/O. Figure 10.4 shows a seven-card expansion chassis as well as a serial bridging PCI card that provides a 5Gbps full-duplex link to the PCI expansion system. Most often, this type of breakout box is a connectivity solution for storage devices, SANs, or network attached storage (NAS).

Figure 10.4 Magma's external PCI expansion chassis and PCI director card.

Installing Network Interface Devices and Drivers

As you're probably well aware, your network interface isn't just about hardware. Software plays an essential role in system performance and stability. From the underlying protocols used in the operating system to the NIC's drivers for the operating system, knowing how to correctly install your network interface devices is a critical skill. Well-implemented driver software can help ensure the stability of your server, and bad driver software can cripple your systems. So yes, the type and version of the network driver you use do make a difference.

Network drivers are among the most heavily used pieces of software on a network computer, so it shouldn't surprise you that driver software tends to get corrupted more easily than other system functions. While architecting Windows 2000 Server, Microsoft found that poorly written or malfunctioning device drivers were the second most common reason for system restarts, lagging only slightly behind human error. So today Microsoft requires that its Data Center Edition use certified NICs and drivers only.

When you install a NIC, your operating system may or may not recognize the card automatically. Not all operating systems can handle plug-and-play, and not all adapters are listed in the operating system's database of device drivers. Therefore, it is always a good idea to check whether you have an up-to-date installation disk from the network card vendor before you begin an installation. Also, you should check your vendor's website to find the current driver version offered online; this will usually be the most up-to-date and current set of drivers available for your NIC.

When you are installing a popular network card, such as NetGear's FA311 or GA311 (Fast and GigE cards), into a popular operating system, chances are that the card's driver is contained in the operating system distribution's installation routine. However, the more exotic the NIC, the smaller the vendor, or the less commonly used the operating system, the less likely that the very latest driver is available or even that any driver is available. You should be sure to have your vendor's device drivers on hand when you install your NIC.

Note

Make life easy on yourself. Instead of trying to physically navigate to your vendor's website, enter a search string such as "GA311 driver download" into your favorite search engine. Chances are that one of the first few matches will take you directly to the page.

Many nonstandard sites maintain libraries of network card drivers, and they are particularly useful when you are trying to locate an older version of a driver.

Tip

A NIC without a suitable driver for your server's operating system is nothing more than toxic landfill. It's the software that makes it work.

It is really important to understand how to install your NIC driver software, but it is perhaps more important to know how to *uninstall* your NIC driver software. The reasoning for this is simple: Many operating systems don't really delete a driver you uninstall; they merely leave the software on disk. When you go to reinstall the software, you may find that you have reverted back to the driver you've just been using. If the driver version number is the same, then it can be impossible to determine that the driver software is the cause of your problem.

Each operating system is a little different in the manner in which it handles NIC and driver installation, but the differences are largely superficial. Let's take a brief look at how two operating systems install a NIC and its driver. We will look at configuring a Windows Server 2003 server and a Red Hat Linux server.

When you install a new NIC into a Windows Server 2003 server, the operating system almost always recognizes that a new card has been detected and tries to match that card to one that is contained within its driver database. During installation of the NOS, many NIC drivers are copied to the Windows system folder (`C:\Windows\Drivers Cache\i386`), and installed drivers are copied to `C:\Windows\System32\Drivers`. There are a few generic system drivers in `C:\Windows\System`, but mostly this folder contains `*.DLL` files. If Windows doesn't find the correct driver for your NIC, it will ask you to provide a path to an installation disk. There's a chance that the driver is the Windows Update website, but very often, if the driver you need is for a NIC, you're not going to have the network or Internet access needed to utilize the Windows Update site. In some cases, you may need to use another system to help facilitate the download.

Note

A DLL file is a file that contains executable code and data bound to a program at load time or runtime. It is used among several programs that share the DLL simultaneously.

On the remote chance that Windows Server 2003 doesn't recognize your device as a plug-and-play device, you can initiate an installation with the Add/Remove Hardware applet found in the Control Panel. After you launch it, this applet searches for new hardware. If it finds more than one new device, it generates a list and asks you to specify whether it has found the correct one. You can instead specify the NIC as the item you want to install and manually provide the driver software. In some instances, vendors make use of their own installation executable or application files and setup routines, but for the large majority of NIC vendors, the preferred choice is to use the routines that the OS provides. You are most likely to encounter vendor installation programs when the network or host bus adapter you are installing comes with associated software such as network management software. In any case, you should consult the manual for your NIC before installing any software.

After you successfully install your NIC, it should immediately be fully operational. It is a good idea to go into the Windows Device Manager to ensure that there are no alerts or warnings next to your new card.

Note

The Device Manager, which is accessible through the System applet within the Windows Control Panel, is a tool that is included with just about every Microsoft Windows operating system in use today. The Device Manager can display and control the hardware attached to a computer running a Windows-based operating system. When a piece of hardware is not working, the offending hardware is identified in the Device Manager, allowing the user to deal with it. Disabled devices are marked with a red X; a yellow exclamation point indicates a failed or malfunctioning device.

Certainly, when you are experiencing difficulties with your network card, one of your troubleshooting stops should be the Device Manager. If you decide to reinstall your driver software, you need to make sure that the driver software currently in use is deleted. Opening up your NIC's properties dialog box and rolling back the driver is not sufficient. Instead, you should use the Add/Remove Hardware applet to completely uninstall all traces of the NIC from the OS. You should then restart your system and reinstall the driver from which you wish to restore. Remember that Windows doesn't automatically delete drivers from its cache.

Driver rollback is a feature in Windows XP and Windows Server 2003 that stores the past driver when you replace a device driver and allows you to revert back to the previous version. Keep in mind that there is only one version of the driver stored, so if you are trying to fix a problem, you should try rollback first before you install a new version in order to fix a problem.

Device Driver Upgrades

If you have a NIC that is commonly used in other systems, chances are that any plug-and-play OS will recognize it. Should you use the version of the driver that your operating system provides or the one that you find on the disk that came with your card? Different people will give you different answers and advice on this issue. Many people prefer to use the device driver with the latest revision number obtained from the vendor's website. If your hardware was purchased significantly later than the last revision of the operating system, then you might want to use the version found on the disk in preference to the version your OS provides. If the OS is newer than the hardware in question, you should use the OS version.

There are no hard-and-fast rules concerning versioning, and you may find that an older version of a driver works better (that is, is faster or more compatible) than a newer one. NICs and their drivers are notoriously difficult to diagnose when problems occur. Therefore, it is always good to have an extra NIC or two handy to substitute for one that is deemed problematic. Having another card to swap in and out can help you troubleshoot a problem by isolating it. If another NIC works, then you know it was the last NIC installed. When considering stocking replacements, you should keep a duplicate card as well as a different model—and preferably a different vendor's card entirely—just in case your problem is a problem with that brand or version of the card.

Troubleshooting a Network Interface

Because a network interface comprises both a hardware component and its related software, your troubleshooting needs to test both aspects of its connectivity. You should go through the troubleshooting process one step at a time. Before you begin other testing, you should open a command prompt and enter the `ipconfig /all` command to determine whether your NIC has an acceptable IP address and is healthy. If your network interface's address is dynamically assigned by DHCP and no address appears or if you are having problems, you can try using `ipconfig /release` followed by `ipconfig /renew` to refresh your connection. In certain instances, such as with Windows XP Professional Edition, this solves many connection problems.

If the information `ipconfig /all` lists is accurate, you can try using the `ping` utility to test your NIC to see if you're able to send and receive data. To do so, you open a command prompt and type the following:

`ping 127.0.0.1.`

You should see a reply from the loopback address of your `HOSTS` file if your card is active. You can also install a loopback adapter as an interface in your system and then use the preceding command to `ping` that interface. It's a common technique that is used to determine whether a network stack is operating properly.

Some systems don't let you install a loopback adapter, so you should make sure that your system does have this feature or install it if it doesn't.

You can also use `ping localhost`, and that command will return a reply. This is because in your `HOSTS` file, 127.0.0.1 maps to the domain name `localhost`.

If either or both of these commands fail, you should suspect that there is a problem with the card itself.

You can try to `ping` by IP address to see if you have network connectivity and by the network client by name to test name resolution. Either test will show you whether data can travel from your PC to another system without error or trouble.

In some environments (perhaps on your corporate network), the `ping` tool may be turned off, so you might not be able to test connectivity. In such instances, `ping` is not really turned off so much as it is blocked. After all, if TCP/IP is installed, then so is the `ping` utility because `ping` uses a protocol called Internet Control Message Protocol (ICMP), which is an extension to Internet Protocol (IP) within the TCP/IP suite of protocols. ICMP produces error messages, test packets, and other informational messages so that you can find problems on your network. Because ICMP can also be exploited by attackers and crackers, it's important that you disable it—for example, by blocking it with an access list on a firewall. If ICMP is blocked, you will not be able to use `ping`.

If ICMP is blocked, open a browser or My Network Places and try to navigate to another system's shared folders if any are available. You should be able to see whether network activity is occurring by looking in the Network Connection dialog box, by seeing a system tray icon, or by using a utility such as Network Monitor, which can capture and analyze data on a network to which it is connected to and configured.

▶▶ For more information on using Network Monitor, see "Windows Network Monitor," p. 846.

If you don't detect a connection, it's time to check out the physical media—that is, your cabling. The first thing to test is that the cable into the NIC is active and functional. The easiest way to test your cable (and everything else behind it) is to move that cable to another network interface and see if that second interface remains active. If it does not, you should go back and swap the cable or swap the connection port on the hub, switch, or other device to try to correct the problem.

Your NIC should indicate its status. You should check that the NIC has link light activity. A healthy NIC should indicate its condition by displaying a lit up link integrity light. For example, a 10/100Mbps card often has two green lights—a 10 LNK (or link) light, a 100 LNK light—and one yellow ACT (activity) light. If the two LNK lights are lit, this indicates that there is a good connection. If the lights are off, there is no connection. Similarly, the lights should be on at the port of the hub or switch to which the cable is connected. The ACT light on the NIC should flash when there is network traffic passing through it, and the flashing should intensify or appear steady if there is heavy network traffic.

A broadcast storm is an excellent indicator of too much network activity. A broadcast storm is the arrival of too many packets at a computer for a period of time. The LNK light on your NIC (or other network infrastructure device) should appear solid. Broadcast storms disable all functionality on most networks, so if your NIC or other device has steady LNK lights on, this may indicate a problem. Contact your network administrator if you suspect that you have a problem.

If the NIC appears active and simultaneously you have no network traffic, the next step is to perform a test from the server itself. To do so, you need to be logged in to the server as an administrator (either in front of or through a terminal session). First, you need to check that the driver software is loaded correctly. For Windows Server 2003, you should do the following:

1. Right-click My Computer on the Start menu and then select Properties.
2. Click the Hardware tab and then click the Device Manager button.
3. Check the status of the network interface and check to see if there are any listings in the Unsupported Devices category.
4. If the interface shows that it is not active by displaying a red X icon, enable the interface by right-clicking it and selecting Enable. If the interface shows a yellow i icon, then the most likely problem is a driver issue or a possible virus.
5. If you can't enable the network interface or if there is a problem shown in the Device Manager, try uninstalling the card and reinstalling the driver. Uninstall the network interface by going into the Add/Remove Hardware applet in the Control Panel and uninstalling the network card.

If the network interface appears active and healthy, you might want to try moving the NIC to a different PCI slot. An interrupt (IRQ) conflict may be the problem.

In very rare instances, the network protocol stack you are using may be corrupted and need to be replaced. This is much more common for modems than it is for NICs, but it does happen. You need to make sure your server's installation disk is handy prior to performing this action. To reinstall the network protocol stack in Windows Server 2003, do the following:

1. Open the Add/Remove Software applet in the Control Panel and click the Add/Remove Windows Components button.
2. Go into the Network Services section and remove the check mark from the particular network service.
3. Then click the Continue button to remove the component.
4. Restart the server.
5. Go back into the Network Services section of the Add/Remove Windows Component applet and put a check mark back on the service (see Figure 10.5).
6. Reinstall the protocol by clicking the check box and then the Continue button.

Removing a protocol stack should be done only as a last resort.

Often, the problems encountered with a network interface do not arise because of a NIC's malfunctioning but due to some network service issue such as inappropriate addressing, security issues, and other software configuration problems. NOSs provide a number of tools that can help you determine whether any of these issues are your problem.

The TCP/IP protocol stack has a rather large collection of useful tools (such as `ping`) that are freely available and are part of all current NOS toolsets that use TCP/IP. Table 10.2 lists some of the most common commands.

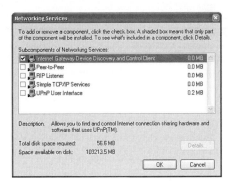

Figure 10.5 The Networking Services window allows you to add and remove various networking components.

Table 10.2   TCP/IP Diagnostic Commands and Utilities

Command	Syntax	Usage
arp	arp [-a [*InetAddr*] [-N *IfaceAddr*]] [-g [*InetAddr*] [-N *IfaceAddr*]] [-d *InetAddr* [*IfaceAddr*]] [-s *InetAddr* *EtherAddr* [*IfaceAddr*]]	Displays and modifies the Address Resolution Protocol cache, which is used to store IP addresses and their related physical network addresses.
finger	finger [-b] [-f] [-h] [-i] [-l] [-m] [-p] [-q] [-s] [-w] [*username*]	Lists information about the user.
getmac	getmac[.exe] [/s *Computer* [/u *Domain\User* [/p *Password*]]] [/fo {*TABLE|LIST|CSV*}] [/nh] [/v]	Finds the MAC address of the NIC(s).
hostname	hostname	Displays the name of the local system.
ipconfig	ipconfig [/all] [/renew [*Adapter*]] [/release [*Adapter*]] [/flushdns] [/displaydns] [/registerdns] [/showclassid *Adapter*] [/setclassid *Adapter* [*ClassID*]]	Determines the network configuration, address, DNS, and DHCP settings.
nbstat	nbtstat [-a *RemoteName*] [-A *IPAddress*] [-c] [-n] [-r] [-R] [-RR] [-s] [-S] [*Interval*]	Examines NetBIOS over TCP/IP statistics and the NetBIOS cache. You can also clear the cache with this command.
netsh	netsh [-a *AliasFile*] [-c *Context*] [-r *RemoteComputer*] [{*NetshCommand*|-f *ScriptFile*}]	Creates a command line that allows you to modify a computer either locally or remotely. You can also use this Windows command to run scripts either singly or in batch, as well as to set a context under which the shell runs.

Table 10.2   Continued

Command	Syntax	Usage
netstat	netstat [-a] [-e] [-n] [-o] [-p *Protocol*] [-r] [-s] [*Interval*]	Shows you which ports on your computer are active and listening to traffic. You can use this command to determine the activity of your Ethernet connection(s) as well as determine your IP routing table.
ping	ping [-t] [-a] [-n *Count*] [-l *Size*] [-f] [-i *TTL*] [-v *TOS*] [-r *Count*] [-s *Count*] [{-j *HostList* | -k *HostList*}] [-w *Timeout*] [*TargetName*]	Lets you verify a connection by sending and receiving a message to another system, using the ICMP protocol. When the echo is returned, you get statistics about your network performance.
recover	recover [*Drive:*][*Path*] *FileName*	Tries to read data from a damaged disk.
route	route [-f] [*command*] [-p] [*destination*] [*MASK*] [*netmask*] [*gateway*] [*METRIC*]	Lets you alter the local routing table.
tracert	tracert [-d] [-h *MaximumHops*] [-j *HostList*] [-w *Timeout*] [*TargetName*]	Determines the pathing used to send and receive a message over TCP/IP to another system, using the ICMP protocol. The path shows the different hops along the route, both there and back.
taskkill	taskkill [/s *Computer*] [/u *Domain\User* [/p *Password*]]] [/fi *FilterName*] [/pid *ProcessID*]| [/im *ImageName*] [/f][/t]	Lets you end a process by ID or name on a Windows system (XP Professional or Server 2003).
tasklist	tasklist[.exe] [/s *computer*] [/u *domain\user* [/p *password*]] [/fo {*TABLE*|*LIST*|*CSV*}] [/nh] [/fi *FilterName* [/fi *FilterName2* [...]]] [/m [*ModuleName*] | /svc | /v]	Displays the current applications and processes in use on a Windows system.
whois	whois [-h *host*] *identifier*	Queries the Internet username directory service to get information on domain names, register, domain owner, and so on.

These commands vary by operating system, so be sure to check the man files or help files of your OS to see whether the command exists and what syntax that version supports.

Note

For a listing of UNIX command programs, see the Wikipedia listing at http://en.wikipedia.org/wiki/List_of_Unix_programs; for DOS command, see http://en.wikipedia.org/wiki/List_of_DOS_commands; and for Windows, see http://en.wikibooks.org/wiki/Guide_to_Windows_commands.

Locating Bottlenecks

Many of the factors described in the preceding section can contribute to or cause network traffic slowdowns. However, because a network slowdown can also be caused by applications and by the network protocol stack, sometimes you need to take a more general approach, involving probing the different protocol layers. Let's take a look at how this is done with TCP/IP, which is representative of many other networking protocols.

The first thing you should determine is whether your latency is due to a problem with the network or whether it's an application-specific issue. For example, you might think you have a latency issue because of your NIC when what is really slowing down the network is the transfer of a large database, the sending and receiving of files via FTP, and so on. The list of examples of what could cause problems on a network is virtually infinite. For example, you could have a bad NIC (commonly known as a *chattering NIC*) that sends endless amounts of data out on your network, causing saturation. In any case, your primary goal is to isolate the problem.

To accomplish this goal, you should do a packet trace during a suspected slowdown. You can send a sample of data to determine the source of latency by using another ICMP-based tool called tracert (for Windows) or traceroute (for UNIX and Linux systems).

To see tracert in action, you should open a command prompt and type the following:

tracert <12.1.1.1>.

You should replace the IP address in this example with one you know or with the hostname of a system you want to check. For instance, you can check latency to your favorite website by sending a ping to Yahoo.com. Because Yahoo allows ICMP to pass its network, you are able to receive a response. If you perform the same test with MSN.com, you will find that ICMP has been disabled. This should show you the importance of understanding how to test and what tools you should use to perform tests.

When you send a tracert to 12.1.1.1, you should see three connect times for the next server in line to the name server as shown here:

```
C:\>tracert 12.1.1.1
Tracing route to 12.1.1.1 over a maximum of 30 hops

1    10 ms    5ms      4ms       142.55.25.1
2    75 ms    15ms     94 ms     11.1.0.43
3    55 ms    82 ms    102 ms    11.1.0.1
Trace complete.
```

An asterisk indicates that your outgoing packet has collided with an incoming packet, called a *data collision*. You see more collisions when network traffic is higher. If all three packets are asterisked, then you may have a dead connection. You should also write a tracefile by using tracert. At the command prompt, you type the following:

tracert <*mydomain.com*> >> C:\text.txt.

The results of your trace will be data that you can analyze. The idea is to figure out who is retransmitting packets—a client or a server? If the client is retransmitting packets, the server isn't acknowledging their receipt. If the server is retransmitting packets and the client doesn't acknowledge them, you know the problem is local. You can use tracert to determine the path a data packet uses and the latency of each hop.

There are also some very sophisticated protocol analyzers you can purchase to analyze network traffic for an enterprise. Such tools come in the form of both software and hardware/software combinations.

Most NOSs also come bundled with packet analyzers. Microsoft's Network Monitor (netmon) is one such tool. Network Monitor ships as a lighter version (with less functionality) in Windows Server 2003 and in a fully functional version as part of the Microsoft Systems Management Server (SMS) package.

The next step is to probe the performance of the TCP stack. If the entire stack has problems (that is, the latency is being experienced across all server applications), you likely have an operating system problem. When only a single application is involved, you can isolate the issue by examining the traffic at the port used by that application. When only one user is affected by the problem, you should suspect that a security issue needs to be resolved.

Note

If you are unsure of the port number a specific application uses, the first place to look is a listing of well-known ports. Port traffic must be registered by application, and you can find a complete listing of well-known ports at www.iana.org/assignments/port-numbers. This may not solve your problem, but it is a good starting point.

If you monitor traffic by port, you can see activity for each port as the application you want to diagnose sends and receives data. You can use a packet sniffer to not only determine the port traffic uses but also look inside the data to see what was sent and received. An example of an application that does port monitoring and sniffing is HHD Software Accurate Network Monitor (see www.hhdsoftware.com/netmon.html), which works with various versions of Windows, including Windows Server 2003. Another example is ObjectPlanet's Network Probe (see www.objectplanet.com/Probe/).

Monitoring an application's traffic also allows you to determine whether a bottleneck is an application or a TCP issue. You should look at the TCP window size advertisements. The TCP window size is the amount of data that can be received and stored in a buffer during a connection. The sending system can only send out that much data before it must stop and wait for an acknowledgement. The advertisement referred to is the communication that indicates the size of the buffer. The size of that window is generally around 8760 or higher. If you see a lower Window size, you are seeing a slow application layer that is trying to take data out of the TCP buffer. When the application is slow, you may find that Window size drops to zero, which means the application is preventing additional data from being transferred. The Window size is a measure of the amount of unacknowledged data that can be transferred, so if a recipient receives a zero-size window, no more data can be sent back.

In diagnosing network slowdowns, you should look for the following issues:

- Large amounts of packet retransmission being sent from the server. In this case, the client(s) will be unable to keep up with sent traffic.
- Large amounts of packet retransmission from clients.
- Unusually high CPU utilization.
- Too many simultaneous connections or client sessions.
- Consumption of the swap file by using memory that is sized too low and high disk space usage that forces disk paging.
- Inaccessibility of shared network resources.

All these problems can cause degradations in network and/or system performance.

Multihoming and Fault Tolerance

When you install two or more concurrently active network interfaces, you have a dual-homed or multihomed system. There are several reasons you might want to have a dual-homed system:

- **Extra network performance**—Having multiple network interfaces provide more network paths or channels to and from your server. With the use of special software, you can manage this additional capability, called *multipathing*. Many multihomed systems are created in order to manage a form of multipathing called *load balancing*. When your software performs load balancing, it is managing the throughput of your network interfaces so that the maximum throughput can be achieved.

  F5's Big IP server (www.f5.com/products/bigip/) is an example of a network switch specifically designed to route TCP/IP traffic intelligently from external networks to the servers in the network behind it. The Big IP intelligent router is performing both multipathing and load balancing. Meant for large enterprise applications such as server farms, Big IP greatly simplifies an enterprise's network architecture and improves network performance.

- **Fault tolerance**—Having multiple network interfaces allows you to fail over network traffic from a damaged or malfunctioning interface to another, thus providing additional fault tolerance.

- **Security through physical or protocol isolation**—Any network router is a dual-homed system. The purpose of a router is to route traffic from one network interface to another. Examples of routers include firewalls, the computer switches that run the Internet, and many other switching applications.

  When you work with a dual-homed system, you have the option of having each network interface belong to a different network and even run different network protocols. Physical isolation (addressing) and protocol isolation (switching transport protocols) make it much more difficult for an intruder to penetrate your internal network. Other software features can enhance your server's security.

Many server motherboards come with two network interfaces. The intent is to provide one network interface for monitoring the motherboard and another for network communication. You might also want to have two interfaces so that you can use one to talk to an external network and the second to communicate to an internal network. Consider, for example, a motherboard that comes with both a GigE port and a Fast Ethernet port. If you are using this board as a firewall server and one of the connections is to the Internet, you can use the Fast Ethernet port to connect to the Internet and the GigE port to connect to your internal network. Unless the server is on an Internet backbone or Internet2, you would rarely be able to saturate a Fast Ethernet network interface.

Configuring a dual-homed system isn't much more difficult than configuring a system with a single network interface. A couple extra issues add complexity, and one issue can be a gotcha. First, to have a dual-homed or multihomed system you need to have two or more network interfaces. When you have multiple NICs installed, they are given default and generic interface names. In Windows Server 2003, that would be Local Area Connection, Local Area Connection 1, Local Area Connection 2, and so forth. These NICs can be renamed for easier identification. For UNIX/Linux (depending on the distribution), that designation is commonly seen as le0, le1, and so forth. These are logical names (just like with Windows), and they can be renamed with more appropriate names, such as External, Internal, or whatever is appropriate. The key is that you have to be able to recognize which network adapter is which. When you have two or more of the same model of NIC installed, that can be a challenge, and you need to be careful.

Many server programs that require two or more active network interfaces for successful operation are likely to include network adapter configuration as part of their routines. This is certainly true of any network "front-facing" server, such as a firewall or network traffic director. Microsoft Internet Security and Acceleration (ISA) Server is also a solid-performing firewall and proxy server solution.

Tip

If your NOS supports plug-and-play and you use exactly the same network card, some operating systems may not recognize that there are two instances of the same card, and they may not properly configure the second card. This is not true of all cards, models, or operating systems, but it comes up from time to time and is an issue you should watch out for when implementing a multihomed system.

Protocols

Protocols are the software standards (quite literally, software agreements) that are used to communicate over a network. There are protocols in all seven layers of the ISO/OSI network model. However, for our purposes, the main protocols of interest are those used by applications and the operating system at the transport layer. You are undoubtedly already familiar with transport protocols because they are the ones that you learn to set up when you add or modify a network computer. Figure 10.6 shows the ISO/OSI seven-layer protocol stack, including the protocols discussed in the following sections.

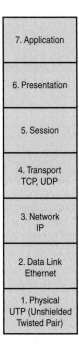

Figure 10.6   The ISO/OSI protocol stack.

Note

For more in depth information on network protocols, refer to *Upgrading and Repairing Networks*.

Transport Protocols

Each NOS comes with a set of transport protocols that support each kind of network client on the network. In the past, you were forced to know a little bit about the nature of multiple transport protocols, but that is no longer really the case. The rise of the Internet and ubiquity of TCP/IP over

Ethernet networking requires that every client be able to run TCP/IP as its transport protocol in order to use a browser or get access to network services such as email or files stored on servers. In a world where printers, scanners, storage, and even refrigerators require TCP/IP addressing, we are now as close to a universal standard as we're likely to get.

Note

NetBEUI was the first of the Windows automated network protocols used for Windows 95. By 1998, Windows 98 was using TCP/IP, but NetBEUI didn't quite disappear. Windows XP was the first version to ship without NetBEUI, which Microsoft no longer supports. If you still are using NetBEUI for Print and File Services, you should consider removing that transport protocol from your network and using one that is supported, such as IPX or, better yet, TCP/IP.

If you are working with a recent NOS, chances are good that you will find that TCP/IP is the only protocol stack installed from a larger set of available transport protocols. If you are supporting Macintosh, UNIX/Linux, or NetWare (and particularly legacy versions of these operating systems), you might need to install other protocols, such as AppleTalk or IPX/SPX in order for those clients to be able to communicate with the server system.

For Windows Server 2003, you should install these other legacy transport protocols by following these steps:

1. Make sure you have access to the Windows Server 2003 installation disks.

2. Select Network Connections from the Windows Control Panel folder.

3. Double-click the named connection to which you want to add a protocol. The Connection Status dialog box appears.

4. Click the Properties button to open the Connection Properties dialog box, which is shown in Figure 10.7.

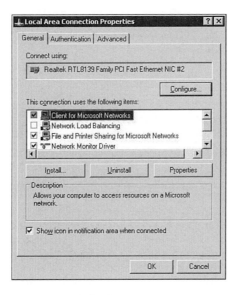

Figure 10.7 The Connection Properties dialog box.

5. Click the Install button to open the Select Network Component Type dialog box, shown in Figure 10.8.

Figure 10.8 The Select Network Component Type dialog box.

6. Select the Protocol component in the list and then click the Add button. The Select Network Protocol dialog box appears, as shown in Figure 10.9.

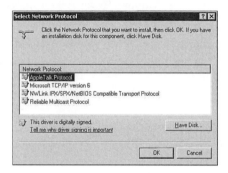

Figure 10.9 The Select Network Protocol dialog box.

7. Click the network protocol you want to install; then click the OK button. The network transport protocols included with Windows Server 2003 Standard Edition are AppleTalk, TCP/IP versions 4 and 6, NWLink/NetBIOS Compatible Transport, and Reliable Multicast Protocol.

8. Close all open dialog boxes and confirm that you want to install the protocol.

9. Verify that you have installed the protocol by double-clicking the network connection to open the Properties dialog box. The protocol should be listed as one of the components.

One transport protocol that doesn't get a lot of press but is widely used in many NOSs, particularly for applications such as streaming media, is User Datagram Protocol (UDP). UDP, like its cousin TCP, runs over the IP network-layer protocol and operates at the transport layer of the ISO/OSI network model. UDP uses a more compact form for data transmission, called a *datagram*, which has only a small amount of header information and which does less data checking to see if the data was correctly transmitted. Whereas missing a section of a document would definitely be a problem, dropping a frame in a movie would not be. UDP is therefore attractive in certain situations. The lightweight nature of UDP makes it faster than TCP because less processing is required to deconstruct and reconstruct the data. UDP traffic uses a separate port from TCP.

You should be judicious in your choices of which transport protocols you install. All network services add additional overhead to a server, so from the standpoint of obtaining maximum performance, you should seek to minimize the number of running services. However, transport protocols also provide a new pathway for exploits, and they represent an additional security path that needs to be monitored and protected.

Note

When running a server, you want to streamline the software used on that server to the absolute minimum. This applies doubly to protocols of any kind. You need to be cautious and always try to understand what is running on your server and why.

From time to time, you should open the Task Manager in Windows or a process list in UNIX/Linux, or you should use some other utility that will show you what applications, processes, and daemons are running on your server. You should then identify which processes to stop or eliminate.

If you are adding the NWLink protocol, you need to be sure to add the Microsoft Client Service for NetWare (CSNW) to provide NetWare access to your server. Windows Server 2003 also provides native file and print services support for Macintosh and UNIX clients.

You can find additional server protocol support from third-party vendors.

Several years ago, servers supporting Macintosh clients would install AppleTalk, those supporting Novell clients would install IPX/SPX, and so forth. While those protocols are still options, they now mainly exist to support legacy clients. The predominance of TCP/IP means that you can support almost any client (except those from before 1998) with TCP/IP alone (supported by other required naming and application services, as detailed in the following section). Thus, having a detailed knowledge of multiple transport protocols is becoming less and less necessary for server administrators.

Application-Layer Protocols

Whereas transport protocols are few, application-layer protocols are many. Some are specific to the NOS you are using, and many can be installed as part of the server's OS distribution that you are using.

Here are some examples:

- You have one IP address to use for your enterprise but many computers to service. The service that provides the dynamic assignment of private IP address is Dynamic Host Configuration Protocol (DHCP).

- You type a URL into a browser, and data is requested from the correct system, either locally or on the Internet. That service is Domain Name System (DNS).

- You search for a printer on your network, and that search is optimized. Here a directory service is used, probably utilizing some variant of Lightweight Directory Access Protocol (LDAP) as its protocol.

Note

TCP/IP, DNS, DHCP, and all the other protocols described in this chapter are big topics that require more space to learn than we have available in this book. Many networking books have been written for beginning, intermediate, and advanced users who need general information about protocols or services or who are trying to solve specific network problems. Among the books you might want to consult are *Upgrading and Repairing Networks* (a companion book in this series), *Sams Teach Yourself Networking in 24 Hours*, *Sams Teach Yourself TCP/IP in 24 Hours*, *Sams Teach Yourself Network Troubleshooting in 24 Hours*, *Local Area High Speed Networks*, and *Networking with Microsoft TCP/IP*.

The aforementioned protocols are generic—that is, a version of each of these services is found in all NOSs, with only slight variations between them. The main idea with these protocols is that they interoperate well between operating systems. You want a DNS request from a Windows server to be able to get an appropriate DNS response, and you want an LDAP request to Active Directory on Microsoft Windows to be able to get an appropriate LDAP response from an eDirectory service running on a Novell NetWare server.

A number of network protocols are specific to particular NOSs but are nonetheless quite important. Chief among them are name resolution protocols. These protocols resolve a friendly, easy-to-remember name, such as Columbia, to its TCP/IP address and vice versa. Currently Windows server technology recommends the use of Network Basic Input/Output System (NetBIOS) or a combination of NetBIOS and Windows Internet Name System (WINS), which is also known as NBT. WINS is an older Windows name resolution service that has been largely replaced on most networks by DNS. NetBIOS is an API that extends network BIOS functions. WINS uses a distributed database listing for name resolution. In fact, you can still find `LMHOSTS` text files with network resource listings, but because these files must be manually maintained, they tend to be used only on small networks or for absolutely essential and nonchanging resources.

Protocol Binding

The addition of protocols to a network interface is called *protocol binding*. The process by which a network interface is created is similar to how drivers are loaded. Protocols load one at a time for each network interface, and the order of binding shown in the network connection is the order in which they are loaded. The important point is that the order in which protocols are bound can affect network performance, and you can modify this binding order.

Consider a situation where your network interface runs both TCP/IP for general networking and IPX/SPX for NetWare connectivity. If IPX/SPX is listed before TCP/IP, switching the order will improve your network interface's performance for most general networking tasks.

To change your protocol binding order in Windows Server 2003, you follow these steps:

1. Select the Network Connections folder from the Control Panel.
2. Select the Advanced Settings command from the Advanced menu in the window.
3. In the Advanced Settings dialog box, select the Adapters and Bindings tab (see Figure 10.10). Then click the network adapter you want to modify and then click the protocol binding you want to change.
4. Use the up- and down-arrow buttons to change the protocol binding order.
5. Click the OK button to make your changes.

You also might want to modify the provider order on the Provider Order tab (see Figure 10.10) of the Advanced Settings dialog box. For example, if you don't use Windows Terminal Services, you can move it to the bottom of the list.

The Advanced Settings dialog box is also a great place to determine what protocols you are using and to get rid of the ones you don't need.

Network Operations Management

Network monitoring and management software encompasses such a large category of software (and hardware) tools that entire books have been written about it. The software can be simple, as in the case of the command prompt utilities you have already seen: `ipconfig` and `ifconfig`, `ping`, `tracert/traceroute`, `nslookup`, and so forth.

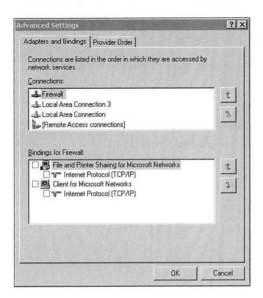

Figure 10.10   The Advanced Settings dialog box.

For larger enterprises managing hundreds and thousands of systems, it is common to see network console applications that have so much functionality that entire books have been written about each one of them. Beyond simple console applications are the network framework products that support many snap-in monitoring and management tools.

Let's consider network utilities by category, according to tasks, in order to get a feel for what tools you might want to acquire for your monitoring and management toolkit. The following are the areas that most commonly require management:

- Command-line TCP/IP utilities or graphical utilities based on them
- Performance Console and Monitor in older versions of Windows and in Sun Solaris and some other versions of Linux
- Port scanners and protocol analyzers (packet sniffers)
- Network discovery (typically Simple Network Management Protocol [SNMP] based), inventory or asset, and mapping software
- Bandwidth management and Quality of Service (QoS) management tools
- Event monitoring and analysis tools
- Network loading, routing, and path analysis tools
- Time synchronization managers
- Remote access management tools
- Wireless networking utilities
- Network security monitors

Consider this list as a starting place for core tools because, depending on the kind of network you have, you might want to deploy additional tools.

Most of these tools are created for use on a single NOS, perhaps with a single protocol, and often come with only with a diagnostic function. (This is not always the case, however.) True network operation management in enterprises where many servers are managed requires both a diagnostic function and a management console. That's where applications such as LANDesk (see Figure 10.11), Alteris, Microsoft Operations Manager and SMS, and Novell ZENworks come into play. You can use these and other applications you find online or in other publications, such as trade magazines.

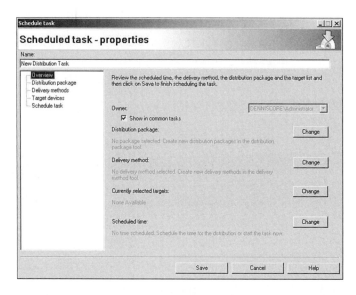

Figure 10.11   LANDesk's central console lets you manage and monitor a network as well as perform a number of related tasks.

The previously mentioned products are integrated solutions characterized by the concept of a central management console. That is, all these applications let you monitor and analyze a network, perform reconfiguration of systems, remotely install software, and more. Not all these capabilities are included in the base version of each product, but you can add additional capabilities as you need them.

There is a lot of overlap in these different products, and there are many more capable products in this area as well. Some products, such as ZENworks, are notable for directory service management, and others, such as LANDesk, are broad and battle tested and have strong Macintosh client support. Alteris uses a Web console approach that is relatively easy to use (when you know the product). These products are not cheap. Depending on the size of the deployment and the types of capabilities you purchase, you are probably looking at a few thousand dollars per deployed server and $300 or $400 dollars per client. But this category of software pays for itself quickly.

Finally, some of the network management tools that can be added to enterprise frameworks are Hewlett-Packard OpenView, Computer Associates Unicenter, and IBM Tivoli. Each of these frameworks is built so that you can add to them applications that are written in a consistent form. The framework helps you navigate to and employ the software that is installed into it, and the software is written in a consistent manner so that, as with a graphical user interface, you already know how to operate the software at a basic level. Frameworks can add all the tool types mentioned here, as well as application services, such as server antivirus and spam elimination utilities, backup, data migration, and many other tools.

CHAPTER 11

Disk Subsystems

As mathematician and pioneering computer scientist John Von Neumann conceptualized it, a computer's architecture is built like a human brain. A server's processors correspond to intelligence or, more precisely, higher logic functions; your RAM and cache perform a function similar to short-term memory; and permanent storage such as disks functions similarly to long-term memory. We don't yet have computers that are massively parallel processed or compute with a fault-tolerant fabric, but one day, in the not-too-distant future, we most certainly will.

Access to massive amounts of storage is a feature of modern computers; and that is true to an even greater degree with servers. What once fit into a very large room now fits on your desktop. Shakespeare's life works is a 1MB text file, and Microsoft's Encarta encyclopedia, which would occupy several linear feet in printed book form, is now 5GB of data, images and multimedia components included. No wonder that EMC, the world's largest maker of enterprise-class shared storage servers has as its slogan "Where Information Lives." Here's a truly remarkable fact: Every year or two, information stored in digital form doubles the amount of all recorded information from the dawn of man on. Because of this exponential growth, a server is called upon to perform more and more tasks that require access to large amounts of storage. Therefore, it's really important for you to have a fundamental appreciation of what the different types of storage can offer and how to manipulate storage to suit your needs. This chapter focuses on the building blocks of storage systems: the different type of drives, connections (cables, backplanes), and host adaptors.

Servers are required to be much more reliable than workstations. Another way to describe reliability is the term *availability*, which is a statistic that can be quantified. If you are in a hospital and your computer provides a mission-critical service, you might require that it be down only five minutes a year (roughly two reboots). That level of fault tolerance translates into a 99.999% availability, also referred to as "five nines." For a departmental server, a more easily achieved level of availability might allow for nine hours of downtime over the course of a year; that availability would be 99.9%, or three nines.

Note

Because the focus of this chapter is on deployment of drives in server environments, it is assumed that you have some familiarity with basic disk drive technology. You should be somewhat familiar with terms such as *platters, cylinders, heads, sectors, format, partitions,* and *addressing modes* before you read this chapter. You should also have a sense for the metrics of disk performance: seek time, latency, transfer rates, and access times. For more information on these subjects, pick up a copy of *Upgrading and Repairing PCs*.

Because availability translates into fault tolerance, a central focus of server disk subsystems is data redundancy. The second half of this chapter examines redundant array of inexpensive disks (RAID). Servers use different types of RAID controllers and different configurations of drive arrays to create fault tolerance. This chapter looks at the definitions of the different types of RAID, as well as the advantages and disadvantages of each RAID level. From an operational standpoint, this chapter also describes procedures for adding drives to arrays, recovering from drive failures, doing maintenance on arrays, and protecting your data on arrays.

This chapter describes nonvolatile storage that is directly attached to a server, what is referred to in the storage industry as *direct attached storage (DAS)*. In addition to disk-based technologies, you will find a variety of other useful nonvolatile storage technologies that are often directly attached to a server, including tape backups, libraries, and optical disk writers and readers (both singly and in the form of optical disk carousels). Because large libraries and carousels are mostly used for backup, hierarchical storage systems (HSS), and near online storage systems, we don't discuss them further in this chapter.

This chapter sets the stage for Chapter 12, "Storage Area Networks," where the focus is on shared storage solutions.

Disk Types

Hard drives became a commodity product in the early 1990s, and the resulting low margins afforded manufacturers the ability to force many hard disk manufacturers out of business or into merger. Currently, there are four major manufacturers of hard drives in the United States, and between them, they control in excess of 90% of the worldwide market:

- **Maxtor**—Maxtor specializes in large-capacity (3.5-inch) consumer and enterprise drives.

- **Seagate**—Seagate is noted for its high-speed enterprise-class SCSI and Fibre Channel drives, but it also has consumer lines in high-capacity drives, notebook drives (2.5-inch), and microdrives.

- **Western Digital**—Western Digital also specializes in high-capacity consumer drives, with additional lines of high-speed drives as well.

- **Hitachi**—Formerly IBM's disk drive division, Hitachi makes desktop, laptop, and server drives, but is best known for its notebook drives (Travelstar brand) as well as its enterprise-class hard drives.

Other vendors you may encounter include Fujitsu, Samsung, and Toshiba.

Note

Regardless of who you buy your disk drives from, the entire industry generally produces reliable products. Consumer drives typically come with anywhere from a three-month to three-year warranty, enterprise-class drives usually start at a three-year warranty. The mean time between failures (MTBF) is usually advertised as around seven years. That may seem like a lot, but remember that this number is a mean. When you purchase drives for a disk array of say eight drives, the chances of one failing are eight times greater than with a single drive. You should expect a drive to fail in the first year or two. That's why you want to have redundancy built into your system, by including extra drives.

Whereas it is common to find a single disk drive in a workstation, servers are a different beast entirely. Modern server motherboards don't look all that different from PC motherboards, except that they tend to be larger in order to accommodate more expansion slots. Other differences are that they often support multiple processors, have onboard RAID and network support, and come in an extended ATX or extended BTX form factor, with features geared toward controlling internal case temperatures. Most server deployments opt to use faster drives and more drives, and they combine those drives in the form of external disk arrays. Arrays provide for both enhanced speed (as measured by data throughput) and higher fault tolerance.

◄◄ For more information on motherboard form factors see, "Motherboard Types and Form Factors," p. 226.

You generally only find the IDE bus and ATA drives used in the low end of the server market, typically in single- or dual-processor systems. You might find that a server's boot drive is an enhanced ATA drive or a two-drive EIDE RAID array, but the business end, with larger amounts of storage, typically uses other technologies. Most of the server industry is currently using one of the following four standard types of 3.5-inch disk drives:

- SCSI
- Fibre Channel
- SATA
- IDE

Each of these types is described in the sections that follow. Because all drives have the same size and form factor, the best way to tell them apart is to look at the back of the drive to see what connectors each has.

IDE and ATA Drives

Integrated Drive Electronics (IDE) has been the storage interface on PC motherboards for many years. The "integrated" part refers to an onboard controller (an ASIC) that offloads processing to the disk, as well as an onboard drive cache.

In Chapter 6, "The ATA/IDE Interface," we already detailed just about all there is to know about the technology behind the IDE interface. In this section, however, we'll recap some of the core details as they pertain to this chapter.

◄◄ See Chapter 6, "The ATA/IDE Interface," for more information on the IDE bus and its characteristics.

These days when people refer to IDE drives, what they really mean is the advanced version of the ATA standard, probably implemented in a proprietary version. ATA-2 is also marketed as Enhanced IDE (EIDE), which was a term Western Digital coined for its hard drives. Seagate was another vendor with an "enhanced" IDE standard; it called its Fast ATA or FAST IDE. Essentially, these names all refer to minor variations on the same theme (ATA-2), and the term *EIDE* is in wide usage. You can expect EIDE drives to be about three or four times faster than the original IDE standard, with data transfer rates between 4MBps and 16.6MBps. The next version of the ATA standard was ATA-3, a minor revision that isn't differentiated from EIDE.

Usually, a server motherboard comes with two or four EIDE connections, with each channel supporting one master device and one slave device. Devices that can connect to IDE are hard drives, optical drives, and tape drives, for the most part. Motherboards with four IDE connections often connect a pair of them to an onboard EIDE RAID chip. You can also purchase EIDE RAID controllers from several vendors. EIDE RAID is discussed later in this chapter, in the section "RAID Controllers."

From the standpoint of using ATA in servers, the next few versions of ATA are of the most interest. After version ATA-3, there followed more versions of the ATA standard. There are currently seven ATA versions. Those that are currently in use are recapped in the following list:

- **Ultra ATA**—This version is sometimes referred to as Ultra DMA (UDMA), and it runs in mode 3 with a throughput of 33MBps. This standard is obsolete.

- **(Ultra) ATA/66**—The ATA/66 standard originally promulgated by Quantum (now part of Maxtor) is also supported by Intel and others. The 66 refers to a throughput of 66MBps. The term "Ultra" is in parenthesis because some vendors use it in their advertising, while others do not. ATA/66 is nearly obsolete.

- **(Ultra) ATA/100**—ATA/100 was released rather recently, offering 100MBps. In consumer-level drives, ATA/100 is in common use. This drive standard takes the 40-pin, 80-wire ribbon connector that you see on the current generation of motherboards.

- **(Ultra) ATA/133**—The current version of ATA, also called ATA-7, features 133MBps throughput and a number of other advanced features. Maxtor calls its implantation FastDrive/133, and it is backward compatible with the ATA/100 standard. However, to get 133MBps performance, you need a controller that supports that speed; otherwise, the drive runs at 100MBps. There's little, if any, performance advantage to be gained from ATA/133 because even an ATA/100 drive can bottleneck your PCI bus.

Note

ATA as *implemented* in real drives is the work of an ad hoc group called the Small Form Factor (SFF) Committee. You can read more about them at www.sffcommittee.com, but the standard itself is specified by Technical Committee T13 of the NCITS (see http://t13.org).

Let's look at some of the features offered by the latest versions of EIDE drives, as these are the ones that are most desirable to use in server deployments. The specs following Figure 11.1 list an abbreviated spec sheet for a Samsung SP1604N 160GB, 7200rpm EIDE hard drive, a drive that is in the SpinPoint P80 series.

Figure 11.1   Most EIDE drives used today are ATA-7 (Ultra ATA/133) drives that spin at at least 7200 rpm.

The SP1604N features the following:

- **The Ultra ATA/133 interface (ATA-7)**—The drive offers a 48-bit address set and 8MB of cache, and it is formatted at 512 bytes per sector.
- **A fluid dynamic bearing spindle motor**—It offers noise-reduction technology (NoiseGuard and SilentSeek).
- **High-speed dual digital signal**—It has an onboard dual-channel digital signal processor.
- **ATA SMART compliance**—Self-Monitoring Analysis and Reporting Technology (SMART) is a feature that looks ahead to predict disk errors and helps you take corrective actions. For a detailed description of SMART, see www.seagate.com/support/kb/disc/smart.html.
- **Management features**—It offers ATA Security Mode Feature Set, ATA Host Protected Area Feature Set, and ATA Automatic Acoustic Management Feature Set.
- **Hot-pluggability and hot-swappability**—This drive is hot-plug and hot-swap capable, which is very desirable in a server drive for RAID applications.

It's very important that server drives be quiet, cool, and power efficient because you multiply these issues many times in server deployments.

From the standpoint of performance, here's what Samsung advertises:

- **Read seek time**—Typically 0.8ms (track-to-track); average 8.9ms; full-stroke 18ms.
- **Average latency**—4.17ms, with a drive ready time of 7 seconds.

- **Data transfer rate**—133MBps media to/from buffer (maximum), 741MBps buffer to/from host (maximum).

- **Reliability**—MTBF 500,000 POH; start/stop cycles 50,000; component design life five years.

- **Power consumption**—Voltage 5V ±5%/12V 10%; Read/write on-track 8.5W; Seek 9.5W; Idle 7.7W; Standby 0.9W; and Sleep 0.9W.

- **Size**—4.0 inches × 1.0 inches × 5.75 inches and 1.4 pounds.

It's still possible to find EIDE models with 2MB of onboard cache or ones that operate at the older 5600rpm speed, but their cost advantage over drives such as the one from Samsung is no longer what it used to be. Consequently, these drives are slowly being phased out.

Serial ATA

Serial ATA (SATA) is the technology that is meant to replace the EIDE interface in desktop systems and workstations. You find SATA connections on nearly all modern motherboards, with two or four onboard connections being common. Some new server boards have as many as eight SATA connections.

The SATA bus standard is similar to Fibre Channel in regard to its ability to fan out and connect not only hard drives but peripherals as well. In terms of the physical drive, a SATA drive is identical to a standard parallel ATA (PATA) drive, except that it uses the serial interface. The ATA or EIDE drives you learned about in the preceding section use a parallel data transfer method, with many channels communicating during each processor cycle. The ATA/100 standard uses a 16-bit channel and requires the ribbon cables we are so familiar with in desktop PCs. It's not uncommon to see ribbon cables with 40 or 80 wires. The form of the wire is flat and wide to eliminate crosstalk between channels. The rounded cables that replace ribbon IDE cables contain a significant amount of shielding.

SATA uses a serial connection, sending data down a single control channel because the serial data stream runs at much greater speeds than the EIDE bus. When SATA was first introduced, the bus clock was sending data down the wire at 1.5GHz, compared to the clock rate of around 100MHz for Ultra ATA/100. That is roughly 150 times as fast, and so even if you reduced the number of wires by a factor of 40 or 80, SATA would be faster than ATA. SATA suffers from fewer data transmission errors, and there's less need to re-send data over an SATA cable than there typically is over an ATA cable. All that, coupled with the fact that the run lengths of SATA can be longer than ATA, adds up to a significant design advantage.

Note

The website of the Serial ATA International Organization, which manages the SATA standard, is www.serialata.org.

Another one of EIDE/ATA's thorny configuration issues, the master/slave relationship, disappears with SATA. An ATA bus master/slave configuration shares the same wire, effectively halving the performance available to each device. In SATA data connections, there is no master or slave. Each device gets a full dedicated 150MBps or 300MBps connection to the SATA host controller, with future transfer rates of 600MBps and faster planned as part of the SATA road map. SATA allows for hot-swappable drives—and more of them than EIDE. This means SATA can compete with SCSI and Fibre Channel when it comes to creating fault-tolerant RAID configurations.

Although SATA was initially thought of as a technology for gamers and for enhanced workstations, it is a very interesting server storage technology, and the industry is keeping a sharp eye on its development.

◀◀ For more information on Serial ATA see, "SATA," p. 424.

SCSI Drives

SCSI has been the drive interface of choice for small computer systems that require fast data transfers and can live with short cable runs. SCSI is notable for being a self-configuring bidirectional bus, with what is now a long history.

The first SCSI standard appeared about the same time as the Macintosh II personal computer and was developed at Apple. Server vendors have made heavy use of the SCSI interface in applications ranging from drives inside the server itself (so-called "captive disk") to DAS applications, as well as the internal drives used in some storage servers (smaller ones, generally) and disk arrays.

◄◄ Chapter 7, "The SCSI Bus," describes the SCSI bus in more detail.

Demystifying SCSI

You learned a lot about the SCSI bus in Chapter 7, "The SCSI Bus," so in this chapter we simply review in brief the different standards and look at the types of SCSI drives that are preferred in server deployments today. You saw seven different iterations of the ATA standard earlier (depending on how you count them); with SCSI, there are even more. Many of these standard revision levels are backward compatible with others, and some are not. The key feature to look for is the pin count of the connector.

SCSI has appeared in the following revision levels or types:

- SCSI-1 (released in 1986)
- SCSI-2 (released in 1994)
- SCSI-3 (released in 1996)

These standards define the command set that any variant of that level of SCSI uses. Chances are that these days, if someone refers to "SCSI," they are talking about some form of the SCSI-2 specification.

The original SCSI was an 8-bit bus standard operating at 4 MBps, using a 25-pin connector. The 8-bit bus offered seven connected devices, IDs 0 through 7. ID 7 usually is the host adapter, by default. (SCSI gives priority to the highest-numbered device on a chain, which is why 7 is used.) Moving to a 16-bit standard (SCSI-2) doubled the number of possible connected devices to 15. A 32-bit 40MBps version of SCSI-2 has been codified but is not yet in use.

Note

A lot of information has been published on the SCSI standard. To begin with, SCSI is defined by the T10 Technical Committee (www.t10.org) of INCITS (InterNational Committee for Information Technology Standards), under the auspices of ANSI (American National Standards Institute; www.ansi.org). The relevant trade organization is the SCSI Trade Association (www.scsita.org). Many vendors maintain an open library of information to aid their customers in buying SCSI disks.

Three other sites you might want to look at are Adaptec's (www.adaptec.com/worldwide/support/supportindex.jsp?sess=no&language=English+US&source=home_tab), Seagate's (www.seagate.com/support/kb/disc/index_faq.html), and Parlan's (www.paralan.com/scsi.html), but there are many others as well.

All of the first sets of SCSI standards until SCSI-2 were 5-volt single-ended standards that used TTL voltage levels to determine the signal. That architecture used only a single wire but required termination and high power. A recent variant of SCSI-3, Ultra 2 SCSI, offered a lower 3-volt voltage double-ended alternative called Low Voltage Differential (LVD) signal; you may find it referred to as LVD SCSI.

The low voltage signal in LVD SCSI allows for a longer cable run (35 feet), and the signal is measured as the difference between the two wires of each channel inside the LVD cable. The advantage of Ultra 2 is that it has modest power requirements and is cheaper to make, and because it has two wires, twice as much data can be transferred. You may see the terms HVD SCSI and LVD SCSI bandied about, and this is what they refer to.

You can't directly connect HVD and LVD SCSI, but it is possible to find an adapter called an LVD-to-HVD converter that makes the necessary conversions. You may also encounter a hybrid called "multi-mode LVD," or LVD/MSE SCSI. That implementation can switch automatically between LVD and single-ended mode.

Things started to get weird when SCSI-2 substituted a 50-pin connector in place of the original 25-pin connector introduced by SCSI-1. The 8-bit standard of SCSI-2's 50-pin connector is sometimes referred to as Narrow SCSI, to differentiate it from the 16-bit 68-pin connector standard called Wide SCSI. Thus the terms Narrow SCSI and Wide SCSI identify not only the width of the standard but to some extent the size of the SCSI connector used.

SCSI Performance

The speed of the SCSI implementation plays a role in what the manufacturer advertises its SCSI as achieving. After SCSI-1, the standards allowed for different speed implementations. After SCSI came Fast SCSI, just like after Ethernet came Fast Ethernet. You will see the Fast standards Fast-10, Fast-20, Fast-40, and Fast-80 SCSI in the literature, where the numbers represent a metric called MegaTransfers/second. For an 8-bit-wide bus, 20 MegaTransfers corresponds to 20MBps, and for the 16-bit bus, 40MBps. That's why each of the Fast standards has two quoted speeds.

These so-called "Fast" speed standards are advertised and known by other names:

- Fast-10 is simply referred to as Fast SCSI.
- Fast-20 is also called Ultra SCSI.
- Fast-40 is Ultra 2 SCSI, which can also run at 80MBps with a 16-bit bus and uses LVD signals.
- Ultra 3 SCSI runs at 160MBps using LVD. Ultra 3 SCSI is also called Ultra 160.
- Ultra 4 SCSI, also known as Ultra320, is the fastest SCSI standard in use, running at 320MBps.

Note

Ultra 3 (or Ultra160) is often promoted as an alternative to Fibre Channel because the throughput speeds are similar. It's a debate that will go on for a while. Fibre Channel has higher numbers of nodes (126 versus 15) and a much longer run length (10km versus 35 feet). Ultra 3 offers better manufacturer interoperability as well as lower costs. These characteristics define where each is used. You don't typically find Fibre Channel inside servers, connecting just a few drives, or connecting arrays that are close to a server—characteristics of small business or departmental servers. For larger deployments with many more nodes and longer cable lengths, Fibre Channel has the advantage.

Let's break this down just a little bit further to see how all these terms come together to form some of the slang surrounding SCSI. Fast-Wide SCSI is the Fast-10 standard using a 16-bit (wide) bus. Wide Ultra SCSI is the 16-bit version of the Fast-20 or Ultra standard.

It's really easy to see how people get confused when talking about SCSI. Let's simplify this by getting down to what you really need to know from a server perspective when it comes to disk drives.

The Suitability of SCSI

These days, when people refer to SCSI, they are usually referring to the SCSI-2 standard. Ultra SCSI and Ultra 2 SCSI are both in wide use and are usually referred to by their correct names. It is very rare to run into terms such as Fast-20 or wide, and when SCSI is HVD, people don't generally differentiate it from all the other common garden varieties of HVD around. Ultra 3 and Ultra 4, on the other hand, are newer and are used in high-performance applications. People who use Ultra 3 generally refer to their implementation as LVD SCSI or U160 (and its variants). Ultra 4 users generally use the term Ultra 320.

For the most part, SCSI standards are interoperable—but not always. If you have two-pin compatible forms of SCSI and plug one into the other, the combination will run at the slower standard's speed. Ultra 2 and Ultra 3, for example, are backward compatible with any of the earlier single-ended versions of SCSI but revert from multimode to single mode when they sense a single-ended device. You need to pay attention to the types of controllers you are using, the cables and terminators they require, and the drives you are purchasing if you want to minimize problems.

Let's now consider suitability to task as it relates to SCSI and servers. Table 11.1 lists SCSI cable lengths, speeds, and connectivity.

Table 11.1   SCSI Standards

Name	Bus Width (bits)	Maximum Cable Length (meters)	Maximum Speed (MBps)	Maximum Number of Devices (IDs)
SCSI-1	8	6	5	8
SCSI-2	8	6	5-10	8
Fast SCSI-2	16	3	10-20	8
Wide SCSI-2	16	3	20	16
Fast Wide SCSI-2	16	3	20	16
Ultra SCSI-3, 8-bit	8	1.5	20	8
Ultra SCSI-3, 16-bit	16	1.5	40	16
Ultra 2 SCSI	8	12	40	8
Wide Ultra 2 SCSI	16	12	80	16
Ultra 3 (Ultra160/m) SCSI	16	12	160	16
Ultra320 SCSI-3	16	12	320	16

From Table 11.1, we see that the following is true:

- Ultra 2, Wide Ultra 2, and Ultra 3 SCSI offer 12-meter connections. This makes those standards suitable for use in connecting a server to storage across the room or a hall.

- Ultra SCSI-3, Fast, and Wide SCSI standards are faster standards with short cable length runs. As such, they are better suited for applications where the SCSI host adapter and SCSI disk drives are in close proximity. You would use this second group of SCSI standards for a captive disk inside a server or for a connection to a storage array that is either in the same case or rack as the server itself, or to an array that is very close by.

Indeed, this is just the pattern of usage you find in the industry. Now that we've reprised and hopefully demystified the various SCSI standards, let's take a look at the disk drives in common usage.

SCSI Drives

SCSI drives are favored for captive disks inside servers, for smaller disk arrays, and in some high-performance disk arrays. SCSI drives are much more expensive than PATA or SATA drives; you can expect to pay a premium that can be as much as two to three times the price of SATA or PATA drives. Two speeds of drives are currently in use today: 10,000rpm, or 10k, disks marketed for mainstream servers, and 15,000rpm, or 15k, disks marketed for high-performance servers. As of this writing, you can purchase SCSI drives in the range of 37GB to 300GB, or you can purchase PATA or SATA drives up to 500GB. SCSI tends to lag a little behind in terms of capacity despite being the leader in performance.

The most common types of SCSI drives currently on the market are Ultra320 LVD SCSI drives in either the 10K or 15K speeds, and these Ultra320 drives come with either 68-pin Wide SCSI or 80-pin SCA-2 (hot-swappable) connectors. Most of the drives sold on the market today ship with 8MB of onboard cache in them. As a general rule, the 10K drives have seek times of around 5ms (microseconds) average, and the 15k drives have a seek time of about 2.75ms to 3.5ms on average.

Earlier, we looked at a 160GB Samsung PATA drive. Now let's compare that drive to the characteristics you would find for a Seagate Cheetah Ultra320 ST3146854LW drive of similar size. Here are some of the specifications:

- **Rotational speed**—15,400rpm
- **Connection**—1 68-pin Ultra320 SCSI LVD-SCSI connector
- **Capacity**—146GB; 8 physical heads, 50,864 cylinders; 4 discs/platters; 512 bytes per sector; 286,749,488 user sectors per drive
- **Seek time**—3.5ms average
- **Buffer (cache)**—8MB
- **Reliability**—MTBF 1,400,000 hour(s) shock tolerance
- **Power**—5V DC input or 12V; input current from 0.6A to 3A, depending on the voltage and operating state; power consumption 11.91W at idle
- **Performance**—Spin rate 15,4000 rpm; data transfer rate 320MBps External Maximum Ultra320 SCSI; track-to-track write typical 0.45ms; track-to-track read 0.27ms typical; full-disc read 7.4ms typical; full-disc write 7.9ms typical; average read 3.5ms typical; average write 4ms typical; latency 2ms average; spinup time 20 seconds; power-on to ready time 3 seconds; track density (TPI) 85,000 tracks/inch; recording density (BPI) 628000 bits/inch maximum; bytes/track 471916 average; internal transfer rate 685Mbps–1142 MBps; formatted internal transfer rate 85MBps–142 MBps
- **Environmental**—Temperature range 5° C (41° F) to 50° C (122° F) under operation; 95% maximum humidity; altitude –1001 feet to 10,000 feet under operation; sound emission 36dB at idle typical
- **Miscellaneous**—Enhanced error correction code, fluid dynamic bearing motor, full duty cycle reliability, SMART error correction
- **Warranty**—Standard warranty 5 year(s) limited, worldwide parts warranty/labor 5 year(s)

This level of performance is particularly impressive given that this drive is two to three times as fast as the Samsung drive detailed earlier. Perhaps the most important comparison is price. The Samsung SP160N's full retail price is a little more than $100, while the Seagate drive is approximately $1,200. Both of these are new drives, but whereas the Samsung will maintain its price over time (it's still a commodity), you will see a large price drop over the next 18 months in a drive like the Seagate one.

Fibre Channel

Fibre Channel is a high-performance serial drive interface that borrows from the SCSI command set to attach to drives using either copper or high-speed optical wires. Fibre Channel has some very desirable features from the standpoint of server/storage deployment.

Originally deployed in mainframes around 1988, Fibre Channel was meant to replace HIPPI. Fibre Channel is the interconnect of choice for large storage devices and SANs. It allows a large number of disks to be connected. You tend to find Fibre Channel employed as the predominant interface type in enterprise-class storage servers such as EMC Symmetrics or Network Appliance NAS servers.

There are three different Fibre Channel topologies or architectures:

- **Fibre Channel Point-to-Point (FC-P2P)**—FC-P2P is implemented with a direct connection between to FC devices.

- **Fibre Channel Arbitrated Loop (FC-AL)**—With FC-AL, a Fibre Channel HBA attaches to a backplane with a printed circuit board. Fibre Channel drives housed in carriers mount directly into the backplane, making a direct connection without a cable. The direct connection makes them more reliable. This topology is used to connect a storage server directly to an application server.

- **Switched Fabric (FC-SW)**—In larger deployments typical of SANs, Fibre Channel connections plug into an intelligent (that is, manageable) switch. That switch can route traffic from one port to another, making data available to a number of servers potentially through different paths.

▶▶ Fabric switch Fibre Channel is covered in detail in Chapter 12.

The wiring used in Fibre Channel from the backplane to the HBA or from the backplane to the switch is either an optical (that is, fiber) or twisted-pair copper cable.

Fibre Channel, like many other transport technologies, borrows from and owes a lot to the SCSI standard. Normally, you see the protocol broken down into a five-layer scheme:

- FC-4—The application layer, where Fibre Channel data is prepared for transport.

- FC-3—A layer with protocols pertaining to Fibre Channel ports.

- FC-2—The network layer, which is the protocol with the Fibre Channel command set.

- FC-1—The data link layer, where signal encoding and decoding are managed.

- FC-0—The physical layer, which involves wiring.

Note

For more information about the Fibre Channel protocol layers, see http://hsi.web.cern.ch/HSI/fcs/spec/overview.htm.

Because Fibre Channel is expensive to deploy and requires separate networking skills, it isn't used in smaller disk deployments. For a server or an array with five or fewer drives, there is no significant performance boost in using Fibre Channel versus SCSI.

Characteristics of Fibre Channel

You learned a lot about Fibre Channel when you learned about SCSI. Fibre Channel borrows many things from the SCSI world. The following factors separate Fibre Channel technology from SCSI and the other drive standards:

- **Speed**—The Fibre Channel interface operates at 100MBps at the drive. HBAs may be found in both the 1Gbps and 2Gbps ranges. 4Gbps, 8Gbps, and 10Gbps standards have been ratified, but the only active product development is in the 8Gbps range. The 10Gbps standard is not backward compatible with prior standards.

- **Longer cable lengths**—Each controller is able to connect up to 30m over copper wire or 10km over optical wiring.

- **Higher device connect count**—The limit for the IDE bus is four drives on two channels; SCSI can connect to up to 15 devices; Fibre Channel can connect up to 126 devices.

- **Loop architecture**—You can create what are called FC-AL as well as dual loops that connect to two different servers at the same time. Dual loops offer advantages in multiple-drive systems implemented in a RAID solution because they allow data on one side of the loop to be seen on the second loop. Each loop of a dual loop gets its own HBA, so the combined data transfer rate can be as high as 200MBps. A dual-loop topology can have 2×126, or 252, devices.

- **Standard serial port implementation**—Just like SATA, Fibre Channel is a standard serial port interface. The Fibre Channel interface is actually an ANSI standard. A Fibre Channel bus requires a backplane (see "Backplanes," later in this chapter), which holds the drives and drive receptacles, a Fibre Channel HBA, and the drives themselves.

- **Hot-swapping (hot-plugging)**—With Fibre Channel, drives can be installed or removed from the bus at any time, even when the server is down. This is not true of SCSI, although it will eventually be implemented as a feature in SATA drives.

Fibre Channel is reliable and well established. Many factors have given Fibre Channel a distinct advantage over other technologies in the past. There is so much investment and expertise in Ethernet infrastructure that developing storage over TCP/IP technologies may steal a lot of Fibre Channel's market share over time.

Arbitrated Loop Topology

One of the major reasons Fibre Channel is so widely deployed is that you can create a topology called an arbitrated loop. As shown in the previous section, FC-AL isn't a loop at all (except topologically speaking); rather, it's a connection through the backplane of drives to the HBA. On the backplane is a port bypass circuit (PPCB) logic board that allows for the fast operation of the loop and for the ability to hot-swap drives.

Although there are 126 assignable addresses (the 127th is the host), in practical terms, you can attach from 45 to 55 disks to an FC-AL before you start getting performance degradation. Performance in these storage systems is typically measured in terms of I/O per second. Often the diagnostic utility of choice is the freeware Intel IOmeter.

FC-AL can use coaxial, twin-axial, or optical cabling, and there are no drive switches or jumpers to set because the interface is self-configuring. In terms of fault tolerance, a backplane is both hot-swappable and double ported. The current standard runs at 100MBps, with a frequency of 1.062GHz.

When Fibre Channel is configured into the dual-loop topography, it picks up not only speed but fault tolerance as well. Dual loops uses two Fibre Channel HBAs connected to each disk drive, allowing each bus to access the same drive. Although only one of the two loops may access a drive at a time, the net result is that you get an overall doubling of throughput. Not only that, but if one of the bus's connections to a disk fails, that disk is still available through the other bus. The ability to share data between two systems provides built-in redundancy that saves you from having to duplicate a data set.

Fibre Channel really has a lot to recommend it, especially when you are trying to build a large shared storage system in a storage area network (SAN).

Installing a Fibre Channel Drive

To install a Fibre Channel drive, follow these steps:

1. Mount the drive into the tray or carrier that is part of your Fibre Channel backplane.

2. Connect the LED pins on the back of the drive to the carrier if you want to observe the signals. The LEDs tell you when there is a fault condition (the Fault LED) and the activity of the disk (the Activity LED). Activities are indicated by the light being on or off, blinking slowly or steadily, or toggling on and off. Table 11.2 describes the status of the lights.

3. Inset the tray or carrier into the backplane connecting the 40-pin Fibre Channel connector on the back of the drive to the mated connector on the backplane.

4. The drive should be recognized at this point. Partition and format it. Most Fibre Channel drives come low-level preformatted, but you may need to do a low-level reformat.

If your Fibre Channel drive doesn't spin up, the most likely problem is that you don't have a good physical connection to the backplane. You should remove the drive and check its mounting and then reinsert it carefully and firmly. If the drive does spin up but isn't recognized by the Fibre Channel HBA, you need to run the host adapter setup utility that ships with your adapter to enable the drive through software.

Table 11.2   Fibre Channel Disk LED Indicators[1]

LED	Status	Indication
Fault LED	On	Both ports failed, there is an internal failure, or the drive receives a fault signal from the host.
Fault LED	Off	No error detected (operation normal).
Active LED	On	Spun down and read or write in progress.
Active LED	Off	Spun up and no disk head activity.
Active LED	Slow blink (20% on/80% off)	Spun down and no read or write activity in progress.
Active LED	Steady blink (50% on and off)	Changing spin rate up or down.
Active LED	Toggles on and off	A format is in progress, the light changes as the cylinder in use changes.

[1]*These settings can change somewhat, depending on the manufacturer. The settings in this table are specific for Seagate's Fibre Channel drives.*

HBAs and RAID Controllers

An HBA is a generic name for bus interface card. A $25 PCI card that adds FireWire or USB 2.0 is called an HBA. From a computer storage standpoint, an HBA is something that can recognize and communicate with a storage device, and therefore all HBAs are "named entities" in the bus or channel type that they participate in. That is to say, every HBA takes an address. Because an HBA is a network interface, there are all manner of HBAs on the market. Your NIC is an HBA, and so are the storage HBAs described in this section and the ones that follow.

An HBA offloads I/O processing from the CPUs and contains not only a command set but often specialized algorithms and intelligent responses. In Ethernet networking, the fastest cards are now the ones that come with TCP/IP offload engines. The intelligence added to storage HBAs is RAID and management technologies.

Depending on the technology, vendor groups coin their own terms for their HBAs (for example, TCA or HCA for InfiniBand). Each of the technologies described so far requires its own particular HBA. The chipset on the HBA contains the commands, logic, timing circuits, and so on that are all part of the bus's specification. HBAs require their own device drivers. For widely available adapters, you will find support for them in your operating system, but for many specialized drivers, you need to get the current software from the adapter's vendor.

Form Factors

HBAs are almost always sold as add-in PCI cards, although you can expect to see more and more HBAs as PCI-X or PCI-Express cards—particularly high-throughput cards like the ones we talk about in a moment. Occasionally, you will find high-performance interfaces that are externally housed or use nonstandard form factors, but these alternate forms are rare for the newer and more advanced HBAs. SCSI has been around for 20 years, and it is possible to find SCSI controllers for all kinds of buses, including ISA, EISA, MCA, PCI, VLB, PCMCIA, and CardBus.

From the standpoint of server-to-storage connections, adding an EIDE card or a SATA card that is simply a drive interface connection with no multidisk array features almost never happens. That's a PC upgrade, not a server upgrade. HBAs sold to server manufacturers or as after-market products almost always have a RAID function. RAID is so inexpensive to add to a product that you will find RAID on your server's motherboard and even on higher-performing PC and workstation boards. You may also find multiple types of RAID—usually EIDE RAID, SATA RAID, and SCSI RAID—on the same board.

Usually, if your server has a motherboard with multiple RAID interfaces, you set up the drive connections and RAID features in your server's BIOS. After a drive has been recognized or an array has been created, you can proceed to partition and format your drive(s), and with the operating system loaded, you can apply different storage management and configuration utilities to your storage devices. Most onboard RAID systems offer limited RAID capabilities: RAID 0, 1, and 10 or 1+0 are most common.

Keep in mind that onboard RAID is not "free." You use up some processor cycles to manage onboard RAID, and the effect is small but noticeable. Because you don't want hard drive I/O to be a bottleneck (and it commonly is, especially in server environments), a high-efficiency HBA on a fast bus is preferable. There is a good reason that servers come with HBAs that often cost as much as a good desktop or laptop PC, and there is a good reason for all the activity with and interest in new forms of interfaces in servers such as PCI-X, PCI-Express, InfiniBand, and others.

Many HBAs offer various levels of RAID or no RAID at all. If your system uses a disk array, but with no RAID implemented, you have a system commonly referred to a JBOD (just a bunch of disks). You use JBOD when storage capacity is your only concern and you don't care about either performance or data protection.

We will return to a more complete description of RAID later in this chapter, but the point for our purposes here is that the terms *HBA* and *RAID controller* are almost synonymous in the industry for servers (and the technologies described in this chapter), and they differentiate only in describing upgrades to older PCs.

▶▶   For more information on RAID technology, see "Introduction to RAID," p. 600.

PATA HBAs

PATA connectors (or EIDE, if you prefer) are included on every server motherboard you can buy, and they will be for the near future. There are changes on the horizon, though. Intel, for one, is intent on replacing parallel ATA with serial ATA in future server motherboards but has not done so yet.

People add HBAs when they need more channels for parallel ATA drives. They do so to create larger JBODs or to build very large-capacity volumes using low-cost drives. ATA RAID can offer you faster performance and fault tolerance, so you sometimes find an EIDE HBA deployed in that manner.

Most of the time people purchase an EIDE RAID HBA because of "RAID lock-in." Say you choose to implement RAID on a captive drive set, using the onboard ATA RAID function that your motherboard offers. That feature might even be one of the reasons you selected the motherboard in the first place.

Onboard ATA RAID chips come from companies such as Adaptec, Highpoint, Intel, and Promise, and their inclusion adds very little to the cost of the motherboard relative to the dramatic improvement in performance they provide to a system. The RAID chips found on good motherboards are the same chips used to power the HBAs sold by these manufacturers, although very often you are buying an onboard RAID chip that has a newer, faster, or more capable brother on the way. Including older chip technology on motherboard chips while providing their latest and greatest chips on separate HBAs is one way for RAID vendors to improve volume or reduce inventory.

This methodology may seem innocuous until one day your server's motherboard or onboard RAID chip fails. Your disk volume contains data you want to use, and although you could reinstall from backup, it is just easier to replace the function. Unfortunately, vendors can charge a premium to provide HBAs based on previous iterations of their chipsets, and at this point, you're locked into whatever cost they want to set. The moral is that when you implement a RAID volume, you may be marrying yourself to a specific RAID HBA vendor.

Aside from RAID lock-in, the other reason that server administrators install RAID adapters is that they give you access to a faster standard for EIDE (perhaps Ultra ATA/133), allowing them to unlock disk performance for the EIDE drives they already possess. EIDE cards are the least expensive cards you can buy with RAID functionality, and they range from costing as little as $50 for a two-channel ATA/100 or ATA/133 RAID HBA from a company such as Startech or SIIG to as much as an absurd $400 for a four-channel Adaptec 2400A HBA with some nice features but only ATA/66 or ATA/100 support.

You should consider using PATA RAID for servers only if you need to keep an investment in legacy equipment. With SATA RAID rapidly displacing EIDE, that network interface would be a better and higher-performing choice for little extra money.

SATA Controllers

Most of the development effort these days for high-capacity, low-cost disk array HBA is in the area of SATA RAID. If you want to build a storage server dedicated to media of any kind, this is the standard to look at. Why? The disks are cheap, arrays are reliable enough to be acceptable for servers, and SATA RAID offers good, albeit not outstanding, performance, especially for the price.

SATA RAID controllers are available from a wide variety of vendors, including 3Ware, Adaptec, Broadcom, Highpoint, Intel, LSI Logic, Promise, and many others. You can choose from PCI, PCI-X, and PCI-Express cards offering a variety of RAID levels.

Let's consider for a moment the application of a SATA RAID card in practice. As an example, let's look at Adaptec's 2810SA eight-port SATA card (shown in Figure 11.2). This card retails for around $600 and is targeted for use by departmental and workgroup servers running video, backup, and web services—all high-capacity applications.

Figure 11.2   The Adaptec eight-port 2810SA PCI-X SATA RAID host adapter.

These are some of the features of this host adapter:

- It has an Intel 80303 100MHz processor with a 64MB cache.
- It offers RAID support (0, 1, 5, 10, and JBOD). These levels are explained in the "Introduction to RAID" section, later in this chapter.
- If offers hot-swapping and online expansion. Hot-swapping means you can add and remove drives. Online expansion allows you to expand volume sizes by using new disks added to the array.
- RAID level migration means you can change one type of RAID to another.
- It has a 1.5GBps transfer rate.
- It offers Windows, UNIX, and Linux support.
- It offers browser-based management software.

These features go well beyond what you would find on most EIDE controllers and are quite similar to the features you would find in an enterprise SCSI or Fibre Channel controller.

The industry has a keen interest in SATA HBAs because an eight-port SATA HBA can attach to cheap capacious hard drives. At today's prices, you could purchase eight 300GB HBAs for about $200 a piece. Your total investment of HBA and disk would run about $2,200, and you would have 2.4 *terabytes (TB)* of storage to work with. Clearly, you would need an enclosure, a processor(s), a motherboard, and other system components to complete your storage server, but even allowing another $1,500 for those components, you would have a massive amount of storage for less than $4,000.

SCSI or Fibre Channel storage servers offer you only a small fraction of this storage at that price level. Although the performance of a SATA HBA won't be as fast as those other two technologies, having that many drives in play makes SATA arrays plenty fast for many applications.

SCSI HBAs

SCSI HBAs were among the first high-performance HBAs sold in large numbers. Originally used for desktop PCs, mass production lowered their prices to the point where the technology became mainstream for servers of all kinds. As discussed earlier in this chapter, SCSI has gone through a range of changes, improving in both speed and performance. But through it all, SCSI has remained a parallel bus, and the principles under which a SCSI bus operates have remained largely the same. Recently, several new technologies have leveraged companies' investments in SCSI, in particular serial attached SCSI (SAS) and iSCSI. Before looking at the alternative technologies and where you would want to use them, let's look at some of the specifics about SCSI HBAs.

A SCSI HBA connects your computer with the SCSI bus. A SCSI HBA that is in a device on the SCSI daisy chain is called a *target controller*. Target controllers can be either internal to the device or created by adding a SCSI card to the device. There can be more than one host adapter on a SCSI bus, which permits peripheral sharing between systems. High-speed SCSI is often used, for example, as the connection between nodes in a cluster and shared storage, as well as the connection to whatever device in a cluster is maintaining the heartbeat of the cluster.

A SCSI bus is a peer network where all devices can initiate and target data requests. From a storage standpoint, the important logical addressing on the SCSI chain is called a logical unit number (LUN). LUNs are the connection to a SCSI device (not just disk), and because storage structures on disks may or may not bear any relationship to the physical disk, LUNs are used to indicate the actual disks in use, regardless of how the data is written.

SCSI uses an LBA scheme, which allows applications such as backup programs to copy data using the address on the disk, without regard to what kind of information it is. If you want a simple explanation that defines the difference between a SAN device and a network attached storage (NAS) device, it is this: SANs move data primarily as blocks, and NAS moves data as files.

Almost all SCSI HBAs come with built-in RAID controllers, powerful RISC (reduced instruction set computer) processors, and lots of cache. RAID controllers are configured in software, which is found in the adapter's BIOS. As your server performs a POST and the bus with the SCSI HBA is enumerated, you see the software load, with a prompt on how to access it. As the SCSI BIOS loads, it communicates with each possible target and enumerates them onscreen.

◄◄   For more information on RISC technology, see "RISC and CISC Chips," p. 58.

A vast number of vendors sell SCSI HBAs into the marketplace. Chief among them are AMI, ATTO, Adaptec, Emulex, FalconStor, Intel, LSI Logic, Mylex, Parlan, and others, as well as all the server vendors, such as Hewlett-Packard, Dell, IBM, and Sun. Emulex is the largest supplier selling to OEMs. Adaptec is the largest supplier selling to the general public, and it most certainly has the widest range of offerings of any vendor.

There are many different SCSI HBAs on the market today, but as far as servers are concerned, only the two highest-performing standards really matter: Ultra160 and Ultra320. An Ultra SCSI board is fine for a workstation or very small server, but unless cost is the primary concern, it is preferable to go with one of the later standards.

Let's consider some of the characteristics of one of the current crop of SCSI Ultra320 HBAs, the Adaptec SCSI RAID 2130SLP (see Figure 11.3), a $500 board that Adaptec aims at entry-level to high-density servers. This is a single-channel 16-bit PCI-X board that can attach to up to 15 disk drives. The primary features of this board are as follows:

- **Interface**—Ultra320 SCSI, PCI-X, 64-bit, 133MHz, and 64-bit capable
- **Performance**—Data transfer rate 320MBps
- **RAID**—1 to 15 drives (1 can be bootable); RAID 0, 1, 5, 10, and 50
- **Connections**—68-pin HD Ultra320 SCSI internal (with active terminator) and 68-pin VHDCI Ultra320 external
- **Power**—5V DC input voltage, 4A at 5V DC current

- **Temperature**—0° C (32° F) to 50° C (122° F)

- **Software**—Storage Manager, BIOS configuration utility, command-line interface, and Adaptec Storage Manager remote storage manager

- **Features**—Online expansion, hot-swapping, hot spare disk support with automatic rebuild, SMART, RAID level migration, 128MB DDR memory

Figure 11.3   The Adaptec SCSI RAID 2130SLP PCI-X HBA.

Many of these features are also available on the Adaptec SATA RAID board, but the Adaptec SCSI RAID 2130SLP PCI-X HBA is a much higher-performing adapter. Key features of the board are not only its performance but its RAID support and software portfolio. Most people who don't have experience in SCSI make a purchase based solely on price and speed, but the management software is a critical feature that is often overlooked.

What should be obvious is that Ultra320 controllers stand alone; that is, they don't offer backward compatibility with previous forms of SCSI. This becomes obvious when you consider the wide variety of shapes and sizes that exists with regard to the various types of SCSI ports and cables that the technology has employed over the years. The Ultra160 Adaptec SCSI controller card comes with a 68-pin LVD SCSI (one internal and one external), a 68-pin Wide Ultra SCSI (internal), and a 50-pin Ultra SCSI connection (internal). The 50-pin Ultra SCSI connection gives this board the ability to preserve your investment in legacy SCSI devices. When purchasing a modern SCSI adapter, you should look for one of the following connection types:

- 68-pin connector, which supports fast/wide 16-bit adapters

- SCA 80-pin connector

- 50-pin high-density connector used by FAST SCSI

Most other connector types, in particular the 25-pin connector, are obsolete. You can find more information on SCSI connectors, including illustrations of each type, in Chapter 7.

Both of the aforementioned SCSI adapters are single-channel devices. Because it is 16-bit, that channel supports up to 15 devices. It is also possible to buy dual-channel SCSI boards, which support up to 30 SCSI devices. For onboard or captive drives inside a server, single-channel SCSI HBAs are desirable since they are both less expensive and easier to implement. When storage server vendors build dense arrays based on the SCSI interface, the preference is to us an HBA that supports a larger number of devices. In those instances, installation of a separate dual-channel board is the way to go.

There is yet one more RAID implementation you might find in low-end servers: a Zero Channel RAID (ZCR) card. This small credit card–sized card goes into a specially designed EMRL (embedded RAID logic, usually seen on Adaptec systems) slot in low form factor 1U or blade servers and lets you add RAID to a server without having to use a PCI slot to do so. Using ZCR is akin to adding a RAID ASIC (application-specific integrated circuit) to your server's motherboard.

Backplanes

RAID arrays, by their very nature, often contain a large number of disks. Those disks generate a lot of heat, take up a lot of room, and present a connection challenge to any RAID controller. The solution that most servers have opted for is to incorporate a *backplane* into the chassis.

A backplane is usually designed to abut a cage, with each drive inserted into the backplane using a carrier. Strictly speaking, the circuit board is the backplane, but it's the whole assembly that makes the system work. Figure 11.4 shows an example of a backplane, cage, and disk in a carrier from a Dell PowerEdge 2400.

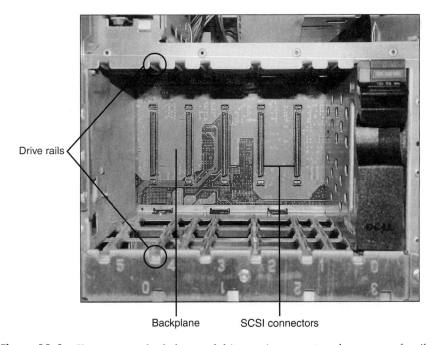

Figure 11.4   You can use a backplane and drive carrier to create a dense array of easily connected drives.

Note

The term *backplane* is used for any circuit board into which other devices can be attached or plugged. Backplanes have been used to describe all manner of things, even a server's motherboard. It is typical to find backplanes described as either active or passive. An active backplane has processing power of its own. A passive backplane offers only a mechanical connection.

Backplanes are helpful in that they allow for strategic placement of fans for heat dissipation, provide a secure and reliable electrical connection, and offer a system by which drives can be removed and added easily without having to open a server.

Redundancy

As mentioned earlier, servers may be rated based on their availability, or the amount of uptime they have. The more reliable a server has to be, the more "insurance" you have to buy for contingencies. Lots of things can go wrong on a server—everything from driver corruption to power supply problems or the failure of an add-in card. To create servers that are truly fault tolerant, vendors go to great lengths to create redundancy as well as seamless failover. In fault-tolerant systems like the ones that Stratus Computer (www.stratus.com) is famous for, essentially every component in the server is duplicated. In such a system, when a component of the server fails, the entire server fails over quickly and seamlessly.

Storage systems, disks, and disk controllers are the components that fail most often in servers. A disk is a mechanical device, and it runs hot and at high speed. You can make these components very reliable, but you can't completely eliminate failure. When you multiply the number of disks to expand your storage capacity, the potential for problems also goes up linearly. Even in servers that don't need to be highly available and can suffer some downtime, protecting your storage assets (that is, data) is paramount.

The popularization of inexpensive disk drive technology provided the impetus to create disk structures that could survive different types of failure, including data corruption, drive failures, host bus failures, and array failures. You do this by creating redundancy, which you can achieve in several different ways:

- If a drive fails, you can switch to another drive with exactly the same data, called a *mirror*.

- If your data spans more than one drive and a drive fails, you can reconstruct your data from additional parity data written to the volume that "fills in" the missing data, provided that the data is spread out evenly (that is, striped) across all the volumes in the array.

- If an HBA fails, you can switch to another HBA—usually one that is managing an array that is a mirror of the one attached to a failed array. This approach also works for array failure.

These are three very different approaches to three very different problems, yet all of them are grouped together under a concept called RAID. The redundancy discussed in the first case involves both hardware (a disk) and data (a data set). In the second case, the data set still exists, but hardware is added (a spare disk), and the data set is reestablished in its original form. The third case also substitutes redundant hardware and a redundant data set to recover from error. RAID can be relatively inexpensive (for example, replace a drive) or very expensive (for example, run duplicate or triplicate data systems for redundancy).

Introduction to RAID

RAID appeared on the scene in 1988, out of the work of Frank Hayes at University of California at Berkeley. As part of a graduate class in computer science, he and his students considered the different ways in which small hard drives could be configured and attached to a Macintosh to improve performance, redundancy, and other beneficial features. The resulting paper, titled "The Case for Redundant Arrays of Inexpensive Disks," argued that a collection of small disks operating together can outperform a single large disk, even one operating at breakneck speed, because the smaller seek paths and larger number of heads possible enhance performance.

The original RAID 1 was written in software and was followed by the higher-performance RAID 2 hardware implementation with redundancy. (These labels bear no relationship to the labels we use now for different RAID types.) You could pull a disk out of RAID 2 while the drives were up and running, which was novel at the time for small systems. (Many of these ideas had preexisting counterparts in the mainframe workspace.) The idea took off, and different types of RAID were proposed and named.

It wasn't long before people realized that although a single array of the small hard drives of the era was "inexpensive," multiple arrays of such drives was not. So the researchers in the field changed the *I* in RAID to the word *independent* instead of *inexpensive*. You can find both definitions in use today.

RAID leads us logically to the concept of storage virtualization, which we consider at the end of this chapter, in the section "Storage Virtualization." RAID as an underpinning storage virtualization tool gives a modern server powerful methods for managing data and can improve operation, availability, and performance immeasurably.

Table 11.3 lists the most popular RAID levels discussed in this chapter.

Table 11.3   Popular RAID Levels

RAID Level	Type	Requires	Fault Tolerance	Usage
RAID 0	Striped	2 drives	No	Graphics, games, non-server applications
RAID 1	Mirror or duplexing	2 drives	Can survive loss of one mirror	Financial and other high-availability applications
RAID 4	Independent disks with shared parity disk	4 drives	Good fault tolerance but slow rebuilds	Filers
RAID 5	Striped with distributed parity blocks	3 drives	Can survive loss of one disk	High-performance applications requiring high availability
RAID 10	Mirrored with striping	4 drives	Can survive the loss of a mirror	High-performance and fault-tolerant applications, but costly

JBODs: Concatenation

As described previously, JBOD is a method for obtaining a larger volume size out of a group of smaller-sized drives. This scheme concatenates the disks so that the addressing scheme extends or spans over the drives in the array, creating a virtual volume, as shown in Figure 11.5.

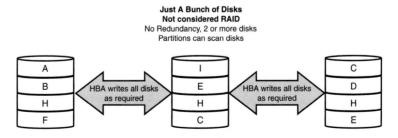

Figure 11.5   JBOD concatenates disks to form larger volumes. The letters on the disks indicate that partitions can be written on any disk and that these partitions are independent (no relationships to) of any others.

JBOD places no restrictions on the size of the drive, its type, its speed, or the bus that it's on. If your operating system can see the disk, you can create a JBOD with it. So you can consume whatever disk you have around with this arrangement.

JBOD isn't RAID, but it does require the use of a controller. Given that most any controller offers RAID of some kind, most people opt for a RAID solution instead of relying on a JBOD methodology. In Windows, for example, you could use the Disk Management snap-in of the MMC (formerly called the Disk Administrator) to create a JBOD. Creating a JBOD in the Disk Manager is just like creating individual partitions on multiple drives that your system can access. To create a JBOD, you do the following:

1. Attach the various drives to your controller and then boot your system.
2. Open the Disk Manager and right-click the first drive in your JBOD. Then select the Initialize Disk command.
3. If a wizard appears, select the size of the partition you want to create, select its file type, and set a drive label. If a wizard does not appear, right-click an unallocated section of the disk and select the Format command then specify the parameters of the partition you wish to create.
4. Repeat step 3 to initialize other disks in the JBOD. Then create the partitions you want.

JBOD doesn't get recommended very often, but because the fact that it is both cheap and easy to implement makes it popular in certain environments. With JBOD, when a disk fails, you can still recover the files on your working disks. However, to reestablish the volume, you need to restore from backup.

RAID 0: Striping, No Parity

RAID has come to be codified into several different levels, which are different configurations or techniques for creating data structures. Let's first look at RAID 0, which is the favorite disk structure for PC gamers who want to inexpensively achieve higher disk performance.

RAID 0 takes any number of disks—let's call that number D^n—and combines those disks into a single container or logical structure. The container is then formatted so that the data is "striped" across all the disks sequentially, as shown in Figure 11.6. As data is written, the disk head proceeds to write one set of blocks on one drive, followed by the head of the second disk writing the same set of blocks on the second, and so forth. At the end of the last drive in the array, the data writing continues on the first drive, picking up at the next set of blocks that followed the previous set. RAID 0 is sometimes referred to as a *striped set*.

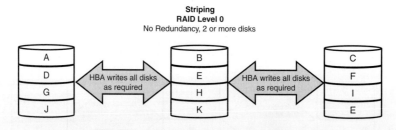

Figure 11.6 How striping works in a RAID 0 implementation. Notice that there is now a consecutive sequence of lettering, indicating that data is written in small sections, switching from disk to disk as those sections get filled. Striping improves performance by bringing more disk heads into play.

Note

Because RAID 0 must stripe across similar-sized areas of a disk, most RAID 0 implementations require that you use the same disk drive size in order to create the array. This isn't always the case, though; some HBAs or disk managers allow you to create the same-sized partition on each drive and stripe across that. Whenever possible, you should always opt for the solution that gives you the maximum amount of flexibility. Because the hard drive of today is the dinosaur of tomorrow, you want to be able to move up in capacity without having to swap out all your drives at once. So it pays to look carefully for the more forgiving RAID implementations.

For a small file, you might find that the data is on one single drive, but in most cases, you will find that the data is actually spread out across two or more drives, maybe even all the drives. For multifile operations, particularly in a multitasked environment, the data is actually spread out randomly among all the drives, and some operations can approach *n* times the performance of a single drive. Sometimes people use RAID 0 to split a collection of disks into a larger set of virtual disks.

RAID 0 imposes a slight performance penalty for write operations because the controller has to manage the move from one disk to another. When it comes to read operations, however, RAID 0 gives you a considerable performance enhancement because you can have multiple heads reading data on multiple disks at the same time, with each of them concurrently sending that data to the host controller. The smaller and more numerous the reads, the more performance is boosted. For large data files that are written sequentially across all the disks, RAID 0 doesn't offer much of a performance boost, even for read operations, because the file still has to be read sequentially, which negates the advantage of having more drive heads accessing the data. RAID 0 is helpful when you have a large NFS server with multiple disks or where the operating system limits you to a smaller number of drive letters, such as the 24-letter limit in Windows.

RAID 0 is the lowest form of RAID, and some people argue that it isn't RAID at all. There's no redundant data being written, and there's absolutely no data protection. You can't pull a disk out of RAID 0 because all disks are part of the data structure, although some RAID systems let you add a disk to RAID 0. In fact, because more disks participate in a single data structure, there is *n* times the MTBF that you will have a disk failure and run into trouble. There are also *n* times the likelihood that a cluster on a drive will fail, and so forth.

If you implement RAID and run into any kind of problem at all, you better be well backed up because you might have to re-create your RAID set and your volume to get back in business. RAID 0 is really "AID," or simply an association of independent disks, because it has no redundancy. Still, RAID 0 at least offers some performance enhancements, and for that reason it is considered RAID where JBOD is not.

RAID 1: Mirroring

RAID 1 is the simplest form of data redundancy you can have, and it is often used for small, entry-level RAID systems. In a RAID 1 configuration, your data is written in two places at essentially the same time, which is where the term *mirror* is derived. When you have a problem with one disk, you can break the mirror and switch over to the second copy on the other disk, which is presumably still functioning normally. When your hardware problem is fixed, usually because you've replaced the malfunctioning drive, you can add the first volume back and rebuild the mirror.

Caution

No version of RAID protects you from software errors; that's what backup and snapshots are for. You need to keep in mind that mirroring is only one form of redundancy, and it won't protect you if the nature of your hardware failure damages each drive in the array (fire or flood damage, for example). Mirroring your data is not a substitute for backing up data to some form of removable storage than can be securely stored.

Many dual-channel SCSI HBAs are specifically used to implement mirrored structures. A mirror can be made of part of a disk—perhaps a volume; or a mirror can be the simple duplication of one whole drive to another. In the former case, the mirror is almost always created and managed by either the operating system or a program running under the operating system. In the latter case, block copying is faster when done in hardware at the HBA.

RAID 1 provides no performance enhancement with either read or write operations. Depending on how mirroring is implemented and the robustness of your controller, most often mirroring doesn't affect your servers' performance at all. Most mirroring implementations done in hardware are fast enough that they don't have to buffer or cache content written to the second disk. Because your want your mirrored disk to be valid, there is some reading of the second disk to determine whether it has the same data at the same place as the first disk. Usually this data validation can be done in the background.

With RAID 1 you get full data protection against drive or array failure, albeit at a high price. If you have two HBAs, one connected to each array (an architecture called *duplexing*), RAID 1 also gives you protection against HBA failure. The cost of this protection is that you have duplicated an entire set of drives and perhaps a controller as well. RAID 1 is almost never implemented because there are more attractive options available with the same collection of storage system elements, as you will see when we discuss RAID 1+0 in a moment.

Business Continuance Volumes

In server technology, it is essential to protect a corporate database that is the core asset of your business. When that database resides on a volume on a storage server, you can create a duplicate volume and then use that duplicate volume to create other volumes if you like. EMC pioneered this approach as a data protection technique on its enterprise-class Symmetrix storage server line, and it called the mirrored or cloned volumes Business Continuance Volumes (BCVs). Figure 11.7 shows the principle behind mirroring and BCVs.

BCVs offer several important advantages. The primary advantage is that you can seamlessly switch over to a BCV when you have a problem with your primary data set, with no downtime that is perceptible to your customers. However, that isn't the only advantage that a BCV offers.

When you split off a BCV from the original data set, you have stopped synchronizing it with the primary volume. You have created a snapshot of your volume in time. Considering that a large volume can take many hours, even days, to back up to tape, you now have a data structure that you can use to back up to a tape library offline. Here's where things get really interesting. If you have a duplicate storage server and create a BCV on it, when you split that BCV off, you then have a test bed you can use to do development work on. More often than not, a large corporation will add additional identical storage servers connected by a LAN (a SAN, actually) or a WAN, in case of either server or site failure, to take over the operation.

A fully loaded, high-end Symmetric server can represent a $1 to $2 million investment for a multi-terabyte system, so the cost of the EMC servers is very often more than the cost of the buildings that surround them. The price of redundancy can be high, but the price of not being redundant can be incalculable.

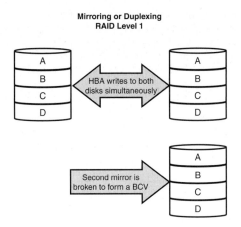

Figure 11.7   A mirrored volume and BCVs.

This technique of BCVs isn't only for the Exxon-Mobils of the world. Regardless of the size of your server, if you can mirror a volume, you can create a BCV. So it pays to think in these terms even if you can't make the solution as seamless as it is in larger enterprise environments.

RAID 10 (or 1+0): Mirroring with Striping

RAID 10, also called RAID 1+0, combines the RAID techniques you've just learned about in the two previous sections in a combination that some people describe as either *nested* or *stacked* RAID levels. RAID 10 gives you the redundancy of a mirrored volume or drive along with the performance benefit of a striped array.

Because RAID 1+0 is nothing more than RAID 1 and RAID 0 combined, you will find that all RAID HBAs, from the cheapest ones you can find to the most expensive ones, offer RAID 1+0. Many people refer to this RAID level as RAID 10 or *mirroring with striping* to reflect the order in which the RAID levels are applied.

Because RAID 10 is both high performance and fully redundant, this particular configuration is recommended for high-transaction-volume applications where you need performance and fast failover to a redundant data set should something fail on the first array. RAID 10 is one of the most popular RAID levels implemented. Large database servers, messaging servers, and webservers often implement RAID 10 for their disk arrays.

You can think of RAID 1+0 as being formed by applying to your physical disks a first layer of RAID (mirroring, in this case). Then you overlay the second RAID level, which stripes data across the mirrored array.

RAID 0+1: Striping with Mirroring

You might ask what the difference is between RAID 1+0 (or RAID 10) and the level of RAID you would create if you striped first and then applied a mirror—or if, indeed, there is any difference at all. There is a difference, and this other RAID level is referred to as RAID 0+1 or *striping with mirroring*. (You usually don't see RAID 0+1 abbreviated as RAID 01 because there is concern that people will get this abbreviation mixed up with RAID 1.)

Figure 11.8 illustrates the difference between RAID 10 and RAID 0+1. In this example, you have a number of disks (D^n) arranged in two equal-sized mirrored volumes. Consider what happens when a drive fails. In RAID 10, you would break the mirror, replace the disk, and rebuild the mirror. A RAID

10 array can survive both the loss of one mirror (any number of disks) and disk failures in both arrays, as long as the failed disks in the two arrays are not the same failed members of the sets. That is, in a four-disk array where A1B1 is mirrored to A2B2, and the As and Bs have the same data, you could fail A1 and B2 or B1 and A2, but not A1 and A2 or B1 and B2.

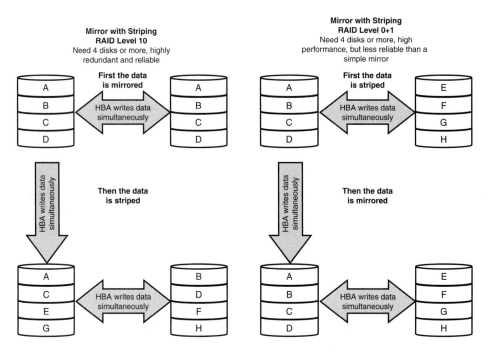

Figure 11.8   RAID 10 versus RAID 0+1. In this figure, the top two disks are A1 and A2, and the bottom two disks are B1 and B2.

Now let's consider RAID 0+1, where first you stripe and then you mirror. When you lose a disk in this configuration, one of your RAID 0 sets has been lost. When you break the mirror and add your new disk, the remaining disks in the stripe no longer correspond to the disks in the other striped mirror. The result is that you actually need to start from scratch and either rebuild the complete stripe from your working drives in the damaged mirror (plus the new one) or, as is often the case, start with a complete set of new drives that match the damaged set being replaced. In this circumstance, RAID 0+1 has to write more data than RAID 1+0.

Writing data is strictly a mechanical process, and except with very large volumes, you may not care if you have to rebuild the entire stripe. However, while RAID 10 survives the loss of disks in both arrays, RAID 0+1 does not. When you lose two or more drives on both mirrors in RAID 0+1 you can no longer rely on RAID to get you going again, and you have to reestablish your array from backups (and invariably some new data is lost). Nothing is perfect in this world, but RAID 10 is a little more perfect than RAID 0+1.

RAID 5: Striping with Parity

RAID 5 is the third most popular RAID level used in the industry. RAID 5 performs block-level striping across the disk set of a volume and writes some redundant information, called *parity data*, that lets you reconstruct missing data if a disk fails. The parity data is written across all the disks so that the array can survive a single disk failure and still be rebuilt. RAID 5 doesn't offer quite the performance of RAID 1 because of the overhead of reading and writing parity data, but it provides some redundancy that you don't find in RAID 1 without having to duplicate the volume as part of a mirror. Thus, if you like, you can think of RAID 5 as poor man's RAID 10.

Let's look a little more closely at how RAID 5 works and what parity is all about. You need three or more disks to create a RAID 5 volume, as shown in Figure 11.9. A block of data is subdivided by partitioning software into sectors, and the number of blocks is determined by the capacity of the disk. The number of sectors is a variable that you can define—usually 256 or fewer sectors. As each block of data is written to disk, the RAID 5 algorithm calculates a parity block that corresponds to the data and then writes the parity block on the same stripe, but not on the same disk. If stripe n in a three-disk RAID 5 volume has the parity block on disk 1, then stripe $n+1$ would have the parity block on disk 2, stripe $n+2$ would place the parity block on disk 3, so that by stripe $n+3$, the parity block would be returned to disk 1 again to start the cycle over, creating a distributed parity block arrangement.

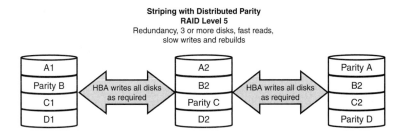

Figure 11.9 How RAID 5 works. In this three-disk array, data is written in small sections on sequential disks, with parity data alternating on disks from stripe to stripe.

RAID 5 imposes some overhead on write operations because in an n disk system, $1/n$ of the data that is written isn't going to be anything you can use, except in the hopefully rare case in which you need to rebuild a RAID 5 array. RAID 5 requires at least three disks because if one of a two disk RAID 5 arrays fails, you would lose half of your data set. The third disk in the RAID 5 set provides the extra redundancy you need to make the system work. To really make RAID 5 perform, you want to have more than three disks. Although there is a write operation penalty, RAID 5 doesn't impose a read operation penalty on your disk I/O because the parity information is ignored. You still have the same benefit of multiple heads on multiple disks reading data at the same time.

Upon a read operation, RAID 5 performs a cyclic redundancy check (CRC) calculation to see if the data is valid. CRC is an algorithm that reads the data and writes a sum, based on the data it contains. When an error is detected, RAID 5 can read the parity block in that stripe, locate the sector with the error, and use the data to reconstruct the sector with the incorrect checksum. This process usually occurs on-the-fly, without your noticing it (though it will post an appropriate error message). If a whole disk fails, RAID 5 can rebuild the missing disk from the data contained in the remaining disks, and it can even do so automatically to a hot spare. In most implementations, RAID 5 arrays can continue to collect data even while rebuilding a failed disk, although at a considerably slower rate because the disk heads are busy with the rebuild. RAID 5 can sustain the loss of a single drive without data loss.

RAID 5 can be intelligent. Some RAID 5 systems have predictive functions that can determine whether a disk is *likely to fail* and initiate a rebuild based on that information. Data such as inaccessible clusters, hot spots on the disk, and other factors can be an indication of an impending disk failure. That predictive capability can be put to good use. In some instances, RAID 5 systems can analyze disk activity, figure out where your hot spots are, and move data around to lessen the stress on that area of the disk as well as to optimize data locations to improve disk head access. It's no wonder that RAID 5 is so popular. It really has a lot of things going for it.

RAID 5 works best when it is used with from 4 to 15 drives. Beyond 15 drives, RAID 5's performance drops, and the risk of data loss increases to unacceptable levels. RAID 5 gives you a slight write penalty (less so with more drives), enough redundancy to recover from a disk failure, and read performance similar to what you can achieve with RAID 0. One of the main attractions of RAID 5 is that you get some of the benefits of mirroring (RAID 1) without having to duplicate the entire disk set of the array.

There are two dual-level, or stacked, RAID 5 arrays in use today. The first is called RAID 1.5 or RAID 15. Here, the first array is mirrored to a second, and each array is written and striped with distributed parity. With RAID 15 you get the performance of reading from two drives at a time (one in each mirror) as well the performance of being able to write continuously (as with RAID 1). RAID 15 is considered to offer high performance, especially for streaming and sequential reads, fast writes, and redundancy. The cost of RAID 5 is high, even greater than that of RAID 10. Most people who can afford RAID 15 opt for RAID 10 in order to achieve faster write performance.

The second type of stacked RAID 5 is RAID 50. With RAID 50 a drive can fail in each of the RAID 5 arrays contained in the array. RAID 50 offers enhanced write performance, but as with all RAID levels that can rebuild an array on-the-fly, you see significant performance degradation when a rebuild is taking place. RAID 50, like RAID 1, is expensive to build. Not only do you have the redundancy of the mirrored drives, but you also have the redundancy of the parity drives with each RAID 5 array. A similar RAID 0+5 type of array is also defined, but although both of these RAID levels are secure and perform well, neither is in wide use.

Nonstandard Single-Level RAID Arrays

A few additional single-level RAID array types have been defined and find occasional use in the industry. Let's take a brief look at them before moving on to nonstandard dual-level RAID and proprietary RAID level definitions described later in this chapter, in the section "Miscellaneous RAID Types."

RAID 2: Bit-Level Striping with Redundancy

RAID 2 is similar to RAID 0 in that it uses a striping technique, but instead of striping blocks, RAID 2 stripes data at the bit level. RAID 2 includes redundancy (which RAID 0 doesn't) by applying a hammering code to determine the validity of the data contained in the array. In RAID 2 the RAID controller synchronizes the data set so that it can write to all disks in the array simultaneously. RAID 2 is not currently in use in any vendor's products.

RAID 3: Bit-Level Striping with Parity

RAID 3 is similar to RAID 5 in that it stripes data, but it does so at a byte level and uses a dedicated parity disk, which reduces processing somewhat. You need at least three drives and a reasonably powerful RAID controller to get good performance out of RAID 3. You won't find RAID 3 created in software because it requires a hardware implementation to obtain reasonable performance.

RAID 3 combines striping with parity, which imparts a performance penalty on any random disk activity (both read and write operations). Thus you don't find RAID 3 used in high-performance transactional systems. Like RAID 5, RAID 3 can survive the loss of a drive in the array, and most implementations also support hot-swaps and automatic rebuilds. Unlike with other RAID levels, rebuilding a lost drive in the array doesn't impart a large performance penalty; however, it does take a long time to rebuild the missing drive because all data across the array must be rebuilt.

RAID 3 is rather similar to RAID 4, and most people implementing this type of solution opt for RAID 4.

RAID 4: Block-Level Synchronized Striping with Parity

RAID 4 is another RAID level that does striping, but it does so at a block level, with a dedicated parity disk. RAID 4 synchronizes data across all disks in the array and offers outstanding read performance for long sequential read operations. Thus RAID 4 finds favor in streaming media applications, or when large files, such as prepress files, are used. In this regard, RAID 4 is very similar to RAID 3 and has the same benefits and penalties. Figure 11.10 illustrates the difference between RAID 3 and 4.

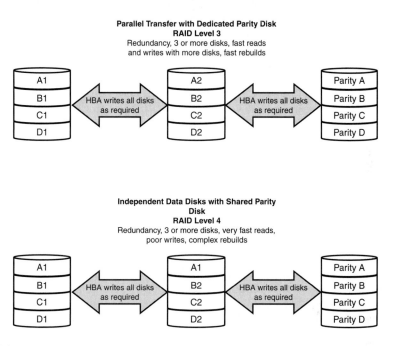

Figure 11.10 RAID levels 3 and 4.

Along with excellent read transaction and aggregate transfer rates, RAID 4 offers little disk loss to parity information storage. The disadvantages are that (like RAID 3) RAID 4 sustains very poor write transaction and aggregate transfer rates, and its block read transfer rate isn't much better than what you would achieve with a single disk. Rebuilds impose a low performance penalty on this type of array but take a long time to process.

Some fairly large arrays are written with RAID 4, even though RAID 4 controllers are rather difficult to design. The most well-known proponent of RAID 4 is Network Appliance, which has pioneered the use of this RAID level in its large FAS series filers. (See www. netapp.com/tech_library/3001.html for a detailed description of how RAID 4 is applied.)

RAID 6: Independent Disks with Dual Parity

RAID 6 is very similar to RAID 5, but it has an extra method of distributed parity, called a *Reed-Solomon* parity scheme. In RAID 6 the data is striped by blocks across the array in the same manner as you would find in RAID 5, but in this case, a second set of parity data is then written over all drives. This RAID level requires the use of two additional drives to write the parity information on (as shown in Figure 11.11), but it provides for both outstanding fault tolerance and high performance. RAID 6 can sustain multiple drive failures.

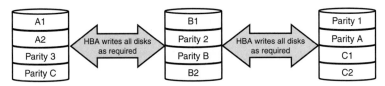

Independent Data Disks with Two
Independent Parity Stripes
RAID Level 6
Highly redundant, 3 or more disks, fast reads
and writes. Similar to RAID 5 (but slower)
Slow rebuilds

Figure 11.11 A RAID 6 array.

RAID 6 may come into wider use over time, but at the moment, RAID 6 is found on very few RAID controllers, and those are usually on the expensive end of the cost spectrum because the design needed to compute the additional parity information is hard to engineer and requires a high-performance design. However, with a fast controller, it is possible to use RAID 6 to approach RAID 5 performance with much better fault tolerance and still at a much lower cost than mirroring allows. To get the most out of a RAID 6 array, you have to deploy it with more drives than you would a RAID 5 array. At a minimum, you need three drives, as shown in Figure 11.11, but performance will be slow. Most RAID 6 implementations choose to use a minimum of four or five drives so that there is less of a performance and disk usage penalty for the redundant RAID information.

Miscellaneous RAID Types

The vast majority of RAID implementations that you will encounter use one of the levels described previously. A few other types of RAID do exist, though:

- **RAID 7**—This RAID level is a proprietary design of Storage Computer Corporation (see www.storage.com/metadot/index.pl). It is similar to RAID 3 and 4, but it adds a data cache, which improves performance somewhat.

- **RAID S or Parity RAID**—This is a proprietary RAID array scheme that appears in EMC's Symmetrix storage servers. To create RAID S, you create a volume on each physical hard drive and then combine the volumes together to create parity information.

- **Matrix RAID**—The term *Matrix RAID* was part of the term coined as part of the Intel ICH6BR BIOS. Matrix RAID partitions a drive with half of the drive assigned as RAID 0 and the other half as RAID 1. You get the performance of RAID 0, and you get redundancy in case your RAID 0 partition fails. Matrix RAID doesn't really provide fault tolerance, and it is really aimed at small, single-disk workstations and home users. Because this isn't a configuration that can survive a disk failure, it isn't really RAID.

Software Versus Hardware RAID

You may think of RAID as a hardware feature because it uses HBAs and disk drives. Oftentimes, RAID doesn't even require your server's operating system to be created or managed because that process is managed by an ASIC on the controller. But RAID isn't a hardware feature: It is essentially a software feature. When you use hardware RAID, the software for RAID is embedded on an ASIC and presented as part of the controller's BIOS. An ASIC is a chip that contains custom programming that supports an application.

Software RAID implements the various RAID functions by using your server's CPUs in place of a RAID controller's ASIC. There is some performance penalty involved in doing so, but RAID is a low-level disk function and doesn't require much processing in order to implement. Today's CPUs are so powerful that software RAID is often faster or at least no slower than the RAID you can achieve with dedicated hardware. When we talk about hardware RAID, in essence we are talking about using a controller that performs RAID offloading.

The best-known example of software RAID is the Veritas Volume Manager, which is available for both Windows and Sun servers. Light versions of the Veritas Volume Manager have appeared in Windows for a while now. Windows 2000 had it in the form of the Microsoft Logical Disk Manager (LDM), which is now the Disk Management snap-in of the MMC. Nearly every operating system offers some form of software RAID. The Linux Software RAID program (see www.tldp.org/HOWTO/Software-RAID-HOWTO.html) and the Solstice Disksuite let you add software RAID to Linux and Solaris, respectively.

Managing RAID

RAID creates an abstraction of the physical disks involved and creates data structures that can be implemented independently of hardware. The prototype RAID systems were built with SCSI, but as you have already seen, you can build RAID arrays with ATA, SCSI, Fibre Channel, and other storage interfaces. In SCSI, as you have learned, the bus can connect to multiple disk drives identified to the bus as LUNs. A LUN is really a connection point to the controller, something that can take part of your array.

Because you now know what RAID is, let's take a look at what you have to do to create, manage, and rebuild or modify a RAID array. We will talk generally using a Windows SATA array as an example, but the principles apply to all RAID systems.

Creating New Arrays

To create a new array, you need to have an HBA or a RAID controller that supports the kind of RAID array you want to create. If that RAID is onboard, you might need to enable the controller in the BIOS. Chances are that if the HBA is an add-in board, you will need to install it.

Implementing RAID involves creating a *container*, which is nothing more than an object that contains the specific LUNs that you assign to it. You create a container in the RAID software. After a container is created, you can partition the container by using partitioning software and then apply formatting to create a file system.

Partitioning is most often done in the operating system, but without the existing container, your operating system may not even recognize that the hard drives are there to work with. In order to partition the storage that is assigned to the container, you need to have an appropriate driver so that the container is recognized. That driver is specific to the operating system being used and to the RAID chip that contains the RAID software that is managing the container. With the correct driver in place, you can proceed to partition and format the storage assigned to the container from the array of disks.

To install your RAID components and create a container, you need to do the following:

1. Turn off your computer and install your RAID controller in the appropriate bus slot (PCI, PCI-X, and so on).

2. Install all the hard drives that you want to be part of the array, attaching them to the bus interface with the RAID controller as follows:

   - If you are creating an IDE RAID array, usually all your drives should be set to master. You might need to consult your motherboard's RAID documentation to see what is required.

   - For SATA drives, there is no master or slave; you simply install the drive.

   - For SCSI drives, you set the SCSI ID for each drive, making sure that each is unique and that the entire SCSI chain is properly terminated.

3. Boot your computer, and if your RAID controller is an onboard controller, press Delete, F1, or whatever other keystroke takes you into your BIOS. (If your RAID controller is an add-on board, proceed to step 5.)

4. Go to the screen for peripheral devices (or a similar screen) and enable your RAID controller. Figure 11.12 shows a screen for an ASUS A7X8N-E motherboard, which offers both IDE and SATA onboard RAID.

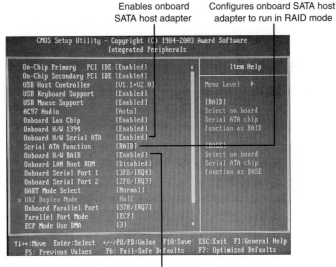

Enables onboard SATA host adapter

Configures onboard SATA host adapter to run in RAID mode

Enables hardware RAID array

Figure 11.12 To enable onboard RAID, you might need to turn it on in the BIOS.

5. Save your changes and exit the BIOS.

6. With either an onboard or add-on RAID controller, start your computer and watch during its boot cycle as the different buses are enumerated. The BIOS of your RAID controller appears and indicates which keystroke to press to enter its BIOS.

7. With the BIOS onscreen, select the drives you want to be part of your array; then use the Create Array command to create a container. You are then asked to enter a name for the array.

   Figure 11.13 shows the BIOS for the SATA RAID controller on a motherboard whose BIOS is shown in Figure 11.12. This controller offers a limited set of RAID options: 0, 1, and 1+0. Your RAID controller's BIOS may offer other RAID options. In controller BIOSs, you can delete arrays, check the health of an array, break mirrors, and so forth.

8. Save your container definition and reboot your system.

What happens next depends on your particular operating system and your RAID controller. Some operating systems automatically recognize a new container, and some do not. If you are installing an operating system into this array (and even if you are not), you need the device driver that lets your RAID controller talk to your operating system. Your motherboard or controller should come with the driver on disk, or you can go to the vendor's website to get the most current driver. You shouldn't count on your operating system to provide the correct driver.

In the case of the SATA RAID controller used as an example here, the Windows Setup installation routine refuses to recognize the container. As far as Windows is concerned, the drives added are simply raw disk. So in order to install Windows into this container, you can use FDISK on a DOS 6.22 disk or another partitioning program to create a partition on the container. At that point, Windows XP can recognize the container's partition and make the entire array available to the installer.

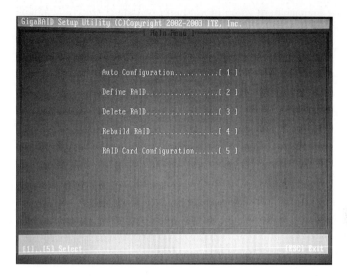

Figure 11.13 A RAID controller's BIOS.

In creating a RAID volume, the two places people get into trouble is that they forget about creating the container and they use the wrong driver. Either can lead to the dreaded "disk not found" warning.

RAID Maintenance

Although RAID protects your data, there are still issues that arise. Most drives don't fail at once. Usually, a drive starts to fail, and a cluster here or there becomes corrupted. When there are a few bad clusters, you can remap your drive, but when the number of bad clusters reaches a certain point, it is best to replace the drives. Depending on your RAID hardware and software, some of this work might be done for you, or you might have to do it manually.

All advanced RAID array systems offer some form of protection in the form of routines that are referred to as *disk scrubbers*. A disk scrubber checks the data on an array to see if it can be read correctly. It also checks the parity data to see if it is still valid. Disk scrubbing goes on in the background, and when errors are reported, those errors are fixed by remapping the data or correcting the data written.

Damaged areas of the disk are cordoned off by a disk scrubber, just as they would be when you run Check Disk in the operating system. With many RAID systems, you can simply restart the array and go through an exhaustive diagnostic.

When you purchase your RAID controller or the program that creates and manages software RAID, one of the things you are paying for is the management utilities that come with that system. Among the features you are looking for are the following:

- Event tracking and problem resolution
- Online volume expansion
- Performance analysis and, if possible, disk utilization optimization

- Automatic disk replacement when failure is detected, if possible
- Data replication
- Multipathing management when more than one data channel is available to your server (as in dual-channel RAID or Fibre Channel)
- Data checking (disk scrubbing)

Rebuilding Failed Arrays

Eventually, all components fail, and disks and RAID controllers are certainly no exception. While these are long-lived components, they are high-performance ones, too, often operating at extreme speeds or high voltages. Mechanical devices fail more often than electrical devices, and really that's what RAID is aimed to protect against. Let's take a look at some of the scenarios for damaged RAID arrays and how you go about rebuilding them.

First of all, there is no cure for a damaged RAID 0 array. The best you can hope for is to rebuild the array and restore your data from a backup. That means that if you are running a RAID 0 array, as many small workstations and home users do, that array should have attached a multilevel backup scheme with a real-time backup system. However, RAID 0 isn't typically used on servers, so we don't need to discuss this further.

RAID 1 data mirroring can survive a failed disk. To re-create a failed mirror, you need to follow these steps:

1. When your operating system or RAID BIOS indicates that a disk has failed, open the volume management utility. For example, if you have created a mirror by using the Windows Disk Management snap-in, open that utility.

2. Select the Break Mirror command or its equivalent to split the mirror and retain the healthy drive. People often use this function to create disks as backups or for testing, similar to BCVs.

3. Shut down your server.

4. Remove the failed or broken mirror drive. This is optional if the drive to be removed is healthy and was simply separated.

5. Add the new drive and restart your computer.

6. Open your disk management tool and format the new disk.

7. Select the healthy drive and use the Add Mirror command (or its equivalent). Depending on your utility, the process may begin immediately, proceed in the background, or be scheduled for another time. The mirror reestablishes itself when this step is complete.

In many instances, a mirror breaks because a disk gets disconnected and is no longer synchronized. You need to reconnect the drive and resynchronize the two drives so that the mirror is reestablished. Usually, this is a two-step process: Issue a Repair Mirror command and then issue a Resynchronize command. Whereas resynchronization may not be a long or processor-intensive operation, creating an entirely new mirror drive generally is. You might want to re-create the mirror at a time of low activity.

When a RAID 5 array fails, the procedure for repairing the array isn't much different from the procedure you saw earlier for RAID 1. However, most systems that offer RAID 5 support employ the use of a hot spare and rebuild the array for you automatically. Chances are you won't have to do anything except live though a period of poor server performance while the missing member of the array is rebuilt.

Storage Virtualization

Before we leave the topic of drives and RAID arrays, it is worth pausing a moment to see where all this technology is leading us. As noted earlier, modern operating systems abstract the data stored on a disk from the actual physical disk by creating named entities called volumes. The intent is to provide a means for moving data around in the server as needed.

There are many reasons you might want to perform a data migration, moving a volume from one place to another. Here are a few of them:

- You have just built a speedy new array and want to get better performance.
- Your array is failing and you have to move the data.
- You need a copy of your volume to perform testing on.
- You want to bring a new, more powerful server online and move your data onto that server.
- You want to move your volume elsewhere to improve capacity utilization.
- You need to move the data to another location in order to perform disaster recovery.

There are many good reasons to move your data or to have the ability to do so. Storage virtualization is a technology that creates a pool of storage that can be managed and made available to network clients and other servers. Virtualization software makes it possible to move volumes around from place to place. SANs and virtualization are powerful tools that make servers even more powerful. Let's now turn to Chapter 12, which explores the topic of SANs for creating distributed storage managed by and stored on specialized servers.

CHAPTER 12

Storage Area Networks

A storage area network (SAN) is a network of managed, shared, and distributed storage assets—a network of storage servers, if you will. You might infer that a SAN must have its own dedicated network, and for the most part, you would be correct, at least historically. As described in the Chapter 11, "Disk Subsystems," SANs are built with Fibre Channel switches and hubs, and the nodes are linked with either fiber-optic or coaxial cabling.

That storage network interfaces to a local area network (LAN) of servers and clients, where each server and client on the LAN connects to the SAN either through a file server or with a connection to the SAN itself. As Ethernet has gotten faster, and as the storage industry has found ways to permit hosts to transfer large amounts of data by offloading the processing required, there has been more and more interest in eliminating separate storage networks and unifying a whole networking enterprise. There's no hard-and-fast definition of what constitutes a SAN—only that it achieves the desired aim of making storage available to clients.

Most SANs are built to network vast amounts of storage data. When you consider that a large EMC, Hitachi Data Systems, IBM, or Hewlett-Packard storage server can contain hundreds of terabytes of data stored on as many as a couple hundred disk drives and that many storage deployments network *petabytes* of data, SANs make a lot of sense. There's an enormous amount of money invested in storage (often it's more than 50% of the IT budget), and it's important to get the most out of that investment.

Note

For a more in-depth discussion of SANs, see *Using Storage Area Networks Special Edition.*

In an era when you can create a RAID array of more than a terabyte from three 400GB hard drives or purchase a network attached storage (NAS) appliance such as LaCie's Bigger Disk Extreme (1.8TB for $1,700), the time has come to consider applying the principles of storage area networking to your own servers and your own network. If you find yourself backing up computers at night in order to keep your LAN from being saturated by backup traffic, or if you find that your client systems have difficulty getting needed files from a central repository—let alone finding them in the first place—you are an ideal candidate for this technology.

SAN Topologies

Figure 12.1 shows the four different topologies you can use to connect to storage. The simplest topology is not a network topology at all but a straightforward bus connection. Here you connect to a disk within your server, which is also called *captive disk*. In high-performance servers, SCSI is the dominant interconnect technology. For low-end servers, captive disk tends to be connected using Serial ATA (SATA) or parallel ATA (PATA) drives. Fibre Channel and Gigabit Ethernet (GigE) rarely play in this space.

You can also connect to external storage by using a point-to-point topology, and that's called direct attached storage (DAS). Many people refer to internal disk as part of DAS, and the two are indeed rather similar.

SCSI dominates the DAS marketplace, but Fibre Channel is also used in many cases. There are fewer instances of DAS using GigE, but that's probably because very-high-speed GigE has only been available for a short period of time. DAS also isn't really a networking topology.With dual-homed Fibre Channel NICs you can create a loop topology, the same topology used in IBM's Token Ring network. A Fibre Channel loop of this kind is called a Fibre Channel Arbitrated Loop or (FC-AL).

With 126 theoretical nodes and 100MBps per channel, FC-AL dominates the market for this kind of topology. The advantages of FC-AL are that it is self-configuring, allows for hot-swapping of devices, and can use the same software as SCSI. With coaxial runs of 30 meters and fiber runs of up to 10km, these advantages have kept Fibre Channel in play, particularly in this simple kind of network. It's not necessary to daisy-chain together a Fibre Channel loop; you can achieve the same result by using a Fibre Channel hub.

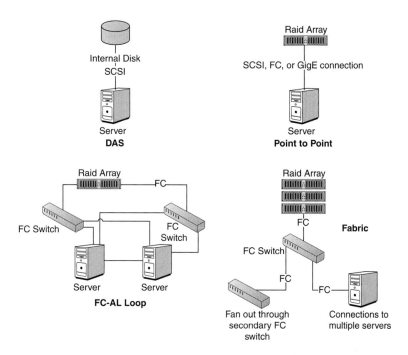

Figure 12.1   Four different storage connection topologies: DAS, point-to-point, loop (with and without a hub), and a fabric topology.

The main problems with Fibre Channel in terms of storage networking are that it is relatively expensive and that it requires some specific expertise that most network administrators don't normally develop. For those reasons, desktop vendors have been promoting FireWire (IEEE 1394) and high-speed USB as desktop alternatives for small bus storage networks. Both of these alternatives are backbones and not loops, and neither offers the fault tolerance or performance of Fibre Channel. No other technology is implemented as a loop structure.

The last topology you find in SANs is a fabric technology. Nearly all modern SANs are built using a fabric connecting Fibre Channel or GigE together using a switch. The advantage of the fabric architecture is that it offers the most flexibility as well as the easiest manageability. Storage APIs located at the switch can act like a traffic cop, which gives the fabric topology a significant advantage over other topologies. When you build a fabric from Fibre Channel, you are creating two separate networks: an out-of-band Fibre Channel network for storage and an in-band Ethernet network for hosts and clients. However, when you build a network using an Ethernet technology, there is only one network for all system devices. This fact has led some people to suggest that the term *storage area network* should be reserved for the dual-network type of solution, whereas the term *systems area network* should be used when all devices are on the same wire protocol (Ethernet). Perhaps this is just semantics, but it is worth noting.

It is worth spending a moment considering how a fabric architecture influences your decision about where to focus your management efforts. A fabric has three intelligent devices: the host or server, the switch, and the storage server. Software can run on any one of these devices, so even if you are viewing the performance of your SAN devices from a host, it may actually be the routines at the switch that are doing the probing and collecting. The host-based software is simply displaying the data. Deciding what kind of software you buy and where your control and management functions for a SAN take place is a fundamental decision. It can be the difference between purchasing a very high-end storage array or a cheaper one, a fully managed switch or an unmanaged switch, and so on. Unfortunately, there are no right and wrong answers here. Each of these three SAN devices has advantages and disadvantages from a management standpoint, so your conclusion may be based entirely on the hardware you already have or are committed to using.

Is a SAN Right for You?

It's best not to think of SANs as being built from any one particular recipe, but instead to think about the list of characteristics your storage deployment requires. Here's a short list of the most important criteria:

- **Can you manage with a simple loop or ring network architecture, or do you need to have the flexibility of a fabric architecture?** Although it's cheaper to build a loop topology, most people opt to build a switched fabric one.

- **Do you require that your storage assets be on their own dedicated network?** A SAN with its own dedicated network is what is referred to as an *out-of-band* network. The LAN that the SAN is connected to is then referred to as the *in-band* network. The two can be managed independently. While creating and managing two separate networks adds both cost and complexity, there are strong performance and security reasons that make a dual-band network solution a very practical solution.

- **How and from where will you manage your storage assets?** In a SAN fabric, it is possible to manage your SAN at your server, at the switch, using an appliance, and even with some storage servers at the storage server itself. Many management programs are now browser based. There is no right or wrong answer to this question, but it is part of your guiding philosophy.

- **What standards will you choose to embrace?** For many years, SANs were recognized as difficult to connect up. Many vendors' devices didn't work with other ones on the market. Because companies tended to create SANs from islands of storage, SANs are often a "Noah's Ark" of servers. It's better now—but not necessarily easy. There are hard choices to make, ones that require you to make good guesses. Mistakes are very expensive to fix, and many aren't even fixable. This reality causes information technology (IT) managers many sleepless nights and often results in SANs being installed by a single vendor—a "captive SAN," if you like.

- **Are you starting from scratch, or are you integrating existing assets?** This criterion speaks to the amount of freedom you have to choose components for your SAN.

- **Do you have a budget?** A SAN is a major capital acquisition that requires an ongoing commitment. Your budget is your eventual limitation on what is possible.

Where to Start with a SAN

What is the minimum investment you can make to create a SAN? All SANs have three common elements:

- **Storage servers**—File servers, NAS, or intelligent arrays
- **Connection device**—Switches, hubs, and so on
- **Transport media**—Fibre Channel, Ethernet, and so on

If you simplify it to just those items, they can form the basis of a nascent SAN. Indeed, it is possible to buy products such as QLogic's SAN-in-a-Box, which is currently packaged under the name SAN Connectivity Kit (see Figure 12.2). The 2GB SAN Connectivity Kit 3000 (see www.qlogic.com/simplify/sck3000.asp) bundles the following:

- An 8-port SANbox 5200 switch
- SANblade 2340 HBAs (with optical interface)
- Four LC 5M fiber-optic cables
- A portfolio of HBA and switch software managers and device APIs

Figure 12.2   QLogic's SAN Connectivity Kit 3000 is the successor to a product called SAN-in-a-Box.

Mix in your own storage server with the QLogic kit, and you have all the ingredients needed to create a small fabric SAN at an attractive price. QLogic bundles this package with instructions that allow an IT professional, even one unfamiliar with these technologies, an easy entry into this technology.

SANs and Standards

The problems with SANs are that there are too many standards, and very often the standards aren't standard at all. Many "standards" are proprietary or are limited to a few vendors, confusing, and don't play well with others. Storage networking's vocabulary is a veritable alphabet soup.

The standards problem—or, really, the lack of real standards—has been recognized as the single biggest issue facing the storage industry. This has led to the formation of industry organizations and working groups to address the problem. Notable among them are the Storage Networking Industry Association (www.snia.org) and the Fibre Channel Industry Association (FCIA; www.fibrechannel.org), but there are many others. These associations try to standardize the different technologies by sponsoring "plugfests," running conferences (Storage Networking World, for example), and seeing that the work of their members is published and publicized. (A plugfest is a meeting of vendors where their equipment, hardware, and software are connected together to check their interoperability.)

Table 12.1 lists some of the most prominent storage industry trade associations and standards committees. Their websites are great places to learn about current and future storage and server networking technologies.

Table 12.1 Storage and Server Trade Industry Organizations and Associations

Organization	Website	Purpose
AIT Forum	www.aitape.com	Sets the standard for software and hardware vendors using this enterprise tape format.
Blade Systems Alliance	www.bladesystems.org	Is a trade organization for small form factor blade servers.
Blue-ray Disk Association	www.blu-raydisk.com	Sets standards for this type of high-capacity optical disc drives. See also www.blu-ray.com/info/ as the bladesystems.org is a German-language site.
DAFS Collaborative	N/A	Creates the standards for the Direct Access File System.
DAT Manufacturers Group	www.datmgm.com	Sets the standard for DDS/DAT tape.
DVD Forum	www.dvdforum.org	Promotes standards for optical disc drives and discs.
Fibre Channel Industry Association	www.fibrechannel.org	Sets standards associated with Fibre Channel networking and components.
HDSA	N/A	Promotes multidrive devices, connectivity, and their relationship to multimedia applications.
IBTA	www.infinibandta.org	Sets the standards for the InfiniBand high-speed bus.
LTO	www.lto.org	Sets standards for a high-density tape format that was created by Seagate, IBM, and Hewlett-Packard and that is a competitor to DLT formats.
MMCA	www.mmca.org	Promotes open-standard small-format removable storage devices.
Open Group	www.opengroup.org	Sets standards for software over InfiniBand.
OSTA	www.osta.org	Promotes rewritable optical disc technology.
PCIMG	www.picmg.com	Promotes PCI products.
PCI Special Interest Group	www.pcisig.com	Is a PCI trade association.
RAID Advisory Board	www.raid-advisory.com	Promotes RAID and has a number of useful resources on its site.
RapidIO	www.rapidio.org	Is developing the standards for backplanes and other circuit boards that will operate beyond the 10Gbps standards.
Recordable DVD Council	www.rdvdc.org	Promotes DVD products that are standardized by the DVD Forum and is a Japanese website.
SATA-IO	www.sata-io.org	The Serial ATA International Organization promotes the SATA bus standard. This URL takes you to the scita.org website mentioned below.
SCSI Trade Association	www.scsita.org	Is responsible for SCSI standards.
Serial Attached SCSI Working Group	www.serialattachedscsi.com	Is defining a serial point-to-point direct attached interface based on the SCSI command set.
Serial ATA Working Group	www.serialata.org	Creates standards for SATA disk drives and SATA interfaces.

Organization	Website	Purpose
SNIA	www.storageperformance.org	Defines storage networking standards, promotes inter-operability among vendors, and creates benchmarks.
USB	www.usb.org	Promotes the USB standard and products.
VMEbus International Trade Organization	www.vita.com	Promotes VMEbus (a fast interconnect standard for storage and clustering) and related PCI products.
XFPMSA.org	www.xfpmsa.org	Develops 10Gbps Fibre Channel and Ethernet connections.

To discuss SANs intelligently and make some sense about what standards are really important, we need a framework to place the various storage networking components in context. In an effort to bring all kinds of storage technologies into a unified theoretical framework, SNIA has developed a storage networking model that is similar in approach to the seven-layer ISO/OSI networking model. Figure 12.3 shows the SNIA shared-storage networking architectural model, which was created by Wayne Rickard, John Wilkes, David Black, and Harald Skadal, along with input from other members of SNIA during a period from 2000 to 2003.

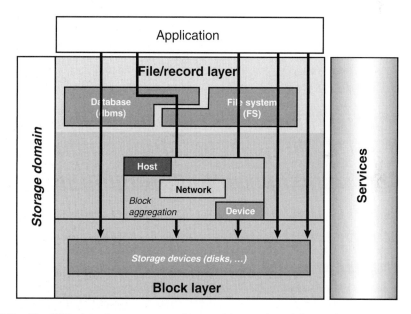

Figure 12.3 The SNIA shared storage networking architectural model provides a context in which to discuss various networking devices and standards. Used by permission of SNIA (www.snia.org).

The SNIA storage model defines a set of architectural layers, functions, and services that are used to network storage. These layers define a set of interfaces: Some of those interfaces are contained within the storage devices themselves, some are conceptual interfaces, and some are actual network interfaces. By using this model, it is possible to describe where services are necessary, pinpoint areas where interoperability is a problem (typically at common interfaces), and describe the advantages and disadvantages of any particular storage networking approach. The SNIA model gives us a vocabulary we can use to compare different approaches and a framework we can use to define hardware and software. We can't use this model to describe whether any particular architecture or product is better than any other—only that if you install a certain device, you will need certain other kinds of hardware and software to complete the solution.

In the SNIA model, the storage domain is the hardware container that stores your data. At the top of the container is organized information in the form of files or information stored in organized containers: fields and records with the associated metadata needed to make sense of what's stored in them. The file/record layer's function is to provide the means to access information and the logic necessary to package information for storage. The logic required involves taking small units of data and associating that data with a naming space allocation scheme in order to construct larger data structures. At the file/record level in the storage model is placed a data cache, which provides a means for data retrieval of commonly or recently used information. Caching data enhances a storage system's performance. Finally, this layer also requires the logic to determine whether the information has been correctly transmitted out of storage or back in—which is often called a system's *coherency*.

The bottom layer of the model shows how information is stored in a storage network. At the lowest level, storage takes the form of blocks that contain data. Blocks have no high-level informational content but are merely locations contained within storage devices, such as hard drives, solid-state devices, tape, or optical discs. Each of these devices must have a way of organizing the blocks it contains (that is, organized pointers to each block). Block aggregation, or block address mapping, allows you to organize information in blocks without regard to where the blocks are located.

The term *aggregation* is synonymous with the concept of *virtualization*, where the definition of *information* is abstracted from the actual physical storage. You saw a number of examples of aggregation in Chapter 11, in the form of RAID. Virtualization also includes the concept of logical units (LUNs) and volumes, and the software you use to manage them, called *volume managers*.

◄◄   See "Introduction to RAID," p. 600.

Because you can attain a performance advantage by caching commonly or recently used blocks, caching is also part of the block layer. On-board cache is the reason that modern enterprise disks ship with 8MB of memory or more.

The third part of the SNIA storage model is the access paths that you see as arrow-headed lines leading from the application layer to the storage devices. Each of the eight possible paths that can be defined represents a different method of data storage and retrieval.

If you examine Figure 12.3 closely, you see that there are four defined networks or interfaces:

- **Application/operating system**—This interface is composed of an API that connects the two layers.

- **Operating system/file layer**—This interface also consists of an API.

- **File layer/block layer**—The file/block layer is the storage network layer.

- **Block layer/storage device**—Blocks and their device storage involve a bus interface such as PCI.

When you hear the word *interface*, you should picture a duck dropping from the ceiling and saying the two magic words: *trouble* and *opportunity*. Interfaces are troublesome (and make IT folk grouchy) because they are where most of the interoperability issues crop up. Interfaces also offer an opportunity because when they are open standards, they allow you to pick different devices above and below them, offer horizontal scaling opportunities, and provide a measure of supplier independence. Thus, if you have storage software written on an industry-standard API, any device that can talk to that API can connect to your SAN at that point in the topology. Thus, it is a widespread trend in the industry to openly publish central APIs, even when (as is the case with EMC, for example) the API is highly proprietary because it allows other vendors to write to that API and extend its value. An important consideration in building any SAN, regardless of the size, is to consider these four interfaces as fundamental building blocks and choose accordingly.

Components of a SAN

You've already seen the minimum components of a SAN: a storage device, a connection device, and physical wiring. You build a SAN because it offers you the flexibility to add many components to a network and turn them into a shared resource at a very high speed. Therefore, you can expect to see all manner of devices attached to a SAN, including the following:

- Application and file servers
- Simple disk arrays and intelligent disk arrays
- NAS (filers)
- Caching servers (such as Microsoft Internet Security and Acceleration Server [ISA])
- Solid-state caching devices
- Tape backup drives and tape libraries
- Optical disc jukeboxes
- Network traffic directors or routers
- Load-balancing appliances
- Distributed file system servers
- Data movers
- Hierarchical storage management (HSM) systems (near online storage)

Storage networking is one of the most dynamic areas of technology around, and many new devices and software products are introduced every year. All these devices can be related to the shared storage model we've been discussing. Let's use some of the vocabulary you've just seen to put some of the various storage networking devices into context.

Block-Oriented Servers

The block layer is where you manage data, create fault tolerance, and organize data for best performance. That means that the following devices are assigned as block-level devices:

- Host (servers) devices, including logical volume mangers and device driver software and HBAs
- The HBA of a specialized storage network appliance
- Storage devices, in the form of RAID or disk controllers

The system of I/O that is used to aggregate blocks passes a vector of block addresses between the file/record layer and the block layer. Thus, a typical block-layer device can span three layers of the model, as shown by the prototypical block-layer device, a disk array (refer to Figure 12.3).

In fact, block-oriented architectures don't even need to be fully contained within the block layer. As you can see in Figure 12.4, a host (or server) connected to a DAS device extends this type of SAN component to other layers, such as the three hosts shown spanning the file/record layer. Block-oriented devices require three components: disk storage, aggregation, and the logic necessary to supply data to applications.

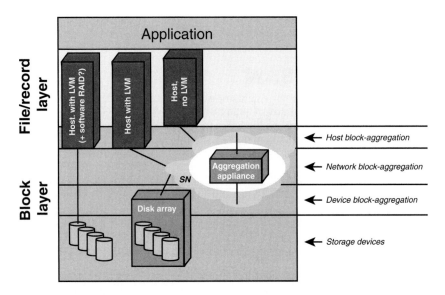

Figure 12.4   Block-oriented devices require a three-layer approach to storage networking. This figure is used by permission of SNIA.

File-Oriented Servers

The file/record layer offers different opportunities for the creation of storage networked devices. What happens at the file/record layer is a mapping function of volumes to files and volumes to tables and tuples, which are essentially the functions of a file system. (This is a different kind of mapping than the block address mapping done in the block layer.)

A file system can be at the operating system level in a host, in a database server or its equivalent, or in a distributed file system, some of which are built around HTTP protocol caches.

SAN components that are file-oriented devices may be any of the following:

- **Host-based devices**—These include not only OS file systems and databases (such as Oracle Parallel Server), but NFS (Network File System) or CIFS (Common Internet File System) file servers and their clients as well. A SAMBA share is an example of one of these client/server systems, but the entire storage system actually must include the client portion as well.

- **A storage networking appliance such as a NAS head**—A NAS head is a server that includes all the logic of a NAS device but not the disk function.

- **A fully configured file-oriented storage server**—This is a NAS with an associated array.

Figure 12.5 shows how file-oriented storage devices are illustrated within the SNIA networking model.

Thus, you can see that even file-oriented storage devices can incorporate various layers in the SNIA model. A NAS server is essentially a SAN in a box; it spans all the layers, from the very lowest block level through the file/record layer that connects directly into the LAN. From a host's point of view, a NAS server appears on the network as any other host would. Similarly, a NAS head also appears as a named server on a network, but unlike a fully contained NAS server, a NAS head requires a connection to a storage network to a disk array to be a fully functional storage device. That is, you can't just plug a NAS head into an Ethernet switch and have it work as soon as you assign a TCP/IP address to it.

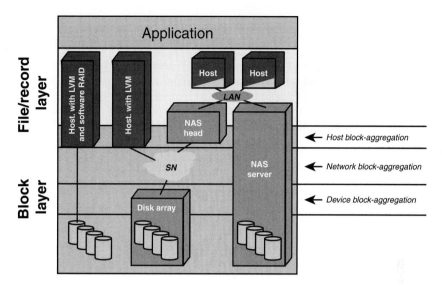

Figure 12.5   File-oriented storage devices. Figure courtesy of SNIA.

Host-oriented, file-based storage devices require not only an HBA to be functional but also a logical volume manager (LVM) to supply the mapping function. Depending on the type of disk controller used, the HBA can be a simple network interface to the storage network (the storage network–attached host on the right in Figure 12.5), or, when the host has either software or hardware RAID, the block mapping function can be moved into the file layer of the host.

At nearly any point in a SAN, it makes sense to place a cache. Referring again to Figure 12.5, which shows the various file-oriented servers, you could put a cache in each of the storage servers, with the exception of the host with LVM and the NAS head. The reason you wouldn't cache those two servers is that you get faster performance from caching the disk array that they both connect to. Caching is a very important application in SANs, and caching appliances are in fact their own category of devices. Network Appliances, for example, has a significant business in cache appliances that are specially tuned filers. From a topological viewpoint, you would place a cache appliance in the network block aggregation layer, directly into the storage network, where it's central location benefits all devices connected to the SAN.

All the aforementioned theoretical discussion brings up the essential point that there are two basic types of storage networking devices: block-oriented and file-oriented servers.

Intelligent disk arrays such as an EMS Symmetrix, an HDS Freedom, or a Hewlett-Packard StorageWorks server are block-oriented servers. The classic examples of NAS servers are Network Appliances's filers (FS series), EMC Celera, and Dell PowerVaults, to name but a few. There are the big boys, very large storage deployment devices, and there are much smaller departmental and personal storage devices that are similarly architected. Each offers a distributed storage solution, but the two different approaches are better at doing different things. A block-oriented server is highly efficient at moving volumes of data, such as backup or in transactional systems. A file-oriented server is best at serving up files, and it is particularly good at serving up *big* files, as you might have for streaming applications.

While this discussion is rather theoretical in nature, it is important because by simply keeping this one fundamental difference between storage server types in mind, it is possible to guess the reasons that different storage network devices or architectures and different software applications hold sway where they do.

Software and Services

A SAN has the same requirements for managing components as any other network does. Therefore, the SNIA model defines a services component that spans all layers of the storage domain. SAN software runs the gamut in size and cost. There's free Open Source software such as the Samba file-sharing software. You often find a lot of software bundled with the hardware you buy; it isn't exactly free, but it is of unknown cost. Software written for SANs—even common server software such as backup programs—tends to be expensive. The most capable packages (for example, SANPoint Control and Foundation) can costs hundreds of thousands of dollars to employ on a SAN.

But here's the thing about SAN software: It is absolutely the most critical part of a SAN and holds the greatest opportunity for both short-term and long-term success, as measured by both performance gains and cost savings. When considering building a SAN, after you decide exactly what functions you need to implement, your next consideration should be the software.

Refer to Figure 12.3, where the SNIA model shows software in the services layer. The following classifications of software would be included as service-layer applications:

- Discovery and monitoring software determines what assets are on the SAN at any moment.

- Resource management and configuration software measures the performance of a SAN's components and allows you to modify them.

- Security and billing applications allow you to secure components as well as bill for SAN usage.

- Redundancy applications include both backup and snapshot software. (Software RAID is considered to be part of the host's block aggregation function and not grouped in this category.)

- High-availability and fault-tolerant applications, such as clustering and failover, are also accommodated as part of the storage networking model. One of the reasons that people build SANs is to make their distributed storage assets highly available. By using software that allows for multinode LVM or a Cluster FS (File System) that is spread over two or more NAS heads (for example), you can perform load balancing and multipathing, features that create high availability and scalability.

- Capacity planning applications let you predict when you need to bring resources online or, better yet, tell you when you can take them offline.

Arrays

Arrays are the stars of the SAN world. That may be because it is in the storage container itself that the most money is spent. However, it is also because the arrays of today come with an unprecedented amount of intelligence, in the forms of built-in capabilities and special software for management and staging as well as many specialized tasks. It's easy to develop a storage-server-centric point of view.

When it comes to storage, people use the term *arrays* rather loosely. An *array* is a storage container that contains multiple storage devices that can be managed as a single entity from either a connected host or a remote point. Some arrays are small—a collection of disks you can count on your hand(s)—and live inside your application server. At the high end are storage servers the size of a very large refrigerator, such as the Symmetrix DMX3000, which can contain up to 584 disks and more than a terabyte of disk space. There's a clear distinction being made in the industry between a simple array and an "intelligent" array. An intelligent array implies a complete server solution.

Most often arrays are based on hard drives, and nearly all arrays support RAID. But solid-state memory caching servers are also configured as disk arrays, and large managed tape libraries are also referred to as *tape arrays*; a few even support what is called *tape RAID*. Any RAID configuration is by definition an array. Depending on your point of view, an enclosure set up as a JBOD may or may not be an array.

To qualify as an array, a storage system should be able to be managed by some form of control software. Control software presents a unified method for defining data structures, executing commands that are carried out in a disk controller or intelligent HBA, or executing logic in the BIOS of the storage server as part of the firmware. Nearly any array you purchase comes with software to manage that array. You can also buy software from third parties to manage various storage arrays.

Raidtec's line of products exemplifies the range of devices to which the term *array* is applied. Raidtec (www.raidtec.com) sells an external DAS array called the Raidtec CS3102, which connects to a server using a dual Ultra 320 LVD SCSI controller. Because it is an entry-level system, the CS3102 is populated with SATA disks. Further up the food chain in Raidtec's DAS offerings is its FlexArray Ultra, which is an Ultra 160 SCSI host independent. Raidtec is known primarily for its smaller systems and has been acquired by Plasmon (www.plasmon.com). However, it also has larger products. Its FibreArray Extreme array with Fibre Channel connectivity is the large server in Figure 12.6. In this figure, there are 1u and 2u devices. Raidtec also sells a NAS box, the SNAZ Pro, a managed NAS server with an integrated Fibre Channel SAN router; the SNAZ Elite; and the large array shown in the figure, which is the FibreArray AA solution. Each of these storage systems qualifies as an array, but each is meant to be used with different applications.

Figure 12.6 The Raidtec family of products spans the range from small DAS arrays up to large enterprise arrays meant for SAN applications.

Raidtec is only an example of what is a very large marketplace of system manufacturers where no vendor really dominates the industry. Other vendors that offer arrays for the server market are listed in Table 12.2. Chances are that when you purchased your server, your server vendor had an array that it wanted you to buy. All server hardware companies either own or partner with companies that make arrays. Dell, for example, has the PowerVault line of products. In some instances, Dell's products are rebranded from vendors such as IBM or EMC, and in others, they are assembled at Dell. Hewlett-Packard and Sun have storage divisions that build storage arrays, and IBM's storage division (which was sold to Hitachi Data Systems) was another OEM. All these vendors offer a very large range of arrays, from small to large.

Table 12.2 Array and Storage Server Vendors

Vendor	Website	Product Types
Adaptec	www.adaptec.com	Fibre Channel arrays, Ethernet NAS, SCSI and iSCSI connections, and JBODs
Adjile Systems	www.adjile.com	SATA RAID and JBOD arrays, storage enclosures
Advanced Computer & Network Corporation	www.acnc.com	JetStor line of arrays and NAS
American Megatrends	www.megatrends.com	StorTrends IP SAN and NAS appliances, as well as backplanes
ATTO	www.attotech.com	Diamond Storage Arrays, which are enterprise-class SATA RAID servers
Aviv	www.aviv.com	DAS, NAS, and SAN arrays
Ciprico	www.ciprico.com	DAS Fibre Channel, SCSI and Fibre Channel RAID arrays, NAS
DataDirect Networks	www.datadirectnetworks.com	Fibre Channel and InfiniBand storage arrays and controllers
Dell	www.dell.com	DAS SCSI and Fibre Channel (EMC partner) arrays, PowerVault NAS servers
Digi-Data	www.digidata.com	STORM line of RAID arrays
Dot Hill	www.dothill.com	SATA, SCSI, and Fibre Channel RAID arrays
EMC	www.emc.com	Array products including the CLARiiON line of midrange arrays and Symmetrix line of enterprise-class arrays and a Celerra line of NAS filers
Enhance Technology	www.enhance-tech.com	Backplanes, desktop enclosures, Terastor SCSI JBODs, and ULTRASTOR RAID appliances
Fujitsu	www.fujitsu.com	EMC storage systems
Gigatrend	www.gigatrend.com	Nexsan enterprise RAID arrays and IDE RAID
Hewlett-Packard/ Compaq	www.hp.com	A complete line of storage arrays under the StorageWorks line from smal up to the enterprise-class StorageWorks XP12000 array, NAS servers, and models in the ProLiant line
IBM	www.ibm.com	Full range of storage arrays, including DAS and SAN solutions; Enterprise Storage Server is one of the large storage deployment systems
Integrix	www.integrix.com	SAN, NAS, and Sun storage servers and arrays

Vendor	Website	Product Types
Medea	www.medea.com	RAID arrays for the A/V market
MicroNet	www.micronet.com	Products best known for small server deployments, including midrange and enterprise=class arrays and NAS
MTI	www.mti.com	EMC storage servers
Network Appliance	www.netapp.com	Full range of NAS servers, caching servers, and near-online solutions
nStor	www.nstor.com	DAS, Serial Attached SCSI (SAS—OneStor), SATA RAID, and SCSI midrange as well as NexStor Fibre Channel enterprise servers
Procom	www.procom.com	NetForce range of NAS filers
Raidsys	www.raidsys.com	Fibre Channel RAID array, backplanes, and controllers
Raidtec	www.raidtec.com	Smaller storage servers
StorageTek	www.storagetek.com	Enterprise-class arrays
Sun	www.sun.com/storage	Full range of disk arrays, from workstation/server level up to the Sun StorEdge 9990 enterprise-class storage server, and NAS and other types of arrays
Western Scientific	www.wsm.com	Fibre Channel and SATA RAID arrays as well as an array appliance
Xiotech	www.xiotech.com	Large, fault-tolerant enterprise-class storage arrays and NAS
Xyratec	www.xyratec.com	Enterprise-class RAID arrays, JBODs, and switched JBOD

When considering an array, you need to consider the following properties:

- **Capacity**—You need to consider the number of disks and the type of disks supported.
- **Connectivity**—You need to consider the array's means to connect to either a host or the SAN.
- **Fault tolerance**—For an array, fault tolerance translates into the elimination of any single point of failure. The array should connect to a host or SAN using multiple connections (multi-pathing), be able to sustain HBA and disk failures, and so forth.
- **Intelligence**—You need to consider where onboard processors and HBAs do the I/O processing.
- **Manageability**—Manageability translates into the ability of the array to be managed in software either locally (at the array), at a switch, or at a host.
- **Interoperability**—Interoperability means that the array can exchange data with other devices on the SAN.

At the higher end of the food chain are a few vendors and some notable product lines. Most people would recognize the lines of the large block-oriented servers: EMC Symmetrix DMX, Hewlett-Packard StorageWorks XP, the Hitachi Data Systems Lightening 9900 or Thunder 9500, or IBM TotalStorage DS arrays. However, the term *array* applies equally well to NAS file servers, such as Network Appliances's FAS980 and EMC's Cellera line, which also contains an array of disks. Figure 12.7 shows a picture of the FAS980. If you take the faceplate off the FAS980, you find that the system is a multidisk RAID array (RAID 4) that contains both an onboard processor and controllers and HBAs. Essentially, the FAS is a fully fledged computer, albeit one that is optimized for file services, and the NetApp boxes come with their own small, proprietary, high-performance operating system. All the products mentioned in this paragraph fall under the category of intelligent disk arrays, and it is only whether they are file- or block-oriented that separates one from another.

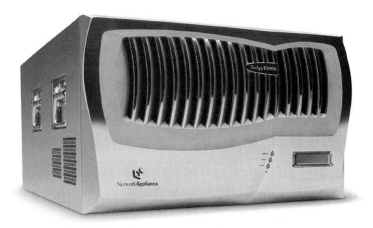

Figure 12.7   The Network Appliances FAS980 is a storage array that is optimized for file services and is a computer or host in its own right.

In purchasing a disk array for your server, you need to be concerned with only a few compatibility issues. A disk array either works with your server and its operating system or it doesn't. In most cases, this compatibility has more to do with the disk or RAID controller than it does with the array hardware itself. As you move up to the very large storage arrays, their use of onboard processors and proprietary operating systems means that you need to be very concerned with their ability to interoperate with other hosts and storage systems. Many companies advertise what they call "open systems storage solutions," which may mean that their servers work with multiple types of hosts, or simply that their servers can connect to various flavors of UNIX.

Fibre Channel SANs

The HBA you use to connect a device to a storage network determines the physical connection type or medium as well as the transport protocol you use. In Chapter 11 we considered some of the most common HBAs—in particular, various forms of SCSI and Fibre Channel—and briefly described their utility in building SANs. Both SCSI and Fibre Channel are used to connect servers to DAS systems. The small number of possible nodes on a SCSI bus and the short-run lengths of that medium limit SCSI to only DAS storage. But Fibre Channel is another story.

◀◀   See "HBAs and RAID Controllers," p. 593.

Fibre Channel is, for the moment at least, the dominant interconnect technology used to create SANs. Although Fibre Channel SANs were originally in the form of arbitrated loops, for the past several years Fibre Channel fabric SANs have dominated. A Fibre Channel bus can support 126 drives or nodes per bus, with a theoretical 40 to 60 nodes in practice, which limits a FC-AL to small storage networks and more often to the internal connections in large storage servers. When you attach a Fibre Channel HBA to a fabric switch, the fan out to other fabric switches allows for 2^{24}, or 16 million, nodes. Although Fibre Channel is still expensive and somewhat difficult to connect correctly, it still accounts for most of the sales in the SAN HBA market.

More About Fibre Channel

Fibre Channel is described as having two layers: a lower signaling level and an upper level of services and protocol mapping. The signaling layer includes the physical interface and media layer (FC-0) on which a transmission or wire protocol is layered (FC-1). Signals are frames that travel in a framing and signaling protocol layer that form the top of the signaling layer (FC-2). In the upper layer are common services (FC-3) on which there is a protocol mapping layer (FC-4), which is where the framing rules are applied. The FC-3 layer transports information about fabric network device discovery, RAID levels, the type of encryption and compression being used. The FC-4 layer allows for mapping bus protocols like SCSI, IP, and VI (virtual interface).

More important in determining compatible hardware is the Fibre Channel class levels. A Fibre Channel class determines the flow control in the FC-2 layer, and that is how Fibre Channel components negotiate with one another. You need to match device classes if you can to optimize performance. Currently, six classes are defined:

- **Class 1**—This class is used for end-to-end connections. Because each frame is verified, in Class 1 there is no negotiation; each device in the point-to-point connection has the full attention of the wire. Class 1 isn't used on any shared storage system because it is a closed system.

- **Class 2**—This class is a frame-switched connection that allows for a shared connection in a fabric. Although Class 2 verifies all frame delivery, it does not require that frames be ordered in any way. Because frames aren't sequential, Class 2 Fibre Channel can't be used for SCSI data, which must be sequential. Some vendors' Class 2 switches support sequential delivery as a proprietary feature. You can tell which switches those are because they support SCSI over Fibre Channel.

- **Class 3**—This class is another frame-switched connection, but here the overhead of frame acknowledgement is removed. It is up to the target and source systems to determine whether a transmission has been successfully accomplished. Class 3 uses the buffer-to-buffer flow control method that is described later in this section. Class 3 Fibre Channel also doesn't sequence frames, but it does include a broadcast feature that can send simultaneous traffic to more than one device.

- **Class 4**—This class allows for fractional bandwidth allocation on a fabric, using what is called a *virtual circuit*. Thus, Class 4 allows for a shared connection but offers some of the advantages of Class 1 Fibre Channel. Class 4 is just coming into use.

- **Class 5**—This class is a definition of isochronous (same time) and just-in-time service. It is unclear whether Class 5 will ever be implemented in products.

- **Class 6**—This class is a proposed multicast fabric service with dedicated connections.

Note

You can find a detailed tutorial on Fibre Channel standards at www.recoverdata.com/fc_tutorial.htm#Class%204.

The most common type of Fibre Channel in use today is the 100MBps variety. Earlier standards of 25MBps and 50MBps were used, and today they are referred to as *quarter-* and *half-speed* Fibre Channel. These slower speeds exist as part of legacy deployments. The road map for Fibre Channel includes 200MBps HBAs and switches (which are just starting to be employed), with 400MBps and 1GBps speeds promised. Given that competitive technologies are being introduced in the 1GBps range and above, it is likely that vendors will ignore 400MBps and jump directly to the 1GBps (and faster) speeds.

In Fibre Channel connections, cables and connectors are passive devices. The signal is transmitted and received by an electronic component called a *transceiver*. Each Fibre Channel connection contains two transceivers, and traffic down each wire flows in one direction. Thus one wire transmits data from one port to another port, while on the second wire connecting these two ports, data is transmitted in the opposite direction. Therefore, Fibre Channel avoids a number of issues that plague other networking technologies, such as Ethernet: signal contention and interference. A two-wire transmission scheme also simplifies the connectors so that they are easier to design and implement. The real advantage that Fibre Channel offers is that a loop or fabric network eliminates a single point of failure because most Fibre Channel HBAs used are dual homed, to take advantage of loop topology.

Switches

Although you can buy Fibre Channel hubs and routers, most Fibre Channel interconnect devices sold are switches. On SANs, switches can be small and unmanaged, but most often they are managed devices with some intelligence. A Fibre Channel SAN switch has the following:

- Onboard processing
- The capability to route storage traffic
- The capability to be both discoverable and manageable through SNMP
- The capability to be programmable through the vendor's API

Entry-level Fibre Channel switches go up to around 16 ports. Brocade (www.brocade.com) dominates the market for entry-level switches with its SilkWorm line. Brocade also does well in the larger workgroup switches space; these devices are most often defined as having 16 to 64 ports. Figure 12.8 shows the highly regarded 16-port SilkWorm 3850 fabric switch, which is a 2Gbps-per-port autosensing switch. This switch is compatible with the slower 1Gbps devices. Brocade's switches go up to the 4Gbps speed and to the higher end of the switch market—64 ports and beyond—where switches are referred to as *director-class* or *director-level* switches.

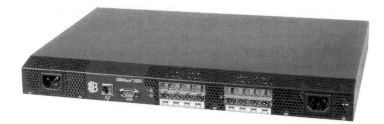

Figure 12.8   The Brocade SilkWorm 3850 16-port 2Gbps Fibre Channel switch.

Brocade is so well entrenched in this marketplace that its API has become something of a standard. Nearly all software management programs, autodiscovery software, and other SAN software offerings support Brocade's products.

Brocade does have competitors, and it is in the workgroup and director-class markets that there is vigorous competition. The company in the director class with the most market share is McData, with its Intrepid switches. Other significant players are Cisco, with its MDS line of switches, and QLogic. Cisco is the 800-pound gorilla of the networking market, but although the company was expected to become a major player in storage networking, it has moved slowly in this marketplace.

A simple FC-AL loop topology can be created by connected all devices to a nonswitching Fibre Channel router or hub. Connecting two FC-ALs together requires having a switched path, and the simplest way to create that is to connect a switching hub on one FC-AL through a Fibre Channel bridge to the second FC-AL. When you connect multiple loops, they share the address space but not the bandwidth: Each loop still has its full rated speed available to its connected devices.

A fabric topology requires (as you saw earlier in this chapter) at a minimum a switch into which all devices are connected. It's easier to build a fabric than a loop topology in that you can connect two switches to one another to grow your network.

Port Types

To understand how SAN connections are made, you need to know a little bit about switch port definition. Each connection on a Fibre Channel switch is called a *port*, and each connection on the Fibre Channel HBA is also called a *port*. Any Fibre Channel device that you hook up using a Fibre Channel cable to a Fibre Channel–based SAN—be it a hub, switch, bridge, or system—is a port on the storage network. The cable attaches to one port on one end and one port on the other end so that for each port there is a single cable connection. The entire system attached to a Fibre Channel HBA is referred to as a *node*.

Fibre Channel defines eight port types:

- B-ports are bridging ports that can connect to additional networks.
- N-ports are used in fabric switches where they both initiate and receive frames.
- L-ports are used in loops.
- NL-ports can be used for both fabrics and loops, and they can be used to connect through a loop to a fabric.
- E-ports are switch ports that connect to other switch ports.
- F-ports are switch ports that connect to N-ports.
- FL-ports are switch ports that connect to NL-ports.
- G-ports are common, or "generic," ports that can be used to connect to E, F, or FL-ports.

All Fibre Channel ports and connections are passive; all the addressing and packaging of frames is done in the controller. Fibre Channel provides a heartbeat so that regular signals are sent between N-ports and F-ports and are received to indicate the port status. Because L-ports were designed to work in loops, they both initiate and control traffic.

Addressing

Fibre Channel has its own addressing and naming scheme, just like Ethernet does. To create a unique network name, Fibre Channel uses the following:

- **World Wide Name (WWN)**—The WWN is a 64-bit identification number that is assigned for each Fibre Channel device by the manufacturer and burned into the device's ROM. You can think of the WWN as Fibre Channel's equivalent of an Ethernet MAC address; when you discover a Fibre Channel port in software, you can inventory what's attached to it using the WWN.

- **Port address**—A port address is a unique 24-bit address that is assigned to a port on a network. You can think of a port address as the Fibre Channel equivalent of an IP address in a TCP/IP network. The 24-bit address space defines 2^{24}, or 16 million (16,777,216), possible addresses. Assignment of port address numbers is determined by the person or organization setting up a Fibre Channel SAN.

- **Arbitrated Loop Physical Address (AL-PA)**—AL-PA is used on loop topologies to define an addressable and unique address. Because loops have a much lower number of connected nodes, an 8-bit address scheme allowing 256 possible addresses, which is the theoretical limit.

Traffic Flow

To mitigate traffic over the network, Fibre Channel manages traffic by using a scheme called *buffer credits*. Each port is given a certain budget of traffic, and when that budget is used up, traffic is switched to the next port. Buffer credits are issued for end-to-end flow control where the destination N-port, L-port, or NL-port sends an acknowledgement that the frame arrived correctly and an additional credit is given to that port because it is now waiting for data. A second form of flow control, called *buffer-to-buffer*, manages a set of credits between adjacent ports. In this form of traffic control, the target port issues a receive ready signal to the sending port.

On a pure FC-AL network, all ports are L type, and this type of loop is called a *private loop*. No other network can access a private loop because it is a closed system. Many FC-ALs are built so that some devices can remain private while other devices are viewable to a connecting network. This sort of loop is called a *public loop*, as shown in Figure 12.9. On a public loop, private devices are still connected to L-ports, public devices are connected through NL-ports, and the arbitrated loop connects to another network via an FL-port connection to a switch.

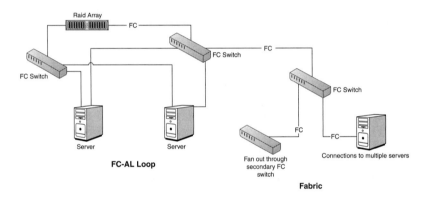

Figure 12.9 A public loop.

For a Fibre Channel loop, the arbitration scheme used is similar to the one that SCSI uses to perform bus arbitration. In this scheme, the port with the highest priority gets priority to send and receive frames. Unlike SCSI, which determines priority based on electronics, on an FC-AL, the priority is done in the command language. As an L- or NL-port on an FC-AL requires loop access, it starts to issue commands that indicate it is ready. As the commands circulate the loop, each node determines its priority in relationship to the node requesting loop control; either that node takes command or passes the control command on.

At some point, the loop becomes available to the arbitrating port, traffic flows or an exchange occurs, and then another higher-priority node assumes command of the loop. Exchanges are a set of data sequences, where the data is sent as a frame and in a prescribed order (thus a sequence). Fibre Channel SANs use a rather small frame size, typically 2KB.

A Fibre Channel frame is similar in construction to other packet frame type networking protocols—that is, the frame has start and end markers, a header that defines the frame, addresses, data, error connection, and a validation data set that performs both acknowledgement and data recovery. A frame is constructed like an envelope. It encapsulates data, just like in other wire protocols, so that Fibre Channel can be constructed so that it maps to other upper-level protocols, such as SCSI, IP, HIPI, FICON, ESCON, 802.2, and Virtual Interface Architecture (VIA).

With a Fibre Channel fabric, a different kind of process is used to determine flow control. A set of nodes and process logons communicate the status of different port types in a fabric network. As each node logs on to the network, initiator and target ports perform a node logon, which establishes the data transfer connection. When different node types exist, the option process login can be used to establish the type of protocol that the transferred data uses. Fabric networks use the FCP (Fibre Channel Protocol) serial SCSI protocol. This kind of process happens for any type of Fibre Channel connections, even direct attached Fibre Channel.

Fibre Channel is almost always installed as a switched fabric for networked storage. However, that doesn't mean that Fibre Channel loops are going to disappear anytime soon. Internal Fibre Channel connections within storage devices such as large storage arrays will continue to be used for the foreseeable future.

TCP/IP Storage Networking

The advantages of TCP/IP storage networks is not only that you can use them to create a unified network but that the infrastructure and trained IT staff are more widely available and that Ethernet adapters, switches, and other hardware offer a great economy of scale—that is, components tend to either be less expensive to start out with or will become so over time.

Storage networking over IP is leveraging the investment that the industry has made in Ethernet. File-oriented storage traffic already travels over IP networks; that's what NAS or filers are designed to do. But these new standards hope that all kinds of storage traffic, even block-oriented, DAS, or Fibre Channel SAN data will function over IP networks. Doing so will expose storage traffic to a whole host of IP-based applications (backup, replication, and so forth) while allowing IP management tools and staff trained in IP methods to manage storage assets more easily.

Ethernet networks have always been used to send and receive storage data. Put aside the fact that NAS filers (NFS and CIFS) are often connected directly to a TCP/IP network, servers and clients are where very important data resides on DAS, and that means that backup traffic must flow from these systems. These historical uses of storage over Ethernet have been largely file based and have not been used to access block-oriented devices. The more recent developments, therefore, have been aimed at making storage traffic over TCP/IP a much more general phenomenon. It is expected that some of the technologies discussed in the next sections will have significant impact in the storage networking marketplace and will to some extent replace Fibre Channel SANs.

There are three approaches to sending storage traffic over IP networks:

- **Fibre Channel over IP (FCIP)**—FCIP uses tunneling to encapsulate Fibre Channel frames within IP packets, sends them over the IP network, and strips the encapsulation off when the packets arrive to restore the Fibre Channel frames. This is a point-to-point technology that has been compared to data transmission across a dedicated dark fibre link, where the initiator and target both have the overhead of encapsulation and removing the encapsulation.

- **iSCSI**—With iSCSI, a SCSI command and data are added to the IP protocol and then sent over the IP network. The processing is done on IP packets at the HBA, so one iSCSI HBA communicates with another. IP enhances SCSI by allowing the data and commands to be sent over a much greater distance, turning DAS into a networked storage asset.

- **iFCP**—Similar to iSCSI, iFCP adds Fibre Channel commands and data to IP packets and then sends the storage traffic as native transport. iFCP uses the Layer 4 Fibre Channel protocol as part of an IP packet, where the transmission of the IP packets is from iFCP gateway to iFCP gateway. Here, the IP infrastructure replaces the Fibre Channel fabric.

FCIP

Fibre Channel, while both scalable and reliable, imposes considerable cost. In addition, a significant amount of overhead is required to map Fibre Channel protocols so that they are compatible with their wrapper, and it is easy to transmit and translate the data when it arrives. When you exceed the distance that Fibre Channel can run (about 1.8km), storage traffic sent over long distances requires a different transport medium, and Fibre Channel is impractical.

What you really want to do is leverage the availability of established IP networks to send Fibre Channel data. Therefore, the industry is developing new standards that allow for WAN transmission of Fibre Channel as well as allow Fibre Channel traffic to use IP LANs when Fibre Channel SANs do not exist. These FCIP technologies are also regarded as a means of solving the problem of connecting "SAN islands"—that is, bridging two separate SANs by using FCIP gateways, whether they are located on different floors in a building, different buildings on a campus, or across the country.

Fibre Channel and IP networking have two very different design principles. Fibre Channel was designed to be fast and highly reliable. IP networks were designed to be fault tolerant but not necessarily fast. That Quality of Service (QoS) difference greatly affects how you can use FCIP technologies. FCIP exposes this difference, especially IP's intrinsic latency.

Many Fibre Channel SANs support high-speed transactional database systems. A transactional system like that can sustain a wait period of a second or so to retrieve some data in order to continue processing, but longer wait periods bring the transactional processing to a halt. When you send FCIP data across the room, there is perhaps one "hop": the latency involved with the path through the switch and the delay in its retransmission. Add a couple more hops to cross a city, and it's unlikely that FCIP is going to connect an OLTP database to primary storage.

Some processes tolerate latency. Backup is one example of where FCIP could be used. In a backup process, data is transmitted from one site to another. If there is latency, the data throughput is simply slower. How much slower? At current speeds, data over an OC-3 IP connection takes about six times as long as over a Fibre Channel SAN.

iFCP replaces the Fibre Channel transport layer with the TCP/IP protocol set and GigE wire transport. It does not create native IP packets, but it does allow for fast point-to-point dedicated connections between two iFCP gateways or switches. The iFCP gateways communicate with Fibre Channel devices and make the necessary conversion. The main market for iFCP deployment is enterprise-class backup, replication, and storage virtualization.

iSCSI

The iSCSI protocol defines a set of rules that determine how to send and receive SCSI-3 commands along with the block storage data on SCSI attached storage over TCP/IP. Because what is being communicated is IP packets, you can send iSCSI over GigE. iSCSI is placed just above the data link layer in the OSI networking model, and it directly interacts with a host's SCSI access method command set. Although any TCP/IP transport is generally defined to work over any TCP/IP network and can even be implemented entirely in software, almost all implementations of iSCSI use a specially constructed HBA that interfaces with GigE.

Not only can iSCSI connect two different IP SANs, it is also possible to use an iSCSI-FC gateway to provide access to storage on a Fibre Channel SAN. Thus iSCSI can link storage over not only LAN but MAN and WAN networks. However, the first iSCSI HBAs from companies such as Adaptec are aimed at getting SCSI storage that is DAS to be made available to other systems in small workgroup or departmental settings. We haven't yet seen enterprise iSCSI devices appear, but the HBAs that should enable this technology started appearing in the market in 2003.

SAN Backup

Any serious storage networking professional knows that backup is the "killer app" of storage networking. Backup is the one application that every SAN runs, and it is considered to be either the most mission-critical application for the organization or nearly so. Many SANs exist solely for the purpose of backup and recovery. And while it's an axiom that no one ever gets promoted for doing a great job on backups, it's also true that the life expectancy of an administrator who can't restore critical data from backups can be clocked with an egg timer.

Backup over a SAN adds significant convenience and additional capability to the task at hand that isn't there when you back up either locally or over a network. With centralized SAN backup hardware and software, you get an economy of scale that you don't have with smaller forms of backup. But the most important reason that backup is such a powerful selling point for SANs is that it removes one of the primary consumers of network bandwidth from your corporate LAN. With SAN backup, you don't have to wait for periods of inactivity to perform a backup, and you can make better use of the backup resources that you do have.

Up until a few years ago, the predominant form of SAN backup was to tape. Tape is a relatively inexpensive storage medium, and tape technologies have steadily improved in performance and capacity over the years. However, the cost and capacity of disk storage have improved even more significantly than those of tape, leading to a situation where the cost of disk capacity is now similar to the cost for the same capacity of tape storage.

Each of these two media offers different capabilities that complement each other. Tape is portable and reliable, but it affords only serial access to data, and it is mind-numbingly slow. Hard disks are faster and offer parallel access to stored data, but they're not portable. Consequently, disk backup is used more often on SANs for first-level backup and snapshots, where the most recent data is stored. Tape has taken the role of near-online backup and archival storage. Taken together, server, disk, and tape offer a multilayered approach to backup that is both flexible and prudent.

Note

You can find a detailed discussion comparing tape to disk backup on UltraBac's website, at www.ultrabac.com/techsupport/50white-papers/UBS_tapevsdisk.asp.

Tape Formats and Libraries

Tape drives have a long and storied past. Space precludes a historical presentation here, but the reality of the current situation is that there are really only three tape formats that are in common use in server/SAN deployments:

- **DLT (Digital Linear Tape) format**—For years, Quantum's DLT was the enterprise tape format of choice. The format originated from technology developed at DEC, and it has the broadest industry support, including Dell, Hewlett-Packard, Maxell, Fujifilm, Exabyte, and many others. The DLT IV version offers a 40GB native tape capacity and a native transfer rate of 3MBps–6MBps. It has been estimated that DLT (as well as SDLT) has a 30-year life span and can sustain one million read/writes.

  SDLT (Super DLT) is a higher-capacity and higher-speed version of the DLT format. The current version is SDLT-320. The road map for Super DLT goes up to DLT VS600 tapes of 600GB.

- **LTO (Linear Tape Open) format**—This format is a joint offering from Hewlett-Packard, IBM, and Seagate, and it is a competitor for SDLT. Several generations of LTO are planned, but the first has tapes with a native capacity of 100GB uncompressed and up to 200GB compressed.

Ultrium is one of the two formats of LTO. There are two versions of Ultrium, Ultrium-1 and Ultrium-2, the latter of which has a 200GB native format and a fast transfer rate of 30MBps. Ultrium-2 puts a small 4KB memory chip onto the tape cartridge, into which is stored the directory of records written on the tape. That directory allows the tape to go to the record on the tape when required without having to first rewind to the directory on the tape for the location.

- **AIT format**—Two versions of this backup format, developed at Sony, exist: AIT-2 and AIT-3. AIT-2 offers tapes of 50GB uncompressed and about two to three times that compressed, with a 6MBps transfer rate. The AIT-2 format is a competitor for DLT, and it isn't a contemporary choice for servers. AIT-2's replacement, AIT-3, offers 100GB native capacity, with a 12MBps transfer rate.

Of course, there are many other tape formats, including VXA, ADR, SLR, Mammoth, Travan, and Accelis, but these are older DAS tape formats. Of the formats mentioned previously, SDLT and LTO are the two that are still deployed on SANs. What makes these two formats the ones of choice is not only that they have high capacities and transfer rates but that the casing for these tape formats was specially ruggedized to withstand the wear and tear of handling in robotic tape libraries. Typically, SDLT-320 drives use Ultra SCSI connections, whereas Ultrium-2 drives are found in both Ultra SCSI and Fibre Channel connections.

The most important tape backup system is the robotic multitape carousel or library. Because modern enterprise tape cartridges duplicate approximately one single hard drive (roughly speaking), tape backup must use a significant number of tapes in order to create archival copies. When snapshots are stored, an even larger capacity is required. Let's consider some representative examples of enterprise tape storage system.

At the low end for SAN tape systems are autoloaders such as the $5,000 Exabyte Magnum 1X7 LTO-2 2u tape system shown in Figure 12.10. A carousel of seven 200GB LTO-2 tapes are passed around a circle and are read/written to by a single tape drive at the back of the unit. The capacity of the system is 1.4TB native and 2.8 compressed, with a throughput of 169MBps, using the two Ultra 320 SCSI ports. Systems of this type can be rack mounted. Exabyte is one of the larger tape system vendors, and it offers a variety of tape systems and formats. The LTO series moves up to more tape heads and more tapes. Exabyte systems come with software that lets you manage them remotely.

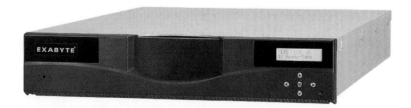

Figure 12.10   The Exabyte LTO-2 Magnum 1X7 autoloader.

Note

When purchasing or intending to use a tape system, make sure that your backup software contains an up-to-date driver for that system.

The next step up from an autoloader is a tape library. Tape libraries look like the kinds of automation you see in science fiction and spy movies. They come in sizes ranging from a desktop model to the more commonly seen size of a file cabinet or refrigerator up to absolutely mammoth systems that fill enormous rooms. One system, built by eMASS (now a part of ADIC) for the Internal Revenue Service, fills an entire building.

Because the only way to make certain that a unit functions correctly is to see the robotics in action, tape libraries often come with see-through doors. Unlike an autoloader, a library comes with multiple tape drives, often not of the same type. Having multiple tape drives operating at the same time enables fantastic throughputs, features such as tape RAID, internal tape calibration, redundant systems, and very broad heterogeneous networking support. Pricing is almost never standard, and it is quoted on a per-system build, depending on the components.

As an example of a tape library, consider the StorageTek 9740 shown in Figure 12.11. This system can contain up to 494 cartridges, 10 tape drives, and 6 slots with a capacity of up to 30TB uncompressed tape when fully populated by DLT, or 60TB compressed. Tape libraries are often expandable, with an extra cabinet added to the side of the starter and with the robotics used to service the combined unit. Companies buy these tape libraries to back up the enterprise-class storage servers described earlier in this chapter. To give this some scale, you could back up roughly 15 EMC Symmetrix DMX servers like the one you saw earlier in this chapter. Companies buy tape libraries to help them archive, do backup and restoration, and to be the last line of defense in a disaster recovery system.

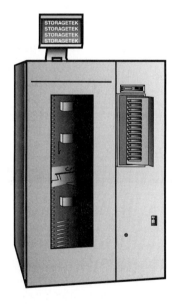

Figure 12.11   The StorageTek Timberwolf 9740 enterprise-class tape library.

Disk Backup Hardware

There are a lot of good reasons people back up their SAN data to disk systems. (Chapter 11 describes some disk backup systems, although it doesn't stress backup.) People use storage arrays and storage servers to back each other up. Internally, arrays can be backed up in hardware RAID, using mirroring and replication techniques. *BCV* (Business Continuance Volume) is just a fancy way of saying disk-to-disk backup. Disk-based backup is more reliable, more fault-tolerant, and a great deal faster than tape.

Of course, some vendors offer storage arrays that are specially outfitted for disk-to-disk backup. For example, consider the DX series from Quantum (see www.quantum.com/am/products/eb/ default.htm). The DX30 array offers 277MBps throughput to up to 16TB of disk. Its bigger brother, the DX100, stores 64TB of disk. Organizations invest in disk-to-disk storage devices because they solve some thorny backup problems. With tape, you are always fighting to keep backups within a reasonable backup window. You can throw more and more tape hardware at the problem, but because tape is so much slower than disk, it's a much more expensive proposition. Using disk arrays to back up your email or large databases lets you restore a system much more quickly while still giving you the opportunity to do versioning using snapshots.

SAN Backup Software and Servers

When you prepare to back up a server over a SAN, typically your server is one of a pool of systems. If your server is to be backed up, it is a matter of adding your server to the backup routine and defining the parameters of the backup. The parameters might include which disk(s) to back up, how often, and using what method (full backup, incremental backup, snapshot, and so on). Some programs let you access the backup program remotely and set up the backup, or you can pop a terminal session and log in to the system. There's nothing substantially different about setting up a system to be backed up over a SAN; the software you use is similar to what you might have used in the past to do local backup. Enterprise backup software has a number of features that are unique, as described later in this chapter.

Much of the real action in SAN backups becomes apparent when your server is one of the "backupers." Backup servers on a SAN run enterprise backup software, and you need to consider a number of factors to get them to perform effectively. Here's a fact for you to ponder: Typically 15% of all servers deployed in an enterprise are deployed as backup servers. Thus for small workgroups or departments, a backup server might be a lone wolf, but more often SAN-level backup requires multiple servers operating cooperatively when backing up other systems. When you select your backup software, you need to look for features such as master backup systems, backup groups, storage groups, backup policy and scripting, and other automation features that make it possible for as few IT staff to run the system as possible. Of course, you also need to look for wide device support within the software package because you never know what you might be called to back up from or to.

The major backup software packages in the SAN marketplace are VERITAS NetBackup, Computer Associates ARCserve, Legato Systems Networker, and Tivoli Systems Storage Manager. However, this is a crowded category with many more players. Smaller vendors such as BakBone, NovaNET, Syncsort, and others all have products in this area. Figure 12.12 shows you the main console from VERITAS's NetBackup software.

You are probably familiar with centralized backup systems, but SANs enable some very interesting backup options, including the following:

- **LAN free backup**—In this type of setup, a host (server) communicates with storage on the SAN, and all backup traffic flows over the Fibre Channel SAN network. This method of backup is one of the main motivators for creating SANs because it eliminates one of the primary consumers of LAN bandwidth.

- **Server free backup**—You may not be familiar with server-free backups, but that's the next step in SAN backup design. In a server-free backup, the host commands a storage server to initiate a backup and gives it the parameters needed to perform the operation. Data from the source storage system is then moved by a data mover application to the backup system, using Extended Copy commands and data mapping operations. That is, backup is done on a block-level basis, and the snapshot image (also called a *point-in-time backup*) is performed, and the data is mapped to physical locations on the target system. Server-free backup requires even less host processing than LAN-free backup, and it is extremely efficient. However, it must be supported by the storage servers involved, and its command set must be supported in the HBA. Consequently, server-free backup is a work in progress and requires careful hardware/software selection to implement.

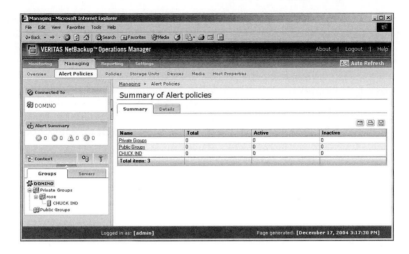

Figure 12.12   VERITAS NetBackup is a market leader in SAN backup software. Shown here is its main console.

You need to consider two other concepts when it comes to backup software over a SAN: hot versus cold backup and vaulting. In a cold backup, you can close the running applications on a server and perform a complete backup, knowing that none of the data will change during the time of your backup or snapshot.

Many application servers that run over a SAN are either mission critical or do not have sufficient free time to enable a backup window to be established. You can't just shut down a corporate email server or a large transactional database. In such a situation, you need to perform a "warm" or "hot" backup. In a warm backup, special software designed for the enterprise application you need to back up quiesces the application so that it is running slowly and performs the backup. A hot backup backs up while the application is running, without slowing down any of the processing. A hot backup picks a point in time, runs the backup, and then examines a transaction log to see what transactions need to be backed up in order to bring the backup successfully to completion. Hot backup software is specific for the application it is backing up—an Oracle database or Exchange Server, for example—and can be quite expensive to implement.

Hot backups lead naturally to the concept of data vaulting. Data vaulting is a backup method that is done remotely so that the data is both duplicated and protected. The transmission is compressed, encrypted, and assembled. You can purchase data vaulting software, or you can buy it as a subscription service. Companies such as LiveVault and CommVault offer special techniques for backing up enterprise applications. The advantage of a vaulting application is that if all else fails, your friendly vaulting application is there to back you up. Vaulting should be viewed in the context of disaster recovery and applied to mission-critical systems and data.

Final Thoughts

In nearly all cases, people who operate servers don't usually install or maintain a SAN. The skill sets for the two tasks are very different. You are likely to need to call in a storage professional or an outside consulting firm to install a SAN. You may, however, need to connect a system or component to an existing SAN, which requires that you have some familiarity with Fibre Channel connection types and a basic understanding of device addressing and how to troubleshoot addressing problems.

Storage management on SANs is a big topic, and because it is storage-centric, we don't describe it fully here. However, as SANs become more widely adopted, and particularly as the components get cheaper, you may find that you are called upon to manage a SAN using specialized software. SAN management software offers autodiscovery technology, topology mapping, device properties drill-down, path analysis, and visualization that makes the job of managing a SAN easier. Some of these software packages are really software suites, bundling in volume managers, backup software, and other capabilities. You'll also find that the major network frameworks, such as Hewlett-Packard's OpenView, IBM's Tivoli, and CA's Unicenter TNG, all offer storage networking, backup, and other applications for managing SANs. Thus if you find yourself involved in working with SANs, you should investigate the capabilities of software in this area.

CHAPTER 13

Fault Tolerance

One of the most significant ways in which servers differ from desktop computers has to do with the importance placed on fault tolerance. *Fault tolerance* means that a problem with software or hardware does not shut down the system, which minimizes the risk of data loss. To achieve fault tolerance, servers use technologies such as the following:

- Error correction for memory
- Self-monitoring of critical components such as memory, disk storage, and network connections
- Redundant memory, disk arrays, power supplies, and network connections
- Management of network hardware

Although many of these topics are covered in detail in other chapters, this chapter is designed to show you how these server technologies help you achieve a truly fault-tolerant network.

Fault-Tolerant Network Topologies

When setting up a network that must remain continuously accessible, one of the most important and often overlooked aspects to consider is the network topology.

Originally, Ethernet networks used a bus topology, which connected all devices to a common bus. If a single device on the bus failed, or if the ends of the network were improperly terminated, the network failed. 10BASE-T and faster networks that use UTP cables use a star topology, in which all devices connect to a central hub or switch. If a device other than the hub or switch fails, other devices can continue to connect to each other. However, if the hub or switch fails, the network fails.

To achieve a truly fault-tolerant network, you should consider one or more of these methods to provide redundant connections between devices on the network:

- **Star topologies featuring teaming and failover connections between servers and backbone switches**—These networks provide high-speed and redundant connections between servers and other network devices.

- **The Hot Standby Router Protocol (HSRP, RFC 2281) and the newer Virtual Router Redundancy Protocol (VRRP, RFC 2338)**—These protocols enable multiple routers to share a single virtual IP address and MAC address for fast recovery from router failure; these protocols also provide the benefit of load balancing.

These topologies and protocols support both copper and fiber-optic media, enabling usage in a wide variety of network situations. If you need to avoid network-related downtime, you should consider these solutions. The following sections provide more details about how these methods work and how to implement them in a new or existing network.

Mesh Configurations: Multiple Network Connections

A *mesh configuration* is designed to provide two or more direct links between networks or devices to create a redundant network of multiple interconnected sites. Because every site is directly connected to every other site, data can travel to any location on the network through a variety of routes that are configured within each site's routers.

To take full advantage of a mesh topology, each router should have multiple routes configured to each location. This allows for one of the lines to be taken down, due to disaster or scheduled maintenance, and still allow traffic to pass via an alternative route.

There are two types of mesh types: full mesh and partial mesh.

Note

If you are considering either a full or partial mesh network topology, you should determine which network nodes are of primary importance and which are secondary. You may decide to emphasize redundancy for primary nodes, in which case a partial mesh network or some other fault-tolerant design may make more sense (and cost far less money).

Full Mesh Networks

In a full mesh network, all network sites are directly connected to each other, as shown in Figure 13.1. This setup provides fault tolerance for every location, so if a line fails, no matter what one it is, all traffic will still be passed to its destination.

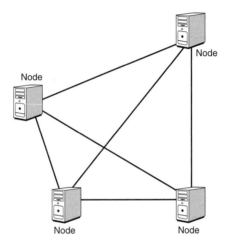

Figure 13.1   A full mesh network with all sites connected.

Although a full mesh configuration sounds like an ideal way to create a fault-tolerant network, it is not feasible in practice except, possibly, for very small networks. A full mesh network actually has several drawbacks, including the following:

- High initial hardware and cabling expenses
- Difficulties in scaling the network

A full mesh network requires at least two connections between each device on the network, with each connected to a different network. This type of configuration is known as dual-homed (two connections) or multihomed (three or more connections) and requires the addition of at least one network adapter to most clients (a few clients have two integrated network adapters). Many switches are required to provide redundant connections between the clients, and two network cables need to be run between each client or server—one each to different switches. The high initial cost of a full mesh network's additional hardware and cabling is magnified if the network needs more servers or clients.

A full mesh wide area network (WAN) is also very expensive due to the cost of the high-speed dedicated lines to connect the nodes. The larger the network gets, the more expensive a full mesh network is. As a result, a full mesh network design is not practical and is usually passed over in favor of a partial mesh network or other types of fault-tolerant network designs.

Partial Mesh Networks

In a partial mesh network, all the critical sites are directly connected together, with the secondary sites connected using a star or ring topology, as shown in Figure 13.2. This setup is a little more common than full mesh because the cost of implementation is lower. This type of network has more points of failure, but if the secondary site is not critical, this is a good, cost-effective option for a network.

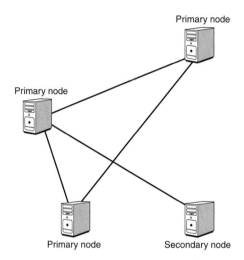

Figure 13.2   A partial mesh network with critical sites connected in a mesh topology and the secondary sites connected in a star topology.

Teaming and Failover

If a network adapter (that is, a NIC) fails in a server that has only one NIC, it loses connection with the entire network. If a multihomed server loses one NIC, it loses connection with the network segment serviced by that NIC. However, if teaming and failover have been implemented, a server can continue to connect to the network, even if one or more NICs have failed.

The following sections discuss how teaming and failover work to help create a fault-tolerant network.

Teaming

Teaming is the process of installing multiple NICs into a server or router and configuring them to work together in one of various ways. Teaming is controlled by the software on the network device that is using the teaming service. A team can include up to eight network ports in a server. This could be up to eight single-port network adapters (card-based or integrated) or a smaller number of multi-port adapters.

Teaming can be used for fault tolerance, and it can also be used to improve network performance by allowing network traffic to be load balanced between all the network cards involved in the network team or to create a faster connection by aggregating the members of the team into a single logical connection. Because teaming can be used for a variety of purposes, you need to be familiar with the process of configuring a team. The following sections discuss how teaming is supported by some of the most popular server and network hardware vendors.

Teaming with Hewlett-Packard ProLiant Servers

Hewlett-Packard ProLiant servers offer a wide range of teaming options that vary by operating system. In addition to automatic teaming and failover, in which the server chooses the best method for keeping a connection alive, you can also choose dual-channel teaming. Dual-channel teaming allows for a team of network cards to be connected to two different switches. This method of teaming allows for a complete network switch failure to occur and the server or network device to stay online, without any downtime.

Switch-assisted load balancing is yet another option that is available for load balancing servers. This option is similar to the dual-channel option, but it allows you to have eight teams of eight network cards that all send and receive data simultaneously.

For automatic teaming and failover, as well as dynamic dual-channel load balancing or switch-assisted load balancing, you must use Windows 2000 Server or Windows Server 2003. Other teaming options are also available with these versions of Windows, as well as with other server operating systems, such as Windows NT 4.0, Red Hat and SUSE Linux Enterprise versions, Novell Netware 4.2 and greater, and various versions of SCO.

Tip

For more information about the teaming options and operating system support of Hewlett-Packard ProLiant servers, see http://h18004.www1.hp.com/products/servers/networking/teaming.html.

Teaming with Intel Advanced Network Services

Intel supports teaming through its Advanced Network Services (ANS) software, which is provided with Intel PRO Server adapters. ANS supports teaming and load balancing with Intel server-class Ethernet network adapters, Intel integrated Ethernet network adapters, and third-party network adapters. Note that at least one of the adapters in the team must be an Intel PRO add-on card or integrated network adapter. Intel ANS supports Windows 2000 Server, Windows Server 2003, and Linux. ANS teaming options include the following:

- **Adapter fault tolerance (AFT)**—Adapters configured for AFT provide automatic redundancy. If one fails, a backup adapter takes over and releases control back to the primary adapter when it comes back online. AFT works with standard switches.

- **Adaptive load balancing**—Adaptive load balancing provides load balancing among teamed adapters as well as fault tolerance with failover. It works with standard switches.

- **Intel link aggregation (Cisco Fast EtherChannel Trunking or Gigabit EtherChannel Trunking)**—Intel link aggregation provides faster throughput for teamed adapters as well as adapter fault tolerance and load balancing, but only when connected to switches that support the specific feature. It requires identical speed and duplex settings.

- **IEEE 802.3ad dynamic link aggregation**—IEEE 802.3ad dynamic link aggregation enables mixing of different speeds of Ethernet adapters for increased throughput, but it does not support fault tolerance. It requires a switch with IEEE 802.3ad support, and all adapters in a team to be assigned the same MAC address.

Tip

Intel provides a guide to using ANS with Linux at www.intel.com/support/network/adapter/1000/linux/ans.htm.

IBM provides a useful visual tutorial for the Intel PROSet network configuration utility and teaming wizard for Windows 2000 at www.307.ibm.com/pc/support/site.wss/document.do?lndocid=MIGR-40983.

Teaming with Broadcom Advanced Server Program

Broadcom, a leading vendor of server-class Ethernet adapters, provides the Broadcom Advanced Server Program (BASP) driver to enable Broadcom adapters to team with other Broadcom-based or third-party vendor network adapters. BASP supports Windows 2000 Server, Windows Server 2003, and Linux. BASP teaming options include the following:

- **Smart load balancing**—Smart load balancing provides load balancing among teamed adapters as well as fault tolerance with failover. It works with standard switches.

- **IEEE 802.3ad dynamic link aggregation**—IEEE 802.3ad dynamic link aggregation enables mixing of different speeds of Ethernet adapters for increased throughput, but it does not support fault tolerance. It requires a switch with IEEE 802.3ad support, and all adapters in a team to be assigned the same MAC address.

- **Generic link aggregation (trunking)**—This is a Broadcom protocol-independent version of IEEE 802.3ad aggregation with failover support.

Tip

For information on BASP, see the "Broadcom Ethernet FAQ's" page at www.broadcom.com/support/ethernet_nic/faq_drivers.php and whitepaper BCM570X: "Broadcom NetXtreme Gigabit Ethernet Teaming" at www.broadcom.com/collateral/wp/570X-WP100-R.pdf.

Failover

When you want to make sure that a server or another network device is constantly available, another technique, called *failover*, can also play an important role in your server network. A failover, which is automatic and transparent to the user, switches you to a backup device in the event of the failure of a server, database, router, or any other network device. You can use failover for emergency situations when you have a device failure or when you need to take a device down for routine maintenance.

Failover requires that you have a duplicate device that is connected and ready to be switched to in the event that the original hardware fails. This can be an expensive option to implement, but if your cost of being down is more than the cost of the redundant hardware, it is well worth it. You can implement many levels of failover, ranging from support for very minor components, such as a network card, to the extreme of having a backup device to everything on your network. Depending on your network's needs, you can decide the level of failover that is right for you.

As you learned in the previous sections, one of the features that NIC teaming supports is failover. Hewlett-Packard ProLiant servers support failover with most types of teaming (except for switch-assisted load balancing and 802.3ad dynamic teaming). With Intel ANS, you can select adapter fault tolerance or adaptive load balancing to set up failover support when teaming adapters. With Broadcom BASP, you can select smart load balancing or generic link aggregation to set up failover support when teaming adapters.

If you use routers that support the Virtual Router Redundancy Protocol (VRRP), you can configure two or more routers to provide redundancy and failover services.

However, failover should not be limited to NIC and router installations. Consider the following lists of devices that require failover support if you want to create a truly fault-tolerant network.

A company that relies on an Internet database should consider failover for the following:

- T1 or Internet connection, usually from two separate providers
- Smartjack

- Firewall
- Router with internal CSU/DSU
- Network switch
- Server
- Server network cards
- Database

A multisite company that relies on information sharing between locations should consider failover for the following:

- Point-to-point lines between each location, usually a T1 line but perhaps a fractional T1 or Frame Relay
- Smartjack
- Firewall
- Router with internal CSU/DSU
- Network switch
- Domain controller
- File server where the shared data resides
- Storage area network (SAN), if one is in use

A single-site company that desires failover only for LAN (not Internet) connections should consider failover for the following:

- Server network card
- Server power supply
- Server cooling fans
- Network switch
- SAN
- Database server (if applicable)

The individual components listed for a single-site company's server should also be considered for servers in large organizations.

▶▶ For more information about redundant power supplies, see "Redundant Power Supplies (RPSs)," p. 675.

▶▶ For more information about implementing other types of hardware redundancy, see "Implementing Hardware Redundancy Options," p. 866.

◀◀ For more information about advanced network adapter configurations such as dual-homing and teaming, see "Network Interface Cards (NICs)," p. 557.

RAID

RAID (redundant array of inexpensive [or independent] disks) is a set of two or more storage devices combined together to provide fault tolerance and/or improve performance.

Not every level of RAID is fault tolerant. Striping (RAID 0) improves the speed of the disk subsystem, but because data is stored across two drives, there is no fault tolerance; if either drive fails, all data is lost. Fault-tolerant levels of RAID include RAID 1 (mirroring), RAID 5, RAID 10, and RAID 50.

◀◀ For more information about RAID levels and RAID configuration, see "Introduction to RAID," p. 600.

Although RAID levels other than RAID 0 provide some level of fault tolerance in that they protect against data loss, you still experience a loss of productivity if you need to shut down the server, remove and replace the failed drive, and rebuild the array. Generally, RAID arrays that use motherboard-integrated ATA/IDE, SATA, or SCSI host adapters are more likely to require you to perform a manual array rebuild. For true fault tolerance, you should consider RAID arrays that permit automatic rebuilding.

Transparently Rebuilding Failed Drives

To permit a server to continue to operate even in the event of a drive failure in a RAID array, your RAID solution needs to incorporate the following fault-tolerant features:

- **Hot drive sparing**—With this feature, a drive not currently in the array is placed in standby mode, ready to take over for a failed drive.
- **Automatic array rebuilding**—This feature swaps the failed drive for the hot spare drive and rebuilds the array without user intervention.
- **Hot drive swapping**—This feature permits failed drive replacement without shutting down the system.

Host adapters that support these features are available for ATA/IDE, SATA, and SCSI hard disks from a variety of vendors, including the following:

- Adaptec (www.adaptec.com)
- HighPoint Technologies, Inc. (www.highpoint.com)
- LSI Logic (www.lsilogic.com)
- Promise Technology (www.promise.com)

◀◀ For more information about RAID troubleshooting and array rebuilding, see "Managing RAID," p. 611.

Improving Network Speed and Reliability

Although improving a server's fault tolerance is critical to the reliability of a network, you should not overlook the design of the network itself or the hardware you use to build the network.

If your network carries different types of traffic to two or more servers, you should divide the network into separate segments to better manage traffic flow. However, a segmented network can also be used to provide fault tolerance if you make sure that one segment can take over for another segment in case of failure.

The following sections discuss segmentation and the selection of switches and routers needed to create a faster and more fault-tolerant network.

Segmentation

Segmentation alleviates network bottlenecks by splitting network traffic loads to different network segments. You can use segmentation to lower the total network traffic that is passed on a network by splitting up the traffic as shown in Figure 13.3. If one set of systems need to communicate with each other and not the rest of the network (for example, different departments), you can segment them into different networks. You can also use network segmentation if you have multiple locations that all need to access the same server but no other resources on the other segment (for example, if multiple locations all share the same email or file server).

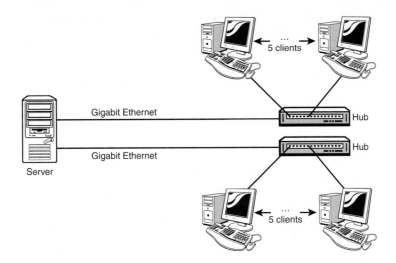

Figure 13.3   Using network segmentation.

Segmentation can be used to improve a network's fault tolerance. By configuring a server's NICs to connect to different network segments (dual-homing) and using a router or Layer 3 switch to connect the segments, you enable the router to maintain a connection to all network segments, even if a direct connection to one segment fails.

Switches and Routers

You use switches and routers to create the network topology you prefer. As you have learned, the network topology can also help create a network with enhanced levels of fault tolerance. To achieve the desired level of fault tolerance at the network level, you need to understand how switches and routers can be used in a fault-tolerant installation.

Switches

If your network uses hubs to connect network nodes, there are several good reasons to upgrade to switches. Compared to hubs, switches don't generate unnecessary network traffic. Instead of broadcasting data frames to all ports, a switch transmits the packets directly to the destination port. Hubs subdivide total network bandwidth among connected devices (for example, a 10-port 100Mbps Fast Ethernet hub provides only 10Mbps bandwidth to each port), whereas switches provide full bandwidth to each connected device. Also, most recent switches, even on small networks, support full-duplex operation. Thus, a nominally 100Mbps Fast Ethernet connection becomes a 200Mbps Fast Ethernet connection if all devices in the connection (network adapters and switches) support full-duplex operation. Many switches now support Gigabit Ethernet (1000Mbps) connections for servers as well as 10/100Mbps connections for client PCs and other devices.

Intelligent network switches can also be configured to improve network reliability, using a protocol called *spanning tree* that provides fault tolerance for the switch. A spanning tree reroutes traffic through the secondary switch if it detects a failed network connection or a bad NIC. In this configuration, you use two switches connected to two separate NICs in your server to provide fault tolerance and redundancy for your server's NICs and your network traffic.

Routers

Routers are specialized pieces of hardware that connect at least two separate networks, sending all of the network traffic on the Internet or any other WAN connection to its correct destination, choosing among thousands of available pathways. Routers use routing tables to determine the best pathway to the destination and then send the information to the next hop in the very long data train. The next hop is usually another router that looks up the data's destination point in its routing table. The router then determines the best path to the destination and sends the packet on to the next hop. This continues to happen from router to router until the final router sends the data to the correct server or network device. The data may traverse thousands of geographical miles, but the process takes but a few seconds to complete.

Because routers are a vital component in connecting networks in different locations to each other (and to the Internet, the world's largest network), keeping routers working is essential if your network depends on those connections.

You can use routers to help provide a fault-tolerant connection in several ways. One method is to set up separate routers to connect your network to the Internet via different network segments. By using dual-homed network adapters in your server, you can maintain a connection to the other network or the Internet, even if one connection fails. The major expense in this type of redundancy is the cost of an additional leased line or ISP service.

If you have a reliable connection but are concerned about router failure, you can use routers from Cisco, Nortel, or others that support VRRP; you can also use Cisco routers that use Hot-Swap Router Protocol (HSRP) or similar methods for setting up multiple routers to appear as a single router to the network.

Tip

Although you can buy routers from SOHO vendors such as Linksys, D-Link, and others, most vendors that sell into the SOHO space do not provide routers with support for VRRP, HSRP, or similar standards.

Providing Redundancy in Server Hardware

Redundancy is a principle of fault tolerance that has many applications for servers and networks. As you have learned in this chapter, you can use redundant network adapters, routers, and hard disks in a RAID array to provide automatic failover and recovery in the event of primary device failure.

However, other parts of a server should also be protected with redundancy whenever possible. Depending on the component, it may not always be possible to arrange for automatic failover, but you should provide for as much redundancy in installed equipment as possible, and you should have spare hardware readily at hand for other types of server components.

Major component areas to consider for built-in redundancy or, at minimum, redundancy through in-stock spare parts include the following:

- Power supplies
- Fans
- Memory
- Processors

The following sections provide details.

Note

Standard servers provide integrated redundancy for only select onboard components. However, fault-tolerant servers that incorporate replicated hardware that processes instructions at the same time as the primary hardware are available from Stratus Technologies (www.stratus.com), NEC Solutions (America), Inc. (www.necsam.com), and other vendors. Essentially, fault-tolerant servers provide two complete servers that operate in parallel in a single chassis. If the primary hardware fails in a fault-tolerant server, the replicated hardware takes over automatically.

Power Supplies

A power supply is one of the most vulnerable pieces of hardware in a server or other network device. Power supplies are always carrying a load, and with the type of work they perform, they are usually one of the first major pieces of hardware in a server or other network device to fail. If you have no redundancy in place for this device, that failure will bring down everything drawing power from it.

Because of the severity of having a power supply go out, you can usually order your major network equipment and almost all servers with dual (redundant) power supplies. It's a very good idea to spend the extra money on the option for redundant power supplies in any major network device.

Note

If your server does not include an option for a redundant power supply (RPS) but you can use off-the-shelf power supplies in your server chassis, you can purchase an RPS from any one of a number of vendors as a retrofit.

▶▶   For more information about RPSs, see "Redundant Power Supplies (RPSs)," p. 675.

Power supplies are relatively inexpensive, especially compared to the loss of productivity that results when a power supply failure takes a server offline, so you should consider keeping at least one spare power supply unit for your server on hand. This is especially important if your servers are rack mounted. 3U, 2U, and 1U rack-mounted servers use power supplies customized to each form factor size.

Fans

Keeping systems cool is a crucial step in keeping a network up and running. Electronics of all types generate heat, and all of them run much better the cooler they are. You can look at almost any electronic component and see at least one fan, and most computer equipment, including network devices such as routers and switches, has at least two fans.

Servers usually have at least four or more fans, and having a redundant fan in place is a very good idea. You usually have at least one or two fans in each of your power supplies, and as you just read, you should have two power supplies. You will also have at least two system fans. You should definitely have one for each processor in the system: Your video card could have a fan on it, and some systems even have fans on the system boards. The fans for which you should consider having redundancy are the system fans. You can have online redundant system fans for some servers that will automatically switch on if another fan goes out. You should also consider keeping a spare active heatsink (processor fan) onsite because most servers will not boot if the active heatsink's fan fails.

Note that whereas tower chassis can often use standard 80mm to 120mm fans, fans in 1U, 2U, and 3U chassis are usually special models that are not sold at normal computer parts stores. Similarly, active heatsink specifications for some server processors (such as the 90nm-manufacturing process Intel Xeon) may be substantially different from those used by desktop processors. You should keep a spare or two handy to avoid unnecessary downtime.

To determine whether an onboard fan is failing, you should check the system management software installed on your server or the BIOS System Monitor.

Memory

Like most pieces of hardware for a server, you should also have redundant memory. Although this practice is the least used of the redundant items listed in this chapter, it is yet another way of preventing downtime. Some servers come with a redundant memory bank, but you must enable this feature in the system BIOS before it will work. Redundant memory is known as *memory sparing*. In addition to memory sparing, some systems support hot-plug RAID memory, which creates a memory array similar to a RAID 5 disk array.

◄◄ To learn more about hot-plug RAID memory and other methods used by servers to improve memory reliability, see "Advanced Error Correction Technologies," p. 391.

Physical Maintenance

There are many types of software can help you maintain your servers, but if you don't take care of the physical components of your servers, all the software in the world will be of no use to you. Because your servers need to be kept clean and in the proper operating conditions, you should take time periodically to take your servers down during off-hours in midmonth and perform a complete hardware maintenance check on them. During your hardware check, you need to do the following:

▶▶ For more information on maintaining servers, see, "Routine Maintenance," p. 854.

- Use compressed air and blow out your system. When using the compressed air, make sure that you clean all parts of the server, including the fans, power supply, memory banks, hard drive cage, and cooling slots in the case. Before using compressed air, move the server outside or use a vacuum system to remove dust from the air before it can be sucked into another server or client PC nearby.

- Remove and reseat the cards in the server, including the system's memory modules.

- Pull the hard drives and reseat them. While the drives are out, blow out their connectors with compressed air.

- Make sure that all indicator lights on the system are functioning properly.

- If you have redundant parts, such as power supply or fans, make sure that they are functioning properly.

Note

Sometimes redundant hardware failures may only be reported during initial system startup. Thus, it can be useful to shut down a server occasionally, maintain it, and restart it to check for these types of failures.

- Check your server room for any water leaks in the ceiling or any other environmental conditions that would be hazardous to your server.

- Check you battery backup meter to make sure that your battery isn't overloaded or reading as bad.

- Test your battery backup. You should make sure that your battery backup system lasts the duration for which it is rated before its battery dies. Your UPS should have a serial or USB cable to your server to allow for a smart system shutdown before your UPS battery dies, and you should make sure that your UPS can properly shut down your server. For more information, see Chapter 14, "Power Protection."

Note

UPS software usually gives you the option to shut down your server X minutes before your battery dies, where X is determined by the server administrator. When you set this up, it might take three minutes for your server to shut down, so setting this option to five minutes is sufficient. Over time, adding more items to your server could cause your server to take a considerably longer time to shut down. When this happens, your UPS will run out of battery life before it gets to shut down your server, causing your server to crash.

To avoid unnecessary downtime for your network, you should schedule routine maintenance during off hours.

The Server Environment

To keep your servers running smoothly, you should make sure that the environmental conditions within the server room are optimal for your servers' performance. A common cause of server failure is improper server room environments. Sometimes server rooms are literally closets that people put their servers in. Without modifications suited to a particular server, these types of environments are asking for trouble.

▶▶ For more information on sever rooms, see Chapter 17, "Server Rooms."

Because poor environmental conditions can cause server instability, maintaining the proper conditions for your server's operation is just another reason you need to make sure your servers are as fault tolerant as your budget will allow.

Server Software Updates

Another important defensive maintenance tool is software updates. The most important software updates are for a server's operating system. If you are running a Microsoft Windows server operating system, you are probably all too aware of the frequent updates that Microsoft releases.

Although it is true that occasionally these updates can cause some problems of their own, overall, they are far more beneficial for your server's reliability and security than they are a risk to your server's stability. These updates will keep your systems protected from recently discovered security vulnerabilities, they frequently add new features that Microsoft has developed and added to its toolbox, and they often slam the front door on new viruses that are capable of attacking holes in Microsoft's operating systems.

There are two ways to install Microsoft's latest updates onto your server: using auto-updates and using Microsoft's Windows updates website. It is generally a better idea to install updates manually than to use auto-updates; that way, you know what you are installing, just in case an update causes a problem for your system. Installing Windows updates after verifying that they will work properly with your server is a good item to add to your defensive maintenance plan.

Tip

Sometimes Microsoft patches for Windows Server 2003, Windows 2000 Server, and Windows clients cause problems. To find out whether a particular patch or update is worth installing or should be avoided, we recommend visiting the Patch Watch column in the Windows Secrets Newsletter. Io subscribe, go to http://windowssecrets.com.

Hardware Drivers and BIOS Updates

Another good tool to add to your defensive maintenance plan is hardware updates. You can check your hardware manufacturer's website to see if there are any updates for your server or your server's hardware. These updates can fix minor flaws and compatibility issues with your hardware. If your server is a name-brand server such as Compaq or Dell, getting these updates is a relatively easy task. You just go to the appropriate support website and look for updates for your particular system. If you have built your server(s) from scratch, using industry-standard components, you should keep a list of the support site for each component and visit these sites regularly to look for updates.

You should upgrade hardware drivers or BIOS code under the following circumstances:

- When current versions are known to be defective
- When updates are required before other updates (such as processor updates) can be performed

In addition to these guidelines, you should follow these recommendations:

- Use only production-level drivers or BIOS code; avoid using beta (prerelease) drivers or BIOS.
- If possible, install the updates on a test server identical to production systems and test the updates under typical and exceptional circumstances before installing the updates on production hardware. Keeping your server's OS and hardware drivers up-to-date helps you avoid running into compatibility issues as well as make sure your server gives you the best possible performance for as long as it can.

▶▶ For more information on operating systems and drivers for your server, see "Server Hardware and Drivers," p. 776.

◀◀ For more information on BIOS updates, see "Upgrading a Flash BIOS," p. 314.

Server Management Software

Many software packages on the market today allow you to monitor your servers and the rest of your network for performance and hardware issues to try to help catch a problem before it becomes a failure. In the following sections, we look at some of the features that come with Microsoft servers and then explore some of the third-party products on the market today. You can learn more from Chapter 21, "Server Testing and Maintenance," about various performance monitors and establishing baseline performance for your systems. Note that Microsoft's Windows 2000 Server and Server 2003 include useful server management features.

Server Management with Active Directory Group Policies

In Windows you can use Active Directory group policies to manage almost everything within your domain (see Figure 13.4). A huge number of policy features can be configured—too many to list them all here—but the following is a list of the most basic and commonly used configurations for a server environment:

- Manage user account policies, including the following:
  - Minimum password length
  - Maximum password age
  - Password lockout period
- Use Local system policy.
- Redirect folders. You can redirect users' folders to the server so that to the user, everything seems local on his or her machine, but in reality, the folders are sent to and from the server. This is mainly used for users' desktop settings or the My Documents folder. How it works is a user saves files to his or her My Documents as usual, but instead of a file being stored locally on the user's workstation, there is a folder on the server for the user's documents, and the files are

sent to that folder. This is used so that all the files are saved in one location and so they can be backed up without having to back up each user's workstation.

■ Remotely install software. There are two types of remote software installations through group policy:

- ■ **Published applications**—Published applications are sent to the user's PC and are available for installation through the Add/Remove Programs option or by clicking on a file that needs the program that is published.

- ■ **Assigned applications**—Assigned applications are installed on the user's PC the next time they log in to the network. When you assign an application to a user, that person does not have a choice of having the program installed; it is done automatically.

■ Block or set up Windows automatic updates.

■ Control what rights a user has for Internet Explorer.

■ Remove or disable features from a user's Start menu or taskbar.

■ Remove or disable features from a user's desktop.

■ Disable the Add/Remove Programs feature or block certain items with Add/Remove Programs.

■ Lock a user's desktop background and screensaver.

■ Disable a user's ability to add or remove printers.

■ Disable or prevent the use of offline files.

■ Disable a user's ability to lock or log off a computer.

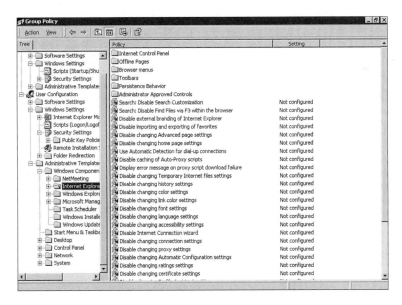

Figure 13.4 Windows 2000 Active Directory group policy configuration.

These are just some of the options available through group policy. For a detailed look at all the available options, you can download Microsoft's whitepaper from http://download.microsoft.com/download/5/2/f/52f3dbd6-2864-4d97-8792-276544ad6426/grouppolwp.doc.

Command-Prompt Tools for Network Troubleshooting

Other network tools available through the Windows operating system include command prompt tools such as

- **ping**—Tells whether a specified IP address or URL can be contacted.
- **telnet**—Provides remote access to a server or other device for management.
- **tracert**—Traces the route between the current system and a remote URL or IP address.
- **nslookup**—Looks up the IP address of a specified URL or a URL for a specified IP address.
- **netstat**—Lists active connections and listening ports.
- **net commands**—Displays and modifies network configuration settings.
- **netsh commands**—Displays and modifies the network configuration for the current or specified remote server; they can work with DHCP, IP, network bridge, routing, RPC, WINS, diagnostic, and other network components and features and can create scripts.
- **ipconfig commands**—Displays IP address, MAC address, and other IP settings for the current system.

These are just a few of the most commonly used command-line tools, but there are many more. For more information about TCP/IP and networking command-line tools available with Windows Server 2003, go to www.microsoft.com/technet/prodtechnol/windowsserver2003/library/TechRef/. If you would like to explore the many commands available from the Windows command prompt, you can go to www.computerhope.com/msdos.htm#02.

Third-Party Software

For a truly proactive approach to managing your servers and your entire network, you can try some of the great third-party software packages available. The following sections look at two different packages that can each give you a truly proactive network. These types of packages can monitor all aspects of your servers, as well as other critical network devices, to notify you of any degradation of your devices before they become critical, causing network outages. These programs will also notify you if your devices fail so that you can get the problem resolved as quickly as possible.

Intel's Server Management

Intel's Server Management software comes in three different versions, all of which offer comprehensive local and centralized system management. You get continuous monitoring of pivotal server hardware and system resources to maintain a truly proactive approach to keeping your network up and running smoothly. The following are some features offered by Intel's Server Management software:

- **Fault management and event handling**—Server Management provides a proactive notification of current or potential hardware failures. Event notification allows users to be notified via email, pager, or SMS gateway if one of the user-configured policies is triggered. This allows an administrator to configure policies to notify them if predetermined events are listed in the server's event viewer. The administrator can therefore know about critical system events as soon as they occur, which eliminates the need for an administrator to constantly check a server's Event Viewer.
- **Unified multisystem management**—This feature allows for a true central management server. From one server, an administrator can issue a command that will initiate the command on multiple servers or nodes. This feature eliminates tedious one-at-a-time operations on each server. The integration of Intel's single-system-aware tools makes the management server multisystem aware, allowing all the systems to execute simultaneous commands on multiple nodes.

- **Data collection and inventory reports**—This feature enables users to prepare detailed inventory reports for all managed devices by performing detailed system scans and hardware inventory detection.

- **Web browser and command-line interface**—Intel's software gives an administrator the ability to use either a web browser for interactivity or a command line for automation. This ensures that Intel's Server Management fits well with the existing management processes.

This list gives you an overview of the features and functionality available with Intel's Server Management. Intel offers the Server Management software in three versions: Standard, Professional, and Advanced. Table 13.1 lists the functions available with each version of Server Management.

Table 13.1   Intel Server Management Features

Function	Standard	Professional	Advanced
Upgrade Options			
Web Management Console	Yes	Yes	Yes
Access Modes	LAN	LAN, serial, modem	LAN, serial, modem
Console Redirection	Text-based (VT100)	SOL (VT-UTF8)	SOL (VT-UTF8) KVM
BMC Features			
ICMB	No	Yes	Yes
Sensor support	Limited to 32	Limited to 256	Limited to 256
System event log	92 entries	3,000 entries	3,000 entries
IPMI support	1.5	2.0	2.0
Embedded webserver	No	No	Yes
SNMP support	PET traps	PET traps	Full SNMP access
Out-of-band management NIC	NIC TCO port	NIC TCO port	NIC TCO port
Out-of-band embedded email alerting	No	No	Yes
Software Features			
SNMP baseboard agent	Yes	Yes	Yes
Agent-less management	Yes	Yes	Yes
In-band email alerting	Yes	Yes	Yes
Command-line interface	Yes (reduced feature set)	Yes	Yes
SCSI/RAID instrumentation	Yes	Yes	Yes
PCI hot-plug	No	Yes	Yes
Power management instrumentation	No	Yes	Yes
Memory RAS	No	Yes	Yes
KVM remote viewer	No	No	Yes

If you decide to upgrade to the Professional or Advanced version, you need to purchase Intel's add-on monitoring cards.

For more information, see the Intel Server Management page, at www.intel.com/design/servers/ism/.

Summit Digital Networks's RMS

Summit's RMS service is a monthly service that is offered to customers as a proactive monitoring service. The benefit of this RMS program is that Summit offers a wide range of service plans. Most companies that offer monitoring services require a minimum number of devices to be monitored to make it worth their setup. Summit offers its monitoring services for any number of devices. This means that small companies with just one or two devices to monitor can take advantage of the same great monitoring features as large corporations with hundreds of devices that need to be monitored.

Summit Digital Networks's RMS package works by using a central server at Summit's headquarters, combined with hardware or software probes onsite and remote monitoring agents on at least one server onsite. Using a multilocation monitoring system allows administrators to be notified even if their networks are completely down. The notifications are sent from Summit's central server at its office, so even if your servers are down, you will still receive your notification. Even if you suffer a phone or Internet failure, which is how most software notifies the administrator, you will still receive your notifications. The service is billed on a monthly fee basis for the total number of devices that you want monitored. The only upfront cost is for the hardware or software probe licenses and a server or workstation for the probes to reside on.

The RMS service is capable of monitoring almost anything on your network. You can also customize the software by setting the notification thresholds to be whatever is acceptable to you for your particular needs. You can monitor items such as your Internet service, your email service, your routers, or your server's processor usage. The following is a more detailed list of items you can monitor with this service:

- Network services
- Local services
- SNMP services
- Security services
- System services

Other major features include the following:

- Antivirus activity and update tracking for major products, including McAfee, Symantec, Sophos, and TrendMicro
- Server processor, disk space, and physical/virtual memory usage
- Connectivity, DNS service, Ethernet errors, Frame Relay, FTP, HTTP, HTTPS, NNTP, Telnet, and other network features
- Email and messaging services, including POP, Exchange Server, SMTP and IMAP
- Monitoring for Veritas Backup Pro, Microsoft IIS, Microsoft SQL Server, and Citrix Metaframe Server for thin clients
- Server processes for Windows, Linux, Solaris, and Novell servers
- Event, system change, security, and other logs
- Intrusion detection, security, and firewalls
- Patch management for Windows servers

This list should give you a good idea of the power of the Summit Digital Networks RMS service. For more information, see the Summit Digital Networks website, at www.summitnetworking.net.

Troubleshooting and Documentation

One of the most difficult, most stressful, and most common tasks for a network administrator is troubleshooting problems. No matter how well your network is designed and runs, sooner or later, you will have to troubleshoot some sort of network or server issue. If you stay calm and follow a step-by-step, logical plan to track the problem, you should be able to get the issue resolved as quickly as possible. Here is an outline, based on the CompTIA Network+ troubleshooting methodology, to follow to help resolve your issues:

1. Identify and document the symptoms.

2. Determine the severity of the problem and which users are affected. For example, is the entire network down, are just the users on a particular switch down, or is everyone who uses a specific database down?

3. Determine what has changed on the network (hardware, software, driver or operating system patches, and so on). Jerry Pournelle's classic question, "What changed since the last time [the network] worked?" is a useful way to summarize this step.

4. Determine the most likely cause of the problem. Make sure users understand how to use the network (user errors often cause problems), and check physical and logical connections on the network. To determine whether you have discovered the actual cause of the problem, re-create it and apply your suggested solution on a test network (if possible). If the re-creation and solution appear to work, proceed to step 5.

5. Implement the solution developed in step 4.

6. Test the solution on working systems.

7. Recognize the side effects of the solution and prepare to deal with them. Examples include client software updates and IP address type changes.

8. Document the solution and make sure support and management staff understand the problem and the solution. Make the information available through an online database or a FAQ list, or via some other manner that is easily accessible.

Tip

If you are managing a network, you should consider using a system for tracking tech support calls and solutions. This type of software is sometimes referred to as a *trouble ticket system*. Some examples include the following:

- Open Ticket Request System (OTRS; http://otrs.org)
- AnswerTrack trouble ticket system (www.answertrack.com/marketing/trouble_ticket_system.html)
- Trouble Ticket Express (www.troubleticketexpress.com)

In finding solutions to almost any problem with your server or network, documentation is a precious resource. In fact, documentation is one of the most important tools when you are trying to troubleshoot or upgrade a network. A network administrator needs to have everything documented for ease of use and to be as efficient as possible in everyday administration, but even more so when there are problems. You can know everything there is to know about your network when things are calm, but when something goes wrong and all the pressure is on your shoulders, you tend to forget some of the little details, and your thinking can sometimes be a little less reliable than usual. For this reason, it is nice to have network diagrams and documentation to help keep a clear picture of what is going on.

If you decide to upgrade items on your network or add features and servers to your network, your network documentation can help you avoid having problems. For example, you could run into little problems such as an IP conflict that could take a little bit of time to track down, but if you have your documentation handy, you could quickly look and see what IP addresses are available and make sure that you never run into that issue to begin with. You could use your documentation to make sure that you continue using the same naming context for your devices. When running a network, attention to details and all the little things really make your network run smoothly in the long run.

Tip

Network documentation software can help you easily diagram and capture network information. Some leading titles include the following:

- Neon Software's LANsurveyor (www.neon.com)

- SmartDraw Technical Edition (www.smartdraw.com)

- Microsoft Visio (www.microsoft.com); note that many vendors make add-ons for use with Visio, including Altima NetZoom (www.altimatech.com) and Neon Software LANsurveyor for Visio (www.neon.com)

If you have a network that is not large enough to require a network administrator, your documentation could be even more important. Good network documentation can help you solve problems without needing to call in network consultants. However, even if a network problem becomes so difficult that you need to bring in a network consultant, you will save time and money by providing the consultant with accurate and up-to-date network documentation. Otherwise, the consultant will need to determine how your network is configured. At typical rates of $150 to $250 per hour, the time needed to determine configuration information can add up quickly.

CHAPTER 14

Power Protection

Power-protection systems do just what the name implies: They protect equipment from the effects of power surges and power failures. In particular, power surges and spikes can damage server and client PC hardware, and a loss of power can result in lost data or, at the very least, lost productivity. Because servers store data used by departments or entire companies, the threat of data loss looms potentially much larger than even hardware damage. These threats to computer hardware and equipment correspond to three major types of power protection for servers:

- **Battery backup systems (usually referred to as uninterruptible power supplies [UPSs])**— Battery backup systems protect against power reductions (brownout) and power loss (blackout).

- **Surge protection**—Surge protection devices protect against power surges and spikes (overvoltages).

- **Redundant power supplies**—Redundant power supplies (RPSs) protect against power supply failure.

The following sections describe the most important features and uses of each type of power protection.

Caution

All the power-protection features in this chapter and the protection features in the power supply inside your computer require that the computer's AC power cable be connected to a ground. Some older business locations do not have three-prong (grounded) outlets to accommodate grounded devices.

Do not use a three-pronged adapter (that bypasses the three-prong requirement and enables you to connect to a two-prong socket) to plug a surge suppressor, computer, or UPS into a two-pronged outlet. They often don't provide a good ground and can inhibit the capabilities of your power-protection devices.

You should also test your power sockets to ensure that they are grounded. Sometimes outlets, despite having three-prong sockets, are not connected to a ground wire; an inexpensive socket tester (available at most hardware stores) can detect this condition.

If you do not properly ground your equipment, your equipment could be damaged, and surge suppression features might not work properly.

UPS Styles and Manufacturers

Several major technologies are used in UPS units. These are the most important types to consider:

- **Standby**—These UPSs are used primarily for personal computers. This type was previously known as a standby power supply (SPS).

- **Line-interactive**—These are the most common type of UPSs for pedestal or rack-mounted servers.

- **Double-conversion online**—These UPSs are a popular choice for N+1 (redundant) configurations in large data centers and for multiple servers. This type is sometimes referred to as a true UPS.

The following sections provide a list of major vendors, discuss how UPS units are rated, and describe the differences in UPS technologies and the desirable features needed in a UPS solution for a server configuration.

Major UPS Manufacturers

There are several major UPS manufacturers. These manufacturers provide a wide variety of technologies, capacities, and features to choose from. Table 14.1 lists major UPS vendors and highlights their server-oriented product lines up to 30kVA. Note that some of these vendors offer higher-capacity products as well. See Appendix C, "Vendor List," for contact information.

Table 14.1   Major UPS Vendors and Server-Grade Product Lines

Product Line	Technology	Capacity
American Power Conversion		
Smart-UPS	Line-interactive	750–5,000VA
Smart-UPS SC	Line-interactive	420–620VA
Smart-UPS XL	Line-interactive	720–2,200VA, 1.4kVA—5kVA 3U–5U[1]
Smart-UPS RT	Double-conversion online	1–10kVA
Symmetra	Double-conversion online	2–6kVA
Symmetra LX	Double-conversion online	4–16kVA
Eaton Powerware		
Powerware 5115	Line-interactive	500–1,400VA
Powerware 5115RM	Line-interactive	500–1,500VA
Powerware 5125	Line-interactive	1,000–2,200VA
Powerware 5125RM	Line-interactive	1,000–3,000VA, 5,000–6,000VA
Powerware 9120	Double-conversion online	700–3,000VA
Powerware 9125	Double-conversion online	700–2,000VA
Powerware 9125RM	Double-conversion online	700–6,000VA
Powerware 9155	Double-conversion online	8–15kVA
Powerware 9170+, 9170+RM	Double-conversion online	3–18kVA
Powerware FERRUPS, FERRUPS RM	Ferro-resonant	500–18,000VA
Liebert (Emerson Network Power)		
PowerSure PSI	Line-interactive	1,000–3,000VA
UPStation GXT	Double-conversion online	700–3,000VA, 10kVA
UPStation GXT2	Double-conversion online	500–6,000VA
Nfinity	Double-conversion online	4–16kVA, 12–20kVA
MGE UPS		
Pulsar Evolution	Line-interactive	500–2,200VA
Pulsar EX RT	Double-conversion online	700–3,200VA
EX RT	Double-conversion online	5–11kVA
Galaxy 3000	Double-conversion online	10–30kVA
MinuteMan UPS		
Pro-E	Line-interactive	500–1,500VA
SmartSine	Line-interactive	700–2,000VA

Table 14.1   Continued

Product Line	Technology	Capacity
MinuteMan UPS		
Enterprise	Line-interactive	500–3,200VA
XRT	Line-interactive	600–2,000VA
MCP-E	Double-conversion online	700VA–7kVA
MCP	Double-conversion online	6–10kVA
OneAC		
ONePlus	Line-interactive	250–1,000VA
ON Series	Line-interactive	200–5,000VA
Sinergy S Series	Double-conversion online	700–3,000VA
Sinergy SE Series	Double-conversion online	4kVA–20kVA
CP Series Parallel Redundant	Double-conversion online	10kVA–20kVA
Tripp Lite		
VS/AVR Series	Line-interactive	550–1,500VA
OmniSmart	Line-interactive	300–1,400VA
SmartPro	Line-interactive	500–5kVA
SmartOnline	Double-conversion online	1kVA–30kVA

¹kVA=1,000VA

How UPS Systems Are Rated

The most common method used to rate a UPS device is the Volt-Ampere (also known as volt-amp [VA]) rating. The VA rating is used to select an appropriately sized UPS unit. The VA rating indicates how long a UPS unit can provide power to the devices connected to it. Although UPS units below 2,000VA are usually intended to support a single server and its essential peripherals, UPS units with 2,000VA or higher ratings can support multiple units. For these larger UPS units, the higher the VA rating, the greater the number of devices that can be connected to the unit.

Note

A VA rating is derived from the device's wattage rating, which is the method used in Table 14.1. A UPS device's VA rating is 167% of the device's wattage rating. To convert from VA to watts, you multiply the VA rating by 0.6.

A UPS device can provide only a few minutes of runtime if it is connected to a full load (that is, devices that require the entire VA rating of the unit). However, the runtime at half load can be anywhere from 2 to 10 times longer (or more), depending on the device, the size of the batteries, and whether the device can be expanded with multiple battery packs. At a minimum, you should select a UPS device with a runtime sufficient to permit normal shutdown. Later in this chapter, we assume a runtime of 30 minutes or longer for the recommendations made for various configurations. If you want to enable a UPS to power a server through a normal backup process, you need to make sure the UPS has a high enough VA rating to enable the server, its display, and the tape backup unit to run for the time period needed for a backup to be completed or shut down properly.

To find out just how much power your server requires, you can look at the Underwriters Laboratories (UL) sticker on the back of the server and the UL sticker on the back (or bottom) of the external devices that are used along with the server, such as a tape backup, monitor, and Internet access devices, such as analog, cable, or DSL modems or routers. These stickers list the maximum power draw in watts, or sometimes in just volts and amperes. If only voltage and amperage are listed, you can multiply the two figures to calculate the wattage. Note that the wattage listed for the power supply includes a safety factor. If you want to calculate the actual wattage the server uses, you can reduce the power supply wattage by about one third.

Calculating Power Use

If you are building your own "white box" server, you need to make sure your power supply and UPS unit provide enough power for all the devices connected to the power supply. Similarly, if you need to select a UPS device, you need to make sure that the UPS device has a large enough VA rating to provide power for the computer, the display, and any other mission-critical devices connected to the unit.

One method of calculating the wattage levels needed for a UPS is to add up the wattage of each component installed in the PC and then add the wattage of the display and other external devices that will be connected to the UPS, such as tape backups, routers, or modems. You then multiply the result by 1.67, which gives you the minimum VA rating needed for the UPS unit. Although external devices are usually labeled with wattage information, the wattage ratings for internal devices are often not available in the documentation.

Tip

If you know the voltage and the amperage of a particular device, you can calculate the wattage required for that device. You simply multiply amps by volts to determine the wattage. For example, a USB mouse that requires 500mA (0.5 amp) and 5V DC power requires 2.5 watts of power ($0.5 \times 5 = 2.5$).

Fortunately, JCS Custom PCs has created an excellent online calculator (www.jscustompcs.com/power_supply/) that can be used to calculate wattage requirements for Intel-based PCs, AMD-based PCs, and servers based on either Intel or AMD processors.

For example, assume that you have a dual-processor Intel Xeon system running at 3GHz, with PCI graphics, four DDR memory modules, three hard disks, a rewritable DVD drive, a SCSI host adapter card, two PCI network cards, and two internal fans. Table 14.2 lists the estimated (maximum) wattage requirements for each component of this system.

Table 14.2   An Example of a Dual-Processor Server's Wattage/VA Requirements

Component	Maximum Wattage
Motherboard	25w
Xeon 3.0GHz CPU (Socket 604)—1	92w
Xeon 3.0GHz CPU (Socket 604)—2	92w
3.5-inch floppy drive	5w
Processor fan—CPU 1	3w
Processor fan—CPU 2	3w
Keyboard and mouse	3w
PCI video	20w

Table 14.2   Continued

Component	Maximum Wattage
DDR memory—1	10w
DDR memory—2	10w
DDR memory—3	10w
DDR memory—4	10w
SCSI hard disk drive—1	25w
SCSI hard disk drive—2	25w
SCSI hard disk drive—3	25w
SCSI host adapter card	25w
Rewritable DVD drive	25w
PCI NIC	4w
120mm system fan—1	2w
120mm system fan—2	2w
15-inch LCD display	60w
Total wattage (TW)	**468w**
VA requirement (TW×1.67)	**782VA**

You can perform the same type of calculation for your system. If you have information on the power usage for a particular component, you can substitute it for the example given here or use an estimation tool such as the one at the JCS Custom PCs site.

Note

If you are building a server, you need to make sure the power supply you select provides enough power for the components inside the chassis as well as those that are bus powered via USB or IEEE 1394 ports. For more information, see the section "Power Supply Sizing," later in this chapter.

Vendor Help

Vendors provide interactive buying guides for UPS systems that are designed to factor in the server type (often by brand and model number) and the devices that might be connected to the server, such as hard disk drives, a monitor, tape backup, or Internet access devices. The recommendations the vendor makes for a particular combination of server hardware are designed to provide you with a range of runtimes and other features. These calculations are based on estimates of typical wattage requirements, using a calculation method similar to the one shown in Table 14.2.

Note

The highest-capacity UPS sold for use with a conventional 15-amp outlet is about 1,400 watts. If it's any higher, you risk tripping a 15-amp circuit breaker when the battery is charging heavily and the inverter is drawing maximum current.

If you need higher capacity for rack-mounted systems or a server cluster, you should make sure you have 20-amp or 30-amp outlets, use a UPS that can be connected to multiple electrical outlets, or use a UPS that can be wired directly into the building's electrical system. This type of UPS is known as a *hard-wired* UPS. To learn more about hard-wired UPS devices, see the websites for the UPS vendors listed in Table 14.1

The specifications for a particular UPS unit indicate what type of outlet or wiring is required.

Although a VA rating high enough to permit you to shut down your server without losing data is essential, it is only one of several considerations in choosing a UPS unit.

UPS Technologies

As discussed in the following sections, the technology used by a UPS unit is important in improving reliability. The following sections discuss a number of UPS technologies:

- Standby UPS (SPS)
- Line-interactive UPS
- Double-conversion online UPS
- Ferro-resonant UPS

These UPS technologies support individual servers and the requirements of small to medium-sized server rooms. Other technologies, such as delta-conversion online UPS, are designed for very large server installations and are beyond the scope of this book.

Standby UPS (SPS) Technology

Most low-end battery backup devices made for personal computers use the standby design. A standby UPS is known as an *offline device*: It functions only when normal power is disrupted. A standby UPS system uses a special circuit that can sense the AC line current. If the sensor detects a loss of power on the line, the system quickly switches over to a standby battery and power inverter. The power inverter converts the battery power to 120V AC power, which is then supplied to the system. Figure 14.1 provides a conceptual diagram of standby UPS technology.

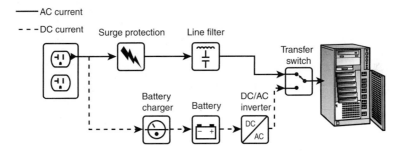

Figure 14.1   A typical standby UPS system suitable for PC workstations.

Modern standby UPS devices are designed to store a small amount of power in a transformer and deliver it to connected devices during the switchover time from AC to battery power. This acts as a buffer on the power line, giving the standby UPS almost uninterruptible capability. You should look at the line/battery transfer (switch) time specifications and make sure the unit can switch in 6ms or less between AC and battery power. A longer transfer time could cause your PC to crash. You should also look at the minimum voltage level used for switching between AC and battery power. Typical units switch to battery power at 99 volts AC (120V AC current), which is well within the range at which a 120V AC power supply can produce adequate DC power.

A standby UPS cannot provide power conditioning unless it includes separate power-conditioning hardware because it passes AC power through to the server and other connected devices in normal operation. (The standby UPS diagrammed in Figure 14.1 does include surge suppression and line conditioning.)

The battery is used only when AC power fails. Although standby UPS devices are not recommended for server use because they have limited VA capacity (1.5kVA/1,500VA maximum), high-performance units (700VA or higher) are recommended for mission-critical client PCs.

Line-Interactive UPS Technology

Line-interactive UPS devices are the most common type of UPS devices used for individual servers. In a line-interactive UPS, the system is run by the AC/DC inverter, which also charges the battery. When the AC current supplying the battery charger fails, the inverter is already in operation, and it simply reverses direction to provide DC power from the battery for conversion into AC power.

There is no interruption in power because the inverter is used at all times to run the system, whether AC power is available or not. When the line power returns, the battery charger begins recharging the battery, again with no interruption. Figure 14.2 illustrates how a typical line-interactive UPS system works.

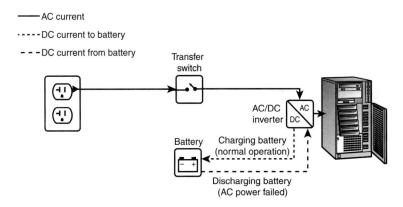

Figure 14.2 A typical line-interactive UPS system.

Most line-interactive UPS devices are designed to regulate voltage to prevent unnecessary use of the battery and to avoid overvoltages going to the server. Line-interactive units are available with capacities up to 5,000VA/5KVA.

Double-Conversion Online UPS Technology

Although line-interactive technology can support capacities up to 5,000VA, most UPS units with capacities of 2,000VA or higher use a double-conversion design. A double-conversion design converts power from AC to DC (using a rectifier) to charge the battery and then converts power from DC back to AC with a DC/AC inverter. The inverter is the source of AC power for the server, whether power is flowing normally or is interrupted. However, unlike with a line-interactive UPS, with a double-conversion online UPS, it is not necessary for the inverter to reverse directions. This enables the unit to respond even faster than with a line-interactive design. For this reason, double-conversion online UPS devices are sometimes referred to as true UPS devices. Figure 14.3 illustrates how a double-conversion online UPS device works.

Power Factor Correction and UPS Technologies

One way to measure the efficiency of a UPS is in terms of power factor correction (PFC). A perfectly efficient power supply has a PFC of 100% (1.0), while older double-conversion units were limited to 85% (.85) PFC. Filtering devices and other improvements enable recent designs to reach over 90% (.9)

PFC in high-performance mode. If you use auxiliary generators to provide backup power, you should keep in mind that under some circumstances, double-conversion UPS units connected to light loads can interfere with proper operation of the generator. If you use a generator to keep your servers online in the event of an AC power failure, you should look for UPS units designed to work with a generator.

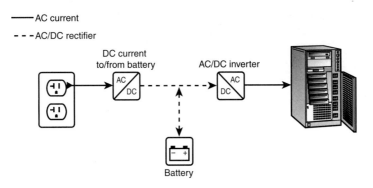

Figure 14.3 A typical double-conversion online UPS system.

One advantage of double-conversion online UPS over line-interactive and standby technologies is their ability to cope with poor-quality input power. A double-conversion online UPS can handle AC power that is not at a constant frequency without unnecessary switchovers to battery power.

Tip

Be sure to check the amperage rating and AC connection type needed to run a double-conversion online UPS. Models with output of up to 2,200VA require a 20-amp outlet, while units with output of 2,400–5,000VA require a 30-amp outlet. Higher-capacity UPS devices must be hard-wired, and models from 20,000VA and up use three-phase wiring.

Ferro-Resonant UPSs

A few UPS devices still use the ferro-resonant (also known as *standby ferro*) technology. Ferro-resonant UPS units include a ferro-resonant transformer. This type of transformer provides built-in voltage regulation and line conditioning (unlike in standby UPS units) and provides power stored by the transformer for a brief period after an AC outage occurs. At that point, the unit switches rapidly to battery power. Ferro-resonant UPS devices don't produce much heat, which makes them suitable for environments in which cooling could be a problem. However, double-conversion online UPS devices provide comparable power-conditioning features in a more compact form factor with greater efficiency.

UPS Features

Although choosing a UPS with a sufficient VA rating for your server is important, the VA rating is not the only consideration. You also need to consider issues of management, interface between the server and UPS, and the UPS's flexibility. The following are some of the essential features to look for in UPS units suitable for use with servers:

- **Support for server management**—The UPS must be able to signal the server when AC power is lost so that the server can begin a shutdown process. UPS units use the server's serial or USB port for signaling, and, depending on the unit or user preference, they might use the built-in UPS software in Windows or the vendor's own UPS management software.

■ **Support for your server operating system**—If your server uses an operating system other than Windows, you need to make sure the UPS includes management software that is compatible with your operating system (Linux, Solaris, Novell NetWare, UNIX). In some cases, you might need to download the management software after you purchase the device. You can learn more about operating systems in Chapter 18, "Server Platforms: Network Operating Systems."

Tip

The Network UPS Tools (NUT) site, at www.networkupstools.org, is an excellent resource for UPS users. It provides drivers, cable pinouts, documentation, and other aids to help you get your UPS working with Linux.

■ **Support for your preferred I/O port type**—Traditionally, UPS devices communicated with servers through the serial (COM) port. However, most recent UPS units include a USB port, either in addition to or instead of a serial port.

■ **Appropriate form factor**—If you use a rack-mounted server, you will probably prefer to use a rack-mounted UPS. Otherwise, a tower or mini-tower form factor will work. Some UPS units can be converted to work as either tower or rack-mounted units. Note that some vendors' product lines have different VA ratings for tower and rack-mounted UPS units in the same product line.

■ **Power conditioning**—Power conditioning is native to a double-conversion online unit but requires additional hardware in a line-interactive UPS design.

■ **Network manageability**—If UPSs will be located in a server room away from users, you should look for UPS units that can be upgraded with a network management interface. Most interfaces support 10/100 Ethernet networking, but some also include an analog modem for remote dial-up connections. The network management interface can add as much as $300 to the cost of the UPS unit.

■ **Voltage transfer point adjustment**—If the input power varies a great deal from the 120V or 240V standard, you should look for UPS units that permit you to adjust the minimum voltage for switching to battery power.

■ **Generator compatible**—Some UPS units are not designed to work with a generator providing AC power. If you need this capability, you should be sure to look for UPS units that work with a generator.

■ **Hot-swappable batteries**—If your area suffers frequent electrical interruptions, it's useful to be able to swap the UPS battery without shutting down the unit.

■ **Optional battery packs**—If you plan to protect multiple servers with a single UPS, you should look for models that support additional batteries. As more capacity is needed, you can just add another battery.

■ **Automatic restart**—UPS units with this feature can automatically restart devices using AC power after power is restored.

▶▶   See "UPS Specifications and Considerations," p. 678, for more information on applying these considerations to your UPS purchase.

Surge Protection

Virtually every UPS unit suitable for server use includes surge protection. Thus, it is not necessary to use a separate surge protector on a server connected to a UPS. Surge protectors are designed to absorb the high-voltage transients produced by nearby lightning strikes and power equipment. Such spikes can easily destroy sensitive computer equipment.

Because surge protectors help protect computers and other electronic devices, you should connect devices not attached to the UPS, such as printers, to their own surge protectors.

Surge protectors use several devices, usually metal-oxide varistors (MOVs), that can clamp and shunt away all voltages above a certain level. MOVs are designed to accept voltages as high as 6,000V and divert any power above 200V to ground. MOVs can handle normal surges, but powerful surges such as direct lightning strikes can blow right through them. MOVs are not designed to handle a very high level of power, and they self-destruct while shunting a large surge. These devices therefore cease to function after either a single large surge or a series of smaller ones.

Because MOVs eventually fail, you should make sure that you specify only surge protectors that are designed to stop providing power to the outlets when the MOVs have failed. A protection status light is also useful, so you can tell at a glance if the unit is still working.

UL has produced an excellent standard, UL 1449, that governs surge suppressors. Any surge suppressor that meets this standard is a very good one and definitely offers a line of protection beyond what the power supply in your PC already offers. The only types of surge suppressors worth buying, therefore, should have two features:

- Conformance to the UL 1449 standard
- Automatic shutdown of the surge protector when the MOVs have failed, along with a status light indicating whether the device is working.

Units that meet the UL 1449 specification say so on the packaging or directly on the unit. If this standard is not mentioned, it does not conform. You should avoid any unit that doesn't conform to the specification.

Other useful features include the following:

- **Double-sided outlet design**—If outlets are located at both sides of a surge protector, it's more likely that all outlets will be usable.
- **Increased spacing for AC/DC converters**—Many peripherals, such as broadband and dial-up modems and some types of printers, are powered by AC/DC converters (also known as power blocks, or briquettes). Surge suppressors that provide extra spacing between outlets enable all outlets to be used, even when some are occupied by power blocks.
- **Surge suppression for data lines**—If you have an all-in-one or fax machine connected to a phone line, don't overlook the possibility of phone line surges. Phone lines carry power (enabling the phone to be used during a power blackout), so they can also transmit a damaging surge to the modem or the server. Surge protectors with RJ-11 ports provide protection against phone line surges. A few surge protectors on the market now offer surge protection for RJ-45 Ethernet and RG-6 coaxial cables as well.
- **Built-in circuit breaker**—In a unit that has a built-in circuit breaker, the breaker protects your system if it or a peripheral develops a short.

To protect data lines going directly into your server, such as RJ-11 phone, RJ-45 Ethernet, or RG-6 coaxial for video, you should use surge protectors that connect to the data lines. Some UPS units include this feature, either standard or as an option. If your preferred UPS does not, you should look for standalone units available from vendors such as Black Box Network Services (www.blackbox.com), Connect Technologies (www.connecttech.net), and others.

Redundant Power Supplies (RPSs)

A number of server chassis are designed to use, either as standard or as options, RPSs. Essentially, an RPS is two or more power supply modules plugged in to a common connection to the motherboard, drives, and other devices. If the primary module fails, the reserve module takes over.

Figure 14.4 illustrates a typical RPS designed to fit in place of a standard SSI power supply. Other types of RPS units have form factors suitable for use in various sizes of rack-mounted servers.

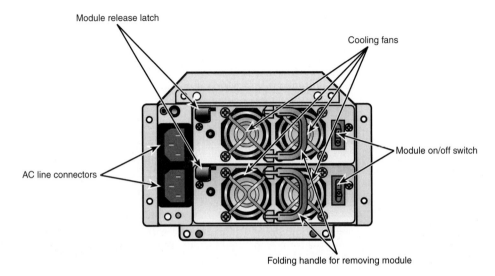

Figure 14.4 A typical redundant power supply that can be used in place of a standard SSI power supply.

Preconfigured servers from major vendors often include RPS capability as either a standard or optional feature in both pedestal and rack-mounted server form factors. However, you can also retrofit existing pedestal, tower, and rack-mounted servers with an RPS. Note that standard power supply vendors do not typically manufacture RPS designs. The following are some RPS vendors:

■ CyberResearch (www.cyberresearch.com)

■ Orbit Micro (www.orbitmicro.com)

■ Rackmount.com (www.rackmount.com)

Some RPS units use a common AC power source for all modules. While this type of design provides protection against power supply module failure, it does nothing to protect against AC power interruptions. This type of RPS should be used only if a UPS unit is used with the server.

A better design, such as the one shown in Figure 14.4, uses a separate AC power source for each module. This type of design is especially valuable if you can connect each module to a different circuit. In the event of a power failure to one circuit, the RPS can continue to receive power from the other circuit and can continue to operate. For maximum protection, a separate UPS should be used for each AC power source.

Note

Hewlett-Packard offers a useful document that outlines best practices for providing power to a server that contains RPS units. You can download "Creating High-Availability Power Solutions for the ProLiant ML570 Server: Best Practices" from http://h200000.www2.hp.com/bc/docs/support/SupportManual/c00257380/c00257380.pdf.

You need to be sure that any RPS solution you use can be hot-swapped. Hot-swapping means that you can remove the failed RPS module and replace it with a spare without shutting down the server.

High-quality RPS modules usually indicate a failure via an alarm (audible, visual, or both). Most server management programs are designed to alert you to a failed RPS.

Power Supply Sizing

Whether you are using an RPS or a standard power supply in your server, it's important to make certain it provides enough power to operate the internal components inside your server as well as those that receive power from the server's USB or IEEE 1394 ports. The calculations used to determine the size of the power supply are similar to those used to determine the appropriate rating for a UPS unit (refer to Table 14.2, earlier in this chapter). The differences include the following:

- Power supplies do not need to provide power to displays or to most other external devices, such as tape backups or external SCSI RAID arrays, so the wattage requirements for those devices are not included.

- Power supplies do not always operate reliably under full load. For safety's sake, it's best to select a power supply that provides at least 20% more wattage than the calculated requirement. For example, if you determine that your server's components need 350 watts of power, a high-quality 425 watt or larger power supply would be recommended.

Table 14.3 provides a typical example of calculating the power supply requirements for a dual-processor server.

Table 14.3   An Example of a Dual-Processor Server's Power Supply Requirements

Component	Maximum Wattage
Motherboard	25w
Xeon 3.0GHz CPU (Socket 604)—1	92w
Xeon 3.0GHz CPU (Socket 604)—2	92w
3.5-inch floppy drive	5w
Processor fan—CPU 1	3w
Processor fan—CPU 2	3w
Keyboard and mouse	3w
PCI video	20w
DDR memory—1	10w
DDR memory—2	10w
DDR memory—3	10w
DDR memory—4	10w
SCSI hard disk drive—1	25w
SCSI hard disk drive—2	25w
SCSI hard disk drive—3	25w
SCSI host adapter card	25w
Rewritable DVD drive	25w
PCI NIC	4w
120mm system fan—1	2w
120mm system fan—2	2w
Total wattage (TW)	**408w**
Wattage with 20% safety factor	**490w**

Note that each module in an RPS must provide the wattage rating needed. For example, in the calculation in Table 14.3, a RPS for the sample system would need two 490w or higher-rated modules. Note that standard power supply sizes are 300w, 350w, 400w, 425w, 450w, 500w, 510w, 550w, 600w, and higher. You should use the next higher-wattage power supply if your calculation does not exactly match a standard size.

Tip

To make power supply sizing easier, try these resources:

- PC Power and Cooling provides a list of wattage ranges for components at www.pcpowercooling.com/ technology/power_usage/ and an interactive power supply selector at www.pcpowercooling.com/products/ power_supplies/selector/.

- Tom's Hardware provides a list of typical internal devices and wattage ratings at www.tomshardware.com/ 2002/10/21/inadequate_and_deceptive_product_labeling/page3.html.

UPS Specifications and Considerations

Selecting the right UPS for a server or server room is not a trivial issue. The greater the number of servers you need to protect, the more complex the task can become. Although most UPS vendors provide online interactive buying guides to help you through the selection process, it's still useful to understand the factors that go into a vendor's recommendations. These include the following:

- Server capacity and purpose
- Voltages
- Runtimes
- Batteries
- AC connectors
- Safety ratings

The following sections discuss each of these factors.

Server Capacity and Purpose

The first question you need to answer before you select a UPS is, "How is this server being used?" If you fail to answer this question first, you will not be able to make an informed choice of UPS. Here's why this question is important:

- A server that can be shut down at any time can use a relatively small UPS. However, a server that provides critical 24/7 services, such as medical information, emergency dispatch, telecom, or utility management, needs enough power to keep working for as long as possible—perhaps several hours. You have two options for extending power: buy a UPS unit with a larger VA rating or buy a UPS unit designed to connect to multiple batteries.

- The number of devices connected to the server that must be powered by the UPS is also an important consideration when configuring a UPS. The power requirements of devices such as dial-up or broadband modems, external hard disk arrays, and backup devices must also be considered. However, printers and other non-essential devices should not be connected to the UPS.

You need to think about these considerations before you purchase a UPS.

Note

Some UPS vendors offer special models optimized for medical environments. These units meet UL 60601-1 medical electrical equipment standards for minimal current leakage. You should specify this type of UPS if you need to place a UPS in an environment sensitive to current leakage, such as hospitals, air traffic control, and laboratories.

Some UPS vendors offer special models designed to handle industrial environments such as those specified in MIL-STD-810. You should specify this type of UPS if the unit will be used on a loading dock or in another rough environment.

Voltages

If you are selecting a UPS for use with a standard x86 or 64-bit server, the UPS you use will be designed for either 120V/60Hz AC (U.S./Canada) or 240V/50Hz AC (Europe/Asia). If your server room has 208V AC power, which is used by telecom equipment and midrange systems, you can select UPS units that accept 208V AC incoming voltage and step it down to 120V AC.

Some UPS devices do not permit much, if any, adjustment of input voltage ranges. If your location is subject to a lot of variation in input voltage, a UPS with limited or no ability to adjust the voltage at which the device switches to battery power could result in unnecessary use of the battery. This can lead to premature battery failure or to a UPS not yet being fully recharged when total loss of AC power takes place.

UPS models that can be configured to work with a wide range of incoming voltage are recommended if your location has substandard or overstandard voltage.

Runtimes

The runtime for a particular combination of UPS and connected hardware is determined by three factors:

- How much wattage the devices draw
- The VA rating of the UPS device
- The number of batteries connected to the unit

The actual wattage your server uses is *not* the same as the server power supply's wattage rating. The server's power supply (like a PC's power supply) is designed to provide power well in excess of the server's requirements. However, each external device connected to a server also has a wattage rating that must also be taken into account.

You can determine the size of UPS you should purchase for your server based on its load or its devices. Some vendors offer both methods. The easiest way to calculate the power used by a server is to use a vendor's UPS selector calculator, assuming it's detailed enough. You should be able to specify the following:

- Server brand and model number
- Processor type
- Number of processors
- Number and type of hard disk drives
- Peripherals (tape backup, modems, optical drives, and so on)
- Monitor type and size
- Operating voltage

- Number of servers connected to the UPS
- Amount of headroom for future expansion
- Desired runtime
- Form factor (rack-mounted or tower)
- Redundancy
- Voltage

Before displaying recommended configurations, many vendors display the calculated wattage based on your selections. If you know the wattage ratings of your server and attached peripherals, you can use the "configure by load" option (if offered by the UPS vendor) to create a list of recommended UPS configurations. Typically, vendors provide two or more UPS configurations that satisfy the device or load requirements you provide.

Tip

Include only essential devices (or the wattage loads they require) when you use a UPS selector wizard. Printers are not essential devices: A printer (particularly a laser printer) can run down even a large UPS unit very quickly and should not be connected to the UPS. However, external devices such as hard disk arrays, tape backups, and monitors should be included.

When you view the vendor's list of suggested configurations, you might notice that the same UPS device is listed more than once with different runtimes. This indicates that the device is listed with both its standard single-battery configuration and with additional batteries.

Batteries

If you plan to connect more than one server to a UPS, or if you want to add additional components to a server connected to a UPS, choosing a UPS that can be connected to multiple batteries is a good idea.

Although you cannot increase a UPS unit's VA rating (which specifies the maximum load it can support) by connecting additional batteries to the UPS, you can connect additional batteries to increase runtime, and doing so permits a UPS to handle a load closer to its maximum while still providing adequate runtime.

For example, an APC Smart-UPS XL 750VA (120V version) connected to an Intel SC5250-E server with four internal SATA drives, a 15-inch CRT, and an external tape backup (about 387 watts or 553VA) offers a runtime of 35 minutes when used with its internal battery, according to APC's online UPS selector. However, the same battery backup unit provides a runtime of up to 160 minutes when an external battery pack (SUA24XLBP) is added to the basic configuration.

If you opt for UPS units that support multiple batteries, you should try to standardize on products that can use the same additional battery pack. For example, Tripp Lite's BP48V24-2U external battery pack works with a variety of 2,200VA–3,000VA Tripp Lite UPS systems. By using different UPS models that use a common additional battery pack, you make handling capacity issues and swapping parts in case of failure far easier than if you don't use interchangeable battery packs.

Even if you choose a UPS that does not support multiple batteries, choosing a unit that supports hot-swap batteries makes sense. A UPS with hot-swap battery support enables you to swap a failed battery or one that is not fully charged for another battery without shutting down the UPS or the server. Note that you cannot swap out a battery if the UPS has only one battery and the battery is currently powering the server.

Batteries for server-class UPS units are typically based on sealed lead-acid technology. If you need to store a UPS unit for an extended period of time, you should reconnect the unit to AC power and recharge the battery every three to six months to enable the battery to receive and retain a full charge. For additional battery-conditioning tips, consult the UPS manufacturer's instruction manual.

AC Connectors

The UPS unit you select must have enough AC connectors to support the devices you need to connect to it. For example, if your server has an external tape backup, a broadband modem, and a broadband router, you need a total of five connectors, one each for the server, the monitor, the tape backup, the broadband modem, and the broadband router.

Some UPS systems offer two or more individually switchable load banks. If you use the management software provided with the UPS, one bank can be configured to drop less critical loads to extend runtime for more critical loads. For example, you could plug the server and tape backup into one load bank and the other devices into a second load bank. The second load bank could be configured to shut off if necessary to provide longer runtime for the devices in the first load bank.

You need to make sure the UPS you select is designed to connect with the electrical outlets available in the area. 120V AC units with up to 1,400VA can plug in to a standard 15-amp outlet. However, units with larger VA ratings must be connected to 20-amp or 30-amp outlets or must be hard-wired, depending on the VA rating of the device. You should be sure to check the specifications for incoming power and outlet type used in your location before you specify a UPS.

Safety Ratings

You need to make sure the UPS unit you buy meets the relevant safety ratings for your country or region. You should check the product's specifications or product manual to determine the safety ratings for a particular product.

Common Server/UPS Configurations

With so many UPS units with different capacities on the market, there are an almost unlimited number of server and UPS configurations possible. However, they can be broken down into a few categories. The following sections show the details of the following typical configurations:

- Pedestal server and UPS
- Single rack-mounted server and UPS
- Multiple rack-mounted servers and UPS

Note

The calculations in the following sections are based on the APC UPS Selector, located at www.apc.com/tools/ups_selector/. Other vendors offer similar online configuration tools.

Pedestal Server and UPS

Typically, you use a tower or mini-tower UPS with a pedestal server (such units are also suitable for use with a tower server). Table 14.4 lists some typical pedestal server configurations and the VA ratings needed to sustain a runtime of 30 minutes or longer with at least a 30% margin for future expansion. Items in Table 14.4 are listed in order of wattage and recommended VA ratings.

Table 14.4   Typical Pedestal Server UPS Configurations

Server Brand, Model	Processor Type (Qty)	Internal Drives	Other Hardware	Watts	Minimum Recommended VA Rating (Estimated Runtime)
IBM xSeries 236	Xeon (2)	6	Tape drive, 15-inch CRT	472	1,500VA (44 min.)
SuperMicro SuperServer 8050	PIII Xeon (2)	6	Tape drive, 15-inch LCD	524	2,200VA (35 min.)
HP Integrity rx8620-32	Itanium 2 (8)	10	Tape drive	1,530	5,000VA (78 min.)[1]

[1]*With additional battery.*

If the server has RPSs, you should connect each power supply AC cable to a separate port on the UPS unit.

Single Rack-Mounted Server and UPS

Typically, if you use a rack-mounted server, you also want to use the rack-mounted server for other components, including your UPS. Table 14.5 lists some typical rack-mounted server configurations and the VA ratings needed to sustain a runtime of 30 minutes or longer with at least a 30% margin for future expansion. Items in Table 14.5 are listed in order of wattage and recommended VA ratings.

Table 14.5   Typical Rack-Mounted Server and UPS Configurations

Server Brand, Model (Form Factor)	Processor Type (Qty)	Internal Drives	Other Hardware	Watts	Minimum Recommended VA Rating (Estimated Runtime)
IBM xSeries 336 (1U)	Xeon (2)	4	Tape drive	359	750VA (39 min.)
HP ProLiant DL580 (4U)	Xeon (4)	4	Tape drive	626	1,500VA (33 min.)
Sun SunFire V40Z (3U)	Opteron (4)	6	Tape drive, cable/DSL modem, cable/DSL router	667	1,500VA (30 min.)

If the server has redundant power supplies, connect each power supply AC cable to a separate port on the UPS unit.

Multiple Rack-Mounted Servers and UPS

One of the attractions of the rack-mounted server form factor is the ability to place multiple servers into the same rack. This saves a great deal of floor space compared with what pedestal servers with comparable features would require. In such situations, it makes sense to use a single higher-capacity UPS to provide backup power to all the servers in a rack. Table 14.6 lists the recommended VA ratings for the same rack-mounted servers shown in Table 14.5, in quantities of two, three, and four units.

Table 14.6   Typical Configurations for Multiple Rack-Mounted Servers and UPS

Server Brand, Model (Form Factor)	Watts per Server Cfg (Table 14.5)	Minimum Recommended VA Rating (Estimated Runtime)		
		Two Units	**Three Units**	**Four Units**
IBM xSeries 336 (1U)	359	2,200VA (43 min.)	2,200VA (85 min.)[1]	3,000VA (58 min.)[1]
HP ProLiant DL580 (4U)	626	2,200VA (70 min.)[1]	3,000VA (51 min.)[2]	5,000VA (39 min.)[1]
Sun SunFire V40Z (3U)	667	2,200VA (64 min.)[1]	3,000VA (48 min.)[2]	5,000VA (35 min.)[1]

[1]*With additional battery.*
[2]*With two additional batteries.*

Each server should be connected to a separate load bank on the UPS. If a server has RPS units, you should connect each RPS to the same load bank if only one UPS is used. If additional UPS units are used, you can connect each RPS to a separate load bank.

Using and Maintaining UPS Documentation

The more complex a UPS unit is, the more important it is to keep documentation available for ready reference. A high-capacity line-interactive or any double-conversion online UPS unit might have several components, each with its own documentation:

- The UPS unit itself
- One or more built-in battery modules
- Additional battery modules
- UPS management software
- Remote network management interface cards

If you do not want to keep the original documentation with the UPS unit, you can usually download PDF versions from the vendor's website. These can be printed out for reference and stored in a binder next to the UPS unit.

In addition to keeping the manufacturer's documentation available for use, you should also record changes you have made to the default settings of the UPS unit or its accessories, such as the following:

- How often the automatic self-test is run
- The ID of the UPS unit on the network
- The battery replacement date
- The minimum capacity before the battery can be used to power up the system after shutdown
- Voltage sensitivity
- Audible alarm
- Shutdown delay timing
- The low battery warning interval

- The synchronized turn-on delay
- The high and low voltage transfer points
- The IP address of the network management module
- The password used to access the network management module

If you print a copy of the original documentation, you can use a highlighter to indicate the selected options and write down the date the option was selected.

Note

If you have only one UPS that you manage through the network, you could keep the default name. If you have more than one, you should develop a name strategy and use the next available name for each new UPS you add to the network.

For example, if the first UPS unit is named "BattBkup" by default, you should consider changing the name to "BattBkup01" and numbering other units sequentially, starting with "BattBkup02." Alternatively, you could assign names that indicate the location, such as "UPS_ServerRM01" or the server being protected, such as "UPS_CommSvr." See the documentation for your UPS unit for details.

Installing a New UPS

The process of installing a new UPS on a server involves several steps. You can use the following list as a general guide to the process, in conjunction with the documentation provided by your UPS vendor:

1. **Connect the battery**—Many UPS units are shipped with the battery disconnected from the unit. To connect an internal battery, open the unit and connect the cables as directed in the documentation. To connect additional batteries, look for the external battery connector on the base unit and connect the additional battery to it. Each additional battery includes a connector for another battery pack, enabling you to daisy-chain the batteries.

2. **Install the network management card or management cable (serial or USB)**—If the UPS unit will be managed remotely, install the network management card or connect the unit to a network cable. If the unit will be managed from the server, connect the USB or serial cable to the appropriate port on the unit and to the server. Note that the serial cable (if used) must be specially designed for use with the UPS.

3. **Connect the UPS unit to AC**—Connect the UPS unit to AC and verify that the unit is charging. Signal lights on the front of the unit indicate the status of the unit.

4. **Turn on unit after charging is complete**—When the signal lights indicate that the unit's battery (or batteries) is completely charged, turn on the unit.

5. **Connect the unit to the server**—If you opted in step 2 to manage the unit at the server, connect the USB or serial cable from the UPS unit to the server. If you use USB, you can hot-plug the cable. If you use the serial cable, you should shut down the server, plug in the serial cable, and restart the server.

6. **Install the drivers provided with the UPS**—Windows 2000 Server and Windows Server 2003 automatically detect a USB-based UPS unit. Provide the driver disk or CD when prompted to complete installation. For serial port units, see the documentation provided with the UPS unit.

7. **Configure the server to manage the UPS**—With Windows 2000 Server and Windows Server 2003, you can use the UPS tab in the Power (or Power Options, in Windows Server 2003) properties sheet in the Control Panel to manage APC and other third-party UPS units that use the serial port. However, the UPS service does not work with USB-based UPS services. In such cases, use the software provided by the vendor instead. Use vendor-provided software if you use other server operating systems.

8. **Install vendor-provided software on the client PC**—If the UPS unit is managed over the network, install vendor-provided software on the client PC that will be used for UPS management.

9. **Log in to unit via the network**—View the default settings. If they are suitable, keep them. Otherwise, configure the unit as desired and record the configuration.

Troubleshooting Power-Protection Problems

The following sections list typical problems that occur with UPS units, surge suppressors, and RPS units. They also discuss the possible solutions or sources for more information.

UPS Does Not Charge Battery When Plugged In

If the UPS unit is new, the battery pack is probably disconnected for shipping. Reconnect the battery pack per the manufacturer's instructions. If the battery is more than two or three years old, replace the battery.

If the battery is connected to the unit through an external port, double-check the connections between the battery and the UPS unit.

Windows Server 2003 Does Not Transmit UPS Alerts

Windows Server 2003 uses the Messenger server to send UPS alerts, but it does not run the Messenger service by default. Messenger needs to be configured to run automatically at startup before UPS alerts can be run. For details, see http://support.microsoft.com/default.aspx?scid=kb;en-us;828286.

System Does Not Restart After AC Power Is Restored

To enable a server connected to a UPS unit to restart automatically after AC power is restored, the BIOS setting for handling power-off events needs to be changed to Always On rather than the typical defaults of Stay Off, Last State, or Auto. This setting is usually found in the Power or Power-On menu of the system BIOS. For details, see http://support.microsoft.com/default.aspx?scid=kb;en-us;819038.

COM Port Conflicts

Windows Server 2003 may shut down unexpectedly after you install a serial-port–based UPS. This can happen if you specify the same serial port already in use by another device, such as a modem. Make sure the serial port specified is only used by the UPS. Move other serial-port–based devices to other serial ports. For details, see http://support.microsoft.com/default.aspx?scid=kb;en-us;815268.

New Services Configuration in Windows Server 2003

If you have problems getting the UPS service working in Windows Server 2003, it could be due to changes in how this version of Windows works with services and user accounts. For a list of these changes, see http://support.microsoft.com/default.aspx?scid=kb;en-us;812519.

Linux Power Management Software Can't Start After Installation

Different Linux distributions use different default folders for utilities (daemons) provided by UPS vendors for use with Linux. If an incorrect folder is used, copy the files used by the daemon to the correct folder for your distribution. For an example, see www.minutemanups.com/support/lnx_tech.php.

General Linux UPS Issues

The UPS HowTo page at The Linux Documentation Project provides useful advice on selecting, configuring, and using UPS devices with Linux servers. Find it at www.tldp.org/HOWTO/UPS-HOWTO/.

UPS Service Shuts Down System

If your UPS software shuts down your server after installation and you are unable to disable it in normal mode, restart your server in Safe Mode. After the server is running in Safe Mode, right-click My Computer, select Manage, open Services and Applications, open Services, and scroll down to Uninterruptible Power Supply Service. Disable the service and reboot your system.

After the server restarts, contact the vendor for updates. Remove the existing software and install the updated version.

UPS Tab Is Missing After Installing a USB-Based UPS and Drivers

The UPS tab provided by Windows 2000 Server and Windows Server 2003 in the Power (Power Options) icon in the Control Panel may be replaced by Alarms and Power Meter after you install a USB-based UPS and its drivers. The UPS service provided with these versions of Windows is only for serial-port–based UPS units.

When you install a USB-based UPS in Windows, you must use the software provided by the vendor. For an example of how to configure an APC UPS, see http://forums.pcworld.co.nz/printthread.php?t=51729.

Devices Don't Work When Plugged In to Surge Protector

A surge protector might not appear to work if the devices plugged into it are turned off or not properly plugged in to the line cord going to the surge protector. If the surge protector is itself not plugged in to a working AC outlet, no device plugged in to it will work. Surge protectors have on/off switches; if the unit is turned off, it will not work.

If the surge protector is turned on and properly connected to AC current, and if all devices are turned on and properly connected, but they do not work, check the surge suppressor's circuit breaker. Turn off the unit and reset it and then turn it back on. If the circuit breaker in the surge protector trips, one of the devices connected to the unit might be malfunctioning. Shut off the surge protector, disconnect all devices, and restart the unit. If the circuit breaker trips again, replace the unit.

If the surge suppressor works with no devices plugged in to it, shut it down. Plug one device at a time in to the unit, turn on the unit, and turn on the device. Repeat until you find a device that trips the surge protector. Replace that device. If no devices trip the surge protector's circuit breaker, but they do not operate when plugged in to the surge protector, the surge protector has failed. Replace it.

RPS Doesn't Switch to Good Module When First Module Fails

An RPS contains two or more power supply modules. When the first module fails, the RPS is designed to automatically switch to the second or subsequent module. If it does not, check the following:

- **Is the RPS module properly connected to AC power?**—Many RPS units have a separate AC power cord for each module. With the server shut down, make sure the cord is properly plugged in to the module and plugged in to a working electrical outlet in the server's UPS.

- **Is the RPS module turned off?**—Some RPS modules have on/off switches. Make sure the module is turned on.

- **Is the RPS module completely plugged in to the RPS enclosure?**—With the server shut down, remove and reinsert the module, verifying that the module is making full contact with the connector inside the enclosure.

Replace a defective RPS module. Check the AC line cord (if additional modules use their own cords); also check the on/off switch on the module, and remove and reinsert the module.

CHAPTER 15

Chassis

Next to the motherboard, the chassis is one of the most important components in a server. The chassis determines how many expansion slots and internal drives the system can use and whether the system can be rack-mounted or must use up valuable floor space in a server room. There are more chassis options today than ever before, but some motherboard form factors may limit your chassis selection. You can use this chapter, along with Chapter 4, "Server Motherboards and BIOS," to help create a server with the right form factor for your needs.

Chassis Types

Although low-end servers might use the same mainstream ATX and slowly emerging BTX standard chassis as desktops, there are abundant reasons to consider using a chassis optimized for server use when you specify or build a server.

Chassis built for server use offer several advantages compared to desktop chassis forced into the server role:

- Server chassis are designed to handle the larger form factors used by server motherboards, such as the SSI-EEB 3.0 and 3.5 standards.
- Some server chassis can be used in either pedestal (vertical) or rack-mounted configurations, enabling a single chassis design to be used in a wide variety of circumstances.
- Server chassis provide better cooling than most desktop cases do, leading to better reliability.
- Rack-mounted server chassis in the 1U to 3U form factors can be used as wall-mounted units for situations in which a standard rack-mounted frame is not available.

◀◀   For more information about SSI-EEB server motherboard form factors, see "The EEB Form Factor," p. 235.

▶▶   For more information about the rack-mounted U (unit) standard, see "Universal Racks," p. 713.

The following sections discuss the entire range of server chassis types, including pedestal, rack-mounted, wall-mounted rack, ATX, and BTX form factors.

Pedestal Chassis

At first glance, the differences between a pedestal chassis (see Figure 15.1) and an ATX tower chassis might be hard to distinguish. Both use a vertical form factor with front-mounted disk drives and a power supply mounted on the top-rear corner of the case, as seen from the front. However, a closer look reveals several differences:

- With few exceptions, typical ATX tower chassis are designed for standard-size ATX motherboards. Pedestal chassis are designed for larger form factors, such as the Server System Infrastructure Entry-Level Electronics Bay (SSI-EEB) version 3.0 and later. Table 15.1 compares typical dimensions.
- Pedestal chassis are designed to accommodate external header cables for SCSI drives and other motherboard integrated devices without using up expansion slots.
- Pedestal chassis are designed to support passive cooling of the processor as a lower-noise alternative to active cooling, while most ATX chassis are designed for active cooling only.

Table 15.1 compares the dimensions and features of two typical pedestal server chassis, Intel's Entry Server Chassis SC5295-E and SC5250-E, with a typical ATX tower case built for standard ATX motherboards, the Antec SLK1650. The dimensions shown in Figure 15.1 are taken from the values listed for the Antec SLK1650 and the Intel SC5295-E in Table 15.1.

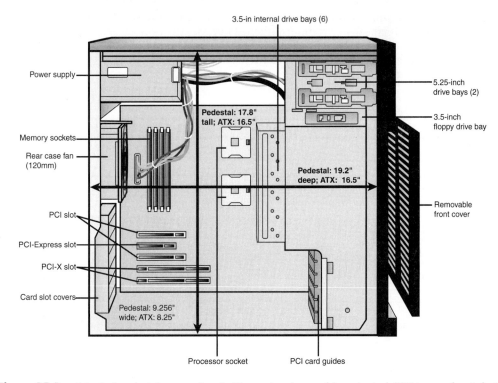

3.5-in internal drive bays (6)

Power supply

5.25-inch
drive bays (2)

Pedestal: 17.8"
tall; ATX: 16.5"

3.5-inch
floppy drive bay

Memory sockets

Rear case fan
(120mm)

Pedestal: 19.2"
deep; ATX: 16.5"

PCI slot

PCI-Express slot

PCI-X slot

Card slot covers

Removable
front cover

Pedestal: 9.256"
wide; ATX: 8.25"

Processor socket   PCI card guides

Figure 15.1 A typical pedestal server chassis (shown here) resembles a typical ATX tower chassis but is taller, wider, and deeper. The dimensions shown here are from Table 15.1 and might vary, depending on the chassis being compared.

Table 15.1   Server and Standard ATX Chassis Compared

	Antec SLK1650	Intel SC5250-E	Intel SC5295-E
Height	16.5 inches	17.75 inches	17.8 inches
Width	8.25 inches	9.28 inches	9.256 inches
Depth	16.5 inches	19.1 inches	19.2 inches
Motherboard Form Factor	ATX	SSI-EEB 3.0	SSI-MEB (also known as SSI-EEB 3.5)[1]
5.25-Inch HH Drive Bays	Four	Two	Two
3.5-Inch Drive Bays	Four	Seven	Seven
Front Fans	80mm (one)	80mm (one)	80mm (one)[2]
Rear Fan	120mm (one)	120mm (one)	120mm (one)
Supports Passive CPU Cooling	No	Yes	Yes
Supports Rack-Mounting	No	No	Yes (5U form factor)

[1]The actual SSI-EEB 3.5 motherboard specification supports motherboards the same size as those supported by the SSI-EEB 3.0 specification (see Table 15.2), but vendors often use this identifier to indicate that the board is larger than SSI-EEB 3.0. The dimensions of such boards are actually those of the old SSI-MEB form factor.

[2]An 80mm cooling fan is installed as part of the optional 3.5-inch hard disk drive hot-swap kit.

As Table 15.1 makes clear, the biggest single difference between a pedestal chassis and an ATX chassis is the size of the motherboards that can be installed in each. The pedestal chassis is taller and deeper, enabling it to handle the larger SSI-EEB and SSI-MEB motherboard form factors used by most server motherboards. Table 15.2 compares the dimensions of standard ATX, extended ATX, SSI-EEB 3.0, and SSI-MEB motherboards.

Table 15.2   Server and Standard ATX Motherboard Form Factors

	Standard ATX	Extended ATX	SSI-EEB 3.0	SSI-MEB
Length[1]	12 inches	12 inches	12 inches	13 inches
Depth[1]	9.6 inches	13.05 inches	13 inches	16 inches

[1]*Because motherboards are mounted vertically in standard ATX and pedestal chassis, compare the length of the motherboard to the height of the chassis and compare the depth of the motherboard to the depth of the chassis.*

◀◀ To learn more about the differences between motherboard form factors, see "ATX Motherboards," p. 228, and "SSI Form Factor Specifications," p. 234.

Some pedestal server chassis can be converted to rack-mounted servers. Typically, pedestal server chassis that can be converted to rack-mounted servers are midrange to high-end models. To convert the Intel SC5295-E server chassis listed in Table 15.1 to a 5U rack-mounted form factor, for example, you must do the following:

1. Remove the left side cover, feet (if installed on the bottom of the unit), any installed PCI cards, and the PCI card guide.

2. Attach rails to what were formerly the top and bottom of the pedestal chassis and matching outer rails to the rack assembly.

3. Install the rack-mounted server into the rack. This step requires two people.

4. Reinstall PCI cards and the PCI card rack after the server is mounted in the rack-mounted server.

You can find complete details in Intel's online product user guide at www.intel.com/support/motherboards/server/chassis/sc5295-e/sb/cs-021099.htm. For other convertible chassis, see the chassis documentation.

Figure 15.2 shows what the Intel SC5295-E chassis looks like in its default pedestal (left) and rack-mounted (right) configurations.

Rack-Mounted Chassis

If your organization has a server room, it probably contains one or more rack frames. You can save space by using rack-mounted servers instead of pedestal servers. Rack-mounted servers are available in a variety of U factors, from 1U to 5U.

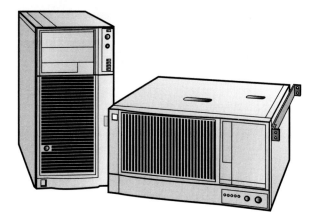

Figure 15.2   The Intel SC5295-E chassis can be used as a pedestal (left) or 5U rack-mounted (right) server.

Note

All rack-mounted devices are classified by their vertical height, or U factor. 1U = 1.75 inches. Thus, a 2U device is 3.5 inches high, a 3U device is 5.25 inches high, a 4U device is 7 inches high, and a 5U device is 8.75 inches high. Servers that can be converted from pedestal to rack-mounted form factors are usually 4U or 5U when converted. Standard rack frames hold 19-inch wide components. Common depths include 13, 20, 25, and 30 inches.

Rack-mounted servers have the same major components as pedestal servers but differ in several ways:

- The slim-line construction used by 1U and 2U servers limits internal expansion. Riser cards are typically used to provide expansion card support (see Figure 15.3).

- 1U servers support only one expansion slot (see Figures 15.3 and 15.4). 2U servers support two slots. 3U and larger servers are tall enough not to need riser cards (which block expansion slots). Thus, up to seven expansion slots are available.

- Some rack-mounted servers might not include standard I/O ports, such as legacy parallel, PS/2 mouse and keyboard, USB, or VGA video ports. Servers without standard I/O ports must be managed remotely via network or serial connections. Rack-mounted server chassis designed for use with standard server motherboards provide standard I/O ports.

Figures 15.3 and 15.4 illustrate the front, rear, and internal views of a typical 1U server.

1U and 2U rack-mounted servers are typically used in server clusters, where a large number of servers in a small space is desirable. 1U and 2U servers can also be wall-mounted when a rack is not available. Some vendors sell convertible server chassis that can be switched between pedestal and rack-mounted form factors. These are generally found in 4U or 5U form factors.

Many vendors produce rack-mounted servers using both Intel and AMD processors. Table 15.3 lists the major specifications for rack-mounted server chassis made by Intel for use with Intel processors.

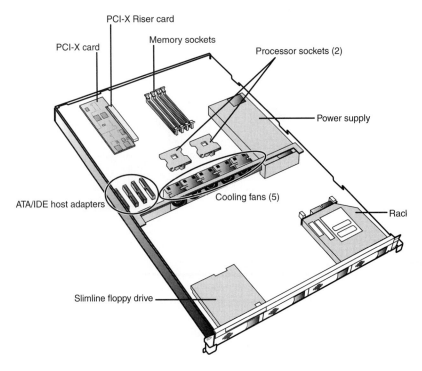

Figure 15.3 Interior view of a typical 1U server.

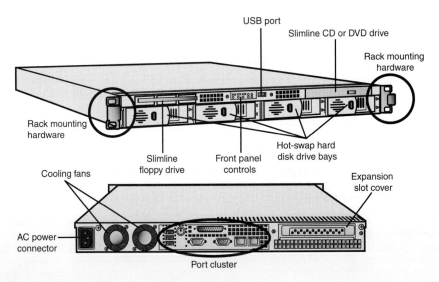

Figure 15.4 Front and rear views of typical 1U servers.

Table 15.3   Intel Rack-Mounted Server Chassis Comparison[1]

Model	Form Factor	MB Form Factors	Optimized for Intel MB	HD Drive Bays	System Cooling Fans (Number)	Power Supply	PS Cooling (Number)
SR1400	1U	SSI TEB 3.1	SE7520JR2	Three	56mm DR (4); 28mm (1)	500W	28mm (2)
SR1450	1U	SSI TEB 3.1	SE7520JR2	Three	56mm DR (4); 28mm (1)	520W redundant	56mm DR (2)
SR2400	2U	SSI TEB 3.1	SE7520JR2, SE7320VP2	Six	60mm (4 standard; 8 optional)	700W redundant	40mm (2 per PS module)
SC5295-E	2U[2,10]	SSE TEB 3.1	SE7230NH1-E[3], SE7320EP2[4,5], SE7525RP2[4,5], SE7520BD2	Four[3,4], Six[5,6]	120mm, 50mm memory cooling fan[6]	350W[3] 420W[4] 500W or optional redundant 500W[5] 600W[6]	Integrated fan
SC5300	5U[2,10]	SSI MEB	SE7320SP2, SE7525GP2, SE7520BD2, SE7520AF2	Six[7] 10[8]	Varies with config-uration[9]	600W[7] 730W redundant[8]	Varies with config-uration[9]

[1]Key: TEB = Thin Electronics Bay; MB = motherboard; DR = dual-rotor; PS = power supply; and HD = hard disk.

[2]Convertible from pedestal configuration.

[3]SC5295UP configuration.

[4]SC5295DP configuration.

[5]SC5295BRP configuration.

[6]SC5295WS configuration.

[7]SC5300BASE chassis.

[8]SC5300BRP, SC5300LX chassis; user must purchase a second PS module for redundancy.

[9]SC5300BASE and SC5300BRP include one 120mm and one 92mm fan; 80mm PS fan (one per PS module in SC5300BRP). SC5300LX includes two 120mm and two 92mm fans; 80mm PS fan per PS module.

[10]Convertible from pedestal configuration.

Wall-Mounted Rack Chassis

Rack-mounted server chassis can be mounted on a wall. A wall-mounted rack makes sense if you want a compact server form factor but don't need to set up a full-size rack for other components. Various vendors produce wall-mounted server racks. See Appendix C, "Vendor List," for details.

A typical wall-mounted rack for a 1U server resembles the one shown in Figure 15.5. A server can be directly attached to the side brackets on the rack, or standard rails can be attached to the side brackets. Rails enable easy access to the server for upgrades or replacement of a failed server or component and improve cooling.

Many wall-mounted racks feature optional covers that can be used to protect the top of the server (which faces outward on a wall rack) from damage and to protect the server from unauthorized tampering.

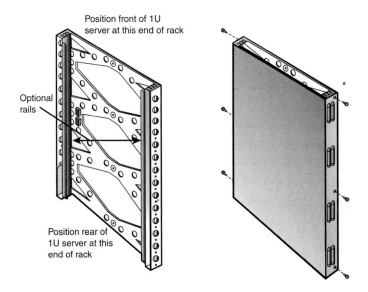

Position front of 1U
server at this end of rack

Optional
rails

Position rear of
1U server at this
end of rack

Figure 15.5   A typical wall-mounted rack for a 1U server (left) with its optional cover (right).

Wall-mounted racks for larger servers are usually built in a cabinet form with a swing-out cover. Some vendors produce wall-mounted racks up to 12U.

Tip
_____

Wall-mounted racks can also be used for network hardware such as switches, routers, wireless access points, and their AC adapters.

_____

ATX Chassis

If you are on a tight budget, you might plan to use a server motherboard that fits in a standard Advanced Technology Extended (ATX) chassis. Many standard ATX tower chassis have enough expandability to support a low-end server.

◄◄   To learn more the ATX form factor, see "ATX Motherboards," p. 228.

Before choosing an ATX chassis, you need to make sure the motherboard you want to use will fit in the chassis. Any full-size ATX chassis can be used with standard ATX or smaller ATX family motherboards. However, only a few ATX chassis are deep enough to handle extended ATX motherboards (similar in size to SSI-EEB 3.0-compatible server motherboards).

At a minimum, an ATX chassis used for a server (see Figure 15.6) should have the following features:

- Large intake and exhaust fans: 120mm is recommended for better cooling than with 80mm or 92mm models. Larger fans can turn more slowly than smaller fans and still provide adequate cooling for the system.

- Four or more 5.25-inch half-height drive bays. These can be used for tape backup, optical drives, and hard disks.
- Four or more 3.5-inch half-height internal drive bays for hard disks.

A motherboard tray (not shown in Figure 15.6) is also a desirable option to look for because it makes motherboard installation and replacement easier than if the motherboard must be installed directly into the case.

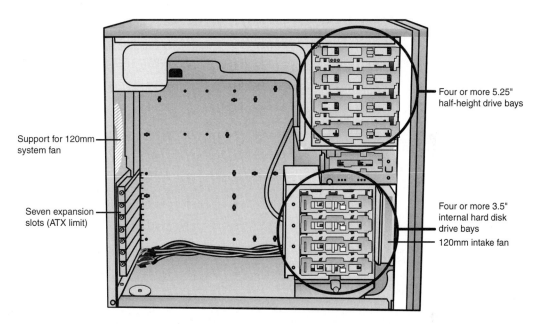

Figure 15.6   Desirable features in an ATX chassis to be used for a server.

If you need support for hot-swapped drives, extended ATX or SSI-EEB motherboards, or other advanced features, you should consider a pedestal chassis instead of an ATX chassis.

BTX Chassis

Intel introduced the Balanced Technology Extended (BTX) form factor in 2003. BTX is designed to improve cooling and make it easier to develop thin form factor systems, such as 1U servers. As you learned in Chapter 4, BTX systems use a component layout that's a mirror image of that used by ATX and are opened from the right side, rather than the left, as with ATX. BTX systems also locate devices that generate the most heat, such as processors and memory modules, in the middle of the motherboard.

For these reasons, BTX motherboards require BTX-specific chassis. Although a few vendors currently manufacture BTX chassis, early BTX products have been aimed at the desktop market. The first vendor to introduce complete BTX servers was Gateway, which introduced its E-9220T series in 2005. However, it is uncertain whether BTX will become a widely popular form factor because Intel is moving to processors that produce less heat than current and recent models. Thermal issues are one of the major reasons for the BTX design. If BTX does become popular, we likely cannot expect significant quantities of BTX server motherboards and chassis for do-it-yourself integration to become available until mid-2006 or later.

◀◀   To learn more about the BTX form factor, see "BTX Motherboards," p. 241.

Chassis Specifications and Considerations

Whether you purchase a preconfigured server or build one yourself from an existing chassis and motherboard, you should consider factors such as airflow through the system, physical security, electromagnetic interference (EMI) and electrostatic discharge (ESD) potential, and safety requirements. The following sections deal with each of these issues.

Airflow

When you select or configure a server chassis, either as part of a complete server or for integration with a motherboard of your choice, airflow concerns should be at the top of your list. Heat is the number-one enemy of reliability, and many of today's high-speed server processors run much hotter than their predecessors. However, processors aren't the only heat source in a modern server. 10,000rpm and faster hard disks produce a great deal of heat, as do memory modules and even the North Bridge or memory controller hub chip.

Server chassis vendors have developed several strategies for dealing with heat buildup, including the following:

- Larger intake and exhaust case fans
- Multiple fans for slim-line 1U and 2U rack-mounted servers
- Server-specific active and passive processor heatsinks
- Air ducts

The following sections examine each of these strategies.

Intake and Exhaust Case Fans

Almost all servers include one or more exhaust fans at the rear of the case, and most pedestal servers include (or have provision for) an intake fan at the front of the case. The exhaust fans work along with the processor fan to pull air from the front of the case past heat-producing components to the rear of the case and out.

One of the benefits of using the latest pedestal or ATX tower chassis is the ability to use 120mm exhaust and intake fans. 120mm fans (refer to Figure 15.1) move more air per minute (CFM) than the 80mm and 92mm fans that are common in older chassis, at substantially lower RPMs. The result is a cooler, more stable, and quieter system.

Note

The Silent PC Review website has a useful Microsoft Excel file that lists fans in various sizes from 65mm up to 120mm. Revolutions per minute (rpm), cubic feet per minute of airflow (CFM), noise, and decibel (dBA) information is provided for each model at various voltage levels and system configurations. You can download the file from www.silentpcreview.com/files/fanspecs/fanspecs.xls. For links to the PDF version and additional technical notes, go to www.silentpcreview.com/article25-page1.html.

If you need to improve cooling in an existing system, you should make sure you have both intake and exhaust fans. Some server chassis provide mounting areas for intake fans, but the fans are an extra-cost option. It's worth the few extra dollars to add additional fans supported by your chassis.

When you look at cooling your system, you should not overlook the impact that high temperatures can have on hard disk and system reliability. 10,000rpm enterprise SATA or SCSI hard disks get very hot, and 15,000rpm SCSI hard disks get even hotter. Heat is radiated out through the top of the hard disk assembly. If the heat is not moved away from the hard disk, it could cause problems with reliable hard disk operation and could shorten the life of the hard disk and the system.

There are several ways to cool hard disks:

- If you don't need to use every internal hard disk mount, leave empty spaces between the hard disks you install.
- If the chassis has provision for a fan to blow air across the hard disk array, install it.
- If the chassis is designed to support hot-swap drives, install an intake fan behind the hot-swap drive array.

Figure 15.7 illustrates a standard 3.5-inch hard disk drive bay designed to handle an 80mm intake fan. The fan (when installed) will pull air past the hard disks to cool them.

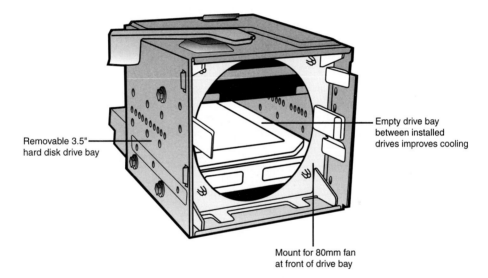

Removable 3.5"
hard disk drive bay

Empty drive bay
between installed
drives improves cooling

Mount for 80mm fan
at front of drive bay

Figure 15.7   Preparing to add a cooling fan to an internal hard disk drive bay.

Note that the most common sizes of case fans on ATX power and SSI-EEB pedestal chassis are 80mm, 92mm, and 120mm. Some chassis use a larger exhaust fan at the rear of the chassis and one or more smaller intake fans at the front of the chassis.

Fan Arrays for 1U, 2U, and 3U Servers

1U, 2U, and 3U servers are not tall enough to support 120mm cooling fans. Instead, multiple smaller fans must be used to provide adequate cooling. Typically, these fans are located in the middle of the system, drawing air through openings in the front of the case and blowing air across the processors and memory modules. Figure 15.8 illustrates the position of a typical five-fan configuration in a 1U server.

A 1U server can support fans up to 56mm, while 2U servers can support fans up to 80mm, and 3U servers can support fans up to 90mm. If you need to replace a fan in a 1U, 2U, or 3U server, you should consult the manufacturer for recommended fan models. Fans used in these servers are generally not the same as those available for standard chassis.

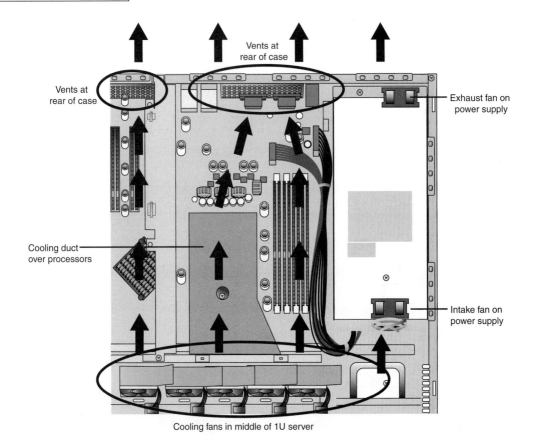

Vents at
rear of case

Vents at
rear of case

Exhaust fan on
power supply

Cooling duct
over processors

Intake fan on
power supply

Cooling fans in middle of 1U server

Figure 15.8   This typical 1U server uses five small fans to cool the memory sockets, processor(s), and other components.

Active and Passive Processor Heatsinks

The battle against overheating a server begins with the processor heatsink. Depending on the processor you use in your server and the chassis you use it in, you might use an active heatsink, a horizontal or vertical fan, a passive heatsink ducting air from an intake fan, or a passive heatsink ducting air to an exhaust fan.

The standard heatsink supplied with boxed Intel Xeon processors is known as the processor wind tunnel (PWT). The PWT incorporates a passive heatsink, a small duct that fits tightly over the passive heatsink, and a fan that pulls air from the front of the system across the passive heatsink (see Figure 15.9).

Some systems, primarily 1U servers, use a specially designed duct to distribute air from cooling fans past the processor's passive heatsink. However, passive cooling is not limited to 1U servers. If your server motherboard and chassis permit, you can use passive cooling with larger systems as well.

For example, if you use the Intel Server Chassis SC5250-E and the Intel Server Board SE7505VB2 with two processors, you can install the Workstation Cooling Kit (Intel part number 858795) to provide passive cooling. This option requires a BIOS update to version 1.08 or greater.

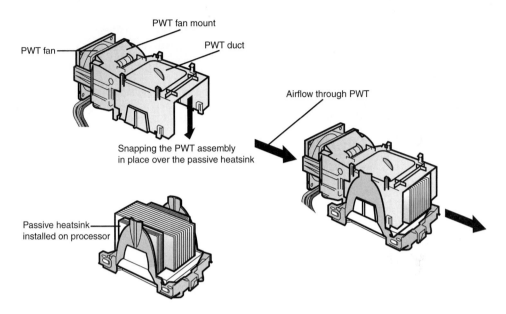

Figure 15.9   The standard PWT heatsink for boxed Intel Xeon processors pulls air past the processor horizontally.

The Workstation Cooling Kit requires the entire PWT assembly, original passive heatsink, and retention mechanism to be removed. Thermal grease must also be removed from the processor before the new cooling kit can be installed.

Tip

If you are planning to use any type of nonstandard cooling for a processor in a new server installation, you should *not* install the standard cooling solution (heatsink and fan). Instead, you should choose the optional cooling solution you prefer and install it. Installing a standard solution first leads to more work because you must remove it before installing the new solution.

To install the Workstation Cooling Kit, you must install new retention brackets on each processor socket, a new (taller) passive heatsink on each processor, with new retaining clips (different clips are used for the 400MHz FSB and 533MHz FSB versions of the Xeon processors) and a new air duct. The air duct fits over both processors' heatsinks and is connected to the rear case fan. The Workstation Cooling Kit also requires that the fan at the front of the hard disk drive bays be mounted on spacers to provide some additional airflow to cool the processors.

Air Ducts

Many server chassis incorporate various types of processor air ducts or air dams. These plastic devices are designed to guide airflow from the front of the system over the areas of the motherboard that are most likely to become overheated.

Some air ducts are built into the left side (as viewed from the front) access panel on a pedestal server, but most air ducts must be installed after the server has been configured with a motherboard.

You need to be sure to follow the chassis vendor's instructions for installing air ducts or air dams provided with the chassis in a particular configuration. For example, when the Intel server chassis

SC5295-E is used with the SE7320EP2 or SE7525RP2 motherboards, a small air duct must be installed along with the large air duct used by all chassis/motherboard configurations.

Security: Locks/Keys

Physical security is another important feature to consider as you specify a server chassis. If your servers are located in an area that makes server or component theft a possibility, protecting the server chassis itself as well as access to the interior of the chassis should be high on your list of required features.

Intel server chassis typically offer three methods for providing physical security:

- A security lock loop located at the rear of the chassis enables the chassis to be locked in place with a standard computer security cable and padlock.

- A key lock located on the front bezel of most models enables the interior of the chassis to be secured against unauthorized access.

- A chassis intrusion switch is tripped when the chassis is opened. This switch has a header cable that must be plugged in to the motherboard's chassis intrusion switch header. The switch is monitored by Intel server monitoring software.

Many, but not all, third-party chassis and servers support some or all of these physical security features. Be sure to check the server or chassis manual for information. If you use a non-Intel motherboard in your server, check with the motherboard manufacturer to determine whether a chassis intrusion switch is supported by your motherboard.

Tip

The Bulldog security kit from Belkin (#F8E500) is an example of a kit that can be used to retrofit servers that lack a security lock loop. This kit contains a locking cable, a padlock, large and small security lock loops, adhesive, and a cleaning wipe to prepare the chassis for application of the adhesive to hold the security lock loop in place. This kit also contains a screw-in security lock loop.

EMI and ESD Considerations

There are two categories for rating the potential for EMI for electronics components in the United States:

- FCC Part 15 Class A is a standard that applies to business-class (commercial) electronics hardware, including most servers. Equipment that receives the FCC Class A rating is not to be used in residential environments because it could interfere with radio, TV, and other residential-class electronics devices.

- FCC Part 15 Class B is a more stringent standard than FCC Class A. FCC Class B devices can be used in residential areas because they emit lower amounts of interfering signals than Class A devices.

Most server chassis and preconfigured servers meet FCC Class A standards. Thus, they should not be used in a residential environment or in other sensitive environments that require FCC Class B–compliant hardware, such as locations near airports or ATM machines and in hospitals.

All components in a server must meet FCC Class B standards for the device to be considered FCC Class B compliant. If you need a server that meets FCC Class B standards, you should follow these steps:

1. Use an FCC Class B–rated chassis. Generally, these chassis use smaller-diameter cooling vents than FCC Class A chassis. Other differences might include positive grounding of metal chassis components to others via spring-loaded contacts and gaskets to eliminate EMI leakage. For a detailed look at the changes needed to enable a particular rack-mounted chassis to meet FCC Class B standards, see "Case Study: Taking a Chassis to the FCC B Standard" at www.cotsjournalonline.com/home/article.php?id=100058.

2. Check the FCC Part 15 rating for each component, including the motherboard, optical drives, hard disks, add-on cards, and power supply. Replace Class A–rated hardware with Class B–rated hardware.

3. Reattach the removable EMI shields provided with some server chassis after installing internal hard disks. EMI shields are usually placed in front of a chassis's 3.5-inch removable hard disk drive bays (see Figure 15.10).

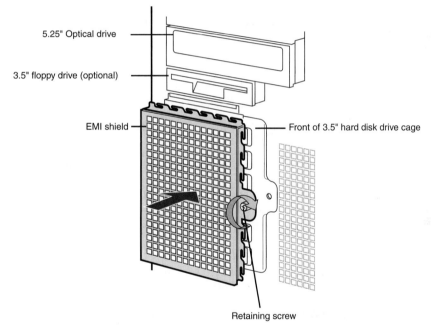

Figure 15.10   Reinstalling the EMI shield after installing internal 3.5-inch hard disk drives.

If EMI appears to be caused by the server when it is running, you should perform these steps:

1. Install a ferrite choke on the AC power cable leading to the server.

2. Install a ferrite choke on each shielded peripheral cable coming from the server, such as external SCSI, USB, FireWire, video, parallel, serial, audio, and coaxial cables.

Figure 15.11 illustrates a typical snap-together ferrite choke being installed.

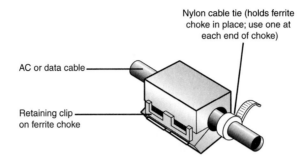

Figure 15.11   Installing a snap-on ferrite choke.

Tip

A ferrite choke contains compressed ferrite (iron) powder. When it is clamped around a cable, it stops, or "chokes," RF energy that may be present in the cable from entering the device connected to the cable. The choke should be located close to the cable connector going to the server. You might also want to add another near the opposite end of the cable. The Radio Shack (www.radioshack.com) #273-105 snap-together ferrite choke core can be used for AC and larger-diameter data cables, such as SCSI, video, parallel, serial, and coaxial. The Dataq Instruments (www.dataq.com) FC-1 snap-on ferrite choke is designed for USB cables. These snap-together ferrite chokes resemble the one illustrated in Figure 15.11.

When servicing a server chassis, either during initial integration with components or later, you need to be sure to take ESD precautions. ESD can take place whenever the server and another object (such as the technician or the tools he or she is using) have different electrical potentials. ESD takes place from the object with higher potential to the object with lower potential, to equalize potential. The human body can discharge thousands of volts safely, but the equipment subjected to ESD might not fare so well.

Although Intel server chassis are designed to withstand up to 15kV (1500V) per the *Intel Environmental Standards Handbook* (#662394-05), this limit is considerably above the 200V limit (sometimes less) that can damage CMOS chips on the motherboard, add-on cards, hard disks, and other components. While these components are protected from ESD when the chassis is closed, when the chassis is open, ESD poses a major risk of damage. Note that while ESD limits on other brands of server chassis might vary, the components in any server are at risk of damage from ESD when the chassis is open for service.

To reduce the possibility of damage from ESD, technicians should always wear an antistatic wrist strap similar to the one shown in Figure 15.12 when working inside a server chassis or with components such as add-on cards, memory, and motherboards. An antistatic wrist strap equalizes electrical potential between the wearer and the server chassis, helping to prevent ESD.

The wrist strap must be securely wrapped around the wrist of the user. Most wrist straps use hook-and-loop fasteners to hold the strap in place. The metal contact plate must make contact with the wrist. The wrist strap is snapped into the coiled cable. One end of the cable contains a one-megohm resistor and a swivel snap. The other end has an alligator clip. You attach the alligator clip to a metal portion of the server's chassis. The resistor stops high-voltage electricity from injuring the wearer.

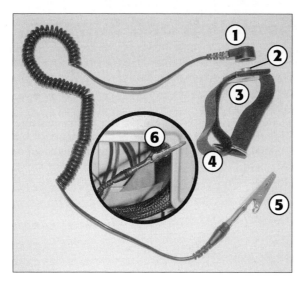

1. One-megohm resistor and
   swivel snap on coiled cable
2. Snap for coiled cable
3. Metal plate used for grounding user
4. Hook and loop closure
5. Alligator clip
6. Alligator clip connected to server chassis

Figure 15.12   A typical wrist strap designed to prevent ESD.

Safety

A server chassis should be approved by the relevant safety regulation organization for your country or region. Some examples of these organizations are listed in Table 15.4.

Table 15.4   Server Product Regulation Compliance Organizations

Country or Region	Product Regulatory Body	URL for More Information
United States	Underwriter's Laboratory (UL)	www.ul.com
Canada	Canadian Standards Association (CSA)	www.csa.ca
European Union	Conformance European (CE)	www.ce-marking.org
Germany	Geprüfte Sicherheit (GS)	www.ul.com/mark or www.us.tuv.com/product_testing/ tuv_rheinland_gs_mark/
Russia	Gosudarstvenii Standart (GOST)	www.ul-asia.com/services/ps_eu_non.htm
Japan	Voluntary Control Council for Interference by Information Technology Equipment (VCCI)	www.vcci.or.jp/vcci_e/index.html
Australia	Australian Communications Authority (C-Tick)	www.acma.gov.au

If you do not see the relevant safety/regulator markings on a chassis itself, you should check the manual for the chassis.

Server Chassis Documentation and Support

Whether you integrate a motherboard and chassis of your choice to create a server or use a commercially manufactured server, you need to obtain the documentation available for your server chassis and have a means to obtain professional technical support for that chassis.

The Importance of Documentation

You can obtain documentation for a separately purchased chassis from the chassis manufacturer. This information might be as brief as a mechanical drawing and a marked list of components, or it might be much more in-depth. Generally, chassis manufactured for a particular server motherboard or series of server motherboards tend to be better-documented than those made for a wide variety of server motherboards. The documentation for a particular server chassis might include some or all of the following information:

- Motherboards supported (either by form factor or specific models)
- Drive bays
- Whether hot-swap SCSI or SATA drives are supported
- Cooling fan sizes and locations
- Optional hardware (hot-swap adapters, passive processor coolers, and so on)

If the chassis is included as part of a preconfigured server, you can contact the server manufacturer for detailed documentation. Intel and Supermicro (www.supermicro.com), for example, provide separate chassis and server documentation.

Intel uses the chassis model number as part of the server platform model number. (Intel uses the term *server platform* to refer to a particular combination of motherboard and chassis.) Here are some examples:

- **SR2400JR2**—This server is based on the SR2400 2U rack-mounted chassis.
- **SR1425BK1-E**—This server is based on the SR1425-E11 1U rack-mounted chassis.
- **SC5300AF2**—This server platform is based on the SC5300LX pedestal rack-mounted chassis.

The component list for each Intel server platform clearly identifies which chassis was used, and the documentation for each chassis is available separately from the Intel website (www.intel.com).

Other major server vendors, such as Hewlett-Packard (www.hp.com), Tyan (www.tyan.com), and Dell (www.dell.com) provide chassis information as part of the documentation for their servers. Sometimes the chassis documentation is part of a maintenance and service guide for a particular server model.

Generally, major chassis and server manufacturers make their documentation available as an Adobe PDF file that you can download and view before you purchase a server or server chassis.

Manufacturer Policies on Opening Chassis

If you assembled a server motherboard and chassis, you are the manufacturer, and there are no restrictions on your ability to open the system and service it as needed. Generally, for most pedestal and rack-mounted servers, manufacturers recommend that only technically skilled users open the system and replace or upgrade components.

Before you open a preconfigured system to perform maintenance or upgrading, you should be sure to check with the vendor to determine whether you must use an authorized technician to perform service. If the vendor requires you to use an authorized technician and you fail to do so, you could void your warranty.

How to Remove the Intel SC5295-E Chassis

The Intel SC5295-E chassis is a typical pedestal chassis, closely resembling an ATX tower chassis in many ways. It can also be converted into a 4U rack-mounted chassis. However, the following sections deal with chassis removal, as it applies to the default pedestal configuration.

This particular chassis, like many recent Intel chassis, is designed to be opened without special tools, making access to the interior easier than with older chassis. Before removing any part of the chassis, you need to be sure to shut down the system, disconnect it from AC power, and put on a wrist strap.

Removing the Left Side Panel

As with ATX tower chassis, you must open the SC5295-E's left side (as seen from the front) to gain access to the interior. After the left side is removed, you can replace the motherboard, install memory, and perform other types of maintenance.

To remove the left side panel, follow these steps:

1. Remove two screws from the back edge of the panel.

2. Push in on the latch near the top of the panel.

3. Pull the panel toward the rear of the system (see Figure 15.13).

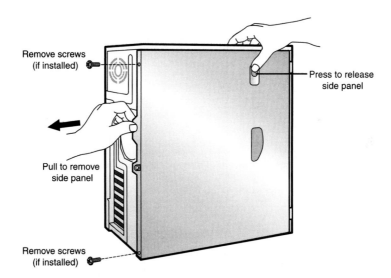

Figure 15.13 Removing the left side panel of the Intel SC5295-E server chassis.

4. After the left side panel is open, attach the alligator clip from the wrist strap to a metal portion of the chassis.

◄◄ To learn more about using a wrist strap to avoid ESD, see "EMI and ESD Considerations," p. 700.

Removing the Front Bezel Assembly

Some versions of the Intel SC5295-E server chassis use a two-piece bezel, while others use a one-piece bezel (see Figure 15.14). In either case, follow these steps to remove the bezel after the left side cover is removed:

1. Push inward on the two bezel clips on the left side of the bezel to release them.

2. Turn the bezel slightly to the left.

3. Push inward on the three bezel clips on the right side of the bezel.

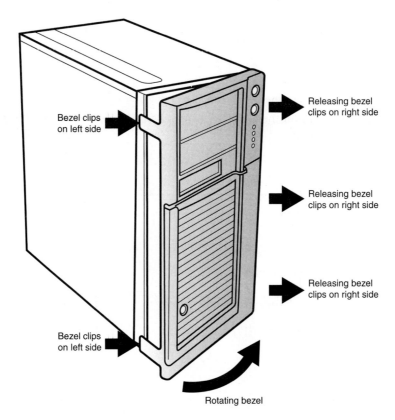

Figure 15.14   Removing the front bezel of the Intel SC5295-E server chassis.

If the bezel is wired to the motherboard, try to place the bezel close enough to the server that you don't need to disconnect motherboard wires. Otherwise, note the position of the wires and disconnect them. You will need to reconnect them later.

Removing the Air Ducts

Most versions of the Intel SC5295-E server chassis have removable air ducts (except for the UP version, which has the air ducts built into the left side panel). Before you can install a processor or motherboard, you must remove the air ducts. The left side panel must be removed first.

If the server chassis uses a small air duct as well as a large air duct, it must be removed first. Unscrew it from the area behind the 3.5-inch internal drive bay and remove it. The small air duct is labeled "Part B."

To remove the large air duct ("Part A"), remove the two mounting screws (see Figure 15.15).

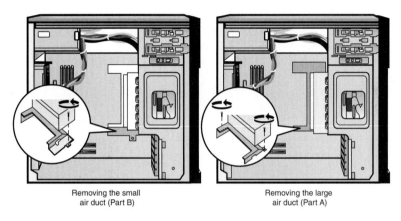

Removing the small
air duct (Part B)

Removing the large
air duct (Part A)

Figure 15.15   Removing air ducts from an SC5295-E server chassis.

Removing the Drive Cage EMI Shield

You must remove the drive cage EMI shield before you can do any of the following:

- Install a new motherboard
- Install 3.5-inch hard disk drives
- Install a hot-swap drive array

The drive cage EMI shield is located behind the front bezel. The front bezel must be removed first.

To remove the EMI shield, unscrew the hold-down screw on the right side of the EMI shield and pull the shield forward (see Figure 15.16).

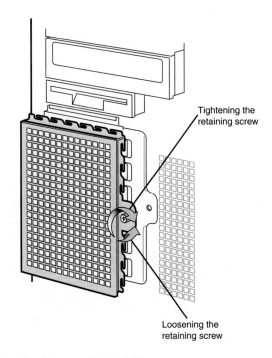

Tightening the
retaining screw

Loosening the
retaining screw

Figure 15.16   Removing the drive cage EMI shield.

CHAPTER 16

Server Racks and Blades

As an organization grows, the size and the number of servers it deploys grows as well. Some applications lend themselves to deployment on larger and larger servers, while other environments benefit from the deployment of larger numbers of servers. You scale up to larger systems when processing is the main consideration, as might be the case with an enterprise database server, such as DB2, Oracle, or SQL Server. You scale out when the primary consideration is the amount of I/O you can supply. Examples of applications that benefit from scaling out are the server farms you see deployed in web-servers, such as Apache, Microsoft IIS, iPlanet, and Zeus.

If you are situating a large multiprocessor server, such as a Unisys ES7000 Orion 560 (shown in Figure 16.1), you can simply roll that server into a secure room that has the right cooling, the correct power hookup, raised flooring, and humidity (or environmental) control, and you are set. The Orion 560 is a 32 Itanium processor system that has physical dimensions of 49 inches wide by 48 inches deep by 69 inches tall, which is a double-rack construction. What might not be obvious from Figure 16.1, but would be if the doors were open, is that systems like this one are constructed around racks with components that fit into those racks.

Figure 16.1 The Unisys ES7000 Orion 560 is an example of a large server system where the rack construction is hidden by a shell. *Image courtesy of Unisys Corporation.*

You can see the rack construction in another Unisys product, the Clear Path Plus Libra 590 server, which is a single-rack system. When you open the Libra's door, you see that this server is a single-rack system with a number of components bolted into it. The system dimensions are 22 inches wide by 47 inches deep by 69 inches tall. On the bottom are a couple 2U disk arrays, in the middle is a management station (laptop) with a KVM switch, above that are a couple optical drives, and at the top are some multiprocessor chassis that take blade servers, as shown in Figure 16.2. (Later in this chapter, in the section "Universal Racks," you'll learn what the term U, as in 2U, means and how that translates into the racks you can purchase for yourself.) For now, though, it suffices to say that 1U is the vertical dimension of the smallest-sized chassis that can be bolted onto a universal rack and that large-sized chassis are simply multiples of this height. A 1U height is roughly the height of a standard audio-phile's hi-fi receiver.

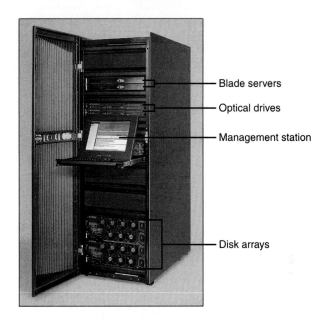

Blade servers

Optical drives

Management station

Disk arrays

Figure 16.2 The Clear Path Plus Libra 590 is shown here with the front door open.

The Libra 590 demonstrates many of the features of server rack construction that are discussed in this chapter. Its standard-size rack takes standard-size components, allowing you to mix and match parts to build the server you need.

The Libra 590 can take up to 56 processors, arranged in 8-processor units, where each processor is a blade in the chassis. Blade servers will play an increasingly prominent role in server architectures in the future, and you will learn later in this chapter about the advantages blades can offer.

Because it can have up to 56 processors, a system such as the 590 lets you run multiple-server systems within the same rack, each with its own operating system. Because you need a way to manage all these servers without having to have multiple monitors, mouse devices, and keyboards hanging off the rack, any multiserver deployment requires the use of a KVM switch to control all the servers. A KVM switch takes the place of multiple keyboards, video displays, and mouse devices, switching from one computer system to another so that you can use a single keyboard, monitor, and mouse to control any number of systems.

You might think that rack mounting is something only for data centers, but that is not the case. Racks are available at moderate cost for small and medium-sized businesses. You can purchase a simple open rack for as little as $175, with the more professional models costing from $1,000 to $1,500. Racks and casings such as the ones shown here typically cost around $3,500 to purchase in one-off quantity.

There are many good reasons for setting up a rack-based server system. Here are some of the most common reasons:

- They better utilize space than standalone server systems.
- The modular design allows you to put infrastructure components in a rack.
- The modular design makes it easy to add and remove components, as needed.

- A rack is easier to physically protect from intrusion or damage than the larger number of servers it replaces.

- A rack can provide needed electromagnetic interference (EMI) and radio frequency interference (RFI) shielding for systems in a dense server environment.

- Cables are out of sight and can be bundled together.

- Rack-mounting designs often are more attractive to look at than a large number of standalone server systems.

Types of Racks

Racks come in many types, and often the terms *rack* and *cabinet* are used to describe the same thing. You may also encounter the terms *LAN racks*, *network racks*, and *computer racks* as alternate terms for this type of server room furniture.

Other industries, such as the telecom industry, have slightly different designs; you'll find racks for that industry called *relay racks*, an example of which is shown in Figure 16.3. Relay racks are used in the telecom industry to stack large numbers of switches. ISPs can also use this kind of rack for large router installations.

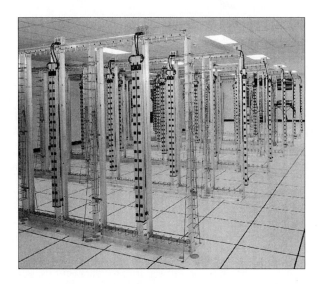

Figure 16.3   This DAMAC open rack system is installed over a raised computer floor.

The following are among the areas and industries that use rack-mounted solutions:

- Control rooms
- High-performance computing applications
- Hospital and medical industry
- Manufacturing industry
- Research centers
- Telecom and networking industry

Some racks are open and very flexible to configure. Other designs are tightly sealed and locked cabinets. Different industries have different needs and standards. And, of course, different budgets allow for different features. The system shown in Figure 16.3 is considered to be a standard server rack, as specified by the Electronic Industries Alliance (EIA), as part of its EIA 310D standard.

There are really two basic kinds of racks:

- **Closed racks or cabinets**—A rack that comes with four vertical rails and that is usually enclosed within a cabinet.
- **Open racks**—A rack that comes with two vertical rails and that is left open.

Because you can't lock an open rack, it is most common to find a rack of this type in a secure server room. A closed-bay rack can be secured with a lock, and although these systems tend to be more expensive, they are better choices when you use the server(s) outside a server room or in another non-secure location. Not only can you secure a closed rack, but you also have greater control over its environmental system, including the filters, cooling devices, and so forth.

Sizes of Cabinets

In specifying a cabinet size, you need to consider the amount of equipment that you want to put into the rack, which speaks to the rack's intended use. Racks come in some standard sizes, but you can also purchase racks in custom sizes. Most people opt for standard-size racks because they want standard-size components to fit into them.

Cabinet size is usually measured from the outside of the cabinets. Figure 16.4 shows how you measure a standard rack or cabinet, using codified A, B, and C measurements:

- Dimension A is the depth of the server, just out from the front rail.
- Dimension B is the depth of the server from the front of the front rail to the back of the server.
- Dimension C represents the total depth of the server.

The rack depth is the distance from the front of the front rail to the back of the back rail. (Figure 16.4 shows a side view.)

Not only does the internal rack dimension need to take into account the size of the components that fit into it, but there needs to be room in the back of the cabinet to run all the different wire connections that each component needs. Exterior dimensions must fit within the parameters of the room into which the rack will be installed. A server rack is a big, heavy beast, with some cabinets running as high as 7 feet tall and weighing as much as 300 pounds. Not only do you need to make sure that you can get the rack into your server room, you also must ensure that it will fit through any openings along the way, including elevators and doorways.

Most rack frames are built to be rugged, and few of the ones you'll find in a data center will break down into smaller racks. The less expensive racks that are used in non–data center environments do often break down into their components or are shipped as small modules that can be rapidly snapped or bolted together.

Universal Racks

U, for *rack unit*, is an EIA standard unit of measure for most of the rack-mountable equipment on the market. The great majority of networking equipment and rackable servers all conform to this standard. Most large enterprise server and storage vendors offer standard, or universal, racks as part of their product lines. Figure 16.5 shows a Hewlett-Packard 5642 server rack as an example.

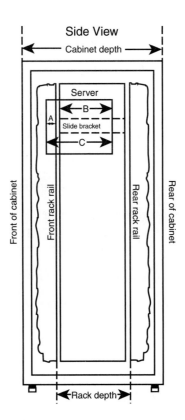

Figure 16.4   How to measure the dimensions of a server rack.

A universal rack unit has the following dimensions:

- **Height**—A 1U component is 1.75 inches in height. A 2U unit is 3.5 inches high, and a 42U rack measures 73.5 inches of rackable space. A 42U rack itself is a little larger because of its horizontal framing elements. Usually you have leeway in deciding what height rack to use.

- **Width**—There are two dimensions to width: the internal width of the cabinet (that is, from mounting rail to mounting rail) and the external dimension of the cabinet, from side to side.

  For the EIA standard, the most commonly used internal width is 19 inches, which you often seen referred to as an EIA 19-inch rack. A 19-inch rack often carries anywhere from a 1.5- to 2.5-inch frame on each side, making the rack's external dimension anywhere from 22 inches (like the server shown in Figure 16.5) to the more common 24 inches. The EIA 19-inch standard is far and away the most commonly used one for servers; Sun servers, for example, are designed to fit into 19-inch rack mounts. However, you will also find vendors selling EIA 23-inch and 24-inch "standards."

- **Depth**—The depth of a server rack is the one dimension that you have some control over: The depth can be can any size you want, so it can accommodate things as thin as status meters to as deep as your rack will allow you to support. The vast majority of universal server racks sold have a dimension of 900mm, or just under 36 inches. Servers from Hewlett-Packard, Dell, and IBM all fit into this size. Because most universal racks exhaust air from the back of the rack, you want to maintain enough space in the back for adequate ventilation.

Figure 16.5   Hewlett-Packard's 5642 server rack is an example of a standard, or universal, rack.

Custom Racks

Many vendors can and do build custom racks for specific applications on a build-to-order basis. Therefore, you will find several places where you can download a library of shapes that let you create your own rack designs. Most often these shapes are standard sizes and units of measures.

The following are some of the companies that sell custom racks:

- **Connect-Tek**—www.connect-tek.com, 718-729-3700
- **DSI Enterprise**—www.dsienterprises.com, 512-447-5869
- **Information Support Concepts**—www.iscdfw.com, 800-458-6255
- **Mainline**—www.mainlinecomputer.com, 800-686-5312
- **President Enclosures**—www.presidentenclosures.com, 800-750-7535
- **Rackmount Solutions**—www.rackmountsolutions.net, 866-207-6631
- **RackSolutions.com**—www.racksolutions.com, 903-453-0801
- **Server Racks Online**—www.server-rack-online.com, 866-722-5776
- **Star Case**—www.starcase.com/rack.htm, 800-822-STAR
- **TechRack Systems**—www.techrack.com, 888-266-3577

Wire Shelving

Many organizations, particularly smaller ones, opt for open wire shelving on which to place their servers. Wire shelving offers considerable flexibility in terms of placement of components as well as in portability within a location. Many companies offer this type of shelving.

The classic stainless steel wire shelving is Metro shelving (www.metro.com), which is used in all kinds of industries. For example, Metro shelving is often used in fine food stores, hospitals, restaurants, kitchens, and even clean rooms where very low particulate counts are required. You can recognize Metro shelving by the trademark wavy "MMMM" rod that encircles the shelf. Figure 16.6 shows a Metro shelf system in use in a server deployment.

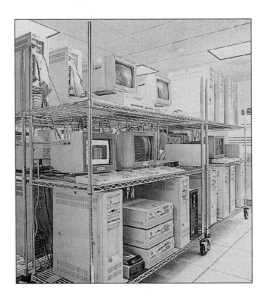

Figure 16.6 Using wire shelving, like this system from Metro, is a very popular way to deploy servers.

A very large number of vendors sell wire shelving for computer applications. In specifying a wire shelf system, the following factors are important:

- **Material of construction**—The ideal material is stainless steel, which is sturdy, easy to clean, and corrosion resistant. Other materials you may find in a wire shelf are steel, aluminum, chrome, and plastic. Aluminum is both lightweight and strong but can be expensive. Chrome is a good alternative to stainless steel and is somewhat cheaper. Plastic shelving is a low-cost option when the equipment being supported is light enough for the plastic shelving to safely support it.

- **Shelf dimensions**—You need to specify length and width.

- **Carrying capacity**—The size, material of construction, pole types, and number of shelves determine the weight of equipment that the shelf can support. Metro shelving, for example, is rated at 800 pounds per shelf, so a two-shelf system is able to hold 1,600 pounds.

- **Pole construction**—Poles are used to bear the weight of the shelves and the components placed on them. A system of locking is required that allows for flexible placement of the shelves at various heights. Pole lengths also determine the height of the shelf system. You will find shelves available up to 93 inches in the Metro system and more commonly up to 72 inches in height for most wire shelf systems meant for server deployment. Metro shelving has a set of grooves placed every inch on the poles that allow for referenced placement.

- **Accessories**—Many shelf systems offer bins and baskets, keyboard trays, wire management systems, shelf liners, and other convenience features.

- **Mobility features**—Most shelf systems come with casters or wheels that you can use to move the system around. A locking caster is an important feature that is worth the extra money.

Rack Specifications and Considerations

Most large server rack deployments are custom built and installed by value-added resellers (VARs) who specialize in this technology. Even simple single-rack installations done for small workgroups require some forethought in terms of their specification. You need to know where to place the rack, what facilities are required, and how many related safety considerations are involved.

Many issues surround the choices you make when you purchase racks and the equipment that fits into them. Some rack systems are very basic affairs—essentially a set of posts or poles with regular holes where you bolt in your equipment. However, some rack systems come with fully developed ventilation systems, electronic monitoring equipment, a selection of walls and doors, and so forth.

Your first constraint is likely to be the size of the rack. That size determines how much equipment your rack can support, but it is only one factor for you to consider. If you are populating a rack with equipment from a specific vendor, you will certainly want to consider that vendor's recommendations for the type of equipment. Racks are an important part of large OEM systems, and you can find a number of tools online to help specify and populate a rack system. The sections that follow describe some of the considerations involved.

Location

The first consideration when determining the proper location for a server rack or set of racks is the flooring. Will it be able to hold the static load, plus additional weight that constitutes your margin of safety? If you are installing the rack(s) into a room with a raised floor, you need to arrange the racks so that the flooring's own supports also lend stability to the rack.

Part of your design calculation should be an estimation of the maximum weight of your rack. With that information in hand, it's useful to consult an architectural engineer to determine the carrying capacity of the room and the specific location where you plan to place your rack(s). That information may lead you to space your racks or may determine the maximum size of the rack you can use. You may also find that your site requires additional support or that some other change in your site is necessary. Unfortunately, there is no standard safety margin, and each building has its own weight tolerance.

Assuming that a cabinet is approximately 3 feet by 4 feet, or 12 square feet, you need to leave at least a 3-foot clearance in the front and the back of the cabinet for convenient access and for heat dissipation. Server racks are constructed so that they don't require much space between them. However, if you have several racks lined up side-by-side, then every few racks, there should be enough room for an administrator or a support technician to access the back of the cabinet.

When you populate a rack, one of the calculations you should make is the amount of heat the rack will produce. It's best to determine the maximum amount of heat that could be generated and then build the appropriate level of cooling into your location. Part of the specification of each component that you put into the rack should be its heat dissipation. For any component that doesn't specify the amount of heat that is given off, you can assume that the power rating of the power supply included in the equipment represents an upper limit for the heat that can be generated. That is, if your equipment is powered by a 500-watt power supply, then the power rating should be the upper limit of the heat that must be accommodated.

If you don't know exactly how your rack is going to be populated, or if the rack is only partially populated when it is deployed, you need to make an assessment without having all the information you need to calculate the amount of heat that must be cooled. Consider the types of equipment that are to be used in your server racks, determine which unit uses the most power, and then multiply that power by the number of units that can be deployed in a server rack. Then you can use that number as your working estimate for the amount of heat you need to accommodate.

When you are estimating heat dissipation, you need to be sure to include the equipment in your server room that supports each rack system. Equipment such as UPCs, lighting, and other external devices contributes to your heat assessment.

Most companies with large server rack deployments install their racks in aisles or rows. With rows that are laid out perpendicularly, with cooling intakes on one side of the aisle and air returns on the other, you get the maximum amount of airflow. Server racks are most often cooled internally front to back, and then from bottom to top at the rear of the cabinet. When hot air rises, the cooler airflow into the bottom of the rack forces the hot air out of the exhaust at the top of the rack and into the room.

To better facilitate airflow, it is recommended that you place your air-conditioning so that the airflow alternates in one direction down an aisle and in the opposite direction down adjacent aisles.

Safety

Large server racks have a number of features that can be safety issues. Some of these we've already touched on, while others will be discussed in more detail in the sections to follow. The following checklist is a short list of safety concerns you should keep in mind when implementing a server rack:

- **Size and weight**—When a server rack is unstable and topples over, the impact can be, shall we say, quite damaging to both people and facilities. Server racks in earthquake zones require special precautions.

- **Power consumption**—Server racks can consume a significant amount of power. Power in that quantity requires careful handling and conditioning, and it also requires adequate backup in the event of a power failure.

- **Heat**—Server racks generate considerable heat—enough to overwhelm cooling systems that aren't adequately designed to accept the load.

- **RFI and EMI emissions**—The level of RFI and EMI emissions in a sever room needs to be monitored because servers can be quite sensitive to this form of pollution. If you find that your server room has high emissions, you may want to install shielding, or—better yet—call in an expert to determine which component is causing the problem and replace it with a safer component.

- **Noise**—All mechanical devices emit noise; electronic components do not generally add much to the noise level. Components such as power supplies, hard drives, and optical drives can add a significant amount of noise to a server room. Careful selection of components can be very helpful in limiting the amount of noise that fills your server room.

- **Fire**—Electronic equipment under high voltage poses a risk of fire when flammable materials are used nearby. The solution to this problem is to eliminate all flammable material in or near your servers, as well as to make provisions for control and suppression of any electrical fires that do occur.

Fire Extinguishers

Fire extinguishers are rated for the types of fires they can suppress. Class C extinguishers are rated for electrical fires, and the indication C means that the agent is nonconductive. Class A extinguishers are for ordinary combustible materials such as wood; Class B extinguishers are used on flammable liquids; and Class D extinguishers may be used on flammable metals. Class D extinguishers are often rated for a specific metal.

Some fire extinguishers are rated for multiple types of fires. The most commonly used server room extinguishers are probably carbon dioxide extinguishers, or CO_2 extinguishers. These extinguishers are rated for Class B and Class C fires and work by cooling the fire and by removing oxygen from the area. Another commonly used server room extinguisher type uses halon, which is a chlorinated or fluorinated hydrocarbon. Halon extinguishers are popular for electrical fires because they are nontoxic, and when the halon evaporates, it leaves no residue.

Large server racks can be quite heavy. Prior to designing and setting up a server rack, it's important to determine the static load of your flooring. If your flooring is the building's flooring, then the static load of the floor may be part of the design specification. At any rate, you should consult with a design architect or, better yet, a qualified structural engineer to obtain this information prior to making any commitments to purchase equipment. If you are installing a server rack(s) onto a raised data center floor, you need to check the static load capacities of both the raised floor and the building.

If your server racks are deployed in an earthquake zone, you need to take special precautions when you set them up. Server racks should not be set up in an earthquake zone on standard raised flooring. Special flooring with honeycombs instead of simple framing should be used. It may also be prudent to support server racks with bracketing that allows the rack to shake or sway but limits the rack's motion in such a way that it can't tip over.

Server racks contain some very power-hungry devices. Many servers, but not all, are left running on a 24×7 basis. Some people turn their server racks off overnight or during the weekend. When you power up a server rack, there can be a considerable power surge on your electrical system. It's a good idea to put a power sequence on your server rack to minimize the effect. Using a power sequencer—which fires up one outlet at a time, waiting a second or two between powering up one outlet and proceeding to the next one—is a good way of avoiding power surges that can knock out systems in your server room.

While on the subject of power, one consideration you need to address when specifying the components of a rack system is how you handle power outages or brownouts. In some ways, a brownout can actually be worse than a power outage because during a brownout, system components are still working, but with reduced power and at additional stress. Your server is more likely to have a component fail under those conditions. The best way to deal with power outages and brownouts is to install a UPS system for your servers and equipment, as covered in Chapter 14, "Power Protection."

As mentioned earlier, EMI and RFI emissions are another issue that you should consider when designing your deployment. All computers sold in the United States must be certified as emitting radiation below a certain level. That level is such that it should be possible to get AM/FM or cell phone reception from a distance that is not too far away from the server itself. The U.S. Federal Communications Commission (FCC), as specified in its Part 15 Rules, defines A and B classes for all commercially operated electronic equipment. Class A is designated as what is acceptable in an industrial or commercial environment, and Class B is the acceptable standard for home or residential operation.

Be aware that not all electronic components that you might want to use in your server rack will be properly certified. Although server racks are designed to create a Faraday cage effect and keep most, if not all, EMI and RFI emissions from escaping the cabinet, the interference of one component with another may be a feature that you might want to minimize. Any devices known to radiate EMI or RFI are best kept out of a server cabinet and housed in their own separate and shielded containers.

Many companies build server racks or cabinets with special environmental controls to enhance and improve their safety. EMC Symmetrix storage servers ship with a number of sensors that can detect temperature, vibration, and other factors. A simple modem can call back to EMC's control room when there is a problem. During an earthquake in Japan in the late 1990s, several EMC Symmetrix systems detected the vibrations of the impending earthquake before it occurred. In other instances, temperature sensors have detected server room fires before the companies where the storage servers are deployed were even aware of them.

Designing a Rack System

If you plan on setting up a server rack system, it's a good idea to design which components fit into the rack and where. A server rack can contain tens of thousands of dollars of equipment, and you want to make full use of your investment. Having a design also allows you to consider issues such as heat flow, where the rack's center of gravity is located, what cable runs you are going to need, and where to place not only hot running components but the fans and other systems needed to cool them.

Visio Designs

There are many places you can go to create designs for server racks. The one program that often gets discussed in this context is Microsoft's Visio, a drawing/entry CAD program that is now part of Microsoft Office. Visio has components in the PC & Peripherals, General Manufacturer Equipment, and Network Devices stencils that are designed to illustrate a standard rack environment.

Several websites also provide libraries of Visio shapes that you can use to lay out a rack design. An example of this approach can be found at http://techrepublic.com.com/5100-6265-1039784.html, where Rick Vanover has provided a set of downloadable stencils you can use to design a standard rack design. The set includes the following:

■ 20U, 22U, 34U, 36U, 41U, 42U, and 47U racks

■ Blade servers

■ 1U–6U rack-mountable servers

■ Management stations, monitors, and KVM components

■ Paneling

Another source of Visio stencils can be found at Remtech (www.remtech.uk.com/shapes.html). Remtech's stencils let you design a rack in metric scale, with shapes such as shelves, cable trays, and rack-mounted systems, all of which are smart Visio shapes that snap into position on the rack. You should also visit the Visio Café and check out Bruce Pullig's stencils of Sun and EMC servers and other related equipment (www.visiocafe.com/brucepullig.htm). The Visio Café also lists other stencils you might want to explore.

After you design your racks, you might want to use your designs to lay out the server room in which you place the racks. Visio has a set of room layout shapes that are in the Solutions>Business Diagrams>Office layouts. You'll want to lay out the room in an overview or plan view. After you've created the room's scaled shape, you need to populate the room with doors, electrical power rails, HVAC, and any other features of the room that will affect where you can place your server racks.

Server Vendor Rack Design Tools

Beyond the generic approach of documenting the design of a rack deployment, you will find that many server vendors offer online tools that allow you to create racks containing their specific products. Dell, Hewlett-Packard, and IBM all have online tools of this type. They can be found at the following locations:

- **Dell**—The Dell Rack Advisor may be downloaded from http://support.dell.com/support/downloads/format.aspx?releaseid=R73797&c=us&l=en&s=gen&cs. The file download includes a different language version, with EN representing the English language version.

- **Hewlett-Packard**—The Hewlett-Packard Customer Builder Online tool is part of the configurator system found at http://h30099.www3.hp.com/configurator/eco-cb/CustomBuilder.asp. You must register to use this tool, but it's a convenient web-based tool system for building Hewlett-Packard /Compaq rack solutions.

- **IBM**—You can download the IBM Rack Configurator at www-307.ibm.com/pc/support/site.wss/BBOD-3MDQFF.html?lang=en_US&page=brand&brand=IBM+PC+Server&doctype=Downloadable+files&subtype=All. With this tool, you select your rack, add components and cables, and then validate your design.

Figure 16.7 shows an example of a rack built using the Dell Rack Advisor, which is an online tool that lets you use a Dell rack or another standard rack design and populate it with Dell servers, storage components, and other parts.

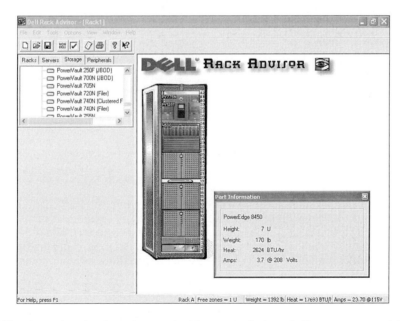

Figure 16.7 The Dell Rack Advisor lets you build server racks from Dell components and from its partners. It offers a limited facility to add non-Dell parts to your design.

By using Rack Advisor, you can select the rack model you want (Figure 16.7 shows a 42U rack from Dell) and then populate the rack with components. The rack shown in Figure 16.7 has three 6U Dell servers, an array, a tape library, and a keyboard, among other things. Components are shapes that you drag and drop from the shape library. When a shape doesn't fit in the rack, the tool posts a message to that effect. When you try to add a component that has requirements that the rack can't support, such as a large UPS system, the tool posts a notice to that effect and doesn't let you add the component. When you have a valid design, you can save it or print it, as needed.

Rack Features and Components

Server racks are custom designed, and you need to give some thought to the features you need in your racks to support the components they contain. Among the special considerations are the components that dissipate heat, fans, HVAC systems, and rack placement. You also need to consider how to mount systems into the racks, and if the server wasn't made specifically to be rack mounted, you need to consider how to convert the server so that it can be made to fit. You will learn about rails, mounts, and conversion kits in the sections that follow.

Fans and Airflow

When you think of a rack of servers, you should think in terms of each processor being the equivalent of a 100-watt light bulb. Not only do rack-mounted servers throw off a lot of heat, but they consume a significant amount of power. Mechanical devices such as hard drives add more heat, as do power supplies and other components. A dense server rack can give off more heat per square foot than an oven, which means that anyone contemplating this kind of deployment must pay particular attention to fans, airflow, and the cooling plant used. Whereas a standard server design might give off something like 2kW (kilowatt) to 4kW, a dense server rack could give off 15kW to 20kW.

The amount of air that a server rack can draw is often specified by a manufacturer. An alternate specification calls for maintaining a specific temperature inside the rack, as measured by a temperature probe. In hot server rooms, it can be difficult to maintain temperature, so it is important to pay attention to the components you use in server racks, how the racks are vented, and how much forced cooling is required.

You often have control over the number of fans and their placement in a server rack—whether the enclosure is sealed or missing a wall—and other factors. Many server rack designs allow you to use ceilings and/or floors that accommodate fans. Many rack designs, even the ones that are enclosed, offer the option of perforated doors or adjustable vents.

It's not just that racks require cooling in the servers themselves; the whole environment must be cooled. In many rooms containing rack servers, the top of the rack is 10°F to 15°F hotter than the floor.

Because high temperatures shorten equipment lifetimes and diminish system performance, there's a lot of incentive to lower server room temperatures. Indeed, many computer systems are designed to partially turn off by lowering the number of clock cycles that are executed as a certain temperature is reached. Today, cooling solutions within a rack are fan based, but some companies are considering switching dense rack solutions to a water-cooling system, something the mainframes of old used to use.

Many companies try to address the heat problem by using raised floors and running cooling systems under the floor. Server racks can add so much extra heat to a server room that large airflows through the ceiling may be required to achieve enough cooling to avoid system failure (and overheated IT staff).

As a rule of thumb, you should figure that each kW of heat generated should be dissipated by about 2 to 3 cubic feet of air per second. A completely populated 42U server rack might therefore require as much as 15 to 25 cubic feet per second. That velocity of airflow requires that modern server rooms with rack-mounted servers pay particular attention to good airflow design by reducing obstructions such as ceiling pipes and obstructions under a raised floor.

With so much air flowing, it is actually possible to create a Venturi effect, in which large airflow under the floor prevents air from flowing upward and instead simply pulls air into the raised floor. Without an upward flow of air, the air at the top of the room doesn't mix with cooler air and stays overheated. If this is problem in your server room implementation, you probably need to consult a specialist to help you design an appropriate solution.

Conversion Kits

Not all servers are built to fit into server racks. In fact, most servers aren't. If you have server rack envy, despair not: Several companies sell rack conversion kits that add to your server the necessary railing and brackets to it to allow it to be mounted in a universal rack. The price for a kit of this type is usually between $100 and $200.

One company selling these types of solutions is RackSolutions (www.racksolutions.com). One example of a RackSolutions kit is the one shown in Figure 16.8, which can be pulled out of the rack enclosure via a set of rails. This particular conversion kit is meant to fit into a relay frame and can support the 165 ProLiant DL760 D2.

Figure 16.8 RackSolutions offers a number of rack conversion solutions that let you make a tower or desktop server rack mountable.

Some conversion kits, like those covered in the next section, are nothing more than simple rail additions.

Rails

Mounting rails are another standard component of server racks. Universal mounting rails come with square holds, and the EIA standard mounting rails come with round holes that are 0.3125-inch tapped and are spaced apart in the following sequence:

- 0.5 inch between holes 1 and 2
- 0.625 inch between holes 2 and 3
- 0.5 inch between holes 3 and 4
- 0.625 inch between holes 4 and 5
- 0.5 inch between holes 5 and 6
- 0.625 inch between holes 6 and 7
- 0.5 inch between holes 7 and 8 (and so forth)

If you have rack-mountable equipment, you can use the measurements listed here to figure out whether your equipment will fit into a standard rack and which holes you must use.

The standard server rack unit 1U is measured as the distance from halfway between holes 1 and 2 and halfway between holes 4 and 5. The standard server rack unit 2U is measured as the distance from halfway been holes 1 and 2 and halfway between holes 7 and 8. Figure 16.9 illustrates this measurement.

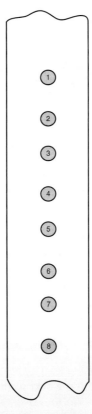

Figure 16.9   Hole spacing on a universal rail is related to standard rack sizes.

Most of the networking and server equipment you can buy conforms to the spacing requirements of the EIA standard mounting rail's hole spacing, but often you can fit equipment into a universal mounting rail by using a set of cage nuts and screws with washers.

Cable Management

Dense server deployment has one special problem associated with it that anyone with a PC and lots of accessories can appreciate: There are so many wires that need to be connected to the servers that it can be almost impossible to connect them all, let alone keep track of which wire goes to which server, which wire connects to which server port, which wire connects to which switch, and so forth.

The solution to this problem is called *cable management*, and it's every bit as important as any other design consideration when it comes to this form of deployment. Pity the poor IT admin who has to find a broken connection without some sort of system in place.

Cable management solutions for data centers often use different colors of wires. Each color is bundled together. In a good cable management system, each wire is also labeled with an identification number that aids in the quick location of any particular instance of a connection. Of course, all assignments need to be documented so that the people using the system later on can use it effectively.

Blade Servers

Several years ago it became possible to reduce a standard PC to a single board that can fit into a specially designed chassis that accommodates 6, 12, or more cards. From this simple concept was born a form factor that has come to be called *blade servers*. A blade server contains the processor, Northbridge and Southbridge chipsets, an Ethernet interface, and memory—and not a whole lot more.

Companies such as Cubix (www.cubix.com) began almost 10 years ago to offer chassis that at first were large boxes containing shared storage and I/O. Eventually, blade server designs shrank to standard 3U (5.25 inches) chassis, then 2U (3.5 inches), and finally even 1U (1.75 inches) chassis. Today Cubix offers a product called the BladeStation, shown in Figure 16.10, that is a 6U chassis or backplane that can stack up to seven dual Xeon processor blades, four SCSI drives, and an appropriately sized power supply into each system. Starting with a single blade, you can buy a BladeStation system for an entry price below $3,000.

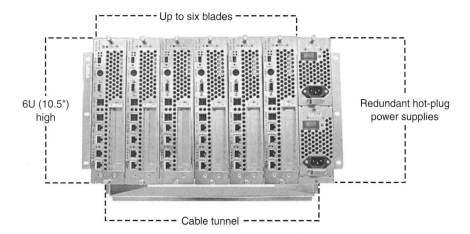

Figure 16.10   The 6U Cubix BladeStation shown here in front view can take up to six dual Xeon blades.

Today you can visit many data centers that maintain large server farms, such as the ones ISPs and search engine sites maintain, and walk down aisle after aisle containing rack after rack of blade servers, with hundreds or thousands of servers. Blades are the perfect answer for webserver applications where scale-out is necessary to get sufficient I/O to support a large number of client connections and where there is a system of load balancing in place to maximize the efficiency of the hardware, using an IP director such as F5 Networks's BIG IP.

What blade servers do, of course, is provide for extraordinary densification of the data center. Blades come in two form factors:

- Stackable pizza boxes
- Chassis with slide-in blades

Figure 16.11 shows a Dell PowerEdge 1850, which is a pizza box 1U server. This type of server is attached directly into the rack. Figure 16.12 shows a Dell PowerEdge 1855, which uses a 6U chassis arrangement to stack 10 blades within the chassis.

Figure 16.11 The Dell PowerEdge 1850 is a 1U pizza box server that stacks horizontally in a universal rack.

Figure 16.12 The Dell PowerEdge 1855 is a 6U cabinet that holds 10 blade servers.

The blade server architecture does even more than that, though. Blade servers provide a means to better utilize shared components, such as power supplies, UPS devices, optical drives, and storage arrays. They even make it easier to reduce the overall cable count and are an ideal form factor for creating fault-tolerant server systems. When a blade fails, the system shifts its computing load over to the working blades, allowing you to pop out the failed blade and pop in a replacement. Such an incident may incur a performance hit for network resources accessing the server, but that is far better than having the entire system crash.

Figure 16.13 shows a Hewlett-Packard ProLiant BL35p server blade. The blade contains a hard drive in the front, dual processors, and a network interface at the back.

Figure 16.13   The Hewlett-Packard ProLiant BL35p dual processor blade is a complete server.

Almost all the major server hardware companies now offer blade server designs. Some examples are IBM's heavily advertised eServer BladeCenter designs, some entries in the Dell PowerEdge series, NEC's Express series, and some entries in the Hewlett-Packard ProLiant series. There are no standard designs for blade server cards, so when you buy an eServer, for example, you are committed to buying cards from IBM. You usually find that blade server chassis offer some standard PCI-X or PCI slot(s) so that you can add a firewall or other standard component.

KVM Switches

A *KVM switch* is a switch that consolidates the keyboard (K), video (V), and mouse (M) for a number of servers into a single switch. A KVM switch makes it possible to use one keyboard, monitor, and mouse to control one server at a time, via a keystroke or an onscreen command. A KVM switch is a very important component in a server rack because there is no other way to accommodate a number of monitors, keyboards, and mouse devices in the physical space available. Not only can you free up space, but you can eliminate heat, lower the complexity of cabling, and lock down your servers by controlling them from a secure room, using a single console.

Many network operating systems now allow what is called *headless operation*, which is just a fancy way of saying that you can remotely control the system without a monitor. However, there are issues that make remote sessions problematic. When the server crashes, or when you need to change a setting in the server's BIOS, you cannot fix these problems via a remote session.

The server shown in Figure 16.3 has a KVM switch built into the it, with the KVM part installed as part of the rack-mounted keyboard, using a feature called an OSD (onscreen display). The OSD is part of the KVM switch, so even when the server itself isn't available, you can still access the OSD, and the OSD can access a server's BIOS as it starts up. A KVM switch, on the other hand, offers you access to each and every server's physical port and therefore direct access to the BIOS. That makes using a KVM switch the preferred means of controlling multiple servers when you can be in reasonable proximity to them.

With today's KVM technologies, the boxes look more like dense network switches, and with cable run lengths of as long as 1,000 feet, you can use a KVM switch in another room or another floor of a building. You can find switches with as many as 32 connections, and you can extend that number even higher because many of these switches have the ability to stack and connect multiple switches to one another. Some KVM switches come with very sophisticated management features, mimicking features you find on networks.

An example of KVM management software is Avocent's DSView Management software (see www.avocent.com/web/en.nsf/Content/DSView3Software). This software can manage KVM-connected devices over an IP network or internetwork, and it gives you BIOS-level access to your servers. That means that if a server fails, you can reboot it, enter the BIOS, and modify its settings. With this type of software, you can autodiscover servers, authenticate users and systems, perform scripts and macros, and handle other tasks.

KVM switches can be as small as a deck of cards, as is the case with most two-port and four-port models. As the KVM switches control more servers, the physical connections required to connect each server to the switch's backpanel connection require that the KVM switch grow in size. It's possible to purchase large rack-mounted KVM switches with 50 and more connections for dense server deployments. Those larger systems are housed in 2U or 4U rack-mounted panels. Some KVM networks can provide a fan-out with theoretical connections of up to 64,000 servers.

In purchasing a KVM switch, you should look for the following features:

- **Heterogeneous OS compatibility**—You need to make sure that any KVM switch you purchase is compatible with the operating systems in use on your servers. Even if a switch advertises that it is compatible with a range of system types, there may be problems in practice that require optional converters, and these converters add cost and eat precious server rack space.

- **Keepalive features**—A keepalive feature allows a switch to continue to send signals to servers, using the server's power, if the primary power to the KVM switch fails.

- **Firmware upgradabilty**—Some systems can have their BIOS upgraded, often remotely and automatically.

- **Video bandwidth**—The video bandwidth of KVM switches varies, and it can depend on cable run lengths.

- **Software and hardware switching**—A KVM switch should allow switching in both hardware and software.

- **Scanning features**—Scanning displays one server at a time so that you can periodically check all your servers at regular intervals. Some scanners display multiple servers' output onscreen at one time, with regular refreshes, and allow you to switch to any server of interest.

- **Scalability and flexibility**—KVM switches should allow you to fan out to add more connections as well as reduce connections, as needed. It's best if this can be done as a hot-swap operation.

- **Security features**—Some KVM switches provide encryption, password protections, and physical key access.

As more and more rack-mounted servers require remote administration, there has been a need to create remotely accessible KVM switches. Thus a number of vendors now offer KVM over IP solutions. What makes a KVM over IP solution so useful is that if a server crashes or if you need to make configuration changes in the BIOS, a KVM over IP switch allows you to reboot the system and access the system's BIOS. You can access the BIOS by using KVM over IP, just as you can when you are standing in front of the input devices attached to the KVM switch.

Raritan (www.raritan.com) is one well-known enterprise KVM switch manufacturer. Its Paragon II analog KVM series can be purchased and stacked, and it allows up to 64 simultaneous users to access up to 10,000 servers. Raritan's enterprise class one- to four-digital-channel KVM over IP appliance, the Dominion KX, offers KVM over IP remote access technology. It allows you to remotely administer 32 servers and other devices from a browser anywhere and still view the BIOS of the connected systems. Among the features of this unit are encryption, remote power control, dual-homed Ethernet connections, LDAP, RADIUS, Active Directory, syslog integration, and Web management of the switch.

One important feature for KVM over IP systems is that you can remotely access them when your network is down. You want secondary access through a modem so that you can perform out-of-band management. When you have this, you can reboot your servers even when the network connection is down and you can't get it up because the network connection depends on a computer such as a firewall.

Among the companies offering KVM switches are AMI, APC, Avocent, Belkin, Black Box, Minicom, Network Technologies, Inc., Raritan, Rose, StarTech, and Tripp Light. Of these companies, Avocent and Raritan are considered to be market leaders in the enterprise KVM switch space.

Cable Management Using KVM Switches

Many KVM switches are mounted in a server rack just as any other component is. Larger switches may take up to 2U of space, but some are thin 1U models. After you have installed the KVM switch, the next step is to connect the switch to the servers in the rack.

In a 72U server rack that contains 24 2U servers, you need to connect the following cables for your servers:

- 24 to 48 one- or two-network cables per server (for dual-homed systems)
- 24 to 48 power connections (for dual power supplies)
- 24 to 48 server-to-storage connections (1 for SCSI, 2 for Fibre Channel)
- 24 keyboard connections
- 24 mouse connections
- 24 video connections
- 24 USB-to-UPS connections

This means that for just the servers, you are connecting approximately 200 cables. Add connections for KVM switches, UPS devices, storage arrays, tape drives, and any other components you have in the rack, and the number probably approaches 250 for a server rack of this type.

It is absolutely critical that you organize these connections and that you use consolidated components such as KVM switches to bundle together different connections to individual servers as much as possible. KVM switch cables are usually bundled together into a single wire for each system and are color coded for the RJ-45 connections for mouse and keyboard. Most KVM switch vendors set up their switches so that a proprietary connector is used to connect the switch to the switch cable.

KVM switches can be connected to a keyboard, a mouse, and a monitor in a system tray at a comfortable level in the server rack. Many data centers prefer to connect KVM switches to remote consoles, and that requires special KVM output wires and extenders for analog KVM switches. Although mouse devices and keyboard signals can run several hundred feet, video signals tend to degrade over cable—hence the need for extenders. For KVM over IP switches, the long runs are over CAT5 UTP cable, the signal is digital, and there is no degradation because the video is rebuilt at the controller system at the other end of the wire.

CHAPTER 17

Server Rooms

Server rooms are an essential design component to any successful server deployment. A server room provides shared secure space, environmental monitoring, special connectivity features, cooling, conditioned power, backup power, redundant systems, and many other features that make it easier to run and protect vital systems. Servers can be deployed in closets, small rooms, large rooms, larger rooms, incredibly large rooms the size of football fields, and entire buildings. Depending on your point of view, a small room might be called a server room; somewhere between large and larger rooms and above, people start to call those spaces data centers. These days you can stuff a closet with a dense rack of blade servers, so it is possible to put the power of what not very long ago was a mainframe into the footprint of a clothing closet. What is a server room and what is a data center is really a question of your imagination and is rather unclear these days.

Many of the principles explored in this chapter apply whether you are building out the office next door or you are going to run the next Google.com. With careful planning, it is possible to protect your systems in case of a facilities failure, to make the best use of the space that you have, and to build and budget effectively. You may not have an unlimited budget to build a data center (few people do), but after reading this chapter, you should have a better idea how to best spend the money you do have and what you might have to do to get started.

Server Room Designs

When designing a server room or even an entire data center, it's best to keep things as simple as possible. The smaller the number of components you introduce into your server room, the easier it is to design. If you can standardize on a particular raised flooring standard, or a particular size and type of server rack, or a particular standard of HVAC (heating, ventilation, and air-conditioning) system, you can design your entire space in a consistent and easy-to-understand manner.

If you can control your design so that you build sections in modules, when you need to expand your capacity, it is often a simple matter of adding another module. Simplicity has many benefits. When you use fewer system types, the number of spare parts you have to keep on hand also drops. Fewer systems also means that you can afford to have a smaller support staff to administer them.

Unfortunately, many server rooms, particularly smaller ones, aren't designed with servers in mind. Smaller server rooms tend to be designed to fit the equipment that is already on hand. Even if you aren't constrained to a small server room, it still behooves you to take a minimalist approach to the range of new equipment you adopt because you generally already have the expertise to run and manage the equipment you have.

Most larger server rooms are designed and built by companies that specialize in this sort of construction. Whatever company you hire to construct your server room, you need to check it out just as you would any other company that does a big project for an organization. That means that you should check references, visit sites to see their past work, and have the work monitored. Building a server room is a lot like building a house: It requires many different skills to construct the systems in the room, and rarely does one company do it all. For most designs and construction, a consultant or consulting firm should act as the general contractor for the work. Whatever design you end up selecting, there should be a project specification document that details the design, sets milestones, and provides oversight.

Chances are that whoever you choose to be your primary contractor, if your server room is large or if you are designing a data center, your contractor may be managing the following types of experts:

- **Architects**—To draw the building or room.
- **Structural engineers**—To evaluate the building's qualities and determine structural parameters, such as floor carrying capacity.

- **Electricians**—To manage the placement of power lines, install distribution panels and conduit, run wiring, and set up fire and smoke alarms, as well as power backup systems.

- **HVAC specialists**—To design and install an HVAC system, including the HVAC plant equipment, and run and return piping, heat exchangers, and other related equipment.

- **Interior designers**—To select furnishings consistent with the purpose of the room(s).

It's rare that any one firm has all these skills in-house. As part of the design phase, you should expect to get a set of CAD drawings with associated financials and time lines that provide a roadmap to the construction phase of the project.

Of course, in the spirit of the 21st century, if you are creating a small server room, you can play all the roles yourself.

Converting Existing Rooms to Server Rooms

In many cases server rooms aren't new construction. A server room may start out as a classroom, a stockroom, a laboratory, an office, an anteroom, or something else. Just about any kind of room can be converted into a server room. This isn't a planned process, like starting from scratch designing a large facility is; it's growth by happenstance. It might begin with the arrival of a single server, and soon, without any planning at all, you might find several servers, storage arrays, and all sorts of systems.

When does a room become a server room, and when does it cease being any other kind of room? You have a server room when the following are true:

- The room needs air conditioning to keep it cool.

- A 220V electrical line needs to be wired into the room.

- You put a special lock on the door.

- You put a surveillance camera in the ceiling.

- You try to move large pieces of equipment from another part of the building into the room.

- Your first thoughts during a hurricane are to rescue the backup tapes in the room.

If you are lucky, you get to choose which room becomes a server room. Part of the planning has the site accommodate the necessary infrastructure to make your job easier. If there is no selection process for the room and you take what you can get, then you must retrofit your facility in order to have the infrastructure accommodate the site. It is typically true that accommodating a site is more difficult and more expensive than planning a site. Let's look first at a room selected by choice and then consider a retrofit project where you have no control over the site.

When you are offered a choice of rooms that can be used as a server room, it is best to draw up a list of characteristics that you need in your ideal server room. You can then rank each room as to how well it offers each of the properties a good server room should have. Here's a partial list of desirable characteristics:

- Good location for managing security issues

- Adequate access to loading docks or elevators

- Preexisting electrical and telecommunications infrastructure

- Adequate or extensible HVAC capabilities

- Ability of the room to carry the physical load (weight imposed)

- Protection from water damage, earthquakes, or other natural disasters

This list isn't much different from what you would use in the design process for a complete data center, but it is scaled down and weights each of the factors in a different way. In order to convert a specific room to a server room, you may find that you have to compromise on one of the characteristics that is desirable. It may be that in order to get the appropriate wiring, you will not be able to use a room near an elevator, for example. However, with planning, you can maximize your server room's capabilities while minimizing the overall cost.

Now let's look at an instance in which you have no control over the room, its location, or any of the other characteristics or properties of the room. In this case, you should create a document that lists the room's facilities: electrical, HVAC, and so forth. That document should then detail the equipment you are going to put into the server room, as well as equipment you want to eventually add. After you specify the equipment, you can then determine the facilities that will have to be added to the room to support the equipment.

The main problem with ad hoc placement of equipment is that in most instances, when the equipment grows to a certain point, it ends up getting relocated. The reason for this is simple: It becomes cheaper to relocate than it does to invest in some needed requirement. You don't want to be in a situation where you've made major investments getting a room ready to be a server room only to find out down the line that the investments were a waste of money. By specifying what you need to support what you intend to use, you can balance cost and a time line so that your server room gives you a strong return on investment. In other words, with some thought and planning, you can maximize your server room's utility while avoiding making unadvised investments in infrastructure.

Server Closets

All mechanical devices make noise. Some, such as dot matrix printers, make a lot of noise. Given that it's possible to build a small data center into a rack and put that rack into an enclosed space, you might want to consider whether that's really a good idea.

Many companies start by building a server rack that they maintain in their office. As the rack gets more fully populated, it gets more valuable and noisier, and it needs more physical protection. For these reasons, companies consider moving their racks into small, enclosed spaces. It's not a new idea: For many years, network connection patch panels and junction boxes have been located in closets. Moving a server or set of servers into a small space is along the same lines.

Unlike with a closet for switching equipment, the main problem for a server closet is environmental control. You don't have to condition a server closet so it can be habitable by people, which lessens the HVAC requirements you might otherwise have. The main HVAC requirement is that your equipment operate in a certain temperature range, and that sets your HVAC thresholds.

Server Room Specifications and Considerations

The design specifications for your server room are where your requirements meet your budget. Your design may be determined by the scope of the capabilities that need to be established; but your ability to add additional redundancies, establish different services, and support maintenance contracts is constrained by the budget you have to build the room as well as the budget you have to support it. Because no one ever has all the funds needed to build everything desired, it's important to make the right set of compromises.

In considering the compromises, you need to try to determine the answers to the following questions:

- Can you start with a subset of your desired installation and complete the plan later on?

- What systems are essential, and what systems are optional?

- How much fault tolerance (provided by redundancy) is desirable, and how much can you afford?

- Does your budget support your project scope, and is there enough flexibility to reassign funds, if needed?
- Does your design leave room for expansion and upgrading?
- Does your server room's annual operating budget support the required number of staff and services?

Perhaps the best investment you can make in designing a server room is to write a formal project specification document. The money you spend planning your building will likely be returned several times over, in the form of less waste and more user satisfaction. Indeed, in any large project, the specification document is considered to be the first phase of the work.

Determining Location

The first step in designing a server room is to site it. In many instances, you don't have control over where you locate your servers, but when you do, there are a number of criteria you can apply to choose the best location. Selecting a location is a balance between cost, convenience, and availability, and your choices should be influenced by the server room's purpose. For network systems that just can't go down, considerations such as network, power, and environmental services may be the deciding factors in choosing a location. When you can tolerate some downtime, you might choose to pick a location with a lower cost.

It's useful to create a matrix of your server room's design elements (as rows), and rank them against each location (the columns). In addition, you should have two columns that estimate your expected installation cost as well as your yearly projected budget for each component. A spreadsheet of this type can really help you decide on a site and other design elements. You might want to develop this document as part of your preliminary thinking or assign it as part of the initial design specification part of your project.

Macro-Level Location Concerns

As the cliché goes, location, location, and location are the three primary factors that offer success in the real estate business. Location also matters when you are determining where to place your server. You certainly wouldn't want to place your server room directly over an active earthquake fault, in an area that floods, or high up in a tall skyscraper. These are all locations with obvious issues that can cause you significant trouble. However, there are ways to deal with these kinds of difficult environments:

- In a seismic zone, at the very least, you can expect vibrational tremors, and you need to constrain all movable items to something solid, using mounting devices. If you build a server room in an earthquake zone, you might make the decision not to use a raised floor, under the assumption that a solid floor offers a better and more secure foundation for your equipment.
- A server room in a tall building also has concerns regarding sway and vibration. Your main concern for a server room located in a tall building might be access. Unless there has been adequate planning done in the construction of the building, it may be difficult to route a cable from one part of the room to another or from one floor to another.
- A flood zone construction may require that you place your server room significantly above historical flood levels in a building, have adequate pumping capabilities, and locate your wiring above the server room (rather than underneath it). You might also have to design your facility to be sealed in a way that prevents water or moisture from intruding.

No one would prefer to locate their equipment in areas such as these, but if you go to San Francisco's West Bay area, New York City's Wall Street, or downtown New Orleans, you will find many companies running server rooms in those areas. You'll also find that with advanced network connectivity, many of those same types of firms choose to locate their data centers miles away, in less problematic and more cost-effective locations.

Micro-Level Location Concerns

The macro-level concerns about where you locate a server room have micro equivalents that should guide your choice for the location of your server room.

A server room should be centrally located in a building, to minimize the amount of cable necessary to connect to other systems in the building. A central building location also has the least temperature and humidity fluctuations. If your server room is on the outside of the building and surrounded by large glass windows, hot temperatures and sunny days or cold temperatures mean that you have to be more careful about cooling and heating the room.

You don't want your server room to flood, so putting a server room in a basement or the ground-floor level of a building isn't as good an idea as moving the room further up in the building. Coastal regions and the effects of global warming aside, the most common way to flood a server room isn't from a nearby body of water flooding its banks; a flood is most likely to be the result of a water pipe bursting. Therefore, you need to eliminate all runs of piping through the server room or in the ceiling above it. If the floor above has a bathroom, then undoubtedly there are water pipes leading into it. Either the bathroom or the server room should be moved. Water and electricity are not a good combination. At the very least, if you can't move piping away from your server room, you should plan for disaster by installing a water barrier on the ceiling of your server room. This water barrier is usually a curtain or an impermeable plastic material that can route water away from your room and equipment, a little like a horizontal shower curtain—albeit a lot bigger. In humid climates, a good vapor barrier should also be installed.

Note

You can find a list of companies that provide waterproofing materials at www.thebluebook.com/cl/stall4670.htm.

Another location consideration is security. Some locations lend themselves better to being protected than others. If your server room is near areas with a large amount of foot traffic, it is harder to secure the room than it would be if it were located in an area where fewer people are located. Lobbies, common rooms, cafeterias, and auditoriums are areas that get a lot of traffic and are unsuitable neighbors for a server room.

The Planning Phase

The sad truth is that no matter where you locate your equipment, each location has issues with temperature, humidity, access, and other factors that are unique for that location and must be planned for. The important task, therefore, is to recognize what issues you face and build solutions for those problems into your design.

These are the essential issues you must plan for with any installation:

- **Size or capacity**—The location must have enough floor space, and the floor must have enough carrying capacity to hold your equipment. If you plan on expansion someday, you should plan to be able to access additional adjacent space when required.

- **Energy**—Servers and the equipment necessary to support them require a lot of power, so it's important that you be able to obtain the power you need when you need it. You also need to plan to condition the power so that it's suitable for use, as well as plan for outages.

- **Network connections**—It's essential to have reliable network connections of sufficient bandwidth. Often, data centers purchase two or three Internet connections from different ISPs, each on separate network trunks, for availability.

- **HVAC**—Cooling, heating, airflow, and humidification are requirements for any server room. Cooling in particular is an issue because servers run hot, and they shut down when they reach a certain temperature.

- **Security**—Systems must be put into place that restrict access to both hardware and software systems.

- **Physical access**—Doors, elevators, conduits, the size of aisles, and other physical attributes of the room(s) must be accounted for.

When you have a design in mind and have a plan drawn up, if you are building a new building or an extension to an existing business, you should check with the local government to ensure that all your plans are within the requirements of the local building codes. The approval process requires that you get two levels of approval: one for the design plans and the second for the completed project. You should also check with your insurance company to determine whether the room or building you are planning alters your coverage in any way.

Determining Size and Capacity

The size of your server room or data center is a gating factor in the type and distribution of equipment you can employ there. Bigger rooms offer the advantages of more space and potentially lower server density, but they also require correspondingly more facilities, such as HVAC. When they are properly designed, you can also get better airflow with bigger spaces, albeit at a higher cost.

A good place to begin laying out the design of a server room is with a design tool such as Visio. When you have the room size and shape laid out on your design surface, you can start to add room features, such as doors and windows, structural columns, and any other features that might affect where you place your system components. Visio contains a number of stencils that provide standard shapes of equipment types, and you can purchase third-party stencils of server room equipment. Figure 17.1 shows some of the stencils dedicated to network and server room design in Visio.

The next step in designing the room is to subdivide the room into squares the size of the server racks that you intend to deploy. Your grid squares can be the size of the panels used in your raised flooring as shown in Figure 17.2, or they can be a standard size, such as 3 feet by 3 feet, which is close to the size of a small server rack.

You need to create rows of servers on your design surface, and between the tows should be open aisles that are as wide as each equipment row. It's possible to use as little as 40% open aisle space and 60% equipment row space, but it's much better to have an equal size, so you have some leeway for accommodating oversized equipment if you decide to deploy some at any point.

◀◀ For more information on using Visio for implementing server rack design, see "Visio Designs," p. 720.

Bob Snevely, in his book *Enterprise Data Center Design and Methodology*, ISBN 0130473936, which is part of the Sun Microsystems *Blueprints* series, developed the concept of rack location units (RLUs). An RLU assigns a weighting factor to the total requirements of the components of a rack system, with respect to the following demands:

- Physical space
- Connectivity
- Power

- Weight
- Cooling
- Functional capacity

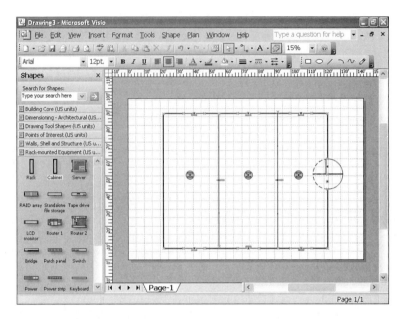

Figure 17.1   Visio, which has many dedicated equipment stencils, is a great tool for developing a space plan for a server room. You can also purchase third-party shape libraries of common server room equipment.

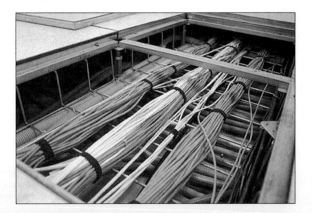

Figure 17.2   Shown here is raised flooring with bundled networking cable.

The idea behind this approach is that you want to distribute dense server racks across the server room so that you don't overload the capacity of any one section with respect to any of the aforementioned factors. Let's say that you have a section of five server racks aligned side-by-side in a row. In this scenario, you would need to create a table that combined all five of those servers into one set of requirements, such as the following:

- Physical space, including not only the size of the five server racks, but the size of the aisles that surround them, the size of any service columns or poles, and the size of row breaks and any additional space required to cool the assembly.

- The number and type of Ethernet CAT5 cable, fiber-optic cable, or coaxial cables that must be run to the different servers in the group.

- The amount of total power—the kind of power in volts, amps, single- or three-phase, and outlet type required.

- The point load and total tile load (for raised flooring) and the total floor load for the space being used. The total floor load should not exceed the carrying capacity of the floor.

- The cooling requirement in British thermal units (BTU) per hour.

- Functional capacity, which is a metric that defines how much computing power or storage capacity the assemblage has. The idea is that you can use the functional capacity to measure whether you have enough assets deployed to support a particular project or business goal.

Measuring Load Capacity

Load capacity is measured in a number of different ways. The first measure is the point load. If your server rack rolls on four metal casters or rollers, the server's load is distributed at four different points. A fully loaded large server can weigh as much as 3,200 pounds, so with such a server on four casters, each caster is has a load of 800 pounds; this is called the *point load* on an area of perhaps 1 square inch.

The second load capacity metric is the static load. *Static load* is the weight that an area of floor must be able to support. Say you have a 4-foot-square floor segment that supports 60% of the weight of a server rack. Because the rack is larger than that square, the static load for a 3,200-pound server would be 60%×3,200 pounds/4, or 480 pounds per square foot.

Finally, the last metric you need to concern yourself with is the *rolling load*. As your rack system moves across the floor, its rolling load is similar to its static load, but the distribution of the weight varies, depending on how the rack is located. If you are using a raised floor, different locations on the raised flooring load tiles differently, depending on the location.

In some situations, a raised floor can support a static load, but the rolling load can lead to the collapse of a panel when too many points on the rack are located on the same tile. It's important to be aware of this problem and replace perforated tiles with stronger, solid tiles along the route of travel if that is required.

With all these measurements in hand, you can then sum them all to create a superset RLU that defines the assemblage. Your five racks might have the following specifications, among others:

- Weigh 4,800 pounds
- Require five 30A 220V outlets and one 40A 480V three-phase power connection, for a total of 12,000 watts
- Need 82,000BTU per hour

If any one particular area can't support these requirements, you should move a dense server out of the group and place it somewhere else. To simplify the process of mixing and matching racks, you might assign a label to the different types of racks and use that label to balance your design. You could assign weighting factors to each requirement, such that your label might be RLU-142331, where each number is the overall assignment of each factor.

When you sum five different RLUs, you get a composite number that lets you determine whether you have distributed servers appropriately. Sneveley's assignment uses a simpler scheme of RLA-A, RLA-B, and so forth, but it's possible and probably preferable to extend this idea to make it a little more quantitative. The total RLUs determine what is called the "in-feed capacities" of the system. This total is not the complete story, of course. Your calculations need to account for not only the amounts of each resource but their types as well.

Planning for Cable Management

Chapter 16, "Server Racks and Blades," briefly touches on the number of cables that run in and out of dense server racks. As you may recall, a server rack with 24 servers can have from 200 to 250 cables going into the connections at the back of the server. Without some form of organization and identification, it can become impossible to find a broken connection or modify your current connections.

The rules for cable management are few:

- Label everything and document what you have labeled. Label your cables *on both ends*, near the connectors. (Some experts recommend labeling cable every 6 to 10 feet, in case you need to troubleshoot the connection under raised flooring.) Use a numbering scheme that allows for sufficient cable count so that you can accommodate growth.

- Keep it simple and keep it organized. Wires going to the same locations should be bundled either below a raised floor, above your equipment, or on cable runs or using some other organization tool.

- Use colored cables and document what the colors mean.

- Avoid using excess cable lengths and never leave open or disconnected cabling. Excess and unused cable is an invitation for the creation of spaghetti cabling, which is both dangerous and a waste of time.

- Use patch panels effectively. Patch panels support CAT5 Ethernet, Fibre Channel, coaxial, fiber-optic cable, and often a custom mix. Label connections at the patch panel, and, if possible, use matching color coding for the wires that connect to them.

- Bundle all cables leading to and away from patch panels. There are different methods for bundling cable, including using cable ties (which come in different colors), routing pipes, wire hooks, and so forth. You can purchase entire cable management systems from several vendors.

- Whenever possible, minimize the number of cables used because each cable and connection represents a potential point of failure. However, maintain redundancy in your cabling scheme so that if a path fails, another path is still open. Obviously, these two rules must be balanced with good common sense.

- Use good-quality insulated cables and keep them away from heat and electromagnetic sources. Don't mix data transmission cables with power cables. Insulate power cables whenever possible.

In a disorganized system, changes that should take seconds can take many minutes, if it's possible to effect the change at all. Without cable management, you can have a rat's nest of wires that impedes airflow and can be a hazard. If you want to know how professional an IT organization is, one of the simplest ways to tell is to look at its cable management scheme on the back of its servers.

The simplest cable management systems are those that have a hook or basket arrangement. One site that offers a number of cable management solutions is Cableorganizer.com (www.cableorganizer.com). You can install cable management systems above head height and out of the way. Many server racks come with cable management systems that run at the top of the server rack, as you can see in the APC InfraStruXure rack series shown later in this chapter, in Figure 17.5.

If you install a raised floor (see "Considering Raised Flooring," later in this chapter), you are likely to install cable trays as part of your floor support. Cable trays are U-shaped wire baskets onto which the wire is placed. Cable trays are placed so that the wires run parallel to the aisles, thus allowing you to have access to the trays at any point along the run.

Determining Power Needs

Electrical consumption is one of the metrics that you need to plan for. As a general rule, you should figure on about 50 watts of power per square foot for a small server to as much as 100 watts per square foot for denser deployments.

In addition to specifying the individual rack power requirements, you also need to specify the total room's power needs. For 10 racks, that figure would be 720 amps. Of course, other equipment in a server room can significantly draw on power. Among the larger consumers of power in a server room are HVAC, switches, printers, lighting, and UPS devices. Therefore, you should consider all those factors when allowing for your power requirements.

If you have a server rack with 36 1U servers in it, and you figure that each server draws approximately 2 amps, then one rack would consume 72 amps. Current power consumption for servers is averaging over 90% of the server's stated load. Given that you want extra capacity for a rack of this type, you might want to allow for twice the amount of amperage during power bursts—say, 150 amps—because most racks include other devices, such as arrays, tape backups, rack ventilation, and so forth.

Note

Large power lines generate magnetic fields that can be a problem for network communications. You need to shield any large power lines so that they don't affect other systems. Many server rooms choose to shield their power wiring inside flexible steel pipe or conduits, often encased in braided copper wire sheaths in order to minimize electromagnetic interference (EMI).

Also keep in mind that elevators often have large motors with magnetic mechanisms in them and that you can have problems from that source as well. When possible, you shouldn't have an elevator near a server room. If you have EMI, you might want to invest in electromagnetic shielding material and use it to line your server rooms' walls.

As much as possible, you should have redundant power inputs to your equipment. In such a system, if one circuit supplying power fails, the second circuit picks up the load. While redundancy is an overriding theme in this chapter, many data centers do not provide duplicate power inputs to their equipment, relying on their UPS equipment to switch on when there is a power failure and to provide for enough time for admins to switch manually over to the second power circuit or to fix the problem.

According to the American Power Conversion (APC) whitepaper "Guidelines for Specification of Data Center Power Density," a typical 5,000-square-foot data center has a power draw of around 50kW at 480 volts, with the following electrical requirements:

- 50% cooling system (where it is assumed that 1kW use requires 1kW cooling)
- 36% critical loads (servers and other systems)
- 11% UPS inefficiencies and battery charging
- 3% electrical lighting

Analysis of a server room or data center's power needs starts with determining the amount of power drawn as part of the critical load. You could start by enumerating the average power requirements of each piece of equipment in the room and add an extra cushion for peak loads. The manufacturer of the equipment should list power consumption either on its specification sheet or on a nameplate that is placed on the equipment. Enumeration can be tedious, particularly when you are dealing with server racks containing different manufacturer's equipment.

Note

You might wonder how kilowatts (kW) relate to kilovolt amps (kVA), as both are used in power measurements. *Kilowatts* are the real power that can be drawn from a system. *Kilovolt amps* include the power you can draw plus the residual power in the system that you can't draw out. Therefore, a UPS device is often rated as kW/kVA, which is called the *power factor*. A computer's ability to draw (that is, its power factor) approaches 1.0 or unity, but modern UPS devices have power ratings in the range of 0.8 to 0.9, depending on the design type. Some designs have a rating as low as 0.65, so this is one factor to take into account. A device with a rating of 0.65 at 200kVA supplies only 1.3kW of power.

When you have determined what your current and future electrical requirements are, you need to multiply that figure by a factor from 25% to 50% to leave sufficient overhead to deal with peaks. The amount of overage you need may be designated as part of your building code, so you need to check. Most power comes into a facility as 480V three-phase AC in the United States and 230V phase AC elsewhere. Where a critical load of 1.25X is used, the current required for critical load is as follows:

Amps needed = (kW×1,000)/(Volts×1.73)

The cooling factor needs to be equal to at least the critical load at peak, with a certain amount of reserve. That's why a 36% critical load requires 50% cooling.

The rated load of the power equipment used may be as much as four times the critical load, while the steady state load is rated at 1.25X. At this point, it should be possible to estimate the size and type of any backup power generators as well as the size and nature of your UPS equipment.

In summary, you need to take the following steps to determine your power requirements:

1. Determine the power requirement of each individual component in your server room for its peak load.
2. Find the total and multiply it by the overage factor that your building codes or your site requires.
3. Determine the type of power that is required and where access to the power must be located.
4. Determine the cost and location of the resources needed to deliver these power requirements.
5. Determine the amount of backup power you need, as required by both your electrical draw and the amount of time you want to be able to be on backup power.

Determining your power needs and how to deploy your electrical connections is definitely something you don't want to do by yourself. This is an area where it makes sense to consult an electrical engineer in order to make sure that each piece of equipment gets the power it needs and is properly protected. You need help figuring out just where to place your outlets, whether you need to deploy flexible power cable outlets (sometimes called power whips), as well as the nature of the type of power supplied to your systems. Some larger systems that draw power need more heavy-duty power supplies, such as three-phase 480V power. It's really important to try to balance the power needs of your equipment across your electrical circuits, and that definitely influences where you put your densest server racks and more powerful systems.

Calculating UPS Needs

As discussed in more detail in Chapter 14, "Power Protection," UPS (uninterruptible power supply) is a backup battery system that provides power when your main power fails. Every server should be backed up by some kind of UPS system, so it is helpful to know a little bit about the kinds of UPS systems on the market as well as how to calculate how much UPS capacity you need.

In an age when power brownouts are common during peak demand, UPS systems are also often called on to condition the power supply. By *conditioning* we mean that the power is monitored and maintained within a certain tolerance so that it is always at a constant voltage and frequency. You will certainly want to check the quality of the power in your building and determine whether it conforms to American National Standards Institute (ANSI) standards for power quality. If it doesn't, you should look for this feature in your UPS devices or invest in special power conditioning equipment.

In calculating UPS capacity, you want to balance the amount of backup powered time available against the cost of the system. For absolutely mission-critical servers, the solution isn't a UPS system but a backup power system, with a UPS perhaps serving to allow for successful transition to the backup power. APC has a UPS product selector at www.apc.com/tools/ups_selector/index.cfm.

UPS devices come in several different types:

- **Standby**—This is the type of UPS used on PCs and workstations, as well as on small servers. A standby UPS device contains a surge suppressor and a voltage filter, in line with a switch that power can flow through. As long as power is available, most of it flows down this circuit, with a little of the current being used to keep the battery topped up. When the power fails, the transfer switch moves the connection from the power on circuit to the battery circuit, where a DC-to-AC converter puts the power into a form that computers and monitors can use.

- **Line-interactive**—This type of UPS is used to back up small groups of computers. In this design, the power line goes first through a transfer switch and then flows through the inverter, which supplies power to the computer(s) and to the battery for charging. When the power fails, the transfer switch opens and the power in the battery discharges. The advantage of a line-interactive UPS is that it offers better voltage regulation and larger battery sizes. You'll find this to be the dominant design for the 0.5kVA to 5kVA range.

- **Standby-ferro**—This type of UPS isn't commonly used anymore, but it is a reliable system that offers superior line filtering. The main electric line runs through a transfer switch to a transformer and then on to the computers. The secondary power line runs through a battery charger, charges a standby battery, runs through an AC/DC converter and then onto the transformer and the computers. Standby-ferro UPS systems have problems supplying the kinds of loads that current computer systems generate. A server's power draw requires a smooth AC power, but a ferro-resonant UPS's transformers create a current that lags the voltage, resulting in a ringing power signal that can cause power surges. While this used to be the dominant UPS in the 3kVA to 15kVA range, it has been replaced by the double conversion online UPS described next.

- **Double conversion online**—This type of UPS is the most commonly used UPS for power ratings above 10kVA. In a double conversion system, the main power runs through an AC/DC power rectifier, charges a battery, and proceeds through an AC/DC inverter on its way to computers. A second line bypasses all these components, going directly from input to output with a static bypass switch. When power fails, this design doesn't throw the transfer switch, and because the battery is on the main power line, there is no transient transfer time for the backup power to kick in. The advantage of this system is that it has very good electrical characteristics, but this design also has the disadvantages of having large component stress as well as sometimes drawing large amounts of powers from the building's power system.

- **Delta conversion online**—This UPS technology fixes some of the deficiencies of the double conversion online design. This design has an inverter that supplies the load voltage, as well as an added delta converter that also adds a power circuit to the inverter's output. When power fails, the design operates similarly to a double conversion system, but a delta converter conditions the input power so that it is sinusoidal, and it also controls the input current so that the battery charge doesn't overwhelm the electrical system. Today the delta conversion system is the dominant large UPS system, and it is used for power ranges from 5kVA to 1.6mW.

Figure 17.3 illustrates the power circuits for the different kinds of UPS devices, and Table 17.1 shows the different types of UPS systems.

Table 17.1   The Different Types of UPS Systems

Type	Power (kVA)	Voltage Conditioning	Cost per VA	Efficiency	Inverter	Used with
Standby	0–0.5	Low	Low	Very high	No	PCs, workstations
Line-interactive	0.5–5	Design dependent	Medium	Very high	Design dependent	Racks, stand alone servers, and poor power environments (most popular UPS)
Standby-ferro	3–15	High	High	Low to medium	No	Banks of redundant UPS systems (not widely used)
Double conversion online	5–5,000	High	Medium	Low–medium	Yes	Banks of redundant UPS systems
Delta conversion online	5–5,000	High	Medium	High	Yes	Widely used in all types of server environments

Now that you know what kinds of UPSs are available, you need to specify which kinds of UPSs and how much capacity you need. For standard servers, you can get by with a single backup system, referred to as an *N topology*, where there are no redundancies. An *N* topology should be able to supply a full load (100%) to critical systems for the amount of time you deem necessary. To add redundancy you might want to move up to an *N+1 topology*, where an additional UPS device is added to any number (*N*) of UPSs.

While a server can run at 90% load, a UPS cannot. If a double conversion or delta conversion UPS surges over its stated load, the device shuts down and goes into a utility bypass mode. Power to backed-up systems is lost. UPS devices are very unforgiving in that way.

Finally, for mission-critical systems, you might have a *2N topology*, where each and every UPS system is backed up by another UPS system. However, for mission-critical systems, what you really want is a backup generator to keep them going. A UPS for a mission-critical system is your very last line of defense and should give you enough time to repair or replace a generator.

Considering Raised Flooring

There was a time when old mainframes were put into chilled rooms with raised flooring because these mainframes contained a large number of mechanical devices, vacuum tubes, and other equipment that ran very hot. Raised flooring was just one of the ways of keeping those behemoths cool. While times have changes in many ways, using a raised floor and the correct ventilation are still effective means of greatly increasing airflow in a room, by perhaps 50% or more. Raised floors are usually from 12 inches to 24 inches off the ground. That allows duct work to flow to the air intakes that many cabinets and racks have, which in turn makes for greatly enhanced airflow.

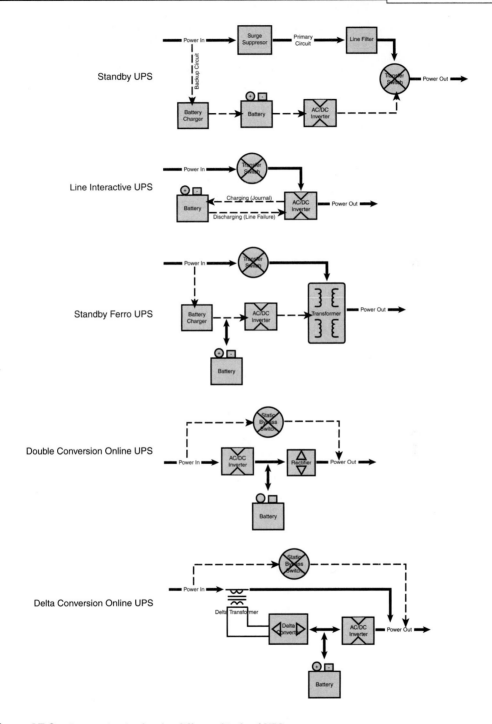

Figure 17.3   Power circuits for the different kinds of UPS systems.

A raised floor is generally constructed by placing a metal load-bearing framework or support grid onto the server room floor. The assembly looks a little bit like an erector set. Most raised floors use tiles or panels that are 2 feet by 2 feet, or 4 feet square. The space below the panels is called the *plenum*, and tiles can be either solid, perforated, or grated. One of the nicest features of raised flooring is the ability to shape your cooling system flow by using the floor panels. Raised flooring requires additional ceiling height in the server room of as much as 2 feet, which can add to building costs.

Raised flooring also offers additional benefits such as providing a place to run cabling and to remove power lines from sight. However, many people find that raised flooring results in poor cable management due to difficulty of access, and that can lead to a situation where cables that are not in use are simply left in place. Therefore, some thought should be given to how the raised flooring is used and what kinds of access features it has. While you still find raised flooring in the smaller data centers and in control rooms, there's been a trend in data centers to avoid putting in raised flooring. Larger data centers tend to avoid that additional complexity and instead invest their time and effort in more robust heat dissipation and electrical facilities.

When using a raised floor, it is important to remove any under-the-floor obstructions as well as to seal the floor below the subfloor; doing this improves the flow of cool air to the hot-running systems above the floor. Because you are counting on the floor to provide airflow, all open or missing floor tiles should always be replaced, and any cable cutouts should either be sealed or replaced. Cable cutouts are a major source of air leak. You want the cold air to flow up and through your systems, so flooring in aisles should be closed tiles, and that under the equipment should be open.

With server racks that are large and heavy, you need to be concerned with the weight-bearing capacity of the raised flooring. The load-bearing capacity of a raised floor today, using cast aluminum tiles, is rated at more than 1,500 pounds, even when you use tiles that are 55% perforated. If you use metal flooring, you should ensure that the floor is nonconductive. Also, you should avoid using as flooring any material that traps dust and dirt or that creates particles. You wouldn't want to use carpet-covered panels, for example, even though carpet would provide the electrical isolation you might want.

If you plan on deploying a set of large server racks, you might find that you require a room height of nearly 10 feet in order to accommodate the floor, server, and ceiling fixtures.

Another issue associated with raised flooring is that it doesn't permit the use of locked cages in large data centers. Many ISP and collocation facilities rent out capacity in a data center and use cages or wire fencing to separate the different areas of servers in the data center. In such a case, raised flooring doesn't work.

Although raised floors continue to be deployed in server rooms, it seems that fewer and fewer data centers are using them as time goes by because they do have a number of drawbacks.

Planning for HVAC and Airflow

As server farms stuff more and more blades into bigger and bigger racks, the problem with heat dissipation has raised its ugly head once more, with a vengeance. High-density blade servers can generate 10kW to 20kW per large rack, but the kinds of cooling solutions that use to be delivered through raised floor plenum typically was designed to provide at most 3kW per rack.

As warm air rises and cold air falls, putting adequate cooling at the bottom of a room and exhaust at the top of the room should handle the heat load. Cooling equipment, like power equipment, should be redundant. You don't want your servers to burn up because an HVAC unit has failed. Most data centers invest in larger cooling capacity and UPS equipment rather than having redundant cooling.

To calculate the amount of air-conditioning required for a server rack, you need to figure that every kW of power used will generate slightly more than 3,400BTU/hr, or 0.28 ton of refrigeration, referred to as a *tonref*. Most air-conditioners are specified in the United States by the BTU/hour rating. Thus a server rack of 36 1U servers, each consuming about 0.2kW of power, requires the dissipation of 7.2kW, or 24,480BTU, per hour.

It probably makes sense to maintain your HVAC equipment on its own power circuit and not on the same circuit as your servers. HVAC equipment tends to be more tolerant of voltage fluctuations than server equipment. If you are trying to determine the amount of refrigeration and the power needed to run that equipment, you might want to go to the American Society of Heating, Refrigerating, and Air-Conditioning Engineers (ASHRAE) website, at www.ashrae.org, where you can find information on how to estimate data center and server room environmental requirements. Most data centers run at temperatures ranging from 67°F to 73°F (19°C to 23°C), and the recommended humidity is between 40% and 55%.

A rack that accommodates 36 1U servers is considered to be a medium to larger rack size in a data center today, but server racks that are coming to market will consume as much as 20kW. Typically the average rack-based server system consumes a little less than 3kW. There's no getting around the numbers: To keep the temperature stable, each 1kW of power consumed requires 1kW of cooling to remove excess heat.

How you distribute your servers can also affect how well your HVAC system works. If you put all your servers together side-by-side, you can overwhelm your cooling system's ability to cool that area. In general, you should distribute servers throughout your server room. In a fully loaded server room, where you may not have the luxury of ideal spacing, you should distribute all your hottest-running racks as best you can.

Even more important from the standpoint of airflow is to design your server rack distribution scheme so that hot and cool aisles alternate with one another. What this means is that because racks tend to exhaust air from the back of the server, a hot aisle is one where the servers on both sides of the aisle have the rear of their racks facing the aisle. A cool aisle would be one where the fronts of both servers face the aisle. Aside from having the benefit of better airflow, this arrangement gives you the benefit of not requiring people to be in hot aisles most of the time. Because servers' controls are typically in the fronts of the units, most of the time personnel work on the servers in the server room will be spent in cool aisles.

Figure 17.4 illustrates a hot aisle/cool aisle arrangement where cooling is distributed to improve airflow and heat dissipation. Even with a scheme such as the one shown here, when you have adequate HVAC in place, you still may not have enough airflow to make the system work properly. To improve airflow, you can place air distribution units to move additional air from location to location. These units should be protected from power loss in the same way as your other HVAC components.

Note

Many server personnel think that having one aisle hot and the next one cool is a design defect. Therefore, they use more cooling vents than they should in hot aisles and more hot returns in cool aisles, thus defeating what is intended to be a design feature. It is important to make clear to personnel in a server room that the hot aisles were designed to be hot and should be left that way.

The ultimate solution to these hot-running systems is to implement direct cooling to them. Cool air should flow into the server racks at the bottom and be directed out at the top of the rack. Because unused vertical space in a rack can provide a way for hot air to recycle within a cabinet, it is important to install blanking panels and make sure that your cable management doesn't interfere with cooling.

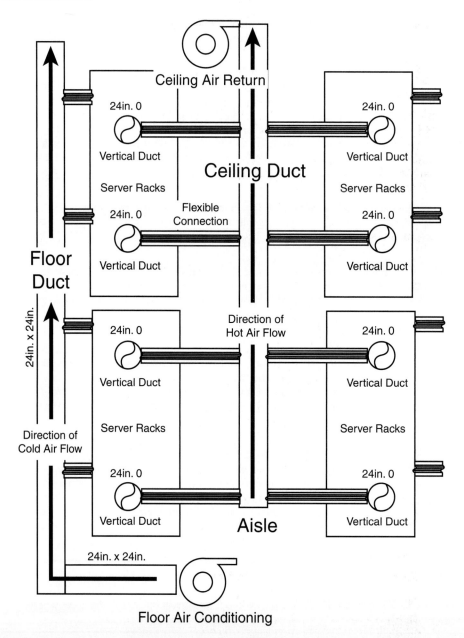

Figure 17.4   This airflow design uses the cool aisle/hot aisle approach.

When you design an HVAC system, keep in mind that the further you move away from the air intake into the room, the lower the air pressure. The forced air flowing into a server rack close to your HVAC system is therefore stronger than the air flowing into a server rack a few feet away, which in turn is stronger than the air pressure in a server rack further down the line. You can improve the situation by using one of these solutions:

- In flooring near the HVAC system, use panels with a smaller number of holes than in the panels further away.
- Use smaller-diameter pipes closer to the HVAC system than further away.

It's best to measure the airflow directly and, if possible, have some form of active flow control. Keep in mind that airflow changes over the course of a day, as the temperature changes and as a function of other factors as well.

Figure 17.5 illustrates APC's (www.apc.com) InfraStruXure design for a 20-server rack system. Notice that cables run along the top of the servers, backs of servers face backs of servers, and a built-in system of air handling vents out the top pipe. APC sells racks and has a rack configuration that lets you specify systems such as this. In addition, you can buy fans to place at the bottom of racks, fans that slide into a rack just as any other component would, fan units that run the whole vertical height of a rack (in the back) with intake at the bottom and exhaust at the top, and completely autonomous rack systems that integrate full cooling, electrics, and other components completely into the rack design.

Figure 17.5 APC's InfraStruXure solution with integrated cooling is shown here in a 20-server rack configuration. *Image courtesy of APC.*

You should measure your HVAC system's performance from time to time to determine whether it is keeping up. Among the places you should measure the temperature are at your HVAC system's cooled input, at the exhaust of the return air, at several places in hot and cool aisles, and at various heights. If possible, it is best to set up an automated monitoring system. It's also important to institute a regular maintenance scheme for changing filters, checking coolant, recalibrating thermometers, and doing other servicing.

Building in Safety

You can't always prevent disasters, but you can plan for them. When you plan for a range of disasters that could conceivably occur, there are two basic tasks you need to do. First, you need to train your staff on what to do when a specific situation occurs. Second, you need to have appropriate safety equipment on hand to mitigate the problem.

These are some of the problems you might encounter:

- Fires
- Flooding
- Earthquakes
- Hazardous fumes (usually as a result of fire)
- Winds due to hurricanes or tornados
- Excessive noise
- Building failures

It's possible to imagine all sorts of disasters, but the problem encountered most frequently is fire. Fires start due to electrical equipment troubles, mechanical failures, and all sorts of other problems. So it is the one hazard you should especially take special care to protect against. You should consider the following safety features as part of your server room deployment:

- Active and automated smoke alarms that conform to the National Fire Protection Association (NFPA) 72E standard for automated fire detection systems. The NFPA 72E standard is an ANSI standard for the application of protective fire alarms and signaling equipment. To get a copy of the standard, go to www.techstreet.com/cgi-bin/detail?product_id=1034981&sid=goog.

- A fire suppression system in the form of a halon release system that is heat activated. (Water sprinkler systems are not the best solutions in rooms full of expensive and highly charged electrical systems.) You should also place portable fire extinguishers in appropriate locations throughout the room.

   The recommended system for fire suppression is an FM200 heptafluoropropane gas dispersion system. This system uses the coolant gas to cool all hot materials and douse the fire. FM200 is used because it doesn't damage hardware, doesn't require cleanup, and has been shown to be safe for personnel in the area when it is discharged. FM200 replaces the older Halon 1301 systems that have been shown to use ozone depleting gases.

Caution

In order to use some fire extinguishers safely, you need to think about special considerations and equipment. For example, although halon is not toxic, when it is used, it displaces the air in the area and makes it difficult to breathe. Therefore, you need a breathing system in order to use halon fire extinguishers. Other fire suppressants have the same issue (CO_2, for example), but not to the same extent. The FM200 halon system is recommended in a data center.

- Breathing systems for use when hazardous fumes are present.
- Fire blanket protectors.
- A well-maintained emergency response system and a fire response plan that is part of a general disaster response plan. Your server room or data center should have an easily understood evacuation plan.

A server room or data center is not a good place to keep combustible materials. Large piles of paper, chemicals, storage packaging materials, and other combustibles should be removed from the area. Smoking should be forbidden both from a fire prevention standpoint and from a particulate contamination standpoint.

Safety also means that all your systems should be inspected and periodically maintained according to manufacturers' specifications. One area where fires often begin is in HVAC systems, when dust has collected in areas where the system is heated, such as reheating coils.

Planning for Physical Security and Access

The best security software available can't defeat an insider who can gain physical access to a system. Even if a person can't log in to the system, physical access makes it possible to damage systems or to remove data in its physical form for later access. You can't eliminate improper use of equipment by authorized personnel, and you also can't eliminate many accidents, but you can lower the risk of non-authorized or inexperienced users getting access to facilities that they are not supposed to have access to. Given that more than 60% of downtime is attributed to operator error, anything you can do to lower the risk is worth considering.

The first line of defense in a physical security scheme is to require users to reliably identify themselves. There are a variety of ways to do this, including using fingerprints, hand scans, eye scans, facial scans, and physical keys such as smart cards. These systems identify the user requesting access, but they do not identify why the user is trying to access the room.

The second level of physical security is to define the perimeter of the area that needs to be protected. The following areas can be security boundaries:

- The entire location
- The building
- The floor or portion of the building that contains sensitive equipment
- Any waiting areas
- The computer room
- The utility room
- Individual computer systems

Because physical security of a server room also includes the facilities necessary to make your systems work, access to UPS and power systems, as well as HVAC systems, may also need to be protected. When designing security systems, many consultants try to establish a set of concentric security perimeters, with increasingly secure methods of validating a person's access as he or she moves to inner perimeters. Thus while a maintenance person might have access to offices and common areas, only personnel with greater clearance, such as vetted maintenance personnel, IT staff, and management, would have access to the data center area. To gain access to the actual server room, the number of personnel would be even more limited, to many fewer people, eliminating most if not all maintenance staff, most of the IT staff, and probably most if not all of the management staff, with the exception of high-level IT managers.

In selecting identification and access systems, you should think in terms of functionality. You could broadly categorize devices into the following types:

- **Physical token**—In locking down a facility, the least reliable ID devices are the ones that identify a person by some physical thing that the person carries, be it a card, a key, or some other device. Those items, often called *tokens*, can be stolen or lost, and systems that rely on those devices don't know the difference between the correct individual and someone else using that person's token.

  Among the token technologies in use are magnetic-strip cards, barium ferrite cards (which have small magnetic fields), Weigand cards (with coded magnetic stripes), bar code cards, infrared shadow bar code cards, proximity (or "prox") cards, and (the ultimate) smart cards along with smart card readers.

- **Information access**—A piece of information that you know and that no one else has access to, such as a computer password, a code, or a method for opening a lock or physically verifying the

ID of a card is more reliable than a token in that it cannot usually be stolen. However, simple passwords can be cracked, using password tables and brute force. This level of access can also be breached if an ID is shared with someone else or discovered on a written reminder. Still, these methods are better than physical tokens.

Information access devices include keypads and coded locks on which a personal access code or personal ID number is entered.

Note

It is possible to purchase computer software and DVDs that contain several million passwords, systematically constructed to include all letter and symbol combinations. These programs, called *crackers*, start by testing single-character passwords, two-character passwords, three-character passwords, and so on. The longer the password, the harder it is to crack. Some of these programs test for lowercase letters only before adding in uppercase letters and then symbols.

Using this type of software is a brute-force approach, but it can be amazingly quick. An eight-character password that consists of lowercase letters only can usually be cracked in a few minutes, using a standard desktop PC. When you mix in uppercase letters, the amount of time rises, but not substantially. It isn't until you have eight letters with a combination of upper- and lowercase letters as well as ASCII symbols that the time to crack an eight-character code rises to the point where most people would give up.

- **Personal identification**—The most secure method of access is by something that is unique to an individual and only that individual. The ultimate method is a DNA sequence, but that technology is off in the future somewhere. In today's market, it is possible to purchase fingerprint ID systems and systems that identify iris and retina patterns (eye color and eye blood vessel distribution, respectively), hand shape, facial geometry, and voice matching. All these are unique or nearly unique to one particular individual. Some people put handwriting analysis on the list; this type of security is not concerned with the actual letters being written but with the pattern of the motion of the pen. However, with careful study, a person can learn to imitate someone else's handwriting patterns.

  Most personal ID equipment falls into the category of biometric devices. Although this technology has a high rate of accuracy, it is not perfect technology. Biometric devices can take an unacceptably long time to return a match and can have failures due to false acceptance or false rejection.

All the aforementioned devices can authenticate a user but do nothing to protect against a second person getting access by following closely behind an authenticated user, called piggybacking or tailgating. To prevent this type of access, you may need to use entry doors that physically allow only one person to pass through at a time. Another way to monitor this type of entry is through camera surveillance or the use of a guard.

CHAPTER 18

Server Platforms: Network Operating Systems

In the Dark Ages, a Slavic king invited representatives of each of the major religions—Roman Catholicism, Greek Orthodoxy, Islam, Judaism, and others—to visit him. He wanted them to make their religions known to him so that he could pick a religion for his country to follow. Eventually he chose the Greek Orthodox religion, which is a story for another time. That parallel to this chapter becomes clear only if you've ever seen users jumping up and down over some new announcement at a MacWorld or Windows World conference. If you've witnessed to that kind of scene, you can't help but be reminded that adopting an operating system (OS) is a little bit like adopting a religion.

When you pick a network operating system (NOS)—or any OS, for that matter—you face the same dilemma the Slavic king faced. All mature NOSs come with the necessary tools to support many different types of clients; a host of network services such as Dynamic Host Configuration Protocol (DHCP), Domain Name System (DNS), Transmission Control Protocol/Internet Protocol (TCP/IP); a variety of file systems; and many other industry standards. In many ways Microsoft Windows Servers, Novell NetWare, Sun Solaris, Hewlett-Packard UNIX, and a variety of Linux flavors are more alike than they are dissimilar. A desktop user selects one or two OSs to run on his or her workstation, gets the religion, and lives a happy, blissful, comfortable life. If you are "lucky" enough to be in a company that has rigorously enforced a one-state computing solution on its people, life is similarly blissful. You can continue on, oblivious to the outside world.

Many companies and organizations don't have the luxury of enforcing the one-NOS solution. Their graphics and marketing departments may run on Apple Macintosh, accounting may run an Oracle software solution on UNIX, engineering may have a little of everything, from Windows Server to Linux and even older systems running MS-DOS that can't be replaced, and so on. Therefore, system administrators find themselves having to support a little bit of everything, as well as trying to make good decisions for future technology purchases. If that doesn't make things complex, then consider when Organization A merges with Organization B, and each runs different NOSs. With complexity comes a lot of headaches and chaos, but you also get some real opportunities to make decisions that can give your organization best-of-breed systems. Some choices can substantially lower a company's computing costs. Other choices may lower support costs or offer other opportunities.

This chapter presents a high-level discussion of the major NOSs in use today and describes how they might fit into a modern heterogeneous network where different types of servers are called upon to work together. The discussion in this chapter focuses on some of the known advantages and disadvantages of different server OSs, how to determine what represents a best-of-breed solution, how to make the many application directory services interoperate, and how to best manage your servers so that you aren't running around from server to server, applying fixes like the proverbial chicken with its head chopped off.

Major Features of NOSs

All major NOSs share certain features in common. Common features found in all of the NOSs include the following:

- Computer and user identification services
- Logon services
- File and print services

- Standard network transport support, mainly TCP/IP version 4
- Network addressing and name resolution services, primarily DHCP and DNS
- Web services, in the form of Hypertext Transfer Protocol (HTTP) and browser support
- Messaging, in the form of POP3 and IMAP
- Heterogeneous client support

All the OSs that are described in this chapter have most, if not all, of these features. In addition, each of the features listed here are based on industry standards (which makes them less proprietary) and are fully implemented into each respective NOS. As an example, TCP/IP (the protocol most widely used on the Internet and beyond) is based on widely accepted industry standards and is implemented into every NOS or OS released today. Before TCP/IP was so widely used, software and hardware vendors used proprietary solutions such as IBM's System Network Architecture (SNA) protocol, Apple Macintosh used the AppleTalk protocol, and Novell NetWare used the Internet Packet Exchange/Sequenced Packet Exchange (IPX/SPX) protocol. And that's just to name a few. All three of these proprietary protocols worked like TCP/IP, but they needed to be translated for each other, which caused significant configuration and management issues. Therefore, standardizing on using one protocol—TCP/IP—between all systems made sense. For example, each of the NOS supports DNS. They have to, because if they didn't their DNS wouldn't work properly with the service on the Internet. In the past, when you purchased a NOS such as Novell NetWare or Apple Macintosh, you were buying into using IPX/SPX or AppleTalk as a native protocol. While there is still support for these protocols to support legacy clients, today the native transport for all NOSs is TCP/IP.

So if all these NOSs are so similar, what exactly are the differences that would help you decide to choose one over another? Differentiation between NOSs is a function of the following:

- Pricing and delivery models
- Third-party developer support, as evidenced by available server applications (what we refer to in this chapter as an application server or overall as an application platform)
- Integration with heterogeneous clients
- Directory services
- Policies
- Management tools and style

Table 18.1 lists some of the characteristics of the different server NOSs so that you can compare them quickly; Table 18.2 is a general rating of the major NOSs described in this chapter, by features.

Table 18.1   Server NOS Features

NOS	Owner	Version	Architectures	Cost	License
NetWare	Novell	6.5	x86	$184	Proprietary, moving to open source Linux
Open VMS	Hewlett-Packard	8.2	VAX, Alpha, IA-64	—	Proprietary
OS/2	IBM	4.5	x86	—	Proprietary
Red Hat Linux	Red Hat	4.1	x86, AMD64, Alpha, PPC, SPARC, and others	$349 ES basic, $749 ES standard, $1499 AS standard, $2499 AS Premium	—
Solaris	Sun Microsystems	10	SPARC, SPARC64, x86, IA-64, AMD64	—	CDDL
Windows Server 2003	Microsoft	5.2 SP2	x86, IA-64, AMD64	$999 (5 CALs)	Proprietary

Table 18.2   Server NOS Ratings

	Linux	NetWare 6.5	Solaris	Windows Server
Entry Cost	Excellent	Very good	Good	Good
Overall cost	Very good	Very good	Good	Very good
Range of services	Very good	Good	Excellent	Excellent
Range of hardware supported	Good	Good	Good	Excellent
Native management tools	Fair	Excellent	Very good	Excellent
GUI Management tools	Fair	Very good	Very good	Excellent
Command Line Interface tools	Excellent	Good	Excellent	Very good
Third party applications	Good	Good	Very good	Excellent
Open source applications	Excellent	Very good	Very good	Good
Domain services	Good	Very good	Very good	Very good
Logon services	Good	Excellent	Very good	Very good
Directory services	Good	Excellent	Excellent	Very good
File	Very good	Excellent	Very good	Very good
Print	Fair	Very good	Good	Excellent
Messaging	Good	Good	Very good	Very good
Security	Good	Very good	Excellent	Good

Platform	GUI	Kernel	File Systems	Package Management	Update Method	APIs
Servers	—	Hybrid kernel	NSS, NWFS, FAT, NFS, AFP, UDE, ISO 9660	Binary update	Proprietary	Proprietary
Server	—	Monolithic with module extensions	Files-11, I SO-9660, NFS	PCSI, UNIX like VMSINSTALLS	UNIX like	
Desktop, server	WARP	Feature Installer	—	—	Proprietary	—
Servers and desktops	—	Monolithic kernel, extended using modules	ext2, ext3, FAT, NFS, ISO 9660, ReiserFS, etc.	—	POSIX	POSIX
Workstation, servers	Servers no, workstation GNOME	Monolithic with module extensions	UFS, ZFS, ext2, FAT, UDF, NFS, ISO 9660 and more, SysV packages (pkgadd)	—	Sun Update Connection	SysV POSIX
Servers	Windows desktop	Hybrid	NTFS 5, FAT32, FAT	MSI, custom installers	Windows Update	Win32

	Linux	NetWare 6.5	Solaris	Windows Server
PKI/Kerberos support	Very good	Excellent	Excellent	Very good
Stability	Very good	Excellent	Excellent	Very good
Scalability	Good	Good	Excellent	Excellent
Fault tolerance	Good	Very good	Excellent	Very good
Internet services	Good	Very good	Excellent	Excellent
Development platform	Fair	Fair	Excellent	Excellent
Support	Very good	Very good	Very good	Excellent
Heterogeneous client support	Fair	Excellent	Very good	Excellent
Windows client support	Good	Excellent	Good	Excellent
Storage systems support	Fair	Fair	Excellent	Excellent
Backup/Snapshot/Shadow	Good	Good	Very good	Excellent
Terminal/remote services	Fair	Good	Very good	Very good
Scripting/OS programming	Good	Good	Excellent	Very good
Application/OS healing			Yes	Yes
Java Support	Very good	Very good	Excellent	Good

With all this information in hand it begs the question: Does the type of NOS you use matter? The short answer to this question is both yes and no. Because all NOSs offer the same basic functions, and those functions are based on industry standards, each NOS has enough tools to let you run a successful network. No matter which NOS you choose to implement, you will be able to create most standard services. There's less difference between all the NOSs than their respective vendors would care to admit.

If you are choosing a server platform to run only one significant network service or application, your decision may hinge on whether the application you want to run exists on the platform of your choice or on whether you want to use a different application that runs only on a different platform. Consider a situation in which you want to create a website, and you are considering which platform to use for this. After comparing different webservers, you may decide to implement Apache. This isn't an endorsement of Apache as the best-of-breed webserver, but you think that Apache has a number of advantages going for it. One of Apache's advantages is that there are versions of Apache that run on nearly all NOSs. Chances are that you wouldn't implement Apache on Windows Server 2003 (or 2000) because Microsoft's Internet Information Server (IIS) has a number of special advantages on that platform that cater to the underlying NOS. However, you'd be equally well served (for different reasons) running Apache on Linux, Solaris, or some other NOS server platform.

The NOS definitely does matter when it comes to some specialized application or service that just isn't available on another platform. That would be the case for an application such as Novell's eDirectory, or Microsoft's Commerce Server. Selection of either of those products would in effect limit your choice to those two NOSs. If you decided that you wanted to install an ERP (enterprise resource planning) package like SAP's solution, you would be opting for either a UNIX or Windows server because that is what the vendor supports. A choice between those two platforms for SAP would boil down to which of the two platforms made the most sense in terms of integration into your established infrastructure.

NOS vendors do their best to lock you into a single solution, their servers, and their desktops. Their rationale is that by investing in a single solution, you minimize your support costs and eliminate a lot of complexity. There's merit in that argument. However, if you are building an industry-standard server, such as a file server built on the open source package Samba 3, then once the server is set up, it is probably going to be left as is for some time to come. There's some initial setup penalty but little extra grief once you are past those problems, generally speaking.

Server NOSs

The sections that follow provide a more detailed discussion of each of the major server NOSs, with more explanation as to why each NOS is rated as it is. You'll also find references to resources for further reading.

Windows Servers

Microsoft Windows Server (www.microsoft.com/windowsserver2003/default.mspx) is probably the dominant application server platform on the market today, and it maintains a large minority of the servers in use today. On the desktop Microsoft reigns supreme, with perhaps 85% or 90% of the market share.

Three versions of Windows Server are currently deployed:

- Windows Server 2003 R2, which is the most current version and is an enhanced version of Service Pack 1
- Windows 2000 Server, which is currently at Service Pack 4
- Windows Server NT 4.0, which is currently being retired in phases but for which updates will still be available until 2007

The Windows NT kernel was based on the architecture of DEC VMS, which isolates devices using device drivers and organizes memory in a manner superior to previous Windows OSs. Windows 2000 Server incorporates Active Directory (AD). Just like NetWare 4, which incorporated Novell Directory Services (NDS)—now called eDirectory—from its bindery days, Windows 2000 Server represented a major challenge to existing sites that needed to migrate their user and computer accounts from the NT 4.0 security system to the Windows Security Accounts Manager (SAM) subsystem security database of newer models (such as 2000 and 2003). Windows 2000 supported the concept of a mixed-mode domain where some of the systems could participate in Windows 2000's AD services, while others running older versions of the OS (both servers and clients) would only be able to participate in some of the AD features. When a complete Windows 2000–only domain was established, the domain could be transformed to what is called "native mode," and the full complement of AD would be available for all network systems that were able to use it.

Windows Server 2003 added to Windows 2000 the graphical user interface (GUI) of Windows XP, enhanced the management tools and group policy features, and updated core components such as the IIS webserver service. Windows Server 2003 also enhanced AD and improved the components necessary to support the .NET web service initiative and framework. Microsoft publishes a major network management tool called the Microsoft Operations Manager (MOM), as well as System Management Server (SMS), currently up to version 2003. Some of the best network management tools available for Windows server systems are from third parties, including the following:

- LANDesk Management Suite
- Altiris Management Suites
- CA TNG Unicenter
- IBM Tivoli
- Argent
- Novell ZENworks

Microsoft considers the strength of its Windows Server platform to be that it's an integrated server environment. That is, Microsoft bundles many of the core servers and services into the OS's distribution. Thus, when you install Windows Server 2003, you automatically install AD if the server is the domain server (called the domain controller [DC]). You also install the IIS webserver for many application services, such as HTTP and FTP. You may also install and activate Windows Terminal Services so that clients can connect remotely to the server using the Microsoft Remote Desktop Protocol (RDP). All these services are installed through a single installation routine.

One of the primary differences between Windows and UNIX and Linux has been that the latter NOSs come with a much more fully developed command-line interface (CLI). While for the end user, a CLI is a clumsy, arcane interface that is difficult to make any use of, for an administrator it offers the ability to fine-tune a server much more quickly and efficiently than would be possible from a typical GUI.

Windows Server 2003 is available as several different editions:

- **Standard Edition**—This offering supports up to four processors and comes with the management suite as well as the Internet webservers and terminal servers. It supports up to 4GB of RAM. The cost is $995, with five client access licenses (CALs). Additional CALs may be required for OS clients as well as application clients such as Exchange.

- **Web Edition**—The Web Edition is a hosting and web application platform that sells for a little less than $400. You can use this version of the OS to develop websites and web services. It comes with IIS 6.0, ASP.NET technologies, and a 10-connection client limit.

- **Enterprise Edition**—The Enterprise Edition of Windows Server 2003 supports up to 8 processors, supports eight node clusters with failover, and has 32GB of memory. There is a 64-bit version of this OS for Itanium systems.

- **Datacenter Edition**—With support for up to 32 processors and 64GB of RAM in its 32-bit version, this OS is available for OEMs and VARs who qualify for Microsoft's certification program. The 64-bit version of this edition can scale up to 128-way SMP systems and 512GB of RAM, and it can be configured for up to eight node clusters. Included in this OS are load balancing and a system management utility called the Windows System Resource Manager.

Note

For a comparison chart of the features in the four different editions of Windows Server 2003, go to www.microsoft.com/windowsserver2003/evaluation/features/compareeditions.mspx.

Microsoft sells two versions of its OS that are really application servers, although it doesn't call them that:

- **Microsoft Small Business Server 2003 (SBS)**—This product supports a single domain with no trust relationships, supports up to 75 connected users (provided that you purchase the CALs), and comes with a suite of applications, including Exchange, SharePoint, and a basic firewall. The premium version of this product adds both SQL Server and Internet Security and Acceleration (ISA) Server, which is a proxy, firewall, and caching server. SBS is aimed at the small office environment, and it isn't really suitable for a workgroup in a larger system because of the trust limitations.

- **Windows Storage Server 2003**—This is a highly tuned version of a file and print server. As with the Datacenter Edition of Windows Server 2003, you can't buy this version of the OS alone: You can only purchase it from a certified VAR or OEM as a hardware software bundle. The pricing for Windows Storage Server is aggressive, and this version doesn't require connected clients to obtain CALs.

Of the NOS vendors described in this chapter, Microsoft has the most complete line of application servers. The list of Microsoft servers that you can purchase as standalone applications that run on top of Windows Server 2003 or that Microsoft markets as part of a "solution" is extensive. Space precludes a full treatment of these servers here, but you can find a jump page at www.microsoft.com/technet/prodtechnol/servers.mspx and more information at www.microsoft.com/windowsserversystem/wss2003/default.mspx.

Among the most popular of Microsoft's server NOSs are Microsoft BizTalk Server, Microsoft Commerce Server, Microsoft Host Integration Server, Microsoft Identity Integration Server, Microsoft MapPoint Location Server, MOM, Microsoft Mobile Server, and Microsoft Windows Media Server, although the list goes on and continues to grow each year. Several of these servers are essentially unique offerings in the industry. Only Sun Solaris can compete with this list of application servers, but Sun's list would have to include many more third-party offerings to attain the breadth of application servers that Microsoft supports in-house.

The bottom line with Windows is that it is a safe play for many corporations due to Microsoft's excellent support setup. Other OSs, such as freeware versions of UNIX and Linux, have entry cost advantages over Windows, and although Microsoft argues that the support costs make Windows Server comparable, it's an argument that makes some assumptions. When you want to implement a unique Microsoft server or want more seamless integration with a set of Windows desktop clients, Windows Server has some pervasive advantages.

However, when the server you want to run is a standard (even an open source standard), other OS advantages come into play that can make the other NOSs better choices. For example, implementing any open source server application is more straightforward on Linux/UNIX/Solaris than it is on Windows, even though almost all versions of major open source applications have been ported to Windows. Furthermore, NetWare's sophisticated management applications argue for that NOS's consideration. Many consider Novell's eDirectory (formerly NDS) to be the state-of-the-art directory service, and that, along with superior security, makes NetWare very attractive. Also, NetWare has the widest compatibility with other OS in a heterogeneous environment—something that Novell stresses.

People argue about Windows Server's scalability and vulnerability, but there is really both less and more there than meets the eye. Windows scalability has been largely proven with the work Microsoft has done on Windows 2000 Server and Datacenter Edition. Microsoft now holds several significant performance benchmarks. However, the ability to buy a Sun Solaris server package is very attractive when it comes to scaling up systems and for mission-critical applications. Sun servers and Windows servers are considered to be the two standards that are supported by the storage industry for storage area network (SAN) applications. From a performance point of view, there isn't that much difference between these two platforms.

As to the security issue, it is undoubtedly true that Windows gets the lion's share of the efforts of hackers and sustains more exploits. The reasons for this are simple: There are many more users on Windows systems, Microsoft has tried to keep its systems open to encourage development on its platform. This has led to exploiters getting more bang for their buck in terms of the effort required to hack into the OS.

Novell NetWare 6.5

In the early 1980s, Novell NetWare was *the* name in PC networking. Although Novell lost much of its market share, and Novell as a company has had its ups and downs, Novell has redefined itself as a company. It has also positioned NetWare to be a very interesting and valuable server platform, directory system, and a wide variety of applications uniquely made to run on just about any NOS created, including Linux, which it also just acquired with the acquisition of Germany's SUSE Linux.

Novell's long history in the NOS and directory industry means that their file and print servers are solid and reliable and support a vast array of printing devices; their NDS is among the best platforms for heterogeneous client support; and their network management tools for servers are among the best in the industry. In well-established companies with long IT histories, you may be lucky enough to find a NetWare graybeard or two, but if you are new to networking and to servers, you should take a moment to consider some of Novell's offerings, particularly if you are in a heterogeneous environment.

NetWare was one of the last of the major enterprise networking platforms to accept TCP/IP as its native protocol, although Apple's Macintosh was also late in moving to TCP/IP as a native transport. (NWIP) was used. It was a modified and somewhat proprietary version of the IP Stack. With later NetWare version releases of version 5 and then 6, TCP/IP became the protocol for all core services, such as file and print services and directory services, and it was finally based on the industry standard. That version of the OS also introduced NDS. NetWare 5.0 predated Windows 2000 Server's introduction by about a year.

Note

You can find Novell NetWare's home page at www.novell.com/products/netware. At this site, the company offers a number of introductions and position papers describing its products.

Novell NetWare's current version is 6.5, and Novell advertises it as "the most reliable foundation for deploying business critical, open source-enabled solutions." Novell bundles the Novell Cluster Services solution into version 6.5, which allows you to create two node server clusters, both locally and as a failover to a remote location. Other new features that distinguish NetWare 6.5 are its native support for iSCSI, which is a server migration wizard and server consolidation utility, and the NOS built-in snapshot backup tool.

NetWare has offered a highly regarded directory service for well over a decade. NDS has been renamed and repositioned as a full-service, Internet-enabled directory called Novell eDirectory. NetWare 6.5 comes with a 250,000-user license for eDirectory, which supports AIX, HP-UX, Linux, NetWare, Solaris, and Windows.

With eDirectory you can store information about network users, employees, customer accounts, and so forth. NetWare 6.5 extends its file and print services with what Novell calls the Virtual Office. With Virtual Office, your users can set up an Internet print service (iPrint), a virtual online folder (iFolder), web file backup, web publishing, and email and password management.

NetWare also comes bundled with a browser-based network management tool that Novell calls iManager, which can inventory your network clients and servers. iManager includes tools for managing the DirXML tool that is used to exchange data with another directory service, such as AD.

The push to position NetWare as a very friendly, open source server has NetWare 6.5 bundling the following server software: the Apache webserver, the MySQL database, the Perl scripted programming language, and Jakarta Tomcat, which is the Apache Java-enabled webserver project. iManager can be used to manage these open source tools running on NetWare servers. NetWare also ships with the exteNd Application server (see www.novell.com/products/extend/), which is a Java 2 Enterprise Edition (J2EE) certified solution, and the Workbench application, which allows you to develop web applications on NetWare in the visual Integrated Development Environment (IDE) of exteNd Composer and exteNd Director. Java applications can then be ported to other NOS platforms based on the Java standard.

Novell has worked hard to position itself as the heterogeneous system and directory service provider of choice. In doing so, it has created a set of products aimed at supporting Windows and Linux/UNIX server/clients. Novell's desktop solution is Novell Linux Desktop (NLD) 9, which comes with the Novell Edition of OpenOffice.org, Novell Evolution which is an open source collaboration client, the Mozilla Firefox browser, and a multivendor instant messaging client for AOL, Yahoo!, and MSN. Novell's Linux solution is based on the SUSE Linux distribution, which is one of the better distributions for servers and corporate Linux.

Among the types of server products available for NetWare are the following:

- **GroupWise**—This is the NetWare messaging platform.
- **ZENworks**—ZENworks is one of the best heterogeneous network management platforms available today.
- **eDirectory**—This directory service is lauded for large-scale Internet identity management but can be deployed on networks of all sizes.
- **Desktop Management, Linux Management, Server Management, Handheld Management, and Asset Management (inventory) packages**—These packages represent capabilities that you purchase for other management suites, such as LANDesk or Altiris.
- **Novell File System Factory**—This product extends the NetWare File System into a policy-based storage management system with provisioning capabilities. With this solution comes load

balancing, logging and auditing, and integration of storage assets with the Nsure Identity Manager and LDAP directories.

- **Nsure SecureLogin**—This is Novell's highly regarded single-signon or single-login tool.

The bottom line with NetWare is that it is a superior platform for network management, directory services, and file and print services. As an application server for open source applications, NetWare is better than Windows but no better than Solaris or a good enterprise version of Linux.

Sun Solaris

Sun Solaris, also called the Sun OS, is arguably the best-supported version of UNIX in the PC server marketplace. Many other vendors offer UNIX server platforms, but what makes Solaris special is that there are more applications running on Solaris than all the other UNIX versions combined—on the order of 10,000 or more. Sun has paid a lot of attention over the years to developers, particularly the ones developing network-based applications. That makes Solaris the only NOS that can compete with Microsoft Windows as an application server platform, with Windows being far and away the larger platform in terms of numbers of applications for desktop systems. This is a matter of opinion, of course; some think that IBM AIX may be the best-supported version of UNIX at the moment.

▶▶ Sun Solaris is described in detail in Chapter 19, "Sun Microsystems Servers." This section overviews the Solaris NOS versus other NOSs.

Solaris really got its boost from Sun's early adoption of the Internet as a strategic server platform, which predated Microsoft's Internet push by a year or two. At one point, webservers running Sun Solaris had a predominant share of the market, but this is no longer true today. Still, when you lump Solaris with other forms of UNIX and throw in Linux, it is still true that the large majority of servers on the Internet are UNIX- or Linux-based servers.

There's been a perception in the industry that UNIX in general and Solaris in particular is more stable, more secure, and better performing than Microsoft Windows Server. Sun has actively pursued performance benchmark records in the database and webserver arenas as proof of this superiority. With the introduction of Windows 2000 Server, Microsoft successfully bridged the performance gap between itself and UNIX and was also able to improve stability and security. However, UNIX is still the leading platform in terms of stability and security for all classes of servers, with the exception of mission-critical or data center servers.

Sun Solaris's biggest advantage is that it is sold into the marketplace as a hardware/software package. All the other enterprise server NOSs described in this chapter are sold as software packages only. When you buy from Sun's line of servers and run Solaris, you are running hardware that has been certified by Sun to be compatible with its NOS.

Note

Chances are that when you buy a Windows, NetWare, UNIX, or Linux server, you are buying that server as a package sold by a reseller, a value added reseller (VAR), or OEM. In those instances, you rely on your system vendor to certify that its hardware package is compatible with the OS it is selling.

Solaris comes in two versions: one that runs on the SPARC and UltraSPARC processors and one that runs on the Intel x86 processor platform. The vast majority of Solaris systems are deployed on Sun SPARC servers, and the bulk of the Intel x86 deployments are reserved for desktop systems and smaller servers. The exception to this rule is that Solaris 10 can be deployed on x86 64-bit systems, and there has been a considerable effort to market Solaris 10 x86 on entry servers running AMD 64-bit Opteron CPUs. Solaris 10 began to incorporate Linux APIs and can also natively run Linux binaries on the x86 platform.

The Sun OS is released under what is called the Common Development and Distribution License (CDDL), based on the Open Source Initiative (OSI) license model. Early versions of the Sun OS were based on BSD UNIX. When the code base moved to System V UNIX, the company adopted the name Solaris 2 and described major version releases as point releases. Thus version 2.8 is Solaris 8, 2.9 is version 9, and the current version of Solaris is 2.10, or 10. Common practice usually refers to Solaris by the point number only (for example, Solaris 10).

OSI is a nonprofit corporation dedicated to managing and promoting the Open Source definition for the good of the community, specifically through the OSI Certified Open Source Software certification mark and program. OSI tries to ensure that its certification mark and program allows you to be confident that software really is open source. OSI also makes copies of approved open source licenses and posts them at its site, www.opensource.org.

Note

For a jump page to a description of key features of Solaris 10 and a number of other learning resources, go to www.sun.com/software/solaris/ds/index.jsp.

There is no functional difference between installing Sun on a large server and on a desktop system. Pricing does change, of course, as do the services you activate on each platform. However, the installation is essentially the same. The Sun desktop environment started out using an OpenWindows GUI but switched to a Common Desktop Environment GUI in versions 6 through 9. Version 10 bases its Java Desktop System on the GNOME GUI, in an effort to make Solaris more friendly to Linux desktop users.

Sun's unique value proposition is that by combining a UNIX solution with hardware that Sun sells and supports, Sun has been able to develop solutions that scale and integrate particularly well. As Sun servers scale to larger numbers of processors, Sun has been able to get better performance out of more of its processors than other vendors have. In addition, a variety of leading-edge network services, such as IPv6, various streaming protocols, and 10Gbps Ethernet, appear on Solaris before they show up on other NOSs. However, Sun does make you pay a premium for its NOS on its equipment. The proficiency of Sun servers as network servers has an historical basis. Earlier generations of Sun servers were the routers of choice on the early Internet, and although that function has been replaced by specialized Cisco (and other vendors') routers. ISPs chose Sun servers because the Sun Solaris network stack was efficient, highly refined, and feature filled. The Sun/Solaris platform is still recognized for this networking strength.

Solaris 10 concentrated on adding a number of new networking features. Among the main new features added were an improved dual IP stack, better IPv6 support, Layer 3 multipathing (which offers better network redundancy), better streaming and session support, an improved Solaris Network Cache Accelerator (NCA), and a new technology called Solaris Containers (previously called N1 Grid Containers); these new features help implement a shared distributed processing model. Solaris comes with an NFS file server, an email server, and a DNS server (using BIND 8 or BIND 9 with IPv6).

IPv6 support also means that there is better support for the Solaris IPSec secure communications protocol and with the Internet Key Exchange (IKE) infrastructure. Sun likes to advertise Solaris as a "more secure" platform, which may be true in as far as Sun servers tend to be attacked or hacked less frequently than Windows servers are.

Note

For a list of Sun server applications, go to the jump page at www.sun.com/software/.

Sun's work on Java and in creating portable web applications means that Sun is one of the best web developer platforms on the market. Sun absorbed many of Netscape's server applications, giving the company a range of Internet servers that it has been able to build on. Thus Sun's directory servers, webservers, and applications servers are well-implemented and mature solutions.

Sun's product for integrating PC servers and clients into the Solaris network is Solaris PC NetLink. Using NetLink, you can have Sun servers play the role of Windows domain controllers, Windows file and print servers, and even Windows application servers. The implementation is for a Windows NT 4.0 server domain, which supports clients up to Windows XP, as well as both Windows NT 4.0 and Windows 2000 Server systems.

The integration of Linux into Sun's plans as both a desktop and server platform should help Sun better compete with other versions of Linux, whose growth in the market has largely taken place at the expense of Solaris. Linux users will find that they can now run the Java Desktop System and Java Enterprise System on Linux, as well as run Linux and Solaris on the same AMD Opteron and Intel X-86 systems.

Sun Solaris's unique value proposition is that it offers a stable, secure form of UNIX on supported hardware. Sun has an excellent network service suite and is a very strong network application and Internet platform (that is, a large number of third-party applications are available for the Solaris platform).

Solutions on Solaris tend to be more expensive than those on other platforms, and because you are buying proprietary hardware, there is a narrower choice of hardware from which to choose. Integration of network applications with desktop systems also tends to be not as smooth as it might be with Windows servers, simply because there are so many more Windows desktops deployed today. Sun and Microsoft are finally working together on interoperability issues, which means that Solaris's Windows support will probably improve over time. Sun lags behind Novell badly in this area of heterogeneous network management. It remains to be seen how well Sun will be able to entice Linux users to the Solaris platform over time, which is another important issue for this platform.

Linux

Linux is an interesting proposition as a server NOS platform because it has been embraced by almost all major server hardware vendors, including IBM, Hewlett-Packard, Novell, and others. The Linux OS is an open source project and is loosely based on UNIX, but it has its own kernel, which is what the name Linux actually refers to.

Most Linux commands are similar to their UNIX counterparts, but the internal architecture of the Linux kernel is unique. Anyone who distributes the Linux OS and conforms to the GNU GPL license is free to modify, sell, or give away his or her own version of Linux. GNU stands for "GNU's not Unix" and refers generally to software distributed under the GNU Public License (GPL). For more information about GNU, see www.gnu.org. Among the countries with major investments in Linux used in the enterprise are China and Brazil.

Linux runs on a variety of processor platforms, but it most often appears on the Intel X86 processor platform. The original version ran on the Intel 80386, but the Advanced Server version runs on 64-bit processors such as the AMD Opteron found in the Cray XD1 SMP systems. Linux's low cost has given the OS a position in small, embedded systems such as set-top boxes, PDAs such as the Symbian OS, phones, routers and firewalls from companies such as Linksys, and even the TiVo personal video recorder (PVR).

There are perhaps as many as 300 distributions of Linux (see http://lwn.net/Distributions/), ranging from packages such as Mandriva (formerly Mandrake) that are meant for desktop users to Novell's SUSE Linux Enterprise Server 9, which is sold as a server platform. The Red Hat Linux version of Linux dominates the sales of this platform for server applications.

The reason that Red Hat has been able to be as successful with their version in the past as it has been is that the company has arguably done the best job building a support organization to service its customers. Red Hat was one of the companies to go public during the Internet bubble, and it was able to leverage its IPO as well as investments for hardware partners to achieve this position. Red Hat also has one of the smoothest installation packages available for a Linux distribution, which is another factor in its success.

All that said, many companies have caught up to Red Hat in terms of Linux support; in particular, IBM and NetWare represent suitable, even better alternatives to Red Hat in many instances.

Other applications, such as Perl, a development language written by Larry Wall and widely adopted by the UNIX/Linux community, is sometimes replaced by PHP or Python, which are two additional widely deployed applications. PHP is a widely used general-purpose scripting language that is especially suited for web development (see www.php.net), and Python is a freeware open source, object-oriented, cross-platform, interactive, and interpreted scripting language (see www.python.org).

Although it's true that compared to the other OSs, Solaris and Windows have many more applications available to them, if you are installing an application server, you are probably doing it for one or two purposes at most. In addition to the open source programs mentioned earlier, Red Hat Enterprise Linux Server version 4 (RHEL 4; see www.redhat.com/software/rhel/) will run Oracle databases, IBM DB2, many VERITAS applications (but in particular the VERITAS backup suite), and BEA's management software. This is just a partial list of what's available, so you should check Red Hat's website (www.redhat.com) for more details.

Red Hat used to sell both a desktop and a server version of Linux but dropped out of the desktop market for a while after version 9 to concentrate on its server product. The desktop version of Red Hat is now developed and distributed as part of the Fedora project. However, Red Hat now offers what it calls Red Hat Enterprise Linux WS (for workstation) and Red Hat Desktop in 10 and 50 packs or bundled with Red Hat Network Proxy and Satellite Server. The WS client version is aimed at users creating software and those with high-performance computing needs such as graphics or CAD.

RHEL 4 comes with the Linux 2.6.9 kernel, which has improved the speed of the product over previous versions. Red Hat markets RHEL 4 in two versions: a base server NOS and an Advanced Server version. RHEL 4 AS is the version that is meant to run on large SMP and 64-bit processor systems.

One of the main improvements in RHEL 4 was the introduction of the Security Enhanced Linux (SELinux) kernel modification. When you install RHEL 4, SELinux is automatically compiled into the OS so that it is always included by default. One thing you may notice if you work with this OS is that it eliminates the vulnerabilities associated with the superuser or root user and the way in which other passwords and privileges are managed. The kernel is designed to directly manage server applications and allows the administrator to control and manage even privileged services. This prevents a user from gaining root user status and running a process that can exploit an entire server. RHEL 4 may have some issues with older applications, but there are workarounds to these issues that involve modifying some of the SELinux parameters.

One thing you may also notice is that SELinux allows you to set policies, although in its first version, reviewers have reported that policy management on RHEL 4 isn't anywhere near as smooth as it is in NetWare 6 or even AD's Group Policy management scheme. Consider this a work in progress.

One of the major criticisms of Linux is that it can be difficult to obtain stable Linux device drivers. Support for many items that servers rely on normally depends on the work of the open source community. However, because Red Hat has been able to achieve a central market position, most of the vendors who intend for their equipment to run on Linux servers—RAID controllers, iSCSI adapters, Gigabit NICs, and so on—all certify their products against Red Hat Linux. It's considered to be the de facto standard in the industry for enterprise Linux. Red Hat has put a lot of effort into making its Anaconda installer's hardware detection routines as robust as those of any of the other major NOS platforms, and version 4 not only dramatically added to the number of devices recognized but also resolved issues with some of the more troublesome devices, such as embedded motherboard controllers and a wider range of NICs.

RHEL 4 uses the ext3 file system, but RHEL 4 also offers the Global File System for clustered 64-bit large-scale deployments. RHEL 4 added support for Sun NFS version 4, adopted Samba 3 file and print services for Windows clients, and added upgraded versions of most of the bundled enterprise server applications that shipped previously with the product.

Red Hat has begun to delve heavily into the application server market, selling solution-type products. It advertises a modular web-based Linux management and infrastructure platform called the Red Hat Network (RHN) that has access to RHN Update Module and the Management and Provisioning module. You can deploy this internally or use all or part of it as a hosted solution. Among the application servers that Red Hat sells are Red Hat Application Server, a J2EE 1.4 application server that features Tomcat and EJB Container and is based on JOnAS. You can deploy the Global File System as a server for databases and grid applications, and you can use GFS for support of the Red Hat Cluster Suite. Some large and powerful cluster applications have been built using Red Hat Linux servers and high-speed interconnect technologies. Finally, Red Hat also offers a developer's suite as a server, and the Red Hat IDE is based on the Eclipse tools.

Most organizations adopt Linux servers for two main reasons: the lower cost of licensing the OS and the modest equipment demands of Linux. Although RHEL 4 makes strides at bridging the gap between Linux as a management platform by improving AD interoperability and adding policy management, most organizations choose Red Hat Linux servers as a platform for running open source server applications, such as Apache. As an application server platform RHEL 4 is better than Novell's NetWare for open source applications, but it is not nearly as strong as either Sun Solaris or Microsoft Windows Server for the depth and breadth of the server applications available.

If you are considering RHEL, you should be aware that Novell has an enterprise Linux platform in the market and that Sun will be releasing a Linux-based server product in the near future. In 2006 and beyond there will be more and stronger competitors in this market for Red Hat to compete with.

Directory Services and Interoperability

NOSs collect information into a specialized database called a *directory*. Directories are optimized to be fast to access, to be flexibly organized, to be rich in content, and to have access to the information carefully controlled. Nearly all the modern network directories in use today store information into an *object database* schema. Entries in the database are named entities with numerous properties associated with them, as well as the ability to create new properties for each.

The directory service is the application that runs on the server that accesses the stored information. You can think of a directory service as an object database and the directory as its data store. The service is optimized for fast searches and reads. Because a directory contains most of the personalized information about systems and users, an important part of any directory service is that it is the authentication authority for access to network resources based on identities, personalities, and their relationships to the resources they are trying to access.

Although directory services share many of the properties of a relational database, there are some significant differences. Most databases balance reads and writes, have lots of tuple relationships, and attempt to reduce the amount of data redundancy to a minimum—a process called normalization. Directories don't allow for tuple or many-to-many relationships, and they don't provide a means to revert or roll back changes or transactions. The fundamental difference, though, is that the attributes of an object in a directory would be broken apart into independent values if they were stored in a relational database.

At any one time, there is a considerable amount of authentication going on at the directory server as well as authentication traffic passing over the network. In order to lessen the impact of directory network traffic on a LAN and especially on a WAN, most directories are designed to be distributed across both multiple servers and sites. Changes to the directory are replicated using one of many replication topologies, but most often, a topology with a single- or multiple-master directory server(s) is employed.

X.500

There's a problem with directory services: In any large enterprise, server OSs and enterprise applications are all running their own directory services. It is common for large, heterogeneous networks to run many directory services. Companies often have as many as 20 or 30 directory services running at a time. Interoperation between all these services would be impossible were it not for some industry-standard naming conventions and some specialized tools that different OSs and third-party vendors offer.

Objects in a directory are named according to a set of rules that provide a mapping of the resource name to the physical address of the resource. The universe of all possible named objects (even those objects that don't yet exist) is known as the service's *namespace*. Each object has a unique and unambiguous name in the namespace, something that is called its *distinguished name* (DN).

An example of a DN is cn=George Washington,ou=people,dc=encyclopedia,dc=com, which describes an entry for the first U.S. president in a listing describing people listed in the directory www.encyclopedia.com (a hypothetical example). In this example, an ou is an object, and George Washington is an attribute, encyclopedia is the directory, and .com (the Internet commercial nameserver) is the repository of the namespace. The hierarchical schema thus describes people in a listing that is often used in whitepaper schema, similar to a phone book.

X.500 is a complete directory service specification. It outlines how logical schema are related and how directory access can be achieved. Directory access is how stored objects can be queried, accessed, and replicated to other directory systems. The X.500 definition includes three transport protocols:

- **Directory Access Protocol (DAP)**—DAP specifies how an application can access stored information in an X.500-compliant directory.

- **Directory Service Protocol (DSP)**—DSP specifies how to propagate requests for information from one directory server to another directory server in a hierarchy of directory servers.

- **Directory Information Shadowing Protocol (DISP)**—DISP describes the rules under which objects and information can be replicated. Replication requires that a master copy exist and that copies of that data be distributed on multiple servers so that the directory service response time can be acceptable and so the system has improved fault tolerance.

LDAP

Because DAP is a very resource-intensive protocol, lighter-weight protocols have been developed. The best known is Lightweight Directory Access Protocol (LDAP), which is now in version 2. With LDAP you can access data in any X.500-compliant database, but you do so over TCP/IP, without having to incur the overhead that is in DAP.

As Table 18.3 indicates, many implementations of LDAP are available, both from NOS vendors such as Microsoft and Novell, and from database vendors such as Oracle. LDAP implementations have also been created by the opensource community.

Lightweight is really something of a misnomer because LDAP contains a detailed specification for naming and mapping. LDAP is based on the X.500 ISO/ITU directory service, which itself is based on the original DAP, but LDAP has a life of its own. Developments in LDAP have contributed to later versions of X.500 and influenced several other Internet standards.

LDAP was developed for browser applications and then extended to network management services and applications. Services based on LDAP are so widely used in modern networks that they are almost ubiquitous. DNS servers are based on LDAP. You are already familiar with LDAP because we all use it frequently in many forms. For example, in LDAP version 3 the mailing address name@domain.com is in a UTF-8 format. Eventually LDAP will become the directory-to-directory communication protocol standard. However, LDAP can't replace an X.500-type directory service, which is where network directory servers come in.

What makes LDAP particularly useful is that it defines interoperability and transport over TCP/IP, it defines relatively simple directory searches and updates, and it is supported by most modern NOS services. Any directory service that uses LDAP and understands how to access objects labeled with X.500 identifiers is termed an LDAP directory. How the directory service implements LDAP features is left entirely up to the developers; thus there is no such thing as a standard LDAP directory. LDAP first appeared out of work done at the University of Michigan, where OpenLDAP was created. Eventually LDAP was codified into a protocol and popularized by Netscape.

Table 18.3 lists some of the better-known and important directory services.

Table 18.3   Directory Services

Service	Vendor	Description
Active Directory	Microsoft	The directory service of Windows 2000 and 2003 servers. For a description of AD, see www.microsoft.com/windows2000/server/evaluation/features/dirlist.asp.
Apache Directory Server	Apache Software Foundation (open source)	An X.500 and LDAP directory with an administrative server back end. It uses the MINA framework and implements industry-standard protocols such as Kerberos.
Open Directory	Apple Computer	Open Directory is based on the OpenLDAP open source implementation and ships with Apple Mac OS X Server. Among its features are Windows support, Kerberos, NT Domain services, Samba 3, and LDAP account integration. With these features, a Mac OS X server can function as a Windows domain server.
DirX server	SiemansAG	See www.siemens.com/directory.
eDirectory	Novell	An LDAP directory and management system that is best known for successful large enterprise deployment (although it is installable in enterprises of all sizes). For more information, see http://www.novell.com/products/edirectory/ and http://en.wikipedia.org/wiki/Novell_Directory_Services.
Fedora Directory Service (FDS)	Red Hat	Originally developed at Netscape, FDS ships with Red Hat Linux server.
Kerberos	Novell	This is Novell's LDAP implementation, described in more detail earlier in this chapter. See www.novell.com/products/edirectory/ for more information.
Domain Name Service (DNS)	Internic/ICANN	DNS is the Internet name service. ICANN also maintains the reverse directory lookup WHOIS.

Table 18.3   Continued

Service	Vendor	Description
GroupWise	Novell	GroupWise is Novell's email name and address book service.
Notes	Lotus/IBM	The Name and Address Book is an application-specific directory service.
Exchange Address Book	Microsoft	This is a first implementation of AD.
Network Information Service (NIS)	Sun Microsystems	NIS appeared first as Sun's UNIX Yellow Pages. Eventually, Sun rolled NIS into the iPlanet directory service acquired from Netscape. iPlanet eventually became Sun ONE and is now part of Sun's current offering, Sun Java Enterprise.
Novell Directory Service (NDS)	Novell	NDS is marketed as a heterogeneous directory service that can support UNIX, Windows, Linux, NetWare, and even AS/400. Novell has had some success marketing NDS to large Internet websites, including CNN.com. The NDS logo appears on sites that use this service.
Open Directory Project (ODP)	Open source/ community maintained	ODP or Directory Mozilla (DMoz) is an open directory project that indexes content linked to on the web through Time Warner.
OpenLDAP	open source	OpenLDAP is used as the model for a number of vendors' directory services. See www.openldap.org.
Internet Directory	Oracle	Internet Directory is used in Oracle's database and business applications.
Samba	open source	Samba can be a domain controller, with LDAP and Kerberos support.
StreetTalk Directory	Banyan	This is one of the first full-featured enterprise network directory services to appear.

Table 18.3 is only a partial list of directory services; many more could be listed. What is common to all these services is that they are able to exchange information with other directory services, using either X.500 or a subset or, much more commonly, LDAP. Whether they can exchange information natively or whether they require additional help is the topic of the next section.

A careful examination of the directory services in Table 18.3 indicates that there are four basic categories of directory services:

- X.500, LDAP, and other standards-based, general-purpose directory services
- NOS directories, such as AD, iPlanet, and StreetTalk
- Application-specific directories, such as the messaging directories of Notes, Exchange, and GroupWise, as well as databases such as Oracle, and many others
- Special-purpose directories, such as the Internet's DNS

The Microsoft Management Console (MMC) offers a view into many of the aspects of Windows AD. Figure 18.1 shows the policy console. Often there are better tools available for manipulating directory services than those that come natively with NOSs.

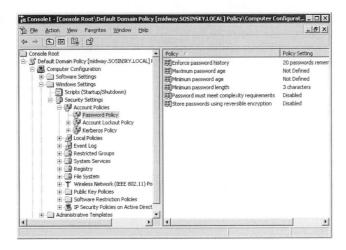

Figure 18.1 The MMC, showing some of the policy assignments that have been made. Note that the left panel lets you choose from a number of AD areas, using MMC snap-ins. The framework is extensible so that other vendors can add their solutions to the MMC.

Directory Services Interoperability

We are most concerned here with NOS directories and, more specifically, with the ability of a NOS directory service to be able to talk with the three other types of directory services. What LDAP can't do—that is, support many of the features of X.500—the NOS directory services can do. NOSs began to support directory services when Banyan Vines StreetTalk appeared, and this was one of the reasons Vines had such success early on in large enterprises.

Hopefully you've noticed that your favorite NOS or enterprise application is on the list in Table 18.3. It's hard not to be impressed by how central directory services are in making modern network services operate efficiently and effectively. The trick is to get all these services to work together seamlessly. Strong interoperability should be a key factor when you decide to adopt an application or an OS.

Interoperability is a must in two central areas: security and information or personalization sharing. These two areas are intimately related. A user or an administrator shouldn't be able to access information unless he or she is authorized to do so, and authorization should be tied to the personalization or profile of that user.

The ultimate system would allow a single central data repository with a single secured logon for all users. If you intend to run an enterprise with best-of-breed components, you aren't going to be using a single data repository, and single-signon is difficult to achieve. How well you can achieve single logon depends on how well integrated security services can be made to be, and that is a function of the security standards that are in place (Kerberos, X.509 certificates, and others) as well as the access control protocols in use.

Novell NetWare's approach to directory management has been to create a tool originally called Novell DirXML, which is bundled as a starter pack with NetWare 6.5. DirXML has drivers that can let a NetWare server exchange data from Microsoft AD with Novell's eDirectory. Another feature of DirXML is that it can synchronize passwords with a Windows domain. Recently Novell has renamed DirXML Novell Nsure Identity Manager (see www.novell.com/products/nsureidentitymanager/) to emphasize this capability of the product. Nsure Identity Manager is one of the tools you can manage with Novell's browser-based iManager system tool, which is also bundled with NetWare.

FDS is based on directory server technology that Red Hat acquired from AOL in 2004. It is managed as part of the Fedora project and is advertised as being compatible with Fedora Core 3, Solaris 2.8 and 2.9, Windows 2000 Server, and HP-UX 11i. FDS comes as an LDAP definition service, with management tools offered to users in binary form. FDS is supported by the Fedora community, while RedHat offers a commercially supported version known as RedHat Directory Service (RDS).

Other Considerations in Selecting a Server Platform

When people think in terms of servers, they often tend to think that a server is a monolithic entity. Nothing could be further from the truth. Usually servers are deployed so that they provide one or perhaps two main network services, at most. This is the case because you can get better performance from a server when it is tuned for the specific function it is providing. In any large enterprise application, you adjust the storage system, size and type of memory and processors, and other functions to suit the application at hand.

▶▶ For more information, see "Capacity Planning," p. 828.

The sections that follow describe the different types of servers that are available, from a network services point of view.

The Purpose of a Server

In the past, computers providing network services were often categorized as minicomputers, mainframes, or supercomputers. With the introduction of general-purpose microprocessors that are used both in PCs and for shared services, the term *server* has come to be used for any system that is microprocessor based and provides network services.

The purpose of a server is to provide reliable and predictable network services to clients. Either the OS or some software application runs a process that provides the service to software that is usually running on another computer, called the *client*. For example, Microsoft Exchange running on a server that uses the Windows Server 2003 OS collects messages for Outlook clients of that system. However, you can just as well open a copy of Outlook on the server itself, and then your client is running on the same system. It's good to keep in mind that a client represents just a piece of software and not necessarily another system.

Note

Not all systems use the terms *clients* and *servers* the same way. In X Window, as discussed shortly, the server is the software receiving the information from the client. It's a little confusing, but it's important to keep in mind for each particular OS.

Server Categories

Servers are generally described as belonging to one of the following categories:

- **General-purpose server**—A general-purpose server is an enhanced PC that is capable of being configured to be able to run a variety of applications.

- **Application server**—An application server's primary purpose is to run a specific application.

- **File and print server**—File and print services are most often OS functions, so a file and print server is a general-purpose server that is tuned specifically to serve files or interface to printers or virtual printers.

- **Mail or messaging server**—A messaging server uses the POP or IMAP protocol to store and send mail messages.

- **Collaboration server**—A real time communication server such as one managing Voice over IP (VoIP) traffic would be included in this category of servers.

- **Database server**—Most enterprise servers use some implementation of the SQL standard, and most are relational. However, there are a broad range of database server types in use, including object databases.

- **Domain or logon servers**—All NOSs establish their credentials by using a domain or logon server. However, it is often possible to replace or supplement authentication services by using other servers' products.

- **Backup servers**—Backup servers copy data from clients or other servers to another location. Backup servers range in type from a general-purpose server to specialized appliances fitted with a backup program.

- **Proxy server or firewall**—When set up as a proxy server or firewall, a server is configured as a router. Two or more network interfaces maintain physical and logical isolation of one network from another. Often these types of servers are set up and sold as routers.

- **Storage server**—A storage server can be as simple as an appliance with an embedded OS, to a specialized network file server, to a large block-oriented intelligent disk array.

- **Appliances**—An appliance is a server with a very specialized purpose and with limited management functions. The term *appliance* is best applied to a system that can be essentially plugged in to a network and turned on with little or no effort.

From this list you can see that servers fulfill a huge range of roles in a network environment, and many serve multiple roles. A domain server with a shared network resource, for example, provides the NOS server function of authentication as well as the server function of file services. It's best to take a holistic view when considering what is meant by the term *server*.

Servers Versus Clients

Consider the situation of a terminal service running on a server. Terminal services essentially run instances of the server OS on the server, and they do so by sharing open resources. Terminal servers are typically put into place to run applications that can be viewed through a low-bandwidth connection on a client system or on a computer terminal. Clearly, the terminal server is a server in its own right. The application running inside the server uses the terminal server as a client but would be considered part of the terminal server service to the window that you open on a workstation or terminal. Most people ignore the complexity here and consider the view into the terminal server running the application as a single server service.

It gets more interesting when you consider how a server based on the X Window System is named. The applications running on an X Window server are called *clients*. The command session(s) running on a terminal or workstation are called the *server*. X Window systems are, by design, a client/server architecture. It's possible to run both a client and a server on the same computer, but from the standpoint of networking, the X protocol can use the command set from any terminal or workstation (the server) to issue commands to the client system that actually does the processing.

Because X Window is designed as a network architecture, you might wonder how it's possible to run both server and client on the same computer. When a single computer runs both components, either the UNIX local socket or a loopback interface is used to simulate the network component that is part of the transport process. That is, X Window considers these elements to be a transparent network connection for the service. As far as the X Window System is concerned, the server's command is transmitted to these elements, and then the reply is returned by them.

Just keep in mind that for all other NOSs described in this chapter, the X Window System uses exactly the opposite naming convention. It's simply a matter of definition, and of course, point of view.

Web Services

The term *server* has recently acquired an even more general usage, as many vendors are rushing to create web-based services. The draw to providing web services is that vendors can provide sophisticated services from servers located anywhere in the world for low cost. Because they can sell these services to a larger audience by using a per-usage model, the margins behind this kind of business model can be enormous.

To implement a successful web service, a vendor or standards organization must publish and have accepted a set of standards for programming languages and program construction, protocols, and API against which applications can be written to run on a variety of platforms. The most successful web services to date have been based on Sun's Java platform, but with everything from Microsoft's .NET servers, Novell's exteNd strategy, Google's web services API, Amazon Web Services—to name but a few—exploding onto the scene, the server marketplace is changing once again.

Essentially what web services do is let a small server (perhaps your web server) behave as if it were a much bigger and more capable server. You don't need a local authentication server because that service runs remotely. You don't need an accounting package because that service runs remotely; you don't need an inventory module, a database engine, a messaging server, an Unreal Tournament server—you get the idea—because these services all run on a server remotely. You only need to have data pass from client to server securely and reliably to have this work. When done correctly, the service is transparent, and the user doesn't know or need to know the location of the server that is doing the work.

Note

For a nice description of web services and Novell's positioning, see www.novell.com/collateral/4621359/ 4621359.html. For information about Microsoft's efforts, you can go to http://msdn.microsoft.com/webservices/. You can find a jump page with whitepapers and tutorials at http://msdn.microsoft.com/webservices/understanding/ webservicebasics/default.aspx.

When a client makes a request of a web service, a program such as PHP, JSP, ASP, or a COM object makes a service request on the web service server. That request gets processed, and data is returned. When you log on to Hotmail or log in to Microsoft's Passport service to authenticate yourself, you are running a web service.

A successful web service relies on a set of standards being uniformly accepted so that it can be implemented by developers in a consistent way. You only need to consider the history of Java or the way browser technologies have developed to know that even when standards organizations are involved, it is rarely the case that all vendors implement the same standard in a consistent way. Standards committees rely on industry vendors to create products that implement their standards, and in most cases to extend the standards to create new capabilities. If fonts in browsers are step one, one vendor might think stylesheets are the next thing and implement them prior to the process of clearing an RFC. By the time that issue gets worked out, perhaps the next extension is moving stylesheets to XML.

Acceptance of networking standards is clearly a moving target. This process has affected how successful web services have been so far. To combat these problems, standards committees such as W3C, WS-I, OASIS, and others have chosen to isolate them by codifying individual protocols and standards and then working on trying to get them all to communicate successfully with one another. You are already probably familiar with the elements of the web service architecture. Figure 18.2 shows how these elements interact.

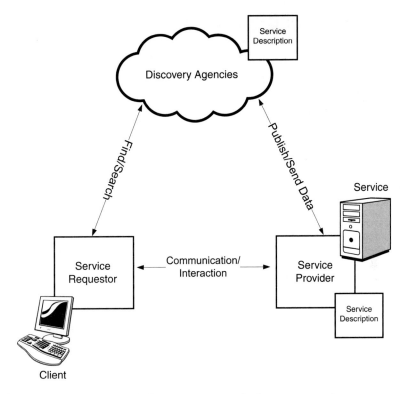

Figure 18.2 Servers implementing web services use standard components that must communicate with one another to be successfully deployed.

Web service component standards include the following:

- **Protocols**—Protocols include the common transport protocols, such as HTTP, SMTP, FTP, and XMPP, as well as a web service protocol "stack" that is used to implement specific web services.

- **Interchange formats**—The exchange format with the most juice is XML. Data in XML can be transported using protocols such as Microsoft SOAP, JAX-RPC, and even XML-RPC. SOAP is at the heart of Microsoft's .NET initiative.

- **Interface**—The Web Services Description Language (WSDL) is the best-known interface. It is an XML communications service.

- **Security protocols**—The OASIS standard for security is the WS-Security protocol, which is used to authenticate requests and maintain data security for communications.

- **Publication protocol**—The most commonly used protocol to transmit the information provided by servers running web services is UDDI.

The key advantage of building, deploying, or using servers running web services is that doing so allows applications to become portable and much more interoperable. Because web services are based on an open standard with common transport mechanisms, you can utilize existing infrastructure without having to create or deploy any special hardware, software, or security to get it to work. All that said, the main problem behind web services is that they are still not standardized, they are slow, and web transport is not as secure as internal network protocols. Negatives aside, web services are still the future, and you may find yourself implementing such server applications frequently.

Server Hardware and Drivers

Depending on the NOS you use, your server solution will either come as a software-only package that gets installed on industry-standard equipment or as a hardware/software bundle that the OS vendor provides. There are advantages and disadvantages to both approaches.

Software-Only NOSs and the Microsoft Experience

Microsoft's server OSs, Windows 2003 and, prior to that, Windows 2000 and NT, are software-based approaches to building a NOS. Microsoft relies on its industry associations with companies such as Intel, but others such as Advanced Micro Devices (AMD) instead create what is best called an industry-standard PC and server-based architecture. The size of Microsoft's market actually helps create a diverse hardware standard to support different versions of the OS. This approach is quite helpful when it comes to seeding the desktop and laptop markets with a number of different compatible designs, but it can have unintended consequences when it comes to server hardware.

Windows NT grew in popularity in the late 1990s but was burdened with a reputation in the industry of being unreliable. As Microsoft set about designing and debugging its code for Windows 2000, the company developed and acquired a set of testing tools designed to test memory leaks, check variables at the time of a crash, and perform other analyses that could help understand why people were having to reboot their servers so often. The information gleaned from this experience has led to some interesting conclusions and a number of new directions for Microsoft. The lessons learned apply to all server OSs.

As it turned out, the number-one cause of server failure was termed "human error." Often, server operators restarted their servers for the following reasons:

- They didn't know how to end a process correctly.
- They made a mistake in a command at the command line.
- They installed software incorrectly.
- They set a system setting incorrectly.
- They attempted to "refresh" their server (that is, return to a known state) by restarting the server instead of fixing an underlying problem that they didn't understand.
- They attempted to clear out a log that was full by restarting their system.

Something on the order of a little more than 50% of all system restarts fall into one of these categories.

The second most significant cause of failures was device driver errors—that is, either the wrong device driver was installed, the device driver was poorly written in some way, or there was an interaction between the device driver and the OS that led to a crash. In many cases, the error involved the device driver trying to write to protected memory in the system. In a very small number of cases, problems in the OS were traced back to memory leaks.

A memory leak occurs when a driver or other software program writes to memory that is assigned to a system process or to another application. When the system tries to use the "corrupted" memory contents, it may hang or cause some other unpredictable result. This can happen when the software is written in a nonstandard way and becomes unsupported in future versions of the OS or simply due to poorly written code.

With this experience, Microsoft changed its tactics somewhat, moving from a "PC Standard Architecture" to a "Certified for Windows XXX" program, where peripherals, software, and device drivers go through quality assurance testing in order to attain this status.

If you have installed a video card, tuner, USB hub, storage device, or almost any other type of peripheral, you may have encountered a dialog box that says "This software is not certified for use with Windows XP...." In most instances, the vendor's documentation tells you to ignore the warning and install the software anyway. The Windows certification program costs a vendor thousands of dollars in fees. For a low-priced item such as a USB hub, most vendors don't bother to go to the trouble. Higher-priced items such as RAID controllers almost always seek this type of certification.

The Certified for Windows program is not all that valuable for a Windows workstation, but it carries added significance for servers. When you want a server to be more reliable, careful selection of the drivers, software, and peripherals that you use is part of "hardening" the server. Hardening is the process by which the server is made more reliable or more secure.

Microsoft committed to a Datacenter Server program, where large SMP computers of 16, 32, and 64 processors are running in the enterprise, so the Datacenter certification is an essential element of any deployment. The Datacenter program actually went further than that. You can only obtain a Windows Datacenter system from a certified vendor, and the vendor is required to certify the systems that they ship as well as to strictly use items that are approved on the Datacenter hardware compatibility list. Essentially, this means that for large Datacenter systems, Microsoft moved to an OS/hardware platform combination, even if Microsoft itself isn't the one delivering the system.

A large number of other OSs are software-only solutions that rely on industry-standard PC or server hardware platforms. In this category are Linux and its many flavors, Sun Solaris for Intel, Novell NetWare, DOS, and a whole host of real-time and other specialized OSs.

Selecting a NOS that is software based is a compromise: You trade a certain level of supposed reliability for access to a much larger universe of hardware. More often than not, it is less expensive to create a NOS server than it is to buy a complete proprietary solution. However, it is certainly possible and often straightforward to build servers with software NOS and even with open source applications such as the webserver Apache or the file server Samba and have them run very reliably for very long periods of time.

Hardware/Software Packaged NOSs

Many computer companies prefer to deliver their OSs as part of a hardware-packaged solution. There are two reasons for this. First, a NOS vendor can ensure a certain level of reliability if it controls not only the OS software but the hardware as well. This rationale has worked well in the server sector, with vendors' products as diverse as IBM AS/400, Sun Solaris, Apple Macintosh, and others. The second reason a bundled server solution makes sense from the vendor point of view is that it allows the vendor to achieve acceptable profit margins on hardware that isn't possible for commodity hardware sold on the open market.

Thus hardware/NOS bundles usually offer better reliability than software-only solutions, provided that you stay within the limits of the software the vendor recommends. You pay for this reliability by having to pay a premium on the hardware you buy as well as by having fewer hardware choices available should you try to upgrade your server. Does this compromise mean that choosing a hardware/NOS bundle is a more reliable than choosing a software-only NOS? Not necessarily.

Right out of the box, most hardware/NOS bundles are rigorously tested and reliable, for the most part. As you start to add additional applications to a server, add peripherals, and change the software on the server, chances are that any hardware/NOS bundle's reliability won't be any better than a carefully chosen software-based NOS solution. Anyone who has loaded large number of extensions on a Macintosh desktop knows that third-party software lowers the reliability of the desktop, often in ways that aren't predictable.

Server Installation/Administration Requirements

As your network grows, it becomes impossible to manage each system individually. Therefore, management tools play a central role in how well one NOS can serve a network's needs. These tools have a direct impact on your bottom line because most organizations find that their number-one IT cost is the salary and overhead of the IT staff. If you can't measure the savings in terms of the salary saved, consider that the time your IT staff spends performing what is essentially maintenance tasks limits the attention that they can pay to implementing new systems. That cost is really a measure of lost opportunity, and the impact is often that your business doesn't grow or you don't achieve economies that a NOS should allow.

Let's briefly look at some of the management tools that should affect your thinking when considering an NOS.

Server Upgrade and Patch Management

All NOS vendors are constantly revising their software to take advantage of advances in hardware design, add new features, and provide services that are becoming standards in the industry. The large NOS vendors typically release major OS upgrades every two to three years, with point releases every six months or so.

Not all NOS versions are equal. Although the latest release may give you the most features, it may not be the most stable version of the NOS for your server. There are sweet spots in the technology, and wise IT staff know, often through word of mouth or through personal experience, which versions those are. Most analysts following the computer industry generally advise their clients to be very wary of deploying major version releases—and particularly so when there are significant changes in the technologies.

An example of a major release where the NOS changed substantially was Novell NetWare 5 and Microsoft Windows 2000. What they both have in common is that they were the versions of those two NOSs where the vendors introduced directory services: NDS in March 1997 and AD in February 2000, respectively.

Typically, the first versions of these breaks in technology have a low adoption rate, often no more than 15% in the first year or 18 months because extra effort is needed to migrate software and settings into the new version. As a general rule, the second release of a NOS is significantly better than the first release. Thus, many people tend to wait and are advised to wait for a Service Pack 2 or a .1 release before moving to a new NOS platform. Many enterprise applications running on stable and established NOSs never get upgraded at all because it is cheaper and less troublesome to simply replace the equipment and the NOS at the same time, migrating data as needed.

Whatever policy you decide to adopt regarding system upgrades, it's important to have a clear policy regarding system software patches, given that you are much more likely to be enticed to apply a patch to solve any current system issues than to replace the NOS. There are three approaches:

- Install all system patches and upgrades as soon as they become available in order to stay current. Most NOS vendors want their customers to be current, and the rationale that is used is that doing so lets the company close any security holes, improve performance, and remove any error conditions they find.

- Install only selected patches or upgrades after waiting an appropriate amount of time to determine stability. Many IT administrators feel that waiting an appropriate amount of time for a service pack or an upgrade to prove itself is a cautious approach that is less likely to cause them trouble.

It is certainly true that some patches cause more problems than they actually fix. Many NOS vendors simply don't apply the same amount of resources to certifying their patches' compatibility as they do to the version upgrades of their releases.

■ Stay with a version of the NOS that is stable and well known. If you have a production server that is operating correctly and reliably, an argument can be made for leaving the server alone and not changing anything. In situations where a server is operating well and is well protected behind up-to-date corporate firewalls, it is reasonable to believe that you already have enough protection in place to keep out intruders and for your server to do its job.

What upgrade rules should you employ? There isn't a correct answer to this question. If you have an intimate connection to both your NOS and enterprise application vendor, then it may make sense to stay current and rely on your VAR or vendor to help you through any difficulties.

However, and this is a big drawback, many upgrades are expensive to apply. If an upgrade falls outside your service contract, working that upgrade into your budget may cause you to forgo additional equipment, software, or services that are needed elsewhere.

Note

There is one inviolable rule for any organization that adopts a strategy of staying current with upgrades and patches: to always make sure you can revert to a previous version of the OS. For example, when Windows offers you the option of saving your previous OS files in order to uninstall an upgrade, you should accept that option. Or when you install a patch into Sun Solaris, that patch should appear in the Patch Manager and give you an uninstall option. Failing that, it is absolutely critical that you create a fully functional image backup of your server prior to applying any system software upgrade or patch. Many IT administrators would also argue that the same is true anytime you upgrade or patch your main server application(s).

The middle course of sticking to known good versions of a NOS is a conservative choice but one that acknowledges that the system software tends to get better over time. If you choose this course of action, then a rule of thumb might be to wait until the second patch of a major upgrade before upgrading or to wait three or four months from the time a significant patch is released before you apply that patch. Those three or four months will give you time to consult with colleagues, watch the online forums or blogs, and consult with system vendors to determine whether any significant problems have occurred. The only downside to this approach is that you won't get the full lifetime of the upgrade or patch that you're paying for. Given that an enterprise application has about a three-year life span at most, a four-month delay will cost you about 10% of the working life of the service.

The last course of action falls into the category of "If it's not broken, don't fix it." Its advantage is that you minimize both your additional costs for upgrades and the potential labor costs necessary to support an upgrade. Although vendors want to sell you the next great thing, you really have to ask yourself if this is money and effort well spent. If you are thorough and put together a cost–benefit analysis, in most cases upgrading a stable and reliable server or server application isn't worth doing. Many companies opt to leave their systems in place and intact until they are forced to or required to do a complete system upgrade. There's some chance that you will have a system that will no longer be supported by the original vendors, but there's always someone who will service a legacy system come what may.

A NOS's ability to manage upgrades and patches intelligently is a significant value-added proposition. Of all the NOSs, Microsoft provides probably the best-developed update site (www.microsoft.com/isaserver/default.mspx; see Figure 18.3). It's automated and has both notification and a push capability. Sun's upgrade site is also well implemented, although it's not quite as automated as Microsoft's.

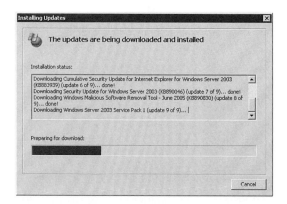

Figure 18.3 Microsoft Windows Update is a refined service for upgrading both desktops and servers. Here, SP1 is being applied to a Windows Server 2003 server running the Microsoft Internet Security and Acceleration (ISA) server.

Software Security Limitations

You need to consider several important aspects of software security when implementing both an application and a NOS. First, there is the issue of how authentication is done. The OS contains its own native authentication mechanism. However, depending on the application, any one of the following may be true:

- The application implements its own security scheme and logon.
- The application relies on the security scheme and logon services of the NOS.
- The application passes its logon and security scheme through to the NOS—the so-called pass-through identification scheme.

Each of these options carries unique benefits and risks. A single-logon scheme is less complex and easier to manage, but when it is compromised, it allows universal access to any security-dependent application. A multiple-logon scheme is more complex and requires more overhead to support. One part of your system can be compromised without the entire system being compromised.

A number of companies, including some of the NOS vendors, offer single-logon or single-signon servers. Most of these servers use industry-standard protocols such as Kerberos to create session tickets that can be used to validate a user and his or her session. Anyone who has used Kerberos knows that not all implementations of the standard are the same, and the small differences can lead to problems when you are trying to make different platforms interoperate. Still, single-logon servers offer you the potential of being able to work with many of these differences, and most of these products are very good at servicing both Windows and UNIX requests.

Single-signon or single-logon is not a feature that NOS vendors really want third-party tools to perform. Authentication is at the heart of what NOSs are meant to provide. That's why over time each NOS incorporates more and more heterogeneous logon support for clients. As much as is possible, NOS vendors also lead their application developers to rely on their particular directory service for their authentication needs.

No software can be 100% secure. The more applications that exist, the more users who use an NOS, and the more systems that are deployed, the greater the risk is for a NOS to be attacked. It's a fact that of the NOSs discussed in this chapter, the greater proportion of viruses, worms, denial of service, spyware, and other attacks are aimed at the Windows server platform. That this is largely a function of greater opportunity, but some people make an argument that it is also due in part to the way Microsoft enables its software to be manipulated by users. Be that as it may, the following general advice on software security is worth considering:

- Keep your servers simple; don't run any services that you don't need.
- Keep your servers up-to-date with patches and updates.
- Keep your servers physically secure. Don't allow physical access to a server to anyone who doesn't need to have it.
- Protect your server's software by using good password management practices.
- Employ appropriate antivirus, spyware, and intrusion-detection software.
- Set up and actively maintain a strong firewall.
- Be vigilant about securing your systems from internal users as well as external ones.
- Keep active logs that can be analyzed for problems.
- Have your security audited by reputable outside consultants and companies on a regular basis.

Server Documentation and Support

Supporting a server is considerably different from supporting a desktop system. Whereas a desktop is used by one user or a limited number of users and perhaps supported by one administrator, servers may be touched or modified by a large number of staff or outside support personnel. This fact argues for a different handling of a server system—handling that provides in-place tools for documentation of the server.

It's a good idea to document a server's contents so that if you or another staff member must access or maintain the server, you will know what the server contains. Nearly all motherboards ship with a decal showing the layout of the motherboard, and the board manufacturers expect you to paste that decal someplace where you will see it when needed. A great location for a motherboard diagram is on the removable side panel of a server housing, on the bottom of the server, or on the case somewhere. If none of those locations are convenient, you should consider attaching a plastic mailing window like the ones used to enclose invoices on packages to the outside of your server. If your motherboard does not come with a schematic or if that schematic is lost, you can print the layout from the server's user's guide. These guides are often posted on the vendors' sites as PDF files.

Many people also create a label that contains pertinent information about the system that an administrator would need to know, such as name, IP address (if a static address is assigned), NIC MAC addresses, and so on. That information is very useful when you are looking for a specific system in a room full of servers or in a server rack. At the very minimum, the name of the server and its logical network location should appear on the front of the server, in plain view. You might want to create a list similar to the one shown in Table 18.4.

Table 18.4   Server System Information

Component	Assignment
System name	DNS assignment
Domain name	The text name assigned to a specific IP or set of IP addresses on the Internet. Domains are listed in a set of databases on name servers (.com, .net, .org, and so on)
Fully qualified domain name	UNC path

Table 18.4   Continued

Component	Assignment
System model number	Type, version number, and ID
OS in use	Version number
Motherboard	Type and ID
CPU(s)	Type and speeds
Memory	Amount and type
IP address	Static assignment or dynamic
NIC(s)	MAC addresses, logical network assignment
Video card	Resolution
Expansion cards enumerated	List of PCI, PCI-x, and other cards in the server
Storage devices	The amount of storage contained and type
RAID information	Any RAID implementation as well as drivers used
Device drivers in use	A list of device drivers would for mission-critical systems
Location of backups or images	Information on how to restore part or all of the system, if required
Date placed in service	Date
Service contract holder	VAR or service provider
Help line	Phone number or website
Person responsible	Administrator
Contact information	Phone and email
Secondary contact	Backup person
Secondary contact information	Phone and email

Your list might contain additional or fewer pieces of information. If you set up a database or spreadsheet for all your servers, you can put this information in a very convenient and searchable format. It's time-consuming to set up this system, but it's much more time-consuming to figure out these details after the fact.

CHAPTER 19

Sun Microsystems Servers

Sun is one of the most important server manufacturers in the industry. The company has been a major player in Internet deployments and has been instrumental in developing some of the most important software used in websites, such as the Java language and portable applications based on Java. This chapter provides an overview of Sun's server offerings, Sun's role in enterprise storage, and the most important management applications that Sun offers.

The Solaris operating system runs on all Sun computers, from the smallest desktop up to the largest enterprise server (Sun's equivalent of a mainframe). Solaris 10 has a number of server management tools that are described in this chapter. These management tools aren't simply for local system management. In fact, many of these tools are aimed at making a Solaris system your management console of choice.

In addition to playing a central role in Internet deployments, Sun plays a central role in the storage industry, as a hardware vendor, as a software vendor, and with its systems as a strategic management console for system area networks (SAN) and other large storage deployments. For several years now, Sun has been able to claim a number of industry performance standards, such as the TPC-C benchmarks, running large system databases such as Oracle, DB2, SQL Server, and others on their enterprise-class servers.

While financial setbacks have slowed Sun's advance in some areas, such as blade servers and server appliances, recently the company has begun to broaden its product line into Linux and to improve its systems' interoperability with other platforms. Sun will remain an important player in the server market for the foreseeable future.

Sun, Servers, and SPARC

Sun Microsystems made its reputation in the mid-1980s by building a line of highly regarded UNIX workstations with the Sun OS, based on a version of the Berkeley Software Distribution of UNIX. Starting in 1982, Sun's servers offered the TCP/IP protocol suite. By 1985 Sun had its IPO, and by 1987 it was the industry leader in the workstation market. Sun had one of the fastest and most successful runs in the computer hardware market.

By 1988 Sun had introduced its SPARCstation 1, the first "pizza box" design. In some ways, 1991 was a watershed year for the company. That year, Sun introduced the Solaris 2 operating system for RISC processors, a version of the operating system that was designed for symmetric multiprocessing (SMP) systems. The SPARCstation 10, which appeared in 1992, was the first SMP desktop system. In that year, Sun shipped more RISC systems than any other UNIX vendor had ever shipped.

The popularization of the Internet really fueled Sun's surge into the server market. ISPs needed routers, switches, and firewalls for their networks and Sun was one of the players. When many of them began comparing the cost and power of servers made by other vendors to the cost and power of Sun workstations, many opted for the much less expensive Sun workstations. As the Internet market grew, Sun workstations and then Sun servers became the dominant platform for not only routers and switches but for webservers and other application servers as well. Eventually Cisco would displace Sun from the router market, but Sun continued to offer more and more powerful systems until it became the dominant Internet server vendor.

In 1996 Sun introduced systems based on its first 64-bit processor, the UltraSPARC. That was the same year that Java was first introduced, and it was when Sun contributed to the development of XML. A year later Sun introduced its first high-end server system, the Sun Enterprise 10000, which was really a mainframe-class system. That system set TCP-C benchmark records on all the leading databases. From the standpoint of servers, the next big introductions were smaller systems meant to be building blocks in horizontally scaled applications, such as the Netra t1 servers and the Sun Ray 1 enterprise appliances in 1999 and the Sun Fire "midframe" systems in 2001.

All of Sun's server offerings ran RISC architectures and Solaris exclusively until 2002, at which point the Sun LX50 server, a general-purpose server that could run either Solaris or Linux, appeared. Sun began to broaden its approach to deploying servers in 2002, first with the N1 architecture, in which "the network is the computer," and later in 2003, with a push into grid computing. Grid computing uses multiple network computers to solve the same problem (see http://en.wikipedia.org/wiki/Grid_computing). This chapter spends a significant amount of time discussing Sun's approach to blade servers, but the company has had a modular approach to systems for quite some time. It's the natural expression of the company's workstation heritage. The most recent trends in their server strategy are the broadening of Sun's product line into Linux, a serious push to attain server interoperability with other network operating systems (something the company didn't strive for until recently), and its initiative into a web services model that Sun calls "utility computing," which is a form of pay-as-you-go services.

The RISC Architecture

Broadly speaking, there are two approaches to building computer processors: complex instruction set computer (CISC) and reduced instruction set computer (RISC). They aren't actual processor designs; they are more like design philosophies. A CISC processor has a larger set of commands, and those commands can be more complex than those in a RISC processor. CISC allows commands that can span several processor cycles to be executed.

In the 1970s, when chip designers took a close look at exactly which instructions developers were using in their programs, they found that the much greater majority were simple commands. Even when a more complex command was used, it was often a combination of simpler commands. A well-known example of this is the VAX INDEX command, which turned out to be slower to execute than using a larger set of simpler commands, looped in code to create the same data structure. The compound instructions called orthogonal addressing modes were ignored, and the additional instructions were converted with compilers rather than the programs being written in assembly language; today compiling code is the standard step taken prior to running a program.

RISC processors use fewer commands in their instruction set than CISC processors, but they try to optimize those commands so that they run more efficiently. An instruction in a CISC processor that might be a combination of four simpler instructions and run over eight processor cycles, when executed on a RISC processor, would become four individual instructions that might still take eight processor cycles, but because the instructions are smaller, there is greater efficiency in getting the instructions processed with fewer lost cycles. That's the difference, in theory.

RISC processors offer a few additional benefits that make them popular in high-performance systems. First, because there are fewer instructions in a RISC processor's instruction set, the design of the processors can be simpler. A simpler design means that the chips can be less expensive or include additional features at the same price as a more complex chip. Also, with simpler commands, less memory is consumed storing the instructions as the code executes. Given that CPUs operate much faster than memory, less memory consumption is a very desirable feature.

In RISC processors, you may find the following:

- Very large internal caches
- Additional registers, which tend to be more homogeneous than CISC registers
- Built-in I/O control and timers for use in controller applications
- Next-generation features implemented into older chip designs, thus using old fabrication facilities to create new series processor
- Built-in graphics routines

- Parallelism implemented through pipelining or by superscalar technologies
- A lack of some features in order to decrease the energy consumption of the chip

Examples of CPUs with RISC architectures are Sun's SPARC and UltraSPARC, IBM PowerPC, MIPS (see http://en.wikipedia.org/wiki/MIPS_architecture), and DEC Alpha chips.

One additional feature is that it's easier to develop RISC chips with larger internal buses than to develop CISC chips, and indeed you need a wider bus if you are going to beat the clappers out of your processor, pushing small instructions through the logic unit. RISC processors and the operating systems that run them reached 64-bit internal buses in the late 1990s. With wider buses, you also get better performance out of the chip at lower frequencies and thus have lower heat issues. This also means that the compiler—the software that translates programs into instructions that the processor understands—is easier to create and more efficient in a RISC-based CPU.

It sounds like RISC is better than sliced bread, doesn't it? Well, not so fast. CISC offers developers the benefits of having a much richer development environment, it is easier to program for, and it has a very long history of development and optimization. If you are a developer and you need an instruction that does four things, do you really want to have to remember which four things they were? Wouldn't it be better to simply give the single instruction and spend your time figuring out if your code does what you want it to do? The best example of CISC processors is the Intel x86 architecture, and we all know how successful those processors have been. Starting with the Pentium Pro, Intel began introducing RISC features into its CPUs, so its current technologies are really something of a hybrid, as are most of the other CPUs on the market today.

As technology has developed, it isn't really possible to say that one chip is a pure CISC chip and the other is a pure RISC chip. RISC chips may have reduced instruction sets, but they are large instruction sets. Chip vendors are optimizing their designs so that you now find RISC features in CISC chips and CISC features in RISC chips. Which design is better is hard to say. As mentioned earlier, these two approaches are design philosophies, and each represents a set of compromises.

SPARC and UltraSPARC

The SPARC processor arose out of RISC processor design work done at Berkeley in the early 1980s. SPARC stands for Scalable Processor Architecture, and although SPARC is most closely associated with Sun Microsystems, it is in fact a registered trademark of SPARC International, Inc. (see www.sparc.com), which promotes and standardizes it as an open system architecture. So you not only find processors using SPARC built by Sun but by Cypress Semiconductor, Fujitsu, Texas Instruments, and in the open source implementation called LEON from Gaiser (see www.gaisler.com/index.html).

Note

You can find a nice repository of CPU statistics and pictures of SPARC processors at www.cpu-collection.de/?tn=1&l0=cl&l1=SPARC.

SPARC is a big-endian processor architecture, unlike the x86 architecture, which is little-endian. That's one reason why you simply can't recompile a program written for x86 onto SPARC and vice versa. Programs that travel from one platform to another are a complete port.

One of the most recognizable features of SPARCs, something that is consistent with RISC processors in general, is their use of general purpose registers (GPRs). SPARC can use as many as 128 GPRs, of which 8 are for global use and 24 form a register window that can be used for function calls in the register stack. A register window of 8 local registers shares 8 registers with nearby register windows. Shared registers pass parameters and return values, whereas local registers store values used by multiple function calls. Only 32 registers (8 + 24) are available for use by programs in the SPARC architecture, but the architecture is called *scalable* because programs can use up to the full allotment of 32 windows or as few as just 1. When you use more windows in memory, you suffer more context switching because memory must page in and out for instructions, but you do have more instructions loaded in memory.

Table 19.1 lists the essential characteristics of the different generations of SPARC processors.

Table 19.1   SPARC Series Processors

Model	Freq. (MHz)	Year	Process (µm)	Transistors (millions)	Size (mm?)	I/O Pins	Power (W)	Voltage (V)	Dcache (KB)	Icache (KB)	Scache (KB)
				Version 8							
microSPARC I	50	1992	0.8	0.8	225	288	2.5	5	4	2	0
SuperSPARC I	33–65	1992	0.8	3.1	NA	NA	14.3	5	16	20	1,024
microSPARC II	60–125	1992	0.5	2.3	233	321	5	3.3	8	16	0
SuperSPARC II	75–90	1994	0.8	3.1	299	NA	16	NA	16	20	2,048
TurboSPARC 1	60–180	1995	0.35	NA	NA	416	7	3.5	16	16	1,024
				Version 9							
UltraSPARC I	140–200	1995	0.5	5.2	315	521	30	3.3	16	16	1,024
UltraSPARC II	250–480	1997	0.25	5.4	156	521	21	3.3	16	16	8,192
UltraSPARC IIi	270–480	1998	0.25	5.4	148	587	21	1.9	16	16	2,048
UltraSPARC IIe	400–500	2000	0.18 AL	NA	NA	370	13	1.7	16	16	256
UltraSPARC IIi+	550–650	2002	0.18 Cu	NA	NA	370	17.6	1.7	16	16	512
UltraSPARC III	600–1200	2001	0.13	29	330	1368	53	1.6	64	32	8,192
UltraSPARC IIIi	1064–1593	2003	0.13	87.5	206	959	52	1.3	64	32	16,384
UltraSPARC IV	1050–1350	2004	0.13	66	356	1368	108	1.35	64	32	16,384

The current versions of the SPARC standard are versions 8 and 9. Version 8 uses 16 double-precision floating-point registers. Each register can be used in different ways. You can use a register to store two single-precision values, which equates to having 32 single-precision registers, or you can couple an odd and an even double-precision register together, which can create up to 8 quad-precision registers. Alternatively, you can use the 32 registers as standard double-precision registers.

SPARC version 9 is notable in that it was the first 64-bit version of the architecture. Version 9 added 16 additional double-precision registers to the architecture to support the internal 64-bit data bus. Of course, even if a processor runs internally at 64 bits, a system's I/O bus still runs at 32 bits. There are plenty of examples of systems running a 64-bit internal CPU bus and a 32-bit I/O bus, as well as the opposite case of a 32-bit internal CPU bus over a 64-bit I/O bus.

Server Categories

Sun classifies its hardware offerings based on the number of clients a server can service. That roughly translates with other server vendors into the number of processors in the server. However, in a world where a 1U server is meant to be densely stacked into a large rack, or where a blade can be stacked 16 or 20 blades to a cabinet ("server shelf"), Sun takes a longer view of the situation. Thus Sun uses the following classifications for the servers it sells:

- **Entry-level servers**—An entry-level server is a one- or two-processor system that is meant to provide a network service(s) to as few as one client/user up to as many as a workgroup. Many entry-level servers are used in horizontally deployed applications.

- **Midrange servers**—The midrange server offerings are viewed as department-level servers or servers that can provide network service(s) to 10 clients/users up to 250 clients/users for large applications. For simpler network services, such as DNS, a server of this class might service thousands of users.

- **Enterprise servers**—An enterprise server is a PC-based server equivalent of a mainframe. Sun's systems in this area scale to hundreds of processors and are used for applications such as data-bases that best scale vertically.

- **Blade servers**—A blade server is a motherboard that has been modified so that it fits into a chassis and can be hot-swapped. Sun's current line of blade servers is in flux, with a new line slated for 2006. The Sun Galaxy line of servers introduced in September 2005 will include a blade server option from mid-2006 on.

- **Appliances**—An appliance server is a special-purpose server that requires little maintenance and/or management. Sun had a line of appliances that included caching servers, firewalls, small file servers and webservers, and small workgroup general-purpose servers. Sun is restructuring its line of appliances, having removed the entire line of Cobalt appliances from the market. It is expected that Sun will reintroduce some of its appliances in 2006.

- **Carrier-grade servers**—This line of servers offers NEBS Level 3 (Network Equipment Building System, an industry standard; see www.telcordia.com/services/testing/nebs/) solutions for the telecommunications industry and for back offices.

- **Storage servers**—Sun is a major supplier of storage arrays, tape backup systems, and storage software, through its StorEdge line. Sun's business is mostly to Sun server customers, but it also plays a central role as a management console of choice for storage area networks (SANs). In 2005, Sun's storage business (about $400 million) put Sun slightly ahead of Dell.

With these categories in mind, let's now take a look at the specific models currently offered at the time of this writing.

Entry-Level Servers

An entry-level server is generally one that is a general-purpose server. Compared to other vendors, Sun's entry-level servers offer the widest range of options in terms of the operating systems supported. Sun's entry-level servers come with both Opteron and UltraSPARC processors (the III and IIIi series); the Opteron processors can run not only on Solaris but on Linux, Windows, and VMware as well. For many people, Sun's entry-level servers offer an economical platform that they use to scale their applications horizontally.

All of Sun's entry-level servers carry the Sun Fire series labels, with the lone exception of Sun's iForce VPN Firewall Appliance. Another common characteristic of all the entry-level servers is that they are all rack-mountable, low-profile servers, in 1U to 4U sizes. Sun makes these entry-level servers with the Internet marketplace in mind. These rack-mounted servers are meant for applications that scale hori-zontally, such as server farms used for websites.

Sun's entry-level servers run the gamut from several single-processor systems to a couple dual-proces-sor systems—all the way up to the 4U eight-processor-capable Sun Fire V880 server. (It's hard to call an eight-processor server entry level, but Sun does.) Table 19.2 compares some of the central features of the current models of the Sun Fire series of entry-level servers. You can find a more complete list at www.sun.com/servers/family-comp.html.

Table 19.2   The Sun Fire Series of Entry-Level Servers

Model	CPUs	Clock Speed	OS Version
Sun Fire V20z	1–2 AMD Opteron 200 Series	Models 244, 248, 250, 252	Solaris OS, Red Hat Enterprise Linux, SUSE Linux Enterprise Server, Microsoft Windows, or VMware
Sun Fire V40z	2–4 AMD dual- or single-core Opteron 800 series	Models 844, 858, 850, 852, 875	Solaris OS, Red Hat Enterprise Linux, SUSE Linux Enterprise Server, Microsoft Windows, or VMware
Sun Fire V100	1 UltraSPARC III	550MHz–650MHz	Solaris 8 update 2/02 and later, Solaris 9
Sun Fire V120	1 UltraSPARC III	650MHz	Solaris 8 update 10/01 and later, Solaris 9
Sun Fire V210	1–2 UltraSPARC III	1.34GHz	Solaris 8 hardware release 12/02 and later, Solaris 9 update 04/03 and later
Sun Fire V240	1–2 UltraSPARC IIIi	1GHz or 1.1.34/1.5GHz	Solaris 8 hardware release 12/02 and later, Solaris 9 update 4/03 and later
Sun Fire V440	2–4 UltraSPARC III	1.28GHz or 1.593GHz	Solaris 8 hardware release 7/03 and later, Solaris 9 update 12/03 and later
Sun Fire V480	2–4 UltraSPARC III Cu	1.05GHz or 1.2GHz	Solaris 8, Solaris 9
Sun Fire V880	2–8 UltraSPARC III	1.2GHz	Solaris 8 update 10/01 and later, Solaris 9

In 2004 Sun had a line of server appliances that was derived from the product line of its acquisition of Qube. Along with its Cobalt appliance line and caching appliances, only one of these systems survived the company's financial difficulties. Of these systems, only the Sun Control Station has a proposed next-generation product listed, and by all appearances, Sun's appliance line has retrenched into a software-based strategy, best exemplified by the iForce VPN, which can run on a variety of systems.

Note

The latest entry-level servers from Sun are the Galaxy series. The Sun Fire X2100 features one Opteron processor; the X4100 and X4200 feature one or two Opteron processors. All Galaxy series servers support both single-core and dual-core Opteron processors. For details, see www.sun.com/servers/index.jsp.

Sun's entry-level systems form the basis for an enterprise computing solution based on the grid model of computing, which is useful in areas as diverse as statistics, graphical analysis, structural analysis, and molecular and computational chemistry. The Sun Grid Rack System is populated with Sun Fire V20z or V40z servers, which are Opteron systems.

Grid computing offers the ability to spread a computational load over multiple systems while still maintaining the flexibility to work on smaller problems on a single computer in the grid. Rather than thinking of a grid system such as Sun's Grid Rack System as a cluster or distributed system, it's best to think of grid computing as a way of performing massively parallel processing projects. To enable grid computing, systems ship with management tools as well as software that acts to manage the processing load among the systems that are part of the grid. It is anticipated that grid computing may become part of pervasive computing technologies, where computer processing is available wherever a person goes.

You can read more about Sun's grid solution at www.sun.com/servers/ index.jsp?cat=Compute%20Grid&tab=3.

Midrange Servers

In Sun's view, a midrange server is meant to be a powerful system that offers high performance at a reasonable price. What differentiates a midrange system from an entry-level system is that a midrange server offers improved fault tolerance and high availability. Midrange servers also ship with support for more management tools. Table 19.3 lists the current members of the Sun midrange server line.

Table 19.3   Sun's Midrange Servers[1]

Model	CPU	Clock Speed (GHz)	I/O Slots	Memory Max (GB)	Domains	Storage Max	Resource Utilization[2]
Sun Fire V480	to 4 UltraSPARC III	1.2	6 PCI	32	1	NA	SC
Sun Fire V490	to 4 UltraSPARC IV	1.05/1.35	6 PCI	32	1	NA	SC
Sun Fire V880	to 8 UltraSPARC III	1.2	9 PCI	64	1	NA	SC
Sun Fire V890	to 8 UltraSPARC IV	1.2/1.35	9 PCI	64	1	NA	SC
Sun Fire V1280	to 12 UltraSPARC III	1.2	6 PCI	96	1	NA	SC
Sun Fire E2900	to 12 UltraSPARC IV	1.05/1.2/ 1.35	6 PCI	96	1	17TB	SC
Sun Fire 4800	to 4 UltraSPARC III	1.05/1.2	16 PCI or 8 PCI+	96	1–2	35TB	DSD, SC
Sun Fire E4900	to 12 UltraSPARC IV	1.05/1.2/ 1.35	16 PCI+	96	1–2	36TB	DSD, SC
Sun Fire 6800	to 24 UltraSPARC III	1.05/1.2	32 PCI/ 16 PCI+	192	1–4	NA	DSD, SC
Sun Fire E6900	to 24 UltraSPARC IV	1.05/1.2/ 1.35	32 PCI+	192	1–4	77TB	DSD, SC

[1]*Key: SC = Solaris Containers and DSD = Dynamic System Domains.*
[2]*All systems are compatible with Solaris 8 and later.*

High-End Servers

Sun's high-end servers are positioned as mainframe replacements. These servers can support from 36 to 72 UltraSPARC processors and are sold into the marketplace as highly fault-tolerant, mission-critical data center servers. Sun's high-end servers are meant to run without downtime, and they come with a number of features that allow them to be reconfigured while they are operational. Sun's high-end servers come with hot-swappable components and bus structures. Dynamic Reconfiguration (DR), which shipped with Solaris 8, lets you reconfigure a core component while Solaris and the applications that run on the system continue to function. With DR you can replace memory boards, PCI cards, CPUs, and other components dynamically, which means basically on-the-fly. DR works in concert with a feature called Dynamic System Domains, which lets you run instances of the Solaris operating system and applications on the same server.

Table 19.4 list the four current members of Sun's high-end server line.

Table 19.4   Sun's High-End Servers[1]

Model	CPU	Clock Speed	I/O Slots[2]	Max Memory	Domains	Storage	Resource Utilization[3]
Sun Fire 12K	to 52 UltraSPARC III	1.05/1.2	36 PCI	288	1–9	120TB	DSD, SC
Sun Fire 15K	to 106 UltraSPARC III	1.05/1.35	72 PCI	576	1–18	250TB	DSD, SC
Sun Fire E20K	to 36 UltraSPARC IV	1.05/1.2	36 PCI+	288	1–9	120+TB	DSD, SC
Sun Fire E25K	to 82 UltraSPARC IV	1.05/1.2/ 1.35	72 PCI+	576	1–18	250+TB	DSD, SC

[1]*Key: SC = Solaris Containers and DSD = Dynamic System Domains.*

[2]*PCI+ is hot-swappable PCI.*

[3]*All systems are compatible with Solaris 8 and later.*

Sun also resells the Fujitsu PRIMEPOWER line of enterprise-class SPARC64-V computers. There are currently seven systems in this new product line: PRIMEPOWER 250, 450, 650, 850, 900, 1500, and 2500. For details on this product line, which is sold only in certain geographical areas so that it doesn't compete with Fujitsu, go to www.sun.com/servers/index.jsp?cat=PRIMEPOWER%20Servers&tab=3.

Blade Servers

Sun's blade server strategy was an important part of Sun's scalable server architecture marketing until June 2005, when Sun discontinued its line of blade servers, including the Sun Fire B1600 chassis system, Sun Fire B100s, Sun Fire B100x Sun Fire B200, Sun Fire B10n Content Load Balancing Bridge, Sun Fire B10p SSL Proxy Blade, and Sun N1 Blades Starter Pack. Sun plans to reintroduce new blade server models in early 2006. Although the exact configuration of the new blade servers has not yet been fully revealed, it appears that Sun will reintroduce two new classes of blades:

- Blade servers that will run AMD's x86 Opteron chips and the Linux operating system
- Blade servers that will run UltraSPARC chips and the Solaris operating system

The expected price of blade servers will average around $1,000, while the cabinet or chassis—what Sun refers to as a "shelf"—will probably run between $6,000 and $7,000.

It is believed that a number of the new blade servers will be dual-processor capable and that they will include more built-in networking and management features, such as switches and perhaps InfiniBand interconnect. With a new management console, it should be possible to turn blades on and off at will, to fail over from blade to blade, to monitor a blade's current condition, and to have each blade's identification be autorecognized. Sun officials have stated that each of these next blade servers will come with a built-in management chip and switch.

Blade servers are important to Sun and other hardware vendors because they allow for a system to be horizontally scaled as needed; this architecture is very important in some of Sun's key markets: high availability clusters, Internet, telecommunications, and others. A number of enterprise applications that run on Sun servers are being redesigned to run on blade servers. This includes IBM DB2 and Oracle, among many others.

A blade configuration essentially packages a computer motherboard so that it is a plug-and-play hot-swappable component in a blade chassis. That chassis shares the power supply and air cooling functions among the installed blades. With blade servers, a data center can create some very dense processing racks with as many as 200 servers in the size of a home refrigerator, thus delivering the power of mainframes.

The current problem with blade servers is that the systems have not yet been completely standardized. There's a rush among server vendors to sell blades, but the market is still relatively young. Therefore, the complete feature set of a blade varies from OEM to OEM.

Storage Servers

Sun is one of the most important players in the storage marketplace, from a hardware perspective, but particularly from a server platform perspective. Sun sells a range of storage devices from small devices up to enterprise-class intelligent storage arrays, as well as accompanying software. However, Sun's real importance in the storage industry is as a strategic server platform. In a data center, only two management server platforms matter: Microsoft Windows servers and Sun Solaris servers. Almost every significant enterprise storage application or storage server that claims to be multiplatform or heterogeneous supports these two server platforms. Much of the most important storage server software has started out on Sun Solaris first before moving to other operating systems.

Note

You can find Sun's storage home page at www.sun.com/storage/.

Sun has grown its storage offerings by building them and converting its servers into storage platforms. It has also acquired a number of companies in the storage market, including HighGround for its storage resource management software, Cobalt for its appliances, and in the summer of 2005, one of the storage industry's pioneering enterprise hardware vendors, StorageTek.

Table 19.5 provides a short list of Sun's storage hardware offerings.

Table 19.5   Sun Storage Servers

System	Features	Capacity	OS
StorEdge 9990 Array	Data center–class storage with crossbar switch	1,152 drives, to 330TB	Solaris, Tru64 Unix, HP-UX, AIX, NetWare, Red Hat Linux, SGI IRIX, Linux, Windows
StorEdge 9985 Array	Storage virtualization	72TB	Solaris 7+, Tru64 Unix, HP-UX, AIX, IRIX, Red Hat Linux, IBM zOS, Windows
StorEdge 9980 Array	High-density footprint, fault tolerant	1,024 drives, to 147TB	7+, Tru64 Unix, HP-UX, AIX, IRIX, Red Hat Linux, Windows
StorEdge 9970 Array	High-density footprint, fault tolerant	128 disks, to 17.5TB	Solaris, Tru64 UNIX, HP-UX, AIX, SGI IRIX, NetWare, Red Hat Linux, SGI IRIX, Windows

System	Features	Capacity	OS
StorEdge 6920 Array	Midrange array, heterogeneous storage virtualization	146TB (base cabinet)	Solaris 8+, Windows, AIX, HP-UX, Red Hat Linux
StorEdge 6130 Array	Midrange array, FC and SATA	112 drives, to 41.2TB	Solaris 8+, Windows, HP-UX, AIX, Linux AS/WS Enterprise Ed., SUSE Linux ES Enterprise Edition, SUSE Linux, NetWare
StorEdge 6120 Array	Midrange array, high availability	12.3TB	Solaris 8+, Windows, HP-UX, AIX, Red Hat Linux
StorEdge 3511 FC Array with SATA	Workgroup near line and secondary 2U storage array	28.8TB	Solaris 8+, Windows, Red Hat Linux, NetWare, SUSE Linux, NetWare, HP-UX, AIX
StorEdge 3510 FC Array	Workgroup 2U server with 2GB FC with 12 FC ports	3.6TB	Solaris 8+, Windows, Red Hat Linux, SUSE Linux ES, NetWare, HP-UX, AIX
StorEdge	Workgroup hot-swap RAID controller, NEBS	68.4TB	Solaris 8+, Windows, Red Hat Linux, SUSE Linux ES, NetWare, HP-UX, AIX
StorEdge 3120 SCSI Array	Workgroup 1U dense SCSI NEBS	4 drives, to greater than 1TB	Solaris 8+, Windows, Red Hat Linux, SUSE Linux ES, NetWare, HP-UX, AIX
StorEdge S1 Array	Workgroup 1U SCSI NEBS	438GB	Solaris 2.6+
StorEdge 5210 NAS	Heterogeneous client support, journaled file system, replication/mirror	6.1TB	Operating system storage optimized
StorEdge 5310 NAS	Heterogeneous client support, journaled file system, replication/mirror, archiving software, cluster capable	65TB FC or 179 SATA	Operating system storage optimized
StorEdge Open SAN Architecture	NA	Fabric boot, 2Gbps, Brocade/McData operability, failover, high-performance SAN file system	Solaris 8+, Windows, HP-UX, AIX, Red Hat Linux EE
StorEdge DAT 72 Tape Drive	Rack-mount or desktop	72GB per DAT tape	Solaris 8+, Red Hat Linux, Windows
StorEdge Desktop Tape Drive	SDLT 600 tape drive or LTO2 or LTO3	300GB for SDLT, 200GB for LTO2, or 400GB for LTO3 per tape	Solaris 8+, Red Hat Linux, Windows

Table 19.5   Continued

System	Features	Capacity	OS
StorEdge L8 Tape Autoloader	LTO2, 2U rack, 8 slot autoloader	1.6TB LTO2 or 1.28 SDLT 320	Solaris 8+, Red Hat Linux, Windows
StorEdge L100 Tape Library	Robotic library	5.0TB LTO2, 10.0TB LTO3, 3.36 SDLT 320, 6.3TB SDLT 600	Solaris 8+, Red Hat Linux, Windows
StorEdge L180 Tape Library	Robotic library	174 tapes, to 34.8TB SDLT 320	Solaris 2.6+
StorEdge L500 Tape Library	FC or SCSI, 2 to 18 drives, Web interface	395 tapes, 79TB LTO-2	Solaris 8+
StorEdge L700 Tape Library	Hot plug drives, small footprint	678 tapes, to 136TB	Solaris 2.6+
StorEdge L8500 Tape Library	Multidrive-type support, connects to libraries	Up to 6,500 tapes, to 1.3PB	Solaris 8+

Sun's StorEdge storage servers are popular with Sun's server customers but aren't as popular with organizations that have large investments in EMC, Hewlett-Packard, or other vendors' storage solutions; they are also not very popular with organizations that are trying to maintain open systems storage solutions. As shown in Table 19.5, Sun offers a wide variety of systems under the StorEdge brand, including a number of systems that are built by other vendors and relabeled by Sun. This is a very common practice in the storage industry.

A number of data management applications are bundled with Sun storage servers. Sun's software portfolio includes the following areas of technology:

- **Sun Java StorEdge**—This software includes Consolidation Suite, Continuity Suite, Content Suite, and Compliance Suite.

- **Data management**—This software includes StorEdge QFS, StorEdge SAM-FS, and the optional VERITAS Storage Foundation, File System, and Volume Management programs.

- **Data protection**—This software includes StorEdge Availability Suite, StorEdge Enterprise Backup, StorEdge Data Snapshot, StorEdge Data Mirror, StorEdge Data Replication, and StorEdge Archiving, as well as the optional VERITAS NetBackup and NetBackup Enterprise Server.

- **Storage management**—This software includes StorEdge Enterprise Storage Manager, StorEdge Traffic Manager, Storage Automatic Diagnostic Environment, and StorEdge Pool Manager Software.

Sun Clusters

Sun Cluster is an integrated hardware/software platform that can cluster up to 16 nodes of Sun servers, running either on the SPARC or x86 platform. Sun Cluster 3.1, which is the latest version of the software, runs on top of the Solaris operating system and is sold as a complete solution with a set of interconnect technologies, storage, and Sun services to keep the whole thing running. Cluster 3.1 uses the Solaris IP Multipathing (iPMP) software, which allows servers to be multihomed and support multiple network interfaces, to improve I/O and overall performance.

Sun Cluster 3 supports the dynamic reconfiguration of cluster hardware, including the addition or removal of CPUs, memory, I/O boards, and other devices. Thus you can pull processor boards out of a Sun server and replace them with faster units without having to bring down either the server or the cluster. Sun calls its on-the-fly reconfiguration DR; the DR software intervenes when it detects a problem with the addition or removal of devices.

Sun clusters can add servers in up to 16 nodes, which means it's possible to build mainframe-class applications by using Sun Cluster 3.1. Some very large databases have been built on this platform, running Oracle9i RAC (Real Application Cluster).

Sun's cluster management application software is called SunPlex Manager, and it manages a cluster as if it were a single system. In the Sun Management Center, Solaris's graphical management utility software, a Sun Cluster module can detect the condition of elements of Sun Cluster through Simple Network Management Protocol (SNMP) traps, using a set of SNMP agents. There are also third-party SNMP agents and utilities that you can use to monitor and manage Sun Cluster.

Sun's servers are packaged along with a set of applications as a platform called the Sun Java Enterprise System, which comes with the following:

- Webservers/web services
- Application servers, including calendaring
- Network Identity (what Sun calls an access and authentication service)
- Communications, messaging, and collaboration services
- Portal building (a Web interface to multiple services)
- Security services
- Directory services
- Availability services

The Java Enterprise System can be used on nonclustered versions of Sun servers, but it you build these applications on a cluster, you can scale them higher and give them greater fault tolerance. In that regard, Sun Cluster 3.1 is the basis for a long-distance connectivity solution that Sun sells, called the Sun Enterprise Continuity Solution. This solution allows nodes in Sun Cluster to be located as far away as 200km. So when a cluster node in a data center goes offline, the cluster can fail over to a remote node.

In addition, Sun has a web service called the Sun Cluster Global Network Service that allows you to build an application on top of a Sun cluster, distribute that application, and then use this free service to load balance your application and make it available. The use of the Sun Cluster Global Network Service means that even if your cluster nodes are geographically separate, you don't need to worry about establishing a load-balancing service and making it fault tolerant because Sun's service is available over the Web. Other consolidated services include Global Network Service, Global Devices, and Global File Services; all the "globals" simply translates into a unified management view of these assets within the cluster management software. You can also use the UFS or the VERITAS VxFS as your cluster file system in place of Global File Service.

Sun Custer 3 technology has some unique features. The Sun cluster can inventory memory, and with remote shared memory (RSM), it can let an application use fast-interconnect technology to directly access memory directly in the cluster, even if the cluster nodes are disbursed. RSM uses the Scalable Coherent Interconnect (SCI-PCI) technology to bypass transport over Ethernet. RSM is useful in building high-performance database applications. Another feature, called Application Traffic Striping, allows IP traffic to be striped across multiple interconnects.

NEBS-Certified Servers

The Telcordia (formerly Belcore) Network Equipment–Building System (NEBS) is a telecommunications standard that defines what equipment can be used in a telecommunications network as part of an ILEC or Regional Bell Operating Company (RBOC) central office. The standard has been around since the 1970s and is used as a design goal by server vendors wishing to sell into this very large marketplace. Verizon, Qwest, SBC, and AT&T all ascribe to this standard, which is driven by Telcordia's software, used in both wired and wireless networks. Certification involves submission of a sample of a company's server product to a certification agency.

Sun makes a line of servers that network equipment providers use for their central office installations. That line of equipment runs the gamut from 1U blade servers through the 12U Netra 1280 server. Among the recommended uses are application servers, control points, gateways, location registers, network management platforms, streaming media servers, switching, voice and VoIP, and webservers and caching. For a table that lists the current generation of Sun NEBS-compliant servers and their intended uses, go to www.sun.com/servers/index.jsp?cat=Netra%20Carrier%20Grade%20Systems&tab=3.

The Solaris Operating System

The Solaris operating system for the SPARC platform was Sun's only offering for much of its early history. Sun started offering an x86 or Intel version of its Solaris operating system, but there was talk before Solaris 9 was released in May 2002 about phasing out the Intel version of Solaris. The popularization of Linux and the success of Linux servers, mainly at the expense of Sun's server line, have influenced Sun to continue developing Solaris on Intel as well as release a number of Intel architecture servers based on the AMD Opteron CPUs discussed earlier in this chapter.

Note

The Solaris operating system version has a somewhat convoluted relationship to the Sun OS version. To convert the Solaris version number to the Sun operating system number, you add to it the prefix Sun OS 5. Thus Solaris 8 is Sun OS 5.8 and Solaris 10 is Sun OS 5.10. Most people now simply refer to the Solaris version as the current OS name.

The Solaris operating system is sometimes referred to as the Solaris operating environment, particularly when Solaris is running applications on Sun equipment. Although the Intel architecture comes with the same set of management tools and interface as the SPARC platform, many features are available on UltraSPARC Solaris systems that aren't found on the Solaris-on-Intel version. Although Sun ported Solaris 2.5.1 to PowerPC, that port died a fast death in the marketplace.

Today Solaris 10 runs on the following architectures:

- SPARC
- x86
- x86-64

With Solaris 10's release in February 2005, Sun has paid a lot of attention to architecting the operating system so that it is optimized for 64-bit computing on Intel architecture systems. At this point in the company's development, it appears that Sun is equally committed to Solaris on SPARC and on Intel.

Solaris is available for free download from Sun's site, at www.sun.com/software/solaris/get.jsp. Restrictions on the use of downloaded copies of Solaris change from time to time, but basically, if you aren't using Solaris for commercial use, you can acquire a free license to run the software. For current license requirements under the Common Development and Distribution License, see www.openso-laris.org. Sun has a version of Solaris called OpenSolaris that is based on Solaris 10 and has some built-in restrictions that allow for open source development work.

The original Solaris graphical interface was based on OpenWindows, and many of Sun's applications still share that origin. OpenWindows is built as a graphical front end to the X Window System. Starting with Solaris 2.6, Sun made the Common Desktop Environment (CDE), a Motif variant, its default GUI. The current default interface in Solaris 10 is called the Java Desktop System (JDS), which is based on the GNOME software project. Figure 19.1 shows the CDE interface of Solaris 2.6 through Solaris 9, and Figure 19.2 shows the JDS interface.

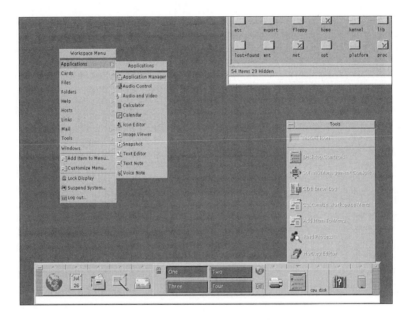

Figure 19.1   The CDE is the GUI in Solaris 2.6 through Solaris 9.

Solaris is unique among network operating systems that you've read about in this book in that it pro-vides the best support for Java applications, as well as probably the best-supported version of UNIX, running on the broadest range of equipment. Sun Java System Directory Server, Sun Java System Application Server, and Sun Java System Message Queue are server technologies that run on top of the Solaris operating system. In the Solaris 10 distribution, Sun offers almost 200 free or open source pro-grams compiled to run on Solaris. Notable among them are the following:

- Apache, Tomcat, and Zebra network servers and webservers
- Bison, Perl, Python, and GCC (GNU Compiler Collection) programming tools
- The GNOME GUI, Mozilla browsers, and Evolution desktop usability software
- IP Filter, TCP wrappers, and secure shell (SSH) utilities

These applications are found on the Solaris Software Companion CD-ROM.

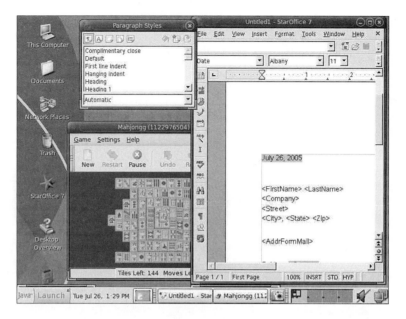

Figure 19.2 The current desktop of choice in Solaris 10 is the JDS, a variant of GNOME.

PC NetLink Integration Software

Solaris PC NetLink software is interoperability software that allows a Solaris system to serve the function of a Windows server in a Windows-based domain but without the added cost of having to obtain Windows client access licenses (CALs). The software is based on AT&T Advanced Server for UNIX. With NetLink, it is possible to have a Solaris system participate in Windows Active Directory services, Windows logons, and as a Windows file and print server. From a client standpoint, and particularly a Windows client standpoint, Sun Solaris systems running PC NetLink appear in a Windows network as any Windows server would appear.

A PC that runs PC NetLink can do the following:

- Perform the duties of a backup domain controller (but not a domain controller in a native Active Directory domain)
- Act as a SAM/SID security/authentication server
- Act as a file and print server for the NTFS file system
- Act as a network browser
- Use NetBIOS and WINS naming services

Solaris systems can support a full range of Windows clients, but they only replicate the capabilities of a Windows NT 4.0 server by running the network services shown in this list. Figure 19.3 shows how the PC NetLink services are layered on top of the Solaris operating system. On a Sun Fire 15K server running PC NetLink, Sun has demonstrated more than 20,000 concurrent Windows connections.

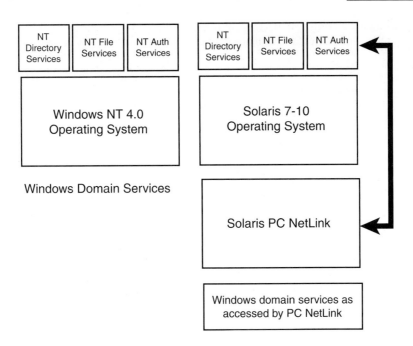

Figure 19.3   PC NetLink software runs Windows network services on top of the Solaris operating system.

Reliability and Scalability

When you scale systems larger, your risks of failure grow simply because the numbers of components are increased. These two trends work at cross-purposes. You can scale your systems and maintain reliability by duplicating components, which greatly improves your fault tolerance—but often at a high price. Who wants to pay twice the cost of a system just to ensure that the system will stay up and running? Some highly fault-tolerant systems do duplicate all components, but they tend to be higher-end systems.

Another approach to improving reliability while you scale your systems is to abstract your physical resources into logical units so that if a physical asset such as a processor or disk fails, the system simply stops asking it to participate in the service being provided. As enterprises continue to build larger systems, often from small building blocks such as blades, this approach offers many benefits. Chapter 11, "Disk Subsystems," describes how RAID can abstract disk assets into volumes and protect the data of a group of disks by writing redundant information. With servers, you can also abstract your servers into a logical pool of resources, which is the essence of Sun's vision of server virtualization.

Server virtualization offers three benefits:

- **Server resource optimization**—When an application demands more processing resources, you can add those resources to the container.
- **Fault isolation**—When a server or processor fails, it is removed from the container.
- **Security isolation**—Because a container is an operating system object, you can apply security constraints to it, thereby restricting or allowing access to users and groups, as required.

Sun introduced DSD in 1996. When you define a domain in DSD, each domain runs an instance of Sun Solaris. When an application fails or an error occurs in one instance of the domain, the other domain continues to operate, unaffected. Unlike what was done in mainframe technology, DSD can be dynamically reapportioned. If a domain requires more resources, those resources can be reallocated.

DSD runs multiple instances of the Sun Solaris operating environment (but not the Sun OS), which is a waste of system resources. The next step in server virtualization is to abstract resources under a single instance of Solaris. That's what SC does. Figure 19.4 shows a schematic of these two different virtualization schemes.

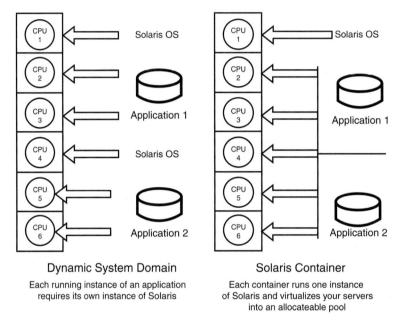

Dynamic System Domain
Each running instance of an application
requires its own instance of Solaris

Solaris Container
Each container runs one instance
of Solaris and virtualizes your servers
into an allocateable pool

Figure 19.4   DSD and SC are logical entities that allow you to manage system resources dynamically, reconfiguring them as the servers are running.

SC, formerly called N1 Grid Containers, allocates processor resources to applications, creating a logical unit called a *container*. Just as you can concatenate volumes into a single volume, with Solaris containers, you can add and remove processors or entire servers from the container that is used to service an application. Essentially, you use software to create hardware resource boundaries that you can then flexibly apply to your processing needs. You can even manage your software applications running under one instance of Solaris by using a Solaris container, and each container runs in isolation from the other. SC is available to software developers to incorporate and manage within their products.

Solaris Management Tools

Solaris ships with a number of management tools that you can use to modify local services as well as remote ones. The sections that follow describe the Solaris Management Console, SyMON, and SunVTS—three of the key tools that let you change system and security settings, monitor performance and tune your server, and run diagnostic tests to determine whether your hardware will allow

Solaris to implement its fault tolerance features. The sections that follow also include a discussion of the Solstice AdminSuite tool, as well as the Sun Enterprise Backup tool and Java Web Start.

Keep in mind that all these graphical tools incorporate commands that you can issue at the command-line interface (CLI). In some instances, the commands contain switches and preferences that aren't expressed in the user interface, making their specification from the CLI more powerful than what you see in the GUI. You might want to consult the man files when working with some of the Solaris management commands to learn their full syntax.

Several tools aren't covered in the sections below but are rather useful:

- **Solaris Patch Manager**—This tool allows you to update Solaris, applying patches as needed or when you want to back out of a patch by removing it.

- **Solaris Print Manager**—This graphical tool allows you to add printers and printer drivers and to manage your printers.

- `admintool`—This tool, for managing users and groups as well as other security features, has been phased out.

- **Solaris Product Registry**—This tool records installed products.

To get more information about Solaris' management tools, go to the jump page at http://docs.sun.com/app/docs/doc/817-1985/6mhm8o5j3?a=view.

The Solaris Management Console

Solaris 7 came with three management tools—admintool, Solstice AdminSuite, and Solaris Management Tools—all of which were supported in Solaris 8. Sun began phasing out these tools in Solaris 9, which supported only admintool and Solaris Management Tools 2.1. Solaris 10, in contrast, continues support for only Solaris Management Tools 2.1.

The key management tool within Solaris 10 is the Sun Management Center (SMC) version 3.5, Update 1. This software is installed as part of the base Solaris installation, but you can add additional modules for added functionality. Over the past couple versions of Solaris, more and more of Solaris's configuration tools have been integrated into the SMC GUI tool, which Sun refers to as an "element management system." From within the SMC, you can monitor both SPARC and x86 Solaris and Linux systems and applications. From the console you can manage a network of servers by using the Java application or from within a standard web browser. Figure 19.5 shows the Solaris 10 SMC.

You can download the SMC, which also comes bundled in the Solaris Media Kit, from Sun's website, at www.sun.com/software/solaris/sunmanagementcenter/get.xml. Although you can install and use the SMC as is, commercial use of this software requires a server license. To view and purchase current licenses for the SMC, go to http://store.sun.com/CMTemplate/CEServlet?process=SunStore&cmdViewProduct_CP&catid=95175.

The SMC consolidates several functions that you find in various tools in Windows Server: performance management, event logging and reporting, and system diagnostics. You can set up automated alarms based on your defined system thresholds, perform scripts from within the console, and run diagnostics on hardware. Like the Windows Microsoft Management Console (MMC), the SMC is both extensible with third-party applications and add-on modules and can be customized to give a defined view of your resources. One of the neatest features is the SMC's ability to give you system information by letting you working with a realistic physical view of your Sun server.

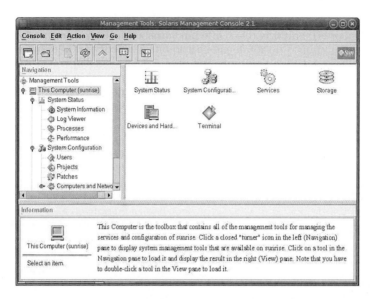

Figure 19.5 The SMC provides a detailed view and system management function for Solaris and Linux.

These are the basic functions of the SMC:

- Installation GUI wizard, patch manager, and deployment system
- Hardware discovery through SMNP
- Web console and custom console views
- Physical view of your server and its components, illustrating current conditions
- Event monitoring and alarms
- Configurable agents
- Direct access to Solaris's CLI

Additional management tools integrate into the Sun Management Center but aren't part of the standard Solaris installation and must be installed as special add-on packages:

- **Advanced System Monitoring**—This tool is part of a value pack and adds some advanced kernel monitoring features, as well as a Solaris health monitoring module, as well as a set of hardware tests called the Hardware Diagnostic Suite.

- **Performance Reporting Manager**—The Performance Reporting Manager adds event counters and logging capabilities to Sun servers. You can use this tool to help perform baseline studies, discover and map network assets through SNMP, do capacity planning, and chart current resource consumption.

- **Service Availability Manager**—You can use this module to monitor network services such as HTTP, FTP directories, and mail and calendar services.

- **Solaris Container Manager**—This tool allows you to configure and manage Solaris containers across your network.

- **System Reliability Manager**—Among the functions that this tool provides are patch (upgrade) management, script launching, file watch capabilities, and an OS crash dump analyzer.

These tools require the following:

- A *server layer* that runs on Solaris 8 and later.

- An *agent layer* that run on Solaris 2.6 and later, Red Hat Linux AS/ES/WS, and SUSE Linux ES. You need to install the Sun Management Center Agent for Linux 1.0 to bring information from Linux systems into the SMC.

- A *console layer* that can run on Solaris 2.6 and later (SPARC), Solaris 9 and later (x86), and Windows XP/2000/NT/98.

For more detailed information on these value pack add-on SMC modules, go to www.sun.com/software/solaris/sunmanagementcenter/index.xml.

SyMON

Sun SyMON is an open system monitoring and management tool based on Java and SNMP. The system monitor utility is a diagnostic tool that is used to provide detailed information about the configuration of and components contained within a Sun server. It is purchased as a standalone product from Sun, unlike some of the built-in commands, such as sar, that are used for performance testing. SyMON is a much more capable application than the built-in command-line tools used for performance testing and event logging.

Among SyMON's capabilities are the following:

- **Operating system management**—You can use SyMON to monitor resources, loads, network statistics, and disk usage.

- **System management**—You can use SyMON to monitor the condition of your component boards, power supplies, disks, and any other hardware that provides SNMP traps that can be monitored.

- **Application management**—You can set up SyMON to monitor the performance of your server's applications in real-time, detecting events, logging security, and so forth.

- **Scalability**—You can use SyMON to view the performance of systems in several domains in your enterprise. Thus you can apply SyMON to determine whether your systems and the software that is running on them have been configured correctly and respond to user requests normally.

SyMON is a Motif GUI application that can be run on a workstation but that can monitor one server at a time. The SyMON server runs on the monitored server, but SyMON agents can be distributed across multiple systems or can monitor different components on the same system. Figure 19.6 shows the components of SyMON's architecture. Not all systems are supported, however. Systems on which you can use SyMON are UltraSPARC systems, Ultra 1 and Ultra 2 workstations, and enterprise servers.

SyMON collects data based on the events that have occurred on that server. The results are displayed in a hierarchical browser view. SyMON allows the user to set the operational limits of the server and to issue an alarm when that server starts to operates beyond those limits. Errors can include temperature variations, detection of high rates of memory or disk errors, and so forth. The alerts you define are rule based and can pass SNMP traps along to other network management packages. The color graphical display lets you view a strip chart of the performance over a couple hours or as a graphed display. There is also an event log viewer within this utility. One really cool feature of SyMON is its ability to display a physical view of your server with a photo-realistic presentation of the server's front, side, and back views. Clicking a component displays detailed information about the condition of that component, as monitored by SyMON's agents.

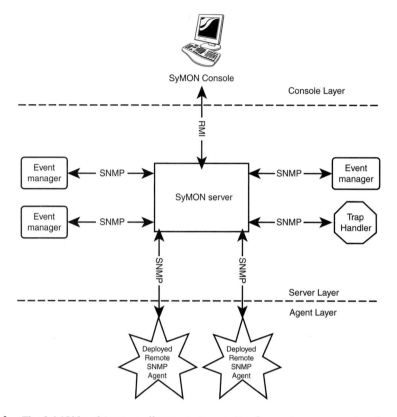

Figure 19.6 The SyMON architecture allows you to monitor Sun systems on a network.

SyMON is a primary tool for not only performance monitoring but system tuning as well. You can use SyMON to determine the result of making changes to software, the operating system, hardware, and other factors. It's possible to diagnose system bottlenecks by using SyMON to compare the differences in several of the server subsystems while you change one subsystem's configuration at a time. You can also use SyMON to create a system benchmark by analyzing performance over time.

SyMON is a performance monitoring tool, similar in its use to Hewlett-Packard's GlancePlus or to a more developed version of the Windows Performance Monitor utility such as the one Microsoft includes with SMS Server. Other tools in this area include Hewlett-Packard's MeasureWare and ViewPoint by Datametrics, which can be used on UNIX-based systems.

SunVTS

The Sun Validation Test Suite (SunVTS) is a series of tests used to determine whether hardware running on Sun servers operates correctly. OEMs, service providers, engineers, and other quality assurance personnel use it to determine whether hardware reacts correctly to system calls, whether software drivers' communication with hardware performs correctly, and whether hardware can be "failed" correctly. SunVTS is used for hardware validation as well as for verifying whether a repair to a Sun server was performed correctly. Sun gives the SunVTS test suite to people who purchase SPARC motherboards or CPUs in order to test their products.

You can use SunVTS in three different modes:

- **Connectivity mode**—In this test mode, the server is tested for its availability and connectivity while running under load. SunVTS uses a fast testing scheme that provides a low risk for disruption of the service.

- **Online mode**—In this set of tests, a more complete list of capabilities is tested than with the connectivity suite. This test mode is meant to test the systems while operational but to leave running applications on the system unimpeded.

- **Offline mode**—In the offline mode, the system's applications are shut down, and any test in SunVTS may be used to test the system.

SunVTS also simulates hardware faults and defects that components might encounter, and therefore it tests whether a component is suitable in a fault-tolerant system. You can run SunVTS within an OPEN LOOK or CDE interface or from a terminal session. It provides support for Solaris 2.5 and greater. To download the SunVTS software, toolkit, and documentation for various versions of the Solaris operating system, go to www.sun.com/oem/products/vts/index.html#vtsdesc.

Solstice AdminSuite

Solstice AdminSuite is an X Window System GUI that serves as a central management console for a number of central system management functions.

To open Solstice AdminSuite you can either open a terminal session on a local system and enter $ `solstice &` or enter $ `solstice -display` on a remote system. In either case, the Solstice Launcher is displayed. To open one of the management tools, you double-click the icon in the Solstice Launcher window. The different AdminSuite tools allow you to use the following:

- **Group Manager**—To create, edit, and delete UNIX groups
- **User Manager**—To create, edit, and delete user accounts
- **Printer Manager**—To add printer software and drivers for print servers and clients
- **Database Manager**—To edit your system's database files, including your `hosts` file, `aliases`, and others
- **Storage Manager**—To create and manage disk slices and `fdisk` partitions (using Disk Manager); works with file systems (using File System Manager)
- **Host Manager**—To view server information; manage servers and diskless and dataless clients; standalone servers; as well as AutoClient
- **Serial Port Manager**—To install and manager serial port software used by terminals and modems

Host Manager plays a central role in determining your Sun server's identification on the network. For one thing, it is where you select which name service your system will use. To select a name service, do the following:

1. Start Solstice Launcher.
2. Double-click the Host Manager icon.
3. Select Name Service and then either NIS+, NIS, or None. (When you select None, your system uses the `/etc` files on the local system to determine which name service is used.)
4. Enter the name of the domain in the Domain text box.
5. Click OK or press Enter.

AdminSuite was a primary management tool for Solaris 7, and less so for Solaris 8. For Solaris 9 and 10, you should use Solaris Print Manager for managing printers, Solaris Patch Manager for installing upgrades, and the SMC for most other functions.

Volume Manager

A volume manager is a software utility that creates disk structures and logical volumes from physical disks. Solaris has shipped with a volume manager since version 7, although the software has been integrated into the Solstice Storage Manger GUI. Solaris Volume Manager (SVM) is now known as the Solstice DiskSuite. You can administer SVM from within the SMC in the Enhanced Storage tool. As shown in Figure 19.7, the Enhanced Storage tool shows you your volumes, hot spaces, state database replicas, and other storage components. This tool also provides a means of modifying your volumes through a set of wizards. The second method for modifying volumes in Solaris is through the extensive command set at the CLI.

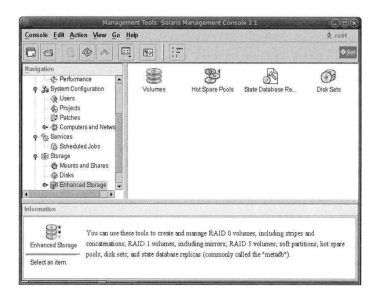

Figure 19.7   The SVM in the Enhanced Storage tool of the SMC.

To open the SVM GUI, do the following:

  1. At the command prompt in a terminal window, enter % /usr/sbin/smc.

  2. Double-click Storage This Computer in the Navigation pane.

  3. Double-click the Storage icon in the Navigation pane and then double-click the Enhanced Storage icon, which loads SVM (refer to Figure 19.7).

  4. If you are asked to log in to the utility, either log in with root privileges or log in as a user with a storage modification role.

  5. Double-click the storage volume you want to manage.

Different volume managers offer different capabilities, but the intent of all volume managers is to provide a means to manage your disk space flexibly, even when you have large amounts of disk space and multiple volumes.

DiskSuite 4.2.1 is capable of the following:

- Creating logical volumes of various sizes, adjusting their sizes, and concatenating (appending) volumes.
- Performance enhancement through disk striping.
- Data protection, using mirroring (RAID 1) and striping with redundancy (RAID 5). You can use DiskSuite to replicate a failed slice (partition).
- Creating file systems and modifying their properties.
- Enabling file system logging.
- Administering SPARC storage arrays. By using DiskSuite's GUI, you can start and stop entire trays of disks in an array and modify volumes created in NVRAM.
- Monitoring and tuning your volumes, as well as using the DiskSuite SNMP capabilities to integrate alerts using the SunNet Manager.

Not only can you manage the volume manager from within the GUI, but you can manage it with a large number of CLI commands.

The Sun Volume Manager was authored in part of VERITAS and is contained in VxM, a subset of the VERITAS Volume Manager for Sun Solaris. VERITAS's VxM became part of the VERITAS Foundation Suite, which was one of the most popular applications sold for Sun Solaris. VxM contains capabilities that weren't part of the original Sun volume manager. Over time, Sun has improved its version of the volume manager, especially for its enterprise server offerings. VERITAS (which is now part of the Symantec empire) continues to sell the Foundation Suite at www.veritas.com/Products/www?c=product&refId=203.

The Foundation Suite also includes the VERITAS File System, which is an alternative to Sun's UFS file system. The VERITAS Storage Foundation, which is a somewhat different bundling of these software packages, allows an administrator to move data between storage arrays, move management of the volumes between different operating systems, and provide advanced multipathing capabilities so that I/O can be managed across multiple network paths. Another part of VERITAS's software portfolio in the storage area is a series of replication products that allow data to be moved to other locations to increase availability and improve fault tolerance.

Prior to the release of Windows Server 2000, Sun's Volume Manager and, by extension, VERITAS's Foundation Suite, gave the Sun server platform an enormous advantage over Windows servers. Microsoft, working with VERITAS, improved the Windows volume manager, incorporating a lot of VERITAS's features into its bundled utility. The VERITAS Volume Manager and other VERITAS products became available for Windows with Windows 2000 Server and narrowed (and perhaps eliminated) the gap between Sun servers and Windows server.

Sun Enterprise Backup

The Sun StorEdge Enterprise Backup software is an integrated software application that can back up data from large storage servers in heterogeneous operating system environments onto tape drives and disk-based backup systems. This software works with SAN environments, network attached storage (NAS), RAID arrays, tape libraries, silos, and even JBODs (just a bunch of disks).

Formerly called Solstice Backup, Sun Enterprise Backup offers the following capabilities:

- **Snapshots**—A snapshot is a point-in-time copy of the contents of a drive. Snapshots differ from backups in that only changes to the drive content since the last snapshot are recorded. A log of the contents and changes allows the system to reconstruct the backup's condition at any point in time that you specify. Thus you can choose to restore a snapshot at any time you had one run, and the system doesn't require that the full disk contents be backed up.

- **Advanced indexing architecture**—You can create a single metadata index that spans different backup systems.

- **LAN-free and serverless backup capability**—In LAN-free and serverless backup, a backup job is specified, and the backup is performed as a bit-level, block-oriented backup over a dedicated FC, SCSI, or SAN connection, without having data transported over the network.

- **Network Data Management Protocol (NDMP) support**—This is an open backup standard that is administered by SNIA (see www.ndmp.org/info/faq.shtml) and was originally developed by Network Appliances for direct tape backup.

- **Dynamic tape drive sharing**—This feature allows different storage nodes to be shared and managed on a SAN from within the software in order to use the tape drives more effectively.

- **Automated media management**—This feature supports autochangers, in which tapes are switched in and out of the tape reader, as well as supports for silos. From within the software you can specify how media is moved, specify when to use a cleaning cartridge, read an electronically labeled or bar-coded tape cases, and verify that the media is in good working order.

- **High-speed parallel backups**—In a high-speed parallel backup, the multiple clients are backed up to storage devices concurrently.

As in other enterprise backup solutions, there's direct control from within StorEdge Enterprise Backup over tape drives and robotic tape libraries. As discussed earlier in this chapter, Sun offers a number of these systems for sale under the StorEdge brand, but it also supports other vendors' devices as well.

A most important part of enterprise backup solutions is the ability to back up enterprise applications, such as Oracle, Microsoft SQL Server, IBM DB2, IBM Informix, Sybase, Microsoft Exchange, IBM Lotus Notes/Domino, and SAP while they are operating, also called *hot backup*. Because many of these products run on Sun clusters, this backup software is also cluster aware and capable of backing up software running on a cluster.

Java Web Start

Java Web Start (see http://java.sun.com/products/javawebstart/) is a framework that lets developers deploy Java 2 applications from within a browser interface. When an application is launched through Web Start, it offers the same desktop and interface features that a standard application running on Solaris offers. From a user's point of view, the spreadsheet or video windows in Web Start have the same characteristics as those in any other application. Web Start also helps administrators because it offers a new way to install and update applications on client systems. Java Web Start isn't a distribution system, as is Marimba or any other push application; it is a Java 2 *application launcher*. Note that Web Start does not work with older versions of Java such as version 1.1.

You get Java Web Start as part of the Java Runtime Environment (JRE; see http://java.sun.com/j2se/desktopjava/jre/index.jsp) or as part of the download of J2SE (Java 2, Standard Edition) 5.0 (see http://java.sun.com/j2se/1.5.0/download.jsp). You can also utilize Web Start applications by installing a plug-in into your browser. You run into Java Web Start in a number of places. Some web pages may request that you install a plug-in to make their applications work, and you may see Java Web Start show up when you try to install a program. The Solaris installation routine can include opening Web Start to allow you to install additional applications when your OS has been loaded.

When you launch a program with Java Web Start, the program downloads resources and caches them on your local drive. When all applications run, they use the resource in the local cache rather than download the components they need from the Internet. In addition, the program provides a transparent transport mechanism as well as a secure execution facility. When a software update is detected, Java Web Start can initiate the required download and then update the application.

What makes Web Start so useful is that it provides an OS-independent development environment that can be used to deploy applications directly from the web. Users can open any web browser that understands Java through the Java Runtime Environment and then launch applications from within that application. A user navigating to a particular web page launches the application, and the application runs on the user's system. Because the application is stored elsewhere on the web, the version of the application being used is always the most current one.

A Windows user would download Java Web Start and then click the icon for that application on his or her desktop to launch the Application Manager utility, which has a list of the applications downloaded and used and which serves as an application launcher. Versions of Windows that support Web Start include Windows 95/NT/2000/XP, as well as Linux/i486, and Solaris (SPARC and x86). Apple supplies a version of Java Web Start with Macintosh OS X. The intent of Web Start is to provide an OS-independent application platform for all types of clients.

A Java Web Start application server needs only a standard webserver to be hosted, and it communicates by using the standard HTTP protocol. The launching technology is called the Java Network Launching Protocol (JNLP), and it has been standardized and added to the Java standard. Sun encourages developers to build Web Start–compliant applications using JNLP and its API. For information about third-party tools, go to http://java.sun.com/aboutJava/communityprocess/jsr/jsr_056_jnlp/html.

Hardware Compatibility with Server Platforms

Sun does not certify SPARC-based systems to run the Solaris OS. However, in order to work with vendors in open systems, the company does maintain a certification scheme as well as a compatibility list for both x86 and x86-64 systems.

Sun maintains a registration program for Solaris hardware compatibility that has three levels:

- Sun Certified and listed on the Solaris Hardware Compatibility List (HCL; see www.sun.com/bigadmin/hcl/).
- Test Suite Certified, where the hardware has been tested using the Hardware Certification Test Suite (HCTS). This testing is performed by a Sun partner or the vendor itself. You can download the HCTS at www.sun.com/bigadmin/hcl/hcts/hcts.html.
- A "Reported to Work" list of components from the Sun Software Express program for Solaris.

The Solaris HCL is a searchable listing, and Sun has a mechanism by which you can submit an entire system for verification as well as submit a component to the HCL team. A separate compatibility list for the JDS is also maintained for JDS Release 2 and Release 3.

Sun also runs a certification program for independent hardware vendors; in this program, a vendor's systems are certified to run the Solaris OS on x86 platforms. Two levels of certification are offered: Level 1 and Level 2 certification. Each has different test suite diagnostics that it must satisfy. To see what these levels entail, go to www.sun.com/bigadmin/hcl/hcts/.

The BigAdmin System Administration Portal

BigAdmin is Sun's resource and community website for Solaris administrators. During the installation of earlier versions of Solaris, the installer sees a browser with BigAdmin as its home page while installation proceeds. BigAdmin's Web Start wizards let you install software on your system during your installation or at a later time.

To learn more about Solaris or to get help from expert users, you should make BigAdmin one of your first visits. You can find BigAdmin, shown in Figure 19.8, at www.sun.com/bigadmin/.

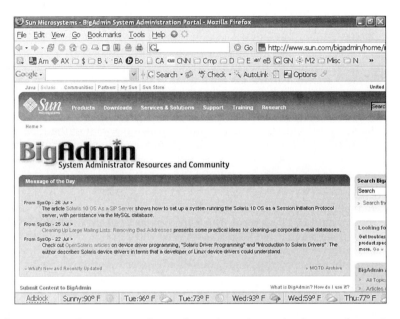

Figure 19.8   Sun's BigAdmin site is replete within information on hardware and on software and configuration.

Among BigAdmin's offerings are links to discussion and newsgroups, documentation, lists of FAQs, information about current patches, freeware and shareware, additional Sun software packages, and service and training.

CHAPTER 20

Building, Upgrading, and Deploying Servers

Now that you've had a chance to explore many of the subsystems of modern servers—including processors, motherboards, buses, and network interfaces—it's time to get your server(s) deployed. With what you have learned already, it should be possible to make a good selection of server type. However, knowing what server you want and choosing the right server for the job at hand is something of an art form. That selection entails choosing a server that allows you to service the number of clients you have, not way too many and certainly not too few—something that is often referred to as *right sizing* or *capacity planning*. This chapter describes some of the considerations involved in trying to size your systems correctly, as well as some of the tools available to help.

When you select a server to deploy, you essentially choose a platform to build on. It's quite possible that you will buy a specialized server designed for a purpose such as a network attached storage (NAS), deploy that server, and then never change that server's hardware or base network operating system in any significant way.

You might buy a server with a contract, and in this case, whenever something goes wrong or you need to beef up the system, your value-added reseller (VAR) sends over Vinny, who keeps your server in line or gives it a shot of what it needs.

It's just as common to deploy a general-purpose server and evolve that system over time. If you go this route, you need to look at your deployment with an eye to the future. For a general-purpose server—or any other server—you need an upgrade path if you intend to keep that server in service for an extended period. The period that a server can be in service translates directly to your organization's return on investment and to its profit. So there is a strong incentive to make some good choices that will give your server added life. This topic is discussed further in this chapter.

In the past, few people built their own servers. Most chose to purchase a server from a large original equipment manufacturer (OEM) or from a company that built no-named servers, called *white boxes*. As more and more server technologies have become mainstream, performance desktop computers have begun to feature many of the same technologies in their builds that servers traditionally had. It has become much easier for a person with basic computer-building skills to construct a custom-built server from standardized parts. You might not want to build an enterprise-class eight-way SMP system from scratch, but a dual- or even a quad-processor system is within the capabilities of most people who read books like this one.

To successfully build a server, you need to create balance between your expectations of the server's purpose and the components necessary to achieve that purpose. You shouldn't expect to save money by choosing to build your own server. The primary benefits of building your own server don't lie in cost, but rather in the customization and upgrade potential of a home-built server, as well as the ability to service it yourself. We'll describe some of the pluses and minuses of building a server and whether you should attempt to build your own.

Finally, you need to take into account a number of other considerations when you deploy a server. Servers have different licensing requirements from desktop computers, as do the applications running on them. You need to know whether your quad processor needs one, two, or even four operating system licenses. At the moment, it appears that vendors are only requiring that a dual-core processor have only a single license for software and hardware. Some software products have licenses that don't use processor counts at all; instead, their licenses are based on the number of connections or some other factors. Some licenses can be mixed and matched. Licenses are a recurring nightmare for any but the smallest of shops. You are definitely not in Kansas anymore! This chapter addresses how you can comply with license terms and discusses management software to help you with all this complexity.

Purchasing Considerations

To build or buy a new server? That is the question. As with all other IT decisions, there are pluses and minuses to doing either. If you can build a PC, you can build a server. The *Upgrading and Repairing PCs* series from Que Publishing offers just about all the know-how you need to build a system, and this chapter does not seek to replicate its content. However, simply because you can do something doesn't necessarily mean you should. So let's look a little more closely at the considerations related to building and buying.

Reasons to Buy from First-Tier OEMs

Buying a server from a first-tier vendor such as Hewlett-Packard, IBM, Dell, or some other large vendor is a straightforward proposition. Your entry costs into the system are known, as are your potential support costs. Chances are that buying a server from a large OEM is going to be your least expensive solution; the companies' high volume assures that.

You can also be sure that the company will keep you up-to-date with new BIOS and drivers as soon as they become available. Also, because these types of companies build a lot of the same models of servers, they will undoubtedly have experienced any problem you may encounter in your server's lifetime. Large vendors reduce the number of variables by narrowing the range of options to the ones they test extensively. It's difficult (but not impossible) these days to buy a server from a large vendor and have a truly miserable experience. However, there are only a limited number of options and customizations you can get from large OEMs, unless you have a very large order that is serviced either by the company's IT services branch or by some affiliated large VAR.

Because many people feel that server models from large OEMs are a safe choice, resale value of these systems tends to be higher than for systems that are custom built. Resale value on any computer system should not be a first priority in your selection, however, because the values drop quite significantly rather quickly.

Many people buy from first-tier vendors because they believe that these companies are going to be in business forever, although these days you never know. Still, there are good margins in servers relative to the PC industry, so it's an almost certain bet that some large company will service your specific model come what may.

When you buy a server from a large vendor, not all aspects of the transaction are good. Servers from first-tier vendors tend to use proprietary cases and motherboards, and they may require that you buy very specific kinds of memory that aren't widely available and are therefore quite expensive. This effectively locks you into the hardware you have purchased. As the server ages, you may find that upgrades and service contracts purchased from these types of OEMs can be expensive. This type of "lock-in" is a standard practice for large OEMs.

Reasons to Build

Compared to buying a server, when you build your own, you have more control over the components and their manufacturers, and you can choose your own server standards. You can find a wide range of server motherboards on the market to choose from, in a variety of form factors: BTX and ATX in both standard and extended form factors, low-profile boards for 1U servers, and perhaps, in time, micro boards. (Chapter 4, "Server Motherboards and BIOS," covers server motherboards in more detail.)

Until recently, building a server yourself meant that you were limited to dual-processor systems. However, major server motherboard vendors such as SuperMicro and Tyan now offer a variety of four-way motherboards using Intel Xeon MP processors. Tyan also offers four-way and eight-way motherboards that support AMD Opteron 8xx processors. These vendors and many others also supply one-way and two-way motherboards. An increasing number of motherboards also support the latest dual-core server processors from Intel and AMD. Consequently, you can now build a powerful server yourself.

Keep in mind that your costs to build a server are probably going to be about 15% to 20% higher than purchasing an equivalent system from a first-tier vendor, and resale of your server later on will be more difficult. However, your costs moving forward for system upgrades and hardware support will be lower, and chances are that if you can build a server, you can provide adequate system support.

Reasons to Opt for a White Box

There is a third viable option for obtaining your server: About 40% of the server market is in the form of "white boxes," or unbranded systems put together by smaller VARs or OEMs. Some vendors buy white boxes from first-tier vendors, and these are essentially standard models in unbranded (thus "white") cases. More often, though, white boxes are servers assembled from standard components in just the same way that you might build the server yourself. White box vendors have the advantage of building more servers than you might and can build to order a system based on your specifications. Most VARs of this type sell these servers as part of solutions, and they package hardware, software, and service as a total package.

A white box server is hard to price effectively because it is usually part of a larger package. If you could separate out the hardware portion—and you usually can't—you'd find that the server would cost a little more than it would from a first-tier vendor, but the resale value would be similar to that of a system you build yourself. However, you are buying hardware, a solution, and support, so you are in effect sourcing out this IT function to people who specialize in their particular technology.

For a lengthy discussion on the advantages and disadvantages of buying a nonbranded white box PC, take a look at Daniel Dern's lengthy article on Informit.com, at www.informit.com/articles/article.asp?p=170498&seqNum=3&rl=1.

Comparing Building and Buying a Server

Table 20.1 summarizes the various options you have when it comes to buying versus building a server. Keep in mind that these evaluations are generalities and that some members of each group will be substantially better or worse than the ratings listed in this table.

Table 20.1   Advantages and Disadvantages of Building Versus Buying a Server

	First-Tier OEM	Home Built	VAR White Box
Entry cost	Very good	Fair	Good
Long term cost	Good	Very good	Good
Upgrade potential	Fair	Excellent	Very good
Vendor support	Fair	Good	Very good
Resale value	Excellent	Fair	Fair
Range of server types	Excellent	Very good	Very good
Reliability	Very good to excellent	Good, improving with time	Very good

Building Your Own Server

Most readers of this book would think nothing about building their own PCs. The hardware is nearly fully standardized across the industry, the choices of component selection are straightforward, and the method for assembly is extremely well documented in numerous books and articles. The pitfalls are few.

However, when it comes to building a server, many of these same people hesitate. When building a server, there are more choices to make, and the equipment is more expensive than that for a PC, but the results can be equally satisfying. Because you've now read a number of chapters that describe how to select a motherboard, what the advantages are of one bus over another, and how casing influences your system configuration, we don't repeat that information here. Instead, the sections that follow speak to what kinds of servers are straightforward to build and why you might want to build your own.

If you are considering building a server, you shouldn't do so because you intend on saving a lot of money. You usually don't. You often can't build a PC for less than you'd spend on a major first-tier OEM, such as Dell or Hewlett-Packard. Components are a commodity, and OEMs buy them by the container load. The best you can hope for is to approach their pricing with your costs. Servers, on the other hand, tend to have higher markups. So it is possible to save some money building your own server. But saving money is still not the best reason to build a server.

The best reason to build your own server is that you can pick and choose your own components in a way that buying someone else's system doesn't allow. When you build your own server, you have more control over the setup of the system, and you are more likely to know what to do or replace when things go wrong. A home-built server is generally rather flexible to configure because you use industry-standard parts and not some proprietary type of casing, memory, or motherboard that will block your upgrade path in the future. Building your own server often results in equipment that has a longer duty cycle because it is more upgradable.

Building your own server makes sense for another reason: Although system builders make their servers competitively priced at purchase time, everything else they sell you—from service to upgrade parts and even their shipping—is priced at whatever the market will bear.

Server Purposes and Form Factors

If you have decided to build a server, the first place to start is determining the intended purpose of the server. That purpose should guide many of your selections. A good rule of thumb when building any system is to try to build a balanced system but oversize that system for any task that is the primary function of the server. A balanced system is one where each subsystem of the server is powerful enough to allow you to avoid bottlenecks. If the purpose of the server is to serve files, then the I/O subsystem needs to be emphasized.

Let's talk a little bit about balanced systems. It's impossible or at least too costly to size subsystems so that they *never* present a bottleneck. When a system gets a job that requires a lot of processing, chances are that the CPU is going to be 100% utilized until the job is near completion. The goal is to allow acceptable performance in those circumstances as well as to maintain a good average CPU utilization rate. That's one advantage that servers offer. If you find that your CPU utilization goes up, if you've selected the right motherboard, you can upgrade your processor or add another processor. What typically separates a server from either a workstation or PC is that servers are built with more upgrade options.

Realistically there are only a few different types of servers that are practical for most people to build themselves:

- A basic server, which is really a souped-up PC
- A workgroup server, featuring dual or four-way CPU boards

- An SMB, or "small or medium-sized business" server, which is typically a dual processor system but built with a lower-performing I/O system
- A thin rack-mountable system

It's possible to build a thin form factor system using readily available components for rack-mounted units. Two types of servers are difficult to build, given the current retail model:

- SMP systems with more than four processors on the motherboard
- Blade systems

Neither of these two types of system is standardized enough and in great enough demand from the average system builder that companies stock the parts needed to build them. If you intend to build either a large SMP or a blade system, you will find yourself spending time talking to the original parts manufacturers themselves. Chances are that for a single board or a limited number of boards, they aren't going to be much help to you.

Server Components

You've seen a wide variety of components described in this book. What are the features that a server requires from its components in order to provide a stable and dependable service to network clients? Intel markets server building to its system builders, using the marketing term "Real Server." A server should include the following:

- **Two- or four-way SMP support**—It is a good idea to have at least a two-CPU system, even if you choose to populate just one of the sockets. Having additional CPU sockets allows your system to grow over time.
- **A high-performance server chipset**—The motherboard chipset is of central importance to the overall performance of your system.
- **Large memory capacity and I/O bandwidth**—The amount of memory determines the number of clients you can support, as does your I/O bus.
- **High-performance network interfaces**—Without a strong network interface, you create an unnecessary bottleneck getting data in and out of your server.
- **Management features**—Because a server is supposed to be up and running reliably, it's important to be able to view what's happening on the system and make changes both locally and remotely.
- **A server operating system**—You don't want to limit the number of connections or any other properties of your system because you've used a desktop- or workstation-oriented operating system. Your equipment should be selected with the operating system in mind.

The preceding list represents a checklist for selecting your basic server components. They are necessary to create a server but are probably not sufficient for most purposes. Servers are differentiated from workstations or desktops through the addition of these features:

- **Redundant components that allow for graceful failover**—Redundant components used are power supplies, fans, and hard drives.
- **Hot-swappable components**—The most important hot-swappable components are disks, but it's valuable to be able to swap out other components.
- **High-performance and high-capacity storage**—The purpose of your server determines the amount of storage (and memory) that you need.

■ **Intelligent RAID arrays that allow for advanced volume management**—RAID arrays make so many important volume operations possible that they are really a requirement for most servers these days.

All these requirements speak to the fundamental differences between workstations/desktops and servers. Servers must be much more dependable, must be higher performing, and must be flexible and have room to grow. Servers require a significantly higher investment than standard PCs, so you want to maximize your investment in them by selecting components that support the features described in this section.

Assembling a Server

When you have chosen your components, the next step is to assemble the system. In most respects, there isn't much difference between assembling a server and assembling a PC. There are a few critical differences, however, so in the following sections we discuss the building of a hypothetical server system step by step.

Installing Core Components

Let's begin by walking through the casing assembly, assuming that you've bought a case with no pre-assembled components already installed in it. Begin as follows:

1. On a good work surface with adequate lighting, open your system case and remove any of the included screws, mounting brackets, disk cages, and other components that you will be populating with parts.

2. Take a good look at your case to familiarize yourself with the design of the case and determine some fundamental issues, such as where the power supply goes and how many fans you need and of what type.

3. Install the power supply. Don't skimp on the power supply. Your power supply should be sufficiently powerful to run all your components well below its stated operating limit and should have good thermal properties as well as being quiet. You can pay a lot for a server power supply, but it is money well spent.

4. Install all your fans. The goal of your cooling system should be to create airflow through the case that removes heat. A lot of system builders position their fans so that intake is from the front of the case, and exhaust is out the back of the case. Some units, such as drive cages, may require their own fans.

5. Install your motherboard into the case, as well as any backplane that your system might have.

6. Install your CPU and then attach your cooler or heat sink on your CPU and plug it in to your motherboard CPU connection. Some people advise that you use a conductive wrist band in order to prevent static discharge from damaging memory or CPUs. Simply grounding yourself to a metallic surface (your case, for example) is sufficient.

7. Attach your case's front panel connections (power, power LED, restart, HD LED, and speaker) to the connections on the motherboard. Visually inspect the connections close up to make sure that they are on the correct posts and that the polarities are correct.

8. Insert one stick of memory into your system, usually on the slot closest to the CPU. (A system using a dual-channel memory controller may require that sticks of RAM be installed in matched pairs.)

9. If your motherboard does not have a video chipset built in, install your video card into the appropriate slot: AGP, PCI-x, and so on.

10. Attach a keyboard, a video monitor, and a mouse to your system or attach the appropriate leads to your KVM switch. KVM switches are covered further in Chapter 16, "Server Racks and Blades."

11. Turn on your system and check that it proceeds to BIOS and stops at the point where it cannot find a boot device.

It's a good idea to test the basic system at step 11 because it becomes increasingly difficult to diagnose problems later on, when there are more potential causes. At this point, if there is an issue, you can try switching the memory or changing slots, swapping out the CPU or video board, changing power supplies, and reexamining your connections. In your initial boot to BIOS, you can determine whether your power LED is functioning, whether your restart button operates, and whether you are getting beep sounds.

Installing the Remaining Components

After you have installed the core components, you can add peripheral devices. It's a good idea to add two or three components at a time and then test the boot process to ensure that the additions aren't causing any problems. If you have the time and patience, you may prefer to test one component at a time. Here are a some of the steps you need to follow, but the order isn't as critical as in the prior list:

1. Add the remaining memory. Memory is one of the most problematic components. It's a good idea to test your system again at full memory load to make sure there are no incompatibilities. If your BIOS is not going through a full display, turn off the fast BIOS startup and let the routine enumerate and check your entire memory.

2. (Optional) Install your floppy drive, being sure that the red wire in the floppy connection is closest to the floppy power connection. (Not all floppy drives have this requirement.)

3. Install any optical drive desired and connect the ATA/IDE, SATA, or USB connection, the audio connection, and the power connection to it.

4. If you are installing a USB flash storage reader or any other USB storage device, install it but do *not* connect that device to your USB bus. The reason you don't want to connect the device is to avoid your operating system from grabbing a set of drive labels for these devices until you are done assigning devices to your more common drives.

5. Install any PCI, PCI-x, or PCI-Express boards into the correct slots and connect any supported devices (such as hard drives) to those boards.

6. Test your system to make sure all devices are recognized and enumerated by the BIOS.

At this point your server is fully populated and ready for configuration. If you are using hardware RAID, follow these steps:

1. During the boot process, go into the RAID BIOS and create the RAID container.

2. Add all drives that you intend to use in your RAID array and designate any additional drives that you want to keep as spares.

3. After you create the container, use the RAID BIOS to create the hardware RAID type: RAID 5, RAID 1+0, and so on.

The process of creating the container is fast, but striping a large array can take some time.

Installing an Operating System

After your RAID has been configured, it is time to install your operating system and complete the installation. To install the operating system, follow these steps:

1. Insert the operating system installation disc into your optical drive and then start your system.

2. As your system proceeds past the BIOS and into the installation routine, make sure to specify correctly what your boot device will be and that you have the correct driver in hand to install so that your operating system will recognize the device.

   In many instances, an operating system may come with the correct driver, but whenever possible, you should try to install the very latest driver from the vendor's website. If you are installing a RAID system, try to have that driver on hand for your operating system. For example, when Windows Server's installation routine starts up, it asks you to press F6 in order to load a driver(s). If you don't press that key in time, you may need to rerun the installation.

3. As part of the installation routine, specify the boot partition and the type of drive formatting you wish to have on it. With Windows Server, you probably want NTFS; with Linux or UNIX, you may need to specify not only the partition and its type but also the number and definitions of any slices on the drive. Formatting a large volume takes some time, so this is a good time to attend to other tasks.

4. Proceed through the installation, specifying the details of your network connections as well as the particular system components that you want to install.

Note

It is possible to bypass any installation step and install and configure system components and settings later on, after your server's operating system has completed its work.

5. When your operating system is installed, shut down the system and connect your USB connections for any USB drives.

In building a server, the steps most people seem to have trouble with are creating the RAID container and not having the correct device driver in hand. Many RAID boards are poorly documented, and if you haven't done a system build before, you might not realize that you need to create a container *first* and stripe it prior to installing the operating system and then formatting the volume. The container and its striping are a hardware feature, separate from the formatting the operating system does.

With your server up and running, it's a good idea to let it burn in for 48 hours, monitoring your system temperature, which can usually be done using capabilities built into modern motherboards. In particular, you should monitor your CPU temperature to make sure it is not overheating.

Project Phasing

Nearly one out of every two large IT projects ends in failure. Failure takes many forms. A project can fail because it doesn't do what it was supposed to do for its users. It can fail because it runs out of money or out of support from project champions. It can fail because technology moves on past it. It can fail because the necessary personnel aren't found to implement or staff the project. The field is full of some amazing horror stories, including stories about IT projects that sank entire large companies because they affected primary business systems.

The bigger the project and the longer a deployment takes, the harder it is to make that project succeed. There are so many ways a project can fail that sometimes it's a wonder that wonder how projects do succeed, in spite of all the things that can possibly go wrong.

However, many large server deployments do succeed, and a few of them even come in close to budget. A few common themes seem to run through all successful deployments. The projects that are successful are carefully planned and implemented in stages, using an iterative approach. That's true for the smallest data room up to huge SAP or PeopleSoft systems that integrate several enterprise database applications running on hundreds of servers.

A project has the highest chance for success when it has the following separate phases:

1. Project specification phase

2. Budget phase and time lines

3. Testing phase

4. Implementation phase

5. Review phase

The following sections take a little closer look at what these different phases entail.

The Project Specification Phase

During the project specification phase, you collect the requirements for the system. When a good database consultant sets out to design a custom database for a client, he or she goes through a project specification phase that involves interviewing all the appropriate knowledge experts, collecting every possible form or input screen, and talking with different classes of potential users. The consultant is on a fishing expedition to find all the information possible to use as input into the project.

For server deployment, the project specification phase should consist of many of the same common elements. During this phase, you need to set the requirements of the system, based on the expectation of management and users. This is a critical step and one that often isn't handled very well by people who have done a few deployment projects already. First of all, the interested parties involved often either have no idea what they need or expect, or have an unrealistic idea. So it is up to you to set the expectations in consulting with these users so that what's possible intersects with what's desired.

The second glitch that's commonly encountered in specifying a server deployment involves the hubris of the project developer, or (worse yet) that of management. To make a server deployment work, you want as many of the people who will use the system to sign onto the project as possible. If you take the attitude that you know best, or that it is "your" money because you control the budget, you will lose valuable, maybe even critical, input from knowledge experts. Worse still, people may not use the expensive systems you deploy.

However you come by the information, you need to develop a working hypothesis as to what the system(s) specifications should be. To meet those expectations, you should consider the characteristics of similar working systems. Usually there are two approaches to a first cut at the system configuration:

■ One is based on models developed by vendors and their previous clients.

■ The second is based on historical data that you collect in-house.

With this information, it should be possible to draw up an initial project specification document that offers a reasonable road map from your wish list to a final implementation and installation of system(s) to be deployed. An initial project specification should not be carved in stone but be approached as a hypothesis that is meant to be tested. All deliverables should be spelled out in this document.

The project specification phase is probably the most important part of any deployment. Every dollar you spend planning your deployment will result in many more dollars in savings and often a much faster deployment time. If you are hiring outside consultants to deploy a system, it is a good idea to insist on a project specification that results in both a budget and a time line. Any consulting firm that doesn't do a project specification is either going to seriously pad the budget to protect itself against overruns or won't be in business long enough to complete your project.

The person or people who are going to deploy your system(s) aren't necessarily the ones who need to do the project specification. The project specification can be done in-house by staff and, when it's completed, the specification can be offered to all interested parties in order to request quotes. You may also want to call for an RFP (request for proposal), a process that matches your specification to what each person thinks he or she can achieve with the new system. The RFP wrestles with the budgetary aspects of the project and tries to match your requirements to a budget that can do the job. The more complete a set of requirements you can provide at this stage, the more precise the RFP should be.

Many consulting firms want to charge for the RFP process because they expend significant resources to create an RFP. If you think you can get a fully developed project specification from an RFP you pay a consultant to create, it may be more economical and more successful go this route than to do it yourself. If you decide to give someone a commission, you should make no commitments to implement the project with the firm preparing your specification, and you should make sure that you have free rights to use the plan the firm produces as you see fit.

Wise consulting firms recognize that a project specification is a unique selling tool that gives them a leg up on the competition when it comes time to bid on the work. Indeed, Dave Rothfield from Creative Sales + Management (www.csm4tqs.com), a marketing consulting firm, has likened creating a project specification to docking a large ocean liner. When an ocean liner gets close to the dock, hands onboard throw down small ropes with large knots on the end, called monkey paws. Those small ropes are attached to the larger ropes that are then pulled in and fastened to the dock to secure the liner. Similarly, a small project specification can often lead to larger things.

The Budget Phase and Time Lines

A project specification should lead naturally to the second phase, which is where the budget is set for the project. You might find that the budget constrains your project so that some resources you hoped to deploy can't be deployed, or you might find that your budget can support more of the resources that you first specified, resulting in a larger project. Budgets are often negotiated. You might find that an initial budget results in rewriting the project specification to match a new reality, and that is all to the good. The more iterative the process, the more accurate and smooth the results.

A project specification should end up with the budget and time line appended to the back of the proposal and with signature sign-offs by all the significant parties concerned. The purpose of having a complete project specification sign-off on the budget and the time line is that it limits the project so that it doesn't run wild with what is often called "scope creep" or "feature creep," where additional functions are created, resources are deployed, and contractor time is spent beyond what the budget calls for. Feature creep is the single most common reason software projects run well over budget or fail.

For large deployment projects, you should use project management software such as Microsoft Project. When multiple resources are required to complete a deployment, and where one phase of the project is dependent on other related parts of the projects, there is too much activity going on for progress against a time line and budget to be manually tracked.

Note

Microsoft Project is probably the best-known project management software, but it is far from being the only product. Many other commercial products are available; some of them are web based, and others are shareware or open source products. For Yahoo's Project Management Software jump page, go to http://dir.yahoo.com/business_and_economy/ business_to_business/computers/software/business_applications/Project_Management/.

Good project management software tracks costs versus budgets, tracks activities, and measures progress against project milestones. The most valuable feature of project management software is the identification of the critical path of the project. The *critical path* is the set of tasks that determines the overall progress of the project and affects its overall completion time. Identification of the critical path is essential in keeping many large projects on budget. If other people and project resources are inactive and waiting for critical tasks to be completed, your deployment will undoubtedly accrue additional costs for which you didn't plan.

It's important to realize that any deployment has two separate budgets. The first budget is the actual deployment, and the second budget (which is often ignored) is the annual operating costs. Many people simply don't take into consideration the annual costs, which can lead to some very nasty surprises later on.

A good project specification not only identifies the primary budget for deployment but projects the annual costs two or three years out. To create an operational budget, you have to make some assumptions about the following:

- **Reliability**—Server hardware is pretty reliable, but components do fail, and if you don't have a warranty covering the full replacement, you need to pay for replacements or warranties.

- **Cost of services being used**—As best you can, you should break down the budget so that each item in the project is budgeted individually. It's good project management to phase your project so that payments are made based on project milestones.

- **Electricity and other utilities**—These costs may include space rental if you are deploying servers in leased space, such as a cage at an ISP.

- **Support staff**—Of all of the aforementioned factors, IT support staff can be the most expensive component of a deployment. It is critical that staffing be accurately gauged and accounted for.

The electricity you use, the portion of floor space, and the amount of staff time needed to manage the system are knowable factors, even if you don't know what the exact cost of these things will be a year, two, or three from now. So be sure to include them in your specification.

The Testing Phase

A multiserver deployment should proceed to a testing phase in order to establish whether it is possible to meet the project specifications by using the hardware and software technologies selected during the project specification phase. The test bed you deploy should be a realistic microcosm of the larger system. The testing phase serves as a reality check.

If it's possible to stage your deployment so that your test bed is a module in a set of replicated modules, then there are fewer surprises when the deployment is implemented. However, that's not always possible.

Consider an example in which you are establishing a website with your deployment. The site will eventually have 50 blade servers in a couple racks. As a first pass, you decide to deploy two blade servers to test your design assumptions. Those webservers are loaded with traffic from a client load simulator or from actual users, and you derive your parameters from that experiment. You want to know how many simultaneous connections you can use, how much traffic the two blades support, the impact of adding more memory or changing disk configurations, and so forth.

Describing performance testing in detail would require an entire book. For now, you need to know that a load simulator will allow you to run your two servers at their full load but may not really be representative of the traffic that your servers will actually encounter when they are deployed. Therefore, a better test might be to select an appropriate subset of users whom you think will be representative of the actual loading in practice.

What you may come to realize in your testing is that your design requires that the webservers be fronted by an IP director that routes webserver requests to the least active webserver. To fully utilize the IP director you chose, you need to have it front 5 blade servers; however, when you create this design, you find that your 5 blade servers are now 20% more efficient than your original specifications thought they'd be. So this is an iteration of your project specification that needs to be accounted for: You need to change the design to add 8 IP directors and reduce your blade server count by 10, to 40.

Now not only does your project specification changed, but your test bed setup changes as well. In order to get the correct performance characteristics, you need to have a test bed setup that has one IP director fronting five blade servers. That test bed represents a base module that you can expand when you are confident that the system works.

The point is that your test bed phase should be a positive feedback loop. You alter your test bed to get the best results you can; then you change your budget accordingly. As you learn more about the system, you can go through another round to more precisely specify the system.

The most important criterion for running a test bed and getting the results you need is to be as accurate as you can. Creating a test bed with a representative sample of your actual users is preferred over running a client load simulator and trying to guess what loading your users will actually present to your system. If you can locate your test systems in the domain in which they are going to be positioned, you can determine the effects that the domain's security features have on your website's potential performance. Little things mean a lot, so if you can discover that the router in front of your IP directors is underpowered for the job in the test phase, you can save yourself that much extra grief later on.

The Implementation Phase

If you are deploying a single server or a small number of servers, chances are that your test phase and implementation are one and the same thing. However, for larger systems, implementation is the phase of deployment in which what was once small is made large. You know that the theory of your system is correct because you've verified it with a test setup. However, practice is not theory, and anything that involves money and people can still go very wrong.

Implementation is where your resource planning pays off. If your project planning is well done, then the equipment should be available when you need it, the people necessary to install and manage the equipment should be there when you need them, and the money to pay the bills should be available when it is needed. In this dream scenario, the bills don't appear until after the money is available. In the real world, it is never possible to choreograph all the dependent resources perfectly. Things just tend to go wrong, and you have to make the best of your situation.

The key to making an implementation work well is to recognize early on just which part of the deployment is going to be troublesome and plan around it. Not all troubles affect your deployment's schedule or budget. If you have a contractor who is slow but whose work is acceptable, and the person's work doesn't affect anyone else's work, then the contractor's speed is more an issue for his or her bottom line and not yours. Your real troubles appear when a task on the critical path for your deployment goes wrong. Because most people don't bother to analyze what their critical path is, you are already ahead of the game if you've thought this through.

The arrival of the servers you ordered is often one of the steps on any project's critical path. You can't set up your racks or install your applications until the servers are in place. So if you anticipate a problem with the delivery of the servers, you could tie a certain date into your contract with the OEM so that if the servers don't arrive because they take a new kind of high-speed memory that isn't readily available, for example, you can replace them with a similar model from another vendor. Alternatively, you could switch to a similar model in the original vendor's line that doesn't use that kind of memory. Or, you could take delivery of the originally specified model, using an older memory type, and then swap it out when the new memory becomes available. The point is that whatever you decide to do, you need to build into your project a set of contingencies that allow you to work around the problem.

One aspect of implementation involves making decisions about single-, dual-, or multisourcing. Single-sourcing is when you use only one vendor to supply a system, part, service, or even the entire project. A vendor that is your single-source partner for server deployments is essentially a master contractor, and you transfer the issues of selection to that vendor. Single-sourcing works well when the vendor has both the resources and track record to give you a high degree of certainty of the project's success.

Not all companies are comfortable with single-sourced projects, and for good reason. Even the very best contractor can run into trouble, for all the same reasons that you can. Most people want more control over their business and destiny. Therefore, having a second vendor as a backup or even as a minor participant, ready to take over in case of a problem, is prudent. Your chances of success are larger when you have a good backup plan. Many companies insist on having a second vendor for all their parts, simply because they don't want to build a product and have their business be dependent on a single partner.

Finally, many deployments are multivendor affairs that can be managed in-house by your IT staff, by a consultant, or by a firm that specializes in this kind of work. Multivendor deployments are more complex and difficult by nature to manage, but they offer the advantage of allowing you to pick the best vendor for the task, with *best* defined by some combination of quality, cost, and speed.

The Review Phase

The final phase in any planned project should be a review of what is accomplished. Often organizations are too busy with the work at hand to spend the time necessary to frame the lessons learned. However, if your server deployment is something that will be reproduced or extended later on, if you fail to create a final review, many of the lessons learned will be lost.

Even if you are only deploying a single server, it is valuable to record the original assumptions in selecting the equipment and software you did—and how those assumptions were borne out in practice. Chances are that at some point in the future, you will be called on to upgrade the software or the server, or possibly replicate the application in another location.

After deployment, someone familiar with the entire project should be called upon to record the results obtained. A good place to start a review cycle is to begin circulating the project specification among selected IT staff and users. Many people scout around for document review software, and indeed there is a large category of that kind of software. However, you can use office productivity software such as Microsoft Word to generate a review, post a discussion in SharePoint, or even start an email chain letter to get the results you need. The point is that you need to be inclusive in obtaining feedback on the projects results from many different points of view.

You should ask people to comment on how the system compares with what was projected by annotating the document and by giving you comments to a number of pertinent questions, such as these:

- Did the deployment meet its functionality and performance objectives?
- What areas of the system(s) require improvement?
- In hindsight, if you could change aspects of the project, what would those aspects be?
- Are there any improvements to the system that should be considered moving forward?

- How manageable is the system for IT staff?
- How easy is it to use the system for users?
- Do you have any general comments?

Your list of questions will undoubtedly be different from this, and it may involve evaluating specific contractors or employees, as well as delving into politics and other aspects of the project that you feel are important to document for projects to come. You might need to publish one form of the document while reserving sensitive matters for people who may have a need to know.

Software Licensing and Upgrades

You buy and deploy servers to run software. When you install software, the creator of the software or the distributor holds a copyright and a license to the software that binds you in some way to the manner in which you can use the software. In essence, a *license* is an enforceable contract. Licenses bestow upon you certain rights and permissions but require your compliance with their terms. When you buy a commercial software package or get a server with software installed, you are given a copy of the software's EULA (end-user license agreement).

EULAs run the range of providing free use of the software to restricting the use of the software so that it runs only on one processor on the system it was purchased for and installed on. EULAs are often transferable, but as the industry moves from a perpetual license based on a single purchase to a subscription service model, EULA terms of use are constantly shifting. If you actually sit down and read through the legalese of some of these EULAs, you'll see that they contain all manner of restrictions of use. Some EULAs actually restrict the content that you can use or data you can collect with the software. It is unclear how much of any particular EULA is actually enforceable in the courts.

Note

For a contrarian view of EULAs, see the article on the Electronic Frontier Foundation's website, at www.eff.org/wp/eula.php.

License Types

You'll find that licenses make the following types of demands on you for compliance:

- **Per-processor or per-system usage license**—Microsoft Windows XP Professional and Windows Server 2003 have a license that lets you install them on a two-processor system (dual packages). If you add additional processors, you need additional licenses.

- **Client licenses**—Many client/server software systems require not only a license for the server software but licenses for the clients that connect to the server. Messaging systems such as Domino and Exchange are examples of this type of dual-system license structure.

- **Per-user license**—Each user accessing the software needs to have his or her own account. Subscriptions, research access, and accounting software often requires a per-user license.

- **Connection licenses**—A connection license allows for a particular number of simultaneous connections to a server. In some instances, each connected client requires a connection license, but in most cases, a company purchases a pool of connection licenses. When one client closes a session, the connection is returned to the pool for use; this is similar to the kinds of leases that DHCP offers. Enterprise databases often use connection licenses.

- **Upgrade license**—These sorts of licenses search your system for a previous version, and if one is found, they install the upgrade.

- **Academic license**—Many companies discount software sold to schools and students. Academic licenses require that you validate your academic connection.

- **Downgrade and transfer licenses**—A *downgrade license* lets you purchase a current version of a piece of software, such as Windows XP, and use that license to run Windows 98 instead. A *transfer license* is a license granted to someone else that you either sell or donate your software to. Transfer licenses sometimes require formal application to the vendor.

- **Open source licenses**—An opens source license allows you to use the software however you see fit, royalty free. You are even allowed to modify the source code, provided that you publish any changes you make in the source code for others to see. A very substantial pool of open source enterprise software for servers is available.

- **Free license**—Freeware provides royalty-free use of the software but most often restricts any changes you make to the software's code. You use the software usually at your own risk.

- **Shareware**—Shareware is *not* freeware; it is more aptly described as "trialware." Most shareware either times out without being purchased and registered or restricts your feature set until you purchase the product.

License Management Software

Regardless of the individual terms of any license, it is important to monitor your licenses. If you give your best effort to stay in compliance with your software vendor's terms, you should be able to pass any compliance audit. The licenses that are software instances are fairly straightforward to inventory, but the licenses that bind software to a particular hardware instance are more difficult and may need to be monitored with a software management utility such as LANDesk, Altiris, or Microsoft MOM.

If you think that licensing is a rat's nest, you are not alone. You may have some luck manually managing compliance when you have a few servers and clients. However, when you reach dozens or hundreds of systems, the task is not cost-effective or accurate enough to do manually.

Whatever software you install on your server, you need to monitor your license compliance for all installed commercial software. Many enterprise server software packages, such as Microsoft Terminal Server, Citrix MetaFrame, Oracle, and so on, come with their own license compliance utilities. Some operating systems can even be inventoried with tools from their developers. Figure 20.1 shows an example of SQL Server's license compliance tool. However, for the most part, license compliance across a range of software and systems involves so many of these kinds of tools (when they exist) that using them individually is a truly thankless task.

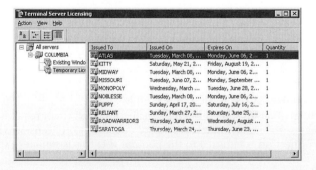

Figure 20.1   The Microsoft Terminal Server license compliance tool helps you manage your compliance for remote session connections in Microsoft Windows servers.

Note

Software license compliance is too complex and time-consuming a task to do by using manual methods. You should use a network management solution to do this task and regularly run the software and spot-check the results to see if they are accurate.

There is a large category of software on the market today that you can use to inventory your hardware and software. The most popular packages are entire software management suites, such as LANDesk, Altiris, and Novell ZENworks, which specialize in not only network systems management but also in application deployment. Each of these products has an associated asset management module or tool offered as an option in the suite.

In addition, all the large enterprise frameworks, such as Hewlett-Packard OpenView, IBM Tivoli, and CA Unicenter TNG have products in the license management area. However, this category of software is actually quite large, and there are simpler and cheaper network software programs that you can use to help you with license management if you don't want to employ a framework solution. Commercial solutions range in their utility from simply inventorying the software that runs on each system to matching software characteristics with a licensing database to determine compliance. You can also employ a consulting firm to assay your license compliance and help you manage it.

Upgrades

At some point all software products are upgraded. Software programs are like sharks: They must constantly move forward to the next version or die. This is as true for operating systems as it is for server applications. Part of any deployment, therefore, must take into account how upgrades will be handled as they occur.

Consider that operating systems and application software get revised every two to three years. Any large deployment during its natural course is going to have to make some decisions about which version(s) of software to deploy. There is a high probability that one or more key software components will need to be upgraded. The following are the essential factors that need to be considered in deciding which software version to deploy:

- Stability and reliability
- Life cycle and life span
- Features
- Costs
- System requirements

How you rate these different factors depends on your situation as well as the application(s) involved. Stability and reliability are especially important because they lower management costs. Also, a long life cycle and life span are primary considerations when it comes to calculating a system's return on investment. Features, costs, and system requirements are factors that don't tend to be as important, provided that they don't negatively affect the project to any great extent. Of course, your lists and rankings may be rather different from this and may vary from application to application.

Generally, when an application has been revised a number of times, as is the case with many enterprise applications on the market, it has reached a point where it is stable and has a mature feature set. Chances are that OurWebServer version 8.0 isn't going to be all that much different from OurWebServer version 7.0. In such a case, you might not wait for a beta version of version 8.0 to appear before beginning your development. For an application that does not have a long revision history or for any major operating system revision, it is important that you do your testing on the most advanced form of the software that you can get access to. You should be aggressive in pursuing the latest operating system versions because doing so provides the longest life cycle for any server deployment and, more importantly, is your best bet in order to secure your systems against current threats.

Chances are that whatever versions you choose for your software, whatever versions you test, and whatever versions you deploy, you are going to be faced with software upgrades further down the line. Most organizations tend to be very conservative in installing upgrades beyond operating system patches to their server deployments. You have to give some measure of faith that your operating system vendor won't break your system with the latest patch, although sometimes that does happen. If you are installing an operating system patch, you should do so in a manner that lets you uninstall the patch if needed. Most operating systems provide an uninstall patch feature. If your operating system doesn't have an uninstall routine, then you should find a patch manager to use or utilize a snapshot backup utility that allows you to return your server's operating system to the state it was in before it was upgraded.

Tip

The Golden Rule of software upgrades is to take small steps and evaluate.

Application upgrades are another story entirely. Most organizations with large investments in optimizing an application for a server platform are very conservative about moving their application to a new version. Studies that measure the percentage of servers that are migrated from an older version to a newer version reveal that usually fewer than 50% of application servers are migrated for most applications. If an application's new version requires a new file format or extensive data reorganization, or if it requires significant code rewriting, often the migration percentages are lower than 20%. Most organizations opt to live with what they have and do a fresh server deployment rather than upgrade their software in place.

It's really best to think of an in-place software upgrade as a fresh deployment anyway. If you intend to migrate to a new version and can run a pilot to uncover any of the issues involved, it may make sense to do so. A pilot for migration works best when one of your working application servers can be upgraded in place and then used going forward for a representative set of users. If the new version of the application doesn't interoperate with the older version of the application, then you probably should try a migration but seek to test a fresh deployment.

Capacity Planning

Capacity planning, also called *right sizing*, is a process by which you develop a working model or hypothesis for the amount of loading that is placed on your server and the power of the server necessary to balance that load. When you successfully determine the right size for your server(s), you will have achieved the following five goals, in order of their importance:

1. **Adequate service levels**—Your server will be able to service the clients for the service it was intended to provide, not only for average loads but for peak loads as well.

2. **Reasonable excess overhead**—You don't want to buy too much server and have much of your investment lay idle.

3. **Appropriate fault tolerance**—The server should be operational enough of the time to be satisfactory to your users. Additional redundancies cost additional money, so right sizing your server requires that you take this factor into consideration.

4. **An upgrade path**—If your service grows over time, you may need to increase your server's capacity. This might mean that you need additional processors or memory, more network connections, and so forth.

5. **An appropriate life cycle**—An appropriate life cycle is one that makes your investment in the server reasonable. A server that was deployed for Windows 2000 (for example) and then upgraded to Windows 2003 has a longer potential life cycle than one stuck at Windows 2000. The average useful life of a first-line server is somewhat longer than that of a PC because server motherboards have more upgrade options. Most PCs are written off after about three years of service in corporations. Servers typically have four to five years of life.

Knowable, Unknowable, Known, and Unknown

As you might rightly suppose, it is hard to completely balance all the factors involved in capacity planning. There are known unknowns, such as the following:

- How will your business activity change in the future?
- Will you need to support additional users?
- Will future operating systems or application upgrades make additional demands on your server?

There are also unknown unknowns, such as these:

- Will your company merge, and will your server be asked to support an entirely new operating system or application?
- Will your design specifications be made redundant (so to speak) by a required change in availability?
- Will the budget change in a way that adversely affects your ability to upgrade or manage your server?

Let's face it: Capacity planning is a very difficult task because no one can predict the future, and technology advances are uncertain.

Let's start on some solid ground, what we defensively call the *knowable knowns*. There are two basic approaches to capacity planning, and they hinge on whether you have or can get established historical data for your usage pattern. If you can't, you must rely on the experience of others in similar circumstances who are using a server like the one you intend to deploy in a situation that is similar or at least can be extrapolated to the situation you are in. When you can establish historical data, you are in more control over the design you choose and the result you can achieve. Let's look at these two situations in a little more detail.

The "art" of capacity planning is one that can yield to statistical analysis, although many people find that it is easier to determine whether a certain type of server will not be able to maintain a load than whether that server can support that load. Consider a situation in which you have a server with a disk system capable of 250 IOPS (inputs/outputs per second), but you need to attain 500 IOPS. You know that your system won't give you the performance you want, but what you don't and can't know is whether if you double the number of disks you can achieve the rate you want. At some point in the system's design, you are going to max out your I/O bus, and you can't know if that point will be reached somewhere between 250 and 500 IOPS or beyond.

Here is one fact that you can absolutely take to the bank, no matter how powerful your server: Your users and staff will find a way to consume all of its resources at some point. This is a variant of Parkinson's Law (www.heretical.com/miscella/parkinsl.html): "Work expands so as to fill the time available for its completion."

Sizing Tools

When you are attempting to configure a server for a particular purpose, you can assume that all operating systems and applications make different demands on your server. Because software architectures vary widely, you need to characterize the capability of the operating system and the application to determine what it is capable of supporting. A hypothetical database application might be multi-threaded and able to distribute a load among a number of processors; this would argue strongly for one or a few large SMP multiprocessor boxes. With similar large databases in existence, you find that I/O isn't often the problem; rather, raw computing power is. The system crunches a lot of data from a short question to return to the client an answer that doesn't have much data in it. Applications that require persistent connections, channels, or sockets are good candidates for scale-up server consolidations.

Upon closer inspection, you might find that published data by the vendor shows that a particular operating system/database application scales performance linearly from one to four processors but starts to loose multithreaded efficiency as the number of processors goes above four. By the time you get to eight processors, those eight processors run at 60% efficiency. This is in fact a very common scenario, and it comes up because the crossbar architecture that couples two quad processor sets together to make an eight-way system isn't 100% efficient and doesn't scale perfectly. So with that information, you have a first cut at right sizing your server, and you see that a quad server or an eight-way is the limit beyond which you do not want to go.

Consider a webserver deployment, the traditional "scale-out" instead of scale-up application where very little processing is done at the server but where I/O requirements are extreme. Any application that doesn't require or can't maintain a persistent connection isn't going to benefit the most from a faster server; it will benefit more from having more network connections and more available servers to connect to. That's why webservers tend to be deployed in server farms.

With a webserver, much of the processing gets done on the client side. When you examine the metrics of the particular webserver/operating system combination that you intend to use, you may find that the application can't make good use of more than two processors (this is another common scenario). Therefore, this system architecture begs for a solution in which many more computers are used and the amount of I/O that can flow through the network interface is the key bottleneck.

Note

IBM has a redbook called "IBM e-server pSeries Sizing and Capacity Planning: A Practical Guide" that you can download from their site, at www.redbooks.ibm.com/abstracts/SG247071.html?Open. This book contains a lot of conceptual material, including benchmarks, guidelines for application-specific sizing, a listing and description of available sizing tools, and IBM's Balanced System Guidelines. Although the redbook is aimed at selecting a pSeries server, the principles of sizing apply to other servers as well.

In order to decide how to size your server without being able to characterize the potential system loading, you need to look at similar systems that are deployed in the field. If you are lucky, you may know other places running servers and applications similar to the one you are running, and you can piggyback on their experience. Chances are, though, that you don't or that the other companies aren't willing to share them with you, so the next logical place to start to develop your capacity plan is with the server vendor selling you the system or with the application vendor selling you the software. IBM, for example, has a tool for this called the eConfig configuration that is available only to IBM and IBM Business Partners.

If you are purchasing a server from a large OEM such as Hewlett-Packard, IBM, or Dell, you might find that the company has developed online sizing tools that can aid your selection of a particular server from that manufacturer. For example, here are some sizing tools that you can use for different applications:

- **Dell sizing tools**—If you visit www1.us.dell.com/content/topics/global.aspx/alliances/en/ sizing?c=us&cs=19&l=en&s=dhs, you can download a number of applications, including sizing tools for Microsoft SQL Server 2000, Microsoft Exchange Server 2000 and 2003, Microsoft Windows 2000 Active Directory, People Software JD Edwards, SAP, and Dell's Rack Adviser.

- **Hewlett-Packard ActiveAnswers tools**—The site http://h18001.www1.hp.com/partners/ microsoft/utilities/storagesystem.html provides a number of sizers, including those for Apache Web Server for Linux, Backup Solution, BroadVision One-to-One Enterprise 6.0 for Windows 2000, Citrix MetaFrame XP and Windows 2000 Terminal Services, Commerce One Enterprise Buyer Desktop Edition 2.0 for Windows NT or 2000, Microsoft Commerce Server for Windows 2000, Microsoft BizTalk Server 2000 on ProLiant DL360, Microsoft BizTalk Server 2000 on ProLiant DL320, Microsoft Internet Information Server for Windows NT, Microsoft Internet Information Services for Windows 2000, and Microsoft Solution for Internet Business.

Although these systems identify only particular models from Dell and Hewlett-Packard, you can be relatively certain that if a dual-processor server handles the load that the sizer suggests, someone else's dual-processor system or even your own home-built one will probably be in the right ballpark.

Capacity Planning Principles

It is possible to be a lot more precise when you have historical data guiding your selection of a server. In a real case scenario, you can determine the parameters necessary to get optimum performance by examining logs from the previous generation of server(s). With a running system, you can analyze how resources are utilized and where any bottlenecks might be, and you can determine the nature of the I/O for which you need to tune your system. Figure 20.2 shows the common steps in a capacity planning project.

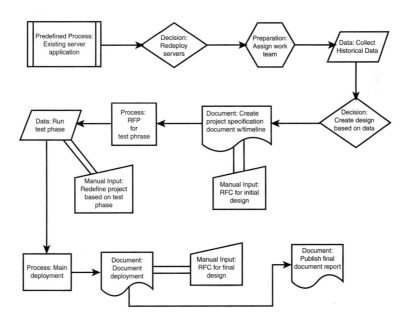

Figure 20.2   A right sizing flowchart is a very useful tool when you are involved in a server resizing project.

Let's consider an example of how a capacity planning project might proceed.

The principles involved in capacity planning based on historical data are as follows:

- **Understand your application**—You need to know your application's characteristics, including how it uses network bandwidth, RAM, disk sector size for I/O, and other important factors. If you don't know this information and can't find it in your application's documentation, you can probably get the information from your vendor.

- **Tune your drive**—If you can set up your disk drive's characteristics so that they match your application's I/O characteristics, you can not only lower the amount of disk space you use, but you can dramatically improve your performance.

- **Abstract your storage from your servers**—If you use a consolidated storage server, such as an intelligent array, you can dramatically lower your costs and improve your fault tolerance.

- **Obtain historical data to identify your maximum system load**—You need to know not only what level high system loads achieve, but the days, times, and reasons this loading is high.

- **Balance your system**—Any one component of a system can be a bottleneck. Try not to under-size the performance of one subsystem in order to emphasize another. IBM has an entire program and related set of calculations called Balanced System Guidelines that is a server sizing tool, but this tool is available only internally at IBM.

- **Determine your ROI**—Any server deployed should have a return on investment calculation done in order to justify its deployment.

An Example of Historical Data

At Company XYZ the decision is made to consolidate a large number of Microsoft Exchange 2000 servers at several sites into a smaller number of more powerful systems at a single site—a scale-up consolidation project. The rationale for this approach is that fewer servers offer fewer points of failure and lower costs of management. Exchange is an application which requires that four persistent connections (sockets or channels) be made to clients, which makes it a good candidate for a scale-up project.

The project manager is tasked with right sizing the system(s) to be purchased and developing the parameters under which the system is operational. The company had determined that instant messaging (IM) reduced its total cost of ownership (TCO) and wanted to add additional server resources to its Exchange operation. There was also the concern that as messages attached more and more rich content, their storage needed to be consolidated in order to handle the additional requirements.

The first step in the analysis was to collect data on the volume of email and the types of email in use by the company. It turns out that logging is turned on and a set of reports are generated that summarize email traffic in 48 increments each day (every 30 minutes). From these data the following can be determined:

- **The volume of email**—You can determine the volume of email, per each half-hour, both in terms of number of messages and the amount of transferred data that the system processes every time period.

- **The average volume**—You can determine the average volume that each individual, group, or site is using on the system.

- **When peak periods of email occur**—The collection of historical data analyzed the message stream and determined that maximum loads were attained on Monday mornings, 9:00–9:30 a.m. EST, when the largest group of company employees checked their mail from over the weekend. Another period of high load was Friday afternoons, 3:30–4:00 p.m. EST.

- **Average message size**—The average email message was 50KB, but the mean email message was actually much lower. Approximately 70% of all emails were 5KB or less, with 5% being emails with attachments.

- **Average size of messages written to disk**—Most messages written to disk were between 3KB and 4KB in size.

- **Messaging volume**—Messaging volume was increasing approximately 50% per year.

Based on these characteristics, the project set the following goals:

- Reduce the number of servers by a factor of four.

- Run at 99.2% uptime or greater.

- Eliminate all Exchange replication traffic on the corporate WAN.

- Make all Exchange data bulletproof by moving them off of SCSI attached storage and onto consolidated intelligent storage arrays.

- Create a backup and recovery scheme that reduces both backup time and data recovery to a period of no more than a two-hour window.

- Establish a design that can be replicated easily to scale the original deployment.

Exchange 2000's database engine is tuned to read and write in 8KB blocks, or extents. (That's not always the case, however: Other applications, such as SQL Server, are designed to use 16KB blocks.) The idea for disk tuning is that you try to match the READ/WRITE characteristics of the server to the application. For Exchange, the two most important characteristics—the ones that the performance logs and literature recognize as bottlenecks—are the READ to WRITE ratio and the I/O loading, known as the *request rate*.

The actual ratios as read by utilities such as IOMeter or IOBench were 3 to 1 READs to WRITEs (on average). From the Windows Performance Monitor and other utilities, you can measure IOPS, which is a measure of the storage system loading. The two relevant disk counters were Pending I/O Disk Requests and Average Disk Queue Length. These factors define the average I/O per user, approximately 1.5 IOPS per user. Memory counters also defined server RAM as a potential bottleneck.

System Selection

With all the aforementioned design parameters and application characteristics, it was possible for the people who are specifying the server consolidation project to make various system selections. The original dual-processor servers were replaced with eight-way servers in a ratio of 4 to 1. This size server was expected to support 3,500 users with the user characteristics described in the previous section. The Exchange messaging system was installed in a single domain on the same data center network.

A large storage array system was chosen, and each Exchange data store was placed onto a large single-volume server with a 4KB cluster size specified. This cluster size was a little larger than the mean message, allowing most clusters to be completely filled by a message of mean size without wasting much additional disk space. To attain the desired I/O, the number of 15,000rpm dual-homed Fibre Channel disks required was calculated based on the storage vendor's performance data; also, a disk cache size was established so that the desired throughput and an additional margin for growth could be achieved.

Note

In selecting system components, the general rule of thumb is to determine which component is going to cost the most money and/or which component is going to be the most difficult one to fix if it isn't correctly sized for the project. That component should then be selected in order to best meet the needs of the project. For the Exchange project described in the Company XYZ example, that evaluation could have led the project manager to pay particular attention to either the servers (the most difficult to correct) or to the large disk arrays (the most expensive). Usually the most expensive component is the one that is also the most difficult to correct.

Because WRITES are slow and represent a large portion of the disk I/O, Company XYZ chose a RAID 0+1 array, which provides the speed of striping with the first-line redundancy of mirroring. It also decided to back up each data store with a BCV (business continuance volume) for failover in case of primary disk storage array failure. Backups were collected as snapshots, with a full backup made of a BCV every week and stored to tape. It was also established that snapshots average around two hours to take and that switching over to a BCV upon system failure could be effected within two hours, with most of the time taken up by bringing the BCV up-to-date with transaction logs.

In this particular example, it was found that the system had a life cycle of around 3.5 years. There were also some surprises. It was found that virus scanning software had an unexpected impact on performance, that adjusting the disk quota size for a user affected what is called the *single instance ratio* (a single file is stored on disk with many pointers to it from users' mailboxes), and that the system could be successfully scaled.

Although this project is based on an Exchange server consolidation project, which means the data are probably not useful to your project, the principles it exposes are useful to anyone trying to deploy a right-sized server. That is, by understanding your application's characteristics, measuring performance bottlenecks and key characteristics, and extrapolating correctly, using your particular loading, it is possible to make good equipment selections. As with all large projects, if your deployment installs multiple systems, it is prudent to create a test bed to determine whether your assumptions are borne out by fact before proceeding to add additional systems.

Note

At this point, any deployment project should have produced a project specification that everyone involved has signed off on. The last thing you want to have happen is to deploy a server that is sized to service 3,500 users and have a high-level manager say that he or she said "5,500 users" or, worse yet, "350 users."

Having management sign off on a document ameliorates these kinds of problems, and it lays out all the assumptions you've made when you can't establish a completely factual model. Therefore, any good specification should document any caveats, establish a risk analysis, and make promises about performance in a conservative way.

A project specification document doesn't need to be Department of Defense fighter-jet long; it can be a spreadsheet and an email message, but it's something you need to create whenever you are spending someone else's money.

Routine Maintenance

You neglect routine maintenance tasks at your peril. Tasks such as backup, virus and spyware scanning, archiving, disk maintenance, data replication, and other services that secure your network services can consume a considerable percentage of your resources and budget. Still, the potential damage that can occur due to hardware or software errors greatly outweighs the cost of the insurance you purchase by staying on top of these services.

Note

The key to making routine maintenance work for you is to automate as many of these tasks as you possibly can. You shouldn't rely on manual methods for routine maintenance. Backups should be scheduled, as should all the other tasks involved in routine maintenance. You might need a scripting tool or scheduler utility to automate these tasks, but many of the utilities in this class come with their own schedulers as part of the package.

Backups

It's a little-appreciated fact that the average organization uses approximately 15% of its servers for backing up its corporate data. This means that 3 out of every 20 servers are backup servers. Therefore, backup should be one of the first services you deploy, and it should be one of the components that is fully specified with any server deployment. Every server should have at least two different backups that you can fall back on in case of problems. This is in addition to any hardware redundancies you build into the system.

Not too long ago, servers and workstations came with their own tape backup drives as part of the build. That's less true today, although it is still possible to incorporate tape systems such as LTO or SuperDLT to back up modern high-capacity disk drives and RAID systems. More often, you install tape libraries or tape carousels as tape systems. However, the large size of data now stored and the faster performance hard disks offer has tended to popularize disk-to-disk backup as the primary first-level backup system in use. As per-gigabyte disk prices have fallen so dramatically over the past few years, the price of disk-to-disk backup has begun to approach that of tape storage.

Disk backup can be mirrored, but more often a backup writes data by using a snapshot technology. A mirrored disk can provide failover, but a snapshot provides a historical record that you can fall back to. You aren't simply held captive to the current state of data on your disk; you can go back and restore to the data that existed on a particular date and time. A second-level backup can be archival to tape, but if you have the budget, it is best to have a second-level backup that provides a faster response time than that.

Among the market leaders in the backup software category are the following:

- VERITAS Backup Exec
- VERITAS NetBackup
- EMC Legato NetWorker
- EMC Dantz Retrospect
- Computer Associates BrightStor ARCserve
- CommVault Galaxy
- IBM Tivoli Storage Manager
- BakBone NetVault
- St. Bernard Software's Open File Manager

Backup systems for enterprise applications are a little different from just standard XCOPY or block-oriented backup technologies. Many applications maintain system locks on their data files that make backups a more problematic proposition. To back up databases and messaging systems, you need to purchase software or specialized extensions for your backup software that can perform open file backup. These software packages are most often sold as packages aimed for particular applications, such as Microsoft Exchange, and they tend to command a higher price than general backup software—often two to five times the price of general backup software. Sometimes you can find software agents that are essentially client-side (even though they run on both servers and client systems) software modules for backup server applications.

Backup isn't sexy, but it is essential. If you find that backup services and the infrastructure necessary to support them don't represent at least 15% of your proposed budget either for an individual server's deployment or for a fleet of them, you need to go back to your project specification and take a careful look at whether you have really protected yourself.

Virus Scanning and Spyware Detection

Other essential routine network services these days are virus scanning, spyware detection, and problem removal. These services should run at all times, and it's best to take a multilevel approach to them. That is, you should employ these services on front-facing servers such as firewalls as your first-level detection, on your servers, and on your clients. Desktop systems can be scanned across the network or from a webservice, and many do not require that client software run locally on them; however, any system, such as a laptop, that travels should be protected by its own firewall, virus, and spyware programs. As with all other routine maintenance tasks, every system should have an automated system for running the service at regular and appropriate intervals.

Many of the vendors who sell antivirus software for PCs sell a version designed specifically for servers. Actually, in many cases, the opposite is true: Companies start out with a server antivirus program that then gets pushed out to the desktop. You'll find packages for servers that are specifically package to monitor email or databases, as well as those that are part of firewalls. This is a large category of software, and the following is a representative list of the better-known server-class antivirus solutions:

- Trend Micro's ServerProtect
- Data Fellows F-Secure Anti-Virus
- Symantec's Corporate AntiVirus
- Computer Associates's eTrust Antivirus
- Alladdin's eSafe
- F-Secure Anti-Virus
- Kaspersky Lab's Anti-virus
- McAfee's Anti-Virus
- Panda Software's Titanium Anti-Virus
- Sophos Anti-Virus

All these companies have Microsoft versions of their product, and almost all sell their products for other operating systems, such as Linux, NetWare, and others. You will also find that companies differentiate their product by market. Thus there may be a version for the desktop, one for small business users, another for enterprise-class deployments, some for firewalls and gateways, and versions for specific applications, such as Exchange or Domino.

Note

Microsoft maintains a list of antivirus partners that you can use as a jump page. It is found at www.microsoft.com/security/partners/antivirus.asp.

While viruses, worms, Trojans, and other security threats were and are early concerns, the growth of spyware software has become a more recent concern. Spyware sets up a monitoring situation or creates a security hole that can then be exploited (see for example, www.securitypipeline.com/56900521). Spyware is thus an extension of the antivirus threat. That being the case, you will often find antivirus products bundled with spyware-scanning software and other security utilities into what the vendors are calling "security suites."

The following are some of the products that include spyware-scanning capabilities:

- Aluria Software's Paladin
- Ashantipic Ltd.'s Spyware Defense
- Blue Coat Systems's Proxy SG/Proxy AV, Spyware Interceptor, and WinProxy 6.0
- Citadel Security Software's Hercules 3.5
- Computer Associates's eTrust PestPatrol Anti-Spyware
- Eset Software's NOD32
- Intrusion's SpySnare
- LANDesk Software's LANDesk Security Suite
- Lavasoft Ad-aware SE Enterprise
- McAfee's Anti-spyware Enterprise
- PC Tools Software's Spyware Doctor
- Sunbelt Software's CounterSpy and Counterspy Enterprise
- SurfControl pic's SurfControl Enterprise Threat Shield
- Tangent Computer's Packet Hawk
- Webroot Software's Spy Sweeper and Spy Sweeper Enterprise
- Websense's Websense Web Security Suite Lockdown Edition
- Webwasher AG's (Cyberguard) Webwasher CSM Suite

Note

Network World maintains a database of networked security products. See its listing of spyware products at www.networkworld.com/bg/2004/spyware/results.jsp?_tablename=antispy_live.

Disk Defragmentation

Another common routine maintenance task is disk defragmentation (or defrag). Some server operating systems have built-in defragging technologies, but most don't. Windows is one operating system that does have built-in defragmenting; it's a scaled-back version of Executive Software's Diskeeper. A host of software products are available for disk defragmentation, but only a few—such as Raxco Software's PerfectDisk, Diskeeper, and Defrag Commander—are really geared to server systems.

Disk defragmentation software for servers isn't often necessary. A server's storage system employs multiple disk heads that access multiple disks for multiple users. Having contiguous files doesn't always make all that much difference in this instance, although it does make some difference when files are smaller, contiguous, and not already in memory. Some published studies suggest performance improvements of 7% to 11%, which, although not negligible, isn't substantial. If you run a background defrag service, you will probably negate this advantage, so if you do choose to defrag your disk system, you should only do so when fragmentation is high and at times of low server usage.

Redundancy and Deployment

One of the most important aspects of a server deployment is the decisions you make about the level of fault tolerance you need to build into the system. When people think about fault tolerance, they tend to think in terms of the equipment or servers in the room or building. You can build fault tolerance into equipment with duplication and failover, as discussed in Chapter 17, "Server Rooms," but you do so at a cost. The real trick in determining what kind of redundancy you need is to determine how much risk you can realistically afford and to build your deployment appropriately. If you don't need a mission-critical system where your uptime is 99.999% or more, then buying or building a system that has less than five minutes of downtime per year is a waste of money that would be better spent on other resources.

Your project specification should include a description of the intended levels of fault tolerance that you expect for the different systems involved. You should spell out the rationale that explains why you chose that level so that it is clear why you are making the investment in the equipment you have selected. These are fundamental assumptions, and they affect overall system costs dramatically, so it's a really good idea to explain the assumptions early on in the process and seek comment from the people involved in the project (managers, users, and other designers) about whether those assumptions are within their expectations.

The following is a list of factors that should play into your selection of system redundancy:

- Cost of downtime, as a function of time
- Number of workers or amount of business affected
- Systems that can be purchased with the budget available to fund the project
- Additional staffing and operational complexity required to maintain a level of fault tolerance
- Ability to respond in a timely fashion to a failure

A few years back, a set of Sun servers at eBay's main data center went offline without a sufficient off-site server failover capability, crashing the entire site for several hours. The next day, eBay's stock value fell $5 billion, down 21% from the day before. This loss, albeit a temporary one, is a dramatic example of the issue that many organizations face when their IT systems fail: The amount of money lost due to system failure can be many times the cost of the entire IT system.

Tip

It's a good idea to perform an analysis to determine the level of risk associated with specific levels of downtime for the systems to be deployed. That analysis, as well as the business assumptions involved with accepting some level of risk, should be spelled out in your completed project specification.

Not every system outage leads to huge losses, nor does a system failing necessarily kill someone, as it might do to a critical care patient at the hospital. So your level of risk may be relatively low. Because the level of risk is essentially a business decision, the business managers of the funding sources should play a central role in setting a deployment's level of redundancy. At one large company, it was decided that the email system was a critical system but didn't require mission-critical status. The business decision was made that an outage of a couple hours every so often was the maximum risk that could be tolerated. After longer than two hours of downtime, it was found that division managers would start to send their employees home or put an end to various business processes. An analysis of the costs of downtime for that particular system was performed, and it was found that after two hours of system downtime, the costs of business lost climbed exponentially, and within four hours, the cost exceeded the entire cost of all the systems and servers that were part of the deployment.

When you have decided on an appropriate level of fault tolerance, you must determine how to assess what your equipment's actual fault tolerance will be. That information isn't always easy to come by, but there is one guiding principle: Any system's fault tolerance is no better than the component with the lowest level of fault tolerance. That is a standard calculation of risk; in any complex system, your level of risk can be no better than the factor with the highest level of risk. Therefore, when you want to improve the reliability of any system, the first step is to address the fault tolerance of the weakest part of the system.

Generally, in modern computer systems, the items with the shortest average mean lifetimes are the mechanical devices (for example, disk drives). That's why RAID is such an important feature in server systems that are expected to have high fault tolerance. Anything that moves—optical drives, tape systems, mechanical switches, and so on—is a candidate for a backup system.

Vendors quote reliability figures, but those numbers don't really provide significant guidance when you're attempting to address the issue of how much fault tolerance to purchase. A vendor's disk drives may have a nominal rating of five years MTBF (mean time between failures). That number is usually valid when you are measuring thousands of drives, randomly scattered among a number of production runs, but failures tend to run in streaks when some problem arises in one particular production run. An MTBF of five years per disk won't be particularly helpful to you if 10% of a 50-drive array fails at about the same time because they were all part of the same production run.

There's really no easy answer to the problem of average failure rates versus failures of specific instances. In some cases, it is possible to distribute components in such a way that your risk is spread out. You could, for example, move disk drives from any one purchase into a number of separate arrays systematically so that there aren't too many of the same production together. However, when you do that, you may be simply spreading your problems around to more systems and making more work for yourself. Chasing this problem is a fool's errand. However, when this kind of consideration crops up, the most appropriate consideration is whether to purchase drives with a higher level of MTBF, moving up in reliability from drives with a five-year average to ones with perhaps seven years.

Sample Project Specification for Deployment

This chapter covers a lot of different topics and makes various suggestions about the different elements of a project specification that you might want to consider. Table 20.2 summarizes this discussion by listing the elements of a complete project specification that you can use as a checklist for your own work.

Table 20.2 Elements of a Complete Deployment Project Specification

Part	Purpose
Executive Summary	One-page overview of the project's goals, time line, and budget.
Table of Contents	Necessary for any long document.
Proposal Process	Identifies who participated and how decisions were made.
System Requirements	Describes the working parameters of the system, including the following: ■ **Servers**—Specifies numbers and types. ■ **Clients**—Specifies numbers and types. ■ **Storage systems**—Specifies numbers and types. ■ **Network requirements**—Identifies network systems, ISPs, network topologies, and other factors. ■ **Backup systems**—Describes the backup systems chosen, including servers for backing up storage and software, UPS devices, and so on. ■ **Maintenance**—Describes the systems used for routine maintenance.

Table 20.2   Continued

Part	Purpose
Equipment Deployed	A list of the equipment described in the previous sections.
Software Deployed	The rationale for the selection of the software systems to be used, including the following: ■ **Operating system**—Describes the version and distribution of operating system types. ■ **Applications**—Describes the types of application software and their distribution. ■ **Management software**—Describes how systems are managed, upgraded, and controlled. ■ **Custom applications**—Describes custom applications, which are software that needs to be coded to support your deployment. This can include full-blown applications, custom database solutions, or even scripts.
Vendors and Contractors	List of vendors and contractors, with any second sourcing available.
Site Description	Location of deployment, generally and specifically.
Risk Analysis	Rationale for the level of fault tolerance and redundant systems.
Project Time Line	Description of the deployment's individual parts. This may be best shown in project management software diagrams, Gantt diagrams, and illustrated time lines. It includes the following: ■ **Project phases**—Typical phases include the test phase, review, implementation, and final review. ■ **Milestones**—This describes significant events that mark either the beginning or end of a phase. ■ **Resources and staffing**—The people participating in the deployment are identified. They should be part of a Gantt chart that is part of your project plan, indicating how resources are deployed throughout the project. ■ **Identification of the critical path**—The critical path is the steps along the project that affect the overall time line.
Budget	A listing of the budget, with significant line items broken out. The budgets include the deployment budget, project operational budgets, software and hardware licenses, and staffing requirements.
Sign-off	The sign-off is proof that the project was approved by those who signed it.

CHAPTER 21

Server Testing and Maintenance

To get the most out of your servers, you need to know how well they are operating, what is "normal" behavior, and what to change when your server(s) don't operate normally. Part of good management practice is the collection of performance data because with that data you can better tune your servers, plan for upgrades, and know when to upgrade your systems.

This chapter describes some of the tools and techniques you can use to test and monitor your servers. Modern operating systems and server applications provide some powerful tools that you can use to help in this area. Performance monitoring is accomplished by using small code snippets called *counters* that trap and measure when system events occur. Windows, UNIX, NetWare, and other server operating systems come with a large array of counters for measuring the resource consumption of key system components, such as processors, memory, disk space, and more. Beyond simple consumption, you can also get information about the efficiency of your system, speeds, throughputs, and more. When you install a server application, it may install additional counters for you to use. You can track the results of your performance measurements by using performance monitors or by executing a number of commands from the command line.

The second area of server testing is troubleshooting, and one of the primary tools for troubleshooting is the collection and analysis of system events. In an event-driven programming environment, a system is constantly reacting to events, and a typical system may generate hundreds, if not thousands, of events each second. Many events, such as screen redraws, may not be particularly significant, but an event such as a user logon is a valuable event to record. Systems store a number of different logs you can use, including application, security, and system logs. This chapter looks at events and event logs and discusses how to get more information about logs as well as how to determine which events are significant. You can build different redundancies into your servers to get different levels of fault tolerance. By paying attention to good backup strategies and building redundancy into your servers, you can give your systems a fault tolerance that will help you survive any disaster that could conceivably happen.

Finally, this chapter presents the topic of disaster recovery. Disaster recovery involves planning and preparation, coupled with having an understanding of the kinds of things that can go wrong.

Gathering Baseline Performance Data

There are three good reasons to collect data on the baseline performance of your servers:

- To know where they've been
- To know where they are now
- To figure out where they will be sometime in the future

The only way to really know any of these three things is to have reliable data that you can use to relate one state to the other. You collect data on your servers so that you can establish a *baseline*—that is, a measured level of performance of that server at a point in time. A baseline study can include a number of key measurements, including the following:

- **Speed**—How fast key components such as your backup to disk are operating
- **Consumption**—How much of a resource, such as memory or disk space, is being consumed
- **Throughput**—The rate or speed/time of a key component such as your disk I/O or the number of messages/second that your Exchange Server sent and received
- **Efficiency**—The overall success the system is having at best utilizing a resource, such as your processor or the amount of data your system gets from RAM cache versus the amount of data that is retrieved from disk cache (page files)
- **Availability**—The percentage of time that your system is up and running or the percentage of time a database transaction succeeds

When you benchmark a server, you establish the baseline for normal performance, or what passes for normal at that particular moment. If you don't know what "normal" is, then you are hard pressed to resolve problems when your system is behaving in a manner that isn't normal. The tools used to create benchmarks and establish baselines are system and event monitors. These tools create data that is written to a log file, and you can export that log file to a standard spreadsheet or database format for further analysis.

You can use benchmarks for three tasks:

- To troubleshoot problems when they arise
- To optimize your system or a component of your system in order to get the best performance possible
- For capacity planning so that you can use trends to predict the future

Benchmarking should be part of everyday administration practice because collecting meaningful data takes a long time. Modern operating system and application vendors build into their software useful tools for benchmarking, so you don't have to look far to find a tool that will help you get started. Solaris, NetWare, Windows, and others network operating systems come with their own performance monitor and event logging applications. These tools are included because they are among the first tools that developers need when they are creating the software you will eventually use.

Most of the various performance monitors are configured for real-time analysis of a system. That is, they collect data on the CPU, disk, and so on. This occurs as often as several times a second to every few seconds so that the tools can display the current behavior of your system. Although that is useful when you want to know what's happening immediately in front of you, it is way too much data over much too short a time to be valuable when you are benchmarking your system. You need to change the default time interval in your performance monitor so that it collects only a few data points per hour so that your log file is able to maintain a meaningful record.

For most purposes, you want to collect from 1 to around 20 data points for each hour. The number you should collect is a function of how representative of the condition the instantaneous measurement you are making is. If you are measuring something that varies over the course of a day, such as email traffic, then a measurement every 10 or 15 minutes will probably be sufficient. You should measure the growth of your log file and determine how much data is stored for each data point. Knowing the frequency and the size of each data point allows you to change the default log size so that you can collect a meaningful data set without the data being overwritten.

When you are benchmarking a system, you should start a new benchmark log. Every change should also register an entry in your work diary so that you know when your system has changed and how. Significant changes include adding or removing software or hardware. Because those changes should alter your performance, creating a new benchmark log makes it easier to figure out where in the logs the changes were made. As a rule of thumb, you should consider starting a new benchmark log every time you might consider creating a restore point.

Tip

It's a good idea to start a notebook in which you put printouts of your trend and activity data over time. When it comes time to justify a server upgrade or you need to plan for additional equipment or set up a resource allocation, you have the information available at your fingertips. If your server room has gone paperless, consider using an Excel spreadsheet or other software tool (preferably a tool that allows you to create graphs).

You should consider creating a new benchmark study whenever you have upgraded your server or creating a new log for each of the additional servers added to your system. Other changes, such as switching from 100BaseT to 1000BaseT (GigE) on your network or replacing a central network switch, are also good points at which to create a new benchmark study.

Benchmarks are a little like backups. You should store a library of benchmarks for your future use, and you should preferably store those benchmarks on removable storage. Benchmarks are so valuable in planning and troubleshooting that you should protect them the same way you protect your company's documents.

Operating systems provide two major tools to measure baseline activity: counters that measure performance by trapping events and an activity log of significant events that are trapped by your operating system or server application.

You should create a baseline of the following components as a function of time:

- **CPU utilization**—A server's CPU utilization might run at 30% normally. All systems respond with 100% peak utilization when larger tasks are presented. However, if your server consistently runs at about 75% CPU utilization, there probably isn't enough overhead to run your system when a significant load occurs. Instead, your system will just grind to a halt.

- **Cache buffer utilization**—Your cache is first-level memory and can greatly improve your system's performance when needed data is found in RAM cache instead of in your system RAM or, worse, on your hard disk. A good level to aim for is when your cache buffer is around 65% to 75% of your available server memory. There's no penalty other than component cost for a larger cache, but you might find that your server's performance suffers at a level of 45%.

- **File reads and writes**—The amount of disk I/O is a measure of the activity of your system. If you find that you are getting an increased number of server-busy notices sent to your clients or if your I/O queue length is growing or is too high, that's an indicator of a disk I/O bottleneck and may require that you upgrade your storage system with a faster controller or a different disk or array type.

- **Volume utilization**—The number of drives that are allocated and no longer available for reads and writes is a measure of your server's capacity to accommodate more users, applications, and tasks. It's a useful capacity planning feature to know your disk consumption over time. Modern operating systems can run with disk utilization as high as 85% to 90%. However, when you consume this much disk capacity or more, you start to eat into your page file allocation. Therefore, when you see that your disk utilization is greater than 75%, it's a good idea to create more free space or add more storage.

Note

Much of the data stored on your servers' disks is useless information. If you run a storage resource manager to categorize your data, you will find data that is duplicated, data that belongs to users who no longer belong to your organization, old and unused files, and files such as MP3s or JPEGs that don't belong on your system.

- **Processes that are running on your server (both services and applications)**—It's a really good idea to create a process map that details what each process is that is running on your server, as well as a standard level of CPU utilization of each. You can view processes in Windows by using the Task Manager (by pressing Ctrl+Alt+Del) and in Linux/Solaris/UNIX by using the process -ls command. (Some operating systems use the ps command or some other utility.) When you understand which processes are legitimate, you can close any rogue processes and make rational decisions about which processes to turn off and which help your system perform better. The latter is one of the best methods for tuning a server for a particular purpose.

These five factors are the measures of the critical system resources: processing, I/O throughput, storage resources, and the standard state of your server. When we say that you need a baseline as a function of time, we mean time in two dimensions: You need to establish the variation of your server's activity as a function of your organization's standard work cycle (usually a week) and how that standard work cycle is changing over the course of months and years. That information gives you a feeling for the normal variation in system resource usage, and it allows you to determine how that variation is trending.

Using Windows Server 2003 Diagnostic Tools

Windows Server offers two primary diagnostic tools for servers: Performance Monitor and Windows Event Viewer. A third tool that you might want to use to diagnose your server is Network Monitor. All three of these tools are discussed in the following sections.

◀◀ For more general information on Windows 2003, see "Windows Servers," p. 758.

Windows Performance Monitor

Performance Monitor is a real-time monitoring tool that offers a wide range of counters for you to monitor. The utility is offered up as a graphical tool, most often shown in strip chart form, but you can configure it in several additional ways. When you run Performance Monitor, you can save the results to a file, and those results can be useful for tuning and for benchmarking studies. Figure 21.1 shows a sample run of Performance Monitor.

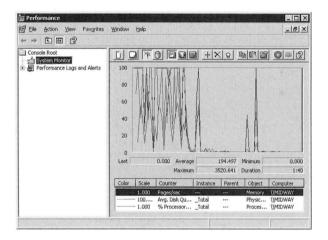

Figure 21.1   A sample run of Performance Monitor.

To open Performance Monitor, do one of the following:

■ Press Windows+R (or select Start, Run), enter perfmon in the dialog box that appears, and then press the Enter key.

■ Select Performance from the Administrative Tools folder of your Program submenu of the Start menu.

Note

Both Windows Performance Monitor and Windows Event Viewer are self-documented tools. That is, if you select their help commands, you find a relatively complete description on how to use these tools and the various capabilities they offer.

Windows Event Viewer

Windows Event Viewer is a window into the contents of the Windows event logs, and can be view within the Microsoft Management Console (MMC). This utility shows the logs in the left pane and the events in the right pane. To open Event Viewer, do either of the following:

- Press Windows+R (or select Start, Run), enter eventvwr in the dialog box that appears, and then press the Enter key.
- Select Start, All Programs, Administrative Tools, Event Viewer.

The Event Viewer is a self-documented tool. If you open the Help system, you will find a detailed description of how to use the tool and what all the different symbols mean. In examining events, you should pay attention to not only error events but also the sequence in which events occur. The sequence of events is often an important clue as to what generated an error.

The Windows event IDs are not always well described in the Event Viewer. Therefore, you may need to consult the Microsoft Knowledge Base or one of the websites devoted to Windows events in order to decode them.

When you are finished with the Event Viewer, you can press Ctrl+F to close the program.

Windows Network Monitor

A third tool that you might want to use to diagnose your server is the Network Monitor, or netmon.

◄◄ For more information on Network Monitor, see "Locating Bottlenecks," p. 571.

To open and view the Network Monitor, do either of the following:

- Press Windows+R (or select Start, Run), enter netmon in the dialog box that appears, and then press the Enter key.
- Select Start, All Programs, Administrative Tools, Network Monitor.

With Network Monitor, you should be able to determine what the throughput levels for your NICs and determine how many errors your NIC sees. If you are getting a large number of network errors, you should follow up on it because it may indicate that you have either a configuration problem or a hardware problem. NICs sometimes fail, and when they do, they often don't just go dead—that would be too easy. When NICs fail, they get flaky first, perhaps dropping their connections at irregular intervals.

Note

If Network Monitor doesn't appear to be installed on your version of Windows Server or is missing drivers or other components, you may need to install it by using Add/Remove Software and specifying it in the Windows Components section. The version of Network Monitor found in Windows Server is not as complete as the version that ships with Windows SMS (Systems Management Server).

Windows Server 2003's diagnostic tools are a capable, if not elegant, set of utilities for establishing system and networking benchmarks. The Performance tool (formerly called the Performance Monitor) can be used to create a strip chart that records various system parameters, not only on a per-server basis but on networks as well. You can often correlate the behaviors you see with events that you see in the event log. With Network Monitor, you can correlate the network traffic you see with network performance to determine the actual types of traffic, their origins, and their target on the network.

Using Sun Solaris Diagnostic Tools

Solaris is replete with performance management tools, borrowing many from the UNIX bag of tricks and also including a few developed at Sun. Many of these tools are command-line tools, but you can find graphical utilities that you can either display the data in or redirect the data to. The following sections describe some of the most commonly used command-line tools.

◄◄ For more general information on Sun Solaris, see "Sun Solaris," p. 763.

The perfmeter Command

The most obvious graphical tool is `perfmeter`, which is the Solaris performance monitor. Actually, `perfmeter` is an OpenWindows XView utility. `perfmeter` creates a graphical display of your system resource consumption, either in the form of a strip chart or as a set of analog dials. The following are some of the performance factors it measures:

- **cpu**—Percentage of CPU utilized
- **pkts**—Ethernet packets per second
- **page**—Paging activity, in pages per second
- **swap**—Jobs swapped per second
- **intr**—Interrupts per second
- **disk**—Disk I/O per second
- **cntxt**—Context switches per second
- **load**—Average number of processors running over the previous minute
- **colls**—Ethernet collisions per second detected
- **errs**—Errors detected in received packets per second

While `perfmeter` is very useful for real-time analysis and troubleshooting, other UNIX commands are more useful for logging information to a file and for creating a baseline or benchmark study.

One commonly used tool for measuring performance is the `vmstat` utility, which measures the use of virtual memory in a system. With `vmstat` you can determine how much your CPU is being utilized, the amount of disk swapping, the number of page faults, and the amount of memory usage.

The `vmstat` command can use the following syntax:

```
vmstat [-cipqsS] [disks] [interval[count]]
```

You can use a number of switches with the `vmstat` command to get useful output, including the following:

- **-c**—Reports the cache flushing. This switch is now obsolete.
- **-I**—Reports the number of interrupts per device.
- **-p**—Reports the paging activity. A variety of paging actions can be specified.
- **-q**—Does not report messages that the system generates during a state change.
- **-s**—Reports the number of system events since the system boot.
- **-S**—Reports the amount of disk swapping.
- **count**—Reports the number of times that your specified switches are repeated.
- **disks**—Lets you determine which disks are measured.
- **interval**—Reports the time period, in seconds, that `vmstat` runs its statistics.

For a more detailed explanation of the `vmstat` command, see the Solaris man pages at http://docs.sun.com/app/docs/doc/816-5166/6mbb1kqjv?a=view.

The `mpstat` Command

The second performance command you can use to measure processor performance in a multiprocessor Solaris system is `mpstat`. The syntax of this command is as follows:

```
/usr/bin/mpstat [-a] [-p| -P set] [interval [ count]]
```

The `mpstat` command returns a table of results of processor statistics. Each row in the table represents a single processor, and each column represents a different processor performance attribute. For a more detailed explanation of the `mpstat` command, you can view the Solaris man pages at http://docs.sun.com/app/docs/doc/816-5166/6mbb1kqjv?a=view.

Note

Keep in mind that there are often slight, and in rare cases significant, differences in the command syntax and the options and switches available in commands in different versions of UNIX.

With `mpstat`, each processor is listed consecutively, and the command provides information on a number of factors. You can see your overall processor load, the number of interrupts used on each processor, the amount of processor time being used by each user, and how long each processor had to wait while an I/O was in progress. In a typical `mpstat` table, you might see the follow columns:

- **minf**—Minor faults
- **mjf**—Major faults
- **xcal**—Interprocessor cross-calls
- **intr**—Interrupts
- **ithr**—Interrupts as threads
- **csw**—Context switches
- **icsw**—Involuntary context switches
- **mig**—Thread migrations to a different processor
- **smtx**—Spins on mutexes or locks not acquired on first attempt
- **srw**—Spins on reader/writers locks or locks not acquired on the first try
- **syscl**—System calls
- **usr**—Percentage of user time
- **sys**—Percentage of system time
- **wt**—Percentage of wait time
- **idl**—Percentage of idle time

Which of these columns you see depends on what options and switches you used with the `mpstat` command.

When you see a large difference in interrupts between processors—say a couple thousand—you can redistribute the load by moving your add-in cards around. The time a processor spends servicing a user's process should be around 85%. You should also see that the amount of time any processor has to wait should be less than around 20%. If you see that the processor spends more than 40% of its time waiting for an I/O operation to complete, you have a bottleneck in your I/O system.

The `iostat` Command

Yet another command-line utility is `iostat` (see http://docs.sun.com/app/docs/doc/816-0211/6m6nc6715?a=view), which measures the efficiency of a system's I/O. With `iostat`, you see a combined summary of activity in the first column, as you do with both `vmstat` and `mpstat`. The information listed is the activity since the last time your system started up, which is also true for `vmstat` and `mpstat`. The most valuable columns in the `iostat` command output are wait, actv, %b, and svc_t. Those columns describe the number of requests for disk writes in the queue, the number of requests pending in the disk volume, how busy the disk is in terms of a percentage, and the time it takes, in milliseconds, for any I/O request to be taken out of the queue and be processed.

Note

Each of the three commands **vmstat**, **mpstat**, and **iostat** is fully documented in the Solaris **man** files, and each has a number of switches that can modify the output of the command.

The `proc` Command

If you want to see what is actually using your system, then you should run a variant of the `proc`, or process, command. You can also see just the processes with the highest utilization by using the `top` command. There are three common uses of the `proc` command:

- **% ps -eo pid,pcpu,args | sort +1n**—This command lists processes with the greatest CPU utilization

- **% ps -eo pid,vsz,args | sort +1n**—This command lists processes with the greatest memory allocation

- **% /usr/ucb/ps aux |more**—This command lists processes that have both the highest CPU utilization and memory allocation.

You will probably find that you need to use the | pipe in order to freeze the screen one screen at a time. The output of the `proc` command can be quite long and will scroll off your screen if you don't use |.

The `sar` Command

Solaris has a command that can collect system information. The sar, or system activity report, command is turned off by default and must be enabled. You follow these steps to enable sar:

1. Open the `crontab` entries for the user sys.
2. Uncomment the entries for that user.
3. Open the `/etc/init.d/perf` file and uncomment the lines in that file.
4. Execute the script `/etc/init.d/perf` from the command line or do so after your system reboots to get a full listing of a complete system session.

The sar command writes the data it collects into a set of files created daily and located at var/adm/sa. The files are consecutively numbered sa*xx*, where *xx* is the day of the month. Unless you remove files that are a month old, they get overwritten by new files. sar output contains information that you can use to benchmark your system. Check the man page for sar for information on how to set the interval between data points, as found at http://docs.sun.com/app/docs/doc/816-5165/6mbb0m9rc?a=view.

Using NetWare Diagnostic Tools

On a NetWare server running ZENworks, you can set the threshold values for services in ConsoleOne and identify trends. You can also modify server files by using the Management Agent for NetWare or by using the Management Agent for Windows. Server agents record the initial values for thresholds and trends when they are installed. Whenever you add a new object to be monitored, NetWare creates a new trend file. You can view the trends in the NTREND.INI file.

When the management agents are running, you can use ConsoleOne to modify both the threshold and trend values. If your server reboots, ZENworks reestablishes the trends and thresholds, using the last values in the trend files. If the trend files are deleted or if a new monitored component is added to the server, the initial threshold and trends are reestablished.

The trend file for NetWare is NTREND.INI, and the trend file for Windows is N_NTTREN.INI. The trend value sets the sample interval, which is the amount of time that goes by for which data is kept. A collection of trend data is called a trend bucket, and each line in the file is a separate data point. ZENworks allows you to alter the sample interval, enable or disable a trend file, and use a backup function to copy out your trend data. You should generally set a trend bucket to the length of your organization's standard work cycle.

The following are some of the server management tasks that ZENworks for Servers (ZfS) offers:

- Getting server configuration information
- Getting summary data
- Trending data
- Altering sampling parameters
- Altering server's operational settings
- Issuing server commands

ConsoleOne is similar to the MMC in terms of its organization. A two-panel window shows organizational or summary information on the left pane and detailed information in the right pane.

Using Third-Party Benchmarking Tools

Using benchmarking tools is a way to establish the relative performance of one system or platform against that of another. All sorts of benchmarks are available for you to measure server performance. Some tests are hardware-only measurements, while others measure a server running a particular operating system or an operating system/application coupling. Many benchmarks are free and easy to deploy, and others are costly both to purchase and to test against.

There are many open and freely available benchmarks, some of which are distributed by industry standards groups such as SPEC, TPC, and Mindspring. As benchmarks get older, they are often released into the public domain either because the group sponsoring them has lost interest in them, gone defunct, or made the benchmark obsolete by producing another (usually more complex) test.

You can find benchmarks that have been created by testing organizations, such as Ziff Davis's NetBench, ServerBench, and WebBench tests. Some very useful benchmarking tests are created by operating system vendors to help OEMs test their systems for capacity planning; Microsoft's MAPI Messaging Benchmark (MMB3) is an example. With an MMB3 workload for the LoadSim 20003 Exchange test suite (see www.microsoft.com/exchange/evaluation/performance/mmb3.mspx), it is possible to benchmark one Exchange server against another. Another example from Microsoft is the inetload tool for testing Web, proxy, caching, directory services, and messaging over Internet servers. Another test from Microsoft is the WCAT test. Table 21.1 lists some of the most commonly used server benchmarks.

Table 21.1   Server Benchmarking Tools

Tool	Sponsor	Purpose	Reference
Apache JMeter	Apache.org	Java application testing	http://jakarta.apache.org/jmeter/index.html
Iometer	Intel	Disk performance	www.iometer.org
LMbench	Bitmover.com	UNIX system benchmarks	www.bitmover.com/lmbench
NetBench	Ziff Davis	Network file server testing	www.veritest.com/benchmarks/netbench/default.asp
NetPerf	Netperf.org	Server network testing (for UNIX mostly)	www.netperf.org
SPECWeb2005	SPEC	Webserver testing	www.spec.org/web2005
stress		CPU, memory, and disk I/O testing	weather.ou.edu/~apw/projects/stress/
TPC-C	TPC	OLTP or data warehouse testing	www.tpc.org/tpcc/default.asp
TPC-H	TPC	Database query transactions	www.tpc.org/tpch/default.asp
WebBench	Ziff Davis	Webserver testing	www.veritest.com/benchmarks/webbench/home.asp
WebStone	Mindcraft	Webserver testing	www.mindcraft.com/webstone/

Benchmarking is best done when you are comparing two or more systems under identical conditions. Most frequently, however, that is not the case. Moving from platform to platform, moving from application to application, and dealing with equipment modifications, even when they are minor, can skew the results of a benchmark toward one vendor or another. Therefore, several industry standards groups were formed to create tests that could be developed over time, lead to meaningful comparisons, and be policed when necessary. The following sections take a look at three of these standards and testing organizations: SPEC, TPC, and Mindcraft.

SPEC

The SPEC benchmarks (see www.spec.org) are a set of standardized tests that measure systems under what are meant to be real-world testing conditions. SPEC was originally formed as a cooperative in 1988 by several workstation vendors, and later it spun off as an independent corporation called the Standard Performance Evaluation Corporation. The goal of the SPEC tests, which are constantly under revision, is to establish a standard code base that allows different operating systems running on different equipment to be measured in a meaningful way, one against another. Most often you see SPEC benchmark results described for very high-end workstations, servers, and even supercomputers in an effort to set the performance record for a particular SPEC benchmark. SPEC benchmarks not only measure system performance, but they often set standards for price/performance standards as well. That's why companies like to quote the different SPEC results in their marketing information when it suits their purposes.

There are currently SPEC benchmarks for the following systems and components:

- **CPU**—The CPU2000 benchmark measures the performance of a processor for floating-point operations. The CINT2000 test measures straight integer performance.

- **Graphics/applications**—SPEC has a set of six different graphics tests that measure a variety of operations: vector and bitmapped drawing, 3D rendering, shading, and others.

- **High Performance Computing, OpenMP, and MPI**—These benchmarks are aimed at measuring the performance of large systems running enterprise applications, where the advantages of a parallel or distributed architecture can make a meaningful contribution to performance. MPI is a standard based on a Message Passing Interface application.

- **Java client/server**—Three main Java tests run specific Java applets or applications in a client/server environment: jAppServer2004, JBB2005, and JVM98 (some older variations exist). The JBB2005 benchmark measures a Java business application where an order-processing application of a wholesale supplier is set up and measured on a Java Virtual Machine (JVM).

- **Mail servers**—The MAIL2001 benchmark measures the performance of a mail server to send and receive SMTP and POP3 mail. Throughput and response are measured under standard client mail workloads, with specified network connections and disk storage systems. The SPECimap benchmark measures IMAPI servers that run the SMTP and IMAP4 protocols.

- **Network file systems**—This SFS97 benchmark, now at version 3.0, measures the performance of a network file server running NFS.

- **Webservers**—The latest benchmark in this area is the WEB2005 test, which sends HTTP GET requests for both JSP and PHP pages over a broadband connection. There are work loads that measure a banking site using HTTPS, an e-commerce site using HTTP/HTTPS, and a help desk site using standard HTTP. Older versions of this standard, such as WEB99, measured straight client/server throughput, and the WEB99_SSL standard used the SSL protocol.

The purchase price of SPEC benchmarks ranges from around $100 up to as much as $2,000. The disparity in pricing is due to the complexity of the work necessary to both create the benchmark as well as the personnel and equipment needed to verify compliance of the results.

The problem with the SPEC benchmarks has been that they allow vendors to implement the tests in ways that favor their particular systems and thus they aren't as standardized as they might seem. However, this is by design. SPEC endeavors to allow vendors the freedom to run the benchmarks in a way that allows them to demonstrate the advantages of their system. So although the SPEC benchmark uses standard source code that is based on existing applications that have already been created by members of the organizations, it is up to the benchmarker to take the benchmark, compile the source code, and tune its system to obtain the best results. Thus there are inherent differences between test results.

To consider how benchmarking might work, consider a test based on a specific webserver such as Apache. Apache exists on most major operating system platforms, and certainly on any of the ones you are likely to consider working with if you are reading this book. Although Apache's code is the same in any case, when you compile it for Linux, Solaris, HP-UX, or even Windows, you get different versions of the software. Even the compiler you use can make a slight difference in performance. That's the first level of differences. In addition, each vendor can tune its system so that it provides the best performance possible for that particular application. So if one vendor is smarter than another in how it tunes its disk system, that's yet another advantage. SPEC is replete with these potential advantages and disadvantages.

Still, SPEC measures systems by using standard applications, and the results that vendors get are real results. So even if one vendor is able to achieve a new benchmark standard, that benchmark is a legitimate performance measurement. SPEC publishes several hundred of its members' benchmark results every year.

TPC

The Transaction Processing Performance Council (TPC; see www.tpc.org) is an industry group that consists of nearly all the major server vendors. The tests that TPC sponsors focus on transaction processing and database benchmarks. These tests define a set of transactions that would be of interest to a business. The kind of transactions the tests create are meant to be similar to the ones you create when you withdrew money from a checking account at an ATM. Similar types of transactions are used to update a database system when you make an airline reservation or when a warehouse ships or purchases inventory items.

In many large-scale enterprise deployments, TPC benchmarks are often requested. This is because TPC benchmarks simulate actual deployments and let a buyer evaluate a system as a whole rather than one subsystem at a time. Large government and corporate projects often request these tests for their larger systems, so many of the TPC benchmarks that are run are never published or publicized. In these instances, the vendor running the benchmark may choose to customize the benchmark to make it more suitable for the project that is being evaluated. As you might imagine, it's relatively easy for vendors to modify the TPC tests in ways that give their systems an unfair advantage over other vendors. The TPC has established a fair-use policy as well as an audit process to make sure that its benchmarks aren't misused.

The TPC sponsors four main benchmarks:

- **TCP-App**—The TCP-App benchmark sets up a test platform using application servers and a web service. It uses applications that are commercially available, including messaging servers and databases such as Exchange, Domino, SQL Server, and Oracle. A client workload is generated against this system so that the performance of multiple sessions in a managed environment can be measured. TCP-App sessions try to make use of the latest technologies, so XML documents and SOAP are used for data exchange, and transactions are managed in a multitiered distributed architecture. The databases used have a variety of tables and relationships, and their integrity (that is, ACID properties) is also established.

- **TCP-C**—TPC-C v5 is one of the most well known of all the large server benchmarks. TPC-C was first established in 1992, and it has been the standard measurement for large-scale online transaction processing (OLTP). The TPC-C benchmark creates a complex database that simulates an order-entry system against which a large number of users create several kinds of transactions, such as orders, payments, status checks, and warehouse management functions. This is exactly the kind of system that enterprise management systems or enterprise resource planning (ERP) applications such as SAP/R3, PeopleSoft, Oracle Applications, and others are meant to address. TPC-C benchmarks give two results: one that measures performance in tpm-C (transactions per minute) and one that measures the price performance in $/tpm-C. Thus vendors quote success in TPC-C benchmarks for each of these two different factors.

- **TCP-H**—The TCP-H benchmark is an ad hoc decision support database that allows users to generate queries against the database and make modifications based on the results. The results of this benchmark are expressed in terms of the TPC-H price/performance measurement and expressed in terms of $/QphH@Size (query per hour at a certain database size).

- **TCP-W**—TPC-W is a web e-commerce benchmark application. In this benchmark, a transactional webserver application is subjected to a transactional load, using standard TCP/IP transport and browsers. The environment generates on-the-fly, dynamic, data-driven web pages against a complex database system where transaction integrity must be maintained and where there is contention for access to the database as well as for data modifications. The result of the TPC-W benchmark is expressed in terms of a shopping metric (WIPS), a browsing metric (WIPSb), and a web-based order-entry metric (WIPSo). When all these are measured, the result leads to the overall measure of the WIPS rate and its associated price/performance measure of $/WIPS, which is the actual quoted benchmark. A new version of TCP-W is in development.

Note

To view the top 10 results for each of the TPC benchmarks, go to www.tpc.org/information/results.asp.

TPC tests are often very involved affairs; not only are the tests relatively expensive to buy, but they can be very expensive to run. Vendors sometimes stage tests with million-dollar pieces of equipment, so it's not unheard of for some of the more involved tests, such as data warehousing tests, to run into six figures or more. However, when a server vendor is trying to sell a top-level business manager on a system that will run a significant part of his or her business—and often a mission-critical part—many vendors believe it is well worth spending the money.

Mindcraft

Mindcraft (see www.mindcraft.com) is an independent testing laboratory that was created in 1985 by people already involved with SPEC. Mindcraft does both contract benchmark testing and creates its own benchmarks. Among the tests that Mindcraft has developed are the following:

- **DirectoryMark**—This is a test for the performance of Active Directory on both Windows Server 2003 and Windows Server 2000 domain servers, as well as Active Directory running on an application server. This test is available for free download, as is its source code, and it's available for both Windows and Solaris servers. This benchmark measures the performance of a server that is running a Lightweight Directory Access Protocol (LDAP) 3 sever. Data is transferred in LDIF format, and it is possible for vendors running this benchmark to create their own special scripts that execute the kinds of directory transactions that their systems will use.

- **AuthMark**—This benchmark tests products that authenticate access to web-based products. One simulation tested is called the Login scenario, which measures how long it takes for a user to request and download a web page from a secure webserver. The second tested configuration, called the Extranet scenario, has a login scenario that measures the time it takes external users (for example, customers or suppliers) to request and get information from a private website. These two scenarios are measured under different loads.

- **iLOAD MVP**—This tool creates loading for systems being benchmarked. The tool can be used not only for benchmarking but also for capacity planning, and it can also be used as a regression testing tool.

- **WebStone**—This is probably the best known of Mindcraft's tests. WebStone 2.5 is downloadable for free from Mindcraft's website, as is its source code. The WebStone benchmark was first developed by Silicon Graphics to measure their systems' performance as webservers. Mindcraft acquired the rights to the benchmark from Silicon Graphics and has enhanced the tests and modified the workloads that the WebStone test runs. The benchmark places a client load on a webserver, which requests (through HTTP commands) that pages and files be returned to clients' browsers. The test provides performance data for how well HTML commands are processed, how fast CGI scripts run, and how well the webserver's API performs as a function of load. Mindscape has WebStone running on Microsoft Internet Information Server's (IIS's) ISAPI and Netscape's NSAPI.

Mindcraft has become the repository of a number of older benchmarking standards that the company continues to develop. Several of these benchmarks are available in an open standard format, meaning that both the application and the source code are available for download.

Routine Maintenance

Servers are meant to run without much attention the great majority of the time. Therefore, you might think that there isn't much regular maintenance involved. That's largely true, but there are tasks that you need to do on a regular basis in order to protect your data. As your server chugs along, you have to pay attention to its status by doing a regular reading of the server's vital signs, its performance trends, and its event logs.

When it's time to do routine maintenance on your server, chances are that the work will disrupt the service that the server is doing for your clients/users. This results in the dreaded "Server is down for maintenance" message. Timing and notice are, of course, important. You should notify all users with reasonable notice prior to bringing down any essential service. Given how busy people are these days, it's not a bad idea to start giving daily notices about a week prior to maintenance. On the day of maintenance, you should probably post a couple notices during the day.

There's some contention about when is the best time to perform server maintenance. Most people recommend after-hours, and often late at night, because that will affect the fewest people. Many people recommend doing maintenance on Friday and Saturday nights because if something goes wrong, you still have at least one weekend day to fix the problem before the work week begins. A minority recommendation is that Monday nights are the best time because if there is a problem, you are in the beginning of a work week, and you have additional help and service resources available to you to fix the problem.

Backup and replication are probably the most important pieces of routine maintenance. With modern server technologies, you shouldn't have to bring a server offline to perform a backup. However, a backup will affect your server's performance. Therefore, you should also do backup and replication at low-activity time.

The sections that follow look at a few additional routine maintenance tasks:

- Drive and media testing
- Routine cleaning
- Virus and spyware checking
- Disk defragmentation

Drive Testing

If your server starts to experience read or write errors, or if you see stop errors from the operating system or random weird behavior, it's not a bad idea to test your hard drives to see if there is a problem with a drive or with some portion of it. In a high-end RAID or storage solution, diagnostic software is usually included as part of the package. If you are lucky, that software runs in the background or runs periodically. However, you might need to run such a utility manually.

All modern operating systems ship with a diagnostic disk utility for testing a drive, the file system that's on it, and the data structures contained on the drive, such as indexes. Because your operating system actually formats the disk, writes the file system, and writes the files, it's a good idea to start drive testing by using the tools that the operating system supplies.

It's good practice to run a disk checking utility from time to time because even if you aren't experiencing a problem at the moment, the utility can find damaged sectors and mark them so that they can't damage future files or I/O. It may take a while to do a disk check on a large drive, so it's best to perform these tasks at time of low workload. Also, if your system is highly available, you may have to remove the volume to test your drives, and despite the hassle, you should do so from time to time. Let's briefly look at a couple of examples of how this is done, first with Windows Server 2003 and then with Sun Solaris.

Checking a Disk in Windows Server 2003

When Windows uses a hard drive, particularly a system drive, it puts a lock on the drive, preventing it from being low-level tested on a bit-by-bit basis. The original DOS CHKDSK disk checking utility was modified in Windows and is now called Check Disk. However, just like CHKDSK, Check Disk has to be run from outside Windows on an unmounted volume. It's most often run at startup.

You run Check Disk by doing the following:

1. Open My Computer, right-click the drive to be tested, and then select Properties.

2. Click the Tools tab and then click the Check Now button in the Error Testing section. The Check Disk dialog box appears, as shown in Figure 21.2.

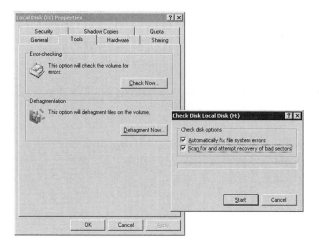

Figure 21.2   The Check Disk dialog box shown in Windows Server 2003.

3. Click on both the Automatically Fix File System Errors and the Scan for and Attempt Recovery of Bad Sectors check boxes and then click OK.

4. When the Check Disk utility posts a dialog box, asking you if you would like to schedule the check when Windows next restarts, click Yes.

5. Close all dialog boxes and restart your system. Scanning a large drive can take some time, so it's best left for periods when the system will be lightly used, if at all.

Note

In the Windows 2000 operating system, the Check Disk utility is referred to as ScanDisk.

Checking a Disk in Sun Solaris

With Sun Solaris, the disk check utility fsck is rather similar to its Windows equivalent. It is fully documented in the Solaris man pages, and you can find its procedure for use at www.cs.manchester.ac.uk/solaris/sun_docs/C/solaris_9/SUNWaadm/SYSADV1/ p145.html#FSTROUBLEFSCK-28. In a nutshell, fsck checks the file system for data integrity. The drive being tested needs to be unmounted, and some file systems aren't supported. (However, UFS is supported.) fsck can be used with a number of switches, and those switches differ, depending on the version of UNIX you use.

One good utility for disk repairs and testing is Gibson Research's SpinRite 6.0 (see http://grc.com/spinrite.htm). This utility finds bad sectors, predicts the ones that are likely to fail, reads the data out of that region, and then marks off the problem areas. SpinRite is a replacement for the original DOS CHKDSK command and does a read-only surface scan when run. ScanDisk also does a read-only scan and can mark off a bad sector, but SpinRite does data pattern testing, defect scrubbing, data relocation, and sector repair and recovery in addition. At a price around $100, SpinRite pays for itself many times over and works with Windows, Linux, and other file systems.

When a disk starts to fail, you should start to see more read and write errors in your event log. It's a good idea to set up an alert system so that when one of these factors starts to increase beyond what's normal, you get a message. At that point, you should run your standard disk diagnostics and make sure that your backups are in good order.

Disk checking utilities have some significant limitations. For one thing, they don't work on a mounted volume. Also, they work only on drives that your operating system manages. Your operating system cannot perform a low-level disk check on any drive attached to a disk controller. For those types of disks, you need to use a compatible utility. SpinRite, for example, can work with some RAID 0 or RAID 1 configurations, where the RAID is an on-board chip and isn't managed by its own processor. As a general rule, SpinRite's maker says that if DOS can recognize a RAID volume, then SpinRite can check that volume. Chances are that any controller you buy has an on-board processor on it.

Defragmentation

Disk defragmentation is among the most common tasks that administrators perform. Although you can experience measurable performance improvement when you defragment a single user's single-disk workstation, when you move to a server with multiple users running software on multiple disks, the benefit of disk defragmentation becomes less apparent. Most servers run RAID configurations that stripe their files across several disks, and multiple heads access those disks to satisfy a complex workload, so rearranging files to make them contiguous doesn't have a lot of impact.

Note

Keep in mind that when you copy a disk's contents to another location on a file-oriented—or file-by-file—basis, the target system is automatically defragmented. This is not true of a bit-level or **XCOPY** operation, where each bit is copied bit-by-bit and each sector is copied sector-by-sector. In that case, the fragmentation is preserved. Server backup programs fall under both categories: file oriented and bit oriented. If you do a file-level backup, you end up with a defragmented disk if you did a disk-to-disk copy. If you have backed up to tape, then a restore from tape will also result in a defragmented disk.

In studies of server systems running older versions of Windows server systems, system performance improvements of between 7% and 11% have been achieved. That's not insignificant, but it isn't dramatic either. When many more disks are involved, the performance improvement is even smaller. Still, there is little downside to defragging your disk system other than the load that the operation places on your system: When you perform the operation at a time of low activity (at night, for example), the benefits justify the effort.

Keep in mind that most defragmentation tools need to have 15% of the drive free in order to perform a defragmentation.

Antivirus and Firewall Software and Systems

Unfortunately, it has become necessary to deploy antivirus software at several levels in the enterprise. Antivirus software should be costed into any server deployment and should be on virtually every computer on your network.

Many analysts believe the following:

- General antivirus server software should be deployed at all firewalls (perimeter protection). The best protection is achieved using software that provides virus scanning capability and enforces a set of policy rules. When an antivirus software program scans a system's files, it is looking for the signatures of known viruses. Those signatures can be code snippets, registry entries, filenames, file types, file locations, and so forth.

■ Domain servers should be locked down as much a possible.

■ Application servers should run specialized antivirus software that may be effective in preventing viruses from attacking that type of application. Antivirus vendors sell specialized software for messaging applications such as Exchange and Domino; databases such as SQL Server, Oracle, and DB2; complete office solutions such as Microsoft Small Business Server; and so forth.

■ Antivirus software and personal firewalls should be installed on desktops and workstations. It's important to keep this software up-to-date so that it can detect current threats and so its scanning protection is enabled.

■ Antivirus software and personal firewalls *must* be installed on laptops, handheld PDAs, and networked wireless devices, as well as any traveling systems.

This four-pronged approach to virus management is illustrated in Figure 21.3.

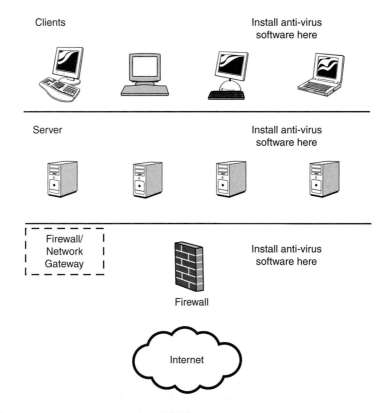

Figure 21.3   Antivirus software should be deployed at several layers of a network in order to provide protection from attack from without and attack from within.

The two most important places to stop viruses and spyware are at the firewall and at the desktop. If you can stop viruses and spyware before they gain entry to your network, you can save your systems from performing a lot of extra work. The desktop is also very important because it is impossible to stop 100% of all threats; mistakes and accidents happen. By being vigilant at the client level, you can catch problems before they make it through to the entire network.

In the past, most large ISPs considered virus and spyware protection to be something that their clients must do, and not the responsibility of the ISP itself. However, as the industry has matured and become even more competitive, many ISPs are now offering virus and spyware protection tools as part of their standard packages—to businesses as well as to consumers. Some companies offer a prescanning service either by redirecting traffic through their servers or as part of their hosting package. It's worth seeking out this additional protection.

It's useless to spend large sums of money installing antivirus software on servers if you don't install the appropriate firewalls that allow a worm or Trojan Horse to gain access to your system through a back door. Similarly, it is useless to position firewalls and antivirus software on your servers to protect the front end of your network if you have mobile systems that can propagate viruses and other malware when they are reattached to your network. Failure to protect mobile systems is one of the major errors many companies make when they implement security systems. (Failure to properly back up mobile systems is another issue that doesn't get enough attention from network administrators.)

Antivirus software and firewalls that use a packet-sniffing approach have two cost components. The first cost is the up-front cost of the software and the yearly subscription costs for servers and clients. The second cost, one that most people don't account for, is the reduction in server performance for any server that is forced to run this type of software. You can figure that antivirus software will reduce your server's performance anywhere from 5% to 15% in most cases. However, when you are under attack, you may find that your antivirus software's consumption of server resources goes up dramatically.

Note

One common method for virus propagation is through network shares. When some viruses detect a network share that they can copy themselves, they take full advantage of the opportunity. Propagation of the virus then proceeds when the virus searches for other network shares and copies executable software to those directories. When you set your shares' permissions, you should make this type of propagation mechanism difficult or impossible.

Rather than just guess, it's a good idea to measure the impact of your antivirus software by using a performance monitoring tool to gauge the increase in activity for your CPU(s), the increased memory usage, and, to a much lesser degree, disk I/O. Keep in mind that unusual situations occur when you are under attack. If you are experiencing an attack of an email worm or mass mailing, your messaging server's antivirus software may consume considerably more resources than it would under normal conditions.

More and more appliances are becoming available for front-end networks and server systems. Few companies put their most significant firewalls on their application or domain servers these days. The trend toward self-contained appliances probably means that more products will move their antivirus programs off servers. In fact, many higher-end firewalls also come with antivirus software that is either built in or can be activated with payment of an additional fee. If you deploy a system like that, be sure that your firewall's antivirus program doesn't interfere with anything you are deploying on workstations, desktops, or laptops. Often firewalls download client antivirus software (and in some cases, firewall clients as well), and they can interfere with other products. It's good to test these issues before you commit to a vendor's product.

Keeping Case Fans and Filters Clean

Very little attention is paid to keeping servers clean inside. For the most part, you can get away with negligence because modern electronics are often sealed devices and relatively impervious to dust.

However, neglecting to keep a server clean may get you in trouble when you write to an optical disc inside the server, where a dust particle can interfere with the laser that is writing to the disc. Other components, particularly mechanical components, can fail. Also, dirty heat sinks aren't nearly as effective as clean surfaces at shedding heat.

The heat modern processors throw off is truly amazing. In demonstrations, people have cooked eggs on working processors. That may not be something you actually want to do, but it does speak to the temperatures involved. You only have to consider Intel's BTX replacement platform for the ATX casing, what Intel refers to as the "heat advantaged chassis." In the BTX form factor–compliant cases, large (massive?) heat sinks sit on top of the processors and pull air in from outside the case to cool the processor.

Very few modern cases and fans filter the air coming into the case. You can dramatically lower the amount of dust and dirt in a system if you follow these simple rules:

- Make sure your air flows in one direction. Systems usually have air flowing from the front of the case to the back of the case, with fans blowing in at the entrance point and fans blowing out at the exit point.
- Close all holes in the case that don't have significant airflow out of them. Don't leave the opening of an expansion slot uncovered, for example.
- Place filters so that all air coming into the system is filtered.

Filtered fans can be a little hard to find, and many server OEMs don't go to the trouble to use them. Still, it's worth the effort to add them. You can find fan filters at a number of online stores because they tend to be popular with gamers. A filter is a flat panel that screws onto the outside of your case, in front of the fan.

Tip

To filter incoming air in a low-cost way, consider cutting out an appropriate-sized cardboard frame and then gluing to it a cut piece of nylon panty hose. Don't stretch the nylon when you are fitting it to the frame; it's a more effective filter when the pores are smaller sized.

When you're adding fans to a server case or replacing a stock heat sink or CPU cooler, size matters. Bigger fans can move more air, even when they rotate more slowly than smaller fans. Therefore, bigger fans are quieter. Similarly, bigger heat sinks can absorb more heat, and they can shed more heat than smaller heat sinks. When looking for high-efficiency cooling solutions for CPUs, you should try to mate the two: large heat sinks with large but slower-moving fans. For sound absorption, you can get good (but not great) results by adding to systems sound absorption panels from manufacturers such as Asaka.

At some point, you need to open your server and physically remove the dust that has accumulated inside it. The best way to do this is by using a canister of compressed gas specifically sold for dust removal. This canister should come with a long plastic tube spout that can be aimed into cramped spaces. It's important that the product you use leaves no residue. To see whether your compressed gas leaves a residue, spray it on a very clean piece of glass or a clean window and observe whether a film or particles are left behind. If the product you are considering using leaves a residue, you should replace it immediately with a better dust removal product.

When you are dusting out your case, it is fine to vigorously dust nonmechanical parts. Memory, hard drives, and other components aren't likely to be displaced or damaged by a stream of gas, and because they are enclosed, they can't be damaged. However, you should make sure you don't displace a wire or connection. More importantly, if you aim a stream of compressed air into a mechanism that is open, such as the door of a floppy disk drive, you can cause the drive to malfunction.

When you are trying to remove dust from a server, you need to be extremely careful when you are trying to clean an optical or mechanical drive. DVDs, CD-ROMs, tape drives, and floppy disk drives, among other components, contain delicate internal equipment such as aligned laser heads that can be damaged or misaligned if disturbed too vigorously. You should therefore clean internal drives like these with products that are designed for them. You can find tape cleaning cartridges for all types of tape drives, specially designed optical disks for cleaning CD/DVD drives, and so forth.

Error Logging and Tracking

In the event-driven programming environments that are a feature of all modern network operating systems, event logging is a standard capability. Not only does the operating system log events, but so do major server applications, which log events in their own proprietary logs. Events can be either hardware or software related, or they can be a function of both. The following kinds of events are stored in event logs:

- Error condition
- Alert or warning issued
- Status update
- Successful monitored condition
- Unsuccessful monitored condition

Event logging imposes a certain amount of overhead on a server and on the applications that run on it. That's why many of the logging capabilities of a network operating system or a server application are not used. In some cases, entire logs are always on by default; this is the case with Windows Server logs. In other cases, you have to explicitly turn on logging; for example, you might have to do this with an application log.

The snippets of software code used to trap events and record their existence are called *counters*. Counters are available to measure CPU utilization, the number of active processing threads, aspects of memory usage, and on and on. When you install an application, you may install with it a whole new set of counters, many of which aren't activated by default. If you logged all the counters that were actually available to log, the overhead would slow your system to a crawl. Therefore, many counters are left off by default.

One set of counters you have to turn on is the Windows server disk counters in Windows 2000; they are turned off by default in that operating system because using them affects disk I/O performance.

To turn on the disk performance counters in Windows Server 2000, you do the following:

1. Select Start, Run, enter cmd in the dialog box that appears, and then press Enter.
2. Enter the command diskperf -y for standard IDE or SATA drives, or enter diskperf -ye for software RAID and mirrored drives. (Note that hardware RAID is not affected by this command.)

Note

The **diskperf** disk counters are turned on in Windows Server 2003 by default.

3. Open the Windows Performance Monitor by entering perfmon in the Command window and then press Enter.
4. Verify that the disk performance counters are now available from the list of counters.

Different operating systems and different applications offer additional counters that are turned on (and off) either using command-line tools or through the use of graphical interface tools. You need to consult those products' documentation for details.

The Purpose of Event Logging

The purpose of event logging is to provide a means of analyzing the state of your system as well as provide you with a historical record of the system's performance. When you examine an event log, you see the type of events listed, and each event is identified by its source and some kind of an ID number. The sequence of events is often a key to understanding why something on your system doesn't work properly or how you can change your system to make it perform better. Many people turn to event logs when things go wrong.

Typical scenarios where you would want to examine your event logs include the following:

- **Hardware failure**—If you are experiencing problems such as an intermittent network connection or a disk error, you should check your event logs.

- **System performance issues**—If your system or application doesn't seem to run as well as it should, and you suspect some kind of resource issue such as a memory leak or errant daemon, you should check your event logs.

- **Security issue**—If you want to check who has logged on to your network or one particular server or who has logged on to a database application, you should check your event logs.

- **Resource access**—If you have a network share that can't be accessed and you want to find out whether the issue is a permissions problem, hardware problem, or some other issue, you should check your event logs.

- **State of an application**—If you initiated a system backup and want to know how long it took and whether it is finished, you should check your event logs.

As you can see, event logs can be very useful even when your system seems to be running correctly.

Proper analysis of your event logs can offer you all sorts of valuable information; they are veritable gold mines of information. And that's the real problem: With so many recordable events that it is possible to record, it is hard to keep track of them all, correlate them with behavior, manage the information they contain, and, most importantly, figure out which event has particular significance. No wonder the area of event analysis and management has given rise to a whole host of management tools that monitor events, collect events, analyze events, alert you when an event occurs, and more.

Many events just keep on happening. When your mouse button sticks, it sticks. If your event log records MouseDown events, your log is going to be getting a lot of MouseDown events to record. Chances are that you only need to see a few of these events to figure out the cause.

Many network, network operating system, and application operations repeat themselves. Give a command, and chances are that if it doesn't successfully complete, the application will continue to execute the command, if only to determine whether the resource required is simply busy and not permanently unavailable. When you examine an event log, you should see that it is loaded with large numbers of similar events, and this can be overwhelming at first. Any event log or product that manages events requires a good search filter utility to aid in finding events of interest. Smart products must be able to differentiate between multiple instances of the same event and related events that occur in an escalating chain. Understanding the relationships is one of the best troubleshooting tools for a server administrator.

You need to keep in mind that event logs of operating systems and event logs of applications are almost always in different formats. In most instances, you can export all event logs to database files and then analyze them in a database. However, when you try to pull all the information from multiple sources, you may find that you can't because all the different data isn't organized in the same way. Therefore, to work with the combined data from multiple event logs coming from different sources, you need to do considerable work up front to make the data compatible. This is an area where you need to rely on third-party tools to help you out, such as Kane Security Analyst's Event Log Analyzer Tool. One tool you can try is Microsoft's free LogParser 2.0, which is a command-line utility that lets you execute a SQL query against an event log file.

Event Logs

The Windows Server 2003/2000 operating system comes with several different event logs that system administrators can use. Which logs exist depends on the type of Windows server you have. All Windows servers come with three logs, and additional event logs are maintained for domain and DNS servers. Figure 21.4 shows the Windows Event Viewer.

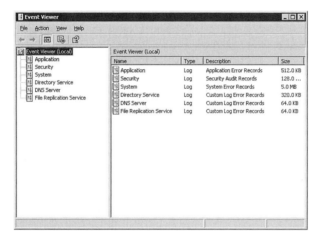

Figure 21.4 The Windows Event Viewer.

These are the standard system logs for Windows servers:

- **Application log (AppEvent.evt)**—This log, found on all Windows servers, contains information for all counters that applications install and all others that they enable.

- **Directory Service log (NTDS.evt)**—This log, found on Windows domain controllers only, records the events associated with the Windows Active Directory service.

- **DNS Server log (DnsEvent.evt)**—This log is found on all DNS servers, whether they are domain servers, application servers, or even standalone servers.

- **File Replication log (NtFrs.evt)**—This log, found only on Windows domain servers, records replication events associated with domain controllers.

- **Security log (SecEvent.evt)**—This log, found on all Windows servers, contains information that is set by the Windows security audit policies.

- **System log (SysEvent.evt)**—This log, found on all Windows servers, contains information about the operating system and hardware components.

To view any of the specific log files, you should look for them located in your Windows directory, at `%systemroot%\system32\config`.

By default, the Windows event logs maintain a fairly small log size and overwrite older events on a first-in, first-out basis. You may find that the default settings for log size are inappropriately small and that a log doesn't maintain a record of events long enough to maintain an appropriate historical record.

To change the behavior of the different Windows event logs for Windows servers on a network, you can open the Windows Group Policy Editor and click the event log settings. These settings let you control the size, access to, retention methods, and other policies for the Application, Security, and System logs. Figure 21.5 shows the Group Policy Object Editor event log settings.

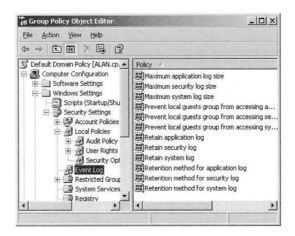

Figure 21.5   The Group Policy Object Editor event log settings.

You can access the Application, Security, and System logs from the Event Viewer utility. To access the event log, you select Start, All Programs, Administrative Tools, Event Log (refer to Figure 21.4). To view a specific event, you click the log you want to view in the left panel and then double-click the specific event you want to view. Figure 21.6 shows a sample event from the System log—one that logs a DHCP error condition. The specific event properties list a variety of information, including when and where the error happened, the source of the error, and what the specific type or ID of the error is. The event log is well known to almost all Windows administrators. A little less well known is what to do with specific errors after you view them.

The problem with many event logs and with Microsoft's logs in particular is that they offer explanations that can often be difficult to decipher. Over the years, the messages have gotten somewhat better, but they still have the ability to confuse and confound. They also don't offer much in the way of practical advice on how to fix the problem in question. So the first step in most cases where you are diagnosing a Windows issue from the event log is to get more information about the event in question. At the end of an event's description (refer to Figure 21.7) is a hyperlink to Microsoft's event library. When you click the link, you are asked if you will allow the information to be sent to Microsoft so that it can match the event's ID. If you agree, the Windows Help and Support Center opens a browser window with more details on the event in question, as shown in Figure 21.7 If you liked the description of the event in the event log, chances are that you will like the description in the Help Center.

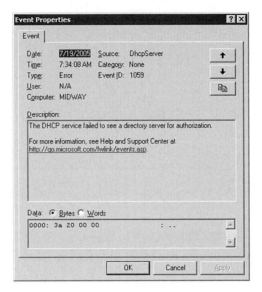

Figure 21.6   A particular event's description.

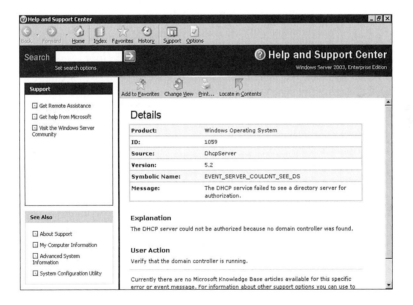

Figure 21.7   Windows Help and Support Center information on an event.

You might want to look at additional sources of information to help decipher different event IDs. One of them is EventID.Net (see www.eventid.net), which is run by the consulting group Altair Technologies. When you enter an event ID and its source into the EventID.Net search field, you get an alternative description of the event. The EventID.Net database contains a collection of event descriptions and also descriptions of the experiences of a number of contributors. If you scroll further down the page, you see comments, questions, and answers detailing experiences with this particular event, which can really be useful.

Novell maintains specialized event logs for security audits, as a management platform for Windows events, and with many of its applications, such as the GroupWise messaging server.

Solaris has several log files that you may want to check:

- **/etc/system**—This log lists your kernel configuration parameters.
- **/var/adm/messages syslog**—This log is the daemon log. Problems are listed with flags such as warnings, errors, panics, reboots, and so on. This is the most important Solaris log to examine.
- **/etc/release**—This log lists your OS version information.

Note

Sun offers a concise performance monitoring tutorial at http://sunsolve.sun.com/pub-cgi/show.pl?target=content/content3&ttl=article.

Implementing Hardware Redundancy Options

The purpose of a server is to provide reliable network services to clients. In order for a server to be reliable, it must be available a large percentage of the time. Not every service must be operated 24 hours a day, 7 days a week, 52 weeks a year—but in the age of global commerce and the Internet, many do. It's a fact that sooner or later, system components fail, and the more components you have in a system, the greater the chance of failure. Therefore, in order to build a more perfect server, you need to build in redundancies and have the capability to fail over to those systems when problems arise.

The purpose of having hardware redundancies is to provide greater availability, which is another way of describing a server's fault tolerance. People measure the fault tolerance of their servers in terms of the amount of time that the server is available to clients. Thus a server that can be accessed 9 days out of 10 is 90% available, which is also referred to as "one nine" availability. You probably don't think you need to do much to have a server run 9 days out of 10, and you're right. If a hard drive fails, you can probably restore it within 1 day, and chances are that any network outage isn't going to last more than 1 day, either. An availability of "two nines," or 99.0%, is also something that isn't all that hard to achieve, as it means that your server is down only approximately 87.7 hours a year, or 3 days, 15 hours, and roughly 40 minutes. Most departmental servers with standard RAID systems run in the range of from 98% up to around 99% of the time, depending on what applications they run.

Let's say that your website must be running 99.9% of the time, or "three nines." You've done the calculation that shows that if your system goes down for longer than that period, your business will lose so much money that you could have replaced your server entirely. With three-nines availability, your window to fix potential problems or outages shrinks to only 8 hours 45 minutes *each year*, which is uncomfortably close to just one single working day. You might be able to replace a drive once a year, but if your network goes down for longer than a working day, you've lost more money than your company can afford to lose. Therefore, additional measures are called for: extra drives, redundant network connections, readily available duplicate data sets, and so forth.

Now let's consider the next step up: "four nines," or 99.99%. A system that is available at the level of four nines is referred to as "highly available." With a system of this type, your allowable downtime shrinks to just under an hour, or around 53 minutes. That's not enough time to deal with a network outage; it's probably not enough time to replace a disk and rebuild its data set. If your system *must* achieve four-nines availability and doesn't, you have just about enough time to catch lunch and consider new career options. To get to this level of availability, not only must every subsystem associated with the server be fully duplicated but failover to the redundant systems must be swift. At this level, you could sustain maybe one reboot a month or so. Many people refer to this level of availability as "mission critical," and almost all organizations can get by with four nines. This is the level that the big banks and financial houses aim for as their minimum.

In rare instances, four nines isn't good enough: A system may be required to be up 100% of the time. This is the case when a system is needed for a life-and-death situation and when the cost of a system's downtime is so large that no downtime is really acceptable. Some of the very largest OLTP financial institutions that process millions of dollars of transactions each hour fit into that category. At this level, "five nines," your window for downtime is a little more than 5 minutes a year, which translates to roughly one reboot. At this level of fault tolerance, it is not adequate to duplicate all computer sub-systems. The entire computer itself must be duplicated, as you might do in a clustered server system. A small number of companies sell servers that have been engineered to be "fault tolerant." Probably the best known of them are the Tandem (now part of Hewlett-Packard) NonStop systems (see http://h20223.www2.hp.com/nonstopcomputing/cache/76385-0-0-0-121.aspx), Stratus Computer's VOS and FT systems (www.stratus.com), and Marathon Computers (www.marathontechnologies.com). FTvirtual server is another example of a fault-tolerant system.

Table 21.2 summarizes the basics of server fault tolerance.

Table 21.2   Different Levels of Server Fault Tolerance

Availability	Downtime	Purpose	Requirements
90%	36 days, 12 hours, 36 min.	Standard PC/server	No fault tolerance required
99%	3 days, 15 hours, 40 min.	Departmental server	RAID storage system
99.9%	0 days, 8 hours, 46 min.	Highly available	RAID, duplicate data
99.99%	0 days, 0 hours, 52.6 min.	Mission critical	All subsystems and data duplicated, fast failover
99.999%	0 days, 0 hours, 5.26 min.	Fault tolerant	Entire computer and data duplicated, very fast failover

Integrated NICs, Memory, and Power Supplies

When your buy server hardware, you should expect to pay extra for the parts you purchase. Some of that additional cost goes into hardening the equipment so that it is less likely to fail. Drives meant for servers are manufactured to a higher standard than drives meant for desktops and laptops. Another factor that adds cost is redundancies built into the equipment you buy.

Server motherboards can contain a number of redundant features. One very useful feature is a dual set of memory banks. With such a system, when a memory stick fails or is about to fail, a diagnostic utility in the server BIOS detects the problem and takes that bank offline and enables the available spare memory. Not all server motherboards have this feature, but it's a very useful one.

Another feature on some server motherboards is dual integrated NICs. The first generation of these multihomed cards comes with one fast NIC port and one slower NIC port, typically a GigE port and a Fast Ethernet port. The manufacturer intends for you to use the fast port for your standard network connection to the server and to use the slow port as a management connection. Even when you purchase a motherboard with two NICs integrated into it, you should still install an extra NIC into your server. The rationale for this is that NICs do not consume much power or system resources, and integrated NICs seem to have a high failure rate. With an extra NIC installed, you can more easily switch over to the extra card. You can also install a second GigE card if you need a second fast port for throughput, as you might if you were building a proxy server or a router. Today's enterprise OSs support fault-tolerant NICs that work as failover devices or clustered devices. They can be embedded, PCI, or PCI-X cards in many cases.

It is possible to find servers that support multiple power supplies, which allows for failover if one supply stops working. Power supplies have a relatively long lifetime, but when they fail, they don't tend to simply stop working. Their output starts to vary, and you may find that your server starts to experience some very bizarre behavior. You may start getting STOP errors, see blue screens, have applications fail, and experience other problems that may seem to be unrelated. Having a second power source lets you swap over and diagnose the problem a lot more easily. Not many server motherboards support dual power supplies, but it's a great feature to have, and it is highly recommended for any critical server in your organization.

Load Balancing

The highest level of availability is achieved when you duplicate entire computer systems. There are two approaches to creating this type of fault tolerance:

- **Load balancing**—Many computers work together, providing the same service with service requests apportioned out to the most available server.

- **Clustering**—Two or more computers are logically grouped together as if they were a single computer.

With load balancing, each server is a member of a domain, and the system is front-ended by a routing service either in hardware (such as a BigIP box) or implemented in software through a cluster service. An example of a cluster service is Microsoft Clustering Services (see www.microsoft.com/windowsserver2003/technologies/clustering/default.mspx), which appears in Windows Server 2003 as the Cluster service and Network Load Balancing service.

A load-balanced set of computers is commonly referred to as a "server farm." When a computer fails in a server farm, the load balancing service simply removes the faulty server from the overall aggregate of servers. A user would notice a drop in service performance only if the server were operating at or near its rated load. When convenient, a new server can be added to the server farm to replace the one that was removed, and then it can be registered with the load balancing service. Figure 21.8 illustrates how load balancing works.

Load balancing is best used when a system is I/O limited and when you want to scale the system up by scaling out. A server farm is a highly reliable system with great redundancy. Server farms do not fail because of server failure; they typically fail because of problems with the infrastructure (for example, network connection or power failures). You can find server farms in enterprise websites such as Yahoo! or Google, in telecommunications systems where computers serve as switches and routers, and in many other places.

Every network operating system you have read about in this book has a load balancing solution available for it either from the operating system vendor itself or from a third party. With NetWare 6.5, load balancing is built directly into the operating system. There are load balancing solutions for network operating system services such as DNS, DHCP, and others, as well as for applications running on servers.

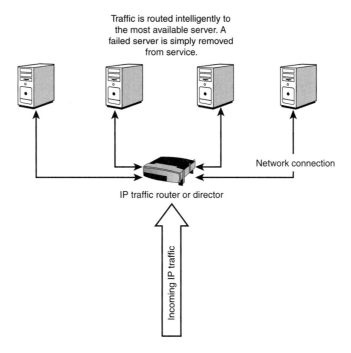

Figure 21.8 How load balancing works.

Because you can implement load balancing in both hardware and software, a very wide range of solutions are available in this area. Among the most notable solutions are the following:

- `balance` (http://balance.sourceforge.net)—This is an open source TCP proxy.

- **Citrix MetaFrame (www.citrix.com)**—MetaFrame is a load balancing arrangement of Windows terminal servers that offers a large portfolio of additional services, such as application launching and management.

- **Coyote Point Systems's Equalizer series (www.coyotepoint.com)**—This is a software application traffic load balancer for Windows server applications.

- **F5 Networks's BigIP (www.f5.com)**—BigIP is a hardware solution that routes requests to servers based on their availability. It is OS independent.

- **Netscaler Application Delivery Systems (www.netscaler.com)**—This is a hardware switch/gateway for routing requests to different applications, such as Oracle, PeopleSoft, SAP, Siebel, and web applications.

- **Linux Virtual Server (LVS; www.linuxvirtualserver.org)**—This is open source load balancing software for Linux.

- **Load Sharing Facility (LSF; www.platform.com)**—This is a load balancing software solution for Sun Solaris.

- `Queue` (www.gnu.org/software/queue)—This is a GNU load balancing application with batch processing.

- **Sybase EAServer (www.sybase.com)**—This is an example of an application-level load balancing application for Sybase's enterprise database. Many server applications come with this capability.

- **Windows Server 2003**—All versions of Server 2003 come with Network Load Balancing.

This list includes only a very small portion of the available load balancing applications that are on the market today and is meant to be representative of the range of possibilities.

Load Balancing Versus Clustering

Many people confuse load-balanced servers with clusters because both utilize multiple servers to the same end. Most of the time, when you load balance servers, each server retains its own separate identity as a computer, and when you cluster servers, they appear on the network as if they were a single computer. (We say *most of the time* because there are instances in which the software abstracts the different systems in a server farm from view, making it appear as if they are a single system; there are also times when a cluster appears to be multiple systems on the network, even if for the purpose of clustering only one logical entity can be addressed.)

So if the situation is so cloudy, where is there a clear distinction? The answer lies in the mechanism involved in fault tolerance. In load-balanced situations, the system *doesn't fail over* when a member server fails; the capabilities of the failed server are simply removed from the service. A cluster, on the other hand, *always fails over* when a member server fails. The ability to always fail over quickly that characterizes a cluster also means that the mechanism for failover requires that the cluster have a rapid means of communications by which a failed server can be identified as failed and the control and activity of the cluster is then passed on to another server in the cluster. Different clustering products have different methods of communicating, but the predominant method is to have members of a cluster share a common bus and have a "heartbeat" signal poll the status of the cluster on a second-by-second basis. Figure 21.9 shows how a clustering works.

High-Performance Clusters

Many different types of clusters are available in the market today, from two-node clusters on up. Broadly speaking, clusters can be classified into one of the following categories:

- **Share-nothing**—With this type of cluster, two or more servers that are set aside for the same purpose work independently. In some instances, a server is maintained to provide "hot backup" for a server when it fails; some clusters, such as IBM's x-architecture, maintain a "spare" unused cluster node that's activated when another node fails.

- **Share-something**—With this type of cluster, two or more servers share a critical component such as a RAID array and use a communications method to determine when a server has failed. These servers can be in peer-level relationships or in master/slave relationships.

- **Share-everything**—A share-everything arrangement duplicates all aspects of a computer system, has all components operating under load, and simply removes a failed component from the operational mix when a failure occurs. Tandem's NonStop systems, Stratus's FT servers, and others fall into this category.

Let's consider these different possibilities a little more. The simplest cluster is a two-node cluster with failover. Examples of this architecture can be built with Microsoft Cluster Server and Linux-HA software. In the arrangement of a two-node cluster shown in Figure 21.10, two nodes of a cluster share a common RAID array where the data is stored. The RAID array is usually protected by being a 0+1 RAID level, which allows for both performance (0—striping) and failover (1—mirroring).

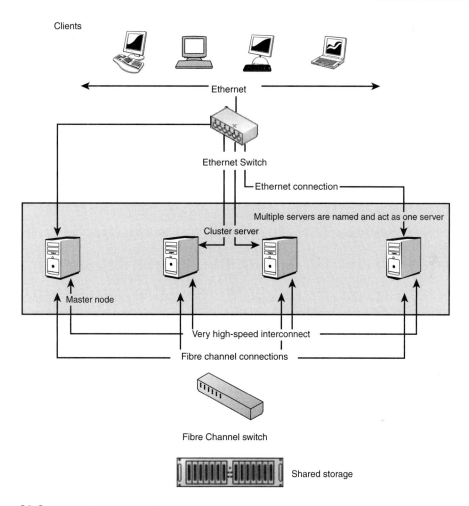

Clients

Ethernet

Ethernet Switch

Ethernet connection

Multiple servers are named and act as one server

Cluster server

Master node

Very high-speed interconnect

Fibre channel connections

Fibre Channel switch

Shared storage

Figure 21.9 How clustering works.

A second SCSI bus connects one node directly to another, with a heartbeat signal running over that bus. When a server fails in this two-node arrangement, the second server takes over the host responsibility for the storage array and assumes the other duties of the cluster. The failed member is removed from the logical association until the administrator replaces it and adds the newly working system back into the cluster. The concept of polling in a cluster is called a "quorum" and can be extended to include a multinode cluster of any size. For more information about quorums, see www.windowsnetworking.com/articles_tutorials/Cluster-Quorums.html.

A share-nothing cluster implies that the servers in a cluster operate independently, but a mechanism exists that allows failover of the cluster to another cluster node when a fault is determined. Share-nothing clusters are a variation on simple load balancing. Not many systems are built with the share-nothing approach because it is an expensive architecture, and for the cost, OEMs prefer to build share-everything systems.

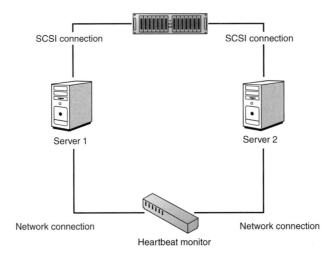

SCSI connection   SCSI connection

Server 1   Server 2

Network connection   Network connection

Heartbeat monitor

Figure 21.10   An example of a two-node cluster with a shared storage array.

High-performance clusters are often built with many connected computer systems. These types of systems aren't new, but their application on lower-costs PC server platforms has popularized them. As early as 1977, Datapoint had developed ARCnet as a commercial cluster. The best known of the early implementations probably were the VAX/VMS VAXClusters that appeared in the 1980s.

When you move beyond two nodes in a cluster, the most important characteristic of the cluster technology becomes the high-performance interconnect technology. Clusters and high-speed networking are intimately related. In a high-speed network, each cluster node on the network requires some sort of CPU offload technology to move network processing to very-high-speed ASICs on the networking card. Among the technologies that power the larger clusters today are GigaNet's CLAN, Myrinet, Quadrics, InfiniBand, and Tandem's ServerNet, among others. These networking technologies typically work in the 2Gbps range and are expected to move to the 10Gbps range in the near future. Working clusters with more than 100 servers have been built in the past.

Note

The Top500 organization publishes a list of the highest-performance computer systems in the world at www.top500.org/lists. The current list at the time of this writing had the following five systems at the top:

1. DOE/NNSA/LLNL's IBM eServer Blue Gene Solution
2. IBM Watson Research Center's eServer Blue Gene Solution
3. DOE/NNSA/LLNL's IBM ASC Purple eServer pSeries p575
4. NASA/Ames Research Center/NAS's Silicon Graphics Altix 1.5GHz, Voltair InfiniBand
5. Sandia Labs' Dell Thunderbird

The top system used 131,072 processors to achieve a rating of 280.6 Tflop/s, which is a measure of how fast these system run the LINPACK Benchmark. LINPACK is a set of linear equations that measure the floating-point performance of a system. See www.top500.org/lists/linpack.php for more information.

As you peruse this list, notice that quite a few of the listed supercomputers are built using PC-based servers as their building blocks, along with very-high-speed interconnect technologies.

Among the products used to cluster PC servers are the following:

- **Beowulf (www.beowulf.org)**—This is an open source project for application clustering.
- **LinuxHPC (www.linuxhpc.org)**—This is an open source project for Linux super computing.
- **Microsoft Cluster Server (www.microsoft.com/technet/prodtechnol/windowsserver2003/ technologies/genclust.mspx)**—The Cluster service was a standalone product but is now part of Microsoft Windows Server 2003. The Cluster service is included in Server 2003 Enterprise Edition and Datacenter Edition, but not in Standard Edition or Web Edition. You can cluster up to eight systems by using this technology.
- **Novell Cluster Services (NCS) 1.7 for NetWare 6.5 (www.novell.com/products/ clusters/ncs/)**—With NCS you can manage up to 32 NetWare 6.5 nodes with up to 32 processors per server. It provides support for iSCSI and Fibre Channel SAN connects, can pool free disk space, and has both failover and fallback capabilities. NCS supports dynamic configuration of clusters and storage volumes without rebooting.
- **Sun Cluster 3.1 (www.sun.com/software/cluster/)**—Offering up to 16-node support on both SPARC and x86 Solaris, this software ships with a management suite.
- **Red Hat Cluster Suite (RHCS; www.redhat.com/software/rha/cluster/)**—RHCS offers both application/server failover and IP load balancing. It supports up to eight cluster nodes. Features include NFS/CIFS failover, shared storage (required), SCSI and Fibre Channel support, and automated failover. The product can run on Red Hat Enterprise Linux ES on x86, AMD64/EM64T, and Itanium processors.

The next step beyond simple clusters is grid computing. What differentiates grid technology from traditional clusters is that although a grid gives you distributed processing through large numbers of computers, it is still just collections of computers that don't operate as a unit, don't form a domain or share security credentials, and don't have the fast failover of a high-performance computing (HPC) cluster.

Disaster Recovery Planning

Eventually every system fails, and occasionally systems fail in very unpredictable ways, such as the following:

- A construction crew cuts through the main optic cable line and disables all data communication to your city.
- Your building is struck by an act of terrorism.
- A water main leak or hurricane floods your entire data center.
- Your building is swallowed up by the earth during an earthquake.
- A computer virus destroys all of your systems' boot files or a hacker gets into the system and takes control.
- Solar flares knock out a power station in Ontario, which disables the entire North American power grid.
- Someone causes a fire in your building.
- Mergatroid in IT successfully upgrades your domain controllers but fails to migrate all the user accounts before overwriting all the information. Heavens!

All the aforementioned qualify as disasters, and we all pray that we are spared problems like these. However, good practice necessitates that organizations do disaster planning to keep critical business processes working or to recover from these problems as quickly and as cost-effectively as possible.

The Purpose of Disaster Recovery Planning

When disaster strikes, your first inclination when trying to address the problem is likely to be wrong, and in fact may make things worse. In an emergency, there's a very strong tendency to act first and think second. A well-thought-out disaster recovery plan is an essential component of any well-run computing center. In some locales, planning for business continuity is not just good business practice—it is the law.

The purpose of disaster planning is to codify a set of rules and actions that are to be followed when a problem occurs. Disaster recovery takes time to plan, and if disaster doesn't strike, it's a cost in time and salaries you might be tempted to forgo. A plan is a lot like insurance: If you don't need it, it's a waste of money, but when you do need it, it can save your organization a considerable amount of money, improve the quality of the recovery, and greatly diminish your downtime.

Disaster recovery planning is part of an overall fault tolerance strategy. It's where you utilize all your backup systems and test your strategies. However, you don't have time to fix any deficiencies in your systems at the time a disaster occurs. Therefore, it is absolutely critical that every system that you count on for recovery be tested beforehand. Just as is the case for data backups themselves, it is absolutely critical that you know the integrity of your systems by doing the following:

- If you have a data backup system you count on, do a restore from that system.
- If you have a mirrored disk system, test it by taking one-half of the mirror offline, running from the second mirror, and then reestablishing the mirror.
- If you have a clustered server system, try removing one of the nodes.
- If you have a backup power system, pull the plug on your main system.
- If there are people who are important in the chain of notification, call them to see if they respond.

There are many different tests that you can perform to test the viability of your recovery plan. The point is that none of them are any good if you decide to test them at the time a disaster strikes. So as part of your recovery plan, you need a set of regular action items to test the systems you count on.

An Example of a Disaster Recovery Plan

A disaster recovery plan should be an ongoing effort that results in a working document. Every year, at the appointed time, the document should be brought out and revised. People at every significant level of the organization should review and sign off on the plan. Disaster planning is not just an IT exercise; the level of loss that an organization is willing to endure or the amount of money that an organization is willing to pay to avoid a loss is really a business decision. There should be a reasonable calculation made to quantify the decisions made in the disaster recovery plan.

A disaster recovery plan should be written in the same way that any project plan is written. The plan should start with a clear and concise description of its purpose, there should be a table of contents for the issues the plan covers, and each issue should be written up in its own section. Sections should not only describe the issue and its potential solution(s) but designate who is responsible for action.

Note

A disaster plan needs to be readily accessible when needed. If your disaster plan is found only on a computer system, it isn't going to do you any good if that system goes down. A disaster plan should be a paper document that is stored with emergency equipment, with a copy or set of copies stored offsite in logical locations.

Disaster recovery plans are a little different than a lot of other project plans. They don't include definite time lines, although they may specify how long operations should take. They must also specify how problems are identified and how to escalate actions to the next level when issues aren't resolved. A good disaster recovery plan should include flowcharts that illustrate how actions should flow.

Table 21.3 shows an example of the parts of a disaster recovery plan.

Table 21.3 The Parts of a Disaster Recovery Plan

Section	Contents
Title page	The title of document, with the names of the recovery managers, along with their titles, phone numbers, cell phone numbers, pager numbers, and email addresses. The point of the page is that even if someone doesn't open the document, he or she has enough information to take the next step.
Action summary	A one-page description of the purpose of the document. The summary describes the problems that are discussed in the document, how these issues are addressed (the chain of execution), and how the document is organized. It is important that *the action summary be one page only* and that there is enough information on that page to allow the reader to bring a problem to the attention of the person responsible.
Table of contents	A list of topics covered.
Topic title page	A one-line description of the problem.
Short description page	A description of how the problem can be detected and what the scope of the problem includes.
Notification page	A list of the persons to be notified for this particular issue, with an order that shows quickly how notification gets escalated.
System isolation page	A description of how systems should be taken offline if necessary or what steps should be taken immediately by the person onsite to avoid further damage.
Repair sequence page	A description of the proposed remedies, in the order which they should be performed, along with the conditions that represent restoration of the service.

With a fully developed disaster recovery plan, if and when a disaster strikes, you will be in a much better position to minimize the damage, contain the costs, and bring your systems and services back online much more quickly. At times of great difficulty, it is best not to have to spend time thinking through complex responses.

Glossary

This glossary contains computer and electronics terms that are applicable to the subject matter in this book. The glossary is meant to be as comprehensive as possible on the subject of upgrading and repairing servers. Many terms correspond to the latest technology in disk interfaces, modems, video and display equipment, and standards that govern the server industry. Although a glossary is a resource not designed to be read from beginning to end, you should find that scanning through this one is interesting, if not enlightening, with respect to some of the newer server technology.

The computer industry is rife with abbreviations used as shorthand for a number of terms. This glossary defines many abbreviations, as well as the terms on which the abbreviations are based. The definition of an abbreviation is included under the acronym. For example, *video graphics array* is defined under the abbreviation *VGA* rather than under *video graphics array*. This organization makes looking up a term easier; for example, even if you do not know in advance what *IDE* stands for, you can quickly find that it is an abbreviation for *integrated drive electronics*.

The following websites can also help you with terms not included in this glossary:

www.webopedia.com

whatis.techtarget.com

1X–50X CD-ROM maximum speeds in relation to the speed of a music CD (1X = 150KBps). At speeds of 16X or above, most drives are CAV and reach their rated speeds only on the outer edges of the disc. See also *CLV* and *CAV*.

3GIO The original name for PCI Express, a replacement for existing PCI connections. See also *PCIe (PCI Express)*.

8mm video See *Video 8*.

10BASE-2 An IEEE standard for baseband Ethernet at 10Mbps over RG-58 coaxial cable to a maximum distance of 185 meters. Also known as Thin Ethernet (Thinnet) or IEEE 802.3.

10BASE-5 An IEEE standard for baseband Ethernet at 10Mbps over thick coaxial cable to a maximum distance of 500 meters. Also known as Thick Ethernet or Thicknet.

10BASE-T A 10Mbps CSMA/CD Ethernet LAN that works on Category 3 or better twisted-pair wiring, which is very similar to standard telephone cabling. 10BASE-T Ethernet LANs work on a star configuration, in which the wire from each workstation routes directly to a 10BASE-T hub. Hubs can be joined together. 10BASE-T has a maximum distance of 100 meters between each workstation and the hub.

24x7 Continuous 24 hours per day, 7 days per week computer or services operation.

56K The generic term for modems that can receive data at a maximum rate of 56Kbps. See also *V.90, V.92, X2, K56flex*.

64-bit processor A processor that has 64-bit registers. The Intel Itanium and Itanium 2 processors for workstations and servers, which can also emulate 32-bit Intel processors; the AMD Athlon 64 desktop and Opteron server/workstation processors; and Intel EM64T versions of the Intel Xeon, Pentium 4, Pentium Extreme Edition and Pentium D, are some of the 64-bit processors now available.

100BASE-T A 100Mbps CSMA/CD Ethernet LAN that works on Category 5 twisted-pair wiring. 100BASE-T Ethernet LANs work on a star configuration in which the wire from each workstation routes directly to a central 100BASE-T hub. This is the current standard for 100Mbps Ethernet, replacing 100BASE-VG.

100BASE-VG The joint Hewlett-Packard–AT&T proposal for Fast Ethernet running at 100Mbps. It uses four pairs of Category 5 cable, using the 10BASE-T twisted-pair wiring scheme to transmit or receive. 100BASE-VG splits the signal across the four wire pairs at 25MHz each. This standard has not found favor with corporations and has been almost totally replaced by 100BASE-T.

286 See *80286*.

386 See *80386DX*.

404 A website error code which indicates that the specified page is not found. Some websites display a customized error message instead of the standard 404 code.

486 See *80486DX*.

586 A generic term used to refer to fifth-generation processors similar to the Intel Pentium, such as the AMD K6 series and the VIA Cyrix MII.

640KB barrier The limit imposed by the PC-compatible memory model using DOS mode. DOS programs can address only 1MB total memory, and PC compatibility generally requires the top 384KB to be reserved for the system, leaving only the lower 640KB for DOS or other real-mode applications.

802.11 The family name for various wireless Ethernet standards. See also *IEEE 802.11 family*.

1000BASE-T A 1,000Mbps Ethernet LAN that runs over four pairs of Category 5 cable. Popularly known as Gigabit Ethernet, 1000BASE-T can be used as an upgrade to a properly wired 100BASE-T network because the same cable and distance limitations (100 meters) apply.

1394 See *FireWire*.

8086 An Intel microprocessor with 16-bit registers, a 16-bit data bus, and a 20-bit address bus. This processor can operate only in real mode.

8087 An Intel math coprocessor designed to perform floating-point math with much greater speed and precision than the main CPU. The 8087 can be installed in most 8086- and 8088-based systems, and it adds more than 50 new instructions to those available in the primary CPU alone.

8088 An Intel microprocessor with 16-bit registers, an 8-bit data bus, and a 20-bit address bus. This processor can operate only in real mode and was designed as a low-cost version of the 8086.

8514/A An analog video display adapter from IBM for the PS/2 line of personal computers. Compared to previous display adapters, such as EGA and VGA, it provides a high resolution of 1,024×768 pixels, with as many as 256 colors or 64 shades of gray. It provides a video coprocessor that performs two-dimensional graphics functions internally, thus relieving the CPU of graphics tasks. It uses an interlaced monitor and scans every other line every time the screen is refreshed.

80286   An Intel microprocessor with 16-bit registers, a 16-bit data bus, and a 24-bit address bus. It can operate in both real and protected virtual modes.

80287   An Intel math coprocessor designed to perform floating-point math with much greater speed and precision than the main CPU. The 80287 can be installed in most 286- and some 386DX-based systems, and it adds more than 50 new instructions to what is available in the primary CPU alone.

80386   See *80386DX*.

80386DX   An Intel microprocessor with 32-bit registers, a 32-bit data bus, and a 32-bit address bus. This processor can operate in real, protected virtual, and virtual real modes.

80386SX   An Intel microprocessor with 32-bit registers, a 16-bit data bus, and a 24-bit address bus. This processor, designed as a low-cost version of the 386DX, can operate in real, protected virtual, and virtual real modes.

80387DX   An Intel math coprocessor designed to perform floating-point math with much greater speed and precision than the main CPU. The 80387DX can be installed in most 386DX-based systems, and it adds more than 50 new instructions to those available in the primary CPU alone.

80387SX   An Intel math coprocessor designed to perform floating-point math with much greater speed and precision than the main CPU. The 80387SX can be installed in most 386SX-based systems, and it adds more than 50 new instructions to those available in the primary CPU alone.

80486   See *80486DX*.

80486DX   An Intel microprocessor with 32-bit registers, a 32-bit data bus, and a 32-bit address bus. The 486DX has a built-in cache controller with 8KB of cache memory as well as a built-in math coprocessor equivalent to a 387DX. The 486DX can operate in real, protected virtual, and virtual real modes.

80486DX2   A version of the 486DX with an internal clock-doubling circuit that causes the chip to run at twice the motherboard clock speed. If the motherboard clock is 33MHz, the DX2 chip will run at 66MHz. The DX2 designation applies to chips sold through the OEM market, whereas a retail version of the DX2 sold by Intel and designed for use as an upgrade was sold as an Overdrive processor.

80486DX4   A version of the 486DX with an internal clock-tripling circuit that causes the chip to run at three times the motherboard clock speed. If the motherboard clock is 33.33MHz, the DX4 chip will run at 100MHz.

80486SX   An Intel microprocessor with 32-bit registers, a 32-bit data bus, and a 32-bit address bus. The 486SX is the same as the 486DX, except that it lacks the built-in math coprocessor function, and it was designed as a low-cost version of the 486DX. The 486SX can operate in real, protected virtual, and virtual real modes.

80487SX   An Intel microprocessor with 32-bit registers, a 32-bit data bus, and a 32-bit address bus. Although the name implies that the 80487SX adds floating-point math capabilities, in reality, the 487SX is the same as the 486DX, except that it uses a modified pinout and must be installed in a special 80487SX socket. When installed, the 80487SX replaces the 80486SX for all processing tasks. The 487SX can operate in real, protected virtual, and virtual real modes.

A+   CompTIA A+ certification, a vendor-neutral certification for computer hardware technicians. A+ certification exams test knowledge of basic hardware and software skills. The A+ certification can be used as part of the exam requirements for the Microsoft Certified System Administrator (MCSA) credential.

abend (abnormal end)   A condition that occurs when the execution of a program or task is terminated unexpectedly because of a bug or crash.

absolute address   An explicit identification of a memory location, device, or location within a device.

AC (alternating current)   Electricity whose frequency is measured in cycles per seconds (cps) or hertz (Hz). The standard value running through the wall outlet is 120 volts at 60Hz through a fuse or circuit breaker that usually can handle about 15 or 20 amps.

accelerator board   An add-in board that replaces the computer's CPU with circuitry that enables the system to run more quickly. See also *graphics accelerator*.

access light   The LED on the front of a drive or other device (or on the front panel of the system) that indicates the computer is reading or writing data on the device.

access mechanism   See *actuator*.

access time The time that elapses from the instant information is requested to the point at which delivery is completed. It's usually described in nanoseconds (ns) for memory chips and in milliseconds (ms) for disk drives. Most manufacturers rate average access time on a hard disk as the time required for a seek across one third of the total number of cylinders plus one half the time for a single revolution of the disk platters (latency). Also known as disk access time.

accumulator A register (temporary storage) in which the result of an operation is formed.

acoustic coupler A device used to connect a computer modem to a phone line by connecting to the handset of a standard AT&T-style phone. The audible sounds to and from the modem are transmitted to the handset through the coupler while the handset is resting in the coupler. Although often thought of as obsolete, an acoustic coupler can be used to ensure the availability of a modem connection when traveling and access to an RJ-11 jack is unavailable.

ACPI (Advanced Configuration and Power Interface) A standard developed by Intel, Microsoft, and Toshiba that is designed to implement power management functions in the operating system. ACPI is a replacement for APM. See also *APM*.

ACR (Advanced Communication Riser) An alternative to CNR, advocated by the ACR Special Interest Group (www.acrsig.org). ACR, like CNR, is designed to allow motherboard designers to add low-cost network capabilities to motherboards but uses the same PCI connector used by PCI expansion cards.

Acrobat An Adobe program for creating and reading cross-platform documents created in Adobe's PDF file format. Many computer and component manuals are available online in Acrobat format. Acrobat Reader can be downloaded free from Adobe's website.

active heatsink A heatsink that includes a fan. Active heatsinks are commonly used to cool processors and North Bridge/MCH chips.

active high Designates a digital signal that must go to a high value to be true. Synonymous with positive.

active low Designates a digital signal that must go to a low value to be true. Synonymous with negative.

active matrix A type of LCD screen that contains at least one transistor for every pixel on the screen. Color active matrix screens use three transistors for each pixel—one each for the red, green, and blue dots. The transistors are arranged on a grid of conductive material, with each connected to a horizontal and a vertical member. See also *TFT*.

active partition Any partition marked as bootable in the partition table. See also *boot manager*.

actuator The device that moves a disk drive's read/write heads across the platter surfaces. Also known as access mechanism.

adapter (1) A device that serves as an interface between a system unit and the devices attached to it. It's often synonymous with circuit board, circuit card, or card. (2) A connector or cable adapter that changes one type of connector to another.

add-in board See *expansion card*.

address (1) An identifier that refers to where a particular piece of data or other information is found in the computer. (2) An identifier that refers to the location of a set of instructions.

address bus One or more electrical conductors used to carry a binary-coded address from the microprocessor throughout the rest of the system.

ADF (adapter description files) The setup and configuration files and drivers necessary to install an adapter card, such as a network adapter card. Primarily used with MCA bus cards.

ADSL (asymmetric digital subscriber line) A high-speed transmission technology originally developed by Bellcore and now standardized by ANSI as T1.413. ADSL uses existing UTP copper wires to communicate digitally at high speed between the telephone company central office and the subscriber. ADSL sends information asymmetrically, meaning it is faster one way than the other. The original ADSL speed was T-1 (1.536Mbps) downstream from the carrier to the subscriber's premises and 16Kbps upstream. However, ADSL is now available in a variety of configurations and speeds. See also *DSL*.

AdvancedTCA (Advanced Telecom Computing Architecture) A new series of standards for telecom processor blades and chassis. Also known as the PICMG 3.0 specification. See also *PICMG*.

AGP (accelerated graphics port)   Developed by Intel, a fast, dedicated interface between the video adapter or chipset and the motherboard chipset North Bridge. AGP is 32 bits wide; runs at 66MHz base speed; and can transfer 1, 2, 4, or 8 bits per cycle (1x, 2x, 4x, or 8x modes), for a throughput of up to 2132MBps.

AHA (Accelerated Hub Architecture)   An Intel technology used on its 800-series chipsets to transfer data between the MCH, which is equivalent to the North Bridge, and the ICH, which is equivalent to the South Bridge. AHA transfers data at 266MBps, twice the speed of the PCI bus previously used.

AIX   IBM's implementation of the UNIX operating system. The current version, AIX 5L, supports eServer p5 systems that run the 64-bit POWER5 and POWER5+ processors. See also *UNIX*.

aliasing   Undesirable visual effects (sometimes called artifacts) in computer-generated images caused by inadequate sampling techniques. The most common effect is jagged edges along diagonal or curved object boundaries. See also *antialiasing*.

allocation unit   See *cluster*.

alphanumeric characters   A character set that contains only letters (A–Z) and digits (0–9). Other characters, such as punctuation marks, also might be allowed.

AMD (Advanced Micro Devices)   The number-two PC processor maker. AMD makes the popular K6, Athlon, Opteron, and Duron series of processors, as well as chipsets and flash memory devices.

AMD64   AMD-developed 64-bit extensions to the standard IA-32 system architecture; originally known as x86-64. AMD64 is supported by AMD Opteron, Athlon 64, and other AMD 64-bit processors.

ampere   The basic unit for measuring electrical current. Also called amp.

AMR (Audio/Modem Riser)   An Intel-developed specification for packaging modem I/O ports and a codec chip into a small card that can be installed into an AMR slot on a motherboard. Although many motherboards have AMR slots, AMR risers have not been popular, and the CNR specification has largely replaced AMR. See also *CNR*.

analog   The representation of numerical values by physical variables such as voltage, current, and so on; continuously variable quantities whose values correspond to the quantitative magnitude of the variables.

analog loopback   A modem self-test in which data from the keyboard is sent to the modem's transmitter, modulated into analog form, looped back to the receiver, demodulated into digital form, and returned to the screen for verification.

analog signals   Continuously variable signals. Analog circuits are more subject to distortion and noise than are digital circuits but are capable of handling complex signals with relatively simple circuitry. See also *digital signals*.

analog-to-digital converter   An electronic device that converts analog signals to digital form.

AND   A logical operator having the property that if P is a statement, Q is a statement, R is a statement…, then the AND of P, Q, R…is true if all statements are true and is false if any statement is false.

AND gate   A logic gate in which the output is 1 only if all inputs are 1.

animation   The process of displaying a sequential series of still images to achieve a motion effect.

ANSI (American National Standards Institute)   A nongovernmental organization founded in 1918 to propose, modify, approve, and publish data processing standards for voluntary use in the United States. It's also the U.S. representative to the ISO in Paris and the IEC. For more information, see www.ansi.org.

answer mode   A state in which a modem transmits at the predefined high frequency of the communications channel and receives at the low frequency. The transmit/receive frequencies are the reverse of those of the calling modem, which is in originate mode. See also *originate mode*.

antialiasing   Software adjustment to make diagonal or curved lines appear smooth and continuous in computer-generated images. See also *aliasing*.

antistatic mat   (1) A pad placed next to a computer on which components are placed while servicing the system to prevent static damage. (2) A large mat below an entire computer desk and chair that discharges static from a user before he or she touches the computer.

antivirus   Software that prevents files containing viruses from running on a computer or software that detects, repairs, cleans, or removes virus-infected files.

APA (all points addressable)   A mode in which all points of a displayable image can be controlled by the user or a program.

aperture grille   A type of shadow mask used in CRTs. The most common is used in Sony's Trinitron monitors, which use vertical phosphor stripes and vertical slots in the mask, compared to the traditional shadow mask that uses phosphor dots and round holes in the mask. See also *shadow mask*.

API (application programming interface)   A system call (routine) that gives programmers access to the services provided by the operating system. In IBM-compatible systems, the ROM BIOS and DOS together present an API that a programmer can use to control the system hardware.

APIC (advanced programmable interrupt controller)   A controller that replaces the 8259 interrupt controllers in multiple-processor PCs, starting with the Pentium. APIC must also be provided by the chipset and BIOS to enable APIC interrupt handling. Systems with virtual IRQs above 15 for PCI devices have working APIC support.

APM (Advanced Power Management)   A specification sponsored by Intel and Microsoft that was originally proposed to extend the life of batteries in battery-powered computers. It is now used in desktop computers as well. APM enables application programs, the system BIOS, and the hardware to work together to reduce power consumption. An APM-compliant BIOS provides built-in power-management services to the operating system. The application software communicates power-saving data via predefined APM interfaces. APM is replaced in newer systems by ACPI. See also *ACPI*.

application   End-user–oriented software, such as a word processor, spreadsheet, database, graphics editor, game, or web browser.

Application Layer   In the OSI reference model, the layer that is responsible for program-to-program communication. See also *OSI model*.

arbitration   A method by which multiple devices attached to a single bus can bid or arbitrate to get control of that bus.

archive bit   The bit in a file's attribute byte that sets the archive attribute. It tells whether the file has been changed since it last was backed up.

archive file   A collection of files that has been stored (often in a compressed format) within a single file. Zip and CAB files are the most common types of archive file formats used with Windows-based PCs. See also *zip file* and *CAB file*.

archive medium   A storage medium (floppy disk, tape cartridge, or removable cartridge) to hold files that need not be accessible instantly.

ARCnet (Attached Resource Computer Network)   A baseband, token-passing LAN technology that offers a flexible bus/star topology for connecting personal computers. Operating at 2.5Mbps, it is one of the oldest LAN systems and was popular in low-cost networks. It was originally developed by John Murphy of Datapoint Corporation. Although ARCnet (www.arcnet.com) is no longer used for office networking, it is still a popular choice for networking embedded systems, such as heating and air-conditioning systems.

areal density   A calculation of the bit density (bits per inch [BPI]) multiplied by the track density (tracks per inch [TPI]), which results in a figure that indicates how many bits per square inch are present on the disk surface.

ARQ (automatic repeat request)   A general term for error-control protocols that feature error detection and automatic retransmission of defective blocks of data.

ASCII (American Standard Code for Information Interchange)   A standard 7-bit code created in 1965 by Robert W. Bemer to achieve compatibility among various types of data processing equipment. The standard ASCII character set consists of 128 decimal numbers ranging from 0 to 127, which are assigned to letters, numbers, punctuation marks, and the most common special characters. In 1981, IBM introduced the extended ASCII character set with the IBM PC, extending the code to 8 bits and adding characters from 128 to 255 to represent additional special mathematic, graphics, and foreign characters.

ASCII character   A 1-byte character from the ASCII character set, including alphabetic and numeric characters, punctuation symbols, and various graphics characters.

ASME (American Society of Mechanical Engineers)   An organization that has nearly 600 codes and standards in print. ASME's (www.asme.org) many committees involve more than 3,000 individuals, mostly engineers but not necessarily members of the society. Its standards are used in more than 90 countries throughout the world.

aspect ratio The measurement of a film or television viewing area in terms of relative height and width. The aspect ratio of most modern motion pictures varies from 5:3 to as large as 16:9, which creates a problem when a wide-format motion picture is transferred to the more square-shaped television screen or monitor, whose aspect ratio is 4:3. See also *letterbox*.

assemble To translate a program expressed in an assembler language into a computer machine language.

assembler language A computer-oriented language whose instructions are usually in one-to-one correspondence with machine language instructions.

asymmetrical modulation A duplex transmission technique that splits the communications channel into one high-speed channel and one slower channel. During a call under asymmetrical modulation, the modem with the greater amount of data to transmit is allocated the high-speed channel. The modem with less data is allocated the slow, or back, channel. The modems dynamically reverse the channels during a call if the volume of data transfer changes.

asynchronous communication Data transmission in which the length of time between transmitted characters can vary. Timing depends on the actual time for the transfer to take place, as opposed to synchronous communication, which is timed rigidly by an external clock signal. Because the receiving modem must be signaled about when the data bits of a character begin and end, start and stop bits are added to each character. See also *synchronous communication*.

asynchronous memory Memory that runs using a timing or clock rate different from (usually slower than) the motherboard speed.

AT clock Refers to the Motorola 146818 RTC and CMOS RAM chip, which first debuted in the IBM AT and whose function has been present in all PC-compatible systems since. Keeps track of the time of day and makes this data available to the operating system or other software.

ATA (AT Attachment) An IDE disk interface standard introduced in 1989 that defines a compatible register set, a 40-pin connector, and its associated signals. See also *IDE* and *SATA*.

ATA-2 The second-generation ATA specification, approved in 1996. This version defines faster

transfer modes and logical block addressing schemes to allow high-performance, large-capacity drives. Also called Fast ATA, Fast ATA-2, and EIDE.

ATA-3 Published in 1997, an ATA standard that defines 8-bit DMA transfers and SMART support for drive failure prediction.

ATA/ATAPI-4 The fourth-generation ATA specification, published in 1998. ATA/ATAPI-4 incorporates ATAPI and adds UDMA/33 (33MBps) transfer mode; APM support; an optional 80-wire, 40-pin cable; support for CompactFlash memory devices; and enhanced BIOS support for larger drives.

ATA/ATAPI-5 Approved in 2000, an ATA standard that includes UDMA/66 support, mandates the 80-wire cable for UDMA/66, detects the cable type, and allows UDMA/66 or faster speeds only if the 80-wire cable is present.

ATA/ATAPI-6 The latest draft ATA standard, which includes UDMA/100 (100MBps) support and increases the ATA drive size limit to 144.12PB (petabytes). See also *petabyte*.

ATAPI (AT Attachment Packet Interface) A specification that defines device-side characteristics for an IDE-connected peripheral, such as a CD-ROM or tape drive. ATAPI is essentially an adaptation of the SCSI command set to the IDE interface. ATA-4 and newer ATA standards include ATAPI standards.

Athlon An AMD sixth-generation processor family roughly comparable to the Intel Pentium III and Pentium 4. Later models (beginning with the Thunderbird core) include on-die L2 cache running at full core speed. It includes MMX and AMD 3DNow! instructions for multimedia performance. Originally available in a Slot-A cartridge package, all Athlons are now available only in the Socket-A (462-pin) package. The Mobile Athlon XP, which replaced the Athlon 4, is designed for mobile applications, the Athlon MP is designed for workstation/server multiprocessor configurations, and the Athlon XP is designed mainly for single-processor applications. All three use the improved Thoroughbred core and 3DNow! Professional multimedia extensions. The Athlon XP processors include AMD's new QuantiSpeed design for faster internal operation and are rated by their performances relative to the Intel Pentium 4 rather than by their clock speeds. For example, the Athlon XP 2600+, which performs comparably to the Pentium 4 2.6GHz processor, runs at a clock speed of about 2.1GHz.

Athlon 64   An AMD processor that uses a 64-bit internal design. The Athlon 64 also emulates 32-bit x86 processors from Intel and AMD. It uses Socket 754 or Socket 939; an integrated DDR memory controller (instead of using the North Bridge for memory control); an improved version of the AMD-developed HyperTransport connection to AGP, PCI, and other components; and an improved heatsink-mounting solution. It supports MMX and AMD 3dNow! instructions for multimedia and uses a performance-rating system similar to that used by 32-bit Athlon processors. See also *Athlon, Socket 754*, and *Socket 939*.

Athlon 64 FX   An AMD processor based on the Athlon 64 that offers an integrated dual-channel memory controller, faster clock speeds, and a 1MB memory cache. Initial versions used Socket 940, but later models use Socket 939. See also *Socket 939* and *Socket 940*.

Athlon 64 X2   A dual-core version of the AMD Athlon 64 processor that features a separate L2 memory cache for each core and an integrated crossbar memory switch for fast transfer of information between each core. This processor uses Socket 939. See also *Socket 939*.

ATM (asynchronous transfer mode)   A high-bandwidth, low-delay, packet-like switching and multiplexing technique. Usable capacity is segmented into fixed-size cells consisting of header and information fields, allocated to services on demand.

attribute byte   A byte of information, held in the directory entry of any file or folder, that describes various attributes of the file or folder, such as whether it is read-only or has been backed up since it last was changed. Attributes can be set via the DOS ATTRIB command or through Windows Explorer.

ATX   A motherboard and power supply form factor standard designed by Intel and introduced in 1995. It is characterized by a double row of rear external I/O connectors on the motherboard, a single keyed power supply connector, memory and processor locations that are designed not to interfere with the installation of adapter cards, and an improved cooling flow. The current specification, ATX 2.0, was introduced in December 1996.

audio   A signal that can be heard, such as through the speaker of the PC. Many PC diagnostic tests use both visual (onscreen) codes and audio signals.

audio frequencies   Frequencies that can be heard by the human ear (approximately 20Hz–20,000Hz).

auto-answer   A setting in modems that enables them to answer incoming calls over the phone lines automatically.

auto-dial   A feature in modems that enables them to dial phone numbers without human intervention.

auto-disconnect   A modem feature that enables a modem to hang up the telephone line when the modem at the other end hangs up.

auto-redial   A modem or software feature that automatically redials the last number dialed if the number is busy or does not answer.

AUTOEXEC.BAT   A special batch file that DOS and Windows 9x execute at startup. It can contain any number of DOS commands that are executed automatically, including the capability to start programs at startup. See also *batch file*.

autoloader   A tape or Iomega REV-based drive that contains multiple media cartridges and a mechanism for removing and inserting cartridges as each cartridge is filled.

automatic head parking   Disk drive head parking performed whenever the drive is powered off. It is found in all modern hard disk drives that have voice-coil actuators.

available memory   Memory currently not in use by the operating system, drivers, or applications, which can be used to load additional software.

average access time   The average time it takes a disk drive to begin reading any data placed anywhere on the drive. This includes the average seek time, which is when the heads are moved, as well as the latency, which is the average amount of time required for any given data sector to pass underneath the heads. Together, these factors make up the average access time. See also *average seek time* and *latency*.

average latency   The average time required for any byte of data stored on a disk to rotate under the disk drive's read/write head. Equal to one half the time required for a single rotation of a platter.

average seek time   The average amount of time it takes to move the disk drive's heads from one random cylinder location to another, usually including any head settling time. In many cases, the average seek time is defined as the seek time across one third of the total number of cylinders.

AVI (audio video interleave) A storage technique developed by Microsoft for its Video for Windows product that combines audio and video into a single frame or track, saving valuable disk space and keeping audio in synchronization with the corresponding video. AVI files are widely supported by media players and video production programs.

AWG (American Wire Gauge) A U.S. standard for measuring the thickness of copper and aluminum wire for electrical and data-transmission use. Thinner wire is used to save space and for short distances, but thicker wire has less resistance and is better for long wire runs.

B channel (bearer channel) In an ISDN network, the channel that is used to carry data at a rate of 64KBps. See also *BRI*.

backbone The portion of Internet or WAN transmission wiring that connects the main Internet/WAN servers and routers and is responsible for carrying the bulk of the Internet/WAN data.

backplane A rarely used motherboard design in which the components typically found on a motherboard are instead located on an expansion adapter card plugged in to a slot. In these systems, the board with the slots is the backplane. The PICMG single-board computer designs for rack-mounted systems are the primary users of backplane designs today.

backup The duplication of a file or library onto a separate piece of media. Backups are good insurance against the loss of originals. Depending on how a backup was made, the data might need to be restored with a special program before reuse.

backup disk A disk that contains information copied from another disk. It is used to ensure that original information is not destroyed or altered.

backward compatibility The ability of software and hardware to work with previous versions of the same software or hardware.

bad sector A disk sector that can't hold data reliably because of a media flaw or damaged format markings.

bad track table A label affixed to the casing of an ST412/506 or ESDI hard disk drive that tells which tracks are flawed and incapable of holding data. The listing is entered into the low-level formatting program. Modern ATA (IDE) and SCSI drives are low-level formatted during manufacture and don't have (or need) a bad track table.

balanced signal A signal that consists of equal currents moving in opposite directions. When balanced or nearly balanced signals pass through twisted-pair lines, the electromagnetic interference effects—such as crosstalk caused by the two opposite currents—largely cancel each other out. Differential signaling (used by some types of SCSI interfaces) is a method that uses balanced signals.

balun (balanced/unbalanced) A type of transformer that enables balanced cables to be joined with unbalanced cables. Twisted-pair (balanced) cables, for example, can be joined with coaxial (unbalanced) cables if the proper balun transformer is used.

bandwidth (1) Generally, the measure of the range of frequencies within a radiation band required to transmit a particular signal. The difference between the lowest and highest signal frequencies. The bandwidth of a computer monitor is a measure of the rate at which a monitor can handle information from the display adapter. The wider the bandwidth, the more information the monitor can carry and the greater the resolution. (2) A measure of the data-carrying capacity of a given communications circuit or pathway. The bandwidth of a circuit is a measure of the rate at which information can be passed.

bank The collection of memory chips or modules that make up a block of memory that is readable or writable by the processor in a single cycle. This block, therefore, must be as large as the data bus of the particular microprocessor. In server systems, the processor data bus (and therefore the bank size) is usually 32 or 64 bits wide. Optionally, some systems also incorporate an additional parity or ECC bit for each 8 data bits, resulting in a total of 936 or 72 bits (respectively) for each bank. Memory in a server always must be added or removed in full-bank increments. The number of memory chips or modules that make up a bank varies with the width of the memory in bits, the size of the processor's data bus, and whether the system uses dual-channel memory. On single-channel systems with 64-bit data buses that have DIMMs, which are also 64 data bits wide, a bank is one DIMM. However, a dual-channel system uses two DIMMs. Some systems that use memory sparing or memory arrays might require additional modules per bank.

bar code A code used on consumer products and inventory parts for identification purposes. It consists of bars of varying thickness that represent characters and numerals that are read with an optical reader. The most common version is called the UPC.

base 2 The computer numbering system that consists of two numerals: 0 and 1. Also called binary.

base 16 See *hexadecimal*.

base address The starting location for a consecutive string of memory or I/O addresses/ports.

base memory The amount of memory available to the operating system or application programs within the first megabyte, accessible in the processor's real mode. Also known as conventional memory.

baseband transmission The transmission of digital signals over a limited distance. ARCnet and Ethernet LANs use baseband signaling. See also *broadband transmission*.

BASIC (Beginner's All-purpose Symbolic Instruction Code) A popular computer programming language originally developed by John Kemeny and Thomas Kurtz in the mid-1960s at Dartmouth College. Normally, BASIC is an interpretive language, meaning that each statement is translated and executed as it is encountered, but it can be a compiled language, in which all the program statements are compiled before execution. Microsoft Visual Basic, a popular development environment for Windows, is not related to BASIC.

batch file A set of commands stored in a disk file for execution by the operating system. A special batch file called AUTOEXEC.BAT is executed by DOS each time the system is started. All DOS and Windows batch files have a .BAT file extension.

baud A unit of signaling speed that denotes the number of discrete signal elements that can be transmitted per second. The word *baud* is derived from the name of J.M.E. Baudot (1845–1903), a French pioneer in the field of printing telegraphy and the inventor of Baudot code. Although technically inaccurate, *baud rate* commonly is used to mean *bit rate*. Because each signal element, or baud, can translate into many individual bits, bits per second (bps) usually differs from baud rate. A rate of 2,400 baud means that 2,400 frequency or signal changes per second are being sent, but each frequency change can signal several bits of information. For example, 33.6Kbps modems actually transmit at only 2,400 baud.

Baudot code A 5-bit code used in many types of data communications, including teletype (TTY), radio teletype (RTTY), and telecommunications

devices for the deaf (TDD). Baudot code has been revised and extended several times. See also *baud*.

bay An opening in a computer case or chassis that holds disk drives.

BBS (bulletin board system) A computer that operates with a program and a modem to enable other computers with modems to communicate with it, often on a round-the-clock basis. Although BBSs were once the primary means of distributing information and software, the Internet has almost completely replaced BBSs.

benchmark A test or set of tests designed to compare the performance of hardware or software. A popular set of benchmarks for PC hardware is the *PC Magazine* benchmarks, such as Business Winstone, WinBench, and others. You can order CDs or download selected benchmarks from www.veritest.com/benchmarks/pcmbmk.asp.

bezel A cosmetic panel that covers the face of a drive or some other device.

Bézier curve A mathematical method for describing a curve, often used in illustration and CAD programs to draw complex shapes.

BGA (ball grid array) A packaging technology used by Socket 478 Pentium 4 and Celeron processors, as well as many recent motherboard chipsets and video card memory chips. BGA uses small solder balls instead of pin connectors to enable more signaling paths to exist in a smaller space and improve signal accuracy.

bidirectional (1) Refers to lines over which data can move in two directions, such as a data bus or telephone line. (2) Refers to the capability of a printer to print from right to left and from left to right alternately.

binary See *base 2*.

BIOS (basic input/output system) The part of an operating system that handles the communications between the computer and its peripherals. Often burned into ROM chips or rewritable flash (EEPROM) memory chips found on motherboards and expansion cards, such as video cards and SCSI and ATA/IDE host adapters. See also *firmware*.

bipolar A category of semiconductor circuit design that was used to create the first transistor and the first IC. Bipolar and CMOS are the two major transistor technologies. Almost all personal computers use CMOS technology chips. CMOS uses far less energy than bipolar.

bisynchronous (binary synchronous control)
An early protocol developed by IBM for software applications and communicating devices operating in synchronous environments. The protocol defines operations at the link level of communications—for example, the format of data frames exchanged between modems over a phone line.

bit (binary digit)   Represented logically by 0 or 1 and electrically by 0 volts and (typically) 5 volts. Other methods are used to represent bits physically (tones, different voltages, lights, and so on), but the logic is always the same.

bit density   Expressed as bits per inch (BPI), a measure that defines how many bits can be written onto one linear inch of a track. Sometimes also called linear density.

bit depth   The number of bits used to describe the color of each pixel on a computer display. For example, a bit depth of two (2^2) means the monitor can display only black-and-white pixels; a bit depth of four (2^4) means the monitor can display 16 different colors; a bit depth of eight (2^8) allows for 256 colors; and so on.

bit rate   The speed at which a device transmits or receives data. Also known as the data transfer rate. The bit rate is usually expressed in bits per second (bps). For example, Fast Ethernet supports a transfer rate of 10Mbps.

bitmap   A method of storing graphics information in memory, in which a bit devoted to each pixel (picture element) onscreen indicates whether that pixel is on or off. A bitmap contains a bit for each point or dot on a video display screen and enables fine resolution because any point or pixel onscreen can be addressed. A greater number of bits can be used to describe each pixel's color, intensity, and other display characteristics.

blackout   An AC supply voltage drop in which the power shuts off entirely.

blade server   A thin circuit board that contains processors, memory, and, often, storage, which plugs into a special rack-mounted chassis. Multiple blade servers can occupy a single chassis.

BladeCenter   A blade server design developed by IBM that may become the basis for a de facto blade architecture standard.

blank, or blanking, interval   A period in which no video signal is received by a monitor while the videodisc or DVD player searches for the next video segment or frame to display.

block   A string of records, words, or characters formed for technical or logic reasons and to be treated as an entity.

block diagram   The logical structure or layout of a system in graphic form. It does not necessarily match the physical layout and does not specify all the components and their interconnections.

Blue Book   The standard for enhanced CDs (CD-E). CD-E media contains both music (for play on standard CD players) and computer content. Developed by Philips and Sony in 1995.

Bluetooth   An emerging short-range networking standard that is designed to enable PCs, mobile phones, input devices, and PDAs to exchange data with each other. Bluetooth uses the same 2.4GHz frequency range used by some types of wireless phones and by the IEEE 802.11b Wi-Fi wireless Ethernet network. Bluetooth has a speed of 1Mbps or 2Mbps, depending on the version.

BMP   A Windows graphics format that can be device dependent or independent. Device-independent BMP files (DIB) are coded for translation to a wide variety of displays and printers.

BNC (Bayonet-Neill-Concelman, British-Naval-Connector, Baby-N-Connector, or Bayonet-Nut-Coupler)   A bayonet-locking connector is noted for its excellent shielding and impedance-matching characteristics, resulting in low noise and minimal signal loss at any frequency up to 4GHz. It is used in Ethernet 10BASE-2 networks to terminate coaxial cables. It is also used for some high-end video monitors. BNC is named for its connection type (bayonet) and its co-developers.

bonding   In ISDN, the joining of two 64Kbps B-channels to achieve 128Kbps speed. Bonding can also be used with analog modems that use the Multilink Point-to-Point protocol that is supported by Windows 98 and newer versions but by only a few ISPs.

Boolean operation   An operation in which each of the operands and the result takes one of two values. A Boolean search can be performed with many search engines used on websites and help files, using operators such as AND, OR, and NOT.

boot   To load a program into a computer. The term comes from the phrase "pulling a boot on by the bootstrap."

boot manager   A program that enables you to select which active partition to boot from. Often supplied with aftermarket disk-partitioning programs, such as PartitionMagic, or installed by default when you install a Windows upgrade into a separate disk partition instead of replacing your old version. See also *active partition*.

boot record   The first sector on a disk or partition, which contains disk parameter information for the BIOS and operating system as well as bootstrap loader code that instructs the system how to load the operating system files into memory, thus beginning the initial boot sequence to boot the machine. Also known as boot record.

boot sector   See *boot record*.

boot sector virus   A virus designed to occupy the boot sector of a disk. Any attempt to start or boot a system from this disk transfers the virus to the hard disk, after which it is subsequently loaded every time the system is started. Many older PC viruses, particularly those spread by infected floppy disks, are boot sector viruses.

bootstrap   A technique or device designed to bring itself into a desired state by means of its own action. The term is used to describe the process by which a device such as a PC goes from its initial power-on condition to a running condition without human intervention. See also *boot*.

boule   Purified, cylindrical silicon crystals from which semiconducting electronic chips, including microprocessors, memory, and other chips in a PC are manufactured. Also known as ingot.

bps (bits per second)   The number of bits transmitted per second. Sometimes confused with baud.

branch prediction   A feature of fifth-generation (Pentium and higher) processors that attempts to predict whether a program branch will be taken and then fetches the appropriate following instructions.

BRI (basic rate interface)   A form of ISDN used in home and small business applications. A 2B+1D BRI service has two B channels and a single D channel for signaling and control uses.

bridge   (1) In LANs, an interconnection between two similar networks. (2) The hardware equipment used to establish an interconnection between two similar networks.

broadband transmission   A term used to describe analog transmission. It requires modems for connecting terminals and computers to the network. Using frequency division multiplexing, many signals or sets of data can be transmitted simultaneously. The alternative transmission scheme is baseband, or digital, transmission. See also *baseband transmission*.

brownout   An AC supply voltage drop in which the power does not shut off entirely but continues to be supplied at lower-than-normal levels.

BSOD (blue screen of death)   A system crash in Windows that replaces the normal desktop with a blue screen with white text reporting the problem and locks up the system. This condition can be triggered by defective memory, file system errors, and other system problems.

BSRAM (Burst Static RAM)   A common type of static RAM chip used for memory caches where access to subsequent memory locations after the first byte is accessed takes fewer machine cycles.

BTX (Balanced Technology Extended)   A PC and server architecture introduced by Intel in 2003 that is designed to improve internal cooling by placing memory and processors in line with cooling fans.

bubble memory   A special type of nonvolatile read/write memory introduced by Intel in which magnetic regions are suspended in crystal film and data is maintained when the power is off. A typical bubble memory chip contains about 512KB, or more than four million bubbles. Bubble memory failed to catch on because of slow access times measured in several milliseconds. It has, however, found a niche use as solid-state "disk" emulators in environments in which conventional drives are unacceptable, such as in military or factory use.

buffer   A block of memory that is used as a holding tank to store data temporarily. A buffer is often positioned between a slower peripheral device and the faster computer. All data moving between the peripheral and the computer passes through the buffer. A buffer enables the data to be read from or written to the peripheral in larger chunks, which improves performance. A buffer that is x bytes in size usually holds the last x bytes of data that moved between the peripheral and CPU. This method contrasts with a cache, which adds intelligence to the buffer so that the most often accessed data, rather than the last accessed data, remains in the buffer (cache). A cache can improve performance greatly over a plain buffer. See also *cache*.

bug   An error or a defect in a program; it can be corrected through program patches (for applications or operating systems) or firmware updates (for BIOS chips).

burn-in   The operation of a circuit or equipment to establish that its components are stable and to screen out defective ports or assemblies.

BURN-Proof (buffer underrun error-proof)   A technology developed by Sanyo to prevent buffer underruns during the creation of CD-Rs. BURN-Proof, which has been licensed to many CD-RW drive makers, enables a drive to pause the burning process and continue after sufficient data is available in the drive's buffer. The drive and CD-mastering software must both support BURN-Proof for this feature to work. Ricoh's JustLink works in a similar fashion. See also *lossless linking*.

burst mode   A memory-cycling technology that takes advantage of the fact that most memory accesses are consecutive in nature. After setting up the row and column addresses for a given access, using burst mode can then access the next three adjacent addresses with no additional latency.

bus   A linear electrical signal pathway over which power, data, and other signals travel. A bus is capable of connecting to three or more attachments. A bus is generally considered to be distinct from radial or point-to-point signal connections. The term comes from the Latin *omnibus*, meaning "for all." When used to describe a topology, bus always implies a linear structure.

bus mouse   An obsolete type of mouse used in the 1980s that plugs in to a special mouse expansion board (occasionally incorporated into a video card) instead of a serial port or motherboard mouse port. The bus mouse connector looks similar to a motherboard mouse (sometimes called PS/2 mouse) connector, but the pin configurations are different and not compatible.

busmaster   An intelligent device that, when attached to the Micro Channel, EISA, VLB, or PCI bus, can bid for and gain control of the bus to perform its specific task without processor intervention. Most recent motherboards incorporate busmastering ATA/IDE host adapters, but this feature must be enabled in both the BIOS and through the installation of Windows drivers to be effective.

byte   A collection of bits that makes up a character or other designation. Generally, a byte is 8 data bits. When referring to system RAM, an additional parity (error-checking) bit is also stored (see also *parity*), making the total 9 bits.

C   A high-level computer programming language frequently used on mainframes, minis, and PC computer systems. C++ is a popular variant.

C3   A Socket 370–compatible processor developed by VIA Technology from the Cyrix "Joshua" after VIA purchased Cyrix from National Semiconductor. The C3 is noted for its very small die size and cool operation, making it a suitable choice for portable computers and embedded computers.

CAB file (cabinet file)   An archive file type used by Microsoft to distribute recent versions of Windows and applications. Some recent versions of WinZip can be used to manually extract files from a CAB file; you can also open CAB files within Windows Explorer with Windows 98 after you install the Windows 98 Plus! package and with Windows Explorer in Windows 2000, Windows Me, and Windows XP.

cable modem   A broadband Internet device that receives data through the cable TV system. A cable modem can be a one-way device (using a conventional analog modem for dialing and uploading) or a two-way device.

CableLabs Certified Cable Modem   A cable modem that meets the DOCSIS standards for modulation and protocols. Various brands and models of modems meet this standard on cable networks that also meet this standard. DOCSIS/CableLabs Certified Cable Modems can be purchased as well as leased.

cache   An intelligent buffer. By using an intelligent algorithm, a cache contains the data accessed most often between a slower peripheral device and the faster CPU. See also *buffer, disk cache, L1 cache,* and *L2 cache*.

cache coherency   A method of managing processor caches in multiprocessor systems to ensure that data is not lost when it is moved from a cache to main memory.

caddy   A cartridge designed to hold a CD or DVD disc. Some CD drives use caddies, particularly in harsh or industrial environments. A DVD-RAM drive also uses a caddy to protect the disc.

CAM (Common Access Method)   A committee formed in 1988 that consists of several computer peripheral suppliers and is dedicated to developing standards for a common software interface between SCSI peripherals and host adapters.

capacitor   A device that consists of two plates separated by insulating material and is designed to store an electrical charge.

card   A printed circuit board that contains electronic components that form an entire circuit, usually designed to plug in to a connector or slot. Sometimes also called an adapter.

card edge connector   See *edge connector*.

CardBus   A PC Card (PCMCIA) specification for a 32-bit interface that runs at 33MHz and provides 32-bit data paths to the computer's I/O and memory systems, as well as a shielded connector that prevents CardBus devices from being inserted into slots that do not support the latest version of the PC Card (PCMCIA) standard. CardBus slots can also be used with normal 16-bit PC Card (PCMCIA) devices.

carpal tunnel syndrome   A painful hand injury that gets its name from the narrow tunnel in the wrist that connects ligament and bone. When undue pressure is put on the tendons, they can swell and compress the median nerve, which carries impulses from the brain to the hand, causing numbness, weakness, tingling, and burning in the fingers and hands. Computer users get carpal tunnel syndrome primarily from improper keyboard and mouse ergonomics that result in undue strain on the wrist and hand.

carrier   A continuous frequency signal that is capable of being either modulated or impressed with another information-carrying signal. It is the reference signal used for the transmission or reception of data. The most common use of this signal with computers involves modem communications over phone lines. The carrier is used as a signal on which the information is superimposed.

carrier detect signal   A modem interface signal that indicates to the attached DTE that it is receiving a signal from the distant modem. It is defined in the RS-232 specification and is the same as the received line-signal detector.

CAT (Category)   The ANSI/EIA 568 wiring standards used for data transmission. The most common CAT standards include CAT3 (16Mbps maximum data rate, suitable for 10BASE-T Ethernet) and CAT5 (used for 100BASE-T Fast Ethernet or 1000BASE-T Gigabit Ethernet).

CAV (constant angular velocity)   An optical disk recording format in which the data is recorded on the disk in concentric circles. CAV disks are rotated at a constant speed. This is similar to the recording technique used on floppy disk drives.

CAV limits the total recorded capacity compared to CLV, which is also used in optical recording. See also *CLV*.

CBT (computer-based training)   The use of a computer to deliver instruction or training; also known as computer-aided (or assisted) instruction (CAI), computer-aided learning (CAL), computer-based instruction (CBI), and computer-based learning (CBL).

CCITT (Comité Consultatif International de Télégraphique et Téléphonique)   The International Telegraph and Telephone Consultative Committee or the Consultative Committee for International Telegraph and Telephone. Renamed ITU. See also *ITU*.

CCS (common command set)   A set of SCSI commands specified in the ANSI SCSI-1 Standard X3.131-1986 Addendum 4.B. All SCSI devices must be capable of using the CCS to be fully compatible with the ANSI SCSI-1 standard.

cd (candela)   The standard unit of measurement for luminosity. The brightness of LCDs and other types of displays is sometimes measured in cd units.

CD (compact disc or compact audio disc)   A 4.75-inch (12cm) optical disc that contains information encoded digitally in the CLV format. This popular format for high-fidelity music offers 90 decibels signal/noise ratio, 74 minutes of digital sound, and no degradation of quality from playback. The standards for this format (developed by NV Philips and Sony Corporation) are known as the Red Book. The official (and rarely used) designation for the audio-only format is CD-DA (compact disc–digital audio). The simple audio format is also known as CD-A (compact disc–audio). A smaller (3-inch) version of the CD is known as a CD-3 or minidisc.

CD burner   Refers to either a CD-R or CD-RW drive. See also *DVD burner*.

CD-DA (compact disc–digital audio)   See *Red Book*.

CD-E (enhanced CD)   See *Blue Book*.

CD+G (compact disc+graphics)   A CD format that includes extended graphics capabilities, as written into the original CD-ROM specifications. Includes limited video graphics encoded into the CD subcode area. Originally developed and marketed by Warner New Media (later Time Warner Interactive), it's a popular choice for self-contained karaoke systems.

CD-I (compact disc–interactive) A compact disc format released in October 1991 that provides audio, digital data, still graphics, and motion video. The standards for this format (developed by NV Philips and Sony Corporation) are known as the Green Book. CD-I did not catch on with consumers and is now considered obsolete.

CD+MIDI (compact disc+musical instrument digital interface) A CD format that adds to the CD+G format digital audio, graphics information, and MIDI specifications and capabilities. Originally developed and marketed by Warner New Media (later Time Warner Interactive).

CD-R (compact disc–recordable, sometimes called CD-writable) CDs that can be recorded and read as many times as desired. CD-R is part of the Orange Book standard defined by ISO. CD-R technology is used for mass production of multimedia applications. CD-R discs can be compatible with CD-ROM, CD-ROM XA, and CD audio. Orange Book specifies multisession capabilities, which enable data recording on the disc at various times in several recording sessions. Multisession capability enables data such as digital photos, digital music, and other types of data files to be added to a single disc on different occasions. The original capacity of CD-R media was 650MB (74 minutes), but most recent CD-ROM and compatible optical drives support the larger 700MB (80-minute) media.

CD-ROM (compact disc–read-only memory) A 4.75-inch laser-encoded optical memory storage medium with the same CLV spiral format as audio CDs and some videodiscs. CD-ROMs can hold about 650MB of data and require more error-correction information than the standard prerecorded compact audio discs. The standards for this format (developed by NV Philips and Sony Corporation) are known as the Yellow Book. See also *CD-ROM XA*.

CD-ROM drive A device that retrieves data from a CD-ROM disc; it differs from a standard audio CD player by the incorporation of additional error-correction circuitry. CD-ROM drives usually can also play music from audio CDs.

CD-ROM XA (CD-ROM Extended Architecture) A standard developed jointly by Sony, Philips, and Microsoft in 1988 that is now part of the Yellow Book standard. XA is a built-in feature of newer CD-ROM drives and supports simultaneous sound playback with data transfer. Non-XA drives support either sound playback or data transfer, but not

both simultaneously. XA also enables data compression right on the disk, which can also increase data transfer rates.

CD-RW (compact disc–rewritable) A type of rewritable CD-ROM technology defined in Part III of the Orange Book standard that uses a different type of disc that the drive can rewrite at least 1,000 times. CD-RW drives can also be used to write CD-R discs, and they can read CD-ROMs. CD-RWs have a lower reflectivity than standard CD-ROMs, and CD-ROM drives must be of the newer multiread variety to read them. CD-RW was initially known as CD-E (for CD-erasable).

CDV (CD Video) A CD format introduced in 1987 that combines 20 minutes of digital audio and 6 minutes of analog video on a standard 4.75-inch CD. Upon introduction, many firms renamed 8-inch and 12-inch videodiscs CDV in an attempt to capitalize on the consumer popularity of the audio CD. The term fell out of use in 1990 and was replaced in some part by *laser disc* and, more recently, *DVD*. See also *video-on-CD*.

CD-WO (compact disc–write once) A variant of CD-ROM that can be written to once and read many times; developed by NV Philips and Sony Corporation. Also known as CD-WORM (CD–write once/read many), CD-recordable, or CD-writable. Standards for this format are known as the Orange Book.

CD-WORM See *CD-WO*.

CDMA (code division multiple access) A popular family of wireless protocols used in cellular phones for Internet and email access.

CEB (Compact Electronics Bay) An SSI form factor for rack-mounted servers. See also *SSI*.

Celeron A family of processors that are low-cost versions of the Pentium II, Pentium III, and Pentium 4 processors. The major differences include a smaller amount of L2 cache and lower clock speeds.

Centronics connector One of two types of cable connectors used with either parallel (36-pin edge connector) or SCSI (50-pin edge connector) devices.

ceramic substrate A thin, flat, fired-ceramic part used to hold an IC chip (usually made of beryllium oxide or aluminum oxide).

CERN (Conseil Européen pour la Recherche Nucléaire; The European Laboratory for Particle Physics) The site in Geneva where the World Wide Web was created in 1989.

CGA (color graphics adapter) A type of PC video display adapter introduced by IBM in 1981 that supports text and graphics. Text is supported at a maximum resolution of 80×25 characters in 16 colors, with a character box of 8×8 pixels. Graphics are supported at a maximum resolution of 320×200 pixels in 16 colors or 640×200 pixels in 2 colors. The CGA outputs a TTL (digital) signal with a horizontal scanning frequency of 15.75KHz and supports TTL color or NTSC composite displays.

channel (1) Any path along which signals can be sent. (2) In ISDN, a divisions of data bandwidth. The two B-channels bear data, and one D-channel carries information about the call.

character A representation—coded in binary digits—of a letter, number, or other symbol.

character set All the letters, numbers, and other characters a computer can use to represent data. The ASCII standard has 256 characters, each represented by a binary number from 1 to 256. The ASCII set includes all the letters in the alphabet, numbers, most punctuation marks, some mathematical symbols, and other characters.

charge coupled device A light-sensing and storage device used in scanners and digital cameras to capture pixels.

chassis The case used by a desktop PC or server. A server platform includes a chassis, a motherboard, a processor(s), and other components.

checksum (summation check) A technique for determining whether a package of data is valid. The package, a string of binary digits, is added up and compared with the expected number.

chip Another name for an IC. Housed in a plastic or ceramic package, a chip is a carrier device with pins for making electrical connections.

chip carrier A ceramic or plastic package that carries an IC.

chipkill An advanced form of ECC memory correction that can correct multiple-bit failures in a single memory module. Also known as Advanced ECC. See also *ECC*.

chipset A single chip or pair of chips that integrates into the clock generator, bus controller, system timer, interrupt controller, DMA controller, CMOS RAM/clock, and keyboard controller. See also *North Bridge* and *South Bridge*.

CHS (cylinder head sector) The term used to describe the nontranslating scheme used by the

BIOS to access IDE drives that are less than or equal to 528MB in capacity. See also *LBA*.

CIF (common image format) The standard sample structure that represents the picture information of a single frame in digital HDTV, independent of frame rate and sync/blank structure. The uncompressed bit rate for transmitting CIF at 29.97 frames per sec is 36.45Mbps.

CIOB One of a series of I/O bridge chips used by the Broadcom ServerWorks series of server chipsets.

circuit A complete electronic path.

circuit board A collection of circuits gathered on a sheet of plastic, usually with all contacts made through a strip of pins. A circuit board is usually made by chemically etching metal-coated plastic.

CISC (complex instruction set computer) A traditional computer that operates with a large set of processor instructions. Most modern computers, including the Intel 80xxx processors, are in this category. CISC processors have expanded instruction sets that are complex in nature and require several to many execution cycles to complete. This structure contrasts with RISC processors, which have far fewer instructions that execute quickly.

clean room (1) A dust-free room in which certain electronic components (such as chips or hard disk drives) must be manufactured and serviced to prevent contamination. Rooms are rated by class numbers. A Class 100 clean room must have fewer than 100 particles larger than 0.5 microns per cubic foot of space. (2) A legal approach to copying software or hardware in which one team analyzes the product and writes a detailed description, followed by a second team that reads the description written by the first and then develops a compatible version of the product. When done correctly, such a design methodology will survive a legal attack.

client/server A type of network in which every computer is either a server with a defined role of sharing resources with clients or a client that can access the resources on the server.

clock The source of a computer's timing signals. It synchronizes every operation of the CPU.

clock multiplier A processor feature in which the internal core runs at a higher speed than the motherboard or processor bus. See also *overclocking*.

clock speed A measurement of the rate at which the clock signal for a device oscillates, usually expressed in millions of cycles per second (MHz).

clone (1) Originally, an IBM-compatible computer system that physically as well as electrically emulates the design of one of IBM's personal computer systems. (2) More currently, any PC system running an Intel or compatible processor in the 80x86 family.

cluster A group of one or more sectors on a disk that forms a fundamental unit of storage to the operating system. Cluster size is determined by the operating system when the disk is formatted. Larger clusters generally offer faster system performance but waste disk space. Also known as an allocation unit.

CLV (constant linear velocity) An optical recording format in which the spacing of data is consistent throughout the disk and the rotational speed of the disk varies, depending on which track is being read. In addition, more sectors of data are placed on the outer tracks compared to the inner tracks of the disk, which is similar to zone recording on hard drives. CLV drives adjust the rotational speed to maintain a constant track velocity as the diameter of the track changes. CLV drives also rotate more quickly near the center of the disk and more slowly toward the edge. Rotational adjustment maximizes the amount of data that can be stored on a disk. CD audio and CD-ROM use CLV recording. See also *CAV*.

CMOS (complementary metal-oxide semiconductor) A type of chip design that requires little power to operate. In PCs, a battery-powered CMOS memory and clock chip is used to store and maintain the clock setting and system configuration information. See also *MOS*.

CMYK (cyan, magenta, yellow, black) The standard four-color model used for printing.

CNR (Communications and Networking Riser) A technology developed by Intel as a replacement for AMR. CNR enables motherboard makers to offer low-cost modem, networking, and audio features through a special expansion slot. Unlike AMR, a CNR slot can be built as a shared slot with a PCI slot. See also *AMR*.

coated medium A hard disk platter coated with a reddish iron-oxide medium on which data is recorded.

coaxial cable A data-transmission medium noted for its wide bandwidth, immunity to interference, and high cost compared to other types of cable. Signals are transmitted inside a fully shielded environment in which an inner conductor is surrounded by a solid insulating material and then an outer conductor or shield. Coaxial cable is used in many LAN systems, such as Ethernet and ARCnet. Also known as coax cable.

COBOL (Common Business-Oriented Language) A high-level computer programming language used primarily by some larger companies. It has never achieved popularity on personal and small business computers.

code page A table used in DOS 3.3 and later that sets up the keyboard and display characters for various foreign languages.

code page switching A DOS feature in versions 3.3 and later that changes the characters displayed onscreen or printed on an output device. It is primarily used to support foreign-language characters. It requires an EGA or better video system and an IBM-compatible graphics printer.

codec (coder-decoder) (1) A device that converts voice signals from their analog form to digital signals acceptable to more modern digital PBXs and digital transmission systems. It then converts those digital signals back to analog so you can hear and understand what the other party is saying. (2) Compression/decompression software used in the creation of digital audio and video files, such as MP3 and MPEG, and for videophone programs.

coercivity A measurement in units of oersteds of the amount of magnetic energy to switch, or "coerce," the flux change in the magnetic recording media. High-coercivity disk media require a stronger write current.

cold boot To start or restart a computer from a powered-off state. If the system is on, this requires cycling the power off and then back on. A cold boot causes all RAM to be forcibly cleared. See also *warm boot*.

collision In a LAN, a situation in which two computers transmit packets of data at the same time on the network and the data becomes garbled.

collision detection/avoidance A process used on a LAN to prevent data packets from interfering with each other and to determine whether data packets have encountered collisions and initiate resends of the affected packets.

color palette The colors available to a graphics adapter for display.

COM port A serial port on a PC that conforms to the RS-232 standard. See also *RS-232*.

COMDEX The largest international computer trade show and conference in the world, managed by MediaLive International, Inc. See www.comdex.com for the latest information.

command An instruction that tells a computer to start, stop, or continue an operation.

COMMAND.COM An operating system file that is loaded last when the computer is booted. It is the command interpreter or user interface and program-loader portion of DOS.

command interpreter An operating system program that controls a computer's shell or user interface. The command interpreter for MS-DOS (and the command-line sessions in Windows 9x/Me) is COMMAND.COM; the command interpreter for the graphical shell in Windows versions through 9x/Me is WIN.COM; the command interpreter for NT-based versions of Windows (including Windows 2000 and Windows XP) is CMD.COM.

common The ground or return path for an electrical signal. If it's a wire, it is usually colored black.

common mode noise Noise or electrical disturbances that can be measured between a current- or signal-carrying line and its associated ground. Common mode noise is frequently introduced to signals between separate computer equipment components through the power distribution circuits. It can be a problem when single-ended signals are used to connect different equipment or components that are powered by different circuits.

CompactFlash An ATA flash memory card physical format approximately one third the size of a standard PC Card. Often abbreviated CF or CF+, CompactFlash cards are identical in function to standard ATA Flash PC Cards (PCMCIA) but use 50 pin connectors instead of 68. An ATA flash card contains built-in disk controller circuitry to enable the card to function as a solid-state disk drive. CF cards can plug into a CompactFlash socket or with an adapter into a standard Type I or II PC Card (PCMCIA) slot. CF cards are used by many types of digital cameras.

CompactPCI The PICMG standard for PCI-based industrial computers, A CompactPCI board plugs in to a 220-pin IEC-1076 bus.

compatible (1) In the early days of the PC industry, when IBM dominated the market, a term used to refer to computers from other manufacturers that had the same features as a given IBM model. (2) In general, software or hardware that conforms to industry standards or other de facto standards so that it can be used in conjunction with or in lieu of other versions of software or hardware from other vendors in a like manner.

compiler A program that translates a program written in a high-level language into its equivalent machine language. The output from a compiler is called an object program.

complete backup A backup of all information on a hard disk, including the directory tree structure.

composite video Television picture information and sync pulses combined. The complete waveform of the color video signal, composed of chrominance and luminance picture information; blanking pedestal; field, line, and color-sync pulses; and field-equalizing pulses. Some video cards have an RCA jack that outputs a composite video signal. See also *RGB*.

compressed file A file that has been reduced in size via one or more compression techniques. See also *archive file*.

computer A device that is capable of accepting data, applying prescribed processes to the data, and displaying the results or information produced.

CONFIG.SYS A file that can be created to tell DOS how to configure itself when the machine starts up. It can load device drivers, set the number of DOS buffers, and so on.

configuration file A file kept by application software to record various aspects of the software's configuration, such as the printer it uses. Windows uses .INI files and the Windows Registry to control its configuration.

console The unit, such as a terminal or a keyboard, in a system with which you communicate with the computer.

contiguous Touching or joined at the edge or boundary, in one piece.

continuity In electronics, having an unbroken pathway. Testing for continuity usually means testing to determine whether a wire or other conductor is complete and unbroken (by measuring 0 ohms). A broken wire shows infinite resistance (or infinite ohms).

control cable The wider of the two cables that connect an ST-506/412 or ESDI hard disk drive to a controller card. It is a 34-pin cable that carries commands and acknowledgments between the drive and controller.

controller   The electronics that control a device, such as a hard disk drive, and intermediate the passage of data between the device and computer.

controller card   An adapter that holds the control electronics for one or more devices, such as hard disks. It ordinarily occupies one of the slots in a computer.

conventional memory   See *base memory.*

convergence   The action of a color monitor to focus the three colored electron beams on a single point. Poor convergence causes the characters onscreen to appear fuzzy and can cause headaches and eyestrain.

coprocessor   An additional computer processing unit that is designed to handle specific tasks in conjunction with the main or central processing unit.

copy protection   A hardware or software scheme that prohibits making illegal copies of a program.

core   An old-fashioned term for computer memory.

core speed   The internal speed of a processor. With all modern processors, this speed is faster than the system bus speed, and that speed relationship is regulated by the clock multiplier in the processor.

CP/M (Control Program for Microcomputers, originally Control Program/Monitor)   An operating system created by Gary Kildall, the founder of Digital Research. It was created for the old 8-bit microcomputers that used the 8080, 8085, and Z-80 microprocessors. It was the dominant operating system in the late 1970s and early 1980s for small computers used in business environments.

cps (characters per second)   A data transfer rate generally estimated from the bit rate and character length. At 2,400bps, for example, 8-bit characters with start and stop bits (for a total of 10 bits per character) are transmitted at a rate of approximately 240cps. Some protocols, such as V.42 and MNP, employ advanced techniques such as longer transmission frames and data compression to increase cps.

CPU (central processing unit)   A computer's microprocessor chip; the brains of the outfit. Typically, it is an IC using VLSI technology to pack several functions into a tiny area. The most common electronic device in the CPU is the transistor, of which several thousand to several million or more are found.

crash   A malfunction that brings work to a halt. A system crash is usually caused by a software malfunction, and ordinarily you can restart the system by rebooting the machine. A head crash, however, entails physical damage to a disk and probable data loss.

CRC (cyclic redundancy check)   An error-detection technique that consists of a cyclic algorithm performed on each block or frame of data by both sending and receiving modems. The sending modem inserts the results of its computation in each data block in the form of a CRC code. The receiving modem compares its results with the received CRC code and responds with either a positive or negative acknowledgment. In the ARQ protocol implemented in high-speed modems, the receiving modem accepts no more data until a defective block is received correctly.

crossbar   A type of memory controller that interchanges data between different memory paths. It is used in some server chipsets and advanced graphics processors.

crosstalk   The electromagnetic coupling of a signal on one line with another nearby signal line. Crosstalk is caused by electromagnetic induction, where a signal traveling through a wire creates a magnetic field that induces a current in other nearby wires. Various methods, including twisting wire pairs and placing ground wires between data wires, are used to combat crosstalk and create more reliable data communications.

CRT (cathode ray tube)   A device that contains electrodes surrounded by a glass sphere or cylinder and displays information by creating a beam of electrons that strike a phosphor coating inside the display unit. This device is most commonly used in computer monitors and terminals.

CS (cable select)   A method for configuring ATA/IDE hard disks in which the position of drives on the cable is used to determine the master (end of cable) or slave (middle of cable). Requires that ATA/IDE hard disks be jumpered for cable select and are connected to an 80-wire Ultra ATA cable. Also known as CSEL.

current   The flow of electrons, measured in amperes.

cursor   The small, flashing line that appears onscreen to indicate the point at which any input from the keyboard will be placed.

cycle   The time for a signal to transition from one leading edge to the next leading edge.

cylinder The set of tracks on a disk that are on each side of all the disk platters in a stack and are the same distance from the center of the disk. It is the total number of tracks that can be read without moving the heads. A floppy drive with two heads usually has 160 tracks, which are accessible as 80 cylinders. A typical 120GB hard disk physically has about 56,000 cylinders, 6 heads (3 platters), and an average of about 700 sectors per track, for a total of about 235,200,000 sectors (120.4GB).

Cyrix Originally a Texas-based maker of Intel-compatible math coprocessor chips, a company that later developed low-cost, plug-compatible 6x86 and 6x86MX Pentium-class processors that were manufactured by IBM and other fabricators. Cyrix also developed the first chipsets with integrated audio and video (the MediaGX series). Cyrix was later absorbed into National Semiconductor, which retained the MediaGX technology when it sold Cyrix to VIA Technologies. See also *C3* and *VIA Technologies*.

D-channel In ISDN, a 16Kbps channel used to transmit control data about a connection.

DAC (digital-to-analog converter) A device that converts digital signals to analog signals. VGA-based displays are analog, so video cards that connect to them include a DAC to convert the signals to analog to drive the display. See also *RAMDAC*.

daisy-chain To string up components in such a manner that the signals move serially from one to the other. Most microcomputer multiple disk drive systems are daisy-chained. The SCSI bus system is a daisy-chain arrangement, in which the signals move from computer to disk drives to tape units, and so on. USB and IEEE-1394 devices also use the daisy-chain arrangement when hubs are used.

daisywheel printer An impact printer that prints fully formed characters one at a time by rotating a circular print element composed of a series of individual spokes, each containing two characters that radiate from a center hub. It produces letter-quality output but has been replaced by laser and LED printers.

DAT (digital audio tape) A small cassette containing 4mm-wide tape used for storing large amounts of digital information. DAT technology emerged in Europe and Japan in 1986 as a way to produce high-quality digital audio recordings, and it was modified in 1988 to conform to the digital data storage (DDS) standard for storing computer

data. Raw/2:1 compressed capacities for a single tape are 2/4GB for DDS, 4/8GB for DDS-2, 12/24GB for DDS-3, 20/40GB for DDS-4, and 36/72GB for DAT 72, the latest standard.

data A group of facts processed into information. A graphic or textual representation of facts, concepts, numbers, letters, symbols, or instructions used for communication or processing.

data bus A connection that transmits data between the processor and the rest of the system. The width of the data bus defines the number of data bits that can be moved into or out of the processor in one cycle.

data cable Generically, a cable that carries data. Specific to HD connections, the narrower (20-pin) of two cables that connects an ST-506/412 or ESDI hard disk drive to a controller card.

data communication A type of communication in which computers and terminals can exchange data over an electronic medium.

data compression A technique in which mathematical algorithms are applied to the data in a file to eliminate redundancies and therefore reduce the size of the file. See also *lossless compression* and *lossy compression*.

Data Link Layer In networking, the layer of the OSI reference model that controls how the electrical impulses enter or leave the network cable. Ethernet and Token-Ring are the two most common examples of Data Link Layer protocols. See also *OSI model*.

data separator See *endec*.

data transfer rate The maximum rate at which data can be transferred from one device to another.

daughterboard Add-on board to increase functionality and/or memory that attaches to the existing board.

dB (decibel) A logarithmic measure of the ratio between two powers, voltages, currents, sound intensities, and so on. Signal-to-noise ratios are expressed in decibels.

DB-9 A 9-pin D-shell connector, primarily used for PC serial ports.

DB-25 A 25-pin D-shell connector, primarily used for PC parallel ports.

DC (direct current) Electrical current such as that provided by a power supply or batteries.

DC-600 (Data Cartridge 600) A data-storage medium invented by 3M in 1971 that uses a .25-inch-wide tape 600 feet in length.

DCE (data communications equipment) The hardware that performs communication—usually a dialup modem that establishes and controls the data link through the telephone network. See also *DTE*.

DD (double density) An indication of the storage capacity of a floppy drive or disk in which eight or nine sectors per track are recorded using MFM encoding. See also *MFM encoding*.

DDE (dynamic data exchange) A form of interprocess communication used by Microsoft Windows to support the exchange of commands and data between two applications running simultaneously. This capability has been enhanced further with OLE.

DDoS (distributed denial of service) A type of denial-of-service attack that uses multiple computers that have been taken over by an intruder to attack a targeted system. See also *DoS*.

DDR (double data rate) A type of SDRAM that allows two accesses per clock cycle, doubling the effective speed of the memory. The most common types of DDR include PC2100 (also known as DDR 266MHz), PC2700 (also known as DDR 333MHz), and PC3200 (also known as DDR 400MHz). See also *SDRAM*.

DDR2 (double data rate 2) A type of SDRAM that enables two accesses per clock cycle, doubling the effective speed of the memory. DDR2 has more robust signaling and is faster than conventional DDR. The most common types of DDR2 include PC2-3200 (also known as DDR2-400MHz), PC2-4300 (also known as DDR2-533MHz), PC2-5400 (also known as DDR2-667MHz), and PC2-6400 (also known as DDR2-800MHz). See also *DDR* and *SDRAM*.

DDS (digital data storage) A series of standards for using digital audio tape (DAT) for computer storage. See also *DAT*.

de facto standard A software or hardware technology that is not officially made a standard by any recognized standards organization but that is used as a reference for consumers and vendors because of its dominance in the marketplace.

DEBUG The name of a utility program included with DOS and used for specialized purposes, such as altering memory locations, tracing program execution, patching programs and disk sectors, and performing other low-level tasks.

dedicated line A user-installed telephone line that connects a specified number of computers or terminals within a limited area, such as a single building. The line is a cable rather than a public-access telephone line. The communications channel can also be referred to as nonswitched because calls do not go through telephone company switching equipment.

dedicated servo surface In voice-coil–actuated hard disk drives, one side of one platter given over to servo data that is used to guide and position the read/write heads.

default (1) Any setting that is assumed at startup or reset by the computer's software and attached devices and that is operational until changed by the user. It is an assumption the computer makes when no other parameters are specified. When you type DIR without specifying the drive to search, for example, the computer assumes you want it to search the default drive. (2) In software, any action the computer or program takes on its own with embedded values.

defect map A list of unusable sectors and tracks coded onto a drive during the low-level format process.

defragmentation The process of rearranging disk sectors so files are stored on consecutive sectors in adjacent tracks.

degauss (1) To remove magnetic charges or to erase magnetic images. Normal applications include CRT monitors and disks or tapes. Most monitors incorporate a degaussing coil, which surrounds the CRT, and automatically energize this coil for a few seconds when powered up to remove color or image-distorting magnetic fields from the metal mask inside the tube. Some monitors include a button or control that can be used for additional applications of this coil to remove more stubborn magnetic traces. (2) To erase or demagnetize a magnetic disk or tape using a special tool called a degaussing coil.

density The amount of data that can be packed into a certain area on a specific storage medium.

desktop A personal computer that sits on a desk.

device driver Originally, a memory-resident program loaded by CONFIG.SYS that controls an unusual device, such as an expanded memory board. Windows also uses device drivers, but they are loaded through the Windows Registry or .INI files.

DHCP (Dynamic Host Configuration Protocol)
A protocol for assigning dynamic IP addresses to devices on a network. With dynamic addressing, a device can have a different IP address every time it connects to the network. Routers, gateways, and broadband modems can function as DHCP hosts to provide IP addresses to other computers and devices on the network.

Dhrystone   A benchmark program used as a standard figure of merit indicating aspects of a computer system's performance in areas other than floating-point math performance. Because the program does not use any floating-point operations, performs no I/O, and makes no operating system calls, it is most useful for measuring the processor performance of a system. The original Dhrystone program was developed in 1984 and was written in Ada, although the C and Pascal versions became more popular by 1989.

DHTML (Dynamic HTML)   A collective term for Cascading Style Sheets, layering, dynamic fonts, and other features encompassed in standard HTML 4.0, Netscape Navigator 4.x and above, and Internet Explorer 4.x and above. Because of differences in how browsers interpret particular DHTML features, many developers incorporate browser-checking code into their web pages to enable or disable certain features, depending on the browser being used to view the page.

diagnostics   Programs used to check the operation of a computer system. These programs enable the operator to check the entire system for any problems and indicate in which area the problems lie.

dialup adapter   In Windows, a software program that uses a modem to emulate a NIC for networking. They are most commonly used to connect to an ISP or a dialup server for remote access to a LAN.

DIB (dual independent bus) architecture   A processor technology with two independent buses on the processor—the L2 cache bus and the processor-to-main memory system bus. The processor can use both buses simultaneously, thus getting as much as two times more data into and out of the processor than a single bus architecture processor. The Intel Pentium Pro, Pentium II, and newer processors from Intel and AMD (such as the AMD Athlon and Duron) have DIB architecture.

die   An individual chip (processor, RAM, or other IC) cut from a finished silicon chip wafer and built

into the physical package that connects it to the rest of the PC or a circuit board.

differential   An electrical signaling method in which a pair of lines are used for each signal in "push–pull" fashion. In most cases, differential signals are balanced so that the same current flows on each line in opposite directions. This is unlike single-ended signals, which use only one line per signal, referenced to a single ground. Differential signals have a large tolerance for common-mode noise and little crosstalk when used with twisted-pair wires, even in long cables. Differential signaling is expensive because two pins are required for each signal.

digital camera   A type of camera that uses a sensor and internal or removable flash memory in place of film to record still images. The quality of the photos digital cameras take is usually rated in megapixels. See also *megapixel.*

digital loopback   A test that checks a modem's RS-232 interface and the cable that connects the terminal or computer and the modem. The modem receives data (in the form of digital signals) from the computer or terminal and immediately returns the data to the screen for verification.

digital signals   Discrete, uniform signals. In this book, the term refers to the binary digits 0 and 1.

digital signature   An electronic identifier used to authenticate a message or the contents of a file. Windows 98 and above are designed to prefer digitally signed device drivers (drivers approved by the Windows Hardware Quality Labs) and will warn you if you try to install an unsigned device driver.

digitize   To transform an analog wave to a digital signal that a computer can store. Conversion to digital data and back is performed by a DAC, often a single-chip device. How closely a digitized sample represents an analog wave depends on the number of times the amplitude of a wave is measured and recorded (the rate of digitization), as well as the number of levels that can be specified at each instance. The number of possible signal levels is dictated by the resolution, in bits.

DIMM (dual inline memory module)   A series of memory modules used in Pentium and newer PCs. They are available in many different versions, including those with SDRAM, DDR or DDR2, 3.3V, 2.5V or 1.8V, buffered, unbuffered or registered, and in 64-bit (non-ECC/parity) or 72-bit (ECC/parity) form. See also *DDR, DDR2,* and *SDRAM.*

DIP (dual inline package) A family of rectangular, integrated-circuit flat packages that have leads on the two longer sides. Package material is plastic or ceramic.

DIP switch A tiny switch (or group of switches) on a circuit board. Named for the form factor of the carrier device in which the switch is housed.

Direct Rambus DRAM See *RDRAM*.

directory An area of a disk that stores the titles given to the files saved on the disk and serves as a table of contents for those files. It contains data that identifies the name of a file, the size, the attributes (system, hidden, read-only, and so on), the date and time of creation, and a pointer to the location of the file. Each entry in a directory is 32 bytes long. Windows refers to subdirectories (directories beneath the root directory) as folders.

DirectX A set of graphics-related drivers and APIs that translates generic hardware commands into specific commands for particular pieces of hardware. Developed by Microsoft, DirectX enables graphical or multimedia applications to take advantage of specific features supported by various graphics accelerators.

disc A flat, circular, rotating medium that can store various types of information, both analog and digital. *Disc* is often used in reference to optical storage media, whereas *disk* refers to magnetic storage media. *Disc* also is often used as a short form for videodisc or compact disc (CD).

disk An alternative spelling for *disc* that generally refers to magnetic storage media on which information can be accessed at random. Floppy disks and hard disks are examples.

disk access time See *access time*.

disk cache A portion of memory on a PC motherboard or on a drive interface card or controller that is used to store frequently accessed information from the drive (such as the file allocation table [FAT] or directory structure) to speed up disk access. With a larger disk cache, additional data from the data portion of a drive can be cached as well. See also *cache, L1 cache,* and *L2 cache*.

disk partition See *partition*.

display A device used for viewing information generated by a computer. Also called a monitor or a screen.

display adapter An interface between a computer and a monitor that transmits the signals that appear as images on the display. This can take the form of an expansion card or a chip built in to the motherboard.

dithering The process of creating more colors and shades from a given color palette. In monochrome displays or printers, dithering varies the black-and-white dot patterns to simulate shades of gray. Grayscale dithering is used to produce different shades of gray when the device can produce only limited levels of black or white outputs. Color screens or printers use dithering to create additional colors by mixing and varying the dot sizing and spacing. For example, when converting from 24-bit color to 8-bit color (an 8-bit palette has only 256 colors compared to the 24-bit palette's millions), dithering adds pixels of different colors to simulate the original color. Error diffusion is a type of dithering best suited for photographs.

DLC (Data Link Control) Refers to the Data Link Layer in the OSI model. Every NIC has a unique DLC address or DLC identifier (DLCI) that identifies the node on the network. For Ethernet networks, the DLC address is usually called the MAC address.

DLT (digital linear tape) A tape drive technology that writes data in multiple linear tracks as tape is wound forward and backward. It supports native/2:1 compressed capacities of up to 80/160GB. See also *SDLT*.

DLL (dynamic link library) An executable driver program module for Microsoft Windows that can be loaded on demand, linked in at runtime, and subsequently unloaded when the driver is no longer needed.

DMA (direct memory access) A process by which data moves between a disk drive (or other device) and system memory, without direct control of the CPU, thus freeing it up for other tasks.

DMI (Desktop Management Interface) An operating-system– and protocol-independent standard developed by the Desktop Management Task Force (DMTF) for managing desktop systems and servers. DMI provides a bidirectional path to interrogate all the hardware and software components within a PC, enabling hardware and software configurations to be monitored from a central station in a network.

DMI (Direct Media Interface) A 2GBps high-speed bus used by Intel in its E7xxx server and 9xx desktop chipsets. Also known as Integrated Hub Architecture (IHA) 2.0.

DNS (domain name system [or service]) An Internet service that translates domain names into numeric IP addresses. Every time you use a domain name, a DNS server must translate the name into the corresponding IP address.

docking station Equipment that enables a laptop or notebook computer to use peripherals and accessories normally associated with desktop systems.

DOCSIS (Data over Cable Service Interface Specification) See *CableLabs Certified Cable Modem*.

doping Adding chemical impurities to silicon (which is naturally a nonconductor) to create a material with semiconductor properties that is then used in the manufacturing of electronic chips.

DoS (denial of service) An Internet attack on a resource that prevents users from accessing email, websites, or other services. It usually exploits security shortcomings in email or webservers. See also *DDoS*.

DOS (Disk Operating System) A collection of programs stored on the DOS disk that contain routines enabling the system and user to manage information and the hardware resources of the computer. DOS must be loaded into the computer before other programs can be started.

dot pitch A measurement of the width of the dots that make up a pixel. The smaller the dot pitch, the sharper the image.

dot-matrix printer An impact printer that prints characters composed of dots. Characters are printed one at a time by pressing the ends of selected wires against an inked ribbon and paper.

double-conversion online UPS An advanced UPS design that converts AC power to DC for UPS battery charging and back to AC. This type of UPS provides excellent power conditioning and supports long run times and multiple servers with a single unit.

download To receive files from another computer.

downtime Operating time lost because of a computer malfunction.

DPMI (DOS Protected Mode Interface) An industry-standard interface that allows DOS applications to execute program code in the protected mode of the 286 or later Intel processor. The DPMI specification is available from Intel.

DPMS (Display Power Management Signaling) A VESA standard for signaling a monitor or display to switch into energy conservation mode. DPMS provides for two low-energy modes: standby and suspend.

DRAM (dynamic random access memory) The most common type of computer memory, which can be manufactured very inexpensively compared to other types of memory. DRAM chips are small and inexpensive because they normally require only one transistor and a capacitor to represent each bit. The capacitors must be energized every 15ms or so (hundreds of times per second) to maintain their charges. DRAM is volatile, meaning it loses data with no power or without regular refresh cycles.

drive A mechanical device that manipulates data storage media.

driver A program designed to interface a particular piece of hardware to an operating system or other standard software.

drum The cylindrical photoreceptor in a laser printer that receives a document image from the laser and applies it to the page as it slowly rotates.

DSL (digital subscriber line) A high-speed digital modem technology. DSL is either symmetric or asymmetric. Asymmetric provides faster downstream speeds, which is suited for Internet usage and video on demand. Symmetric provides the same rate coming and going. See also *ADSL*.

DSM (digital storage media) A digital storage or transmission device or system.

DSP (digital signal processor) A dedicated, limited-function processor often found in modems, sound cards, and cellular phones.

DTE (data terminal [or terminating] equipment) A device, usually a computer or terminal, that generates or is the final destination of data. See also *DCE*.

dual cavity pin grid array Chip packaging designed by Intel for use with the Pentium Pro processor that houses the processor die in one cavity of the package and the L2 cache memory in a second cavity within the same package.

dual-core processor A processor that contains two distinct physical processor cores in a single package. This type of processor provides most of the benefits of dual-processor designs at lower cost.

dual-ported RAM See *VRAM*.

dual scan display   A lower-quality but economical type of LCD color display that has an array of transistors running down the x and y axes of two sides of the screen. The number of transistors determines the screen's resolution.

dumb terminal   A screen and keyboard device with no inherent processing power connected to a computer that is usually remotely located.

duplex   Indicates a communications channel capable of carrying signals in both directions.

Duron   A low-cost version of the Athlon processor with less L2 cache. It is available in the Socket A (462-pin) chip package.

DVD (digital versatile [or video] disc)   A high-capacity CD-ROM disc and drive format with up to 28 times the capacity of a standard CD-ROM. A DVD is the same diameter as a CD-ROM but can be recorded on both sides and on two layers for each side. Each side holds 4.7GB on a single-layer disc, whereas dual-layer versions hold 8.5GB per side, for a maximum of 17GB total if both sides and both layers are used, which is the equivalent of 28 CD-ROMs. DVD drives can read standard audio CDs and CD-ROMs.

DVD burner   A popular term for a rewritable DVD drive, particularly one that uses DVD-R/RW or DVD+R/RW media.

DVD-A   A DVD format designed to support high-quality music and audio. DVD-A uses 24-bit sampling at 96KHz, significantly better than CD audio (16-bit at 44.1KHz). Unlike DVD, DVD-A discs can be played on conventional CD players but produce the highest quality only when played on DVD-A players.

DVD-R   A writable DVD format that is compatible with standalone DVD players and DVD-ROM drives. DVD-R was introduced by Pioneer and was released to the DVD Forum (www.dvdforum.org) in 1997. It uses a wobbled-groove recording process to store 4.7GB of data and is optimized for sequential data access. See also *DVD-RW*.

DVD-R DL   A dual-layer DVD format based on DVD-R that supports up to 8.5GB of data. See also *DVD-R*.

DVD+R   A writable DVD format compatible with standalone DVD players and DVD-ROM drives. DVD+R was developed by the DVD+RW Alliance (www.dvdrw.com), whose members include Microsoft, Sony, Hewlett-Packard, and Dell. In addition, it is supported by second-generation DVD+RW drives and holds 4.7GB of data.

DVD+R/RW are the only recordable DVD formats that fully support the Mt. Rainier (also called EasyWrite) standard to be used in Windows Vista. This enables discs to be used right out of the box, with automatic background formatting and no additional packet-writing software required. DVD+R/RW are the most compatible, fastest, most capable, and most popular of all the recordable DVD formats. See also *DVD+RW*.

DVD+R DL   A dual-layer DVD format based on DVD+R that supports up to 8.5GB of data. See also *DVD+R*.

DVD-RAM   A rewritable DVD format developed by Panasonic, Toshiba, and Hitachi and supported by the DVD Forum. DVD-RAM is the oldest DVD rewritable format, but because the medium uses a caddy and has a lower reflectivity than normal DVD media, DVD-RAM discs are not compatible with other types of DVD drives or with standalone DVD players. Older DVD-RAM drives used media in caddies, but newer drives do not use caddies.

DVD-RW   A rewritable DVD format developed by Pioneer and released to the DVD Forum in 1999. It uses a phase-change technology similar to CD-RW. As with most CD-RW media and drives, the entire disc must be formatted before it can be used. Its write speed is also lower than that of DVD+RW, and the entire disc must be erased before it can be used to store new data. See also *DVD-R*.

DVD+RW   A rewritable DVD format developed by the DVD+RW Alliance, first released in 2001. DVD+RW uses a phase-change technology similar to CD-RW and DVD-RW. DVD+R/RW are the only recordable DVD formats that fully support the Mt. Rainier (EasyWrite) standard to be used in Windows Vista. This enables discs to be used right out of the box, with automatic background formatting and no additional packet-writing software required. DVD+R/RW are the most compatible, fastest, most capable, and most popular of all the recordable DVD formats. See also *DVD+R*.

DVD±RW   A DVD drive capable of reading and writing to both DVD+R/RW and DVD-R/RW media. Some of these drives also support some or all of these media types: DVD+R DL, DVD-R DL, and DVD-RAM.

DVI (Digital Video Interactive)   A standard that was originally developed at RCA Laboratories and sold to Intel in 1988. DVI integrates digital motion, still video, sound, graphics, and special effects in a compressed format. DVI is a highly sophisticated hardware compression technique used in interactive multimedia applications.

DVI (Digital Visual Interface) The current de facto standard for LCD displays developed by the Digital Display Working Group in April 1999. DVI-D provides digital signals only, whereas DVI-I (which is more common) provides both digital and analog signals. A DVI-I connector can be converted to VGA with an external adapter.

Dvorak keyboard A keyboard design by August Dvorak that was patented in 1936 and approved by ANSI in 1982. It provides increased speed and comfort and reduces the rate of errors by placing the most frequently used letters in the center for use by the strongest fingers. Finger motions and awkward strokes are reduced by more than 90% in comparison with the familiar QWERTY keyboard. The Dvorak keyboard has the five vowel keys, AOEUI, together under the left hand in the center row and the five most frequently used consonants, DHTNS, under the fingers of the right hand.

dynamic execution A processing technique that enables the processor to dynamically predict the order of instructions and execute them out of order internally if necessary for an improvement in speed. It uses three techniques: multiple branch prediction, data flow analysis, and speculative execution.

E2000 (Energy 2000) A Swiss-developed standard for power management that calls for computer monitors to use only 5 watts of power when in standby mode.

EBCDIC (Extended Binary Coded Decimal Interchange Code) An IBM-developed 8-bit code for the representation of characters. It allows 256 possible character combinations within a single byte. EBCDIC is the standard code on IBM minicomputers and mainframes, but not on the IBM microcomputers, where ASCII is used instead.

ECC (error correcting code) A type of system memory or cache that is capable of detecting and correcting some types of memory errors without interrupting processing.

ECP (enhanced capabilities port) A type of high-speed parallel port jointly developed by Microsoft and Hewlett-Packard that offers improved performance for the parallel port and requires special hardware logic. An ECP uses both an IRQ and a DMA channel. See also *IEEE 1284*.

ED (extra-high density) An indication of the storage capacity of a floppy drive or disk in which 36 sectors per track are recorded using a vertical recording technique with MFM encoding.

edge connector The part of a circuit board that contains a series of printed contacts that is inserted into an expansion slot or a connector.

EDO (extended data out) RAM A type of RAM chip that enables a timing overlap between successive accesses, thus improving memory cycle time.

EEB (Entry-Level Electronics Bay) A specification for pedestal servers developed by SSI. See also *SSI*.

EEPROM (electrically erasable programmable read-only memory) A type of nonvolatile memory chip used to store semipermanent information in a computer, such as the BIOS. An EEPROM can be erased and reprogrammed directly in the host system without special equipment. This is used so manufacturers can upgrade the ROM code in a system by supplying a special program that erases and reprograms the EEPROM chip with the new code. Also called flash ROM.

EGA (enhanced graphics adapter) A type of PC video display adapter first introduced by IBM in 1984 that supports text and graphics. Text is supported at a maximum resolution of 80×25 characters in 16 colors, with a character box of 8×14 pixels. Graphics are supported at a maximum resolution of 640×350 pixels in 16 (from a palette of 64) colors. The EGA outputs a TTL (digital) signal with a horizontal scanning frequency of 15.75KHz, 18.432KHz, or 21.85KHz, and it supports TTL color or TTL monochrome displays.

EIA (Electronic Industries Association) An organization that defines electronic standards in the United States. See www.eia.org for more information.

EIDE (Enhanced Integrated Drive Electronics) A specific Western Digital implementation of the ATA-2 specification. See also *ATA-2*.

eight-way server A server that contains eight processors.

EISA (Extended Industry Standard Architecture) An extension of the ISA bus developed by IBM for the AT. The EISA design was led by Compaq Corporation. Later, eight other manufacturers (AST, Epson, Hewlett-Packard, NEC, Olivetti, Tandy, Wyse, and Zenith) joined Compaq in a consortium founded September 13, 1988. This group became known as the "gang of nine." The EISA design was patterned largely after IBM's MCA in the PS/2 systems, but unlike MCA, EISA enables backward compatibility with older plug-in adapters. EISA products became obsolete after the development of the PCI slot architecture. See also *PCI*.

ELF (extremely low frequency)   A very low-frequency electromagnetic radiation generated by common electrical appliances, including computer monitors. The Swedish MPR II standard governs this and other emissions. Also called VLF (very low frequency).

email (electronic mail)   A method of transferring messages from one computer to another.

EM64T   Intel's implementation of the AMD64 64-bit processor architecture. See also *AMD64.*

embedded controller   In disk drives, a controller built in to the same physical unit that houses the drive rather than on a separate adapter card. IDE and SCSI drives both use embedded controllers.

embedded servo data   Magnetic markings embedded between or inside tracks on disk drives that use voice-coil actuators. These markings enable the actuator to fine-tune the position of the read/write heads.

EMM (expanded memory manager)   A driver that provides a software interface to expanded memory. EMMs were originally created for expanded memory boards but also can use the memory management capabilities of 386 or later processors to emulate an expanded memory board. `EMM386.EXE` is an example of an EMM that comes with DOS and Windows 9x.

EMS (Expanded Memory Specification) Sometimes also called the LIM specification because it was developed by Lotus, Intel, and Microsoft, a specification that provides a way for microcomputers running under DOS to access additional memory. EMS memory management provides access to a maximum of 32MB of expanded memory through a small (usually 64KB) window in conventional memory. EMS is a cumbersome access scheme designed primarily for pre-286 systems that could not access extended memory.

emulator   A piece of test apparatus that emulates or imitates the function of a particular chip.

encoding   The protocol by which data is carried or stored by a medium.

encryption   The translation of data into unreadable codes to maintain security.

endec (encoder/decoder)   A device that combines or encodes data and clock signals by using a particular encoding scheme into a single signal for transmission or storage. The same device also later separates or decodes the data and clock signals

during a receive or read operation. Also called a data separator.

Energy Star   A certification program started by the Environmental Protection Agency. Energy Star–certified computers and peripherals are designed to draw less than 30 watts of electrical energy from a standard 110-volt AC outlet during periods of inactivity. Also called Green PCs. See also *E2000.*

e-PCI-X   The PICMG 1.2 embedded PCI-X specification for passive backplane computers. See also *PICMG.*

EPIC (Explicitly Parallel Instruction Computing) The RISC-based 64-bit processor architecture used by the Intel Itanium and Itanium 2 processors. EPIC is not the same architecture as AMD64 or EM64T. See also *RISC.*

EPP (enhanced parallel port)   A type of parallel port developed by Intel, Xircom, and Zenith Data Systems that operates at almost ISA bus speed and offers a tenfold increase in the raw throughput capability over a conventional parallel port. EPP is especially designed for parallel port peripherals, such as LAN adapters, disk drives, and tape backups. See also *IEEE 1284.*

EPROM (erasable programmable read-only memory)   A type of ROM in which the data pattern can be erased to allow a new pattern. EPROM is usually erased by ultraviolet light and recorded by a higher-than-normal voltage programming signal.

equalization   A compensation circuit that is designed into modems to counteract certain distortions introduced by the telephone channel. Two types are used: fixed (compromise) equalizers and those that adapt to channel conditions (adaptive). Good-quality modems use adaptive equalization.

error control   Various techniques that check the reliability of characters (parity) or blocks of data. V.42, MNP, and HST error-control protocols use error detection (CRC) and retransmission of error frames (ARQ).

error message   A word or combination of words to indicate to the user that an error has occurred somewhere in the program.

ESCD (extended system configuration data)   An area in CMOS or flash/NVRAM where plug-and-play information is stored.

ESD (electrostatic discharge)   The grounding of static electricity, a sudden flow of electricity between two objects at different electrical potentials. ESD is a primary cause of IC damage or failure.

ESDI (Enhanced Small Device Interface) A hardware standard developed by Maxtor and standardized by a consortium of 22 disk drive manufacturers in 1983. A group of 27 manufacturers formed the ESDI steering committee in 1986 to enhance and improve the specification. A high-performance interface used primarily with hard disks, ESDI enables a maximum data transfer rate to and from a hard disk of between 10Mbps and 24Mbps. ESDI was replaced by IDE and SCSI interfaces. ESDI drives use the same 34-pin and 20-pin cables used by ST412/ST506 drives.

Ethernet A type of network protocol developed in the late 1970s by Bob Metcalf at Xerox Corporation and endorsed by the IEEE. One of the oldest LAN communications protocols in the PC industry, Ethernet uses a collision-detection protocol to manage contention. Ethernet is defined by the IEEE 802.3 standard. See also *10BASE-T*.

expanded memory Memory that conforms to the EMS specification. It requires a special device driver and conforms to a standard developed by Lotus, Intel, and Microsoft. Also known as EMS memory. See also *EMS*.

expansion card An IC card that plugs in to an expansion slot on a motherboard to provide access to additional peripherals or features not built in to the motherboard. Also referred to as an add-in board.

expansion slot A slot on a motherboard that physically and electrically connects an expansion card to the motherboard and the system buses.

extended memory Direct processor-addressable memory addressed by an Intel (or compatible) 286 or more advanced processor in the region beyond the first megabyte. It is addressable only in the processor's protected mode of operation.

extended partition A nonbootable DOS partition (also supported by Windows) that contains DOS volumes. Starting with DOS v3.3, the FDISK program can create two partitions that serve DOS: an ordinary, bootable partition (called the primary partition) and an extended partition, which can contain as many as 23 volumes, from D: to Z:.

external device A peripheral installed outside a system case.

FAQ (frequently asked questions) A list of popular questions and answers covering any particular subject.

Fast Ethernet Popular term for 100BASE-T and other 100Mbps versions of Ethernet. Fast Ethernet uses CAT5 cable.

Fast Page Mode RAM A type of RAM that improves on standard DRAM speed by enabling faster access to all the data within a given row of memory by keeping the row address the same and changing only the column.

Fast-ATA (Fast AT Attachment Interface) Also called Fast ATA-2, a specific Seagate and Quantum implementation of the ATA-2 interface. See also *ATA-2*.

FAT (file allocation table) A table held near the outer edge of a disk that tells which sectors are allocated to each file and in what order.

FAT32 A disk file allocation system from Microsoft that uses 32-bit values for FAT entries instead of the 16-bit values used by the original FAT system, enabling partition sizes up to 2TB (terabytes). Although the entries are 32 bits, 4 bits are reserved, and only 28 bits are used. FAT32 first appeared in Windows 95B and is also supported by Windows 98, Windows Me, Windows 2000, and Windows XP.

fault tolerance The capability of a computer to withstand a failure. Many levels of fault tolerance exist, and fault tolerance can be applied to several components or systems in a computer. For example, ECC memory is considered fault tolerant because it is typically capable of automatically identifying and correcting single bit errors.

fax/modem A peripheral that integrates the capabilities of a fax machine and a modem in one expansion card or external unit. Almost all 14.4Kbps and faster modems sold for use in desktop or portable PCs include fax capabilities.

FCC (Federal Communications Commission) Part 15 The section of the FCC regulations governing emissions from electronics devices. FCC Part 15 Class A devices are suitable for business, but not residential, use because they emit more interference than FCC Part 15 Class B devices (which are safe in residential areas). Most server components are FCC Part 15 Class A devices.

FC-PGA (flip-chip pin grid array) A type of chip packaging first used in the Socket PGA370 version of the Pentium III where the raw processor die has bumped contacts spaced on the face of the die and is mounted facedown to a pin grid array carrier. The heatsink is then directly attached to the back of the raw silicon die surface.

FDISK The name of the disk-partitioning program under several operating systems, including DOS and Windows 9x/Me, to create the master boot record and allocate partitions for the operating system's use.

feature connector On a video adapter, a connector that enables an additional video feature card, such as a separate 3D accelerator, video capture card, or MPEG decoder, to be connected to the main video adapter and display.

ferro-resonant UPS A type of UPS design noted for excellent power conditioning but also for its bulk and inefficient use of power. Largely replaced by double-conversion online UPS units. See *double-conversion online UPS*.

fiber optic A type of cable or connection that uses strands or threads of glass to guide a beam of modulated light. It allows for very high-speed signaling and multiplexing, as well as the combining of many data streams along a single cable.

FIFO (first-in, first-out) A method of storing and retrieving items from a list, table, or stack so that the first element stored is the first one retrieved.

file A collection of information kept somewhere other than in RAM.

file attribute Information held in the attribute byte of a file's directory entry.

file compression See *compressed file*.

filename The name given to a disk file. For DOS, it must be from one to eight characters long and can be followed by a filename extension, which can be from one to three characters long. Windows 9x and above ease these constraints by allowing filenames of up to 255 characters, including the directory path.

firewall A hardware or software system designed to prevent unauthorized access to or from a private network.

FireWire A serial I/O interface standard that is extremely fast, with data transfer rates up to 400MBps, 800MBps, or 3.2GBps, depending on the version of standard used. (Most current implementations use the 400MBps IEEE 1394a version.) Also called IEEE 1394 or i.Link.

firmware Software contained in a ROM device. A cross between hardware and software, firmware can be easily updated if stored in an EEPROM or flash ROM chip. See also *EEPROM*.

fixed disk See *hard disk*.

flash ROM See *EEPROM*.

flicker A monitor condition caused by refresh rates that are too low, in which the display flashes visibly. This can cause eyestrain or more severe physical problems.

floppy disk A removable disk that uses flexible magnetic media enclosed in a semirigid or rigid plastic case.

floppy disk controller The logic and interface that connects a floppy disk drive to a system.

floppy tape A tape standard that uses drives connecting to an ordinary floppy disk controller, such as QIC-80 or Travan-1.

floptical drive A special type of high-capacity removable disk drive that uses an optical mechanism to properly position the drive read/write heads over the data tracks on the disk. This enables more precise control of the read/write positioning and therefore narrower track spacing and more data packed into a smaller area than with traditional floppy disks. The LS-120 and LS-240 SuperDisk drives are examples of floptical drives.

flow control A mechanism that compensates for differences in the flow of data input to and output from a modem or other device.

FM (frequency modulation) encoding An outdated method of encoding data on the disk surface that uses up half the disk space with timing signals.

FM (frequency modulation) synthesis An audio technology that uses one sine wave operator to modify another and create an artificial sound that mimics an instrument.

folder In a GUI, a simulated file folder that holds documents (text, data, or graphics), applications, and other folders. A folder is similar to a DOS subdirectory.

footprint Describes the shape of something. See also *form factor*.

form factor The physical dimensions of a device. Two devices with the same form factor are physically interchangeable. The IBM PC, XT, and XT Model 286, for example, all use power supplies that are internally different but have exactly the same form factor.

format To prepare a disk so the computer can read or write to it. Formatting involves checking the disk for defects and constructing an organizational system to manage information on the disk.

FORMAT The DOS/Windows format program that performs both low- and high-level formatting on floppy disks but only high-level formatting on hard disks.

formatted capacity The total number of bytes of data that can fit on a formatted disk. The unformatted capacity is higher because space is lost in defining the boundaries between sectors.

FORTRAN A high-level programming language developed in 1954 by John Backus at IBM primarily for programs dealing with mathematical formulas and expressions similar to algebra and used primarily in scientific and technical applications.

four-way server A server that contains four processors.

FPU (floating-point unit) See *math coprocessor*.

fragmentation The state of having a file scattered around a disk in pieces rather than existing in one contiguous area of the disk. Fragmented files are slower to read than files stored in contiguous areas and can be more difficult to recover if the FAT or a directory becomes damaged.

frame (1) A data communications term for a block of data with header and trailer information attached. The added information usually includes a frame number, block size data, error-check codes, and start/end indicators. (2) A single, complete picture in a video or film recording. A video frame consists of two interlaced fields of either 525 lines (NTSC) or 625 lines (PAL/SECAM), running at 30 frames per second (NTSC) or 25 frames per second (PAL/SECAM).

frame buffer A memory device that stores, pixel by pixel, the contents of an image. Frame buffers are used to refresh a raster image. Sometimes they incorporate local processing capability. The "depth" of the frame buffer is the number of bits per pixel, which determines the number of colors or intensities that can be displayed.

frame rate The speed at which video frames are scanned or displayed: 30 frames per second (fps) for NTSC and 25 fps for PAL/SECAM.

FTP (File Transfer Protocol) A method of transferring files over the Internet. FTP can be used to transfer files between two machines on which the user has accounts. Anonymous FTP can be used to retrieve a file from a server without having an account on that server.

full duplex Signal flow in both directions at the same time. In microcomputer communications, it also can refer to the suppression of the online local echo. 100BASE-TX network cards capable of full-duplex operations can run at an effective speed of 200Mbps when full-duplex operation is enabled.

full-height drive A drive unit that is 3.25 inches high, 5.25 inches wide, and 8 inches deep. Equal to two half-height drive bays.

full-motion video A video sequence displayed at full television standard resolutions and frame rates. In the United States, this equates to NTSC video at 30 frames per second.

function keys Special-purpose keys that can be programmed to perform various operations. They serve many functions, depending on the program being used.

G.lite A popular form of ADSL that can be self-installed by the user. Also referred to as the G.992.2 standard.

gas-plasma display Commonly used in portable systems, a type of display that operates by exciting a gas—usually neon or an argon-neon mixture—through the application of voltage. When sufficient voltage is applied at the intersection of two electrodes, the gas glows an orange-red. Because gas-plasma displays generate light, they require no backlighting.

gateway (1) Officially, an application-to-application conversion program or system. For example, an email gateway converts from SMTP (Internet) email format to MHS (Novell) email format. (2) Slang for router. See also *router*.

GB (gigabyte) A unit of information storage equal to 1,000,000,000 bytes. The value formerly called a binary GB (1,073,741,824 bytes) is now called a gibibyte. See also *gibibyte*.

gender The shape of a PC connector. Connectors are described as male if they have pins or female if they have receptacles designed to accept the pins of a male connector.

genlocking The process of aligning the data rate of a video image with that of a digital device to digitize the image and enter it into computer memory. The machine that performs this function is known as a genlock.

Ghost A popular utility program sold by Symantec that can be used to create a compressed version of a drive's contents and clone it to one or more PCs over a network or via CD storage.

GHz (gigahertz)   A measurement of the clock frequency of high-performance processors. The first 1GHz desktop processor was introduced by AMD (a 1GHz Athlon) in 2000.

gibi-   A prefix equal to 1,073,741,824. Abbreviated Gi.

gibibyte (GiB)   A unit of information storage equal to 1,073,741,824 bytes (1,024×1,024×1,024 equals a Gi). Formerly known as a binary gigabyte. See also *GB* and *KB*.

GIF (Graphics Interchange Format)   A popular raster graphics file format developed by CompuServe that handles 8-bit color (256 colors) and uses the LZW method to achieve compression ratios of approximately 1.5:1 to 2:1. You can reduce the size of a GIF file even more by dropping unused colors from the file.

giga-   A prefix indicating one billion (1,000,000,000) of some unit. Abbreviated g or G. The binary giga (1,073,741,824) is now referred to as a gibi. See also *gibi-*.

Gigabit Ethernet   See *1000BASE-T*.

GPU (graphics processing unit)   A 3D graphics chip that contains advanced 3D rendering features, such as hardware, vertex, and pixel shaders. NVIDIA's GeForce 3 and GeForce 4 Ti series; the ATI Radeon 7xxx, 8xxx, and 9xxx series; and the Matrox Parhelia series are typical GPUs. See also *hardware shader*, *pixel shader*, and *vertex shader*.

graphics accelerator   A video processor or chipset specially designed to speed the display and rendering of graphical objects onscreen. Originally, accelerators were optimized for 2D or 3D operations, but all current graphics accelerators, such as NVIDIA's GeForce and ATI's RADEON series, accelerate both types of data.

graphics adapter   See *video adapter*.

Green Book   The standard for CD-I. Philips developed CD-I technology for the consumer market to be connected to a television instead of a computer monitor. CD-I is not a computer system but a consumer device that made a small splash in the market and disappeared. CD-I discs require special code and are not compatible with standard CD-ROMs. A CD-ROM can't be played on the CD-I machine, but Red Book audio can be played on it.

GUI (graphical user interface)   A type of program interface that enables users to choose commands and functions by pointing to a graphical icon using either a keyboard or pointing device,

such as a mouse. Windows is the most popular GUI available for PC systems.

half duplex   Signal flow in both directions but only one way at a time. In microcomputer communications, half duplex can refer to activation of the online local echo, which causes the modem to send a copy of the transmitted data to the screen of the sending computer.

half-height drive   A drive unit that is 1.625 inches high, 5.25 inches wide, and 8 inches deep. See also *full-height drive*.

halftoning   A process that uses dithering to simulate a continuous tone image, such as a photograph or shaded drawing, using various sizes of dots. Newspapers, magazines, and many books use halftoning. The human eye merges the dots to give the impression of gray shades.

handshaking   The process of exchanging information about speeds and protocols between analog modems to establish a dialup connection. If a modem's volume is high enough, you can hear handshaking as a series of distinct tones at the start of a modem-to-modem call.

hard disk   A high-capacity disk storage unit characterized by a normally nonremovable rigid substrate medium. The platters in a hard disk are usually constructed of aluminum or glass/ceramic. Also sometimes called a fixed disk.

hard error   An error in reading or writing data caused by damaged hardware.

hard reset   A reset of a system via the hardware, usually by pressing a dedicated reset button wired to the motherboard/processor reset circuitry. It does not clear memory like a cold boot does. See also *cold boot*.

hardware   Physical components that make up a microcomputer, monitor, printer, and so on.

hardware shader   A general term describing the processing of vertex or pixel shading in a GPU's hardware. GPUs such as the ATI 8xxx and 9xxx series or the NVIDIA GeForce 3 and GeForce 4 Ti-series GPU chips have hardware shaders compatible with DirectX 8 and above.

HD (high density)   An indication of the storage capacity of a floppy drive or disk, in which 15 or 18 sectors per track are recorded using MFM encoding.

HDLC (High-Level Data Link Control)   A standard protocol developed by the ISO for software applications and communicating devices operating in synchronous environments. It defines operations at the link level of communications—for example, the format of data frames exchanged between modems over a phone line.

HDTV (high-definition television)   A video format that offers greater visual accuracy (or resolution) than current NTSC, PAL, or SECAM broadcast standards. HDTV formats generally range in resolution from 655 to 2,125 scanning lines, having an aspect ratio of 5:3 (or 1.67:1) and a video bandwidth of 30MHz–50MHz (more than five times greater than the NTSC standard). Digital HDTV has a bandwidth of 300MHz.

head   A small electromagnetic device inside a drive that reads, records, and erases data on the medium.

head actuator   A device that moves read/write heads across a disk drive's platters. Most drives use a stepper-motor or voice-coil actuator.

head crash   A (usually) rare occurrence in which a read/write head strikes a platter surface with sufficient force to damage the magnetic medium.

head parking   A procedure in which a disk drive's read/write heads are moved to an unused track so they will not damage data in the event of a head crash or other failure.

head seek   The movement of a drive's read/write heads to a particular track.

heatsink   A mass of metal attached to a chip carrier or socket for the purpose of dissipating heat. Some heatsinks are passive (relying on existing air currents only), but most heatsinks on processors are active (including a fan). Many video card accelerator chips and motherboard North Bridge chips are also fitted with heatsinks today.

helical scan   A type of recording technology that has vastly increased the capacity of tape drives. It was invented for use in broadcast systems and is now used in VCRs. Conventional longitudinal recording records a track of data straight across the width of a single-track tape. Helical scan recording packs more data on the tape by positioning the tape at an angle to the recording heads. The heads spin to record diagonal stripes of information on the tape. Helical scan is used by DAT/DDS, Exabyte, and AIT drives.

hexadecimal   A system of numbers encoded in base 16, such that digits include the letters A–F and the numerals 0–9 (for example, 8BF3, which equals 35,827 in base 10).

HFC (hybrid fiber coaxial)   A network (such as that used by digital cable TV and two-way cable modems) that uses fiber-optic cabling for its backbone, with coaxial cable connections to each individual computer or TV.

hidden file   A file that is not displayed in DOS directory listings because the file's attribute byte holds a special setting.

High Sierra format   A standard format for placing files and directories on CD-ROMs, proposed by an ad hoc committee of computer vendors, software developers, and CD-ROM system integrators. (Work on the format proposal began at the High Sierra Hotel in Lake Tahoe, Nevada.) A revised version of the format was adopted by the ISO as ISO 9660. You can use the ISO 9660 format to create cross-platform CD-R recordings.

high-level formatting   Formatting performed by the DOS FORMAT program. Among other things, it creates the root directory and FATs.

history file   A file created by utility software to keep track of earlier use of the software. Many backup programs, for example, keep history files describing earlier backup sessions.

hit ratio   In describing the efficiency of a disk or memory cache, the ratio of the number of times the data is found in the cache to the total number of data requests. 1:1 is a perfect hit ratio, meaning that every data request was found in the cache. The closer to 1:1 the ratio is, the more efficient the cache.

HMA (high memory area)   The first 64KB of extended memory, which typically is controlled by the HIMEM.SYS device driver. Real-mode programs can be loaded into the HMA to conserve conventional memory. Normally, DOS 5.0 and later use the HMA exclusively to reduce the DOS conventional memory footprint.

HomePNA   A home networking standard that uses existing home or office telephone wiring to obtain speeds of up to 11Mbps.

HomeRF   A wireless home networking system that uses radio waves to obtain speeds of up to 11Mbps.

horizontal scan rate   In monitors, the speed at which the electron beam moves laterally across the screen. It's normally expressed as a frequency; typical monitors range from 31.5KHz to 90KHz, with the higher frequencies being more desirable.

host   The main device when two or more devices are connected. When two or more systems are connected, the system that contains the data is typically called the host, and the other is called the guest or user.

HPA (host protected area)   A technique used in ATA-7 and newer ATA drive specifications for reducing the reported size of the hard disk. The space not reported is used to store system recovery data.

hotfix   A software patch for a Microsoft application or operating system. Hotfixes can be downloaded individually from the Windows Update website or as a service pack. Microsoft also calls them quick fix engineering (QFE) files.

hot-plug RAID memory   A memory technology used on servers to permit hot-swapping of defective memory modules without loss of memory contents. Memory modules form a RAID array similar in operation to a RAID 5 disk array.

hot-swapping   The removal and replacement of equipment without shutting down the server.

HPT (high-pressure tin)   A PLCC socket that promotes high forces between socket contacts and PLCC contacts for a good connection.

HP-UX   Hewlett-Packard's implementation of UNIX for its HP-9000 series of business servers. See also *UNIX*.

HST (High-Speed Technology)   The now-obsolete U.S. Robotics proprietary high-speed modem-signaling scheme, developed as an interim protocol until the V.32 protocol could be implemented in a cost-effective manner.

HT (hyperthreading) technology   A method developed by Intel for running two different instruction streams through a processor at the same time. Introduced in 2002, HT technology was first used in the Intel Xeon processor with HT technology, with speeds starting at 2.8GHz; the first HT technology–enabled desktop processor was the 3.06GHz Pentium 4.

HTML (Hypertext Markup Language)   A language used to describe and format plain-text files on the Web. HTML is based on pairs of tags that enable the user to mix graphics with text, change the appearance of text, and create hypertext documents with links to other documents. See also *DHTML*.

HTTP (Hypertext Transfer Protocol)   A protocol that describes the rules a browser and server use to communicate over the World Wide Web. HTTP allows a web browser to request HTML documents from a webserver. See also *hypertext*.

hub   A common connection point for multiple devices in a network. A hub contains a number of ports to connect several segments of a LAN together. When a packet arrives at one of the ports on the hub, it is copied to all the other ports so all the segments of the LAN can see all the packets. A hub can be passive, intelligent (allowing remote management, including traffic monitoring and port configuration), or switching. A switching hub is also called a switch. See also *switch*.

Huffman coding   A technique that minimizes the average number of bytes required to represent the characters in text. Huffman coding works for a given character distribution by assigning short codes to frequently occurring characters and longer codes to infrequently occurring characters.

hypertext   A technology that enables quick and easy navigation between and within large documents. Hypertext links are pointers to other sections within the same document; other documents; or other resources, such as FTP sites, images, or sounds.

HyperTransport   AMD's high-speed technology for connecting the North Bridge and South Bridge or equivalent chips on a motherboard. HyperTransport runs at six times the speed of the PCI bus (800MBps versus 133MBps for PCI). The original name was Lightning Data Transport (LDT). Several chipset makers, including AMD and NVIDIA, use HyperTransport.

Hz (hertz)   A frequency measurement unit used internationally to indicate one cycle per second. Named after Heinrich R. Hertz, a German physicist who first detected electromagnetic waves in 1883.

i.Link   Sony's term for IEEE 1394/FireWire. See also *FireWire*.

I/O (input/output)   A circuit path that enables independent communication between the processor and external devices.

I/O port (input/output port)   A port used to communicate to and from another device, such as a printer or disk.

IA-64   Intel's 64-bit processor architecture, first used in the Itanium processor for servers.

IBMBIO.COM   One of the DOS system files required to boot the machine in older versions of PC-DOS (IBM's version of MS-DOS). The first file loaded from disk during the boot, it contains extensions to the ROM BIOS.

IBMDOS.COM   One of the DOS system files required to boot the machine in older versions of PC-DOS (IBM's version of MS-DOS). It contains the primary DOS routines. Loaded by IBMBIO.COM, it in turn loads COMMAND.COM.

IC (integrated circuit)   A complete electronic circuit contained on a single chip. It can consist of only a few or thousands of transistors, capacitors, diodes, or resistors, and it generally is classified according to the complexity of the circuitry and the approximate number of circuits on the chip. Small-scale integration (SSI) equals 2–10 circuits, and medium-scale integration (MSI) equals 10–100 circuits. Large-scale integration (LSI) equals 100–1,000 circuits, and very-large-scale integration (VLSI) equals 1,000–10,000 circuits. Finally, ultra-large-scale integration (ULSI) equals more than 10,000 circuits.

ICH (I/O controller hub)   Intel's term for the chip used in its 8xx chipsets to interface with lower-speed devices, such as PCI slots, USB ports, ATA drives, and other devices traditionally controlled by the South Bridge chip. ICH chips connect with the MCH (the 8xx chipsets' replacement for the North Bridge) through a high-speed hub interface. Current ICH chips used by Intel 8xx–series chipsets include the ICH2 and ICH4. See also *MCH*.

IDE (Integrated Drive Electronics)   A hard disk with the disk controller circuitry integrated within it. The first IDE drives commonly were called hard cards. Also refers to the ATA interface standard—the standard for attaching hard disk drives to ISA bus IBM-compatible computers. IDE drives typically operate as though they were standard ST-506/412 drives. See also *ATA*.

IEC (International Electrotechnical Commission)   An international organization that sets electrical and electronics standards. For more information, see www.iec.ch.

IEEE (Institute of Electrical and Electronics Engineers)   An organization that sets many standards for electrical, electronics, computer, and networking fields. For more information, see www.ieee.org.

IEEE 802.3   See *10BASE-2*.

IEEE 802.11 family   A family of wireless network standards commonly known as wireless Ethernet, the most popular of which are 802.11a (54Mbps using 5GHz signaling), 802.11b (11Mbps using 2.4GHz signaling), and 802.11g (54Mbps using 2.4GHz signaling). See also *Wi-Fi*.

IEEE 1284   A series of standards for parallel ports. IEEE 1284 includes EPP and ECP configurations as well as the older bidirectional and 4-bit compatible parallel port modes. Printer cables that can work with all modes are referred to as IEEE 1284–compliant cables. See also *EPP* and *ECP*.

IEEE 1394   See *FireWire*.

illegal operation   A command sent to Windows or the processor that can't be performed. Illegal operations can be triggered by software bugs or conflicts between programs in memory; although the name is reminiscent of a penalty in football, an illegal operation is hardly ever caused by the computer user. In most cases, you can continue to work and might even be able to restart the program without rebooting.

IMB (Inter-Module Bus)   A proprietary high-speed bus used by the Broadcom ServerWorks chipsets. It runs at various speeds, depending on the chipset.

impedance   The total opposition a circuit offers to the flow of alternating current, measured in ohms.

INCITS (InterNational Committee on Information Technology Standards)   An organization (originally known as Accredited Standards Committee X3) that sets and maintains various technology standards. For more information, see www.incits.org.

incremental backup   A backup of all the files that have changed since the last backup.

inductive   A property in which energy can be transferred from one device to another via the magnetic field generated by the device, even though no direct electrical connection is established between the two.

.INF file   A Windows driver and device information file used to install new drivers or services.

ingot   See *boule*.

initiator   A device attached to the SCSI bus that sends a command to another device (the target) on the SCSI bus. The SCSI host adapter plugged in to the system bus is an example of a SCSI initiator.

inkjet printer   A type of printer that sprays one or more colors of ink on the paper; it can produce output with quality approaching that of a laser printer at a lower cost.

input   Data sent to a computer from the keyboard, the telephone, a video camera, another computer, paddles, joysticks, and so on.

InstallShield   A popular program used to create installation and uninstallation routines for Windows-based programs.

instruction   A program step that tells a computer what to do for a single operation.

interface   A communications device or protocol that enables one device to communicate with another. It matches the output of one device to the input of the other device.

interlacing   A method of scanning alternate lines of pixels on a display screen. The odd lines are scanned first, from top to bottom and left to right. The electron gun goes back to the top and makes a second pass, scanning the even lines. Interlacing requires two scan passes to construct a single image. Because of this additional scanning, interlaced screens often seem to flicker unless a long-persistence phosphor is used in the display. Interlaced monitors were used with the IBM 8514/A display card but are now obsolete for desktop computers.

interleave ratio   The number of sectors that pass beneath the read/write heads before the "next" numbered sector arrives. When the interleave ratio is 3:1, for example, a sector is read, two pass by, and then the next is read. A proper interleave ratio, laid down during low-level formatting, enables the disk to transfer information without excessive revolutions due to missed sectors. All modern IDE and SCSI drives have a 1:1 interleave ratio.

interleaved memory   The process of alternating access between two banks of memory to overlap accesses, thus speeding up data retrieval. Systems that require only one memory module per bank to operate can work more quickly when two are installed if the system supports interleaved memory.

internal command   In DOS, a command contained in COMMAND.COM that prevents any other file from being loaded so that the command can be performed. DIR and COPY are two examples of internal commands. In Windows 2000 Server and Windows Server 2003, an internal command is contained in CMD.EXE.

internal device   A peripheral device installed inside the main system case in either an expansion slot or a drive bay.

internal drive   A disk or tape drive mounted inside one of a computer's disk drive bays (or a hard disk card, which is installed in one of the computer's slots).

Internet   A computer network that joins many government, university, and private computers together over phone and high-speed lines. The Internet traces its origins to a network set up in 1969 by the Department of Defense. You can connect to the Internet through many online services, such as CompuServe and America Online, or you can connect through local ISPs. Internet computers use the TCP/IP communications protocol. Several million hosts exist on the Internet; a host is a mainframe, mini, or workstation that directly supports the Internet Protocol (the *IP* in *TCP/IP*).

Internet Explorer   Microsoft's line of web browsers for Windows and Macintosh computers. Most websites are optimized to display best on systems running recent versions of Internet Explorer.

interpreter   A program for a high-level language that translates and executes the program at the same time. The program statements that are interpreted remain in their original source language, the way the programmer wrote them—that is, the program does not need to be compiled before execution. Interpreted programs run more slowly than compiled programs and always must be run with the interpreter loaded in memory.

interrupt   A suspension of a process, such as the execution of a computer program, caused by an event external to that process and performed in such a way that the process can be resumed. An interrupt can be caused by internal or external conditions, such as a signal indicating that a device or program has completed a transfer of data. Hardware interrupts (also called IRQs) are used by devices, whereas software interrupts are used by programs. See also *IRQ*.

interrupt vector   A pointer in a table that gives the location of a set of instructions the computer should execute when a particular interrupt occurs.

IO.SYS   One of the DOS/Windows 9x system files required to boot a machine. The first file loaded from disk during the boot, it contains extensions to the ROM BIOS.

IP address An identifier for a computer or device on a TCP/IP network. The format of an IP address is a 32-bit numeric address written as four numbers separated by periods, in which each number can be 0–255. TCP/IP routes messages based on the IP address of the destination.

IPv6 (Internet Protocol version 6) A new version of IP that expands the range of IP addresses from 32 bits to 128 bits, which relieves the strain on the current universe of IP addresses. IPv6 is backward compatible with IPv4 to allow its gradual adoption.

IPX (Internetwork Packet Exchange) Novell NetWare's native LAN communications protocol (primarily in versions 4.x and earlier) used to move data between server and/or workstation programs running on different network nodes. IPX packets are encapsulated and carried by the packets used in Ethernet and the similar frames used in Token-Ring networks.

IrDA An infrared communications standard established by the Infrared Data Association in 1993. IrDA is currently used primarily for data transfer between portable computers and to allow portable computers to print to a printer with an IrDA port.

IRIX Silicon Graphics's implementation of UNIX. IRIX is used on SGI's 64-bit Origin servers. See also *UNIX*.

IRQ (interrupt request) Physical connections between external hardware devices and the interrupt controllers. When a device such as a floppy controller or a printer needs the attention of the CPU, an IRQ line is used to get the attention of the system to perform a task. On PC and XT IBM-compatible systems, eight IRQ lines are included, numbered IRQ0–IRQ7. On the AT and PS/2 systems, 16 IRQ lines are numbered IRQ0–IRQ15. IRQ lines must be used by only a single adapter in the ISA bus systems, but MCA adapters and most PCI-based systems can share interrupts. IRQ sharing with modern systems requires a system with PCI cards and Windows 95B or above. Windows 2000 and XP are better at sharing IRQs than are Windows 9x and Me. See also *virtual IRQ*.

ISA (Industry Standard Architecture) A bus architecture introduced as an 8-bit bus with the original IBM PC in 1981 and expanded to 16 bits with the IBM PC/AT in 1984. ISA slots are occasionally found in PC systems today, but the latest chipsets have eliminated them.

ISA bus clock A clock that normally operates the ISA bus at 8.33MHz.

iSCSI (Internet SCSI) An implementation of SCSI that uses Ethernet networks using TCP/IP to transfer data in both directions between a server and a SCSI drive or drive array.

ISDN (Integrated Services Digital Network) An international telecommunications standard that enables a communications channel to carry digital data simultaneously with voice and video information.

ISO (International Organization for Standardization) An organization based in Paris that develops standards for international and national data communications. The U.S. representative to the ISO is ANSI. See also *High Sierra format*.

ISO 9660 An international standard that defines file systems for CD-ROM discs, independent of the operating system. ISO 9660 has two levels: The first level provides for DOS file system compatibility, whereas the second level allows filenames of up to 32 characters. See also *High Sierra format*.

ISP (Internet service provider) A company that provides Internet access to computer users. Most ISPs originally provided dialup analog modem service only, but many ISPs now provide various types of broadband support for DSL, cable modem, or fixed wireless Internet devices. Some ISPs, such as America Online, also provide proprietary content.

Itanium An Intel eighth-generation processor, codenamed Merced, that is the first 64-bit instruction PC processor from Intel. It features a new EPIC architecture for more performance when running optimized code. Also, it features internal L1/L2 and L3 ECC caches to improve throughput and reliability. It was designed initially for the server or high-end workstation market. The improved Itanium 2 processor offers faster clock speeds and faster cache memory. See also *L3 cache*.

ITU (International Telecommunications Union) Formerly called CCITT, an international committee organized by the United Nations to set international communications recommendations—which are frequently adopted as standards—and to develop interface, modem, and data network recommendations. The Bell 212A standard for 1,200bps communication in North America, for example, is observed internationally as CCITT V.22. For 2,400bps communication, most U.S. manufacturers observe V.22bis, whereas V.32,

V.32bis, V34, and V34+ are standards for 9,600bps, 14,400bps, 28,800bps, and 33,600bps, respectively. The V.90 standard recently was defined for 56Kbps modems.

J-lead J-shaped leads on chip carriers, which can be surface-mounted on a PC board or plugged in to a socket that then is mounted on a PC board, usually on .050-inch centers.

jabber An error condition on an Ethernet-based network in which a defective network card or outside interference is constantly sending data, preventing the rest of the network from working.

Java An object-oriented programming language and environment similar to C or C++. Java was developed by Sun Microsystems and is used to create network-based applications.

JavaScript A scripting language developed by Netscape for web browsers. JavaScript can perform calculations and mouse rollovers, but it doesn't require the web browser to download additional files, as does Java.

Jaz drive A proprietary type of removable media drive with a magnetic hard disk platter in a rigid plastic case. Developed by Iomega, Jaz drives were discontinued in 2002, but media is still available for both 1GB and 2GB versions of the drives.

JEDEC (Joint Electron Devices Engineering Council) A group that establishes standards for the electronics industry. JEDEC established the original PC66 SDRAM standard.

Joliet A Microsoft extension of the ISO 9660 standard for recordable/rewritable CDs. Joliet is designed for use with 32-bit Windows versions that support long filenames, but it supports file/folder names up to 128 bytes (128 European or 64 Unicode characters) only. Some very long folder/filenames might need to be truncated when stored on a Joliet-format CD.

joule The standard unit of electrical energy, frequently used to measure the effectiveness of surge suppressors.

joystick An input device generally used for game software, usually consisting of a central upright stick that controls horizontal and vertical motion and one or more buttons to control discrete events, such as firing guns. More complex models can resemble flight yokes and steering wheels or incorporate tactile feedback.

JPEG (Joint Photographic Experts Group) An international consortium of hardware, software, and publishing interests that—under the auspices of the ISO—has defined a universal standard for digital compression and decompression of still images for use in computer systems. JPEG compresses at about a 20:1 ratio before visible image degradation occurs. It is a lossy data compression standard that was originally designed for still images but also can compress real-time video (30 frames per second) and animation. Files stored in the JPEG format have the extension .jpg or .jpeg. See also *lossy compression*.

JScript Microsoft's equivalent to JavaScript. See also *JavaScript*.

jukebox A type of CD-ROM drive that enables several CD-ROM discs to be in the drive at the same time. The drive itself determines which disc is needed by the system and loads the discs into the reading mechanism as needed.

jumper block A small, plastic-covered metal clip that slips over two pins protruding from a circuit board. Sometimes also called a shunt. When in place, a jumper block connects the pins electrically and closes the circuit. By doing so, it connects the two terminals of a switch, turning it "on." Jumper blocks are commonly used to configure internal hard drives and motherboard settings.

K6 The popular line of Socket 7 and Super Socket 7 processors developed by AMD. Members included the K6, K6-2, and K6-III.

K56flex A proprietary standard for 56Kbps modem transmissions developed by Rockwell and implemented in modems from a variety of vendors. It was superseded by the official V.90 standard for 56Kbps modems. See also *V.90, V.92, and X2*.

KB (kilobyte) A unit of information storage equal to 1,000 bytes (decimal) or 1,024 bytes (binary). Binary KB are now called kibibytes. See also *kibi-*.

Kermit A protocol designed for transferring files between microcomputers and mainframes. Developed by Frank DaCruz and Bill Catchings at Columbia University (and named after the talking frog on *The Muppet Show*), Kermit was widely accepted in the academic world before the advent of the Internet.

kernel An operating system core component.

key disk In software copy protection schemes popular during the 1980s, a distribution floppy disk that must be present in a floppy disk drive in order for an application program to run.

keyboard   The primary input device for most computers, consisting of keys with letters of the alphabet, digits, punctuation, and function control keys.

keyboard macro   A series of keystrokes automatically input when a single key or a key combination is pressed.

keychain drive   A popular term for small solid-state devices that uses flash memory and connects to a PC through the USB port. Such devices are recognized as drive letters and have typical capacities ranging from 32MB to over 1GB. Most have a fixed capacity, but some have provision for upgradeable memory with SD or other small-form-factor flash memory. Also known as thumb drives.

keylock   A physical locking mechanism to prevent internal access to a system unit or peripherals.

kibi-   A prefix indicating 1,024 of some unit. Abbreviated Ki. See also *gibi-*.

kilo-   A prefix indicating one thousand (1,000) of some unit. Abbreviated k or K. When used to indicate a number of bytes of memory storage, the multiplier definition changes to 1,024. One kilobit (Kb), for example, equals 1,000 bits, whereas one kilobyte (KB) equals 1,024 bytes.

kludge   An inelegant but workable solution for a software or hardware problem.

KVM (keyboard-video-mouse) switch   A device that permits a single keyboard, display, and mouse to control two or more PCs or servers.

L1 (Level 1) cache   A memory cache built into the CPU core of 486 and later generation processors. See also *cache* and *disk cache*.

L2 (Level 2) cache   A second-level memory cache external to the processor core, usually larger and slower than L1. It is normally found on the motherboards of 386, 486, and Pentium systems and inside the processor packages or modules in Pentium Pro and later Intel processors, AMD K6-III processors, and Athlon and Duron processors. Cartridge-based caches used in the Pentium II, early Celeron, Pentium III, and Athlon processors run faster than motherboard cache but at speeds of up to only one-half the CPU speed. Modern socket-based processors that include L2 cache contain the L2 cache inside the CPU die, enabling the L2 cache to work at the full speed of the processor. See also *cache*, *disk cache*, and *SEC*.

L3 (Level 3) cache   A third-level memory cache external to the processor core. Some server-class processors, such as the Intel Itanium, Itanium 2, and some Xeon models, as well as some RISC processors, incorporate L3 cache. L3 cache in the processor die runs at full CPU speed. L3 cache external to the processor typically runs at slower speeds. See also *cache* and *disk cache*.

LAN (local area network)   The connection of two or more computers, usually via a network adapter card or NIC. A LAN is a network contained within a building. Both home and office networks are considered LANs. Ethernet, Fast Ethernet, Gigabit Ethernet, and Wireless Ethernet are used in office LANs, whereas home LANs might use Ethernet, Fast Ethernet, HomePNA, HomeRF, or Wi-Fi Wireless Ethernet.

landing zone   An unused track on a disk surface on which the read/write heads can land when power is shut off. The place a parking program or a drive with an autopark mechanism parks the heads.

LAPM (Link-Access Procedure for Modems)   An error-control protocol incorporated in CCITT Recommendation V.42. Similar to the MNP and HST protocols, it uses CRC and ARQ to ensure data reliability.

laptop computer   A computer system smaller than a briefcase but larger than a notebook that usually has a clamshell design in which the keyboard and display are on separate halves of the system, which are hinged together. These systems normally run on battery power. Many vendors use the terms *notebook* and *laptop computer* interchangeably.

large mode   A translation scheme used by the Award BIOS to translate the cylinder, head, and sector specifications of an IDE drive to those usable by an enhanced BIOS. It doesn't produce the same translated values as LBA mode and is not recommended because it is not supported by other BIOS vendors.

large-scale integration   See *IC*.

laser printer   A type of printer that is a combination of an electrostatic copying machine and a computer printer. The output data from the computer is converted by an interface into a raster feed, similar to the impulses a TV picture tube receives. The impulses cause the laser beam to scan a small drum that carries a positive electrical charge. Where the laser hits, the drum is discharged. Toner, which also carries a positive charge, is then applied to the drum. This toner—a fine black powder—sticks to only the areas of the drum that have been discharged electrically. As it rotates, the drum deposits the toner on a negatively charged sheet of paper. Another roller then heats and bonds the toner to the page. See also *LED printer*.

latency (1) The amount of time required for a disk drive to rotate half a revolution. It represents the average amount of time to locate a specific sector after the heads have arrived at a specific track. Latency is part of the average access time for a drive. (2) The initial setup time required for a memory transfer in DRAM to select the row and column addresses for the memory to be read/written.

LBA (logical block addressing) A method used with SCSI and IDE drives to translate the cylinder, head, and sector specifications of the drive to those usable by an enhanced BIOS. LBA is used with drives that are larger than 528MB, and it causes the BIOS to translate the drive's logical parameters to those usable by the system BIOS.

LCC (leadless chip carrier) A type of IC package that has input and output pads rather than leads on its perimeter.

LCD (liquid crystal display) A display that uses liquid crystal sealed between two pieces of polarized glass. The polarity of the liquid crystal is changed by an electric current to vary the amount of light that can pass through. Because LCD displays do not generate light, they depend on either the reflection of ambient light or backlighting of the screen. The best type of LCD, the active-matrix or TFT LCD, offers fast screen updates and true color capability.

LED (light-emitting diode) A semiconductor diode that emits light when a current is passed through it.

LED printer A printer that uses an LED instead of a laser beam to discharge the drum.

legacy port An I/O port used on a system before the development of the multipurpose USB port. Serial, parallel, keyboard, and PS/2 mouse ports are legacy ports.

letterbox Refers to how wide-screen movies are displayed on TV or monitor screens with normal aspect rations of 4:3. Because widescreen movies have aspect ratios as high as 16:9, the widescreen image leaves blank areas at the top and bottom of the screen. This area is sometimes used for displaying subtitles on foreign-language films. See also *aspect ratio*.

LGA (land grid array) A type of chip socket that moves the pins from the processor to the motherboard. The pins ("lands") connect to pads on the back side of the processor. The first LGA design is Socket 775.

Li-ion (lithium-ion) battery A portable system battery type that is longer-lived than either NiCad or NiMH technologies, can't be overcharged, and holds a charge well when not in use. Lithium-ion batteries are also lighter-weight than the NiCad and NiMH technologies. Because of these superior features, Li-ion batteries have come to be used in all but the very low end of the portable system market. See also *NiCad battery* and *NiMH battery*.

LIF (low insertion force) A type of socket that requires only a minimum of force to insert a chip carrier.

LIFO (last-in, first-out) See *stack*.

light pen A handheld input device with a light-sensitive probe or stylus connected to the computer's graphics adapter board by a cable. It is used for writing or sketching onscreen or as a pointing device for making selections. Unlike mouse devices, light pens are not widely supported by software applications.

line-interactive UPS A UPS design that uses a two-way AC/DC inverter to charge the battery and provide power from the battery after AC power fails. It is the simplest type of UPS suitable for server use.

line voltage The AC voltage available at a standard wall outlet, nominally 110V–120V in North America and 220V–230V in Europe and Japan.

Linux An operating system similar to UNIX that can be run on a wide range of server, desktop, and portable computers. Linux distributions are customized to provide support for different processors and server platforms. See also *UNIX*.

local bus A generic term used to describe a bus directly attached to a processor that operates at the processor's speed and data transfer width.

local echo A modem feature that enables a modem to send copies of keyboard commands and transmitted data to the screen. When the modem is in command mode (not online to another system), the local echo is usually invoked through an ATE1 command, which causes the modem to display the user's typed commands. When the modem is online to another system, the local echo is invoked by an ATF0 command, which causes the modem to display the data it transmits to the remote system.

logical drive A drive, as named by a DOS drive specifier, such as C: or D:. Under DOS 3.3 or later, a single physical drive can act as several logical drives, each with its own specifier. A primary partition can contain only one logical drive; an extended partition can contain one or more logical drives. See also *extended partition* and *primary partition*.

lossless compression A compression technique that preserves all the original information in an image or other data structures. PKZIP and Microsoft CAB files are popular applications of lossless compression.

lossless linking A technique used by DVD+RW drives to enable the DVD+RW video writing process to pause and continue as data is available. Lossless linking enables DVD+RW video media to be read by standalone DVD video players and DVD-ROM drives.

lossy compression A compression technique that achieves optimal data reduction by discarding redundant and unnecessary information in an image. Lossy compression permanently discards unnecessary data, resulting in some loss of precision. MP3, MPEG, and JPEG are popular examples of lossy compression.

lost clusters Clusters that have been marked accidentally as "unavailable" in the FAT even though they don't belong to any file listed in a directory. See also *cluster*.

low-level formatting Formatting that divides tracks into sectors on the platter surfaces. It places sector-identifying information before and after each sector and fills each sector with null data (usually hex F6). It specifies the sector interleave and marks defective tracks by placing invalid checksum figures in each sector on a defective track.

LPT (line printer) port A parallel printer port. Common LPT port numbers range from LPT1 to LPT3.

LPX A semiproprietary motherboard design used in many Low Profile or Slimline case systems. Because no formal standard exists, these typically are not interchangeable between vendors and are often difficult to find replacement parts for or upgrade.

LSI (large-scale integration) See *IC*.

LTO (linear tape-open) A family of open standards for tape backups whose first products were introduced in mid-2000. LTO was jointly developed by Seagate, IBM, and Hewlett-Packard. Ultrium format products have capacities of up to 800GB (2:1 compression). The faster but smaller-capacity Accelis format was never manufactured. See also *Ultrium*.

luminance A measure of brightness usually used in specifying monitor brightness.

LUN (logical unit number) A number given to a device (a logical unit) attached to a SCSI physical unit and not directly to the SCSI bus. Although as many as eight logical units can be attached to a single physical unit, a single logical unit typically is a built-in part of a single physical unit. A SCSI hard disk, for example, has a built-in SCSI bus adapter that is assigned a physical unit number or SCSI ID, and the controller and drive portions of the hard disk are assigned a LUN (usually 0). See also *PUN*.

LZW (Lempel Ziv Welch) A lossless compression scheme used in the GIF and TIFF graphic formats, named after its co-creators, Abraham Lempel, Jacob Ziv, and Terry Welch.

MAC (Media Access Control) address A unique hardware number assigned to network hardware, such as NICs and routers. The MAC address assigned to the WAN side of some broadband Internet routers can be changed to equal the MAC address of the NIC previously used to attach to a broadband device, such as a cable modem.

machine address A hexadecimal location in memory.

machine language Hexadecimal program code a computer can understand and execute. It can be output from the assembler or compiler.

macro A series of commands in an application that can be stored and played back on demand. Many applications from various vendors support Microsoft Visual Basic for Applications as their macro language.

macro virus   A computer virus that uses a scripting language to infect Microsoft Word document templates or email systems.

magnetic domain   A tiny segment of a track just large enough to hold one of the magnetic flux reversals that encode data on a disk surface.

magneto-optical recording   An erasable optical disc recording technique that uses a laser beam to heat pits on the disk surface to the point at which a magnet can make flux changes.

magneto-resistive   A technology originally developed by IBM and commonly used for the read element of a read/write head on a high-density magnetic disk. It is based on the principle that the resistance to electricity changes in a material when brought into contact with a magnetic field—in this case, the read element material and the magnetic bit. Such drives use a magneto-resistive read sensor for reading and a standard inductive element for writing. A magneto-resistive read head is more sensitive to magnetic fields than inductive read heads. Giant magneto-resistive heads are an improved version that store more data in the same space.

mainframe   A somewhat vague distinction that identifies any large computer system normally capable of supporting many users and programs simultaneously.

mask   A photographic map of the circuits for a particular layer of a semiconductor chip used in manufacturing the chip.

master boot sector   See *MBR*.

math coprocessor   A processing chip designed to quickly handle complex arithmetic computations involving floating-point arithmetic, offloading these from the main processor. It was originally contained in a separate coprocessor chip, starting with the 486 family of processors. Intel now has incorporated the math coprocessor into the main processors in what is called the FPU. Also called a numeric coprocessor.

MB (megabyte)   A unit of information storage equal to 1,000,000 bytes. Also called a decimal megabyte. The value 1,048,576 bytes has been called a binary megabyte but is now known as a mebibyte. See also *mebibyte*.

MBR (master boot record)   On hard disks, a one-sector-long record that contains the master boot program as well as the master partition table containing up to four partition entries. The master boot program reads the master partition table to determine which of the four entries is active (bootable) and then loads the first sector of that partition, called the volume boot record. The master boot program tests the volume boot record for a 55AAh signature at offset 510; if it's present, program execution is transferred to the volume boot sector, which typically contains a program designed to load the operating system files. The MBR is always the first physical sector of the disk, at Cylinder 0, Head 0, Sector 1. Also called master boot sector.

MCA (Micro Channel Architecture)   An architecture developed by IBM for the PS/2 line of computers and introduced in 1987. Its features include a 16- or 32-bit bus width and multiple master control. By allowing several processors to arbitrate for resources on a single bus, the MCA is optimized for multitasking, multiprocessor systems. It offers switchless configuration of adapters, which eliminates one of the biggest headaches of installing older adapters. MCA systems became obsolete after the development of the PCI bus.

MCGA (multicolor graphics array)   A type of PC video display circuit introduced by IBM in 1987 that supports text and graphics. Text is supported at a maximum resolution of 80×25 characters in 16 colors, with a character box of 8×16 pixels. Graphics are supported at a maximum resolution of 320×200 pixels in 256 (from a palette of 262,144) colors or 640×480 pixels in 2 colors. The MCGA outputs an analog signal with a horizontal scanning frequency of 31.5KHz and supports analog color or analog monochrome displays.

MCH (memory controller hub)   Intel's term for the chip used in its 8xx-series chipsets to connect the processor with high-bandwidth devices such as memory, video, and the system bus. It replaces the North Bridge chip. MCH chips connect with the I/O controller hub (the 8xx chipsets' replacement for the South Bridge) through a high-speed hub interface. See also *ICH*.

MCI (media control interface)   A device-independent specification for controlling multimedia devices and files. MCI is a part of the multimedia extensions and offers a standard interface set of device control commands. MCI commands are used for audio recording and playback and for animation playback. Device types include CD audio, DAT players, scanners, MIDI sequencers, videotape players or recorders, and audio devices that play digitized waveform files.

MDA (monochrome display adapter)   A type of PC video display adapter introduced by IBM on August 12, 1981, that supports text only. Text is supported at a maximum resolution of 80×25 characters in four colors with a character box of 9×14 pixels. Colors, in this case, indicate black, white, bright white, and underlined. Graphics modes are not supported. The MDA outputs a digital signal with a horizontal scanning frequency of 18.432KHz and supports TTL monochrome displays. The IBM MDA card also includes a parallel printer port. Also known as a mono graphics adapter (MGA).

MEB (midlevel electronics bay)   A SSI form factor originally developed for use with slot-based server processors, now used for four-way and larger designs. Sometimes erroneously referred to as EEB 3.5.

mebi-   A prefix indicating 1,048,576 of a unit of measurement. Abbreviated Mi.

mebibyte (MiB)   A unit of information storage equal to 1,048,576 bytes (1,024×1,024 equals 1Mi). This value was previously called a binary megabyte. See also *MB* and *KB*.

medium   The magnetic coating or plating that covers a disk or tape.

mega-   A prefix indicating one million (1,000,000) of some unit. Abbreviated m or M. Traditionally, mega has also been defined as 1,048,576 (1,024 kilobytes, where a kilobyte equals 1,024) in applications such as memory sizing or disk storage applications (as defined by many BIOSs and by FDISK and other disk preparation programs). The term mebi is now used for 1,048,576. See also *mebi-*.

megapixel   A unit of digital camera resolution equal to approximately 1,000,000 pixels. A 1-megapixel camera has a resolution of approximately 1,152×864; a 2-megapixel camera has a resolution of approximately 1,760×1,168. A 3-megapixel camera has a resolution of approximately 2,160×1,440. 1-megapixel or lower-resolution cameras are suitable for 4-inch×6-inch or smaller snapshots only, whereas 2-megapixel cameras produce excellent 5-inch×7-inch enlargements and acceptable 8-inch×10-inch enlargements. 3-megapixel or higher-resolution cameras produce excellent 8-inch×10-inch and 11-inch×14-inch enlargements. The higher the megapixel rating, the more flash memory space is used by each picture, and the longer it takes each picture to be recorded to flash memory.

memory   A component in a computer system that stores information for future use.

memory caching   A service provided by extremely fast memory chips that keeps copies of the most recent memory accesses. When the CPU makes a subsequent access, the value is supplied by the fast memory rather than by the relatively slow system memory. L1 and L2 caches are memory caches found on most recent processors. See also *L1 cache*, *L2 cache*, and *L3 cache*.

memory scrubbing   A task performed by many servers that involves repeatedly reading memory contents during idle time and correcting errors when possible. Noncorrectable errors are reported to the server management software so the defective module can be replaced.

Memory Stick   A Sony-developed flash memory device that's about the size of a stick of gum. It is used by digital cameras, camcorders, digital music players, and voice recorders—primarily those made by Sony.

memory-resident program   A program that remains in memory after it has been loaded, consuming memory that otherwise might be used by application software.

menu software   Utility software that makes a computer running DOS easier to use by replacing DOS commands with a series of menu selections.

MFM (modified frequency modulation) encoding   A method of encoding data on the surface of a disk. The coding of a bit of data varies by the coding of the preceding bit to preserve clocking information. MFM is used only by floppy drives today because it stores less data than other types of encoding, such as RLL. See also *RLL*.

MGA (mono graphics adapter)   See *MDA*.

MHz (megahertz)   A unit of measurement indicating the frequency of one million cycles per second. One Hz is equal to one cycle per second.

MI/MIC (mode indicate/mode indicate common)   A mode provided for installations in which equipment other than the modem does the dialing. In such installations, the modem operates in dumb mode (with no auto-dial capability) yet must go off-hook in originate mode to connect with answering modems. Also called forced or manual originate.

micro- A prefix indicating one millionth (1/1,000,000 or .000001) of some unit. Abbreviated µ.

micron A unit of measurement equaling one millionth of a meter. Often used in measuring the size of circuits in chip manufacturing processes. Current state-of-the-art chip fabrication builds chips with 0.13- to 0.15-micron circuits. The symbol µ is often used for microns.

microprocessor A solid-state CPU much like a computer on a chip. It is an IC that accepts coded instructions for execution. Also called a processor.

microsecond (µs) A unit of time equal to one millionth (1/1,000,000 or .000001) of a second.

MIDI (musical instrument digital interface) An interface and file format standard for connecting a musical instrument to a microcomputer and storing musical instrument data. Multiple musical instruments can be daisy-chained and played simultaneously with the help of a computer and related software. The various operations of the instruments can be captured, saved, edited, and played back. A MIDI file contains note information, timing (how long a note is held), volume, and instrument type for as many as 16 channels. Sequencer programs are used to control MIDI functions such as recording, playback, and editing. MIDI files store only note instructions and not actual sound data. MIDI files can be played back by virtually all sound cards, but old sound cards might use FM synthesis to imitate the musical instruments called for in a MIDI file. Recent sound cards use stored musical instrument samples for more realistic MIDI playback.

MII A Socket 7–compatible processor originally developed by Cyrix and now sold by VIA Technologies as the VIA Cyrix MII.

milli- A prefix indicating one thousandth (1/1,000 or .001) of some unit. Abbreviated m.

MIME (Multipurpose Internet Mail Extensions) A standard that allows Internet and email services to exchange binary files and select the proper program to open the file after it's received.

minitower A type of PC system case that is shorter than a full- or midsized tower. Most low-cost computers sold at retail stores use the minitower case combined with a Micro-ATX motherboard.

MIPS (million instructions per second) Refers to the average number of machine-language instructions a computer can perform or execute in 1 second. Because various processors can perform different functions in a single instruction, MIPS should be used only as a general measure of performance among various types of computers.

MMDS (Multichannel Multipoint Distribution Service) The most common form of so-called "wireless cable TV." MMDS is also used for two-way wireless Internet service. One of the leading MMDS technology manufacturers is Navini Networks (www.navini.com).

MMO (mobile module) A type of processor packing from Intel for mobile computers consisting of a Pentium or newer processor mounted on a small daughterboard along with the processor voltage regulator, the system's L2 cache memory, and the North Bridge part of the motherboard chipset.

MMX An Intel processor enhancement that adds 57 new instructions designed to improve multimedia performance. MMX also implies a doubling of the internal L1 processor cache on Pentium MMX processors compared to non-MMX Pentium processors. Later processors also include MMX along with other multimedia instructions.

mnemonic An abbreviated name for something used in a manner similar to an acronym. Computer processor instructions are often abbreviated with a mnemonic, such as JMP (jump), CLR (clear), STO (store), and INIT (initialize). A mnemonic name for an instruction or operation makes it easy to remember and convenient to use.

MNP (Microcom Networking Protocol) An asynchronous error-control and data-compression protocol developed by Microcom, Inc., and now in the public domain. It ensures error-free transmission through error detection (CRC) and retransmission of erred frames. MNP Levels 1–4 cover error control and have been incorporated into CCITT Recommendation V.42. MNP Level 5 includes data compression but is eclipsed in superiority by V.42bis—an international standard that is more efficient. Most high-speed modems connect with MNP Level 5 if V.42bis is unavailable. MNP Level 10 provides error correction for impaired lines and adjusts to the fastest possible speed during connection. MNP Level 10EC is an improved version of MNP Level 10, adding more reliability and support for cellular phone hand-offs.

MO (magneto-optical) Drives that use both magnetic and optical storage properties. MO technology is erasable and recordable, as opposed to CD-ROM (read-only) and WORM (write-once) drives. MO uses laser and magnetic field technology to record and erase data.

modem (modulator/demodulator) A device that converts electrical signals from a computer into an audio form transmittable over telephone lines or vice versa. It modulates, or transforms, digital signals from a computer into the analog form that can be carried successfully on a phone line; it also demodulates signals received from the phone line back to digital signals before passing them to the receiving computer. To avoid confusion with other types of Internet connection devices, such as cable modems, modems are often called analog modems or dialup modems.

modulation The process of modifying some characteristic of a carrier wave or signal so that it varies in step with the changes of another signal, thus carrying the information of the other signal.

module An assembly that contains a complete circuit or subcircuit.

MOESI (Modified Owned Exclusive Shared Invalid) A cache coherency protocol used by AMD Opteron processors.

monitor See *display*.

MOS (metal-oxide semiconductor) The three layers used in forming the gate structure of a field-effect transistor (FET). MOS circuits offer low-power dissipation and enable transistors to be jammed closely together before a critical heat problem arises. PMOS, the oldest type of MOS circuit, is a silicon-gate P-channel MOS process that uses currents made up of positive charges. NMOS is a silicon-gate N-channel MOS process that uses currents made up of negative charges and is at least twice as fast as PMOS. CMOS, complementary MOS, is nearly immune to noise, runs off almost any power supply, and is an extremely low-power circuit technique.

MESI (Modified Exclusive Shared Invalid) A cache coherency protocol used by Intel processors.

motherboard The main circuit board in a computer. Also called planar board, system board, or backplane.

mouse An input device invented by Douglas Engelbart of Stanford Research Center in 1963 and popularized by Xerox in the 1970s. A mechanical mouse consists of a roller ball and a tracking mechanism on the underside that relays the mouse's horizontal and vertical position to the computer, allowing precise control of the pointer location onscreen. The top side features two or three buttons and possibly a small wheel used to select or click items onscreen. Old-style optical mouse devices sold in the 1980s used a single optical sensor and a grid-marked pad as an alternative to the roller ball. The latest optical mouse devices use two optical sensors and can be moved across virtually any nonmirrored surface.

MPC (Multimedia Personal Computer) A specification developed by Tandy Corporation and Microsoft as the minimum platform capable of running multimedia software. In 1995, the MPC Marketing Council introduced an upgraded MPC 3 standard. The MPC 1 specification defines the following minimum standard requirements: a 386SX or 486 CPU; 2MB RAM; 30MB hard disk; VGA video display; 8-bit digital audio subsystem; CD-ROM drive; and systems software compatible with the APIs of Microsoft Windows version 3.1 or later. The MPC 2 specification defines the following minimum standard requirements: 25MHz 486SX with 4MB RAM; 160MB hard disk; 16-bit sound card; 65,536-color video display; double-speed CD-ROM drive; and systems software compatible with the APIs of Microsoft Windows version 3.1 or later. The MPC 3 specification defines the following minimum standard requirements: 75MHz Pentium with 8MB RAM; 540MB hard disk; 16-bit sound card; 65,536-color video display; quad-speed CD-ROM drive; OM-1–compliant MPEG-1 video, and systems software compatible with the APIs of Microsoft Windows version 3.1 and DOS 6.0 or later. Virtually all computers sold since 1995 exceed MPC 3 standards.

MPEG (Motion Picture Experts Group) A working ISO committee that has defined standards for lossy digital compression and decompression of motion video/audio for use in computer systems. The MPEG-1 standard delivers decompression data at 1.2MBps–1.5MBps, enabling CD players to play full-motion color movies at 30 frames per second. MPEG-1 compresses at about a 50:1 ratio before image degradation occurs, but compression ratios as high as 200:1 are attainable. MPEG-2 extends to the higher data rates (2Mbps–15Mbps) necessary for signals delivered from remote sources (such as broadcast, cable, or satellite). MPEG-2 is designed to support a range of picture aspect ratios, including 4:3 and 16:9. MPEG compression produces about a 50% volume reduction in file size. See also *lossy compression* and *MP3*.

MP3   The audio layer portion of the MPEG-1 standard, which provides a wide range of compression ratios and file sizes for digital music storage, making it the de facto standard for exchanging digital music through sites such as Napster and its many rivals.

MPR   The Swedish government standard for maximum video terminal radiation. The current version is called MPR II, but most monitors also comply with the newer and more restrictive TCO standards. See also *TCO*.

ms (millisecond)   A unit of time equal to one thousandth (1/1,000, or .001) of a second.

MSDOS.SYS   One of the DOS/Windows 9x system files required to boot a machine. It contains the primary DOS routines. Loaded by IO.SYS, it in turn loads COMMAND.COM.

MSI (medium-scale integration)   See *IC*.

Mt. Rainier   An emerging standard for CD-RW and DVD+RW drives that provides for native operating system support of CD-RW and rewritable DVD media. Drives and operating systems that support the Mt. Rainier standard (www.mt-rainier.org) can read or write Mt. Rainier–formatted CD-R/RW or DVD+R/RW media without the need for proprietary packet-reading software such as Roxio's UDF Volume Reader for DirectCD-formatted media (www.roxio.com).

MTBF (mean time between failures)   A statistically derived measure of the probable time a device will continue to operate before a hardware failure occurs, usually given in hours. Because no standard technique exists for measuring MTBF, a device from one manufacturer can be significantly more or significantly less reliable than a device with the same MTBF rating from another manufacturer.

MTTR (mean time to repair)   A measure of the probable time it will take a technician to service or repair a specific device, usually given in hours.

multimedia   The integration of sound, graphic images, animation, motion video, and text in one environment on a computer. It is a set of hardware and software technologies that is rapidly changing and enhancing the computing environment.

multisession   A term used in CD-ROM recording to describe a recording event. Multisession capabilities allow data recording on the disk at various times in several recording sessions. Kodak's Photo CD is an example of multisession CD-R technology. See also *session (single or multisession)*.

multitask   To run several programs simultaneously.

multithread   To concurrently process more than one message by an application program. OS/2 and 32-bit versions of Windows are examples of multi-threaded operating systems. Each program can start two or more threads, which carry out various inter-related tasks with less overhead than two separate programs would require.

multiuser system   A system in which several computer terminals share the same CPU.

nano-   A prefix indicating one billionth (1/1,000,000,000, or .000000001) of some unit. Abbreviated n.

nanosecond (ns)   A unit of time equal to one billionth (1/1,000,000,000 or .000000001) of a second.

NAS (network attached storage)   A hard disk–based storage device or array that plugs in to a network and has its own IP address.

NetBEUI (NetBIOS Extended User Interface)   A network protocol used primarily by Windows NT and Windows 9x and most suitable for small peer-to-peer networks. NetBEUI is not supported by Microsoft in Windows XP and above but can still be manually installed for use in troubleshooting computers.

NetBIOS (Network Basic Input/Output System)   A commonly used network protocol originally developed by IBM and Sytek for PC LANs. NetBIOS provides session and transport services (Layers 4 and 5 of the OSI model).

NetWare   Novell's server-based network for large businesses. NetWare 5 and NetWare 6 are designed to work well with IP-based networks.

network   A system in which several independent computers are linked to share data and peripherals, such as hard disks and printers.

Network Layer   In the OSI reference model, the layer that switches and routes packets as necessary to get them to their destinations. This layer is responsible for addressing and delivering message packets. See also *OSI model*.

NIC (network interface card)   An adapter that connects a PC to a network.

NiCad (nickel cadmium) battery   The oldest of the three battery technologies used in portable systems. NiCad batteries are rarely used in portable systems today because of their shorter life and sensitivity to improper charging and discharging. See also *NiMH battery* and *Li-ion battery*.

NiMH (nickel metal-hydride) battery A battery technology used in portable systems. NiMH batteries have approximately a 30% longer life than NiCads, are less sensitive to the memory effect caused by improper charging and discharging, and do not use the environmentally dangerous substances found in NiCads. NiMH batteries can sometimes be used in place of NiCads. Newer Li-ion batteries are far superior to both NiCad and NiMH batteries. See also *Li-ion battery* and *NiCad battery*.

NLX A new low-profile motherboard form factor standard that is basically an improved version of the semiproprietary LPX design. It is designed to accommodate larger processor and memory form factors and incorporate newer bus technologies, such as AGP and USB. Besides design improvements, it is fully standardized, which means you should be able to replace one NLX board with another from a different manufacturer, which is not normally possible with LPX.

node (1) A device on a network. (2) Any junction point at which two or more items meet.

noise Any unwanted disturbance in an electrical or mechanical system.

noninterlaced monitor A desirable monitor design in which the electron beam sweeps the screen in lines from top to bottom, one line after the other, completing the entire screen in one pass. Virtually all CRTs sold recently for desktop use are noninterlaced.

North Bridge The Intel term for the main portion of the motherboard chipset that incorporates the interface between the processor and the rest of the motherboard. North Bridge contains the cache, main memory, and AGP controllers, as well as the interface between the high-speed (normally 66MHz or 100MHz) processor bus and the 33MHz PCI or 66MHz AGP buses. The functional equivalent of the North Bridge on the latest 8xx-series chipsets from Intel is the MCH. See also *chipset*, *ICH*, *MCH*, and *South Bridge*.

NOS (network operating system) An operating system designed primarily to support network operations. Current server and client operating systems provide NOS functionality as part of their function.

notebook computer See *laptop computer*.

NTSC (National Television Standards Committee) A committee that governs the standards for television and video playback and recording in the United States. The NTSC was originally organized in 1941, when TV broadcasting first began on a wide scale in black and white, and the format was revised in 1953 for color. The NTSC format has 525 scan lines, a field frequency of 60Hz, a broadcast bandwidth of 4MHz, a line frequency of 15.75KHz, a frame frequency of 1/30 second, and a color subcarrier frequency of 3.58MHz. It is an interlaced signal, which means it scans every other line each time the screen is refreshed. The signal is generated as a composite of red, green, and blue signals for color and includes an FM frequency for audio and a signal for stereo. PAL and SECAM are incompatible systems used in Europe. See also *composite video*, *PAL*, and *SECAM*.

null modem A serial cable that is wired so that two DTE devices, such as PCs, or two DCE devices, such as modems or mouse devices, can be connected. Also sometimes called a modem-eliminator or a LapLink cable. To make a null-modem cable with DB-25 connectors, you wire these pins together: 1-1, 2-3, 3-2, 4-5, 5-4, 6-8-20, 20-8-6, and 7-7.

numeric coprocessor See *math coprocessor*.

NVRAM (nonvolatile random-access memory) RAM whose data is retained when power is turned off. ROM, EPROM, and EEPROM (flash) memory are examples of NVRAM. Sometimes NVRAM is retained without any power whatsoever, as in EEPROM or flash memory devices. In other cases, the memory is maintained by a small battery. NVRAM that is battery maintained is sometimes also called CMOS memory (although CMOS RAM technically is volatile). CMOS NVRAM is used in IBM-compatible systems to store configuration information. True NVRAM often is used in intelligent modems to store a user-defined default configuration loaded into normal modem RAM at power-up.

NVRAM disk A RAM disk powered by a battery supply so that it continues to hold its data during a power outage.

object hierarchy A situation in a graphical program in which two or more objects are linked and one object's movement is dependent on the other object. This is known as a parent–child hierarchy. In an example using a human figure, the fingers would be child objects to the hand, which is a child object to the arm, which is a child to the shoulder, and so on. Object hierarchy provides much control for an animator in moving complex figures.

OC (optical carrier) rates   Various data rates for optical fiber used in Internet backbones, based on the OC-1 rate of 51.84Mbps. You multiply the OC rate by 51.84Mbps to derive the data rate. For example, OC-12 is 622.08Mbps (51.84×12).

Occam's Razor   A popular name for the principle that the simplest explanation is usually the correct one—a very useful principle in computer troubleshooting. Also spelled Ockham's Razor.

OCR (optical character recognition)   An information-processing technology that converts human-readable text into computer data. Usually a scanner is used to read the text on a page, and OCR software converts the images to characters. Advanced OCR programs, such as OmniPage, can also match fonts, re-create page layouts, and scan graphics into machine-readable form.

ODI (Open Data-link Interface)   A device driver standard from Novell that enables multiple protocols to run on the same network adapter card. ODI adds functionality to Novell's NetWare and network computing environments by supporting multiple protocols and drivers.

OEM (original equipment manufacturer)   A manufacturer that sells its product to a reseller. OEM usually refers to the original manufacturer of a particular device or component. Most Hewlett-Packard hard disks, for example, are made by Seagate Technologies, which is considered the OEM. OEM products often differ in features from retail products and can have very short warranty periods if purchased separately from their intended use.

OLE (object linking and embedding)   An enhancement to the original DDE protocol that enables the user to embed or link data created in one application to a document created in another application and subsequently edit that data directly from the final document.

online fallback   A feature that enables high-speed error-control modems to monitor line quality and fall back to the next lower speed if line quality degrades. Some modems fall forward as line quality improves.

open architecture   A system design in which the specifications are made public to encourage third-party vendors to develop add-on products. The PC is a true open architecture system, but the Macintosh is proprietary.

OpenVMS   A high-performance server operating system originally developed by Digital Equipment Corporation (DEC) for VAX computers. OpenVMS is now used on Hewlett-Packard's AlphaServer and Itanium-based Integrity servers.

Opteron   An AMD single-core and dual-core processor built for workstation and server tasks. Opteron supports AMD64 64-bit extensions. It can be scaled to eight-way operation and beyond. It uses Socket 940 or Socket 939. Dual-core Socket 939 versions of Opteron can be installed in existing systems built for single-core Socket 939 processors after a BIOS update. See also *AMD64*, *Socket 940*, and *Socket 939*.

optical disc   A disc that encodes data as a series of reflective pits that are read (and sometimes written) by a laser beam.

Orange Book   The standards for recordable (CD-R) and rewritable (CD-RW) compact discs.

originate mode   A state in which a modem transmits at the predefined low frequency of the communications channel and receives at the high frequency. The transmit/receive frequencies are the reverse of the called modem, which is in answer mode. See also *answer mode*.

OS (operating system)   A collection of programs for operating a computer. Operating systems perform housekeeping tasks, such as input and output between the computer and peripherals and accepting and interpreting information from the keyboard. Windows XP and MacOS X are examples of popular OSs.

OS/2   An operating system originally developed through a joint effort by IBM and Microsoft Corporation and later by IBM alone. Originally released in 1987, OS/2 is a 32-bit operating system designed to run on computers using the Intel 386 or later microprocessors. The OS/2 Workplace Shell, an integral part of the system, is a graphical interface similar to Microsoft Windows and the Apple Macintosh system. OS/2 Warp 4 is the most recent one and is used primarily as a server or in back-office functions today.

OSI (Open Systems Interconnection) model A reference model developed by the ISO in the 1980s that splits a computer's networking stack into seven discrete layers. Each layer provides specific services to the layers above and below it. From the top down, the Application Layer is responsible for program-to-program communication; the Presentation Layer manages data representation conversions. Next, the Session Layer is responsible for establishing and maintaining communications channels, and the Transport Layer is responsible for the integrity of data transmission. The Network Layer routes data from one node to another, the Data Link Layer is responsible for physically passing data from one node to another, and finally, the Physical Layer is responsible for moving data on and off the network media.

OTP (one-time programmable) See *PROM*.

output (1) Information processed by a computer. (2) To send information processed by a computer to a mass storage device, such as a video display, printer, or modem.

overclocking The process of running a processor or video card at a speed faster than the officially marked speed by using a higher clock multiplier, faster bus speed, or faster core clock speed. Overclocking is not recommended or endorsed by processor or video card manufacturers. See also *clock multiplier*.

OverDrive An Intel trademark name for its line of upgrade processors for 486, Pentium, and Pentium Pro systems. Although Intel no longer sells OverDrive processors, similar products are available from Evergreen Technologies and PowerLeap Products, Inc., for these processors plus Pentium II, Pentium III, Pentium 4, and Celeron-based systems.

overlay Part of a program that is loaded into memory only when it is required.

overrun A situation in which data moves from one device more quickly than a second device can accept it.

overscanning A technique used in consumer display products that extends the deflection of a CRT's electron beam beyond the physical boundaries of the screen to ensure that images always fill the display area.

overwrite To write data on top of existing data, thus erasing the existing data.

package A device that includes a chip mounted on a carrier and sealed.

packet A message sent over a network that contains data and a destination address.

packet writing A recording technique that sends data to a CD-R or CD-RW disc in multiple blocks, enabling normal writing processes in Windows Explorer to be used instead of a CD-mastering program. Compatible packet-reading software, such as Roxio's UDF Reader for DirectCD, must be used on systems that don't have a CD-R or CD-RW drive to enable the media to be read. See also *Mt. Rainier*.

pairing Combining processor instructions for optimal execution on superscalar processors.

PAL (Phase Alternating Line) system Invented in 1961, a system of TV broadcasting used in England and other European countries (except France). PAL's image format is 4:3, 625 lines, 50Hz, and 4MHz video bandwidth, with a total 8MHz of video channel width. With its 625-line picture delivered at 25 frames per second, PAL provides a better image and an improved color transmission over the NTSC system used in North America. As a consequence, PAL and NTSC videotapes aren't interchangeable.

PAL (programmable array logic) A type of chip that has logic gates specified by a device programmer.

palmtop computer A computer system smaller than a notebook that is designed so it can be held in one hand while being operated by the other. Many are now called PDAs.

parallel A method of transferring data characters in which the bits travel down parallel electrical paths simultaneously—for example, eight paths for 8-bit characters. Data is stored in computers in parallel form but can be converted to serial form for certain operations.

parity A method of error checking in which an extra bit is sent to the receiving device to indicate whether an even or odd number of binary 1 bits was transmitted. The receiving unit compares the received information with this bit and can obtain a reasonable judgment about the validity of the character. The same type of parity (even or odd) must be used by two communicating computers, or both may omit parity. When parity is used, a parity bit is added to each transmitted character. The bit's value is 0 or 1, to make the total number of 1s in the character even or odd, depending on which type of parity is used. Parity checking isn't widely supported on recent systems, but memory with parity bits can be used as ECC memory on systems with ECC-compatible chipsets. See also *ECC*.

park program   A program that executes a seek to the highest cylinder or just past the highest cylinder of a drive so the potential of data loss is minimized if the drive is moved. Park programs are not interchangeable between drives and are no longer required on most drives 40MB and above because these drives self-park their heads for safety.

partition   A section of a hard disk devoted to a particular operating system. Most hard disks have only one partition, devoted to DOS. A hard disk can have as many as four partitions, each occupied by a different operating system. DOS v3.3 or later can occupy two of these four partitions. A boot manager enables you to select the partition occupied by the operating system you want to start if you have multiple operating systems installed in different partitions. See also *boot manager*.

Pascal   A high-level programming language named for the French mathematician Blaise Pascal (1623–1662). Pascal was developed in the early 1970s by Niklaus Wirth for teaching programming, and it was designed to support the concepts of structured programming.

passive heatsink   A heatsink that does not include a fan. Passive heatsinks used on processors are usually larger than active heatsinks, and they rely on case fans to dissipate heat. Many North Bridge or MCHs on recent motherboards also use passive heatsinks.

passive matrix   Another name for a dual-scan, display-type LCD.

PATA (parallel ATA)   Another name for ATA. See also *ATA* and *IDE*.

PC Card/PCMCIA (Personal Computer Memory Card International Association)   A credit card–sized expansion adapter for notebook and laptop PCs. PC Card is the official PCMCIA trademark; however, both PC Card and PCMCIA card are used to refer to these standards. PCMCIA cards are removable modules that can hold numerous types of devices, including memory, modems, fax/modems, radio transceivers, network adapters, solid-state disks, hard disks, and flash memory adapters.

PCI (Peripheral Component Interconnect)   A standard bus specification initially developed by Intel in 1992 that bypasses the standard ISA I/O bus and uses the system bus to increase the bus clock speed and take full advantage of the CPU's data path. The most common form of PCI is 32 bits wide, running at 33MHz, but 66MHz and

64-bit wide versions of PCI are frequently used on servers.

PCIe (PCI Express)   A high-speed serial I/O interconnect standard being developed by the PCI-SIG (www.pcisig.com) as a replacement for the original PCI standard. The initial version of PCI Express supports 0.8V signaling at 2.5GHz.

PCI-X (Peripheral Component Interconnect Extended)   A faster 64-bit version of PCI with speeds of up to 133MHz. PCI-X is backward compatible with PCI but also supports fault-tolerant features such as automatic reinitializing or disabling of faulty add-on cards.

PCL (Printer Control Language)   A language developed by Hewlett-Packard in 1984 as a language for the Hewlett-Packard LaserJet printer. PCL is now the de facto industry standard for PC printing. PCL defines a standard set of commands, enabling applications to communicate with Hewlett-Packard or Hewlett-Packard–compatible printers and is supported by virtually all printer manufacturers. Various levels of PCL are supported by Hewlett-Packard and other brands of laser and inkjet printers.

PCM (powertrain control module)   The computer in most modern automobiles.

PCM (pulse code modulation)   A technique for digitizing analog signals by sampling the signal and converting each sample into a binary number.

PDA (personal digital assistant)   A handheld, palm-sized computer that functions primarily as a personal organizer and can be combined with a cellular phone or pager. Leading examples include the Palm series, Windows-based PalmPCs, and the Handspring (which also runs the Palm OS). See also *palmtop computer*.

PDF (Portable Document Format)   A file format that can be read with the Adobe Acrobat Reader. See also *Acrobat*.

pedestal   A server chassis that resembles a tower chassis but is wider, taller, and deeper, to permit use of larger motherboards. Some pedestal server chassis include wheels, and some can be converted to a rack-mounted form factor.

peer-to-peer   A type of network in which any computer can act as both a server (by providing access to its resources to other computers) and a client (by accessing shared resources from other computers).

pel   See *pixel*.

Pentium An Intel microprocessor with 32-bit registers, a 64-bit data bus, and a 32-bit address bus. The Pentium has a built-in L1 cache, segmented into a separate 8KB cache for code and another 8KB cache for data. The Pentium includes an FPU or math coprocessor. It is backward compatible with the 486 and can operate in real, protected virtual, and virtual real modes. The MMX Pentium has a 16KB cache for code, has a 16KB cache for data, and adds the MMX instruction set.

Pentium 4 The first Intel seventh-generation processor, it's based on a 32-bit microarchitecture that operates at higher clock speeds because of hyper pipelined technology, a rapid execution engine, a 400MHz system bus (later boosted to 533MHz and 800MHz), and an execution trace cache. The system bus runs at four times the processor bus speed. The floating-point and multimedia units have been improved by making the registers 128 bits wide and adding a separate register for data movement. Finally, SSE2 adds 144 new instructions for double-precision floating-point, SIMD integer, and memory management. The original Socket 423 version (Willamette) was later replaced by Socket 478 (Northwood) and finally by Socket 775 (Prescott), running at up to 3.6GHz. 800MHz system bus versions also support HT technology.

Pentium 4 Extreme Edition A high-speed version of the Pentium 4 that includes 2MB of L3 cache. The original versions ran at 3.46GHZ and were made in Socket 478 and Socket 775. Later versions boosted the system bus to 1066MHz from 800MHz, used the Prescott core, and ran at 3.73MHz. Pentium 4 Extreme Edition has been replaced by Pentium Extreme Edition.

Pentium D An Intel seventh-generation processor (codenamed Smithfield) that includes two Pentium 4 Prescott processor cores in the same processor die. The Pentium D fits into Socket 775 but uses different chipsets than the Pentium 4. The Pentium D includes EM64T architecture. See also *AMD64* and *EM64T*.

Pentium II An Intel sixth-generation processor similar to the Pentium Pro but with MMX capabilities and SEC cartridge packaging technology. It includes L2 cache running at half-core speed.

Pentium III An Intel sixth-generation processor similar to the Pentium II but with SSE added. Later PIII models (codenamed Coppermine) include on-die L2 cache running at full-core speed. Pentium III is available in both cartridge (Slot 1) and chip package (Socket 370) versions.

Pentium Extreme Edition A seventh-generation EM64T-compatible dual-core processor based on the Pentium D, but with HT Technology enabled. Dual-processor–enabled operating systems treat this chip as having four logical processors when HT Technology is enabled. The Pentium Extreme Edition requires a different chipset than the Pentium 4. See also *AMD64*, *EM64T*, and *Pentium D*.

Pentium Pro An Intel sixth-generation (P6) processor with 32-bit registers, a 64-bit data bus, and a 36-bit address bus. The Pentium Pro has the same segmented L1 cache as the Pentium but also includes 256KB, 512KB, or 1MB of L2 cache on a separate die inside the processor package. The Pentium Pro includes an FPU or math coprocessor. It is backward compatible with the Pentium and can operate in real, protected, and virtual real modes. The Pentium Pro fits into Socket 8.

peripheral A piece of equipment used in computer systems that is an attachment to a computer. Disk drives, terminals, and printers are all examples of peripherals.

persistence In a monitor, the quality of the phosphor chemical that indicates how long the glow caused by the electrons striking the phosphor will remain onscreen.

peta- A prefix indicating one thousand trillion (1,000,000,000,000,000) of some unit. Abbreviated p or P.

petabyte (PB) A measure of disk capacity equaling 1,000,000,000,000,000 bytes.

PFC (power factor conversion) An expression of how efficient a power supply or UPS is at providing power. A device that provides 100% of its rated output has a PFC of 1.0. In practice, high-quality power supplies and UPS units have PFCs in the 90%–97% range (.90–.97 PFC).

PGA (pin grid array) A chip package that has a large number of pins on the bottom, designed for socket mounting.

PGA (professional graphics adapter) A limited-production, high-resolution graphics card for XT and AT systems from IBM.

phono connector See *RCA jack*.

phosphor A layer of electroluminescent material applied to the inside face of a CRT. When bombarded by electrons, the material fluoresces, and after the bombardment stops, it phosphoresces.

phosphorescence The emission of light from a substance after the source of excitation has been removed.

Photo CD A technology developed by Eastman Kodak and Philips that stores photographic images on a CD-R. Images stored on the Photo CD can have resolutions as high as 2,048×3,072 pixels. Up to 100 true-color images (24-bit color) can be stored on one disc. Photo CD images are created by scanning film and digitally recording the images on CDs. The digitized images are indexed (given a 4-digit code), and thumbnails of the images on the disc are shown on the front of the case, along with their index numbers. Multisession capability enables several rolls of film to be added to a single disc on different occasions.

photolithography The photographic process used in electronic chip manufacturing that creates transistors and circuit and signal pathways in semiconductors by depositing different layers of various materials on the chip.

photoresist A chemical used to coat a silicon wafer in the semiconductor manufacturing process that makes the silicon sensitive to light for photolithography.

physical drive A single disk drive. DOS defines logical drives, which are given a specifier, such as C: or D:. A single physical drive can be divided into multiple logical drives. Conversely, special software can span a single logical drive across two physical drives.

Physical Layer In the OSI reference model, the layer that is responsible for moving data on and off the network media. See also *OSI model*.

PICMG (PCI Industrial Computers Manufacturers Group) A trade association that develops standards for single-board and industrial computers. Its standards include AdvancedTCA, CompactPCI, and others. See also *AdvancedTCA* and *CompactPCI*.

Picture CD A simplified version of Photo CD that stores scanned images from a single roll of film on a CD-R. Images on Picture CDs, unlike those on Photo CDs, are stored in the industry-standard JPEG file format and can be opened with most photo-editing programs. See also *Photo CD*.

PIF (program information file) A file that contains information about a non-Windows application, specifying optimum settings for running the program under Windows 3.x. These files are called property sheets in 32-bit Windows.

pin The lead on a connector, chip, module, or device.

PIN (personal identification number) A personal password used for identification purposes.

pin compatible Chips having the same pinout functions. For example, a VIA C3 processor is pin compatible with an Intel Celeron (Socket 370 version).

pinout A listing of which pins have which functions on a chip, socket, slot, or other connector.

PIO (programmed input/output) mode The standard data transfer modes used by IDE drives that use the processor's registers for data transfer. This is in contrast with DMA modes, which transfer data directly between main memory and the device. The slowest PIO mode is 0, and the fastest PIO mode is mode 4 (16.66MBps). Faster modes use UDMA transfers. See also *UDMA*.

pipeline A path for instructions or data to follow.

pixel (picture element) Any of the tiny elements that form a picture on a video display screen. Also called a pel.

pixel shader A small program that controls the appearance of individual pixels in a 3D image. Most recent midrange and high-end GPUs such as NVIDIA's GeForce 3 and GeForce 4 Ti series and the ATI 8xxx and 9xxx series have built-in pixel shaders. See also *GPU*, *hardware shader*, and *vertex shader*.

PKZIP The original ZIP-format compression/decompression program developed by the late Phil Katz. His company, PKWARE, continues to develop PKZIP for popular operating systems, including Windows.

planar board A term equivalent to motherboard that IBM uses in some of its literature.

plasma display A display technology that uses plasma (electrically charged gas) to illuminate each pixel. Plasma displays are much thinner than conventional CRT displays but are much more expensive than CRTs or LCD displays. Several vendors now sell HDTV plasma displays that can also be connected to computers with VGA or DVI video connectors.

plated media Hard disk platters plated with thin metal film medium on which data is recorded.

platter A disk contained in a hard disk drive. Most drives have two or more platters, each with data recorded on both sides.

PLCC (plastic leaded-chip carrier) A chip-carrier package with J-leads around the perimeter of the package.

PnP (Plug and Play) A hardware and software specification developed by Intel that enables a PnP system and PnP adapter cards to automatically configure themselves. PnP cards are free from switches and jumpers and are configured via the PnP BIOS in the host system or via supplied programs for non-PnP systems. PnP also allows the system to detect and configure external devices, such as monitors, modems, and devices attached to USB or IEEE-1394 ports. Windows 9x, Me, 2000, and XP all support PnP devices.

polling A communications technique that determines when a device is ready to send data. The system continually interrogates polled devices in a round-robin sequence. If a device has data to send, it sends back an acknowledgment, and the transmission begins. Polling contrasts with interrupt-driven communications, in which the device generates a signal to interrupt the system when it has data to send. Polling enables two devices that would normally have an IRQ conflict to coexist because the IRQ is not used for flow control.

port (1) A plug or socket that enables an external device, such as a printer, to be attached to the adapter card in the computer. (2) A logical address used by a microprocessor for communication between it and various devices.

port address One of a system of addresses used by a computer to access devices such as disk drives or printer ports. You might need to specify an unused port address when installing an adapter board in a system unit.

port replicator For mobile computers, a device that plugs into a laptop and provides all the ports for connecting external devices. The advantage of using a port replicator is that the external devices can be left connected to the replicator, and the mobile computer can be connected to them all at once by connecting to the replicator, rather than connecting to each individual device. A port replicator differs from a docking station in that the latter can provide additional drive bays and expansion slots not found in port replicators. Traditionally, port replicators have plugged in to a proprietary bus on the rear of a portable computer, but so-called universal models might attach to the PC Card (PCMCIA) slot or to a USB port.

portable computer A computer system smaller than a transportable system but larger than a laptop system. Very few systems in this form factor are sold today, but companies such as Dolch still produce them. Most portable systems conform to the lunchbox style popularized by Compaq or the briefcase style popularized by IBM, each with a fold-down (removable) keyboard and built-in display. These systems characteristically run on AC power and not on batteries, include several expansion slots, and can be as powerful as full desktop systems.

POS (Programmable Option Select) A Micro Channel Architecture system that eliminates switches and jumpers from the system board and adapters by replacing them with programmable registers. Automatic configuration routines store the POS data in battery-powered CMOS memory for system configuration and operations. The configuration utilities rely on ADF that contain the setup data for each card.

POST (power-on self-test) A series of tests run by a computer at power-on. Most computers scan and test many of their circuits and sound a beep from the internal speaker if this initial test indicates proper system performance.

PostScript A page-description language developed primarily by John Warnock of Adobe Systems for converting and moving data to the laser-printed page. Instead of using the standard method of transmitting graphics or character information to a printer and telling it where to place dots one-by-one on a page, PostScript provides a way for the laser printer to interpret mathematically a full page of shapes and curves. Adobe Acrobat converts PostScript output files into files that can be read by users with varying operating systems. See also *Acrobat*.

POTS (plain old telephone service) Standard analog telephone service.

power management Systems used initially in mobile computers (and now also used in desktop systems) to decrease power consumption by turning off or slowing down devices during periods of inactivity. See also *ACPI* and *APM*.

power supply An electrical/electronic circuit that supplies all operating voltage and current to a computer system.

PPGA (plastic pin grid array) A chip-packaging form factor used by Intel as an alternative to traditional ceramic packaging.

PPP (Point-to-Point Protocol) A protocol that enables a computer to use the Internet with a standard telephone line and high-speed modem. PPP has largely replaced the Serial Line Internet Protocol (SLIP) because it supports line sharing and error detection.

precompensation A data write modification required by some older drives on the inner cylinders to compensate for the higher density of data on the (smaller) inner cylinders.

Presentation Layer In the OSI reference model, the layer that is responsible for managing data representation conversions. See also *OSI model*.

primary partition An ordinary, single-volume bootable partition. See also *extended partition*.

printer A device that records information visually on paper or other material.

processor See *microprocessor*.

processor speed The clock rate at which a microprocessor processes data. A typical Pentium 4 processor, for example, operates at 2GHz (2 billion cycles per second).

program A set of instructions or steps that tell a computer how to handle a problem or task.

program module See *subroutine*.

PROM (programmable read-only memory) A type of memory chip that can be programmed to store information permanently—information that can't be erased. Also referred to as OTP.

proprietary Anything invented by a company that uses components available from only that one company. Especially applies to cases in which the inventing company goes to lengths to hide the specifications of the new invention or to prevent other manufacturers from making similar or compatible items. Proprietary is the opposite of standard or open architecture. Computers with nonstandard components that are available from only the original manufacturer, such as Apple Macintosh systems, are proprietary.

protected mode A mode available in all Intel and compatible processors except the first-generation 8086 and 8088. In this mode, memory addressing is extended beyond the 1MB limits of the 8088, and real mode and restricted protection levels can be set to trap software crashes and control the system.

protocol A system of rules and procedures governing communications between two or more devices. Protocols vary, but communicating devices must follow the same protocol to exchange data. The data format, readiness to receive or send, error detection, and error correction are some of the operations that can be defined in protocols.

proxy server A computer that acts as a gateway between the computers on a network and the Internet and also provides page caching and optional content filtering and firewall services to the network. Some home network software solutions for Internet sharing, such as WinProxy, use proxy servers.

PS/2 mouse A mouse designed to plug in to a dedicated mouse port (a round, 6-pin DIN connector) on the motherboard rather than plug in to a serial port. The name comes from the fact that this port was first introduced on IBM PS/2 systems.

PUN (physical unit number) A term used to describe a device attached directly to the SCSI bus. Also known as a SCSI ID. As many as eight SCSI devices can be attached to a single SCSI bus, and each must have a unique PUN or ID assigned, from 7 to 0. Normally, the SCSI host adapter is assigned the highest-priority ID, which is 7. A bootable hard disk is assigned an ID of 0, and other nonbootable drives are assigned higher priorities. See also *LUN*.

QAM (quadrature amplitude modulation) A modulation technique used by high-speed modems that combines both phase and amplitude modulation. This technique enables multiple bits to be encoded in a single time interval.

QDR (quad data rate) A high-speed SDRAM technology (www.qdrsram.com) that uses separate input and output ports with a DDR interface to enable four pieces of data to be processed at the same time. See also *DDR*.

QIC (Quarter-Inch Committee) An industry association that sets hardware and software standards for tape backup units that use quarter-inch–wide tapes. QIC, QIC-Wide, Travan, and Travan NS drives are all based on QIC standards.

QoS (quality of service) A general term for various methods of prioritizing voice, video, audio, and other types of data traveling over a network to ensure that streaming data is granted a higher priority than other types of data when necessary.

Quantum Formerly a major maker of hard disk drives and now a major maker of attached network storage devices. Quantum-brand disk drives are now sold and supported by Maxtor.

QWERTY keyboard   The standard typewriter or computer keyboard, with the characters Q, W, E, R, T, and Y on the top row of alpha keys. Because of the haphazard placement of characters, this keyboard can hinder fast typing.

rack   An open framework that enables servers and other types of network equipment to be stacked for maximum efficiency. Many racks are designed to permit fast insertion and removal of rack-mounted equipment. Rack vertical dimensions are measured in rack units (RU). Racks are 20.125 inches wide, to support standard 19-inch rack-mounted hardware. See also *rack-mounted server* and *U*.

rack-mounted server   A server that fits into a rack. Typical sizes range from 1U to 5U. See also *U*.

radial density   See *track density*.

RAID (redundant array of independent [or inexpensive] disks)   A storage unit that employs two or more drives in combination for fault tolerance and greater performance, used mostly in file server applications. Originally used only with SCSI drives and host adapters, many motherboards now feature ATA/IDE or SATA RAID implementations.

rails   Plastic or metal strips attached to the sides of disk drives mounted in IBM ATs and compatibles so that the drives can slide into place. These rails fit into channels in the side of each disk drive bay position and might be held in position with screws or snap into place. In server rooms, rails are used to permit rack-mounted servers and other equipment to be quickly inserted and removed.

RAM (random-access memory)   Memory that is accessible at any instant (randomly) by a microprocessor.

RAM disk   A "phantom disk drive" in which a section of system memory (RAM) is set aside to hold data, just as though it were a number of disk sectors. To an operating system, a RAM disk looks and functions like any other drive.

RAMDAC (random-access memory digital-to-analog converter)   A special type of DAC found on video cards. RAMDACs use a trio of DACs—one each for red, green, and yellow—to convert image data into a picture. RAMDACs were formerly separate chips but are now integrated into the 3D accelerator chips on most recent video cards.

random-access file   A file in which all data elements (or records) are of equal length and written in the file end-to-end, without delimiting characters between. Any element (or record) in the file can be found directly by calculating the record's offset in the file.

raster   A pattern of horizontal scanning lines normally on a computer monitor. An electromagnetic field causes the beam of the monitor's tube to illuminate the correct dots to produce the required characters.

raster graphics   A technique for representing a picture image as a matrix of dots. It is the digital counterpart of the analog method used in TV. Several raster graphics standards exist, including PCX, TIFF, BMP, JPEG, and GIF.

RCA jack   A plug and socket for a two-wire coaxial cable used to connect audio and video components. The plug is a 1/8-inch-thick prong that sticks out 5/16 inch from the middle of a cylinder. Also called a phono connector.

RDRAM (Rambus dynamic random-access memory)   A high-speed dynamic RAM technology developed by Rambus, Inc., that is supported by Intel's 1999 and later motherboard chipsets. RDRAM transfers data at 1GBps or faster, which is significantly faster than SDRAM and other technologies and which is capable of keeping up with future-generation high-speed processors. Memory modules with RDRAM chips are called RIMMs. Rambus licenses its technology to other semiconductor companies, which manufacture the chips and RIMMs. RDRAMs are used by some of Intel's midrange and high-end chipsets for the Pentium III and Pentium 4 desktop processors and their server counterparts.

read-only file   A file whose attribute setting in the file's directory entry tells DOS not to allow software to write into or over the file.

read/write head   A tiny magnet that reads and writes data on a disk track.

real mode   A mode available in all Intel 8086–compatible processors that enables compatibility with the original 8086. In this mode, memory addressing is limited to 1MB.

real-time   The actual time in which a program or an event takes place. In computing, real-time refers to an operating mode under which data is received and processed and the results are returned so quickly that the process appears instantaneous to the user. The term is also used to describe the process of simultaneous digitization and compression of audio and video information.

reboot   To restart a computer and reload the operating system.

Red Book   One of four CD standards. Red Book got its name from the color of the manual used to describe the CD-audio specifications. The Red Book audio standard requires that digital audio be sampled at a 44.1KHz sample rate, using 16 bits for each sample. This is the standard used by audio CDs and many CD-ROMs. Also known as CD-DA.

redundancy   Including server or network equipment that will automatically take over if the primary equipment fails. On a typical server, redundant hardware might include hard disks in a RAID array, memory, or a power supply. Some servers are built to provide redundancy for all components. This type of server is known as a fault-tolerant server.

refresh cycle   A cycle in which a computer accesses all memory locations stored by DRAM chips so that the information remains intact. DRAM chips must be accessed several times per second; otherwise, the information fades.

refresh rate   Another term for the vertical scan frequency of monitors.

register   A storage area in memory that has a specified storage capacity—such as a bit, byte, or computer word—and is intended for a special purpose.

Registry   The system configuration files used by Windows 9x, Windows Me, Windows NT, Windows 2000, and Windows XP to store settings about installed hardware and drivers, user preferences, installed software, and other settings required to keep Windows running properly. Replaces the WIN.INI and SYSTEM.INI files from Windows 3.x. The Registry structure varies between Windows versions.

remote digital loopback   A test that checks the phone link and a remote modem's transmitter and receiver. Data entered from the keyboard is transmitted from the initiating modem, received by the remote modem's receiver, looped through its transmitter, and returned to the local screen for verification.

remote echo   A copy of the data received by the remote system, returned to the sending system, and displayed onscreen. Remote echo is a function of the remote system.

rendering   Generating a 3D image that incorporates the simulation of lighting effects, such as shadows and reflection.

resident program   See *TSR*.

resolution   (1) A reference to the size of the pixels used in graphics. In medium-resolution graphics, pixels are large. In high-resolution graphics, pixels are small. (2) A measure of the number of horizontal and vertical pixels that can be displayed by a video adapter and monitor.

REV   A proprietary hard-disk-based removable-media drive made by Iomega. REV has a native/2.6:1 compressed capacity of 35/90GB per cartridge. REV can be used for backup or primary storage. An autoloader is also available. See also *autoloader.*

reverse engineering   The act of duplicating a hardware or software component by studying the functions of the component and designing a different one that has the same functions.

RFI (radio frequency interference)   A high-frequency signal radiated by improperly shielded conductors, particularly when signal path lengths are comparable to or longer than the signal wavelengths. The FCC now regulates RFI in computer equipment sold in the United States under FCC Regulations, Part 15, Subpart J.

RGB (red, green, blue)   A type of computer color display output signal comprised of separately controllable red, green, and blue signals. RGB monitors offer much higher resolution and sharper pictures than composite monitors, in which signals are combined prior to output. See also *composite video.*

ribbon cable   A flat cable with wires running in parallel, such as those used for internal IDE or SCSI.

RIMM (Rambus inline memory module)   A type of memory module made using RDRAM chips. See also *RDRAM.*

RISC (reduced instruction set computer)   A computer whose processor has a simple instruction set that requires only one or a few execution cycles. These simple instructions can be used more effectively than CISC systems with appropriately designed software, resulting in faster operations. See also *CISC.*

RJ-11   The standard two-wire connector type used for single-line telephone connections.

RJ-14   The standard four-wire connector type used for two-line telephone connections.

RJ-45   A standard connector type used in networking with twisted-pair cabling. Resembles an RJ-11 or RJ-14 telephone jack, but RJ-45 is larger, with more wires.

RLL (run-length limited) A type of encoding that derives its name from the fact that the techniques used limit the distance (run length) between magnetic flux reversals on the disk platter. Several types of RLL encoding techniques exist, although only two are commonly used. (1,7) RLL encoding increases storage capacity by about 30% over MFM encoding and is most popular in the very highest-capacity drives due to having a better window margin, whereas (2,7) RLL encoding increases storage capacity by 50% over MFM encoding and is used in the majority of RLL implementations. Most IDE, ESDI, and SCSI hard disks use one of these forms of RLL encoding.

RMA (return-merchandise authorization) number A number given to you by a vendor when you arrange to return an item for repair. The RMA is used to track the item and the repair.

ROM (read-only memory) A type of memory that has values permanently or semipermanently burned in. These locations are used to hold important programs or data that must be available to the computer when the power initially is turned on.

ROM BIOS (read-only memory basic input/output system) A BIOS encoded in a form of ROM for protection.

ROM shadowing See *shadow RAM*.

root directory The main directory of any hard or floppy disk. It has a fixed size and location for a particular disk volume and can't be resized dynamically the way subdirectories can.

router A device that is used to connect various networks to intelligently route information between them. A router is used to internetwork similar and dissimilar networks and can select the most expedient route based on traffic load, line speeds, costs, and network failures. Routers use forwarding tables to determine which packets should be forwarded between the connected networks. A cable or DSL modem is an example of a simple router that connects the Internet to a LAN. Many routers include firewall capability to block suspect packets from being transmitted between networks.

routine A set of frequently used instructions. It can be considered a subdivision of a program with two or more instructions that are related functionally.

RPS (redundant power supply) A power supply with two or more modules, one of which is in service at a time. If the primary module fails, another automatically takes its place. An RPS might be designed into a server or could be retrofitted later.

RS-232 An interface introduced in 1969 by the EIA. The RS-232 interface standard provides an electrical description for connecting peripheral devices to computers. Originally, RS-232 (serial) ports on computers used a 25-pin interface, but starting with the IBM AT, most use a 9-pin interface.

RTC (real-time clock) A battery-powered clock included on the motherboard of 286-class and newer computers. The contents of the RTC are read at startup time to provide the time display in the operating system's clock. It's often part of the NVRAM chip.

RTF (Rich Text Format) A universal file format suitable for exchanging formatted text files between different word processing and page layout programs.

S/N (signal-to-noise) ratio The strength of a video or an audio signal in relation to interference (noise). The higher the S/N ratio, the better the quality of the signal. The latest high-end sound cards have an S/N ratio of 100:1.

S/PDIF (Sony Philips Digital Interface) An interface that provides digital I/O on high-end sound cards and multimedia-capable video cards. Might use either an RCA jack or optical jack; some devices support both types of S/PDIF connectors.

S-Video (Y/C) A type of video signal used in the Hi8 and S-VHS videotape formats in which the luminance and chrominance (Y/C) components are kept separate, providing greater control and quality of each image. S-video transmits luminance and color portions separately, thus avoiding the NTSC encoding process and its inevitable loss of picture quality.

SAN (storage area network) A high-speed local or remote network that connects servers with storage devices. SANs often use fiber-optic connections.

SAS (Serial Attached SCSI) A high-speed serial implementation of SCSI adopted in 2003 that combines backward compatibility with SATA drives, current performance of 300MBps, and future improvements to data rates up to 1200MBps.

SATA (Serial ATA) A high-speed serial interface designed to replace the current PATA and Ultra ATA drive interface standards. Serial ATA 1.0 uses a seven-wire data/ground cable and supports direct point-to-point connections to host adapters at initial speeds of up to 150MBps, which is faster than Ultra ATA-133. SATA 3GBps hardware is now available. See also *UDMA*.

scalable Capable of being scaled so that a person can add capacity to a system or network as needed while maintaining performance.

scan codes The hexadecimal codes sent by a keyboard to a motherboard when a key is pressed.

scan lines The parallel lines across a video screen, along which the scanning spot travels in painting the video information that makes up a monitor picture. NTSC systems use 525 scan lines to a screen; PAL systems use 625.

ScanDisk The default Windows 9x/Me drive-testing program, which might be referred to as error checking in the Drive properties screen. Windows NT, Windows 2000, and Windows XP use CHKDSK to test drives.

scanner A device that reads an image and converts it into computer data.

scanning frequency A monitor measurement that specifies how often the image is refreshed. See also *vertical scan frequency*.

scratch disk A disk that contains no useful information and can be used as a test disk. IBM has a routine on the Advanced Diagnostics disks that creates a specially formatted scratch disk to be used for testing floppy drives.

SCSI (small computer system interface) A standard originally developed by Shugart Associates (then called SASI, for Shugart Associates System Interface) and later approved by ANSI in 1986. SCSI-2 (now called SPI-2) was approved in 1994, and Ultra 3 SCSI (now called SPI-3) was approved in 2000. Ultra 4 SCSI (now called SPI-4) was approved in 2002 . 8-bit (narrow) versions of SCSI typically use a 50-pin connector and permit multiple devices (up to 8, including the host) to be connected in daisy-chain fashion. Some low-cost narrow SCSI devices might use a 25-pin connector. Wide and Ultra Wide versions of SCSI use a 68-pin connector and can support up to 16 devices, including the host. An 80-pin connector is used on hot-swap SCSI drives used in RAID arrays.

SCSI ID See *PUN*.

SDLC (Synchronous Data Link Control) A protocol developed by IBM for software applications and communicating devices operation in IBM's SNA. SDLC defines operations at the link level of communications—for example, the format of data frames exchanged between modems over a phone line.

SDLT (Super DLT) An enhanced version of the DLT tape standard that supports faster data transfer and native/2:1 compressed capacities up to 300/600GB.

SDRAM (synchronous DRAM) RAM that runs at the same speed as the main system bus.

SEC (single edge contact) An Intel processor packaging design in which the processor and optional L2 cache chips are mounted on a small circuit board (much like an oversized memory SIMM), which might be sealed in a metal and plastic cartridge. The cartridge is then plugged in to the motherboard through an edge connector called Slot 1 or Slot 2, which looks similar to an adapter card slot. Several variations on the SEC cartridge form factor exist: The single edge contact cartridge (SECC) has a cover and a thermal plate; the single edge contact cartridge 2 (SECC2) has a cover but no thermal plate; and the single edge processor package (SEPP, which is used only with Celeron processors) has no cover or thermal plate. In implementations with no thermal plate, the heatsink is attached directly to the processor package or die.

SECAM (Sequential Couleur A Mémoire) "Sequential color with memory," the French color TV system, also adopted in Russia. The basis of operation is the sequential recording of primary colors in alternate lines. The image format is 4:3, 625 lines, 50Hz, and 6MHz video bandwidth, with a total 8MHz of video channel width.

SECC (single edge contact cartridge) See *SEC*.

SECC2 (single edge contact cartridge 2) See *SEC*.

sector A section of one track defined with identification markings and an identification number. Most sectors hold 512 bytes of data.

security software Utility software that uses a system of passwords and other devices to restrict an individual's access to subdirectories and files.

seek time The amount of time required for a disk drive to move the heads across one third of the total number of cylinders. The seek time represents the average time it takes to move the heads from one cylinder to another randomly selected cylinder. Seek time is a part of the average access time for a drive.

self-extracting file   An archive file that contains its own extraction program. You open such a file in a file manager, such as Windows Explorer, to uncompress the files it contains. Because all types of files, including trojans, can be distributed as .exe files (the extension also used by self-extracting files), you should consider using a program such as WinZip to examine the contents of an .exe file before you open it.

semiconductor   A substance, such as germanium or silicon, whose conductivity is poor at low temperatures but is improved by minute additions of certain substances or by the application of heat, light, or voltage. Depending on the temperature and pressure, a semiconductor can control a flow of electricity. Semiconductors are the basis of modern electronic-circuit technology.

SEPP (single edge processor package)   See *SEC*.

sequencer   A software program that controls MIDI file messages and keeps track of music timing. Because MIDI files store note instructions instead of actual sounds, a sequencer is needed to play, record, and edit MIDI sounds. Sequencer programs enable recording and playback of MIDI files by storing the instrument, note pitch (frequency), duration (in real-time) that each note is held, and loudness (amplitude) of each musical or sound-effect note.

sequential file   A file in which varying-length data elements are recorded end-to-end, with delimiting characters placed between the elements. To find a particular element, you must read the whole file up to that element.

serial   The transfer of data characters one bit at a time, sequentially, using a single electrical path.

serial mouse   A mouse designed to connect to a computer's serial port.

serial port   An I/O connector used to connect to serial devices. See also *RS-232*.

server   A computer in a network that enables resources such as files and printers to be shared by multiple users.

server room   A room used by operational servers and support hardware such as external storage and backup devices and management consoles. A server room may also contain a wiring closet.

ServerWorks   A major developer of server chipsets for use with Pentium III Xeon and Xeon/Xeon MP processors. Now owned by Broadcom.

servo   The mechanism in a drive that enables the head positioner to adjust continuously so that it is precisely placed above a given cylinder in the drive.

servo data   Magnetic markings written on disk platters to guide the read/write heads in drives that use voice-coil actuators.

session (single or multisession)   A term used in CD-ROM recording to describe a recording event. In a single session, data is recorded on a CD-ROM, and an index is created. If additional space is left on the disc, another session can be used to record additional files along with another index. Some older CD-ROM drives do not expect additional recording sessions and therefore are incapable of reading the additional session data on the disc. The advent of Kodak's Photo CD propelled the desire for multisession CD-ROM XA drives.

Session Layer   In the OSI reference model, the layer that is responsible for establishing and maintaining communications channels. See also *OSI model*.

settling time   The time required for read/write heads to stop vibrating after they have been moved to a new track.

shadow mask   A thin screen full of holes that adheres to the inside of a color CRT. The electron beam is aimed through the holes in the mask onto the phosphor dots. See also *aperture grille*.

shadow RAM   A copy of a system's slower-access ROM BIOS placed in faster-access RAM, usually during the startup or boot procedure. This setup enables the system to access BIOS code without the penalty of additional wait states required by the slower ROM chips. Also called shadow ROM or ROM shadowing.

shell   The generic name for any user interface software. COMMAND.COM is the standard shell for DOS; 32-bit Windows uses Windows Explorer as a graphical shell and either COMMAND.COM (Windows 9x/Me) or CMD.EXE (Windows NT/2000/XP) as the command-line shell.

shock rating   A rating (usually expressed in G force units) of how much shock a disk drive can sustain without damage. Usually two specifications exist for a drive: powered on and powered off.

shunt   See *jumper block*.

silicon   The base material for computer chips. The element silicon (symbol Si) is contained in the majority of rock and sand on earth and is the second most abundant element on the planet, next to oxygen.

SIMD (single instruction multiple data)   A term used to describe the MMX and SSE instructions added to the Intel processors. These instructions can process matrixes consisting of multiple data elements with only a single instruction, enabling more efficient processing of graphics and sound data.

SIMM (single inline memory module)   An array of memory chips on a small PC board with a single row of I/O contacts. SIMMs commonly have 30 or 72 connectors.

single-ended   An electrical signaling method in which a single line is referenced by a ground path common to other signals. In a single-ended bus intended for moderately long distances, commonly one ground line exists between groups of signal lines to provide some resistance to signal crosstalk. Single-ended signals require only one driver or receiver pin per signal, plus one ground pin per group of signals. Single-ended signals are vulnerable to common mode noise and crosstalk but are much less expensive than differential signaling methods.

SIP (single inline package)   A DIP-like package with only one row of leads.

skinny dip   Twenty-four– and 28–position DIP devices with .300-inch row-to-row centerlines.

sleep   See *suspend.*

SLIP (Serial Line Internet Protocol)   An Internet protocol that is used to run IP over serial lines, such as telephone circuits. IP enables a packet to traverse multiple networks on the way to its final destination. SLIP has largely been replaced by PPP. See also *PPP.*

slot   A physical connector on a motherboard to hold an expansion card, a SIMM or a DIMM, or a processor card in place and make contact with the electrical connections.

Slot 1   A motherboard connector designed by Intel to accept its SEC cartridge processor design used by the Pentium II and early Celeron and Pentium III processors.

Slot 2   A motherboard connector for Pentium II and Pentium III Xeon processors intended mainly for file server applications. Slot 2 systems support up to four-way symmetric multiprocessing.

SMART (Self-Monitoring Analysis and Reporting Technology)   An industry standard for advance reporting of imminent hard drive failure. When this feature is enabled in the BIOS and a SMART-compliant hard drive is installed, detected problems can be reported to the computer. This enables the user to replace a drive before it fails. Programs such as Norton System Works and Norton Utilities are compatible with SMART status messages.

SMBIOS (system management basic input/output system)   A BIOS that incorporates system management functions and reporting compatibility with the DMI.

SMM (System Management Mode)   Circuitry integrated into Intel processors that operates independently to control the processor's power use, based on its activity level. It enables the user to specify time intervals after which the CPU will be powered down partially or fully and also supports the suspend/resume feature that enables instant power-on and power-off.

SMPTE (Society of Motion Picture and Television Engineers) time code   An 80-bit standardized edit time code adopted by SMPTE. The SMPTE time code is a standard used to identify individual video frames in the video-editing process. SMPTE time code controls such functions as play, record, rewind, and forward of video tapes. SMPTE time code displays video in terms of hours, minutes, seconds, and frames for accurate video editing.

SNA (Systems Network Architecture)   A proprietary IBM network architecture that defined common user access, programming interface, and communications support standards. SNA is now part of IBM's Open Blueprint.

snow   A flurry of bright dots that can appear anywhere onscreen on a monitor.

SO-J (small outline J-lead)   A small DIP package with J-shaped leads for surface mounting or socketing.

socket   A receptacle, usually on a motherboard, although sometimes also found on expansion cards, into which processors or chips can be plugged.

Socket 1–8   The Intel specifications for eight different sockets to accept various Intel processors in the 486, Pentium, and Pentium Pro families.

Socket 370   A 370-pin socket used by socketed versions of the Celeron and Pentium III and the VIA C3 processors.

Socket 423   The socket used by the initial versions of the Pentium 4.

Socket 462 See *Socket A.*

Socket 478 A 478-pin socket used by the Northwood versions of the Pentium 4.

Socket 603 A 603-pin socket used by Intel Xeon processors based on the Pentium 4 design.

Socket 604 A 604-pin socket used by Intel Xeon processors based on the Pentium 4 design. It is backward compatible with Socket 603 processors.

Socket 754 A 754-pin socket used by the AMD Athlon 64 and some versions of the Sempron.

Socket 775 A 775-land socket used by the latest Intel Pentium 4 processors, as well as the Pentium 4 Extreme Edition, Pentium D, and Pentium Extreme Edition. Also known as Socket T.

Socket 939 A 939-pin socket used by recent versions of the Athlon 64 FX and Athlon 64 and all Athlon 64 X2 processors.

Socket 940 A 940-pin socket used by the AMD Opteron processor and early versions of the Athlon 64 FX processor.

Socket A A 462-pin socket used by socketed versions of the AMD Athlon, all AMD Athlon MP, Athlon XP, Duron, and most versions of the AMD Sempron. Also called Socket 462.

Socket T See *Socket 775.*

SODIMM (small outline dual inline memory module) An industry-standard 144-pin memory module designed for use primarily in laptop and portable computers.

soft error An error in reading or writing data that occurs sporadically, usually because of a transient problem, such as a power fluctuation.

software A series of instructions loaded in a computer's memory that instructs the computer on how to accomplish a problem or task.

Solaris Sun Microsystems's operating system for its SPARC and x86-based servers and workstations. Solaris is based on UNIX.

sound card An adapter card with sound-generating capabilities.

South Bridge The Intel term for the lower-speed component in the chipset that has always been a single individual chip. It has been replaced in the 8xx-series chipsets by the ICH. The South Bridge connects to the 33MHz PCI bus and contains the IDE interface ports and the interface to the 8MHz ISA bus (when present). It also typically contains the USB interface and even the CMOS RAM and real-time clock functions. The South Bridge

contains all the components that make up the ISA bus, including the interrupt and DMA controllers. See also *chipset, ICH, MCH,* and *North Bridge.*

SPARC (Scalable Processor Architecture) Sun Microsystems's 32-bit and 64-bit RISC processor architecture for workstations and servers. See also *RISC.*

SPI (SCSI parallel interface) An alternative name for common SCSI standards. See also *SCSI.*

spindle The central post on which a disk drive's platters are mounted.

spindle count In notebook and laptop computers with interchangeable drives, the number of drives that can be installed and used at the same time.

splitter A device used in DSL and cable modem service to separate Internet signals from those used by the existing telephone (DSL) or cable TV service.

SRAM (static random access memory) A form of high-speed memory. SRAM chips do not require a refresh cycle, as do DRAM chips, and they can be made to operate at very high access speeds. SRAM chips are very expensive because they normally require six transistors per bit. This also makes the chips larger than conventional DRAM chips. SRAM is volatile, meaning it will lose data with no power. SRAMs are often used for cache memory.

SSE (streaming SIMD extensions) The name given by Intel to the 70 new MMX-type instructions added to the Pentium III processor when it was introduced. See also *MMX* and *SIMD.*

SSI (Server System Infrastructure) A series of power supply, motherboard, and chassis standards developed by Intel for servers.

ST-506/412 A hard disk interface invented by Seagate Technology and introduced in 1980 with the ST-506 5MB hard drive. IDE drives emulate this disk interface.

stack An area of memory storage for temporary values that normally are read in the reverse order from which they are written. Also called LIFO.

stackable hub or switch A hub or switch that can be connected to another hub or switch to increase its capacity. The uplink port on the existing hub or switch is used to connect the new hub or switch.

stair-stepping A jagged raster representation of diagonals or curves. It is corrected via antialiasing.

standby   An optional operating state of minimal power reduction with the shortest recovery time.

standby UPS (uninterruptible power supply)   A UPS that quickly switches into operation during a power outage.

standoffs   In a motherboard and case design, small nonconductive spacers (usually plastic or nylon) used to keep the underside of the motherboard from contacting the metallic case, to prevent short-circuits of the motherboard.

start/stop bits   The signaling bits attached to a character before and after the character is transmitted during asynchronous transmission.

starting cluster   The number of the first cluster occupied by a file. It is listed in the directory entry of every file.

stepper motor actuator   An assembly that moves disk drive read/write heads across platters by a sequence of small partial turns of a stepper motor. Once common on low-cost hard disk drives of 40MB or less, stepper motor actuators are now confined to floppy disk drives.

stepping   The code used to identify the revision of a processor. New masks are introduced to build each successive stepping, incorporating any changes necessary to fix known bugs in prior steppings.

storage   A device or medium on or in which data can be entered or held and retrieved at a later time. Synonymous with memory.

STP (shielded twisted-pair)   UTP network cabling with a metal sheath or braid around it to reduce interference, usually used in Token-Ring networks.

streaming   In tape backup, a condition in which data is transferred from the hard disk as quickly as the tape drive can record the data so the drive does not start and stop or waste tape.

string   A sequence of characters.

subdirectory   A directory listed in another directory. Subdirectories themselves exist as files.

subroutine   A segment of a program that can be executed by a single call. Also called a program module.

superscalar execution   The capability of a processor to execute more than one instruction at a time.

surface mount   Chip carriers and sockets designed to mount to the surface of a PC board.

surge protector   A device in the power line that feeds the computer and provides protection against voltage spikes and other transients.

suspend   Refers to a level of power management in which substantial power reduction is achieved by the display or other components. The components can have a longer recovery time from this state than from the standby state.

SVGA (Super VGA)   A video adapter or monitor capable of 800×600 resolution.

SWEDAC (Swedish Board for Technical Accreditation)   A regulatory agency establishing standards such as MPR1 and MPR2, which specify maximum values for both alternating electric fields and magnetic fields and provide monitor manufacturers with guidelines in creating low-emission monitors.

switch   Also called a switching hub, a type of hub that reads the destination address of each packet and then forwards the packet to only the correct port, minimizing traffic on other parts of the network. Unlike a regular hub, which wastes network bandwidth by copying packets to all ports, a switch forwards packets to only their intended recipients, immediately reducing network traffic jams and improving overall efficiency for the entire network. Many switches also support full-duplex service, effectively doubling the speed of full-duplex network cards attached to the switch. See also *hub*.

SXGA (Super XGA)   A video adapter or monitor capable of 1280×1024 or greater resolution.

synchronous communication   A form of communication in which blocks of data are sent at strictly timed intervals. Because the timing is uniform, no start or stop bits are required. Some mainframes support only asynchronous communication unless a synchronous adapter and appropriate software have been installed. See also *asynchronous communication*.

system board   See *motherboard*.

system crash   A situation in which a computer freezes up and refuses to proceed without rebooting. Usually caused by faulty software, a system crash is unlike a hard disk crash because no permanent physical damage occurs.

system files   Files with the system attribute. They are usually the hidden files that are used to boot the operating system. The MS-DOS and Windows 9x system files include IO.SYS and MSDOS.SYS; the IBM DOS system files are IBMBIO.COM and IBMDOS.COM.

tape drive   A data storage drive that uses tape as the storage medium.

tape library   An array of tape drives that can be partitioned into multiple logical libraries. Tape libraries incorporate autoloaders. See also *autoloader.*

target   A device attached to a SCSI bus that receives and processes commands sent from another device (the initiator) on the SCSI bus. A SCSI hard disk is an example of a target.

T13 Technical Committee   The committee that is responsible for developing ATA and SATA standards. See www.t13.org.

TCM (Trellis-coded modulation)   An error-detection and correction technique employed by high-speed modems to enable higher-speed transmissions that are more resistant to line impairments.

TCO   The Swedish Confederation of Professional Employees, which has set stringent standards for devices that emit radiation. See also *MPR.*

TCO (total cost of ownership)   The cost of using a server or other hardware, such as a computer or network. It includes the cost of the hardware, software, and upgrades, as well as the cost of the in-house staff and consultants who provide training and technical support.

TCP (tape carrier package)   A method of packaging processors for use in portable systems that reduces the size, power consumed, and heat generated by the chip. A processor in the TCP form factor is essentially a raw die encased in an oversized piece of polyamide film. The film is laminated with copper foil that is etched to form the leads that will connect the processor to the motherboard.

TCP port number   A logical port number used by TCP to communicate between computers—for example, web browsing (http://) uses TCP port 80. POP3 email uses TCP port 110. Some firewalls require you to manually configure open TCP port numbers to allow certain processes and programs to work.

TCP/IP (Transmission Control Protocol/Internet Protocol)   A set of protocols developed by the U.S. Department of Defense to link dissimilar computers across many types of networks. This is the primary protocol used by the Internet.

TEB (Thin Electronics Bay)   An SSI-developed standard for rack-mounted servers.

temporary backup   A second copy of a work file, usually having the extension .BAK. It is created by application software so you easily can return to a previous version of your work.

temporary file   A file temporarily (and usually invisibly) created by a program for its own use.

tera-   A prefix indicating one trillion (1,000,000,000,000) of some unit. Abbreviated t or T. A binary tera (now called a tebi) is 1,099,511,627,776.

terabyte (TB)   A unit of information storage equal to 1,000,000,000 bytes.

terminal   A device whose keyboard and display are used for sending and receiving data over a communications link. It differs from a microcomputer in that it has no internal processing capabilities. It is used to enter data into or retrieve processed data from a system or network.

terminal mode   An operational mode required for microcomputers to transmit data. In terminal mode, the computer acts as though it were a standard terminal, such as a teletypewriter, rather than a data processor. Keyboard entries go directly to the modem, whether the entry is a modem command or data to be transmitted over phone lines. Received data is output directly to the screen. The more popular communications software products control terminal mode and enable more complex operations, including file transmission and saving of received files.

terminator   Hardware or circuits that must be attached to or enabled at both ends of an electrical bus. A terminator functions to prevent the reflection or echoing of signals that reach the ends of the bus and to ensure that the correct impedance load is placed on the driver circuits on the bus. They are most commonly used with the SCSI bus and Thin Ethernet.

TFT (thin film transistor)   The highest-quality and brightest LCD color display type. TFT is a method for packaging one to four transistors per pixel within a flexible material that is the same size and shape as the LCD display, which enables the transistors for each pixel to lie directly behind the liquid crystal cells they control.

thick Ethernet   See *10BASE-5.*

thin Ethernet   See *10BASE-2.*

thin-film media   Hard disk platters that have a thin film (usually three-millionths of an inch) of medium deposited on the aluminum substrate through a sputtering or plating process.

Thinnet   See *10BASE-2*.

through-hole   Chip carriers and sockets equipped with leads that extend through holes in a PC board.

throughput   The amount of user data transmitted per second without the overhead of protocol information, such as start and stop bits or frame headers and trailers.

thumb drive   See *keychain drive*.

TIA (Telecommunications Industry Association)   A trade group that develops network and telecom standards. See www.tiaonline.org for more information.

TIFF (tagged image file format)   A way of storing and exchanging digital image data, developed by Aldus Corporation, Microsoft Corporation, and major scanner vendors to help link scanned images with the popular desktop publishing applications. TIFF supports three main types of image data: black-and-white data, halftones or dithered data, and grayscale data. Compressed TIFF files are stored using lossless compression.

time code   A frame-by-frame address code time reference recorded on the spare track of a videotape or inserted in the vertical blanking interval. The time code is an eight-digit number that encodes time in hours, minutes, seconds, and video frames.

Token-Ring   A type of LAN in which the workstations relay a packet of data called a token in a logical ring configuration. When a station wants to transmit, it takes possession of the token, attaches its data, and then frees the token after the data has made a complete circuit of the electrical ring. It transmits at speeds of 16Mbps. Because of the token-passing scheme, access to the network is controlled, unlike with the slower 10BASE-X Ethernet system, in which collisions of data can occur, which wastes time. A Token-Ring network uses STP wiring, which is cheaper than the coaxial cable used by 10BASE-2 and 10BASE-5 Ethernet and ARCnet.

toner   Ultrafine, colored, plastic powder used in laser printers, LED printers, and photocopiers to produce the image on paper.

tower   A personal computer that normally sits on the floor and is mounted vertically rather than horizontally.

TPI (tracks per inch)   A measurement of magnetic track density. Standard 5.25-inch 360KB floppy disks have a density of 48TPI, and 1.2MB disks have a 96TPI density. All 3.5-inch disks have a 135.4667TPI density, and hard disks can have densities greater than 3,000TPI.

track   One of the many concentric circles that hold data on a disk surface. A track consists of a single line of magnetic flux changes and is divided into some number of 512-byte sectors.

track density   A measure of how many tracks are recorded in 1 inch of space, measured radially from the center of a disk. Track density is expressed as TPI. Sometimes also called radial density.

track-to-track seek time   The time required for read/write heads to move between adjacent tracks.

transistor   A semiconductor device invented in 1947 at Bell Labs (released in 1948) that is used to amplify a signal or open and close a circuit. In digital computers, it functions as an electronic switch. It is reduced to microscopic size in modern digital ICs, which contain 100 million or more individual transistors.

Transport Layer   In the OSI reference model, the layer that controls the sequencing of the message components and regulates inbound traffic flow when more than one packet is in process at any time, such as when a large file must be split into multiple packets for transmission. See also *OSI model*.

transportable computer   A computer system larger than a portable system and similar in size and shape to a portable sewing machine. Most transportables conform to a design similar to the original Compaq portable, with a built-in CRT display. These systems are characteristically very heavy and run only on AC power. Because of advances primarily in LCD and plasma-display technology, these systems are obsolete and have largely been replaced by portable and laptop systems.

troubleshooting   The task of determining the cause of a problem.

true-color image   A 24-bit color image in which each pixel is represented by 24 bits of data, allowing for 16.7 million colors. The number of colors possible is based on the number of bits used to represent the color. If 8 bits are used, 256 possible color values (2^8) exist. To obtain 16.7 million colors, each of the primary colors (red, green, and blue) is represented by 8 bits per pixel, which enables 256 possible shades for each of the primary red, green, and blue colors or $256\times256\times256 = 16.7$ million total colors.

TrueType   An Apple/Microsoft-developed scalable font technology designed to provide a high-performance alternative to PostScript Type 1 fonts. TrueType fonts are supported by both Windows and MacOS, but a particular TrueType font must either be made in both MacOS and Windows versions or support the cross-platform OpenType font format to be used on both platforms.

TSR (terminate-and-stay-resident)   A program that remains in memory after being loaded. Because they remain in memory, TSR programs can be reactivated by a predefined keystroke sequence or other operation while another program is active. They are usually called resident programs. TSR programs are often loaded from the AUTOEXEC.BAT file used at startup by DOS and Windows 9x.

TTL (transistor-to-transistor logic)   Digital signals displayed on a monitor that accepts digital input at standardized signal voltage levels.

TWAIN   An imaging standard used to interface scanners and digital cameras to applications such as Photoshop and other image editors. TWAIN enables the user to scan or download pictures without exiting the image-editing program.

TweakUI   An unsupported software utility provided by Microsoft for 32-bit Windows users. TweakUI allows users to change the user interface and adjust Registry settings without manually editing the Registry.

twisted pair   A type of wire in which two small, insulated copper wires are wrapped or twisted around each other to minimize interference from other wires in the cable. Two types of twisted-pair cables are available: UTP and STP. UTP wiring commonly is used in telephone cables and 10BASE-T, 100BASE-TX, and 1000BASE-T networking and provides little protection against interference. STP wiring is used in some networks or any application in which immunity from electrical interference is more important. Twisted-pair wire is much easier to work with than coaxial cable and is cheaper as well.

two-way server   A server with two separate processors. A server running a dual-core processor offers performance close to, but not quite matching, the performance of a two-way server.

typematic   A situation in which the keyboard repeatedly sending a keypress code to the motherboard for a key that is held down. The delay before the code begins to repeat and the speed at which it repeats are user adjustable through MODE commands in DOS or the Windows Control Panel.

U (unit)   A standard unit of vertical measurement for racks and rack-mounted server/network equipment. 1U equals 1.75 inches.

UART (Universal Asynchronous Receiver/Transmitter)   A chip device that controls the RS-232 serial port in a PC-compatible system. Originally developed by National Semiconductor, several UART versions are in PC-compatible systems: The 8250B is used in PC- and XT-class systems, and the 16450 and 16550 series are used in AT-class systems. The 16650 and higher UARTs are used for specialized high-speed serial communication cards.

UDF (Universal Disk Format)   The disk format used by packet-writing software, such as Adaptec DirectCD. See also *Mt. Rainier* and *packet writing*.

UDMA (Ultra DMA)   A protocol for transferring data to an ATA interface hard drive. The UDMA/33 protocol transfers data in burst mode at a rate of 33MBps, and the even faster UDMA/66 protocol transfers at 66MBps. UDMA/66 also requires the use of a special 80-conductor cable for signal integrity. This cable is also recommended for UDMA/33 and is backward compatible with standard ATA/IDE cables. The fastest UDMA modes are UDMA/100 (supported by most recent chipsets) and UDMA/133 (introduced by Maxtor in 2001). Also known as Ultra ATA.

ULSI (ultra-large-scale integration)   See *IC*.

UltraXGA (UXGA)   A screen resolution of 1,600×1,200.

Ultrium   The high-capacity implementation of the LTO standard. LTO-3 Ultrium is the highest-capacity version currently available, with native/2:1 compressed capacity of 400/800GB.

UMA (upper memory area)   The 384KB of memory between 640KB and 1MB. See also *UMB*.

UMB (upper memory block)   A block of unused memory in the UMA, which is the 384KB region between 640KB and 1MB of memory space in the PC. BIOS chips and memory buffers on add-on cards must be configured to use empty areas of the UMB; otherwise, they will not work. See also *UMA*.

unformatted capacity The total number of bytes of data that can fit on a disk. The formatted capacity is lower than the unformatted capacity because space is lost defining the boundaries between sectors. For example, some vendors have referred to the high-density 1.44MB floppy disk as a 2.0MB disk (2.0MB is the unformatted capacity). However, because most media is preformatted today, this issue is fading away.

Unicode A worldwide standard for displaying, interchanging, and processing all types of language texts, including both those based on letters (such as Western European languages) and pictographs (such as Chinese, Japanese, and Korean).

UNIX An operating system originally developed at Bell Labs and now used in various implementations by most RISC-based servers. Linux is based on UNIX. See also *Linux*.

unzipping The process of extracting one or more files from a PKZIP or WinZip-compatible archive file.

UPC (universal product code) A 10-digit computer-readable bar code used in labeling retail products. The code in the form of vertical bars includes a five-digit manufacturer identification number and a five-digit product code number.

update To modify information already contained in a file or program with current information.

UPS (uninterruptible power supply) A device that supplies power to a computer from batteries so power will not stop even momentarily during a power outage. The batteries are recharged constantly from a wall socket.

URL (uniform resource locator) A name used to identify a particular site or file on the World Wide Web. URLs combine information about the protocol being used, the address of the site where the resource is located, the subdirectory location at the site, and the name of the particular file (or page) in question.

USB (Universal Serial Bus) A high-speed port standard that has largely replaced serial, parallel, and PS/2 ports on servers and PCs. USB version 1.1 is a 12Mbps (1.5MBps) interface over a simple four-wire connection. The bus supports up to 127 devices and uses a tiered star topology built on expansion hubs that can reside in the PC, any USB peripheral, or even standalone hub boxes. USB 2.0, also called High-Speed USB, runs at 480Mbps and handles multiple devices better than USB 1.1.

utility A program that carries out routine procedures to make computer use easier.

UTP (unshielded twisted pair) A type of wire often used indoors to connect telephones or computer devices. It comes with two or four wires, twisted inside a flexible plastic sheath or conduit, and uses modular plugs and phone jacks.

V.21 An ITU standard for modem communications at 300bps. Modems made in the United States or Canada follow the Bell 103 standard but can be set to answer V.21 calls from overseas. The actual transmission rate is 300 baud and employs frequency shift keying (FSK) modulation, which encodes a single bit per baud.

V.22 An ITU standard for modem communications at 1,200bps, with an optional fallback to 600bps. V.22 is partially compatible with the Bell 212A standard observed in the United States and Canada. The actual transmission rate is 600 baud, using differential-phase shift keying (DPSK) to encode as much as 2 bits per baud.

V.22bis An ITU standard for modem communications at 2,400bps. It includes an automatic link-negotiation fallback to 1,200bps and compatibility with Bell 212A/V.22 modems. The actual transmission rate is 600 baud, using QAM to encode as much as 4 bits per baud.

V.23 An ITU standard for modem communications at 1,200bps or 600bps, with a 75bps back channel. It is used in the United Kingdom for some videotext systems.

V.25 An ITU standard for modem communications that specifies an answer tone different from the Bell answer tone used in the United States and Canada. Most intelligent modems can be set with an ATB0 command so that they use the V.25 2,100Hz tone when answering overseas calls.

V.32 An ITU standard for modem communications at 9,600bps and 4,800bps. V.32 modems fall back to 4,800bps when line quality is impaired and fall forward again to 9,600bps when line quality improves. The actual transmission rate is 2,400 baud using QAM and optional TCM to encode as much as 4 data bits per baud.

V.32bis An ITU standard that extends the standard V.32 connection range and supports 4,800bps; 7,200bps; 9,600bps; 12,000bps; and 14,400bps transmission rates. V.32bis modems fall back to the next lower speed when line quality is impaired, fall back further as necessary, and fall forward to the next higher speed when line quality improves. The actual transmission rate is 2,400 baud using QAM and TCM to encode as much as 6 data bits per baud.

V.32terbo A proprietary standard proposed by several modem manufacturers that will be cheaper to implement than the standard V.32 fast protocol but that will support transmission speeds of up to only 18,800bps. Because it is not an industry standard, it is not likely to have widespread industry support.

V.34 An ITU standard that extends the standard V.32bis connection range, supporting 28,800bps transmission rates as well as all the functions and rates of V.32bis. It was called V.32fast or V.fast while under development.

V.34+ An ITU standard that extends the standard V.34 connection range, supporting 33,600bps transmission rates as well as all the functions and rates of V.34.

V.42 An ITU standard for modem communications that defines a two-stage process of detection and negotiation for LAPM error control. Also supports MNP error-control protocol, Levels 1–4.

V.42bis An extension of CCITT V.42 that defines a specific data-compression scheme for use with V.42 and MNP error control.

V.44 The ITU-T designation for a faster data-compression scheme than V.42bis. V.44 can compress data up to 6:1. V.44 is included on most V.92-compliant modems. See also *V.92*.

V.90 The ITU-T designation for defining the standard for 56Kbps communication. It supersedes the proprietary X2 schemes from U.S. Robotics (3Com) and K56flex from Rockwell.

V.92 The ITU-T designation for an improved version of the V.90 protocol. V.92 allows faster uploading (up to 48Kbps), faster connections, and optional modem-on-hold (enabling you to take calls while online). Most V.92 modems also support V.44 compression. See also *V.44*.

V-Link A VIA Technologies high-speed (266MBps) bus between the North Bridge and South Bridge chips in VIA chipsets, such as the P4X266 (for Pentium 4) and KT266/266A (for Athlon/Duron). V-Link is twice as fast as the PCI bus and provides a dedicated pathway for data transfer.

vaccine A type of program used to locate and eradicate virus code from infected programs or systems.

vacuum tube A device used to amplify or control electronic signals, it contains two major components: a cathode (a filament used to generate electrons) and an anode (a plate that captures electron current after it flows through one or more grids). Largely replaced by transistors and ICs in most small electronics applications, vacuum tubes in the form of CRTs are still used to make conventional monitors. The Aopen AX4B-533 Tube motherboard uses vacuum tubes for higher-quality integrated sound. See also *CRT*.

VBI (vertical blanking interval) The top and bottom lines in the video field, in which frame numbers, picture stops, chapter stops, white flags, closed captions, and more can be encoded. These lines do not appear on the display screen but maintain image stability and enhance image access.

VCPI (virtual control program interface) A 386 and later processor memory management standard created by Phar Lap software in conjunction with other software developers. VCPI provides an interface between applications using DOS extenders and 386 memory managers.

vertex The corner of a triangle in 3D graphics. The plural of vertex is vertices. See also *vertex shader*.

vertex shader A graphics processing function built in to recent 3D graphics chips that manipulates vertices by adding color, shading, and texture effects. Recent GPUs such as the NVIDIA GeForce 3 and GeForce Ti and the ATI Radeon series incorporate vertex shaders. See also *GPU*, *hardware shader*, and *pixel shader*.

vertical scan frequency The rate at which the electron gun in a monitor scans or refreshes the entire screen each second.

VESA (Video Electronics Standards Association) An association founded in the late 1980s by NEC Home Electronics and eight other leading video board manufacturers, with the main goal to standardize the electrical, timing, and programming issues surrounding 800×600 resolution video displays, commonly known as SVGA. VESA has also developed the VL-Bus standard for connecting high-speed adapters directly to the local processor bus. The most recent VESA standards involve digital flat-panel displays and display identification.

VFAT (virtual file allocation table)   A file system used in Windows for Workgroups and Windows 9x. VFAT provides 32-bit protected-mode access for file manipulation and supports long filenames of up to 255 characters in Windows 95 and later. VFAT can also read disks prepared with the standard DOS 16-bit FAT. VFAT was called 32-bit file access in Windows for Workgroups. VFAT is not the same as FAT32.

VGA (video graphics array)   A type of PC video display circuit (and adapter) first introduced by IBM in 1987 that supports text and graphics. Text is supported at a maximum resolution of 80×25 characters in 16 colors, with a character box of 9×16 pixels. Graphics are supported at a maximum resolution of 320×200 pixels in 256 (from a palette of 262,144) colors or 640×480 pixels in 16 colors. The VGA outputs an analog signal with a horizontal scanning frequency of 31.5KHz and supports analog color or analog monochrome displays. VGA also refers generically to any adapter or display capable of 640×480 resolution.

VHS (Video Home System)   A popular consumer videotape format developed by Matsushita and JVC.

VIA Technologies   A popular vendor of chipsets for AMD Athlon and Intel Pentium 4–based systems; it's also the maker of the VIA C3 processor.

video   A system of recording and transmission of primarily visual information by translating moving or still images into electrical signals. The term *video* properly refers to only the picture, but as a generic term, *video* usually embraces audio and other signals that are part of a complete program. Video now includes not only broadcast television but many nonbroadcast applications, such as corporate communications, marketing, home entertainment, games, teletext, security, and even the visual display units of computer-based technology.

Video 8   A video format based on the 8mm videotapes popularized by Sony for camcorders. Also known as 8mm video.

video adapter   An expansion card or chipset that is built in to a motherboard and provides the capability to display text and graphics onscreen. If the adapter is part of an expansion card, it also includes the physical connector for the monitor cable. If the chipset is on the motherboard, the video connector is on the motherboard as well.

video graphics array   See *VGA*.

video-on-CD   A full-motion digital video format that uses MPEG video compression and incorporating a variety of VCR-like control capabilities. Also known as video CD. See also *White Book*.

virtual disk   A RAM disk or "phantom disk drive" in which a section of system memory (usually RAM) is set aside to hold data, just as though it were several disk sectors. To DOS, a virtual disk looks and functions like any other "real" drive.

virtual IRQ   A PCI IRQ higher than 15 (the end of the standard IRQ listing). Windows XP, Service Pack 1, and later and Windows 2003 Server machines assign PCI devices that share hardware IRQs virtual IRQ numbers in Device Manager. See *IRQ*.

virtual memory   A technique by which operating systems such as 32-bit Windows versions load more programs and data into memory than they can hold. Parts of the programs and data are kept on disk and are constantly swapped back and forth into system memory. The applications' software programs are unaware of this setup and act as though a large amount of memory is available.

virtual real mode   A mode available in all Intel 80386-compatible processors in which memory addressing is limited to 4,096MB, restricted protection levels can be set to trap software crashes and control the system, and individual real-mode compatible sessions can be set up and maintained separately from one another.

virtual tape library   A disk-based backup device that emulates a tape library. See also *tape library*.

virus   A type of resident program designed to replicate itself. Usually at some later time when the virus is running, it causes an undesirable action to take place.

VL-Bus (VESA Local Bus)   A standard 32-bit expansion slot bus specification used in 486 PCs. The VL-Bus connector was an extension of the ISA slot, and any VL-Bus slot is also an ISA slot. Replaced by the PCI bus, the VL-Bus slot was used on only a very few early Pentium systems.

VLF (very low frequency)   See *ELF*.

VLSI (very-large-scale integration)   See *IC*.

VMM (Virtual Memory Manager)   A facility in Windows enhanced mode that manages the task of swapping data in and out of 386 and later processor virtual real-mode memory space for multiple non-Windows applications running in virtual real mode.

vmstat A command-line Linux program that can be used to view server performance and look for bottlenecks.

voice-coil actuator A device that moves read/write heads across hard disk platters by magnetic interaction between coils of wire and a magnet. It functions somewhat like an audio speaker, from which the name originated. It is the standard actuator type on hard drives.

volatile memory Memory that does not hold data without power. Both DRAM (the main RAM in a computer) and SRAM (used for cache memory) are considered volatile memory. See also *NVRAM*.

voltage reduction technology An Intel processor technology that enables a processor to draw the standard voltage from the motherboard but run the internal processor core at a lower voltage.

voltage regulator A device that smoothes out voltage irregularities in the power fed to the computer.

volume A portion of a disk signified by a single drive specifier. Under DOS v3.3 and later, a single hard disk can be partitioned into several volumes, each with its own logical drive specifier (C:, D:, E:, and so on).

volume label An identifier or name of up to 11 characters that names a disk.

VPN (virtual private network) A private network operated within a public network. To maintain privacy, VPNs use access control and encryption.

VRAM (video random-access memory) Modified DRAMs on video boards that enable simultaneous access by the host system's processor and the processor on the video board. A large amount of information therefore can be transferred quickly between the video board and the system processor. Sometimes also called dual-ported RAM. It has been replaced by SDRAM, SGRAM, and DDR SDRAM on recent high-performance video cards.

VxD (virtual device driver) A special type of Windows driver that runs at the most privileged CPU mode (ring 0) and enables low-level interaction with the hardware and internal Windows functions.

W3C (World Wide Web Consortium) A group that sets standards for HTML, XML, and the Web.

wafer A thin, circular piece of silicon either 8 inches (200mm) or 12 inches (300mm) in diameter from which processors, memory, and other semiconductor electronics are manufactured.

wait states One or more pause cycles added during certain system operations that require the processor to wait until memory or some other system component can respond. Adding wait states enables a high-speed processor to synchronize with lower-cost, slower components. A system that runs with "zero wait states" requires none of these cycles because of the use of faster memory or other components in the system. The widespread use of L1 and L2 memory caches has made the issue of wait states largely irrelevant. See also *L1 cache* and *L2 cache*.

WAN (wide area network) A LAN that extends beyond the boundaries of a single building.

warm boot To reboot a system by means of a software command rather than by turning the power off and back on. See also *cold boot*.

wave table synthesis A method of creating synthetic sound on a sound card that uses actual musical instrument sounds sampled and stored on ROM (or RAM) on the sound card or in system RAM. The sound card then modifies this sample to create any note necessary for that instrument. It produces much better sound quality than FM synthesis.

Web See *WWW*.

webcam An inexpensive (usually less than $100) video camera that plugs into a USB or an IEEE 1394/FireWire port for use with video chat, websites, or email programs.

WEP (Wired Equivalent Privacy) The original security standard used by IEEE 802.11 (Wi-Fi) wireless networks. WEP uses fixed-length encryption keys, making it vulnerable to attacks. WPA is recommended instead of WEP for equipment that supports WPA encryption. See also *WPA*.

Whetstone A benchmark program developed in 1976 and designed to simulate arithmetic-intensive programs used in scientific computing. It remains completely CPU bound and performs no I/O or system calls. It was originally written in ALGOL, although the C and Pascal versions became more popular by the late 1980s. The speed at which a system performs floating-point operations is often measured in units of Whetstones.

White Book   A standard specification developed by Philips and JVC in 1993 for storing MPEG standard video on CDs. It is an extension of the Red Book standard for digital audio, Yellow Book standard for CD-ROM, Green Book standard for CD-I, and Orange Book standard for CD write-once.

Whitney technology   A term referring to a magnetic disk design that usually has oxide or thin film media, thin film read/write heads, low floating-height sliders, and low-mass actuator arms that together allow higher bit densities than the older Winchester technology. Whitney technology was first introduced with the IBM 3370 disk drive, circa 1979.

Wi-Fi (Wireless Fidelity)   The IEEE 802.11–compliant network hardware that also meets the interoperability standards of the Wireless Ethernet Compatibility Alliance (WECA). Despite the presence of Wi-Fi approval for various brands of hardware, achieving the simplest setup and operation is still easier if you purchase Wi-Fi wireless NICs and access points that support the same standard (802.11a, b, or g) from the same vendor. See also *802.11*.

Winchester drive   Any ordinary, nonremovable (or fixed) hard disk drive. The name originates from a particular IBM drive in the 1960s that had 30MB of fixed and 30MB of removable storage. This 30–30 drive matched the caliber figure for a popular series of rifles made by Winchester, so the slang term *Winchester* was applied to any fixed-platter hard disk.

Winchester technology   Any disk with a fixed or nonremovable recording medium. More precisely, the term applies to a ferrite read/write head and slider design with oxide media that was first employed in the IBM 3340 disk drive, circa 1973. Virtually all drives today actually use developments of Whitney technology. See also *Whitney technology*.

Wintel   The common name given to computers running Microsoft Windows using Intel (or compatible) processors. It is a slang term for the PC standard.

wire frames   The most common technique used to construct a 3D object for animation. A wire frame is given coordinates of length, height, and width. Wire frames are then filled with textures, colors, and movement. Transforming a wire frame into a textured object is called rendering.

wiring closet   The central servicing point for the cables in a network. So named because the cables are usually connected to a switch or router inside a closet or similar confined space.

word length   The number of bits in a data character, without parity, start, or stop bits.

workstation   (1) A somewhat vague term for any high-performance, single-user computer that usually has been adapted for specialized graphics, computer-aided design, computer-aided engineering, or scientific applications. (2) A computer connected to a server.

WORM (write-once, read-many [or multiple])   An optical mass-storage device capable of storing many megabytes of information but that can be written to only once on any given area of the disk. A WORM disk typically holds more than 200MB of data. Because a WORM drive can't write over an old version of a file, new copies of files are made and stored on other parts of the disk whenever a file is revised. WORM disks are used to store information when a history of older versions must be maintained. Recording on a WORM disk is performed by a laser writer that burns pits in a thin metallic film (usually tellurium) embedded in the disk. This burning process is called ablation. WORM drives are frequently used for archiving data. WORM drives have been replaced by CD-R drives, which have a capacity of 650MB–700MB but have similar characteristics to WORM drives.

WPA (Wi-Fi Protected Access)   An improved security standard for IEEE 802.11/Wi-Fi wireless networks. WPA supports better data encryption, periodic changes to keys, and optional user authentication. WPA should be used instead of WEP unless some equipment on the network cannot be updated to support WPA. See also *WEP*.

write precompensation   A modification applied to write data by a controller to partially alleviate the problem of bit shift, which causes adjacent 1s written on magnetic media to read as though they were farther apart. When adjacent 1s are sensed by the controller, precompensation is used to write them more closely together on the disk, thus enabling them to be read in the proper bit cell window. Drives with built-in controllers typically handle precompensation automatically. Precompensation is usually required for the inner cylinders of now-obsolete oxide media drives.

write protect   To prevent a removable disk or Sony Memory Stick from being overwritten by means of covering a notch or repositioning a sliding switch, depending on the medium.

WWW (World Wide Web) A graphical information system based on hypertext that enables a user to easily access documents located on the Internet. Also called the Web.

X2 A proprietary modem standard developed by U.S. Robotics (since acquired by 3Com) that enables modems to receive data at up to 56Kbps. X2 has been superseded by the V.90 standard. See also *V.90* and *V.92*.

x86 A generic term referring to Intel and Intel-compatible PC microprocessors. Although the Pentium family processors do not have a numeric designation because of trademark law limitations on trademarking numbers, they are later generations of this family.

XA (Extended Architecture) Refers to the ability of a CD to store audio, video, and computer data on the same disc. Pressed CDs that support this feature are known as CD-ROM XA discs. XA is the basis for the Photo CD, Video CD, and CD-Extra standards.

Xeon Intel's family name for its server processors derived from the Pentium II, Pentium III, and Pentium 4 desktop processors. The Pentium II Xeon and Pentium III Xeon use Slot 2, whereas Xeon (the Pentium 4 version does not have a numerical designation) uses the Socket 603 or Socket 604. All Xeon processors have larger caches and memory addressing schemes than their desktop counterparts. Some Xeon processors support EM64T 64-bit extensions, and a dual-core version of Xeon with EM64T support was introduced in early 2006.

Xeon MP A version of the Intel Xeon made especially for four-way and larger server implementations. Some versions of the Xeon MP support EM64T 64-bit extensions, and a dual-core version with EM64T support was introduced in early 2006.

XGA (extended graphics array) A type of PC video display circuit (and adapter) first introduced by IBM on October 30, 1990, that supports text and graphics. Text is supported at a maximum resolution of 132×60 characters in 16 colors, with a character box of 8×6 pixels. Graphics are supported at a maximum resolution of 1024×768 pixels in 256 (from a palette of 262,144) colors or 640×480 pixels in 65,536 colors. The XGA outputs an analog signal with a horizontal scanning frequency of 31.5KHz or 35.52KHz and supports analog color or analog monochrome displays. XGA is

also used to refer generically to any adapter or display capable of 1024×768 resolution.

XML (Extensible Markup Language) A standard for creating and sharing data and data formats over the Internet and other networks. XML, like HTML, uses markup tags to control the page, but XML tags control both appearance and the uses of the data and can be extended with new tags created by any XML user. See also *W3C*.

XMM (extended memory manager) A driver that controls access to extended memory on 286 and later processor systems. HIMEM.SYS is an example of an XMM that comes with DOS and Windows 9x.

XModem A file transfer protocol, with error checking, developed by Ward Christensen in the mid-1970s and placed in the public domain. It was designed to transfer files between machines running the CP/M operating system and using 300bps or 1,200bps modems. Until the late 1980s, because of its simplicity and public-domain status, XModem remained the most widely used microcomputer file-transfer protocol. In standard XModem, the transmitted blocks are 128 bytes. 1KB-XModem is an extension to XModem that increases the block size to 1,024 bytes. Many newer file transfer protocols that are much faster and more accurate than XModem have been developed, such as YModem and ZModem.

XMS (Extended Memory Specification) A Microsoft standard that provides a way for real-mode applications to access extended memory in a controlled fashion.

XON/XOFF Standard ASCII control characters used to tell an intelligent device to stop or resume transmitting data. In most systems, pressing Ctrl+S sends the XOFF character. Most devices understand Ctrl+Q as XON; others interpret the pressing of any key after Ctrl+S as XON.

Y-connector A Y-shaped splitter cable that divides a source input into two output signals.

Y-mouse A family of adapters from P.I. Engineering that enables a single mouse port to drive two devices. P.I. Engineering also makes the Y-see adapter for dual monitors and the Y-key adapter for dual keyboards.

Yellow Book The standard used by CD-ROM. Multimedia applications most commonly use the Yellow Book standard, which specifies how digital information is to be stored on the CD-ROM and read by a computer. XA is currently an extension of the Yellow Book that enables the combination of various data types (audio and video, for example) onto one track in a CD-ROM. Without XA, a CD-ROM can access only one data type at a time. Many CD-ROM drives are now XA capable. See also *CD-ROM*.

YModem   A file-transfer protocol first released as part of Chuck Forsberg's YAM (yet another modem) program. It is an extension to XModem designed to overcome some of the limitations of the original. YModem enables information about the transmitted file, such as the filename and length, to be sent along with the file data, and it increases the size of a block from 128 bytes to 1,024 bytes. YModem-batch adds the capability to transmit batches, or groups, of files without operator interruption. YModemG is a variation that sends the entire file before waiting for an acknowledgment. If the receiving side detects an error midstream, the transfer is aborted. YModemG is designed for use with modems that have built-in error-correcting capabilities.

Z-buffering   A 3D graphics technique used to determine which objects in a 3D scene will be visible to the user and which will be blocked by other objects. Z-buffering displays only the visible pixels in each object.

zero wait states   See *wait states*.

ZIF (zero insertion force)   Sockets that require no force for the insertion of a chip carrier. This is usually accomplished through movable contacts. ZIF sockets are used by 486, Pentium, Pentium Pro, and other socketed processors (including the latest Pentium 4 and AMD Athlon and Duron models).

ZIP (zigzag inline package)   A DIP package that has all leads on one edge in a zigzag pattern and that mounts in a vertical plane.

Zip drive   An external drive manufactured by Iomega that supports 100MB, 250MB, or 750MB magnetic media on a 3.5-inch removable drive.

zip file   A file created using PKZIP, WinZip, or a compatible archiving program.

zipping   The process of creating a PKZIP or WinZip-compatible archive file. See also *unzipping*.

ZModem   A file transfer protocol commissioned by Telnet and placed in the public domain. Like YModem, it was designed by Chuck Forsberg and developed as an extension to XModem to overcome the inherent latency when using Send/Ack-based protocols, such as XModem and YModem. It is a streaming, sliding-window protocol.

zoned recording   A system that splits the cylinders in a hard drive into groups called zones, with each successive zone having more and more sectors per track, moving out from the inner radius of the disk. (In hard drives, one way to increase the capacity of a hard drive is to format more sectors on the outer cylinders than on the inner ones.) All the cylinders in a particular zone have the same number of sectors per track.

ZV (zoomed video)   A direct video bus connection between the PC Card adapter and a mobile system's VGA controller, enabling high-speed video displays for videoconferencing applications and MPEG decoders.

List of Acronyms and Abbreviations

A

a-Si	hydrogenated amorphous silicon
ABC	Atanasoff-Berry Computer
AC	alternating current
ACL	access control list
ACPI	Advanced Configuration and Power Interface
ACR	advanced communications riser
ADC	analog-to-digital converter
ADF	adapter description files
ADPCM	adaptive differential pulse code modulation
ADR	advanced digital recording
ADSL	asymmetric digital subscriber line
AFC	antiferromagnetically coupled

AGC	automatic gain control
AGP	accelerated graphics port
AHA	Accelerated Hub Architecture
AHRA	Audio Home Recording Act
AIT	advanced intelligent tape
ALDC	advanced lossless data compression
ALi	Acer Laboratories, Inc.
AMD	Advanced Micro Devices
AMI	American Megatrends, Inc.
AMR	anistropic magneto-resistant or Audio/Modem Riser
ANSI	American National Standards Institute
APA	all points addressable
API	application programming interface
APIC	advanced programmable interrupt controller
APM	Advanced Power Management
APS	analog protection system
ARCnet	Attached Resource Computer Network
ARLL	advanced run length limited
ARQ	automatic repeat request
ASCII	American Standard Code for Information Interchange
ASME	American Society of Mechanical Engineers
ASPI	Advanced SCSI Programming Interface
AT	Advanced Technology
ATA	Advanced Technology Attachment
ATAPI	Advanced Technology Attachment Packet Interface
ATF	auto tracking following
ATM	asynchronous transfer mode
ATX	advanced technology extended
AVI	audio video interleave
AWG	American Wire Gauge

B

BASIC	Beginner's All-purpose Symbolic Instruction Code
BBS	bulletin board system
BBUL	bumpless build-up layer
BEDO RAM	burst extended data out RAM
BF	bus frequency

BGA	ball grid array
BiCMOS	bipolar complementary metal-oxide semiconductor
BIOS	basic input/output system
BLER	block error rate
BMP	bitmap
BNC	Bayonet-Neill-Concelman or British-Naval-Connector or Bayonet-Nut-Coupler
BOOTP	bootstrap protocol
bps	bits per second
BRI	basic rate interface
BSOD	blue screen of death
BSRAM	Burst Static RAM
BTB	branch target buffer
BTX	Balanced Technology Extended
BURN-Proof	buffer underrun error-proof

C

CAB	cabinet file
CAI	computer-aided (or assisted) instruction
CAL	computer-aided learning
CAM	Common Access Method
CAM ATA	Common Access Method Advanced Technology Attachment
CAP	carrierless amplitude/phase
CAS	column address strobe
CAT	category
CATV	community access television
CAV	constant angular velocity
CBI	computer-based instruction
CBL	computer-based learning
CBT	computer-based training
CCITT	Comité Consultatif International de Télégraphique et Téléphonique
CCS	common command set
CD	compact disc
CD-DA	compact disc–digital audio
CD+G	compact disc+graphics
CD-I	compact disc–interactive
CD+MIDI	compact disc+musical instrument digital interface
CD-MO	compact disc–magneto-optical

CD-R	compact disc–recordable
CD-ROM	compact disc–read-only memory
CD-ROM XA	compact disc–read-only memory extended architecture
CD-RW	compact disc–rewritable
CD-WO	compact disc–write once
CDMA	code division multiple access
CDSL	consumer DSL
CEB	Compact Electronics Bay
CERN	Conseil Européen pour la Recherche Nucléaire
CF	CompactFlash
CFCs	chlorofluorocarbons
CGA	color graphics adapter
CHAP	Challenge-Handshake Authentication Protocol
CHS	cylinder head sector
CIF	common image format
CIRC	cross-interleave Reed-Solomon code
CISC	complex instruction set computer
CLKMUL	clock multiplier
CLV	constant linear velocity
CMOS	complementary metal-oxide semiconductor
CMYK	cyan, magenta, yellow, black
CNR	Communications and Networking Riser
COBOL	Common Business-Oriented Language
COC	chip on ceramic
codec	coder-decoder
CP/M	Control Program for Microcomputers (originally Control Program/Monitor)
cps	characters per second
CPU	central processing unit
CRC	cyclical redundancy check
CRT	cathode ray tube
CS	cable select or central switch
CSA	Canadian Standards Agency
CSEL	cable select
CSMA/CD	carrier sense multiple access/collision detect
CSS	contact start stop or content scramble system
CTFT	color thin film transistor

D

DAC	digital-to-analog converter
DAE	digital audio extraction
DASD	direct access storage device
DASP	drive action/slave present
DAT	digital audio tape
db	decibel
DBB	dynamic bass boost
DBR	DOS boot record
DC	direct current
DCC	direct cable connection
DCE	data communications equipment
DD	double density
DDE	dynamic data exchange
DDMA	distributed direct memory access
DDoS	distributed denial of service
DDR SDRAM	double data rate synchronous dynamic random-access memory
DDR2 SDRAM	double data rate 2 synchronous dynamic random-access memory
DDS	digital data storage
DDWG	Digital Display Working Group
DFP	digital flat panel
DFT	drive fitness test
DHCP	Dynamic Host Configuration Protocol
DHTML	Dynamic Hypertext Markup Language
DIB	dual independent bus
DIMM	dual inline memory module
DIN	Deutsches Institut für Normung e.V.
DIP	dual inline package
DIVX	Digital Video Express
DLC	Data Link Control
DLL	dynamic link library
DLT	digital linear tape
DMA	direct memory access
DMI	Desktop Management Interface or Direct Media Interface
DMM	digital multimeter

DMT	discrete multitone
DNS	domain name system (or service)
DOCSIS	Data over Cable Service Interface Specification
DoS	denial of service
DOS	Disk Operating System
DPMI	DOS protected mode interface
DPMS	display power-management signaling
DRAM	dynamic random-access memory
DSK	Dvorak simplified keyboard
DSL	digital subscriber line
DSLAM	digital subscriber line access multiplier
DSM	digital storage media
DSP	digital signal processor
DSTN	Double-layer SuperTwist Nematic LCD
DTE	data terminal (or terminating) equipment
DVD	digital versatile (or video) disc
DVD-A	digital versatile (or video) disc–audio
DVD-R	digital versatile (or video) disc–recordable
DVD-R DL	digital versatile (or video) disc–recordable dual-layer
DVD-RW	digital versatile (or video) disc–phase change rewritable
DVI	Digital Video Interactive or Digital Video Interface

E

E2000	Energy 2000
EAX	environmental audio extensions
EBCDIC	Extended Binary Coded Decimal Interchange Code
ECC	error correcting code
ECP	enhanced capabilities port
ED	extra-high density
EDD	enhanced disk drive
EDO RAM	extended data out random-access memory
EEB	Entry-Level Electronics Bay
EEPROM	electronically erasable programmable read-only memory
EFM	eight to fourteen modulation data encoding
EFS	encrypted file system
EGA	enhanced graphics adapter

EIA	Electronic Industries Association
EIDE	Enhanced Integrated Drive Electronics
EISA	Extended Industry Standard Architecture
ELF	extremely low frequency
EMI	electromagnetic interference
EMM	expanded memory manager
EMS	Expanded Memory Specification
ENIAC	Electrical Numerical Integrator and Calculator
e-PCI-X	embedded Peripheral Component Interconnect-X
EPIC	Explicitly Parallel Instruction Computing
EPP	enhanced parallel port
EPROM	erasable programmable read-only memory
ESCD	extended system configuration data
ESD	electrostatic discharge
ESDI	Enhanced Small Device Interface

F

FAP	Fair Access Policy
FAQ	frequently asked questions
FAT	file allocation table
FC-PGA	flip-chip pin grid array
FCC	Federal Communications Commission
FDDI	Fiber Distributed Data Interface
FDIV	floating-point divide
FIC	flex interconnect cable
FIFO	first-in, first-out
FM	frequency modulation
FPM DRAM	fast page mode dynamic random-access memory
FPT	forced perfect termination
FPU	floating-point unit
FSB	front-side bus
FSK	frequency-shift keying
FST	flat square tube
FTP	File Transfer Protocol
FUD	fear, uncertainty, and doubt
FWH	firmware hub

G

GB	gigabyte (1,000,000,000 bytes)
GHz	gigahertz
GiB	gigabinary byte
GIF	Graphics Interchange Format
GMCH	graphics memory controller hub
GMR	giant magnetoresistive
GPA	graphics performance accelerator
GPU	graphics processing unit
GUI	graphical user interface

H

HAN	home area network
HD	high-density
HD-ROM	high-density read-only memory
HDA	head disk assembly
HDD	hard disk drive
HDLC	High-Level Data Link Control
HDTV	high-definition television
HER	hard error rate
HFC	hybrid fiber/coax
HFS	hierarchical file system
HID	human interface device
HLF	high-level formatting
HMA	high memory area
HP	Hewlett-Packard
HPA	host protected area
HPFS	high performance file system
HPT	high-pressure tin
HRTF	head-related transfer function
HST	High-Speed Technology
HT	hyperthreading
HTML	Hypertext Markup Language
HTTP	Hypertext Transfer Protocol
HVD	high-voltage differential
Hz	Hertz

I

I/O	input/output
IC	integrated circuit
ICH	I/O controller hub
iCOMP	Intel Comparative Microprocessor Performance
ICS	Internet Connection Sharing
IDE	Integrated Drive Electronics
IE	Internet Explorer
IEC	International Electrotechnical Commission
IED	ID error detection
IEEE	Institute of Electrical and Electronics Engineers
IMA	Interactive Multimedia Association
IMAPI	image mastering application programming interface
IMB	Inter-Module Bus
IML	initial microcode load
INCITS	InterNational Committee on Information Technology Standards
IOS	input/output supervisor
IP	Internet Protocol
IPv6	Internet Protocol, version 6
IPL	initial program load
IPS	in-plane switching
IPX	Internetwork Packet Exchange
IR	infrared
IrDA	Infrared Data Association
IRQ	interrupt request
ISA	Industry Standard Architecture
iSCSI	Internet SCSI
ISDN	Integrated Services Digital Network
ISO	International Organization for Standardization
ISP	Internet service provider
ITU	International Telecommunication Union

J–K

JEDEC	Joint Electron Devices Engineering Council
JPEG	Joint Photographic Experts Group
Kb	kilobit (1,000 bits)

KB	kilobyte (1,000 bytes)
KHz	kilohertz
Kib	kibibit (1,024 bits)
KiB	kibibyte (1,024 bytes)
KVAR	kilovolt-amperes-reactive
KVM	keyboard, video, mouse
KW/KVA	working power/apparent power

L

L1	Level 1
L2	Level 2
L3	Level 3
LAN	local area network
LAPM	Link-Access Procedure for Modems
LBA	logical block addressing
LCC	leadless chip carrier
LCD	liquid crystal display
LED	light-emitting diode
LGA	land grid array
LIF	low insertion force
LIM	Lotus-Intel-Microsoft
LLF	low-level formatting
LPT	line printer
LSI	large-scale integration
LTO	linear tape-open
LUN	logical unit number
LVD	low-voltage differential
LZW	Lempel Ziv Welch

M

MAC	Media Access Control
MAU	media access unit or media attachment unit
Mb	megabit (1,000,000 bits)
MB	megabyte (1,000,000 bytes)
MBR	master boot record
MC	microcartridge
MCA	MicroChannel Architecture

MCGA	multicolor graphics array
MCH	memory controller hub
MCI	media control interface
MCM	multichip module
MDA	monochrome display adapter
MEB	midlevel electronics bay
MESI	modified exclusive shared invalid
MFM	modified frequency modulation
MFT	master file table
MGA	monochrome graphics adapter
MHz	megahertz
MI/MIC	mode indicate/mode indicate common
Mib	mebibit (1,048,576 bits)
MiB	mebibyte (1,048,576 bytes)
MIC	memory in cassette
MIDI	musical instrument digital interface
MIME	Multipurpose Internet Mail Extensions
MIPS	million instructions per second
MMC	MultiMediaCard
MMDS	Multichannel Multipoint Distribution Service
MMO	mobile module
MMU	memory management unit
MMX	multimedia (or matrix math) extensions
MNP	Microcom Network Protocol
MO	magneto-optical
modem	modulator/demodulator
MOESI	Modified Owned Exclusive Shared Invalid
MOS	metal-oxide semiconductor
MOV	metal-oxide varistor
MP	megapixel
MPC	Multimedia Personal Computer
MPEG	Motion Picture Experts Group
MPS	Multiprocessor Specification
MR	Microid Research
MRH-R	memory repeater hub Rambus dynamic random-access memory–based
MRH-S	memory repeater hub synchronous dynamic random-access memory–based

MS	Microsoft
MS-DOS	Microsoft disk operating system
MSAU	multistation access unit
MTBF	mean time between failures
MTH	memory translator hub
MTTF	mean time to failure
MTTR	mean time to repair
MVA	multidomain vertical alignment

N

NAS	network attached storage
NDP	numeric data processor
NEAT	New Enhanced Advanced Technology
NetBEUI	NetBIOS Extended User Interface
NetBIOS	Network Basic Input/Output System
NIC	network interface card
NiCad	nickel cadmium
NiFe	nickel ferrite
NiMH	nickel metal hydride
NMI	nonmaskable interrupt
NOS	network operating system
NRTC	National Rural Telecommunications Cooperative
NRZ	non-return to zero
NTFS	New Technology File System
NTSC	National Television Standards Committee
NVRAM	nonvolatile RAM

O

OC	optical carrier
OCR	optical character recognition
OD	overdrive
ODI	Open Data-link Interface
OEM	original equipment manufacturer
OLE	object linking and embedding
OLGA	organic land grid array
OS	operating system
OSI	Open Systems Interconnection

OSO	overscan operation
OSTA	Optical Storage Technology Association
OTP	one-time programmable or opposite track path

P

P3	Pentium 3
P4	Pentium 4
P4EE	Pentium 4 Extreme Edition
p-Si	low-temperature polysilicon
PAC	Peripheral Component Interconnect/accelerated graphics port controller or pin array cartridge
PAL	Phase Alternating Line or programmable array logic
PARD	periodic and random deviation
PATA	parallel Advanced Technology Attachment
PB	petabyte (1,000,000,000,000,000 bytes)
PC-DOS	personal computer disk operating system
PCA	power calibration area
PCI	Peripheral Component Interconnect
PCI-X	Peripheral Component Interconnect Extended
PCIe	Peripheral Component Interconnect Express
PCL	Printer Control Language
PCM	pulse code modulation
PCMCIA	Personal Computer Memory Card International Association
PDA	personal digital assistant
PDF	Portable Document Format
PFA	predictive failure analysis
PFC	power factor correction
PGA	pin grid array
PH	Peripheral Component Interconnect controller hub
PI	parity inner
PICMG	Peripheral Component Interconnect Industrial Computers Manufacturers Group
PIF	program information file
PII	Pentium II
PIIX	Peripheral Component Interconnect ISA IDE Xcelerator
PIO	programmed input/output
PLCC	plastic leaded-chip carrier

PLGA	plastic land grid array
PMA	power memory area
PnP	Plug and Play
PO	parity outer
PoP	point of presence
POP3	Post Office Protocol 3
POS	programmable option select or point-of-sale
POST	power-on self-test
POTS	plain old telephone service
PPD	parallel presence detect
PPD file	PostScript Printer Description file
PPGA	plastic pin grid array
PPI	Programmable Peripheral Interface
PPP	Point-to-Point Protocol
PQFP	plastic quad flat pack
PRI	primary rate interface
PRML	Partial-Response Maximum-Likelihood
PROM	programmable read-only memory
PSK	phase-shift keying
PTP	parallel track path

Q

QAM	quadrature amplitude modulation
QDR	quad data rate
QEGA	quantum extended graphics array
QFE	quick fix engineering
QIC	Quarter-Inch Committee
QoS	quality of service

R

RAB	RAID Advisory Board
RAID	redundant array of independent (or inexpensive) disks
RAM	random-access memory
RAMAC	Random Access Method of Accounting and Control
RAMDAC	random-access memory digital-to-analog converter
RBOC	regional Bell operating company
RCA	Radio Corporation of America

RDRAM	Rambus dynamic random-access memory
RF	radio frequency
RFI	radio frequency interference
RGB	red, green, blue
RIAA	Recording Industry Association of America
RIMM	Rambus inline memory module
RISC	reduced instruction set computer
RLL	run-length limited
RMA	return-merchandise authorization
RNG	random number generator
ROM	read-only memory
ROM BIOS	read-only memory basic input/output system
RPC	regional playback control
RPS	redundant power supply
RRIP	Rock Ridge Interchange Protocol
RS	recommended standard
RTC	real-time clock
RTC/NVRAM	real-time clock/nonvolatile memory
RTF	Rich Text Format

S

SACD	super audio compact disc
SAL	soft adjacent layer
SAN	storage area network
SAS	serial attached small computer system interface
SASI	Shugart Associates System Interface
SATA	Serial Advanced Technology Attachment
SCAT	Single Chip Advanced Technology
SCMS	serial copy management system
SCSI	small computer system interface
SD	super density or secure digital
SDLC	synchronous data link control
SDLT	Super DLT
SDRAM	synchronous dynamic random-access memory
SDSL	symmetrical digital subscriber line
SE	single ended

SEC	single edge contact
SEC-DED	single-bit error-correction–double-bit error detection
SECAM	Sequential Couleur A Mémoire
SECC	single edge contact cartridge
SECC2	single edge contact cartridge 2
SEP	single edge processor
SEPP	single edge processor package
SER	soft error rate
SGRAM	synchronous graphics random-access memory
SIMD	single instruction multiple data
SIMM	single inline memory module
SIP	single inline package
SIPP	single inline pin package
SiS	Silicon Integrated Systems
SLIP	Serial Line Internet Protocol
SMART	Self-Monitoring Analysis and Reporting Technology
SMBIOS	system management basic input/output system
SMI	system management interrupt
SMM	System Management Mode
SMPTE	Society of Motion Picture and Television Engineers
SNR	signal-to-noise ratio
SODIMM	small outline dual inline memory module
SOJ	small outline J-lead
SPD	serial presence detect
SPDIF	Sony/Philips Digital Interface
SPGA	staggered pin grid array
SPI	small computer system interface parallel interface
SPS	standby power supply
SPSYNC	spindle synchronization
SRAM	static random-access memory
SSE	Streaming Single Instruction Multiple Data Extensions
SSI	Server System Infrastructure
STP	shielded twisted pair
SVGA	super video graphics array
SWAP	Shared Wireless Access Protocol
SWEDAC	Swedish Board for Technical Accreditation
SXGA	Super Extended Graphics Array

T

TAD	telephone answering device
TAO	track-at-once
TAPI	telephone application programming interface
TCM	Trellis-coded modulation
TCO	total cost of ownership
TCP	tape carrier packaging
TCP/IP	Transmission Control Protocol/Internet Protocol
TDMA	transparent direct memory access or time-division multiple access
TEB	Thin Electronics Bay
TFT	thin film transistor
TIFF	tagged image file format
TIP	trouble in paradise
TLB	translation lookaside buffer
TPI	tracks per inch
TTL	transistor-to-transistor logic or through-the-lens
TSOP	thin small outline package
TSR	terminate-and-stay-resident

U

U	unit (of vertical measurement for racks and rack-mounted hardware)
UART	Universal Asynchronous Receiver/Transmitter
UDF	Universal Disk Format
UDMA	ultra direct memory access
UI	user interface
UL	Underwriters Laboratories
UMA	unified memory architecture or upper memory area
UMB	upper memory block4
UNIVAC	Universal Automatic Computer
UPC	universal product code
UPI	Universal Peripheral Interface
UPnP	Universal Plug and Play
UPS	uninterruptible power supply
URL	uniform resource locator
USB	Universal Serial Bus
USN	update sequence number

UTP	unshielded twisted pair
UXGA	Ultra Extended Graphics Array

V

VAFC	Video Electronics Standards Association Advanced Feature Connector
VBI	vertical blanking interval
VBR	volume boot record
VCPI	virtual control program interface
VESA	Video Electronics Standards Association
VESA VIP	Video Electronics Standards Association Video Interface Port
VFAT	virtual file allocation table
VFC	video feature connector
VGA	video graphics array
VHS	Video Home System
VID	voltage identification
VIS	viewable image size
VL-Bus	Video Electronics Standards Association local bus
VLF	very low frequency
VLSI	very-large-scale integration
VM	virtual machine
VMC	Video Electronics Standards Association Media Channel
VMM	Virtual Memory Manager
VoIP	voice over IP
VPN	virtual private network
VRAM	video random-access memory
VRM	voltage regulator module
VRT	voltage reduction technology
VxD	virtual device driver

W–X

W2K	Windows 2000
W3C	World Wide Web Consortium
WAN	wide area network
WAP	Wireless Application Protocol
WBR	wireless broadband router
WEP	wired equivalent privacy
Wi-Fi	Wireless Fidelity

WORM	write-once, read-many (or multiple)
WPA	Wi-Fi Protected Access
WWW	World Wide Web
XA	Extended Architecture
XGA	extended graphics array
XML	Extensible Markup Language
XMM	extended memory manager
XMS	Extended Memory Specification

Y–Z

Y2K	year 2000
ZBR	zoned-bit recording
ZIF	zero insertion force
ZIP	zigzag inline package
ZV	zoomed video

Vendor List

One of the most frustrating things about supporting servers is finding a specific adapter board, part, driver program, or whatever you need to make a system work. If you are supporting or installing products, you need access to technical support or documentation for products you might not have purchased. Over the years, we have compiled a list of companies whose products are popular or whose products we have found to work exceptionally well. We use these contacts regularly to provide information and components that enable us to support PC and server systems effectively.

Alphabetical Vendor List

Many of the companies listed in this appendix have been mentioned in this book, but others not specifically mentioned have been added here. These companies carry many computer products you will have contact with or that we simply recommend. We have tried to list as many vendors as possible. These vendors are important in day-to-day work with PC and server systems and can supply documentation for your components, provide parts and service, and be used as a source for new equipment and software. This list is alphabetical and as up-to-date as possible, but companies move and go out of business all the time. If you find any information in this list that is no longer accurate, please send Scott Mueller a message at scottmueller@compuserve.com.

Although originally exclusively the domain of computer enthusiasts, today almost all companies use Internet websites to provide a high level of technical support. Through a company-run website, you can receive detailed technical support on that company's products and download product literature and reference materials. Each vendor listing in this appendix includes the company's website and a description of its major product lines. Visiting a company's website is the fastest way to learn how to contact the company, even if you plan to call or email the company.

#1-PC Diagnostics Company (the ESD Division of Windsor Technologies, Inc.)

www.tufftest.com

This company manufactures #1-TuffTEST-Pro, an excellent high-end, service-technician-level, PC diagnostics, and troubleshooting program that can be downloaded from its website. Other diagnostic products available include the #1-TuffTEST automatic PC testing program and the free #1-TuffTEST-Lite.

3Com Corp.

www.3com.com

This company manufactures network switches and NICs for enterprise and small-business customers; Wi-Fi–compliant wireless LAN hardware; networked telephony solutions; and Bluetooth, 10/100 Ethernet, and 56Kbps modem/LAN PC Cards. It also offers IP-based telecommunications infrastructures and service platforms through its wholly owned subsidiary CommWorks Corporation (www.commworks.com).

3D Labs

See *Creative Labs, Inc.*

3Dfx Interactive, Inc.

This former creator of Voodoo-series 3D accelerator chipsets went out of business in late 2001 and no longer provides any technical support. The following websites provide the latest available drivers, including beta and third-party–developed drivers for Windows XP:

www.voodoofiles.com

www.windrivers.com

A.K. Stamping Company, Inc./Globe Manufacturing Sales

www.akstamping.com

This company manufactures assorted PC adapter card brackets, connector shells, Compact PCI, PC Card kits, and board-level shields sold by its sales arm, Globe Manufacturing Sales, Inc. (www.globe-brackets.com).

Aavid Thermalloy LLC

www.aavidthermalloy.com

The first ISO-certified heatsink manufacturer in North, Aavid Thermalloy manufactures a line of excellent CPU and graphics chip heatsink products, including versions with built-in ball-bearing fan modules, as well as cooling products for other electronics products.

ABIT Computer (USA) Corporation

www.abit-usa.com

This company manufactures an excellent line of PC motherboards in ATX form factors for use with Intel and AMD CPUs. It also manufactures multimedia speaker and I/O devices and graphics cards based on ATI Radeon chipsets.

Accurite Technologies, Inc.

www.accurite.com

This company manufactures floppy drive diagnostic products, PC Card (PCMCIA) diagnostic products; compact USB and IEEE 1394 hubs; CompactFlash (CF) adapters; PC Card (PCMCIA), USB, and IEEE 1394-based hard drive subsystems; PC Card (PCMCIA)-based floppy and LS-120 SuperDisk drives, CF and PC Card development products; and ZigBee development and diagnostic products. Its floppy drive diagnostic products include the Accurite Drive Probe and Drive Probe Advanced Edition floppy drive diagnostics programs; HRD, DDD, and AAD industry-standard test disks; and a reference disk for certifying floppy disk testing hardware. Its PC Card (PCMCIA) products include the PC ExtenderCard, the PC ReportCard (a PCMCIA diagnostic card), the HeadstartCard (a PCMCIA developers' kit), the Travel Floppy (a PCMCIA interfaced floppy drive subsystem), the Travel 120 (a SuperDisk LS-120 PC Card interfaced high-capacity floppy drive), and the Travel HD (a 10GB or larger external hard disk available with PC Card, USB, or IEEE 1394 interfaces).

Acer United States

http://us.acer.com

This company is the U.S. arm of one of the top 10 branded worldwide PC vendors. Acer manufactures complete desktop and notebook systems, tablet PCs, servers, and monitors.

For motherboards and components, see *Aopen, Inc.* For scanners, optical drives, keyboards, and projectors, see *BenQ Corporation.*

Acme Electric/Electronics Division

www.acmeelec.com/electronics

This company manufactures custom electronics for OEM suppliers.

Acterna, LLC

www.acterna.com

Acterna is the world's largest provider of test and management solutions for optical, transport, access, and cable networks. It provides test and management products for all major network types, including ATM, FDDI, Fast Ethernet, Gigabit Ethernet, wireless, DSL, and many others.

Adaptec

www.adaptec.com

Adaptec is a leading supplier of high-performance I/O solutions, including a broad array of SCSI: SCSI, Serial ATA and ATA RAID, iSCSI, Serial Attached SCSI, TCP offload, USB 2.0, and IEEE 1394 host adapters, video capture and creation products, and the SnapAppliance line of NAS devices, as well as high-performance storage expansion and software products. Its SCSI host adapters have become a de facto standard and have an enormous amount of third-party support. Its USBXchange and

USB2Xchange allows USB 1.1 and 2.0 ports to attach to external SCSI peripherals. It also acquired Future Domain and DPT (Distributed Process Technology) and supports their products.

For former Adaptec-brand software, such as Easy CD Creator Platinum and others, see *Sonic Solutions*.

Adobe Systems, Inc.

www.adobe.com

This company manufactures (and created) the PostScript language and a variety of graphics software for web, print, animation, and ePaper uses, as well as Type 1 PostScript fonts. It is the publisher of PageMaker, Illustrator, Acrobat, FrameMaker, InDesign, GoLive, PhotoDeluxe, Photoshop, Photoshop Elements, TypeManager and PostScript fonts (for DOS and Macintosh systems), AfterEffects, Premiere, Streamline, and other titles.

Advanced Digital Information Corporation

www.adic.com

This company manufactures high-capacity tape libraries, storage network appliances for SANs, and software for HSM and archiving.

Advanced Personal Systems

www.syschk.com

This company manufactures the excellent SysChk diagnostics program, which provides valuable information about devices installed in a system.

Advisor Media, Inc.

www.advisor.com

This company publishes a wide variety of magazines and journals for programmers and developers. It also sponsors live events and offers Advisor Academy CD-based training courses.

Aladdin Knowledge Systems, Inc.

www.esafe.com

This company is the developer of eSafe antivirus, antispyware, and antispam devices for corporate networks, as well as HASP software licensing devices and eToken authentication and password management.

Alienware Corporation

www.alienware.com

This company is a leading manufacturer of desktop, small-form-factor, and portable computer systems for hard-core gamers (the Area 51 series). It also manufactures systems designed for general users, CAD, digital video editing, and Windows XP Media Center.

ALPS Electric (USA), Inc.

www.alpsusa.com

This company manufactures tactile-feedback keyboard switches, mouse devices, touchpads, LCD displays, printers, Bluetooth modules, and other components for OEM sales.

Altex Electronics, Ltd.

www.altex.com

This company supplies retail and mail-order computer, networking, and electronics parts.

Altiris Americas

www.altiris.com

This company provides support, configuration, asset management, remote control, software distribution, and other services for new computers and for IT organizations.

Amazon.com, Inc.

www.amazon.com

Amazon is an online bookstore and much more. Millions of people in more than 220 countries have made Amazon the leading online shopping site. It has a huge selection of products, including millions of books, CDs, videos, DVDs, toys and games, and electronics.

AMD (Advanced Micro Devices)

www.amd.com

This company manufactures Intel-compatible desktop, server, and mobile CPU chips, including the Sempron, Athlon XP, Athlon 64, and Opteron. AMD also produces motherboard chipsets, embedded processors, flash memory, and connectivity chipsets.

America Online

www.corp.aol.com

This company provides a popular online service that allows access to its own network and the Internet. It is the owner and marketer of CompuServe online service and Netscape products and services. It also owns the ICQ and AOL Instant Messenger Internet messaging products, Digital City portal service, AOL Moviefone movie ticketing service, MapQuest online driving map service, and Winamp MP3 player and online music site. America Online is a division of AOL Time Warner.

American Power Conversion (APC)

www.apc.com

APC manufactures popular lines of power protection, monitoring, and management equipment for workstation and network use.

AMI (American Megatrends, Inc.)

www.ami.com

As a core technology provider, AMI develops and provides superior system-level technologies, including SCSI RAID products, AMIBIOS, motherboards, IDE host adapters, server management solutions, enterprise KVM over IP switches, NAS, and diagnostics utilities, such as AMIDiag for DOS, AMIDiag Suite for Windows, and the PC Defender series.

Andromeda Research Labs

www.arlabs.com

This company manufactures an excellent EPROM and electronic device programmer (EPROM+) that runs from a PC parallel port. The device can program up to 16M UV and Flash EPROMS, plus more. The included software runs under DOS, Windows 3.1, Windows 9x/Me, and Windows 2000/XP on any PC-compatible computer. A low-cost optional BIOS Backup & Repair Kit enables you to make a backup copy of your flash BIOS.

ANSI (American National Standards Institute)

www.ansi.org

The ANSI committees set standards throughout the computer industry. Copies of any ANSI-approved standard can be ordered from the ANSI website.

Antec, Inc.

www.antec.com

This company manufactures a popular line of system enclosures for standard and rack-mounted systems. It also manufactures power supplies with capacities up to 550 watts, cooling, and case customization products.

Anvil Cases

www.anvilcase.com

This company manufactures heavy-duty equipment shipping and transit cases, and it custom-engineers cases to customers' requirements.

Aopen, Inc.

http://usa.aopen.com

This company manufactures a popular line of PCs and components, including motherboards, cases, monitors, power supplies, all types of add-on cards, optical storage, keyboards, and mouse devices. It is a popular source used by many "white box" system vendors. It is the manufacturer of the first motherboards with vacuum-tube audio for richer sound.

Apple Computer, Inc.

www.apple.com

Apple manufactures several lines of personal computers under the iMac, iBook, PowerMac, and PowerBook brand names. It also makes peripherals such as the large-screen LCD Cinema Display and DVD recorder and software, including QuickTime, MacOS, AppleWorks, and the i-series of multimedia programs. It is the manufacturer of the very popular iPod line of music, photo, and video players.

Arco Computer Products, LLC

www.arcoide.com

This company manufactures disk-to-disk (D2D) backup devices, disk mirroring and copying devices (EZ series), and ATA/SATA RAID host adapters and drive enclosures.

ARI Service

www.ari-service.com

This company provides information, drivers, and remaining replacement parts for AST-brand hardware purchased before February 1999. Its parent company, InteliSol, Inc. (www.intelisol.com), specializes in outsourcing warranty, repair, and tech support services.

Arrow Electronics

www.arrow.com

This company is a distributor of millions of computer parts and components. It offers online ordering of parts by manufacturer and part number.

Arrowfield International, Inc.

www.arrowfieldinc.com

This company manufactures the SIDEKICKS series of disk drive brackets, rails, slides, cable adapters, bezels, cabinets, and complete drive upgrade and repair assemblies for standard PC-compatibles, notebook computers, and popular PC and server brands.

Association of Shareware Professionals (ASP)

www.asp-shareware.org

ASP sets standards for shareware products and acts as an ombudsman for disputes between users and authors. It also provides marketing information for shareware authors and distributors.

AST Computer, Inc.

This company is out of business. For drivers and information on AST-brand hardware purchased before February 1999, see *ARI Service*.

Astec Power

www.astec.com

This company, a division of Emerson, manufactures high-end power supplies for PC systems and many other applications. Astec power supplies are used as OEM equipment in many of the top manufacturers' systems, including those of IBM.

ASUS Computer International America (ASUSTeK)

http://usa.asus.com

This company manufactures a popular line of PC-compatible motherboards, bare-bones servers, notebook computers, graphics accelerators, Wi-Fi and Fast Ethernet cards, Internet broadband (cable modem, DSL, and VoIP) devices, and optical drives.

ATI Technologies, Inc.

www.ati.com

This company manufactures a popular line of high-performance PC video adapters based on RADEON X1K, RADEON X, RADEON 9xxx, and Mobility RADEON X and 9xxx chipsets. It also makes the Fire GL series workstation adapters based on IBM and RADEON chipsets; TV tuners, integrated All-in-Wonder multimedia cards, motherboard and motherboard chipsets, and server graphics chipsets. ATI board-level and chipset products are found in desktop and notebook computers, servers, and set-top boxes from many manufacturers around the world.

Autodesk, Inc.

http://usa.autodesk.com

This company manufactures AutoCAD software, related industry-specific titles, Autodesk Inventor 3D design software, Autodesk VIZ 3D design visualization, video encoding and media management programs, and the Discreet series of professional digital graphics editing and color correction software.

Autotime Corporation

www.autotime.com

This company manufactures Hypercable, which transmits high-speed parallel data up to 200 feet. Hypercable-1284 supports IEEE 1284 (EPP/ECP) devices up to 100 feet away. Autotime also sells the DIMM ID (with optional SO-DIMM adapter) and Processor Protector accessories for service technicians, GeoFlex32 Geode-based single-board computer, and the Syke Headphone Headband, which provides stereo music under extreme sports conditions.

Avocent

www.avocent.com

This company is a leading provider of desktop and network KVM switches and remote server management products and software.

Award Software International, Inc.

See *Phoenix Technologies, Ltd.*

AZ-COM, Inc.

www.az-com.com

This company manufactures a complete line of Bus-Extender cards for AGP, Compact PCI, PCI, PCI-X, miniPCI, ISA, EISA, MCA, VESA VL-Bus, NuBus, and MicroChannel. It also makes the three-part CompactPCI Backplane Protection System. These extenders allow you to easily insert and remove adapter cards for testing with the power on.

BakBone Software, Inc.

www.bakbone.com

This company is a developer of NetVault backup and data protection software for Windows, UNIX, Linux, and MacOS X platforms.

Barracuda Networks

http://barracudanetworks.com

This company is a developer of network antivirus, antispam, and firewall devices.

Belden CDT Electronics Division

http://bwcecom.belden.com

This company manufactures cable, fiber optic, and wire products for AV, LAN, industrial, home automation, and PC uses.

BenQ Corporation

www.benq.com

This company, formerly Acer Peripherals America and Acer Communications and Multimedia, produces a popular line of display products (LCD, CRT, plasma, and projectors), scanners, digital cameras, optical drive products (CD-ROM, DVD-ROM, and CD-RW drives), keyboards, mouse devices, cell phone products, broadband, and peripherals.

Berkshire Products

www.berkprod.com or www.pcwatchdog.com

Berkshire Products manufactures the PC Watchdog system monitor series for ISA, PCI, USB, and serial port interfacing, including temperature alarm. These boards and external devices can automatically restart a server or other system that has locked up. The ATX Reset Adapter lets you reset ATX-based systems that lack a reset header on the motherboard.

Bitstream, Inc.

www.bitstream.com

This company manufactures TrueType and Type 1 fonts and font management for web developers, software developers, and end users. It also developed the ThunderHawk 2.0 wireless web browser solution for web-enabled cell phones and PDAs.

Black Box Network Services

www.blackbox.com

This company is a leading direct marketer of computer communications and networking products and services, including voice and data network equipment, specialized power protection, cables, racks, tools, and connectors for a variety of applications.

Borland Software Corporation

www.borland.com

This company is a developer of a wide variety of application development, management, and middleware tools, including JBuilder, StarTeam, Core SDP, Delphi, C++ Building, C# Builder, Borland Enterprise Server, and InterBase.

Bose Corp.

www.bose.com

This company manufactures speakers, integrated amplifiers, and the famous Bose WaveRadio and WaveRadio CD systems.

Breece Hill

www.breecehill.com

This company manufactures backup libraries and devices, including iStoRA disk-to-disk-to-tape (D2D2T) devices; MaxOptix magneto-optical and blue laser drives; autoloaders based on AIT, Super AIT, Super DLT, and LTO Ultrium technologies; and software.

Brooktree Corporation

See *Conexant Systems, Inc.*

Buerg Software

www.buerg.com

This company manufactures an excellent line of shareware utility programs, including the popular LIST Plus and List Enhanced file-scanning programs.

Business Objects

www.businessobjects.com

This company, formerly Crystal Decisions, manufactures a line of business-intelligence products, including the Business Objects series, Crystal Reports, and others.

Byte Runner Technologies

www.byterunner.com

This company manufactures high-speed ISA-bus and PCI-bus RS-232/422/485 serial and parallel cards; PCI-bus USB and IEEE 1394 cards; distinctive ring routers; and specialized USB adapters for network, Internet phone, and infrared use. The RS-232 serial port cards feature FIFO 16550, 16650, 16750, or 16950 UARTs, and both parallel and serial port cards can be set to a wide range of 8-bit and 16-bit IRQs to avoid conflicts; some models also allow IRQ sharing.

CableOrganizer.com, Inc.

www.cableorganizer.com

This company sells a wide variety of cable management devices, server racks and cabinets, cable-testing products, electrical generators, and power distribution devices.

Cables to Go

www.cablestogo.com

This company, formerly CTG, manufactures and distributes a variety of cable, connector, power, testing, and switch products for PC, network, video, PDA, premise wiring, SCSI, and other uses.

CAIG Laboratories

www.caig.com

This company manufactures and sells cleaners and lubricants for electronic applications, including R5 PowerBooster deoxidant, DeoxIt Gold (formerly ProGold) contact enhancer for plated contacts and connectors, and others.

Canon USA, Inc.

www.usa.canon.com

This company manufactures a popular line of inkjet and laser printers, multifunction devices, image scanners, video projectors, digital cameras and film cameras, and micrographics equipment.

Casio, Inc.

www.casio.com

Casio manufactures digital cameras, Pocket PCs, personal data systems, label printers, projectors, and digital watches (including GPS- and MP3-compatible models). It also sells software for personal PCs.

CBT Direct

www.cbtdirect.com

This company manufactures IT training courses delivered online, through CBT, and as self-paced testing. Formerly known as SmartForce, it merged with SkillSoft (www.skillsoft.com) in 2002.

CDW (Computer Discount Warehouse)

www.cdw.com

CDW is a leading computer retail superstore and mail-order/online catalog outlet.

Centon Electronics, Inc.

www.centon.com

This company manufactures memory enhancement kits, SDRAM, DDR and DDR2 SDRAM modules, RAMBUS modules, flash memory, and USB and PCMCIA memory cards.

Chemtronics

See *ITW Chemtronics*.

Cherry Electrical Products

www.cherrycorp.com

This company manufactures a line of high-quality standard and specialized data-acquisition keyboards for PC systems, including models with built-in pointing devices, integrated card readers, biometrics, and other functions. It also manufactures keyswitches, other types of electrical switches, speed and proximity sensors, and automotive modules.

Chicago Case Company

www.chicagocase.com

This company manufactures equipment-shipping and travel cases, including custom designs.

Ci Design Company

www.cidesign.com

This company manufactures server and storage rack chassis and removable drive trays for hard disk drives, universal drive mounting kits for floppy and hard drives, and notebook drive caddies. It supports major brands of server and desktop computers.

Cirrus Logic, Inc.

www.cirrus.com

This company manufactures a line of chipsets for magnetic storage, optical storage, video recording, networking, consumer audio, professional audio, data acquisition, embedded processors, and communications circuits. Some products are sold under the Crystal, Maverick, and 3Ci brand names. Standard and enhanced (Windows 98/2000) drivers for former Cirrus Logic video card products are now supplied by Integrated Software and Devices Corporation (www.isdcorp.com).

Cisco Systems, Inc.

www.cisco.com

Cisco is the leading manufacturer of network hardware, software, and services.

Citizen America Corporation

www.citizen-america.com

This company manufactures a line of bar-code, dot-matrix, and portable printers for retail purchase; it also produces OEM printer components.

CMSProducts, Inc.

www.cmsproducts.com

This company manufactures a line of portable and desktop external backup hard disk drives in USB, IEEE 1394a, and SATA form factors, featuring BounceBack Professional backup software; portable and desktop hard disk upgrades; BouceBack Professional backup and disaster recovery software for Windows 2000, Windows XP and MacOS; portable memory; and USB devices.

CNET Networks

www.cnetnetworks.com

CNET Networks is the parent company of CNet Shopper, Download.com, Computer Shopper, GameSpot, MP3.com, TechRepublic, and many other popular web and print publications for technology users.

Columbia Data Products

www.cdp.com

This company manufactures the Persistent Storage Manager (PSM), which creates multiple point-in-time backup images for Windows NT Server, 2000 Server, XP, and Windows Server 2003. It also makes the Open Transaction Manager (OTM) disk/volume backup software for Windows XP/2000/NT/2003 and SnapTO data protection for Microsoft-GreatPlains accounting applications. SnapBack products are now sold and supported by SnapBack U.K. (www.snapback.com).

CommVault Systems, Inc.

www.commvault.com

CommVault Systems is the developer of the Galaxy family of backup and data management products for major network operating systems and databases.

Compaq Computer Corporation

See *Hewlett-Packard Company*.

CompTIA (Computing Technology Industry Association)

www.comptia.org

This nonprofit trade association sponsors the A+ Certification, Network+ Certification, i-Net+, Server+, Linux+, IT Project+, e-Biz+, CTT+, Convergence+, RFID+, Security+ and Certified Document Imaging Architect (CDIA) certification programs. Microsoft's Microsoft Certified System Administrator (MCSA) certification accepts A+, Network+, and Server+ exams as electives.

CompUSA, Inc.

www.compusa.com

This company has computer retail superstores, mail-order, and online stores.

CompuServe Interactive Services, Inc. (CIS)

www.compuserve.com

This is a leading online information and messaging service oriented to business users. It is owned by America Online.

Computer Associates International, Inc.

www.ca.com

This company develops computer security, antivirus, antispyware, PC–Mac connectivity, firewall, backup, desktop management, business modeling, and other products for enterprise, small to medium business, network, and home office users. CA brands include BrightStor ARCServe Backup, Unicenter, AllFusion, eTrust, and Advantage CA, among others.

Computer Graphics World

http://cgw.pennnet.com

This industry magazine covers graphics hardware, software, and applications. It is Part of the PennWell (www.penwell.com) family of technical publications.

Computer Hotline

www.computerhotline.com

This publication features advertisers offering excellent sources of replacement and repair parts and new and used equipment at wholesale prices. It is part of the Trader Publishing Company line of magazines.

Computer Technology Review

www.wwpi.com

This is an excellent monthly technical magazine and website for systems integrators, value-added resellers, and OEMs. Subscriptions are free to those who qualify.

Condor D.C. Power Supplies, Inc.

www.condorpower.com

This company, a subsidiary of SL Industries, manufactures the Condor line of power supplies for computer, server, medical, telecom, and other uses.

Conexant Systems, Inc.

www.conexant.com

This company manufactures a wide range of chipsets for home, office, and high-speed networking, digital imaging, cellular phones, wireless devices, standard cable and xDSL modems, VoIP, set-top boxes, and modems. It also manufactures embedded communication software.

Connect Technologies

www.connecttech.net

This company sells a wide variety of cables, KVM switches, and adapters for PC, network, and data-com uses.

Corel Systems, Inc.

www.corel.com

This company manufactures the CorelDRAW!, Corel Designer Technical Suite, and PaintShop Pro graphics programs; Ventura desktop publishing; the WordPerfect Office integrated office suite (various versions incorporate WordPerfect, Quattro Pro spreadsheet, Presentations, and some include Paradox relational database); and graphics utilities such as KnockOut, KPT, and Visual Creation Studio (for digital A/V production).

Creative Labs, Inc.

www.creative.com

This company is the U.S. arm of Singapore-based Creative Technology Ltd. This company manufactures the Sound Blaster X-Fi, Sound Blaster AUDIGY, AUDIGY 2, and AUDIGY 4 series of audio cards for multimedia and sound applications. It also manufactures a popular line of MP3 and media players; video webcams; headphones; speakers; digital cameras; mouse devices; keyboards; MIDI keyboards; gaming controllers; small-form-factor PCs; CD-ROM, CD-RW, combo CD-RW/DVD, and DVD drives; wireless, broadband, and analog modems; and graphics cards based on ATI chipsets. It owns Cambridge Sound Works (speakers); E-MU/Ensoniq (audio chipsets); Silicon Engineering (chipsets); Broadxent, formerly Digicom Systems (DSL and telecom); and Ectiva (Internet appliances). It also owns 3D Labs (www.3dlabs.com), which creates 3D graphics accelerator chipsets and cards, including the Wildcat series and Oxygen series for CAD and graphics workstations. It also creates embedded solutions for specialized real-time environments, from jet fighters to cellphones, featuring the GLINT Gamma G2, GLINT R4, and Permedia chipsets.

CRN

www.crn.com

CRN, formerly called *Computer Reseller News*, is an excellent industry trade weekly news magazine and website featuring news for computer professionals involved in value-added reselling of computer equipment. Subscriptions are free to those who qualify.

CRU Acquisitions Group, LLC

www.cruinc.com

This company manufactures the CRU line of removable hard drive modules, the original patented American-made DataPort. DataPort supports all hard drive interfaces and has special cooling for complex, high-RPM drives; some models feature encryption. DataPort backplanes support multiple SCSI hard disk drives. DataPort external enclosures support one to seven drives. DataPortable external enclosures support 2.5-inch through 5.25-inch drives. CRU also manufactures various types of disk array enclosures for use with RAID, LVD, and SCSI drives and cooling fans for desktop drive bays.

Crucial Technologies

www.crucial.com

This company, a division of Micron Technologies, is a direct marketer of memory upgrades for servers, PCs, printers, Macintosh, and other computing devices; USB drives; and flash memory made by Micron Technologies. It also sells graphics cards based on ATI Radeon chipsets.

CS Electronics

www.cselex.com

This company manufactures a very high-quality line of cables, converters, and drive adapters for all types of SCSI, LVD, Fibre Channel, fiber-optic, RAID, SAN, Gigabit Ethernet, and GBIC uses. It offers custom lengths, connectors, and impedances for a proper match with an existing installation, and it uses the highest-quality raw cable available.

CST

www.simmtester.com

This company manufactures memory/SIMM/DIMM testers and the DocMemory memory testing program.

CTS Corporation

www.ctscorp.com

This company manufactures a line of excellent passive CPU heatsink products.

CTX International, Inc.

www.ctxintl.com

This company manufactures a line of high-performance CRT and LCD monitors, display projectors, industrial displays, flash memory recorders, speakers, and video capture devices.

CyberResearch

www.cyberresearch.com

This company sells redundant power supplies (RPSs), industrial computers, KVM switches, motion control devices, PC and network cables and wiring, and other products for network engineering.

Cypress Semiconductor Corporation

www.cypress.com

This company manufactures many different types of chipsets and other semiconductor devices.

D.W. Electrochemicals, Ltd.

www.stabilant.com

This company manufactures and sells Stabilant 22 contact enhancer and treatment (previously sold by another company as Tweek). Stabilant 22 is the gel concentrate, Stabilant 22A is a 4-to-1 iso-propanol diluted form, and Stabilant 22E is the ethanol diluted form.

Da-Lite Screen Co.

www.da-lite.com

This company manufactures a line of projection screens, easels and accessories, projector mounts, and computer furniture.

DakTech

www.daktech.com

This company manufactures and sells custom-configured PCs, laptops, and servers based on Intel processors.

Dallas Semiconductor

www.maxim-ic.com

This company, a wholly owned subsidiary of Maxim Integrated Products, manufactures real-time clocks, nonvolatile RAM modules, and many other electronic components used by a number of OEMs. Its parent company designs linear and mixed-signal ICs for PCs, peripherals, process control, wireless and fiber communications, and other uses.

DAMAC Products, Inc.

www.damac.com

This company manufactures a line of racks, enclosures, cabinets, and other accessories for rack-mounted servers and devices.

Datamation

www.datamation.com

This excellent online industry publication features articles on networking, communications, enterprise, and computing management. It is part of the Earthweb family.

Dell Computer Corporation

www.dell.com

Dell manufactures a line of high-performance PC computer systems and accessories, including notebooks, desktops, servers, and network storage devices and appliances. It also provides consulting services.

DEX (Data Exchange Corporation)

www.dex.com

DEX specializes in contract manufacturing, end-of-life support, depot repair, logistic services, call center services, returns management, and spare parts and unit sales. It's a complete repair and refurbishment facility, providing ISO 9002–certified depot repair of high-tech electronics and computer-related products from all major manufacturers.

Diamond Flower, Inc. (DFI)

www.dfiusa.com

This company manufactures a line of industrial, touchscreen-based, all-in-one, tower, rack-mounted, and desktop PCs with touchscreens and LCD panels, specializing in restaurant and retail POS uses. Visit www.dfi.com for motherboard products.

DigiBuy

www.pslweb.com

This company is a distributor of high-quality public-domain and shareware software on CD-ROM. Its library is the most well researched and well tested available. It also offers the DigiBuy secured shareware registration and online shopping cart services.

Digi-Key Corporation

www.digikey.com

This company sells an enormous variety of electronic and computer components, tools, and test equipment.

DisplayMate Technologies Corp.

www.displaymate.com

This company manufactures the DisplayMate series of video display utilities and diagnostic programs for Windows and MS-DOS. DisplayMate exercises, troubleshoots, and diagnoses video display adapter, LCD and CRT, and monitor problems; it is excellent for optimizing analog LCD displays. Versions are also available for TV, projector, HDTV, and similar devices attached to computers.

Diversified Technology

www.dtims.com

This company, an Ergon Company, manufactures industrial and rack-mounted PC-compatible systems and a variety of backplane-design CPU boards, multifunction adapters, and single-board computer products, based on the embedded PCI-X, ETX, PICMG PCI/ISA, CompactPCI, and AdvancedTCA form factors.

D-Link Systems, Inc.

www.dlink.com

This company manufactures a popular line of consumer and business-class wireless and wired network and Internet sharing products, including switches, access points, routers, gateways, video conferencing, print servers, VPN, firewall, VoIP, Power over Ethernet, and network adapters. It also manufactures KVM switches, USB hardware, and multimedia hardware.

Dot Hill Systems Corporation

www.dothill.com

This company manufactures high-performance storage area network (SAN) disk storage products based on SATA, Fibre Channel, and SCSI; as well as SANScape and SANpath storage software.

DTK Computer, Inc.

www.dtk.com.tw

This company manufactures PC-compatible motherboards and add-on cards, small-form-factor bare-bones PCs, and PICMG-based single-board computers.

Dukane Corporation

www.dukcorp.com

Dukane's AudioVisual division manufactures a complete line of high-intensity overhead projectors, CRTs, LCD and plasma panels, ImagePro data/video projectors, and the ConVA media control system. It specializes in portable high-brightness overhead projector units designed for LCD-panel projection applications. The website features an interactive calculator that helps you select the correct projector for your desired room and image size.

Duracell, Inc.

www.duracell.com

This company manufactures high-performance consumer, technical OEM, and B2B industrial batteries, including alkaline, lithium, and standard-sized nickel-metal hydride rechargeable batteries.

East/West Manufacturing Enterprises, Inc.

www.ewme.com

This company manufactures the Aeronics line of highest-quality active and forced-perfect terminators for use in SCSI-bus systems. It's known for solving problems with longer distances or multiple-SCSI devices. It also provides useful SCSI tutorials and connectors guides.

Eaton Powerware Division

www.powerware.com

This company manufactures an excellent line of computer power protection equipment, from high-end ferroresonant UPS systems to line conditioners and standby power protection systems.

EETimes

www.eetimes.com

This is an excellent industry trade weekly news magazine (formerly known as *Electronic Engineering Times*), featuring news for engineers and technical management. Subscriptions are free to those who qualify.

Electrocution Technical Publishers

www.electrocution.com

This company publishes Phil Croucher's *The BIOS Companion*, an invaluable book on CD-ROM that covers in detail the various BIOS versions on the market, including detailed setup, configuration, and diagnostics information. It also sells the Tech Support CD set (which includes an A+ Certification reference guide, software patches, and drivers), and publishes reference guides on helicopter and fixed-wing aviation.

Electronic Industries Alliance (EIA)

www.eia.org

EIA is a national trade organization for electronics manufacturers of all sizes. It is the co-sponsor of the Internet Security Alliance (www.isalliance.org). EIA works to develop improved polices on broadband access, recycling, and other industry concerns.

Electronic Products

www.electronicproducts.com

This is an excellent industry trade magazine, featuring engineering-type information on electronic and computer components and in-depth technical articles. Subscriptions are free to those who qualify.

Electronics Supply and Manufacturing

www.my-esm.com

This is an excellent industry trade weekly magazine and website (formerly known as *Electronic Buyers' News*), featuring news and information for those involved in electronics purchasing, materials, and management. Subscriptions are free to those who qualify.

Elitegroup Computer Systems, Inc.

www.ecusa.com

This company is one of the largest PC motherboard manufacturers in the world. It also manufactures notebook computers, bare-bones systems, graphics cards, and peripherals.

EMC Dantz

www.dantz.com

EMC Dantz is the developer of the Dantz Retrospect line of backup software for Windows desktop and server versions, MacOS X, and Novell NetWare. It also manufactures EMC RepliStor replication software for Windows servers.

Emerson & Cuming

www.emersoncuming.com

This company, a National Starch and Chemical company, manufactures structurally, thermally, and electronically conductive epoxy and silicone adhesives, coatings, and encapsulates. It also manufactures room-temperature, heat-cured, and UV-cured systems and circuit board fabrication materials, including various solder replacements and surface-mount and film adhesives.

Endl Publications

www.rahul.net/endl

This company publishes CD_Access, a subscription-based CD-ROM guide to SCSI, ATAPI, and similar interface standards. It also publishes the "Endl Letter," a monthly guide summarizing conferences, standards activity, and industry meetings on storage standards from both engineering and marketing perspectives. Subscribers can call on Endl for additional research. It also publishes the *SCSI Series*, which provides extensive technical guidance and organization to the growing world of SCSI and related interface technologies.

Epson America, Inc.

www.epson.com

This company manufactures popular lines of dot-matrix, laser, and high-resolution inkjet printers, scanners, digital cameras, all-in-one devices, projection systems, and media.

eSupport.com, Inc.

www.esupport.com

This company provides BIOS upgrades for motherboards with Award, AMI, Phoenix, or Microid Research (MR) BIOS chips. It offers free downloadable BIOS Agent software to determine the correct BIOS upgrade for your system. It is owned by TouchStone Software (www.touchstonesoftware.com). It also distributes POST cards, CardWare, and Millennium Pro LBA assist cards.

Eurosoft (U.S.) Inc.

www.eurosoft.com

This company manufactures test and diagnostic products, including QA+WIN32, QA+FE Service Center, PC-Check, Virtual QA+ and Virtual PC-Check for hardware OEMs, CD-Check, Preferred POST board PCI/ISA, PC-Check PRO Bundle, and accessories.

eWeek

www.eweek.com

This weekly magazine and companion website feature industry news and information; free subscriptions are given to those who qualify.

Exabyte Corporation

www.exabyte.com

This company manufactures high-performance network storage solutions featuring 8mm (Mammoth), AIT, VXA, and LTO/Ultrium tape backup systems and automated tape libraries.

Extron Electronics

www.extron.com

This company manufactures computer–video interface products used to connect PCs to large-screen video projectors and monitors. It also manufactures VGA, Mac, and RGB distribution amplifiers and switchers used to connect multimedia classroom and boardroom equipment and makes VGA- and Mac-to-NTSC/PAL converters for recording computer information and graphics on videotape. It also sells the former Inline, Inc., line of AV products.

F-Secure

www.f-secure.com

This company develops a line of antivirus and intrusion protection software and devices for enterprise networks, small to medium businesses, and home office PCs.

FCI

www.fciconnect.com

This company manufactures electronic connector products for computers and electronics devices.

Fedco Electronics, Inc.

www.fedcoelectronics.com

This company manufactures and distributes a large variety of computer, data terminal/scanner, utility meters, and UPS batteries under the Energy+ brand as well as chargers and accessories for notebook and desktop models.

First International Computer America

www.fica.com

This company is the U.S. branch of First International Computer, the largest Taiwan-based manufacturer of PC-compatible motherboards. It also manufactures PC systems, mobile access devices, and graphics cards.

Fluke, John Manufacturing Company, Inc.

www.fluke.com

This company manufactures high-end digital troubleshooting tools, network analysis devices, and digital multimeters.

FSI Computer GmbH

www.pciii.de/UKSeiten/index.htm

This company manufactures the Atlas and PCIII lines of bare-bones and fully configured portable cases that combine standard ATX motherboards with LCD displays in ABS (PCIII) or aluminum (Atlas) cases.

Fujitsu Computer Products of America, Inc.

www.fcpa.com

This company manufactures SCSI, SAS, and mobile hard disk drives. It also manufactures scanners, rewritable magneto-optical drives, and a palm vein biometrics authentication device.

Futuremark Corporation

www.futuremark.com

This company is the U.S. division of Finland's Futuremark Oy. Formerly known as MadOnion.com, it develops and sells a very popular series of system and 3D graphics benchmarks, including 3DMark, PCMark, and SPMark (for smartphones). It also distributes benchmarks developed by BAPco.

Gateway, Inc.

www.gateway.com

This company manufactures popular lines of desktop, notebook, handheld, and server PC systems, wide-format LCD screens, projectors, PDAs, speakers, digital cameras, MP3 players, and accessories, sold directly to the public.

Giga-Byte Technology Co., Inc.

www.giga-byte.com

This company is one of the 10 largest Taiwan-based motherboard manufacturers. It manufactures PC and server/workstation motherboards; Nvidia and ATI-based graphics cards; desktop and notebook PCs; components; rack-mounted, appliance, and traditional servers; wireless and wired network hardware; and set-top boxes.

GigaTrend, Inc.

www.gigatrend.com

This company manufactures high-capacity tape drives, tape libraries, RAID tape arrays, backup appliances, and integrated RAID hard disk/tape arrays in 4MM, DAT, AIT, and LTO formats. GigaTrend also manufactures devices for SANs, NAS, and specialized storage devices for video editing.

Global Engineering Documents

http://global.ihs.com

This company is a division of IHS Engineering. It is a source for various ANSI and other industry-standard documents, including SCSI-1, 2, and 3; ATA IDE; ESDI; and many others. Unlike ANSI, it sells draft documents of standards that are not yet fully ANSI approved. It also sells technical standards and publications for aerospace, automotive, construction, and other industries.

Golden Bow Systems

www.goldenbow.com

This company manufactures VOPT for Windows 9x, Me, NT, 2000, and XP and MS-DOS. VOPT is one of the best and fastest disk optimizer software programs available.

HALLoGRAM Publishing

www.hallogram.com

This company is an excellent resource for bar-code, POS, database, and other programmers. It distributes dSalvage Pro, the leading database editor and repair tool for Xbase (dBase, Foxpro, Clipper, and similar languages) as well as many other tools for other development languages.

Hauppauge Computer Works, Inc.

www.hauppauge.com

This company manufactures a wide variety of analog and digital video TV receivers and editing devices in PCI and USB form factors. Its Eskape Labs division (www.eskapelabs.com) produces video capture devices for Macintosh systems.

Heathkit Educational Systems

www.heathkit.com

This company sells courses and training materials for learning electronics, telecom, and computer technologies, including training for CompTIA's A+, Network+, and Server+ certifications for computer technicians.

Hewlett-Packard Company

www.hp.com

This company manufactures notebook, desktop, and handheld PCs for home and office; laser and inkjet printers; scanners and imaging products; all-in-one devices; network servers, storage, hardware, and software; and tape backup, DVD, CD-RW, magneto-optical, SCSI hard disks, disk arrays, and magneto-optical subsystems.

Hitachi Global Storage Technologies

www.hitachigst.com

A joint venture between IBM and Hitachi, Hitachi Global Storage Technologies produces the Ultrastar, Deskstar, Travelstar, Endurastar, and Microdrive hard disk product lines for enterprise network, desktop, mobile, and digital media uses.

Hitachi, Ltd.

www.hitachi.us.

This company manufactures memory and semiconductor devices and computer peripherals, including digital graphics products, magnetic and optical storage products, and LCD projectors. It also manufactures enterprisewide office and document automation software.

Hynix Semiconductor America, Inc.

http://hsa.hynix.com

This company makes DRAM, SDRAM, flash, and MCP memory and system IC chips for OEM markets.

IBM Corporation

www.ibm.com

This company sells popular lines of server computers, printers, and accessories. IBM Software manufactures WebSphere server software; the Rational software development platform; the Tivoli application and business management software; DB2 information management; Lotus products, including Lotus 1-2-3, Lotus Organizer, Lotus SmartSuite, Lotus Enterprise Integrator, Lotus Notes, the Lotus Domino family, Lotus Workflow, Lotus QuickPlace team collaboration software, and Lotus Sametime live-collaboration software; and the Learning Space distance education platform. For ThinkPad and ThinkCentre PCs, see *Lenovo*.

IBM Semiconductor Solutions

www.ibm.com/chips

This IBM division is responsible for developing, manufacturing, and marketing semiconductor and electronic packaging products, services, and solutions.

Illinois Lock

www.illinoislock.com

This company, a division of the Eastern Company, manufactures keylocks used in many PC systems.

Imation Corp.

www.imation.com

This company manufactures popular lines of floppy disk drives and media; flash memory drives; CD and DVD optical media; tape media in all popular formats; the Micro hard disk; specialty papers; CD and DVD media management products; and the Ulysses hard disk-based tape drive emulator.

Infineon Technologies AG

www.infineon.com

This company is a manufacturer of memory and system IC chips for computers, consumer electronics, wireless, and other electronics applications.

InfoWorld

www.infoworld.com

This magazine and website feature excellent product reviews, news, and information about personal and enterprise computing. Free subscriptions are available to those who qualify.

Inline, Inc.

See *Extron Electronics*.

Integrated Device Technology, Inc.

www.idt.com

This company manufactures chipsets and other semiconductor devices for computer, electronics, and telecom applications.

Intel Corporation

www.intel.com

This company manufactures microprocessors used in PC and server systems, including the Pentium D, Celeron D, Pentium M, Pentium 4, Celeron, Xeon, and Itanium. It also manufactures a popular line of motherboards for desktops and servers; digital home technologies; small business and enterprise networking products; motherboard bridge, graphics, and I/O chipsets; flash memory; and software development tools.

Iomega Corporation

www.iomega.com

This company manufactures Zip and REV removable-cartridge drives; CD-RW and DVD rewritable optical drives; external hard disks; flash memory USB drives; the Screenplay hard disk for video and photo playback on TVs; and network hard disk and autoloader backup solutions. It also provides iStorage online storage and backup services; ActiveDisk programs that run directly from storage devices; and Hotburn and Hotburn Pro CD and DVD mastering software.

ITW Chemtronics

www.chemtronics.com

This company, an Illinois Tool Works company, manufactures and sells a complete line of computer and electronic-grade chemicals, materials, and supplies, as well as solder wick and clean-room items.

It also manufactures and sells the Coventry line of clean-room swabs for use in servicing computer disk drives.

Jameco Computer Products

www.jameco.com

This company supplies computer components, integrated circuits, parts, peripherals, and test/measuring equipment.

JDR Microdevices

www.jdr.com

This company is a vendor for chips, disk drives, and various computer and electronic parts and components.

Jensen Tools, Inc.

www.jensentools.com

This company is a catalog and online distributor of networking tools and PC testing equipment.

JVC America/Professional

http://pro.jvc.com

This company manufactures LCD and other projection and presentation equipment, digital broadcast and video equipment, and video security/imaging systems.

Kaspersky Lab

www.kaspersky.com

This company is a developer of antivirus, antispam, and security products for corporate networks, businesses, and home users.

Kensington Computer Products Group

www.kensington.com

This company, an ACCO Brands company, manufactures and supplies computer accessories, including digital PC cameras, mouse devices and pointing devices, computer security, ergonomic accessories, and others.

KeyTronicEMS

www.keytronic.com

This company manufactures a variety of high-quality keyboards—including models incorporating smart card readers, biometric fingerprint scanners, Ergo technology (different force levels to match the strength of each finger), and Citrix thin clients—and mouse devices for PC-compatible systems. It sells mouse devices based on Honeywell's patented design that never needs cleaning and doesn't use a removable roller; some models also feature interchangeable button layouts. It supplies Microsoft and other vendors with keyboards and performs contract design and manufacturing services, engineering services, and custom molding and tooling.

Kingston Technology Corporation

www.kingston.com

Kingston is the world's largest vendor of memory modules. It also manufactures flash card and USB flash memory. For StorCase, see *StorCase Technology, Inc.*

Kontron

www.kontron.com

This company, which purchased Dolch Computer Systems in 2005, continues to sell the former Dolch line of rugged portable computers. It also sells various single-board PCs based on COTS, various PICMG standards, and other types of components, software, industrial I/O devices, and customized thin-panel devices.

Labconco Corporation

www.labconco.com

This company manufactures a variety of clean-room cabinets, hood blowers, and clean benches for use in hard disk drive and other sensitive component repair.

Labtec Enterprises, Inc.

www.labtec.com

This company is a manufacturer of multimedia speakers, computer and telephony microphones and headsets, music headsets, wireless and wired keyboards and mouse devices, and webcams.

Lantronix

www.lantronix.com

This company manufactures a variety of specialized network hardware, including device servers, terminal servers, network time servers, remote access servers, console servers, and print servers.

LapLink Software, Inc.

www.laplink.com

This company manufactures the LapLink Gold series of remote control and file-transfer programs, PCMover system transfer, and Filemove file transfer. It also manufactures PDAsync software for synchronizing Palm and Windows CE–based PDAs with popular Windows applications. It provides Sharedirect folder sharing and Laplink Everywhere remote access and control services.

LearnKey, Inc.

www.learnkey.com

This company produces and distributes high-quality computer technology and certification training courses on CD-ROM and through the Internet and intranets.

Lenovo

www.lenovo.com

China's largest PC maker, Lenovo was originally known as Legend, and it acquired the former IBM Personal Computer division in 2005. This company manufactures and sells the former IBM ThinkPad notebook, ThinkCentre desktop, and ThinkVision display brands.

Lexmark

www.lexmark.com

This company manufactures a line of laser, inkjet, and dot-matrix forms printers, as well as multifunction network devices.

LG Electronics

http://us.lge.com

This company manufactures LCD color monitors, CD-RW and DVD optical drives, flash memory cards, and USB drives. It also manufactures plasma, LCD, and projection TVs; digital audio and video products; mobile phones; and home appliances.

Libi Industries, Ltd.

www.libi.com

This online computer superstore sells many lines of hardware and software to individuals and as a business-to-business distributor.

Liebert

www.liebert.com

This company, a division of Emerson Network Power, manufactures network, telecom, and industrial power-protection and site-protection devices and software.

Linksys

www.linksys.com

This company, owned by Cisco Systems, manufactures a popular line of Ethernet, Fast Ethernet, and Gigabit Ethernet network cards, hubs, switches, print servers, NAS, routers, and cable modems. This company manufactures Wi-Fi–compatible IEEE 802.11b, 802.11a, and 802.11g adapters, wireless access points, routers, and multimedia and gaming devices. It also manufactures HomePNA and HomePlug-compatible network hardware.

Linux Online, Inc.

www.linux.org

This company is a leading information and resource site for Linux users at all levels.

LionBRIDGE

www.lionbridge.com

This company provides content localization and testing services for companies around the world. Its Veritest division (www.veritest.com) developed and published the popular *PC Magazine* benchmarks, such as Winstone and Winbench, and it currently develops various tests and benchmarks for a variety of clients.

LiteON Technology Corporation

www.liteon.com

This company is a leading producer of CD-RW and DVD rewritable drives sold at retail and produced for many OEMs. It also sells most other types of PC and network components and accessories. Its component division manufactures various types of PC and electronics components. It owns MaxiSwitch, a popular manufacturer of keyboards bundled with many popular computer brands and sold by various OEMs.

Logitech

www.logitech.com

This company manufactures a popular line of corded and cordless mouse devices, trackballs, and keyboards, as well as game controllers, webcams, and speakers. Logitech is also the OEM producer for the mouse devices used by many popular brands of computers.

Lone Star Software

www.cactus.com

This company is a developer of backup and disaster recovery software for Linux and UNIX, including Line-TAR, Rescue-Ranger, and LTX.

Lotus Software

See *IBM Corporation.*

LSI Logic, Inc.

www.lsilogic.com

This company manufactures motherboard logic and chipsets for SCSI, networking, telecom, A/V, digital cameras, digital signal processing, ADSL CoreWare system-on-a-chip, and other uses; these products are used by many OEMs. LSI Logic manufactures a line of SCSI, RAID, multifunction SCSI/Ethernet, Ethernet, and Fibre Channel host adapters and accessories; it also manufactures PCI riser cards. It owns the former NCR Microelectronics.

MA Labs, Inc.

www.malabs.com

This company is a leading distributor of CPUs, memory modules, PC boards, hard disk drives, floppy drives, motherboards, and other PC and network components.

Macworld Communications, Inc.

www.macworld.com

This company produces an excellent website and publication, covering news in the Macintosh universe.

MAG InnoVision

See *Proview Technology, Inc.*

MAGNI Systems, Inc.

www.magnisystems.com

This company manufactures a line of scan converters, which convert VGA graphics screens to either NTSC (VHS) or S-video (S-VHS), as well as video monitoring and measurement equipment for TV production.

MapInfo Corporation

www.mapinfo.com

> This company produces desktop, embedded object, and Internet/intranet mapping, routing, and geocoding software and associated data for public- and private-sector information discovery.

Matrox Graphics, Inc.

www.matrox.com/mga

> This company manufactures high-performance PC graphics adapters optimized for 2D and multiple-monitor applications (including CRT and DVI LCD displays). Other divisions of its parent company (www.matrox.com) produce video capture and editing equipment and scientific and industrial imaging products.

Maxell Corporation of America

www.maxell-usa.com

> This company manufactures magnetic media products, including floppy, Zip, and SuperDisk disks and tape cartridges for DDS, QIC, Travan, AIT, DLT, and LTO drives, as well as optical products, including CD-R, CD-RW, DVD-RAM, and magneto-optical media. It also produces batteries and consumer video and audio magnetic tape products.

Maxoptix Inc.

> See *Breece Hill*.

Maxtor Corporation

www.maxtor.com

> This company manufactures large-capacity, high-quality SCSI, Fibre Channel, SAS, SATA, and ATA/IDE hard disk drives; Shared Storage network drives; OneTouch I/II/IIIUSB, and IEEE 1394 storage devices; QuickView hard disks for consumer media DVRs; and media centers.

McAfee, Inc.

www.mcafee.com

> This company provides a wide range of personal, small-business, and enterprise antivirus and security products. It also manufactures VirusScan, Personal Firewall Plus, AntiSpyware, SpamKiller, Privacy Service, and Wireless Home Network Security Suite.

Media Live International

www.mili.com

> This company produces the world's leading computer tradeshows, including Comdex, Seybold Seminars, Interop, VoiceCon, Mobile Business Expo, Web 2.0, and others. It also produces *Business Communications Review* (www.bcmag.com) and *The Seybold Report* (www.seyboldreports.com).

Meritec

www.meritec.com

> This company manufactures a line of SCSI 8-bit to 16-bit (Wide SCSI) adapters in a variety of configurations. These adapters allow Wide SCSI devices to be installed in a standard 8-bit SCSI bus and vice

versa. It also manufactures PCI and AGP slot test connectors and other standard memory and inter-face connectors for system boards and add-on cards, as well as custom cable assemblies.

Meterman Test Tools

www.metermantesttools.com

This company, formerly Wavetek-Meterman, manufactures digital multimeters and other testing instruments.

Methode Electronics, Inc.

www.methode.com

This company manufactures and sells a complete line of SCSI terminators and adapters; USB, fiber-optic, Fibre Channel, Compact Flash, and PCMCIA products; and custom/standard cable assemblies.

MGE UPS Systems

www.mgeups.com

This company is a manufacturer of UPS units, surge suppressors, and power management products for residential, small to medium businesses, telecom, networking, and data center uses.

Micro 2000, Inc.

www.micro2000.com

This company manufactures the MicroScope, Universal Diagnostics Toolkit, and USB-Scope PC diag-nostics programs; the RemoteScope network administration tool; the EraserDisk drive wiping pro-gram; and the POSTProbe Universal diagnostics card, which works in PCI, ISA, VL-Bus, and EISA slots. It also sells training programs for PC hardware and A+ certification.

Micro Accessories, Inc.

www.micro-a.com

This company manufactures a variety of cables, disk drive mounting brackets, removable drive adapters, enclosures, and accessories (including drive adapter kits for popular brands of servers and notebook computers). It also sells SCSI and IDE/ATA cables, Cisco cables, and SCSI terminators.

Micro Computer Cable Company, LLC

www.mc3llc.com

This company manufactures a complete line of network and computer cables, connectors, switch-boxes, and cabling accessories. It also manufactures custom cables.

Micro Design International, Inc. (MDI)

www.mdi.com

This company manufactures the SCSI Express driver software for integration of SCSI peripherals in a variety of environments, along with solutions for server and storage consolidation, backup and disas-ter recovery, NAS, and iSCSI.

Micro Industries Corporation

www.microindustries.com

This company manufactures PC-compatible motherboards for OEMs—including single-board, passive-backplane, PICMG, Compact PCI, and NLX products—using the latest CPUs and technologies.

Micro Warehouse

See *CDW (Computer Discount Warehouse)*.

Micron Technologies, Inc.

www.micron.com

The parent company of Crucial Technology, Micron is one of the world's leading producers of semi-conductor memory products, including QDR/DDR SDRAM, SDRAM, DRAM, SRAM, flash memory, and memory modules of all types. It also produces CMOS image sensors and bare-die products.

Microsoft Corporation

www.microsoft.com

This company manufactures Windows Server 2003; Windows XP; other Windows server and desktop operating systems; Microsoft Office; Microsoft Works; and many other titles. It also manufactures a popular line of keyboards, mouse devices, game controllers, the TV Photo Viewer, and the Xbox video game system.

MicroSolutions, Inc.

www.micro-solutions.com

This company manufactures the LockBox external hard disk with biometric (fingerprint) access; RoadStar and RoadStor Pro photo-to-CD or -DVD burner/digital photo viewer/DVD-drive; BackPack rewritable DVD, CD-RW/DVD combo, DVD-ROM, CD-ROM, hard disk, and floppy disk drives; and BackPack wireless workgroup storage and print server. BackPack drives attach via one or more of these interfaces: USB, PC Card, or parallel port.

MicroSystems Development Tech, Inc.

www.msdus.com

This company manufactures a line of excellent hardware diagnostics products, including Post Code Master POST board (available in mini-PCI, PCI, and ISA versions) and Test Drive diagnostics for floppy drives. It also sells EPROM emulators for USB and parallel ports and provides engineering services.

Microway, Inc.

www.microway.com

This company manufactures a line of workstations, servers, and clusters, based on Intel, AMD, and Alpha processors; RAID storage; FastTree InfiniBand switches; storage products, including SAS, SATA, NAS, SCSI, and ATA RAID; tape drives, loaders, and libraries; and chassis products. It also installs and configures popular open-source and commercial clustering and applications-development software.

Minicom

www.minicom.com

This company is a manufacturer of network KVM switches and management devices, AV extenders and video splitters, and computer-based training (CBT) products.

Mitsumi Electronics Corporation

www.mitsumi.com

This company manufactures a line of CD- and DVD-based optical drives, floppy drives, USB drives, keyboards, and mouse devices. It also manufactures electronic components.

Modem Doctor

www.modemdoctor.com

Modem Doctor manufactures the Modem Doctor serial port and modem diagnostics programs for Windows 9x/Me/NT/2000/XP, Windows 3.1, and MS-DOS.

Molex, Inc.

www.molex.com

This company manufactures a variety of connectors used in PC and server systems; it also sells cable assemblies, structured wiring, terminal blocks, and other products for electronics uses. It also produces fiber-optic transceivers.

Mosel Vitelic (MVC)

www.mvc.com

This company manufactures memory modules, DRAMs, SRAMs, and flash memory.

Motorola Embedded Communications Computing

www.motorola.com/computers

This company manufactures a wide variety of single-board and industrial-type computer mother-boards and embedded products, including PMC, AdvancedTCA, CompactPCI, and VMEbus products for the Intel and PowerPC platforms, as well as software and telecom products. For other Motorola products, see the Motorola site, at www.motorola.com.

MPC Computers, LLC

www.buympc.com

This company, formerly owned by Micron Technologies, manufactures a line of desktop, notebook, and server PC systems.

MSI Computer Corporation

www.msicomputer.com

This company, the U.S. division of Micro-Star International, is one of the 10 largest Taiwan-based motherboard manufacturers. It also manufactures slimline PCs, notebook computers, servers, home theater PCs, portable audio and multimedia players, portable storage, and 3D graphics accelerators.

Mueller Technical Research

This is Scott Mueller's company, which offers the best in custom onsite PC hardware and software technical seminars and training, specializing in all aspects of PC hardware, software, and data recovery. It can present a custom seminar for your organization. Contact Scott at scottmueller@compuserve.com, or call 847-854-6794.

Mushkin, Inc.

www.mushkin.com

This company manufactures and sells a wide variety of standard and high-performance SDRAM, DDR, and DDR-2 memory modules for desktop and notebook computers.

Mylex Corporation

See *LSI Logic, Inc.*

Myoda Computer Center

www.myoda.com

This company assembles PC desktop and server systems for retail sale. It also sells a complete line of PC components for build-it-yourself systems and upgrades.

National Semiconductor Corporation

www.national.com

This company manufactures a variety of chips for PC circuit and other electronics applications. It is known especially for its UART and Super I/O chips.

NEC Display Solutions of America, Inc.

www.necdisplay.com

A merger of Mitsubishi and NEC's display product lines, this company manufactures a line of CRT and LCD displays for business, consumer, medical, and information uses. Mitsubishi projectors and widescreen LCD monitors for information display are now available from Mitsubishi Digital Electronics America (www.mitsubishi-presentations.com).

NEC Electronics, Inc.

www.necel.com

This company manufactures memory, microprocessors, other semiconductor devices, batteries, high-speed I/O port chipsets, and other components used by many OEMs.

NEC Packard Bell

www.packardbell.com

This company manufactures a popular line of low-cost PC systems and peripherals sold in most portions of the world outside North America. For support for Packard Bell products formerly sold in the United States, go to www.priorityonesupport.com.

NEC Solutions America

www.necsam.com

> This company manufactures servers, enterprise software, CD- and DVD-based optical drives, floppy drives, projectors, and solutions aimed at public safety, retail, health care, and other specific applications.

Netgear Inc.

www.netgear.com

> This company manufactures a popular line of wireless and wired network and Internet sharing products, including switches, access points, routers, gateways, print servers, and network adapters.

Network Associates, Inc.

> See *McAfee, Inc.*

Network Technologies, Inc. (NTI)

www.networktechinc.com

> This company manufactures a wide range of KVM and network KVM switches and splitters, server monitoring products, video splitters and extenders, rack-mounted monitors, and other products for server rooms.

Newark InOne

www.newark.com

> Formerly Newark Electronics, this company is owned by Premier Farnell plc. It is an electronic component and product supplier with a huge catalog of products.

NextPage

www.nextpage.com

> This company provides the NextPage 2 document collaboration service, which is designed to ensure that multiple users working on a document are working with the most up-to-date version.

Novell, Inc.

www.novell.com

> This company manufactures the NetWare 6 LAN operating system. It also manufactures Novell Identity Manager, Open Enterprise Server, GroupWise, ZENworks, SUSE Linux, SUSE Linux Enterprise Server, and many other network/Internet management, collaboration, and communications products.

Nvidia Corporation

www.nvidia.com

> This company is a leading provider of 3D graphics processor chips, such as the GeForce 7xxx, GeForce 6xxx, and GeForce FX series, which are used in many OEM-branded graphics adapters. It also produces the Quadro series of workstation graphics accelerator chips; the nForce Professional, nForce4, and nForce3 motherboard chipsets; and GeForce Go notebook graphics chipsets.

Oak Technology, Inc.

See *Zoran*.

Oki Data Americas, Inc.

www.okidata.com

This company is a manufacturer of color and monochrome LED printers, Microline dot-matrix impact printers, fax machines, and workgroup-level color print-scan-copy-fax multifunction peripherals.

OneAC

www.oneac.com

OneAC, a Chloride Power Protection Company, manufactures UPS, power conditioning, data line surge protection, DC power shelves, and power filter products.

Ontrack Data Recovery

www.ontrack.com

Ontrack Data Recovery is a world leader in data recovery services and software. It manufactures the EasyRecovery line of data-recovery programs; Ontrack PowerControls for copying data from Microsoft Exchange databases; Disk Manager disk installation and maintenance software (also widely distributed through OEM hard disk drive vendors); DataEraser disk deletion software; and Data Advisor system and drive diagnostics.

Opti, Inc.

www.opti-inc.com

This company manufactures chipsets for popular PC subsystems, including IEEE 1394, USB, LCD display panels, and PCI bridge products.

Orbit Micro

www.orbitmicro.com

This company sells a wide variety of desktop and network hardware, including RPS, single-board computers (SBC), rack-mounted network appliances, and standard peripherals.

Overland Storage

www.overlanddata.com

This company manufactures Ultamus protection storage devices, Reo disk2disk backup, data management software, Neo tape libraries, autoloaders, and external tape drives based on SDLT, DLT, and LTO technologies. It formerly manufactured, sold, and serviced Ditto, Travan, and DDS drives through its Tecmar subsidiary (www.tecmar.com); it offers web-based tech support only for Tecmar products.

Pacific Digital Corporation

www.pacificdigital.com

This company produces a popular line of DVD- and CD-rewritable drives, Memory Frame LCD digital media frames, and SATA RAID host adapters and chipsets.

Panasonic Corporation of North America

www.panasonic.com

This company is the U.S. division of Matsushita Electric. Panasonic manufactures a wide range of consumer and professional products, including digital cameras, notebook computers, DVD media, flash memory cards, webcams, workgroup scanners, telephones, and multifunction printers.

Panda Software

www.pandasoftware.com

This company is a developer of antivirus, antispam, and security software and appliances for corporate networks, business and home office networks, and desktops.

Para Systems, Inc

www.minutemanups.com

This company is the manufacturer of the MinuteMan line of UPS units for desktops, networks, and server rooms.

Parallel Technologies, Inc.

www.lpt.com

This company manufactures USBInfo performance testing and troubleshooting software, direct connection cables for parallel and USB data transfer with Windows or Norton Ghost, 802.11g network adapters, Net-LinQ USB connection cables, and USB 2.0 flash memory drives.

PARTS NOW! LLC

www.partsnowinc.com

This company sells a large variety of laser printer parts for Hewlett-Packard, Canon, and Lexmark laser printers; it also performs laser printer repairs, sells printers, and sells printer repair training resources and training classes. Back issues of its *Service Today* newsletter, providing printer repair tips, are available at the company website.

PC Connection

www.pcconnection.com

PC Connection is a major mail-order superstore for hardware and software.

PC-Doctor, Inc.

www.pc-doctor.com

This company, previously known as Watergate Software, manufactures the excellent PC-Doctor series of diagnostic programs for PC troubleshooting and repair, which are used by many leading system manufacturers. PC-Doctor Service Center 5 includes hardware test devices and tests all versions of Windows and MS-DOS. Other versions support Linux, factory pretesting, or customized versions for specific requirements.

PC Magazine

www.pcmag.com

> This Ziff-Davis magazine and companion website feature product reviews, comparisons, and technical tips.

PC Power & Cooling, Inc.

www.pcpowercooling.com

> This company manufactures a line of high-quality, high-output power supplies and cooling fans for PC systems, including special models for Dell computers. Its products are known for high-power output and quiet fan operation. PC Power & Cooling also sells a high-quality line of overheat-alarm devices, power supply testers, and ATX 12V adapters.

PC World Communications

www.pcworld.com

> Part of the IDG network of technology publications, this company is the publisher of *PC World*, a monthly magazine and companion website featuring product reviews and comparisons.

PCI Special Interest Group

www.pcisig.com

> Formed in 1992, this group is the industry organization that owns and manages PCI. PCI-X, and PCI-Express high-speed bus specifications. More than 900 industry-leading companies are PCI SIG members. The organization is chartered to support new requirements while maintaining backward compatibility for all PCI revisions. It also maintains the specification as an easy-to-implement, stable technology and contributes to the technical longevity of PCI and its establishment as an industrywide standard.

PCMCIA (Personal Computer Memory Card International Association)

www.pcmcia.org

> This independent organization with more than 200 member companies maintains the PC Card (PCMCIA) standard for credit card–sized expansion adapters. It also publishes and maintains the CardBus, ExpressCard (see www.expresscard.com), Miniature Card, and SmartMedia card standards.

PCWIZ, Inc.

www.datadepo.com

> This company, formerly Data Depot, manufactures the PocketPOST diagnostic card for ISA and EISA systems and several other excellent diagnostics hardware and software products, including the PC Clinic series for hands-on and remote system testing.

Phoenix Technologies, Ltd.

www.phoenix.com

> This company designs Phoenix TrustedCore security, asset management, and BIOS software for all types of PCs, including servers, desktops, and mobile and embedded systems. It also sells Phoenix

First BIOS Pro and Phoenix First BIOS, Phoenix BIOS, and Award BIOS PC BIOS software for all types of PC and server systems and processors. It also sells FirstWare series of system-recovery programs and Phoenix ImageCast. It sells to OEM manufacturers. For BIOS upgrades, see *eSupport.com, Inc.*

Pioneer Electronics Inc.

www.pioneerelectronics.com

This company manufactures a popular line of rewritable DVD drives, DVD library systems, and many other consumer and business electronics products.

Pivar Computing Services, Inc.

www.convert.com

This service company specializes in data and media conversion.

PKWare, Inc.

www.pkware.com

PKWare originated and introduced the Zip file compression format. PKWare manufactures data compression products such as SecureZIP and PKZIP for Windows. It also makes PKZIP versions for Linux, UNIX, Windows servers, iSeries and zSeries midrange systems, DOS, OpenVMS, VM, and VSE. It is widely used on the Internet and by manufacturers for software distribution.

Plasmon

www.plasmon.com

This company manufactures UDO 30GB blue-laser archival WORM and rewritable storage devices; DVD libraries; Raidtech NAS, SCSI, and FC-based storage devices; management software; and backup media.

Plextor

www.plextor.com

This company manufactures a line of high-performance DVD rewritable and CD-RW drives and digital video capture devices. It introduced the first CD-RW drive with Sanyo's BURN-Proof technology to eliminate buffer underruns even while multitasking.

PNY Technologies, Inc.

www.pny.com

PNY Technologies manufactures a popular line of memory products for computers and digital cameras. It also sells flash card memory and readers; USB flash drives; graphics cards based on Nvidia GeForce 7, 6, and FX series chipsets; professional graphics cards based on Nvidia Quadro FX and NVS chipsets; digital audio players; Nvidia Personal Cinema; and SATA RAID adapters.

PowerLeap, LLC

www.powerleap.com

PowerLeap is a U.S. distributor of FriendTech (www.friendtech.com) processor upgrades and adapters for certain systems with Socket 478 (Celeron, Pentium 4), Socket 423 (early Pentium 4), Socket 370 (Celeron, Pentium III single or dual-processor), Slot 1 (Pentium II, Pentium III, Celeron), Slot 2

(Pentium II/III Xeon), or Socket 5/7 (Pentium, Pentium MMX, AMD K6). It also sells a wide variety of PC components for upgrading systems.

PowerQuest Corporation

See *Symantec Corporation*.

Processor

www.processor.com

Processor is a publication and companion website that offers excellent sources of replacement and repair parts and new, used, and refurbished PC, server, midrange, mainframe, workstation, networking, and telecom equipment at discount prices. It is part of the Sandhills family of computer publications.

Promise Technology, Inc.

www.promise.com

Promise Technology is a leading manufacturer of SATA RAID, SCSI RAID, and iSCSI RAID external enclosures; SATA and ATA RAID and non-RAID host adapters; and SATA and ATA chipsets.

Proview Technology, Inc.

www.proview.com

Proview Technology is one of the top five computer monitor makers in the world. It manufactures a wide range of LCD and CRT monitors sold at retail and by various OEMs. It also manufactures LCD and plasma TVs.

QLogic Corporation

www.qlogic.com

This company manufactures SAN Pro and SAN Express Fibre Channel and iSCSI SAN solutions for enterprise and small/medium business. It also manufactures ICs for use by leading server, networking, and storage OEMs, Fibre Channel adapters, iSCSI adapters, and SANSurfer SAN management software.

Qualitas, Inc.

www.qualitas.com

This company manufactures the Qualitas RAMexam, a popular memory diagnostic software program used by NASA and Micron Technologies. It also manufactures the Qualitas C.Y.A. Windows Registry backup and protection utility and the Qualitas Q.E.D. (Qualitas Enhanced Display) utility for enlarging Windows dialog boxes.

Quantum Corporation

www.quantum.com

Quantum is the world's largest tape drive manufacturer. It manufactures a line of tape drives using Travan, DDS, DAT 72, DLT, and LTO Ultrium technologies. It also manufactures a line of autoloaders, tape libraries, and hard-disk and disk-based backup devices that emulate tape libraries. It sold its 3.5-inch hard disk business and QuickView home-entertainment hard drive business to Maxtor in 2000. For Quantum's former SnapServer products, see *Adaptec*.

Quarter-Inch Cartridge Drive Standards, Inc. (QIC)

www.qic.org

> This independent industry group developed various Quarter-Inch Cartridge (QIC) tape drive standards for backup and archiving purposes. The organization is no longer active, but the website is maintained for reference purposes.

Que Publishing

www.quepublishing.com

> This imprint of Pearson Technology Group publishes the highest-quality computer software and hardware books in the industry.

Rackmount.com

www.rackmount.com

> Rackmount.com is a developer of rack-mounted products, including servers, chassis, storage, RPS, rails, and SBC backplanes.

Radio Shack

www.radioshack.com

> Radio Shack electronics stores sell numerous electronics devices, parts, and supplies. Radio Shack also manufactures a line of computer accessories and supplies. Tandy Corporation, parent company of Radio Shack, changed its name to Radio Shack Corporation in 2000.

Rambus Inc.

www.rambus.com

> This company is the developer and licensor of RDRAM (Rambus DRAM), a high-speed memory technology that has been used by Intel and other vendors in high-end systems; XDR, the world's fastest DRAM solution; and DDR memory controllers. It also develops interfaces for PCI Express, Fibre Channel, SATA, SerDes high-speed backplanes, Gigabit Ethernet, and other computer and networking technologies.

Ramtron International Corporation

www.ramtron.com

> This company manufactures a line of NVRAM chips and logic that use ferro-electric (FRAM) technology.

Rancho Technology, Inc.

www.rancho.com

> This company designs and manufactures SCSI expander, converter, repeater, and extender products, such as single-to-differential–ended converters, extenders, LVD SCSI, and ASIC products. It also manufactures SAS and SATA enclosures and accessories. It also specializes in custom (OEM) solutions.

Raritan Computer, Inc.

www.raritan.com

This company manufactures a line of KVM and network KVM switches, secure console servers, remote management devices, long-distance KVM devices, and remote power control devices.

Red Hat

www.redhat.com

This company is the developer of one of the leading enterprise-level Linux distributions. It also sponsors the freeware open-source Fedora project for desktop operating systems and applications.

Rip-Tie Company

www.riptie.com

This company manufactures standard and custom cable management products made from Velcro, including plenum-rated cable ties for use with plenum network and data cables.

Rockwell Semiconductor Systems

See *Conexant Systems, Inc.*

Roland Corporation U.S.

www.rolandus.com

This company manufactures a variety of musical equipment and MIDI interfaces for computers, as well as digital music keyboards, CD-based recording equipment, guitars, and many other musical products.

Rose Electronics

www.rose.com

This company manufactures a line of KVM switches, including network and fiber KVM switches and KVM accessories.

Royal Consumer Information Products, Inc.

www.royal.com

This company manufactures Royal products, including PDAs, personal organizers, calculators, cash management systems, shredders (including CD-rated models), and other products. It is owned by Olivetti Office USA.

RTC Books Division of the RTC Group

www.rtcbooks.com

This technical book publisher publishes former Annabooks titles as well as other titles on memory and PC architecture, including PCI, PCI-X, PC Card, Internet, USB, and Windows. Its parent company, RTC Group (www.rtcgroup.com), is a leader in the embedded technology industry, sponsoring real-time and embedded computing conferences and publishing *COTS Journal* and *RTC* magazine.

RuppSoft

www.ruppsoft.com

This company specializes in software for the Sharp Zaurus and Wizard PDAs, including the RuppLynx family that synchronizes various PDAs with popular email and contact clients such as Microsoft Outlook, Outlook Express, ACT!2000, Goldmine, Lotus Organizer, and others.

S3 Graphics Co, Ltd.

www.s3graphics.com

This company is a joint venture between SONICblue (the former S3 company) and motherboard chipset maker VIA Technologies. It produces the GammaChrome PCI-Express GPU, DeltaChrome AGP 8x GPU, and UniChrome integrated video found in many recent VIA Technologies chipsets. It also produced the Savage and AlphaChrome lines of desktop, mobile, and integrated graphics products.

Safeware, The Insurance Agency, Inc.

www.safeware.com

This insurance company specializes in insurance for computer equipment.

Sams Publishing

www.samspublishing.com

Sams publishes technical books on web development, programming, and other intermediate to advanced computer topics.

Samsung

www.samsung.com

Samsung is the world's largest manufacturer of memory components. It manufactures DRAMs, SRAMs, graphics and flash memory, EEPROMs, ASICs, microcontrollers, and LCD display panels. It also manufactures a popular line of LCD and CRT monitors, hard disk drives, CD- and DVD-based optical drives, multifunction devices and laser printers, as well as consumer electronics.

Seagate Technology

www.seagate.com

Seagate is one of the largest hard disk manufacturers in the world. It offers the most extensive product line of any disk manufacturer, ranging from low-cost units to the highest-performance, -capacity, and -quality hard disk and network storage units available, including the first 15,000rpm drives for Ultra160 and Ultra320 SCSI and Fibre Channel servers. It also offers external USB hard drives in a variety of capacities. For Seagate's former line of tape drives, see *Quantum Corporation*.

Sencore

www.sencore.com

This company manufactures a line of electronic testing instruments for computer monitors, digital video, cable, gaming, home automation, and many other markets.

Sharp Electronics Corporation

www.sharpusa.com

This company manufactures a wide variety of electronic and computer equipment, high-quality LCD active matrix color displays and panels, LCD and DLP projectors, as well as fax machines, multifunction devices, color printers and copiers, and notebook computer systems.

Sharp Microelectronics of the Americas

www.sharpmeg.com

This company manufactures LCD flat panels, memory, microcontrollers and RF, imaging, optoelectronics, power devices, and other semiconductor devices.

Sigma Data

www.sigmadata.com

This company is a manufacturer and distributor of computer add-on and peripheral products, specializing in hot-swap drives for IBM NetFinity servers; drives for IBM/Lenovo ThinkPad notebooks; memory for IBM servers, workstations, and IBM/Lenovo desktops and ThinkPad notebooks; ThinkPad batteries; USB 2.0 hard disks and flash memory drives; and hard drive upgrades for notebook and desktop computers.

Silicon Image

www.siimage.com

This company manufactures DVI and HDMI transmitters for PCs and displays; receivers for LCD displays; high-resolution digital video controllers; LCD panel controllers; SATA, Fibre Channel, and ATA controllers; and support ICs. It also produces transmitters, receivers, and digital video processors for use in various consumer electronics video devices.

Silicon Integrated Systems Corp. (SiS)

www.sis.com

SiS manufactures PC motherboard and mobile chipsets that support Intel and AMD processors; wireless and Ethernet controllers; South Bridge, SATA controller, and video bridge chips; and information appliance chipsets.

Simple Technology

www.simpletech.com

This company manufactures OEM and retail products, including memory upgrades for standard desktop, server, notebook, and workstation systems; Flash Disk Module products; hard drive upgrades for notebook computers; and network storage devices. It also makes hard drive upgrades for ATA, SmartMedia, USB, and CompactFlash PC Card storage; and media readers for notebook and desktop computers.

SiSoftware

www.sisoftware.co.uk

This company develops the SiSoftware Sandra series of diagnostic, hardware reporting, and benchmarking software for Windows desktops and servers, including x64 and Itanium.

Smart Cable, Inc.

www.smart-cable.com

This company manufactures the SmartCable Universal serial RS-232 cable and several other intelligent cables, as well as a wide range of standard computer and network cables and custom cables.

SMC Networks, Inc.

www.smc.com

This company manufactures standard and PC Card NICs, hubs, switches, and other network hardware based on the Ethernet, Fast Ethernet, Gigabit Ethernet, Enhanced Ethernet, Fibre Channel, IEEE 802.11a/b/g, and HomePlug PNA standards for home and business use. It also manufactures cable broadband modems and routers.

Smith Micro Software, Inc.

www.smithmicro.com

This company sells the QuickLink Mobile series of communications software for consumer and enterprise use. It also sells the CheckIt series of computer diagnostic programs; fax hardware and software; VideoLink videoconferencing; and the WebDNA Internet application generator. It also provides professional services and web hosting. It owns Allume (www.allume.com), producer of ZipMagic Deluxe, StuffIt Deluxe, and other utility programs for Windows and MacOS.

Sonic Solutions

www.sonic.com

This company manufactures and distributes digital media programs, including Easy Media Creator, MyDVD, RecordNow, BackUp MyPC, and others. It also produces professional DVD authoring programs, including DVDit Pro, DVD Producer, eDVD, and others. For the Mac market, it produces Popcorn, Toast, Toast with Jam, and Boom Box. Some of its products were originally developed by Adaptec and later sold by the Adaptec subsidiary Roxio. Sonic purchased Roxio in 2004.

Sony Corporation of America

http://b2b.sony.com

This company manufactures all types of high-quality electronic and computer equipment, including LCD and CRT monitors, VAIO notebook computers, and magnetic- and optical-storage devices and media, including AIT and SAIT tape drives and libraries.

Sophos PLC

www.sophos.com

This company develops antivirus, antispam, and security software for enterprise and small businesses.

SOYO Group, Inc.

www.soyousa.com

This company is one of the 10 largest Taiwan-based motherboard manufacturers. It also manufactures bare-bones systems, internal media readers, and a unique adapter (the KiKi X-series) that allows PlayStation controllers to attach to a PC's USB port. The SY-TechAID debug card plugs into a PCI slot to display POST codes and motherboard voltage levels.

Specialized Products Company

www.specialized.net

This company distributes a variety of tools and testing equipment for computer, network, and tele-com use, including customized toolkits made to a customer's specifications.

Sprague Magnetics, Inc.

www.sprague-magnetics.com

This company distributes a unique and interesting magnetic developer fluid that can be used to view sectors and tracks on a magnetic disk or tape. It also repairs computer tape drives, hard drives, and other types of magnetic storage devices.

St. Bernard Software

www.stbernard.com

This company is a developer of Open File Manager backup software and other security and network management products.

Standard Performance Evaluation Corporation (SPEC)

www.spec.org

This company develops and sells a popular line of benchmark tests, including SPECCPU (including SPECint and SPECfp), SPECjAppServer, SPECViewperf, HPC2002 (designed for high-performance computers running industrial-style applications), WEB2005, and others.

ST Microelectronics

www.st.com

This company manufactures a variety of memory and semiconductor devices.

Standard Microsystems Corporation (SMSC)

www.smsc.com

This company manufactures I/O, PCI bridge, LAN, USB, IEEE 1394, Device Bay, and embedded chipsets for computers and other devices. For network cards, see *SMC Networks, Inc.*

Star Micronics, Inc.

www.starmicronics.com

This company manufactures a line of forms printers, receipt printers (some with wireless, USB, and Ethernet capabilities), and visual card systems. It also manufactures machine tools, precision products, and audio components, such as buzzers and transducers.

StarTech

www.startech.com

This company sells a line of KVM switches, AV switches, video converters, video amplifiers, RPSs, and other computer and server room parts.

StorageSoft Solutions, Inc.

See *Phoenix Technologies, Ltd.*

StorCase Technology, Inc.

www.storcase.com

This company is a sister company to Kingston Technology. It manufactures InfoStation and DataSilo storage chassis for SATA, SCSI, and Fibre Channel drives; DataExpress removable drive enclosures; DataStacker expansion chassis for SCSU Ultra160 drives; and RhinoJR external drive enclosures for all popular drive interfaces.

Supermicro Computer, Inc.

www.supermicro.com

This company manufactures a high-quality line of server-class rack-mounted, tower, and pedestal servers; RPSs; chassis; backplanes; accessories; and motherboards for Intel Itanium 2, Xeon, Xeon MP, Pentium D, Pentium 4, and Pentium III processors.

Superpower Supply, Inc.

www.superpower.com

This company manufactures PC and server cases, many of which feature easy-assembly options.

Sykes Enterprises, Inc.

www.sykes.com

This company provides a wide range of customer care management solutions for computer and other industries.

Symantec Corporation

www.symantec.com

This company manufactures a popular line of security, backup, antivirus, communications, and utility software and appliances for Windows desktops, network clients, and servers. Some of its products also support Linux, UNIX, or NetWare servers, Macintosh computers, and handheld devices. Its product families include Norton, Symantec, LiveState, Ghost, Partition Magic, pcAnywhere, WinFax Pro, BackupExec, and Symantec Manager. It purchased enterprise backup and security vendor Veritas Software in 2005.

Syquest Repair.com

www.syquest.com

This company provides repair services for SyQuest drives, and it sells cartridges, drives, and accessories.

Tadiran

www.tadiranbat.com

This company manufactures a variety of lithium thionyl chloride batteries for computer and other applications.

Tandberg Data

www.tandbergdata.com

This company is a leading manufacturer of tape backup drives, autoloaders, libraries, D2D backup, and backup appliances based on LTO Ultrium, DLT and SDLT, and Tandberg's own SLR technologies.

Tanisys Technology, Inc.

www.tanisys.com

This company manufactures memory test systems for RAMBUS, DRAM, SDRAM, Flash, USB DDR, and DDR-2 memory modules and devices.

Tatung Company of America, Inc.

www.tatungusa.com

This company manufactures CRT and LCD monitors for computer, kiosk, and industrial use, as well as consumer electronics.

TDK Electronics Corporation

www.tdk.com

This company manufactures a line of magnetic and optical media, including disks, recordable and rewritable optical media, and tape cartridges. It also manufactures the Indi DV and VeloCD ReWriter CD-RW drive series, USB floppy drives, speakers, video capture devices, analog and digital video and audio products, semiconductors and electronic components, and magnetic card systems.

Teac America, Inc.

www.teac.com

This company manufactures floppy, tape, CD-RW, DVD, and hard disk drives for desktop and portable systems. It also makes a line of optical disk printers.

Tech Data Corporation

www.techdata.com

This company distributes a complete line of computer systems, peripherals, and computer supplies.

Tech Spray, LP

www.techspray.com

This company manufactures a complete line of computer and electronic cleaning chemicals and products.

Technology Data Exchange, Inc.

www.oemtechnology.com

This company publishes *OEM Technology News*, which provides OEM sources for electronics products. It provides links to online sourcing sites for parts.

Tekram Technologies

www.tekram.com

> This company manufactures a complete line of SCSI and SATA RAID subsystems, SCSI and SATA RAID host adapters, SCSI and Fibre Channel host adapters, IEEE 1394 and USB host adapters, and FIR and SIR IrDA adapters.

Teleplan International

www.teleplan.com

> This company specializes in depot-level in-warranty and out-of-warranty repairs and component swapping (fulfillment) of CRT and LCD displays, notebook computers, digital cameras, drives (floppy, hard disk, optical, tape, printed circuit boards), printers and scanners, networks, cell phones, and consumer electronics. It also provides supply chain management (SCM) and reverse SCM (RSCM) services, including call centers.

Test and Measurement World

www.reed-electronics.com/tmworld/

> *Test and Measurement World* is a magazine and companion website for quality control and testing in the electronics industry. It is free for those who qualify. Its parent company, Reed Electronics Group (www.reed-electronics.com), publishes many magazines and websites and also provides information through trade shows and events. It is owned by Reed Elsevier (www.reedelsevier.com), a worldwide event provider and publisher of book, online, magazine, and CD-based information in science, medical, legal, educational, and business categories.

Texas Instruments, Inc.

www.ti.com

> This company manufactures semiconductor devices, including digital signal processors (DSPs), analog and mixed-signal processors, speech and graphics processors, programmable logic, ASICs, and others.

Toshiba America, Inc.

www.toshiba.com

> This company manufactures a popular line of notebook and tablet computers, as well as data projectors, hard disk drives for notebook computers and smaller-form-factor markets, rewritable DVD and other optical drives, semiconductors, barcode printers and POS devices, digital cameras, digital camcorders, and other electronic devices.

TouchStone Software Corporation

www.touchstonesoftware.com

> This company owns BIOS upgrade specialist eSupport (formerly Unicore Software). See *Smith Micro Software, Inc.*, for the CheckIt and FastMove product lines.

Trace Research and Development Center

www.trace.wisc.edu

> This organization is a leading interdisciplinary research, development, and resource center on technology and disability.

Trend Micro

www.trendmicro.com

This company is a developer of antivirus, antispyware, and network security solutions for enterprise, small to medium business, and home office settings.

Trident Microsystems, Inc.

www.tridentmicro.com

This company manufactures a line of video processing chips used in digital TVs and multimedia notebook computers.

Tripp Lite Manufacturing

www.tripplite.com

This company manufactures a complete line of computer and server power-protection devices, including UPS and surge protection. It also manufactures network and data cables, network cabinets, KVM switches, line conditioners, and isolation transformers.

True Query, Inc.

www.truequery.net

True Query is a subscription-based index that offers full-text access to a two-year archive of more than 100 technology-specific publications. It owns the assets of the ComputerSelectWeb/eShaman database formerly owned by Shaman Corporation and Gale Group.

Twinhead Corporation

www.twinhead.com

This company manufactures notebook computer systems.

Tyan Computer Corporation

www.tyan.com

This company manufactures an excellent line of server, workstation, and ATX-format motherboards based on Intel and AMD CPUs. It also manufactures rack-mounted server systems and network security appliances.

Tyco Electronics

http://connectors.tycoelectronics.com/

Tyco Electronics makes connectors for electronic, computer, video, and telecom uses, including the famous AMP brand used by many OEMs, as well as other brands, such as Elcon, Greenpar, HTS, Microdot, and Hellstern.

ULi Electronics, Inc.

www.uli.com.tw

Formerly ALi Corporation, this company manufactures chipsets for PC motherboard, multimedia, USB, RS-232, and RTC applications.

Ultra-X, Inc.

www.uxd.com

This company manufactures the excellent P.H.D. PCI 2, Hummer IP, QuickPost PCI, RAM Stress Test Pro II and Mini-PCI , and QuickTech USB 2.0 lines of diagnostic hardware, as well as the QuickTech PRO, QuickTech Personal, and Win Stress Test and RAM Stress Test (RST) diagnostic software packages, among others.

Underwriters Laboratories, Inc.

www.ul.com

This company is the leading third-party product safety certification organization in the United States, with a growing worldwide presence. Established in 1894, it offers an online searchable database of certifications and registration.

Unicomp, Inc.

www.pckeyboard.com

This company manufactures and sells keyboards based on the Lexmark (previously IBM) keyboard technology it purchased from Lexmark in 1996. Unicomp's keyboards are available with the same clicky feel (buckling-spring design) as classic IBM keyboards, or you can choose the quieter rubber-dome design in some models. Many models are available, including designs with a TrackPoint-integrated pointing device, programmable keys, an integrated trackball, reduced footprint, terminal emulation, wireless with TrackPoint pointing device, and others. Unicomp also stocks new IBM-brand and Lexmark-brand keyboards.

Unicore Software, Inc.

See *eSupport.com, Inc.*

UNISYS

www.unisys.com

This company is a popular supplier of e-business solutions, servers for Windows and Linux, data center solutions, financial printers, disk and tape drives, tape libraries, midrange and mainframe computers, computer software, and management services to federal and state governments as well as large corporations.

U.S. Robotics, Inc.

www.usr.com

This company makes a popular line of analog modems, broadband Internet devices, and Ethernet and wireless network and VoIP products.

V Communications, Inc.

www.v-com.com

This company manufactures the Commander series of disk copying, disk partitioning, boot management, and security programs. It also manufactures Fix-It Utilities, Web Easy and Web Easy Professional, PowerDesk Pro, Media Easy, AutoSave, and FinalBid.

Varta Batteries, Inc.

www.varta.com

This company manufactures a complete line of computer batteries as well as consumer and automotive batteries.

Verbatim Americas

www.verbatimcorp.com

This company manufactures a line of storage media, including optical and magnetic disks and tapes, and flash memory devices. It is a subsidiary of Mitsubishi Chemical Corporation.

Veritas Software Corporation

See *Symantec Corporation.*

VESA Standards

www.vesa.org

This company is the leading worldwide video standards trade association, with more than 125 member companies. VESA's mission is to promote and develop open, interoperable, and international interface standards for the video, audio, and graphics interfaces of computers. Recent standards include VESA-2005-3 (19-inch LCD monitor panel), VESA 2005-5 (Flat Panel Display Measurement Version 2 update and Monitor Control Command Set Version 2 Revision 1).

VIA Technologies, Inc.

www.viatech.com

This company manufactures a popular line of high-performance chipsets for AMD and Intel desktop and mobile processors. Other products include EPIA embedded motherboards (see VIA Embedded Platform, at www.viaembedded.com), VIA C-series and M-series processors, video display chipsets, high-performance audio chipsets, network chipsets (see VIA Networking Technologies, Inc., at www.vntek.com), and peripheral controller cards.

ViewSonic

www.viewsonic.com

ViewSonic manufactures a line of high-quality CRT and LCD monitors; LCD and DLP projection units; large-screen LCD and plasma TVs; wireless media; and network devices.

Viziflex Seels, Inc.

www.viziflex.com

This company manufactures Viziflex Seels form-fitting clear keyboard and Tablet PC covers and other computer accessories, including static control products and medical lab organizer products. It purchased Amherst-Merritt, International, manufacturer of SafeSkin keyboard protectors, in 2004.

Watergate Software

See *PC-Doctor, Inc.*

Wavetek-Meterman

See *Meterman Test Tools*.

Western Digital Corporation

www.westerndigital.com

Western Digital is the leader in information storage management, providing a broad array of hard drives in ATA/IDE, SATA, USB 2.0, and i.LINK/IEEE 1394 products for personal, mobile, network, and enterprisewide computing. It also manufactures the CE series for digital video recorder (DVR) applications.

Winbond Electronic Corporation

www.winbond.com

This company manufactures memory chips, I/O chipsets, digital speech processing chipsets, LAN and peripheral chipsets, and other types of ICs.

WordPerfect

See *Corel Systems, Inc.*

Wyse Technology

www.wyse.com

This company manufactures Wyse Winterm Windows-based thin clients, Wyse 550 Video Client, and general-purpose terminals under the Wyse and Link brands.

Xerox Corporation

www.xerox.com

This company manufactures an extensive line of inkjet and laser printers, scanners, multifunction devices, and copiers, ranging from personal-use to networked devices. Xerox purchased Textronix in 2000 and now manufactures the Phaser line of revolutionary solid-ink color printers. It also manufactures document-management software.

XFree86

www.xfree86.org

XFree86 is the developer of the leading X Window implementation for Linux, UNIX, and other operating systems.

Xircom

See *Intel Corporation*.

Y-E Data Company

www.yedata.com

This company manufactures a line of internal, USB, and PC Card external floppy disk drives, media readers, and network printers for OEM and retail markets.

Yosemite Technologies, Inc.

www.yosemitetech.com

This company is the developer of Yosemite Backup, a line of backup software for desktops and networks.

Zoom Telephonics, Inc.

www.zoomtel.com

Zoom Telephonics manufactures a line of VoIP devices; DSL, cable, ISDN, and analog modems; Bluetooth adapters; and automatic dialers sold under the Zoom and Hayes, and Global Village brand names. Some of its products are also sold through OEM channels. Zoom introduced the first analog modems that support the V.92 standard for faster uploads and call-waiting support.

Zoran

www.zoran.com

Zoran is a manufacturer of a wide range of IP core, DVD, mobile technology, digital TV, and imaging ICs. It purchased Oak Technology in 2003.

Vendors by Product or Service Category

If you are looking for a product or service but don't know a specific vendor that provides it, use this part of the vendor list to find a vendor that provides what you need. Then you can look up the vendor's contact information in the alphabetical listing in the first part of this appendix.

Audio Adapters (Sound Cards)

Creative Labs, Inc.

Backup Software

BakBone Software, Inc.

Columbia Data Products

CommVault Systems, Inc.

Computer Associates International, Inc.

EMC Dantz

Lone Star Software

Sonic Solutions

St. Bernard Software

Symantec Corporation

Yosemite Technologies, Inc.

Batteries

Duracell, Inc.

Fedco Electronics, Inc.

Maxell Corporation of America

NEC Electronics, Inc.

Panasonic Corporation of North America

Sigma Data

Tadiran

Varta Batteries, Inc.

BIOS

AMI (American Megatrends, Inc.)

eSupport.com, Inc.

Micro Firmware, Inc.

Phoenix Technologies, Ltd.

Books, Magazines, and Documentation

Advisor Media, Inc.

Computer Graphics World

Computer Hotline

Computer Technology Review

CRN

Datamation

EE Times

Electrocution Technical Publishers

Electronic Products

Electronics Supply and Manufacturing (formerly *Electronic Buyers' News*)

Endl Publications

eWeek

Global Engineering Documents

InfoWorld

Macworld Communications, Inc.

PC Magazine

PC World Communications

Processor

Que Publishing

Sams Publishing

Test and Measurement World

Cables, Connectors, and Cable Management

Arrowfield International, Inc.

Autotime Corporation

Belden CDT Electronics Division

Black Box Network Services

CableOrganizer.com, Inc.

Cables to Go

Connect Technologies

CS Electronics

CyberResearch

FCI

Meritec

Methode Electronics, Inc.

Micro Accessories, Inc.

Micro Computer Cable Company, Inc.

Molex, Inc.

Parallel Technologies, Inc.

Rip-Tie Company

Smart Cable, Inc.

Tripp Lite Manufacturing

Tyco Electronics

Cases/Chassis

Antec, Inc.

Aopen, Inc.

Ci Design Company

Intel Corporation

Microway, Inc.

Rackmount.com

Supermicro Computer, Inc.

Superpower Supply, Inc.

CD/DVD Drives and Media

Aopen

Apple Computer

ASUS Computer International America (ASUSTeK)

BenQ America Corporation

Creative Labs, Inc.

Hewlett-Packard

Imation

Iomega

JVC America/Professional

LG Electronics

Maxell Corporation of America

Mitsumi Electronics Corporation

NEC Solutions America

Panasonic Corporation of North America

Plextor

Pioneer Electronics, Inc.

TDK Electronics Corporation

Samsung

Sony Corporation

Toshiba America, Inc.

Verbatim Americas

Chipsets

AMD (Advanced Micro Devices)

ATI Technologies, Inc.

Cirrus Logic, Inc.

Conexant Systems, Inc.

Creative Labs, Inc.

Cypress Semiconductor Corporation

Integrated Device Technology, Inc.

Intel Corporation

LSI Logic, Inc.

National Semiconductor Corporation

NEC Electronics, Inc.

Nvidia Corporation

Opti, Inc.

QLogic Corporation

S3 Graphics, Inc.

Silicon Integrated Systems Corp. (SiS)

Standard Microsystems Corporation

Trident Microsystems, Inc.

ULi Electronics, Inc.

VIA Technologies, Inc.

Winbond Electronic Corporation America

Zoran

Diagnostics Software and Hardware

#1-PC Diagnostics Company

Accurite Technologies, Inc.

Advanced Personal Systems

AMI (American Megatrends, Inc.)

Comtech Publishing Ltd.

CST

DisplayMate Technologies Corp.

Electrocution

Eurosoft (U.S.) Inc.

Fluke, John Manufacturing Company, Inc.

Golden Bow Systems

McAfee.com Corporation

Micro 2000, Inc.

MicroSystems Development, Inc.

Modem Doctor

Ontrack Data Recovery

Parallel Technologies, Inc.

PC-Doctor, Inc.

PCWIZ, Inc.

Qualitas, Inc.

SiSoftware Sandra

Smith Micro Software, Inc.

Symantec Corporation

Tanisys Technology, Inc.

TriniTech, Inc.

Ultra-X, Inc.

Distributors

Arrow Electronics

Libi Industries, Ltd.

Mini Micro Supply

Tech Data Corporation

Floppy Drives

Accurite Technologies, Inc.

ALPS Electric

Citizen America Corporation

MA Laboratories, Inc.

MicroSolutions, Inc.

Mitsumi Electronics Corporation

Panasonic Corporation of North America

Teac America, Inc.

Toshiba America, Inc.

Y-E Data America, Inc.

Graphics Adapters and Chipsets

ABIT Computer (USA) Corporation

Aopen America, Inc.

ASUS Computer International America (ASUSTeK)

ATI Technologies, Inc.

Elitegroup Computer Systems, Inc.

FIC of America (FICA)

Giga-Byte Technology Co., Inc.

Matrox Graphics, Inc.

MSI Computer Corporation

Nvidia Corporation

SOYO Tek, Inc.

Tyan Computer Corporation

Hard and Removable Disk Drives, Drive Controllers, and Network Storage

Adaptec

AMI (American Megatrends, Inc.)

ASUS Computer International America (ASUSTeK)

Breece Hill

Fujitsu Computer Products of America, Inc.

Hewlett-Packard Company

IBM Corporation

Iomega Corporation

LSI Logic, Inc.

MA Laboratories, Inc.

Maxtor Corporation

Quantum Corporation

QLogic Corporation

Seagate Technology

Silicon Image

SYQT, Inc.

Tekram Technologies

Toshiba America, Inc.

Western Digital Corporation

Hardware (Screws, Mounting Brackets, and So On)

Ci Design Company

Jameco Computer Products

JDR Microdevices

Radio Shack

Keyboards

ALPS Electric

Aopen America, Inc.

Belkin

BenQ

Cherry Electrical Products Division

KeyTronicEMS

Labtec Enterprises, Inc.

LiteOn Technology Corporation

Logitech

Microsoft Corporation

Mitsumi Electronics Corporation

Unicomp, Inc.

KVM Switches

AMI

APC

Avocent

Belkin

Black Box

Minicom

Network Technologies, Inc

Raritan Computer

Rose Electronics

StarTech.com

Tripp Lite

Memory

AMD (Advanced Micro Devices)

Centon Electronics, Inc.

Crucial Technologies

Dallas Semiconductor

Hitachi America, Ltd. (Semiconductor and IC Division)

Hynix Semiconductor America, Inc.

IBM Semiconductor Solutions

Intel Corporation

Kingston Technology Corporation

MA Laboratories, Inc.

Micron Technologies, Inc.

Microprocessors Unlimited, Inc.

Mosel Vitelic (MVC)

NEC Electronics, Inc.

Panasonic Corporation of North America

Ramtron International Corporation

Samsung Semiconductor, Inc.

Sharp Microelectronics of the Americas

Sigma Data

Simple Technology

ST Microelectronics

Winbond Electronic Corporation

Mouse Devices

ALPS Electric

Aopen America, Inc.

Kensington Technology Group

KeyTronicEMS

Labtec Enterprises, Inc.

Logitech

Microsoft Corporation

Mitsumi Electronics Corporation

Miscellaneous

Aavid Thermalloy LLC

Anvil Cases

AZ-COM, Inc.

Berkshire Products

Byte Runner Technologies

Casio, Inc.

Chicago Case Company

CTS Corporation

Curtis Computer Products

Da-Lite Screen Co.

DEX (Data Exchange Corporation)

Digi-Key Corporation

Extron Electronics

FCI

Heathkit Company, Inc.

Hypertech, Inc.

IBM Corporation

Illinois Lock

Labconco Corporation

LearnKey, Inc.

MAGNI Systems, Inc.

Molex, Inc.

Pivar Computing Services, Inc.

Radio Shack

Rip-Tie Company

Safeware, The Insurance Agency, Inc.

Specialized Products Company

Sprague Magnetics, Inc.

StorCase Technology, Inc.

Trace Research and Development Center

Viziflex Seels, Inc.

Wyse Technology

Modems (Analog, DSL, Cable Modem, Broadband)

3Com Corp.

ASUS Computer International America (ASUSTeK)

Creative Labs, Inc.

Intel Corporation

Linksys

Simple Technology

SONICblue

SMC Networks Worldwide

U.S. Robotics, Inc.

Zoom Telephonics, Inc.

Monitors and Display Devices

Acer United States

Aopen America, Inc.

BenQ

CTX International, Inc.

DTK Computer, Inc.

Dukane Corporation

Extron Electronics

Hewlett-Packard Company

Hitachi America, Ltd.

LG Electronics

NEC Display Solutions of America, Inc.

NEC Solutions America

Panasonic Corporation of North America

Philips Electronics North America

Proview Technology, Inc.

Sharp Electronics Corporation

Sony Corporation of America

Tatung Company of America, Inc.

Toshiba America, Inc.

ViewSonic

Motherboards

ABIT Computer (USA) Corporation

AMI (American Megatrends, Inc.)

Aopen America, Inc.

ASUS Computer International America (ASUSTeK)

Diamond Flower, Inc. (DFI)

DTK Computer, Inc.

Elitegroup Computer Systems, Inc.

First International Computer America

Giga-Byte Technology Co., Inc.

Intel Corporation

MA Labs, Inc.

Micro Industries Corporation

Motorola Embedded Communications Computing

MSI Computer Corporation

SOYO Tek, Inc.

Supermicro Computer, Inc.

Tyan Computer Corporation

VIA Technologies, Inc.

Networking

3Com Corp.

Black Box Network Services

Byte Runner Technologies

CDW (Computer Discount Warehouse)

Cisco Systems, Inc.

Dell Computer Corporation

D-Link

Gateway, Inc.

Hewlett-Packard Company

IBM Corporation

Intel Corporation

Lantronix

Lexmark

Linksys

Matrox Graphics, Inc.

Netgear

SMC Networks Worldwide

U.S. Robotics, Inc.

Zoom Telephonics, Inc.

Online Services

America Online

CompuServe Interactive Services, Inc. (CIS)

Optical Drives and Media

Acer United States

Aopen America, Inc.

ASUS Computer International America (ASUSTeK)

Breece Hill

Fujitsu Computer Products of America, Inc.

Hewlett-Packard Company

Hitachi America, Ltd.

Imation Enterprises Corp.

Iomega Corporation

LG Electronics

Maxell Corporation of America

Micro Design International, Inc. (MDI)

Panasonic Corporation of North America

Philips Electronics North America

Pioneer Electronics

Plasmon

Plextor

Sony Corporation of America

TDK Electronics Corporation

Verbatim Americas

Power Protection and UPSs

Acme Electric/Electronics Division

American Power Conversion (APC)

Black Box Network Services

Invesys Powerware Division

Liebert

MGE UPS Systems

OneAC

Para Systems

Tripp Lite Manufacturing

Power Supplies and Redundant Power Supplies

Antec, Inc.

Astec America, Inc.

CyberResearch

Orbit Micro

Panasonic Corporation of North America

PC Power & Cooling, Inc.

Rackmount.com

Printers, Printer Parts, and Supplies

ALPS Electric

Canon USA, Inc.

Citizen America Corporation

Epson America, Inc.

Fujitsu Computer Products of America, Inc.

Hewlett-Packard Company

Lexmark

NEC Technologies, Inc.

Oki Data Americas, Inc.

Panasonic Corporation of North America

PARTS NOW!, LLC

Sharp Electronics Corporation

Star Micronics America, Inc.

Y-E Data America, Inc.

Processors and Processor Upgrades

AMD (Advanced Micro Devices)

Intel Corporation

MA Laboratories, Inc.

Motorola

PowerLeap, LLC

VIA Technologies, Inc.

RAID

Adaptec

AMI (American Megatrends, Inc.)

Arco Computer Products, LLC

GigaTrend, Inc.

LSI Logic, Inc.

Microway, Inc.

Pacific Digital

Plasmon

PNY Technologies

Promise Technology, Inc.

Silicon Image

Supermicro Computer, Inc.

Tekram Technologies

Removable Media

Imation Enterprises Corp.

Iomega Corporation

Maxell Corporation of America

Sony Corporation of America

TDK Electronics Corporation

Verbatim Americas

Repair Services

Arrowfield International, Inc.

CompUSA, Inc.

InteliSol

DEX (Data Exchange Corporation)

PARTS NOW! LLC

Sprague Magnetics, Inc.

Syquest Repair.com

Teleplan International

Retail and Direct Mail

Altex Electronics, Inc.

Black Box Network Services CompUSA, Inc.

CDW (Computer Discount Warehouse)

Dell Computer Corporation

Gateway, Inc.

IBM Corporation

Jameco Computer Products

JDR Microdevices

Jensen Tools, Inc.

Myoda Computer Center

Newark Electronics

PC Connection

SCSI Accessories

Adaptec

East/West Manufacturing Enterprises, Inc.

LSI Logic, Inc.

Methode Electronics, Inc.

Micro Accessories, Inc.

Micro Design International, Inc. (MDI)

QLogic Corporation

Rancho Technology, Inc.

Software

Adobe Systems, Inc.

Apple Computer, Inc.

Autodesk, Inc.

Bitstream, Inc.

Borland Software Corporation

Buerg Software

Casio, Inc.

Columbia Data Products

Comtech Publishing Ltd.

Conexant Systems, Inc.

Corel Systems, Inc.

Crystal Decisions

Dot Hill Systems Corporation

eSupport.com, Inc.

Golden Bow Systems

Hewlett-Packard Company

Hitachi America, Ltd. (Semiconductor & IC Division)

IBM Corporation

Iomega Corporation

LapLink.com

LSI Logic, Inc.

MapInfo Corporation

McAfee, Inc.

Micro Design International, Inc. (MDI)

Microsoft Corporation

MicroWay, Inc.

Modem Doctor

Motorola

NextPage

Novell, Inc.

Ontrack Data Recovery

Parallel Technologies, Inc.

PC-Doctor, Inc.

PCWIZ, Inc.

PKWare, Inc.

Plextor

PSL

Qualitas, Inc.

Rupp Technology Corporation

Silicon Image

Smith Micro Software, Inc.

Sonic Solutions

Symantec Corporation

Ultra-X, Inc.

V Communications, Inc.

Xerox Corporation

Speakers

Bose Corp.

Creative Labs, Inc.

Labtec Enterprises, Inc.

Logitech

Philips Electronics North America

Standards Bodies and Organizations

ANSI (American National Standards Institute)

Association of Shareware Professionals (ASP)

CompTIA (Computing Technology Industry Association)

PCI Special Interest Group

PCMCIA (Personal Computer Memory Card International Association)

Quarter-Inch Cartridge Drive Standards, Inc. (QIC)

Underwriters Laboratories, Inc.

VESA Standards

Supplies (Chemicals, Cleaners, and So On)

CAIG Laboratories

Curtis Computer Products

D.W. Electrochemicals, Ltd.

Emerson & Cuming

ITW Chemtronics

Tech Spray, LP

Systems (Desktop, Server, and Mobile)

Acer United States

Aopen America, Inc.

Apple Computer, Inc.

ASUS Computer International America (ASUSTeK)

DakTech

Dell Computer Corporation

Diamond Flower, Inc. (DFI)

Diversified Technology

DTK Computer, Inc.

Everex Systems, Inc.

Fujitsu Computer Products of America, Inc.

Gateway, Inc.

Giga-Byte Technology Co., Inc.

Hewlett-Packard Company

IBM Corporation

Intel Corporation

Microway, Inc.

MPC, LLC MSI Computer Corporation

Myoda Computer Center

NEC Solutions America

Panasonic Corporation of North America

Rackmount.com

Radio Shack

Sharp Electronics Corporation

Supermicro Computer, Inc.

Toshiba America, Inc.

Tyan Computer Corporation

UNISYS

Tape Drives, Autoloaders, Libraries, and Media

Advanced Digital Information Corporation

Breece HillExabyte Corporation

GigaTrend, Inc.

Hewlett-Packard Company

Imation Enterprises Corp.

Maxell Corporation of America

MicroSolutions, Inc.

MicroWay, Inc.

Overland Storage

Plasmon

Quantum Corporation

Sony Corporation of America

Tandberg Data

TDK Electronics Corporation

Teac America, Inc.

UNISYS

Verbatim Americas

INDEX

Installing the DVD

The DVD accompanying this book is playable on both a standalone DVD player (DVD player attached to your television/home theater system) and a DVD drive installed in or connected to your PC.

Standalone DVD Video Players

To play the videos on this DVD, insert the DVD into your standalone DVD video player and navigate the menus using your DVD player's remote, just as you would do with any DVD.

Note

The DVD is region-free. The extra features using Internet (Web) links are not active links; you must enter the specified URLs into your Web browser directly. Extra features and Windows Media Player–formatted videos are also available on Scott's Web site at www.upgradingandrepairingpcs.com.

PC-Based DVD Drives

To play the DVD video content, do the following:

1. Insert the DVD into your PC's DVD drive.
2. Run your previously installed DVD player application and select Play.
3. Navigate the DVD menus as you would any standard DVD video.

Most DVD drives include a decoder/player application. If you do not currently have a DVD decoder/player installed on your system, you can do one of the following:

- Play the disc in a standard set-top DVD player.
- Use an existing DVD decoder with Windows Media Player 9 or later (visit www.microsoft.com/windows/windowsmedia).
- Purchase a DVD decoder to use with Windows Media Player.
- Purchase a complete decoder/player combination, such as PowerDVD by CyberLink (www.gocyberlink.com), or WinDVD by Intervideo (www.intervideo.com).

Here's how to access the Technical Reference files, previous editions of the book, and any other files on the DVD-ROM:

1. Insert the DVD into your PC's DVD drive.
2. Open My Computer.
3. Right-click the icon for the DVD drive containing the disc.
4. Select Explore.
5. Navigate through the folders and files just as if you were viewing files stored on your computer's hard drive.

Note

Many of the documents included in the Extras section of the DVD are in PDF format, which requires Adobe Acrobat to view. Acrobat is freely available at www.adobe.com.

System Requirements for DVD-ROM Video

The minimum system configuration is as follows:

- Intel Celeron/Pentium or AMD Duron/Athlon processor, 400MHz
- Windows 98 Second Edition, Me, 2000, or XP
- 64MB of RAM (Windows 2000 and XP require 128MB of RAM)
- 4MB graphics card, 800×600 resolution, 16-bit color
- Direct Sound–compatible sound card
- 4X DVD-ROM drive (UDMA enabled)
- Direct Show–compliant DVD decoder/player software installed
- Direct X 7.0
- Internet Explorer 5.0

Access to DVD Content Without a DVD Player or DVD Drive

If you do not have a set-top DVD player or DVD drive, you can still access all the files included on the DVD-ROM by visiting www.upgradingandrepairingpcs.com. To access these materials on the Web, follow these steps:

1. Remove the DVD from the package insert and note the password on the DVD label.
2. Visit www.upgradingandrepairingpcs.com and follow the DVD link from the home page.
3. Enter your password as included on the DVD label.
4. You can then download any of the files provided there, including Windows Media Player versions of the videos, multiple previous editions in PDF format, a hard drive specification database, a vendor database, and more.

License Agreement

By opening this package, you are agreeing to be bound by the following agreement:

You may not copy or redistribute the entire media as a whole. Copying and redistribution of individual software programs on the media is governed by terms set by individual copyright holders.

The installer and code from the author(s) are copyrighted by the publisher and author(s). Individual programs and other items on the media are copyrighted by their various authors or other copyright holders. Some of the programs included with this product may be governed by an Open Source license, which allows redistribution; see the license information for each product for more information.

Other programs are included on the media by special permission from their authors.

This software is provided as is without warranty of any kind, either expressed or implied, including but not limited to the implied warranties of merchantability and fitness for a particular purpose. Neither the publisher nor its dealers or distributors assume any liability for any alleged or actual damages arising from the use of this program. (Some states do not allow for the exclusion of implied warranties, so the exclusion may not apply to you.)